Presidential Sheet Music

An endeavor of this magnitude by necessity
becomes a collaborative effort. The testimony to this
can readily be seen from the wealth
of individual and institutional support I received
during the twelve years it took to compile the catalogue.

Three very special individuals, each in his or her own way,
share credit for this effort, however, and it is to them,
with my most sincere thanks,
that this book is gratefully dedicated:
David J. Frent, Beverly A. Hamer, Lawrence Zimmerman.

Presidential Sheet Music

*An Illustrated Catalogue of
Published Music Associated with
the American Presidency and
Those Who Sought the Office*

Danny O. Crew

McFarland & Company, Inc., Publishers
Jefferson, North Carolina, and London

ACKNOWLEDGMENTS. *Individuals*—Dr. Stephen J. Adelson; Joseph Albertson; Don and Edith Allen; Teresa Ammons; Gillian B. Anderson; Mrs. M.L. Anderson; Isabella W. Athey; Ruben Babich; James C. Bernard; Linda Solow Blotner; Larry Brokofsky; James Nelson Brown; Kenton Broyles; Wayland Bunnell; Kenneth Bush; Kenneth A. Carley; Nelson Chubb, Jr; Robert M. Clifford; Donald Coney; Lois Cordrey; Meg Cortright; Rosemary Cullen; Jenny Creighton; Linda Grant De Pauw; Sam DeVincent; Dorothy Field; Dr. George Foreman; Tom French; David and Janice Frent; Soloman Goodman; Margaret Goostray; Bob Goshorn; Ronnie Grossfeld; Beverly Hamer; J. Samuel Hammond; Leeta Hardin; Patricia Harpole; Winnie Hartke; Pinky Herman; Charles A. Hunter; Tom Huston; Millard Irion; Howard Kanetzke; David Jason; Philip H. Jones; Craig Lacy; Norma Jean Lamb; William R. Lee; Sandy and Dennis Marrone; Charles H. McCall; Robert V. McCarthy; William Miles; John Miley; Deborah D. Miller; John K. Moody; Janet I. Nichol; Dr. Terry Parish; Joseph Patrarca; Leslie Patterson; Nelson Rice, Jr; Michael J. Rogan; Jackie Ryberg; Harris Saunders; Peter Scanlan; Linda Scates; Karen Schneider; Charles B. Seton; Bobbie and Henry Shaffner; Dr. Leonard B. Smith; Dr. Rex Stark; Kurt Stein; Susan Stokes; Carol Ann Strahl; Dr. Edmund B. Sullivan; Elwyn A. Taylor; Jean Thompson; Cynthia S. Wall; Lucille Wehner; Jim Wiemers; Steven M. Wilson; Lawrence Zimmerman; Michael Zinman. **Institutions/Organizations**—American Political Item Collectors Association, Inc; Boston, Public Library; Boston University (John Hay Library); Brown University; Buffalo and Erie County, New York, Public Library; Calvin Coolidge Memorial Foundation; Centre College of Kentucky; Central Michigan University (Clarke Historical Library); Cincinnati Historical Society; Detroit Concert Band; Duke University Library (Wm. R. Perkins Library); Harvard University (The Eda Loeb Music Library) and Harvard College Library (The Theodore Roosevelt Collection); Indiana State Library; The Johns Hopkins University (The Milton S. Eisenhower Library); The Library of Congress (Music and Rare Books Divisions); Indiana University (Lily Library); Lincoln Memorial University (The Abraham Lincoln Museum); Louis A. Warren Lincoln Library And Museum; Maryland Historical Society; Massachusetts State Library; Massachusetts Historical Society; Minnesota Historical Society; The Museum of the Confederacy (The Eleanor S. Brockenborough Library); The Newberry Library; New York City Public Library; New York Historical Society; City of Pompano Beach, Florida, Public Library; The Smithsonian Institution; The State Historical Society of Wisconsin; United States Marine Band Library; University of Georgia (Hargrett Library); University of Illinois Library, Chicago (Joseph Jacobs Collection); University of Hartford; University of Kentucky; University of Scranton; Utica, New York, Public Library; Yale University.

Library of Congress Cataloguing-in-Publication Data
Crew, Danny O., 1947–
Presidential sheet music : an illustrated catalogue of published music associated with the American presidency and those who sought the office / Danny O. Crew.
p.   cm.   Includes bibliographical references and indexes.
ISBN 0-7864-0928-2 (library binding : 50# alkaline paper) ∞
1. Presidents — United States — Songs and music — Bibliography.
2. Presidential candidates — United States — Songs and music — Bibliography.
3. Campaign songs — United States — Bibliography.   I. Title.
ML128.P66C74   2001   016.7815'99'0973   dc21   00-52530
British Library cataloguing data are available

©2001 Danny O. Crew. All rights reserved. Manufactured in the United States of America

No part of this book may be reproduced or transmitted in any form or by any means, electronic or mechanical, including photocopying or recording, or by any information storage and retrieval system, without permission in writing from the publisher.

McFarland & Company, Inc., Publishers, Box 611, Jefferson, North Carolina 28640
www.mcfarlandpub.com

Table of Contents I: Candidates and Parties [By Sheet Music Code]

Acknowledgments iv
Table of Contents I: Candidates and Parties [By Sheet Music Code] v
Table of Contents II: Candidates and Parties, in Order of Candidacy vii
Table of Contents III: Candidates and Parties, Alphabetically ix
Preface xi
Key to Symbols and Abbreviations xvi
Music and the Presidency: A Brief History 1

The Catalog of Sheet Music: Candidates and Parties [By Sheet Music Code]

Alton B. Parker (ABP)	33
Alfred E. Smith (AES)	34
Andrew Jackson (AJK)	42
Andrew Johnson (AJN)	48
Abraham Lincoln (AL)	51
Alfred M. Landon (AML)	100
Anti-Masonic Party (AMP)	104
Adlai E. Stevenson II (AS)	104
Benjamin F. Butler (BFB)	106
Benjamin F. Harrison (BFH)	108
Barry M. Goldwater (BMG)	121
Chester A. Arthur (CAA)	122
Clinton B. Fisk (CBF)	124
Calvin Coolidge (CC)	124
Charles E. Hughes (CEH)	131
Communist Party (CP)	132
Douglas A. MacArthur (DAM)	132
Dwight D. Eisenhower (DDE)	138
Daniel Webster (DW)	150
De Witt Clinton (DWC)	153
Eugene V. Debs (EVD)	154
Franklin D. Roosevelt (FDR)	155
Franklin Pierce (FP)	199
George H.W. Bush (GB)	200
George B. McClellan (GBM)	201
(Stephen) Grover Cleveland (GC)	210
George C. Wallace (GCW)	227
Gerald R. Ford (GRF)	228
George S. McGovern (GSM)	229
George Washington (GW)	230
Henry A. Wallace (HAW)	295

Table of Contents I

Henry Clay (HC)	297	Miscellaneous (MISC)	404
Herbert C. Hoover (HCH)	308	Michael S. Dukakis (MSD)	424
Horace Greeley (HG)	315	Martin Van Buren (MVB)	424
Hubert H. Humphrey (HHH)	319	Nathaniel Banks (NB)	426
Henry Krajewski (HK)	320	Neal Dow (ND)	426
Horatio Seymour (HS)	320	Peter Cooper (PC)	427
Harry S Truman (HST)	322	Prohibition Party (PP)	427
John Adams (JA)	326	Rutherford B. Hayes (RBH)	428
James A. Garfield (JAG)	329	Robert M. La Follette (RML)	435
James Buchanan (JB)	341	Richard M. Nixon (RMN)	436
John Bell (JBL)	344	Ross Perot (RP)	441
James Birney (JBR)	345	Ronald Reagan (RR)	441
James B. Weaver (JBW)	346	Stephen A. Douglas (SAD)	446
John C. Breckenridge (JCB)	348	Silas C. Swallow (SCS)	448
John C. Fremont (JCF)	348	Samuel J. Tilden (SJT)	448
Jefferson Davis (JD)	353	Socialist Labor Party (SLP)	451
James E. Carter (JEC)	360	Socialist Party (SP)	452
John F. Kennedy (JFK)	361	Thomas E. Dewey (TED)	453
James G. Blaine (JGB)	370	Thomas Jefferson (TJ)	457
John G. Schmitz (JGS)	380	Theodore Roosevelt (TR)	465
James K. Polk (JKP)	381	Ulysses S. Grant (USG)	506
Joshua Levering (JL)	383	Walter F. Mondale (WFM)	535
James M. Cox (JMC)	383	Warren G. Harding (WGH)	535
James Madison (JMD)	385	William H. Harrison (WHH)	542
James Monroe (JMN)	387	William H. Taft (WHT)	557
John M. Palmer (JMP)	390	William J. Bryan (WJB)	564
John Q. Adams (JQA)	390	William J. Clinton (WJC)	573
James R. Cox (JRC)	391	William Lemke (WL)	575
Jacob S. Coxey (JSC)	392	Wendell L. Willkie (WLW)	575
John St. John (JSJ)	392	William McKinley (WM)	582
John Tyler (JT)	393	Winfield Scott (WS)	616
John W. Davis (JWD)	394	Winfield S. Hancock (WSH)	621
Lyndon B. Johnson (LBJ)	395	(Thomas) Woodrow Wilson (WW)	626
Lewis Cass (LC)	399		
Lester G. Maddox (LGM)	400	Zachary Taylor (ZT)	652
Millard Fillmore (MF)	400		

Appendix: Publishers by City	660
Bibliography	710
Title Index	712
Composer Index	766

Table of Contents II: Candidates and Parties, in Order of Candidacy

Acknowledgments	iv
Table of Contents I: Candidates and Parties [By Sheet Music Code]	v
Table of Contents II: Candidates and Parties, in Order of Candidacy	vii
Table of Contents III: Candidates and Parties, Alphabetically	ix
Preface	xi
Key to Symbols and Abbreviations	xvi
Music and the Presidency: A Brief History	1

The Catalog of Sheet Music: Candidates and Parties, in Order of Candidacy

Major Party Candidates

George Washington (GW)	230
John Adams (JA)	326
Thomas Jefferson (TJ)	457
De Witt Clinton (DWC)	153
James Madison (JMD)	385
James Monroe (JMN)	387
John Q. Adams (JQA)	390
Andrew Jackson (AJK)	42
Martin Van Buren (MVB)	424
William H. Harrison (WHH)	542
John Tyler (JT)	393
Henry Clay (HC)	297
James K. Polk (JKP)	381
Lewis Cass (LC)	399
Zachary Taylor (ZT)	652
Millard Fillmore (MF)	400
Winfield Scott (WS)	616
Franklin Pierce (FP)	199
John C. Fremont (JCF)	348
James Buchanan (JB)	341
Stephen A. Douglas (SAD)	446
George B. McClellan (GBM)	201
Abraham Lincoln (AL)	51
Andrew Johnson (AJN)	48
Horatio Seymour (HS)	320
Horace Greeley (HG)	315
Ulysses S. Grant (USG)	506
Samuel J. Tilden (SJT)	448
Rutherford B. Hayes (RBH)	428
Winfield S. Hancock (WSH)	621

Table of Contents II

James A. Garfield (JAG)	329	George H.W. Bush (GB)	200
Chester A. Arthur (CAA)	122	William J. Clinton (BC)	573
James G. Blaine (JGB)	370		
Benjamin F. Harrison (BFH)	108	***Minor Party Candidates***	
(Stephen) Grover Cleveland (GC)	210	Anti-Masonic Party (AMP)	104
William J. Bryan (WJB)	564	Daniel Webster (DW)	150
William McKinley (WM)	582	James Birney (JBR)	345
Alton B. Parker (ABP)	33	John C. Breckenridge (JCB)	348
Theodore Roosevelt (TR)	465	John Bell (JBL)	344
William H. Taft (WHT)	557	Jefferson Davis (JD)	353
Charles E. Hughes (CEH)	131	Nathaniel Banks (NB)	426
(Thomas) Woodrow Wilson (WW)	626	Peter Cooper (PC)	427
		Socialist Labor Party (SLP)	451
James M. Cox (JMC)	383	Neal Dow (ND)	426
Warren G. Harding (WGH)	535	Benjamin F. Butler (BFB)	106
John W. Davis (JWD)	394	Clinton B. Fisk (CBF)	124
Calvin Coolidge (CC)	124	Prohibition Party (PP)	427
Alfred E. Smith (AES)	34	John St. John (JSJ)	392
Herbert C. Hoover (HCH)	308	James B. Weaver (JBW)	346
Alfred M. Landon (AML)	100	Joshua Levering (JL)	383
Wendell L. Willkie (WLW)	575	Socialist Party (SP)	452
Franklin D. Roosevelt (FDR)	155	John M. Palmer (JMP)	390
Thomas E. Dewey (TED)	453	Silas C. Swallow (SCS)	448
Harry S Truman (HST)	322	Eugene V. Debs (EVD)	154
Adlai E. Stevenson II (AS)	104	Robert M. La Follette (RML)	435
Dwight D. Eisenhower (DDE)	138	Jacob S. Coxey (JSC)	392
John F. Kennedy (JFK)	361	James R. Cox (JRC)	391
Barry M. Goldwater (BMG)	121	William Lemke (WL)	575
Lyndon B. Johnson (LBJ)	395	Communist Party (CP)	132
Hubert H. Humphrey (HHH)	319	Henry A. Wallace (HAW)	295
George S. McGovern (GSM)	229	Douglas A. MacArthur (DAM)	132
Richard M. Nixon (RMN)	436	Henry Krajewski (HK)	320
Gerald R. Ford (GRF)	228	George C. Wallace (GCW)	227
James E. Carter (JEC)	360	John G. Schmitz (JGS)	380
Walter F. Mondale (WFM)	535	Lester G. Maddox (LGM)	400
Ronald Reagan (RR)	441	Ross Perot (RP)	441
Michael S. Dukakis (MSD)	424	Miscellaneous (MISC)	404

Appendix: Publishers by City	660
Bibliography	710
Title Index	712
Composer Index	766

Table of Contents III: Candidates and Parties, Alphabetically

Acknowledgments iv
Table of Contents I: Candidates and Parties [By Sheet Music Code] v
Table of Contents II: Candidates and Parties, in Order of Candidacy vii
Table of Contents III: Candidates and Parties, Alphabetically ix
Preface xi
Key to Symbols and Abbreviations xvi
Music and the Presidency: A Brief History 1

The Catalog of Sheet Music: Candidates and Parties, Alphabetically

Adams, John (JA)	326
Adams, John Q. (JQA)	390
Anti-Masonic Party (AMP)	104
Arthur, Chester A. (CAA)	122
Banks, Nathaniel (NB)	426
Bell, John (JBL)	344
Birney, James (JBR)	345
Blaine, James G. (JGB)	370
Breckenridge, John C. (JCB)	348
Bryan, William J. (WJB)	564
Buchanan, James (JB)	341
Bush, George H.W. (GB)	200
Butler, Benjamin F. (BFB)	106
Carter, James E. (JEC)	360
Cass, Lewis (LC)	399
Clay, Henry (HC)	297
Cleveland, (Stephen) Grover (GC)	210
Clinton, William J. (WJC)	573
Clinton, De Witt (DWC)	153
Communist Party (CP)	132
Coolidge, Calvin (CC)	124
Cooper, Peter (PC)	427
Cox, James M. (JMC)	383
Cox, James R. (JRC)	391
Coxey, Jacob S. (JSC)	392
Davis, Jefferson (JD)	353
Davis, John W. (JWD)	394
Debs, Eugene V. (EVD)	154
Dewey, Thomas E. (TED)	453
Douglas, Stephen A. (SAD)	446
Dow, Neal (ND)	426
Dukakis, Michael S. (MSD)	424
Eisenhower, Dwight D. (DDE)	138

Table of Contents III

Fillmore, Millard (MF)	400	Monroe, James (JMN)	387
Fisk, Clinton B. (CBF)	124	Nixon, Richard M. (RMN)	436
Ford, Gerald R. (GRF)	228	Palmer, John M. (JMP)	390
Fremont, John C. (JCF)	348	Parker, Alton P. (APB)	33
Garfield, James A. (JAG)	329	Perot, Ross (RP)	441
Goldwater, Barry M. (BMG)	121	Pierce, Franklin (FP)	199
Grant, Ulysses S. (USG)	506	Polk, James K. (JKP)	381
Greeley, Horace (HG)	315	Prohibition Party (PP)	427
Hancock, Winfield S. (WSH)	621	Reagan, Ronald (RR)	441
Harding, Warren G. (WGH)	535	Roosevelt, Franklin D. (FDR)	155
Harrison, Benjamin F. (BFH)	108	Roosevelt, Theodore (TR)	465
Harrison, William H. (WHH)	542	St. John, John (JSJ)	392
Hayes, Rutherford B. (RBH)	428	Schmitz, John G. (JGS)	380
Hoover, Herbert C. (HCH)	308	Scott, Winfield (WS)	616
Hughes, Charles E. (CEH)	131	Seymour, Horatio (HS)	320
Humphrey, Hubert H. (HHH)	319	Smith, Alfred E. (AES)	34
Jackson, Andrew (AJK)	42	Socialist Labor Party (SLP)	451
Jefferson, Thomas (TJ)	457	Socialist Party (SP)	452
Johnson, Andrew (AJN)	48	Stevenson II, Adlai E. (AS)	104
Johnson, Lyndon B. (LBJ)	395	Swallow, Silas C. (SCS)	448
Kennedy, John F. (JFK)	361	Taft, William H. (WHT)	557
Krajewski, Henry (HK)	320	Taylor, Zachary (ZT)	652
La Follette, Robert M.(RML)	435	Tilden, Samuel J. (SJT)	448
Landon, Alfred M. (AML)	100	Truman, Harry S (HST)	322
Lemke, William (WL)	575	Tyler, John (JT)	393
Levering, Joshua (JL)	383	Van Buren, Martin (MVB)	424
Lincoln, Abraham (AL)	51	Wallace, George C. (GCW)	227
MacArthur, Douglas A. (DAM)	132	Wallace, Henry A. (HAW)	295
Maddox, Lester G. (LGM)	400	Washington, George (GW)	230
Madison, James (JMD)	385	Weaver, James B. (JBW)	346
McClellan, George B. (GBM)	201	Webster, Daniel (DW)	150
McGovern, George S. (GSM)	229	Willkie, Wendell L. (WLW)	575
McKinley, William (WM)	582	Wilson, (Thomas) Woodrow (WW)	626
Miscellaneous (MISC)	404		
Mondale, Walter F. (WFM)	535		

Appendix: Publishers by City	660
Bibliography	710
Title Index	712
Composer Index	766

Preface

> "Was it not burning as with a red-hot iron when Whig songs were so riveted upon the mind of hard-shell Democrats, that they can correctly quote from memory, that which was so distasteful after a lapse of forty-eight years? When men, women, and children did nothing but sing.... The writer can remember of many wives and daughters of Democrats joining in the singing, and how mad the husbands and fathers were, and ... all to no purpose; the singing went on..."
>
> A.B. Norton in 1888, on the Campaign of 1840

In this hectic and news hungry world of the 21st century, it is difficult to conceive of a time when the front page of the daily newspaper was filled with poetry and music and the principal forms of mass political and social communication were books, periodicals, pamphlets, and published sheet music. This was, nevertheless, the America of little more than a hundred years ago.

Historians studying pre-electronic politics have traditionally interpreted the thoughts and actions of that era through contemporary printed word, principally books, periodicals, letters, diaries, and speeches. There is, however, one source of printed material that has not received as much attention and scholarship as might be expected considering that such a large quantity of material is available. That source is published music, i.e. sheet music, song books, songsters, and broadside ballads.

What research on political music has been undertaken, by and large, has been confined to the music of the American Revolution, the Civil War, and those politicians directly involved in each. *Songs and Ballads of the American Revolution* (1855) by Frank Moore, *Uncertain Glory: Folklore and the American Revolution* (1971) by Tristram Potter Coffin, and *The Singing Sixties* by Willard A. and Porter W. Heaps are good examples of such works. Music scholarship on our political system in general, and on our presidents in particular, is more difficult to find.

Early works that touch on political themes include Lester Levy's *Grace Notes in American History* (1967) and *A History of Popular Music in America* (1948) by Sigmund Spaeth. In her 1975 study of American patriotic music entitled *Music for Patriots, Politicians, and Presidents: Harmonies and Discords of the First Hundred Years* (1975), Vera

Brodsky Lawrence combined narrative, illustration, and lyrics to paint a broad picture of such music and its role in the American political arena. In 1971, Irwin Silber's *Songs America Voted By* took an exclusive look at the presidential-related song, systematically following the history of the campaign song from election to election, from George Washington to Richard Nixon. As limited chronological reviews, both the Silber and Lawrence works provide only a glimpse of the wealth of material available to researchers and historians.

More complete, though limited exclusively to songbooks and songsters, is William Mills' 1990 book *Songs, Odes, Glees and Ballads: A Bibliography of American President Campaign Songsters*. Mills' work is the first dealing with political music in an exhaustive manner, albeit a limited focus.

It is the goal of this present work to present a comprehensive listing of all of the thousands of pieces of Presidential-related music, in all forms, that are available. It is my hope that through knowledge of their existence, additional scholarship will be initiated utilizing these resources, expanding our understanding of political communication and discourse throughout American history.

In order to provide an identifiable reference to each candidate, a system of sheet music codes has been employed in the organization of the book. The letters in the alphanumeric code generally follow the candidate's initials (e.g., the code for Abraham Lincoln is "AL"). The number part of the coding system provides a unique address within the candidate code.

There are three tables of contents and multiple indices provided so that the user may choose the method of reference that is easiest. The collector may be most used to thinking about this sheet music in chronological terms, so an alternate table of contents has been provided in the order of the candidacy with the minor party candidates in a separate sequence from the major party candidates. To serve the general reader, the book has been arranged so that the user can go straight from the indexing (alphanumeric entry codes) to the catalog and quickly find what they need without having to know anything besides the entry code. Both the general reader and the sheet music collector may also use an alternate table of contents that is organized alphabetically by the candidate's last name. To access a specific known place, an alphabetical title index is provided at the end of the book.

Every effort has been made to make this work as comprehensive as possible; however, given the strictures of time, space and funding under which this work was produced, and the several audiences it was designed to reach, certain compromises were made as to both form and content. I sincerely hope that these limitations will be only minor irritations to the vast majority of readers for whom this work was conceived.

Most of the music illustrated in this catalogue was reviewed firsthand; however in some cases, documentation of an item's existence was limited to a review of a photocopy of the cover only or to a photograph found in a collectors publication or auction catalog. In a few instances, reference to a piece of music was taken from another catalog or sales list only. Whatever the circumstance, each entry is as complete as was possible given the availability of the source material.

Music Included in This Catalogue

• Music which illustrates on its cover, names in its title or is dedicated to a President (including Jefferson Davis) or Vice President. This includes music published prior, during and after the individual held office, and memorial and other posthumous music.

• Music which illustrates on its cover, names in its title, or, is dedicated to a candidate for President or Vice President, including third parties, and those for whom votes were cast in Electoral balloting.

• Music which illustrates on its cover, names in its title, or, is dedicated to a member of the immediate family of either of the above.

• Music which illustrates on its cover, names in its title or is dedicated to a hopeful or a fantasy candidate for President or Vice President *and* the title, cover illustration or dedication indicates the race for the Presidency.

• Music about a Presidential party (Democratic, Republican, Whig, Prohibition, etc.).

• Individual songs per the above that are contained in otherwise non-political songsters and song books. Partisan political songsters are cataloged under the appropriate individual or party.

• Songs printed in newspapers or magazines when they contain musical notation.

Music Not Included in This Catalogue

• Music in which a verse(s) is about a person or party, but does not indicate this in the title, dedication or in the cover illustration.

• Individual song contents of political songsters, song books and song sheets.

• Music generally associated with a particular President, but for which no "special edition" meeting the criteria was published.

• Songs printed in newspapers or magazines where a "Tune" or "Air" is indicated in lieu of musical notation.

Although music falling within these latter categories is generally not listed in the catalogue, a limited number of exceptions have been made. These exceptions fall into one of two groupings:

(1) Where little music of any type exists for a particular individual, in order to give the user of the catalogue a feel for the man and his environment through song, a limited amount of material otherwise beyond the scope of the catalogue was included, and

(2) Where a particular piece of music illustrates a significant concept, theme, or other important aspect concerning an individual which, if left out, would significantly detract from the overall musical-related history of the individual, it was included.

Below are a few examples of these exceptions along with the reasoning behind their inclusion:

• Example #1: JKP-1: ***La Polka***: This piece is a non-illustrated song about the dance — the polka. It does however, contain one verse about President Polk,

Preface

making use of the coincidence of the dance's name and his. This piece was included primarily due to the paucity of Polk-related music.

- Example #2: GW-55: **Hail Columbia**: It is generally accepted that this song was written for George Washington and is so closely associated with him that to omit it from the catalogue would seriously distort the record of music associated with him.
- Example #3: GRF-2: **Win**: While this piece is not linked to President Ford by specific reference, its relationship to him is nonetheless direct. The "Whip Inflation Now" campaign was started by Ford in response to the double-digit inflation of the mid-1970s. Because of his short tenure in the White House, the inclusion of this piece provides critical insight into his musical legacy.

In order to provide continuity and preclude repetition of certain statistical data, certain editorial assumptions have been incorporated into the catalog. These are listed below and generally apply unless otherwise noted.

(1) Music before 1919 is approximately 10¾" × 13¾".

(2) Music from 1919 to the present is approximately 9" × 12".

(3) Copyright is held by the publisher.

(4) Date given is the copyright date, not the publishing date.

(5) Sheet music with multiple songs listed *on* the cover, or where only the title changes from one cover to another, are generally identified as sub-numbers of one reference number: BFH-12(A), (B), (C).

(6) Editions which are identical except for color, publisher, size or non-music related content such as advertising, are generally identified by variation numbers: [V-1: Published by Lee & Walker] [V-2: Published by Oliver Ditson].

(7) Non-illustrated covers are black and white unless otherwise noted.

(8) The following criteria are used to determine placement of music with multiple Presidents or candidates named or illustrated:

A. Even though a piece of music lists, names or illustrates several persons, it was obviously written for a specific person. For example: **WW-22: *I Think We've Got Another Washington And Wilson Is His Name***. This song relates to both Washington and Wilson but, as a WWI song, it directly relates to Wilson, thus is listed there. (*Note*: As with all multiple person covers, a cross reference is provided at the end of each section.)

B. Even though a piece of music lists, names in its title or illustrates an earlier President, it is dedicated to a current individual. For example: **GBM-10: *The Flag Of Washington*** is "Dedicated to Maj. Gen. George B. McClellan." Since the reference to Washington is secondary to its contemporary purpose of promoting McClellan, it is listed under McClellan.

C. Even though a song lists or illustrates several people, it was written for an event or purpose contemporary with a specific person. For example: **WW-31: *We're Bound To Win With Boys Like You***. This piece illustrates Washington, Grant, and Wilson, but is a WWI piece and directly relates to Wilson.

D. When multiple candidates are illustrated, the item is listed under the winning candidate. For example: **WM-5:** *1900 Campaign March*, illustrates William Jennings Bryan and William McKinley. It is listed under McKinley as he won that year.

E. In the absence of a specific purpose or event linking a song to a particular person, it is generally listed under the earliest individual such as **GW-271:** *Mr. Yankee Doodle Are We Prepared?* which illustrates Washington and Jackson but is not directly related to either.

F. In some instances, the relationship is so remote that the item has been listed in the Miscellaneous section. For example: **GW-275:** *Mt. Rushmore Memorial March*. This piece illustrates the four presidents on Mt. Rushmore but has no special relationship to the term of any specific President.

G. In the case of Vice-Presidents, they are listed under the President or candidate with whom they served or ran unless rule (H) below applies. For example: **FDR-104:** *Cactus Jack*. John (Jack) Garner was FDR's Vice President and was never nominated on his own, thus it is listed under Roosevelt.

H. In the case of a Vice-President who later became President or who was a nominee on his own at a different time, the piece is listed under his own Presidential listing unless it also shares a title or illustration with the earlier Presidential candidate. For example **AJN-11:** *The Wreath*, a Gubernatorial item for Andrew Johnson is listed under Johnson and not Lincoln; but **AL-91:** *Liberty's Call Or Hurrah For Abraham & Andy*, an Andrew Johnson vice-presidential item that names both Lincoln and Johnson in the title, thus is listed under Lincoln.

I. General party music that can be related to a specific campaign or individual is listed under the Presidential listing during which it was copyrighted. For example: **WW-117:** *When You're All In Down And Out*. This piece is "Dedicated to the Democratic Administration in Washington" and copyrighted during the Wilson years, thus it is listed under Wilson. If such general party music cannot be related to a specific administration or candidate, it is listed in the Miscellaneous section.

J. Third party music has been catalogued by candidate and listed in a separate section following the main candidates.

K. Music associated with hopeful and fantasy candidates is listed in a Miscellaneous section at the end of the catalogue. Only hopefuls for which a special "For President" edition of the music was published are listed. For example: **MISC-7:** *Our Bonus And Our Beer*. This song was written about Royal S. Copeland, Senator from New York, for his abortive attempt to secure the 1924 Democratic nomination. On the cover of the music it states "Copeland Is Our Choice For President."

Also included in the Miscellaneous section is material of a more generic nature related to the Presidency. This includes music about the White House, the Presidency in general, political party music that could not be related to any specific individual or election and music about First Ladies in general.

Key to Symbols and Abbreviations

General Key

a.	Arranged by
ab.	About
Adm.	Admiral
Adv.	Advertisement
Ave.	Avenue
Bet.	Between
Bro.	Brother
Bros.	Brothers
c.	Compiled by
ca.	Circa
Co.	Company
Cor.	Corner
Corp.	Corporation
Demo.	Democratic
e.	Edited by
Eng.	Engraving
Etc.	Etcetera
Hon.	Honorable
Inc.	Incorporated
Incl.	Including
Ltd.	Limited
m.	Music by
Obv:	Obverse (Front)
Op. ###	Opus number
Opp.	Opposite
pp.	Pages
Pub.	Publishing
Repub.	Republican
Rev.	Revised
Rev:	Reverse (Back)
Sq.	Square
St.	Street
Sts.	Streets
U.S.	United States
w.	Words by
&	And
&c	Etcetera
[ ]	Information not found on the music itself
( )	Information found on music
" "	Quoted exactly as on music
' '	Quote within a quote or emphasis as on music

Color Key

Be	Beige
Bk	Black
Bl	Blue
B/w	Black & White
Br	Brown
Gd	Gold
Gn	Green
Gy	Grey
Ma	Maroon
N/c	Natural Color
O	Orange
Pk	Pink
Pl	Purple
R	Red
R/w/b	Red, White & Blue
S	Silver
W	White
Y	Yellow

Reference Key

[S/U, p.#]   Sonneck/Upton Reference: Sonneck, Oscar George Theodore, and William Treat Upton. *A Bibliography of Early Secular Music [18th Century]*. Washington: Library of Congress, 1945.

[W-####]   Wolfe Reference: Wolfe, Richard J. *Secular Music in America 1801–1825 (A Bibliography)*. New York: New York Public Library, 1964.

[H-###]   Hoogerwerf, Frank W. *Confederate Sheet-Music Imprints*. Brooklyn: Brooklyn College, 1984.

[M-###]   Mills, William. *Songs, Odes, Glees and Ballads: A Bibliography of American President Campaign Songsters*. Westport: Greenwood Press, 1990.

Music and the Presidency: A Brief History

Cataloging sheet music has always proceeded on the basic assumption that its value lies principally in either the music itself, or its relationship to the composer. While this is certainly true enough for classical and sacred music, it is not always the case with secular sheet music. To those involved in the methodical world of music cataloging, the notion that the actual music or composer is of little or no value per se can be quite unsettling, but to those involved in the collecting of old sheet music, it comes as no surprise at all. With some notable exceptions both as to musical content and authorship, the real historical value of most secular sheet music is to be found on the cover or in the subject matter of the work, and not necessarily in its musical content.

Two trends in music publication had begun to surface by the late 1700s. First was the rise of socially significant lyrics. Beginning with the *Liberty Song* in 1768, music began to be a force in stirring the soul. By the 1840s, a catchy tune and lyrics that spoke to the heart (or the prejudices as the case may be) soon became inseparable from the American political campaign.

Concurrent with this development was the increasing use of attractive, illustrated sheet music covers. By the early 1800s, enterprising politicians and their supporters realized that a well placed illustration of their candidate on the cover of a piece of music might be a good way to boost his cause. By the mid 1800s, the sheet music cover had become a major component of pre-industrial mass media.

Until recently, much of this interesting and historically significant material has been lost in the archives of libraries and museums, catalogued (if at all) in ways that made it virtually impossible to locate items by their subject matter. *Presidential Sheet Music* is the first book to offer a new way of looking at these American musical resources. Dozens of other important musical subjects remain to be culled from the files of libraries and collectors and organized in such a way as to facilitate scholarship. The great social movements and historical events such as abolition, suffrage, prohibition, temperance, war, the rise of the Ku Klux Klan, the coming of automobile, sports events and many, many more all cry for scholarly attention.

Another virtually untapped subject which is just waiting to be mined from old sheet music is the cover illustration and its associated artist. For example, two of America's greatest artists began their careers as sheet music illustrators — James Whistler and Winslow Homer. Add to this the likes of Rockwell, Flagg, Armstrong, Vargas, De Tackas, Barbelle and Pfiffer, and you begin to understand the potential resources available.

Historians should delight in the compilation of such a vast body of virtually unknown material. It is hoped that *Presidential Sheet Music* will expand the study of the American presidency. It also adds a new dimension to the study of published music, and in particular, its non-musical attributes.

Major Party Candidates

THE LIBERTY SONG

Music in America did not always play a socio-political role in everyday life. From the 17th to the mid-18th centuries, published music was predominately sacred in nature. What secular music there was generally originated in Europe, mainly England and Ireland, and dealt principally with sentimental subject matter. It wasn't until the 1760's and the hated Stamp Act that music began to assume an American socio-political character. With the publication of **The Liberty Song** in 1768, music formally became an instrument of political expression in America.

The continuing deterioration of relations between the Colonies and England, and the repression of political dissent gradually led to music as a principal outlet for political expression. Old English folk songs were appropriated and given new anti-English or pro-American lyrics. By the time the country entered into war with England, the political ballad was an established fixture in the Revolutionary arsenal.

It should come as no surprise that America's first political superstar — George Washington — would have been the subject of many of these tunes. Music written for and about Washington first appeared during the Revolutionary War, usually in the form of new verses added to existing tunes such as **Yankee Doodle** and **God Save The King**; however, new songs specifically praising Washington were also to be found. Since sheet music in the form we know it today was not yet common, most of these early songs were printed on single page leafs known as "broadsides," or were printed in newspapers, almanacs, and magazines.

Washington's inauguration in 1789 provided the first post-war occasion of importance celebrated in music. These early songs and marches gave expression to the country's gratitude toward Washington and to the hope of a new nation under his guidance.

One of the first tunes written specifically for President Washington was entitled **Chorus Sung Before Gen. Washington** and was composed by Alexander Renegale. It was published in sheet music form and included this inscription printed after the title: "Sung before Gen. Washington as he passed under the Triumphal Arch raised on the bridge at Trenton, April 21st, 1789..." It provides the earliest reported use of music linked to a presidential event.

The most popular of musical compositions dating from the Federal period was **The President's March** composed by Philip Phile. Written around 1793, it was an instant success. In 1798, Judge Joseph Hopkinson added appropriate lyrics and the resulting piece was renamed **Hail Columbia**. It became so popular that it served as our nation's unofficial national anthem for over one hundred years.

Because of Washington's unique place in American history, virtually every facet of his life has been celebrated in music over the past 200 years. His birthday was first celebrated musically in 1793 when A. Stoddard wrote **The President's Birth Day Ode** to the tune of **God Save The King**. Virtually every major anniversary of his birth since has been an occasion for new musical expression. **The Baltimore Centennial March** by George F. Cole, **Washington's Birthday March (And Quickstep)** by Edward L. White, **Washington's Grand Centennial March** by Oliver Shaw and **Grand Centennial March** by Adolph Schmitz are a few examples from the 1832 celebration.

The 200th anniversary celebration of his birth in 1932 spawned even more musical tributes including some by the era's most famous songwriters such as **George Washington Bicentennial March** by John Philip Sousa, and **Father Of The Land We Love** by George M. Cohan. The latter was published by The United States George Washington Bicentennial Commission and featured a cover illustration of Washington by the great American illustrator James Montgomery Flagg.

The expression of patriotism during time of war is vital to any nation's morale. Music has consistently played an important role in bolstering the morale both on the battlefield and the homefront. These times have also been fertile events for musically evoking memories of the great Washington. While this was a common practice during all of our nation's military episodes, World War I represented the peak of this phenomenon, coming as it did near the end of the pre-radio era and at the mid-point of the Tin Pan Alley publishing rage.

Examples of such songs are numerous: The cover of **From Valley Forge To France** by Mary Earl depicts modern American soldiers being led by Washington on horseback; **It Must Be The Spirit Of '76** by William Jerome and Arthur N. Green features cover drawings of a World War I soldier and sailor and a vignette of George Washington; and **Just Like Washington Crossed The Delaware, General Pershing Will Cross The Rhine** by Howard Johnson and George W. Meyer uses a cover photograph of General John Pershing, commander of the American forces in Europe, superimposed over the famous Emanuel Leutze painting of George Washington crossing the Delaware River.

STAR SPANGLED MELODY

In addition to **Hail Columbia**, a second important presidential-related song was composed in the year 1798. This was **Adams And Liberty** by Thomas Paine. As was the custom of the day, Paine set his words to the melody of an existing song. In this case, he used an old English tune called **Anacrean In Heaven**. With the subsequent popularity of **Adams And Liberty**, other songwriters borrowed the melody again and again. Fourteen years later, it was the use of that same melody, in combination with Frances Scott Key's poem *In Defense Of Fort McHenry*, that gained it timeless fame as **The Star Spangled Banner**.

JEFFERSON AND LIBERTY

From the earliest days of the Washington administration, two distinct political factions began to emerge in American politics. The first, known as "Federalists," included John Adams and Alexander Hamilton. The second, referred to as "Republicans" or "Democratic-Republicans" included Thomas Jefferson and James Madison. If there is any doubt that a party system was developing, one only has to look at the music of the times to see the polarization and personal animosity developing along these party lines.

By 1800, Federalist sentiment against Thomas Jefferson was so strong that Federalist newspapers constantly slandered his administration and his policies. Personal attacks against him were numerous and vicious. Typical of these attacks is a song from the September 23, 1802, *Boston Gazette* newspaper entitled **A Philosophic Love Song**. It was based on rumors of Jefferson's liaison with one of his slaves, Sally Hemings. As if Jefferson himself were its author, the song declares that "Black's the hue for me!" It is ironic that only a few years earlier, under the Federalists' Alien and Sedition Acts, Jefferson's followers were jailed for speech much milder.

In 1809, James Madison was inaugurated as our fourth President, continuing the Democratic-Republican tradition begun with Jefferson. Although his term of office is principally noted for the War of 1812, his tenure is also important for two musically related milestones. First, and most importantly, our national anthem was written during his administration. The second milestone was Madison's 1809 inauguration itself. This marked the first time that a presidential inaugural ball was held. The event has since become the crown jewel in Washington social circles, spawning dozens of songs and marches over the years. It was reported that at this first ball, both **Jefferson's March** and **Madison's March** were played.

MONROE'S GRAND MARCH

The 1820 election was, in its own way, one of the more interesting in our nation's history. It might be said that it was really a non-election. By this time, the Federalist Party had completely disappeared from the American political scene. A Democratic-Republican Congressional caucus was called to make a nomination, which was the custom at the time, but less than 50 members gathered. Officially, they voted not to make any nomination for President because, in their words, "It was inexpedient to do so." Technically, official slates for Madison were filed with the various states, and in electoral balloting, he received 231 of 232 electoral votes.

THE HUNTERS OF KENTUCKY

Andrew Jackson, the hero of the battle of New Orleans during the War of 1812, was one of those personages who elicited strong feelings among both supporters and detractors. His loss of the presidency to John Quincy Adams in 1824, despite winning a plurality of both the popular votes and the electoral votes, embittered his supporters and ignited one of the ugliest campaigns in American history four years later.

Prior to the 1828 election, running for the Presidency bore little resemblance to campaigning today. Nominations were made by Congressional caucuses, and state presidential electors were chosen by the various state legislatures. While the first, true modern campaign was not until 1840, unmistakable signs of change were evident in 1828. Accusations by the Jackson forces against Adams included such crimes as his "Corrupt Bargain" with Henry Clay that threw the 1824 election to John Quincy Adams, and even charges that Adams had served as a pimp for the Czar of Russia while he was posted there. Jackson on the other hand, was accused by Adams' supporters of murder, being the son of a prostitute, and of being a bigamist (his wife's divorce had not been granted at the time of his marriage).

Aside from the low nature of this and the 1832 campaign, the election of 1828 saw one campaign music milestone — the first use of a "theme" song. As a result of Jackson's heroic victory over the British at the Battle of New Orleans in 1815, numerous songs were written celebrating the victory and the victor. In 1824, using the battle as its theme, William Blondell composed **The Hunters Of Kentucky**. It was reportedly used as the unofficial theme song for Jackson's 1824 campaign and its use during the 1828 campaign was widespread.

TIPPECANOE AND TYLER TOO!

The election of 1840 was a watershed in American political history. It was the first campaign to fully integrate the philosophies and tactics that characterize the modern political campaign, into an active national party strategy. As one Whig contemporary of the time, Thomas Elder, suggested: "Passion and prejudice, properly aroused and directed, would do as well as principle and reason in a party contest."

To say that music ever won an election might be somewhat overstating its role in American political history, but if an argument for this proposition could be made, it would be for the 1840 campaign. To quote an anonymous Democrat of the day, upon losing the election: "We have been sung down, lied down [and] drunk down."

As in the election of 1840, music continued to play an important role in the election of 1844. The previous three years under Whig President John Tyler, a former Democrat, had been marked by continual bickering between Tyler and the Congressional Whigs. It came as no surprise when Henry Clay received a unanimous vote as party nominee over Tyler. New Jersey Senator Theodore Frelinghuysen of New Jersey was chosen as his running mate, inspiring one of the most popular campaign songs ever — **Clay And Frelinghuysen**.

In addition to dozens of popular songs, Clay's music publishers established several important "firsts" in political music publishing history. A pro-Clay songster, **The Kentucky Minstrel and Jersey Warbler**, was the first piece of published campaign music to feature the correct likenesses of both the presidential and vice presidential candidates together on the cover. This is a trend that continues to this day.

A second important publishing first was the use of multi-color lithography, or chromolithography, to illustrate campaign sheet music covers. However, despite all the songs and musical innovations, Clay and Frelinghuysen lost the election to Democratic "dark horse" candidate James K. Polk.

THE ROUGH AND READY QUICK STEP

Having captured the White House in 1844, the Democrats believed that the Whig party was dead. At their 1848 Baltimore convention, they nominated Senator Lewis Cass of Michigan for President and General William O. Butler of Kentucky for Vice President. The idea of the death of the Whig party was evident in a pro-Cass ballad entitled **Freedom Of The Seas**. It graphically depicted a procession of animals marching in the "The funeral of Federal principles" and featured the Whig symbols for the late William H. Harrison (the log cabin), and for Henry Clay (the raccoon), along with the quote: "The remains of the Whig principles of 1840 and 1844." Unfortunately for Cass and Butler, Whig nominee "Old Rough and Ready" Zachary Taylor proved that rumors of the demise of the Whig Party were one election premature.

There is one note of musical importance associated with the Cass and Butler campaign. In 1848, a song called **The Boat Horn**, composed by General William O. Butler and C.H. Thornbecke was published in sheet music form. In this instance, a poem by Butler was set to music by Thornbecke. The published edition featured a black and white lithograph of Gen. Butler on the title page and a dedication to Mrs. James K. Polk. This is the first account of a presidential or vice presidential candidate actually being associated with the composition of a published musical work.

KNOW NOTHING POLKA

The election of 1856 holds a special place in American political history. It marked the end of two major political movements, the Whig Party and the American Party ("Know Nothings). It also marked the beginning of a new major political party—the Republicans.

The "Know Nothings" were originally founded in 1849 as a secret order, complete with all of the usual trappings of secret societies including passwords, secret handshakes and the ceremonial rituals. The Know Nothing movement grew out of the earlier Nativist philosophy of intolerance towards foreigners, Catholics, and other "non-pure," non-American elements. Calling themselves "Sam" and always answering questions with a standard "I Don't Know," they soon became a formidable political power. By 1855, they had elected seven governors, five senators and 43 members of the House of Representatives. In their one and only try for the presidency in 1856, they nominated former President Millard Fillmore to head their ticket. Not surprisingly, most Know Nothing song titles reflected their slogans such as **Where Is Sam** and **I Don't Know**.

Freiheitslied der Deutschen Republikaner

With the demise of the Whigs, the Republican Party was founded in 1854 on the principle of opposition to the extension of slavery. At their first national nominating convention in 1856, western explorer John C. Fremont was given the party's presidential nod. Fremont's popularity, explorations, military service and his party's catchy slogan — "Free Soil, Free Speech, Free Men, Fremont and Victory" — were all easily translated into music.

The 1856 election furnished several interesting developments in political music history. The first was a Fremont campaign song entitled ***Freiheitslied Der Deutschen Republikaner***. It marked the first example of political sheet music designed to appeal to the immigrant vote.

The second involves a significant milestone sheet music cover art. By 1840, much of the political and secular music in America was characterized by the use of a lithographed illustration to adorn the cover pages of individual pieces of sheet music. By mid-century, many music publishers had entered into creative alliances with engraving and lithography firms to provide these illustrations. One of the most respected and well known of these lithography firms at the time was that of John H. Bufford of Boston. In 1856, five of these assignments were given to a young Bufford apprentice. These were: ***Fremont's Great Republican March***, ***There Is A White House Yonder (A Fremont Campaign Song)***, ***Buchanan's Grand Union March***, ***The Wheelbarrow Polka*** (a Buchanan-related piece), and ***The Wreath***, a musical tribute to Governor Andrew Johnson of Tennessee. All of these pieces were profusely illustrated. This young apprentice, at the beginning of his career, was Winslow Homer, the great American artist.

Honest Old Abe

With the approaching Civil War, music took on the urgent cause of trying to keep the county united. Songs such as ***Song Of The Union*** and ***The Constitution*** were dedicated to President Buchanan in a vain hope that they might rally the nation to remain together. But this was not to be.

By the time of the 1860 election, the country was split along regional lines. Abraham Lincoln, the Republican nominee, captured all the northern and western states, while his Democratic rival, Stephen A. Douglas won only Missouri. Two splinter parties headed by John Breckenridge (Southern Democrats) and John Bell (Constitutional Union), carved up the South.

Music played an important role in introducing the public to Abraham Lincoln. Before his nomination, Lincoln was a Congressman of little note outside Washington circles. Many people had not even heard of him, let alone seen him. Tunes such as ***Honest Old Abe, Lincoln Quick Step*** and ***The Wigwam Grand March***, with bold lithographs of a gaunt, serious and beardless Lincoln, were but a few of the many pieces of sheet music that introduced him to the public. Other pieces such as ***Lincoln Quick Step*** by Charles Grobe and ***Republican Song Book*** by Thomas Drew, emphasized Lincoln's simple, hard working background through lithographic images of Lincoln splitting rails and polling a river boat. Probably the most popular of the Lincoln songs was **Lincoln and Liberty**, composed and sung by the abolitionist Hutchinson Family Singers.

By 1864, many believed that Lincoln's popularity had peaked. The North was tired of war and many people still harbored resentment toward Lincoln for his earlier dismissal of General George McClellan as commander of the Union armies. In a late August convention, the Democrats nominated McClellan in the hopes of capitalizing on these dissatisfactions. Though Lincoln himself had doubts as to his re-election chances, McClellan went down in a massive defeat, carrying only the states of New Jersey, Delaware, and Kentucky.

One interesting campaign song for the McClellan ticket was **Little Mac! Little Mac! You're The Very Man**. Although it was attributed to composer Stephen Foster, he had died the previous year. It is more logical to assume that the lyrics were written by his sister to a previously unpublished Foster melody.

Our Brutus

The assassination of Lincoln in 1865 sent shock waves of sorrow throughout the nation. Dozens of funeral marches, laments and dirges were composed in an effort to assuage a grief stricken public. Songs such as **Live But One Moment**, and **Little Tad**, both composed by J.W. Turner, described the poignancy of Mrs. Lincoln's reference to their son Tad in her desperate deathbed attempt to get her husband to speak: "O! Bring our Tad here! for he loves Tad so well that I know he will speak to him." At least four composers wrote memorial music entitled **Oh! Why Should The Spirit Of Mortal Be Proud**, using a line from Lincoln's favorite poem for inspiration.

While most of the nation mourned for their beloved President, not everyone shared this feeling. One particular musical effort stands out in this regard. **Our Brutus** by E.B. Armand (a pseudonym for New Orleans music publisher A.E. Blackmar), praises John Wilkes Booth, who, like Brutus, downed a tyrant. As is noted on an inside page of the sheet music: "This poem was written at the time when it was proposed to bury its illustrious subject [Booth] in the ocean, so that no trace of his resting place could be found by those who might wish to honor his remains." The sheet music cover features a handsome lithograph of Booth.

Upon the death of Lincoln, Vice President Andrew Johnson ascended to the presidency. Initially, Johnson was honored through musical composition. No less that six marches and songs were written and dedicated to him in his first year; however, by 1866, things had changed. The use of the presidential veto became Johnson's weapon of choice to manage a Congress looking to punish the South. One interesting pro-Johnson piece of music features a cover illustration depicting Johnson riding a white horse named "Constitution," trampling on radical Republican Congressmen and abolitionists. The work was aptly named **The Veto Galop!** and was written under the pseudonym of "Make Peace."

More common, however, were songs belittling Johnson. Songs such as ***Andy Veto, Ye Tailor Man*** and ***Where Is Our Moses?*** were composed as ridicule. ***Ye Tailor Man*** by E.W. Foster makes use of Johnson's one time occupation (as a tailor) to mock his policies. On the cover of the sheet music is the following dedication: "Respectfully inscribed to ye DEAD DOG of ye White House." The Moses reference in ***Where Is Our Moses?*** is a satire on former slaves' reference to Lincoln as their Moses, leading them to freedom.

Andrew Johnson's impeachment by the House of Representatives also provided songwriters abundant grist for unsympathetic tunes. One wry tune — ***The Impeachment Polka*** by Charles Blake, used what is generally considered a lighthearted musical form — the polka — to reflect the prevailing mood of the majority in Congress in what one would normally consider a serious circumstance.

Grant Us a Hero

Less than a year before the 1868 election, Ulysses S. Grant, the nation's great war hero, was being considered for the Democratic Party's nomination; however, his break with Andrew Johnson ensured that he would run as a Republican. Grant's Democratic opponent was Horatio Seymour, the wartime Governor of New York. General Francis P. Blair, Jr. of Missouri was Seymour's running mate.

Seymour was known as a Copperhead. Blair on the other hand, had recently broken with the Republicans over his opposition to Radical Reconstruction. This election would be the first opportunity for much of the South to express their feelings in the post war era. One rather chilling campaign song for Seymour and Blair — ***The White Man's Banner*** by F.M. Bigney and Theo. von LaHache, mirrored the feelings of many of their contemporaries in the South.

Grant's musical supporters emphasized his strong points, in particular, his great military victories. Another popular theme was his famous quote: "Let us have Peace." One of the more interesting Grant-related pieces is the ***Mammoth Ox Grand March*** by D. Frank Tully. The sheet music cover features a lithograph of a giant ox named "Gen: Grant." The music was dedicated to the "President-Elect."

The 1872 election is notable for the fact that it is the only time in American history that a nominee for president, Horace Greeley, died prior to electoral balloting. Greeley was both the Liberal Republican Party and Democratic Party candidate for President. For years Greeley had been a critic of the Democrats and, while editor of *The Log Cabin*, had written a number of pro-Whig, pro-Harrison campaign songs during the 1840 election. A number of these 1872 pieces took note of Greeley's trademark white hat. Songs such as George Wiegand's ***Horace Greeley's March***, and Harry Birch's ***Oh Horace*** both featured a cover lithograph of Greeley wearing his hat. H.T. Merrill even published a song titled ***The Old White Hat***.

Centennial Reform March

If one word could be used to characterize the Grant presidency, it was "corruption." Scandal after scandal rocked his appointees. The Democrats, sensing victory in a nation fed up with political immorality, chose "honesty and reform" as their campaign theme for 1876. Their candidate was New York Governor Samuel J. Tilden, fresh from his victory against Tammany Hall's Boss Tweed.

Music associated with the Democratic campaign reflected the reform theme with such tunes as **Honest Sam Tilden**, **Tilden And Reform**, and **Tilden And Hendricks' Centennial Reform March**. However, the most interesting of the Tilden songs is **Tilden And Hendricks' Democratic Centennial Campaign March With Radical Accompaniments** by A. Lutz. Both the front and back covers of the latter are decorated with cartoon-like depictions of various Republican scandals, each with the head of the politician involved set onto the body of an animal (rats were popular). Next to each illustration is an appropriate saying, the most ironic being a twist on Grant's famous quote "Let us have peace," which is altered to read — "Let us have (A) piece" referring to a piece of the graft. In addition to more drawings, the back cover lists over 35 scandals ascribed to the Republicans.

Rutherford B. Hayes and the Republicans also climbed on the reform bandwagon in their campaign. Songs such as **Hurrah For Hayes And Honest Ways** by E.W. Foster and **Hayes The True And Wheeler Too** were direct appeals to separate Hayes from the previous Grant administration. One dramatically illustrated Hayes song — **Roll Along, Roll Along, Shout The Campaign Battle Song** by Thomas Peppergrass and "Y.D." featured a handsome J.H. Bufford's Sons lithograph of a horse-drawn wagon traveling on the road to Washington. Riding on the wagon is Uncle Sam along with a sign that reads: "A Good Honest Load of HAYes on the way to Washington."

Ironically, Tilden was right about the country being ready for a change. For the second time in less than one hundred years, the candidate with the most popular votes lost the election. To make matters worse, this is the first election in our nation's history in which a candidate actually received over 50% of the popular vote and still lost. The South, which had expected a Tilden-Hendricks victory to end Reconstruction, nevertheless got their wish. In an unprecedented deal, General Hayes' congressional supporters agreed to pull Federal troops out of the South in return for allowing the Hayes victory to stand.

Why Should They Kill My Baby?

The election of 1880 did not have the drama of the 1876 campaign. Once again the Republicans, led by James Garfield and Chester Arthur, won; however, out of some nine million votes cast, their winning margin over Democrat Winfield Scott Hancock was by less than 2,000 votes. With both the Democrats and Republicans fielding ex-Civil War generals, much of the political sheet music featured illustrations of the candidates in military uniform and was generally uninspiring. It was Garfield's assassination by Charles Guiteau in 1881 that produced the most interesting music.

As evidenced after Lincoln's assassination, music once again helped a sad nation deal with the loss of their president. ***Slowly And Sadly***, a song by Miss Arabella Root, featured a cover lithograph of both Garfield's mother and his wife. Others repeated this family theme: ***President Garfield Died Last Night, Break The News To His Mother*** by Griswald and Rosewig, ***Why Should They Kill My Baby!*** by W. Carlton and C.T. Coenial and ***Mother In The Doorway Waiting*** by James Murray are good examples. This latter piece featured a drawing of Garfield's mother sitting on her front porch reading the Bible.

Finally, there was a small group of songs that can only be described as representing the more primal urge of an angry nation — revenge. Featuring a spectacular cover illustration, ***The Verdict March*** by Eugene Blake has a full page lithograph of the actual members of the jury that convicted Guiteau. A second piece, ***Guiteau's March To Hades*** by H.W. Stratton, features a pathetic Guiteau being escorted to the gates of hell by the Devil.

Ma, Ma, Where's My Pa

With President Chester Arthur never really in contention for the Republican nomination, the election of 1884 finally provided perennial Republican hopeful James G. Blaine of Maine, with his opportunity to head the ticket. With running mate, General John A. Logan, the father of Memorial Day, they faced off against New York's Democratic Governor, Grover Cleveland and his running mate, Indiana Senator Thomas Hendricks.

Blaine's nickname, "The Plumed Knight," provided great inspiration for sympathetic songwriters. Two pieces composed by the young John Philip Sousa, ***We'll Follow Where The White Plume Waves*** and ***The White Plume March*** along with ***The Plumed Knight Of Maine*** by J.A.M. Harned and Walter Wheeler, are excellent examples of the "plume" genre.

Neither Blaine nor Cleveland forces hesitated to use music for mockery. Cleveland was accused of fathering an illegitimate child and, although he did not admit paternity, he did assume financial responsibility. This was all that the Blaine forces needed. H.R. Monroe captured the affair in the infamous song entitled ***Ma, Ma, Where's My Pa (Up In The White House Dear)***.

Not to be out done, pro-Cleveland songwriter Ben Warren took the old Irish tune ***Mary Blane***, and altered the title to ***Mary Blaine***. The publisher added a satirical illustration of James Blaine in a woman's dress, and numerous graphic reminders of alleged Blaine scandals.

With Cleveland's victory, music related to him soon took a domestic turn. In 1886, he married his former ward — Francis Folsom. This was the first ever White House wedding, and numerous songs and marches were written in honor of the occasion. Tunes such as ***Wedding March*** by Adam Geibel, ***Cleveland's Luck And Love Grand March*** by Miss Ida, and ***President Cleveland's Wedding March*** by Charles D. Blake, helped express the nation's joy and excitement about the event.

One piece of Cleveland wedding music, ***President Grover Cleveland's Wedding March***, deserves special note.

Written by Isidor Witmark, it was reportedly published by him on a basement music press in the Witmark brothers home. Many scholars give this piece of music the distinction of being the first of what would eventually become millions of pieces of music published in New York City's "Tin Pan Alley."

Tippecanoe and Morton Too!

Musically speaking, the 1888 campaign was interesting on both sides. Pro-Republican songwriters attempted to recapture the excitement of the 1840 campaign by dusting off nominee Benjamin Harrison's grandfather's old "Tippecanoe" slogan for reuse. With former New York Congressman, Levi P. Morton as his running mate, "Tippecanoe and Tyler Too" became "Tippecanoe and Morton Too."

With the death of Vice President Thomas Hendricks in 1885, the Democrats chose former Senator Allen Thurman of Ohio to fill the second slot. Thurman's claim to fame was the distinctive red bandanna he used in public to assist in his snuff pinching habit. This colorful symbol adorned a number of music covers including **Waive High The Red Bandana**, **The Grand Old Red Bandana** and **The Old Roman March**, the latter being the 75 year old Thurman's nickname.

The election of 1888 once again proved that popularity was not necessarily enough to be President. Cleveland won the popular vote by over 90,000 votes. Harrison on the other hand, won the all important Electoral vote majority and with it, the election.

However, even in defeat, Cleveland continued to inspire music. In 1891, the ex-First Family had their first child, Ruth Cleveland. This was a national event commemorated in music. One song, **The Coming Woman** by Monroe Rosenfeld, featured a full-cover illustration of the ex-President holding his daughter. A second group of tunes however, helped ensure the event a permanent place in history.

It was a custom of the time to use the term "Baby" as part of the child's name. In this case, the new child became an instant celebrity as "Baby Ruth" Cleveland. Songs such as **Baby Ruth** by T.L. Weaver, **Baby Ruth Schottische** by A. Mirault, and **Baby Ruth's Slumber Song** by George Schleiffarth helped celebrate the occasion and endear her to the public. Baby Ruth died in 1904 at the of age 12, but she was so adored that some 16 years later, the Curtiss Candy Company named a new candy bar in her honor — The Baby Ruth bar.

The 1892 campaign was a rematch of 1888, with President Benjamin Harrison facing ex-President Grover Cleveland. History records the campaign as rather dull, and so too was the musical output. One interesting piece of music was published by the Williams and Carleton Manufacturing Company of Hartford, Connecticut, manufacturer of Williams Extract (Root Beer). The published music took the form of a one-sided broadside with two vertical columns. At the top of each column respectively, was a lithograph of Benjamin Harrison and Grover Cleveland. Below each illustration were lyrics to the same song, with only slight variations to fit the appropriate candidate. Of course, the basic thrust of the lyrics was to show that William's Root Beer was appreciated by both parties.

GIVE US SILVER JOLLY SILVER

Only once in our nation's history has one of the two major parties nominated the same man for President three times and subsequently, he lost each time. This dubious honor belongs to William Jennings Bryan, the Democratic nominee in 1896, 1900 and 1908.

Only 36 years old at the time of the 1896 Democratic convention, initially Bryan was not a serious contender for the nomination. This changed dramatically when, as the final speaker on the debate over whether the party should endorse retention of the gold standard or support the unlimited coinage of silver and gold at the legal ratio of 16 ounces of silver to one ounce of gold, Bryan electrified the convention. He ended his speech with one of the most famous lines in American political oratory: "You shall not press down upon the brow of labor this crown of thorns, you shall not crucify mankind upon a cross of gold." Silver won the day and Bryan won the nomination.

Cries of "Free Silver" and "16-to-1" became synonymous with the Democratic campaign. The **Bryan Free Silver March** by L.M. French, **Give Us Silver, Jolly Silver** by Arnold Watson, **The Silver Knight Of The West** by Lucius West, and **Silver Regiment March** by Annie Pekin, are a few of the many "silver" tunes composed for Bryan. A number of "16-to-1" songs were also composed for the campaign: **Sixteen To One Campaign Song** by Lount and Reid, **Sixteen To One Two-Step** by A.F. Jacobs, and the **Sixteen To One Galop** by F.H. Rollison. The latter featured a cover illustration of a scale with a 16-ounce bar of silver on one side balancing a one-ounce bar of gold on the other.

The Republicans held their convention in St. Louis in June of 1896. A number of candidates were touted as possibilities. Al G. Mark, a local composer and music publisher composed his **Republican National Convention March** for the occasion. The sheet music edition featured a cover illustration of a large American flag with oval portraits of four of the leading candidates: William McKinley, Thomas Reed, William Allison and Levi Morton. Actually, McKinley's selection had been assured long before the June convention. Marcus A. Hanna, McKinley's campaign manager, had been working for over a year securing pledges. By convention time, he had more than enough votes to put McKinley over the top on the first ballot.

McKinley was a popular candidate, especially in the Northeast and upper Midwest. Because of his wife's epilepsy, McKinley spent little time on the campaign trail, preferring instead to hold rallies at his home in Canton, Ohio. His "front porch" campaign proved more than enough for victory. Music for the McKinley campaign reflected the Republican themes of "Sound Money" (maintaining the gold standard), "Protection to American Industries" (high tariff), and the "Full Dinner Bucket" (prosperity).

The lunch pail or dinner bucket was an especially popular theme for Republican composers. A.M. Bruner wrote a tune entitled **The Little Dinner Bucket Song**. It featured a cover illustration of a workingman's lunch pail. Two other "dinner pail" pieces featured actual pictures of the members of local McKinley glee clubs formed to promote the ticket. The cover to *We Are Just From The Mills*, by J. Franklin Gill, uses a drawing of a large mill as backdrop to a drawing of the members of "The Full Dinner Pail Quartette" of Lockport, New York. *The Full Dinner Pail* by Henry Tyrrell features a real photograph of the "McKinley Glee Club, Howard, Kans." On the reverse of the photo are the lyrics to the song.

MACK AND TEDDY

Four years of relative prosperity found the nation feeling pretty good about itself as the election of 1900 approached. Times were good and the nation had just acquired Cuba, Puerto Rico and the Philippine Islands as a result of a short, four month war with Spain. McKinley got the credit.

The most difficult task facing the Republicans was to find a suitable running mate for McKinley as Vice President Garret Hobart had died late the year before. Ultimately, the Party turned to the young Spanish-American War hero, New York Governor Theodore Roosevelt. The choice however, was not made because of his tremendous public popularity or his sweeping reforms while Police Commissioner of New York City or as Governor of New York. To the contrary, he was chosen by the New York Republican Party bosses to get him out of their way. As Republican Senator Thomas Platt stated: "I want to get rid of that bastard. I don't want him raising hell in my state any longer." Roosevelt understood what was happening and fought the nomination as long as possible. Roosevelt is quoted as saying upon his selection: "I do not expect to go any further in politics."

To the public, the choice of Roosevelt was very popular as evidenced by the abundant music written for the campaign. *That's The Ticket March* by Edward Rice, featured bold photographs of the candidates on the cover as did *Mack And Teddy* by Leopold Kessler, and *McKinley And Roosevelt March* by Fred Spencer. One interesting piece of music, *We Are For Bliss* by Harry Zickel, was a campaign song written for Aaron T. Bliss, Republican candidate for Governor of Michigan. On the back cover of this sheet music were portraits of McKinley and Roosevelt. This is the first instance in sheet music format, of a candidate for one office attempting to ride to victory on the coattails of the national ticket. It worked.

YOUNG JOSHUA

On September 13, 1901, a week after being shot by an anarchist while visiting the Pan-American Exposition in Buffalo, President McKinley died. For the third time in less than 40 years, the nation grieved for their President. Meanwhile, shock waves within the Republican establishment had only just begun. To quote Mark Hanna: "Now look, that damned cowboy is President of the United States."

Long before Roosevelt became President, his deeds had been set to music. Over 50 songs and marches celebrated the exploits of his famous Rough Riders during the Spanish-American War. Tunes such as *Gov.*

Roosevelt's Rough Riders March by B.W. Phillips, ***The Hero Of San Juan*** by Nicholson and Arnette, and ***Teddy's Terrors*** by Warner Crosby, quickly helped establish Roosevelt as an American folk hero.

Roosevelt's promise to Mark Hanna that he would carry on the policies of McKinley was short lived. Within months of assuming office, Roosevelt began his campaign against illegal corporate trusts, most of which were controlled by such Republican big money men as J.P. Morgan, John D. Rockefeller, Jay Gould and Edward Harriman among others. Roosevelt's highly public battles with big business garnered him a reputation as the defender of the working man, protector of fair play, and the father of "the square deal." Songs such as ***Young Joshua*** by J.B. Herbert, drawing on a Biblical analogy, ***The Square Deal March And Two Step*** by H. Maybaum and ***Teddy's For The People*** by Benj. F. Nysewander reflect the nation's high regard for Roosevelt as a fighter against the odds.

Presidents and their children were always a popular theme for composers. Roosevelt's children, particularly his daughter Alice, were no exception. In her teens during most of his first term, "Princess Alice" as she was often called, was the essence of the liberated woman. She slid down White House banisters in front of heads of state; she terrorized guests with a live garter snake she liked to carry in her purse; she roller skated in the White House halls; and publicly smoked cigarettes (something no proper lady of the time would do). Once asked why he couldn't control her, Roosevelt's now famous reply was: "I can be President of the United States or I can control Alice. I cannot possibly do both."

Alice was a songwriter's dream. Her popularity with the public, coupled with her 1906 White House wedding, was easily turned into musical profit. ***Daughter Of The Nation*** by Charles Kuebler, ***The American Girl*** by Harold Frankensteen, and ***A Daughter Of Uncle Sam*** by Roger Halle, reflected the nation's love for her and her father. Songs such as ***Alice Blue Waltzes*** by Abbie Ford, ***Alice, The Bride Of The White House*** by Anita Comfort-Brooks, and ***Nick And Alice*** by Berton Maddux, are a sampling of the music composed for her wedding.

No discussion of Theodore Roosevelt would be complete without a mention of his famous 1901 trip to Mississippi to settle a boundary dispute and draw a new state line between the states of Mississippi and Louisiana. While there, he was invited to do a little hunting. Story has it that hunting was not particularly good, so a small bear cub [or malnourished adult] was captured for him to shoot. Roosevelt declined, stating that it was unsportsmanlike.

Clifford Berryman, a noted cartoonist of the day, heard the story and published a cartoon with the double entendre title *Drawing the line in Mississippi*. It featured T.R. in Rough Rider attire, rifle in one hand with the other outstretched signaling a resolute No! to shooting a little bear cub tied to a tree. The nation may not remember Roosevelt for the Panama Canal or his Nobel Peace Prize or his trust-busting campaign, but he will forever be remembered in the heart of every child as the father of the "Teddy Bear." That single event spawned hundreds of Teddy Bear toys, books, postcards, and of course, Teddy Bear music — at least 60 pieces.

From the purely political perspective, at least three Roosevelt-related songs were published featuring Teddy Bears: **Parade Of The Teddy Bears** by George Cobb featured a gorgeous color illustration of a Teddy Bear band marching with their instruments and carrying a large banner with a likeness of T.R. and the phrase — "De-Lighted," one of Roosevelt's most popular sayings. A second piece, associated with his 1912 campaign, was composed by Mildred Hibbs and titled **Teddy's In The Ring**. This piece featured a drawing of a Rough Rider hat and two Teddy Bear cowboys shooting their pistols. The third piece, **Dee-Lighted** by Clinton Kiethley and Charles Musgrove, depicted a grinning Teddy Bear holding the famous Roosevelt "Big Stick."

After leaving office in 1909, Roosevelt began a series of trips abroad, the most celebrated being a big game hunting trip to Africa. As with almost every other aspect of his career, this too generated wide publicity and plenty of music. **Teddy We're Glad Your Here** by Vivian Russell, featured a cover photo of Roosevelt surrounded by wild game animals (who were probably not quite as happy to see the gun-toting Roosevelt as the title suggests). Other interesting songs were: **Since Bwano Tumbo Came From Jumbo Land** by Francis Rivarde, **African Hunter** by Edwin F. Kendall, and **Cannibal Isle** by Olive Fields and Harry Newman.

Roosevelt's final claim to widespread notoriety and musical posterity came, with the election of 1912 and Roosevelt hand-picked a successor for the Republican nomination in 1908, his close friend William H. Taft. He believed that Taft would carry on established Roosevelt programs; however by 1912, Roosevelt had become disillusioned with Taft's policies and, declaring himself "fit as a bull moose," went after Taft for the Republican nomination. Taft however, emerged from the convention with the nomination, so Roosevelt accepted a draft by the new Progressive or "Bull Moose" Party, as it was popularly called.

One song heard over and over at the Progressive Convention was **They Are Calling From The Mountains (We Want Teddy)** by Dan Wall and W.S. Mason. The sheet music edition featured an illustration of a large moose on the cover. The moose was featured prominently on the cover of other pieces as well: **Bull Moose March** by E.P. Hartman, **The Bull Moose Glide** by Will Callahan and Will Morrison, **Bull Moose March** by Brookes Peters and **Triplicity (Or The Donkey, Moose Or Elephant)** by Shelley Sutton and Paul Baltinke. It can be fairly said that no other President or candidate enjoyed a more varied musical legacy than Theodore Roosevelt.

Possum Bill

As the 1908 election approached, Roosevelt felt obligated to honor a 1904 election promise not to seek another term. Instead, his efforts went to securing the nomination and election of his friend William H. Taft. "Bill Big"

Taft, who weighed some 350 pounds, never wanted to be President, and at the end of his four years, was happy to step down. [It wasn't until 1921 that President Warren Harding gave him the one job he really wanted — Chief Justice of the Supreme Court].

Taft's musical legacy is chiefly known for two things. One is the Harry Kerr and Abe Holtzman campaign tune **Get On The Raft With Taft**. Its popularity as the quintessential campaign song has given it a measure of immortality. The other interesting musical theme found in Taft's campaign music revolves around the use of his nickname – "Possum Bill" — as inspiration for "Possum" songs much like Roosevelt and his "Teddy Bear" music. **Possum (The Latest Craze)** by G.A. Scofield and J.B. Cohen, featured two cover vignettes: One of a man eating a possum at the dinner table and another of a possum in front of the White House. Other tunes such as **Billy Possum March** by Bert Lowe and **The Billy Possum Barn Dance** by H.S. Taylor, combined illustrations of possums with Taft's first name.

Wilson Has a Winning Way

As the Democratic National Convention met in Baltimore in June, 1912, most observers believed that House Speaker James Beauchamp "Champ" Clark would secure the nomination. Dr. Woodrow T. Wilson, former President of Princeton University and Governor of New Jersey was his chief rival. On the first ballot, Clark received 440 1/2 votes to Wilson's 324 votes. By the 10th ballot, Clark had secured 556 votes, a majority of the convention, but still short of the two thirds needed for nomination. By the 30th ballot, however, Wilson had surpassed Clark. Finally, on the 46th ballot, the tide broke and Wilson captured the nomination.

Wilson ran on a platform known as "The New Freedom," a progressive theme in which government regulation would free the nation of illegal trusts and monopolies and ensure fair competition in the marketplace. Little music was written for the Democrats in 1912. **Wilson March** by Victor LaSalle, and **March Progressive** by Amy Titus Worthington, are two examples, the latter reflecting Wilson's conversion to the progressive cause.

Wilson's first term had been marked by several spectacular and popular policy successes. He had lowered the high Republican tariff, opening the market to greater competition, created the Federal Reserve System placing the nation's banking system under Federal regulation, and had managed to keep the United States out of the on-going European war despite such German provocations as the sinking of the Lusitania in 1915.

Wilson's second campaign in 1916 against New York's Republican Governor Charles Evans Hughes, produced considerable musical expression, much of which reflected his policy of neutrality. **We'll Vote For The Man Who Kept Us Out Of War** by M.A. Jones, **We Stand For Peace While Others Stand For War** by W.R. Williams, and **Neutrality** composed by J. Patrick Doyle, and "Dedicated to the person and policy of Woodrow Wilson" are good examples of this theme.

In April of 1917, with a final peace effort rebuffed by the Germans, Wilson asked Congress for a declaration of war stating that "The world must be made safe for Democracy." Because he had tried so hard to maintain the peace, he received the nation's support for war. From Tin Pan Alley to Omaha to Indianapolis and Denver, big publishers and small geared up for the home front musical war.

One of the most popular tunes in this genre was **It's Time For Every Boy To Be A Soldier** by Alfred Bryan and Harry Tierney. The cover illustration of this piece featured a drawing of a soldier with vignettes along side of Abraham Lincoln and Woodrow Wilson. **World Wide Democracy March** by William Rehm, and **Where Our Wilson Shines Democracy** by Michael Perna, emphasized the loftier side of the conflict. There were also a number of not-so-serious "novelty" songs such as **When Wilson Called The Kaiser's Bluff** by L.F. Newman, and **Bing! Bang! Bing 'Em On The Rhine** by Jack Mahoney and Allen Flynn.

It is ironic that Wilson's greatest achievement, and his greatest defeat, were one in the same — his proposal for a League of Nations. His tireless efforts and refusal to compromise at having the League's creation incorporated into the Treaty of Versailles which ended the war, garnered him the Nobel Peace Prize, but also cost him his health, his political support, and ultimately League approval itself when the Senate failed to ratify the Treaty.

Surprisingly, a number of songs were penned supporting the League concept, the most famous of these being Lou Spero and Gerald Peck's **Good-Bye, Shot And Shell**. This number was published by Joseph W. Stern, a stalwart of Tin Pan Alley, and featured a large photograph of Wilson and a dedication to Wilson "and his [policy of] peace through [a] League of Nations." Other League-related songs include: **Give Us A League Of Nations** by Jere De Graff, **The American Marseillaise** by Felix Schreiber, and **Hope Of The World — America** by Walter Carruth and Cal O'Chaters.

Gimmy Jimmy

The concept of a League of Nations figured in the 1920 presidential election as well. Cover drawings of the Democratic presidential nominees, Governor James M. Cox of Ohio and his running mate, the virtually unknown Assistant Secretary of the Navy, Franklin D. Roosevelt, were prominently featured on the cover of a campaign song by George Barlow — **League Of Nations Song (The American Marseillaise)**. The Democratic National Committee issued a League-related song also — **The League Triumphant** by Felix Lake and Ella Zimmerman.

Meanwhile, the Republican ticket, consisting of Ohio Senator Warren G. Harding and Vermont Governor Calvin Coolidge, would have nothing to do with the League, choosing instead to run on a theme of returning "normalcy" to the nation. Songs such as **A Man And A Credit To The Nation** by H.C. Talbert and John Stuart, which touted Harding as "Upright and honest; Fearless and Bold" hit a responsive chord in a country tired of war.

As with Grant before him, Harding's administration was chiefly known for its corruption. Like Grant, Harding was not personally involved. The most notorious of these scandals was the Teapot Dome oil reserve incident where Harding's Secretary of the Interior, Albert B. Fall, leased military oil reserves at Teapot Dome, Wyoming, to private parties in return for some $150,000 in "loans." Fall eventually went to jail for the fraud. Several musical numbers were penned featuring this scandal including ***Tea Pot Blues*** by Leona Lovell. For better or worse, Harding would not have to answer for his friends' misconduct. He died on August 2, 1923, before the full extent of the scandals came to light. With Harding's death, Vice President Calvin Coolidge assumed the presidency.

Keep Cool and Keep Coolidge

In a rather quiet 1924 convention, Coolidge was nominated on the first ballot without any serious competition. Former Budget Director and Major General Charles G. Dawes was nominated as Vice President. The story was far different on the Democratic side. Two issues dominated the convention: The first was religion (hopeful Al Smith was Catholic), and the second was whether the party platform should denounce the Ku-Klux-Klan. The battle between Smith and William McAdoo of California lasted 99 ballots with neither able to secure the needed 2/3 majority. Finally, on the 103rd ballot after McAdoo and Smith withdrew, John W. Davis, former Congressman, Ambassador, and Wall Street lawyer carried the convention. William Jennings Bryan's brother, Nebraska Governor Charles W. Bryan was nominated to fill the vice presidential slot.

For all his supposed lack of personality, the Coolidge candidacy inspired a good number of songs. While ***Coolidge And Dawes For The Nation's Cause*** by Zeph Fitz-Gerald, billed itself as the "Official Campaign Song," ***Keep Cool And Keep Coolidge*** by Ida Cheever Goodwin and Bruce Harper, credit their tune as being "The official campaign song of the Home Town Coolidge Club of Plymouth, Vermont," Coolidge's home. One interesting edition of the Cheever-Harper song was printed on a flat piece of fan-shaped cardboard called a "Rooter-Phone." Also printed on the fan were instructions on how to fold cardboard to create the Rooter-Phone, a megaphone device for instant use at the rally of your choice.

The Davis campaign also published practical song devices. To help their supporters beat the heat while singing their favorite campaign tunes at hot rallies and stuffy convention halls, the Democratic National Committee published one of their theme songs—***In Democracy We Trust***—on the back of a hand-held cardboard fan.

Coolidge was a man of few expressions and fewer words. In 1927, he created quite a stir when he announced, "I do not choose to run for President in 1928." The statement was so unusual for a politician, that even Tin Pan Alley took notice. Charles Kenny and Tom Dennis wrote a novelty tune of the same title—***I Do Not Choose To Run***, featuring comic verses about various things not running—a Horse, a clock, a car, a snail, and of course, a politician.

Coolidge's vice president, General Charles G. Dawes, also made musical history. In 1912, long before serving as Vice President, Dawes wrote and published his ***Melody***. This is the only instance in which a president or vice president actually wrote and published music as opposed to lyrics. An instant success, it attained even greater fame when, in 1951, words were added by Carl Sigman and the title changed to ***Its All In The Game***. Over the years it has been performed by the likes of Fritz Kreisler, Henry Jerome, Tommy Edwards, Cliff Richard, and the Four Tops.

When, in 1928 Calvin Coolidge uttered his famous phrase "I Choose not to run," the Republicans turned to Secretary of Commerce Herbert Hoover to lead their ticket. The Democrats, wanting to avoid another deadlocked convention like 1924, gave Al Smith the nomination on the first ballot. The election, however, was not close. Eight years of prosperity under Republican administrations translated into an easy Hoover victory.

The Smith campaign did enjoy success in the musical arena however. Very few songs appropriated for political use have ever approached the identification with an individual as did Al Smith's official campaign song ***The Sidewalks Of New York***. Written in 1894 by Charles B. Lawlor and James W. Blake, special campaign verses were added in 1928 by Al Dubin. Other popular Smith tunes included two by America's top songwriter, Irving Berlin—***We'll All Go Voting For Al*** and ***Better Times With Al***, and a piece called ***Oily Blues*** by A.A. Granger and Raymond Francis. This latter piece featured a cover drawing of the Capitol dome and the Statue of Liberty sitting in a pool of oil and a Democratic donkey kicking a Republican elephant. The elephant has a "Teapot" tied to its tail.

Music associated with Hoover can be divided into three eras: World War I, his 1928 campaign, and his 1932 campaign. The latter two produced the standard campaign-type tunes, certainly nothing of the hit magnitude of his opponent's ***Sidewalks Of New York***; however, the former did leave an interesting musical legacy.

After the outbreak of World War I, Hoover was appointed head of the United States Food Administration. He had been involved in a private food-aid organization for war-torn Europe for several years and was well suited to lead the U.S. food effort. For Americans of that era, to "Hooverize" will always be associated with his famous call to save food. Tin Pan Alley had a ball with the theme. One example, ***I Want To Thank You Mr. Hoover (That's The Best Day Of The Year)*** by Clarence Gaskell, was a lighthearted look at Hoover's program to save food by abstaining from certain items each day. The cover sported a drawing of Hoover standing over an empty dinner table and in front of a calendar in which the days of the week had been changed to "Meatless," "Wheatless," "Lightless," "Heatless," "Bill-less," "Kiss-less," "Sweetless," "Rideless," and "Wifeless." Other musical efforts included Debbie Peterson and Ed. Denny's ***Mr. Hoover Don't Give Us A Loveless Day*** and Madelyn Sheppherd's ***Hooverize***.

Let's Re-Re-Re-Elect Roosevelt

Many of our Presidents have made history, altered history, or, exerted a profound influence on history. However, three have the distinction of unalterably changing not only history, but changing that almost indefinable essence of what it means to be American: These were George Washington, Abraham Lincoln and Franklin Delano Roosevelt. By the end of each of their terms, America was a fundamentally different country than before they took office. It is not surprising then, that such monumental transformations of society would be amply reflected in the music of the times.

Roosevelt went to the 1932 Democratic National Convention with a majority of delegates but short of the two-thirds needed for nomination. His chief rival was the party's 1928 nominee, Al Smith. By the fourth ballot however, Roosevelt claimed the nomination. The Democratic platform stressed unemployment relief, public works, tariff adjustment, and repeal of prohibition. In his acceptance speech to the convention, Roosevelt promised "a new deal for the American public."

The Democrat's themes were reinforced in their music. **The Unemployment Blues** by Will Striker and G.L. Fisher, featured a photo of F.D.R. on the cover along with the notation that the song was "Endorsed by James A. Farley, Chairman, Democratic National Committee." Kenneth Warrdell wrote his campaign song, **We Want A Man Like Roosevelt**, decorated the cover with a drawing of F.D.R., and, in bold letters in each corner was printed one of the major Democratic platform planks: "REPEAL"—"EMPLOYMENT"—"STATES RIGHTS"—"TARIFF ADJUSTMENT."

Roosevelt's first 100 days as President were unlike any other in American history before or since. In that short time, the core of his "New Deal" was enacted. These included: The Emergency Banking Relief Act; The Economy Act; The Beer-Wine Revenue Act; The Civilian Conservation Corps; The Federal Emergency Relief Act; The Agricultural Adjustment Administration; The Emergency Farm Mortgage Act; The Tennessee Valley Authority; The Truth-In- Securities Act; The Farm Credit Administration; The Federal Deposit Insurance Corporation; The Home Owners Loan Corporation; The National Industrial Recovery Act; The National Recovery Administration; and The Works Project Administration.

While Republicans decried the programs as "Fascist," "Socialist" and even "Communist," the nation's songwriters celebrated their creation in song. **A Real Depression Buster** by Bob and Evie Lewis, featured a cover illustration of a smiling Roosevelt surrounded by the "alphabet" symbols of his New Deal—NRA, CCC, CWA, PWA. A similar approach was used for **Virginia Waltz** by Raffaele Capecelatro, which had a serious looking photograph of Roosevelt surrounded by the slogans: "Prosperity—Security—NRA—FERA." One of the more popular topics for such songs was the NRA, or the National Recovery Administration. This Act provided for codes of fair competition and practices for industry, and protection of labor's right to organize and to bargain collectively. The symbol of the NRA was a blue eagle. This symbol was found in the windows of businesses, on newspapers and magazines, and became a symbol of hope for a generation of Americans.

NRA blue eagle songs were everywhere: **The N.I.R.A.** by G.W. Mc-

Causlin; ***The Spirit Of The NRA*** by Kock and Walter; ***Blue Eagle*** by Olive Coleman; ***Under The Big Blue Eagle*** by George Field; and ***L'acquila Blu (A Patriotic Sicilian-American Song)*** by Pierina Palumbo, are just a few examples. As usual, Tin Pan Alley songwriters and publishers got into the act. One of their best offerings was ***I've Got Another Day From The NRA To Love That Baby Of Mine*** by Pierre Norman, Charlie Tobias and Henry Tobias. The cover featured a photograph of the great Eddie Cantor.

Roosevelt's reelection in 1936 was a given, only the margin was in question. His opponent, Governor Alfred M. Landon of Kansas, ultimately went down to the greatest electoral defeat in American history (carrying only the states of Vermont and Maine). Landon's campaign music often reflected the conservative's belief that Roosevelt was a despot spending the country into the poorhouse. One interesting tune — ***Long Live King Franklin The First*** by G.A. Cleveland Shrigley, reflected this viewpoint. ***Have You Ever Tried To Count To A Billion (A Song Burlesque)*** by J.F. Bridges and Dr. H.J. Reynolds, takes a lighter look at the Roosevelt money spigot, while ***Humanity With Sanity*** by William R. Seiffert, tries to project Landon's more reasonable approach to solving the nation's troubles. This latter piece would be recycled for the 1960 campaign, substituting photographs of Richard Nixon and Henry Cabot Lodge for those of Landon and his running mate Frank Knox, on the cover.

By the 1940 election, Roosevelt had suffered several major setbacks in Congress and with the public. His gross miscalculations in trying to "pack" the Supreme Court and, in the 1938 Congressional elections, of trying to punish Democrats who had opposed some of his programs, left him vulnerable, at least so the Republicans believed. They also felt they had one other issue going for them; no President had ever run for a third term. Even the official Republican plank took a stand on the third term issue, proposing a Constitutional Amendment to limit the President to two terms. The Republicans nominated a former Democrat, Wendell L. Willkie to head their ticket.

Willkie's campaign theme song was ***On The Banks Of The Wabash*** by Paul Dresser with special 'Willkie' campaign choruses by John W. Bratton. His most interesting music revolved around two other themes: Roosevelt's third term and Roosevelt's son Eliott. At least two Willkie "third term" songs were written: ***When A Third Term Bug Gets Drafted*** by J.E. Knight, featuring a dramatic cover photograph of Willkie and his running mate Charles McNary, and ***That No-3rd Term Tradition*** by E.B. Leiby, written to the tune of ***Give Me That Old Time Religion***. Although it was not illustrated, this latter piece carried a short narrative outlining the Republican viewpoint of Roosevelt's third term attempt: "George Washington and Thomas Jefferson could have had third terms but refused on grounds that this would lead to a dictatorship (The return to a king). Andrew Jackson would not countenance an attempt to give him a third term…"

The other interesting Willkie musical theme that also spawned several songs was the Army's granting of a Captaincy to Roosevelt's son Elliott. ***Elliott, I Wanta Be A Cap't Too!*** by C.R. Huff, Grace Justus, and Jack Maclean, featured a drawing by Bill Wall of an envious G.I. looking at Captain Elloitt Roosevelt in new uniform. ***I Want To Be A Captain*** by Herbert Teale and Harold Healy had a cover drawing of a soldier in a fox hole sitting beside his pay pouch marked "$30 — You." On the back cover was a different drawing. This one featured Captain Elliott Roosevelt sitting at a desk with his feet up, reading a newspaper with his pay pouch marked: "$200 + $116" and the comment: "A Captain's Pay — Just 23 days before the draft."

In their pro-Roosevelt campaign song — ***Willkie Should Stay In Wall Street***, songwriters Henry Eckmann and Bob Day correctly predicted the electoral outcome: Roosevelt won in a landslide victory. Unfortunately, he had little time to savor his victory. Less than a year after his inauguration, the United States entered the on-going European and Pacific wars. The nation's music once again turned patriotic, and our Commander-In-Chief featured prominently in many of the songs.

One interesting theme of war inspired music was that related to our special relationship with England. ***Let's Stand Behind Great Britain*** by Abner Silver and Mann Curtis, was written in response to Roosevelt's call to help the people of Great Britain. A composer's note on the cover states: "The writers of this song have donated their royalties to Bundles For Britain." Another tune in this category was ***Carry On! Old England*** by Al Sherman, was illustrated with drawings of Franklin Roosevelt, George Washington, Abraham Lincoln, Theodore Roosevelt and Woodrow Wilson. A cover note states that the song was "Officially sponsored by the British American Ambulance Corps." Other Anglo-American entries included: ***Mister Franklin D. And Mister Winston C.*** by Harry Patouhas and Morris, ***The Churchill — Roosevelt Swing*** by Gerard Bryant and George Posford, and ***Hands Across The Sea*** by S. Stoddon, the latter two being published in London.

To the strains of ***Don't Change Horses***, by Al Hofman and Milton and Jerry Livington, Roosevelt ran for a fourth term in 1944. The Convention dumped liberal Vice President Henry Wallace in favor of Missouri Senator Harry S Truman. New York Governor Thomas Dewey was the Republican choice to head the ticket. Perhaps Alice Roosevelt Longworth summed up Dewey's chances best when she said: "How can you vote for a man who looks like the bridegroom on a wedding cake?" Although this was the closest of the four Roosevelt elections, his popular and electoral winning margins were comfortable. Then, three months after his fourth inauguration, he died.

I'M JUST WILD ABOUT HARRY

Harry S Truman, when once told that he had shown that he would rather be right than President, responded that "I'd rather be anything than President." From the day he assumed office, he faced crisis after crisis: The use of the atomic bomb; the creation of the United Nations; post-war price controls; massive strikes in the coal and railroad industries; initiation of the cold war; the Berlin blockade. Add to this the defection of both his party's left wing, lead by Henry Wallace, and its right wing, lead by Strom Thurman. Wallace jumped to head the Progressive Party ticket while Thurman became the States Rights Party's nominee. Almost no one, except Truman himself, thought he would win reelection.

With little financial or party support, Truman undertook one of the most amazing personal campaigns in our nation's history. He embarked on a series of "Whistle-Stop" train trips, lecturing from the rear platform of the train at each stop. The Democratic Congressional Wives Forum even published a song for the trips—**Song Of The Whistle Stop**. On election night, the nation went to bed with President Thomas E. Dewey, and woke up the next morning with President Truman again. *I'm Just Wild About Harry*, an old Broadway tune by Noble Sissle and Eubie Blake, was re-issued with "Special Truman Victory Lyrics."

I LIKE IKE

Although he did not want to run for president, Adlai Stevenson II, Democratic Governor of Illinois, was tapped by his party in both 1952 and 1956 to head their ticket. The grandson of Grover Cleveland's vice president, he was given the mission of defeating a national hero, General Dwight D. Eisenhower. Stevenson, always articulate and witty, remarked upon losing the 1952 election "I was happy to hear that I had even finished second."

Published music for Stevenson is scarce, but there were several interesting pieces. *We're Madly For Adlai* by Gilbert S. Watson, used the obvious rhyme to sell its message. **Don't Let Them Take It Away** by Robert Sour and Bernie Wayne, emphasized the programs for working Americans resulting from 20 years of Democratic presidents. One tune, simply called **Stevenson** and written by Morrie Allen, was published in 1960 in the hope of securing Stevenson a third try for the presidency.

As for Eisenhower, he was so popular with both parties following the end of World War II, that even President Truman once offered to help him capture the 1948 Democratic nomination for President. It wasn't until shortly before the 1952 Republican Convention that Eisenhower's party choice was even known. The race against Stevenson was never close. "I Like Ike" was truly a national tribute to a real American hero and "Ike" music was everywhere.

Irving Berlin used the catchy phrase as the title to his 1952 musical campaign tribute to Eisenhower, and later used a variation—**They Like Ike**—in the Broadway play *Call Me Madam*. Other songwriters chose the "Ike" theme also: **Hike With Ike** by Jack Gould; **Let's O-K Ike** by Nora Bell, Irwin M. Cassel and Mana-Zucca; **We Want Ike** by Arthur Herbert, Dan Michaud and Bob Ecton; and **Out Of The Wilderness With Ike** and **Get Ike**, both by Kenneth Barnum, are only a few examples.

The 1956 election was a repeat of 1952 with the even more popular Eisenhower again facing Adlai Stevenson. Campaign music was also largely a repeat of 1952. Irving Berlin wrote a new tune—***Ike For Four More Years***, but, in general, there was little of consequence. During his second term however, one interesting Eisenhower-related song was written—***There's Still Time Brother!*** by Paul S. Vance and Jacob Segal. This 1959 tune featured a cover photograph of Eisenhower and Nikita Khrushchev and the notation: "Inspired by the Stanley Kramer [film] production *On The Beach*." Eisenhower tried in vain for a U.S.-Soviet accord on nuclear testing, but this would have to wait for his successor.

High Hopes

The election of 1960 pitted Senator John F. Kennedy against Vice President Richard Nixon. Both of these choices were unusual. This was only the fifth time in Electoral history that an incumbent Senator had been nominated for the presidency, and only the third time since nominating conventions were established in 1831 that a sitting Vice President was chosen to head a ticket. Campaign sheet music for both candidates was scarce, reflecting its declining role as a meaningful campaign tool. ***We're Voting For Nixon (To Keep The Country Strong)*** by Walt Marsh and Dave Thornton appealed to the voter to continue with the accomplishments of the Eisenhower-Nixon era. The cover featured a photograph of Nixon among drawings of various military and industrial scenes. This is the first piece of campaign music to add a rocket to the usual military hardware symbols.

Music relating to Kennedy was a little more common, undoubtedly reflecting the excitement surrounding this youthful candidate. Kennedy would be the youngest candidate ever elected to the presidency. Several songs were written reflecting his campaign theme that the United States was "on the verge of a new frontier," the phrase that came to symbolize his legislative agenda. Other songs emphasized his Massachusetts roots such as Lawrence Stutto's ***Massachusetts Is Our Home*** and ***Massachusetts My Home State (M-A-Double S-A-C-H-U-S-E-Double T-S)*** by John Redmond. One song, ***P.T. 109*** by Marijohn Wilkin and Fred Burch, became a minor hit when country singer Jimmy Dean recorded the tune on Columbia Records.

Although Kennedy's time in office was short, it did inspire several pieces of music of note: ***Theme For Jacqueline*** written and recorded by Russell Faith enjoyed wide radio air play, and ***Walkin' Down To Washington*** by Dick Sanford and Sammy Mysels, was performed by Mitch Miller. Two novelty songbooks were published featuring comic songs relating to the Kennedy Administration. One of these was ***Sing Along With Jack*** by Milton M. Schwartz and Danny Hurd, and was billed as "Hit songs from the New Frontier." It contained such titles as: ***I Dream Of Jackie With The Bouffant Hair***, ***Vive La Dynasty***, ***The Peace Corps Goes Rolling Along*** and ***Oh, Bring Back Dick Nixon To Me***.

As with Lincoln, Garfield, and McKinley before him, the assassination of Kennedy stunned the nation and sparked an outpouring of musical tribute, some two dozen songs in all. Two of these tunes attained considerable recording popularity: ***In The Summer Of His Years*** by Herbert Kretzmer and David Lee, was published immediately after the assassination. A song written by Dick Holler and recorded by Dion in 1968 after the assassination of Martin Luther King and Robert Kennedy, entitled **Abraham, Martin And John** was even more popular. This latter piece was a musical tribute to John Kennedy, Martin Luther King, Robert Kennedy and Abraham Lincoln. The sheet music edition featured an illustration of Mt. Rushmore with their likenesses substituted for the original carvings.

One additional interesting musical effort related to the assassination was a song entitled **History Repeats Itself** written and recorded by Buddy Starcher. Starcher's approach was to use a recitation over a musical background featuring the tune **America**. The text described the strange life parallels between the John Kennedy and Abraham Lincoln.

ALL THE WAY WITH L.B.J.

Vice President Lyndon B. Johnson completed Kennedy's term and, in 1964, ran for the presidency in his own right, picking Minnesota Senator Hubert H. Humphrey as his running mate. The Republicans chose conservative Arizona Senator Barry Goldwater as their standard bearer.

Pro-Goldwater campaign music was very limited. Only three pieces in true sheet music format are known to have been published, though several additional tunes in lead sheet format exist. One anti-Goldwater piece of sheet music enjoyed contemporary success when it was recorded by the Chad Mitchell Trio, a popular folk group of the time. The song, **Barry's Boys** by June Reizner, lampooned Republican's commie-hunting mentality — "Let's investigate the P.T.A."- and reactionary longings — "We're the kids with a cause, yes a government like grandma's."

Music for the Democratic cause was also limited, though total Johnson-related music published during his five years in office was abundant by modern standards. Campaign music included such slogan-oriented songs as **All The Way With LBJ**, a title used by two different composing teams, Billy Hays and Eddie Bonnelly, and Eli Schaff and Bee Walker. The most popular of Johnson campaign tunes was **Hello Lyndon**, an appropriation of the popular Broadway melody **Hello Dolly** by Jerry Herman.

In addition to campaign songs, several other pieces of Johnson-related music are noteworthy. **The Great Society** by Frederick Braun and Bobby Gregory musically portrays the hopes embodied in Johnson's legislative program of the same name. **Aren't There Black Angels In Heaven Too?** by Christopher Smart and Gregory Stone, relates the poignant story of a little girl who asked her father this question and his only answer is "a flood of tears." The plain black and white cover of the sheet music has the notation: "Inspired by President Lyndon B. Johnson's Historic Address to Congress on Negro Voting Rights." Finally, there was an interesting piece of music written by Frank Keith and Samuel Starr entitled **Lady Bird Cha Cha Cha**. This piece was "composed by the authors for our First Lady who cares about the beautification of the United States" and featured a cover illustration of Lady Bird Johnson by noted American illustrator Norman Rockwell.

NIXON'S THE ONE

The year 1968 was a tumultuous year in politics: The assassinations of Martin Luther King Jr. and Robert Kennedy, the dramatic primary victories of Eugene McCarthy, Lyndon Johnson's announcement that he would not run for reelection, the halting of the bombing of North Vietnam, and the resurrection of Richard M. Nixon. When all the dust had settled, it was to be a fight to the finish between Democratic nominee Vice President Hubert H. Humphrey and, back for a second try, former Vice President Richard M. Nixon. Unable to separate himself from Johnson's Vietnam nightmare, and faced with Nixon's "secret plan" to end the war, Humphrey fought an uphill, and ultimately, loosing battle. By less than one percent of the popular vote, Nixon captured the presidency.

Campaign music for both Humphrey and Nixon is uncommon. More sheet music was written for Humphrey's unsuccessful try for the Democratic nomination in 1960 against John Kennedy, and for Nixon's loosing effort in 1960, than in their respective campaigns in 1968. This continued to hold true for Nixon in 1972.

If Nixon campaign music was rare, music for his 1972 Democratic challenger, Senator George McGovern, was non-existent. Although a fair number of McGovern phonograph records were issued, not one piece of McGovern sheet music has been located. The 1972 Democratic National Convention did issue an **Official Song Sheet** for use during their Miami Beach convention. It included many patriotic tunes and old familiar Democratic campaign songs including **Wilson, That's All**; **High Hopes — JFK '60**; **Adlai's Gonna Win**; **Row, Row, Row For Roosevelt**; **Jefferson And Liberty**; and **Hello Lyndon**.

The most interesting piece of music associated with the Nixon years is a series of four pieces published under the title **Let's Sing For The President**. Henry Tobias composed the four songs in 1974 at the height of the Watergate hysteria which were intended to show support for the embattled president.

W.I.N.

On August 9, 1974, Nixon gave up the fight and resigned. Gerald R. Ford became the nation's 38th president. He had been picked as vice president in 1973 when Vice President Spiro Agnew resigned after pleading "no contest" to income tax evasion charges. Ford was the first person so chosen under the succession provisions of the 25th Amendment to the U.S. Constitution. Subsequently, he chose New York Governor Nelson Rockefeller as his Vice President under the same provision.

Born Leslie King, Jr. in Omaha, Nebraska, in 1913, Ford's mother remarried when he was two and gave him the new family name. He was first elected to Congress in 1948 where he served until appointed vice president. Despite being the first appointed vice president and the nations only appointed president, Ford managed to secure the Republican nomination for 1976. Although the public generally respected Ford, lack of party enthusiasm and his pardon of Nixon in 1974, contributed to his loosing the election.

Though a couple of presidential marches were composed in his honor, no campaign music for Ford seems to exist. One interesting piece of music was composed for Ford's famous WIN program [Whip Inflation Now] — **WIN** by Meredith Willson. Willson was the composer of music for the Broadway musical *The Music Man*, and several earlier presidential-related songs.

The Democrats turned to a peanut farmer from Georgia to lead their ticket in 1976. To the cries of "Jimmy Who?," the party nominated the generally unknown Governor of Georgia, James E. "Jimmy" Carter to head their ticket. In a close electoral victory, Carter prevailed.

Surprisingly, the Carter campaign and presidency spawned a number of musical efforts. Belle Dowdall composed a song entitled **Jimmy Who?**, taking advantage of the phrase that seemed to be on everyone's lips in the early days of the campaign. Other songs of interest relating to Carter were **Born Again (The Man From Plains, Georgia)** by Harry Simeone, reflecting Carter's declared status as a born-again Christian; **Amy Doesn't Live Here Anymore**, a song by Herman (DOC) Silvers about Carter's precocious daughter Amy; and an inaugural song entitled **Jimmy Carter** composed by Henry and Bobbie Shaffner, using the famous Civil War song **The Battle Cry of Freedom** by George F. Root, as the basis for it's melody.

The magic of 1976 did not repeat for Carter in 1980 thanks to a number of intervening events, not the least of which was the Iranian hostage crisis. Vice President Walter Mondale continued as Carter's running mate. The Republicans chose the 69 year old former actor and former Governor of California Ronald Reagan. Texas Congressman George Bush was picked for the number two slot. When the votes were counted, Reagan had won the popular vote by almost 8 1/2 million and had captured ten times the electoral votes as Carter.

BEDTIME FOR BONZO

Musically, the Reagan campaign generated a number of interesting campaign songs. **Hello Ronnie, Good-Bye Jimmy** by Herman "Doc" Silvers and Cornel Tanassy, **Stand Up And Cheer For Ronald Reagan** by E.F. Moss, and **Ronald Reagan March** by Sterling D. Stone, all featured cover photographs of Reagan. For his Inauguration, the 1981 Presidential Inaugural Committee issued its own piece of music — **Thumbs Up America**. Composed by J. William Middendorf II, former Secretary of the Navy, with lyrics by Sammy Cahn, President of the Song Writers Hall of Fame, the music featured a gorgeous color photograph by Mark Meyer of Ronald Reagan on the cover.

Much in the way that Zachary Taylor, Ulysses Grant and Theodore Roosevelt's pre-presidential careers had generated a significant musical legacy, so too did Ronald Reagan's movie career. While not every movie in which he played had published music issued, many did, including several with his picture on the cover. These films included **Bedtime For Bonzo**, **Million Dollar Baby**, and **The Girl From Jones Beach**. On seven others, his name was imprinted on the cover as part of the cast.

The Reagan/Bush reelection victory margin in 1984 over former Vice President Walter Mondale and this running mate Geraldine Ferraro dwarfed even the large 1980 margins. The popular vote plurality approached 17 million votes, and in electoral balloting, Reagan carried all but one state and the District of Columbia.

Published music for Mondale is virtually non-existent. Two pieces were published in lead-sheet format by Joseph Erdelyi, Jr. Erdelyi had earlier published campaign songs for George Wallace and John Schmitz, and in 1984, composed several pieces for Ronald Reagan. According to a note on the front of his song *All The Way With Mondale*, he states that the song is: "Dedicated to the Honorable Mario Cuomo, who encouraged the Author to write a song for the Democrats." His other Mondale tune—*We Need A Change In Washington*—is also in lead-sheet format and features small photographs of Erdelyi and a Mondale campaign button.

Dukakis Has Got It

With the end of the Reagan era, the Republicans chose Vice President George Bush to carry forth their agenda in the 1988 campaign while the Democrats nominated Massachusetts Governor Michael Dukakis to head their ticket. As the election returns clearly indicated, the nation was eager for another four years of Republican leadership. Promising a "kinder and gentler America," Bush swept all but two states in his lopsided victory.

For 1988, published campaign music remained an elusive commodity. One Dukakis tune in the lead sheet format was written by Henry and Bobby Shaffner—*Dukakis Has Got It*—it was also published as a cassette tape—and one song sheet was issued in photocopy form by Pinky Herman featuring new Dukakis words substituted for his earlier 1940 F.D.R. adaptation of *Happy Days Are Here Again*. There appears to be no Bush-related campaign music published. Andrea and Ervin Litkei, veteran presidential march composers, did publish their *President George Bush March* featuring an official White House color photograph of Bush on the cover, but no other published Bush music has been located.

Don't Stop Thinking About Tomorrow

The elections of 1992 and 1996 continued the tradition of new music written for the election. Several pieces related to Bill and Hillary Clinton have emerged, though so far, music for Bob Dole has not surfaced. Clinton, an avid saxophone musician himself, made use of a popular "Fleetwood Mac" song as his 1992 campaign theme – *Don't Stop Thinking About Tomorrow*, and even managed to engineer a reunion of the group. No specific campaign edition appears to have been published.

Meet the Future President

Although presidential-related sheet music continues to be published, the latter part of the 1950s decade essentially marked the end of published music as anything more than an interesting anachronism. Survivors of the Tin Pan Alley generation are few, and their children and grandchildren are products of the record, CD, and video generations.

The decline of published music however, does not mean the end of music in the presidential cause. Music will continue to play a significant, albeit more sub-conscious role, in generating excitement and setting the tone for almost every presidential activity from receptions to conventions and from campaign stops to campaign commercials.

As history clearly demonstrates, strong personalities and important events will most assuredly continue to stir the soul of songwriters. Only the medium of musical expression changes.

Introduction to Third Party Nominees

When we think of presidential campaigns, we generally think in terms of the major party nominees. However, our electoral history offers us a number of examples of third party campaigns that have played a significant role in the presidential selection process. While third parties have never actually altered the result of an election, they have often been responsible for changing the issues and emphasis of a campaign. Part 2 of this catalogue presents individual third party nominees and third parties which have been on a presidential ballot. Some of these are fairly obscure, while others demonstrated a strong showing at the polls.

The American political arena is decidedly skewed toward the two party system; however, once in a while, an individual or issue can create the momentum necessary to scale the structural barriers to a third party run. The closest that a third party has actually come to the White House was in the election of 1912 when the third party candidate actually finished second. Numerous examples of these pieces can be found under the Theodore Roosevelt section. They include such tunes as *They Are Calling From The Mountains, We Want Teddy* by Dan J. Wall and W.S. Mason, *Progressive Battle Hymns* by C.H. Congdon, and *The Bullmoosers* by Captain Fritz Duquesne.

The importance and power of third parties in American politics has not historically been in its quest for the top spot, but rather in its shaping of the political agenda. Most third parties are one-issue oriented, and their popularity and strength arises from this fact. History has demonstrated over and over that if they in fact, have a popular issue, the major parties co-opt that issue into their own philosophy, thus sapping the very foundation of the 3rd party appeal.

Third party music began in with what is still the most interesting third party piece ever conceived, *Corner-Stone March.* Composed by Charles Zeuner in 1832, it featured a dramatic comic illustration by noted 19th century illustrator David C. Johnston, of a scene at the "Antimasonic Convention in Valdimor [Baltimore]." It featured drawings of talking animals making fun of the Anti-Masonic Party. Throughout the years, third party candidates and their music, have represented every stripe of political belief. *Ode To Birney* by Elizur Wright supported abolitionist James Birney in 1844. *A Battle Song*, supporting the candidacy of Independent Greenback Party candidates Peter Cooper and Sam'l. F. Cary was printed on the back of a facsimile dollar bill.

Socialist Party candidate Eugene Debs had several songs praising him.

One of the best was ***We Will Follow Brave Debs To The End* by** Ellis B. Harris. The sheet music cover illustration featured Debs' photograph superimposed on a red flag. Around his head was the phrase, "Workers of the world unite, You have nothing to lose but your Chains." Conservative candidates are also represented in song. ***We're Strong For George Wallace* by** Dr. Julius Radke Finn and Joe Murphy touted former Governor George Wallace, and ***Rhythm Of Reform: Song Lyrics For Reform Party Volunteers*** by Linda Grant De Pauw, were written for Ross Perot's 1996 campaign.

Miscellaneous Presidential Related Sheet Music

There is an old saying which goes: Many are called, but few are chosen. If its original context was not presidential politics, it well should have been. For example, in the presidential election of 1976, no fewer than 400 individuals registered with the Federal Elections Commission as "candidates." While most of these could scarcely be called legitimate, dozens of others could. Music written for such pre-convention hopefuls is scarce, especially where the music itself makes reference to the race or campaign. Example of hopeful music include ***Jim Reed From Old Missouri*** by Rose Donegan, ***Song Sheet For Taft Demonstration*** (Robert Taft), and ***This Man Was Ment For You And Me*** by James A. Frankus (Eugene McCarthy).

In addition to "hopefuls," there is another class of presidential candidate represented through music: They are called "fantasy candidates." Fantasy candidates, as the name implies, encompasses those candidacies that can only be characterized as "wishful thinking." These are generally non-serious attempts to elect an individual, but more often, are a vehicle used to promote and idea, position or personal quality. Fantasy candidates can be divided into two sub-categories: The first refers to actual persons who are touted for nomination by supporters, often without permission and or even knowledge of the person in question. Songs such as ***Will Rogers For President*** by Marvin Burton Gordon, and ***Come Back, General Pershing, We'll Make You President*** by Dr. Smiles, fall into this category.

The other sub-category of fantasy candidates involves either real or purely fictional individuals who are offered for consideration just for fun. Often these "campaigns" are mounted for advertising purposes, or to make fun at the real candidates. Once in a while, however, they are pursued so as to actually make a point about a quality or trait that would be desirable in the real candidates. ***Elvis Presley For President*** by Norman Henry, Ruth Roberts and Bill Katz and ***Vote For Gracie*** by Charles Henderson are songs in this category.

Finally, there is a modest body of music which has a generic relationship to the Presidency. This includes music which is associated with the office, like ***Hail to the Chief*** by James Sanderson, and music which is incidentally related to former Presidents such as ***Are You Half The Man, Your Mother Thought You'd Be*** by Leo Wood and Harry De Costa which features illustrations of many famous persons, including former presidents. It also includes music which uses the office to ridicule or to promote ideas and fads like *I'd Rather Be Mr. Murphy Than The President* by Boyle Woolfolk.

There are also a number of entries relating to a political parties that are not directly connected to a specific candidate or President such as *Republicans Will Win This Fall* by C.P. Siegfried, and *I'm A Member Of The G.O.P.* by Red Mescara and Parke Frankenfield. Lastly, music related to the White House and to First Ladies is included. Examples of these include *The White House Is The Light House Of The World* by Isador Caesar and Alfred Bryan, and *The President's Lady* by Alfred Newman.

The Catalog of Sheet Music: Candidates and Parties [By Sheet Music Code]

ALTON B. PARKER

ABP-1 Pull Together Boys (A Campaign Song). w. George Hayden Bromby, F.S.A. Published by Sol Bloom, New Amsterdam Theatre Building, New York, NY. 1904. B/w photo of Alton B. Parker, flowers, geometric design border. "Inscribed by Permission to the Hon. Alton Brooks Parker, LL.D., Democratic Candidate for the Presidency." 6pp. Page 2: Blank. Page 3: "Democratic National Campaign Song." Page 6: Advertising.

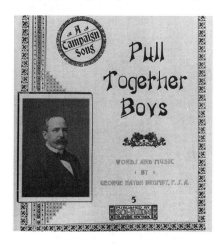

ABP-1

ABP-2 Democratic Presidential March. m. E.O. Fletcher. Published by Empire Music Publishing Company, New York, NY. 1904. B/w photo of Alton B. Parker, facsimile signature. R/w/b drawing of eagle, shield, flags. 6pp. Page 6: Blank.

ABP-3 Good-By [sic]**, Teddy! You Must March! March! March!** (Democratic Marching Song). w. Paul West. m. John W. Bratton (Composer of *The Pearl and the Pumpkin*, &c). Published as a musical supplement to the *New York World*, August 21, 1904. B/w photo by Pach of "Alton B. Parker." Y/w floral designs. Music begins on page one. "Written and Composed Especially for the *Sunday World*." 4pp.

ABP-4 Parker! Parker! (You're the Moses Who Will Lead Us Out of the Wilderness) (March Song). w.m. Paul Dresser. Published by Jas. H. Curtin, New York, NY. 1904. Br/w drawing of Alton B. Parker, geometric design border. 6pp. Pages 2 and 6: Blank.

ABP-5 Iroquois Campaign Song. m. "To the tune of *Good bye, My Lover, Good bye*." [3 1/2" × 6 3/4"]. [1904]. Non-pictorial. "In the 2d, 3d and 4th chorus, use the words 'King Teddy' instead of 'Dear Teddy.'" 2pp. Page 2: Song—*America*.

(AES) ALFRED E. SMITH

ABP-4

ABP-6 Parks' Democratic Campaign Songs. c. James Asher Parks. Published by J.A. Parks Company, York, NE. 1904. 34pp. [M-393].

ABP-7 Parker Campaign Songster, 1904. e. Logan S. Porter. Published by The Home Music Company, Logansport, IN. 1904. O/bk litho of Alton Parker and Henry Gassaway Davis. 32pp. [M-394].

See also TR-193; TR-292.

ALFRED E. SMITH

AES-1 The Sidewalks Of New York (East Side, West Side). w.m. Charles B. Lawlor and James W. Blake. Published by Paull-Pioneer Music Company, No. 119 Fifth Avenue, New York, NY. 1928. Y/br/w with photo of Al Smith, facsimile signature. "Complete with Campaign Choruses." "Hon. 'Al' Smith's Official Campaign Song." "Published for Band and Orchestra." 6pp. + two page Insert. Page 2: Extra choruses. Page 6: Advertising for other Paull-Pioneer music.

AES-2 The Sidewalks Of New York (East Side, West Side). w.m. Charles B. Lawlor and James W. Blake. Published by Paull-Pioneer Music Company, No. 119 Fifth Avenue, New York, NY. 1928. O/br/w with photo of Al Smith. "Complete with Campaign Choruses." "Hon. 'Al' Smith's Official Campaign Song." "Published for Band and Orchestra." 6pp. + 2 page insert arranged for Solo Saxophones. Page 2: Extra choruses. Page 6: Advertising.

AES-3 Our AL. w.m. Bobby Shoemaker and Pastor Guerrero. Published by Miller and Shoemaker, Music Publishers, No. 745 Seventh Avenue, New York, NY. 1928. Bl/w drawing of the Capitol building, star. Br/w photo of Al Smith. 6pp. Page 6: Advertising.

AES-4 Alfred E. Smith (The Man You'll Appreciate). w.m. Tom Romley and Jack Donahue. Published by Romley-Donahue, Cambridge, MA. 1928. B/w photo by International News Reel of Al Smith, geometric design border. "With Ukulele Arrangement." 6pp. Pages 2 and 6: Blank.

AES-5 The Sidewalks Of New York (East Side, West Side, All Around the Town). w.m. Charles B. Lawlor and James W. Blake. [V-1: Published by Pioneer Music Publishing Company] [V-2: Published by Paull-Pioneer Music Company], No. 119 Fifth Avenue, New York, NY. 1928. Br/w photo of Al Smith, facsimile signature—"Hon. Gov. 'Al' Smith of the 'Empire' State." "Respectfully Dedicated to Hon. Gov. Al Smith of the State of New York." [V-1: "With Ukulele Arrangement"] [V-2: "With Ukulele and Saxophone Arrangements"] [V-2: 6pp. + 2 page Insert for "Saxophone"]. 6pp. Pages 2 and 6: Advertising for other music.

AES-6 March To Democracy. w.m. Francis P. Loubet. Published by Fine Arts Opera Company, Inc., No. 1425 Broadway, New York, NY. 1928. Br/w clay-like sculpture of Al Smith, Statue of Liberty, eagle, people. 6pp. Page 2: [Numbered Page "1"] : "Dedicated to

Gov. Alfred E. Smith, Candidate for the Presidency." Pages 5 and 6: Blank.

AES-7 He's Our Al. w.m. Albert Von Tilzer and Seymour A. Brown. Published by Broadway Music Corporation, No. 1600 Broadway, New York, NY. 1928. Ma/w photo of Al Smith, geometric designs. "Respectfully Dedicated to Hon. Alfred E. Smith." "As successfully introduced by Frank McCormack in the *Anvil Chorus Show, 1928*." 6pp. Page 6: Advertising.

AES-8 Al For All And All For Al. w.m. Billy Peyers and Sam Wanger. Published by Riley, Wilson and Company, Music Publishers, No. 30 Chapel Street, Albany, NY. 1928. Br/w photo of Al Smith. "Campaign Song." 6pp. Page 2: Blank. Page 6: Advertising.

AES-9 (Good Times with Hoover) Better Times With Al. w.m. Irving Berlin. Published by Irving Berlin, Inc., Music Publishers, No. 1607 Broadway, New York, NY. 1928. R/w/bk drawing of farmer, factory, train, ship, geometric designs. B/w tinted photo of Al Smith. 6pp. Page 6: Advertising for other music.

AES-10 Good-Bye Cal, Hello Al! w. George Daly and Ed. Mason. m. Gene Cullinan and Billy Hickey. Published by Henry Peters Company, Publishers, No. 7005 Percy Terrace, Brooklyn, NY. Copyright 1928 by Gene Cullinan. B/w photos of Daly and Mason. "Successfully introduced by Daly and Mason." 6pp. Page 2: Blank. Page 3: "Respectfully Dedicated to Our Next President, Hon. Alfred E. Smith." Page 6: Advertising for other Peters music.

AES-11 Better Times With Al. w. Irving Berlin. Published as a "Supplement, *Philadelphia Record*, October 14, 1928." Copyright 1928 by Irving Berlin. [6 7/8" × 10 3/8"]. Br/be drawing of cheering crowd, banners inscribed "Our Al," "Smith." Br/be photo of Alfred E. Smith. "Song Hit of the Campaign." 4pp. Page 4: Br/w photo by I.P.E.U. of and testimonial by Irving Berlin on Al Smith.

AES-12 We're For You Mister Smith. w. N.P. Beck. m. Gene Rautenberg. Distributed by Music Arranging Bureau, No. 523 Wells Street, Milwaukee, WI. Copyright 1928 by N.P. Beck and Gene Rautenberg. Bk/w/bl cover. B/w photo of Alfred Smith. 4pp. Page 4: Blank.

AES-13 Yankee Dood-"Al". w. Samuel A. Bergman. m. Air: "To be sung to the tune of *Yankee Doodle*." Published by Cayuga Democratic Club (19th Assembly District), No. 2043 7th Avenue, New York, NY. [1928]. [4 1/4" × 7"]. Br/be non-pictorial broadside. 2pp. Page 2: Blank.

AES-14 "Al". w. William J. Macdonald. m. Al Frazzini. [V-1: Published by Popular Music Company, No. 181 Tremont Street, Boston, MA] [V-2: "Victory Song of the Convention"]. 1928. R/w/b crossed flags. B/w photo of Al Smith. 6pp. Page 2: Poem by William J. Macdonald. Page 6: Blank.

AES-15 Dixie Land For "Al". w. Samuel A. Bergman. m. Air: "To be sung to the tune of *Dixie's Land*." Published by Cayuga Democratic Club (19th Assembly District) 2043 Seventh Avenue, New York, NY. [1928]. [4 1/4" × 7"]. Br/be non-pictorial broadside. 2pp. Page 2: Blank.

AES-16 Our "Al" From Tammany. w.m. Jack Maharon. Published by Edward B. Marks Music Company, No. 225 West 46th Street, New York, NY. 1927. Bl/w Underwood and Underwood photo of parade, shield, geometric design border. "Dedicated to Gov. Alfred E. Smith." 6pp. Page 2: Blank. Page 6: Advertising for other Edward B. Marks music.

AES-17 Statutes And Statuettes [Program and Song Book]. Published by Albany Legislative Correspondents' Association, Albany, NY. 1925. N/c drawing by Fred O. Seibel of "Venus DeMilo

Smith," other politicians as historical figures. "A Private Presentation of Immortal Images and Matchless Masterpieces From the 1925 Legislative Louvre Frivolously Fashioned in Political Pigments and Capitoline Colors and Featuring Etchers and Fetchers, Chisels and Fizzles, Hues and Hewitts, G.O.P. Gargoyles, Democratic Dorics, Prohibition Pastels, Lowman Landscapes and McGinnies Models, Combined with a Superficial Squint into the Gallery of Gee-Gaws, Freaks and Flim Flam." "Viewed at Ten Eyck Hotel, Albany, N.Y., on the Evening of March 12, 1925, Seven O'clock." 20pp.

AES-18 Oily Blues. w. A.A. Granger. m. Raymond Francis. Published by Granger and Francis, Suite 3, No. 107 West University Avenue, Champaign, IL. 1928. R/w/bl/gy drawing by Hugh Leslie of the U.S. Capitol dome resting in "Oily Blues" water, oil dripping on the Statue of Liberty, donkey kicking elephant out of Capitol dome, "teapot" tied to elephant's tail. 4pp. Page 4: Arrangement for Quartet.

AES-19 Good-Bye Cal, Hello Al. w.m. Florence Hanick. Published by Hanick Music Company, No. 52 Musical Art Building, St. Louis, Mo. 1928. Bl/w photo of Alfred E. Smith. R/w/b crossed flags. 4pp. Page 4: Blank.

AES-20 Al Smith. w. E.E. Aspinwall. m. Henry J. Donovan. Published by E.E. Aspinwall, Pawtucket, RI. 1928. R/w/b cover design by E.S. Fisher of flag, shield, eagle. B/w photo of Alfred E. Smith. 6pp. Pages 2 and 6: Blank.

AES-21 We'll All Go Voting For Al. w.m. Irving Berlin. Published by New York State Committee for the Nomination of Gov. Alfred E. Smith, Prudence Building, Madison Avenue at 43rd Street, New York, NY. [1928]. R/w/b drawing of Capitol dome. Bl/w photo of "Alfred E. Smith." 6pp. Page 2: Blank. Page 6: Narrative — "Why Governor Alfred E. Smith Will Be Nominated and Elected President of the United States."

AES-22 Our Pal. w.m. Harry R. Franks. Published by Franks and Tucker, No. 299 Underhill Avenue, Brooklyn, NY. 1927. B/w photo of "Governor Alfred E. Smith," geometric designs. "Campaign Manager of Song — Thomas A. Tucker." 6pp. Pages 2 and 6: Blank.

AES-23 Good-Bye Cal Hello Al! (C From Cal Leaves Al). w.m. Edward Laska. Published by The Democratic Song Company, No. 205 West 57th Street, New York, NY. Copyright 1928 by Edward Laska. Br/o/w Pfeiffer geometric designs. Br/w photos of Alfred E. Smith, facsimile signature, "Miss Melvena Passmore of the Civic Opera Company who was the Convention's Prima Donna." "The Song Hit of the National Democratic Convention in Houston sung by Miss Passmore with the Graymare Band immediately After the Nomination of Alfred E. Smith for the Presidency and was broadcast throughout the Country by the National and Columbia Broadcasting Networks and announced by Graham McNamee and Major White." 6pp. Page 2: Blank. Page 6: Advertising for this song.

AES-24 Let's Make Al Smith Our President For Nineteen Twenty Nine. w.m. C.J. O'Hara. Published by C.J. O'Hara, No. 111 East 88th Street, New York, NY. 1928. B/w geometric designs. Ma/w photo of Alfred E. Smith, facsimile signature, geometric designs. 6pp. Pages 2 and 6: Blank.

AES-25 (There'll Be A) Big Brown Derby (In the White House) (Song). w.m. C. Akey. Published by Violet Music Publishers, No. 528 Broadway, Milwaukee, WI. 1928. B/w drawing by Shurtleff Studios of Alfred E. Smith at the U.S. Capitol building with handbag and derby. 6pp. Pages 2 and 6: Advertising.

AES-26 Get Yourself A Nice Brown Derby (And Fall In Line for Al).

w.m. Walter Goodwin (Writer of *Back In The Old Neighborhood*). 1928. Br/w photos of "Alfred E. Smith," "T.J. Crowe," "James M. Whalen," "Henry A. Berger" and "Ald. Ross A. Woodhull (To fill vacancy)." 4pp. Page 4: Biographies of "Democratic Nominees for Trustees Sanitary District of Chicago." "For Your Health's Sake."

AES-27 I'm Going To Vote For Al. Smith! m. Air: *East Side-West Side*. Published as a postcard. [1928]. Obv: Gy/bk/bl/be drawing of Al Smith. Lyrics. Rev: Blank.

AES-28 The Happy Warrior (When We Make "AL" President). w.m. Joseph W. and John J. McQuaid. Published by J.W. and John McQuaid, Publishers, No. 5311 Larchwood Avenue, Philadelphia, PA. 1928. B/w photo of Al Smith. Bl/w drawing of flowers. "Dedicated to the Hon. Alfred E. Smith, Governor of New York." 6pp. Page 6: Blank.

AES-29 The Democrats (Democrat's Marching Song). w.m. Charles J. Lennox. Published by Charles J. Lennox, No. 92 Warren Street, Carteret, NJ. 1928. B/w photos by World Wide Photo of "Governor Alfred Smith" and "C.J. Lennox." R/w drawing of two little girls, star, geometric designs. 4pp. Page 4: B/w photo of "C.J. Lennox, Aurthor [sic] of Poems, Songs, recitations, &c., &c." Advertising.

AES-30 AL Smith (Song and Chorus). w.m. James Rooney. Published by Frank Harding's Music House, No. 228 East 22nd Street, New York, NY. Copyright 1928 by James Rooney. Br/w photo of Al Smith, wings, star, geometric designs. Bl/w/br border. "Dedicated to His Excellency, Governor Alfred Smith." 6pp. Page 2: Blank. Page 6: Advertising for other music.

AES-31 You Cant' Keep A Good Man Down (Waltz Song With a Chorus). w.m. Michael Flanagan. Published by Flanagan Brothers, New York, NY. 1928. B/w photo of Alfred E. Smith, wings, star, geometric designs. R/w cover. "Respectfully Dedicated to our Governor, Alfred Smith." 6pp. Page 2: Blank. Page 4: B/w photo of Flanagan Brothers. Advertising.

AES-32 From The Sidewalks Of New York To Washington. w.m. Lee White, Evelyn Butler and Jerry Alexander. Published by The White Music Publishing Company, Publishers, No. 507 West 50th Street, New York, NY. 1928. Bl/w photo of Al Smith. R/w/b stars, geometric designs. 4pp. Page 4: R/w logo, geometric designs.

AES-33 Open The Gates Of The White House. w.m. Johnny Rossi. a. William Fleer. Published by J.P. Rossi, Wheeling, WV. 1928. Bl/w drawing of Al Smith. "Respectfully Dedicated to Hon. Alfred E. Smith." 4pp. Page 4: Blank.

AES-34 Good Luck. w. A.J. Handley. m. Rene D'erson. Copyright 1928 by A.J. Handley. B/w non-pictorial geometric design border. "Dedicated to the Hon. Alfred E. Smith." 4pp. Page 4: Blank.

AES-35 We're With Al Smith (Our Peerless Al and Sam His Pal). w.m. Mark Kenney. Published by Mark Kenney, Marquette Hotel, St. Louis, MO. 1928. R/w/b drawing of Thomas Jefferson, Uncle Sam, eagle, shield. Bl/w photo of Al Smith. "Dedicated to All One Hundred Per Cent Americans." "The vocal compass of the ballad is such that if one can talk one can sing it." 6pp. Page 2: Verses. Page 6: Bl/w photo of Al Smith. R/w/b drawing of eagle, shield.

AES-36 Good Luck. w. A.J. Handley. Copyright 1933 by A.J. Handley. B/w non-pictorial, geometric design border, facsimile handwritten title. "Dedicated to the Hon. Alfred E. Smith." 4pp. Page 4: Blank.

AES-37 Alfred E. Smith The Happy Warrior (Patriotic March Song). w. Donald Bain. m. Ernest A. Schulze. Published by Ernest A. Schulze, No. 1003 Washington Street, Evanston, IL. 1928.

(AES) ALFRED E. SMITH

B/w photo by The Associated Press of Al Smith. "Campaign Song Endorsed by Democratic National Committee, New York." "The sentiment in the campaign song *Alfred E. Smith, The Happy Warrior* composed by you is deeply appreciated by the Governor — Charles Greathouse, Secretary, Democratic National Committee." "First printed in *The Buffalo Times*, Norman E. Mack of the Democratic National Committee, Owner-Editor." "'The Happy Warrior' Who is He? Franklin D. Roosevelt called him 'The Happy Warrior' in 1920 at San Francisco. Again Roosevelt called him 'the Happy Warrior' in Madison Square Garden in 1924. And the Democratic National Convention, at Houston, on June 29th accepted Roosevelt's 'Happy Warrior' as the Presidential standard bearer — Alfred E. Smith, Governor of New York State.— *The Buffalo Times*." 4pp.

AES-38 Oh, Al You Are My Pal. w.m. Ruth Cashen-Lippert, No. 8007 St. Lawrence Avenue, Chicago, IL. Published as a supplement to *The Buffalo Times*, April 28, 1928. B/w photo of Al Smith. 4pp. Page 4: Versus.

AES-39 From The City Streets. w. John Mellor. m. M.G. Kennedy. Published by John Mellor & Sons, Inc., Music Printers and Publishers, Nos. 120-134 Forty-Sixth Street, Pittsburgh, PA. 1928. B/w photo by Underwood and Underwood of Al Smith, facsimile signature. "The Song Hit of 1928." "Professional Copy — Warning!" "Dedicated to Governor Alfred E. Smith." "New York Distributors: Walter Kane, Inc., 1595 Broadway, NY." 4pp. Page 4: Advertising.

AES-40 Happy Warrior Al. w. Leo Donaghue. m. Frank J. Donaghue. Published by Leo Donaghue and Frank J. Donaghue. Composers, Bridge Street, Mahanoy Plane, PA. Copyright 1928 Leo Donaghue. Photo of Al Smith, Capitol building. "Dedicated to the Honorable Alfred E. Smith." 6pp. Page 6: Blank.

AES-41 Sure Al Is Meant For Pres-i-dent (When We A-Votin' Go) (Fox-Trot). w.m. Roy Pauley. Published by The Our Next President Company, Publishers, Albany, NY. 1924. B/w photos of Al Smith, The White House. 8pp.

AES-42 Our Al Is Meant For Pres-i-dent (In-19-20-8) (Fox-Trot). w.m. Jack McCauley and Duke Morris. Published by The Our Next President Company, Publisher, Schenectady, NY. 1928. B/w photos of Al Smith, The White House. 8pp. Page 4: Blank.

AES-42

AES-43 If Smith Sits In The Presidential Chair (Topical Song). w.m. Robert Hickey and Harry Tigue. a. Carl Tischendorf. Published by Hickey and Tigue, No. 527 Ellicott Square, Buffalo, NY. 1928. B/w non-pictorial geometric designs. 4pp. Page 4: Extra choruses.

AES-44 The Honorable Alfred Smith (March). w.m. Franklin Summers. Published by Hamilton Music Publishing Company, No. 419 86th Street, Brooklyn, NY. Copyright 1928 by Franklin Summers. Pl/w photo of Alfred Smith. 6pp. Page 6: Blank.

AES-45 The Next President (Freedom In the Land). w.m. Professor Joseph "DOC" Frank. Published by Prof. Joseph Frank Music Publishing Company, Rooms 1131-1136, No. 127 North Dearborn Street, Chicago, IL. 1928. B/w photos of Al Smith and "Prof. Joseph Frank." R/w/b drawing of crossed flags. "Flag of the Free Through our Al—Al Smith President." 6pp. Page 6: Blank.

AES-45

AES-46 Al Smith We Are All For You. w.m. Thomas Murray & James McCarty. Published by Murray and McCarty Music Publishing Company, No. 101 Hoffman Avenue, Columbus, OH. 1928. R/w/bl/br drawing of Al Smith, stripes. B/w photos of "Thomas Murray" and "James McCarty." 6pp. Page 2 and 6: Blank. Page 3: "Dedicated with deep respect to Gov. Alfred E. Smith, Governor of New York and Hon. James Walker, Mayor of New York City."

AES-47 Al, My Pal. Photo of Alfred Smith.

AES-48 Our "Al" Smith (Presidential Fox Trot for 1928). w.m. D. Simmon and Joseph Szigeti. Copyright 1928 by D. Simmon. Photo of Al Smith in star. Drawing of dancing couples.

AES-49 Make Al Smith President. w.m. George D. Lacey and Wilber S. Wesner. 1928. Non-pictorial "Professional Copy." Copyright "Warning." 4pp. Pages 1 and 4: Blank.

AES-50 A-L Smith (Song). w.m. Ben Shanley (Writer of the famous Holy Cross College Song *Chu-Chu*). Published by Ben Shanley, Music Publisher, No. 46 Academy Hill, Southington, CT. 1928. Bl/w stars, line border. "Words and Music by Ben Shanley Who Was Kidnapped on the Sidewalks of New York!" 4pp. Page 2: Long narrative from *The Meriden Journal* on song history.

AES-51 Always Everywhere Smiling (Alfred E. Smith). w.m. Ben Breslow. Published by Ben Breslow, No. 1215 East 13th Street, Brooklyn, NY. 1928. R/w/b drawing of Al Smith, flag, eagle, Capitol building. 6pp. Pages 2 and 6: Blank.

AES-52 Let's All Be For Al (Booster Song). w. Harvey E. Tripp. m. Carrie E. Slade. Published by The Los Angeles Music Publishing Company, No. 520 Broadway, Los Angeles, CA. 1928. Br/w photo of "Governor Al Smith, New York." B/w cover. 6pp. Pages 2 and 6: Blank.

AES-53 Al Smith, Al Smith (The Great Song and Chorus). Published by Frank Harding, Publisher, New York, NY. Copyright 1928 by James Rooney, No. 51 Felix Street, Providence, RI. [6 5/16" × 9 13/16"]. Non-pictorial. "Sing This Chorus." "Al Smith." "For sale at all music stores." 2pp. Page 2: Blank.

AES-54 He's Our Al. w.m. Albert Von Tilzer and A. Seymour Brown. Published by Broadway Music Corporation, No. 1600 Broadway, New York, NY. 1928. Non-pictorial "Professional Copy." Copyright "Warning." 4pp.

AES-55 Al! Al! Al! w. Mary Ryan Cahill and Irene Ryan Gerhard. m. Irene

Ryan Gerhard. Printed by J.A. Welch Company, Print. Copyright 1928 by Irene Ryan Gerhard. B/w photo by I.P.E.U. of Alfred Smith. B/w stars, geometric design border. 4pp. Page 4: Blank.

AES-56 We're For Al. w.m. R.J. "Dinty" Moore, Oklahoma City, OK. 1928. Bl/w photo by I.P.E.U. of Al Smith. "Played by 'Dinty' Moore's Band at Houston Convention." 4pp. Page 3: B/w litho of a rooster. Page 4: "Democratic National Convention 1928."

AES-57 Just Our Al The Workingman's Pal. w.m. George H. Perkins. a. Wally Ives. Published by George H. Perkins, No. 40 Court Street, Boston, MA. 1928. B/w photo of Al Smith. Bl/w drawings of a workingman, "White House," road sign inscribed "To The White House." 6pp. Pages 2 and 6: Blank.

AES-57

AES-58 Al Smith. w.m. Thomas A. Murray and James J. Mullan. Published by Thomas A. Murray, No. 3861 Fairmount Avenue, Philadelphia, PA. 1928. B/w photo of Al Smith. R/w drawings of house, roses, flowers. 6pp. Pages 2 and 6: Blank.

AES-59 The Answer To Heflin. [1928]. [3 1/2" × 5 1/8"]. O/bk non-pictorial. "The New Song Hit." 2pp.

AES-60 We Want Al Smith (For the Presidential Chair). w. J. Calvin Stewart. m. Chas. A. Meyers. Published by Independent Music Publishers, No. 6044 8th Avenue, Kenosha, WI. 1928. Br/w photo of "Al E. Smith." Bl/w cover. 6pp. Page 2 and 6: Blank.

AES-61 Al Smith To Lead Us On. w. Jack O'Brien (of the Al Smith Club of South Boston, Mass). m.a. Jack O'Brien ("To the Tune of *Curley for Four Years More*"). Published by the Al Smith Club of South Boston, Boston, MA. Copyright 1928 by Jack O'Brien. [3 11/16" × 5 1/2"]. Bl/bk non-pictorial card. "Learn this and sing it every day." Advertising. 2pp. Page 2: Narrative — "This song card is presented to you with the compliments of The Al Smith Club of South Boston, Mass. — A live wire 100% Al Smith organization made up of men and women of a district known all over the United States for its loyalty to the City, State and Nation at all times, and absolutely to be depended upon in the great cause of—'Al Smith To Lead Us On!'"

AES-62 Our Al To Succeed Cal (Campaign Song). w. Eddie Machugh. m. Air: "Old Welsh Air." Published by Edward Machugh Boston, MA. 1928. Non-pictorial. "Order for any number with 2 ct. stamp enclosed, may be mailed to Democratic State Headquarters, 75 State Street, Boston, Mass." "Note: Take this copy home. Don't Destroy it, Sing it. Singing helped to win the War. Let this song help to elect 'Al.'" At top of music — "(Spoken) Our Al, To Succeed Cal, The Friend of Bigger Business and the Poor Man's Pal." "Professional copy herewith presented with compliments of the Democratic State Committee of Mass., 75 State St., Boston." 2pp.

AES-63 For President Gov. Al-

fred E. Smith [Song Sheet]. m. Popular tunes. Printed in Louisville, KY. [1928]. [5 1/2" × 8 1/2"]. O/bk litho of Al Smith. "When the Band Plays — Sing, Folks, Sing!" Song: **Al Smith**. 2pp. Page 2 Song: **Sidewalks Of New York**.

AES-64 Let's Make Al Smith Our President In Nineteen Twenty Nine. w.m. C.J. O'Hara. Published by C.J. O'Hara, Publisher, No. 111 East 88th Street, New York, NY. 1927. B/w nonpictorial geometric designs. 6pp. Pages 2 and 6: Blank.

AES-65 The Bacchanal Of 1919 [Program and Song Book]. Published by The Legislative Correspondents' Association of New York, Albany, NY. 1919. [7 3/4" × 10 1/2"]. N/c drawing by Fred O. Seibel of the "Last Chance Cafe," sign — "Headquarters Hard Liquor Club," "Senator Sage" as bellboy, and "Al Smith Tonight" on sign marquee. "A Product of the Capitoline Vineyard, Staged for the Delertation of People Still on Earth by The Legislative Correspondents' Association at The Ten Eyck, Albany, the Night of April 3, 1919." [Songs about Al Smith].

AES-66 Fourth Internationale [Program and Song Book]. Published by The Legislative Correspondents' Association of the State of New York, Albany, NY. 1920. [8" × 11 1/4"]. N/c drawing by Fred O. Seibel of a statue of House Speaker Thaddeus "Sweet" on horseback, "Governor's Chair," "Assemblyman Roosevelt," other politicians. "A Session of Soviets, Seething with Socialism, Sweetism, Sedition, Seven-Cent Fares, School-Ma'ams, Soda-Water, Slams, Slander, Simps and Strangulation, and Bristling with Booms, Boobs and Bunk." "Called by The Legislative Correspondents' Association of the State of New York, at The Ten Eyck, Albany, April 22, 1920." Page 5: "Toast List" including "Comrade Alfred E. Smith, Dictator of the Proletariat." [Songs about Al Smith].

AES-67 Al S. In Wonderland [Program and Song Book]. Published by The Albany Legislative Correspondents' Association of New York State, Albany, NY. 1924. [8 1/2" × 10 1/2"]. N/c drawing by Fred O. Seibel of Statue of Liberty with Beer, "Al Smith," Calvin "Coolidge" as a dragon, other politicians. "A Jocose Junket in Phantom Pullmans to that Roisterous Realm, where Hectic Hopes, Hocus-Pocus Harmonies, Folly, Froth and Flim Flam Blend Blithely with Becalmed Booms, Budget Butchers, Bubbles, Blunders and Barters." "Departing from at Ten Eyck Hotel Terminal, Albany, NY., at 7 O'clock, Eastern Time, on the evening of Thursday, March, 27, 1924." [Songs about Al Smith].

AES-68 Old Hokum Week [Program and Song Book]. Published by The Albany Legislative Correspondents' Association of New York State, Albany, NY. 1926. N/c drawing by Fred O. Seibel of Statue of Liberty with Beer, Al Smith, Coolidge, other politicians. "A Rousing Reunion of Ravenous and Rampant Republican Rajahs, Rallying Round Resolution to Raid and Ravish, Recapture and Replenish, and Reeking with Hungry Hordes, Head-Hunters, Hughes and Hydro and Hewitt-Hutchinson Hocus Pocus, Plus a Peek Into the Puppet-Shows and Pow-Wows of Pap-Greedy, Picket-Fence Plum-Seekers." "Held Somewhere Near Geneseo, N.Y. Train leaves Ten Eyck Hotel for Rural Rendezvous at Seven-thirty o'clock the evening of Thursday, March, Twenty-fifth, 1926." [Songs about Al Smith].

AES-69 Rounders And Showdowns [Program and Song Book]. Published by The Albany Legislative Correspondents' Association, Albany, NY. 1928. [8" × 11 3/4"]. N/c drawing labeled "Ride Her, Cowboy" of "Al" Smith on bucking horse — "Solid Dixie Vote," James "Cox," John "Davis," other politicians — "Heflin, Reed, Ritchie," pennant — "The Great Houston Rodeo." "A Rollicking Rodeo and Sizzling Stampede, Laid in the Light of Western Stars and Set to the Hammer of Heifrer Hoofs, Plus a Perspiration-proof Potpourri of Presidential Piffle and Proxy Prattle, Topped by the Miniature Mirthquake, 'Who's Who in Houston.'" "Ride Her, Cowboy!" "Staged at The Ten Eyck, Albany, The Evening of March 8, 1928." 20pp.

AES-70   Democratic Song Book. Published by Charles W. Stewart, 439 Arlington Place, Chicago, IL. July 21, 1928. [3 3/4" × 6 1/8"]. Non-pictorial. "Dedicated to sane government and honest administration with 'Life, Liberty and The Pursuit of Happiness' without blue laws or fool laws. The most damnable tyranny is the tyranny of small things. 'Give me the writing of a nation's songs and I care not who writes its laws.' The best way to cure a fool of his folly — to Laugh him out of it." "Sing Brother Sing!" 6pp. Christian and anti-prohibition sayings throughout — "Would Christ have joined the Ku Klux Klan or the Anti-Saloon League?, &c. [M-418].

AES-71   Sidewalks Of New York. [1928]. [3 1/8" × 6 5/16"]. Non-pictorial. "For Happiness and Prosperity Sing this Song and Vote for Alfred E. Smith." 2pp.

AES-72   Brown Derby March. m. Peter C. Riley, Jr. Published by Riley, Wilson and Company, Music Publishers, No. 30 Chapel Street, Albany, NY. 1928.

AES-73   It's Al Smith (A Popular Song). w.m. Dayve B. De Waltoff, M.D. (Brooklyn, N.Y.). 1928. Br/w drawing of Al Smith. Br/w photo of Mrs. Frances Malley — "Sung by." "Dedicated to The Hon. John H. McCooey, the Leader of Democracy in the County of Kings, State of New York." "Other songs by same writer *The Bride's Prayer, New York Town, The Seasons, Wie Lang, O Gott, Prayers, Brooklyn My Brooklyn, Erwach Mein Folk, Rejoyce,* etc, etc." "At All Leading Music Stores." 4pp. Advertisement.
See also HCH-4; HCH-44; HCH-53; HCH-60; FDR-277; FDR-362; FDR-363.

ANDREW JACKSON

AJK-1   Jackson's Favorite March. m. Wagler. Printed by G. Dobbin & Murphy, Baltimore, MD. [ca. 1830]. B/w litho at page 2 of flags, drum and sword. "As performed by the band in the Washington Theatre." "Copy Right Secured." 4pp. Pages 1 and 4: Blank.

AJK-2   President Jackson's Grand March. a. Mr. Peile. Published by J.L. Hewitt & Company, [V-1: No. 36 Market Street] [V-2: 137 Broadway], Boston, MA. [ca. 1829]. B/w litho V-1: By Pendleton] of Andrew Jackson. "Performed by the Boston Brigade Band." "Arranged for the Piano Forte." 4pp. "Second Edition" at top of cover. Page 2: "Arranged for the Piano Forte by Mr. Peile. Performed by the Boston Brigade Band and presented to them by the Publisher." Page 4: Advertising.

AJK-3   President Jackson's Favorite March And Quick Step. m. Henry Dielman. Published & sold by George Willig, No. 171 Chesnut Street,

AJK-2

Philadelphia, PA. [ca. 1828]. 4pp. Pages 1 and 4: Blank. Page 2: B/w engraving at top of Andrew Jackson, crossed flags, leaves. "Composed for the Piano Forte."

AJK-4   Genl Jackson's March To Pensacola. Published by E. Riley & Company, No. 29 Chatham Street, New York, NY. [181-?]. 2pp. Page 2: Blank.

AJK-5   President Jackson's Parade March. m. "An Amateur of the City of Philadelphia." Published by J.L. Frederick, No. 53 South 4th Street, Philadelphia, PA. [ca. 1830]. Non-pictorial. "Composed and Arranged for the Piano Forte." "Respectfully Dedicated to the Citizens of the U.S." "Entered According to Law." 4pp. Pages 1 and 4: Blank.

AJK-6   General Jackson's New Orleans March. m. Miss Mary Annette V. Thompson. Published by Firth & Hall, No. 1 Franklin Square, New York, NY. [ca. 1830]. Non-pictorial. "In Commemoration of the Battle of New Orleans 8th January 1815." "Respectfully Dedicated to General Andrew Jackson, President of the United States." "Composed and Presented by Miss Mary Annette V. Thompson." 4pp. Page 4: Blank.

AJK-7   King Andrew (Glee). m. "Tune: *Dame Durden*." Published by S.H. Parker, No. 141 Washington Street, Boston, MA. August, 1834. Non-pictorial. "As Sung at the Salem Whig Festival." 4pp. Pages 1 and 4: Blank. [Anti-Jackson].

AJK-8   Come, Sons Of Freedom! (A New National Song). w.m. J.C. Beckel. Published by J.C. Beckel, Philadelphia, PA. 1839. Non-pictorial. "Respectfully dedicated to Ex-President Jackson." "July 4th 1839." 4pp. Pages 1 and 4: Blank.

AJK-9   Jackson's Grand March. m. Kuffner. a. S. Knaebel. Published by Parker & Ditson, No. 107 Washington Street, Boston, MA. 1836. Non-pictorial. "As played at the Boston Democratic Celebration, July 4, 1836, by the Boston Brass Band and by them Respectfully Dedicated with permission to Gen. Andrew Jackson, President of the United States." 4pp. Pages 1 and 4: Blank.

AJK-10   General Andrew Jackson's Presidential Grand March. m. T.W.H.B.B. Published by T. [Thomas] Birch, No. 50 Howard Street, New York, NY. January 8th, 1829. Non-pictorial. 4pp. Pages 1 and 4: Blank.

AJK-11   The Hunter's Of Kentucky. w. S. Woodworth. m. William Blondell. [V-1: Published by T. Birch, No. 235 Chapple near Canal Street, New York, NY] [V-2: Same as V-1 with "Apollo No. 41" added above "Copy Right"] [V-3: Published by George Willig, No. 171 Chestnut Street, Philadelphia, PA]. [ca. 1828]. B/w engraving of two men in buckskin uniforms with long rifles each standing over a saying—"Ye gentleman and ladies fair" and "But here was old Kentucky." "As sung in character by Mr. Petrie with unbounded applause at Chatham Garden Theatre, the Symphonies & Accompaniments by William Blondell." Music begins on page one. Page 2 and 6: Blank. [V-1: W-887] [V-2: W-887A] [V-3: W-887B].

AJK-12   The President's Turkish March. m. J. Kuffner. a. J. Worsley. Published by C. Bradlee, No. 164 Washington Street, Boston, MA. [ca. 1830]. Non-pictorial. "Arranged for the Piano Forte." [V-1: At bottom of page one—"Entered According to Act of Congress."] [V-2: No copyright notation at bottom of page one]. 4pp. Pages 1 and 4: Blank.

AJK-13   General Jackson's Grand March. Published by G.E. Blake, No. 13 South 5th Street, Philadelphia, PA. [1815?]. Non-pictorial. "No. 2 of Blake's Musical Miscellany." Number "6" at top of page. 4pp. Page 1 and 4: Blank. [W-2942?].

AJK-14   President Jackson's Grand March & Quick Step. m. Mr. Braun (Director of Music, Chesnut Street Theatre). Published by John Ashton, No. 197 Washington Street, Boston, MA. [ca. 1829]. Non-pictorial. 2pp.

AJK-15 The Battle Of New Orleans. w.m. J.N. Barker, Esq. Published by G.E. Blake, No. 13 South 5th Street, Philadelphia, PA. March 4th, 1829. Non-pictorial geometric designs. "Sung on the 8th of January at the Democratic Festival." 4pp. Page 1 and 4: Blank.

AJK-16 General Jackson's Favorite March. m. F.A. Wagler. Published & sold by G. Willig, Jr., Baltimore, MD. Feb. 25, 1829. Non-pictorial. "As performed by the Marine Band after the Battle of New Orleans." 2pp. Page 2: Blank.

AJK-17 President Jackson's Inauguration March. Published at W. Geib's Piano Forte & Music Warehouse, No. 219 Broadway, New York, NY. [ca. 1829?]. Non-pictorial. 4pp. Page 3: "Engrd. by T. Birch." Page 4: Blank.

AJK-18 President Jackson's Grand March. m. J.F. Goneke. Published by Geo. Willig, No. 171 Chesnut Street, Philadelphia, PA. [ca. 1829]. Non-pictorial. "As performed at the Chesnut Theatre." "Composed for the Piano Forte." 4pp. Page 4: Blank.

AJK-19 Grand Funeral March. m. A. Metz. Published by G. Willig, Jr., Baltimore, MD. 1845. Non-pictorial black background for "General Jackson." "Composed in Memory of General Jackson." 4pp. Pages 1 and 4: Blank.

AJK-20 Battle Of The Memorable 8th Of January, 1815. m. Philip Laroque (of New Orleans). Printed & sold by G. Willig at his Musical Magazine, Philadelphia, PA. [1815]. B/w engraving of Andrew Jackson on large banner suspended by spears, wreath with a star inside. "The Hero of New Orleans." "Composed for the Piano Forte." "Most respectfully dedicated...to the Fair Sex of America." 16pp. Page 2: Blank. [W-5227].

AJK-21 General Jackson's Grand March. Published by [V-1: J. Paff, New York, NY. ca. 1815] [V-2: W. Dubois, New York, NY. 1817-1821] [V-3: E.S. Mesier, No. 28 Wall Street, New York, NY. 1816-1844]. Non-pictorial. "For the Piano Forte." 4pp. Pages 1 and 4: Blank. [V-1: W-2943] [V-2: W-2943A].

AJK-22 Jackson's Grand March. m. B.S. Clements. Published & sold by G. Willig's Musical Magazine, No. 171 Chesnut Street, Philadelphia, PA. [1818-1819]. Non-pictorial. 2pp. Page 2: Blank. [W-1878].

AJK-23 The Hunter's Of Kentucky (Or the Battle of New Orleans). [w. S. Woodworth. m. William Blondell]. Printed by J. Puitts[?], Chambersburg. [1828?]. [9 1/2" × 10 7/8"]. B/w broadside. Litho of hunter, flowers, eagles, geometric border design. 2pp. Page 2: Blank.

AJK-24 Jackson's Victory Grand March. m. A. Raffelin. Printed for the Author by G.E. Blake, Philadelphia, PA. [1814-1831]. "Composed and Arranged for the Piano Forte." 4pp. Pages 1 and 4: Blank. Page 2: *Waltz*. [W-7287].

AJK-25 The Hunter's Of Kentucky!! w. [S. Woodworth]. m. [William Blondell]. [ca. 1828?]. [7 7/8" × 8 7/8"]. Non-pictorial. 2pp. Page 2: Blank.

AJK-26 President Jackson's Grand March. m. George O. Farmer (Pupil to Mr. Paddon). Published for the Author by C. Bradlee, No. 164 Washington Street, Boston, MA. February 24, 1829. Non-pictorial. 4pp. Pages 1 and 4: Blank.

AJK-27 General Jackson's Waltz. m. C. Meineke. Published & Sold by G. Willig, No. 71 Market Street, Baltimore, MD. [1824?]. "Willig's Musical Miscellany No. 4." [W-5775].

AJK-28 Andrew Jackson And Long May He Live! w. T.F. Archer. m. J. Long. Published by O. Torp, No. 465 Broadway, New York, NY. [1828-1837]. Non-pictorial geometric designs. 4pp. Page 4: Blank.

AJK-29 Jackson's Duett [sic]. Published & Sold by Geo. Willig, No. 171 Chestnut Street, Philadelphia, PA.

[1824?]. Non-pictorial. "For Two Performers." 4pp. Pages 1 and 4: Blank. Page 2: Secundo part. Page 3: Primo part. [W-4592].

AJK-30 Gen'l. Jackson's Triumph Grand March. m. F.L. Abel. Published by G.E. Blake, No. 13 South 5th Street, Philadelphia, PA. [ca. 1828]. Non-pictorial geometric designs. "For Two Performers on the Piano Forte." "No. 18 Blake's Miscellany." 6pp. Pages 2 and 4: Secundo part. Pages 3 and 5: Primo part. Page 6: Blank.

AJK-31 President Jackson's Grand March. Published for the Author by G.E. Blake, No. 13 South 5th Street, Philadelphia, PA. [Copyright ca. 1829 by J.T. Metz]. Non-pictorial. Composed and Arranged Expressly for the Piano Forte and Dedicated to Colonel John Thomas of Baltimore." "Pr. 38 cents." 4pp.

AJK-32 Jackson's Welcome Home. In: *Riley's Flute Melodies, A Collection of Songs, Airs, Waltzes, Cotillions, Dances, Marches, &c., &c. Arranged for the German Flute, Violin and Patent Flageolet, First Volume*, page 86. Engraved, printed & publised [sic] by the Editor [Edward Riley], No. 23 Chatham Street, New York, NY. [1814-1816]. Preceded on page one by *The Wedding Day*. Followed on page by *Surry Hornpipe*. [W-7490].

AJK-33 Grand National March. m. C. Meineke. Published by John Cole, Baltimore, MD. February 24, 1829. B/w litho of "The Hermitage, The Residence of General A. Jackson, Tennessee." "Composed and dedicated to General Andrew Jackson, President of the U. States." 2pp. Page 2: Blank.

AJK-34 General Jackson's Grand March. m. Owen L. Nares. Printed & Sold at Carr's Musical Store, Baltimore, MD. [ca. 1815]. Non-pictorial. 4pp. Pages 1 and 4: Blank. [W-6458].

AJK-35 President Jackson's Grand March. m. T. Segura. Published & sold by Geo. Willig, No. 171 Chestnut

AJK-32

Street, Philadelphia, PA. January 16, 1829. Non-pictorial. "Most Respectfully Dedicated to Him [Jackson] & Composed for the Piano Forte." 2pp.

AJK-36 General Jackson's March. m. Anderson. a. Auvray. Published & Sold at G. Willig's Music Store, Philadelphia, PA. [1816-1817]. Non-pictorial. "Composed in Jackson's Camp While the English were before New Orleans." "Arranged for the Piano Forte." 4pp. Pages 2 and 4: Blank. [W-134].

AJK-37 Andrew Jackson's March. [ca. 1819]. Non-pictorial. 2pp. Pages 1 and 2 numbered "8" and "9" respectively. Page 9: Songs—*Where Roses Wild Were Blowing* and *Oh! Yes, We Often Mention Her.*

AJK-38 Hickory Tree. w. F. Cole. m. "Air: *The Poachers*." Published by Elton, Printer, No. 134 Division Street, New York, NY. [1828?]. B/w engraving of eagle. Followed on page one by **Jackson Song.** m. "Air: *Wha'll Be King But Charlie*." 2pp. Page : Blank.

AJK-39 Old Hickory. w. David Stevens. m. Charles F. Bryan. Published by C.C. Birchard & Company, Boston, MA. 1946. B/w portrait of Andrew Jackson, drawing of hickory branch. 4pp. Page 4: Logo of Norse ship.

AJK-40 The Song Of Democracy. w. Dennis A. Ward. m. Jean Walz. Published by Dennisl A. Ward, No. 516 North Lockwood Avenue, Chicago, IL. 1932. B/w portrait of Andrew Jackson. "Dedicated to General Andrew Jackson."

(AJK) ANDREW JACKSON

6pp. Page 2: Blank. Page 6: Advertising for this song.

AJK-41 Jackson At New Orleans. In: *The Army and Navy Fife Instructor: Containing the Calls, Signals, and the Complete Camp and Garrison Duties as Practised* [sic] *in the Army and Navy of the United States, Including the Volunteer and Regular Service, Containing the National Airs, and a Large Collection of Marches, Quicksteps, Waltzes, Polkas, &c.*, page 47. e.a. Elias Howe. Published by Elias Howe, Agt., No. 103 Court Street, Boston, MA. Copyright 1863 by Willard Howe.

AJK-42 Andrew Jackson (The War of 1812). w.m. Dorothy Gaynor Blake. Published by Theodore Presser Company, No. 1712 Chestnut Street, Philadelphia, PA. 1925. R/w/b drawing of soldiers from various American wars. "Musical Portraits from American History for the Pianoforte." List of other songs in the series including *Abraham Lincoln—The Civil War* and *Theodore Roosevelt—The Spanish American War*. 4pp. Page 4: Advertising.

AJK-43 The Ballad Of Davy Crockett. w. Tom Blackburn. m. George Burns. Published by Wonderland Music Company, No. 477 Madison Avenue, New York, NY. Br/w photo, copyright 1954 by Walt Disney Productions, of "Fess Parker as Davy Crockett." "His early life, hunting adventures, services under General Jackson in the Creek War, electioneering speeches, career in Congress, triumphal tour in the Northern states and services in the Texan War." 6pp. Page 6: Three photos "From the Disneyland Television Production of *Davy Crockett*."

AJK-44 Old Hickory. w. Isobel C. White. m. James Guest. [Published in Pensacola, FL]. [ca. 1960]. R/w/bl/br/bk/y drawing by Clemente of Andrew Jackson in uniform, soldiers, Indians, palm trees. 8pp. Pages 2 and 8: Blank.

AJK-45 The Battle Of New Orleans. w.m. Jimmy Driftwood. Published by Warden Music Company, Nashville, TN. Sole Selling Agent: Keys—Hansen, Inc., No. 119 West 57th Street, New York 19, NY. Copyright 1957 and 1959. R/w photo of Johnny Horton. "Recorded by Johnny Horton on Columbia Records." 4pp.

AJK-46 President A. Jackson's Inauguration March. m. F.A. Wagler. Published by G. Willig, Jr., Baltimore, MD. 1829. Non-pictorial.

AJK-47 The New York Jackson Guards March. m. Ignace Roca. Published by Firth & Hall, No. 358 Pearl Street, New York, NY. June 18, 1829. Non-pictorial. "As performed by the Third Regt. Jackson Band, Composed and Arranged for the Piano Forte, Respectfully Dedicated to Col. Charles W. Sandford, 3rd Reg. NYS. Artillery by Ignace Roca, Leader." 4pp. Pages 1 and 4: Blank.

AJK-48 Ode To General Jackson. m. Air: *Marlbrook*. In: *The London Mathews, Containing an Account of this Celebrated Comedian's Trip to America, Being an Arrival Lecture on Peculiarities, Characters, and Manners, Founded on his Own Observations and Adventures, To Which are Prefixed Several Original Comic Songs*, page 33. Published by Morgan & Yeager, Chestnut Street, Philadelphia, PA. 1824. [3 3/4" × 6 1/4"].

AJK-49(A) Battle Of New Orleans. In: *The American Songster, Containing a Choice Selection of About One Hundred and Fifty Modern and Popular Songs*, page 174. Published by Cornish, Lamport & Company, No. 267 Pearl Street, New York, NY. 1851. Hardback. "Sterotype Edition." [3" × 4 1/8"]. 272pp.

(B) **Hickory Twigs**, page 164.

(C) **Hunters Of Kentucky**, page 57.

(D) **New Jackson Song**, page 110.

AJK-50 An Ode To Gen. Andrew Jackson (Song and Chorus). w.m.

Rev. F.W.E. Peschau (Pastor of the Evangelical Lutheran Church, Nashville, Tenn.). Published by James A. McClure, No. 65 Union Street, Nashville, TN. 1880. B/w litho of flags, statue of Andrew Jackson entitled — "The Federal Union Must Be Preserved." "Respectfully Dedicated to the Tennessee Historical Society." "Hero of New Orleans, 7th President of the U.S." "As sung at the unveiling of the Jackson Equestrian Statue, Nashville, May 20, 1880." 6pp. Pages 2, 5 and 6: Blank.

AJK-51   Tears, Idle Tears (Canatina). w.m. P.O. Bassvecchi. Published by Firth, Pond & Company, No. 547 Broadway, New York, NY. 1856. Non-pictorial geometric designs. "Sung with Great Applause by A Distinguished Lady Amateur at the Grand Concert for the Calhoun Monument Association on May 14th, 1856." "Composed and Dedicated to Miss S.F. Elmore of S.C." 12pp. Page 12: Blank.

AJK-52   The Hunters Of Kentucky. "As sung by Mr. Ludlow, in the New Orleans and Western Country Theatres." In: *The Southern Warbler, A New Collection of Patriotic, National, Naval, Martial, Professional, Convivial, Humorous, Pathetic, Sentimental, Old, and New Songs*, p. 25. Published by Babcock & Company, Charleston, SC. 1845. [3 5/8" × 6 7/8"]. Gold imprinting of a lyre, music page, instruments and eagle on brown hard cover. 330pp.

AJK-53(A)   The Hunter's Of Kentucky or Half Horse And Half Alligator. In: *The American Songbag*, page 427. e. Carl Sandburg. Published by Harcourt, Brace & Company, Inc., New York, NY. 1927.

(B) **Jackson**, page 430.

AJK-54   Jackson At New Orleans. In: *Musician's Omnibus: Containing the Whole Camp Duty, Calls and Signals Used in the Army and Navy; Forty Setts of Quadrilles, Including Waltz, Polka and Schottische, with Calls; and an Immense Collection of Polkas, Schottisches, Waltzes, Marches, Quicksteps, Hornpipes, Contra & Fancy Dances, Songs, &c., for the Violin, Flute, Cornet, Clarionett, &c, containing over 700 Pieces of Music*, page 47. c. Elias Howe. Published by Elias Howe, No. 103 Court Street, Boston, MA. 1861. [8 1/2" × 11"]. O/bk non-pictorial. "Improved Edition." 100pp.

AJK-55   Jackson At New Orleans. In: *Howe's Diamond School For The Violin: Containing, Complete Instructions and Full Directions in Bowing; to which is added A Large Collection of Popular Polkas, Schottisches, Waltzes, Redowas, Marches, Quicksteps, Dances, Hornpipes, Songs,* , page 47. c. Elias Howe. Published by Elias Howe, No. 103 Court Street, Boston, MA. 1861. [8 1/2" × 11"]. Bl/bk non-pictorial. 68pp.

AJK-56   Jackson's Grand March. m. Ludovico Gabici (Leader of the Musical Band of Mount Vernon Musketeers). Published by Johns & Co., corner of St. Charles & Common Streets, New Orleans, LA. 1840. Non-pictorial. "Souvenir of the 8th January, 1815." "Composed and Dedicated to General Andrew Jackson, on his Visit to New Orleans Jany. 8th, 1840." 4pp.

AJK-57   The Hunters Of Kentucky. "As sung by Mr. Ludlow, in the New-Orleans and Western Country Theatres." In: *War Songs of the Blue and the Gray, As Sung by the Brave Soldiers of the Union and Confederate Armies in Camp, on the March and in Garrison, Containing all the favorite Lyrics that are sung with such different feelings of sadness and mirth as they recall the shades and lights of the Great War. There is also included a large variety of old, well known and American Ballads and Songs, both patriotic and sentimental, as sung and played during the stirring times of '76 and 1812*, page 41. Published by Hurst & Co., Publishers, No. 122 Nassau Street, New York, NY. [ca. 1890].

AJK-58   President Jackson's Favorite March. m. H. Dielman. In:

Marches Of The Presidents, 1789-1909, Authentic Marches & Campaign Songs, page 18. A. Carl Miller. Published by Chappell & Co., Inc., No. 609 Fifth Avenue, New York, NY. "By arrangement with Chilmark Press, Inc." 1968. [9" × 12"]. R/w/b litho of eagle, flag. "An Illustrated Piano Folio For All Ages." 72pp.

AJK-59 Jackson's Duet. m. Philip Phile. a. Raynor Taylor (1747-1825). In: *Duets Of Early American Music*, page 14. e. Anne McClenny and Maurice Hinson. Published by Belwin Mills Publishing Company, Rockville Centre, NY. 11571. 1971. R/w/b cover drawing of two women playing piano. "Level Four." "David Carr Glover Piano Library." 36pp.

AJK-60 The Hunter's Of Kentucky. "As sung by Mr. Ludlow, in the New-Orleans and Western Country Theatres." In: *The American Naval and Patriotic Songster: As Sung at Various Places of Amusement, In Honor of the American Naval and Military Heroes; Together with a Variety of the Sentimental and Other Songs*, page 176. No publisher indicated. Published in Baltimore, 1841. [3" × 4 3/8"]. Non-pictorial leather hand bound. Gold title on spine — *Naval Songs*. 328pp.

See also GW-180; GW-181; GW-182; GW-271; MVB-9; JKP-5; MF-12; AL-221; GC-38; GC-46; TR-252; TR-293; WHT-23; WW-19; WLW-41; FDR-158; AS-4; DDE-9; LBJ-1; MISC-36 MISC-127; MISC-167; MISC-169.

Andrew Johnson

AJN-1 President Johnson's Grand Union March. m. G.R. Herbert. Published by Lyon & Healy, corner of Clark and Washington Streets, Chicago, IL. 1865. B/w litho by L. Nelke of a T. Poleni drawing of Andrew Johnson. Inside page numbers are 12-15. 6pp. Page 6: Blank.

AJN-2 Vice President Andrew Johnson's Grand March. m. L.W. Eastman. Published by J. Church, Jr., No. 66 West Fourth Street, Cincinnati, OH. 1864. B/w litho by Ehrgott, Forbriger & Co. of Andrew Johnson. Inside page numbers are 12-15. 6pp. Pages 2 and 6: Blank.

AJN-3 President Johnson's Grand Union March. m. G.R. Herbert. Published by Lyon & Healy, corner Clark and Washington Streets, Chicago, IL. 1865. B/w beige tinted litho of Andrew Johnson. 6pp. Page 6: Advertising for Lyon & Healy's store.

AJN-4 Is That You Andy? Or My Policy. w. Joshua Hutchinson and Walter Kittredge. m. Walter Kittredge. Published by Oliver Ditson & Company, No. 277 Washington Street, Boston, MA. 1866. Non-pictorial geometric designs. "As sung by them in their popular entertainments." 6pp. Pages 2 and 6: Blank. Page 3: Title: **It's No Use Standing There A-Knocking Or My Policy.**

AJN-5 Andy Veto (Song and Chorus). w.m. Henry C. Work. Published by Root & Cady, No. 67 Washington Street, Chicago, IL. 1866. B/w litho of Andrew Johnson caricature, flags, man with hoe labeled "Hail Columbia," clothes "bureau" — "Dedicated to the Freedman's [Bureau]." 6pp. Pages 2 and 6: Advertising.

AJN-6 My Policy Or Johnson On The Brain (Song and Chorus). w. Luke Collin. m. A. Weaver. Published by W.W. Whitney, Palace of Music, No. 173 Summit Street, Toledo, OH. 1866. Non-pictorial. "With profound respect and esteem, this Song is dedicated to Petroleum V. Nasby, late paster uv the church uv the noo dispensashen; P.M. at confedrit x roads (wich is in the State uv Kentucky); and chaplin to the Presidential Western Expedishn" [sic]. 6pp. Page 2: Blank. Page 6: Advertising for other W.W. Whitney published songs.

AJN-7 Impeachment Polka. m. Charles D. Blake. Published by Oliver Ditson & Company, No. 277 Washington

Street, Boston, MA. 1868. Non-pictorial geometric designs. 6pp. Pages 2 and 6: Blank.

AJN-8   God Bless The President (National Song). w. E.N. Lamont (Late Adj. 101st N.Y. Infantry). a. Charles E. White (Late Lieut., 13th Pa. Cavalry). Published by William A. Pond & Company, No. 547 Broadway, New York, NY. 1866. Non-pictorial geometric design border. 4pp.

AJN-9(A)   President Johnson's Grand Quick Step. m. E. Mack. Published by Lee & Walker, No. 722 Chestnut Street, Philadelphia, PA. 1865. Non-pictorial. "Respectfully Dedicated to President Andrew Johnson." 6pp.

(B)   President Johnson's Grand March. m. E. Mack.

AJN-10   Where Is Our Moses? (Song of the Freedman). w.m. J.H. McNaughton. Published by Oliver Ditson & Company, No. 277 Washington Street, Boston, MA. 1866. Non-pictorial geometric designs. "I will be your Moses, and will lead you through the Red Sea of struggle and servitude to a future of Liberty & Peace (Speech to the Freedmen by Andrew Johnson, 1864)." 6pp. Pages 2 and 6: Blank.

AJN-11   The Wreath (March). m. Henry Schwing. Published by Oliver Ditson, No. 115 Washington Street, Boston, MA. 1856. B/w tinted litho by J.H. Bufford's Litho. [by Winslow Homer] of Andrew Johnson, floral wreath. "To His Excellency, Andrew Johnson, Gov. of Tenn." "For the Piano Forte." 6pp. Pages 2 and 6: Blank.

AJN-12(A)   President Johnson's Grand March. m. E. Mack. Published by Lee & Walker, No. 722 Chestnut Street, Philadelphia, PA. 1865. B/w sepia tinted litho by T. Sinclair's Litho. of Andrew Johnson. "Respectfully Dedicated to President Andrew Johnson." 8pp. Pages 2 and 8: Blank. Page 3: Title page.

(B)   President Johnson's Grand Quick Step. m. E. Mack.

AJN-11

AJN-13   Ye Tailor Man (Song and Chorus). w.m. E.W. Foster. Published by Lyon & Healy, Clark and Washington Streets, Chicago, IL. 1866. B/w litho of tailor in various poses forming the first letter of each word in title. "Respectfully inscribed to ye 'Dead Dog' of the White House." 6pp. Pages 2 and 6: Blank.

AJN-14   Impeachment Song. w.m. L.A. Dochez. Published in New York, NY. 1868. Non-pictorial. 4pp. Page 4: Blank.

AJN-15   President Johnson's Grand Union March. m. G.R. Herbert. Published by Lyon & Healy, Clark and Washington Streets, Chicago, IL. 1865. B/w litho of eagle, harp, trumpet, geometric border design. "For the Piano Forte." 6pp. Page 6: B/w litho of Lyon & Healy's store. Advertising.

AJN-16   Our Moses Swinging Round The Circle. w. Charles Haynes. m. J.E. Haynes. Published by H.M. Higgins, No. 117 Randolph Street, Chicago, IL. [ca. 1866]. Non-pictorial. "25 Prize Songs." List of other songs in series, including *Jeff Davis in Crinoline* and *Uncle Abe's Rebellious Boys*. 6pp. Page 6: Adv.

AJN-17 The Veto Galop! m. "Make Peace." Published by McCarrell & Mininger, No. 91 West Jefferson Street, Louisville, KY. 1866. B/w litho by Bennett, Donaldson & Elmes of "Andy" Johnson holding a document inscribed "Veto" and riding a horse named "Constitution" trampling men labeled "Dead Ducks", including "W. Phillips," "Wade," "Stevens, "Fr. Douglass," "Freedmans Bureau;" Crowd cheering—"Hurrah for Andy," "See the Lame Ducks." Litho of building in the background labled "Forney & Co., Dealers in Game." 6pp. Pages 2 and 6: Blank.

AJN-18 President Andrew Johnson's Grand March. m. J. Henry Wolsieffer, Op. 4. Published by Louis Meyer, No. 1323 Chestnut Street, Philadelphia, PA. 1865. B/w litho by G.F. Swain of eagle with ribbon inscribed "E Pluribus Unum," shield, crossed flags. 6pp. Pages 2 and 6: Blank.

AJN-19 Bread And Butter (Illustrative of My Policy). w. Luke Collin. m. A. Weaver. Published by Lyon & Healy, corner Clark and Washington Streets, Chicago, IL. 1866. B/w litho of ribbon inscribed "My Policy," geometric designs 6pp. Page 6: Blank.

AJN-20 The Celebrated Arion Carnival Festival March. m. Carl Faust. a. George Gipner. Published by J. Schuberth & Company, No. 820 Broadway, New York, NY. 1867. Bk/w/m litho from a drawing by Thomas Nast of various heads of State, including Andrew Johnson, and allegorical figures at a pre-Lent masked ball of the Arion Society. Litho titled "Arion Fancy Dress Ball, Wednesday, March 27th, 1867, Academy of Music." "Composed for the Pianoforte." 6pp. Pages 2 and 6: Blank.

AJN-21 The Boys In Blue To The Boys In Grey. w.m. T.N. Caulfield. Published by William A. Pond & Company, No. 547 Broadway, New York, NY. 1866. Non-pictorial geometric design border. "Dedicated to His Excellency President Johnson." 6pp. Pages 2 and 6: Blank.

AJN-22 The Glorious Nineteen. Published by N. Car**?, Washington, DC. [1868]. B/w litho of U.S. flag, eagle with ribbon inscribed "U.S. Supreme Court." Star inscribed "U.S. Constitution." Wreath with the number "19"

AJN-17

AJN-20

within. 6pp. Page 2: "Legend — In 1868 before the nation had time to recover from the effects of the great Rebellion when the hearts of men were still torn, and their minds still confused with the horrors of '64, the reins of government were seized by a fanatical crew, who threatened once more to plunge the country into civil war. All was gloom and despondency, thinking man dreaded the future still more than the past, the Head of the Nation, was arraigned before a partisan tribunal, the Paladium of our liberty was stormed, when seven noble patriots threw themselves into the breach, and striking for God and their Country, scoring alike the threats and imprecations, bribes and promises of their party, pushed forward to the rescue and, by their timely efforts in behalf of law and order and the Rights of the People, gave the nation once more the blessings of Tranquility and Peace." 6pp. Page 6: Blank.

AJN-23 Handy Andy Polka. m. Max Maretzek. Published by Edward L. Walker, No. 142 Chesnut Street, Philadelphia, PA. 1856. B/w non-pictorial design. 10pp. 6pp. Pages 2 and 6: Blank. [Possibly Andrew Johnson as Governor; possibility not political].

AJN-24 President Johnson's March. Published by John Church, Jr., No. 66 West 4th Street, Cincinnati, OH. [1866?]. Non-pictorial. "XX Beautiful Pieces for the Piano by Eminent Authors." List of other titles in series.

AJN-25 Swinging 'Round The Circle (Song and Chorus.). w. S.H.M. Byers. m. P.G. Salis. Published by Lyon & Healy, No. 114 Clark Street, Chicago, IL. 1866. B/w litho of geometric designs, title in circle. 6pp. Page 2: Blank. Page 6: Advertisement for Lyon & Healy.

AJN-26 Swinging Around The Circle. w.m. E.W. Locke. Published by G.D. Russel & Company, No. 126 Tremont, Opp. Park Street, Boston, MA. 1866. B/w non-pictorial geometric designs. "Sung at the Soldiers & Sailors Convention at Pittsburgh, Sept. 1866 by the Author, and received with unbounded applause."

AJN-27 The Dawn of Peace. w.m. Samuel Jarden, Baltimore, Maryland. 1866. Non-pictorial geometric designs. "Respectfully Dedicated to President Johnson." 6pp. Pages 2 and 6: Blank.

AJN-28 President Andrew Johnson's Grand March. m. J. Henry Wolsieffer. In: *Marches Of The Presidents, 1789-1909, Authentic Marches & Campaign Songs*, page 44. A. Carl Miller. Published by Chappell & Co., Inc., No. 609 Fifth Avenue, New York, NY. "By arrangement with Chilmark Press, Inc." 1968. [9" × 12"]. R/w/b litho of eagle, flag. "An Illustrated Piano Folio For All Ages." 72pp.

See also AL-91; AL-117; AL-159; AL-379; AL-402; AL-408; WHT-23; WW-19; FDR-158; DDE-9; LBJ-1; MISC-167.

ABRAHAM LINCOLN

AL-1 President Lincoln's Grand March. m. F.B. Helmsmuller (Leader of 22nd Regiment Band, N.Y.S.M.). Published by E.A. Daggett, New York, NY. 1862. N/c litho by Thomas & Eno of Abraham Lincoln, U.S. flag, two women — "Peace" and "War." "Respectfully Dedicated to the Union Army." 8pp. Pages 2, 7 and 8: Blank.

AL-2 Lincoln Quick Step. Published by J. Church, Jr., No. 66 West Fourth Street, Cincinnati, OH. 1860. B/w beige tinted litho by Ehrgott, Forbriger & Co. of Abraham Lincoln. 6pp. Pages 2 and 6: Blank.

AL-3 Our National Union March. m. Charles Rehm. Published by the Author [Charles Rehm], New York, NY. 1862. N/c litho by Shearman & Hart of Abraham Lincoln, flag, Capitol, man — "War," woman — "Peace." "Most Respectfully Inscribed to Abraham Lin-

AL-1

coln, President of the United States." 8pp. Page 2: Facsimile letter — "Executive Mansion, Washington, February 3, 1862; My Dear Sir, It gives me greatest pleasure acknowledging the receipt of your favor of the 29th January, accompanying copies

AL-4

of your *National Union March*...A. Lincoln." "For sale by J.F. Lovell, 80 Nassau Street and at all the Principal Music Stores." Pages 7 and 8: Blank.

AL-4 **Lincoln Polka**. Published by J. Church, Jr., No. 66 West Fourth Street, Cincinnati, OH. 1860. B/w litho by Ehrgott, Forbriger & Co. of Abraham Lincoln. Page 2: Blank.

AL-5 **Old Abe Polka**. Published for B. Leidersdorf & Company (Manufacturers of Old Abe Tobaccos), Milwaukee, WI. [ca. 187-?]. B/w sepia tinted litho by the Milwaukee Litho Company of Abraham Lincoln, vignettes of slaves, rail splitting, log cabin, three pouches of "Old Abe Tobacco." "We extend our compliments to all friends of Honest 'Old Abe' who is the patron of the 'Old Abe' Chewing & Smoking Tobaccos so popular all over the country. We bespeak your friendship for it and remain yours very truly, B. Leidersdorf & Co., Sole Proprietors and Manufacturers." 6pp.

AL-6 **Lincoln Grand March**. m. F.W. Rauch. Published by F.W. Rauch, No. 82 West 4th Street, Cincinnati, OH. 1860. B/w beige tinted litho of Abraham Lincoln. 6pp. Pages 2 and 6: Blank.

AL-7 **Lincoln Quick Step**. m. Charles Grobe, Op. 1209. Published by Lee & Walker, No. 722 Chestnut Street, Philadelphia, PA. 1860. B/w tinted litho by T. Sinclair's Litho. of Abraham Lincoln, vignettes of flat boat, chopping wood, tools, flowers, &c. "Dedicated to Hon. Abraham Lincoln." 8pp.

AL-8 **Republican Song Book**. c. Thomas Drew (Late Editor of *The Massachusetts Spy*). Published by Thayer and Eldridge, Boston, MA. 1860. [3 7/8" × 5 7/8"]. Br/bk litho of beardless Abraham Lincoln, vignettes of young Lincoln chopping rails, polling raft. 68pp. "The Campaign of 1860, Republican Songs for the People, Original and Selected." Page 2: Litho of Lincoln. Pages 62-64: Republican platform. [M-108].

AL-9 **Honest Old Abe** (Song and

Chorus). w. D. Wentworth, Esq. m. "A Wide Awake." Published by Blodgett and Bradford, No. 209 Main Street, Buffalo, NY. 1860. B/w beige tinted litho by J. Sage & Sons of Abraham Lincoln — "Yours Truly, A. Lincoln" [facsimile signature]. 6pp. Pages 2 and 6: Blank.

AL-10 Inauguration Grand March. Published by Oliver Ditson & Company, No. 277 Washington Street, Boston, MA. 1861. B/w litho by J.H. Bufford's Litho. of Abraham Lincoln. "Dedicated to the President of the United States, Hon. Abrm. Lincoln." "Washington — Illinois." 6pp. Page 6: Blank.

AL-11 The Old Union Wagon. m. Chaplain John Hogarth Lozier. Published by J. Church, Jr., No. 66 West Fourth Street, Cincinnati, OH. 1863. B/w litho by Middleton, Strobridge & Company of Abraham Lincoln driving wagon labeled "Constitution" and "Union" out of the "Secession Mire;" snakes, soldiers marching, Uncle Sam with lever labeled "Emancipation Proclamation" helping free wagon, horses with flags labeled "B.B." [Ben Butler] and "U.S.G." [Ulysses S. Grant]. "Respectfully dedicated to his comrades the 37th Indiana Regiment and all who love our brave soldier boys." 6pp.

AL-12 The Wigwam Grand March. Published by Oliver Ditson & Company, No. 277 Washington Street, Boston, MA. 1860. B/w litho by J.H. Bufford's Litho. of Abraham Lincoln. B/w drawings of Lincoln splitting rails, man on horse." "Washington — Illinois." "Dedicated to the Republican Presidential Candidate." 6pp.

AL-13 Our Country's Flag. w.m. G. Gumpert. a. F. Losse. Published by G. Andre & Company, No. 1104 Chestnut Street, Philadelphia, PA. 1861. N/c litho of Union soldier with U.S. flag, rifles, tents, cannons. "Song Composed and Dedicated to His Excellency Abraham Lincoln President of the United States." 6pp. Pages 2 and 6: Blank.

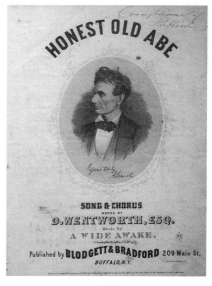

AL-9

AL-14 President Lincoln's Funeral March. m. J.T. Wamelink (Author of *Col. Clark's Triumphal March, Sanitary Fair March, &c*). Published by Wamelink & Barr, Pittsburgh, PA. 1865. B/w sepia tinted litho by Krebs &

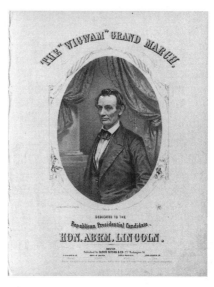

AL-12

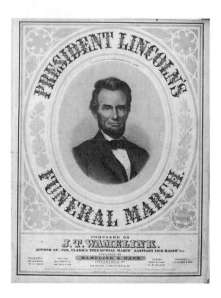

AL-14

Brother of Abraham Lincoln. "Composed on the Announcement of his Death." 6pp. Pages 2 and 6: Blank.

AL-15 We're Coming Fodder Abraham (We're Coming "In a Horn"). w.m. "By an Intelligent Contraband." Published by C.T. Beauman, Nashville, TN. 1863. B/w litho of a large horn with soldiers marching in one end. "To the new American citizens of African descent."

AL-16 The Savior Of Our Country. m. O. Wheelock. Published by John Marsh, Philadelphia, PA. [186-]. B/w beige tinted litho by L.N. Rosenthal of Abraham Lincoln & Son, Willie. "Dedicated to Little Willie."

AL-17 Abe Lincoln's Union Wagon. w. James D. Gay, Army Song Dealer and Publisher, No. 300 North 20th Street, Philadelphia, PA. m. "Air: *Wait For The Wagon* or *Old Virginia Low Lands*." Published by Charles Magnus, No. 12 Frankfort Street, New York, NY. 1864. [5" × 8"]. B/w litho of Abraham Lincoln, star. Hand Colored litho of woman with shield, Capitol building, flags. "All of Gay's Army Songs sent by mail." 4pp. Pages 2, 3 and 4: Lined paper.

AL-18 The Wide Awake Quick Step. m. Max Mayo. Published by A. & D.R. Andrews, No. 85 State Street, Tweddle Hall Music Store, Albany, NY. 1860. N/c litho by Harry Pease of a Lincoln Wide Awake Club member in campaign uniform, Capitol, White House, eagle, flags, "Constitution." "Dedicated to Capt. J. Owen Moore, Comp. A Central Club, Albany, N.Y." "As Performed by Screibers Albany Cornet Band." 6pp. Pages 2 and 6: Blank.

AL-19 President Lincoln's Funeral March. m. E. Mack. Published by Lee & Walker, No. 722 Chestnut Street, Philadelphia, PA. 1865. B/w grey tinted litho by Major & Knapp of Abraham Lincoln, flags, eagle, two women, casket. "Respectfully Dedicated to the People of the U.S." 6pp. Page 2: Blank.

AL-20 The Nation In Tears (A Dirge in the Memory of the Nation's Chief, Abraham Lincoln). w. R.C. m. Konrad Treuer. Published by Wm. Jennings Demorest, No. 39 Beekman Street,

AL-18

New York, NY. 1865. [V-1: Hand Colored] [V-2: B/w] litho of Abraham Lincoln, black border; urn, drape, facsimile signature. "Our martyred President, the friend of man, servant of God, the nation his mourner and the country his monument." "In Memoriam." "May be sung as a Solo, Duet, Trio, or Full Chorus, also arranged for the piano or organ as a Grand March." 6pp. Pages 2, 5 and 6: Blank.

AL-21   The Nation In Tears (A Dirge in the Memory of the Nation's Chief, Abraham Lincoln). w. R.C. m. Konrad Treuer. Published by Wm. Jennings Demorest, No. 39 Beekman Street, New York, NY. 1865. [V-2: 9 1/4" × 11 3/4"]. B/w [V-1: tinted] litho of Abraham Lincoln, striped [V-1: Double] [V-2: Single] border. [V-1: List of Co-Publishers]. "In Memoriam." "May be Sung as a Solo, Trio, Duett [sic] or Chorus." "Arranged for the Piano or Organ." [V-1: 6pp] [V-2: 4pp]. [V-1: Page 5: Tombstone—"In Memory of Abraham Lincoln...Requiescat in Pace [sic]." [V-1: Page 6 and V-2: Page 4]: B/w litho of Lincoln's funeral procession.

AL-22   Toll The Bell Mournfully. w.m. C. Everest. Published by Lee & Walker, No. 722 Chestnut Street, Philadelphia, PA. 1865. B/w litho of Abraham Lincoln, back geometric design border. "Toll the bell mournfully, Toll the bell Slow, Toll the bell Solemnly; Toll the bell Low; The Chief of the land is taken away, The Nation in grief is mourning to-day; Mantle his form with the flag of the land, The symbol of peace, Then place in his hand, Toll the Bell Mournfully, &c." "Written & Composed on the death of President Abraham Lincoln." 6pp. Page 6: Advertising.

AL-23   President Lincoln's Funeral March. m. E. Mack. Published by [V-1: Ditson & Company, Boston, MA. 1865] [V-2: Oliver Ditson Company, Boston, MA. ca. 1892]. B/w tinted litho of Abraham Lincoln, chain link frame, black geometric design border. "Respectfully Dedicated to the People of the United States." 6pp. Pages 2 and 6: Blank.

AL-24   Funeral March (To the Memory of Abraham Lincoln). m. Mrs. E.A. Parkhurst. Published by Horace Waters, No. 481 Broadway, New York, NY. 1865. Major & Knapp litho of Abraham Lincoln. "The Martyr President." "The Nation Mourns." 8pp. Pages 2, 7 and 8: Blank. Page 3: "To the Memory of the Martyr President of the United States of America who died April 15, 1865, in the 57th year of his age." 8pp.

AL-25   Funeral March. m. Donizetti. Published by Oliver Ditson, No. 277 Washington Street, Boston, MA. 1865. B/w gray tinted litho by J.H. Bufford's Litho. of Abraham Lincoln. "To the Memory of Abraham Lincoln." 6pp. Pages 2 and 6: Blank.

AL-26   A Funeral March. m. John K. Paine. Published by Beer & Schirmer, No. 701 Broadway, New York, NY. 1865. B/w gray tinted litho by Major & Knapp of Abraham Lincoln in wreath, crown of stars. "In Memory of President Lincoln." 8pp. Page 2: Blank.

AL-27   Abraham Lincoln's Funeral March. m. W.J. Robjohn. Published by J. Henry Whittemore, Detroit, MI. 1865. B/w Colvert & Company litho of Abraham Lincoln, crossed flags, drape, black border. "Dedicated to the People of the United States." 8pp. Pages 2, 7 and 8: Blank.

AL-28   President Lincoln's Funeral March. m. T.M. Brown. Published by Endres & Compton, No. 52 Fourth Street, St. Louis, MO. 1865. B/w beige litho by A. McLean of Abraham Lincoln in oval frame, woman weeping holding wreath, eagle, shield, flags. 8pp. Pages 2, 7 and 8: Blank. Page 3: Title—**A Tribute To Pres. Lincoln**.

AL-29   Lincoln Quick Step. m. Charles Grobe, Op. 1209. Published by Lee & Walker, No. 722 Chesnut Street,

(AL) ABRAHAM LINCOLN

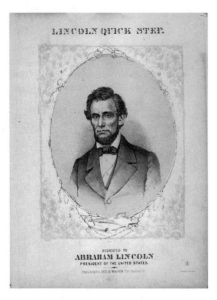

AL-29

AL-30

Philadelphia, PA. 1860. B/w beige tinted litho by T. Sinclair's Litho. of Abraham Lincoln, branch frame, quill, ivy, scroll. "Dedicated to Abraham Lincoln, President of the United States." 8pp. Pages 2 and 7: Blank. Page 3: "Honest Old Abe has split many a rail, He is up to his work, and he'll surely not Fail, He has guided his Flat-Boat thro' many a strait, and Watchful he'll prove at the helm of the State." Page 8: Advertising.

AL-30 Our Brutus. w. La Grosse Democrat. m. E.B. Armand. Published by A.E. Blackmar, New Orleans, LA. 1865. B/w tinted litho of John Wilkes Booth. 6pp. Page 3: History of the poem "Our Brutus." [Pro-Booth].

AL-31 President Lincoln's Funeral March. m. E. Mack. Published by Lee & Walker, No. 722 Chestnut Street, Philadelphia, PA. 1865. B/w beige tinted litho by Thomas Sinclair of Abraham Lincoln, scroll, quill. "Respectfully Dedicated to the People of the United States." 6pp. Page 6: Advertising.

AL-32 Rest Spirit Rest (Grand Requiem March). m. E. Hoffman (Author of *Mocking Bird*, *Trinity Chimes*, &c. &c.). Published by William A. Pond & Company, No. 547 Broadway, New York, NY. 1865. B/w beige tinted litho by Major & Knapp of Abraham Lincoln, facsimile signature, circle of stars. "To the Memory of Abraham Lincoln." 8pp.

AL-33 We Are Coming Father Abraham (300,000 More). w. "From the *New York Evening Post*." a. S.J. Adams. Published by Henry Tolman & Company, Boston, MA. 1862. B/w non-pictorial geometric designs. "To the President." 6pp. Pages 2 and 6: Blank.

AL-34 Our Flag Is Half Mast High! (Song and Chorus). w.m. H.W. Luther. Published by M. Gray, No. 613 Clay Street, San Francisco, CA. [1865]. Non-pictorial black border. "In Memory of Abraham Lincoln, Assassinated April 14, 1865." 6pp.

AL-35 Uncle Abram, Bully For You! (Song and Chorus). w. J. Smith, Jr. m. G.R. Lampard. Published by H.M. Higgins, No. 117 Randolph Street, Chicago, IL. 1862. B/w non-pictorial geometric design border. 6pp. Page 2:

Blank. Page 6: Advertising for other H.M. Higgins published music.

AL-36 We Are Coming Father Abraham (or Three Hundred Thousand More). w. "From *The New York Evening Post*." m. A.B. Irving. Published by H.M. Higgins, No. 117 Randolph Street, Chicago, IL. 1862. Non-pictorial. "Inscribed to our Volunteers." 6pp. Page 6: Blank.

AL-37 Funeral March. m. Bvt. Major General J.C. Barnard. Published by William A. Pond & Company, No. 547 Broadway, New York, NY. 1865. Non-pictorial black line border. "Played at the obsequies of the late President of the United States by the U.S. Marine Band." "Dedicated to the memory of Abraham Lincoln." 6pp. Page 6: Blank.

AL-38 600,000 More (We Are Coming Father Abram!) (Song and Chorus). w.m. "A Volunteer." Published by S. Brainard & Company, No. 203 Superior Street, Cleveland, OH. 1862. B/w non-pictorial geometric design border. "Price 25 cents." 6pp. Pages 2 and 6: Blank.

AL-39 Old Abe Has Gone & Did It, Boys (Song and Chorus). w. S. Fillmore Bennett. m. J.P. Webster. Published by H.M. Higgins, No. 117 Randolph Street, Chicago, IL. 1862. Non-pictorial. 6pp. Page 6: Blank.

AL-40 President Lincoln's Funeral March. m. E. Mack. Published by Oliver Ditson Company, Boston, MA. [ca. 1905]. O/bk/w non-pictorial floral and geometric designs. "Garland of Melodies, First Series." List of other titles in the series.

AL-41 Nomination Song. w. Charles Haynes. m. James Edward Haynes. Published by H.M. Higgins, No. 117 Randolph Street, Chicago, IL. 1864. Non-pictorial geometric designs and border. "Three Offerings to Thee, Goddess of Liberty." "To thee fair goddess our offerings we bring, Accept them though humble they be, For gladly we trust to thy keeping the flag, That waves o'er the brave and the free." List of other titles in series. 6pp. Pages 2 and 6: Blank.

AL-42 Emancipation March. m. Thomas J. Martin (Author of *Persifer Smith's March*). Published by D.S. Crutchley & Company, No. 182 Superior Street, Cleveland, OH. 1863. Non-pictorial geometric design border. "To his Excellency Abraham Lincoln, President of the United States." "Composed for the Piano Forte." 6pp. Pages 2 and 6: Blank.

AL-43 The Martyr Of Liberty. w.m. James G. Clark (Author of *Voice of the Army, Let Me Die With My Face to the Foe, Moonlight and Starlight, Beautiful Annie, &c., &c.*). Published by Horace Waters, No. 481 Broadway, New York, NY. 1865. Non-pictorial geometric design border. "Dedicated to Mrs. Lincoln." "In Memory of President Lincoln." 6pp. Page 6: Advertising.

AL-44 Mourn Not! Oh, Ye People, As Those Without Hope. w. Mrs. M.A. Kidder. m. Mrs. E.A. Parkhurst (Author of *A Home In The Mountain, Richmond Is Ours, President Lincoln's Funeral March, Oh, Send Me One Flower From His Grave, &c.*). Published by Horace Waters, No. 481 Broadway, New York, NY. 1865. Non-pictorial geometric design border. "A Tribute to the memory of Abraham Lincoln."

AL-45 Honest Old Abe's Quick Step. Published by Oliver Ditson & Company, No. 277 Washington Street, Boston, MA. 1860. Non-pictorial geometric designs. "For the Piano." "To the Hon. A. Lincoln."

AL-46 Hold On Abraham (Uncle Sam's Boys Are Coming Right Along) (Song and Chorus). w.m. B. Bradbury (Author of *Marching Along, The Dear Old Flag, Flag of Our Union, &c., &c.*). Published by William A. Pond & Co., No. 547 Broadway, New York, NY. 1862. B/w non-pictorial. "Being a response of Uncle Sam's Boys to the Call for 'Three Hundred Thousand More.'"

"Sung with Immense success by Wood's Minstrels." "To the President of the United States." 6pp. Page 6: Blank.

AL-47 Oh! Why Should The Spirit Of Mortal Be Proud? w. [William Knox]. m. C. Everest. Published by Lee & Walker, No. 722 Chestnut Street, Philadelphia, Pa. 1865. B/w geometric design border. "President Lincoln's Favorite Poem. Copied by F.B. Carpenter, Esq., while our lamented Chief was reciting it." Six printed verses. 6pp. Page 2: Blank. Page 6: Advertising for other Lee & Walker published music.

AL-48 300,000 More! m. George R. Poulton. Published by Joseph P. Shaw, No. 110 State Street, Rochester, NY. 1862. B/w border drawing of small flowers. "To President Abraham." 6pp. Page 2: Blank. Page 6: Advertising for other Joseph P. Shaw published music.

AL-49 The Assassin's Vision (Ballad). w.m. J.W. Turner. Published by S. Brainard's Sons, Cleveland, OH. 1865. Non-pictorial black border. "(Note) This ballad was suggested on seeing the representation of the assassin Booth wildly fleeing the forest on his horse, startled by the apparition of his victim appearing in the trees and around him." 6pp. Pages 2 and 6: Blank.

AL-50 Helmer's Lincoln Song. m. Air: *Happy Land Of Freedom*. Non-pictorial. 2pp. Page 2: Blank.

AL-51 Farewell Father, Friend And Guardian (Song and Chorus). w. L.M. Dawn. m. George F. Root. Published by Root & Cady, No. 67 Washington Street, Chicago, IL. 1865. Non-pictorial black border. "Sung at the funeral ceremonies of President Lincoln buried at Springfield, Ill., May 4, 1865." 6pp. Pages 2 and 6: Advertising for other songs.

AL-52 Requiem March in Honor of President Lincoln. m. W.O. Fiske. Published by Oliver Ditson & Company, No. 277 Washington Street, Boston, MA. 1865. B/w litho of a circle of stars. 6pp. Pages 2 and 6: Blank. Page 3: Inside title—**President Lincoln's Funeral March**

AL-53 He's Gone To The Arms Of Abraham. w.m. Sep. Winner. Published by Johnson, Song Publisher, No. 7 North 10th Street, Philadelphia, PA. [ca. 1862]. [6" × 9 1/4"]. B/w non-pictorial geometric design border. "This song written by Sep. Winner, and Published in Sheet Music by Winner & Company, No. 933 Spring Garden Street. See the music of it." "See Johnson's New Catalogue of Songs." 2pp. Page 2: Blank.

AL-54 Rest, Martyr, Rest (Song and Chorus). w. James E. Glass. m. George P. Graff. Published by H.M. Higgins, No. 117 Randolph Street, Chicago, IL. 1865. B/w geometric design border. "Tribute to Lincoln." 6pp. Page 2: Blank. Page 6: Advertising for H.M. Higgins song book.

AL-55 Song On The Death Of President Abraham Lincoln. w. Silas S. Steele. m. "Tune: *Annie Laurie*." Copyright 1865 by J. Magee, No. 316 Chestnut Street, Philadelphia, PA. [5 1/8" × 8"]. Non-pictorial black border. 2pp. Page 2: Blank.

AL-56 Oh! Why Should The Spirit Of Mortal Be Proud. w. Abraham Lincoln. m. George C. Pearson. Published by H.M. Higgins, No. 117 Randolph Street, Chicago, IL. 1865. Non-pictorial geometric design border. "Poem by Abraham Lincoln, late President of the U.S." 6pp. Pages 5 and 6: Blank.

AL-57 The Republican Campaign Songster For 1860. c. W.H. Burleigh. Published by H. Dayton, No. 36 Howard Street, New York, NY. 1860. [V-1: Gn/bk] [V-2: Y/bk]. "Price 10 cents." 72pp. [M-104].

AL-58 Death And Patriotism Of Abraham Lincoln! w. A.M. Osborn. [1865]. [5 1/2" × 9 13/16"]. Non-pictorial. 2pp. Page 2: Blank. [May not be a song].

AL-59 The Wide Awake Vocalist (Or Rail Splitters' Song Book). Published by E.A. Daggett, No. 333 Broadway, New York, NY. 1860. Non-pictorial geometric design border. "Words and Music for the Republican Campaign of 1860, Embracing a Great Variety of Songs, Solos, Duets and Choruses Arranged for Piano or melodeon; The best collection of Words and Music ever published for a campaign, Every Club and Family should have copies, so as to join in the choruses; The Ladies are invited to join in the choruses at the meetings." 68pp. Page 2: Index. Page 67: Blank. Page 68: Advertising for Horace Waters publications. [M-116].

AL-60 Lincoln Lies Sleeping. w. Nathan Upham. m. "Air: *Under The Willow*." Published by Johnson, Song Publisher, No. 7 North 10th Street, Philadelphia, PA. [1865]. [4" × 8 1/4"]. B/w litho of Abraham Lincoln. "We have Reduced our Wholesale Prices of Songs." 2pp. Page 2: Blank.

AL-61 Funeral Procession Of President Lincoln. m. "Tune: *Star of The Evening, Glory on High*." Published by J.H. Johnson's Card & Job Printing Office, No. 7 North 10th Street above Market, Philadelphia, PA. 1865. [5 3/4" × 9 7/16"]. Non-pictorial. "As it started from the depot in Philadelphia, April 22d, 1865." "Cards, Bill Heads, Circulars, Hand Bills, Labels, Envelopes, Meeting Notices, Ball Tickets, Party Tickets, Ladies Invitations, Programmes, Checks, Badges, Visiting Cards, &c., &c., &c., Neatly Printed." 2pp. Page 2: Blank.

AL-62 The President's Emancipation March. m. George E. Fawcett. Published by Root & Cady, No. 95 Clark Street, Chicago, IL. 1862. Non-pictorial black line border. Quote—"Go ring the bells, and fire the guns, and fling the Starry banner out, Shout 'Freedom' till your lisping ones give back their cradle shout—Whittier." "Dedicated to Abraham Lincoln, A Foe to Tyrants, and my Country's Friend." "Composed for the Piano." 6pp. Page 6: Blank.

AL-63 President Lincoln's Favorite Poem. Published by A.W. Auner, Song Publisher, cor. 11th and Market, Philadelphia, PA. [1865]. [5" × 8 7/8"]. B/w litho of eagle with ribbon inscribed "E Pluribus Unum," flags, shield, black border. 2pp. Page 2: Blank.

AL-64 The Old Chieftain. (Song and Chorus). w.m. Edwin Henry. Published by Lee & Walker, No. 722 Chesnut Street, Philadelphia, PA. 1864. Non-pictorial geometric design border, verse: printed "Old Abe Lincoln is the man for me, However long and lean he may be, He's honest and bold and never fails, He knows how to fight and split old rails, Old Abe Lincoln is the man for me, Old Abe Lincoln is the man for thee, Old Abe Lincoln is the man for all, He can whip old Jeff and old Stonewall."

AL-65 Abe Lincoln's Union Wagon. m. "Air: *Wait For The Wagon* or *Virginia Low Lands*." Published by C.H. Day, [PA]. 1864. [4 1/4" × 6 7/8"]. Non-pictorial broadside. Page 2: Blank.

AL-66 Funeral March. m. Dr. F. Haase. Published by Oliver Ditson & Company, No. 277 Washington Street, Boston, MA. 1865. B/w litho of a wreath. "In Memoriam." "In Honor of President Lincoln." 6pp. Pages 2 and 6: Blank.

AL-67 The Death Knell Is Tolling (A Requiem to the Memory of Our Late Beloved President Abraham Lincoln) (Quartette). w. Honorable H.H. Cody. m. J.F. Fargo. Published by Lyon & Healy, corner of Clark and Washington Streets, Chicago, IL. 1865. Non-pictorial black geometric design border. 6pp. Pages 2 and 6: Blank.

AL-68 The President's Death (A Prayer). m. "Tune: *America*." Published by Tribune Print, Smyrna. [1865]. [2 1/2" × 6 1/2"]. Non-pictorial black border top and bottom. 2pp. Page 2: Blank.

AL-69 Abraham! Our Abraham! (A Rallying Song and Chorus). w. "H." m. Air: "To the Popular Melody *Maryland! My Maryland*!" a. W.F. Sherman.

Published by W.F. Sherman, No. 85 State Street, Albany, NY. 1864. Non-pictorial geometric border. 6pp. Pages 2 and 6: Blank.

AL-70 Abraham Lincoln's Funeral March. m. William Wolsieffer, Op. 7. Published by Louis Meyer, No. 1323 Chestnut Street, Philadelphia, PA. 1865. B/w litho of flags, shields, black drape, tombstone inscribed "In Memory of a Country's Martyred Father." "Composed for the Piano Forte." 6pp. Pages 2 and 6: Blank.

AL-71 Song For Republican Rally, Nov. 1, 1864. w. George A. Kimball. m. "Tune—*America*." Published by Tyler & Seagrave, Printers, No. 212 Main Street, Worcester, MA. 1864. [4 3/4" × 8 3/4"]. Non-pictorial geometric design border. Page 2: Blank.

AL-72 Abraham The Great And Genl. Grant His Mate. w.m. T. Brigham Bishop. Published by John Church, No. 66 West 4th Street, Cincinnati, OH. 1864. Non-pictorial geometric designs. "Sung by T. Brigham Bishop and Troop." "Campaign Song for 1864."

AL-73(A) Lincoln's Grand March. Published by A.C. Peters & Bro., No. 94 West Fourth Street, opposite the Post Office, Cincinnati, OH. 1860. B/w litho by Ehrgott, Forbriger & Co. of Abraham Lincoln. 6pp. Pages 2 and 6: Blank.

AL-74 The President Lincoln Campaign Songster. Published by T.R. Dawley, Nos. 13 and 14 Park Row, New York, NY. 1864. O/bk litho of Abraham Lincoln, vignettes of Lincoln's life. "Price 12 cents." [M-127].

AL-75 We Are Coming Father Abra'am, 300,000 More. w. William Cullen Bryant [John Sloan Gibbons]. m. L.O. Emerson. Published by Oliver Ditson & Company, No. 277 Washington Street, Boston, MA. 1862. Non-pictorial ribbon. 6pp. Pages 2 and 6: Blank.

AL-76 The Nation's Purest Man, Abraham Lincoln (Song and Chorus). w. John H. Cook. e. William B. Broadway. Published for the Author by Louis Tripp, Louisville, KY. 1865. B/w litho of ivy, geometric designs. 6pp. Pages 2 and 6: Blank.

AL-77 Honest Abe's Songster. Published by T.R. Dawley, Publisher for the Million, New York, NY. 1864. Y/bk litho of Abraham Lincoln, vignettes of Lincoln's life. "Dawley's Ten-Penny Song Books." 72pp. [M-122].

AL-78 Funeral March. m. E.C. Davis. Published by Balmer & Weber, No. 56 Fourth Street, St. Louis, MO. 1865. B/w beige tinted litho by A. McLean of Abraham Lincoln, flag, drape, document. "Composed and Dedicated to the Memory of the Pure and Noble Patriot Abraham Lincoln, 16th President of the U.S." 6pp. Pages 2, 4, 5 and 6: Blank.

AL-79 Lincoln Campaign Songster. Published by Mason & Company, Philadelphia, PA. 1864. [2 7/8" × 4 7/8"]. B/w litho of a beardless Abraham Lincoln, geometric design border. 20pp. Pages 2 and 19: Blank. Page 3: Title page. "For the use of Clubs. Containing all of the most popular songs." Page 20: Advertising. [M-125].

AL-80 Grand Funeral March. m. Henry Mayer. Published by William A. Pond & Company, No. 547 Broadway, New York, NY. 1865. B/w tinted litho by Major & Knapp of Abraham Lincoln, facsimile signature, stars. "To the memory of Abraham Lincoln, Born Feby. 12, 1809; Died Apr. 15, 1865." 8pp. Pages 2 and 8: Blank.

AL-81 Lincoln Campaign Songster. Published by Mason & Company, Philadelphia, PA. 1864. [4" × 6 3/8"]. B/w litho of a beardless Abraham Lincoln, bold striped border. 20pp. "For the use of Clubs, Containing all of the most popular songs." [M-126].

AL-82 In Memoriam. w. Mrs. E.J. Bugbee. m. H.T. Merrill. Published by Merrill & Brennan, No. 91 Washington Street, Chicago, IL. 1865. Non-pictorial black border. "Quartette on the Death of Abraham Lincoln, the Sixteenth President of the United States."

AL-83 Requiem. m. M. Keller. Published by Henry Tolman & Company, No. 291 Washington Street, Boston, MA. 1865. B/w litho of black drape, feathers. "Composed & Inscribed To the memory of Abraham Lincoln, the Champion of Universal Liberty." 8pp. Pages 2 and 8: Blank.

AL-84 The National Funeral March. m. C. Everest. Published by Charles W.A. Trumpler, 7th & Chestnut Streets, Philadelphia, PA. 1865. Non-pictorial black border. "In Honor of President Abraham Lincoln." 6pp. Pages 2 and 6: Blank.

AL-85 A Nation Mourns Her Martyr'd Son. w. Alice Hawthorne. m. Sep. Winner. Published by Sep. Winner, No. 933 Spring Garden Street, Philadelphia, PA. 1865. Non-pictorial black border. "An Honest Man's the Noblest Work of God." "In Memory of Abraham Lincoln, Sixteenth President of the United States." 6pp. Page 2: Blank. Page 6: Advertising.

AL-86 Enjolras (The Song of the Patriot). w.m. Edmundus Scotus, R.Q.S. a. George Zoeller. Published by D.P. Faulds, No. 223 Main Street, Louisville, KY. 1865. Non-pictorial geometric design border. "Before everything, but the Republic chastely dropped his eyes. He was the marble lover of Liberty.— Les Miserables." "To the immortal memory of the people's President, Abraham Lincoln, is Mournfully Inscribed this Song, by a Soldier of the Republic." "Arranged for the Piano Forte." 8pp. Pages 2 and 8: Blank.

AL-87 How Are You Greenbacks? m. Air: *We Are Coming Father Abraham.* Published by Johnson, Song Publisher, No. 7 North 10th Street, Philadelphia, PA. 1863. [6" × 8 3/4"]. Non-pictorial geometric design litho border. "The music for this song can be had of Wm. A. Pond & Co., No. 547 Broanway [sic], N.Y." 2pp. Page 2: Blank.

AL-81

AL-88(A) Secretary Chase's Grand March And Quickstep. m. E. Mack. Published by Lee & Walker, No. 722 Chestnut Street, Philadelphia, PA. 1863. Gn/bk/w litho of $50 "Greenback" with picture of Miss Justice, Secretary Chase, eagle, other Greenback notes with likeness of George Washington, woman. "To the Hon. Salmon P. Chase, Secretary of the Treasury." "Composed for the Piano Forte." 6pp. Page 6: Advertising.

(B) Greenback Quick Step.

AL-89 How Are You Green-Backs! w. E. Bowers, Esq. and G.W.H. Griffin. a. Charles Glover. Published by Wm. A. Pond & Company, No. 547 Broadway, New York, NY. [1862]. Gn/bk/w litho of $10 "Greenback" note with picture of Dan Bryant [facsimile signature], George Washington, eagle, Miss Liberty, Indian, Washington Monument. "Dan Bryant's Popular Comic *Song How Are You Green-Backs?* as sung by Him with Immense success at Bryant's Minstrels also by Mrs. John Wood in the grand Fairy Extravaganza *Fair One with the Golden Locks*." 6pp. Pages 2 and 6: Blank. [Lyrics mention George McClellan and Horace Greeley].

AL-90   Greenbacks! (New Song for the Times). w.m. Dan D. Emmett (Author of *Dixie's Land, High Daddy*, &c., &c.). Published by William A. Pond & Company, No. 547 Broadway, New York, NY. 1863. Gn/bk/w litho by Sarony, Major and Knapp of $10 and $20 "Greenback" notes, woman, eagle. "Sung by Bryant's Minstrels." 6pp. Page 6: Blank.

AL-91   Liberty's Call (or Hurrah for Abe and Andy). w. W.S. Blanchard. m. L.B. Starkweather. Published by Oliver Ditson & Company, No. 277 Washington Street, Boston, MA. [ca. 1864]. B/w litho of banner—"Liberty's Call." 6pp. Pages 2 and 6: Blank.

AL-92   Our Noble Chief Has Passed Away (Elegy on the Death of Abraham Lincoln). w. George Cooper. m. J.R. Thomas. Published by Wm. A. Pond & Co., No. 547 Broadway, New York, NY. 1865. B/w litho of column, church, cherubs. 8[?]pp. Page 2: Blank.

AL-93   Lost On The Sultana (Song and Chorus). w.m. James A. Barney (of Morris and Wilson's Opera House). Published by Endres & Compton, No. 52 4th Street, St. Louis, MO. 1865. Non-pictorial black border. "To the memory of the Loved and Lost on the steamer Sultana." "These Beautiful and Patriotic lines were found upon the body of an Officer of one of the Ohio Regiments written upon the back of an Extra announcing the assassination of President Lincoln and addressed to his wife, to whom he was returning after two years of confinement in Southern prisons." 6pp.

AL-94   Strike For The Right! (A Republican Campaign Song). w.m. E.W. Locke. Published by E.W. Locke. Printed by I. Berry & Son, No. 177 Fore, corner of Exchange, Portland, ME. 1860. Non-pictorial broadside. 2pp.

AL-95   Lincoln's Funeral March. m. E.C. Davis (Author of *Only Waiting, Song Of Night, &c.*). Published by Balmer & Weber, No. 311 North Fifth Street, St. Louis, MO. Copyright 1865, 1875 and 1888. Non-pictorial geometric designs, black border. "Composed and Dedicated to the Memory of the Pure and Noble Patriot Abraham Lincoln, 16th President of the U.S." [V-1: 6pp. Page 2: Advertising for *Garfield's Funeral March* by Henry Werner. B/w litho of "Fac Simile of the Hearse that bore Him to Rest." Page 6: Advertising for "The Martyr Sleeps" by H.S. Thompson. B/w litho of "Fac Simile of the Catafalque at Cleveland"] [V-2: 4[?]pp. Page 2: Advertising for funeral marches including *Lincoln's Funeral March* by E.C. Davis, , *Tribute To Lincoln* by T.M. Brown, *Garfield's Funeral March* by H. Werner, and *Webster's Funeral March* by L. von Beethoven.] [V-3: At bottom of page 5—"Be sure to examine complete copies of the beautiful musical tributs [sic] to our martyred President William McKinley]."

AL-96   The President's Hymn. w.m. Dr. Muhlenberg. Published by Root & Cady, No. 95 Clark Street, Chicago, IL. 1863. Non-pictorial. "In response to the Proclamation of the President of the United States recommending a General Thanksgiving on November 26, 1863. When the dedication was proposed to the President, he answered 'Let it be so called.'" "Price 5 cents; 50 cents a dozen." 2pp. Page 2: Blank.

AL-97   The Nation's Honored Dead (Monody on the Death of Our Beloved President). w. Miss M.J. Bishop. m. J.W. Turner. Published by C.C. Clapp & Company, No. 69 Court Street, Boston, MA. 1865. Non-pictorial geometric and black line border. 6pp. Pages 2 and 6: Blank.

AL-98   Funeral March (To the Memory of Abraham Lincoln). m. Mrs.

E.A. Parkhurst. Published by Horace Waters, No. 481 Broadway, New York, NY. 1865. Non-pictorial black border. "The Martyr President of the United States of America who died April 15th, 1865, in the 57th year of his age." "The Nation Mourns." 6pp. Page 2: Blank. Page 6: Advertising for other Horace Waters published music.

AL-99 Washington And Lincoln (Song and Chorus). w.m. Henry C. Work. Published by Root & Cady, No. 95 Clark Street, Chicago, IL. 1864. Non-pictorial geometric design border. 6pp. Pages 2 and 6: Advertising for other Root & Cady published music.

AL-100 A Nation Weeps (Dirge on the Death of Abraham Lincoln). w.m. J.W. Turner. Published by Oliver Ditson & Company, No. 277 Washington Street, Boston, MA. 1865. Non-pictorial geometric design black border. 6pp. Pages 2 and 6: Blank. Page 3: Title: **A Nation Weeps** (or the Death of President Lincoln).

AL-101 Strike For The Right. w.m. E.W. Locke. Published by Oliver Ditson & Company, No. 277 Washington Street, Boston, MA. 1860. B/w litho arrow, ribbon inscribed "Sung with rapturous applause at the Fanueil Hall Ratification Meeting." "To Honest Abe Lincoln." 6pp. Pages 2 and 6: Blank.

AL-102 Funeral March. m. Donizetti. Published by Oliver Ditson & Company, No. 277 Washington Street, Boston, MA. [1865]. Non-pictorial black border. "Performed at the funeral of Abraham Lincoln." 6pp. Page 2 and 6: Blank. Page 3: Title: **Marche Funebre**.

AL-103 Oh! Speak To Me Once More! w. W. Dexter Smith, Jr. m. Henri Cromwell. Published by G.D. Russell & Company, No. 126 Tremont, opp. Park Street, Boston, MA. 1865. Non-pictorial geometric design black border. "Respectfully Dedicated to Mrs. Abraham Lincoln." 6pp. Pages 2 and 6: Blank.

AL-104 Little Tad (Ballad). w.m. J.W. Turner. Published by Oliver Ditson & Company, No. 277 Washington Street, Boston, MA. 1865. Non-pictorial geometric design border. "'TAD' is the pet name of President Lincoln's youngest son. He was a great favorite with his father, as may be inferred from the fact that Mrs. Lincoln while at the bedside of her dying husband, exclaimed, 'O! bring our 'TAD' here! for he loves TAD so well that I know he will speak to him!'" 6pp.

AL-105 Dirge (Our Deeply Lamented Martyred President!). w. O. Wheelock. m. E. Mack. Published by Lee & Walker, No. 722 Chestnut Street, Philadelphia, PA. 1865. Non-pictorial black border. "Very Respectfully Inscribed to Mrs. Lincoln, widow of the late President of the United States, by the Author — with the assurance that he shares the Nation's Condolence." 6pp. Page 6: Advertising.

AL-106 The Martyred Patriot (Grand Funeral March). m. James W. Porter, Op. 473. Published by J. Marsh, No. 1029 Chestnut Street, Philadelphia, PA. 1865. Non-pictorial black border. "Performed on the Reception of the Remains of Our Beloved President Abraham Lincoln at Philad'a April 22, 1865." 6pp. Page 2: Blank.

AL-107 We Are Coming Father Abra'am (Six Hundred Thousand More). w. *New York Evening Post* [James Sloane Gibbons]. m.a. Professor A. Cull. Published by Horace Waters, No. 481 Broadway, New York, NY. 1862. B/w non-pictorial geometric design. 6pp. Pages 2 and 6: Blank.

AL-108 Lincoln's Grave. w.m. Isaiah W. Gougler. Published by William A. Pond & Company, No. 547 Broadway, New York, NY. 1865. Non-pictorial. 6pp. Pages 2 and 6: Blank.

AL-109 The Nation Is Weeping. w. Louise S. Upham. m. "Air: *Under the Willow She's Sleeping*." Published by Charles Magnus, No. 12 Frankfort Street, New York, NY. [1865]. [5" × 8"]. B/w litho of the Lincoln funeral procession in New York City. 2pp. Page 2: Blank.

AL-110 Columbia Mourns For Our President Lincoln. w. A.W. Harmon. [1865]. [6 13/16" × 10"]. B/w litho of Abraham Lincoln in oval frame at top of music. B/w geometric design border. 2pp. Page 2: Blank.

AL-111 The Nation Mourns. Published by Charles Magnus, No. 12 Frankfort Street, New York, NY. [1865]. [5" × 8"]. B/w litho of Abraham Lincoln in oval frame, two women, soldier, flag, black border. 2pp. Page 2: Blank.

AL-112 Lincoln & Hamlin. m. "Air: *Wait For The Wagon*." Published by H. De Marsan, Publisher of Songs and Ballads — Toy-Books, &c., No. 60 Chatham Street, New York, NY. [1860]. [5 1/2" × 9 3/8"]. B/w and hand colored border of soldier, sailor, ship. 2pp. Page 2: Blank.

AL-113 Lincoln & Hamlin. Published by H. De Marsan, Publisher of Songs and Ballads, Toy-books, Paperdolls, No. 60 Chatham Street, New York, NY. [1860]. [6" × 9 1/2"]. B/w hand colored border of soldier, sailor, ship, geometric designs. "Republican Campaign Song." 2pp. Page 2: Blank.

AL-114 Lincoln Lies Sleeping. w. Nathan Upham. m. "Air: *Under the Willow*." Published by H. De Marsan, Publisher, No. 54 Chatham Street, New York, NY. [1865]. [6 3/4" × 10 1/4"]. B/w litho of [V-1: Sword, pillow] [V-2: Flag, house, tomb with woman] border of cherubs, woman. 2pp. Page 2: Blank.

AL-115 Republican Glee For Lincoln & Hamlin. Published by H. De Marsan, Publishers, Songs, Ballads, Toybooks, No. 60 Chatham Street, New York, NY. [1860]. [5 7/8" × 9 1/8"]. B/w litho border [hand Colored] drawings of man, woman, cherubs, banner inscribed "E Pluribus Unum." 2pp. Page 2: Blank.

AL-116 The Wide-Awakes. w. O.P.Q. m. Air: *Washing Day*. Published by H. De Marsan, Publisher, Songs, Ballads, Toy Books, Nos. 58 and 60 Chatham Street, New York, NY. 1860. [6 1/2" × 9 1/4"]. B/w litho border of clowns, knaves, jesters, &c. 2pp. Page 2: Blank.

AL-117 A Voice From The Army. w. R.B. Nicol (Author and Publisher of a Choice Collection of Popular Songs). Published by R.B. Nicol, No. 271 Pennsylvania Avenue, Washington, DC. 1864. [5" × 8 1/16"]. R/w/bl/br litho of eagle, flags [First letter of each line vertically spells "Vote for Lincoln and Johnson"]. 4pp. Pages 2 to 4: Lined writing paper.

AL-118 Live But One Moment (Ballad). w.m. J.W. Turner. Published by [V-1: Henry Tolman & Company, No. 291 Washington Street, Boston, MA] [V-2: S. Brainard's Sons, Cleveland, OH]. 1865. B/w engraving by H.F. Greene of star border on black background. "Live! exclaimed the wife of our lamented President as she stood bending o'er his dying form, Live but for one moment, to speak to me once more, to speak to our children." 6pp. Pages 2 and 6: Blank.

AL-119 Uncle Sam's Menagerie (A Union Campaign Song and Chorus). w.m. J. William Pope. Published by Charles C. Mellor, No. 81 Wood Street, Pittsburgh, PA. 1864. Non-pictorial. Quote — "So wide spread was Treason, so Faithless the President, that all hope was exhausted except the single one that his term would expire Before all was lost, Thank God! Abraham Lincoln became the President before the cause of the Union was totally ruined, and then the work of rescue began — Moorehead." "Respectfully dedicated to Hon J.K. Moorehead, M.C." 6pp. Pages 2 and 6: Blank.

AL-120 Raw Recruits (or Abraham's Daughter). Published by Firth, Pond & Company, No. 547 Broadway, New York, NY. Copyright 1861 by Sep. Winner and 1862 by Firth, Pond & Company. B/w litho by Sarony, Major & Knapp of five black Union soldiers in caricature with one carrying a sign inscribed "Raw Recruits, Capt. Dan Bryant." "As sung with great applause by Bryant's Minstrels of New York." "Wanted to Sing, Raw Recruits." 6pp. Page 6: Blank.

AL-121 We Are Coming Father Abraam 300,000 More. m. Stephen C. Foster. Published by [V-1: S.T. Gordon, No. 706 Broadway, New York, NY. 1862] [V-2: a. Paul Brandrik. Schmitt Music Centers Publications Division, 110 at Fifth Street, Minneapolis, MN. 55403]. Non-pictorial geometric design border. "Respectfully dedicated to the President of the United States." [V-2: 20pp].

AL-122 We Are Coming Father Abraham 600,000 More (Song and Chorus). m. B.F. Baker. Published by Henry Tolman, No. 291 Washington Street, Boston, MA. [ca. 1863]. Non-pictorial. 6pp. Pages 2 and 6: Blank.

AL-123 Grand Marche Des Wide Awakes. m. Victor. Published by H.M. Higgins, No. 117 Randolph Street, Chicago, IL. 1861. Non-pictorial geometric designs. "La Conquete." 8pp. Page 8: Blank.

AL-124 Farewell Father, Friend And Guardian. w. L.M. Dawn. m. George F. Root. [1865]. Non-pictorial black line border. "We mourn the nation's dead." 2pp. Page 2: Blank.

AL-125 We Are Coming, Father Abra'am. w. Duane N. Griffin. "Dedicated to the memory of Abraham Lincoln." In: *The Water Wagon World Express and Other Prohibition Songs and Patriotic Hymns*, page 6. Published by the Smith Linsley Company, Hartford, CT. [ca. 1890]. [5 15/16" × 9"]. 8pp. B/w floral and geometric designs.

AL-126 Vote For Abraham (Campaign Song of '64). w.m. Union. Published by H.L. Story, Burlington, VT. 1864. Non-pictorial geometric designs. "To all true lovers of our common country." 6pp. Pages 2 and 6: Blank.

AL-127 '63 Is Jubilee. w. J.L. Green. m. D.A. French. Published by Root & Cady, No. 95 Clark Street, Chicago, IL. 1863. B/w litho of U.S. flag. 6pp. Pages 2 and 6: Blank.

AL-128 Rest, Noble Chieftain (Song on the Death of President Lincoln). m. C. Archer. Published by Lee & Walker, No. 722 Chestnut Street, Philadelphia, PA. 1865. Non-pictorial black border. 4pp. Pages 2 and 4: Blank.

AL-129 A Nation Mourns Her Chief. w.m. H.S. Thompson (Author of *Lilly Dale, Annie Lisle, Marion Lee, I Am Lonely Since My Mother Died*, &c). Published by Blamer & Weber, No. 56 Fourth Street, St. Louis, MO. 1865. B/w litho of column with urn. Poem — "Twine our flag with death's dark emblem. Mingle crape and laurel leaf. Weep true heart and pay homage. See a Nation mourns her Chief." 6pp. Pages 2 and 6: Blank.

AL-130 Abraham My Abraham (Song and Chorus). w. William K. O'Donoughue, Esqr. a. Charles G. Degenhard. Published by Sheppard & Cottier, No. 215 Main Street, Buffalo, NY. 1863. Non-pictorial geometric designs. "Arranged for the Piano Forte." 6pp. Pages 2 and 6: Blank.

AL-131 Rail Splitter's Polka. m. Harry L. Tatnall. Published by Lee & Walker, No. 722 Chestnut Street, Philadelphia, PA. 1860. B/w litho of hatchet, wedge, mallet. Title made of rails. 6pp. Pages 2 and 6: Blank.

AL-132 Oh! Massa's Gwine To Washington. w. Edmund Kirke (Author of *Among The Pines*). m. Charles S. Brainard. Published by S. Brainard & Company, No. 203 Superior Street, Cleveland, OH. [ca. 1861]. Non-pictorial geometric design border. "To Charles Edmunds, Esq., Boston."

AL-133 Stand! Father Abraham (Song and Chorus). w. S.C. Burdick. m. J.M. Stillman. Published by Oliver Ditson & Company, No. 277 Washington Street, Boston, MA. [186-]. Non-pictorial geometric designs.

AL-134(A) We See The Break Of Day. w.m. Karl Cora. Published by Russell & Tolman, No. 291 Washington Street, Boston, MA. 1860. Non-pictorial geometric designs. "The Campaign — 2 Lincoln Republican Songs." "Words Written Expressly for the Times."
(B) Freeman's Call. w.m. Karl Cora.

AL-135 Away Goes Cuffie (Or Horray for '63). w.m. L.B. Starkweather. Published by Oliver Ditson & Company, No. 277 Washington Street, Boston, MA. 1863. B/w litho of Black man's face, tree, log title "A." 6pp. Pages 2 and 6: Blank.

AL-136 Abraham Lincoln's Funeral March. m. C.H. Bach. Published by H.N. Hempsted, No. 410 Main Street, Milwaukee, WI. 1865. B/w litho by L. Kutz of Abraham Lincoln, drape, eagle with ribbon inscribed "E Pluribus Unum," urns marked "Victory" and "Emancipation."

AL-137 Johnny, Fill Up The Bowl! m. Air: *Johnny Came Marching Home*. Published by Johnson, Song Publisher, Stationer and Printer, No. 7 North 10th Street, Philadelphia, PA. [ca. 1863]. [9 1/4" × 6 1/8"]. B/w litho of a soldier with horn and banner. "See Prof. Brook's Ball Room Monitor, it will give you more instruction in Dancing than any Book ever Published. Sold by Johnson, Song Publisher, No. 7 North 10th Street, Philadelphia, PA. Price 15 cts." 2pp.

AL-138 National Funeral March. m. J.E. Schonacker. Published by John Church, Jr., No. 66 West 4th Street, 3 doors above Market, Cincinnati, OH. Copyright 1865 by J.E. Schonacker. N/c litho by Ehrgott, Forbriger & Company of Abraham Lincoln, weeping angel and woman, flag, drape, Capitol dome, ribbon inscribed "The Nation Mourns." "Dedicated to the Loyal Hearts of America." 6pp. Pages 2 and 6: Blank.

AL-139 President Lincoln's Funeral March. m. W.E.M. Pettee. Pub-

AL-138

lished by J.R. Cory, Providence, RI. 1865. Non-pictorial geometric design border. "As played by Shepard's Cornet Band (of Providence, RI) at the Funeral Obsequies of Abraham Lincoln." Page 2: Blank.

AL-140 Stand By The President (Trio and Chorus). w. G.H. Springs. e. George F. Root. In: *The Bugle Call*, pages 16-17. Published by Root & Cady, No. 95 Clark Street, Chicago, IL. 1863. 64pp. Br/bk geometric design. List of contents on cover. [6 3/8" × 9 3/8"].

AL-141 Abraham's Draft (600,000 More) (Song and Chorus). w.a. J.W. Turner. Published by Oliver Ditson & Company, No. 277 Washington Street, Boston, MA. 1862. Non-pictorial geometric designs.

AL-142 To Arms! Freemen To Arms! (Patriotic Song). w. Dr. J.H. Sullivan, Jr. m. Giovanni Sconcia. Published by Russell and Patee, No. 108 Tremont Street, Boston, MA. 1862. Non-pictorial geometric design border. "Dedicated to His Excellency Abraham Lincoln, President of the United States." 6pp. Pages 2 and 6: Blank.

AL-143 The Ship Of State (Wide

Awake Campaign Song). w. E.W. Locke. m. Air: "An Old Melody Slightly Altered." Published by Root & Cady, No. 95 Clark Street, Chicago, IL. Copyright 1860 by E.W. Locke, Maine. [Approx. 8 1/2" × 11"]. Non-pictorial.

AL-144 Campaign Song. w. B.H. Grierson (of Meredosia, IL). m. "Tune—*Old Dan Tucker*." "Offered for sale by the Meredosia Wide-Awakes." 1860. [7" × 8 1/2"]. Non-pictorial geometric design border. 2pp. Page 2: Blank.

AL-145 Lincoln's Requiem. w. Irene Boynton. m. J.A. Butterfield. Published by H.M. Higgins, No. 117 Randolph Street, Chicago, IL. 1865. Non-pictorial geometric designs and black border.

AL-146 Our Martyr President. w. W. Dexter Smith, Jr. m. Oscar Linden. Published by G.D. Russell & Company, No. 126 Tremont, Boston, MA. 1865. Non-pictorial geometric designs and border.

AL-147 Funeral March. m. E.C. Davis (Author of *Only Waiting, Song of Night*, &c). Published by Balmer & Weber, No. 56 Fourth Street, St. Louis, MO. 1865. Litho of black drape, line border. "Composed and Dedicated to the Memory of the Pure and Noble Patriot Abraham Lincoln, 16th President of the U.S."

AL-148 Our Flag Our Army And Our President (Quartette). w. James T. Dudley. m. William H. Perry. Published by Horace Waters, No. 481 Broadway, New York, NY. 1864. Non-pictorial geometric design border. 6pp. Pages 2 and 6: Blank.

AL-149 Lincoln Schottisch. m. D.C. Roberts. Published by H.M. Higgins, No. 117 Randolph Street, Chicago, IL. 1860. Non-pictorial geometric designs. "Gems of the Ball Room." List of other titles in series. 4pp. Page 4: Blank.

AL-150 Funeral March (In Memory of Our Lamented President Abraham Lincoln). m. Charles Wels. Published by Firth, Son & Company, No. 563 Broadway, New York, NY. 1865. Non-pictorial black border.

AL-151(A) Monody On The Death Of Abraham Lincoln. w.m. J.C. Beckel. Published by J. Marsh, No. 1029 Chestnut Street, Philadelphia, PA. 1865. Non-pictorial black border. "Sixteenth President of the United States, Born Feb. 12th, 1808 [sic], Died by the hand of an assassin, Apr. 15, 1865." "To the Union." "Mourn ye afflicted people-mourn."

(B) Funeral March.

AL-152 Lincoln's Campaign March-Song. m. "Air: *Red, White And Blue*." Sold at Wholesale by Horace Partridge, [Boston, MA]. [1864]. [5 5/8" × 8 1/4"]. Non-pictorial geometric design border. Number "925" at top of title. 2pp. Page 2: Blank.

AL-153 In Memoriam Abraham Lincoln. w. W. Dexter Smith, Jr. m. M. Keller. Published by [V-1 & V-2: Wm. Hall & Son, No. 543 Broadway, New York, NY] [V-3: J. & E. Hoch, Boston, MA]. [V-1: ca. 1865] [V-2: ca. 1866] [V-3: ca. 1866]. Non-pictorial black border. "To a Mourning World." "M. Keller to whom sole permission was given by the Author and publisher of the poem, Messrs. J. and E. Hoch, Boston." "W. Dexter Smith's Exquisite and Popular Poem." 8pp.

AL-154 In Memory Of Abraham Lincoln. m. Karl Formes. Published by Root & Cady, No. 67 Washington Street, Chicago, IL. 1865. Non-pictorial geometric designs. "Three Songs Without Words." List of other titles in series.

AL-155 Good Old Father Abraham. w.m. James M. Stewart. Published by John R. Cory, Providence, RI. 1864. "F" in title is a litho of a rail, hatchet and wedge, geometric designs.

AL-156 We'll Fight For Uncle Abe (Plantation Song and Chorus). w. C.E. Pratt. m.a. Fred Buckley. Published by Oliver Ditson & Company, No. 277 Washington Street, Boston, MA. 1863.

(AL) ABRAHAM LINCOLN

Non-pictorial geometric design litho border. "Sung with great success by C. Pettengill at the concerts of the Buckley Serenaders." 6pp. Pages 2 and 6: Blank.

AL-157 Johnny Fill Up The Bowl! m. Air: *Johnny Came Marching Home*. And Sung by James D. Gay of the Ringold Artillery of Reading, PA, for sale at his residence, No. 300 North 20th above Race Street, Philadelphia, PA. [ca. 1863]. [8" × 5"]. Hand Colored litho of Union soldiers, Zouaves at refreshment tent. "Ten illustrated songs on Notepaper, mailed to any address on receipt of 50 cts. Published by Chas. Magnus, 12 Frankfort St., NY." 2pp. Page 2: Blank.

AL-158 We Are Coming Father Abraham. w. J. Cullen Bryant. m. David A. Warren. Published by David A. Warden, No. 1138 Lombard Street, Philadelphia, PA. 1863. Non-pictorial. "Warden's Popular Songs, Duetts [sic], &c." "Authorized Edition." List of other titles in series. "Copies sent post paid to any part, on receipt of price 15 cts." 4pp. Page 2: At top of music — "Warden's Patriotic Songs No. 3." Inside title — **We Are Coming Father Abra'am**. Page 4: Blank.

AL-159(A) Republican Campaign Song. w. "Our Ned." m. *Ellsworth's Body Lies Mouldering In The Dust*. Published by Mason & Company, No. 58 North Sixth Street, Philadelphia, PA. [1864]. [6 3/8" × 9?"]. B/w litho of Abraham Lincoln. "Dedicated to the Lincoln and Johnson Clubs." Advertising. 2pp. Page 2: Blank.

(B) **Rally Round The Cause Boy's** (Campaign Song). [1860?]. Litho of Abraham Lincoln. Penny song sheet. 2pp. Page 2: Blank.

AL-160 Grand Inaugural Polonaise. m. Charles H. Bach. Published by [V-1: Ziegfield and Willson, at Reed's Temple of Music, No. 69 Dearborn and Nos. 88 and 90 Randolph Streets] [V-2: Root & Cady, No. 67 Washington Street], Chicago, IL. 1865. Non-pictorial. "Performed by the Orchestra of the Milwaukee Musical Society at the Inauguration Ball (New Musical Hall)." 6pp. Page 6: Blank.

AL-161 We Are Coming Father Abraham, 300.000 More (Song or Quartette). m. Ferdinand Mayer. Published by Henry Tolman & Company, No. 291 Washington Street, Boston, MA. 1862. B/w non-pictorial designs. 6pp. Pages 2 and 6: Blank.

AL-162 He's Gone To The Arms Of Abraham (Comic War Ballad). w.m. Sep. Winner. Published by Oliver Ditson & Company, No. 277 Washington Street, Boston, MA. 1863. Non-pictorial geometric design border. "Respectfully Dedicated to E.F. Dixey, Esq." Two verses and the Chorus printed on cover. 6pp. Page 2: Blank. Page 6: Advertising.

AL-163 Arraham's [sic] **Daughter**. Published by Lee & Walker, No. 722 Chesnut Street, Philadelphia, PA. [ca. 186-]. Non-pictorial geometric designs. "Music Sweet for the Piano Forte." "Respectfully Dedicated to Miss Emily H. Winner." List of other titles in series.

AL-164 Our Nation's Captain (Song and Chorus). w. Charles Haynes. m. Edward Haynes. Published by Root & Cady, No. 95 Clark Street, Chicago, IL. 1864. Non-pictorial. 6pp. Pages 2 and 6: Blank.

AL-165 We Are Coming Father Abraam (Three Hundred Thousand More). m. P.S. Gilmore. Published by Russell and Patee, No. 108 Tremont Street, Boston, MA. 1862. B/w non-pictorial geometric design border. 6pp. Pages 2 and 6: Blank.

AL-166(A) We Are Coming, Father Abraham. a. J.A. Getze. Published by Lee & Walker, No. 722 Chestnut Street, Philadelphia, PA. 1863. Non-pictorial black border. "National and Patriotic Songs, Ballads, &c. Arranged for the Piano." List of other titles in series.

(B) **The Old Chieftain** (Song and Chorus). w.m. Edwin Henry.

AL-167 He's Gone To The Arms

Of Abraham (Comic War Ballad). w.m. Sep. Winner. Published by [V-1 & V-3: Winner & Company, No. 933 Spring Garden Street] [V-2: Lee & Walker], Philadelphia, PA] [V-4: O. Ditson, Boston, MA]. 1863. B/w non-pictorial geometric border. [V-1: "Dedicated to E.F. Dixey, Esq."] [V-1 & V-3: Dedicated to "Swain."]. 6pp. Page 2: Blank. Page 6: Advertising.

AL-168 Uncle Abe's Rebellious Boys. Published by H.M. Higgins, No. 117 Randolph Street, Chicago, IL. [ca. 1866]. Non-pictorial. "25 Prize Songs."

AL-169 A Gloom Is Cast O'er All The land! (Song and Chorus). w.m. Henry Schroeder. Published by Horace Waters, No. 481 Broadway, New York, NY. 1865. B/w non-pictorial floral and geometric border design. "To the memory of our lamented President." 6pp. Page 2: Blank. Page 6: Advertising.

AL-170 300,000 More. m. S.L. Coe. Published by Wm. H. Dutton, No. 169 Genesee Street, Utica, NY. 1862. Non-pictorial geometric design border. "To President Lincoln." 4pp. Pages 2 and 4: Blank.

AL-171 Oh, Why Should The Spirit Of Mortal Be Proud. m. A. Sedgwick. Published by William A. Pond & Company, No. 547 Broadway, New York, NY. 1865. B/w non-pictorial geometric design border. Long narrative on history of Abraham Lincoln and this poem. "Composed and Inscribed to the American People." "President Lincoln's Favorite Poem." 6pp. Page 6: Blank.

AL-172 The Serenade Of The 300,000 Federal Ghosts. [Probably published in the South]. [ca. 1862]. [5" × 7 1/2"]. Y/bk non-pictorial geometric design border "Respectfully Dedicated to Old Black Abe." 2pp. Page 2: Blank.

AL-173 We Are Coming Father Abraham, 600,000 More. w.m. "The Wife of a Volunteer." Published by John Church, Jr., No. 66 West 4th Street, Cincinnati, OH. 1862. Non-pictorial.

AL-174 Hold On Abraham! (Uncle Sam's Boys Are Coming Right Along). w. "By William B. Bradbury And Sung with immense success by Wood's Minstrels." m. Published by Johnson, Song Publisher, Stationer & Printer, No. 7 Tenth Street, Philadelphia, PA. [ca. 1862]. [5 1/2" × 9 1/4"]. Non-pictorial. "Published by William A. Pond & Company, No. 547 Broadway, New York, NY." 2pp. Page 2: Blank.

AL-175 Connecticut Wide-Awake Songster. e. John W. Hutchinson (Of Hutchinson Family Singers) and Benjamin Jepson. Published by O. Hutchinson, Publisher, No. 272 Greenwich Street, New York, NY. 1860. [4" × 6"]. Bl/bk non-pictorial line border. "Lincoln and liberty." 76pp. Pages 2, 75 and 76: Advertising. Pages 5 and 6: Contents. Pages 7 to 10: Republican platform. [M-109].

AL-176 To Canaan (Song of the Six Hundred Thousand). a. C.S. Brainard. Published by S. Brainard & Company, Cleveland, OH. 1862. Non-pictorial geometric design border. Chorus — "Where are you going, Soldiers with banner, gun and sword? We're marching South to Canaan to battle for the Lord." "Our Grand Army's new Marching Hymn." 6pp. Pages 2 and 6: Blank.

AL-177 Our American Cousin (Or Sneezing Polka). m. Thomas Baker. Published by John M. Willson, No. 435 Broadway, New York, NY. 1858. B/w non-pictorial geometric designs. "As played at Laura Keene's Theatre." 6pp. Pages 2 and 6: Blank.

AL-178 Our American Cousin Polka. m. Thomas Baker. Published by John M. Willson, No. 435 Broadway, New York, NY. 1859. B/w sepia tinted litho by Endicott & Company of eight vignettes of scenes and stars of the play *Our American Cousin*, including "Laura Keene." "Performed at Laura Keen's Theatre with unbounded applause." Pages 2 and 8: Blank.

AL-179 Our American Cousin Polka. m. Frank Drew, Esq. Published by D.P. Faulds & Company, Louisville, KY. 1859. B/w non-pictorial geometric designs. "To the Patrons and Friends of Asa Trenchard." 6pp. Pages 2 and 6: Blank.

AL-180(A) Our American Cousin Polka. m. Charles Jarvis. Published by Lee & Walker, No. 722 Chestnut Street, Philadelphia, PA. Copyright 1858 by E.S. Lancaster. B/w tinted litho from a photograph by W.L. Germon of "Mr. J.S. Clarke, as he appears in his popular character of 'Asa Trenchard' now performing with unabated success at the Arch Street Theatre." "Respectfully Inscribed to Messrs. Wheatly and Clarke, Managers of the Arch St. Theatre, Philadelphia." Page 2: Blank.

(B) Schottisch.

AL-181 The Lincoln Penny. w. Alfred Kreymborg. m. Elie Siegmeister. Published by Edward B. Marks Corporation, RCA Building, Radio City, New York, NY. 1943. Copper/w drawing of Abraham Lincoln; stars. 6pp. Page 2: Poem "The Lincoln Penny." "Note: This Ballad was first printed by *Colliers* in February, 1942." Page 6: Advertising for other Edward B. Marks' published songs.

AL-182 Abe Lincoln. w. Alfred Hayes, Earl Robinson and Abraham Lincoln. m. Earl Robinson. Published by Bob Miller, Inc., No. 1619 Broadway, New York, NY. 1938. B/w litho of Abraham Lincoln. 6pp. Page 3: "Chorus quotations from Lincoln's first Inaugural address, March 4, 1861."

AL-183 Allegiance (Patriotic Song). w.m. Julia Smith. Published by the D.W. Cooper Publishing Company, No. 224 Tremont Street, Boston, MA. 1918. R/w/b drawing of soldier, sailor, flag. Pledge of Allegiance followed by a blank line for reader to sign their loyalty—"Sign Here." "Dedicated to That Spirit of Americanism As Typified by the Immortal Lincoln." 4pp. Page 4: Advertising for other Cooper published song.

AL-184 Lincoln's Log Cabin March (In Memory of Abraham Lincoln). m. Louis Weber. Published by Weber Brothers, No. 622 Minnesota Avenue, Kansas City, KS. 1915. B/w drawing of Abraham Lincoln. B/w photo of "Louis Weber," Log Cabin. "A Fine March for Schools, Colleges, Lodges, &c." "For sale by all music dealers." 6pp. Page 6: Advertising.

AL-185 Lincoln's Gettysburg Address. w. Abraham Lincoln. m. Peter Tinturin. Published by Mills Music, Inc., No. 1619 Broadway, New York 19, NY. 1941. Bl/w photo of a "sculpture by Max Kalish" of Abraham Lincoln. "Centennial Edition." 12pp. Page 2: Narrative on Gettysburg Address.

AL-186 The Gettysburg Hymn. w. Abraham Lincoln. m. Edward Dunbar O'Brien. Copyright 1944 and 1956 by Edward O'Brien. Bl/w photo of Edward O'Brien in a military uniform. Gettysburg Address printed on cover. "Third Edition, Original Version." 8pp. Page 2: "From *The Civil War Overture*, Overture to Act III, 'The Proclamation.'" Pages 5 and 6: "Story of the *Gettysburg Hym*n." Page 8: Advertising for other music.

AL-187 Lincoln (Song). w.m. Cyrus Simmons. Published by Lyrique Hiroique, Cyrus Simmons, Publisher, P.O. Box 558, Knoxville, TN. 1928. B/w drawing by Shoup of Abraham Lincoln. "Globe Edition." 6pp. Page 2: Blank. Page 6: Advertising for song.

AL-188 Lincoln (A Song for the Nation). w. John J. Nilan. m. Roger Halle. Published by Roger Hale Music Company, No. 173 East 93rd Street, New York, NY. 1910. R/w/b litho of Abraham Lincoln, eagle, shield, geometric design border. 6pp. Page 2: Male quartette. Page 3: "In memory of the Great Emancipator."

AL-189 March Of The Iron Horse. m. Erno Rapee. Published by Belwin, Inc., New York, NY. 1924. [9 1/4" × 12 1/4"]. Bl/w drawings of Abraham

Lincoln, train, two men shaking hands. "Respectfully Dedicated to Mr. William Fox." 8pp. Page 2: Blank. Page 8: Advertising for other Belwin publications.

AL-190 The Gettysburg Address. w. Abraham Lincoln. m. Peter Morgan Thall. Published by Megan Music Company, New York, NY. [ca. 1970?]. Bl/bk/w photo of Lincoln Memorial statue in Washington. "Distributed by Big 3."

AL-191 In The Woods Of Old Kentucky Long Ago. w.m. George W. Hall. a. Mrs. Carrie Rainey. Published by George W. Hall, King City, MO. 1909. Bl/w photos of Henry and Mattie Williams — "Sung by Henry and Mattie Williams." Bl/w drawing of Abraham Lincoln. Bk/w/y drawing of log cabin. 8pp. Page 3: "To the Memory of Lincoln."

AL-192(A) Father Abraham's Reply To The 60,000. m. George Root. Published by S. Brainard's Sons, Publishers, Cleveland, OH. [ca. 1885]. N/c litho by Goes and Quensel of mounted Union soldiers. "Our National War Songs." List of other titles in series.

(B) Washington And Lincoln. w.m. Henry C. Work.

(C) We Are Coming Father Abraham. w.m. Baker.

AL-193 Abraham Lincoln. w. James Martin Fox. m. A. Melvin Crosby. Published by C.L. Partee Music Publishing Company, New York, NY. 1914. O/br/w drawing of flowers, flower pots. Br/w photo of man. 6pp. Pages 2 and 6: Advertising.

AL-194 Abraham. w.m. Irving Berlin. Published by Irving Berlin, Inc., Music Publishers, No. 799 7th Avenue, New York, NY. 1942. R/w/b photos of scenes and stars from movie "Irving Berlin's Hit *Holiday Inn*." "Staring Bing Crosby, Fred Astire. A Mark Sandrich Production-A Paramount Picture." List of songs from movie. Victory imprint — "Buy Bonds and Stamps for Victory."

6pp. Page 2: "From the Paramount Picture." Pages 5 and 6: Advertising.

AL-195 Raw Recruit (Or Abraham's Daughter). Published by Oliver Ditson & Company, No. 277 Washington Street, Boston, MA. [ca. 188-]. Nonpictorial geometric border. "Scenes By Gaslight, A Collection of Comic Songs." List of titles in series.

AL-196(A) Someone You Know. w. Joan Javits. m. Victor Ziskin. Published by Fairway Publishing Corporation. Sole selling agent Chappell & Company, No. 609 Fifth Avenue, New York, NY. 1961. R/w/bk drawing of Abraham Lincoln, cheering crowd, signs inscribed "Vote for Abe." "Arthur Shimkin presents the Little Golden Theatre Production of *Young Abe Lincoln*, Lyrics by Joan Javits, Music by Victor Ziskin, Book by Richard N. Bernstein and John Allen, Special Dialogue and Lyrics by Arnold Sundgaard, Directed by Jay Harnick, Production Manager John Allen, Sets & Costumes by Fred Vollpel." 6pp. Page 2: Blank.

(B) Skip-Hop Dance. w. Arnold Sundgaard. m. Victor Ziskin. 6pp. Pages 2 and 6: Blank.

(C) A Little Frog In A Little Pond. w. Joan Javits. m. Victor Ziskin. 8pp. Pages 2 and 8: Blank.

AL-197 In Dixie's Sunnyland (A Southern Ballad). w.m. Mrs. Jessie Colson. Published by Nostalgia U.S.A., Inc., No. 1502 Pine Circle East, Clearwater, FL. 33516. [ca. 1970?]. R/w/b musical notes, geometric designs. 6pp. Page 2: B/w drawing of Abraham Lincoln and family. Page 6: Blank.

AL-198 For God & Country (Lincoln Memorial Home Mission Day for Sunday School) [Booklet for Memorial Day Program with Recitations, Narratives & Songs]. Published by American Baptist Home Mission Society, New York, NY. 1909. [7" × 9"]. B/w litho of Abraham Lincoln. R/w/b flags, eagle. "Feb. 14, 1909." 12pp. Page 12: B/w litho of Abraham Lincoln, facsimile signature.

AL-199 Old Glory. w. Lieutenant A. Cooper (Author of *In And Out Of Rebel Prison, Sucession, War & Peace,* &c.). m. Prof. J.C. Bell. 1910. R/w/b flag. B/w photo of Lt. A. Cooper. 6pp. Page 2: Song—**Lincoln Centennial**. w. Lt. A. Cooper. m. "Air: *America.*" Page 6: Blank.

AL-200 Lincoln's Gettysburg Address. w. W.C. Handy. m. Jean Stor. Published by Handy Brothers Music Company, Inc., New York, NY. [19—]. Photo of Abraham Lincoln reading. Quote.

AL-201 A Real American. w. W.R. Williams. m. Frederick V. Bowers (The Singing Speaker). Published by Will Rossiter, The Chicago Publisher, No. 173 West Madison Street, Chicago, IL. 1940. B/w drawing "from the etching by Otto J. Schneider" of Abraham Lincoln. 6pp. Page 2: Blank. Page 3: "Dedicated to our friend George Cushing." Page 6: Advertising

AL-202 Gettysburg. w.m. Art Vallee, Edwin Lieberman and Al Semola. Published by Bregman, Vocco & Conn, Inc., No. 1619 Broadway, New York, NY. 1961. B/w drawing of "Abraham Lincoln" and "Jefferson Davis," battle scene, U.S. & Confederate flags. "Gettysburg-July 1-3, 1863." "That these honored dead shall not have died in vain." "Civil War Centennial 1961-1965." "Recorded by Dan Cherry on Roulette Records." 4pp. Page 4: Advertising.

AL-203 The National Prohibition Lincoln-Lee Legion (Supplement No. 1 to the National Prohibition Lincoln-Lee Legion Program Book) [Songster]. Published by The Lincoln-Lee Legion, National Headquarters, Westerville, OH. [ca. 1907]. [6" × 8 3/4"]. B/w drawings of Abraham Lincoln, Robert E. Lee. "Everybody sing, talk, pray and vote for National Prohibition." 16pp.

AL-204 Illinois. w.m. Derby O'Downey. Published by Red, White and Blue Productions, Box 341, Princeton, IL. 61356. 1968. R/w/b drawing of children, Abraham Lincoln. "A Sesquicentennial Song 1818-1968." "Cover art by Mary Win Walter. The sketch is President Lincoln as a young man. It is made from an original daguerreotype given to the artist's great grandmother by Honest Abe, the lawyer, on a trip to Princeton in 1856. This is the first publication of this portrayal." "Collector's Copy. Words and music. This song dedicated to all the people of Illinois, of yesterday, today and tomorrow. Like bread on the waters may it go forth with humility and return as heritage. Speak it, Sing it, March it, Dance it. Make it live. Make it your own." 4pp.

AL-205 Lincoln's College Flag. w. Will A. Heelan. m. J. Fred Helf. Published by J. Fred Helf, No. 136 West 37th Street, New York, NY. 1912. R/w/bl/br drawing of Abraham Lincoln, Flag, log cabin "District School," Lincoln reading by fireplace. 6pp. Page 6: Advertising.

AL-206 The School Where Lincoln Went. w.m. Will Hardy. Published by Bostonia Publishing Company, No. 181 Tremont Street, Boston, MA. Copyright 1910 by Will Hardy. R/w/b drawing of log cabin, eagle, college pennants inscribed with an "H" and a "Y" respectively—"Teddy went to Harvard, Big Bill went to Yale." "Featured by Pierce and Roslyn." 6pp. Page 2: Blank. Page 6: Advertising.

AL-207 (From) Lincoln The Great Commoner. w. Edwin Markam. m. Charles E. Ives. Published by Peer International Corporation, New York, NY. 1952. Non-pictorial. "For Voice and Piano." 6pp. Page 6: Advertising.

AL-208 My Heart Is Buried There. w.m. P.W. McAllister. Published by P.W. McAllister, Minneapolis, MN. 1896. Ma/w photo of Abraham Lincoln. "Grave of Ann Rutledge, Abraham Lincoln's first love," Ann Rutledge was buried in Concord Cemetery, a country burying-ground seven miles northwest of

New Salem, Ill. To this lonely spot Lincoln frequently journeyed to weep over her grave; 'My Heart is Buried There' he said to one of his friends. One stormy night Lincoln was sitting beside William Greene, his head bowed on his hands, while tears trickled through his fingers; his friend begged him to control his sorrow, to try to forget. "I cannot moaned Lincoln: The thought of snow and rain on her grave fills me with indescribable grief." 4pp. Page 4: Blank.

AL-209 Wisconsin Forward Forever (A Marching Song). w. Berton Braley, U.W. '05. m. John Philip Sousa. Published by The Cardinal Press, Madison, WI. Copyright 1907 by T.B. Harms and Francis, Day and Hunter. Gy/r/w drawing of a statue of Abraham Lincoln, school building. "Maxon F. Judell, Presents *Wisconsin Forward Forever*." "Dedicated to the University of Wisconsin Students, Faculty and Alumni." 8pp. Page 8: Blank.

AL-210 Abraham Lincoln And His First Sweetheart Ann Rutledge. w. Dr. W.H. Gilbertson. m. B.B. Beall. a. Harry Jay. Published by W.H. Gilbertson Music Company, Plymouth, PA. 1926. B/w photo of Abraham Lincoln. 6pp.

AL-211 Old Abe Lincoln (Campaign Song for President Lincoln—1860). a. Eric Steiner. Published by Belwin, Inc., Rockville Centre, L.I., NY. 1960. R/w/b drawing of Abraham Lincoln, crowd, signs. "Piano Solo with Words." 4pp. Page 4: Advertising for other music.

AL-212 Young Abe Lincoln. w.m. Abner Silver and Roy Alfred. Published by Planetary Music Publishing Corporation, No. 1619 Broadway, New York 19, NY. 1955. B/w geometric designs, music notes. Bl/w photo of Don Carnell. "Featured by Don Carnell." 6pp. Page 6: Advertising.

AL-213 I Love You Like Lincoln Loved The Old Red-White And Blue. w. William Jerome and Joe Young. m. Jean Schwartz. Published by Harry Williams Music Company, No. 154 West 46th Street, New York, NY. 1914. R/w/b drawing by Pfeifer of Abraham Lincoln, soldiers, young couple. 6pp. Pages 2 and 6: Blank.

AL-214 Where Graves Outnumber The Flowers. w. Henry A. Hancox. m. Charles N. Mayer. Published by Veteran Publishing Company, No. 28 State Street, Room 59, Boston, MA. Copyright 1896 by Henry Hancox. B/w photo of Abraham Lincoln. B/w drawing of flowers, wreath, eagle, flags, drum inscribed "Sixth Mass. Regiment." Scroll inscribed "Dedicated to the Patriot Dead." 4pp. Page 4: Blank.

AL-215(A) Father Abraham's Reply To The 600,000. w.m. George Root. Published by S. Brainard's Sons, Publishers, Cleveland, OH. 1884. O/y/r/w/bl/bk drawing of soldier on horseback. "Our National War Songs." List of other titles in series.

(B) **Farewell Father, Friend And Guardian.** w.m. George Root.

(C) **We Are Coming Father Abraham.**

(D) **Washington And Lincoln.** w.m. Henry Work.

AL-216 [Theme From] Abe Lincoln In Illinois. m. George Fischoff. Published by Saunders Publications, Inc. Sole selling agents: Frank Distributing Corporation, No. 119 West 57th Street, New York 19, NY. 1963. O/bk/w drawing of Abraham Lincoln, flags, drum, cannon, swords. "The Phoenix Theatre, T. Edward Hambleton, Noris Houghton, Managing Directors, presents Hal Holbrook in Robert E. Sherwood's Pulitzer Prize winning play *Abe Lincoln In Illinois*, Directed by Stuart Vaughn, Setting and Lighting by Peter Wexler, Costumes by Alvin Colt, Music by George Fischoff." 4pp. Page 4: Advertising for Losser and Burrows musical.

AL-217 Nancy Hanks. w. Rosemary Benet. m. Elie Siegmeister. Published by Edmund B. Marks Corporation, RCA Building, Radio City, New York, NY. Copyright 1933 by Rosemary Benet. Ma/w drawing by "David S. Ulartin from the photograph by Mathew B. Brady" of Abraham Lincoln & Son. 6pp. Pages 2 and 6: Advertising.

AL-218 American Legends. w.m. Elie Siegmeister. Published by Edward B. Marks Music Corporation, RCA Building, Radio City, New York, NY. 1947. Bk/w/br drawing of Abraham Lincoln & Son. "Six Songs for Voice and Piano as Recorded with the America Ballad Singers on DISC Album 728." 28pp. Page 9: Song—**Nancy Hanks**. Page 24: Song—**The Lincoln Penny**.

AL-219 I Wonder What They're Doing To Night (At Home Sweet Home). w. Bernie Grossman. m. Al Piantadosi. Published by Shapiro, Bernstein & Company, Music Publishers, No. 224 West 47th Street, New York, NY. 1916. O/bl/w drawing by Dunk of father, mother, child at dinner table, clock, cat, portrait of Abraham Lincoln on wall. 4pp. Page 4: Advertising for song book.

AL-220 Freedom Liberty (Is My Prayer). w. Abraham Lincoln. m. Grant Green. Published by Southwest Music Publications, No. 5817 South Arlington Avenue, Los Angeles 43, CA. 1944. Non-pictorial geometric designs, music notes. "Adapted from Abraham Lincoln's Gettysburg Address." 6pp. Page 6: Blank.

AL-221 Give Us Just Another Lincoln [V-1: March] [V-2: Two-Step]. w.m. Paul Dresser (Composer of *The Blue And The Grey, The Green Above The Red, On The Banks Of The Wabash*, and many other successes). Published by Howley, Haviland & Company, Nos. 1260-1266 Broadway, New York, NY. 1900. Bl/w litho of Abraham Lincoln, George Washington, Andrew Jackson, Ulysses S. Grant, Thomas Jefferson. R/w/b drawings by Bert Cobb of two women, shields inscribed "Liberty" and "Independence," soldier, Indian, eagle, flags. 8pp. Pages 2, 6, 7 and 8: Advertising. Page 3: "To Mr. Arthur Brisbane with my compliments—Paul Dresser."

AL-222 The Gettysburg Address. w. Abraham Lincoln. m. Charles George. Published by T.S. Denison & Company, Chicago, IL. 1946. Br/w drawing of family wearing drama masks, geometric designs. "Denison's Musical Readings." List of "selected list of popular Musical Readings." 10pp. Page 10: Advertising.

AL-223 Oh Why Should The Spirit Of Mortal Be Proud. w. William Knox. m. John Philip Sousa. Published by The John Church Company, Cincinnati, OH. 1899. Non-pictorial geometric design border. "President Lincoln's Favorite Hymn." "Compliments of Messr. Klaw, Erlanger and B.D. Stevens, in Commemoration of Abraham Lincoln's birthday." 12pp. Pages 2 and 12: Blank.

AL-224 Abraham's Daughter. a. F.H.H. Oldfield. Published by M. Gray, San Francisco, CA. 1867. Litho by Nahl Brothers of Ben Cotton in Union uniform and blackface. "As sung by Ben Cotton."

AL-225 Allegiance (Patriotic Song). w.m. Julia Smith. Published by Arrow Music Publishing Company, No. 24 Warren Street, Boston, MA. 1918. Non-pictorial. "Dedicated to that Spirit of Americanism As Typified by the Immortal Lincoln." 6pp. Page 6: Blank.

AL-226 (Don't Be Ashamed of) The Name Of Abraham. w.m. Irving Bibo, Howard Johnson and Lew Klein. Published by Ager, Yellen and Bornstein, Music Publishers, Inc., No. 1595 Broadway, New York, NY. 1925. Y/gn/w/bl drawing by Barbelle of a statue of Abraham Lincoln. Bl/w photo of J.C. Flippen. "Successfully sung by J.C. Flippen." "With Ukulele Arrangement." 6pp. Pages 2 and 6: Advertising for other Ager, Yellen & Bornstein published music.

AL-227 Lincoln Memorial March. m. Tom A. Tanner. Published by

ABRAHAM LINCOLN (AL)

Tom A. Tanner, No. 265 Christian Street, Lowell, MA. 1908. Bl/w drawing of crossed U.S. flags. B/w photo of a statue of Abraham Lincoln. "100th Anniversary of the Birth of Abraham Lincoln." "Dedicated to the School Children of Lowell, Mass." 6pp. Pages 2 and 6: Blank.

AL-228 Honest Abe (March). m. Bert Lowe. Published by The New England Music Company, Boston, MA. 1909. Br/w drawing by Bryant of Abraham Lincoln. 6pp. Page 6: Advertising for Krey Music Company music.

AL-229 Lincoln. w. Edwin Liebfreed. m. Robert Braine, Op. 7. Published by Hinds, Hayden & Eldredge, Inc., Publishers, New York, NY. 1923. Y/gn photo of a sculpture of a bust of Abraham Lincoln. 12pp. Page 2: History of sculpture—"Author's note: The head of Abraham Lincoln which appears on the cover of this song, and was its inspiration, is a photo of George Barnard's white marble bust, which is donated to France and is to repose in Luxembourg Gallery in Paris. Due to a clever carving of the eyes, properly lighted gives them the effect of opening and closing, an optical illusion uncanny in realism." Pages 10 and 11: Blank. Page 12: Advertising for other Hinds, Hayden & Eldredge music.

AL-230 Lincoln Centennial (Grand March). m. E.T. Paull. Published by E.T. Paull Music Company, [V-1: No. 46 West 28th Street, New York, NY. 1909. N/c] [V-2: B/w] [V-3: No. 243 West 42nd Street, New York, NY. Post-1919 size. Br/w] drawings of Abraham Lincoln, four vignettes of Lincoln's life—"Lincoln's Tomb, Springfield, Ill," "Lincoln's Birthplace," "Lincoln's Memorial Hall," "Emancipation Statue of Lincoln in Washington." "1809-1909." 8pp. Page 8: Advertising for other E.T. Paull songs.

AL-231 The Ballad Of Abe Lincoln. w. Beatrice Goldsmith. m. George Kleinsinger. Published by Edward B. Marks Corporation, RCA Building, Radio City, NY. 1940. Bk/gd/w drawing of quills. Bl/w photo of Lincoln Memorial statue. "When performing this composition give all program credits to Edward B. Marks Corporation." 8pp. Pages 2, 6 and 7: Blank. Page 8: Advertising for other Edward B. Marks music.

AL-232 The Lincoln Grand March. m. S.L. Bowman. a. J.C. Heed. Published by The Bowman-Burck Music Publishing Company, Newark, NJ. 1905. R/w/b flag with a drawing of Abraham Lincoln in the star field of a flag. "Respectfully Dedicated to the Lincoln Mutual Aid Assn., Newark, N.J." 6pp. Pages 2 and 6: Blank.

AL-233 Abe Lincoln Had Just One Country. w. Oscar Hammerstein II and Otto Harbach. m. Jerome Kern. Published by T.B. Harms Company, New York, NY. "Written at the request of Henry Morgenthau, Jr., Secretary of the Treasury, on behalf of the United States Defense Bonds and Stamps." 1941. Br/w photo of an Abraham Lincoln memorial statue. 6pp. Page 2: Blank. Page 6: Advertising.

AL-234 Liberty Under God. w. Gerard Willem van Loon. m. John Sacco. Published by G. Schirmer, Inc., New York, NY. 1942. R/w/b drawing of Lincoln Memorial statue. "Song for Voice and Piano." 6pp. Page 2: Blank. Page 6: Advertising.

AL-235(A) Monody On The Death Of Ellsworth. w. Mrs. G. Remak. m. J.C. Beckel. Published by Lee & Walker, No. 722 Chestnut Street, Philadelphia, PA. 1861. Non-pictorial geometric designs and black line border. "One of the names that was not born to die." "To Mrs. Abraham Lincoln."

(B) Col. Ellsworth's Funeral March. m. J.C. Beckel. 6pp. Pages 2 and 6: Blank.

AL-236 The Rail Splitter's Polka. m. A. Neuman. Published by Oliver Ditson & Company, No. 277 Washington Street, Boston, MA. 1860.

(AL) ABRAHAM LINCOLN

B/w litho of rails comprising the "R" in the title. "To the Republican Presidential Candidate Hon. A. Lincoln." "For the Piano Forte." 6pp. Pages 2 and 6: Blank.

AL-237 The President's Hymn (Song and Chorus). w. Dr. Muhlenburg. m. J.W. Turner. Published by [V-1: H.M. Higgins, Chicago, IL] [V-2: Oliver Ditson & Company, No. 277 Washington Street, Boston, MA]. 1863. Non-pictorial litho design. 6pp. Pages 2 and 6: Blank.

AL-238 Emancipation Quick Step. m. L.W. Ballard. Published by Henry Tolman & Company, No. 291 Washington Street, Boston, MA. 1863. Non-pictorial. "To the Friends of Freedom." "For the Piano." 6pp. Pages 2 and 6: Blank.

AL-239 We Are Coming Father Abraham, 300,000 More [V-1: Quickstep] [V-2: Song and Chorus]. a. J.A. Getze. Published by Lee & Walker, No. 722 Chestnut Street, Philadelphia, PA. 1862. R/w/b non-pictorial geometric design border. Verse printed below title. 6pp. Page 2: Blank. Page 6: Advertising.

AL-240 De United States Hotel. w. "One of the Boardahs." m. M.C. Bisbee. Published by Bruce & Bisbee, North Seventh Street, Philadelphia, PA. [186-?]. Non-pictorial.

AL-241 President Lincoln's Funeral March. a. Louis Grube. Published by Grube and Metz, No. 163 Atlantic Street, Brooklyn, NY. 1865. Non-pictorial black border. "Respectfully Dedicated to the American People." 6pp. Pages 2 and 6: Blank.

AL-242 Weep Not For The Slain, O Columbia (Song and Chorus). m. Mrs. O.N. Haskins. Published by H.M. Higgins, No. 117 Randolph Street, Chicago, IL. 1865. Non-pictorial geometric border. "Loyal Lyrics." Second song in series listed.

AL-243 Abraham's Daughter (Comic Ballad). w.m. Tony Emmett. Published by Sep. Winner, No. 531 North Eighth Street, Philadelphia, PA. 1861. Non-pictorial geometric design. "Respectfully Dedicated to Wm. Munyan, Esq."

AL-244 We're Rolling. w.m. Fred Roth. Published by Witro Music Publishing Company, No. 1619 Broadway, New York, NY. 1943. Bl/w drawing of military equipment, airplanes, ships, tanks, &c., Statue of Liberty, wheel. "Keep Rolling." 6pp. Page 2: Quote — "And the Government of the People, by the People, and for the People Shall not perish from the Earth — Abraham Lincoln." Page 6: War Bond advertising.

AL-245 Hail To The Spirit Of Freedom (March). m. W.C. Handy. Published by [V-1: Pace and Handy Music, Memphis, TN. 1915] [V-2: Handy Brothers Music Company, Inc., Publishers, No. 1650 Broadway, New York, NY. 1943]. [V-1: O/w/bl] [V-2: B/w photos of "Abraham Lincoln," "Frederick Douglass," flags, eagle, man — "50 years of freedom, ladder with rungs inscribed "Labor, Religion, Education, wealth, art, music, science." "1865-1915," woman with scales and shield — "Ethiopia shall stretch forth her hand." "Souvenir of the Lincoln Jubilee." Bl/w photo of "W.C. Handy." 6pp. Page 2: "Dedicated to the ten million Afro-Americans and to the immortal Lincoln." Lincoln quote — "Let us keep step to the music of the Republic." Page 6: Advertising.

AL-246 Death Of Abraham Lincoln (Solo, Duet or Quartett). w.m. Richard Davis. Published by Richard Davis, No. 105 North Main Street, Scranton, PA. 1913. Bl/w drawings of "Abraham Lincoln," "Ford's Theatre Where Lincoln Was Shot," and "Old Lincoln Cabin in Spencer County, Ind.," flags. Br/w photo of Richard Davis. "National and Most Patriotic Song of America." 6pp. Page 2: B/w photo of Abraham Lincoln. Page 6: B/w drawing of Abraham Lincoln.

AL-247(A) Abraham Lincoln. w.m. Rosemary and Stephen Vincent Benet. m. Arnold Shaw. In: *Sing A Song of Americans*, page 53. Published by Musette Publications, Inc., Steinway Hall, New York, NY. 1941. R/w/b drawings by Mollie Shuger including Theodore Roosevelt. 84pp.
(B) Nancy Hanks. Page 24.

AL-248 Abraham Lincoln (The Civil War). w.m. Dorothy Gaynor Blake. Published by Theodore Presser Company, No. 1712 Chestnut Street, Philadelphia, PA. 1925. R/w/b drawings of soldiers. "Musical Portraits from American History for the Pianoforte." List of other songs in the series.

AL-249 Happy Birthday America (1776-1976 Bicentennial Song Spectacular) [Song Book]. Copyright 1975 by California Music Press, Inc., New York, NY. Distributed by Charles Hansen, No. 1860 Broadway, New York, NY. 10023. [8 1/2" × 11"]. N/c photo of Lincoln Memorial. N/c photo of Lincoln Memorial Statue. Table of Contents printed on cover. 36pp.

AL-250 The True American. w.m. Jacob S. Rosenburg. a. H.A. Hummel. Published by Jacob S. Rosenburg, No. 6011 Quincy Avenue, Cleveland, OH. [ca. 1916]. Bl/w photo of Abraham Lincoln. R/w/b geometric design border. 6pp. Page 2: Bl/w photos of Composers. List of other songs by the Composers. Page 6: Blank.

AL-251 Abraham Lincoln (What Would You Do?). w. Carol Hirsh. m. Baker and Blink. Published by Metropolitan Music Publishing Company, No. 212 1st National Bank Building, Milwaukee, WI. Copyright 1918 by Carol Hirsh. B/w drawing of Abraham Lincoln, woman dressed in U.S. flag. "Roger Graham, Distributor, 143 N. Dearborn St., Chicago." 4pp. Page 4: Advertising.

AL-252 To The Memory Of Abraham Lincoln. m. Mrs. E.A. Parkhurst. a.c. Ervin Litkei (Author of *Presidential Marches of America*). In: *A Tribute To The U.S.A.*, page 14. Published by Loena Music Publishing Company, No. 239 West 18th Street, New York, NY. 10011. Copyright 1985 and 1986. N/c drawing by Edward Moran of the Statue of Liberty celebration in 1886 — "The Statue of Liberty, standing as an eternal symbol of the friendship of the people of France, was presented to the United States in 1886 by its creator, Frederick Bartholdi." Quotes by "Emma Lazarus (1883)," and "President Grover Cleveland (1886)."

AL-253 Old Abe Has Gone And Did It, Boys. w.m. J.P. Webster. Published by H.M. Higgins, No. 117 Randolph Street, Chicago, IL. 1862. Non-pictorial geometric design border. "Western Gems: 100 Songs Composed by J.P. Webster." List of other titles in series.

AL-254 Johnny Fill Up The Bowl. Published by A.W. Auner, Philadelphia, PA. [ca. 1863]. B/w litho of eagle, geometric design border. 2pp. Page 2: Blank.

AL-255 A National Hymn. w. James Nicholson. m. C. Everest. Published by Lee & Walker, No. 722 Chestnut Street, Philadelphia, PA. 1864. Non-pictorial. "To His Excellency Abraham Lincoln, President of the United States." "For 4 Voices with an Accompaniment for Organ or Piano-Forte." 6pp. Page 2: "Respectfully dedicated to Abraham Lincoln, President of the United States." Page 6: Blank.

AL-256 Uncle Joe's Hail Columbia (Song and Chorus). w.m. Henry C. Work (Author of *Kingdom Coming, Nellie Lost and Found, Our Captain's Last Words*, &c.). Published by Root & Cady, No. 95 Clark Street, Chicago, IL. 1862. Non-pictorial geometric design border. 6pp. Page 2: Blank. Page 3: "The Act entitled 'An Act for the release of certain persons held to service or labor in the District of Columbia,' has this day been approved and signed. Abraham Lincoln, Washington, April 16th, 1862." Page 6: Advertising.

AL-257 Lincoln's Funeral March. m. Charles Hess. Published by A.C. Peters and Bro., Cincinnati, OH. 1865. B/w litho of Abraham Lincoln, black oval border. "Performed by Menter's Band." "Dedicated to the Nation." 8pp. Pages 2 and 8: Blank.

AL-258 Lincoln's Dying Refrain. m. M.B. Ladd (Author of *Darling Minnie*, &c). Published by W.R. Smith, No. 135 North Eighth Street, Philadelphia, PA. 1865. Non-pictorial black border. "To the Memory of Abraham Lincoln who died a martyr to the cause of Freedom." "Toll O Mournfully the Bell, Chant the Dirge and Ring the Knell, Let it Throb and Rise and Swell, Up to Heaven, Up to goal Of our Martyred Patriot's Soul." 6pp. Pages 2 and 6: Blank.

AL-259 Lincoln's Funeral March. m. Henry Mayer. Published by William A. Pond & Company, No. 547 Broadway, New York, NY. [ca. 1865]. Non-pictorial. "Piano Forte Folio, A Choice Selection of Brilliant and Instructive Compositions by Favorite Authors." List of other titles in series. 8pp.

AL-260 Lincoln's Grand March. Published by R. Wurlitzer, No. 123 Main Street, Cincinnati, OH. 1867. B/w litho of roses. "Pleasant Dreams for the Piano." List of other titles in series. 6pp.

AL-261 Lincoln Medley Quadrille. m. James W. Porter. Published by W.R. Smith, No. 135 North Eighth Street, Philadelphia, PA. 1874. Non-pictorial geometric design border. "The Figures of this Quadrille are the Plain Polka, Schottische, Polka Mazurka and Waltz. Each figure can be used separately for its respective dance." 8pp. Pages 2 and 8: Blank.

AL-262 Lincoln's Gettysburg Address. w. Abraham Lincoln. m. Bernie Wayne. Published by Peer International Corporation, New York, NY. 1954. Non-pictorial facsimile of Abraham Lincoln's Gettysburg Address handwritten speech. 8pp.

AL-263 Lincoln, Grant & Lee (or The War is Over Many Years). w.m. Paul Dresser. Copyright 1903 by Howley, Haviland and Dresser, New York, NY. Gd/bk/w geometric designs. B/w photos of Abraham Lincoln, Ulysses Grant and Robert E. Lee. 6pp. Pages 2 and 6: Blank.

AL-264 Lincoln (The Pride of Springfield, Illinois). w. William T. Rice. m. F. Berneker. Published by William T. Rice, No. 1512 South 15th Street, Springfield, IL. 1927. Drawing of Abraham Lincoln. 6pp.

AL-265 Lincoln-Union-Victory (March). m. C.O. Lundberg. Published by H.M. Higgins, No. 117 Randolph Street, Chicago, IL. 1864. Litho of vines. "Respectfully dedicated to His Excellency Abraham Lincoln, President of the United States." 6pp.

AL-266 Lincoln (We're Proud of You) (March Song). w.m. Paul Merry and Dave Hanger. Published by United Artists Music Company, Nos. 108-114 North Kickapoo Street, Lincoln, IL. [ca.

AL-257

1930]. Drawing of Abraham Lincoln, geometric design border. "Special Edition." 4pp. Page 4: Advertising.

AL-267   Old Abe's Gallop. m. C. Dotzler. Published by H.M. Higgins, No. 117 Randolph Street, Chicago, IL. [186-]. Non-pictorial geometric designs. "Dedicated to the President of the United States." 6pp. Pages 2 and 6: Blank.

AL-268   The Abe-Iad. w. J.P. McRebel. m. F. Bartenstein. Published by John H. Parrott, Alexandria, VA. 1861. Litho of Confederate flag, Confederate soldier firing cannon at Abraham Lincoln labeled "Catch Who!" "The former place, the changing face, The midnight race, and present place of Honest Abe." 6pp.

AL-269   Abraham's Tea Party (Song and Chorus). w.m. J.H. McNaughton. Published by Firth, Son & Company, No. 563 Broadway, New York, NY. 1864. Non-pictorial geometric designs and black line border. 6pp.

AL-270   Funeral Dirge Of President Lincoln. m. Rose Rynder. Published by Marsh and Bubna, No. 1029 Chestnut Street, Philadelphia, PA. 1866. Non-pictorial black border. "To the American people." Page 3: Title: **Prest. Lincoln's Funeral Dirge**. 6pp. Pages 2 and 6: Blank.

AL-271   Campaign Song For Abraham Lincoln. w.m. J.E. Haynes. Published by H.M. Higgins, No. 117 Randolph Street, Chicago, IL. 1864. Litho of flowers, geometric designs. 6pp.

AL-272   Your Mission (Song). w.m. S.M. Grannis (Author of *Do They Miss Me At Home, What I Live For, People Will Talk, We All Wear Cloaks, Only Waiting, Strike For The Right, &c,*). Published by S, Brainard &Company, No. 203 Superior Street, Cleveland, OH. 1862 [Edition ca. 1866]. Non-pictorial geometric design border. "To Miss L.A. Gillett, Saline, Mich." 6pp. Page 2: Narrative: "At the closing anniversary of the U.S. Christian Commission held at Washington on the 11th February, 1866, the Hon. Shuyler Colfax said: 'At the last anniversary of the Commission on the Sabbath January, 1865, the striking Ode *Your Mission* was sung. Abraham Lincoln, with his tall form, his care furrowed face, and his nobly-throbbing heart, was here, and listened to it; the tears coursing down his cheeks.' Subsequently he sent up a programme which Mr. Colfax exhibited; on which appears the following request in his familiar handwriting—written by that hand now lying cold in the grave—'Near the close, let us have *Your Mission* repeated by Mr. Phillips. Don't say I called for it—Lincoln.' Mr. Phillips, of Cincinnati, then sung, amidst profound silence, this beautiful Ode." Page 6: Music catalog.

AL-273   In Memoriam A Lincoln. w.m. Gertrude I. Ladd. Published by C.M. Tremaine, No. 481 Broadway, New York, NY. 1866. Non-pictorial geometric designs, four circles with initials—"AL." Black border. 6pp.

AL-274   Lincoln (In Memoriam) [sic]. w. William P. Fox. m. Francis Wolcott. Published by John Church, Jr., No. 66 West Fourth Street, Cincinnati, OH. 1865. Non-pictorial black line border. "The words written and dedicated to Col. Theo. S. Case, Qr. M. Genl. of Mo." 6pp.

AL-275(A)   May Rose (Waltz). m. Mrs. Lottie J. Johnson. Published by H.M. Higgins, No. 117 Randolph Street, Chicago, IL. 1865. Non-pictorial geometric designs and border. "Lincoln's Garden Waltzes." "To Miss Georgia Louise Kilbourne." Page 3: Poem at top of music.

   (B)   **Jasmine** (Waltz). 6pp.
   (C)   **Violet** (Waltz).
   (D)   **Water Lily** (Waltz).

AL-276   The Lincoln Boys March. m. Mrs. A.H. Whitney. Published by Lee & Walker, No. 922 Chestnut Street, Philadelphia, PA. 1874. Non-pictorial geometric designs. "To George W. Schock, A.M., Principal of the Lincoln

Boys Grammar School." "For the Piano." 6pp. Page 6: Blank.

AL-277 Lincoln Club March. m. Anna T. Cramer. Published by John Church Company, Cincinnati, OH. [ca. 1880]. Non-pictorial geometric designs. "To Honorable President and Members of the Lincoln Club of Cincinnati, O." 6pp. Page 6: Blank.

AL-278 Tell Her I'm A Soldier And Not Afraid To Die. w.m. W.R. Williams (Author of *He Enlisted With the U.S. Volunteers*— The $5000 Prize Song, *We Can't Forget The Maine, Somebody's Sweetheart*, &c). Published by Will Rossiter, No. 56 Fifth Avenue, Chicago, IL. 1898. Drawing of battle, Abraham Lincoln, Ulysses S. Grant, Robert E. Lee, soldier. "Say good-bye to Mother."

AL-279 Juarez And Lincoln. w. Henry Myers and Edward Eliscu. m. Jay Gorney. Published by Mills Music, Inc., No. 1619 Broadway, New York, NY. 1943. R/w/b drawings of people's faces. "From the musical production *The New Meet the People*, Book, Lyrics and Music by Henry Myers, Edward Eliscu and Jay Gorney, Production Staged by Danny Dare." 6pp. Page 6: Advertising.

AL-280 Prasident Lincoln's Marsch. m. F.B. Helmsmuller. a. Flodoard Hoffmann. Published by Bie Aug. Fr. Cranz., Bremen, [Germany]. [1865]. B/w litho of Abraham Lincoln within wreath, angels weeping, Miss Liberty weeping at coffin, U.S. flag. "Fur Pianoforte." 6pp. Pages 2 and 6: Blank.

AL-281 Abraham's Daughter. Published by H. De Marsan, Publisher, No. 54 Chatham Street, New York, NY. [186-]. [6 1/2" × 9 3/4"]. B/w drawings of flags, soldier, man in border litho. 2pp.

AL-282 That's Whats The Matter With The Purps (A Comic Song). "Published by the Author." "Sold by music dealers in general." [Published by Tripp and Craig, Louisville, KY]. 1865. B/w litho of two dogs with the faces of "Abe" Lincoln and "Jeff" Davis, pulling

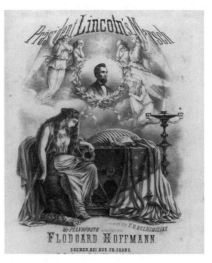

AL-280

in opposite directions on the legs of a black man. 6pp. Pages 2 and 6: Blank. Page 3 title: **Dats Whats, De Matter Wid De Purps**.

AL-283 Monody On The Death Of A. Lincoln [V-1: Song] [V-2: Funeral March]. w.m. J.C. Beckel. Published by J.J. Dobmeyer & Company, Cincinnati, OH. 1865. Non-pictorial black line border. "Sixteenth President of the United States, Born Feb. 12, 1808. Died by the hand of an assassin, April 15, 1865." "To the Union." "Mourn ye afflicted People — Mourn." 6pp. Page 2: Blank. Page 6: Advertising.

AL-284 Song (On the Death of President Abraham Lincoln). w. Silas S. Steele. m. "Tune: *Annie Laurie*." Published by J. Magee, No. 316 Chestnut Street, Philadelphia, PA. [1865]. [5 1/5" × 8"]. R/w/b border and two flags. "Liberty and Union Forever." 4pp. Pages 2 through 4: Lined note paper.

AL-285 Father Abraham's Reply To The 600,000! w. "By the Author of *Sybelle*." m.a. George F. Root. Published by Root & Cady, No. 95 Clark Street, Chicago, IL. 1862. Non-pictorial geometric design border. "I welcome you, my gallant boys, Six Hundred Thousand more." 6pp. Page 6: Advertising.

AL-286 Lincoln's Funeral March. m. Charles Hess. Published by A.C. Peters and Bro., Cincinnati, OH. 1865. B/w litho of flowers, drape inscribed "To the Nation, black line border." "As played by Mentor's Band." "Composed in Commemoration of Abraham Lincoln, President of the United States — Savior of His Country." 8pp.

AL-287 Come To Mammouth Cave In Old Kentucky (Song). w. Jettie Warden and Elliott Turner. m. Ray Hibbeler. Published by Jettie W.E. Turner, No. 407 South Third Street, Paducah, KY. 1921. R/gn/br/w drawings of a Woman and a horse—"Our Kentucky Products;" Inside Mammouth cave—"River Styx, Mammouth Cave;" Log Cabin, White House, Abraham Lincoln—"Lincoln, from a Kentucky cabin rose to the Presidency of our Country," flowers. 6pp. Page 3: "Dedicated to the Kentucky Club of Paducah, Ky."

AL-288(A) Letter To A Mother. w. Abraham Lincoln. m. Sol Berkowitz. Published by Elkan-Vogel, Inc., (A Subsidiary of The Theodore Presser Company), Bryn Mawr, PA. 19010. 1974. [6 7/8" × 10 1/2"]. B/w drawing by Bob Blansky of Abraham Lincoln. "Two Letters From Lincoln." 16pp. Page 2: Facsimile "Reproduction of a Lincoln letter" from Lincoln to Mrs. Bixby upon the death of her five sons.

(B) Letter To A Brother. 28pp. Page 2: Facsimile "Reproduction of a Lincoln letter" from Lincoln to stepbrother John Johnson.

AL-289 Give Thanks All Ye People (The President's Hymn). w.m. Reverend Dr. Muhlenberg. In: *Harper's Weekly*, page 1, Saturday, Dec. 5, 1863, by permission of A.D. Randolph, No. 688 Broadway, New York, NY. B/w engraving of angels, slaves, soldier.

AL-290 President Abraham Lincoln's Quick Step. Published by J. Church, Jr., No. 66 West Fourth Street, Cincinnati, OH. 1864. B/w litho by Ehrgott & Forbriger & Co. of Abraham Lincoln. 6pp. Pages 2 and 6: Blank.

AL-291 Lincoln's March (or On the Road to Washington). m. H.W. Hickok. Published by Oliver Ditson & Company, No. 277 Washington Street, Boston, MA. [1860]. Non-pictorial. "Respectfully dedicated to Abraham Lincoln." 8pp. Pages 2 and 8: Blank.

AL-292 To The Memory Of Abraham Lincoln. m. Mrs. E.A. Parkhurst. a. Ervin Litkei. In: *The Bicentennial March and Presidential Marches of America*. Published by Loena Music Publishing Company, No. 239 West 18th Street, New York, NY. 10011. 1975. R/w/bl/bk drawings of George Washington, Thomas Jefferson, Abraham Lincoln [facsimile signatures], eagle with ribbon inscribed "E Pluribus Unum," flags, Liberty Bell, bunting, official Bicentennial logo. "American Revolution Bicentennial, 1776-1976." "Officially Recognized Commemorative of the American Revolution Bi-Centennial Administration." 40pp.

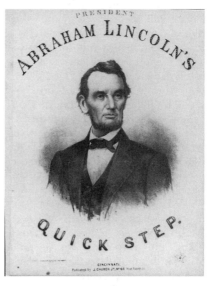

AL-290

(AL) ABRAHAM LINCOLN

AL-293 We Are Coming Father Abra'am (300.000 More). w. [William Cullen] Bryant. m. L.S. Burditt. Published by Oliver Ditson & Company, No. 277 Washington Street, Boston, MA. [1862]. B/w non-pictorial geometric design. 6pp. Pages 2 and 6: Blank.

AL-294 Land Of Lincoln. w.m. Forrest Fish. Published by Fish Music Publications, No. 3541 West 62nd Street, Chicago, IL. Copyright 1954 and 1957. O/w/bl drawing of a Abraham Lincoln statue over the outline of the State of Illinois. 6pp. Pages 2 and 6: Blank.

AL-295 Poor Old Lincoln (Song). m. "Air: *I Have No Mother Now.*" Published as a penny song sheet (Probably in the South). [ca. 1862]. [10 1/8" × 4 5/8"]. B/w litho of a man in uniform, geometric design border. 2pp. Page 2: Blank. [Pro-Jeff Davis].

AL-296 Retreat Of The Sixty Thousand Lincoln Troops (Song). Published as a penny song sheet (Probably in the South). [ca. 1862]. [4 7/16" × 10 7/8"]. B/w litho of a man in uniform, geometric design border. 2pp. Page 2: Blank. [Anti-Lincoln]

AL-297 Old Abe Lincoln! (Song). Published as a penny song sheet (Probably in the South). [ca. 1862]. [4 1/2" × 11 3/8"]. B/w litho of a man in uniform and bugler on horseback, geometric design border. 2pp. Page 2: Blank. [Anti-Lincoln and Winfield Scott].

AL-298 The Republican Campaign Songster No. #1. Published by American Publishing House, No. 60 West Fourth Street, Cincinnati, OH. [1860]. [3 3/4" × 5 3/4"]. B/w litho of Abraham Lincoln. 48[?]pp. Page 2: Advertising. [M-113].

AL-299 Dead March In Saul. m.a. E. Mack. Published by Lee & Walker, No. 722 Chestnut Street, Philadelphia, PA. 1865. Non-pictorial black border. 6pp. Pages 2 and 6: Blank. [Bound with other music published on the death of Lincoln].

AL-300 Honest Abe And Hamlin True. [1860]. [4 5/8" × 8 3/16"]. Non-pictorial. 2pp. Page 2: Blank.

AL-301 The Tears On Lincoln's Face. w.m. Glenn Sutton and Hugh Lewis. Published by Al Gallico Music Corporation, No. 65 West 55th Street, New York, NY. 1970. [8 1/2" × 11"]. Bl/bk photo of Tommy Cash. "Recorded by Tommy Cash on Epic Records." "Produced by Glen Sutton for Epic Records." "Charles Hansen Publication." 4pp. Page 4: Treble clef sign.

AL-302 It's Like The Promised Land. w.m. Eddie Scott. Published by Scott and Scott, No. 2237 East Prairie, Decatur, IL. 1955. Br/w drawings of Abraham Lincoln, log cabin, rail fence, outline of the State of "Illinois" with place names — "Little Egypt," "New Salem," "Springfield," "Chicago," "Lake Michigan," "Mississippi River," "Ohio River," "Wabash River." 6pp. Page 6: Narrative — "Paul Harvey News Broadcast over American Broadcasting Company Network, February 13, 1955" supporting "Lincoln Memorial Center Association, Inc."

AL-303 We Are Coming Father Abraham. In: *War Songs*, page 25. Published by Woolson Spice Company, Toledo, OH. [ca. 1884]. [4 3/4" × 6 7/8"]. N/c litho of war scene, company logos for "Lion Coffee" and "Woolson Spice Co." "Dedicated to the G.A.R., The Woman's Relief Corps and The Sons of Volunteers." 36pp.

AL-304 The Song Of The Abraham Lincoln Battalion. w.m. Jack Peters. Published by The Friends of the Abraham Lincoln Brigade, No. 125 West 45th Street, New York, NY. 1937. Bl/w photo of soldier. "Dedicated to the members of the Abraham Lincoln Brigade fighting for freedom in Spain. All funds from this sale will be used to send comforts to the Americans in Spain." 4pp. Page 4: Advertising.

AL-305 The Coming Election

[Song Sheet]. m. "Air: *Kingdom Coming*." "Written for the Troy Union Glee-Club." [4 1/4" × 9 9/19"]. [1864]. Non-pictorial. 2pp. Page 2: Song—**Four Northern Heroes**.

AL-306 Grand Reunion Descriptive March And Two Step To The Heroes Of 1865. m. C.H.R. Miller. Published by Phelps Music Company, No. 52-54 Lafayette Place, New York, NY. 1896. R/w/b cover. Bl/w photos of a statue of Abraham Lincoln, Ulysses S. Grant and William Stanton—"The War Council" and a statue of two Civil War soldiers. Quote from *The Boston Sunday Globe*—"Mr. Miller's specialty is dance music, and his compositions teem with catchy melodies combined with the right swing and dash to set one's toes tinging." List of 19 songs by C.H.R. Miller. "*Tenting To-Night* used by arrangement with Oliver Ditson & Co., owners of the copyright." "*Marching Through Georgia* used by arrangement with S. Brainard's Sons, owners of the copyright." 6pp. Page 6: Advertising.

AL-307 Nancy Hanks (Song for High Voice with Piano Accompaniment). w. Rosemary Benet. m. Katherine K. Davis. Published by Galaxy Music Corporation, [V-1: New York, NY] [V-2: Boston, MA]. Copyright 1933 and 1941. Non-pictorial. [V-1: "Nancy Hanks, the mother of Abraham Lincoln, never knew of his greatness, as she died when he was nine years old"] [V-2: "Abraham Lincoln's Mother"]. 6pp. [V-1: Page 2: Blank. Page 6: Advertising] [V-2: 4pp.].

AL-308 Get Down On Your Knees, O' America. w.m. Ruth Kablish. a. Dawnmarie Schaefer. Copyright 1970 by Ruth Kablish. R/w/b flag. Bl/w photo "Courtesy *Buffalo Evening News*" of school children praying in class, drawing of hands in prayer. "Blessed is the nation whose God is the Lord—Psalms 33-12." 6pp. Page 2: Narrative—"This beautiful song was written February 12, 1970, on Abraham Lincoln's birthday…" "Program repeated…with Congressman Jack Kemp…" Quotes from Abraham Lincoln, Patrick Henry and Dwight D. Eisenhower. Page 6: "1972 Commemorative issue honoring Lancaster, New York, on its Fifth Annual 4th of July 'God & Country' Celebration." Bl/w photo of marching band. John Adams Quote.

AL-309 The Ballad Of Booth. w.m. Stephen Sondheim. In: *Assassins*, page 7. Published by Rilting Music, Inc., Sole Agents: W.B. Music Corp. Copyright 1990 and 1992. Bl/w star cover by Neal Pozner.

AL-310 Peter Butternut's Lament. w. E.W. Locke (Army Poet and Balladist). m. "Air: *Wait for the Wagon*." Published by E.W. Locke, Maine. 1863. [5 1/2" × 11 13/16"]. Non-pictorial. 2pp. Page 2: Blank.

AL-311 Abraham Lincoln's Gettysburg Address. w. Abraham Lincoln. m. "Musical setting composed by George Mysels, A.S.C.A.P., Op. 4. " Published by Harvey Music Corporation, No. 1619 Broadway, New York, NY. 1940. Br/w drawing of Abraham Lincoln. 8pp.

AL-312 What Does Old Glory Say To The Rest Of The World. w. James B. Gaughen. m. Fred L. Hakel. Published by James B. Gaughen, Music Publisher, No. 4046 3rd Street, San Diego, CA. 1926. [10 3/8" × 13 13/16"]. B/w photos of Abraham Lincoln, world military leaders—"Pershing," "Foch," "Diaz," "Haig." "If you want world peace, keep me on your piano." 12pp. Page 2: "Balboa Theatre Patriotic Week, Sunday, June 13, to Saturday, June 19, San Diego, 1926." Advertising throughout on pages 2, 3, 4, 6, 8, 10, 11 and 12. Many ads for local politicians.

AL-313 Ann Rutledge. w. Edgar Lee Masters. m. Vincent T. Williams. Published by Shattinger, St. Louis, MO. 1954. B/w non-pictorial lines. "From *Spoon River Anthology*. Published by The Macmillian Co., New York. Permission granted by the Estate of Edgar Lee Masters." Lyrics printed on cover. 6pp. Page 2: "Forward — Ann Rutledge, age 22 years, died August 25, 1835. Shortly before her death, Abraham Lincoln, deeply perturbed about her illness, visited her. What was said or what endearing confidences were exchanged between them at this sorrowful, last meeting no one will ever know this. Thus seemingly, the romance was ended and relegated to the past, but like all things spiritual that touch the soul, it must have lived. It is hoped that this musical setting will be found as appropriate and expressive as the poem by Edgar Lee Masters — The Publishers." Page 6: Advertising.

AL-314 Lincoln Two Step. m. J.M. Himelman. In: *Jordan, Marsh & Company's Latest Instrumental Music Collection*, page 128. [ca. 1895]. [10 7/8" × 13 5/8"]. Non-pictorial. "30th Edition, 240,000 Copies Printed." 260[?]pp.

AL-315 Abe Lincoln Had Just One Country. w. Otto Harbach and Oscar Hammerstein II. m. Jerome Kern. Published by T.B. Harms Company, New York, NY. 1941. Bk/w/pl drawing of two military cadets and woman in ball gown. From the play "*Hayfoot Strawfoot* (Play with Music)." List of songs in the production. 6pp. Pages 2 and 6: Advertising.

AL-316 We're Coming Fodder Abraham, We're Coming In A Horn (Comic Song). w. "By an 'Intelligent Contraband.'" Published by Tripp and Craig, Louisville, KY. 1863. Non-pictorial. "To the new American Citizens of African Descent." 6pp. Pages 2 and 6: Blank.

AL-317 Hutchinson's Republican Songster For 1860. e. John W. Hutchinson (of the Hutchinson Family Singers). Published by O. Hutchinson, Publisher, No. 272 Greenwich Street, New York, NY. 1860. B/w floral design border. "Lincoln and Liberty." 76pp. Inside title — **Republican Songster**. [M-110].

AL-318 Union March. m. F. Scala. Published by Oliver Ditson & Company, No. 277 Washington Street, Boston, MA. 1861. Non-pictorial. "As performed by the U.S. Marine Band at the Inauguration of President Lincoln, March 4, 1861." "Composed and respectfully dedicated to Mrs. President Lincoln."

AL-319 National Consecration Chant (Or Hymn). w. Maj. B.B. French. m. Wilson G. Horner. Published by Henry McCaffrey, No. 205 Baltimore Street, Baltimore, MD. 1863. Non-pictorial geometric design border. "The following beautiful lines were chanted at the dedication of the National Cemetery, Gettysburg, Nov. 19, 1863, by the National Union Musical Association of Baltimore, at the close of Mr. Everett's ovation and just before President Lincoln's address. The deep pathos of the poetry, the words of which, being clearly enunciated, were distinctly heard by the assembled thousands — the occasion and surroundings, made it a solemn feature of the day, moving very many to tears." "Respectfully dedicated to the memory of the fallen heroes of Gettysburg."

AL-320 Lincoln (Two Themes for Piano). m. Alan Menken. Published by Warner Bros. Publication, Inc., No. 265 Secaucus Road, Secaucus, NJ. Copyright 1992 and 1993 by Menken Music and Carl Trunksong Music. "From the film by Peter W. Kunhardt, Philip B. Kunhardt III and Peter B. Kunhardt, Jr. "Original Soundtrack on Angel Records." 6pp.

AL-321 [Lincoln Music Corporation]. The Lincoln Music Corporation used a silhouette of Abraham Lincoln as its company logo. The following are a sample of their publications.

(A) **You're Ev'rything Sweet**. w.m. Andy Razaf, Paul Denniker and Charles Bayha. Published by Lincoln Music Corporation, No. 1619 Broadway, New York, NY. 1936. Bl/w small drawing of Abraham Lincoln in company logo at

top and bottom of cover—"Lincoln Songs."
 (B) **Heaven In My Heart**. w.m. Fred Rose and Ed. G. Nelson.
 (C) **Yesterday** (Waltz Song). w. Charles Harrison. m. Monte Wilhite. 6pp. Page 6: Advertising.
 (D) **'Deed I Do**.
 (E) **He May Be Your Man** (But He Comes to See Me).
 (F) **You May Be He May Be Your Man Lonesome** (But You'll be Lonesome Alone).
 (G) **An Old Italian Love Song**.
 (H) **Oh! Look At That Baby**.
 (I) **Truly I Do**.
 (J) **I Wish You Were Jealous Of Me**. (Waltz Song. w.m. Earl Hambrich and Glen Rowel. 8pp. Pages 2 and 8: Advertising.
 (K) **Back In Hackensack New Jersey**.
 (L) **Until The End**.

AL-322 **Lincoln's Land**. w. Bliss Carman. m. Hector Spaulding. In: *Folk Songs and Art Songs For Intermediate Grades, Book II*. Edited by Teresa Armitage. Published by C.C. Birchdale & Company, Boston, MA. 1924. [6 1/4" × 9 7/8"]. Hard cover book. B/w non-pictorial cover. 166pp.

AL-323 **The Gettysburg Address**. w. Abraham Lincoln. m. William Stearns Walker. Published by McAfee Music Corporation, No. 501 East Third Street, Dayton, OH. 45401. Copyrights 1958, 1974 and 1975. [8 7/8" × 11 7/8"]. Bl/bk/w drawing of Abraham Lincoln superimposed over a handwritten copy of the Gettysburg Address. 12pp. Pages 2 and 11: Blank. Page 3: Repeat of title page in B/w. Page 4: B/w photo of Sherrill Milnes. Page 5: "Featured by Sherrill Milnes of the Metropolitan Opera Company." Page 12; Logo.

AL-324 **Abraham Lincoln**. w.m. Edna Mae Burnam. Published by The Willis Music Company, Cincinnati, OH. 1975. B/w drawing of Abraham Lincoln in top hat. Bk/bl drawing of White House, log cabin. "6 Piano Solos About a Great American." 20pp. Pages 2, 18 and 19: Blank. Page 20: Advertising.

AL-325 **Land Of Lincoln** (Concert March for Symphonic Band). m. Paul W. Whear. Published by Ludwig Music Publishing Company, No. 557-67 East 140th Street, Cleveland, OH. 1968. Bl/w seal of the State of Illinois Sesquicentennial 1868-1968." "Ludwig Contemporary Symphonic Band Series No. 133." Full Band Package.

AL-326 **A Lincoln Address** (For Narrator and Band). w. "Text from Abraham Lincoln's Second Inaugural Address." m. Vincent Persichetti. Published by Elkan-Vogal, Inc., Bryn Mawr, PA. 19010. Copyrights 1959, 1967, 1973 and 1974. Br/w cover drawing of Abraham Lincoln giving speech, flag, soldiers. Full parts set for band. Top of score—"Version for Narrator and band Commissioned by Arkansas Polytechnic College in memory of Hallie Belle Witherspoon."

AL-327 **Abe Lincoln Overture**. m. Leland Forsblad. Published by Shawnee Press, Inc., Delaware Water Gap, PA. 1985. [8 1/2" × 11"]. Bk/bl/w drawing of Abraham Lincoln, flag, church. Full parts set for band.

AL-328 **Abraham Lincoln Walks At Midnight**. m. Leland Forsblad. Published by Alfred Publishing Company. 1981. [8 1/2" × 11"]. O/gy/w non-pictorial cover. "Concert Band." Full parts set for band. Top of score—"From poem by Vachel Lindsay."

AL-329 **Three Hundred Thousand More**. m. "Air: *Hurrah for Harry Clay*." Published by T.C. Boyd, Engraver on Wood, No. 228 Montgomery Street, Opposite the Russ House, San Francisco, CA. [ca. 1863]. [6" × 9 3/8"]. B/w litho of two U.S. flags, liberty caps. "10,000 Songs for Sale." 2pp. Page 2: Blank.

AL-330 **We Are Coming Father Abraham**. In: *Patriotic Songs*. [1865]. [15 11/16" × 21 5/8"]. B/w litho of an eagle—

"Your sons and your money on your Country's alter." Also includes **Hail Columbia**. 2pp. Page 2: "Seven Thirty Facts and Figures." Articles on investing in government bonds.

AL-331 Lincoln's Funeral March. m. C.H. Bach. Published by H.N. Hempsted, No. 410 Main Street, Milwaukee, WI. [ca. 1865]. B/w tinted litho of soldiers in battle," geometric designs. "Marches and Quicksteps for the Piano Forte." List of other titles in series.

AL-332 For God & Country. w.m. H. Millard (Author of *Viva L'America, Flag of the Free, &c*). Published by Firth, Son & Company, No. 563 Broadway, New York, NY. 1865. N/c litho by Major and Knapp of a statue of a woman — Miss Liberty — holding U.S. flag, surrounded by Union soldiers. "To His Excellency, The President of the United States." "As a Solo or Quartette." 10pp. Pages 2, 9 and 10: Blank.

AL-333 Lincoln Portrait. w. Abraham Lincoln and Aaron Copeland. m. Aaron Copeland. Published by Boosey & Hawkes, Inc. Copyright 1943 by Aaron Copeland. [Edition ca. 1970]. Be/gn non-pictorial cover. [Conductor's Full Score]. 52pp. Page 3: "For Narrator and Orchestra." Page 4: "Notes for the Speaker." Page 5: Narration. Page 6: "Instrumentation." "*Lincoln Portrait* was commissioned by Andre Kostelanetz and was first performed by the Cincinnati Symphony Orchestra under his direction on May 14, 1942." Page 7: "To Andre Kostelanetz."

AL-334 Deep In The Wildwood. w.m. Raymond B. Elrdred. Published by G. Schirmer, Inc., New York, NY. 1948. Gn/br/be silhouette of Abraham Lincoln. "For Voice and Piano." 6pp. Page 6: Advertising for other G. Schirmer publications.

AL-335 Abraham Lincoln's Birthday. w.m. Ruth Norman. Published by Mills Music, Inc., No. 1619 Broadway, New York, NY. 1952. R/w/b drawing of children. "Action Songs for Special Occasions." 6pp. Page 6: Advertising for other Mills Music Company published music.

AL-336 Death Of President Lincoln. w. James D. Gay. m. "Air: *Sword of Bunker Hill*." Published by James D. Gay, No. 300 North Twentieth Street, Philadelphia, PA. 1865. [6" × 9"]. Non-pictorial geometric design border. "Gay's Illustrated Army Songs Lithographed and Printed on Double Sheet of Letter Paper, sent by mail, price 5 cts. each, or 50 cents per package, his army songs and ballads are sold wholesale by J.W. Barns, No. 503 South Street, Philadelphia." 2pp. Page 2: Blank.

AL-337 Be Glad You're An American. w.m. Catherine Allison Christie. a. Ellen Jane Lorenz. Published by Lorenz Publishing Company, No. 501 East Third Street, Dayton, OH. 1941. B/w drawings of U.S. map, Abraham Lincoln, Betsy Ross, Mayflower, Log Cabin, wagon train, redwood. 4pp.

AL-338 A Nation Mourns Her Martyr'd Son. w. Alice Hawthorne. m. Sep. Winner. Published by A.W. Auner, Song Publisher, N.E. cor. 11th and Market Street, Philadelphia, PA. 1865. [5 1/2" × 8 3/4"]. Non-pictorial black border. "An Honest Man's the Noblest Work of God." "In Memory of Abraham Lincoln, Sixteenth President of the United States." "Sep. Winner's Music Store, No. 933 Spring Garden Street, Phila., Pa." 2pp.

AL-339 Saule-Pleureur (Weeping-Willow) (Marche Funebre du President Lincoln). m. B.A. Whaples. 1865. Published by [V-1: Benson, St. Louis, MO] [V-2: Blelock & Company, New York, NY]. 8[?]pp.

AL-340 Illinois. w. C.H. Chamberlain. m. "Air: *Baby Mine*." Published by Charles F. Carpentier, Secretary of State, Springfield, IL. [1890-1894] [Edition ca. 1970]. [8 1/2" × 11 1/4"]. R/w/b drawing — "Seal of the State of Illinois, Aug. 26th, 1818." 4pp. Page 2: "By permission of

Clayton F. Summy Co." Page 3: Narrative—"The State Song." "By Act of the Fifty-fourth General Assembly the song *Illinois* became the official State song." Page 4: Bl/w outline of state, Abraham Lincoln—"Illinois, Land of Lincoln."

AL-341 Lincoln, The Great Commoner. w. Edwin Markham. m. Charles Ives. e.a. James G. Smith. Published by Fostco Music Press. Sole Agent: Mark Foster Music, Box 4012, Champaign, IL. 1976. [7 1/2" × 10 3/4"]. R/bk reproduction of *The New Liberty Bell*, A Bicentennial Anthology of American Choral Music." 12pp. Page 3: "Although Charles Ives lived to be eighty years old, his creative career was considerably shorter than his life. Born in 1874, he wrote very little new music after the American entry into World War I. *Lincoln, The Great Commoner*, written in 1912, is therefore one of his most mature choral compositions."

AL-342 Gettysburg. w. "Text from Abraham Lincoln's Gettysburg Address." m. Richard Fuchs. Published by Belwin Mills Publishing Corp., Melville, NY. 11747. 1983. [6 7/8" × 10 3/8"]. Bl/w photo of Lincoln Memorial. "Text from Abraham Lincoln's Gettysburg Address." "S.A.T.B. with Piano Accompaniment." 20pp. Page 2: "Performed at the Lincoln Memorial in Washington, D.C. on November 19, 1983, to Commemorate the 120th anniversary of Abraham Lincoln's immortal Gettysburg Address."

AL-343 The Gettysburg Address. w. Abraham Lincoln. m. Georecge Lynn. Published by Theodore Presser Company, Bryn Mawr, PA. 1962. [6 7/8" × 10 1/2"]. B/w non-pictorial designs. "College Choral Series." "Selected by the Beta Chapter of Pi Nu Epsilon at Drexel Institute of Technology, Wallace Heaton, Editor." "S.A.T.B. Baritone Solo, with Piano." 20pp. Page 2: B/w litho of eagle, shield—"The Gettysburg Address delivered by Abraham Lincoln at the dedication of the Gettysburg National Cemetery, November 19, 1963." Page 3: "To Arthur Leslie Jacobs."

AL-344 A Lincoln Letter. w. Abraham Lincoln. m. Ulysses Kay. Published by C.F. Peters Corporation, New York, NY. 1958. [6 7/8" × 10 3/8"]. Be/bk non-pictorial. "Mixed Voices and Bass Solo." 16pp. Page 2: "To Carl Haverlin."

AL-345 Lincoln Speaks. w. Abraham Lincoln. m. W. Lawrence Curry. Published by Elkan-Vogel, Philadelphia 3, PA. 1962. [6 7/8" × 10 3/8"]. Gy/w silhouette of Lincoln Memorial statue. "For Mixed Chorus (SATB) with Narrator." 16pp. Page 2: "To Edwin E. Heilakka."

AL-346 Advice From Honest Abe (Riff). w. Richard Engquist. m. Jack Gottlieb. Published by Theophilious Music. Sole Agent: Boosey & Hawkes, Inc. 1989. [6 7/8" × 10 1/2"]. Non-pictorial. "Presidential Suite, Seven Pieces for Mixed Chorus (SATB) a cappella. 12pp. Page 2: "Presidential Suite is a celebration of America's priceless heritage of liberty. Inspired by the wisdom and whimsy of some of our most colorful presidents, it juxtaposes the eloquence of John F. Kennedy and Franklin Delano Roosevelt, with the journalistic pith of Theodore Roosevelt, Harry S. Truman's blunt common sense, Abraham Lincoln's homespun wit and Thomas Jefferson's irony, plus a legendary quip from the taciturn Calvin Coolidge. This patriotic work combines idealism with light-heartedness, inspiration with a dash of salt." Page 3: "For Eric Johns."

AL-347 Abraham Lincoln. w. F.I. Hosmer. m. W.O. Wilkinson (1895). [5 7/8" × 9"]. "Poem written for Lincoln Celebration, Chicago, 1909." "Used by permission of Presbyterian Board of Publication." Page 11.

AL-348(A) We Are Coming, Father Abra'am. a. Harry Prendiville. In: *The Leaders Joy Band Book*, page 3. Published by Edward A. Samuels, Boston, MA. [ca. 1890]. [6 7/8" × 5"]. Non-pictorial.

(AL) ABRAHAM LINCOLN

"Containing Sixty-One National and Popular Airs." 32pp.

    (B) **Abraham's Daughter**, page 19.

    AL-349 Have You Seen Him? w. Edward Eager. m. Jerome Moross. In: *Three Songs From Gentlemen, Be Seated!*, page 3. Published by Chappell & Company, No. 606 Fifth Avenue, New York, NY. 1964. Bl/gy drawing of soldiers. Page 3: "*Have You Seen Him?* is a tribute to President Lincoln."

    AL-350(A) We Are Coming, Father Abraham. In: *War Songs*, p. 55. Published by Oliver Ditson Company, Nos. 453-463 Washington Street, Boston, MA. 1890. R/w/bl/y drawings of flag, G.A.R. medal. B/w photos of litho of Ulysses Grant, two generals. "Arranged for Male Voices." 100pp.

    (B) **Abraham's Daughter**. Page 50.

    AL-351(A) We Are Coming, Father Abraham. In: *War Songs*, p. 55. Published by Oliver Ditson Company, Boston, MA. 1906. [6 3/4" × 10 3/16"]. N/c photos of Ulysses Grant, two generals, flags. "Arranged for Mixed Voices." 140pp.

    (B) **Abraham's Daughter**, page 50.

    AL-352(A) We Are Coming, Father Abraham. In: *War Songs*, p. 55. Published by Oliver Ditson Company, Nos. 453-463 Washington Street, Boston, MA. 1890. B/w photo of Ulysses Grant, two generals. Drawing of flag, G.A.R. medal. "Arranged for Male Voices." 100pp.

    (B) **Abraham's Daughter**, page 50.

    AL-353 We Are Coming, Father Abraham. In: *Wehman's American National Songs*, page 40. Published by Wehman Bros., New York, NY. 1898. [4 11/16" × 7 1/8"]. Bl/w litho of eagle, flag, stars. 64pp. Page 3: "A Choice Collection of American Patriotic and National Songs."

    AL-354 The People To The President. w. "By A Lady of Washington City." m. "German Melody: *O Tannebaum, O Tannebaum, Wei grun sind deine Blatter*. Air: *Maryland My Maryland*." Hand Colored litho of Abraham Lincoln, women and angel. "Purchase Magnus' Ornamental and Glorious Union Packet, Made up from an endless variety of screens, each Packet will gratify yourself and gladden the hearts of friends at home." 2pp.

    AL-355 Lincoln's Birthday. w. Homer H. Harbour. m. "Netherlands Folk-Song." In: *A Book of Songs, Words and Melodies Only for Unison and Part Singing for Grades IV, V and VI (Student Edition)*, page 24. c.e. Archibald T. Davison, Thomas Whitney Surette and Augustus D. Zanig. Published by E.C. Schirmer Music Company, No. 221 Columbus Avenue, Boston, MA. 1924. [6 12/" × 8 1/2"]. Gn/bk drawing of building, lyres, geometric designs. "Concord Series No. 4." 344pp.

    AL-356 Abraham Lincoln Lives Again. w.m. Lewis Allan. In: *Sing America* [Song Book], page 20. c. Annie Allan. Published by Worker's Bookshop, No. 50 East 13th Street, New York, NY. [ca. 1944]. [4 1/2" × 6"]. Non-pictorial. 68pp.

    AL-357 Alls For The Best. m. "Music Published by Firth, Pond & Co., 547 Broadway, N.Y." Published by Charles Magnus, No. 12 Frankfort Street, New York, NY. [ca. 1863]. [5 1/8" × 8"]. H/c litho of Abraham Lincoln, George McClellan, Union Troops. "Ten Illustrated Songs on notepaper, Mailed to any address on receipt of 50 cts."

    AL-358 The President's Hymn — Give Thanks All Ye People. Published by A.D.F. Randolph, No. 683 Broadway, New York, NY. 1863. [6 3/4" × 9 3/4"]. Non-pictorial. "In Response to the Proclamation of the President of the United States Recommending a General Thanksgiving, on November 26th, 1863." 4pp. Page 4: Blank.

    AL-359 He's Gone To The Arms Of Abraham. w.m. Sep. Winner. Published by J.H. Johnson, Song Publisher, Stationer and Printer, No. 7 North Tenth

Street, Philadelphia, PA. [ca. 1863]. [6 1/8" × 9"]. Non-pictorial geometric designs. "This song is Written by Sep. Winner and Published in sheet music by Winner & Company, No. 933 Spring Garden Street — See the Music of it." 2pp. Page 2: Blank.

AL-360 Lincoln. w.m. Edna G. Young. In: *Merry Songs For Merry Singers, A Collection of Sacred, Secular, Nature and Patriotic Songs for Children*, page 14. e. I.H. Meredith and Grant Colfax Tullar. Published by Tullar-Meredith, No. 265 West 36th Street, New York, NY. 1914. N/c photo of children at flag raising. Gn/w geometric design border. Hard cover book.

AL-361 My Land My Flag. w. A.V. Lewis. m. Hedwig A. Fritsch-Modrzejewska. Published by Hedwig A. Fritsch-Modrzejewska. 1920. [Pre-1919 size]. B/w drawing of Abraham Lincoln. Gn/w drawing of shield, geometric designs. "Reverently Dedicated to the Memory of Abraham Lincoln." 8pp. Page 2: Poem — *My Land — My Flag!* Pages 7 and 8: Blank.

AL-362 Ode To Lincoln. w. Leilia Shipman Tromblee. m. Burt Wallace. Published by The H. Kirkus Dugdale Company, Music Publishers and Dealers, Dugdale Building, Washington, DC. Copyright 1914 by Mrs. Andrew Tromblee. [6 3/4" × 10 5/16"]. B/w litho of Abraham Lincoln. "1873-1913." "Lincoln's Favorite Maxims: Animo Et Fide Deo Duce — By Courage and Faith God Being Our Leader." 4pp. Page 4: Blank.

AL-363 American Missionary Association Concert Exercise For Lincoln Memorial Sunday. [ca. 1920?]. 6" × 8 3/4"]. Non-pictorial. 6pp.

AL-364 The Conscript's Lay. w. George P. Holt. m. "Air: *Kingdom Coming*." Published by Charles Magnus, No. 12 Frankfort Street, New York, NY. 1863. [5" × 8"]. H/c litho of "Review of United States forces by the President, Va., 1863." Followed on page one by: **How Are You Conscript?** w. G.P. Holt. 2pp. Page 2: Blank.

AL-365(A) Lincoln And Liberty. w. Jesse Hutchinson. m. "Tune: *Old Rosin The Beau*." a. John W. Schaum. In: *Music of America, Songs of the Union*, page 6. Published by Schaum Publications, Inc., No. 2018 East North Avenue, Milwaukee, WI. 1961. R/w/b drawings of patriotic scenes. 36pp.

(B) **Abraham's Daughter**, page 7.

(C) **We Are Coming, Father Abraham**, page 13.

AL-366 He's Gone To The Arms Of Abraham. Published by Charles Magnus, No. 12 Frankfort Street, New York, NY. [ca. 1863]. [5" × 8"]. H/c litho of Union soldiers firing a cannon. "Ten illustrated songs on notepaper, mailed to any address on receipt of 50 cts., Charles Magnus, No. 12 Frankfort Street, New York, NY." 2pp. Page 2: Lined notepaper.

AL-367 Wide Awake (Two-Step). m. Lizzie Beach Stevens. Published by The Melody Music Company, Detroit, MI. 1909. R/w/b litho of U.S. flag, wreath. Bl/w drawing of Abraham Lincoln. 6pp. Page 2: Blank. Page 6: Advertising.

AL-368 Come Rally, Freemen Rally (Campaign Song and Chorus). w. John Adams. m. Mrs. Parkhurst (Author of *They Tell Me I'll Forget, A Home on the Mountain, The Soldier's Dying Farewell, Only You & I, Sweet Home of My Earlier Days, The Sigh in the Heart*). Published by Horace Waters, No. 481 Broadway, New York, NY. 1864. B/w geometric designs. 6pp. Page 6: Blank.

AL-369 Gettysburg Address. w. Abraham Lincoln. m. Henry Hadley. In: *Junior Laurel Songs*, page 114. c. M. Teresa Armitage. Published by C.C. Birchard & Company, Boston, MA. 1917. 164pp.

AL-370 About Abe Lincoln. w.m. George Frederick McKay. Drawing of Lincoln Memorial. In: *Our Land of Song*, page 96. Published by C.L. Birchard & Company, Boston, MA. 1947. [6 7/8" × 6 11/16"].

AL-371 Young Abe Lincoln (Rote). w.m. J.W. Beattie. m. Johnny Green. Drawing of boy with axe. In: *The American Singer [V-2 Book 3]*, page 134. Published by American Book Company, New York, NY. 1946. [6 5/8" × 8 3/8"]. R/w/b stars, bars of music.

AL-372 The Gettysburg Hymn (And The 2nd Battle of Gettysburg, O'Brien-Sanatra, See?). w. Abraham Lincoln. m. Edward Dunbar O'Brien. Copyright 1944, 1956 and 1957. Bk/w/gd cover of newspaper clippings. 12pp. Pages 2, 3, 4, 5, 8, 9, 10, 11 and 12: Clippings and typed narratives.

AL-373 Lincoln. w. S.F. Furst. m. "Tune—*Hark, The Herald Angels Sing* or 'The American National Anthem.'" "Written on the occasion of the one hundredth anniversary of the birth of Lincoln." In: *Lincoln Day Souvenir Program*, page 16. Published by Souvenir Publishing Company, Williamsport, PA. 1910. [4" × 6 11/16"]. Bk/gy photo of "Abraham Lincoln." 18pp.

AL-374 Songs For The Great Campaign [Song Sheet]. c. Glenn Collins. Published by *The New York Times Magazine*, page 87, "Endpaper," February 8, 1976. [9 1/4" × 12 1/4"]. B/w photo of Abraham "Lincoln." Five songs, words only, from Lincoln's campaigns.

AL-375 Lincoln's Face. w. Louise Baum. m. Helen S. Levitt. In: *Introductory Music*, page 132. Published by Ginn & Company, Boston, MA. 1923. [6 1/2" × 8 3/16"]. Bl/bk hardback book. 184pp.

AL-376 How Are You Greenbacks? Published by Charles Magnus, No. 12 Frankfort Street, New York, NY. [ca. 1863]. [4 15/16" × 7 15/16"]. Hand Colored litho of Secretary Salmon Chase, printing press. "Music of this song to be had of Wm. A. Pond & Co., 547 Broadway." 2pp. Page 2: Blank.

AL-377 Lincoln. w. Ethel Crowninshield. m. C.H. Rinck. In: *Tuning Up*, page 118. Published by Ginn & Company, Boston, MA. 1936. [6 1/2" × 8"]. Gn/bl hardback book. 184pp.

AL-378 Anne Rutledge. w. Edgar Lee Masters. m. Sam Raphling. Published by Edition Musicus, New York, NY. Copyright 1952 by Mrs. E.L. Masters and Sam Raphling. Gn/w drawing by R. Bernatschke of house, cemetery, trees. "*Spoon River Anthology*. Poems by Edgar Lee Masters. Music for Voice and Piano by Sam Raphling. First Series." List of other songs in the series. 6pp. Page 2: : "To Cathalene Parker." "From *Spoon River Anthology*."

AL-379 The Lincoln And Johnson Union Campaign Songster. Published by A. Winch, No. 505 Chestnut Street, Philadelphia. 1864. [3 7/8" × 6"]. Be/bk lithos of Abraham Lincoln and Andrew Johnson, geometric design border. 58pp. Pages 2, 57 and 58: Advertising. Page 7: "The Union Party Platform." [M-124].

AL-380 Deacon Lincoln Brown. w. Joserh [sic] (Joseph) F. Lyston. m.

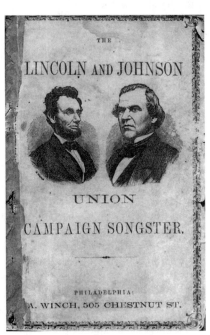

AL-379

Don Loring. Published by H. Kirkus Dugdale, Publisher, Dugdale Building, Washington, DC. Copyright 1913 by Joseph F. Lyston. B/w drawing of a tall, Abraham Lincoln look-a-like man with satchel and Bible. 6pp. Page 2: Blank.

AL-381 Mozart Lincoln. w. John Gilroy. m. Ben M. Jerome. Published by Sol Bloom, New Amsterdam Theatre Building, New York, NY. 1903. Gn/w branches, geometric designs. "The song success of *The Darling Of The Gallery Gods*, Book by George V. Hobart, Music by Ben M. Jerome, Lyrics by Matt C. Woodward, as produced at the Crystal Gardens atop of the New York Theatre under the direction of Mr. George Lederer. List of other songs from the play. 6pp. Page 6: Advertising.

AL-382 The Lincoln And Hamlin Songster (or Continental Melodist). Published by Fisher & Brother, No. 10 South Sixth Street, Philadelphia, PA. 1860. Y/bk litho of a beardless Abraham Lincoln. "Comprising a choice collection of Original and Selected songs, in Honor of the People's Candidates, Lincoln and Hamlin, and Illustrative of the Enthusiasm Everywhere Entertained for 'Honest Old Abe' of Illinois, and the Noble Hamlin of Maine." 72pp. [M-112].

AL-383 Old Honest Abe For Me (Song and Chorus). A. C.D.S. Published by Firth, Pond & Co., No. 547 Broadway, New York, NY. 1860. Non-pictorial geometric designs. "To The Young Men's Republican Club of Rockland, Me. And Republicans Everywhere." "Arranged for the Piano Forte.

AL-384 Lincoln On A Rail (Song). m. "Tune—*Sitting on a Rail*." [4 5/8" × 11 1/4"]. [Probably published in the South]. B/w non-pictorial geometric designs and border. 2pp. Page 2: Blank. [Anti-Lincoln].

AL-385 Abe Lincoln's Battle Cry. Published by James D. Gay (The Celebrated Army Song Publisher and Vocalists), No. 300 North 20th Street, Philadelphia. PA. 1864. [5 1/2" × 9 1/2"]. B/w litho of Abraham Lincoln within frame of two women, cherubs, flowers. 2pp. Page 2: Blank.

AL-386 Lincoln The Liberator. m. Buckley.

AL-387 The Bobolink Minstrel (Or Republican Songster For 1860). e. George Washington Bungay (Author of *Crayon Sketches*). Published by O. Hutchinson, New York, NY. 1860. Br/bk. "Lincoln And Liberty." Verse. 72pp. [M-103].

AL-388 Songs For The Great Campaign Of 1860. e. George W. Civis. Published by *The New York Tribune*, New York, NY. 1860. "Comprising a Choice Collection of Original and Selected Solos, Glees, Choruses, &c., &c., from the Best Authors." "Words and Music." "Single copy 25 cents; One Dozen, $2; One Hundred, $15." 12pp. [M-105].

AL-389 Our Lincoln The Hero Of The Nation. w.m. J.F. Burke. 1916.

AL-390 Union Campaign Songs [Song Book]. 1864. Non-pictorial. 16pp. [M-130].

AL-391 Lincoln And The Starry Flag. m. E.A. Burkes. 1913.

AL-392 Ring The Bell Softly. w. W.D. Smith, Jr. m. E.N. Carlin. 1866.

AL-393 The Clarion Melodist (A New Republican Campaign Songster). Published by The Lincoln Clarion Print, Springfield, IL. 1860. Non-pictorial. "We will have bonfires and illuminations. We will have every Demonstration of Joy, and ten thousand banners shall be borne aloft inscribed with the words 'Lincoln and Hamlin, Union and Victory.'" 32pp. [M-106].

AL-394 The Young Men's Republican Vocalist. w.m.c. William P. Dale. Published by A. Morris, New York, NY. 1860. Be/bk litho of Abraham Lincoln. "By their songs ye know them. Ours are of Freedom." "By order of the Committee for the Campaign of 1860." "Price 8 cents." [M-107].

AL-395 The Death Of President Lincoln. w.m. W. Clifton.

AL-396 Lincoln And Hamlin Campaign Songster (For The Presidential Campaign Of 1860). Published in Ithaca, New York. 1860. Y/bk non-pictorial. [M-111].

AL-397 The Republican Campaign Songster #2. Published by American Publishing House, No. 60 West Fourth Street, Cincinnati, OH. 1860. Litho of Abraham Lincoln. [M-114].

AL-398 Lincoln. w. Stevens. m. J.W. Clokey. 1923.

AL-399 Lincoln Memorial Song. w.m. L.S. Collins.

AL-400 Uncle Abe's Songster. Published by Towne and Bacon, San Francisco, CA. 1860. Non-pictorial. Inside title: **Uncle Abe's Republican Songster for "Uncle Abe's Choir"**. [M-115].

AL-401 Washington Et Lincoln. m. J. Comellas. 1867.

AL-402 The Tremaine Brothers' Lincoln And Johnson Campaign Song-Book. Published by [V-1: C.M. Tremaine] [V-2: The American News Company], New York, NY. 1864. [V-1: Be/bk] [V-2: Y/bk] non-pictorial. 40pp. "Containing 40 Pages of Soul-Stirring Pieces Written Expressly for This Campaign." Page 40: "McClellan's History in three Sentences." [M-129].

AL-403 Abraham Lincoln Schottisch. m. E.S. Cummings. 1860.

AL-404 Song Of Lincoln. w.m. L.B. Durand. 1919.

AL-405 The Republican Songster (For The Campaign Of 1864). Published by J.R. Hawley & Co., Cincinnati, OH. 1864. [V-1: Gy/bk] [V-2: O/bk] non-pictorial. 64pp. [M-128].

AL-406 An Abraham Lincoln Song. w. Whitman. m. W. Damrosch. 1936.

AL-407 Lincoln's Funeral March. m. C.J. Fischer. 1865.

AL-408 Lincoln And Johnson Campaign Song-Book. 1864. 38pp. [M-123].

AL-409 Massa Linkum's Boy. w. Parker. m. M.S. Gordon. 1884.

AL-410 Abe Lincoln. w. Beebe. m. M.C. Hanford. 1912.

AL-411 Songs For The Union. c. Union Congressional Committee. Printed for the Union Congressional Committee by John A. Grey and Green, New York, NY. 1864. Non-pictorial. [M-131].

AL-412 The Flower From Lincoln's Grave. w. Lawrence. m. J. Holberton.

AL-413 Honor You Today, Lincoln Oh Lincoln. w. Douglas. m. K.L. Hoschina. 1906.

AL-414 Abraham Lincoln. w.m. H.F. Kampe. 1865.

AL-415 Abraham Lincoln. w. Briar. m. R. Kountz.

AL-416 We Mourn Our Fallen Chieftain. w.m. M.B. Ladd. 1865.

AL-417 A Lincoln Symphony. m. D.G. Mason.

Al-418 President Lincoln's Funeral March. m. Karl Merz.

AL-419 The President's Grave (Quartette). w. Edwin S. Babbitt. m. L.B. Miller. Published by [V-1: S. Brainard, Cleveland, OH] [V-2: Root & Cady, No. 67 Washington Street, Chicago]. 1865. Non-pictorial geometric designs. 6pp. [V-2: Page 6: Advertisement for Root & Cady music].

AL-420 President Lincoln's Funeral March. m. F. Mueller.

AL-421 Memories Of Lincoln. w. Whitman. m. W.H. Neidlinger.

AL-422 Lincoln. w. Kiser. m. J.A. Parks. 1914.

AL-423 Lincoln. w.m. Charles Provis. 1931.

AL-424 Our Lincoln's Act. w. Benjamin. m. R.M. Price.

AL-425 Lincoln Way Grand March. m. L.P. Reed. 1916.

AL-426 Oh Why Should The

Spirit Of Mortal Be Proud. w. William Knox. m. A.J. Robyn. 1911.

AL-427 Lincoln Centennial. m. Lee Sanford.

AL-428 Lincoln. w. Hanks. m. Schwartz.

AL-429 Lincoln's Birthday. w.m. George L. Spaulding. Published by Theodore Presser, No. 1712 Chestnut, Philadelphia, PA. [ca. 191-]. Non-pictorial geometric design border. "Days We Celebrate, Pianoforte Pieces Introducing Popular Melodies."

AL-430 Our Lincoln. w. Washburn. m. J. Surdo. Published by [V-1: Walnut Hills Music Co., Cincinnati, OH] [V-2: Willis Music Co.] [V-3: Lincoln Centennial Memorial Association, Cincinnati, OH]. [V1 & V-2: 1918] [V-3: 1908]. [V-1: For three equal voices, 32pp] [V-2: On Ode for one, two and three equal voices with piano or orchestra accompaniment, 32pp] [V-3: 31pp].

AL-431 Little Willie's Grave (Ballad).. w. W. Ross Wallace. m. J.R. Thomas. Published by Wm. Hall & Son, New York, NY. 1863. Non-pictorial geometric designs. "To Mrs. Abraham Lincoln, Washington, D.C." 6pp. Pages 2 and 6: Blank.

AL-432 Abraham's Covenant (New Battle Song). w.m. A.B. Tobey. Published by H.M. Higgins, 117 Randolph St., Chicago, IL. 1862. B/w litho of geometric designs. "We're going to fight in earnest boys — Lincoln to the soldiers."

AL-433 On The Lincoln Highway. w.m. Mabel Van Ess. 1915.

AL-434 Good Morning, Master Lincoln. w. Langenschwarz. m. Charles Magnus. Published by Charles Magnus, No. 12 Frankfort Street, New York, NY. 1864.

AL-435 Lincoln And Douglas. w.m. Wilson.

AL-436 Lincoln's Reign. w.m. Wilson.

AL-437 Lincoln's Funeral March. m. P.J. Wires. 1935.

AL-438 Please Mr. Lincoln. w. Roden. m. Max S. Witt. 1900.

AL-439 Lincoln Tune. m. C. Wood. 1912.

AL-440 Lincoln's Fame, Lincoln's Bright Name. m. Wright.

AL-441 Lincoln. w. Tillotson. m. B.D. Ackley. 1916.

AL-442 Lincoln. m. Anderson.

AL-443 America Is Calling Lincoln. m. Andino.

AL-444 We Mourn Our Country's Loss (Marcia Funerale In Memory of Our Late President). w.m. Augustus Buechel. Published by P.A. Wundermann, No. 824 Broadway, New York, NY. 1865. B/w non-pictorial geometric designs, line border. "Composed and Respectfully Dedicated to Mrs. Abraham Lincoln." 6pp. Page 2: Title — **Marcia Funerale In Memory of The Late President Of The United States, Abraham Lincoln.**

AL-445 Lincoln. m. Critelle. 1860.

AL-446 President's Hymn (Give Thanks All Ye People). w. Muhlenberg. m. A.C. Gutterson. 1864.

AL-447 Lincoln Highway March Two Step. m. H.J. Lincoln.

AL-448 Lincoln Highway March Two Step. m. G.B. Lutz.

AL-449 Who Will Care For Old Abe Now? w.m. J.M.

AL-450 Abraham Lincoln. w.m. Ostermeyer.

AL-451 To Arms! To Arms! April 15th, 1861 (Song). w.m. William F. Otten, L.L.D. a. Vanderweyde. w. Published by Thos. Birch & Son, No. 521 Sixth Avenue, New York, NY. 1861. B/w litho by Stackpole of crossed flags, shield, bunting, cannons, floral designs. "Sung by Miss Maria Brainerd." "Respectfully Dedicated to the President of the United States."

AL-452 Funeral March [?]. m. C.E. Rogers. Published by [V-1: O. Ditson, Boston, MA] [V-2 & V-3: S.

(AL) ABRAHAM LINCOLN

Brainard, Cleveland, OH]. [V-1 & V-2: 1865] [V-3: ca. 1893].

AL-453 (Loyal Legion Hymn) Abraham Lincoln. m. H.M. Rogers. 1918

AL-454 Lincoln Highway March. m. F.J. St. Clair. 1914.

AL-455 Lincoln. w. Barnes. m. R.D. Shure. 1864.

AL-456 We Are Coming Father Abraham, 600,000 More. w. Gibbons. m. N.J. Sporle.

AL-457 Abraham Lincoln Jones. w. Mack and Ceil. m. Chris Smith. 1909.

AL-458 Old Abe The Battle Eagle (Song & Chorus). w. L.J. Bates, Esq. m. T. Martin Towne (Author of *Our Boys Are Coming Home*). Published by H.N. Hempsted, No. 410 Main Street, Milwaukee, WI. 1865. N/c litho by Chas. Shober of eagle, shield. "Inscribed to the 8th Wisconsin Regt." Long narrative on "Old Abe, The Battle Eagle."

AL-459 Who Will Care For Old Abe Now? Published by H. De Marsan, Publisher, No. 54 Chatham Street, New York, NY.

AL-460 Let The President Sleep. w. Stewart. m. G.A. Brown. 1865.

AL-461 Abraham Lincoln. m. R.R. Bennett. 1931.

AL-462 Abraham Lincoln. w.m. C. Blamphin.

AL-463 Lincoln Quickstep. m.a. Jessie Brinley. Published by John Church, Jr., No. 66 West 4th Street, Cincinnati, OH. 1865. B/w floral and geometric designs. "Priceless Pearls, A Collection of Beautiful Pieces for Piano." List of other tunes in series.

AL-464 Lincoln (Requiem Aeternam). w. John Gould Fletcher. m. Herbert Elwell. Published by Broadcast Music, No. 580 Fifth Avenue, New York 19, NY. [ca. 1947]. "For Mixed Chorus With Baritone Solo."

AL-465 We Are Coming Father Abram, Full 600,000 More. w. William Cullen Bryant. m.a. Nathan Barker. Published by A.C. Peters & Bro., No. 94 West 4th Street, Cincinnati, OH. 1862.

AL-466 We Are Coming Father Abra'am, 600,000 More. w. William Cullen Bryant. m.a. E.M. Bruce. Published by J.W. Lawton & Company, No. 19 South Eighth Street, Philadelphia, PA. 1862. Non-pictorial geometric designs.

AL-467 We Are Coming Father Abra'am (Song). w. William Cullen Bryant. m.a. N.J. Sprole. Published by Oliver Ditson & Company, No. 277 Washington Street, Boston, MA. [ca. 1862]. B/w litho of scrolls.

AL-468 March Of The 600,000. m. George Root. Published by Strange & Company, Musical Publishers and Importers, No. 120 King Street West, Toronto, Canada. [ca. 1860's]. "The Canadian Musical Library."

AL-469 Camp Songs For The Soldiers And Poems Of Leisure Moments. c. Gen'l. William H. Hayward. Published by Harry A. Robinson, Baltimore, MD. 1864. Non-pictorial. 152pp. [M-121].

AL-470 Lincoln (Study Song). w. Ann Underhill. m. Eleanor Smith. In: *The Music Hour, First Book*, page 40. Published by Silver Burditt Company, New York, NY. Copyright 1927, 1928, 1936, 1937. 120pp.

AL-471 Lincoln. w. F.M. Daniels. m. George A. Boynton. B/w drawing of Abraham Lincoln, crossed flags. In: *The American Singer, Book 7*, page 212. Published by American Book Company, New York, NY. 1947. [7 1/2" × 10 1/8"]. R/w/b stars, bars of music. 238pp.

AL-472 The Last Race Of The Rail Splitter. [Probably published in Baltimore]. [ca. 1861]. Penny songsheet. B/w litho of a runaway slave. "It will not be forgotton that Lincoln, after his election, on his way to Washington, heard at Harrisburg, that a plan was laid to run the cars off, and kill him on the Northern Central Road, or in Baltimore a mere invention, when not a soul thought of hurting a hair on his head,) and to avoid the imaginary danger to himself, he slipped around in the night, in disguise, by the Philadelphia Road, and sent his wife and son by the cars, which were to be smashed up, to be killed in his place." 2pp. Page 2: Blank. [Anti-Lincoln lyrics].

AL-473 Honest Abe. w.m. J. Lilian Vandevere. "Abraham Lincoln called our democracy a "Government of the people, by the people, for the people." In: *We Sing*, page 128. Published by C.C. Birchard aand Company, Boston, MA. [ca. 193-]. [6 7/8" × 8 5/8"]. 200pp.

AL-474 Abraham Lincoln. w. M. Louise Baun. m. Pauline Meyer. In: *Intermediate Music*, page 150. Published by Ginn and Company, Boston, MA. 1924. [6 1/2" × 8 3/16"]. Bl/bk hardback book.

AL-475(A) Abraham's Daughter. w.m. Septimus Winner. In: *Ballads & Songs Of The Civil War*, page 72. c. Jerry Silverman. Published by Mel Bay Publications, Inc., Pacific, MO. 63069. 1998. 276pp.

(B) Abraham's Daughter, II., page 74.

(C) Booth Killed Lincoln, page 83.

(D) Lincoln And Liberty, page 68. w. Jesse Hutchinson. m. *Old Rosin The Beau*

(E) Old Abe Lincoln Came Out Of The Wilderness, page 66. w. Anonymous. m. *Down in Alabam.*

(F) We Are Coming Father Abr'am, page 76. w. James Sloan Gibbons. m L.O. Emerson.

(G) We'll Fight For Uncle Abe, page 80. w. C.E. Pratt. m. Frederick Buckley.

AL-476(A) The Missouri Harmony. "Young Abraham Lincoln and his sweetheart, Ann Rutledge, sang from this book in the Rutledge tavern in New Salem, according to old settlers there." In: *The American Songbag*, page 152. e. Carl Sandburg. Published by Harcourt, Brace & Company, Inc., New York, NY. 1927.

(B) The Brown Girl or Fair Eleanor, page 156. "Little Abe Lincoln, as a child, probably heard *The Brown Girl*, according to persons familiar with Kentucky backgrounds."

(C) Hooser Johnny, page 164. "Lincoln heard it often. It was a favorite of his singing with a friend with the banjo, Ward Hill Lamon."

(D) Lincoln And Liberty, page 167. "This campaign ditty has the brag and extravaganza of electioneering. The tune is from *Old Rosin The Bow* and served earlier for a Henry Clay candidacy in which was the salutation. In a later year when Horace Greeley was running for the Presidency against Gen. U.S. Grant, voters were reminded, 'Then let Greeley go to dickens, too soon he has counted his chickens.'"

(E) Old Abe Came Out Of The Wilderness. "Torchlight processions of Republicans sang this in the summer and fall months of 1860. The young Wide Awakes burbled it as the kerosene dripped on their blue oilcloth capes. Quartets and octettes jubilated with it in packed, smoky halls where audiences waited for speakers of the evening. In Springfield, Illinois, the nation, heard his two boys Tad and Willie sing it at him. The tune is from the Negro spirituals, *When I Come Out De Wilderness* and *Ol' Gray Mare Come Tearin' Out De Wilderness.*"

AL-477 Back To The Days Of Lincoln (Song). w. Z.M. Parvin and A.C. Roche. m. Z.M. Parvin (Author of *The Half Has Never Been Told* (Sacred), *Dearest One, A Little Bird Whispered So, In Grand Old Oregon*). Published by Z.M. Parvin, No, 165 _ Fourth Street, Portland, Oregon 1909. [9 1/2" × 12 1/2"]. R/w/b litho of Abraham Lincoln, eagle with ribbon inscribed "E Pluribus Unum," flag, geometric designs. "Dedicated to the

G.A.R. and All Who Love the Memory of America's Greatest Statesman — Abraham Lincoln." "'That this nation under God shall have a new birth of freedom and that government of the people, by the people, for the people, shall not perish from the earth' — Lincoln at Gettysburg." 4pp. Page 4: "Annual Commencement of the Capitol Normal School, Salem, Oregon, 1909." Order of Exercises and Programme.

AL-478 Abraham Lincoln Walks At Midnight. w. Vachel Lindsay. m. Ellie Siegmeister. Published by Carl Fischer, Inc., No. 62 Cooper Square, New York, NY. 10003. [6 16/16" × 10 1/4"]. 1966. Pl/bk/w drawing of treble clef and music notes. "Coral Score." 34pp. Pages 2, 28-33: Blank. Page 3: "For Mixed Chorus with Piano (or Orchestral) Accompaniment). Page 34: Advertising.

AL-479(A) O Captain! My Captain! w. Walt Whitman. In: *Songs of Purpose, Advanced Music*, page 243. c. Will Earhart and E. Hershey Sneath. Published by The MacMillan Company, New York, NY. 1929. [7 1/4" × 10 1/2"]. Gn/o drawing of couple singing, geometric designs. Hardback book. 320pp.

(B) Washington And Lincoln, page 250. w.m. George F. Root. "Tune: *The Battle Cry Of Freedom*." "Arranged for youthful voices."

AL-480 Save Our Flag (Song and Chorus). w. Mrs. Sara Wolverton. m. J.A. Getze. Published by J. Henry Whittemore, Detroit. 1862. Non-pictorial geometric designs. "Dedicated to the Michigan Volunteers." 6pp. Pages 2 and 6: Blank. [Verse on Abraham Lincoln: "the strong right arm of God."].

AL-481 Old Abe Lies Sick. a. Frances Wellman. In: *Rebel Songster — Songs The Confederates Sang*. Published by Heritage House, Charlotte, NC. 1959. [6 5/8" × 10 3/4"]. R/w/b litho of the Confederate battle flag, crossed rifles. 54pp.

AL-482(A) Lincoln's Address. w. Capt. Patrick F. Kelly. m. "Tune — *Scots wha hae wi Wallace Bled*." In: *Capt. Kelly's Knapsack, Well Packed with a Choice Selection of his Most Popular Songs and Other Small Pieces, also Containing his Celebrated Song of 'The Old Fire Laddie,' all Written and Composed by Himself*, page 16. Published by Capt. P.F. Kelly, No. 39 Beekman Street, New York, NY. 1892. [4 3/16" × 6 9/16"]. R/w/b drawing of stacked rifles, back pack enscribed "N.Y.S. Vol's." "10 Cents." 68pp.

(B) On The Death Of Abraham Lincoln, Our Martyred President, page 21. w. Capt. P. Kelly.

AL-483 Litoria (Campaign College Chorus) and **Upidee** (Campaign College Chorus). w. A.W. Tourgee. Cut from a newspaper in 1860 and pasted in a personal fraternity notebook owned by R.M. Tuttle, No. 16 Canal Street, Rochester, NY, a student at The University of Rochester. Also in the book is a cut lithograph of a beardless Abraham Lincoln with slogan — "The Peoples Candidate for President." [3" × 5 3/8"].

AL-484 Lincoln Lyrics (That All Men May Aspire) (A Choral Suite). w. Edwin Markham. m. George Frederick McKay. Published by C.C. Birchard and Company, Boston, MA. 1949. [7 1/8" × 10 3/8"]. Gn/gn drawing of log cabin, flowers. 72pp.

AL-485 Ole Uncle Abrum's Comin' (Song with Chorus). w.m. A.C. D'Sandie. Published by Bruce & Bisbee, No. 18 North 7th Street, Philadelphia, PA. 1862. Non-pictorial geometric designs. 6pp. Pages 2 and 6: Blank.

AL-486 We Have Another Lincoln And Edwards Is His Name. Photo of Edwards. [19 —].

AL-487 Freedom's Martyred Chief. w. Laura E. Newell. m.a. S.C. Hanson. In: *Golden Glees*, page 98. e. S.C. Hanson. [8 1/2" × 6 1/8"]. [ca. 1880].

AL-488 We Are Coming, Father Abraham. w. Hutchinson. m. L.O. Emerson. In: [V-2: *The New American*

Song Book], *A Century of Progress in American Song*, page 112. c. Marx Oberndorfer and Anne Oberndorfer. Published by Hall & McCreary, Chicago, IL. [V-1: 1933] [V-2: 1941]. [V-1: Pl/s hard cover] [V-2: "Pan American Edition"]. [V-1: 780pp] [V-2: 186pp].

AL-489(A) Abraham's Tea Party. m. "Air — *Oh Susanna!*" In: *Beadle's Dime Knapsack Songster: Containing the Choicest Patriotic Songs, Together with many New and Original Ones, Set to Old Melodies*, page 31. Published by Beadle and Company, No. 141 William Street, New York, NY. 1862. [3 3/4" × 5 3/4"]. Litho of coin — "One Dime, United States of America." 74pp.[?].

(B) Hold On, Abraham, page 46. "Copyright by permission of Firth, Pond & Co., Music Publishers, 547 Broadway, N.Y., owners of the copyright."

(C) We Are Coming, Father Abraham, page 5. "Copied by permission of Oliver Ditson & Co., Music Publishers, 277 Washington St., Boston, owners of the copyright."

AL-490 Abe Lincoln. w. Alfred Hayes. m. Earl Robinson. "The words to the chorus are taken from an address by Abraham Lincoln. The remarks in parentheses are meant to be spoken simply and with conviction." In: *The People's Songbook*, page 50. Published by Oak Publications, New York, NY. 1961. [6 15/16" × 9 15/16"]. Br/bk/w photo of folk singers. 132pp.

AL-491 We Are Coming, Father Abrah'm. w.m. L.O. Emerson. In: *The Most Popular Songs of Patriotism, Including National Songs of All the World*, page 46. Published by Hinds Hayden & Eldridge, Inc., Publishers, New York, NY. 1916. [7 1/8" × 10 5/8"]. 184pp. R/w/bk drawing of national flags, eagles.

AL-492 Give Us Just Another Lincoln. w.m. Paul Dresser. Published by Howley, Haviland & Company, Nos. 1260-1266 Broadway, New York, NY. 1900. B/w non-pictorial "Professional Copy." Copyright "Warning!" 6pp. Page 4: Advertising.

AL-493 We'll Fight For Uncle Abe. In: *Trumpet Of Freedom*. Published by Oliver Ditson & Company, No. 277 Washington Street, Boston, MA. 1864. [6 1/2" × 9 3/4"]. Be/bk litho of Union soldier with trumpet. List of contents. 64pp.

AL-494 Abraham Lincoln Lives Again. w.m. Lewis Allan. "Dedicated to the Abraham Lincoln Battalion." In: *Songs For America, American Ballads, Folk Songs, Marching Songs, Songs of Other Lands*, page 18. Published by Workers Library Publishers, Inc., P.O. Box 148, Station D, New York, NY. 1939. [6" × 9 1/8"]. R/w/bk drawing of a factory. 68pp.

AL-495(A) Abraham's Daughter (Or Raw Recruits). "Copyright 1861 by Sep. Winner." In: *War Songs, For Anniversaries and Gatherings of Soldiers, To Which is Added a Selection of Songs and Hymns for Memorial Day, The Choruses of all the Songs are Arranged for Male Voices*, page 50. Published by Oliver Ditson & Company, Boston, MA. 1888. Non-pictorial gn/bk cover. [6 1/2" × 10"]. 100pp.

(B) We Are Coming, Father Abra'am, page 55. m. L.O. Emerson.

AL-496 Do No Leave Me Mother Darling (Last Words Of Little "Tad" Lincoln) (Song With Chorus Ad Lib). w. Robert B. Johnson. m. Frank M. Davis. 1872. Non-pictorial geometric designs. "To Mrs. Abraham Lincoln."

AL-497 Six Hundred Thousand More. In: *The Star Songster, Containing 48 Patriotic, Sentimental and Comic Songs*, page 30. Published by McMullen & Gates, No. 143 Walnut Street, Cincinnati, OH. [ca. 1865]. [3 5/8" × 5 7/8"]. R/w/b star, geometric design frame. 52pp.

AL-498 Our Flag Shall Wave There! (Patriotic Song). w.m. Robert Hervey. Published by W.R. Smith, No. 135 North Eighth Street, Philadelphia,

(AL) ABRAHAM LINCOLN

PA. 1865. Non-pictorial geometric designs. "Sung With Great Applause by W.W. Batchelor." "Respectfully Dedicated to Abraham Lincoln, President of the United States." 6pp. Pages 2 and 6: Blank.

AL-499 Pro Patria! (A National Song for The Fourth of July, 1862). w.m. Pilgrim John. Published by E.D. D.S. Holmes, No. 67 Fourth Street, Brooklyn, NY. 1862. R/w/bl/be drawings of crossed flags, two domes with flags inscribed "Our Country," hands clasped, geometric designs. 6pp. [?]. Page 2: "Dedication To Abraham Lincoln, President of the United States and His Glorious Retinue of Triumphant Commanding Generals, With all their Noble and Gallant Companions in Arms, for the defense and protection of the just rights and privileges of a great, free, and intelligent people, and the best government in the world: This humble composition of verse and music is Respectfully Dedicated."

AL-500 Republican Rallying Song. m. E.W. Locke. [1864]. Non-pictorial black line border. 2pp. Page 2: Blank.

AL-501 Old Abe's Lament. m. "Tune — *The Campbells Are Coming.*" Probably published in the South. [ca. 1863]. [3 1/2" × 6 1/2"]. "Abolition President" handwritten in ink below title.

AL-502 The Irish Wide-Awake. w. Harry M. Palmer. m. "Air — *Billy O. Rourke.*" Published by H. De Marsan, Nos. 38 & 60 Chatham Street, New York, NY. n.d..

AL-503 Hold On Abraham! (Uncle Sam's Boys Are Coming Right Along). w. Wm. B. Bradbury. Published by Johnson, Song Publisher, No. 7 Tenth Avenue, Philadelphia, PA. [ca. 1863]. B/w non-pictorial geometric design border. "Sung with immense success by Wood's Minstrels." "See Prof. Brooks' Ball Room Monitor, it will give you more Information on Dancing than any book ever published. Sold by Johnson, No. 7 Tenth Avenue, Philadelphia." Sheet music "Published by Wm. A. Pond & Co., No. 547 Broadway, New York, NY."

AL-504 That Same Old Tune. m. "Air — *Vive la Campaignie.*" [1860. [5" × 7"]. Non-pictorial. "As sung by the West Chester Wide Awake Club." 2pp. Page 2: Blank.

AL-505(A) Old Abe Has Gone And Did It, Boys!. w. S. Filmore Bennett. m. J.P. Webster. In: *Patriotic Song Book, For the use of the G.A.R. in their Post-Meeting, Reunions, Camp-Fires, Installation Exercises, Fourth of July Celebrations, and Memorial Service. Also For all Patriotic Occasions*, page 26. Published by Orwell Blake, Des Moines, IA. 1883. [5 15/16" × 9 1/16"]. R/gd litho of a G.A.R. badge. 116pp.

(B) We Are Coming, Father Abraham (Or Three Hundred Thousand More). m. J.B. Irving, page 8.

AL-506(A) We Are Coming Father Abraam, 300,000 More. w.m. Stephen C. Foster. e. Gregg Smith. In: *America's Bicentennial Songs from The Great Sentimental Age, 1850-1900, Stephen Foster to Charles E. Ives*, page 1. Published by G. Schirmer, New York, NY. 1975. [9" × 11 7/8"]. N/c litho of woman with roses, flag, city. 152.

AL-507(A) There's Nothing Going Wrong. "Dedicated to 'Old Abe.'" In: *War Songs of the Blue and the Gray, As Sung by the Brave Soldiers of the Union and Confederate Armies in Camp, on the March and in Garrison, Containing all the favorite Lyrics that are sung with such different feelings of sadness and mirth as they recall the shades and lights of the Great War. [V-2: There is also included a large variety of old, well known and American Ballads and Songs, both patriotic and sentimental, as sung and played during the stirring times of '76 and 1812]*, page 36. Published by Hurst & Co., Publishers, [V-1: No Address] [V-2: No. 122 Nassau Street], New York, NY. [V-1: ca. 1880]. [V-2: ca. 1890]. [V-2: B/w litho of

"Grant, Robert E. Lee, Sherman and Johnston."].

(B) Lincoln's Inaugural Address, page 54. w. [V-1: "By a Southern Rights Man."][V-2: "By a 'Southern Man."] "In Advance of all competition."

AL-508 New Patriotic Songs [Song Sheet]. w. H. Webster Canterbury. m. Popular tunes. [1860]. [12 7/8" × 14 1/2"]. B/w litho of Abraham Lincoln and George Washington, "Price only five cents a sheet." 2pp. Page 2: Blank.

AL-509 March Funebre. In: *Marches Of The Presidents, 1789-1909, Authentic Marches & Campaign Songs*, page 42. A. Carl Miller. Published by Chappell & Co., Inc., No. 609 Fifth Avenue, New York, NY. "By arrangement with Chilmark Press, Inc." 1968. [9" × 12"]. R/w/b litho of eagle, flag. "An Illustrated Piano Folio For All Ages." 72pp.

AL-510 Lincoln And Liberty. Published by the authority of the Wide Awake Club No. 1 of West Chester, PA. [1860]. [5 1/4" × 7"]. Non-pictorial. "Honest Abe Lincoln — born in Kentucky — followed the plow and the path of rectitude in Indiana — and mauled rails and Stephen A. Douglas in Illinois." 2pp. Page 2: Blank.

AL-511 To Whom It May Concern. w. W. Dexter Smith, Jr. m. Carl Lazare. Published by G.D. Russel And Company, No. 126 Tremont, Boston, MA. [ca. 1864]. Non-pictorial geometric design border. "To Abraham Lincoln, President of the United States." 6pp. Pages 2 and 6: Blank.

AL-512(A) Abraham Lincoln. w. Gladys Shelly. m. Ruth Cleary. Bl/w drawing of Abraham Lincoln. In: *Little Patriots, A Book Of American Sons For Children*, page 13. Published by ABC Music Corporation, No. 799 7th Avenue, New York, NY. 1941. [6" × 9"]. R/w/b drawing of child. 44pp.

(B) Abraham Lincoln And His Books, page 21.

AL-513 The People's Advent (A New Quartette For The Times). w. Gerald Massy. m. James G. Clark. Published by H.M. Higgins, No. 117 Randolph Street, Chicago, IL. 1864. B/w non-pictorial geometric designs. "To Abraham Lincoln."6pp. Pages 2 and 6: Blank.

AL-514 I Cannot Support Him! Can You? w. Ladd (Private, 14th Brig. N.Y. Artillery).. m. "Air: *Rosin The Bow*." Published by "James D. Gay, the Celebrated Army Song Publisher and Vocalist, No. 300 North 20th Street, Philadelphia, Pa." 1864. B/w litho of political rally with speaker saying — "Grant's Beverage is Meade." "Union Club supplied with all the best Campaign Songs out." 2pp. Page 2: Blank. [Anti-McClellan].

AL-515 Lincoln & Hamlin (Republicanism). w. Druckenmiller. m. "Tune — *Wait For The Wagon*." In: Unnamed song sheet. Published by Druckenmiller, Mt. Joy, PA. [1860]. [9 1/2" × 12"]. Three song non-pictorial song sheet made to be cut apart. Other songs are *Andrew C. Curtin (Republicanism)* [for Governor] and *Office Hunting*. 2pp. B/w geometric design border around each song sheet. Page 2: Blank.

AL-516 How The Slave Loved Lincoln (Massa Linkum). m. "Tune, "*Lily of the Valley*." B/w litho of Abraham Lincoln, "1856 at Springfield." In: Off For The War, page 8. Published by Major E.W. McIntosh, No. 3321 Davenport Street, Omaha, NE. [ca. 1890]. [5 7/8" × 8 1/2"]. B/w litho of young boy in Union uniform leaving home — "Off for the war, 28th day of April 1861, at Bloomington, Illinois, 17 years of age. Captain Harvy's Co. K, 8th Illinois Infantry for 3 Months." 28pp. Page 28: B/w photo of Major E.W. McIntosh — "Will Play in Vaudeville Anywhere."

AL-517 Abe Lincoln In The White House (A Cantata For Low Voice: Singer/Narrator And Piano). w. Isaac E. Ronch (Original words in Yiddish) and J. and S. Cooperman (English Translated Version). m. Joseph Schrogin (Dedicated to my wife Manya). a. Waldemar Hille. Self published by Joseph Schrogin? [ca. 1930s]. [9 5/16" × 13"]. Pl/w drawing of Abraham Lincoln. 10pp. Page 10: Blank.

See also GW-133; GW-193; GW-197; GW-204; GW-219; GW-237; GW-238; GW-248; GW-282; GW-287; GW-288; GW-293; GW-296; GW-303; GW-304; GW-333; GW-351; GW-352; GW-373; GW-377; GW-462; GW-497; GW-558; GW-570; GW-575; GW-611; TJ-40; TJ-49; AJK-42; JCF-40; SAD-15; GBM-48; AJN-16; USG-34; USG-223; JAG-7; JAG-21; JAG-44; JGB-35; BFH-74; WJB-41; WM-24; WM-63; WM-90; WM-192; WM-226; WM-254; TR-142; TR-314; TR-343; TR-375; WHT-23; CEH-8; WW-16; WW-19; WW-31; WW-39; WW-40; WW-44; WW-58; WW-67; WW-83; WW-85; WW-87; WW-89; WW-106; WW-131; WW-150; WW-158; WW-175; WW-193; WW-201; WW-203; WW-209; WGH-11; WGH-34; CC-10; CC-14; CC-50; CC-53; CC-59; AML-9; WLW-2; WLW-45; WLW-67; FDR-92; FDR-158; FDR-173; FDR-270; FDR-272; FDR-279; FDR-281; FDR-310; FDR-367; FDR-390; FDR-401; TED-3; HST-18; DDE-1; DDE-9; DDE-50; DDE-52; DDE-76; DDE-86; JFK-15; JFK-28; JFK-30; JFK-31; JFK-51; JFK-60; JFK-61; JFK-62; JFK-66; JFK-69; JFK-70; JFK-82; JFK-84; LBJ-1; LBJ-27; RMN-27; RMN-39; GRF-8; JD-47; JD-49; RML-4; WL-1; DAM-54; MISC-42; MISC-76; MISC-77; MISC-78; MISC-79; MISC-90; MISC-93; MISC-94; MISC-97; MISC-101; MISC-109; MISC-112; MISC-126; MISC-127; MISC-130; MISC-139; MISC-146; MISC-150; MISC-156; MISC-157; MISC-167; MISC-168; MISC-171; MISC-186.

Alfred M. Landon

AML-1 Our Landon. w. Maida Townsend (Radio Star). m. Claude Lapham (Victor Red Seal Artist). Published by Lapham and Townsend, No. 1607 Broadway, New York, NY. 1936. Bl/w photos of Alfred M. Landon and Frank Knox. R/w/b eagle, crossed flags, border. 6pp. Page 2: Song: **Our Campaign Hymn**. w. Whittier. m. Dr. Henry S. Cutler. Page 3: "Dedicated to the Volunteers." Page 6: Arrangement for Male Quartette.

AML-2 Have You Ever Tried To Count To A Billion (A Song Burlesque). w. J.F. Bridges (Chicago). m. Dr. H.J. Reynolds (Chicago). Published by Noland Commercial Studios, Publisher, No. 224 South Michigan Boulevard, Chicago, IL. 1936. [7" × 10"]. B/w photo of Alf "Landon" and Frank "Knox." Y/bk sunflower. "For The Republican National Campaign 1936." 4pp. Page 4: Blank.

AML-3 Win With Landon. w.m. Paul Rebere [Aka: Paul Specht]. Published by Forster Music Publishers, Inc., No. 216 South Wabash Avenue, Chicago, IL. 1936. B/w photo of Alfred

AML-2

M. Landon. Y/w/bk sunflower. "Sponsored by the Landon-Knox Clubs." "An Official Republican Campaign Song." 4pp. Page 4: Two facsimile letters from the Republican National Committee.

AML-4 Humanity With Sanity. w.m. William R. Seiffert. Published by William R. Seiffert, National Bank Building, Oceanside, NY. 1936. Photos by Associated Press of "Alf M. Landon" and "Frank Knox." "G.O.P." "For Voice and Piano."

AML-5 Happy Landin' With Landon. w.m. Jack Stern and Sid Caine. Published by Caine and Stern, No. 117 West 9th Street, Los Angeles, CA. 1936. Bl/w photo of Alfred Landon. R/w/b facsimile letter—"Republican National Committee, Chicago, IL., John Hamilton, Chairman; I Have heard the song *Happy Landin' With Landon* and I highly recommend it—John Hamilton [facsimile handwriting]." "The Official Republican Campaign Song." "Phonograph records of this song and *Oh, Susanna* with special Landon lyrics on reverse side, can be obtained from the publisher at $.50 each." 4pp. Page 4: Quartette arrangement. a. Billy Hamer.

AML-6 Let's Land Landon In The White House. w. Thomas R. Johnstone. m. A. Maloof. Published by Carnegie Music Company, Carnegie Hall, New York, NY. 1936. B/w "Photo by permission of Republican National Committee" of Alfred Landon. Bk/y sunflower. 4pp. Page 4: Blank.

AML-7 Happy Days With Landon. w.m. Layne H. Hanes. Published by Layne H. Hanes, Music Publisher, Frantenac Building, Minneapolis, MN. 1936. Br/gd/w drawing by of sunflower. "With Ukulele Accompaniment." 4pp. Page 4: Advertising.

AML-8 Win With Landon (A Campaign Song). w.m. Effie Louise Koogle. Published by School and College Novelty Company, Lebanon, OH. 1936. R/w/b drawing by Shafer "Courtesy of *The Cincinnati Times-Star*" of The Statue of Liberty holding sign inscribed "Save America," flag background design, shield—"Patriotic Song." "Rousing Patriotic Song." 6pp. Pages 2 and 6: Blank.

AML-9 G.O.P. March. w.m. Gust Safstrom. Published by the De Montte Music Company, No. 855 East 75th Street, Chicago, IL. 1936. Bl/w photos of "Gov. Alf Landon—For President" and "Col. Frank Knox—For Vice-President." R/w/b drawing of an elephant, bass drum, eagle, crossed flags, silhouettes of George "Washington," Abraham "Lincoln." "Endorsed by the Illinois Republican State Central Committee, Perry B. McCullough, Chairman." "Sold to Help Finance the 1936 Campaign, Price 10 cents." 4pp. Page 4: Campaign advertising—"Opportunity and Landon-Knox." "Composer of record of President Franklin D. Roosevelt and Gov. Alf M. Landon." List of other Illinois candidates.

AML-10 Oh! Susanna (Song and Fox Trot). w.m. Stephen C. Foster. a. W.C. Polla. Published by F.B. Haviland Publishing Company, Music Publishers, No. 114 West 44th Street, New York, NY. 1923. B/w photos of wagon train scene "Where a trail divides." "Louis Wilson as Molly Wingate, Johnny Foz as Jed Wingate." Hand stamped in large red letters—"The Official Landon Campaign Song." "Song and Fox Trot combined as sung in Jesse L. Laskey's Presentation of *The Covered Wagon*, a Paramount Production by James Cruze—Founded on Emmerson Hough's Story." 6pp. Pages 2 and 6: Advertising.

AML-11 Come Along! w.m. Edward Chambreau. 1936. [6" × 9 7/16"]. Non-pictorial broadside. "US Copyright." 2pp. Page 2: Blank.

AML-12 The Potato Party. w. W.M. Hughes. m. Burrell Van Buren. Published by Hughes Publishing House, Mount Tabor, NJ. 1936. R/w/b drawing of flag, trees, geometric designs. 6pp. Page 2: Blank. Page 6: R/w/b eagles.

AML-13 Landing With Landon (Landon And Knox Campaign Songs 1936) [Song Pamphlet]. w. Mary Bush Lang. m. Popular tunes. Published by Mary B. Lang, Melrose Highlands, MA. 1936. [4" × 9"]. Non-pictorial. "$2.00 per hundred, $15 per thousand." Advertising for "Landon and Knox Campaign Lyrics 1936." 12pp. Page 12: Advertising for "Landon-Knox-lyrics 1936." "For copies apply to above address or to Massachusetts Republican State Committee, 11 Beacon Street, Boston, Massachusetts." [M-422].

AML-14 Oh! Susanna. m. Stephen C. Foster. [1936]. [5 1/2" × 8 9/16"]. Non-pictorial. "Everybody sing." 2pp. Page 2: Blank.

AML-15 Landing With Landon (Landon and Knox Campaign Songs 1936) [Song Pamphlet]. w. Mary Bush Lang. m. Popular tunes. Published by Mary Lang, No. 90 Nowell Road, Melrose Highlands, MA. 1936. [4" × 9"]. Non-pictorial. "Compliments of Massachusetts Republican State Committee." "Landon-Knox-Lyrics 1936." 12pp. [M-422].

AML-16 Long Live King Franklin The First (Lawgiver, Judge, Dictator). w. G.A. Cleveland Shrighey. Published by Bookcraft, Nos. 304-320 East 45th Street, New York, NY. Non-pictorial. 2pp. Page 2: Verses. "Vivat Franklin Rex et Dictator."

AML-17 Landon Boom Song. w. Kay Augusta. m. Hurley Kaylor. Published by Conrad Metz, Jr., No. 514 Pickwick Building, Kansas City, MO. [1936]. Bl/w photo of Alf Landon. R/w/b cover. 6pp. Page 2: "Respectfully Dedicated to Governor Alf M. Landon of Kansas by the Writers." Page 6: R/w/b eagle.

AML-18 America Sings For Americanism. w.m. Popular Airs. Published by the Republican National Committee, No. 41 East 42nd Street, New York, NY. [1936]. [6" × 9"]. B/w drawing of sunflower. 4pp. Page 4: "Victory for the American Way with Landon and Knox." [M-421].

AML-19 He's The Man Of The Hour. w. Richard B. Stauffer and Twila Draper. m. Harry L. Alford. Published by The Stauffer Music Company, Topeka, KS. 1936. Bl/w photo of "Alfred M. Landon, Governor of Kansas." "Ad Astra Per Aspera." 4pp. Page 4: Blank.

AML-20 Everything American Is Good Enough For Me (Republican Campaign Song). w.m. Dr. Frank Albert Davis (Composer of *The Twilight Hour* (Piano), *Lead Me On Dear Savior, Lead Me* (Hymn-Anthem), *I Love New England* (Song), *My Home in Old New Hampshire* (Song*), I Am So Glad to Know Jesus* (Hymn), *Guide Us, Oh Thou Great Jehovah* (Hymn). 1936. B/w drawing of George Washington, geometric designs. 4pp. Page 4: Advertising.

AML-21 The New Deal Review. w. C.I. Rudy. m. Luther A. Clark (Arranger of the Piano part *When It's Springtime In The Rockies*)." Published by C.I. Rudy, Darlington, MO. 1936. R/w/b drawing of U.S. Flag. B/w geometric designs. 6pp. Page 6: Bl/w drawing of a basket of flowers.

AML-22 Lick 'Em With Landon, That's Who! w.m. Robert S. Townsend and Inez Denny. Published by *The Augusta Press*, Augusta, ME. [1936]. Non-pictorial black border. 4pp. Page 4: Blank.

AML-23 Republican Victory Songs [Song Pamphlet]. 1936. [6" × 9"]. B/w drawings of "Alf Landon" and "Frank Knox," eagle, "1936," two shields. 4pp. Page 4: "Pennsylvania — A Landslide for Landon."

AML-24 Three Long Years! w.m. Shelby Darnell. Published by Bob Miller, Inc., Music Publisher, No. 1619 Broadway, New York, NY. 1936. Bl/w drawing by Barbelle of a fat, cigar smoking donkey and a beat-up, bandaged elephant. 4pp. Page 4: Advertising.

AML-25 Federal Follies. w. Mrs.

Mary J. O'Bryon Sibley. m. Stephen C. Foster — "Adapted from *Oh! Susanna.*" Published by Stasny-Lang, Inc., Music Publisher, No. 1619 Broadway, New York, NY. 1936. B/w floral and geometric design by F.S. Manning. "Dedicated to Gov. Alfred M. Landon." "Vocal." 4pp. Page 4: Advertising.

AML-26 Madison Square Garden Rally (Musical Program Booklet]. Published by New York Republican State Committee, [New York, NY]. 1936. [6 1/4" × 10 7/16"]. Y/bk drawing of sunflower, eagle. "For President Alf. M. Landon; For Vice President Frank Knox; For Governor Wm. F. Bleakley; For Lieut. Governor Ralph K. Robertson; For Comptroller John E. May; For Atty. General Nathan D. Pearlman." "Richard W. Lawrence, General Chairman; Carleton Greenwald, Chairman General Arrangements Committee." "Madison Square Garden Rally, October 29th, 1936, under the auspices of New York Republican State Committee." 4pp. Page 2: "George McEverett, Director, Music by Melville Monis Orchestra, Capt. Francis W. Southerland and his 7th (107th) Regiment Band, Soloists, Queena Mario, Sporano [sic] Metropolitan Opera Co., Martio Chamlee, Tenor, Metropolitan Opera Co., Republican Mens Glee Club, University of New York, Arthur Hill, Conductor."

AML-27 Our Campaign Hymn. w. Whittier. m. "Sung to the Old Hymn Tune *Cutler*." Published by The Volunteers, No. 435 North Michigan Avenue, Chicago, IL. as part of a volunteer sign-up card for Landon-Knox. 1936. [10 13/16" × 4 1/16"]. R/w/b printed card in two perforated sections. Obv: Section 1— Volunteer Registration card for the Landon-Knox campaign. Section 2: Membership Card and Campaign song. "An Independent organization of American Citizens banded together under the leadership of Landon and Knox to Save America." "1776-1936." Rev: Section 1: Registration list for contacts. Section 2: "Suggestions to Volunteers."

AML-28 Knox Notification Ceremony [Song Sheet Fan]. m. Popular Tunes. Printed by P.J. Kohl and Company, Chicago, IL. 1936. Cardboard hand-held fan. Obv: Bl/w photo of Frank Knox with r/w/b border. Rev: Four campaign songs. "Knox Notification Ceremony, July 30, 1936, Chicago Stadium."

AML-29 Songs For Landon Day. m. Popular tunes. [1936]. [6" × 9"]. Pk/bk non-pictorial. "Songs for Landon Day." 2pp.

AML-30 Oh! Alf Landon (We're Betting On You). w. F.E. Murray. m. Etta Rotter. Published by Murray and Rotter, Cody, WY. Copyright 1936 by F.E. Murray. Br/w/y drawing of a sunflower. 4pp.

AML-31 Oh! Susanna. w. Campaign lyrics. m. "Tune: *Oh! Susanna*." Pub-

AML-28

lished as a napkin. 13 3/8" × 13 3/8"]. [1936]. Obv: Br/w drawing of Alf Landon, sunflower, pig — "West," Cow — "North," cotton ball — "South," factory — "East."

AML-32 Songs Of Republican Sing To Victory. Published by Delos Owen, Chicago, IL. 1936. 4pp. [M-423].

AML-33 Campaign Songs, 1936. w. Mrs. Walter Q. Taylor. 1936. "Some Fallacies of the New Deal Set Forth in Song. " 2 volumes. [M-424].

See also FDR-83; FDR-96; FDR-134.

ANTI-MASONIC PARTY

AMP-1 Corner-Stone March. m. Ch. Zeuner. Published by C. Bradlee, No. 164 Washington Street, Boston, MA. 1832. B/w litho by David C. Johnston, printed by Pendleton, of a scene at the "Antimasonic Convention in Valdimor [Baltimore]" of animals sitting at table, speaking anti-Masonic sayings — "No Secret Societies," "Mr. President I should like to know what cause we are to pursue with regard to the Presidency. I hope no candidate will be entered who is not a *full blooded* Antimason. Rather than vote for any other I will *run* for the office myself," "Mr. President I agree with my friend opposite. To save my own *bacon* I would not vote for any man who would not go the *whole hog* for Antimasonry," "Mr. President I'm not used to many words. I never spin out a long yarn without getting into a *smart*. I've only to say, that since I have em*barked* in this business, I am resolved to go to the full figure." "As performed by the Boston Brigade Band at the Ceremony of laying the Corner Stone of the Masonic Temple, Boston." "Dedicated to the Fraternity." 4pp. Page 4: Blank.

ADLAI E. STEVENSON II

AS-1 Believe In Stevenson. w. Anne Croswell. m. Ed Scott. Published by Mode Music, Inc., No. 1650 Broadway, New York 19, NY. 1956. Bl/w photo of Adlai E. Stevenson II. 6pp.

AS-2 March On With Adlai & John (A Campaign Song 1952). w.m. I. Dan Danziger. a. Charles J. Cliff. Published by American Free Enterprises, No. 1025 Vermont Avenue NW., Washington, DC. 1952. [6" × 10"]. B/w photos of Adlai E. Stevenson II and John Sparkman. 4pp.

AS-3 Don't Let 'Em Take It Away! (A Democratic Campaign Song). w. Robert Sour. m. Bernie Wayne. Published by Meridian Music Corporation, No. 1619 Broadway, New York 19, NY. 1952. R/w/b photo of a farmer, businessman and trades worker. 6pp. Page 6: Same as cover photo.

AS-4 Be Democrats. w.m. A. Stevens and Maron Web. Published by WAM Publishers, Los Angeles, CA. 1952. R/w/b drawings of Thomas Jefferson, Andrew Jackson, shield, two crossed flags, one is the U.S. Flag and the other is inscribed "To Lead Always." 4pp. Page 4: R/w drawing of a donkey.

AMP-1

AS-2

AS-5 Stevenson. w.m. Morrie Allen. Copyright 1960, Mt. Vernon, NY. B/w photo of "Adlai E. Stevenson" II. Bl/bk/w cover with music and lyrics to the song. 2pp. Page 2: Blank.

AS-6 We're Madly For Adlai. w.m. Gilbert S. Watson. Published by Tweed Enterprises, Inc., P.O.B. 392, Lake Forest, IL. 1956. Bl/w photo of Adlai E. Stevenson II. 4pp. Page 4: Blank.

AS-7 We're For Adlai. w.m. Cyril A. Smack. a. Gertrude Smack Seaman. Published by Cyril A. Smack, No. 30 Beach Street, Sea Bright, NJ. [1952]. B/w photo of "Adlai Stevenson" II. "Let us justify our faith in the future of America by using all we have of character and thought in selecting as our leaders those men and women who know and love the freedom that is ours — Who know how to continue well the building on from the best our Nation's founders and preservers have established, improved and maintained until this day." 4pp. Page 4: Narrative: "The World's Hope Is Democracy. America's Hope is the Democratic Party."

AS-8 We're Madly For Adlai. w.m. Gilbert S. Watson. Published by Tweed Enterprises, Inc., P.O.B. 392, Lake Forest, IL. 1956. B/w photo of Adlai E. Stevenson II. B/w drawing of flag, The White House, ladder with rungs labeled "Our Next President," "Nominee For President," "Governor of Illinois," "Representative To U.N.," Ass't. Secretary of State," "Ass't. to Secretary of Navy," "Private Citizen." Song Lyrics. 2pp. Page 2: Blank.

AS-9 Strike Ike (Keep Your Pay with Adlai). [1952?]. Photos of Dwight D. Eisenhower and Adlai E. Stevenson. Drawing of donkey.

AS-10 We Want Adlai (He Knows the Score). w.m. George (Jeb) Long. Copyright 1948 and 1956 by George (Jeb) Long, Gillespie, IL. [8 1/2" × 11"]. Non-pictorial. 4pp.

AS-12 Climb On This Adlai Train. m. "Set to an Edited Version of the American Folk-Melody *Crawdad Song*." Published by Volunteers for Stevenson, Pittsburgh, PA. [1956]. [8 1/2" × 11"]. Non-pictorial. "Any reprinting, publication or commercial performance of these lyrics is prohibited without express consent of Volunteers For Stevenson, Pittsburgh, Pa." 2pp. Page 2: Blank.

AS-13 [Adlai Song Sheet]. w. Jim Corbett (Director, International Ladies' Garment Workers' Union Chorus). [1956]. [5" × 8"]. Non-pictorial. 2pp.

AS-14 You Must Be There. w. Mike Johnson. [1956]. [5" × 8"]. Non-pictorial. "When It's Time To Cast Your Vote You Must Be There." "Democratic Campaign Songs 1956." 2pp. Page 2: Blank.

AS-11 The Democratic March. w. Herbert Baker and Johnny Green. m. "Adapted from *The Yellow Rose of Texas*." Copyright 1956 by Herbert Baker and

Johnny Green. [5 1/4" × 8 1/4"]. Non-pictorial. 2pp. Page 2: Blank.

BENJAMIN F. BUTLER

BFB-1 Gov. Benjamin F. Butler's Grand March. m. Charles D. Blake. Published by White, Smith and Company, Boston, MA. 1882. B/w litho of Benjamin Butler. "To Columbia's Noble Son, Gov. Benjamin F. Butler." 6pp.

BFB-2 The Carpet Bagger (Comic Song for the Times). w. T.E. Garrett, Esq. m. Alfred von Rochow. Published by Balmer & Weber, No. 206 North Fifth Street, St. Louis, MO. 1868. B/w litho by Welcker of a man with large carpet bag labeled "Reconstruction" full of household items, plantation home, family, palm tree. "As sung with immense eclat by the inimitable Billy Emerson." "To Gen. Ben Butler." 8pp. Pages 2 and 8: Advertising for other Balmer & Weber music. Page 3: Subtitle — "Comic Song with Chorus ad lib." Page 6: Song — **The Carpet Bagger Dance**. m. Alfred von Rochow.

BFB-3 Genl. Butler's Grand March. m. J.V. Hamm. Published by Oliver Ditson, No. 277 Washington Street, Boston, MA. 1863. B/w tinted litho of General Benjamin Butler with horse. "Arranged for the Piano Forte." 6pp. Pages 2 and 6: Blank.

BFB-4 Gen'l Butler's Grand March. m. J.J. Freeman. Published by Richard A. Saalfield, No. 12 Bible House, New York, NY. 1884. B/w litho of Benjamin F. Butler. "To Hon. Ben F. Butler." 6pp. Pages 2 and 6: Blank.

BFB-5 Heifer Dance. w.m. Edward E. Rice. Published by Oliver Ditson & Company, No. 451 Washington Street, Boston, MA. 1876. B/w litho by J.H. Bufford's Sons of Benjamin Butler, men and women, cow dancing. "From the new American Opera Bouffe *Evangeline*." 6pp. Pages 2 and 6: Blank.

BFB-6 Ole Shady (or the Song of

BFB-3

the Contraband). m. "By the Author of *Darling Nelly Gray*." Published by Oliver Ditson & Company, No. 277 Washington Street, Boston, MA. 1861. Non-pictorial. "To Columbia's Noble Son, Maj. Gen. Benj. F. Butler." 6pp. Pages 2 and 6: Blank.

BFB-7 Ole Shady (or the Song of the Contraband). m. "By the Author of *Darling Nelly Gray*." Published by Oliver Ditson & Company, No. 451 Washington Street, Boston, MA. 1861. Non-pictorial geometric design border. "To Columbia's Noble Son, Maj. Gen. Benj. F. Butler." 6pp. Pages 2 and 6: Blank.

BFB-8 Our Governor Still Lives. m. Air: *Cock Robin-'N Is Dead*. Published in Massachusetts, 1883. [5 7/8" × 9 1/4"]. B/w litho of Benjamin F. Butler. "Notice to Relatives — Tom Marsh, French Joe, et. al. Died on the 6th of November, in the year of our Lord, 1883, Funeral on the 7th, as the corpse could not be kept, Burial ground near Park Street Church, all the friends are requested to attend." 4pp. Page 4: Song — **Tewesbury Tan-Yard** (Independent

BENJAMIN F. BUTLER (BFB)

BFB-5

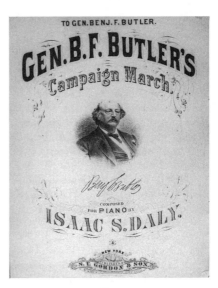

BFB-10

Campaign Song). m. Air: *Susannah*. "[Pamphlet designed as a handout for "The Funeral" of the G.O.P. containing several pro-Butler songs].

BFB-9 The Contraband Schottische. m. Sep. Winner. Published by Lee & Walker, No. 722 Chestnut Street, Philadelphia, PA. 1861. [Probably later edition ca. 1864-1865]. "B/w tinted litho of slave master chasing Black men. "Composed and Respectfully Dedicated to Maj. B.F. Butler." "New edition." 6pp.

BFB-10 Gen. B.F. Butler's Campaign March. m. Isaac S. Daly. Published by S.T. Gordon and Son, No. 13 East 14th Street, near 5th Avenue, New York, NY. 1887. B/w litho of Benjamin Butler, facsimile signature. "Composed for the Piano." "To Gen. Benj. F. Butler." 6pp. Page 6: Advertising.

BFB-11 Campaign Butler Song. m. "Tune—*Yankee Doodle*." [1884]. [4 5/16" × 8 15/16"]. Non-pictorial. 2pp.

BFB-12 God Bless The Soldier. w.m. Charlotte W. Hawes. In: *Butler Souvenir*, page 3. Published as a promotional flyer for *The Butler Book* by A.M. Thayer and Company, Publishers, Boston, MA. 1890. [8 1/2" × 11 1/4"]. Br/w litho of Benjamin F. Butler—"Compliments of Benj. Butler [facsimile handwriting]." Promotional Advertising for "Butler's Book"—"Presented to the members of the G.A.R., W.R.C., and S. of V..." 4pp. Page 2: Be/br litho of "Grand Parade Review of the Union Armies, Washington, D.C. at the close of the War." Page 3: Song. "Dedicated to the Grand Army of the Republic at the 25th National Encampment at Detroit, Mch., 1891 by A.M. Thayer and Company, Boston, Mass., Publishers of *The Butler Book*, the Autobiographical History and Personal Reminiscences of Major Gen. Benj. F. Butler." Page 4: Advertising for "Butler's Book."

BFB-13 Brave Ben Butler. w.m. Waldron Shear. Copyright 1884 by Waldron Shear. B/w litho of a rooster. 2pp. Page 2: Song: **Rare Ben Butler**. w.m. Waldron Shear. Copyright 1884 by Waldron Shear. B/w litho of an eagle with ribbon inscribed "Protection to Labor."

BFB-14 General Butler (Song). m. *Yankee Doodle*. Published as a penny song sheet (Probably in the South). [ca.

1862]. [4 3/8" × 9 5/8"]. B/w litho of ships, cargo — "Edes Print," geometric design border. 2pp. Page 2: Blank. [Anti-Butler].

BFB-15 Benny Butler, Oh! Published by Louis P. Goullurd, No. 108 Tremont Street, Boston, MA. 1878. B/w non-pictorial geometric design border. "A Campaign Song, Dedicated to the Independent Voters of Massachusetts." 4pp. Page 4: Advertising.

BFB-16 Butler Campaign Song. w. E.J. Maloney. [1884]. [5" × 8 1/16"]. Non-pictorial. 2pp. Page 2: Blank.

BFB-17 Ben Butler. m. "Air: *Up In A Balloon*." [ca. 1884]. [12 3/8" × 5 5/8"]. Non-pictorial. 2pp. Page 2: Blank.

BFB-18 Greenback Song-Book. Published by M.S. Cadwell, Grand Ledge, MI. [ca. 1880]. [3 15/16" × 7 15/16"]. Gn/w litho of a "Greenback" bank note. 20pp. Pages 2 and 19: Blank. Pages 3 and 4: "Preface." Page 20: Gn/w litho of a "Greenback" bank note. "The people demand of the United States the repeal of the Resumption Law, the withdrawal of National Bank Notes, a Greenback Currency that shall be legal tender for all debts, Equal Taxation and Rigid Economy in Government affairs, and no fostered monopoly of any kind."

BFB-19 Silverspoons Schottisch. m. Theodore von La Hache. Published by A.E. Blackmar, New Orleans, LA. 1868. B/w litho by H. Wehrmann of Ben Butler pouring booze, pockets filled with "silver" spoons. 6pp. Pages 2 and 6: Blank.

BFB-20 Butler Quick Step. m. E. Mack. Published by J. Marsh, No. 1102 Chestnut Street, Philadelphia. [18—].

BFB-21 Butler, The Beast. m. "Air — *Rory O'More*." In: *Beadle's Dime Knapsack Songster: Containing the Choicest Patriotic Songs, Together with many New and Original Ones, Set to Old Melodies*, page 14. Published by Beadle and Company, No. 141 William Street, New York, NY. 1862. [3 3/4" × 5 3/4"]. Litho of coin — "One Dime, United States of America." 74pp.[?].

BFB-22 Viva L'America. Published by Charles Magnus, No. 12 Frankfort Street, New York, NY. [ca. 1862]. H/c litho of "Major General Butler," map of Louisiana delta. "500 Illustrated Ballads, Lithographed and printed by Charles Magnus, No. 12 Frankfort Street, New York. 2pp. Page 2: Blank.
See also AL-11; JD-37.

BENJAMIN F. HARRISON

BFH-1 Republican Campaign Songs For 1888 [Songster]. w.m. M.H. Rosenfeld. Published by R.M. Collins, Publisher, No. 21 Park Row, New York, NY. Copyright 1888 by M.H. Rosenfeld. [9 1/2" × 11 3/4"]. Bl/bk lithos of "Ben Harrison For President" and "Levi P. Morton For Vice President," axe, leaves, eagle, flags. "Adopted by the Republican National Committee." "In Union is Strength." "Down with the Rag, Up with the Flag! Hurrah for Ben and Levi! The starry Flag is Good Enough for Me, All Cry and No Wool." List of other titles in series. 14pp. Pages 2, 12 to 15: Blank. Page 3: Same as page one. [M-281].

BFH-2 Mother Goose's Campaign Melodies [Songster]. Published by Campaign Publishing Company, Nos. 707 to 709 Filbert Street, Philadelphia, PA. Copyright 1888 by F.B. Greene. [5 1/8" × 6"]. R/w/b crossed flags, drawings of Benjamin Harrison and Levi Morton. 28pp. Page 2: Blank. [Songs and cartoons throughout]. Page 28: Same as page one. [M-263 variation].

BFH-3 To The White House (March). m. George Edw. Jackson. Published by Hitchcock Publishing House, No. 385 Sixth Avenue, New York, NY. Copyright 1888 by W.A. Evans and Brothers. B/w litho of Benjamin F. Harrison, geometric design border. "To my Friend H.R. Johnson." 6pp. Pages 2: Blank. Page 6: Advertising for other songs.

BFH-4 Harrison's Victory March. m. Clifford Hale. Published by P.R. McCargo & Company, Boston, MA. 1888. B/w lithos by George Walker of Benjamin and Levi Morton. "Respectfully dedicated to the Hon. Ben. Harrison, Tippecanoe and Morton Too." 6pp. Page 2: Title—**Gen'l Harrison's Grand March.** Page 6: Blank.

BFH-5 Harrison's Campaign March. m. Clifford Hale. Copyright 1888 by P.R. McCargo, Boston, MA. B/w lithos by George H. Walker & Company of Benjamin Harrison and Levi P. Morton. "Respectfully Dedicated to the Honorable Ben. Harrison—'Tippecanoe and Morton Too!'" "For Piano or Cabinet Organ." 6pp. Page 2: Title—**Gen'l Harrison's Grand March.** Page 6: Blank.

BFH-6 Ben Harrison, Hurrah! (Song and Chorus for Male Voices). w.m. Edward L. Morris. Published by National Music Company, Nos. 215 to 221 Wabash Avenue, Chicago, IL. 1892. B/w litho of Benjamin Harrison, geometric design border. 4pp. Page 4: Advertising.

BFH-7 Harrison's Grand March To The White House. m. C.D. Blake. Published by White, Smith & Company, No. 516 Washington Street, Boston, MA. 1888. R/w/b flags marked "Harrison" and "Morton." B/w litho of Benjamin F. Harrison. "Dedicated to Gen. Benjamin Harrison, Republican Nominee for President of the United States." 6pp. Page 2: Title—**Harrison's Grand March** by Chas. D. Blake (Author of *Clayton's Grand March, Smith's March, &c.*). Page 6: Advertising.

BFH-8 Harrison & Morton Songster (The Tippecanoe Campaign Songster). Copyright 1888 by W.F. Shaw. [5 1/2" × 7 3/4"]. R/w/b litho of flag. Be/bk lithos of Benjamin Harrison and Levi Morton. 68pp. Pages 2 and 67: Advertising. Page 4: Lithos of candidates. Pages 64 to 66: Republican platform and biographies. Page 68: Same as page 1.

BFH-9 Harrison's Campaign March. m. F. Ibach. Published by M.D. Swisher, No. 155 10th Street, Philadelphia, PA. 1888. B/w litho of Benjamin Harrison, oak leaves. 6pp. Pages 2 and 6: Blank.

BFH-10 Benjamin Harrison's Grand March. m. Charles Partello. Copyright 1892 by B.F. Banes & Company. B/w litho of Benjamin Harrison. 6pp. Page 2: Advertising. Page 6: Blank.

BFH-11 Benjamin Harrison's Grand March. m. M. Irving. Published by W.H. Boner & Company, No. 1314 Chestnut Street, Philadelphia, PA. Copyright 1888 by B.F. Banes & Company. B/w litho of Benjamin F. Harrison. 6pp. Pages 2 and 6: Blank.

BFH-12(A) Hail! Benjamin And Whitelaw (Campaign Song and Male Chorus). w.m. E.W. Foster. Published by Oliver Ditson Company, Nos. 453 to 463 Washington Street, Boston, MA. [V-1: 1892] [V-2: 1892]. B/w litho of Benjamin Harrison. 6pp. Page 2: Blank. Page 3: "Dedicated to the Republican Campaign of 1892—Gen. Benjamin Harrison For President, Indiana; Hon. Whitelaw Reid For Vice President, New York." "Solo and Chorus for Male Voices." Page 6: Advertising.

(B) **Harrison's Grand March.** m. M.F. Mullin. Published by Oliver Ditson & Company, No. 451 Washington Street, Boston, MA. 6pp. Page 2: Title—**General Harrison's Grand March.** Page 6: Blank.

(C) **Up With The Stars & Stripes** (Republican Rallying Song for Male Voices) (Octavo). w.m. H.P. Danks.

(D) **We'll Win The Race Again** (Rallying Song and Chorus). w. "Douglass." m. H.L. 6pp. Pages 2 and 6: Blank.

BFH-13 Harrison's March. m. Winnifred Thomas (Winchester, Ind). Published by E. Wulschner, Indianapolis, IN. 1888. B/w litho of Benjamin F. Harrison, geometric design border. "Dedicated to my Dear Father." 6pp. Pages 2 and 6: Blank.

BFH-14 Head-Quarters Republican Glee Book [Songster]. Published by Acme Publishing Bureau, No. 115 South Clinton Street, Syracuse, NY. Copyright 1892 by J.C.O. Redington. [5 1/8" × 6 5/8"]. O/bk litho of Benjamin Harrison and Whitelaw Reid, Uncle Sam, soldier, eagle, flags. "A Well Filled Pocket, Haversack of Loyalty, Glory, Song, Facts and Fun for Every Individual to Read and Study, Whether Singer or Not." Advertising. 68pp. Page 2 and 68: Advertising. Page 3: Title: **The Acme Songs Republican Hand Book For Victory In 1892.** [M-303].

BFH-15 Benjamin & Levi Grand March. m. A. Mirault. Published by Willis Woodward & Company, Nos. 842 and 844 Broadway, New York, NY. Copyright 1888 by A. Mirault. B/w litho of Benjamin Harrison and Levi Morton. "Respectfully Dedicated to Solon W. Stevens, Esq., President of the Lowell Choral Society." "Be sure and get Lauretta Waltz." 8pp.

BFH-16 Harrison's Tariff Campaign March. m. Adam Geibel. Copyright 1888 by The W.F. Shaw Company. B/w litho by W.H. Butler of Benjamin F. Harrison. "Respectfully Dedicated to the Republican candidate." 6pp. Page 2: Blank. Page 6: Advertising.

BFH-17 Washington's Centennial Inaugural March. m. Walter A. Dolane. Published by Spaulding and Kornder, No. 487 Fulton Street, Brooklyn, NY. 1889. B/w litho by George H. Walker & Company of "George Washington, 1789" and "Benjamin Harrison, 1889;" Capitol at Washington, eagle, flags. "Dedicated by Permission to President Benjamin Harrison." 6pp. Page 2: Blank. Page 6: Advertising.

BFH-18 The Harrison Grand March. m. Johann Buchholtz. Published by The Campaign Music Publishing Company, Pittsburgh, PA. 1888. B/w litho of Benjamin F. Harrison, geometric design border. "Protection." "Tippecanoe." "Dedicated to the Republican Candidate for President of the United States by the Composer." "As Played by Gilmore's Celebrated Band." 8pp. Pages 2 and 8: Blank.

BFH-19 Minneapolis Grand March. m. James J. Freeman. Published by Hitchcock Publishing House, No. 385 Sixth Avenue, New York, NY. 1892. B/w lithos of "Benjamin Harrison" and "Whitelaw Reid." "Companion to *Harrison and Reid Campaign Song.*" 8pp. Page 2: Blank. Page 8: Advertising.

BFH-20 Republican Club Campaign Song Book For 1888. a. Thomas Byron. Published by Protection Publication Company, South Central Street, Chicago, IL. 1888. [6 1/8" × 8 7/8"]. Be/bk litho of Benjamin F. Harrison—"For President" and Levi P. Morton—"For Vice-President," eagle, flags, geometric designs. "Thirty Rousing Songs Written to Popular Airs." 36pp. [M-257].

BFH-21 Brave Ben Of Indiana (Campaign Song). w. George E. Hicks. m. Louis Weiler. Published by The

BFH-19

Coupon Music Publishing Company, Lafayette Square, Cambridge, MA. Copyright 1892 by Charles F. Pidgen, Cambridge, MA. Bk/w/y attached photo of Benjamin F. Harrison. Be/bk cover. "Pidgen's Vignette Music, Number 105." 4pp. Page 4: Blank.

BFH-22 Up With The Banner (Campaign Song). w.m. James C. Beckel. Published by M.D. Swisher, No. 149 Wabash Avenue, Chicago, IL. Copyright 1888 by James Bickel. B/w litho of Benjamin Harrison, oak leaves. 6pp.

BFH-23 The Harrison Log-Cabin Song Book Of 1840. e. O.C. Hooper. Published by A.H. Smythe, Columbus, OH. 1888. [4 15/16" × 5 3/4"]. Y/bk litho of log cabin labeled "1840—1888." "Revised for the Campaign of 1888, with Numerous New Songs to Patriotic Airs." 68pp. Pages 2 and 67: Blank. [M-272, 273].

BFH-24 Harrison And Morton's Grand March. m. James J. Freeman. Published by Richard A. Saalfield, No. 41 Union Square, New York, NY. 1888. B/w lithos of Benjamin Harrison and Levi Morton, geometric designs. 6pp. Page 2: Blank. Page 6: Advertising.

BFH-25 Acme Songs, Republican Glee Book, And Cartridge Box Of Truth (Campaign of 1888). Published by The Acme Publishing Bureau, J.C.O. Redington, General Manager, No. 35 University Avenue, Syracuse, NY. Copyright 1888 by J.C.O. Redington. [5 1/6" × 6 13/16"]. Gy/bk lithos of eagle, shield, tent, flag, soldiers, Uncle Sam. "With Music and 20 Illustrations by Nast and others." "Price 10 cents." "Only Book Prepared by Soldiers, The Only Illustrated Campaign Glee Book Ever Printed." "With Music and 20 Illustrations." "Illustrated by Nast and Others." "A Filled Pocket Haversack of Loyalty, Glory, Song, Fun and Facts for Every Individual, Whether Singer or Not." 68pp. [M-255].

BFH-26 Campaign Gavotte. m. Otto J. Goeldner. Published by Chicago Music Company, Chicago, IL. 1892. B/w drawing of Capitol dome, flag, chain border. B/w photo of Benjamin Harrison. "For the Piano." "Respectfully dedicated to Benjamin F. Harrison." Small purple star over the "F" in "Benjamin F. Harrison." 6pp. Pages 2 and 6: Blank.

BFH-21

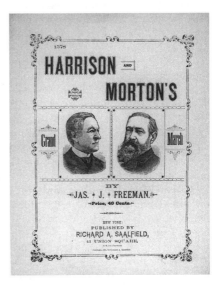

BFH-24

BFH-27 Acme Songs, Republican Glee Book, And Cartridge Box Of Truth, No. 2 (Campaign of 1888). Published by the Acme Publishing Bureau, Syracuse, NY. 1888. Lithos of Uncle Sam, eagle, tent, flag, soldier. "With music and illustrations." "Oct. 10th, illustrated." "Price 5 cents."

BFH-28 Harrison & Morton Flag March. w.m. John Hazel. Published by J. Schott, No. 52 East 4th Street, New York, NY. 1888. B/w litho of flags, eagle, wreath. 6pp. Pages 2 and 6: Blank.

BFH-29 Harrison's Victory March. m. George Schleiffarth. Published by S. Brainard's Sons, Publishers, Cleveland, OH. 1888. R/w/b flag border, stars. 8pp. Pages 2,7 and 8: Advertising for other S. Brainard's Sons music.

BFH-30 When Grover Goes Marching Home (Republican Campaign Songs 1888). a. R. Campaign. Published by S. Brainard's Sons, Cleveland, OH. 1888. Drawing of eagle, flags, stars.

BFH-31 Caroline Gavotte. m. Eduard Holst, Op. 115. Published by N. Weinstein, No. 24 West 23rd Street, New York, NY. 1888. Copper/w litho of flowers. "Dedicated with Permission to Mrs. President Caroline Scott Harrison." 8pp. Page 2: Blank. Page 8: Advertising for other N. Weinstein published songs.

BFH-32 True Blue Republican Campaign Songs For 1888. Published by S. Brainard's Sons, Nos. 145 and 147 Wabash Avenue, Chicago, IL. 1888. [5 3/8" × 7 1/2"]. Bl/bk non-pictorial geometric designs. 36pp. Page 2: Advertising for Democratic Campaign Song Book. Pages 25 and 36: Advertising for other S. Brainard's Sons music. [M-269, 270].

BFH-33 Tippecanoe And Morton, Too (Song). w.m. M.H. Rosenfeld. Published by Hitchcock's Music Stores, No. 11 Park Row, New York, NY. 1888. Bl/w drawing of crossed flags. "To the Republican Party 1888." 6pp. Page 2: Blank. Page 6: Advertising for other Hitchcock published music.

BFH-34 Songs For The Presidential Campaign Of 1888. m. Popular Airs. [8" × 10 5/8"]. B/w non-pictorial. "Wholesale Dry Goods Harrison and Morton Club." "Respectfully Inscribed to the Hon. Benj. Harrison of Indiana For President; Hon. Levi P. Morton, of New York, For Vice-President." 2[?]pp. [M-284?].

BFH-35 Harrison And Reid Campaign Song Book. w. E.J. Seymour. m. Popular Airs. [1892]. [3 7/8" × 5 1/8"]. Bl/gn non-pictorial, stars, geometric designs. 36pp. Pages 2 and 35: Blank. Page 36: Advertising for this song book. [M-316].

BFH-36 Songs For The Presidential Campaign Of 1888. m. Popular Airs. [8 1/4" × 11 3/8"]. 1888. B/w non-pictorial broadside. "Respectfully Inscribed to the Hon. Benj. Harrison, of Indiana, For President; Hon. Levi P. Morton, of New York, For Vice President." "One good Campaign song is equal to a hundred speeches — Senator John Sherman." "Give me the making of the ballads of a nation and I care not who makes the law — A. Fletcher." 4pp. [M-285].

BFH-37 Regina Gavotte (Dance Francaise). m. Henry Lamb. Published by Newhall and Evans Music Company, No. 171 West 4th Street, Cincinnati, OH. 1889. B/w litho of Mrs. Caroline Scott Harrison, facsimile signature, dogwood blossoms. "Pour le Piano." "Dedicated by Permission to Mrs. President Benj. Harrison." 6pp. Page 2: Advertising for other Newhall and Evans music. Page 6: Blank.

BFH-38 Our Emblem! w.m. H.E. Gordon. Copyright 1888 by H.E. Gordon. [6 1/4" × 9"]. B/w non-pictorial geometric designs. "Dedicated to the Republican Invincibles of Norristown, Pa." Page 2: Blank.

BFH-39 The Presidential Polonaise. m. John Philip Sousa (Director of U.S. Marine Band). Published by Harry Coleman, No. 228 North 9th Street,

Philadelphia, PA. 1885. B/w litho of flowers, bow, geometric designs. "As performed by The Band of the United States Marine Corps and Beck's Grand Orchestra of Philadelphia combined at the Inauguration Ball on March 4th, 1889." 6pp. Page 6: Advertising for other Harry Coleman music.

BFH-40   Hush My Baby Go To Sleep (Lullaby). w.m. Blanche Clifton Akin. Published by Sherman, Clay & Company, corner Kearny and Sutter Streets, San Francisco, CA. 1890. B/w litho by Schmidt Label & Litho Company photo of "Baby McKee" Harrison — "Copyright 1889 by C. Parker, Photographer, Wash., D.C.," dogwood blossoms. "Dedicated by Permission of Mrs. President Harrison to Master Benj. Harrison McKee." 6pp. Pages 2 and 6: Blank.

BFH-41   Republican Campaign Songs. 1888. [3 3/8" × 7 9/16"]. B/w litho of eagle. 6pp. [Foldout].

BFH-42   Harrison And Morton Grand March. m. S.J.P. Americus. Published by S. Brainard's Sons, Cleveland, OH. 1888. R/w/b litho of U.S. flag, liberty cap. 6pp. Pages 2 and 6: Blank.

BFH-43   West O' The Wide Missouri. w.m. Richard M. Sherman and Robert B. Sherman. Published by Wonderland Music Company, Inc., No. 800 Sonora Avenue, Glendale, CA. 1967. N/c photo of the cast from motion picture, with poster of Benjamin Harrison in background. "From the Walt Disney Motion Picture *The One and Only, Genuine, Original Family Band.*" 4pp.

BFH-44   Campaign Songs (Harrison And Morton Too!) [Song Sheet]. In: *The New York Tribune*, Extra, No. 107, September, 1888. "Music for the Republican Canvass Against Free Trade." 2pp.

BFH-45   Oh, Benjamin Harrison. w.m. Richard M. Sherman and Robert B. Sherman. Published by Wonderland Music Company, Inc., No. 800 Sonora Avenue, Glendale, CA. 1967.

Copyright 1968 Walt Disney Productions. B/w drawings of the cast from motion picture. "Walt Disney Presents *The One and Only, Genuine, Original Family Band.*" 4pp.

BFH-46   War Veteran's Parade March. m. Edgar H. Sherwood. Published by The Central Music Company, No. 168 Andrews Street, Rochester, NY. Copyright 1889 by Edgar H. Sherwood. B/w litho of "Benjamin Harrison" and "Levi P. Morton," soldiers, ships, tents, G.A.R. badge, flags, eagle with ribbon — "The Grand Army of the Republic Army and Navy of the U.S.A." 8pp. Pages 2, 7 and 8: Blank.

BFH-47   True Blue Republican Campaign Songs For 1892. Published by [V-1: Oliver Ditson Company, Boston, MA] [V-2: The S. Brainard's Son's Company, Chicago, IL]. 1892. [5 3/8" × 7 1/4"]. Bl/bk litho of Benjamin F. Harrison, eagle, flag, geometric designs. 36pp. Page 2: [V-1: Advertising for *Red Hot Democratic Campaign Songster for 1892*] [V-2: Advertising for *World's Fair Songster*]. Page 3: "Quartets for Male Voices," Table of Contents. [M-307].

BFH-48   Up With The Banner. w.m. James C. Beckel. Copyright 1888 by James C. Beckel. R/w/b litho of U.S. flag. Verse — "Up with the Banner, 'Tis no Red Bandana, That Harrison's upholding for you; No Grover can cleave it, You'd better believe it; Three cheers for our banner the Red, White and Blue." "1888 Campaign Song." "Campaign Song 1 — *Not For Grover.* Price 40 cts." 6pp. Pages 2 and 6: Blank.

BFH-49   Harrison And Reid Campaign Songster. Published by The John Church Company, No. 74 West 4th Street, Cincinnati, OH. 1892. [4 1/8" × 5 3/4"]. Be/bk non-pictorial geometric design border. "Including Biographical Sketches & Constitution for Campaign Clubs." 52pp. [M-305].

BFH-50   Republican League Harrison And Morton Song Book,

(BFH) BENJAMIN F. HARRISON

1888. w. P.H. Bristow (Des Moines). m. J. Woollett (Chicago). Printed by Register Press Printing House, Des Moines, IA. Copyright 1888 by P.H. Bristow. [6" × 9 1/4"]. Bl/bk non-pictorial geometric designs, League logo. "The ball it goes rolling from the Gulf to The Lakes, From Maine in the East out to Oregon's peaks, Get out of its way for 'tis rolling along, You tell of its coming, by music & Song." 44pp. Page 44: Bl/bk litho of a log cabin. [M-256].

BFH-51 Harrison And Reid Songster. Copyright 1892 by W.F. Shaw, Philadelphia, PA. [5 13/16" × 8"]. R/w/b litho of Benjamin Harrison and Whitelaw Reid, shield, eagle. 68pp. Page 3: Title: **Harrison And Reid Campaign Songster.** Page 68: Same litho as front cover. [M-306].

BFH-52 Gen. Harrison's Campaign March. m. Charles F. Escher, Jr. Published by [V-1: Charles Escher, Jr., No. 1242 Girard Avenue, Philadelphia, PA] [V-2: No publishing data]. Copyright 1892 by L.C. Gotthold. Litho of flowers. "For Piano or Organ." 6pp.

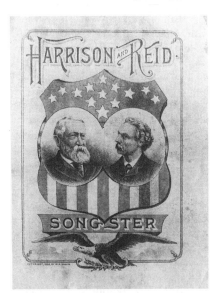

BFH-51

BFH-53 Young Republican Campaign Song Book. c. Henry Camp. Published by the Brooklyn Young Republican Club, Brooklyn, NY. 1888. [4 3/8" × 6 1/2"]. R/w/b litho of a U.S. flag. "Campaign 1888." 100pp. Page 100: Lithos of Benjamin Harrison and Levi Morton. [M-258, 259].

BFH-54 Harrison And Morton Song Book. c.a. W.T. Tredway (Pittsburgh, PA). Published by F.A. North & Company, Publishers, No. 1308 Chestnut Street, Philadelphia, PA. Copyright 1888 by W.T. Tredway. [5 1/4" × 6 3/4"]. R/w/b litho of Benjamin Harrison and Levi Morton, shield, ribbon. 28pp. Page 28: Same as Page one. [M-288?].

BFH-55 President Harrison's Grand Inauguration March. m. Frank Drayton. Published by James C. Beckel, No. 914 Sansom Street, Philadelphia, PA. 1888. B/w litho by Wm. H. Keyser & Company of Benjamin F. Harrison. "March 4th, 1889." 6pp. Pages 2 and 6: Blank.

BFH-56 The National Republican Campaign Song Book. c. Prof. J.M. Hager. Published by J.M. Hager, Brooklyn, NY. 1888. Gy/bk litho of Benjamin F. Harrison and Levi Morton, flags, Capitol dome. "With the Approval of the National Republican Committee." 36pp. [M-264].

BFH-57 Harrison's 1892 Campaign March. m. E. Rose Prime. Published by K. Dehnhoff, No. 44 West Twenty-Ninth Street, New York, NY. 1892. B/w litho of Benjamin F. Harrison with music trimmed around head [as made]. 4pp. Page 4: Advertising.

BFH-58 The Republican League Campaign Song Book. c. Professor J.M. Hager. Published by the Republican League of the United States, No. 202 Fifth Avenue, New York, NY. 1888. [4" × 5 7/8"]. Bk/gy litho of Benjamin F. Harrison and Levi P. Morton, flags, Capitol building. 36pp. Page 36: Advertising for Steinway pianos. [M-265].

BENJAMIN F. HARRISON (BFH)

BFH-57

BFH-59 Harrison's March To The White House. m. Fred Anderson. a. C.L. Beck. Published by National Music Company, No. 266 Wabash Avenue, Chicago, IL. 1892. B/w litho of Benjamin F. Harrison, eagle with ribbon inscribed "National Superior Edition." 4pp. Page 4: Advertising for other music.

BFH-60 Harrison's March To The White House. m. Fred Anderson. a. C.L. Beck. Published by National Music Company, No. 44 East 14th Street, New York, NY. 1892. B/w litho of Benjamin F. Harrison. 4pp. Page 4: Adv.

BFH-61 Harrison's March To The White House. m. Fred Anderson. a. C.L. Beck. Published by [V-1: P.R. McCargo & Company, Boston, MA] [V-2: Hitchcock and McCargo Publishing Company, No. 385 Sixth Avenue, Above 23d Street, New York, NY]. Copyright 1888 by National Music Company of Chicago. B/w litho of Benjamin F. Harrison, geometric design border. 6pp. Page 6: Blank.

BFH-62 Harrison's March To The White House. m. Fred Anderson. a. C.L. Beck. Published by National Music Company, Chicago, IL. 1888. B/w litho of Benjamin F. Harrison, geometric design border. Song title printed parallel to side border. 6pp. Page 6: Blank.

BFH-63 Harrison's March To The White House. m. Fred Anderson. a. C.L. Beck. Published by National Music Company, Chicago, IL. 1888. B/w litho of Benjamin F. Harrison, geometric design border. Song title at angle to side border. 6pp. Page 6: Advertising.

BFH-64 Republican Campaign Songs. w. A.A. Rowley (Beloit, Kas). Published by The Western News Company, Chicago, IL. 1888. [5 1/4" × 7 1/2"]. B/w litho of "The Author, in '63, 17th Illinois Cav." "Original, Pointed and Spicy...Set to Old Familiar Tunes, Suitable for Glee Clubs and Marching Clubs." "Look at it and you will buy it." 36pp. Page 2, 35 and 36: Blank. Page 3: Index. "Composed for the Campaign of 1888 and Set to Old Familiar Airs, Suitable for Glee Clubs and Campaign Clubs." "Respectfully Dedicated to my Comrades of the Civil War, who still vote the way they fought — A.A. Rowley, Beloit, Kan." [M-283].

BFH-65 The Democratic Boat (Republican Campaign Songs 1888) (Male Quartette). a. R. Campaign. Published by S. Brainard's Sons, Cleveland, OH. 1888. R/w/b flag and star border. Bl/w litho of eagle, flags, shield, wreath. 6pp. Pages 2 and 6: Advertising.

BFH-66 Harrison And Reid (Campaign Song). w.m. M. Cooper. Published by Hitchcock's Music Stores, No. 385 Sixth Avenue, New York, NY. 1892. B/w lithos of "Benjamin Harrison" and "Whitelaw Reid." "Companion to the *Minneapolis Grand March.*" 6pp. Page 2: Blank. Page 6: Advertising.

BFH-67 President Harrison's Grand Inauguration March. m. F. Ganter. Published by George Willig & Company, Publishers, Baltimore, MD. 1889. Non-pictorial geometric designs. "As played by All the Leading Bands

(BFH) BENJAMIN F. HARRISON

Arranged for the Piano." 8pp. Page 8: Advertising.

BFH-68 Hip, Hip, Hurrah, Harrison! (Campaign Song). w.m. A.L. Barnes. In: *The New York Tribune*, Extra No. 117, September, 1888, page 2. "Written for the Utica Continental Glee Club."

BFH-69 Our Candidate (March). m. Edward E. Rice. Published by T.B. Harms & Company, No. 18 East 22nd Street, New York, NY. 1896. Bl/w photo of Levi Morton, facsimile signature. R/w geometric designs. "Dedicated to my Friend Mr. Charles A. Hess." 6pp. Page 2: Blank. Page 6: Advertising.

BFH-70 Tippecanoe And Victory Too (Republican Campaign Song). w.m. A. Whilom. Published by The John Church Company, No. 74 West Fourth Street, Cincinnati, OH. 1892. B/w litho of Benjamin F. Harrison. 4pp. Page 4: Blank.

BFH-71 Harrison's Triumphant March. m. Frederic E. White, Op. 19. Published by White-Smith Music Publishing Company, Boston, MA. 1892. B/w litho of Benjamin F. Harrison. "Dedicated to Gen. Benjamin Harrison, Republican Nominee for President of the United States." 8pp. Page 8: Advertising.

BFH-72 Harrison's Victory March. m. Clifford Hale. Copyright 1888 by P.R. McCargo, Boston, MA. Fancy litho arch frame with two lions at top and musical instruments at bottom, geometric designs. "To the Hon. Ben. Harrison — Tippecanoe and Morton too." 6pp. Page 2: Title — **Harrison's Grand Victory March**. Page 6: Advertising.

BFH-73 Republican Campaign March Of 1888. w. Mrs. J. Bona. Published by J.R. Bell, Kansas City, MO. 1888. Non-pictorial geometric designs. "Dedicated to General Benj. Harrison." 6pp. Page 2: Blank. Page 6: Advertising.

BFH-74 National Republican Campaign Songs For 1888. Published by Newhall and Evans, Cincinnati, OH. 1888. [7" × 11"]. B/w litho of eagle, flag. Quotes: "God Reigns and the Nation Lives — Garfield," "A Government of the People, For the People, By the People — Lincoln," "This is a Nation, and Spelled with a great by 'N' — Grant," "Stand up like men, and do not betray your friends, — John Brown," "Its bein' a free man! That's what I'm joyin' for — Uncle Tom," "If any man attempts to pull down the American Flag, shoot him on the spot — Dix."

(A) **Jericho**. w.m. F.L. Bristow.
(B) **The Grand Old Party**. w.m. C. Wegelin.
(C) **Ump-Um Ump!** w.m. F.L. Bristow.
(D) **Don't Worry About That Surplus**. w.m. J.H. Sarchet.
(E) **A Home For Every Flag** (Quartette or Quintette). w.m. F.L. Bristow. 4pp. Page 4: Advertising.
(F) **Shout The Battle Cry!** w.m. W.H. Duane.
(G) **The Spirits Of Our Dead Heroes**. w.m. F.L. Bristow.
(H) **Who Whipped?** w.m. J.H. Sarchet.
(I) **Grover's Lam(o)ent**. w.m. F.L. Bristow.
(J) **Which Nobody Can Deny**. w.m. C.E. Marvin.
(K) **Democratic Clan**. w.m. J.H. Sarchet.
(L) **On, On, On The Boys Are Shouting**. w.m. W.H. Duane.
(M) **Wait Till The Votes Are Counted**. w.m. J.H. Sarchet.
(N) **Forward, March, Republicans**. w.m. George Findet.
(O) **Stand By The Grand Old Party**. w.m. J.J. Sarchet.
(P) **Still We Lead The Nation**. w.m. C.B. Morrell.
(Q) **Star Spangled Banner**.
(R) **America**.
(S) **Hail Columbia**.
(T) **The Democratic Whale**. w.m. J.H. Sarchet.

BFH-75 Reception March. m. Theo. H. Northrup. In: *May-Day Festival Official Programme*, page 4. Published by Grand Army May Day Festival Board, San Francisco, CA. Copyright 1891 by Eclipse Publishing. List of "Board of Management, Chairman of Committees, 1881." B/w lithos of Benjamin F. Harrison, facsimile signature, two G.A.R. Badges. Numerous Advertisements for local businesses. 8pp. Page 2: "Programme, May Day Exercises, Afternoon 2:30 to 5." Advertising. Page 3: Song Title. Advertising. Page 4 and 5: Music. "Inscribed to President Harrison, of U.S.A." Pages 6 to 8: Advertising.

BFH-76 Mother Goose Campaign Melodies. Published by Campaign Publishing Company, Nos. 707 and 709 Filbert Street, Philadelphia, PA. 1888. [5" × 6"]. Bl/w drawings of Harrison and Morton. "True Blue Republican." "Protection to Home Industries." 28pp. Pro-Harrison and anti-Cleveland drawings throughout. [M-263].

BFH-77 Campaign Songs [Song Pamphlet]. [6 3/16" × 2 12/16"]. 1888. Bl/w lithos of Benjamin Harrison and Levi P. Morton. 8pp.

BFH-78 Harrison And Reid Campaign Song Book. w. E.J. Seymour. m. Popular airs. 1892. [3 7/8" × 5 3/8"]. Non-pictorial. 30pp. [M-316].

BFH-79 Republican Club Songs. Published by The Springfield Republican Phalanx, Springfield, MA. 1888. [5 6/8" × 8 3/4"]. Non-pictorial. "Springfield, Mass., November 5th and 6th, 1888." 12pp.

BFH-80 Ben And Levi (Campaign Song and Chorus). w.m. Harry Birch. Published by White, Smith & Company, Boston, MA. 1888. [6 13/16" × 10 9/16"]. R/w/b litho of U.S. flag inscribed "Harrison." "Respectfully Dedicated to Harrison and Morton." 6pp. Pages 2 and 6: Advertising.

BFH-81 Harrison's Second Grand Triumphal March. m. Howard S. Williams. Published by National Music Company, No. 215-221 Wabash Avenue, Chicago, IL. 1892. B/w litho by A. Zeese & Company of Benjamin F. Harrison, geometric designs. 6pp. Page 6: Advertising.

BFH-82 Republican Campaign Song Sheet No. 1. Published by Hitchcock's Steam Printing and Publishing House, No. 385 Sixth Avenue, New York, NY. 1888. [19" × 23 7/8"]. B/w litho of Benjamin F. Harrison and Levi Morton. "Harrison and Morton." Advertising. 2pp. Page 2: Blank.

BFH-83 Harrison And Morton Campaign Songster. Published by The John Church Company, No. 74 West 4th Street, Cincinnati, OH. 1888. [4 1/8" × 5 3/4"]. Non-pictorial geometric design border. "Including Biographical Sketches & Constitution for Campaign Clubs." 52pp. Pages 2, 51 and 52: Advertising. [M-267].

BFH-84 The Burial Of Free Trade (Waltz). m. Thomas M. Thompson. Published by Thomas H. Thompson, Dobbs Ferry, NY. 1889. Non-pictorial. "Dedicated by Thomas M. Thompson to Harrison and Morton." "Published and Sold Exclusively by The Author, Thomas H. Thompson, Dobbs Ferry, New York, Cash or installment dealer in organs and pianos, sheet music and music books, Band and Orchestral instruments and all manner of musical merchandise." 6pp. Page 6: Blank.

BFH-85 Campaign Songs. Published by Wholesale Dry Goods Republican Club, New York, NY. 1892. [5 3/4" × 8 15/16"]. Non-pictorial. "No. 1. *The G.A.R. Song*. Dedicated to President Harrison by the Morris Township Republican Club, by Permission, Grindell Willis, Prest." 8pp. [M-318?].

BFH-86 Under The Banner Of Protection. m. "Tune: *Marching Through Georgia*." Published by The Republican State Committee, Continental Hotel, Philadelphia, PA. [1888]. [5" ×

8"]. B/w litho of U.S. flag. "The Republican State Committee of Pennsylvania sends to the Republican Clubs the above song, which goes exactly to the measure of a patriotic song, and which has already proved very popular. Clubs desiring can be supplied gratis by addressing the Republican State Committee, Continental Hotel, Phila." 2pp. Page 2: Blank.

BFH-87 The Harrison Campaign Songster. w. D.E. Bryer (The Old Campaigner). m. Popular tunes. Published by The Home Music Company, No. 200 Fourth Street, Logansport, IN. 1892. [5 3/4" × 8 1/2"]. Non-pictorial. Table of Contents. 36pp. Page 36: Advertising. [M-301].

BFH-88 True Blue! (Republican Campaign March). m. George Maywood (Author of *World's Exposition March*, *Pauline, &c*). Published by The S. Brainard's Sons Company, Chicago, IL. 1892. R/w/b stripe border. 6pp. Page 2: Blank. Page 6: Advertising for "Campaign Music for 1892."

BFH-89 Still Their Hearts Are Young (Song and Chorus). w. Joshua Smith. m. J.A. Butterfield. Published by Lyon & Healy, No. 161 State Street, Chicago, IL. 1889. B/w litho of eagle, crossed flags, shield, stars, geometric design border. "Dedicated by Permission to Gen. Benj. Harrison, President of the United States." "A Tribute to the Boys in Blue." 6pp. Pages 2 and 6: Blank.

BFH-90 3 Shots More! [Song Sheet]. Published by Lozier Brothers, Mt. Vernon, IA. 1888. [7 3/4" × 10 15/16"]. B/w litho of eagle, shield, flags, stars, flowers, doves. "For Loyalty, Labor and Protection." "From the Cartridge Box of the 'Fighting Chaplain.'" List of contents. "Price 10 cents. By the dozen, one dollar; by the hundred, five dollars. Sent to any address on receipt of price. Address Lozier Brothers, Mt. Vernon, Iowa." 4pp.

BFH-91 Harrison And Morton's March. m. Durkee. Published by Trifet. [ca. 1888]. Non-pictorial geometric design border. "Rondos, Variations, Dances, &c." "Trifet Edition." List of other titles in series.

BFH-92 Hul-Lah For Hal-li-son. w.m. De Yung. 1888. [6 1/8" × 8 1/2"]. Non-pictorial. Chinese writing on the side. "Stick-at-oh, doloroso." 2pp. Page 2: Blank.

BFH-93 The Old Union Wagon. W. Frank M. Jones. Copyright 1888 by Frank M. Jones, Strong City, KS. [5 1/4" × 7"]. Non-pictorial black line border, geometric designs. 2pp. Page 2: Handwriten note: "By mail 5 cts.—$4 per hunded."

BFH-94 Protection Campaign Songs And Recitations. e. Edward Fitzwilliam. Published by Edward Fitzwilliam, Boston, MA. 1888. Pk/bk non-pictorial. [M-261].

BFH-95 Campaign Song Book For The Republican Party, 1888. e. H.E. Gordon. Published by Republican Song Book Committee, Philadelphia, PA. 1888. Litho of Harrison and Morton. "Harrison and Morton." Inside title: **Harrison And Morton Song Book.** 16pp. [M-262].

BFH-96 The Protection Collection Of Campaign Songs For 1888. "Potomac." [e. John Harries]. Published by Gray & Clarkson, Washington, DC. 1888. Gn/bk non-pictorial. 36pp. [M-266].

BFH-97 Tippecanoe Song Book. Published by P.T. Schultz, Steam Book and Job Printer, Cincinnati, OH. Copyright 1888 by P.T. Schultz & Co. Y/bk litho of Benjamin Harrison and Levi Morton. "Harrison And Morton." [M-268].

BFH-98 Western Taps (Republican Campaign Songs). Published by Enterprise Print, Coon Rapids, IA. 1888. 12pp. [M-274].

BFH-99 The Protection Bugle (Songs for the Republican Campaign of 1888). e. William Edward Penney. Published by Shepard and Bonney, New Haven, CT. 1888. 8pp. [M-277].

BFH-100 The Tariff And Campaign Rhymes. w. Olympus. Published as List Number 60, *The Defender*, by The American Protective Tariff League, New York. NY. 1892. "The Yankee Debate. Uncle Sam's Guns Sweep the Whole Field. Free Trade and Sham Democracy Demolished." 26pp. [M-317].

BFH-101 Rough And Ready Campaign Songs. e. Thomas Rourke. 1888. "Dedicated to the Harrison and Morton Glee Club of West New Brighton, S.I. [New York, NY]." 4pp. [M-282].

BFH-102 Republican Campaign Songs. e. A.A. Rowley. Published by W.P. Dunn & Company, Chicago, IL. 1888. Be/bk litho of A.A. Rowley. "Original, Pointed and Spicy. Set to old familiar tunes, suitable for glee clubs and marching clubs. Look at it & you will buy it. Price 10 cents. Supplies at Western News Co., Chicago." [M-283]."

BFH-103 Harrison And Morton Songster. Published by W.F. Shaw, Philadelphia, PA. 1888. Be/bk litho of Benjamin Harrison and Levi Morton. 68pp. Page 3: Inside title—**The Tippecanoe Songster**. "Harrison and Morton, Sketch of Their Lives, and Full Text of the Republican Platform." "Tippecanoe and Morton Too, This is the team to pull us through, 1888." [M-287].

BFH-104 Republican Songs For The Campaign Of 1888. Published by Case, Lockwood & Brainard & Company, Hartford, CT. 1888. B/w litho of arm and hammer. "Wide-Awakes 1860, Re-Union at the Armory, Hartford, November 1, 1888." "For President, Gen. Benjamin Harrison of Indiana; For Vice President, Hon Morgan G. Bulkerley of Hartford. One good campaign song is equal to a hundred speeches—Senator John Sherman." 4pp. Page 4: "The Audience is requested to join in singing the above songs. Each number will be announced before the singing." [M-289].

BFH-105 National Republican Campaign Songs (As Sung by Knight's Famous Campaign Quartette). w.a. Charles H. Chamberlain. Published by The S.B. Bradt Company. Chicago, IL. 1892. Be/bk non-pictorial. "Trade supplied by the Western News Company." 36pp. [M-302].

BFH-106 Business Men's Noon Day Meetings At Museum Hall [Program & Song Sheet]. Published by The Cuyahoga County Republican Party Central Committee, Cleveland, OH. 1892. "For President, Benjamin Harrison; For Vice-President, Whitelaw Reid." "These are Americans for America. Yes, the Democratic party is the party of the poor man, and if he continues to vote that ticket he will never be anything else than a poor man—T.V. Powderly in Knights of Labor Journal, Sept. 22nd, '92." 50pp. "Business Men's Noon Day Meetings At Museum Hall, No. 189 Superior Street. Program—See Last Page. Be sure and register on the first day, Oct. 13th. It will save the Committee a great expense in postage and labor looking up those that fail. Registration days, October 13th, 20th, 28th, 29th. Leader of singing, Prof. A.J. Haywood. Chairman Republican Central Com., Louis Smithnight. Secretary, F.M. Chandler. For Congress, 21st District, Hon. O.J. Hodge, For Congress, 20th District, W.J. White." [M304].

BFH-107 The Republican Campaign Song Book, With Music, 1892. e. Samuel Newall Holmes. Published by Samuel Newall Holmes, Syracuse, NY. 1892. Be/bk non-pictorial. "Composed and especially prepared by Judge S.N. Holmes of Syracuse, N.Y." "Headquarters: Syracuse, N.Y." "Price twenty-five cents." [M-308].

BFH-108 Chaplain Lozier's "Old Glory" Campaign Songs. e. J.H. Lozier, Lozier Brothers, Chicago, IL. 1892. Litho of cats. "Rough on Democrats." "For Use of Republican Campaign Committees and Glee Clubs." 12pp. [M-309].

BFH-109 National Republican Rally Rhymes. Published by Alvah Shelden, *Walnut Valley Times* Print, El Dorado, KS. 1892. Gn/bk non-pictorial. "A Work Designed for the Use of Clubs & Committees in Securing Attendance at Public Meetings, and Teaching Republican Principles and Policy." 52pp. [M-310, 311].

BFH-110 Official Republican Campaign Song Book. Published by Geary Brothers, New Haven, CT. 1892. Also published by "W.A. Pond, New York, NY." 24pp. [M-312].

BFH-111 Not For Grover. w.m. James C. Beckel. Copyright 1888 by James C. Beckel. "Campaign Song 1. Price 40 cts. "

BFH-113 The Republican League Campaign Song Book. 1888. e. Samuel Newall Holmes. Published in New York. 1888. "Composed and especially prepared by Judge S.N. Holmes." "Adopted by the Republican League of the United States." [M-271].

BFH-114 Republican Campaign Songs for 1888. Published by W.A. Vandrecook, Los Angeles, CA. 1888. 24pp. [M-279].

BFH-115 Republican [sic] Campaign Songs. The Echo Music Company, LaFayette, IN. 1888. Br/bk non-pictorial. "The new red, white and blue; Harrison Morton Combine; The flags that we captured are ours; Vote her straight; Hurrah for Harrison and sure to win." 10pp. [M-280].

BFH-116 Songs For The Presidential Campaign of '88. 4pp. "Dedicated to Hon. Benj. Harrison, of Indiana, Hon. Levi P. Morton, of New York & Hon. Robert M. Yardley, by the Young Republican Glee Club of Bristol, PA." [M-286].

BFH-117 The Harrison And Reid Campaign Songster, 1892. c. Sam Booth. Published by Booth & Coffey, *The Mission Journal*, San Francisco, CA. 1892. 32pp. Litho of Benjamin Harrison and Whitelaw Reid. [M-300].

BFH-118 The Heather Bell And Other Poems. w. George L. Reid. Published by George L. Reid, Menasha, WI. 1891. 74pp. [M-313].

BFH-119 Kansas Campaign Songs. w. A.A. Rowley. Published by Geo. W. Crane & Company, Topeka, KS. 1892. Gn/bk non-pictorial. Words by A.A. Rowley. (The Anti-Calamity Poet). 36pp. [M-315].

BFH-120 The Republican Yell Raiser (A Campaign Songster). Published by The Echo Music Company, LaFayette, IN. 1892. Bl/bk non-pictorial. 28pp. [M-314].

BFH-121 Republican Campaign Songs (Good Enough for this Year). Published by J.R. Brodie & Company, Steam Printers, No. 403 Sansome Street, San Francisco, CA. 1888. [3 7/8" × 4 1/2"]. R/w/b flag design. "Harrison & Morton." 20pp.

BFH-122 1888 Campaign Songs. w. H. Thayer, Nashua, IA. 1888. [5 1/4" × 8 7/16"]. Non-pictorial black line border. 2pp. Page 2: Blank.

BFH-123 Republican Campaign Songs. Published by The Echo Music Co., Publishers, LaFayette, IN. 1888. [6 1/16" × 9-3/4"]. Br/bk non-pictorial geometric designs and black line border. Contents listed. "*The New Red White and Blue; Harrison Morton combine; The Flags that we captured are ours; Vote her straight; Hurrah for Harrison and Sure to Win.*" 14pp.

BFH-124 Tippecanoe and Morton Too. w. Wm. Marshall Cook. Published by Lee & Walker, No. 1017 Walnut Street, Philadelphia, PA. 1888. B/w non-pictorial geometric designs. "Respectfully Dedicated to The Harrison Veteran Clubs." No. 1 Popular Series Of Songs For The Great Song Campaign." Advertisements for agents to promote sale of Campaign Songs.

BFH-125 Harrison & Protection (Song & Chorus). w. M.A.M. m. Henry Harding. Published by John

Church Co., No. 74 West Fourth Street, Cincinnati, OH. 1888. Non-pictorial geometric designs. 6pp. Page 6: Blank.

BFH-126 Harrison's Grand March To The White House. m. Charles D. Blake. In: *Marches Of The Presidents, 1789-1909, Authentic Marches & Campaign Songs*, page 54. A. Carl Miller. Published by Chappell & Co., Inc., No. 609 Fifth Avenue, New York, NY. "By arrangement with Chilmark Press, Inc." 1968. [9" × 12"]. R/w/b litho of eagle, flag. "An Illustrated Piano Folio For All Ages." 72pp.

BFH-127 Harrison's Grand March. m. E.H. Erwin. Published by James C. Beckel, 914 Sansom St., Philadelphia, PA. 1889. B/w litho of Benjamin H. Harrison. "To Our President." 6pp.

BFH-128 Benjamin Harrison March. m. Theo. Moelling. 1892. Non-pictorial. Published by C.H. Kimball, Manchester, N.H.

BFH-129 Republican Campaign Songs. Published in Chicago, IL. 1888. Be/bl geometric design border. "As sung by the Marquette Club Quartette."

See also GC-43; GC-97; GC-101; WM-1; WM-48; WHT-23; WW-19; FDR-158; DDE-9; LBJ-1; MISC-167.

BARRY M. GOLDWATER

BMG-1 Barry's Victory March. w.m. Jim MacDonald. Published by Pyramid Music Company, No. 6087 Sunset Boulevard, Hollywood 28, CA. 1964. Bl/w photo of Barry Goldwater. R/w/b drawing of "G.O.P." elephant band. "Net proceeds for Goldwater fund campaign contribution $." 4pp. Page 4: Blank.

BMG-2 The Goldwater Anthem. w.m. LaFayette Sammons. a. Bill Bell. Published by LaFayette Sammons, Publisher, P.O. Box 75, Jonesboro, AR. 1963. [8 1/2" × 11"]. R/w/bl/y photo of Barry M. Goldwater, drawings of The White House, Capitol building, Liberty Bell, flags, shield. 4pp.

BMG-1

BMG-3 Go With Goldwater. w. Tom McDonnell. m. Otis Clements. Published by Vincent Youmans Co., 157 W. 57th Street, New York 19, NY. 1964. Bl/w photo of Barry Goldwater. 4pp. Page 4: Slogans — "A Choice Not An Echo," "For a Stronger Republican Party, For a Stronger America, For a Stronger Free World, Go With Goldwater. The Republican Choice For '64." "Produced by Fuller and Smith and Ross, Inc. for the Goldwater for President Committee, 1101 Connecticut Avenue, N.W., Washington, D.C., Denison Kitchel, General Director."

BMG-4 Barry's Boys. w.m. June Reizner. Published by the B.F. Wood Music Company, Inc., New York 19, NY. 1964. B/w photo of The Chad Mitchell Trio. "Recorded by The Chad Mitchell Trio on Mercury Records." 4pp.

BMG-5 Goldwater. w.m. Hazel Davis (ASCAP). Published by Faith and Freedom Songs, No. 5901 Rose Avenue, Long Beach 5, CA. 1964. Br/w photo of Barry Goldwater. 4pp. Page 4: Blank.

BMG-6 Republican Song Book. w.m.a. Fritz Purnell and Hank Wells.

Published by Bobbs-Merrill Company, Inc. 1964. [9 3/8" × 12 3/8"]. Hardback Book. R/w/bl/gy drawing of elephant, flag. 20pp. Page 20: Rear view of elephant that is on the cover, sign inscribed "Leave Dems Behind." [M-432].

BMG-7 We Want Goldwater. w.m. Michael Herina. Copyright August, 1964. [8 1/2" × 11"]. Non-pictorial. 2pp. Page 2: Blank.

BMG-8 The Goldwater Presidential Campaign Song. w. Bob Saffer (ASCAP). m. "Sing to the *Battle Hymn Of The Republic*." Published by Columbia Advertising Company, No. 133-17 101st Street, Richmond Hill 19, NY. 1964. [7 3/4" × 9 1/4"]. Non-pictorial. 2pp. Page 2: Blank.

BMG-9 Mr. Johnson, The Sandman Said Goodnight. w.m. Michael Hernia. Copyright August, 1964. [8 1/2" × 11"]. Non-pictorial. 2pp. Page 2: Blank.

BMG-10 I'm For Barry. w.m. Ronald M. Feenstra. Published by Ronald M. Feenstra, No. 2184 Tokalon Street, San Diego, CA. 92110. 1964. [8 1/2" × 13"]. Non-pictorial. "Copies available from R.M. Feenstra, Publisher, 10 cts. each, 20 for $1.00, 100 for $4.00, 500 for $15.00, 1000 for $25.00. Add 4% tax in California. Mailed same day received — subject to supply on hand. Max 72 hours from receipt for order. We pay parcel post except on C.O.D. orders." 2pp. Page 2: Blank.

BMG-11 [Hey Look Him Over]. m. Air: "Sung to Tune of *Hey, Look Me Over*." [1964]. [8 1/2" × 5 7/8"]. Gd/bk non-pictorial. 2pp. Page 2: Blank.

BMG-12 The Goldwater Miller Team (For Government Free and Equal). w.m. Bob Saffer. Copyright 1964 by Forward Music Publishing Company and Columbia Advertising Company, No. 133-17 101st Avenue, Richmond Hills 19, NY. [8 1/2" × 11"]. Non-pictorial lead sheet. "Records now available exclusive on Columbia Advertising Company." "Two great songs on one record." "Featured nationally on all T.V. and radio networks. Use for rallies, sound trucks, meetings." "In small 7" L.P." 2pp. Page 2: Second complete Goldwater song — **Let's Put Barry In The White House** (Campaign Song). w. Bob Saffer. m. "Sing to the *Battle Hymn of the Republic*."

BMG-13 Folk Songs For Conservatives. w. Noel E. Parmentel, Jr. and Marshall J. Dodge. Published by Unicorn Press, Inc., No. 790 Madison Avenue, New York, NY. 10021. 1964. [5" × 8 3/8"]. Bl/w drawings of Barry Goldwater, Bill Buckley, Ray Cohn, eagle. List of contents. "Sung by Noel E. Parmentel, Jr. and His Unbleached Muslim, Greatest Political Satirists Since Cohn and Schine." "Right Wing Hootenanny." 36pp.

Chester A. Arthur

CAA-1 President Arthur's Grand March. m. Charles D. Blake. Published by White, Smith & Company, Nos. 188 and 190 State Street, Chicago, IL. [ca. 1881]. B/w litho by C.H. Crosby of Chester A. Arthur. "To Chester A. Arthur." Page 2: Blank.

CAA-2 President Arthur's Grand March. m. L.C. Noles. "For sale by O'Shea Brothers, Nos. 128, 130, 132, 134 and 136 Main Street, Laconia, NH." [ca. 1881]. B/w litho of Chester A. Arthur, flowers, geometric border. 6pp. Pages 2 and 6: Blank.

CAA-3 President Arthur's Grand March. m. C. Carlberg. Copyright 1881 by R.A. Saalfield. B/w litho of Chester A. Arthur. Advertising for "R.H. Macy & Company, 14th Street, Sixth Avenue and 13th Street. We call special attention to our Muslin Underwear for ladies, misses and children. It is all of our own manufacture, and we unhesitatingly say that for variety of design and quality of work it cannot be approached by any other house. Our prices are below all competition. Large assortment of hand embroidered French underwear, our own direct importation, at very attractive prices." 6pp. Page 2: Advertising for song book. Page 6: Advertising for various retail stores in the New York City area.

CAA-4 The Land That We Adore (National Song). w. George Russell Jackson. m. Richard Stahl, Op. 81. Published by P.R. McCargo & Company, Boston, MA. Copyright 1883 by W.A. Evans and Brothers. Non-pictorial. Non-pictorial geometric design border. "Very Respectfully Dedicated to Chester A. Arthur, President of the United States of America." 4pp. Page 4: Blank.

CAA-5 Our Soldiers Return (Grand March). m. Simon Hassler. Published by Lee & Walker, No. 1113 Chestnut Street, Philadelphia, PA. 1885. B/w sepia tinted litho [horizontal format] of President Chester Arthur and other dignitaries reviewing parade of ex-Civil War officers and soldiers. 6pp. Pages 2 and 6: Blank.

CAA-6 President Arthur's March. m. C. Carlberg. Published [V-1: By Richard A. Saalfield, No. 41 Union Square] [V-2: For R.H. Macy's, 14th Street, Sixth Avenue and 13th Street], New York, NY. [Edition ca. 188-]. Non-pictorial geometric design border. "Popular Marches." List of other titles in series. [V-2: Advertising for R.H. Macy & Company]. 6pp. Page 2: Blank. Page 3: Title—**President Arthur's Grand March**. Page 6: Advertising.

CAA-7 President Arthur's Grand March. m. A.H. Rosewig. Published by G. Porter Foster, Geneva, OH. Copyright 1881 by T.A. Bacher. B/w litho of Chester A. Arthur, geometric design border. "Introducing the Beautiful Melody *Onward Christian Soldiers*." "Respectfully Dedicated to His Excellency Chester A. Arthur." 6pp. Page 6: Adv.

CAA-8 President Arthur's Grand March. m. Almon Hougas. Published by H.L. Benham & Company, No.

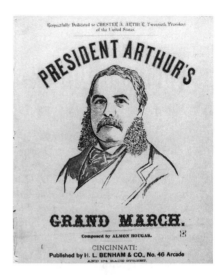

CAA-8

46 Arcade, Cincinnati, OH. 1881. B/w litho of Chester A. Arthur. "Respectfully Dedicated to Chester A. Arthur, Twentieth President of the United States." 6pp. Pages 2 and 6: Blank.

CAA-9 Ex-President Arthur's Funeral March. m. Thorne.

CAA-10 The National Soldiers Reunion Grand March. m. Claxton Wilstach. [1885]. B/w sepia tinted litho [horizontal format] of President Chester Arthur and other dignitaries reviewing parade of ex-Civil War officers and soldiers at "Fairmount Park, Philadelphia, Pa., June 27 to July 6, 1885.".

CAA-11 President Arthur's Grand March. In: *Marches Of The Presidents, 1789-1909, Authentic Marches & Campaign Songs*, page 50. A. Carl Miller. Published by Chappell & Co., Inc., No. 609 Fifth Avenue, New York, NY. "By arrangement with Chilmark Press, Inc." 1968. [9" × 12"]. R/w/b litho of eagle, flag. "An Illustrated Piano Folio For All Ages." 72pp.

See also JAG-1; JAG-3; JAG-20; JAG-22; JAG-27; JAG-37; JAG-41; JAG-47; JAG-50; JAG-59; JAG-62; JAG-66; JAG-82; JAG-94; JAG-101;

JAG-102; JAG-103; JAG-104; WM-31; WHT-23; WW-19; FDR-158; DDE-9; LBJ-1; MISC-167.

CLINTON B. FISK

CBF-1 Laughing Waters. m. Clinton B. Fisk. Published by A.W. Perry's Sons, Sedalia, MO. 1924. B/w photo of a sail boat. Gn/w star border. 6pp. Pages 5 and 6: Advertising.

CBF-2 Vote For Gen. C.B. Fisk. w. Pass Christian, Miss. Published by *Temperance Gazette* Printing House, No. 131 Federal Street, Camden, [NJ]. [1888]. [6 1/2" × 8 15/16"]. Non-pictorial black line border. 2pp. Page 2: Blank.

CBF-3 Prohibition Song. [4 1/4" × 6 15/16"]. Non-pictorial. 2pp. Page 2: Blank.

CBF-4 Battle Songs Of Prohibition. e. A.E. Aldrich. Published by New Era Company, Springfield, OH. 1887. 36pp. [5 1/4" × 6 3/4"]. B/w litho of girls, birds, geometric designs. [M-295].

CBF-5 Prohibition Campaign Songs. Published by Echo Music Company, Publishers, LaFayette, IN. 1888. Be/bk non-pictorial. "For Fiske & Brooks We'll Vote; The No Whisky Party; Election Morning and Vote for Cold Water Boys." [M-296].

CBF-6 Prohibition Campaign Songster. Published by [V-1: John Church Company, Cincinnati, OH] [V-2: Root & Sons Music Co., New York]. 1888. "Including Constitution for Campaign Clubs." 24[?]pp. [M-297].

CBF-7 Blow, Bugler, Blow Up One Note More. w. J.E. Rankin, D.D. m. W.H. Pontis. "Dedicated to Gen. Clinton B. Fiske." In: *Senior Loyal Temperance Legion Song Book Of Marching Songs, Series No. 4*, page 60. e. Anna Adams Gordon. Published by Woman's Temperance Publishing Association, Chicago, IL. [ca. 1901]. [5 15/16" × 7 1/4"]. Gn/bk litho of birds, geometric designs. 68pp.

CALVIN COOLIDGE

CC-1 Keep Cool And Keep Coolidge. w. Ida Cheever Goodwin. m. Bruce Harper. Published by Home Town Coolidge Club, Plymouth, VT. Copyright 1924 by W.S. Tuttle. Br/w photo view of "Plymouth, Vt., Birthplace of President Calvin Coolidge, July 4, 1872." "The Official Campaign Song of the Home Town Coolidge Club of Plymouth, Vermont." "Band, Orchestra, Male Quartet and Mixed Quartet, Arrangement may be obtained from the Publishers." 4pp. Page 4: Br/w photo of "Col. Coolidge seated at the table in the room where he administered the midnight oath to his son."

CC-2 Coolidge And Dawes (For the Nation's Cause). m. Zeph Fitz-Gerald. Published by Zeph Fitz-Gerald Musical Publicity For Coolidge & Dawes, Wrigley Building, Chicago, IL. 1924. Gy/w drawing of eagle, shield. Gy/w photos of Calvin Coolidge and Charles Dawes. "Official Campaign Song." 4pp. Page 4: Arrangement for Quartette.

CC-3 Keep Cool And Keep Coolidge. w. Ida Cheever Goodwin. m. Bruce Harper. Published by the Home Town Coolidge Club, Plymouth, VT. Copyright 1924 by W.S. Tuttle. Br/w photo of "The Home Town Coolidge Club and Quartette presenting to the President and Mrs. Coolidge the first certificates of membership in the Home Town Coolidge Club, Plymouth, Vermont, The White House, Washington, May 3d, 1924." "The Official Campaign Song of the Home Town Coolidge Club of Plymouth, Vermont." "Band, Orchestra, Male Quartet and Mixed Quartet, Arrangement may be obtained from the Publishers." 4pp. Page 4: Br/w photo of "Col. Coolidge seated at the table in the room where he administered the midnight oath to his son."

CC-4 I'd Like To Fish With The President! w. Speed Langworthy (Of

Christofo Columbo Fame). m. Leslie O. Reed. a. Don C. Wilson and Carlton L. Colby. Published by Gene Gamble, Inc., No. 64 East Jackson Boulevard, Chicago, IL. 1927. R/w/gn/br cartoon-like drawing of Calvin Coolidge and old man fishing, large jumping fish. "The Funny Song that makes 'Cal' Laugh!" "On Records and Player Rolls." 6pp. Page 6: Blank.

CC-5 Farmer Ben's Patriotic Song And March To Washington City. w.m. Urania N. Sangster. Published by Urania N. Sangster, Publisher, No. 203 Auburn Avenue, Buffalo, NY. 1924. [Pre-1919 size]. Bl/w photos of "Calvin Coolidge" and "Charles Dawes," drawing of flags. "An honest man is the noblest work of God." "Dedicated to our National Defenders and to the Red Cross Fighting in Behalf of Humanity." 6pp. Pages 2 and 6: Blank.

CC-6 President Coolidge March (March-Song). w. Bartley Costello. m. Roy Carson. Published by Triangle Music Publishing Company, No. 1658 Broadway, New York, NY. 1923. Br/w photo by Edmonston of Calvin Coolidge. Br/w Politzer drawing of eagle, shield, stars. 6pp. Page 2: "Respectfully Dedicated to Hon. Calvin Coolidge." Page 6: Adv.

CC-7 Ride 'Em Cal! (Song). w. Emma Viau Wark and Alexander B. Wark. m. Emma Viau Wark. e. Joseph Viau. Published by Alexander B. Wark, No. 86 East Broadway, Derry, NH. 1924. Ma/be drawing by A.B. Wark and J. Edwards of Calvin Coolidge riding an elephant pushing a donkey off the "Better Road" to the Capitol inscribed "Honest Legislation." 4pp. Page 4: Blank.

CC-8 Coolidge '24. w.m. Warren Carter Foster. Published by Carter Publishing Company, Washington, DC. 1924. B/w photos by Edmonston Studios of "President Calvin Coolidge," Capitol building, The White House. "Let Us Vote For Him." Bl/w cover. 6pp. Page 6: "The Country is Safe with Coolidge." Verses.

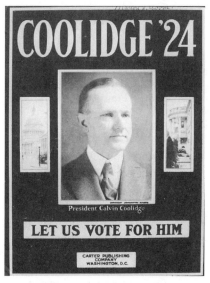

CC-8

CC-9 The Yankee Dood'l Do! w.m. Adaline P. Rundle. m. "Parody on *Yankee Doodle*." Published by Adaline P. Rundle, Greenwich, CT. 1924. B/w silhouette of Calvin Coolidge riding a horse, Capitol building. 4pp. Page 4: Blank.

CC-10 Rally The Standard Of "Abe" Lincoln. w. Mrs. S.R. Artman. m. Roy L. Burtch (Composer of *Guess, One Who Cares for Me*, *The Organ and the Choir*). Published by Halcyon Publishing Company, No. 307 East North Street, Indianapolis, IN. 1924. Br/w photo of Abraham Lincoln, floral designs. "American Campaign March Song." "This song sent by mail anywhere post paid for 25 cts." 4pp. + (2) one page advertising inserts for other Burtch music. Page 4: Blank. [Words on original modified for Coolidge and Dawes].

CC-11 The Open Door. w. Grace Coolidge. m. Robert L. Gannon. Published by Famous Music Corporation, No. 719 7th Avenue, New York, NY. 1932. Br/gy/gd drawing by Jules Gotlieb of Grace Coolidge, church. "Written on the fifth anniversary of the death of Calvin Coolidge, Jr." Verses. 6pp.

CC-12 Keep Cool With Coolidge. w. T.J. Honaker. m. George Crum. Published by T.J. Honaker, Charleston, WV. 1924. R/w/b drawing by Bronstrup "From *The San Francisco Chronicle*" of "President Coolidge" at a ship's wheel. Wheel inscribed "Ship of State." "Miss Columbia" by his side. "Remove violence and spoil, and execute judgement and justice — Ezekiel, 5.9." "Fear not each sudden sound and shock, 'Tis of the wave and not the rock." 6pp.

CC-13 Each As Cool As Coolidge (Campaign Song 1924). w.m. Fred Beck. Copyright 1924 by Fred Beck, Buffalo, NY. [6 7/8" × 10 3/8"]. Non-pictorial. 2pp.

CC-14 Star Spangled Banner. w. Francis Scott Key. m. Air: *Anacreon In Heaven*. Published for L.A. Kennedy Dry Goods Store, Boston, MA. 1926. [9" × 14"]. Cardboard fan. Obv: B/w photos/drawings of Calvin Coolidge, George Washington, Abraham Lincoln and Theodore Roosevelt. R/w/b bunting.

CC-12

"When you look up at old glory, With its colors bold & true, Do you ever stop to think how much it really means to you?" Rev: Advertising. Two songs: **Star Spangled Banner** and **America**.

CC-15 Coolidge And Country (Campaign Song). w. Francesca Carleton Hawes. m. Harold Colonna. Published by Francesca C. Hawes, No. 22 East 31st Street, New York, NY. 1924. Non-pictorial. "Dedicated to the Republican Party." 6pp. Pages 2 and 6: Blank.

CC-16 Presidents On Parade. w.m. Stella Unger and Fred Fischer. Published by Famous Music Corporation, No. 719 Seventh Avenue, New York, NY. 1933. R/w/b flag, stripe. 6pp. Page 5: "Recitation." Page 6: Advertising.

CC-17 [Calvin Coolidge Song Sheet]. [1924]. [4 7/8" × 9 1/8"]. Non-pictorial. [1]: m. "Tune: *Battle Hymn of the Republic*." [2]: m. "Air: *Barney Google*." [3]: m. "Air: *Yes, We Have No Bananas*." 2pp. Page 2: Blank.

CC-18 Northland (Song). w.m. Adolf Hotlen. Published by Four Lakes Music Company, Madison, WI. Copyright 1928 by Adolf Hotlen. Gn/w non-pictorial geometric designs. "Dedicated to President Coolidge's Vacation Land — Wisconsin." 6pp. Pages 2 and 6: Blank.

CC-19 It Is Only A Little Way. w.m. Maria Vrooman Smith. Published by M.V. Smith Publishing Company, No. 369 West 23rd Street, New York, NY. 1926. Bl/w photos of Calvin Coolidge, Jr. and the Capitol building. Gn/bl drawing of a stem of rosemary. "To the memory of Calvin Coolidge, Jr. neath the Rosemary." "A Reverie Beautiful for Us Whose Friends have passed on in the Springtime of Life." 6pp. Pages 2 and 6: Advertising for other music.

CC-20 I Do Not Choose To Run. w. Charles Kenny. m. Tom Dennis. Published by Microfone Music Publishers, No. 148 West 46th Street, New York, NY. 1928. Bl/w photo of Billy Jones and Ernest Hare. "Featured by Billy Jones and Ernest Hare — The Happiness Boys." R/w/b drawings by Doc Rankins of various items that choose not to run — Clock, horse, car, shoes, snail, &c. [Song based on Calvin Coolidge's famous reply to a second term]. 6pp. Page 6: Advertising for other music.

CC-21 It's Coolidge (Waltz Song). w.m. Dr. K.R. Barnum. a. Lena Bell Newkirk. Published by Dr. K.R. Barnum, Sedalia, MO. 1924. [Pre-1919 size]. B/w photo of Statue of Liberty, geometric design border. 6pp. Page 2: Verses. Page 6: Blank.

CC-22 The President's Love Letter. w.m. Adaline P. Rundle. Published by Adaline P. Rundle, Greenwich, CT. 1924. Non-Pictorial. "If it were not for you I should not be here and I want to tell you how much I love you." 6pp. Page 6: Blank.

CC-23 The White House Flower. w. Mrs. E.M. Bishop. m. Yvonna Hudspeth. Published by Yvonna Hudspeth, Rapid City, SD. Copyright 1926 by Virgi Hudspeth. B/w non-pictorial geometric designs. "Dedicated to the First Lady of the Land." 6pp. Pages 2, 7 and 6: Blank.

CC-24 Cushing Academy March Two Step. m. Lieu. Joseph Kiefer (Composer of the famous *Iron Division March*, *Hail Philadelphia March*, &c, &c). Published by The Harry J. Lincoln Music Company, No. 930 North 19th Street, Philadelphia, PA. 1921. B/w photos of "Cushing Academy," "Lieu. Kiefer (Bandmaster of Philadelphia Police Band)." Facsimile letter — "Calvin Coolidge, Governor, The Commonwealth of Massachusetts, Executive Department, State House, Boston, 23d July, 1920 — Dr. Harvey S. Cowell, Cushing Academy, Ashburnham, Mass., My Dear Doctor Cowell: It is a most pleasant duty to be the medium of transmission of this medal given by the Earl of Ashburnham through Mayor Moore of Philadelphia to the boy showing the greatest proficiency in athletics at Cushing Academy. It will be of great value to the one who wins the medal, because it has come from a very noted donor, and because it represents excellence in athletic contests with pupils of one of Massachusetts's most cherished educational institutions of highest traditions, Very Truly Yours, Calvin Coolidge [facsimile signature]." "Respectfully Dedicated to Mr. Louis H. Eisenlohr." "Also published for Band and Orchestra. Can be had for player pianos and talking machines." 4pp. Page 4: Advertising.

CC-25 Keep Cool-idge (Republican Dance). Photo of the "Hon. Calvin Coolidge." Poem. "Composed for the Piano." [1924].

CC-26 C=A=L. w.m. Arthur Schwarz and Robert M. McDonough. Published for The Woman's Republican Club of Rhode Island, Headquarters, Butler's Exchange, Providence, RI. 1924. R/w drawing of eagles, stars, geometric designs. 6pp. Pages 2 and 6: Blank.

CC-27 Amherst Marching Song. m. Edward M. Durban. Published by The Amherst Alumni Association of Philadelphia, Philadelphia, PA. Copyright 1929 by Edward M. Durban. Pl/w logo of Amherst College. "Respectfully Dedicated to Calvin Coolidge." 8pp. Page 8: Blank.

CC-28 Welcome Coolidge (March Song). w.m. William J. Schmidt. Published by Schmidt and Peterson, Milwaukee, WI. 1928. Non-pictorial geometric designs. 6pp. Page 6: Advertising.

CC-29 Coolidge-Dawes Rally Song. w. Ella M. Boston. m. "Tune: *Hold the Fort*." Copyright 1924 by Ella Boston, Washington, D.C. [4 1/4" × 7 1/4"]. Gn/bk lithos of Calvin Coolidge — "For President," and Charles Dawes — "For Vice-President," geometric design border "Endorsed by Mrs. Virginia White Speel, President of the League of Republican Women of the District of Columbia." "September, 1924." 4pp. Pages 2 and 4: Blank.

CC-30 Calvin Coolidge (Song).

w.m. Rufe K. Stanley. Published by R.K. Stanley, Greensboro, NC. 1924. Br/w photo by Purdy of Calvin Coolidge. 6pp. Page 5: Arranged for Quartette. Page 6: Song—**Calvin Coolidge March**.

CC-31 Coolidge And Dawes (For the Nation's Cause). m. Zeph FitzGerald. a. Joe Jordan. Published by Musical Publicity for Coolidge and Dawes, Wrigley Building, Chicago, IL. 1924. [6 15/16" × 10 15/16"]. Br/w woman's face, non-pictorial geometric designs. "Editor's note—Dance orchestras will find this to be an arrangement of real merit with great possibilities for a 'Sock!'" 6pp. foldout. Pages 5 and 6: Blank.

CC-32 Keep Cool And Keep Coolidge. w. Ida Cheever Goodwin. m. Bruce Harper. Published by the Home Town Coolidge Club, Plymouth, VT. Copyright 1924 by W.S. Tuttle. [10 1/2" × 14 1/4"]. Gn/w cardboard, fold-over megaphone. Obv: Two gn/w photos Calvin Coolidge. Song. List of the Home Town Club committee members. "Now sing for Coolidge." "Use the Rooter-Phone with reasonable care." Rev: B/w illustrated directions for folding the "Rooter-Phone." "Patented and manufactured by H.J. Kingsley, Rutland, VT."

CC-33 Our Flag. Photo of Calvin Coolidge.

CC-34 Let Coolidge Carry On (Campaign Song). w. John D. Noble. m. "Tune of Glory, *Glory, Hallelujah, Battle Hymn Of The Republic*." Published by John D. Noble, No. 1966 Broadway, New York, NY. 1924. B/w photo by Walinger of Calvin Coolidge. 4pp. Page 4: Blank.

CC-35 Republican Campaign Song Book. Photos of Calvin Coolidge and Charles Dawes.

CC-36 Let Coolidge Carry On (Campaign and Marching Song). w. John D. Noble. m. "Tune of *Glory, Glory, Hallelujah, Battle Hymn Of The Republic*." a. Al W. Brown. Published by John D. Noble, No. 470 East 161st Street, New York, NY. 1924. Non-pictorial handwritten title. 4pp. Page 4: Blank. Pages 2 and 3: Printed music.

CC-37 Melody. m. Gen. Charles G. Dawes. Orchestrated by Adolph G. Hoffman. Published by Gamble Hinged Music Company, Publishers, Chicago, IL. Copyright 1912 and 1921. [9 1/4" × 12 1/8"]. R/w/b geometric designs. List of arrangements available. "For Violin and Piano." 6pp. + Insert for "Violin." Page 2: "As played by Fritz Kreisler." Page 6: Advertising for other music.

CC-38 Melody. m. Brigadier General Charles G. Dawes. Published by Gamble Hinged Music Company, Publishers, Chicago, IL. Copyright 1912 and 1921. [8 3/4" × 11 5/16"]. Bl/bk/w non-pictorial geometric designs. "Piano Solo." List of arrangements available. 6pp. Pages 2 and 6: Advertising.

CC-39 Melody. m. Charles G. Dawes. Published by Gamble Hinged Music Company, Publishers, Chicago, IL. 1917. R/w/b non-pictorial geometric designs. 6pp. Pages 2 and 6: Advertising.

CC-40 Just You And I. w. Ray Jordan. m. Jacob S. Rosenberg. Published by Jacob S. Rosenberg, No. 805 East 10th Street, Cleveland, OH. 1923. B/w photo of Bernard Landino—"Sung by Bernard Landino, Tenor." Gn/w geometric design border. 6pp. Page 2: B/w photos of Jacob S. Rosenberg and Herman A. Hummel. Facsimile letter written from President Coolidge's secretary to Jacob Resenberg. Page 6: Blank.

CC-41 President Coolidge March. m. M. Azzolina (Composer of *A President Harding March, St. Louis Post Dispatch March, Dreaming Waltz Song*, &c). Published by Christopher Music Publishing Company, DuQuoin, IL. 1924. Br/w drawing of Calvin Coolidge, eagle, shield. 6pp. Page 2: "Respectfully Dedicated to Hon. Calvin Coolidge." Page 6: Advertising.

CC-42 Our Friend And President (A Serenade In Honor of The President of the U.S.A.). m. E. Monroe

Wright. Published by E. Monroe Wright, Manteno, IL. 1928. Br/w photo of Calvin Coolidge. Pl/w geometric designs. 6pp. Page 6: Blank.

CC-43 Coolidge Campaign Songs. Published by Woman's Republican Club of Massachusetts, No. 46 Beacon Street, Boston, MA. [1924]. [6" × 9"]. Non-pictorial. 2pp.

CC-44 Everybody Sing [Song Sheet]. Published by the Republican League of Massachusetts. [1924]. [Folded to 4 1/2" × 17 1/2"]. Non-pictorial. "Coolidge by 50,000." 8pp.

CC-45 It's All In The Game. w. Carl Sigman. m. Gen. Charles G. Dawes. Published by Remick Music Corporation, New York, NY. Copyright 1912 and 1951. [V-1: R/w/b drawing of woman, heart] [V-2: R/w/b drawing of woman, heart. Bl/w photo of Sammy Kaye — "As Featured by Sammy Kaye and His World Famous Swing and Sway Orch."] [V-3: R/w/b drawing of woman, heart. Bl/w photo of Tommy Edwards — "Featured by Tommy Edwards."] [V-4: Gn/r/w drawing of woman, heart. Gn/w photo of Henry Jerome — "Featured by Henry Jerome and His Orchestra"] [V-5: Gn/r/w drawing of woman, heart. Gn/w photo of Vincent Lopez — "Featured by Vincent Lopez and His Orchestra"] [V-6: Gn/r/w drawing of woman, heart. Gn/w photo of Paul Taubman — "Featured by Paul Taubman"]. [V-7: Bl/w photo of Lee Castle — "As Featured By Lee Castle"]. 4pp. Page 4: Advertising.

CC-46 It's All In The Game. w. Carl Sigman. m. Gen. Charles G. Dawes. Published by Warner Bros. Publications, Inc., No. 75 Rockefeller Plaza, New York, NY. 10019. Copyright 1912 and 1951 by Remick Music Corp. [Edition ca. 197-]. Non-pictorial. 4pp. Page 4: Blank.

CC-47 It's All In The Game. w. Carl Sigman. m. Gen. Charles G. Dawes. Published by Warner Bros. Music, No. 488 Madison Avenue, New York, NY. 10022. Copyright 1912, 1951 and 1970. B/w non-pictorial. "Recorded by The Four Tops on Motown Records." "Play along with the record." 4pp. Page 4: Geometric design.

CC-48 Glory (Symphonic Poem). m. Francesco Pozzi. Unpublished manuscript — Conductor's score. Copyright 1924 by Francesco Pozzi. [13 1/2" × 10 3/4"]. R/gd non-pictorial printed velvet cover. "Dedicated to the Honorable Calvin Coolidge President of the U.S. of America." 32pp. + Orchestra parts.

CC-49 Let Me Dream. w.a. Don Wilson. m. "Adapted from the Famous *Melody* by Charles G. Dawes." Published by Gamble Hinged Music Company, Chicago, IL. 1931. N/c drawing by Mari-Mac of woman. 6pp. Pages 2 and 6: Advertising. Page 3: "Adapted from Gen. Charles G. Dawes' famous *Melody in A Major.*"

CC-50 Rally The Standard Of "Abe" Lincoln. w. Mrs. S.R. Artma (Composer of *Guess, One Who Cares For Me, The Organ and The Choir*). m. Roy L. Burtch. Published by Halcyon Publishing Company, No. 307 East North Street, Indianapolis, IN. 1924. Br/w photos of "Calvin Coolidge," "Charles G. Dawes," "Abraham Lincoln" and "Ed Jackson" [Republican nominee for Governor of Indiana], geometric design border. "American Campaign March Song." 4pp. + Insert letter. Page 4: Biographies of candidates and other Republicans from Indiana, including "Ed Jackson, F. Harold Van Orman, Frederick E. Schortmeier, Lewis S. Bohman, Ben H. Urbahns, Arthur L. Gillam, F.M. Thompson, Willard R. Gimmill, Judge Willoughby, E.A. Dausman, Noble Sherwood, Mrs. Edward F. White." Insert — Page 1: Letter from composer to Republican State Committee. Page 2: Advertising.

CC-51 Melody. m. Brigadier General Charles G. Dawes. a. Marie Edwards Von Ritter. Published by The Gamble Hinged Music Company, Chicago, IL. Copyright 1917 and 1921. [Edition ca.

1935]. Gr/bk/w piano keys. List of other arrangements. 6pp. Pages 2 and 6: Advertising for other music.

CC-52 Keep Coolidge In The White House (In The Presidential Chair). w. John J. Bickley. m. Frank Drago. Published by John J. Bickley & Sons, Hartford, CT. 1924. Br/w/bl drawing of The White House. 6pp. Pages 2 and 6: Blank.

CC-53 Calvin's Creed (Softshoe Shuffle). w. Richard Engquist. m. Jack Gottlieb. Published by Theophilious Music, Inc. Sole Agent: Boosey & Hawkes, Inc. 1991. [6 7/8" × 10 1/2"]. Non-pictorial. "Presidential Suite, Seven Pieces for Mixed Chorus (SATB) a cappella. 8pp. Page 2: "Presidential Suite is a celebration of America's priceless heritage of liberty. Inspired by the wisdom and whimsy of some of our most colorful presidents, it juxtaposes the eloquence of John F. Kennedy and Franklin Delano Roosevelt, with the journalistic pith of Theodore Roosevelt, Harry S Truman's blunt common sense, Abraham Lincoln's homespun wit and Thomas Jefferson's irony, plus a legendary quip from the taciturn Calvin Coolidge. This patriotic work combines idealism with light-heartedness, inspiration with a dash of salt…" Page 3: "For Michael Leavitt."

CC-54 Coolidge Song. w.m. J. Matthew Goulbourne. No. 127 East Fourth Street, Newcastle, DE. [1924]. Non-pictorial handwritten manuscript. 4pp. Pages 3 and 4: Blank.

CC-55 Keep Cool And Keep Coolidge. [1924]. [3 1/2" × 5 5/16"]. Card. Obv: Bl/be flag border at top and bottom. "Please all join in last refrain. Keep this copy for future rallies." Rev: Blank.

CC-56 Get Out And Vote! w. Eddie Porray. m. Wright and Bessinger (The Radio Franks). "Compliments of *Corry Evening Journal*." Published by Henry Waterson, Inc., No. 1971 Broadway, New York, NY., Waterson, Berlin and Snyder Co. Selling Agents." "With Ukulele Arrangement." 1924. [5 7/8" × 6 3/4"]. B/w photos of "Calvin Coolidge," "John W. Davis," and "Robert M. La Follette." B/w drawing of Uncle Sam, "Ballot Box." "Released through NEA Service, Inc." 4pp.

CC-57 Keep Cool And Keep Coolidge. w. Ida Cheever Goodwin. m. Bruce Harper. "The Official Campaign Song of the Home Town Coolidge Club of Plymouth, Vt." In: *Calvin Coolidge, Vermonter* (Address by Earle S. Kinsley, State Chamber of Commerce, Burlington, Vermont, March 24, 1924), page 15. Published by Home Town Coolidge Club, Plymouth, VT. 1924. [6" × 9"]. Gn/w drawing of "The Coolidge Homestead." 24pp.

CC-58 Songs For 1924. e. Frank Welling. Published by Ohio State Campaign Committee, Clarence J. Neal, Chairman, Frank Welling, Editor, Columbus, OH. 1924. Bl/r litho of Calvin Coolidge and Charles Dawes. 12pp. [M-417].

CC-59 Let's Sing (Vote For Coolidge And Dawes!) [Song Sheet]. [1924]. [8 1/2" × 13 7/8"]. B/w litho of Abraham Lincoln, William McKinley, Theodore Roosevelt and Warren G. Harding, elephant inscribed "G.O.P.," leaves, geometric designs. "Solo by Miss Gertrude Northrop, Miss Helen Sailors at the piano, popular songs led by Mr. Chet A. Keyes." "Nease Printing Co." 2pp. Page 2: Blank.

See also TJ-49; AL-346; TR-343; WGH-1; WGH-13; WGH-15; WGH-19; WGH-20; WGH-21; WGH-22; WGH-23; WGH-27; WGH-29; WGH-47; WGH-55; AES-10; AES-19; AES-23; AES-62; AES-67; AES-68; FDR-158; FDR-367; HST-22; DDE-9; JFK-27; JFK-61; ; LBJ-1; RMN-39; MISC-101; MISC-110; MISC-167.

Charles E. Hughes

CEH-1 Hughes And Fairbanks Campaign Song Book. c. James L. Feeney. Published by William H. Delaney, Song Publisher, No. 117 Park Row, New York, NY. Copyright 1916 by William W. DeLaney. [8" × 11"]. R/w/b flags, shield. Bl/w photos of "Charles Evans Hughes" and "Charles Warren Fairbanks." "Preparedness, Protection, Prosperity." R/w/b drawing of flags, shield, geometric designs. 20pp. Page 2: Biographies of the Candidates. Page 3: Contents. Pages 19 and 20: Blank. [M-407].

CEH-2 Song Book Of The Campaign Of 1916. w. Felix Fantus. Published by Fantus Brothers, No. 525 South Dearborn Street, Chicago, IL. 1916. [3 7/16" × 6"]. B/w photo of man with music baton — "Everybody sing please." "These stirring lyrics set to well-known melodies are being sung by loyal and patriotic Americans from Maine to Texas, From Florida to Washington. Join the ranks of the Harmony Party-take the song book home." 8pp. Page 2 Title: **Republican Song Review Of 1916.** [M-408, 409].

CEH-3 Charles E. Hughes The American. w.m. William H. Pease. Published by The North Eastern Music Company, New York, NY. 1916. Br/w photo of Charles E. Hughes. "Preparedness, Prosperity and Protection." 4pp.

CEH-4 Prosperity And Hughes (Campaign Song). w. Harry S. Locke. m. H.C. Work. Published by The Song Publishing Company, No. 507 Court Block, St. Paul, MN. Copyright 1916 by Harry S. Locke. Litho of flag, geometric design border. 4pp[?].

CEH-5 Our Choice (National Campaign Song). w.m. Charles A. McCann. Published by Metropolis Music Company, No. 145 West 45th Street, New York, NY. 1916. Br/w photo of Charles E. Hughes. "Dedicated to Charles Evans Hughes." 6pp. Page 6: Advertising.

CEH-6 There Was A Man From New York Town. w.m. Daniel H. Wilson. Published by Daniel H. Wilson, Portland, OR. 1916. Non-pictorial line border. "Republican Campaign Marching Song." 4pp. Page 4: Advertising.

CEH-7 If I Were President. w. C.E. Hughes. m. Wall Street. In: *The Literary Digest*, October 21, 1916, page 1020. B/w drawing of music with hammers for notes, dollar signs as sharps — "Political Sharps," face of Theodore Roosevelt — "With Progressive Expressions." "Sung by Charles Evans Hughes." Cartoon-like man — "Candidate Hughes wants ter [sic] make that th' National Anthem." "Song Without Words." Drawing originally by "Flaschke in *The Louisville Times*."

CEH-8 For Right And Dear Old Glory (An Echo of the Grand War for Humanity — The Song of the Old Volunteer) (Song and Chorus). w.m. Hofwyl Hoorn. Published by American Publishing Company, Indianapolis, IN. Copyright 1916 by J.F. Curtice. Bl/w photos of Charles E. Hughes — "Prosperity at

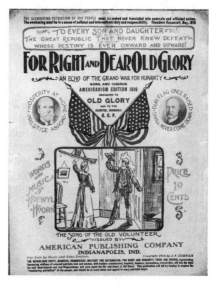

CEH-8

Home, Prestige Abroad," and Charles W. Fairbanks — "Our Flag Once Raised Shall Never Come Down." R/w/b litho of crossed flags, man, woman, gun — "The Song of the Old Volunteer." "Americanism Edition 1916." "Dedicated to Old Glory and to the Reunited, Invincible G.O.P." "The Republican Party, reunited, progressive, militant for nationalism, for right and humanity, tried and proven, representing increasing millions of aroused patriotic men and women, with leaders consecrated, inspired, fearless, harmonious, irresistible, will win the fight for real Americanism and real Preparedness and save again the life and honor of Old Glory! This publication will aid by helping to awaken the 'slumbering patriotism' of the people, and should be in every home and appeal to every patriotic heart." "The stirring patriotism of our People must be awaked and translated into concrete and efficient action. The awakening must be to a sense of national and international duty and responsibility — Theodore Roosevelt, May 1916." "To every Son and Daughter of the Great Republic that never knew defeat and whose destiny is ever onward and upward!" 4pp. Page 4: Patriotic slogans and narrative.

CEH-9 Twelfth Battalion Song — Campaign 1916 [Song Sheet]. [1916]. [4" × 8 9/16"]. Non-pictorial. Four songs. 2pp. Page 2: Blank.

CEH-10 Campaign Song Book. Published by Ohio Republican State Executive Committee, Chas. S. Harfield. 1916. Litho of Charles E. Hughes, Frank B. Willis, Republican candidate for Governor, and Myron T. Herrick, Republican candidate for the Senate. 8pp. [M-406].

CEH-11 The Men for the U.S.A. w.m. Jack Meredith. Published by Lee Publishing Co., No. 717 Majestic Building, Los Angeles, CA. 1916. Photo of Charles Evans Hughes.

See also WHT-12; WHT-27; WGH-5.

COMMUNIST PARTY

CP-1 Jobs, Security Democracy And Peace (Convention Song). w.m. Kenneth Hunter. Published by Worker's Book Shop, No. 50 East 13th Street, New York, NY. 1938. B/w drawing of man in hat, poster reading "10th National Convention of the Communist Party U.S.A., Jobs, Security, Democracy, Peace." "Convention Song." 4pp. Page 2: Subtitle — "Song of the Tenth National Convention of the Communist Party, U.S.A." Page 4: Advertising for song book.

CP-2 Workers Song Book 1934-1. Published by Workers Music League, New York, NY. 1934. [7" × 10 3/16"]. Br/t non-pictorial. 36pp. Page 2: "Music penetrates everywhere. It carries words with it. It fixes them in the mind. It graves [sic] them in the heart. Music is a weapon in the class struggle."

CP-3 Songs Of The People. Published by Workers Library Publishers, Inc., P.O. Box 148, Station D, New York, NY. January, 1937. [6 1/8" × 9 3/16"]. R/be/bk drawing of factory and home. 68pp.

CP-4 Songs Of Struggle. Published by The Workers Book Shop, 50 East 13th Street, New York, NY. [ca. 1935]. [2 5/8" × 4"]. Non-pictorial geometric design border, hammer and sickle. "50 Songs, 5 Cents." "The workers Book Shop carries a full selection of Marxist-Leninist Books — Pamphlets — Periodicals. Write for complete list. Open evenings." 30pp.

DOUGLAS A. MACARTHUR

DAM-1 MacArthur For President. w.m. William Pickford. Published by Pickford Music Company, No. 1674 Broadway, New York 19, NY. 1948. Bl/w photo of General Douglas A. MacArthur. Bl/w drawing of flag. 4pp.

DAM-2 McArthur [sic] **For America In 1952**. w.m. C. Sharp-Minor.

Published by Studio Staff Productions, Hollywood, CA. 1952. Be/bk photo of General Douglas A. MacArthur. "I Pledge Allegiance to the flag of the United States of America, and to the Republic for which it stands, one nation indivisible, with Liberty and Justice for all." 6pp.

DAM-3 Hat's Off To MacArthur (And Our Boys Down There). w.m. Ira Schuster, Paul Cunningham and Leonard Whitcup. Published by Paull-Pioneer Music Corporation, No. 1657 Broadway, New York, NY. 1942. Bl/w/pk photo of General Douglas A. MacArthur. 6pp. Page 6: Advertising.

DAM-4 America And General MacArthur (We Stand By You). w.m. Charles Leont. Published by Charles Leont Publications, No. 953 West Seventh Street, Los Angeles 17, CA. 1952. Gn/w photo of General Douglas A. MacArthur. 4pp.

DAM-5 God Bless You MacArthur. w.m. Anita Lloyd. Published by Croxton Publishing Company, No. 659 South Orange Drive, Los Angeles 36, CA. 1952. Bl/w photo of General Douglas A. MacArthur. Bl/w drawing of the Statue of Liberty. 4pp. Page 4: Advertising.

DAM-6 Fightin' Doug MacArthur. w.m. Buck Ram. Published by T.B. Harms Company, New York, NY. 1942. R/w/b drawing of eagle, shield, stars. 6pp. Pages 2 and 6: Advertising.

DAM-7 Old Soldiers Never Die (They Just Fade Away). w. Douglas A. MacArthur. m. Lt. Barry Drewes (Asst. Bandmaster, United States Military Academy). Published by Charles H. Hansen Music Company, No. 119 West 57th Street, New York, NY. 1951. Bl/w photo of General Douglas MacArthur. 6pp. Page 6: Quote "From the address to Congress by General of the Army, Douglas MacArthur, April 19, 1951."

DAM-8 Old Soldiers Never Die (They Just Fade Away). w. Douglas A. MacArthur. m. Lt. Barry Drewes (Asst. Bandmaster, U.S. Military Academy). Published by Charles H. Hansen Music Company, No. 119 West 57th Street, New York, NY. 1951. [8 1/2" × 11"]. Gn/bk/w drawing of General Douglas A. MacArthur. "I am closing my fifty-two years of military service. I still remember the refrain of the most popular barrack ballads which proclaimed most proudly that old soldiers never die, they just fade away. And like the old soldier of that ballad, I now close my military career and just fade away, an old soldier who tried to do his duty as God give him the light to see that duty, Good By — From the Address to Congress by General of the Army Douglas MacArthur, April 19, 1951." 4pp. Page 4: Star.

DAM-9 MacArthur's Here Again. w.m. Ralph F. Bragg. Copyright 1945 by Ralph F. Bragg, Milo, Maine. Bl/w/y photo of General Douglas MacArthur. Bl/w photos of "Ralph F. Bragg" and "Lt. Alice Zwicker." "Dedicated to Lt. Alice Zwicker." 4pp. Page 4: Y/w drawing of the Statue of Liberty. Advertising for War Bonds — "Buy 'em, War Bonds Speed Victory, Keep 'em."

DAM-10 Hail MacArthur! w. Remo Preziosi. m. Luigi Dell' Orefice. Published by Paragon Music Publishers, New York 3, NY. 1951. Bl/w photo of Jan Peerce — "Best wishes, Jan Peerce" [facsimile handwriting]. "Featured by Jan Peerce." 6pp. Page 2: "To General Douglas A. MacArthur." Page 6: Advertising.

DAM-11 We'll Follow MacArthur (To the End). w.m. Joseph E. Rems, Jr. and E. Brookens. Published by Acme Music Corporation (Del.), No. 1585 Broadway, New York, NY. 1942. Bl/w drawing of military troops, tanks, trucks and aircraft. 6pp. Page 2: Blank. Page 6: Advertising.

DAM-12 MacArthur's Shift. w.m. Virginia M. Sems. Published by Nordyke Publishing Company, Hollywood, CA. 1944. R/w/b drawing of eagle — "The American Eagle." 4pp. Page 4: Advertising.

DAM-13 Here's To You, MacArthur. w. Nat Burton. m. Walter Kent. Published by Shapiro, Bernstein & Company, Inc., Music Publishers, New York, NY. 1952. R/w/bl/ma photo of "General Douglas MacArthur, U.S.A." 4pp. Page 4: Advertising.

DAM-14 Doug MacArthur. w.m. Earl Nunn and Roland Johnson. Copyright 1951 by Acuff-Rose Publications, No. 2510 Franklin Road, Nashville 4, TN. [6" × 9"]. Non-pictorial. 4pp. Pages 1 and 4: Blank.

DAM-15 Old Soldiers Never Die. w.m. Tom Glazer. Published by Warock Music, Inc., No. 1619 Broadway, New York 19, NY. 1951. Bl/w photo of Vaughn Monroe inscribed "As recorded by Vaughn Monroe." 4pp. Page 4: Advertising.

DAM-16 For Brave Men Are They From The Mighty U.S.A. w.m. Billy Jean. Published by Billy Jean, No. 627 Hickory Street, Dayton, OH. 1942. R/w/b drawing of "General MacArthur," soldier, home, shield. 4pp. Page 4: Advertising.

DAM-17 Our Miracle Man. w. Hugh J. Wolfe. m. Wm. D. Sabin. Published by Hugh J. Wolfe, No. 151 Oak Street, Binghamton, NY. [ca. 194-]. Photo of Douglas MacArthur. Drawing of bombers — "To Tokio [sic]." "Most respectfully dedicated to, Gen. Douglas MacArthur. 6pp. Pages 2 and 6: Blank.

DAM-18 The Hills, The Devil And MacArthur. w.m. Russell McLauchlin, Ole B.J. Foerch and Graham T. Overgard. Published by Robbins Music Corporation, No. 799 Seventh Avenue, New York, NY. 1942. Bl/w photo of Barry Wood — "Featured by Barry Wood." R/w/b stripes, Uncle Sam, soldier, War Bond logo — "Buy Bonds and Stamps for Victory." 6pp. Pages 2 and 6: Advertising.

DAM-19 A Toast To General Mac Arthur (And His Men). w.m. Samuel Glasser. Published by Samuel Glasser, No. 557 Birch Street, San Francisco, CA. 1942. Bl/w non-pictorial geometric design border. 4pp. Page 4: Blank.

DAM-20 U.S.A.'s MacArthur. w. Miriam S. Pressey. m. Lew Tobin. Copyright 1942 by Miriam S. Pressey. Non-pictorial. "Dedicated to Gen. Douglas MacArthur." "Professional Copy." "Made in U.S.A. All rights reserved including public performance for profit." 4pp.

DAM-21 Let's Sing For Democracy (Song with Piano Accompaniment). w.m. Dorothy and Sigmund Blackstone. Published by Beacon Music Publishing Company, No. 8215 20th Avenue, Brooklyn, NY. 1942. Bl/w drawing of an eagle, flag. "Dedicated to General Douglas MacArthur and his men." 4pp. Page 4: Blank.

DAM-22 The Stars And Stripes Forever! (March). m. John Philip Sousa. Published by W.H. Paling and Company, Ltd., Sidney, Australia. [1897]. [Edition ca. 1942]. B/w "Department of Information photo" of "General MacArthur, Commander-in-Chief of the Allied forces in the South-Western Pacific Area." B/w drawing of flag. "Piano Solo." "Printed by arrangement with The John Church Company, Theodore Presser Co., Selling Agents, 1712 Chestnut St., Philadelphia." 6pp. Page 6: Advertising.

DAM-23 God Bless President MacArthur. w.m. The Sheik. Published by Home Sweet Home Music Publishing Company, Hollywood, CA. 1948. Bl/br/w drawing of Douglas A. MacArthur in uniform. 4pp. Page 2: At bottom — "This is the song we will be singing." Page 4: Blank.

DAM-24 Until That Rising Sun Is Down. w. Frankie Kelly. m. Roscoe Barnhart and Neale Wrightman. Published by Neale Wrightman Publishers, No. 30 West Washington Street, Chicago, IL. 1942. Y/w/gr drawing of soldiers, Gen. Douglas MacArthur. "Sing the National Campaign Song." "Remember Pearl Harbor." "Buy War Bonds." "Title page courtesy of *American Legion Magazine*." 6pp. Pages 2 and 6: Advertising. Page 3: "Respectfully Dedicated to General Douglas MacArthur."

DAM-25   I Am A Soldier Of The U.S.A. (Song with Piano Accompaniment). w. Pasquale Palma. m. Antonio Misuraca. Published by Carl Fischer, Inc., Kimball Hall, No. 306 South Wabash, Chicago, IL. 1943. Bl/w nonpictorial lines. "Dedicated to General Douglas MacArthur." 6pp.

DAM-26   We're All With You— Oh Doug Mac Arthur (The Mac Arthur Victory Song). w.m. Gene Fifer. Copyright 1945 by Gene Fifer, No. 5614 Chicago Avenue, Chicago, IL. Non-pictorial. "Professional Copy." Copyright notice. 4pp.

DAM-27   Fightin' Doug Mac Arthur U.S.A. w.m. Sheldon "Puss" Donahoo and W.D. "Bill" Spruance. Published by Broadcast Associates, Publishers, No. 431 Clay Street, San Francisco, CA. [194-]. Photo of Douglas MacArthur, palm trees.

DAM-28   America's Hero MacArthur (Spirit of Victory). w.m. Constantino Scotese. Published by Hawaii Conservatory Publishing Company, No. 5002 Melrose Avenue, Hollywood, CA. [194-]. Drawing of Douglas A. MacArthur.

DAM-29   Carry On For General MacArthur (A Marching Song). w.m. Aubrey Stauffer. Published by Laguna Music Prints, No. 472 Popular Street, Laguna Beach, CA. 1942. B/w drawing by Marlin Justice of General Douglas A. MacArthur. "Companion Song to *Journey's End*." "Distributor Morse M. Preeman, Inc., Los Angeles, CA." 4pp. Page 2: "Respectfully Dedicated to the Nation's Hero, General Douglas MacArthur."

DAM-30   Get A Jap Or Two (A Song for Marching Men). w.m. Toby

DAM-23

Keen and Jack Mitchell. Published by Crosby E. Keen and John M. Spargur, No. 12531 Hyde Street, San Francisco, CA. [194-]. Drawing by E.A. Auerbanky of Douglas MacArthur, flag.

DAM-31   MacArthur The Man. Published by Anderson and Lawless, Los Angeles, CA. [194-]. Drawing of Douglas A. MacArthur.

DAM-32   Draft   MacArthur. w.m. E.N. Sanctuary. Published by E.N. Sanctuary, No. 142 West 91st Street, New York, NY. [6 1/4" × 10 1/4"]. [ca. 1952]. Drawing of Douglas A. MacArthur, Civil War soldiers and flags, George Washington, other patriotic symbols. "One Nation Indivisible." Cloth ribbon attached at top. 2pp. Page 2: Music. "The author donates this song. If you think it and the cause are worthy, you can help by contributing to its circulation. Let's win the victory and drive the gloom of the New Deal from our land."

DAM-33   MacArthur And His Minute Men. w.m. Robert H. Pettengill and Lewis K. Caniglia. Published by Pettengill and Caniglia, No. 1242 South 7th

Street, Omaha, NE. 1944. O/w/gn drawing of soldier, ship, planes, palm trees. 6pp. Pages 2 and 6: Blank.

DAM-34 Our Own MacArthur. w.m. Henry Ward, Cora Walker, Dorothy E. Schmiedt, Naomi Hawkins, Lee Starke, and Leslie C. Walker. In: *Songs of Victory, No. 7*, page 32. Published by Westmore Music Corporation, Southwest Ninth Avenue, Portland, ME. 1944. R/w/b stripe cover, "V."

DAM-35 When Douglas Mac Comes Marching Back (To His Boys on Corregidor). w.m. James H. Irving. Published by Pacific Music Sales, Inc., No. 1515 North Vine, Hollywood, CA. 1942. R/w/b eagle and shield. 6pp. Pages 2 and 6: Blank.

DAM-36 (I'd Like to Shake the Hand of) General McArthur [sic]. w.m. Dave Waide. Published by Cosmo Publishing Company, Los Angeles, CA. 1943. [8 1/2" × 11"]. Gn/bk photo of Ted Lewis. Gn/bk/w silhouettes of soldiers, airplanes, Ted Lewis. 6pp. Page 2: Gn/bk photos and narrative on "Ted Lewis." Page 5: Gn/bk photos and narrative on "A Few of Ted Lewis' Proteges — June Edwards, Geraldine DuBoise, Audrey Zimm." Page 6: Gn/bk photo of Ted Lewis.

DAM-37 Old Soldiers Never Die. w.m. Charles R. Campbell. w.a. Alan Campbell. Published by Carl Fischer, Inc., No. 62 Cooper Square, New York 3, NY. [1951?]. R/w/b drawing of bugler and drummer, shield. "This song is based on the Carl Fischer, Inc., band composition of the same title which is used at West Point by the U.S. Military Academy Band." "For Voice and Piano." 6pp. Page 2: Blank. Page 6: Advertising.

DAM-38 MacArthur, The Magnificent. w. Laura Vollmer. m. William David Allison. Published by Allied Publishing Company, No. 357 South Hill Street, Los Angeles 13, CA. 1946. Br/w photo of General Douglas A. MacArthur. 6pp. Pages 2 and 6: Blank.

DAM-39 I Give You A Song, MacArthur. m. Nancy T. Norton. a. Harry Jenks (U.S. Army). Published by Kelton-Romm, Inc., No. 250 West 49th Street, New York, NY. 1942. R/w/bl/br drawing of General Douglas A. MacArthur, flag. 6pp. Page 6: Advertising. Includes a 4 page insert music sheet of same song.

DAM-40 Boys We Love. w. Laura King and Maria Grever. m. Maria Grever. Published by De La Portilla Publications, Inc., No. 871 7th Avenue, New York, NY. 1942. R/w/b drawing of soldiers, sailors, "Gen. Douglas MacArthur," ships, flag. 6pp. Page 2: B/w photo of Maria Grever — "To all of you boys we have with my deepest affection and faith — I humbly dedicate this song." Page 6: Advertising.

DAM-41 Carry On For General MacArthur (A Marching Song). w.m. Aubrey Stauffer. Published in *The Los Angeles Times*, Sunday, page 8, Part III, March 29, 1942. B/w photo by World Wide Photo of General Douglas A. MacArthur. "Companion Song to *Journeys End*." "Respectfully Dedicated to the Nation's Hero, General Douglas MacArthur." "Compliments of *The Los Angeles Times*."

DAM-42 Heaven Watch The Philippines. w.m. Irving Berlin. Published by Irving Berlin Music Company, No. 1650 Broadway, New York, NY. 1945. Non-pictorial stripes. 4pp. Page 2: "Dedicated to General Douglas C. [sic] MacArthur, in commemoration of his liberation of the Philippines."

DAM-43 MacArthur's Hand. w.m. Don Wayne. Published by Tree Publishing Company, Inc., No. 8 Music Square West, Nashville, TN. 1971 photo of Cal Smith — "Recorded by Cal Smith on MCA Records." Bl/w border. "Distributed by Big 3." 4pp.

DAM-44 Journey's End. w.m. Aubrey Stauffer. Published Laguna Music Prints, No. 472 Popular Street, Laguna

Beach, CA. Copyright 1930 by Alfred Hustwick. [Edition ca. 1942]. B/w drawing of General Douglas A. MacArthur. "Companion Song to *Carry On For General MacArthur*." 4pp. Page 4: Advertising.

DAM-45 Mac Arthur Victory March. w.m. Sargent Scotty Allen. Published by Sargent Scotty Allen, No. 3873 California Street, San Diego, CA. 1947. Br/w photo of General Douglas A. MacArthur, inscribed "Douglas MacArthur, Tokyo 1945 [facsimile handwriting]." "A Five Star Song Endorsed by Five Star General Mac Arthur." 6pp. Page 6: Blank.

DAM-46 Give 'Em Hell — Mac Arthur! w.m. Esther Van Sciver and Shelby Darnell. m. Bob Miller. Published by Bob Miller, Inc., Music Publisher, No. 1619 Broadway, New York, NY. 1942. R/w/b drawing by Barbelle of General Douglas A. MacArthur. Title made to look as if cut from newspaper headlines. 4pp. Page 4: Advertising.

DAM-47 Here's To Doug MacArthur, Hero Of Bataan! w. John Morgan Haggard. Published by J.M. Haggard, No. 121 West Wacker Drive, Chicago, IL. 1942. Photo of Douglas MacArthur, geometric designs. 6pp. Pages 2 and 6: Blank.

DAM-48 Old Soldiers Never Die (They Just Fade Away). w. Walter Hirsch. m. Hugo Frey. Published by Leo Fiest, Inc., No. 799 Seventh Avenue, New York 19, NY. 1951. R/w drawing of eagle, stars, scroll. 4pp. Page 4: Advertising.

DAM-49 MacArthur's March (I Shall Return). w.m. G.R. Montemayor and N.C. Villanueva. a. Benny Dacoscos. Printed by Tongg Publishing Company, Honolulu, HI. 1945. Br/w drawing of General Douglas MacArthur, Philippine Islands. 4pp. Page 4: Advertising.

DAM-50 Old Soldiers Never Die. w. Joy Pace. a. Joy Pace. Published by Souvenir Songs, Box 1725, Hollywood, CA. 90028. 1977. R/w photo of

DAM-46

Douglas MacArthur inside a drawing of a picture frame, flags, eagle, shield, stars. Listing of songs from *Fourteen Carat Fool*. 4pp. Page 4: Advertising for other Souvenir published songs.

DAM-51 General MacArthur (He Sure Can Fight) (Patriotic Song) w.m. Henry Ward. a. Mark Rubens. Published by The Patriotic Music Publishing Company, Box 302, Monticello, AR. Copyright 1942 by Henry Ward. [8 1/2" × 11"]. B/w photos of Douglas MacArthur, Statue of Liberty. War bond stamp. 4pp. Page 4: Blank.

DAM-52 Gen. MacArthur And His Men (Military March). w.m. Rodolfo Cornejo (Philipino Composer). Published by Rodolfo Cornejo, General Post Office Box 186, New York, New York. 1942. Br/w drawing of "Gen. Douglas A. MacArthur, soldiers, tree, map of Bataan. 6pp. Page 2: "Dedicated to General Douglas A. MacArthur and his American-Philipino Forces." Page 6: Advertising.

DAM-53 See You In Manila. w.m. G.R. Montemayor and N.C. Villanueva. Published by Tongg Publishing

Company, No. 113 Smith Street, Honolulu 5, HI. Copyright 1943 by G.R. Montemayor and N.C. Villanueva. Br/w drawings of "General Douglas MacArthur," Statue of Liberty—"Freedom," Philippine soldier, airplanes, tank. 4pp. Page 2: "Dedicated to the Filipino Infantry Regiment in California, AUS." Page 4: Advertising.

DAM-54 MacArthur For America (In 1948). w.m. C. Sharpe-Minor. Copyrihjt 1948 by Studio Staff Productions, Hollywood, CA. [5 15/16" × 8 1/4"]. R/w/b litho of "Pillars of American Democracy" including George Washington—"Founder," Abraham Lincoln—"Preserver," Douglas MacArthur—"Defender." "MacArthur for America in 1948." Pledge of Allegiance. R/w/b U.S. flags, eagle. 2pp. Page 2: Music. "Also on C. Sharpe-Minor Recordings."

DAM-55 A Prayer Hymn For Those In Active Service. w. Isabella Stephenson. m. Ethelbert William Bullinger. a. George Arthur Clarke. Copyright 1942 by Whittemore Associates, Inc., No. 16 Ashburton Place, Boston, MA. [4 7/8" × 7 1/4"]. R/w/b American Flag. 8pp. Page 8: B/w photo "Used by permission of Life Magazine" of "General Douglas MacArthur."

DAM-56 Hail MacArthur. w.m. James Moxley and Mal Smith. Published by Nordyke Publishing Company, Hollywood, CA. 1943. R/w/b litho of an eagle, shield inscribed "NPC," geometric designs. "Victory Edition." 4pp. Page 4: Advertising.

DAM-57 MacArthur March. m. Jerry Goldsmith. Published by Dutchess Music Corporation. Sole Selling Agent: MCA Music, a division of MCA, Inc., No. 25 Deshon Drive, Melville, NY. 11746. 1977. N/c drawing of General Douglas MacArthur, MacArthur and men coming ashore. "Gregory Peck as MacArthur, A Richard D. Zanuck/David Brown Production." "Piano Solo." 6pp. Page 5: Blank. Page 6: "Gregory Peck as MacArthur, A Richard D. Zanuck/David Brown Production, Ed Flanders, Dan O'Herlihy, Written by Hal Barwood & Matthew Robbins, Music by Jerry Goldsmith, Directed by Joseph Sargent, Produced by Frank McCarthy—A Universal Picture Technicolor."

DAM-58 Don't Let MacArthur Fade Away. w.m. Lou Leaman. Published by Chas. H. Hansen Music Company, No. 119 West 57th Street, New York 19, NY. 1951. Br/w photo of Douglas A. MacArthur. 4pp. Page 4: Advertising.

DAM-59 Legionnaire (For God And Country). w. Robert Miller. m. Jules Bledsoe. Published by Aeolian Music Publishing Company, Hollywood, CA. Copyright 1942 by Jules Bledsoe. R/w/b American flag. "Respectfully Dedicated to Gen. Douglas MacArthur and all The Marching Men Of America." 6pp. Page 6: Lyrics.

See also HCH-50; FDR-46; FDR-229; FDR-396; DDE-50; DDE-68; FDR-396; FSM-1; MISC-146.

Dwight D. Eisenhower

DDE-1 Ike With Ike! (Eisenhower and Nixon). w.m. Jack Gould (ASCAP). Published by Handy Brothers Music Company, Inc., Publishers, No. 1650 Broadway, New York 19, NY. 1952. Bl/w/o drawings by Barbelle of Dwight D. Eisenhower, Richard M. Nixon, Elephant holding large placard inscribed "A Corollary to our premise of man's Dignity—If our youth, and the generations to come, clearly understand the relationship between individual effort and common good: If they perceive that our privileges and advantages in this great country, won by toil and sacrifice of generations before them, can be retained by only a comparable expenditure on their part; If they appreciate that a corollary to our premise of man's dignity is his individual responsibility to maintain it against threat; then the future of our country is secure — Dwight D. Eisenhower, Civic Responsibility Reception, St. Louis, Mo., Feb. 24, 1947." "Campaign Song." "We publish a musical setting to *Lincoln's Gettysburg Address* and *The Big Stick Blues March* dedicated to Theodore Roosevelt's Big Stick policy." 8pp. Page 2: Three photos of how to dance the *Hike With Ike*. Pages 7 and 8: Advertising.

DDE-2   The Man Of The Hour, General Eisenhower (Song). w.m. James Cavanaugh, John Redmond and Nat Simon. Published by Joe Davis Music Company, Inc., No. 1619 Broadway, New York, NY. 1943. Bl/w stars and stripes with silhouette of Dwight D. Eisenhower in Army uniform, airplanes, truck, Jeep, tank. "A Joe Davis production." 4pp. Page 4: Advertising.

DDE-3   Our President's Waltz. w. John Daifotis. m. Francis Pauly. Published by ART Music Company, P.O. Box 19662, Rimpau Station, Los Angeles 19, CA. 1956. B/w photo of Dwight D. Eisenhower. 4pp. Page 4: Headlines from ART's Tin Pan Alley Magazine.

DDE-4   For Eisenhower. w. Mary Jane Richardson. m. Mischa and Wesley Portnoff. Published by Fifty Seventh Street Music Company, No. 37 West 57th Street, New York 19, NY. 1952. O/bl cover, two music notes. Bl/w photo of Dwight Eisenhower. 4pp.

DDE-5   Look Ahead, Neighbor! w.m. Mann Holiner and Alberta Nichols. Published by The Robbins Company, No. 1619 Broadway, New York 19, NY. 1952. R/w/b flag background. B/w photo of Dwight D. Eisenhower. 4pp. Page 4: History of song title.

DDE-6   We Want Eisenhower For President (Marching Song). w.m. Mayhew Lake. Published by Sam Fox Publishing Company, RCA Building, Radio City, New York 20, NY. 1953. Bl/w photo of Dwight Eisenhower. 4pp. Page 4: Advertising.

DDE-7   We're All For Eisenhower. w.m. Captain Charles Greham Halpine, U.S. Navy (Retired). a. Musician First Class M.P. Magliano, U.S. Naval Academy Band. Published by Charles G. Halpine, No. 1 Taney Avenue, Annapolis, MD. 1952. B/w photo of Dwight D. Eisenhower. "Dedicated to General of the Army Dwight D. Eisenhower." 4pp. Page 4: Blank.

DDE-8   I Like Ike. w.m. Irving Berlin. Published by Irving Berlin Music Corporation, No. 1650 Broadway, New York 19, NY. Copyright 1950 and 1952. R/w/b streamers, stars. Bl/w photo of Dwight D. Eisenhower. 6pp. Page 6: Advertising.

DDE-9   The President Song. w.m. Ruth Roberts and William Katz. Published by Famous Music Corporation, No. 1619 Broadway, New York 19, NY. 1959. Bl/w cover with photos/drawings of all presidents from George Washington to Dwight Eisenhower. Bl/w drawing of man holding photo of Herbert Hoover. Bl/w photo of Jill Corey with photo of Franklin Roosevelt — "Recorded by Jill Corey on Columbia Records." 8pp. Pages 2 and 8: Advertising.

DDE-10   Five Star President. w.m. Peale Sisters. Published by Sunbeam Music Corporation, No. 1619 Broadway, New York, NY. 1953. Pl/w drawing of The White House, five stars. 4pp. Page 4: Advertising.

DDE-11   Dwight D. Eisenhower March. m. Dr. Gorman B. Mance. a. Malcolm Lee. Published by Grand American Freedom Rally Committee and NY State Fair, [Syracuse, NY]. 1952. [8 1/2" × 11"]. R/w/b cover. Bl/w photos of Dwight Eisenhower — "A Great American," "Dr. Gorman B. Mance, Composer-Director, National Championship American Legion Band, Syracuse Post No. 41 under the direction of Dr. Gorman B. Mance." "Dedicated to a great American, Dwight D. Eisenhower." 4pp.

(DDE) DWIGHT D. EISENHOWER

Page 2: "Dedicated at New York State Fair, Sept. 4, 1952." Page 4: Photo of Legion officials. Narrative.

DDE-12 Fore, Ike Is On The Tee. w.m. Helen F. Lengfeld. Copyright 1953 by Helen F. Lengfeld for *The Golfer* magazine and A.W.V.S. Swing Clubs. R/w/b cover. Bl/w drawing of Dwight Eisenhower. R/w photo of *The Golfer* magazine cover. "The Golfer's Song." 6pp. Pages 2 and 6: Blank.

DDE-13 Our Cue For '52 (Let's All Vote Republican). w.m. Walter E. Schneider. Published by Walter E. Schneider, No. 1 West 64th Street, New York, NY. 1952. [8 1/2" × 11"]. Bl/w drawings by C.D. Batchelor of Harry Truman holding music inscribed *Missouri Waltz*, Pendergast-Truman version," elephant holding a cue card inscribed "Cue for '52, Lets All Vote Republican," "GOP," donkey inscribed "Miss Mink." "1952 Republican Campaign Song." "Time to change the Tune." 6pp. Foldout. Page 6: Narrative.

DDE-14 Ike Is A Wonderful Man. w. Cynthia Laraway. m. William D. Barone. Copyright 1957 by William Barone. Bl/w photo of Dwight Eisenhower. 4pp. Page 4: Biographical data.

DDE-15 Go G.O.P. w. H.D. Hirsh. m. Jewel M. Frank. Published by Chappell and Company, RKO Building, New York, NY. Copyright 1952 by Wm. J. Hamilton, Jr. [4 1/2" × 6"]. R/w/b flags. Bl/w photos of "Dwight D. Eisenhower" and "Richard M. Nixon." "Victory Song." "William J. Hamilton, Jr., Chairman, Republican Central Campaign Committee, Philadelphia, Pa." 4pp. Page 4: "Presented by the Allegheny County Republican Committee as a compliment to our Republican friends at Philadelphia."

DDE-16 The Eisenhower March. w.m. Robert Stern. Published by the Bab-El-Bra Publishing Company, Laconia, NH. 1952. R/w/b drawing by G.A. Rollins of Eisenhower. 4pp. Page 4: "The Official Campaign Song of the N.H. State Republican Committee and the Connecticut Republican State Central Committee — Vote Republican! Elect Eisenhower! March on to Victory!"

DDE-17 Army Blue. w. L.W. Becklaw and others. m. George R. Poulton. Published by Shapiro, Bernstein & Company, Inc., No. 666 Fifth Avenue, New York, NY. 10019. Copyright 1911 by Carl Fischer and 1969 by Shapiro, Bernstein. B/w photo of West Point cadets. "Songs of the U.S. Military Academy." Bl/w stars. "Dedicated to the memory of General Dwight David Eisenhower, 1890-1969, 34th President of the United States of America." 4pp.

DDE-18 General Eisenhower March. m. Eddie Ballantine and Lemmy Cohen. Published by Will Rossiter, No. 173 West Madison Street, Chicago 2, IL. 1949. Non-pictorial. 6pp.

DDE-19 Ike For Four More Years. w.m. Irving Berlin. Published by Irving Berlin Music Corporation, No. 1650 Broadway, New York 19, NY. 1956. R/w/b cover. Bl/w *New York Daily News* photo of Dwight D. Eisenhower. 4pp. Page 2: Blank. Page 4: Verse.

DDE-12

DDE-20 There's Still Time Brother! w.m. Paul J. Vance and Jacob Segal. Published by Planetary Music Publishing Corporation, No. 1619 Broadway, New York, NY. Sole Selling Agent: Keys-Hansen, Inc., 119 West 57th Street, New York, NY. 1959. O/bk photo of Dwight D. Eisenhower and Nikita Khrushchev, banner inscribed "There's Still Time Brother." "Inspired by the Stanley Kramer production *On The Beach*." 4pp. Page 4: Advertising.

DDE-21 Mamie. w.m. Jimmie Dodd. Published by Shawnee Press, Inc., Delaware Water Gap, PA. Copyright 1952 and 1953. Bl/w photo of The White House. 4pp. Page 4: Advertising for Shawnee song—*Ike, Mr. President*.

DDE-22 A Prayer For General Eisenhower (And His Men). w. Alice Menaker. m. Laurence Stock. Published by Mutual Music Society, Inc., No. 1270 Sixth Avenue, New York 20, NY. 1945. R/w/bk drawing of flaming sword. B/w photo of General Dwight D. Eisenhower addressing World War II soldiers. 4pp. Page 4: Advertising for other Mutual Music Society music.

DDE-23 Eisenhower (Song Book). [1952]. [5" × 9"]. R/w/b non-pictorial lines. 13pp. 24pp. Ten songs written to popular tunes. [M-430].

DDE-24 Ike, Mr. President. w. Jack Dolph. m. Fred Waring. Published by Shawnee Press, Inc., Delaware Water Gap, PA. Copyright 1952 and 1953. Bl/w photo of The White House. 4pp. Page 4: Advertising for Shawnee the song *Mamie*.

DDE-25 Man Of The Hour. w. John Dunne. m. Charles Osborne. Copyright 1952 by John Dunne. B/w stars. "1952 Campaign Song." "A Snappy March Tune—Words That Mean Something." "Dedicated to Gen. Dwight D. Eisenhower." 4pp.

DDE-26 Dwight D. Eisenhower March. m. Paul Lavalle. Published by Stargen Music Corporation, New York, NY. Sole Agents: Sam Fox Pub. Co., RCA Building, New York, NY. Copyright 1954 and 1955. Bk/w/bl drawing of Capitol building. "Based on Dwight D. Eisenhower's initials D.D.E." "As recorded by Paul Lavalle and the Cities Service Band of America on RCA Victor album 'Paul Lavalle at Work.'" 4pp. Page 4: Advertising for Sam Fox published music.

DDE-27 Gen. Eisenhower's Triumphant March. m. Edgar Williams and P.F.C. James Hornberger. Published by Williams Publishing Company, Dover, NJ. 1947. B/w photo of James Hornberger. 6pp. Page 2: "Dedicated to Gen. Dwight D. Eisenhower." Page 6: Blank.

DDE-28 We Love The Sunshine Of Your Smile. w. Jack Hoffman. m. Jimmy MacDonald. Published by Johnstone-Montei, Inc., No. 1619 Broadway, New York, NY. 1951. Bl/w photo of Dwight D. Eisenhower. R/w/b drawing of elephant band with drum inscribed "G.O.P.," star. 4pp. Page 4: Bl/w photo of Miss Idaho presenting a copy of the record by Mark Carter and His Orchestra to Dwight D. Eisenhower.

DDE-28

DDE-29 I Go For Ike. w. Mann Curtis. m. Vic Mizzy. Published by Noteworthy Music Company, No. 146 West 54th Street, New York, NY. 1956. Bl/w photo of Dwight D. Eisenhower. R/w/b stars and stripes. "An Official Campaign Song for Citizens for Eisenhower." 4pp. Page 4: Excerpts from Eisenhower campaign speech "People and Principles."

DDE-30 Apostle Of Peace (Overture of Honor). m. Henry J. Volz, Op. 1031. Published by Educational Music Publications, Pittsburgh 28, PA. 1960. Br/be photo of Dwight D. Eisenhower. "Dedicated to Dwight D. Eisenhower — U.S.A." "Proceeds from the sale of this sheet music assigned to Heart Fund. Sponsored by Pittsburgh Junior Chamber of Commerce, Inc." 4pp. Page 4: Blank.

DDE-31 The Eisenhower Songs. R/w/b stripes. Photo of Dwight D. Eisenhower. "Ike's Second Term."

DDE-32 All For The U-S-A. m. Henry Dellafield, Op. 54, No. 6. Published by Bach Music Company, Boston, MA. 1954. R/w/b drawing of "President Dwight D. Eisenhower." "Piano Solo." 4pp. Page 2: "To Dwight D. Eisenhower, President of the United States." Page 4: *The Washington Post March* by John Philip Sousa.

DDE-33 The Eisenhower Songs. w. Bruce Cramer. Published by the Audio Center, No. 398 Trumbull Street, Hartford, CT. Copyright 1956 by Bruce Cramer. Y/bk photo of Dwight D. Eisenhower. "Ike's Second Term." 4pp. Page 4: Blank.

DDE-34 Let's O-K, I-K-E. w. Nora Bell and Irwin M. Cassel. m. Mana-Zucca. Published by Congress Music Publications, Miami, FL. 1952. Br/w/bl photo of Dwight D. Eisenhower. 4pp. Page 4: Blank.

DDE-35 Victory In '56 (Campaign Song). w.m. Meyer Davis. Published by Kelton-Romm, Inc., No. 250 West 49th Street, New York 19, NY. Copyright 1956 by Meyer Davis. Bl/w drawing of elephant holding campaign sign with drawing of Dwight D. Eisenhower. 4pp. Page 4: Bl/w drawing of treble clef symbol.

DDE-36 Hail To Eisenhower. w. Dennis Tenney. m. Catherine E. Berry. Published by Townsend Music Printers-Publishers, No. 120 West 7th Street, Kansas City 6, MO. [1952]. R/w/b drawing by A. O'Dorisio of Dwight D. Eisenhower, cheering crowd. 4pp. Page 4: "Critical Comment on Tenney's Writings."

DDE-37 We Will Win With Ike! w.m. Orrice L. Murdock. Copyright 1956 by Orrice L. Murdock, Salt Lake City, Utah. B/w photo of Dwight D. Eisenhower. "Sponsored by Utah Republican State Central Committee." 4pp. Page 4: Blank.

DDE-38 Medal Of Honor March. m. Kathryn Morton Godfrey. Published by Lupal Music Company, No. 501 Madison Avenue, New York 22, NY. 1955. Bl/w/gd photo of the Congressional Medal of Honor. 6pp. Page 3: "Respectfully Dedicated to President Dwight D. Eisenhower."

DDE-39 Mister Eisenhower (He's a Mighty Man). w.m. Henry "Hank" Ward. Published by Henry Ward, YMCA Building, Bremerton, WA. 1954. Bl/w photo of Dwight D. Eisenhower, geometric designs. Page 4: Advertising for another Henry Ward song.

DDE-40 Ike, Mr. President. w. Jack Dolph. m. Fred Waring. a. Harry Simeone. Published by Shawnee Press, Inc., Delaware Water Gap, PA. 1953. [6 3/4" × 10 1/2"]. Non-pictorial black geometric border. "Conductor Condensed Score." "Concert Band Arrangement." List of instrumentation. 12pp.

DDE-41 I Like Ike. w.m. Lilian Cohn. Published by Lilian Cohn. Samuel English, Representative, No. 1658 Broadway, New York City, NY. 1952. B/w photo of Lilian Cohn. "Full permission granted by Copyright Owners to Broadcast, Sing or Play this Song." "Donated as a patriotic contribution by Lilian Cohn." Bulk mail stamp. 4pp.

DDE-42   Dwight D. Eisenhower March. m. Paul Lavalle. Published by Stargen Music. Sole selling agents: Sam Fox Publishing Company, RCA Building, Radio City, New York, NY. 1954. [7" × 10 1/2"]. Ma/w photos "Band of America, Paul Lavelle and Conductor." "Band of America Series." Individual parts for full band. Inside: Biography of Paul Lavalle. Advertising for other music.

DDE-43   That's The Spirit Of G.O.P. w. Sam Goldberg. m. L. Leslie Loth. Published by Goldberg Music Publishers, Box 113 Cross Street, Lakewood, NJ. 1956. R/w/b drawing of an elephant, stars, shield, "Ballot inscribed Eisenhower." 4pp. Page 4: Blank.

DDE-44   General Dwight Eisenhower March. w. Andrea Litkei. m. Ervin Litkei. Published by Loena Publishing Company, No. 239 West 18th Street, New York, NY. 10011. 1965. [8 1/2" × 11"]. Bl/w photo by Fabian Bachrach of Dwight D. Eisenhower. R/w/b shield background. 4pp. Page 4: Geometric design.

DDE-45   A March To Eisenhower. w. Hiram D. Hirsh. m. Jewell M. Frank. Published by Chappell and Company, Inc., RKO Building, Rockefeller Center, New York, NY. 1953. B/w photo of Dwight D. Eisenhower. R/w/b drawing of flag, The White House. "Souvenir of Inauguration 1953." [VI: 4pp. Page 4: Blank] [V-2: Band parts].

DDE-46   The White House Waltz. w.m. Mildred Hoyt. Published by Chappell and Company, RKO Building, New York 20, NY. 1956. Bl/bk/w nonpictorial geometric designs. 6pp. Page 2: Blank. Page 6: Advertising for other music.

DDE-47   Ike Will Lead The Way (March). w.m. Gale Will Callinan. Published by Gale W. Callinan, No. 620 Eddy Street, San Francisco, CA. 1956. R/w/b drawing of Uncle Sam with bugle. 6pp. Pages 6: Blank.

DDE-48   They Like Ike. w.m. Irving Berlin. Published by Irving Berlin Music Corporation, No. 1650 Broadway, New York 19, NY. 1950. R/w/bk/gy drawing by Peter Arno of Ethel Merman. "A New Musical, Leland Hayward presents Ethel Merman in *Call Me Madam* with Paul Lukas; Lyrics and Music by Irving Berlin, Book by Howard Lindsay and Russel Crouse, Directed by George Abbott, Dances and Musical Numbers Staged by Jerome Robbins." List of other songs in show. 8pp. Page 2: Blank. Page 8: Advertising for other songs from show.

DDE-49   General Ike March. m. Arsene Siegel. Published by McKinley Publishers, Inc., No. 797 Eight Avenue, New York, NY. [195-]. Drawing of 5 stars. "Respectfully Dedicated to General Dwight D. Eisenhower." "No. 2517." Advertising for other marches by McKinley Publishers including *General Grant's Grand March* by Mack.

DDE-50   Hold Firm The American Way. w.m. Clarence E. Cunningham. Published by Mountain States Music Company, Somers, MT. 1952. R/w/b drawings of George Washington — "Put none but Americans on guard tonight," Abraham Lincoln — "If danger ever reaches us, it must spring up amongst us," Theodore Roosevelt — "The man who debauches our public life is a foe to our nation," Douglas MacArthur — "Above all else let us regain our faith in ourselves and rededicated all that is within us to the repair and preservation of our free institutions," eagle, ribbon inscribed "For the boys who died for you, for the living and the unborn too." 4pp. Page 4: Bl/w photo of Dwight D. Eisenhower — "Hold Firm the American Way." Ike quote. Pledge to Vote.

DDE-51   Eisenhower. w.m. Vic Knight. Published by Forster Music,

Music Publishers, No. 216 South Wabash Avenue, Publisher, Chicago, IL. 1945. Gn/br/w photo of Eddie Cantor—"Introduced and Featured by Eddie Cantor." 6pp. Pages 2 and 6: Advertising.

DDE-52   Out Of The Wilderness With Ike. w. Kenneth R. Barnum. Published by Townsend Music Printers, No. 120 West 7th Street, Kansas City 6, MO. 1952. B/w photo of "Dwight D. Eisenhower." R/w/b drawings of George "Washington," Abraham "Lincoln," Thomas "Jefferson," "Teddy Roosevelt." "Ask for Damon Record No. 12094." 4pp. Page 4: Other Eisenhower song—**Get Ike**. w.m. Kenneth R. Barnum.

DDE-53   Eisenhower March. w.m. Irving Hamilton. Published by Sweet Music, Inc., No. 6087 Sunset Boulevard, Hollywood 28, CA. 1952? Bk/w/bl drawing by Bruce Russell of Dwight D. Eisenhower. 4pp.

DDE-54   Go G.O.P. w. Hiram D. Hirsh. m. Jewel M. Frank. Published by Chappell and Company, Inc., RKO Building, New York, NY. 1952. Bl/w photo of "Hon. John S. Fine, Pennsylvania's great Governor." R/w/b elephant. 4pp. Page 4: Blank. [1952 Republican National Convention song].

DDE-55   We Want Ike. w.m. Arthur Herbert, Dan Michaud and Bob Ecton. Copyright 1952 by Herb-Mor Music Publishing Company, No. 6000 Sunset Boulevard, Hollywood 28, CA. Bl/w photo of Dwight D. Eisenhower. Bl/w drawing of U.S. map. 4pp. Page 4: "Autographs."

DDE-56   Hike With Ike! w.m. Jack Gould (ASCAP). Published by The Abilene Music Company, No. 342 Madison Avenue, New York 17, NY. Copyright 1943 and 1947 by Jack Gould. [5 1/2" × 8 3/8"]. B/w photo of Dwight D. Eisenhower. "Put Him In The White House." "If this song appeals to you and you feel you or your friends can use more copies of it as campaign material, please contact the publisher for quantity prices." 2pp. Page 2: Blank.

DDE-57   Salute To Eisenhower (Song Sheet). [1953-1960]. [9" × 12"]. R/w/b stars. First song printed on page one—**Thanks, Mr. President**. w. Jack Dolph. m. Fred Waring. 2pp. Page 2: Four additional songs.

DDE-58   Republicans—Our Country Needs You. w.m. Vincent de Paul. Copyright 1952 by DePaul Publications, No. 804 Genessee Bank Building, Flint 3, MI. [9" × 12"]. Drawing of elephant. 4pp.

DDE-59   We Love The Sunshine Of Your Smile. w. Jack Hoffman. m. Jim MacDonald. Published by Hal Leonard Music, Inc., No. 64 East Second, Winona, MN. Copyright 1951 by Jonstone-Montel, Inc. [5 1/2" × 7 1/8"]. B/w photo of Dwight D. Eisenhower. Bl/w drawing of elephants. "Hal Leonard Publication for Band." Full band parts with insert of marching instructions.

DDE-60   Ike For Four More Years. w.m. Irving Berlin. Published by Irving Berlin, No. 1650 Broadway, New York, NY. 1956. Non-pictorial black border. "Four more years, four more years, Give us what we'd like, What we'd like is Ike, For four more years—Three cheers with Ike for four more years." 2pp. Page 2: Music.

DDE-61   Get Ike. w.m. Kenneth R. Barnum. Published by Townsend Music Printers, No. 120 West 7th Street, Kansas City 6, MO. 1952. B/w photo of Dwight D. Eisenhower. R/w/b stars and stripes. "Ask for Damon Record No. 12094." 4pp. Page 4: Other Eisenhower song — **Out Of The Wilderness With Ike**. w.m. Kenneth R. Barnum.

DDE-62   Eisenhower (The Man of the Hour). w.m. Delphia Dorothy Mann. Copyright 1952 by Delphia Dorothy Mann, No. 5919 Pershing Avenue, St. Louis, MO. Distributed by Shattinger, St. Louis, MO. Bl/w photo of Dwight D. Eisenhower. R/w/b stars and stripes. 4pp. Page 4: Blank.

DDE-63   Ike's The Man. w.m. Elvira Stolz. Published by Elvira A. Stolz, No. 21411 Waldron Road, Farmington, MI. 1952. Br/w photo of [V-1: Dwight D. Eisenhower] [V-2: Elvira Stolz]. R/w/b drawing of ballot marked inscribed "Eisenhower," five stars, stripes. 4pp. Page 4: Blank.

DDE-64   Three Cheers For General Ike (Patriotic Song). w.m. Fred C. Bernhardt. Published by Fred C. Bernhardt, Caldwell, NJ. [ca. 1952]. [8 1/4" × 10 1/2"]. B/w photo of General Dwight D. Eisenhower. B/w drawing of U.S. flag, musical notes, geometric designs. 4pp. Page 4: "Note—A short biography of General Ike will be written on this page of the regular copies—Fred C. Bernhardt [facsimile signature]."

DDE-65   When The Boys Come Marching Home. w.m. Eddie Foley (Canada's leading songwriter Honored by Gen. Eisenhower). Published by Edward M. Foley, No. 373 Waverleigh Boulevard, Toronto, Canada. 1943. B/w drawing of soldier, sailor, W.A.C. "The song that all America is now singing, whistling and humming; and the Sweetest Song of the century with a Haunting Melody." "With the Lovely Chorus for the Million Dollar Hit Song." "Easily Eddie Foley's crowning achievement." 6pp. Page 2: Blank. Page 6: Advertising.

DDE-66   Eisenhower (The Man of the Hour). w.m. Ev Garvey and John Finnerty. Copyright 1943 by Ev Garvey and John Finnerty. Bl/w litho of U.S. flag, geometric designs. "As introduced in the LaPointe Employees' Production *Swing to Victory*, June, 8, 9, 10, 1943." 6pp. Page 6: Blank.

DDE-67   Good Evening, Mr. President. w.m. J.H. Van Allen (Rhode Island). Published by Domino Music, Inc., No. 1674 Broadway, New York 19, NY. 1953. [9" × 11 7/8"]. Non-pictorial geometric designs. "Respectfully Dedi-

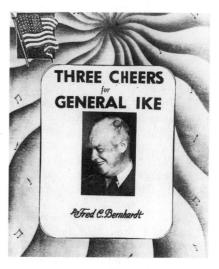

DDE-64

cated to Dwight D. Eisenhower." "Introduced at the Inaugural Ball, Jan. 20, 1953 by Emil Coleman and His Orchestra and Played at the New England 'Forward to '54 Dinner for President Eisenhower." 4pp.

DDE-68   Song Of Heroes. w. Nahum Ben-Horim. m. Jacob Weinburg. Published by National Book Company, No. 505 Fifth Avenue, New York 17, NY. 1944. R/w/bl/pl photos of General Dwight D. Eisenhower, Douglas MacArthur, soldiers, W.A.C., W.A.V.E.—"These Are Our Heroes." "Dedicated to the Gallant Warriors of America." 6pp. Page 6: Advertising.

DDE-69   Take Good Care Of My Heart (IKE's Waltz). w.a. F. Geary Anderson. m. "Adaptation from an old European gypsy air." Published by F.G. Anderson, No. 1015 MacArthur Boulevard, Oakland 10, CA. 1956. Non-pictorial black border. 4pp. Page 4: Song—*A Cross Across a Cross-Road*.

DDE-70   Hail To The Nations United. w.m. Henry Stern. Published by The Songwriters League, Cleveland, OH. Copyright 1955 by Henry Stern. Bl/y/w drawing of soldiers fighting throughout the ages, climbing hill of war—"Ancient wars," "Crusades," "War 1812," "War 1898," "War 1914," "War 1941." Summit labeled—"International Peace." 4pp. Page 2: "Introductory Address" on war, cold war, President Eisenhower and Atoms For Peace.

DDE-71 General Dwight D. Eisenhower March. w. Andrea Fodor Litkei. m. Ervin Litkei. In: *A Tribute To The U.S.A.*, page 8. Published by Loena Music Publishing Company No. 239 West 18th Street, New York, NY. 10011. Copyright 1985 and 1986. N/c drawing by Edward Moran of Statue of Liberty celebration in 1886—"The Statue of Liberty, standing as an eternal symbol of the friendship of the people of France, was presented to the United States in 1886 by its creator, Frederick Bartholdi." Quotes by "Emma Lazarus (1883)," and "President Grover Cleveland (1886)."

DDE-72 Ike, Mr. President. w. Jack Dolph. m. Fred Waring. Published by Shawnee Press, Inc., Delaware Water Gap, PA. 1953. Non-pictorial. "Professional Copy." 4pp. Page 4: Blank.

DDE-73 Mamie. w.m. Jimmy Dodd. Published by Shawnee Press, Inc., Delaware Water Gap, PA. 1952. Non-pictorial "Professional Copy." 4pp. Pages 1 and 4: Blank.

DDE-74 Mamie And Ike. w.m. Meyer Davis. Published by Meyer Davis, No. 119 West 57th Street, New York, NY. 1957. Bl/w photo of President and Mrs. Dwight D. Eisenhower, star border. "Introduced by Meyer Davis and His Orchestra at President Eisenhower's 2nd Inaugural Ball, January 21st, 1957." 4pp. Page 2: Bl/w drawing of Eisenhower at top of music. Page 4: Bl/w photo of Meyer Davis. "President Eisenhower's Second Inaugural Ball is the Sixth Presidential Inaugural Ball played by Meyer Davis and His Orchestra."

DDE-75 Lets Fight For Ike. w.m. Madge Taft. Published by Nordyke Music Publications, Hollywood, CA. 1958. Released by Nordyke, 1960. Drawing of Uncle Sam. 4pp. Page 4: Advertising.

DDE-76 General Dwight D. Eisenhower March. w. Andrea Litkei. m. Ervin Litkei. In: *The Bicentennial March and Presidential Marches of America*, page 24. Published by Loena Music Publishing Company, New York, NY. 1976. R/w/b drawings of George Washington, Thomas Jefferson, Abraham Lincoln, eagle and flags. "American Revolution Bicentennial, 1776-1976." "Officially Recognized Commorative." 40pp.

DDE-77 The Nation Of The People. w.m. Monte Carlo and Alma Sanders. 1955. [8 1/2" × 5 1/2"]. Non-pictorial. "Sung by Charles Simpson, Baritone, Accompanist: Jo Ann Shorch, Houston Lutheran Chorus." 2pp. Page 2: Blank.

DDE-78 A Prayer For General Eisenhower And His Men. w. Alice Menaker. m. Lawrence Stock. Published by Murual Music Society, Inc., No. 1270 Sixth Avenue, New York, NY. 1945. Non-pictorial "Advance Artist Copy." Prayer composed to the letters in "E-I-S-E-N-H-O-W-E-R"—"E'ternal Father, God on High; In Thy Heaven beyond the sky; Stand beside us with Thy might; Ever ours in Thy fight; Never loosing faith in Thee; Help us, Lord, win victory; Once more Thy would make this to be; Weld it strong in liberty; Each man forever free to stand; Rest we this prayer, Lord in Thy hand, amen." 4pp. Page 4: Advertising.

DDE-79 Get On Your Bike And Hike For Ike! w.m. George Glasco and Rosa Donaldson. Published by Sunshine Music Publishing Company, Philadelphia, PA. Sole Selling Agents: David's Ditties, 250 South Broad Street, Philadelphia, PA. 1952. B/w photo of "Dwight D. Eisenhower." B/w drawings of Soldier, Sailor, Airman, Marine, couple kissing. "Sole Selling Agents: David's Ditties, 230 South Broad Street, Philadelphia." 4pp. Page 4: B/w photos of six African-Americans involved in "An

147   DWIGHT D. EISENHOWER (DDE)

DDE-79

Atomic Dramatic Recitation" also composed by Glasco and Rosa Donaldson.

DDE-80   Marching With Ike. w.m. Viola P. Brown. Published by WSAY Artist Bureau, Rochester, NY. 1952. Bl/w photo of Dwight D. Eisenhower. R/w cover. 6pp. Page 2: "Three Fundamental Principles of American Life by Gen. Eisenhower." Page 6: Blank.

DDE-81   We Like Ike's Leadership. w. John Daifotis. m. Francis Pauly. Published by Art Music, 1279 Queen Anne Place, Los Angeles, CA. 1956. Bl/w photos of Dwight Eisenhower and Richard Nixon. 4pp. Page 4: Facsimile letter on Ike's 10 great achievements as President. "For Peace — Prosperity — Progress, Vote For Ike."

DDE-82   Eisenhower Centennial (Concert March). m. James Banes. Published by Southern Music, San Antonio, TX. 1991. Br/w photo "courtesy of Eisenhower Library" of Gen. Dwight Eisenhower. Band Set. Page 2: "Commissioned to all my friends in the 312th U.S. Army Reserve Band."

DDE-83   Aurora March. m. Josef Kaartinen. Copyright by Josef Kaartinen, Helsinki, Finland, 1961. Bl/y/w drawing by Koski of clouds, sunburst. "President Eisenhower's Book — *Crusade In Europe*— inspired the Composer to compose *The Aurora March*." 4pp. Page 2: "Dedicated to President Dwight David

DDE-80

DDE-81

(DDE) DWIGHT D. EISENHOWER   148

Eisenhower, The Greatest Soldier of Modern Times."

DDE-84   Funeral Service For The Honorable Dwight David Eisenhower 1890-1969 [Program Booklet with Songs]. Published by Washington Cathedral, Washington, DC. 1969. [6" × 9"]. Non-pictorial black border. "Monday, March Thirty-first A.D. 1969, Four-thirty o'clock in the afternoon." 8pp. Page 8: Blank.

DDE-85   The First Lady Waltz. w. Betty Comden and Adolph Green. m. Jule Styne. Published by Stratford Music Corporation: Sole Selling Agent: Chappell and Company, Inc., No. 609 Fifth Avenue, New York, NY. 1960. R/w/b drawing of U.S. Capitol building, couples dancing. 6pp. Page 2: Blank. Page 3: "Dedicated to President and Mrs. Eisenhower." Page 6: Advertising.

DDE-86   New New Republicans. w. J.J. Morris. m. Phil Methot. Copyright 1952 by Better Ideas, Inc. R/w/b drawing of elephant with flag. "The Republican March." "The Greatest Song on Earth for God-Country-Fellowman." 4pp. Page 4: Bl/w statue of Abraham Lincoln—"Citizenship My Heritage." Lincoln quote.

DDE-87   Hike With Ike (And Betsy Gay On To Washington) (The Eisenhower March). w.m. J.J. Morris and Helen Gay. Copyright 1952 by Better Ideas, Inc. Bl/w photo of Betsy Gay. R/w/b drawing of two flags. 4pp. Page 4: R/w/b sign advertising music—"Eisenhower The Coordinator," "Voice Your Freedom With Your Vote," "*New New Republicans*, The Greatest Song on Earth For God-County-Fellowman."

DDE-88   It's Got To Be G.O.P. [Song and Song Book]. w.m. Delos Owen. In: *It's Got To Be G.O.P.* [Handmade booklet containing a proposed campaign for the G.O.P. in 1952]. Self published by Delos Owen, No. 215 East Chestnut Street, Chicago 11, IL. 1952. 64pp. Page 13: Song. Page 27-49: Song Book.

DDE-89   Song To Eisenhower. w.m. James Russell Fuller. Published by Clifford and Fuller, Haverhill, MA. 1956. B/w photo of Dwight D. Eisenhower. 4pp.

DDE-90   General Dwight Eisenhower March. e. Andrea and Ervin Litkei. In: *The President's March and Other Songs of the Lone Star State*, page 6. Published by Loena Music Publishing Company, No. 239 West 18th Street, New York, NY. 10011. [ca. 1964]. R/w/bl/bk cover, Presidential seal. "Featuring *President Lyndon Baines Johnson March* and other songs of the Lone Star State." "Pacific Popular Music Books." 36pp. Page 2: Photos of Lyndon Johnson and A. Litkei. Page 35: Photo of Inaugural parade. Page 36: Photo of Lyndon Johnson. Drawings of all presidents.

DDE-91   Keep Ike. w.m. Kenneth R. Barnum. Copyright by Kenneth R. Barnum, No. 1001 Linwood Boulevard, Kansas City, MO. [ca. 1956]. Non-pictorial "Professional Copy—Not To Be Sold." "B.M.I." 2pp. Page 2: Blank.

DDE-92   [Untitled Song For Eisenhower And Nixon]. w. Jackson County Republican Committee. m. "New words for Campaign Song—Either *Eisenhower March* or *Come, On Americans*." Published by Jackson County Republican Committee, Campaign Headquarters, No. 1014 Grand Avenue, Kansas City, MO. [1952]. [8 1/2" × 11"]. Non-pictorial. On Jackson County Republican Committee letterhead. 2pp. Page 2: Blank.

DDE-93   I Like Ike. w. Georgia T. Smith. m. Mack David. [1952]. [8 1/2" × 11"]. Non-pictorial. 2pp. Page 2: Blank.

DDE-94   (We Want) Eisenhower For President. w.m. Mrs. David Levy, 3 Niles Park, Hartford, CT. Copyright 1952. [8 1/2" × 11"]. Bl/w drawing of Dwight D. Eisenhower. Handwritten note—"Corrected Copy of Proof Copy Sent to You Sept. 19th." 4pp. Page 4: Blank.

DDE-95 I Like Ike [Song Pamphlet]. [1952]. [8 9/16" × 5 1/2"]. Non-pictorial. 5pp. [5 stapled songs as handout].

DDE-96 The Inauguration March. m. King W. Baker. Published by King W. Baker, Rumsey, KY. 1952. Photo of Capitol dome. "Dedicated to President Dwight D. Eisenhower." 4pp.

DDE-97 Ike, Mr. President. [w. Jack Dolph]. m. Fred Waring. Published by National Citizens For Eisenhower Congressional Committee. [1953]. [4 1/2" × 6 1/2"]. 2pp. Page 2: Blank.

DDE-98 United Republican Dinner [Program and Song Sheet]. Published by United Republicans of Illinois. [8 1/2" × 11"]. 1958. R/w/b drawing of elephant—"1958." International Amphitheater, Chicago, January 20, 1958. 8pp. Page 8: Patriotic Songs.

DDE-99 'E' Day (Elect Eisenhower). w.m. Frank B. Sohl. a. Bil Doar. Published for the Nassau County Republican Committee. [1952]. [8 11/16" × 11"]. B/w photo of "Dwight D. Eisenhower." B/w drawing of eagle, flag, stripes. "Campaign Song of the G.O.P." "Russel Sprague [facsimile signature], Leader." "William D. Meisser [facsimile signature], Chairman." 4pp. Page 4: Blank.

DDE-100 Young Blood Of The G.O.P. w.m. Patrick Killikelly. Published by Nassau County Republican Committee and Nassau Republican Recruits. [1956?]. Photo of "Dwight D. Eisenhower." Drawing of flag, eagle, stripes. 6pp. Page 2: Narrative—"The Republican Recruits." Page 6: Song lyrics. Narrative—"How Songs Are Made."

DDE-101 This Is Our America. w.m. R. Stephenson. Published by R. Stephenson, No. 1621 Federal Street, Pittsburgh 12, PA. 1953. R/w/b drawings of soldiers, flag, Statue of Liberty, five stars, U.S. map. Page 2: "Dedicated to President Ike Eisenhower and our Brave Soldiers." Page 4: Blank.

DDE-102 They Like Ike. w.m. Irving Berlin. Published by Irving Berlin, LTD, No. 14 George Street, London, England. 1950. R/w/gy non-pictorial. "From Jack Hylton's Production at the London Coliseum, Billie Worth, Anton Walbrook in *Call Me Madam* with Jeff Warren, Donald Burr, Shani Wallis, Lyrics and Music by Irving Berlin, Book by Howard Lindsay and Russel Crouse." List of other songs in show. 6pp. Page 2: Blank. Page 6: Advertising.

DDE-103 Songs For Republican Rallies. Published by Republican Women In Industry & Professions, No. 270 Park Avenue, Building C, Room 613, New York, NY. [ca. 1956]. [3 11/16" × 7 15/16"]. B/w drawing of an elephant with initials "R-W-I-P" and banner inscribed "Republican Women In Industry & Professions." 4pp. [M-431].

DDE-104 Get Ike. w.m. Kenneth R. Barnum, Published by Kenneth R. Barnum, No. 926 McGee, Kansas City, MO. November 21st, 1947. [8 1/2" × 11"]. Non-pictorial. "Not written for profit. May be used anywhere anytime, without tax." 2pp. Page 2: Blank.

DDE-105 Five Stars Are Shining. w.m. Earl L. Cline. Published by Ohio School of Salesa, Box 401, Dover, OH. 1952. R/w/b drawing of The White House, Army officer's hat, five stars. 4pp. Page 4: Blank.

DDE-106 Tell Eisenhower. Published by Souvenir Songs, P.O.B. 1725, Hollywood 28, CA. [ca. 197-].

DDE-107 Vote For Eisenhower. w.m. Halbert W. Hoard. Copyright 1952 by Halbert W. Hoard, 1304 E. Goodrich Lane, Milwaukee, WI. [8 1/2" × 11"]. B/w photo of Dwight D. Eisenhower labled "This is Eisenhower Year." B/w geometric designs. 4pp. Page 4: Blank.

DDE-108 We Want Ike! (Campaign Chant). w.m. Arrety "Rusty" Keefer and L. Ray Fowler. Copyright 1956 by Valley Brook Publications, Inc., No. 112 East 5th Street, Chester, PA. [8" × 10

(DW) DANIEL WEBSTER

1/4"]. 2pp. [Inscribed in ink: "To Tex Gentry, with best wishes, Sat., May 5, '56, L. Ray Fowler"]. [Eisenhower campaign stamp affixed to page one].

DDE-109 (Let's Make It) Unanimous. w.m. Arrety "Rusty' Keefer and L. Ray Fowler. Copyright 1956 by Valley Brook Publications, Inc., No. 112 East 5th Street, Chester, PA. [8" × 10 1/4"]. 2pp. [Inscribed in ink: "To Tex Gentry, with best wishes, Sat., May 5, '56, L. Ray Fowler"]. [Eisenhower campaign stamp affixed to page one].

DDE-110 Get Out And Fight For Ike. w.m. Irma Pepper. Published by Top Tunes. 1952. Bl/w photo of Dwight D. Eisenhower. Bl/w musical notes, geometric designs.

DDE-111 Three Cheers For President Ike. w.m. Fred C. Bernhardt. Published by Star Music, No. 153 Jackson Avenue, Jersey City, NJ. [1956]. [8" × 11"]. B/w photo of Dwight D. Eisenhower. "Photo offset from original manuscript, copyright by Fred C. Bernhardt." 2pp. Page 2 blank.

See also AL-308; FDR-46; AS-9; LBJ-1; RMN-39.

DANIEL WEBSTER

DW-1 Funeral March (In Honor of Daniel Webster). m. Ludwig Von Beethoven. Published by Oliver Ditson, No. 115 Washington Street, Boston, MA. 1861. B/w litho by J.H. Bufford's Litho. of Daniel Webster. [V-1: "Dedicated To the Memory of The Illustrious Patriot and Statesman Daniel Webster"] [V-2: Same but without "Dedicated"]. [V-1: 6pp. Pages 2, 3 and 6: Blank] [V-2: 4pp. Page 4: Blank].

DW-2 Funeral March (In Honor of Daniel Webster). m. Ludwig Von Beethoven. Published by Oliver Ditson & Company, No. 451 Washington Street, Boston, MA. 1861. B/w litho by J.H. Bufford's Sons of Daniel Webster, leaves. "Performed at the obsequies of the Hon. Daniel Webster." 4pp. Page 4: Blank.

DW-3 Funeral March (In Honor of Daniel Webster). m. Ludwig Von Beethoven. Published by Oliver Ditson & Company, Washington Street, Boston, MA. 1861. B/w litho by J.H. Bufford's Litho. of Daniel Webster. "Performed at the obsequies of the Hon. Daniel Webster." 4pp. Page 4: Blank.

DW-4 Webster's Quick Step. m. George Hews. Published by [V-1: Firth, Pond & Company] [V-2: Firth & Hall], No. 1 Franklin Square, New York, NY. [ca. 1849?]. Non-pictorial. "Composed & Arranged for the Piano Forte." [V-1: Number "2243" at bottom of page 2]. 4pp. Page 1 and 4: Blank.

DW-5 Webster's Grand March. m. B. Reiss. Published by the Author, Washington, DC., and for sale by George Willig, Jr., Baltimore, MD. 1842. Non-pictorial. "Composed & respectfully dedicated (by permission) to the Hon. Daniel Webster, Secretary of State." 4pp. Pages 1 and 4: Blank.

DW-6 Webster's Quick Step. m. George Hews. [V-1: Published by Oliver Ditson, No. 115 Washington Street, Boston, MA] [V-2: No publisher indicated]. [ca. 1849?]. Non-pictorial. "Composed and Arranged for the Piano Forte." 4pp. Page 1 and 4: Blank.

DW-7 Webster's Quick Step. m. George Hews. Published at Atwill's Music Saloon, No. 201 Broadway, New York, NY. [ca. 1849?]. Non-pictorial. "Composed and Arranged for the Piano Forte." 4pp. Page 1 and 4: Blank.

DW-8 Funeral March (In Honor of Daniel Webster). m. Ludwig Von Beethoven. Published by Oliver Ditson, No. 115 Washington Street, Boston, MA. [1861]. B/w litho by Bufford's of Daniel Webster, facsimile signature. [No title or publisher listed on cover]. 4pp. Page 4: Blank.

DW-9 Webster's Quick Step. m. George Hews. Published by C. Bradlee, [V-1: No. 135 Washington Street] [V-2: Washington Street], Philadelphia, PA.

[1834-1840]. Non-pictorial geometric designs. "Composed for the Piano Forte." 4pp. Pages 1 and 4: Blank.

DW-10 Webster's Quickstep. George Hews. Published by C. Bradlee, No. 164 Washington Street, Boston, MA. [ca. 1841]. Non-pictorial. "Composed and Respectfully Dedicated to Mrs. Jonathan Hunt." 4pp. Pages 1 and 4: Blank.

DW-11 Webster's Quick Step. m. George Hews. Published by G.E. Blake, No. 13 South Fifth Street, Philadelphia, PA. [1826- 1841]. Non-pictorial geometric designs. "Composed and Arranged for the Piano Forte." 4pp. Pages 1 and 4: Blank.

DW-12 Webster's Quick Step. Published by George Willig, No. 171 Chesnut Street, Philadelphia, PA. [ca. 185-]. Non-pictorial. "Evenings At Home, A Collection of Popular and Esteemed Airs Arranged as Duetts for Two Performers on the Piano Forte." List of other titles in the series.

DW-13 Washington's Tomb (An Ode to the Memory of Washington). w. Mrs. L.H. Sigourney. m. Henry Russell. Published by James L. Hewitt & Company, No. 239 Broadway, New York, NY. 1837. Non-pictorial. "The Music Composed & most Respectfully dedicated to the Hon. Daniel Webster." 6[?]pp. Page 2: Blank.

DW-14 Webster's Grand March & Quick Step. Published by James L. Hewitt & Company, at their Music Saloon, No. 36 Market Street, Boston, MA. [ca. 1840]. Non-pictorial lines. "As performed by the Boston Bands, Arranged for the Piano Forte." 4pp. Pages 1 and 4: Blank.

DW-15 Webster's Funeral March. m. "Air from Beethoven." Published by Oliver Ditson Company, Boston, MA. 1908 edition. O/w/gn floral drawings. "Popular Marches for the Piano." List of other marches in Series III.

DW-16(A) Webster's Funeral [March]. m. Beethoven. Published by S.T. Gordon, No. 538 Broadway, New York, NY. [186-]. Non-pictorial geometric designs. "Camp Favorites, A Collection of Marches and Quicksteps by Various Authors." List of other titles in the series.

(B) Webster's [Quick Step]. m. George Hews.

DW-17 Two Funeral Marches. Published by Oliver Ditson, No. 115 Washington Street, Boston, MA. 1852. B/w litho by J.H. Bufford's Litho. of Daniel Webster, black line border. "In Memoriam." "Performed at the obsequies of the Hon. Daniel Webster." 6pp. Pages 2 and 6: Blank. Page 3: **Funeral March**. m. William C. Glynn. Page 4: **A Dirge**. m. Pleyel.

DW-18 The Minstrel's Return From The War. a. W.R. Coppock. Published by Firth & Hall, No. 1 Franklin Square, New York, NY. 1837. Non-pictorial. "A Favorite Air Arranged as a Rondo for the Piano Forte and Dedicated to Miss Julia Webster." "No. 6 of 12 Airs." 4pp. Page 4: Blank.

DW-19 Webster's Quickstep. m. George Hews. Published by Oliver Ditson & Company, No. 277 Washington Street, Boston, MA. [ca. 1855]. Non-pictorial geometric designs. "Drawing Room Gems, A Collection of Popular Marches, Waltzes, Polkas, Galops, &c." [V-1: Series begins with *Arnold's (Gov) March*] [V-2: Series begins with *Agawam Quickstep*]. List of other titles in the series.

DW-20 Thank God, I Am An American (Song). w.m. Rollin C. Ward. Published by R.C. Ward, No. 1641 Indianola Avenue, Columbus, OH. 1917. Non-pictorial geometric designs. "Immortal words of Daniel Webster." "Song with Piano Accompaniment." "Also Arranged for Male Voices." 4pp. Page 4: Arrangement for "Male Voices."

DW-21 Webster's Quick Step. m. George Hews. Published by [V-1: G. Willig Jr.] [V-2: John Cole], Baltimore,

MD. [ca. 1850]. Non-pictorial. "Composed & Arranged for the Piano Forte." Number "787" at bottom of page three. 4pp. Pages 1 and 4: Blank.

DW-22 Webster's Quick Step. m. G. Hews. [ca. 184-]. Non-pictorial. Page marked "47." 2pp. Page 2: "The Separation" by Charles Jarvis. Page marked "48."

DW-23 Webster's Quick Step. [George Hews]. Published by George P. Reed, No. 17 Tremont Row, Boston, MA. [184-]. Non-pictorial. "Composed for the Piano Forte for the use of Juvenile Performers." Number "70" at bottom of page three. 4pp. Pages 1 and 4: Blank.

DW-24 Webster's Funeral March And Dead March In Saul. Published by Henry Tolman & Company, No. 291 Washington Street, Boston, MA. [ca. 1850]. Non-pictorial geometric design border. "Echoes from the Camp, A Collection of Popular Marches and Quicksteps by Various Authors." List of other titles in series.

DW-25 Webster's Quick Step. m. George Hews. Published by George Willig, No. 171 Chesnut Street, Philadelphia, PA. [ca. 184-]. Non-pictorial. "Composed & Arranged for the Piano Forte." 4pp. Pages 1 and 4: Blank.

DW-26 Webster's Funeral March. m. Ludwig Von Beethoven. [185-]. [8 7/8" × 11 3/8"]. Non-pictorial. "School for the Reed-Organ and Melodeon." Page number "56." 2pp.

DW-27 Webster's Quick Step. m. George Hews. In: *Twelve Popular Quick Steps for the Piano Forte*, page 2. Published by E. Ferrett & Company, No. 68 South Fourth Street, Philadelphia, PA. 1845. Non-pictorial. Listing of quicksteps included. 12pp.

DW-28 Webster's Quick Step. m. George Hews. Published by Millets Music Saloon, No. 375 Broadway, New York, NY. [ca. 1840?]. Non-pictorial. 4pp. Page 4: Blank.

DW-29 Boundary Quick Step. m. T. Bricher. Published by Oliver Ditson, No. 135 Washington Street, Boston, MA. 1842. Non-pictorial geometric designs. "Dedicated to the Hon. Daniel Webster." 4pp. Pages 1 and 4: Blank.

DW-30 Webster's Funeral March. m. Beethoven. Published by D.S. Holmes, No. 67 Fourth Street, Brooklyn, NY. [ca. 1860]. Non-pictorial geometric designs. "Lilies & Violets, A Collection of Popular Melodies by Favorite Composers." List of other titles in series.

DW-31 Union Grand March. m. John Holloway. Published by E.H. Wade, No. 197 Washington Street, Boston, MA. 1851. B/w litho by Tappan & Bradford of Daniel Webster, geometric designs. "As played by the Boston Brigade Band, Composed and Respectfully Dedicated to Hon. Daniel Webster." 6pp. Pages 2 and 6: Blank.

DW-32 Webster's Quick Step. m. George Hews. Published by Keith and Moore, Nos. 67 & 69 Court Street, Boston, MA. [ca. 1850]. Non-pictorial. "Composed for the Piano Forte." Number "13" at bottom of page three. 4pp. Pages 1 and 4: Blank.

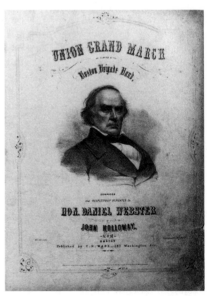

DW-31

DW-33 Webster's Grand March. m. J.C. Beckel. Published by Osbourn's Music Saloon, No. 30 South Fourth Street, Philadelphia, PA. [ca. 184-]. Y/bk non-pictorial. "Composed and respectfully Dedicated to William Morgan, Esqr." Number "79" at bottom of page three. Counter stamp: "G.T. Geslain's Music Store, 357 Broadway, N.Y." 4pp. Pages 1 and 4: Blank.

DW-34 Webster's Funeral March. m. Beethoven. In: *White's School For The Reed Organ, Containing A Full And Comprehensive Method of Instruction*, page 56. e. G.A. White and Chas. D. Blake. Published by White-Smith Music Publishing Company, Boston, MA. 1875. [11 1/2" × 9 1/4"]. B/w litho of a reed organ, geometric designs. Hard cover. 160pp.

DW-35 The Union Forever (A Patriotic Song). a. John H. Hewitt. Published by A. Fiot, No. 196 Chesnut Street, Philadelphia, PA. 1850. B/w stars. "A Patriotic Song Written, Adapted to a Melody From Lucia di Lammermoor and Dedicated to the Hon. Daniel Webster." 6pp. Pages 2 and 6: Blank.

DW-36 Webster's Quickstep. m. C. Hews. In: *Twelve Popular Quick Steps, for the Piano Forte*, page 2. Published by E. Ferrett & Co., No. 68 South Fourth Street, Philadelphia, PA. 1845. Non-pictorial. 14pp.

See also USG-200; WM-31.

DE WITT CLINTON

DWC-1 His Excellency Governor Clinton's Grand March And Quick Step. m. James H. Swindells. [V-1: Published by Geib & Company, No. 23 Maiden Lane, New York, NY. 1817?] [V-2: Published by Geib & Walker, No. 23 Maiden Lane, New York, NY. 1829-1843]. Non-pictorial. 4pp. Page 4: Blank. [W-9181].

DWC-2 Governor Dewitt Clinton's Grand March. m. F. Meline. Published & sold by George Willig, No. 171 Chesnut Street, Philadelphia, PA. [1819-1828]. Non-pictorial. "Composed Expressly for & Dedicated to Him [Clinton]." "For the Piano Forte." "Pr. 37 cts." 4pp.

DWC-3 The Meeting Of The Waters Of Hudson & Erie. w.m. S. Woodworth. Published by [V-1: E. Riley, No. 29 Chatham Street, New York, NY] [V-2: Oliver Ditson, No. 115 Washington Street, Boston, MA]. 1825. Non-pictorial. "Sung by Mr. Keene at the Grand Canal Celebration." "Respectfully Dedicated to His Excellency Dewitt Clinton." [V-1: "Copy Right Secured According to Law, Novr. 1st, 1825"]. 4pp. Page 4: Blank. [W-3039].

DWC-4 Clinton's Triumph (A Grand March). m. William Taylor. Published for the Author by Dubois & Stodart, No. 126 Broadway, New York, NY. [1824?]. Non-pictorial geometric designs. "For the Piano Forte." "Composed and Dedicated to His Excellency Dewitt Clinton by his devoted servant, Wm. Taylor." 2pp. Page 2: Blank. [W-9303].

DWC-5 Clinton's Grand March. m. J. Willson. Published by J. Willson, No. 14 Maiden Lane, New York, NY. [1817]. Non-pictorial. "Composed and Respectfully Dedicated to His Excellency Governor De Witt Clinton." "Engrd. by T. Birch, 38 Vesey St." 4pp. Page 4: Blank. [W-9978].

DWC-6 The Grand Canal March. m. C. Gilfert. Published by Dubois & Stodart, No. 126 Broadway, New York, NY. 1824. Non-pictorial. "For the Piano Forte." "Composed and most Respectfully Inscribed to His Excellency Dewitt Clinton." 4pp. Page 4: Blank. [W-3039].

DWC-7 Dewitt Clinton's Grand Canal March. m. R. Willis (Professor of Music at West Point). Published by [V-1: H. Sage at his Piano Forte and Music Store, No. 214 Broadway, NY., opposite St. Paul's Church] [V-2: A & W Geib at their Piano Forte Warehouse and Wholesale and Retail Music Store, No.

23 Maiden Lane, New York, NY]. [V-1: 1823] [V-2: 1823-1826]. Non-pictorial. "As performed by the West Point Band at the entrance of the first Canal Boat into the Hudson River on the 8th of October, 1823." "Composed for the Occasion." "Copy Right" "Price 25 Cents." 4pp. [V-1: W-9967] [V-2: W-9967A].

DWC-8 Ode For The Canal Celebration. w. Samuel Woodworth. Published by Clayton and Van Norden, Printers, New York, NY. 1825. Non-pictorial. 2pp. Page 2: Blank. "The foregoing *Ode* was printed on a movable stage, on the 4th day of November, 1825, during the procession in honour of the completion of the Grand Western Canal by Clayton and Van Norden, Printers." "Written at the request of the printers of New York."

DWC-9 The Gentleman's Musical Repository (Being a selection from the ancient and modern music of Erin with a number of Scotch and Welsh airs and several original pieces by the compiler. Adapted to violin, flute, flageolet, houtboy and union pipes), page 3. c. P.F. O'Hara, New York, NY. Printed for the Author and sold at his new music store, No. 70 William Street, where may be had a great variety of the most ancient and modern single songs; Also a great assortment of flutes, violins, tambarines [sic], drums and all other musical instruments. 1813. [W-6643].

(A) Dewitt Clinton's Short Troop, Or Waltz. m. O'Hara.

(B) Dewitt Clinton's Grand Slow March. m. O'Hara.

Eugene V. Debs

EVD-1 The Dawning Day (Solo with Chorus Arranged for Male Voices). w. Frank Sence. m. Thomas G. Fudge. Published by Thomas G. Fudge, Terra Haute, IN. 1904. B/w photos of "Eugene V. Debs—Socialist Nominee for President" and "Benjamin Hanford—Social-

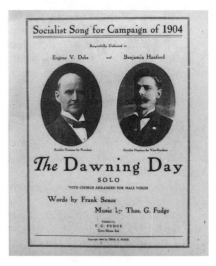

EVD-1

ist Nominee for Vice-President." "Socialist Song for Campaign of 1904." "Respectfully Dedicated to Eugene V. Debs and Benjamin Hanford." 4pp. Page 2: "Join the Socialist Party." Marx quote. Page 3: "Vote for Socialism." Quote.

EVD-2 Spirit Of Gene Debs (March). w. Frank Zeidler. m. John Paulish. Copyright 1938 by John Paulish,

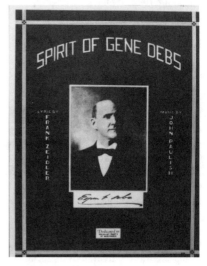

EVD-2

Milwaukee, WI. [8 1/2" × 10 15/16"]. B/w photo of Eugene V. Debs, facsimile signature. "Dedicated to Socialist Party of Wisconsin." 4pp.

EVD-3   We Will Follow Brave Debs To The End. w.m. Ellis B. Harris. Published by New Times Socialist Publishing Company, Minneapolis, MN. Copyright 1897 by Ellis Harris. Pk/bk photo of Eugene V. Debs on red flag inscribed "Workers of the world unite, You have nothing to lose but your Chains." R/pk/bk/w drawing of torch, ribbon inscribed "Good will on Earth, Peace toward men, Equal rights to all, Special privileges to none." "To you, the parents of Eugene, to whom some days and nights were long, to you the faithful wife and queen of his staunch heart, I dedicate my song, to you his followers who gave your helping hands, nor once the banner furled, I give you this, a ballad for the brave, that you may long so and sing it to the world." 6pp. Pages 2 and 6: Blank.

EVD-4   Workers Of The World Awaken! w.m. Joe Hill. Published by Industrial Workers of the World Publishing Bureau, No. 112 Hamilton Avenue, Cleveland, OH. Copyright 1916 by William D. Haywood. O/bk/w sun with rays. "Don't waste any time in mourning, organize — Joe Hill." 4pp. Page 2: "Marching-Song dedicated to all class-conscious workers-everywhere." Page 4: Advertising for "Joe Hill Memorial Edition of I.W.W. Songbook." [Eugene Debs co-founded the I.W.W.].

Franklin D. Roosevelt

FDR-1   The Star Spangled Banner. w. Francis Scott Key. m. John Stafford Smith. a. Robert C. Haring. Published by Skidmore Music Company, Inc., No. 1270 Sixth Avenue, New York, NY. 1941. R/w/b flags, shield, eagle, stars. Bl/w tinted photo by Wide World Studio of Franklin D. Roosevelt. 6pp. Page 6: Pledge of Allegiance.

FDR-2   Roosevelt (Here We Come). w. Ila Dixon Buntz. m. Charles Arthur Ridgway. Published by B & R Publishing Company, No. 646 North Harper Avenue, Los Angeles, CA. 1936. B/w photo of Franklin D. Roosevelt. 6pp. Page 6: Blank.

FDR-3   Friend Roosevelt. w.m. Enrico and Harry del Sordo. Copyright 1934 by Harry del Sordo, Orange, NJ. R/w/b drawings of Franklin D. Roosevelt at ship's wheel inscribed "U.S.S. Ship of State" and taking the oath of office in front of U.S. Capitol building. 6pp. Pages 2 and 6: Blank.

FDR-4   Roosevelt Glide. w.m. Hertha Ann Stein and Vic Lewis. Published by Wayne Music Publishers, No. 115 East Wayne Street, Ft. Wayne, IN. 1932. R/w/bk cover with b/w photo and facsimile signature of Franklin D. Roosevelt. "With 1932 Democratic Campaign Version." 4pp. Page 4: Advertising for dance diagrams for the "Roosevelt Glide."

FDR-5   On With Roosevelt (A Marching Song). w.m. Al Hill, Jr. a. Ted Carmen. Published by Hollywood

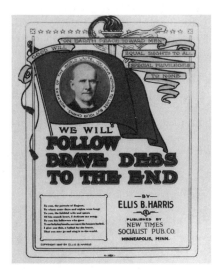

EVD-3

Publishing Company, No. 5426 Sierra Vista Avenue, Hollywood, CA. 1936. B/w drawings by Al Hill, Jr. of a man inscribed "F.D." in boxing gloves knocking out "Old man gloom," sun inscribed "Prosperity." B/w photo of Al Hill, Jr. B/w drawing of Franklin D. Roosevelt. "Dedicated to Franklin D. Roosevelt." 4pp. Page 4: Blank.

FDR-6 A Little Star In The Sky. w.m. Elizabeth Gallagher. a. Burrell Van Buren. Published by Gallagher Publishing House, New York 11, NY. 1935. R/w/b geometric designs. Bl/w drawing of "Franklin Delano Roosevelt." 6pp. Page 2: Blank. Page 6: Advertising for U.S. Savings Bonds.

FDR-7 L'Acquila Blu (The Blue Eagle) (A Patriotic Sicilian-American Song). w.m. Pierina Palumbo. a. Printed and Arranged by Cosmopolitan Music Association, No. 1587 Broadway, New York, NY. Copyright 1933 by Pierina Palumbo, New York, NY. Bl/w drawing of Franklin D. Roosevelt, Capitol building, "NRA" eagle. 6pp. Page 2: Additional Italian-English verses. Page 6: Advertising.

FDR-8 We're For Roosevelt. w.m. William McRae. Published by Consolidated Specialty Company, No. 1209 North LeClaire Avenue, Chicago, IL. 1936. R/w/b drawings of Franklin D. Roosevelt, farmer, worker holding newspaper with the headline "Home Building Comes Back." 6pp. Page 5: Spoken verse. Page 6: Blank.

FDR-9 March On With Roosevelt. w.m. Gene Dabney. a. Dick Rozelle. Published by National Music Publishing Company of Hollywood, California, , No. 312 West First Street, Hollywood, CA. 1936. R/w/b flag design. B/w drawing by Neumann of Franklin D. Roosevelt. 4pp. Page 4: "Respectfully Dedicated to Our Great President and Leader, Honorable Franklin Delano Roosevelt."

FDR-10 Roosevelt Is On The Job. w.m. Jack T. Nelson. Published by Leo Feist, Inc., New York, NY. 1933. Bl/W drawing of U.S. Capitol building, geometric designs. "Popular Edition." 6pp. Page 6: Advertising for other music.

FDR-11 Your Roosevelt And Mine. w. Wesley Ossman. m. Morris Perlman. Published by Triumphant Music, No. 1472 Broadway, New York, NY. Copyright 1932 by Morris Perlman. R/w/b photo of Capitol, flag, crowd. Bl/w tinted photo of Franklin Roosevelt. "Democratic Campaign Song." 6pp. Pages 2 and 6: Blank.

FDR-12 President Roosevelt March (And Chorus). w.m. Theodore A. Metz (World Famous Composer of *There'll Be A Hot Time In The Old Town Tonight*). Published by [V-1: Haviland Publishing Company, No. 112 West 44th Street] [V-2: Music Mail Company, No. 225 West 46th Street], New York, NY. Copyright 1933 by Theodore A. Metz. R/w/b photo of Capitol building, flag, crowd. Bl/w tinted photo of Franklin D. Roosevelt. 6pp. Pages 2 and 6: Advertising.

FDR-13 On The Right Road With Roosevelt. w.m. Robert Sterling. Published by J&M. Novelty Company, Music Publishers, No. 156 West 44th Street, New York, NY. 1932. R/w/b drawing of White House. Bl/w photo of Franklin D. Roosevelt. 6pp. Pages 2 and 6: Blank.

FDR-14 On With Roosevelt (March). w. Margaret B. Code. m. Dina Ablamovicz. Copyright 1936 by Margaret B. Code and Dina Ablamovicz. B/w drawing of Franklin D. Roosevelt. Two verses and the chorus printed on the cover. "Dedicated to Franklin D. Roosevelt, in Sincere Admiration." 4pp. Page 4: Blank.

FDR-15 Our Roosevelt. w.m. Anna Lyons and Helen De Mars. a. Harry Ludwig. Published by James F. Langan, Music Publisher, No. 8219 Woodland Avenue, Cleveland, OH.

FRANKLIN D. ROOSEVELT (FDR)

1933. R/w/b geometric designs. Bl/w photo of Franklin D. Roosevelt. "Dedicated to Franklin D. Roosevelt, President of the United States of America." 6pp. Pages 2 and 6: Advertising for other James F. Langan music.

FDR-16 Roosevelt (March). w. Countess Charrier Milan de Lalande. m. George Lessner and Ray Cameron. Published by Radio Artists' League of America, No. 3105 Chrysler Building, New York, NY. 1934. B/w drawing by Seymore Markus from *The New York World Telegram* of Franklin D. Roosevelt waving hat. 8pp. Page 2: Facsimile letter from Countess Lalande to Birthday Ball Committee. Page 3: "Written especially for Franklin Delano Roosevelt's National Birthday Ball, and dedicated to the Georgia Warm Springs Foundation." Page 8: Another Franklin D. Roosevelt song by same the Composers — **Roosevelt Lullaby**.

FDR-17 We Love Our President Of America (March Song). w.m. Sam Berardini. Published by California Music Company, No. 802 West Eighth Street, Los Angeles, CA. Copyright 1937 by Sam Beradini. R/w/b stripes, stars. Bl/w drawing of Franklin D. Roosevelt 6pp. Pages 2 and 6: Advertising for other California Music Company published music. Page 3: "Respectfully Dedicated to Franklin D. Roosevelt, President of the United States of America."

FDR-18 Roosevelt Is On The Job! (March Fox-Trot Song). w.m. Jack T. Nelson. Published by Leo. Feist, Inc., No. 56 Cooper Square, New York, NY. 1933. Br/w geometric "V" design. Br/w photo of Franklin D. Roosevelt. 6pp. Page 6: Advertising.

FDR-19 Damn The Torpedoes Full Speed Ahead! w.m. Grace Warner Gulesian. Published by R.D. Row Music Company, No. 725 Boylston Street, Boston, MA. 1943. R/w/bk non-pictorial. "The Title of This Song is the Historic Saying of Admiral Farragut and Quoted by President Franklin Delano Roosevelt in his Navy Day Radio Address October 27, 1941." 6pp. Page 6: Blank.

FDR-20 Anchors Aweigh. w. George D. Lottman. m. Charles A. Zimmerman. a. D. Savino. Published by Robbins Music Corporation, No. 799 Seventh Avenue, New York, NY. Copyright 1907, 1930 and 1935. R/w/b drawing of rope, anchor, Naval Academy logo. Bl/w photo of Franklin D. Roosevelt. "The Song of the Navy." "Popular Edition." 6pp. Page 6: Blank.

FDR-21 Hold That Line For F.D.R. w.m. Vernie Hiester. Published by Hiester Publishing Company, Box 82, Reading, PA. 1940. R/w/b flag design. Bl/w photos of "Franklin Delano Roosevelt — For President," and "Henry A. Wallace — For Vice President." 6pp. Page 2: "Words to be Substituted after Nov. 5, 1940." Page 6: R/w/b drawing of eagle, geometric design border. Song — *Star Spangled Banner*.

FDR-22 Virginia (Waltz). m. Raffaele Capecelatro. Published by Raffaele Capecelatro, No. 246 Columbus Avenue, New Haven, CT. 1935. Bl/w photo of Franklin D. Roosevelt, geometric design border. "Prosperity — Security — NRA — FERA." "Respectfully Dedicated To Our President Franklin D. Roosevelt." 6pp. Page 6: Blank.

FDR-23 Hands Across The Sea (Selection of National and Patriotic Airs British & American). a. R.S. Stoddon. Published by B. Feldman & Company, No. 125-9 Shaftesbury Avenue, London, W.C.2. 1941. R/w/b U.S. and British flags. B/w Crown photo of Franklin D. Roosevelt and Winston Churchill shaking hands, military aide. "Contents" listed. "Roland's Pianoforte Tutor — The Best in the World — English Fingering — Continental Fingering." 4pp. Page 4: Advertising.

FDR-24 What A Man! w.m. George M. Cohan. Published by F.B. Haviland Publishing Company, No. 114

West 44th Street, New York, NY. 1934. R/w/b cover, stars, stripes, Capitol building. R/w photo of George M. Cohan, facsimile signature. Bl/w tinted photo by Blank and Stoller of Franklin D. Roosevelt. "Frank Crumit Songs Co." 6pp. Page 6: Note that "Receipts from the sale of this song are being donated by the Composer and the Publisher to the President's Warm Springs Foundation."

FDR-25 Take Me Back To My Daddy. w.m. T.J. Ford. a. Ray L. Adams. Published by T.J. Ford, San Bernardino, CA. 1936. R/w/bl/bk cover, flags. Be/bk photo of Franklin D. Roosevelt. Bl/w photo of battleship. 4pp.

FDR-26 On With Roosevelt [Take Me Back to My Daddy]. w.m. T.J. Ford. a. Ray L. Adams. Published by T.J. Ford, San Bernardino, CA. 1936. R/w/bl/bk cover, flags. Be/bk photo of Franklin D. Roosevelt. Bl/w photo of battleship. R/w/b flags. 4pp. [Inside song is the same as FDR-25].

FDR-27 On With Roosevelt. w.m. Carl S. Kegley. Published by E.B. DuBain Publishing Company, Hollywood, CA. 1938. R/w/b cover. Bl/w drawing of Franklin D. Roosevelt. Bl/w photo of Carl S. Kagley — "Candidate for Attorney General of the State of California." 4pp. Page 4: Blank.

FDR-28 Our President Was Called Away To Heaven. w. Matt Pelkonen. m. Bill Boyd and Lee Mel. Published by Country Music Publishers, No. 20 East Jackson Boulevard, Chicago, IL. 1945. Bl/bk drawing of a church, sunset. Bl/bk photo of Franklin D. Roosevelt. "Franklin Delano Roosevelt January 30th, 1882 — April 12th, 1945." "Sole selling agent: Ashley Music Supply, 1600 Broadway, N.Y." 4pp. Page 4: Adv.

FDR-29 To The Man Of The Hour. w.m. F.W. Thomas. Published by F.W. Thomas Music Publisher, St. Joseph, MI. 1934. R/w/b drawing by Rod Ruth of Franklin D. Roosevelt, mountain, clouds inscribed "Dawn," George Washington pointing the way to mountain top. 4pp. Page 4: Poem by F.W. Thomas dedicated to Roosevelt.

FDR-30 Roosevelt's Campaign Song. w. J.H. Arzich. m. Earl Haubrich. Published by Arzich Bros., Chicago, IL. 1940. [8 1/2" × 10 13/16"]. B/w drawings of men and women carrying banners inscribed "Labor, Youth, Business, Housewife, Farmer, Trade, Professional." B/w photo of Franklin Roosevelt. 4pp. Page 4: "Ask your radio artist to feature this song."

FDR-31 Roosevelt Is The Man. w.m. Kitty Cunningham. Published by Great Western Music Company, No. 442 Plymouth Court, Chicago, IL. 1933. R/w/b shields. Bl/w photo of Bernard Carpenter — "Featured by Bernard Carpenter, Imperial Theatre Organ, Augusta, GA." 4pp.

FDR-32 Remember F.D.R. w.m. Jack Edwards, Harold Potter and Rrod Eddie. Published by Edwards Music Company, No. 1619 Broadway, New York, NY. 1945. R/w/b flag background. Bl/w photo of "Franklin Delano Roosevelt." "A

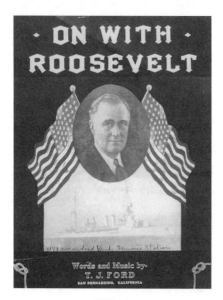

FDR-26

Tribute to a Great Man." 4pp. Page 4: Advertising for other Edwards Music Company published music.

FDR-33 President Roosevelt's Smile. w.m. J.R. Dickinson. Published by J.R. Dickinson, No. 227 West 22nd Street, New York, NY. 1937. B/w photo Franklin Roosevelt. "Hereditary From the Cradle he was Born." 4pp. Page 4: Blank.

FDR-34 The Road Is Open Again. w. Irving Kahal. m. Sammy Fain. Published by M. Witmark and Sons, No. 1657 Broadway, New York, NY. 1933. R/w/b cover, "NRA Member" eagle. Bl/w photo of Franklin D. Roosevelt and Dick Powell. "As sung by Dick Powell in the Warner Bros. and Vitaphone NRA short *The Road Is Open Again* with Warner Bros. most famous stars." 6pp. Page 6: Advertising for other music.

FDR-35 President Roosevelt (Humanity March). m. M.D. Pitt. Published by M.D. Pitt, Morristown, AZ. 1941. B/w photo of Franklin D. Roosevelt, geometric designs. 6pp. Pages 2, 7 and 6: Blank.

FDR-36 We're Going Big For That Big Blanket Code. w.m. Bernard H. Zais. Published by Bernard H. Zias, Fall River, MA. 1933. Bl/w drawing of eagle with ribbon inscribed "E Pluribus Unum," shield, star, wreath, geometric design border. 6pp. Page 6: Advertising.

FDR-37 We Want Roosevelt. w.m. Charles H. Galligan and George Spink. Published by C.H. Galligan, Music Publisher, No. 1587 Broadway, New York, NY. 1932. Br/w drawing of Franklin D. Roosevelt. 4pp.

FDR-38 Row, Row, Row With Roosevelt (On the Good Ship U.S.A.). w.m. Eddie Dowling and J. Fred Coots. Published by Sam Fox Publishing Company, Cleveland, OH. 1932. R/w/b stripe border. Bl/w drawing of "Franklin Delano Roosevelt." "Official Democratic Campaign Song." "Issued by Stage and Screen Division National Democratic Committee." 4pp. Page 4: Facsimile letter to Composers.

FDR-39 On With Roosevelt. w.m. Louise Graeser. Published by G. Burdette & Company, Publishers, No. 111 West Fifth Street, Los Angeles, CA. 1936. R/w/b drawing of Capitol building, factories. B/w photo of Franklin D. Roosevelt. 4pp. Page 2: "1936 Campaign Song." Page 4: Advertising for other G. Burdette songs dedicated to Franklin D. Roosevelt including *The President's Waltz*.

FDR-40 Let's Lend A Hand To Roosevelt. w.m. Gorden Ryan. Published by Illinois Democratic Woman's Division, Blanch Fritz, Chairman. [193-]. [8 9/16" × 11"]. R/w/b eagle, shield, sun, stars. Bl/w photos of Franklin D. Roosevelt and Gordon Ryan[?]. 4pp.

FDR-41 Mr. Roosevelt (Won't You Please Run Again?). w. Henry Myers. m. Jay Gorney. Published by Advance Music, Inc., Markham Building, Hollywood, CA. 1939. Bl/w cover. Br/w drawing of Franklin D. Roosevelt. 4pp. Page 4: Narrative—"History of a Fighter for Democracy, Franklin Delano Roosevelt."

FDR-42 Roosevelt At The Throttle. w. Sam R. McClay. m. Herm DeVol. Published by Sam R. McClay, No. 1300 25th Street NW, Canton, OH. 1936. R/w/b crossed flags. B/w drawing of Franklin D. Roosevelt. Bl/w geometric designs. 6pp. Page 2: Poem: "Our Friend." Page 6: Blank.

FDR-43 A Real Depression Buster! w.m. Bob and Evie Lewis. Published by Music City Publishing Company, No. 219 Taft Building, Hollywood at Vine, Hollywood, CA. 1933. R/w/b drawing by V. Vesely of Franklin D. Roosevelt, U.S. Capitol building, geometric designs. "CCC, NRA, CWA, PWA." 6pp. Pages 2 and 6: Advertising.

FDR-44 The Unemployment Blues (Fox Trot). w. Will Striker. m. G.L. Fischer. Published by Will Striker, No. 1423 Van Buren Street, Missoula, MT. 1932. Bl/w geometric designs. Bk/bl photo of Franklin D. Roosevelt. "Oh, Roosevelt, Oh, Roosevelt, Lets get that Mr. Hoover's Pelt; In politics let's have a change and give the Democrats the reigns; You bet we'll vote for Franklin D. and sing his name from sea to sea; In politics let's have a change and give the Democrats the reigns." "The Democratic Campaign Song endorsed by James A. Farley, Chairman, National Democratic Committee, New York City." 6pp. Pages 2 and 6: Blank.

FDR-45 We Want A Man Like Roosevelt (Democratic Campaign Song). w.m. Kenneth Wardell. a. Charles Coleman. Selling agent Charles Coleman, No. 253 Linden Boulevard, Brooklyn, NY. 1932. R/w/b cover. Bl/w drawing of Franklin D. Roosevelt. "Repeal, Employment, State Rights, Tariff Adjustment." "Popular Music Publication." 6pp. Page 2: "Recitative: 'A Farmer Tells His Son Why He Should Vote For Roosevelt.'" Page 6: Blank.

FDR-46 Freedom's Call. w.m. Felix Schreiber (Founder and Director of the American Institute of Fraternal Citizenship, Inc., Oakland, California). Published by Fraternal Citizens of America and the American Institute of Fraternal Citizenship, Inc., No. 1634 Telegraph Avenue, Oakland, CA. 1945. Bl/w drawing of the Statue of Liberty inscribed "Freedom, Unity and Peace." Bl/w photos "Franklin D. Roosevelt," "General de Gaulle," "Queen Wilhelmina," "Chaing-Kai-Shek," "Joseph Stalin." "Dedicated to the heroes/heroines of Democracy and Peace and to the United Nations." "Compliments and thanks for the heads of the Allied Nations including President Wilson, President Poncare, Marshall Foch, Marshall Jaffe, Field-Marshall Haig, Prime Minister Lloyd George, Ambassador Jusser and President and Mrs. Roosevelt, Prime Minister Churchill, General Eisenhower, General de Gaulle, General MacArthur, Madame Chaing-Kai-Shek and others." "Adopted, in homage, to the air of *Brave and True France*, world's most inspiring and potent air of justice and liberation." "First sung by our boys and girls in France in World War I, it is also helping them now to win Freedom's fight again." 8pp. Foldout. Pages 4 to 7: History. Page 8: Verses.

FDR-47 Three Cheers For Our President (March Song). w. Andy Razaf. m. Joe Davis. Published by Joe Davis Music Company, Inc., No. 1619 Broadway, New York, NY. 1942. R/w/b stripes. Bl/w tinted photo of Franklin D. Roosevelt. 4pp. Page 2: "Respectfully Dedicated to President Franklin Delano Roosevelt." Page 4: Advertising.

FDR-48 The New Deal Rose With Roosevelt. w.m. Clarence L. Bobilya. Published by Bobilya Publishing House, Monroeville, IN. 1936. Bl/w photo of Franklin D. Roosevelt, facsimile signature. "F.D.R.— Full Depression Recovery." 6pp. Page 6: R/w/b eagle, geometric designs.

FDR-49 Roosevelt NRA March Song. w.m. Hellen Witt Tufts and Gertrude H. Brahy. Published by Hellen Witt Tufts and Gertrude H. Brahy, No. 1790 Hague Avenue, St. Paul, MN. 1933. R/w/b stripes, stars, N.R.A. eagle. B/w drawing of Franklin D. Roosevelt. "Introduced in Band Arrangement by the U.S. 3rd Infantry Fort Snelling Band, first in line of march, St. Paul NRA parade, Thursday Afternoon, Aug. 24, 1933. Introduced in Song and Band Arrangement with Community Singing at Democratic Dinner Rally." 6pp. Page 2: "Dedicated by the Composer with deepest admiration to Franklin D. Roosevelt, 32nd President of the United States." Page 6: Blank.

FDR-50 Prosperity Days Are Here. w. S.E. Winstead. m. Lon Frederick Stafford. Published by Lon Frederick Stafford and Company, No. 523 North Geddes Street, Syracuse, NY. 1933. R/w/bl/br Barbelle drawing of farmer, ships, eagle, train, planes. Bl/w photo of

Franklin D. Roosevelt. 6pp. Page 2: Blank. Page 3: "Respectfully Dedicated to President Roosevelt." Page 6: Advertising.

FDR-51 Marching For The NRA. w. Evelyn and Violet Nelson. m. Francis P. Loubet. Published by Fine Art Music Publishers, No. 113 West 57th Street, New York, NY. 1933. R/w/b drawing by Katesman of Franklin D. Roosevelt, woman with flag and horn, band and workers, NRA eagle, signs inscribed "NRA" and "We Do Our Part." 6pp. Pages 2 and 6: Blank.

FDR-52 The Roosevelt Song. w. Sasha Stone. m. Lou Halmy. Published by Sasha Stone, Hollywood, CA. 1940. R/w/b flag, eagle. Bl/w photo of Franklin D. Roosevelt. Slogans based on the letters in "F.D. Roosevelt" — "Fighting for right against all that is wrong; Daring to some, but unfair to none; Rays of sunshine bringing where needed; On is your byword — never defeated; On please don't stop — so on with your work; Serve your Country — bring peace to the world; End all miseries as you wish to do; Voices of millions are praying for you; Efforts are made to discredit what you do; Let them do what they may for they are very few; To ignore the cause of the Red, White and Blue." 4pp. Page 2: "A Tribute to a great humanitarian." Page 4: [V-1: B/w photo of "Honorable Culbert L. Olson, Governor of California for Vice President of the United States"] [V-2: Blank].

FDR-53 President Roosevelt March. e. Andrea and Ervin Litkei. In: *The President's March and Other Songs of the Lone Star State*, page 10. Published by Loena Music Publishing Company, No. 239 West 18th Street, New York, NY. 10011. [196-]. R/w/ bl/bk cover, Presidential seal. "Featuring *President Lyndon Baines Johnson March* and other songs of the Lone Star State." "Pacific Popular Music Books." 36pp. Page 36: Photo of Lyndon Johnson. Drawings of all presidents.

FDR-54 Franklin D. Roosevelt March (With Vocal Trio). w. Irving Caesar. m. William H. Woodin. Published by Miller Music, No. 62 West 45th Street, New York, NY. 1933. [V-1: Standard size] [V-2: 7" × 10 5/8"]. R/w/bl/br drawing of eagle, flag. N/c photo of Franklin Roosevelt. "Dedicated to the 32nd President of the United States of America." [V-1: 8pp] [V-2: "Male Quartett Arrangement included in this orchestration. Band and Orchestra many combine and parts augmented ad libitum"]. Page 2: Letter from Franklin Roosevelt to Composer. Page 7: "Profits from the sale of this composition donated to Warm Springs Foundation." Page 8: Bl/w drawing of an eagle.

FDR-55 To You Roosevelt. m. Ed Bamber. Published by DeVaignie Music Corporation, No. 443 South Dearborn Street, Chicago, IL. Copyright 1935 by Ed Bamber. R/bl drawing of city, boat, cars, train, planes, people. Bl/w photo of Lora Sonderson — "Sincerely yours, Lora [facsimile handwriting]." "With Ukulele Arrangement." 4pp. Page 4: Advertising.

FDR-56 The FRA Of Uncle Sammy (Franklin Roosevelt Administration). w.m. Joseph J. Gallagher. Published by Meryl Prince, Music Publisher, Kress Building, San Francisco, CA. R/w/b "V," eagle, flags, geometric designs. "Successfully featured by Frank McCarthy at Chicago Century of Progress World's Fair, 1933 and Sue Gilman, George Murray, Eugene Mancini, San Jose, KQW." 6pp. Page 3: "Successfully featured at Century of Progress World's Fair, Chicago, 1933." Pages 2 and 6: Advertising.

FDR-57 Fight On With Mr. Roosevelt. w.m. Ben Finger. Published by Jerome Finger, No. 710 Fairmont Place, New York, NY. 1936. B/w photo of Ben Finger — "Featured by Ben Finger and His Fleet Orchestra." 4pp. Page 2: "Dedicated to Hon. Franklin D. Roosevelt, President of the United States." Page 4: Extra verses.

FDR-58 Let's Re-Re-Re-Elect Roosevelt. w. John Dunne. m. Charles Osborne. Copyright 1944 by John Dunne. B/w non-pictorial. "1944 Campaign Song." "A Snappy March Tune—Words That Mean Something." "Dedicated to the Commander-In-Chief." 4pp.

FDR-59 We Want Franklin D. (Democratic Campaign Song—1936). w.m. Lawrence A. Weber. Copyright 1936 by Lawrence A. Weber, Chicago, IL. B/w photo by Underwood & Underwood of Franklin D. Roosevelt, black line frame, stars. "Endorsed by President Franklin D. Roosevelt." 4pp. Page 4: Blank.

FDR-60 Three Cheers For F.D.R. w.m. Barney Young, Leroy (Stuff) Smith, Louis Prima and Edgar Battle. Published by Barney Young, No. 1616 Broadway, New York, NY. 1942. [8 1/2" × 11"]. B/w geometric design border. 4pp. Page 4: Blank.

FDR-61 Viva Roosevelt! (Conga-March). w. Al Stillman (English) and Emillo De Torre (Spanish). m. Xavier Cugat. Published by Edward B. Marks Music Corporation, RCA Building, Radio City, New York, NY. 1942. R/w/bl/y/gn drawing of people in national costumes, flags. 6pp. Page 6: Advertising.

FDR-62 Franklin D.R. (Song). w.m. Mollie Wren Whitman. Published by Carl Fischer, Inc., Cooper Square, New York, NY. 1936. Be/bl geometric design border. "With Piano Accompaniment." 6pp. Page 2: Blank. Page 6: Advertising.

FDR-63 Roosevelt, Garner And Me. w. Al Lewis. m. Al Sherman. Published by Irving Berlin, Inc., Music Publishers, No. 1607 Broadway, New York, NY. 1933. Y/w/bk drawing of sun's rays, Capitol building, three men. B/w photo of Eddie Cantor. "Suggested by Eddie Cantor." "Eddie Cantor, The Kid From Spain [facsimile handwriting]." 6pp. Page 5: Extra verses. Page 6: Advertising.

FDR-64 We Want Roosevelt. w.m. Robert Nicholls. Published by the Progressive Democrats Southern Authority, No. 608 South Hill Street, Los Angeles, CA. Copyright 1936 by C.J. Cullington, Boston, MA. [4 1/4" × 6 1/16"]. Non-pictorial. "Campaign Song." 4pp.

FDR-65 The Texas Waltz. w.m. Lupe Gonzalez. Published by International Music Publishers, No. 1229 Park Row Building, New York, NY. 1936. Br/w photo of "John N. Garner." Bl/w geometric design border. 6pp. Pages 2 and 6: Blank. Page 3: "Respectfully Dedicated to the Hon. John N. Garner and wife." Pages 2 and 6: Blank.

FDR-66 Under The Big Blue Eagle. w.m. George Clayton Field. Published by Field Art Studio Publishers, No. 1720 North 17th Street, Milwaukee, WI. Copyright 1933 by George C. Field. [8 7/16" × 11 1/2"]. R/w/b eagle. "Dedicated by the Employees to their Employers Cutler-Hammer Inc., and to All Other Employers who have so Voluntarily Subscribed to the N.R.A." 6pp. Pages 2 and 6: Blank.

FDR-67 Our President. w.m. Annette Keyser. Published by Keyser, Music Publisher, No. 5337 Sunset Boulevard, Hollywood, CA. 1941. Bl/w geometric design border. "Two Patriotic Songs." 6pp. Page 2: "Dedicated to the Honorable Franklin Delano Roosevelt." Page 4: Song—*The Spirit of America* by Annette Keyser. Page 6: Blank.

FDR-68 America! Let's Go! w. Florence Tarr. m. Fay Foster. Published by Boston Music Company, Boston, MA. 1942. R/w/bl/br eagle, stripes. "Dedicated to our President Franklin Delano Roosevelt." 8pp. Pages 2 and 7: Blank. Page 3: Title: **America! Let's Go!** (America Has Spread Her Wings). Page 8: Advertising for other Boston Music published music.

FDR-69 W.P.A. (Song Novelty). w.m. Jesse Stone. Published by Shapiro,

Bernstein & Company, Inc., Music Publishers, New York, NY. 1940. R/w/b drawings by of man sleeping, raking leaves, sleeping on job, being "Fired." Bl/w photo of Jan Savitt. 6pp. Pages 2 and 6: Advertising for other music.

FDR-70 Three Cheers For Our President (March Song). w. Andy Razaf. m. Joe Davis. Published by Joe Davis Music Company, Inc., No. 1619 Broadway, New York, NY. 1942. Non-pictorial professional copy. "Respectfully Dedicated to President Franklin Delano Roosevelt." 4pp. Pages 1 and 4: Blank.

FDR-71 We've Got The Right Man In The White House Now. w. Carl Dahlin. m. James F. Langan. a. Thomas Rennie. Published by James F. Langan, No. 8219 Woodland Avenue, Cleveland, OH. 1933. R/w/b cover. Photo of Franklin D. Roosevelt and U.S. Capitol building. "Dedicated to Franklin D. Roosevelt, President of the U.S.A." 6pp. Pages 2 and 6: Advertising.

FDR-72 F.D.R. w.m. John E. Cloutier. Distributed by Music Service Company, No. 170A Tremont Street, Boston, MA. Copyright 1942 by John E. Cloutier. [8 1/2" × 11"]. Bl/w drawing of Uncle Sam, geometric design border. "Enthusiastically Dedicated to F.D.R." 6pp. Foldout. Pages 5 and 6: Blank.

FDR-73 Thank You, Mr. President. w.m. Mary Small, Vic Mizzy and Irving Taylor. Published by Santly-Joy-Select, Inc., No. 1619 Broadway, New York, NY. 1942. R/w/b drawing of Franklin D. Roosevelt, shield background, stars. "Introduced by Mary Small and Respectfully Dedicated to the Committee for the Celebration of the President's Birthday." 4pp. Page 4: Advertising.

FDR-74 We'll Win Through We Always Do. w. Irving Taylor. m. Vic Mizzy. Published by Santly-Joy-Select, Inc., No. 1619 Broadway, New York, NY. 1942. R/w/b drawing of Franklin D. Roosevelt, shield background, stars. 4pp. Page 4: Advertising.

FDR-75 He's A Great American. w.m. Roger J. Magee and John C. Wickes. Published by Santly-Joy-Select, Inc., No. 1619 Broadway, New York, NY. 1940. R/w/b drawing of Franklin D. Roosevelt. 6pp. Page 2: Advertising for other Santly-Joy-Select song. Page 6: Advertising for Song Hit Guild.

FDR-76 The Year Of Jubilee Is Here. w.m. Charles Thomas. Published by Charles Thomas, No. 1914 Wilder Street, Philadelphia, PA. 1933. Br/w photo of "Franklin D. Roosevelt," geometric design border. "Poem by Charles Thomas — Fear not, be of good courage, Thy way shall be Prosperous and Successful. I will be with you because, I have sent you, Call on Me, and I will deliver you. My ears are open to Your Cry, Says the Lord God Almighty, All Power is in My Hand. I sent you to bring Prosperity to the People of the World." 6pp. Pages 2 and 6: Blank.

FDR-77 The National Prayer (America's New Anthem). w.m. Louis St. Claire. Harmonized by Irma Wocher Woolen. Published by St. Claire Music Publishing Company, Indianapolis, IN. 1933. B/w photo of Franklin D. Roosevelt. R/w/bl/bk drawing of eagle with ribbon inscribed "Dedicated to Franklin D. Roosevelt," shield inscribed "1933." 12pp. Pages 2, 4, 9 and 11: Blank. Page 3: Same as page 1 except composer's name substituted for the subtitle. Page 5: "Dedication" narrative. Page 8: **The National Prayer** arranged for Quartette. Page 10: R/w/b drawing of an eagle and a shield. Page 12: "The National Prayer" as a poem.

FDR-78 Roosevelt March Song. w.m. George B.L. Braun. Published by Concord Music Publishing Company, San Francisco, Ltd., CA. 1933. B/w photo of Franklin D. Roosevelt, floral and geometric design border. "Dedicated to Franklin D. Roosevelt, President of the United States of America by the Composer." 4pp. Page 4: Advertising.

FDR-79 God Bless Our President. w. Sig. G. Hecht and Monte Carlo. m. Alma Sanders. Published by Mills Music, Inc., No. 1619 Broadway, New York, NY. 1942. R/w/b stars and stripes. 6pp. Pages 2 and 6: Advertising.

FDR-80 You Are The Reason (For My Love Song). w. Sally Gibbs. m. Hilda Emery Davis. Published by Mills Music, Inc., Music Publishers, No. 1619 Broadway, New York, NY. 1937. Gn/bl/w drawing of a silhouette of a man and woman. "Officially Approved as the Dupont-Roosevelt Wedding Song." 6pp. Pages 2 and 6: Advertising for other Mills published music. Page 3: "Dedicated to Ethel and Franklin D. Roosevelt, Jr."

FDR-81 We're With You, Mr. Roosevelt. w.m. Charles J. Kunkel. Published by The Shattinger Piano and Music Company, St. Louis, MO. 1941. R/w/b flag. "We're with you Mister President, In air, on land or sea! We hail our flag, the Stars and Stripes, that pledges liberty; We're millions strong, but stronger still in spirit and our course; The time is here, the challenge clear, we will not lag or pause; So Hi Ho, friends over there, Who Freedom's ring proclaim, So Hi Ho, friends over there, we'll break this iron chain and then put the rising clouds of war, the mirk of present day; Will pass aside, the sun will shine, and Freedom have her say." 6pp. Page 6: B/w drawing of the Statue of Liberty.

FDR-82 Our Leader (Roosevelt Marching Song). w.m. James Hitt, Victor Charles and Charles Dunn. Published by Hitt Music Publishing Company, No. 509 5th Avenue, New York, NY. 1936. B/w drawing of Franklin D. Roosevelt. 6pp. Page 2: Poem: "Our Leader." Page 6: B/w drawing of Franklin D. Roosevelt.

FDR-83 Democratic Campaign Songs, Poems And Jokes (For the 1936 Campaign). c. Ira Craig (Bloomfield, Ind). 1936. [5 13/16" × 8 3/4"]. Non-pictorial geometric design border. "Maude Muller on a summer's day Was out in Kansas raking hay, And at old man Landon laughed in glee, When up his pants leg crawled a bee, Later, they say, he laughed in turn, when a big grasshopper crawled up 'hern.'" [M-419].

FDR-84 Dear Mr. President. w.m. Marie Louise Bunting. Published by Superior Song Studios, Publishers, Passaic, NJ. 1944. R/w drawing of Franklin D. Roosevelt, flag, stars, geometric designs. 4pp. Page 4: Advertising.

FDR-85 Roosevelt I'm For You. w.m. William Ackland. a. "Piano Arrangement by Fredric Watson and Emma Williams." Published by William Ackland, No. 1126 South 51st Street, Philadelphia, PA. 1936. Non-pictorial geometric designs and border. 6pp. Pages 2 and 6: Blank.

FDR-86 Follow The President. w. John W. Bratton. m. Lieut. Gitz Rice (Composer of *Dear Old Pal of Mine*). Published by Bregman, Vocco and Conn, Inc., No. 1619 Broadway, New York, NY. 1942. Bl/w photo of Vaughn Monroe — "Introduced and Featured by Vaughn Monroe and His Orchestra." R/w/b drawing of stripes, workers marching. 8pp. Pages 2 and 8: Advertising.

FDR-87 March On For F.D.R. w.m. Lester Shear and Jeannie Stein. Published by S.S. Publications, No. 1280 Muirfield Road, Los Angeles, CA. 1944. [8 1/2" × 11"]. Non-pictorial geometric design border. "Dedicated to President Roosevelt." 4pp.

FDR-88 Root-Root-Root For Roosevelt (Campaign Song). w. William Lee Mann. m. Rudolph C. Seyman. Published by William Lee Mann Associates, New York, NY. Sole selling agents: Edward B. Marks Music, New York, NY. 1936. R/w/b drawings by Barbelle of soldiers, flags, "Franklin D. Roosevelt — For President." Six patriotic vignettes — "Benjamin Franklin," "Betsy Ross House," "Wm. Penn's House," "Scene of Battle of Germantown," "Chew Mansion," "Independence Hall," and "The

Liberty Bell, Philadelphia." "160 Years of American Independence — Help Us Keep It." 4pp.

FDR-89 Strike Hard, America. w.m. Martha J. Smith. Published by Chappell and Company, Inc., RKO Building, Rockefeller Center, New York, NY. 1943. R/w/b eagle. "America must strike, and strike hard — Franklin D. Roosevelt [facsimile handwriting]." 6pp. Pages 2 and 6: Advertising.

FDR-90 Franklin Roosevelt (There's Nothing the Matter with Him). w.m. Georgina Gordon Keeler, No. 254 Post Road, Fairfield, CT. Copyright 1933 by Georgina Gordon Keeler. R/bl drawing of eagle, stars, geometric designs. 6pp.

FDR-91 President Roosevelt And The NRA. w.m. Ernest L. McCutcheon. Published by New England Publishing Company, Hartford, CT. 1933. Bl/w drawing of Franklin Roosevelt, Statue of Liberty. 6[?]pp.

FDR-92 The Good Old U.S.A. (Double "VV" for Victory March). w. Lt. D.W. Dorsey. m. Johnny Allegro. a. Frank R. Fuller. Published by Jay (JD) Dee Publishing Company, No. 204 Auzerais Avenue, San Jose, CA. Copyright 1945 by Lt. D.W. Dorsey. Bl/w drawings of Franklin Roosevelt, George Washington, Abraham Lincoln, "VV" symbol. 6pp.

FDR-93 Honor To Our President. w. Belle Regas. m. Hugh W. Schubert. Published by [V-1: Kelton-Romm, Inc.] [V-2: Whitney Blake Music Publishers, No. 1585 Broadway, New York, NY]. [ca. 1934]. Bk/w photo of Belle Regas. Bl/bk/w cover. "As sung for President Roosevelt by Belle Regas in 1934." 6pp. Page 2: Advertising for war bonds. Page 6: Advertising.

FDR-94 The President's War, Victory And Marching Song. w.m. Samuel Richards. Published by Samuel Richards, Boston, MA. 1943. R/w/bl/gd drawings of two flags, war scene — "To the Fighting Forces," factory — "To Defense Workers," and crowd scenes — "To the People of the United States of America." "Dedicated to the President of the United States of America, A Forever American War Song." War Bond stamp — "For Victory Buy United States War Bonds and Stamps." 8pp. Page 8: Blank.

FDR-95 F.D.R. Jones. w.m. Harold J. Rome. Published by Chappell and Company, Inc., RKO Building, Rockefeller Center, New York, NY. 1938. R/bk/gy drawing of woman singing, newspaper background. "Max Gordon in association with George S. Kauffman and Moss Hart presents a new revue *Sing out the News*, Music and Lyrics by Harold J. Rome, Conceived and Directed by Charles Friedman, Settings by Jo Mielziner, Dance Ensembles by Dave Gould, Costumes by John Hambleton." List of other songs in show. 8pp. Page 8: Advertising.

FDR-96 Re'lection Day! w.m. Louis J. Parkinson. a. Burrell Van Buren. Copyright 1936 by Louis J. Parkinson. B/w photo of Franklin D. Roosevelt — "1932-1940." B/w drawing of George Washington — "1789-1796." "Dedicated to George Washington's only rival, Franklin Delano Roosevelt." "Keep this song as a souvenir of the Great Democratic victory." 6pp. Page 2: "A Tribute To Our President." B/w drawing of Uncle Sam, woman, donkey, Capitol building, flag. Page 6: Anti-Landon narrative. B/w drawing of Alf Landon — "AML" and Herbert Hoover — "HH." "A Treacherous Paul Revere!" "Uncle Sam says Let's Re-Elect Roosevelt unanimously — Vote American in the Spirit of '36."

FDR-97 Democratic Songs [Song Book]. w. Ira Craig. Distributed by J.F. Keplinger, Jasonville, IN. 1932. [5" × 6 1/4"]. Non-pictorial geometric designs. "Old Mother Hubbard Went to the Cubbard, On her face was a happy expression, But When she got there, The cubbard was bare, It had been hit by Hoover's Depression." "Who are, Who are, Who are We, We are Republicans, Don't you see, Mellon, Watson and Herb all three, Soup House, Poor House, G.O.P." 8pp.

FDR-98 Nation's Prayer For The President. w. Violet Nelson. m. Evelyn Nelson. Published by Evelyn Nelson, Harlan, IA. 1933. B/w photo of Franklin D. Roosevelt. "Dedicated to President Franklin D. Roosevelt." 4pp.

FDR-99 Roosevelt For Mine. w.m. Frederick J. Sutton. Published by Madison Music, No. 965 East Jefferson Avenue, Detroit, MI. [1936?]. R/w/b cover. Photo of Franklin D. Roosevelt. 4pp. Page 4: R/w/b eagle, geometric design.

FDR-100 Our First Ladies' Waltz. m. Jimmy Sheldon. Published by Crow Music Company (BMI), No. 2220 Vista Del Mar, Hollywood 28, CA. 1961. Bl/w photo of Eleanor Roosevelt. "Dedicated to Mrs. Eleanor Roosevelt." 6pp. Page 2: "Recorded by the Composer on Overland Records." Page 6: Bl/w photo of Jimmy Sheldon. "In Honor of all the First Ladies of our land and especially Dedicated to Mrs. Eleanor Roosevelt." Narrative on song history.

FDR-101 We're Comin' Inauguration! w.m. Marie O. Sprinkle. Published by M.O. Sprinkle, Washington, DC. 1925. [8 1/2" × 11"]. B/w drawing of old car full of people, Washington Monument in background. "1933 Edition." 4pp.

FDR-102 President Roosevelt. w.m. Mabel Najarian. Published by Mabel Najarian, No. 177 East Water Street, Rockland, MA. [1933?]. B/w photo by Bachrach of Franklin D. Roosevelt. Bl/w drawing by E.S. Fisher of eagles, crossed flag, stars, sun. 6pp. Pages 2 and 6: Blank.

FDR-103 Our President Of 1933 (Franklin D's Poetry and Melody). w. Clyde L. Guy. m. Louis J. Panella (Two Keystone State Boys). Published by Clyde L. Guy, Jeannette, PA. 1936. B/w photos of Franklin Roosevelt, "Clyde L. Guy." Words by Glyde L. Guy." R/w/bl/s stripes, leaves. "Liberty, Peace, Justice, Happiness." 6pp. Page 6: Poem — "Our President of 1933."

FDR-104 Cactus Jack. w.m. Jack Fox and Rex Lampman. Published by Forster Music Publisher, Inc., No. 216 South Wabash Avenue, Chicago, IL. 1939. R/w/bl/gn/br caricature by John Baer of John N. Garner, cactus. 4pp. Page 4: Advertising for other Forster Music.

FDR-105 The Girl I Love Is A Democrat. w. Tibby Young. m. Rummy Davis. a. Charlie Pearce and Morrey Young. Published by Intercollegiate Music League, Cambridge, MA. 1933. O/bl/w/br drawing of girl with beer mug riding a donkey, Capitol building, sign inscribed "Prosperity." 6pp. Page 6: Advertising for other Intercollegiate Music League music.

FDR-106 Work For The NRA. w.m. E.N.E. Girard. Published by Hazelton Chamber of Commerce, Hazelton, PA. Copyright 1933 by Nicholas Girard. R/w eagle, stripe border. 6pp. Pages 2 and 6: Blank.

FDR-107 Franklin D. March (Campaign Song). w.m. Charles Ryan. a. Don Rocco Colonna. Published by Charles Ryan Publishing Company, No. 136 West 46th Street, New York, NY. 1936. Bl/w drawing of Franklin D. Roosevelt. R/w/b stripe border. 4pp. Page 4: Blank.

FDR-108 Everything Will Be Rosy With Roosevelt. w. Charles E. Dykeman. m. Mitz Witham, Betty Witham and Walton Perkins. Published by Ted Browne Music Company, Chicago, IL. 1932. R/w/b drawing of flowers, geometric designs. Photo of Franklin D. Roosevelt. 4pp. Page 4: Advertising.

FDR-109 The New Deal

(March). m. Emil Hebel. Copyright 1933 by Emil Hebel, No. 7961 77 Road, Glendale, L.I., NY. Bl/w non-pictorial geometric design border. 4pp.

FDR-110 Win With Roosevelt. w.m. Rubin Brodsky. Published by Redstone Publishers, No. 1009 Wilder Building, Rochester, NY. Copyright 1940 by Rubin Brodsky. Bl/w photo of Franklin D. Roosevelt. R/w stars and line border. 6pp. Page 6: Blank.

FDR-111 Mr. President We're A Hundred Per Cent For You! w.m. Pinky Herman, Al Koppell and Eddie Dowling. Published by Bob Miller, Inc, Music Publisher, No. 1619 Broadway, New York, NY. 1940. R/w/bk facsimile letter to the President. "Mail this letter — Instructions on next page." "Mr. Roosevelt: We're a hundred per cent for you, In every little way, In everything you say or do — We'll see you through, We'll follow you where ever you lead; We know you'll succeed, For there's no denyin' that you're always tryin;' Mr. President, Every lady and gent loves you, And every little child we know is simply wild about you, too; You've a great big heart, A smiling face; You're the right kind of man in the right kind of place, Oh! Mr. President, We're a hundred per cent for you! Sincerely yours [space for signature]." 4pp. Page 2: Mailing label addressed to Franklin D. Roosevelt. Instructions to cut off cover and mail it to The White House.

FDR-112 Hip Hip Horray For Roosevelt. w. P. Korecka Masson. m. Wen Talbert and James Lillard. Published by P. Korecka Masson, No. 8902 73rd Avenue, Forest Hills, L.I., NY. [ca. 1936?]. B/w drawing of Franklin D. Roosevelt. 6pp.

FDR-113 Echoes Of Bonneville. w. E.H. Woodward. m. Tom Lyle. Published by Oregon Publishing Company, Portland, OR. 1934. B/w drawing by Fowler of the Bonneville Dam. 4pp. Page 2: "Dedicated to our President Franklin D. Roosevelt." Page 4: Blank.

FDR-114 A Modern Messiah. w.m. Ira B. Arnstein. Published by Ira B. Arnstein. B/w drawing of Franklin D. Roosevelt, geometric design border. "For Mixed Chorus and Orchestra." "Dedicated to our beloved President Franklin Delano Roosevelt." 4pp.

FDR-115 It's Time To Dance (So Others Can Walk). w.m. Walter E. Sickles. Published by Dal E. Haun Company, Music Publishers, No. 2416 Palm Beach Avenue, Pittsburgh, PA. 1942. O/bk/w drawing of a watch, couple dancing, children on crutches. "Dedicated to the Committee for the Celebration of the President's Birthday for the National Foundation for Infantile Paralysis, Inc." 4pp. Page 4: Narrative on Birthday Ball.

FDR-116 It's Time To Dance (So Others Can Walk). w.m. Walter E. Sickles. Published by Dal E. Haun Company, Music Publishers, No. 2416 Palm Beach Avenue, Pittsburgh, PA. 1942. Non-pictorial black border. "Advance Artists Copy." "Dedicated to the Committee for the Celebration of the President's Birthday for the National Foundation for Infantile Paralysis." 4pp. Page 4: Blank.

FDR-117 Mister Franklin D. And Mister Winston C. w.m. Harry Patouhas and Morris Mayhams. Published by Mayhams Music Company, No. 12 West 117th Street, New York, NY. 1940. [9 1/2" × 12 1/2"]. Non-pictorial. 4pp. Page 4: Blank.

FDR-118 God Bless Our Late Commander In Chief (President Franklin Delano Roosevelt Memorial Song). w.m. William Farley. Published by William Farley, No. 600 16th Street, Oakland 12, CA. 1949. Bl/w drawing of Franklin D. Roosevelt, stars. 6pp. Pages 2 and 6: Blank.

FDR-119 He's Doing It Now. w.m. Dr. C.D. Covell. Copyright 1933 by C.D. Covell, San Francisco, CA. R/w/b stripes. Bl/w photo of Franklin D. Roosevelt. "Dedicated to President

Franklin Delano Roosevelt." 6pp. Pages 2 and 6: Blank.

FDR-120   Roosevelt. w.m. Marion Morrison. Published by Frank Harding, Publisher, Nos. 228-232 East 22nd Street, New York, NY. Copyright 1932 by Marion Morrison. R/w/pl drawing of Franklin D. Roosevelt, stars, lyre, floral and geometric design border. "Respectfully Dedicated to Franklin Delano Roosevelt." "Fair and Just, Do Right I Must For Roosevelt is My Name." 6pp. Page 2: Blank. Page 6: "Turn to the Right and Vote for Franklin Roosevelt."

FDR-121   President Roosevelt March (F.D.R., F.D.R., F.D.R. March). w. Andrea Litkei. m. Ervin Litkei. Published by Loena Publishing Company, No. 239 West 18th Street, New York, NY. 10011. 1965. [8 1/2" × 11"]. R/w/b cover. Bl/w photo by Fabian Bachrach of Franklin D. Roosevelt. 4pp. Page 4: Bl/w geographic design.

FDR-122   With A Roosevelt In The White House (Roosevelt's Victory Campaign Song). w. Dayve Boris DeWaltoff. m. Toni Voccoli. Published by D.B. DeWaltoff, No. 451 47th Street, Brooklyn, NY. 1932. B/w drawing of Franklin D. Roosevelt, star. "*With A Roosevelt In The White House* introduced and sung by Evertt D. McCooey." [8 1/2" × 11"]. 4pp. Page 4: Political advertising — "For Mayor Hon. John P. O'Brien." Advertising for book by Dayve Boris DeWaltoff.

FDR-123   There's An "FDR" In Freedom. w.m. Clarence Kelly, Frank H. Stanton and Bob Matthews. Published by Nationwide Songs, Inc., No. 1674 Broadway, New York, NY. 1942. R/w/b flag. Bl/w photos of Franklin D. Roosevelt and Henry Jerome inscribed "Featured by Henry Jerome." Bl/w War Bond advertising. "Pledge Your Support, Buy War Bonds and Stamps." 4pp. Page 4: Advertising for other Nationwide music.

FDR-124   America Marches On (March Song). w. J.B. Richner. m. William W. Taylor. Copyright 1933 by J.B. Richner. R/w/b drawing of Franklin Delano Roosevelt, flags, Capitol dome. "Dedicated to President Franklin Delano Roosevelt." 8pp. Pages 8: Blank.

FDR-125   Song Of The Legionaire. w. Al Lewis. m. Al Sherman. Published by American Music Corporation, No. 745 Seventh Avenue, New York, NY. 1933. R/w/bl/br drawing of Legionaires marching. R/bk photo of "Franklin D. Roosevelt, 32nd President of the U.S." "Respectfully Dedicated to Legionaire Franklin Delano Roosevelt." 4pp. Page 4: Advertising for other songs.

FDR-126   The NIRA Eagle (Song). w.m. G.W. McCauslin. Published by Frank Harding, Publisher, Nos. 228-232 East 22nd Street, New York, NY. Copyright 1933 by G.W. McCauslin. R/w/b drawing of a blue eagle — "NRA Member — U.S., We Do Our Part," geometric designs. 6pp. Page 6: Advertising for other music.

FDR-127   Prosperity March. w.m. D. Carl Gerardo. a. Eugene Platzman. Published by Gerardo Brothers Publishing Company, Elizabeth, NJ. 1933. R/w/b drawings of Capitol building — "March 4, 1933," Beer mug inscribed "April 1933," wine bottle, Bank building — "Bank Holiday March 11th." "Dedicated to Hon. Pres. Franklin Delano Roosevelt and the Democratic Party." "With Ukulele Arrangement." 4pp. Page 4: Blank.

FDR-128   Here's To The Name Of Roosevelt. w.m. Barrington L. Brannan. Published by Brannan Music Publishing Company, Inc., No. 121 West 42nd Street, New York, NY. 1932. Bl/w floral and geometric design border. Bl/w photo of Franklin D. Roosevelt. 6pp. Page 6: Blank.

FDR-129   God's Gift To The U.S.A. w.m. Alita Braun Cameron. Published by Braun Publishing Company, No. 505 Watts Building, San Diego, CA. 1941. Bl/w photo of Franklin D. Roosevelt.

R/w/b drawing of shield. 6pp. Page 6: Blank.

FDR-130 The Spirit Of The N.R.A. w. Carl H. Koch. m. Julius H. Walter. Published by National Music Publishers, San Francisco, CA. 1933. R/w/b drawing of N.R.A. eagle—"U.S.," stripe border. Bl/w photo of Clarence Tolman—"First sung by Clarence Tolman, 'The Cowboy Tenor,' on Coast-to-Coast NBC Broadcast from KGW, The Oregonian, Portland, Oregon." "The New Era Song that crashed into the heart of Broadway over night—The Song that thrilled America over the K.G.W.-NBC Network of stations on the President Roosevelt Program broadcast from Mt. Hood, Oregon, to President Roosevelt at The White House." "Dedicated to President Roosevelt." 6pp. Pages 2 and 6: Narrative on Mt. Hood. Page 2: Bl/w photo of Franklin D. Roosevelt. Page 6: Bl/w photo of Mt. Hood.

FDR-131 Prosperity (U.S.A. Recovery Song). w.m. Clasina L. Poelman. Published by National Music Company, Publishers, Chicago, IL. 1934. R/w/b flag design. B/w photo of Franklin D. Roosevelt, facsimile signature. 6pp. Pages 2 and 6: Advertising for other music.

FDR-132 Roosevelt We Hand The Flag To You! w. William Foster. m. Edna May Foster. Published by Calumet Music Publishers, Gary, IN. 1934. R/w/b eagle, trees, geometric designs. Bl/w photo of Franklin D. Roosevelt. 6pp. [V-1: Pages 2 and 6: Blank] [V-2: Page 2: Advertisement and song for M. Clifford Townsend, Democratic Candidate for Governor of Indiana. Page 6: Advertisement for Carroll Holly for Sheriff].

FDR-133 Around The World With Roosevelt. w.m. George David Mill. Published by DeVaignie Music Corporation, Chicago, IL. 1936. R/bk photo of Stan Ashley's Harmoneers—"Featured by Stan Ashley's Harmoneers of Station WTIC." R/bk drawing of stars, shields, geometric designs. 4pp. Page 4: Advertising for other DeVaignie Music.

FDR-134 Bye-Bye-Landon, Goodbye! w.m. James F. Kiely. Published by Empire Publishing Company, No. 606 Chestnut Street, St. Louis, MO. Copyright 1936 by James F. Kiely. [6 13/16" × 10 7/16"]. Non-pictorial. "The Great Democratic Campaign Song." 4pp. Page 4: Blank.

FDR-135 We Can Win With Roosevelt. w.m. Daniel P. O'Donnell. Published by Indiana Democratic State Central Committee, Fred Bays, State Chairman. 1940. B/w photos of "President Franklin D. Roosevelt" and "Vice-President Henry A. Wallace," Capitol building. B/w drawing of two flags. 6pp. Page 2: Campaign advertising for "Lieut. Gov. Henry Schricker" and "Senator Minton." Page 6: State Democratic ticket.

FDR-136 Our President. w. Monte O. Howard. m. Nelson E. Story and Bert Barber. Copyright 1936 by F.A. Marsh and Bert Barber. Bl/w drawing by McMaster of Franklin Delano Roosevelt. R/w/b stars and stripes design. 6pp. Page 6: Blank.

FDR-137 Thanks, Mister Roosevelt (Song Fox Trot). w.m. Tommie Conner. Published by [V-1 and V-2: B. Feldman & Company, No. 125-9 Shaftesbury Avenue, W.C.2, London, England [V-3 and V-4: J. Albert and Sons, Sidney, Australia]. 1941. [9 3/4" × 12"]. [V-1 and V-2: Bl/bk/w] [V-3 and V-4: R/w/b] flag design. [V-1: B/w photo of Bebe Daniels—"Featured and Broadcast by Bebe Daniels"] [V-2: B/w photo of Geraldo—"Featured and Broadcast by Geraldo and His Orchestra"] [V-3: Bl/w photo of Joy Nichols—"Featured by Joy Nichols"] [V-4: B/w photo of George Nichols—"Sung by George Nichols"]. 4pp. Page 4: Advertising.

FDR-138 New Deal (March Song). w.m. Margaret D. Evans. Published by Margaret D. Evans, No. 35

Brookline Avenue, Youngstown, OH. 1936. R/w/b drawings of Uncle Sam with bugle, music notes, Franklin D. Roosevelt. 6pp. Pages 2 and 6: Blank. Page 3: "Dedicated to President Franklin D. Roosevelt."

FDR-139 There's Something About Franklin D. Roosevelt That Is Fine, Fine, Fine. w.m. Franklin Hugh Ellison. Copyright 1933 by Mills Music, Inc. [8 1/2" × 11"]. B/w photo of "President Franklin D. Roosevelt," stars. 6pp. Page 6: Blank.

FDR-140 Roosevelt-Wallace Campaign Song. [1940]. Non-pictorial black line border. [5 9/16" × 8 1/4"]. 2pp. Page 2: Blank.

FDR-141 Roosevelt (Song). w.m. Felix A. Nolasco. Published by Felix A. Nolasco, New York, NY. 1933. Photo of "Hon. Franklin D. Roosevelt." "Voice and Piano." 6pp. Page 2: "Dedicated to the Honorable Franklin D. Roosevelt." Page 6: Blank.

FDR-142 New Deal March. w.m. Professor Sami Chawa (Member of the Royal Egyptian Academy of Music). Published by Makhoul and Nahmee, No. 574 47th Street, Brooklyn, NY. 1934. Drawing of "Franklin Delano Roosevelt, 1932,"geometric design border. Photo of "Professor Sami Chawa." "Dedicated to President Franklin D. Roosevelt, Father of Labor." "All kinds of Egyptian and Oriental Music Books and Pianolla Rolls for sale at Professor L. Nahmee Studio, 4700 6th Avenue, Brooklyn, NY." 4pp. Page 2: "Dedicated to Franklin D. Roosevelt, Father of Labor." Page 4: Blank.

FDR-143 Roosevelt Victory Song (Fox Trot). w. V.M. Richards. m.a. The Starret System Club. Published by The Starret System Club, New York, NY. Copyright 1933 by V.M. Richards. B/w drawing of "Franklin Delano Roosevelt, 1932." R/w/bk geometric designs, lyre. 4pp. Page 4: Blank.

FDR-144 Governor Roosevelt March. m. Prof. Giacome D'Agostino. Published by Prof. Giacomo D'Agostino, No. 235 Washington Street, Newburgh, NY. 1929. Br/be photo of Professor D'Agostino, geometric design border. "For Violin, E-flat Saxophone and Piano." 6pp. Page 2: Be/br photo of Franklin D. Roosevelt — "To the Honorable Franklin D. Roosevelt, Governor of the State of New York, on the Occasion of his Inauguration Admiringly Dedicated January, 1929." Page 6: Blank.

FDR-145 I've Got Another Day From The N.R.A. (To Love That Baby of Mine). w.m. Charlie Tobias, Pierre Norman and Henry H. Tobias. Published by Famous Music Corporation, No. 1619 Broadway, New York, NY. 1934. Gn/bk drawing of couple. B/w photo of Eddie Canter — "Featured by Eddie Canter." 6pp. Page 6: Advertising for other music.

FDR-146 The Blue Eagle Is Flying High. w.m. Billy Baskette and Theodore Alban. Published by Mason Music Company, No. 1587 Broadway, New York, NY. 1933. Bl/w photo of B.A. Rolfe — "Good Luck to the Blue Eagle, B.A. Rolfe [facsimile handwriting]." 4pp.

FDR-147 America Is On Parade. w.m. Victor A. Tetreault. a. Hal Boorn. Published by Victor A. Tetreault, No. 3821 Montgomery Avenue, Detroit, MI. 1940. R/w/bl/br drawing of Uncle Sam marching with workers, soldiers, &c. 6pp. Page 2: "Dedicated to the President, Franklin Delano Roosevelt and his 'National Defense' Program." Page 6: Blank.

FDR-148 Good-Bye Mr. Hoover (Democratic Victory Song). w.m. Louis Carpino, Lester Perry, Oscar Perry and Riley Altier. Published by Ted Brown Music Company, Chicago, IL. 1932. Bl/bk drawing of cheering crowd throwing "Hooverism" out of The White House. 4pp.

FDR-149 Roosevelt We're For You. w.m. Allen D. Summers. Published by Roosevelt Publishing Company, No. 1741 North Central Avenue, Chicago, IL.

1939. R/bl cover. Bl/w drawing of Franklin D. Roosevelt. 6pp. Page 6: R/w/b eagle logo.

FDR-150 Prosperity Is Returning. w. Blanche R. Snow. m. Sylvia Rowell. Published by Snow Publishing Company, Portland, ME. 1932. R/w/b drawing of Capitol dome, eagle, toy soldiers marching, stars, geometric designs. 6pp.

FDR-151 Here We Come Mr. President (Small Town Boys). w. W. Frank Brown. m. David Lawrence. Published by W. Frank Brown, No. 24 North Fifth, Keokuk, IA. 1943. B/w photo of "W. Frank Brown — Truly Yours [facsimile handwriting]." "I pledge allegiance to my flag, and to the republic for which it stands, one nation, indivisible, with liberty and justice for all." 8pp. Page 8: Advertising.

FDR-152 Here We Come Mr. President (Small Town Boys). w. W. Frank Brown. m. David Lawrence (Hollywood, Calif). Published by W. Frank Brown, No. 24 North Fifth, Keokuk, IA. 1943. R/w/b drawing of Uncle Sam, ribbon, stars. "I pledge allegiance to my flag, and to the republic for which it stands, one nation, indivisible, with liberty and justice for all." 8pp. Page 8: Advertising.

FDR-153 Here We Come Mr. President. w. W. Frank Brown. m. David Lawrence. Published by W. Frank Brown, No. 24 North Fifth, Keokuk, IA. 1943. Non-pictorial. "Professional Copy." "I pledge allegiance to my flag, and to the republic for which it stands, one nation, indivisible, with liberty and justice for all." "Released through La Casa Del Rio Music Publications, 1685 Broadway, New York 19, NY." 8pp.

FDR-154 Play The Game. w.m. Pauline Hope Buttner. Special N.R.A. words and Published by Western Music Arts, Hotel Robins, No. 711 Post Street, San Francisco, CA. [ca. 1934]. Bk/w/y paste-on N.R.A. eagle — "Play The Game, NRA Member, We Do Our Part, Just do Your Part." 6pp. + 2pp. Insert: "N.R.A. Word Version."

FDR-155 Everything's Ding-A-Ling. w. Edward A. Nitram. m. Harry Wagner. Published by Sangamo Music Publishing Company, Springfield, IL. [1933]. R/w/b drawing of Franklin D. Roosevelt, bells, star. 4pp. Page 4: Blank.

FDR-156 The New Deal. w.m. Eliza E. Blanchet. Published by The National Manuscript Bureau, No. 236 West 55th Street, New York, NY. 1934. O/w/bl drawing by P&L Studios of window, sun rising, sun rays, trees. 4pp. Page 4: Advertising.

FDR-157 He Was Your Friend And Mine. w. Tommy MacWilliams. m. Lou E. Zoeller. Published by The Zoeller Music Company, Beverly Hills, CA. 1945. B/w drawing of Franklin D. Roosevelt. R/w/b flag sticker attached. "Introduced and Recorded by Tex Atchison and His Santa Fe Boys, Victory Records No. 124A." "Sole Selling Agents: Pacific Music Sales, 1515 N. Vine St., Hollywood 28, California." 4pp. Page 2: "Dedicated to the Memory of Franklin Roosevelt." Page 4: Advertising.

FDR-158 Hail To Our President. w. Jacqueline Nesbit. m. Herbert J. Smith and Wilma R. Lung. Published by Benearl Publishing Company, No. 299 Heffernan Building, Syracuse, NY. 1940. Bl/w drawings/photos of Franklin D. Roosevelt, George Washington, Abraham Lincoln, Theodore Roosevelt, Woodrow Wilson. R/w/b drawing of flag, Capitol building, eagle, shield. 6pp. Page 2: Song: *Star Spangled Banner*. Page 6: Bl/w photos/drawings of all remaining presidents.

FDR-159 We'll Carry On, On To Victory. w.m. Lew Mel, George Weir and Tommy Carey. a. Belle Schrag. Copyright 1942 by Thomas J. Carey, No. 73 Ridge Avenue, Neptune City, Avon, NJ. [8 1/2" × 11"]. B/w drawing of "Franklin Delano Roosevelt." "Performance rights controlled by Broadcast Music Incorporated." 4pp.

FDR-160 Blue Eagle. w.m. Olive Gorman. Published by Perfection Publishing Company, Omaha, NE. 1933. Drawing of an N.R.A. eagle — "NRA Member — U.S. We Do Our Part." Photo of "Olive Gorman, Composer." "Dedicated to President and Mrs. Franklin D. Roosevelt." 6pp.

FDR-161 No Depression (Fox-Trot Song). w. Diana Gale. m. Jack Edwards. Published by Frank Harding, No. 228 East 22nd Street, New York, NY. Copyright 1933 by Grace E. Dunham. Br/w/bl drawing by A. Gerald of workers walking to factories. "Dedicated to Franklin D. Roosevelt and the N.R.A." "Copies for sale at all music stores or send direct to publisher, price 30 cents per copy." 6pp. Page 6: Advertising.

FDR-162 Another Roosevelt. w. Lawrence L. Foster. m. Ben Gibson. Published by Lawrence L. Foster, Box 15 Rapatee, IL. 1933. B/w drawing by Gibson of Franklin D. Roosevelt, Capitol building, flag. 4pp. Pages 2 and 3: B/w drawings between the lines of the music of people supporting Franklin D. Roosevelt — Cowboy, Farmer, Worker, Crowd, &c. Page 4: Advertising.

FDR-163 There's Something About John N. Garner That Is Fine, Fine, Fine.

FDR-164 Our Flag And You. w.m. Anna Dugan. a. Herman A. Hummel. Published by The Dugan Music Service, No. 244 High Street, Hamilton, OH. 1934. Non-pictorial professional copy. "Dedicated to President and Mrs. Franklin Roosevelt." 2pp.

FDR-165 Roose Franklin. w.m. Janet B. Brooks. Published by Columbian Music Publishers, Ltd., Toronto, Canada. 1938. Drawing of singers, musicians. "Professional Artists Copy." 4pp. Page 4: Blank.

FDR-166 Vote On! Pennsylvania! w.m. Kathryn S. Flohr. Published by Democratic State Committee of PA. 1936. Bl/y cover. B/w drawings of Franklin D. Roosevelt and George H. Earle [Governor]. 4pp. Page 4: The 1936 Democratic Electoral Ticket — "Uphold our President and George H. Earle Our Governor — Vote Straight Democratic!" List of Candidates for local offices.

FDR-167 Ev'eybody Ev'ry Payday. w. Tom Adair. m. Dick Uhl. Published by United States Printing Office, Washington, DC. Copyright 1942 by Henry Morgenthau, Jr., Secretary of the Treasury, Washington, DC. R/w/bl/bk photos of workers, dimes. 4pp.

FDR-168 We're On The March. w.m. Morton Downey, Carl Field and Jack Erickson. Published by M. Witmark and Sons, NY. 1933. Bl/w photo of Morton Downey — "Introduced by Morton Downey, Camel Hour, W.A.B.C." 6pp. Page 6: Advertising.

FDR-169 The March Of Victory. w.m. Carl H. Koch. Published by National Music Publishers, Seattle, WA. 1936. R/w/b drawing of Franklin D. Roosevelt, rose border design. "The Roosevelt National Campaign Song Authorized by the Democratic National Committee." "Original music for the Dance *The Roosevelt Romp.*" "We strive for a better America, and if we shall succeed, as by God's help we will, America will point the way towards a better World — President Roosevelt." 4pp. Page 4: Blank.

FDR-170 We're On The March. w.m. Morton Downey, Carl Field and Jack Erickson. Published by M. Witmark and Sons, NY. 1933. Non-pictorial "Professional Copy." 4pp.

FDR-171 Roosevelt (Song). w.m. James Bracken. Published by James Bracken, No. 23 Kingsley Place, Canton, MA. 1934. Drawing of Franklin D. Roosevelt geometric design border. 4pp.

FDR-172 We're All With You Mister Roosevelt. w.m. Robert Mack. Published by Union Music Company, New York, NY. 1932. Bl/w photo of Franklin D. Roosevelt. 4pp. Page 4: Advertising.

FDR-173 We're All With You Mister Roosevelt (Order Progress, Peace!). w.m. Robert Mack. Published by The Union Music Company, New York, NY. [1940]. B/w photo/drawings of Franklin D. Roosevelt, Henry A. Wallace — "Wallace for Vice-President," George Washington, Abraham Lincoln, Robert Mack, Uncle Sam, flags. 4pp. Page 4: Blank.

FDR-174 President Roosevelt (We Greet You) (March Song). w.m. Mr. and Mrs. John E. Williams. Published by John E. Williams, R.D. #2, Bristol, PA. 1934. B/w photo of Franklin D. Roosevelt. Bl/w drawing of eagle, star and stripe border. 4pp. Page 4: Blank.

FDR-175 Franklin D. Roosevelt's Address To His Forces. w. Patrick Andrew Crorkin. m. Air: *Land O' The Leal*. Published by Hawaii Conservatory Publishing Company, No. 741 South Western Avenue, Los Angeles, CA. 1942. Bl/w drawing of Franklin D. Roosevelt. "Dedicated to General John J. Pershing, U.S. Army." "Melody: Ancient Scottish: Traditionally the Battle Tune of the freedom-defending victorious Scottish Army at Bannuockburn in 1314. Used by the great Robert Burns to celebrate that victory and also used by Lady Narin for her song: *Land O' The Leal*." 4pp. Page 3: "Second Prize: National Patriotic Song Writer's Day, Apr. 22, 1942." Page 4: Facsimile letter from White House.

FDR-176 The Best Known Soldier. w.m. Denver Darling and Vaughn Horton. Published by Rytvoc, Inc., No. 1585 Broadway, New York, NY. 1946. Bl/w drawing of Franklin D. Roosevelt. "Dedicated to the memory of Franklin D. Roosevelt." 4pp. Page 4: Advertising.

FDR-177 (Franklin D., Winston C., Joseph V.) Victory Jones. w.m. Harold Rome. Published by Leeds Music Corporation, RKO Building, New York, NY. 1942. Pl/w drawing of musical notes. Pl/w photo of Sammy Kaye — "Featured by Sammy Kaye and His Orchestra." 6pp. Page 6: Advertising.

FDR-178 What Are You Going To Do In 1932? (Campaign Song). w.m. John H. Trayne. Published by Music Service Company, No. 170A Tremont Street, Boston, MA. 1932. Pl/w drawing by Fisher of a donkey, elephant on crutches. 4pp.

FDR-179 The President's Birthday Ball. w.m. Irving Berlin. Published by Irving Berlin, Inc., No. 799 Seventh Avenue, New York, NY. 1942. R/w/b geometric designs, number "60" within blue diamonds. Bl/w photo of Franklin D. Roosevelt. [V-1: For Piano] [V-2: 7" × 10 1/2"]. [V-1: 6pp. Page 6: Advertising] [V-2: Parts set for Band].

FDR-180 The President's Birthday Ball. w.m. Irving Berlin. Published by Irving Berlin, Inc., Music Publishers, No. 799 Seventh Avenue, New York, NY. 1942. Non-pictorial. "For professional Use Only." Copyright "Warning." 2pp.

FDR-181 Our Heroes (Franklin Delano Roosevelt — Henry A. Wallace) [Song Sheet]. [1940]. Non-pictorial. "Campaign Songs for the Election of Franklin D. Roosevelt, Songs will be introduced by Jula B. Crawford." 2pp. Page 2: Blank.

FDR-182 We're Ridin' To Glory On A Mule. w.m. Frank J. Davis. Published by Dixie Publishing Company, No. 2328 West Seventh Street, Los Angeles, CA. Copyright 1944 by Frank Davis. Bl/w drawing of Franklin D. Roosevelt, others riding donkeys on the road to the Capitol building. 6pp. Page 2 and 6: Advertising for other music.

FDR-183 We're Ridin' To Glory On A Mule. w.m. Frank J. Davis. Published by Dixie Publishing Company, No. 2328 West Seventh Street, Los Angeles, CA. Copyright 1944 by Frank Davis. Bl/bl non-pictorial mimeograph. "Copyright and all other rights reserved and fully protected. Note: The order of the verses can be interchanged at option of

(FDR) FRANKLIN D. ROOSEVELT

performer." 6pp. Obv: Music. Rev: Blank.

FDR-184 Our Friend. w. T.E. Stephenson. m. Air: *What A Friend We Have In Jesus.* [ca. 193-]. Non-pictorial. Two Franklin D. Roosevelt quotes. "Governor Tom Berry of South Dakota Introduced him as 'Our Friend' and when I say 'Our Friend,' I mean it." 2pp. Page 2: Blank.

FDR-185 Roosevelt Day (March Song). w.m. F.W. Grant. Published by Tremont Music Company, Dover, NH. 1933. R/w/b cover with star border. "Souvenir Edition Sponsored by Dover Ind. Textile Workers Union In Honor of It's President John E. McCoole." 4pp. Page 4: Blank.

FDR-186 To Thee America (Cantata For Mixed Chorus and Piano or Orchestra). w. A. Leyeless. m. Lazar Weiner. Published by Transcontinental Music Corporation, New York, NY. 1944. Non-pictorial. "Vocal Score." 44pp. Page 2: "To Franklin Delano Roosevelt and Albert Einstein, Two Great Champions of Liberty and Democracy." Page 44: Advertising.

FDR-187 Sentiments For Franklin D. Roosevelt. w. Marie A. Amberger. m. Leo Richard. Published by Marie A. Amberger, No. 220 Rosalind Avenue, Gloucester, NJ. 1938. Bl/w drawing of water lilies, geometric designs. 4pp. Page 4: Blank.

FDR-188 Toward The Sun. w. Lewis Allen. m. Earl Robinson. Published by Chappell and Company, Inc., RKO Building, New York, NY. 1946. R/w/b drawing of Franklin D. Roosevelt, stars and stripes. "From *The Roosevelt Story.* Produced by Martin Levine and Oliver A. Unger. Released thru United Artists." 6pp. Page 6: Blank.

FDR-189 I Love You O America. w. Dr. Ezekiel Leavitt. m. Samuel Weisser. Published by Metro Music, No. 64 Second Avenue, New York, NY. Copyright 1941 by Samuel Weisser. R/w/b drawing of flag, blue line border. "Dedicated to Franklin D. Roosevelt, President of the United States of America." 4pp. + 4 page insert of song in Yiddish. Page 4: Bl/w photos of Composers.

FDR-190 All Out For America. w. John Adams. m. Mayhew Lake. Published by Sam Fox Publishing Company, Cleveland, OH. 1941. [V-2: 6 7/8" × 10 1/2"]. [V-1: R/w/b drawing of eagle, stars and stripes] [V-2: B/w eagle, stars, border]. "Dedicated to our Commander-in-Chief." "Marching Song of the U.S.A." 4pp. Page 2: [V-2: "Conductor"]. Page 4: Advertising.

FDR-191 The Prosperity Song. w. Estelle B. Page. m. Pierre Page, Sr. Published by Pierre Page, Sr., No. 510 Deming Place, Chicago, IL. 1933. Drawings of old Fort Chicago — "1833," and modern Chicago skyline — "1933." B/w photo of Pierre Page, Jr — "Featured by Pierre Page, Jr. "Piano and Piano Accordion Artist." 6pp. Page 6: Advertising.

FDR-192 Our President. w. W. Jivaraj DeAlwis. m. Vashti Rogers Griffin, L.L. Laugeson and J.W. Stuart. Copyright 1934 by W. Jivaraj DeAlwis. R/w/b drawing of Franklin D. Roosevelt, Capitol building, "Aquarius" sign, globe, geometric designs. "Symbols in Border Design Explained on Back Page." 4pp. Page 2: "Dedicated to Franklin D. Roosevelt." Page 4: "Symbols of cover design explained."

FDR-193 God Bless Our President. w.m. Cordelia Henry. Published by C. Henry, No. 507 North Madison Street, Bloomington, IL. 1940. B/w photo of Franklin Roosevelt. 4pp. Page 4: Drawing of trees, geometric design border.

FDR-194 Don't Change Horses. w.m. Al Hofman, Milton and Jerry Livington. Published by Drake-Hoffman-Livingston, No. 1619 Broadway, New York, NY. 1944. Photo of the Hoosier Hot Shots — "Recorded and featured by The Hoosier Hot Shots." Drawing of man standing on two horses. 4pp.

FDR-195 Stand By Our President. w.m. Joe Carroll. Published by Joe Carroll, No. 2624 Kensington Avenue, Philadelphia, PA. 1944. Bl/w photo of Franklin Roosevelt. R/w drawing of eagle, geometric design border. 6pp. Page 6: Blank.

FDR-196 Hail The President. w.m. L. Frederick Schultz. Published by National Music Company, Chicago, IL. 1936. Bl/w photo of Franklin Roosevelt. R/w/b drawing of trees, geometric designs. 6pp. Page 6: Bl/w eagles.

FDR-197 Songs For Political Action [Song Book]. Published by National Citizens Political Action Committee, No. 205 East 42nd Street, New York, NY. 1944. Drawing of man, guitar, singers. Narrative. 4pp. Songs — Page 1: **He's The People's Choice.** w. Bernice Fields. m. Irma Jurist. Page 2: **Are You Backing Up Your Commander-In-Chief?** w. Henri Meyers, Ed Eliscu. m. Jay Gorney. **My Friend Roosevelt.** w.m. Harold J. Rome. Page 3: **That Man In The White House.** w. Lewis Allen. m. Earl Robinson. Page 4: **Dewey? We Don't.** w. Leo Paris. m. Sylvia Kramer.

FDR-198 Our Fallen Chief. w. Rosa Belle Keith. m. Hal Chanslor. Published by Rosa Keith, No. 1826 Vernon Street, NW., Washington, DC. 1945. Drawing of Franklin Roosevelt, White House. "Dedicated to the late President Franklin Delano Roosevelt, who died April 12, 1945." 4pp.

FDR-199 Franklin Roosevelt, Our President (Waltz Song). w. Livingston Greenwood. m. Pat Guyheen. Published for Roosevelt Men's Democratic Club of Kings County, Washington, Dr. J.P. Binyon, Pres. by Livingston Greenwood, Seattle, WA. 1934. Br/w photo of Franklin Roosevelt, facsimile signature. "Every Promise He's Made Is Not Long Delayed, Every Action Sincerity." 6pp. Page 6: "A Declaration of Loyalty." Membership, Democratic Club of Kings County.

FDR-200 Welcome Mr. Roosevelt. w.m. Eric Karll. Copyright 1934 by Eric Karll, Milwaukee, WI. R/w/b drawing of Franklin D. Roosevelt, map of Wisconsin with cities and products located, NRA eagle. "Compliments of" [V-1: Bagda Motor Company, No. 415 Main Street, Green Bay, WI] [V-2: Lowe Chevrolet Company, 1221 Franklin Street, Manitowoc, WI] [V-3: Two Rivers Beverage Company, Two Rivers, WI]. 6pp. Pages 5 and 6: Advertising — [V-1 and V-2: Chevrolet autos, song — *She's The Sweetheart of the Highways*. Photos of cars] [V-3: Golden Drops Beer, drawing of beer bottle].

FDR-201 The Little White House Down In Georgia. w.m. Margaret Wilson Jones. Published by Southern Music Company, No. 217 Bibb Building, Macon, GA. [ca. 1940]. B/w photo of the Little White House, Warm Springs, GA. 4pp. Page 2: "Dedicated to Hon. Franklin D. Roosevelt."

FDR-202 Our Guiding Star (Franklin D. Roosevelt). w. Charles N. Wuest. m. Clotilde Nagel, San Antonio, TX. Copyright [ca. 1936] by Charles Wuest. [4 3/4" × 6 3/4"]. B/w photo of Franklin Roosevelt. 2pp. Page 2: Blank.

FDR-203 Over Here. w. "A Descendent of New England Pioneers, 1634." m. "A World War Veteran." Published by Patriotic Songs Publications, No. 351 West 52nd Street, New York, NY. 1935. Bl/w drawing of Statue of Liberty, man on hill. "Dedicated To Youth In This World Crisis." 4pp. Page 4: List of crises — "Italy and Ethiopia, League of Nations," "Roosevelt and Red Peril," "Kemal, Dictator of Turkey," "Senator Pope and Anti-Neutrality." "Attention, Immediately write or wire the President, Washington, D.C., Urge America's entrance into the League of Nations."

FDR-204 Roosevelt, Garner And Me (One Step). w.m. Al Lewis and Al Sherman. In: *Universal Dance Folio For Piano, No. 25*, page 20. Published by

Irving Berlin, No. 1607 Broadway, New York, NY. 1933.

FDR-205 Franklin Roosevelt We're With You. w. Maud Michael. m. Charles Gilpin. Published by Maud Michael, 1819 Chestnut Street, Philadelphia, PA. 1935. [5 3/8" × 8 1/2"]. Non-pictorial. "Notice: Endorsed and Sponsored by the Roosevelt Citizens' Committee of Philadelphia, PA. and many Democratic leaders throughout the United States as the Official Democratic Campaign Song for 1936." "Notice: Endorsed by the Atlantic County Democratic Campaign Committee of New Jersey, with a request this song be used to open all Democratic Political Meetings and Public Assemblies, Charles J. Lafferty, Chair." "Notice: Mrs. Mary J. Norton, Democratic Congressman and Chairman of the District of Columbia Committee which supervises local government in Washington, D.C., and the Federal District endorses this song and recommends its use at all Political Meetings and claims it to be a Real Patriotic Promoter." "This song was introduced as the Official Democratic Campaign Song at the Testimonial Dinner of 1200 guests at the Pennsylvania Athletic Club, January 10, 1935, for the Hon. H. Edgar Barnes, Secretary of Revenue of Pennsylvania." "A Meeting without a Song is like a Meal without Salt — It's Flat." 2pp. Page 2: Blank.

FDR-206 National Lament. w.m. Jimmie Lawson and Douglas Venable. Published by Sinclair Publications, No. 2024 South Vermont Avenue, Los Angeles 7, CA. 1945. B/w photo of Franklin Roosevelt, geometric design border. 4pp. Page 4: Blank.

FDR-207 The Face On The Dime. w.m. Harold Rome. Published by M. Witmark and Sons, New York, NY. 1946. R/w/gn non-pictorial. Melvyn Douglas and Herman Levin presents *Call Me Mister*, Music and Lyrics by Harold Rome, Sketches by Arnold Auerbach, Staged by Robt. H. Gordon, Dance Direction by John Wray, Musical Direction by Lehman Engel." 6pp. Page 6: Advertising.

FDR-208 We're Keepin' F.D.R. w.m. Ray Lee. Published by Ray Lee, No. 307 Mississippi Avenue, Joliet, IL. 1936. Non-pictorial. 2pp. Page 2: "Respectfully Dedicated to our President Franklin D. Roosevelt's Official Campaign Song."

FDR-209 Our President. w.m. Joey Hart and E. Cleveland. Published by Joe Hart, Room 608, No. 139 North Clark Street, Chicago, IL. 1936. B/w photo of Franklin D. Roosevelt. Bl/w/bk drawing of trees, geometric designs. 6pp. Page 2: "Respectfully Dedicated to our beloved Franklin Delano Roosevelt." Page 6: Advertising.

FDR-210 The Country's Calling Roosevelt. w.m. Dorothy Alexander. Published by Salt Lake County Democratic Committee, [Salt Lake City, UT]. [1932-1944]. Drawing of an American flag, star and stripe border.

FDR-211 Is It True What They Say About Roosevelt? [w. Irving Caesar]. m. "To the Tune of *Is It True What They Say About Dixie?*" [1936]. [3 3/4" × 6"]. Bl/w non-pictorial geometric border. 2pp. Page 2: Blank.

FDR-212 Franklin D. (You're Good Enough for Me). w. Joseph Gallagher. m. Charles R. Campbell. Published by Joseph Gallagher, Park Theatre Building, Erie, PA. [1932-1940]. Non-pictorial geometric designs.

FDR-213 Let's Re-Re-Re-Elect Roosevelt. [1944]. [5 7/16" × 8 7/16"]. Non-pictorial. 2pp. Page 2: Blank.

FDR-214 Aloha To You Mr. Roosevelt. w.m. Don George. Sponsored by Woodrow Wilson Post No. 10, The American Legion, [Honolulu, HI]. Copyright June 23, 1934, by Don George, Honolulu, HI. R/w/b background. B/w drawings of Franklin D. Roosevelt, hula girl with lei. B/w photo of Don George — "Featured by the Composer at the Princess Theatre." "Dedicated to Our President." 4pp.

FDR-215 I Have A Rendezvous With Life. w. Walter N. Thayer, Jr. m. Geoffrey O'Hara. Published by Music Products Corporation, No. Twenty-Eight East Jackson Boulevard, Chicago, IL. 1938. R/w/bk non-pictorial geometric designs. "To Franklin Delano Roosevelt the man, in appreciation of whose untiring interest in the welfare of the Youth of America this Song is dedicated." 8pp. Pages 2, 7 and 8: Advertising.

FDR-216 Roosevelt Is In (We're Bound to Win) (Song). w.m. P. Waltner, S. Kamholtz and F. Wildau. Published by Franklin Wildau, Publisher, No. 8932 South Manhattan Place, Los Angeles, CA. 1933. Br/w photo of Franklin D. Roosevelt. "Introduced by J. Michelmore." 4pp. Page 4: Blank.

FDR-217 With Roosevelt As The Skipper (Will Sail Along to Prosperity). w. Henry E. Cordell. m. Jean Walz. Published by The Zodiac Publishing Company, Chicago, IL. 1933. Non-pictorial. 4pp.

FDR-218 Roosevelt (We're All for You). w.m. Margaret Scott Penn. Published by Mayflower Music Publishing Company, No. 100 Maryland Avenue NE., Washington, DC. 1933. Bl/w photo of Franklin D. Roosevelt, geometric design border. 4pp. Page 4: Blank.

FDR-219 This Country Of Ours (Flag Day Theme). w.m. Joe Nuccio. Published by Crestwood Music Publications, No. 1585 Broadway, New York, NY. 1945. Bl/w photo of "Franklin Delano Roosevelt." Bl/w drawings by Barbelle of eagle, shield, stars. "Dedicated to Franklin Delano Roosevelt." 6pp. Page 2: Dedication. Page 6: Advertising.

FDR-220 The President's Message. w.m. Vladimir Heifetz. Published by Transcontinental Music Corporation, New York, NY. 1942. [7" × 10 1/2"]. Non-pictorial geometric design border. "Transcontinental Choral Library No. 104." "For Solo, Mixed Voices and Piano (Or Orchestra)." "Vocal Score." 24pp. Page 2: "A Message by Franklin D. Roosevelt." Page 3: "For Mixed Vocals and Piano with Soprano and Baritone Solo." Page 24: Advertising.

FDR-221(A) Franklin D. Roosevelt. w. Lewis Allen. m. "From a Tune from The War of 1812 — *Hey, Betty Martin*." In: *Sing America*, page 54. c. Anne Allan. Published by Worker's Bookshop, No. 50 East 13th Street, New York, NY. [ca. 1944]. [4 1/2" × 6"]. Non-pictorial. 68pp.

(B) Roosevelt And The Four Freedoms. w. L.A. m. "Based on Landon's Campaign Song."

(C) Are You Backing Your Commander-In-Chief? w. Henry Meyers, Edward Eliscu. m. Jay Gorney.

FDR-222 G.O.P. (or Is It GYP?) (Campaign Song). w. Tom Dwyer. m. Air: "With apologies to the Good Democrat who wrote *Oh, Susanna*." [1936]. [8" × 10"]. Non-pictorial. "Ride Right with Roosevelt." "Imagine America like Kansas!" "Good Democrats: Sing this wherever you may to the tune of *Oh Susanna*." "Ask for more where you received this copy. Reproduction for distribution by Democratic organizations and individuals enthusiastically encouraged. Spread 'em!" 2pp. Page 2: Blank.

FDR-223 Elegy. m. Bernard Rogers. Published by Elkan-Vogel Company, Inc., Philadelphia, PA. 1947. [6 7/8" × 10 1/2"]. Non-pictorial. "Elkan-Vogel Orchestra Score Series." "To the Memory of Franklin D. Roosevelt." List of other titles in series. 12pp. Page 2: Advertising. Page 12: Blank.

FDR-224 Prayer For Peace. w. Franklin D. Roosevelt. m. Ralph Matesky. Published by Mills Music, Inc., No. 1619 Broadway, New York, NY. 1947. Non-pictorial geometric designs. "For Mixed Voices S.A.T.B. with Piano or Organ Accompaniment." 30pp.

FDR-225 The Big Three Polka.

(FDR) FRANKLIN D. ROOSEVELT

w. Moe Jaffe and Bickley Reichner. m. Lieutenant Commander Clay A. Boland, U.S.N.R. Published by Mills Music, Inc., No. 1619 Broadway, New York, NY. 1944. R/w/b drawing of a mask, graduation hat, The Mask And Whig Club, University of Pennsylvania, logo. "Mask and Wig presents *Red Points and Blue*, the 56th Annual production of the Mask And Wig Club of The University of Pennsylvania," Lyrics Moe Jaffe and Bickley Reichner, Music by Lieutenant Commander Clay A. Boland, U.S.N.R., Dances by Pete Conlow, Direction by Lou Day, Orchestration and Vocal Arrangements by Lieutenant Commander Clay A. Boland." List of other songs in show. 6pp. Pages 2 and 6: Advertising.

FDR-226 Victory For Democracy (Triunfo de la Democracia). w.m. Fina Morales. Published by Delphina C. Morales, No. 159 West 23rd Street, Los Angeles, CA. 1945. Y/bl/w drawing of Franklin D. Roosevelt, eagle, star, "V" symbol. "In memory of him who kept faith F.D. Roosevelt." "Dedicated to everyone who kept faith with him." 8pp. Page 8: Blank.

FDR-227 Prosperity Is Coming (Thanks to Franklin D). w.m. Dollie Palmer Webb. Published by Dollie Palmer Webb, No. 1506 Jane Street, Flint, MI. 1936. R/w/bk geometric designs. B/w drawing of "Franklin Delano Roosevelt, 1932." 4pp. Page 4: Blank.

FDR-228 They Asked For It And Now They're Gonna Get It. w.m. Samuel Slater and Frank Capano, ASCAP. Published by Tin Pan Alley Publications, No. 1011 Chestnut Street, Philadelphia, PA. 1945. B/w drawing by Harry S. Moskovitz of Franklin D. Roosevelt, stars. 4pp.

FDR-229 The Yankee Doodler. w.m. Fos Carling and Phil Boutelje. Published by Mills Music, Inc., Music Publishers, No. 1619 Broadway, New York, NY. 1942. R/w/b drawings of various people to be used to rhyme words to song, including Franklin Roosevelt, Adolph Hitler and Douglas MacArthur, Benito Mussolini, Tojo. "Refrain — Now we're gonna Fight, Gonna Fight, Gonna Fight, How we're Gonna Fight, Yeah Man! Win this War." Various rhymes — "Hitler's Pay-Beat That Man," "Benito's Jaw-Haw! Haw! Haw!," "MacArthur's Side-Turned the Tide," "President-100%." 6pp. Pages 2 and 5: Blank boxes for rhyming your own words. Pages 3: Music. Page 4: Instructions.

FDR-230 Let's Stand Behind Great Britain. w.m. Abner Silver and Mann Curtis. Published by Lincoln Music Corporation, No. 1619 Broadway, New York, NY. 1941. Ma/w drawing of badge — "Dieu et mon Droit." "Inspired by President Roosevelt's recent broadcast." "The writers of this Song have donated their royalties to Bundles For Britain." 4pp. Page 4: Narrative.

FDR-231 Forward With Roosevelt. w.m. Antun K. Pipin. a. Marcos L. Davalos. Published by Antun K. Pipin, No. 717 North Van Ness Avenue, Hollywood, CA. 1940. Bl/w photo of Franklin Roosevelt. R/w/b drawing by Hazelwood of crossed flags, Statue of Liberty, Bl/w drawing of people lined up at sunset representing "1932." People lined up at sunrise representing "1933." 8pp. Page 8: Same drawing as page 1.

FDR-232 Democratic Campaign Songs. w. Charles von Weise. m. Popular Airs. Published by The Ardmoreite Publishing Company, Inc., Ardmore, OK. 1932. [3 1/2" × 6 3/16"]. B/w non-pictorial geometric design border. "Stirring-Inspiring Vote-Getting." "'Tis the stirring Song and Drumbeat that win wars' — Napoleon." Two page foldover. Inside B/w photos of "Franklin Roosevelt for President," "James N. Garner for Vice President." 16 songs. "Author's Commentary."

FDR-233 Forward With Roosevelt. w.m. Antun K. Pipin. a. Marcos L. Davalos. Published by Antun K. Pipin,

No. 717 North Van Ness Avenue, Hollywood, CA. 1940. Bl/w photo of Franklin Roosevelt. R/w/b drawing by Hazelwood of ship sinking in a storm representing "1932." Ship sailing into sunrise representing "1933." 8pp. Page 8: Bl/w drawing of people lined up at sunrise representing "1933."

FDR-234 Franklin Delano Roosevelt (Patriotic March Song). w.m. J. Grayson Jones. Published by J. Grayson Jones Music Company, P.O. Box 177, Freeland, PA. [1942]. R/w/b drawing of The White House, flag. 4pp. Page 4: Advertising.

FDR-235 Where Did You Get That Hat? [Excerpt] [Campaign Pamphlet]. Published by Republican Service League, No. 920 McCormick Building, Chicago, IL. 1936. [3 13/16" × 9"]. Bl/w photo of "Franklin D. Roosevelt at Democratic State Convention, Syracuse, NY., Sept. 30, 1936." Three bars of music. 4pp.

FDR-236 Blue Eagle March. m. T. Joseph Fredette. Published by Fredette Music Publishing Company, Lowell, MA. 1935. B/w photo of T. Joseph Fredette. Bl/w drawing by Fisher of an eagle, sun, clouds. 6pp. Page 2: "Dedicated to President Franklin D. Roosevelt." Page 6: Blank.

FDR-237 A Ballet Ballade The Elephant Made (And Echoes from the Full Dinner Pail). w.m. Bill Young. Copyright 1931 by William Young, No. 1150 Campbell Avenue, Detroit, MI. Cartoon-like drawing of various Republican follies, scandals — "4 Billion Dollar Treasury Deficit," "Moratoriums for Europeans," &c. 6pp. Page 2: Blank. Page 3: "It required a story writer and a Roosevelt to start the fires of inquiry — under the Chicago Stockyard's Racket. It required a song from the Elephant to start the fires of investigation under Wall Street's Stock (yards) Market, and a Roosevelt to finish it." Page 6: Advertising.

FDR-238 Franklin D. Roosevelt (He's Our President). w.m. Charles Thayer. Published by Charles Willard Publications, Wichita, KS. 1936. B/w drawing of Franklin D. Roosevelt. "Endorsed by the Young Democrats of Kansas." 4pp. Page 4: Blank.

FDR-239 Democratic Victory March. w.m. Val Gerich. Published by Rainbow Music Company, Hollywood, CA. Copyright 1937 by Val Gerich. Bl/w photo of Franklin D. Roosevelt. R/w/b drawing by Coscia of statue of soldiers marching with guns and flags — "Guardian of the Colors." 6pp. Page 6: Advertising.

FDR-240 Franklin Delano Roosevelt (March or Fox Trot). w.m. Bruce Kapustka and Stan Kapustka. 1934. Non-pictorial. 2pp. Page 2: Blank.

FDR-241 The F.D.R. Way. Published by the Liberal Party, [New York, NY]. 1946. [11" × 14"]. Non-pictorial handout. "Liberal Party Rally, Manhattan Center, 34th Street and 8th Avenue, Wed., Oct. 30, 1946." "Singing to be led by Chorus of Local 91, I.L.G.W.U." "Vote the Liberal Party line — Row D." Preceded on page by "Vote The Party Liberal." 2pp. Page 2: Blank.

FDR-242 Democratic Campaign Song. w. G.W. Faulkner. m. "Tune of *Casey Jones*." [1932]. [4 7/8" × 5 11/16"]. Bk/be non-pictorial. 2pp. Page 2: Blank.

FDR-243 Our President (Patriotic Song). w.m. Mollie Wren Whitman. Published by Carl Fischer, Inc., Cooper Square, New York, NY. 1934. Bl/w non-pictorial star and stripe border. 4pp. Page 2: "Dedicated to the President of the United States, Franklin Delano Roosevelt." Page 4: Advertising.

FDR-244 Roosevelt We Do Our Part. w.m. Margaret Scott Penn. Published by Mayflower Music Publishing Company, Cleveland, OH. 1933. Bl/w photo of Franklin D. Roosevelt at desk, NRA eagle — "We Do Our Part." "Dedicated to President Franklin D. Roosevelt and the NRA." 4pp. Page 4: Advertising.

(FDR) FRANKLIN D. ROOSEVELT

FDR-245 Hail! Our Great President (Fox Trot Song). w.m. Jacob H. Kieselmann. Published by Premier Music Company, No. 5031 Margaretta Avenue, St. Louis, MO. Copyright 1934 by Jacob Kieselmann. R/w/b drawing of Revolutionary War soldiers. Bl/w drawing of Franklin D. Roosevelt. 6pp. Pages 2 and 6: Blank. Page 3: "This song suggested by the poem "Hail To Our New President.""

FDR-246 Anthem Of Freedom. w.m. Margaret J. Honn. Published by Hollywood Publishers, Hollywood, CA. 1934. Bl/w photos/drawings of Franklin D. Roosevelt and Upton Sinclair. R/w/b drawing of the Statue of Liberty, stars and stripes. "Dedicated to Franklin D. Roosevelt and Upton Sinclair." 6pp. Page 6: Blank.

FDR-247 Mister President We're For You! w. Homer Hardin. m. Wayne Johnson. Copyright 1939 by Homer Hardin, Joplin, MO. [6 3/4" × 8 7/16"]. Bl/w photo of Franklin Roosevelt. [V-1: R/w/b] [V-2: Bl/w] drawing of Capitol building, bars of music—"Dear Mr. President..." 4pp. Page 4: [V-1: Advertising] [V-2: Campaign advertising for various Missouri politicians].

FDR-248 Homage To Roosevelt. w.m. Roy L. Jones. Published by DeVaignie Music Corporation, Chicago, IL. 1934. R/bk photo of Stan Ashley's Harmoneers — "Featured by Stan Ashley's Harmoneers of Station WTIC." R/bk drawing of shields, geometric designs. "With Ukulele Arrangement." 4pp. Page 4: Advertising.

FDR-249 The Four Freedoms. w. Henry Myers and Edward Eliscu. m. Jay Gorney. Published by Mills Music, Inc., No. 1619 Broadway, NY. 1943. R/w/b drawing of faces. "From the musical production *The New Meet The People*, Book, Lyrics and Music by Henry Myers, Edward Elescu and Jay Gorney, Production staged by Danny Dare." 8pp. Page 8: Advertising.

FDR-250 We Need You Franklin D. w.m. Billy Hays, Charlie Mahoney and Frank Capano. Published by Tin Pan Alley Publications, No. 1001 Chestnut Street, Philadelphia, PA. 1940. B/w drawing by Harry Moskovitz of Franklin D. Roosevelt, stars. 4pp. Page 4: "We Respectfully Dedicate this Song to the Greatest President America Has Ever Had — Billy Hays, Charlie Mahoney and Frank Capano [signed]."

FDR-251 We Need You Franklin D.. w.m. Billy Hays, Charles Mahoney and Frank Capano (ASCAP). Published by Tin Pan Alley Publications, No. 101 Chestnut Street, Philadelphia, PA. 1940. B/w drawing by Harry S. Moskovitz of Franklin D. Roosevelt, stars, lines. 4pp. Page 4: "We Respectfully Dedicate this Song to the Greatest President America Has Ever Had, Franklin Delano Roosevelt — Billy Hays, Charlie Mahoney and Frank Capano [signed]."

FDR-252(A) Rinka Tinka Man. w.m. Lew Kesler and June Sillman. Published by Mills Music, Inc., Music Publishers, No. 1619 Broadway, New York, NY. 1938. O/bl/w caricature drawings of famous people including Franklin D. Roosevelt and Eleanor Roosevelt, Mae West, Clark Gable and others. "Elsa Maxwell presents Leonard Sillman's *Who's Who*, Sketches Mostly by Everett Marcey and Leonard Sillman, Music Mostly by Baldwin Bergersen, James Shelton, Irvin Graham, Paul McGrane, Lyrics Mostly by June Sillman, Irvin Graham, James Shelton, Entire Production Staged & Directed by Mr. Sillman." List of other songs in show. 6pp. Pages 2 and 6: Advertising.

(B) **I Dance Alone** (The Shadow Song). w.m. James Shelton. 4pp. Page 4: Advertising.

(C) **I Must Have A Dinner Coat.** m. James Shelton. 6pp. Pages 2 and 6: Advertising.

(D) **It's You I Want.** w.m. Paul McGrane and Al Stillman. Pages 2 and 6: Advertising.

(E) **Let Your Hair Down With A Bang**. w.m. Baldwin Bergerson.
(F) **The Girl With The Paint On Her Face**.
(G) **You're The Hit Of The Season**.
(H) **Train Time**. w.m. Baldwin Bergersen and June Sillman. Pages 2 and 6: Advertising.

FDR-253 We're Over Here. w. Jimmy Vincent and Al Singer. m. Frank Gilbert. Published by Los Angeles Publishing Company, Los Angeles, CA. Copyright 1935 by Vincent, Singer and Gilbert. R/bl drawing of Franklin D. Roosevelt. R/w/b cover. 4pp. Page 4: Blank.

FDR-254 Return Franklin D. Roosevelt. w.m. Duke Feher. Published by Duke Feher, Passaic, NJ. 1936. Bl/w drawing of Franklin D. Roosevelt. R/w/b flag background. "America's Song Hit." 4pp. Page 4: Blank.

FDR-255 Things Look Rosy With Roosevelt. w.m. Henry Morrow. Published by Henry Morrow, No. 318 Sanford Avenue, Newark, NJ. 1936. Bl/w drawing of "Franklin Delano Roosevelt." R/w/b stripe border. 4pp. Page 4: Blank.

FDR-256 Keep Him There (In the White House Chair). w.m. George A. Losekamp. Published by Harvard Book Company, Publishers, No. 1523 Main Street, Riverside, CA. Copyright 1940 by George A. Losekamp. B/w drawing by Moore of Franklin D. Roosevelt. 4pp. Page 4: Blank.

FDR-257 God Bless Our President. w.m. Cordelia Henry. Published by C. Henry, No. 507 North Madison Street, Bloomington, IN. 1940. B/w photo by Blank & Stoller of Franklin D. Roosevelt. O/w/bk cover. 4pp. Page 4: Drawing of trees.

FDR-258 Oh Roosevelt, Oh Roosevelt. w.m. Emile Winkler. Published by Emile Winkler, R.F.D. #2, Friend, NE. 1935. Pl/w photo of Franklin D. Roosevelt. O/pl/w drawing of trees, geometric designs. 4pp. Page 4: Blank.

FDR-259 Hail Prosperity. w. Robert Buck and Fred E. Reed. m. Jack Fleddermann. a. Charles Midgley. Published by R.H. Buck, Oakland, CA. 1933. R/w/bl/bk drawing of Franklin D. Roosevelt. "Dedicated to President Franklin D. Roosevelt." 6pp. Page 2 and 6: Blank. Page 3: "Dedicated to President Franklin D. Roosevelt."

FDR-260 Hail Prosperity. w. Robert Buck and Fred E. Reed. m. Jack Fleddermann. Published by R.H. Buck, No. 1008 Central Avenue, Alameda, CA. 1933. R/w/b drawing by MacOuillard of Franklin D. Roosevelt, NRA eagle. "Dedicated to President Franklin D. Roosevelt." 6pp. Page 2 and 6: Blank. Page 3: "Dedicated in honor of President Franklin D. Roosevelt."

FDR-261 Hi, Ho Hail The New Deal. w.m. Major A.L. James, Jr. 1935. R/w/bk drawing of James "Farley" conducting choir of people from various walks of life representing New Deal scandals. One man holding a "Slaughtering knife," another holding "B & L Stock." 4pp. Page 4: Blank. [Anti-New Deal].

FDR-262 God, Protect Our President. w. Rev. Dennis J. Cavanagh, S.J. m. Dr. Milton Francis Clark. Published by Milton Francis Clark, No. 10523 Howard Street, San Francisco, CA. 1934. Bl/w photo of Franklin Roosevelt. R/w/b drawing of flags. "To our beloved President Franklin Delano Roosevelt in grateful acknowledgement of what he has done to lead a nation out of the slough of despond, of what he is doing to inspire that nation with hope, and of what, with God's help, he is destine to do to bring about our national recovery." 4pp. Page 4: "In God we trust."

FDR-263 Hurray, Hurrah! (For Roosevelt). w.m. Jason E. Freeman. Published by Jack-Helen Artists Ass'n., No. 11204 Huston Street, North Hollywood, CA. 1944. [8 1/2" × 11"]. Bl/w photo of Franklin Roosevelt. Bl/w cover. "Dedicated to Franklin D. Roosevelt." 4pp.

FDR-264 Roosevelt We Are Following You. w.m. James Della Valle. Published by [V-1: Della Valle Publishing Company, National Headquarters, No. 242 Powell Street] [V-2: America's Song Publishing Company, No. 111 Jones Street] San Francisco, CA. 1935. R/w/b drawing of Franklin D. Roosevelt, crossed flags, skyline, ships, train. 6pp.

FDR-265 There's A Roosevelt In The Chair. w.m. H. Ley. a. Baird Hamlin. Published by H. Lay, No. 1242 Brockton Avenue, Los Angeles, CA. 1933. R/w/b drawing of Franklin D. Roosevelt, flags, skyline, ships, train. "Respectfully Dedicated to Mrs. Franklin D. Roosevelt." 4pp. Page 4: "Endorsements."

FDR-266 Don't Let It Happen Again. w.m. Norma Payne. Published by Charles Ridgway Studios, Hollywood, CA. 1945. B/w photo of Franklin Roosevelt. "We must be sure that when you have won Victory, you will not have to tell your children, that you fought in vain — President Roosevelt's message to Youth — Sept. 3, 1942." 4pp. Page 4: Advertising.

FDR-266

FDR-267 Our Boy Roosevelt He'll Go In (Campaign Song). w.m. Will Sullivan and August Halter. Published by Englewood Music House, No. 516 Englewood Avenue, Chicago, IL. 1932. Bl/gy/w drawing of Franklin D. Roosevelt, floral and geometric designs. 6pp. Pages 2 and 6: Blank.

FDR-268 The Spirit Of Roosevelt The Great. w.m. Andrew J. Petros. Published by Orpheum Publishing Company, Chicago, IL. Copyright 1947 by Andrew J. Petros. B/w photo of Franklin Roosevelt, facsimile signature. 6pp. Page 2: Song — **I Am An American** (March Song). "Dedicated to The Commander-In-Chief President Truman." Page 3: "Dedicated to Franklin D. Roosevelt, the greatest liberator and humanitarian the world has ever seen and the Greatest President America ever had." Page 6: Song: *Chicago Life.*

FDR-269 My Fellow Countrymen (Song For Voice And Piano). w.m. Joseph Schlacht. Published by Joseph Schlacht, No. 440 East 6th Street, New York, NY. 1935. Bl/w drawing of Franklin D. Roosevelt — "March 4, 1933 — President Franklin D. Roosevelt — January 20, 1937." R/w/b lyre, flags. "Compliments of North Pole Tea Company, 440 East 6th Street, NYC." 6pp. Page 6: Advertising. R/w/b drawing of tea box.

FDR-270 Carry On! Old England. w.m. Al Sherman. Published by Fireside Classics, No. 1313 North Highland Avenue, Hollywood, CA. 1941. O/bk/gy/w photos/drawings of Franklin D. Roosevelt, George Washington, Abraham Lincoln, Theodore Roosevelt, Woodrow Wilson, silhouette of ship, airplane, automobiles. "Spirit of Liberty." "Officially sponsored by the British American Ambulance Corps, Carol Wild, Chairman." 4pp. Page 4: R/w photo of ambulance in battle.

FDR-271 Uncle Sam We Promise You. w. Dorothy Hewitt. m. George Rex. Published by Rex Music

Publishers, No. 315 Senaca Street, Seattle, WA. 1942. R/w/b cover. Ma/w photo of Franklin D. Roosevelt. "To the President's challenge—'We are all in it...All The Way,' This Song Is Devotedly Dedicated." 6pp. Pages 2 and 6: Advertising.

FDR-272   Stand Fast Americans. w. Eugene Page and Sara Page. m. Eugene Page. Published by Norman Edwards, Music Publishers, No. 9136 Sunset Boulevard, Hollywood, CA. Sole selling agents: Pacific Music Sales, No. 6425 Hollywood Boulevard, Hollywood, CA. 1942. R/w/b drawing of Franklin Roosevelt, George Washington, Abraham Lincoln, silhouette of a soldier and sailor. 6pp. Page 2: "Dedicated to the Race Relations Commission of the State of California." Page 6: Advertising.

FDR-273   Onward With Roosevelt. w. Frieda Gruss. m. Charles H. Gruss. Published by Red Mountain Springs, Route #1, Box 187, Fallbrook, CA. 1940. [8 1/2" × 11"]. Non-pictorial. 4pp. Page 4: Blank.

FDR-274   America Always Will Love You. w.m. Irene M. Stoffel. Published by Irene M. Stoffel, Dongan Hills, S.I., New York, NY. 1940. Non-pictorial. "Dedicated to Franklin D. Roosevelt, President of the United States." 6pp. Pages 2 and 6: Blank.

FDR-275   Thank God For Franklin Roosevelt. w.m. Wilson J. Gillam. Published by Wilson J. Gillam, Sayville, NY. 1937. Non-pictorial geometric design border. 6pp. Page 6: Advertising.

FDR-276   El Presidente (War Conga). w.m. Marion Sunshine (ASCAP). m. Lazaro Herrera. Spanish lyrics by Don Mario. a. Phil Lang. Published by Pan American Music Company, Inc., RKO Building, New York, NY. 1942. B/w drawing of family listening to Franklin D. Roosevelt speech on radio— "My Friends." "Advanced Artist Copy." 4pp.

FDR-277   Foam Sweet Foam. Published by Albany Legislative Correspondent's Association, Albany, NY. 1933. [8" × 11 3/4"]. N/c drawing by Jerry Costello of Franklin D. Roosevelt, Al Smith and other politicians riding a bottle of beer—"The Lager Limited." "A Rollicking Review Rotating on Resurrection of Bouncing Beverages, Tipsily Tapped at Ten Eyck Hotel Rathskeller, Albany, New York, the evening of Thursday, February 23, 1933, at Seven-Thirty O'clock." 20pp. [Franklin D. Roosevelt and Al Smith songs].

FDR-278   Show Us The Way, Blue Eagle. w.m. Meredith Willson. Published by Sherman, Clay & Company, San Francisco, CA. 1933. Bl/w photo of Meredith Willson. Bl/w drawing of eagle, shield—"Made in U.S.A." 6pp. Page 6: Advertising.

FDR-279   Washington, Lincoln And Franklin D. w. Niederman-Sarnoff. m. Eddie De Luca. Published by De Luca-Niederman-Sarnoff, No. 2222 South 5th Street, Philadelphia, PA. 1945. B/w photo of Arthur Lee Simkins—"Featured by Arthur Lee Simpkins." B/w drawing of flag. "Advance Artists Copy." 4pp.

FDR-280   Onward With Roosevelt (March). w.m. Buster Brocki. Published by Madison Music Publishing Company, No. 965 East Jefferson Avenue, Detroit, MI. 1936. Bl/w photo by Blank and Stoller of Franklin D. Roosevelt. Bl/w geometric designs. 4pp. Page 4: Blank.

FDR-281   There'll Never Be A Stain On Old Glory. w.m. Lou Zoeller and Tom Dempsey. Published by Zoeller Music Company, Music Publishers, Beverly Hills, CA. 1941. R/w/b drawing of flag. Bl/w drawings/photos of Franklin D. Roosevelt, Abraham Lincoln, George Washington. 6pp. Pages 2 and 6: Advertising.

FDR-282   F.D.R. Jones. w.m. Harold J. Rome. Published by Chappell and Company, London, England. 1938.

(FDR) FRANKLIN D. ROOSEVELT

[9 3/4" × 12 1/4"]. B/w photos of Flanagan and Allen — "Sung by Flanagan and Allen." R/w/bk drawing of a dog. "London Palladium…*The Moon The Little Dog Laughed to See*…George Black's Show of 1939." 4pp.

FDR-283 [**The Old G.O.P.**]. w. Sidney J. Catts, Jr. (of the Florida Delegation). m. Air: "Sing to the Tune of *The Old Grey Mare*." 1936]. [8 1/2" × 11"]. Non-pictorial. 2pp. Page 2: Blank.

FDR-284 Our Leader (March). m. Lazarre Jeunehomme. Published by Plains Music Publishing Company, Nos. 24-42 West Bayaud, Denver, CO. 1937. B/w photos of Franklin D. Roosevelt and "L. Jeunehomme — Cornet Soloist and Composer (89th Division, A.E.F.)." "Published for Band." 6pp. Page 2: Blank. Page 3: "Dedicated to President Franklin D. Roosevelt." Page 6: Advertising.

FDR-285 Willkie Should Stay In Wall Street. w.m. Henry Eckmann and Bob Day. Published by Henry N. Eckman, No. 521 East 70th Street, Seattle, WA. 1940. [8 1/2" × 11"]. Bl/w drawing by Roy Tremelling of a bank inscribed "Wall St. Bank," a building inscribed "Power Trust," a "G.O.P." Automobile with an elephant hood ornament, wagon full of money, stocks and bonds, Wendell Willkie with pitch fork — "Wendy making hay in Wall Street." "Souvenir Song of 1940 Presidential Campaign." 4pp. Page 2: "Sponsored by the National Committeewoman Mrs. Jeanette Teste and Margaret Blodgett."

FDR-286 A Good Neighbor. w.m. Alfred Perez and Joseph Maluo. 1938. Bl/w drawing of a house, couple at fence. "Dedicated to Franklin Delano Roosevelt, President of the United States." 4pp. Page 4: Blank.

FDR-287 The President Of The U.S.A. w. Ella Mayfield Dilworth. m. Grace Carroll-Elliot. [ca. 1936]. Non-pictorial. 4pp. Pages 1 and 4: Blank.

FDR-288 The President's Ball. w.m. Polly Berman. Published by Saunders Publications, "Hollywood's First Music Publisher," No. 5617 Hollywood Boulevard, Hollywood, CA. 1938. B/w drawing of a man and woman dancing. 6pp. Page 2: Blank. Page 6: Advertising.

FDR-289 On To Victory We Go (The People's Song). w.m. Isabel "Ma" Lamb. Published by Isabel "Ma" Lamb, No. 6530 Lafayette Avenue, Chicago, IL. 1944. Y/r photos of "President Roosevelt," "Winston Churchill," "Joseph Stalin," "Chiang Kai-Shek." Y/r drawing of chain links — "The Big 4 Unity." "This song is dedicated to the armed forces of the United Nations and their great leaders who so gallantly right what should be right. May a kindly heaven crown their effort with success to bless the world with everlasting peace, Respectfully the Author." 6pp.

FDR-290 I Like My President. w.m. Hon. M.C. Thornton. a. Earl Edwards. Published by Hon. M.C. Thornton, No. 207 Elsby Building, New Albany, IN. 1943. Bl/w non-pictorial line border. "Introduced by Mary Pat Melcher and Bette Wolf at Manzanita Tribes President's Ball with immediate success." 4pp.

FDR-291 President Roosevelt March (F.D.R., F.D.R., F.D.R., March). w. Andrea Fodor Litkei. m. Ervin Litkei. In: *A Tribute to the U.S.A.*, page 30. Published by Loena Music Publishing Company, No. 239 West 18th Street, New York, NY. Copyright 1985 and 1986. N/c drawing by Moran of the 1886 Statue of Liberty celebration.

FDR-292 Row, Row, Row With Roosevelt (On the Good Ship U.S.A.). w.m. Eddie Dowling and J. Fred Coots. Copyright 1932 by Sam Fox Publishing Co., Cleveland, OH. Non-pictorial "Professional Copy." Copyright "Warning." "Official Democratic Campaign Song Issued by Stage and Screen Division — National Democratic Committee." 2pp.

FDR-293   U.S. Flag Is Waiving In Heaven. w.m. Eva R. Weir. Copyright 1945 by Eva R. Weir, No. 399 South Royal, Jackson TN. Bl/w photo of Franklin Roosevelt. Bl/w drawing of flag. 4pp. Page 4: Bl/w shield—"Music for Morale," Minuteman—"Buy a Share in Victory," "V" symbol—"You Can Help Buy U.S. Bonds."

FDR-294   To Our President. w. Anon. m. Benny Thomas. 1940. B/w photo of Franklin Roosevelt. "The President's likeness and title used with kind permission of the White House." 4pp. Page 2: "Note—The following Eulogy, dedicated to our President several years ago, and widely published, was given a musical setting at the suggestion of several friends of the Author. Because of its unfailing recording of the sentiment of Roosevelt admirers and its prophetic sort of character I gladly publish it as a true reflection of the high esteem in which the common people hold their President and champion Franklin D. Roosevelt."

FDR-295   Fun During Recession [Poem, Story and Song Book]. w. Franklin Martin. Published by Franklin Martin, South Orange, NJ. [5 1/4" × 7 5/8"]. 1938. R/w/b drawing of Franklin Roosevelt blowing bubbles. 36pp. [Anti-Roosevelt].

FDR-296   He's My Uncle. w. Charles Newman. m. Lew Pollack. Published by Bergman, Vocco and Conn, Inc., No. 1619 Broadway, New York, NY. 1940. Bl/w photo of Franklin Roosevelt. R/w/b cover. "Distributed in Canada by Gordon V. Thompson, 193 Yonge Street, Toronto." 6pp. Page 2: "Special Version for Canada." Page 3: "Introduced by Dick Powell on the Maxwell House Coffee Time program." Page 6: Blank.

FDR-297   The March Of Free Men! w. I.B. Scheiber and D.S. Mossesson. m. Alexander Laszio. Published by Guild Publications of Art and Music, Inc., No. 202 East 44th Street, New York, NY. 1942. O/bk/w non-pictorial

FDR-296

cover. "Vice-President Henry Wallace—'This is a fight between a slave world and a free world. Just as the United States in 1862 could not remain half slave and half free, so in 1942 the world must make its decision for a complete victory.'" 4pp.

FDR-298   Roosevelt Est Un Peu La! w.m. Madame Edouard Bolduc (Canada). [ca. 1945]. [7" × 11"]. B/w photos of Franklin D. Roosevelt, "Madame Bolduc." "Chanson Dediee au President Roosevelt U.S.A." B/w photo of Madame Bolduc—"Souvenir de la Troupe Madame Ed. Bolduc En Tournee de la Nouvelle Angleterre." "Imprimerie Maarquis." 4pp.

FDR-299   We'll All Be In The Money Now. w. Mary S. Watts. m. Luther A. Clark (Arranger of piano part, *When Its Springtime in the Rockies*). Published by Mary S. Watts, No. 833 South 3rd Street, Omaha, NE. 1936. Ma/w photo of "Franklin D. Roosevelt." O/w/ma cover. 6pp. Page 6: Ma/w roses.

FDR-300   Step Up And Meet The New Champ. w.m. Tommy Rowe and Billy James. Published by Tommy Rowe and Billy James, No. 7823 Mill

(FDR) FRANKLIN D. ROOSEVELT

Road, Elkins Park, PA. 1942. [8 1/2" × 10 13/16"]. B/w non-pictorial geometric design border. "Dedicated to Our President — Franklin D. Roosevelt." 8pp.

FDR-301 The National Recovery March Of The U.S.A. w.m. Harold Edwin Dice (Composer-Bandmaster). a. Harvey H. Kratz. Published by Harold Edwin Dice, No. 335 Cleveland Avenue NW, Canton, OH. 1934. B/w photo of "Franklin D. Roosevelt — Man of the Hour." R/w/b drawings of "Holy Bible — Virtue," "Statue of Liberty — Liberty," Capitol building — "Patriotism," shields, ribbon. "Dedicated to Franklin D. Roosevelt — The N.R.A. — And every American citizen who does his part." "In harmony but not affiliated with The N.R.A." 6pp. Page 6: Blank.

FDR-302 1936 Franklin Roosevelt Song Book. w. Thomas O'Dowd. m. Popular Tunes. Published by Thomas O'Dowd, No. 8 Magaw Place, New York, NY. 1936. Br/w drawing of Franklin Roosevelt. 4pp. Page 4: Advertising. [M-420].

FDR-303 The NRA Song. w.m. George M. Cohan. Published by Gulf Refining Company in Funny Weekly, page 4. Copyright 1933 by George M. Cohan. R/w/b title with blue NRA Eagle. "As Sung Over That Good Gulf Radio Program." "Sponsoring Mr. Cohan's great song over the air and reproducing it in the Gulf Funny Paper is just another part of the whole-hearted cooperation the Gulf Refining Company is giving the President in this time of national emergency, the Gulf Refining Co. is back of the N.R.A. 100%."

FDR-304 Root, Root, Root For Roosevelt (Campaign Song). w. William Lee Mann. m. Rudolph C. Seyman. Copyright 1936 by Edward B. Marks Music, New York, NY. "Professional Copy." Copyright "Warning." 4pp.

FDR-305 Wotta Price Amen. w.m. James J. Fradkin. Published by James Fradkin, Rye, NY. 1939. [8 1/2" × 10"]. R/w/b drawing of faces praying. 4pp. Page 4: Blank. [Anti-WPA song].

FDR-306 Chasing Depression Away (Fox Trot). w. William H. Sheff, Sr. m. Julia Belle Sheff. Published by Frank Harding, Music Publisher and Printer, No. 228 East 22nd Street, New York, NY. 1933. B/w photo by Martin Vos of "Franklin D. Roosevelt." O/w cover. "Popular Music Publication." 6pp. Page 2: Blank. Page 6: Advertising.

FDR-307 God Bless You Mister Roosevelt! (We're With You All The Way). w. Stanley Milton Tudor. m. "Ev" Hunt. Copyright 1933 by Spencer and Tudor, No. 547 Umatilla Street, S.E., Grand Rapids, MI. Non-pictorial. 4pp. Pages 2 and 3: Blank. Page 4: "Franklin D. Roosevelt — A man possessed of implicit faith in God. With a genuine love in his heart for his fellow-man. A keen sense of justice, quick to analyze a situation — swift of action and with courage to follow his honest convictions, even to his own personal disadvantage. What A President!— S.M.T."

FDR-308 Roosevelt, You're The Pride Of The U.S.A. (Grand March

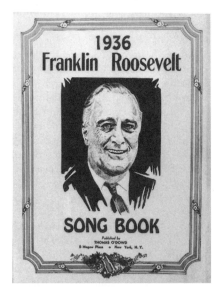

FDR-302

Song). w. William H. Sheff, Sr. m. Julia Belle Sheff. Published by Frank Harding's Music Publishing House, No. 228 East 22nd Street, New York, NY. 1933. B/w photo by Martin Vos of "Franklin D. Roosevelt." R/w geometric designs. 6pp. Page 2: Blank. Page 6: Advertising.

FDR-309 America (Franklin D! 'Tis For Thee). w. William Harrison Dempsey (Jack Dempsey) and Franklin Hugh Ellison. m. Air: *America*. Published by The Roosevelt "My Friends" Legion, No. 428 54th Street, Brooklyn, NY. Copyright 1936 by F.H. Ellison. B/w drawing of Franklin D. Roosevelt, Uncle Sam, stars. "My Friends and Your Friends." 2pp.

FDR-310 President Roosevelt March (F.D.R., F.D.R., F.D.R. March). w. Andrea Litkei. Ervin Litkei. In: *The Bicentennial March and Presidential Marches of America*. Published by Loena Music Publishing Company, New York, NY. 1976. R/w/b drawings of George Washington, Thomas Jefferson, Abraham Lincoln, eagle, flags. "American Revolution Bicentennial, 1776-1976." "Officially Recognized Commorative." 40pp.

FDR-311 The Churchill — Roosevelt Swing. w. Gerard Bryant. m. George Posford. Published by Francis, Day & Hunter, Ltd., Nos. 138-140 Charing Cross Road, London, W.C.2. 1942. [9 1/8" × 12 1/2"]. R/w/b cover with music notes, geometric designs. Bl/w photo by The Associated Press of Franklin D. Roosevelt. Bl/w photo by Sport E. General Press Agency of Winston Churchill. 4pp. Page 4: Advertising.

FDR-312 All Hail To Our Great Leader. w. Madeline Santarello. w. Italian words by John Santarello. m. A.D. Rowe. Published by Madeline Santarello, No. 303 Hobson Street, San Jose, CA. 1934. Pk/gn photo of Franklin D. Roosevelt. Pk/gn drawings of two flags, eagle. 6pp. Page 6: Blank.

FDR-313 (Roosevelt, Stalin, Churchill and Co.) Canners. w.m. Bryan Chadsee. Published by Bryan Chadsee, Williamstown, KY. 1944. Bl/w drawing of Franklin D. Roosevelt, Joseph Stalin and Winston Churchill cooking Adolph Hitler and Hirohito in a large iron pot labeled "Axis Stew." 4pp. Page 4: Blank.

FDR-314 Thank You, Mr. Roosevelt! w.m. Eric Karll. Published by Jack Carr, Inc., Milwaukee, WI. 1934. [8 1/2" × 11"]. B/w drawing of Franklin Roosevelt. "Souvenir of Wisconsin Tercentenary." Bl/w "NRA Member" eagle — "U.S. We Do Our Part." 4pp.

FDR-315 Christmas Gifts For A King. w.m. Miss Antoinette Bandre and Dr. Dick Grant. Harmonized by Federico Kramer. Copyright 1929 and 1944 by Dick Grant, Havana, Cuba. Published in Havana, Cuba. Bl/w photos of "The Honorable Franklin Delany [sic] Roosevelt, President of the U.S.A." and "Eleanor Delany [sic] Roosevelt, the 'First Lady' of America." 6pp. Page 2: Dedication narrative on "The Greatest President of America." Page 6: Narrative on the "Legend of 'Christmas Gifts for a King.'"

FDR-316 N=R=A Song. w.m. Edwin H. Barnes. Published by Edwin H. Barnes, No. 404 Delaware Avenue, Wilmington, DE. 1938. 4pp. B/w floral and geometric design border. Page 2: "Dedicated to President Franklin D. Roosevelt and the National Recovery Administration." Page 6: Blank.

FDR-317 Home On The Range (Texas Cowboy Song). a. David W. Guion. Published by G. Schirmer, Inc., New York, NY. 1930. [Edition: 1933-1945]. Br/gn/w cover, drawing of a cowboy on horseback. "Guion's Home on the Range." "With Added Original Melody." "President Franklin D. Roosevelt's Favorite Song." "Victor Record No. 1525, Sung by John Charles Thomas." 8pp. Page 2: Blank. Page 8: Advertising.

FDR-318 Flag Song (March Song). w.m. Y.J. Nyvall. Copyright by

Y.J. Nyvall, San Pedro, CA. 1936. R/w/b drawing by Kimberlin of soldiers, flag. "Lead Mighty Throng." 6pp. Page 6: R/w/b eagle, flag. Typed narrative within circle—"Compliments of Roosevelt Presidential Club #2, Los Angeles, California, Franklin P. Buyer, President, Councilman 15th District."

FDR-319 Is It True What They Say About Roosevelt? w. Irving Caesar (New York). m. "Air: *Is it true what they say about Dixie?*" Published for the National Democratic Convention, Philadelphia, PA. 1936. [3 7/8" × 6 1/16"]. Non-pictorial r/w/b border. "Donated in admiration of a great American Citizen, Franklin D. Roosevelt—Irving Caesar, New York." 2pp. Page 2: Blank.

FDR-320 Roosevelt, Guffy And Earle. w.m. Mary E. Duffy. Copyright 1934 by Mary E. Duffy, Philadelphia, PA. [8 1/2" × 11"]. Non-pictorial "Professional Copy." Copyright "Warning." 4pp. Pages 1 and 4: Blank.

FDR-321 On To Victory (March). m. Jack Broza. Published by Disraeli Lodge No. 4, Judaic Union, Philadelphia, PA. 1942. R/w/b non-pictorial cover. "Dedicated to Our Commander-in-Chief Franklin D. Roosevelt." 6pp. Page 6: Narrative—"Disraeli Lodge to the Front for Our Boys at the Front."

FDR-322 Helping Hands Across The Seas. w.m. Rex Ford. Copyright 1941 by Ruby Music Publishing Company, No. 1674 Broadway, New York, NY. [8 1/2" × 11"]. Non-pictorial. "Dedicated to President Franklin D. Roosevelt." Page 1 numbered "3." 4pp. Page 4: Blank.

FDR-323 Oh What A Man. w. Robert E. Hartly. m. Alvin Beveir. a. Charles Wolff. Published by Robert E. Hartly, No. 4435 South Dearborn Street, Chicago, IL. 1933. B/w drawings of leaves. "Democracy on Parade." "Sing Brother, Sing." 4pp. Page 4: Advertising.

FDR-324 The New Sunrise (A Song of the New Deal). w. Louis Marshall. m. Jos. Saunders. Published by Damaso Publishing Company, No. 47 West 76th Street, New York, NY. 1933. B/w drawing of Franklin D. Roosevelt. R/w/b drawing of eagle with flag, sunrise. "Dedicated to President Franklin D. Roosevelt." 6pp. Page 2: Facsimile letter from The White House to Louis Marshall. Page 6: Blank.

FDR-325 Tory, Tory Hallelujah [Program and Song Book]. Published by Albany Legislative Correspondent's Association, Albany, NY. 1936. [8" × 11 3/4"]. N/c drawing of Franklin D. Roosevelt, other politicians dressed as Revolutionary soldiers in battle scene—"A Dashing Delirious Drama, Lampooning Loyalists and Liberty Leaguers, Daggering Despots, Dictators and Dummy Donkey-Drivers to music by Red-Coats and Lyrics by Turn-Coats, the Combat Being Played Against a Spangled Back-Drop." "Furiously Fought at Ten Eyck Hotel, Albany, New York, The Evening of Thursday, March 12, 1936, at Seven-Thirty O'clock."

FDR-326 He's On Our Side. w.m. Elliott Buckner. Copyright 1936 by Elliott Buckner. B/w photo of "Franklin D. Roosevelt, Democrat." Bl/w geometric designs. "The Nation's song goes marching on, No court will dare put-in reverse." "Profits to Party." 4pp. Page 4: Blank.

FDR-327 No Blue Eagle Blues. w. Jack Kirkwood. m. Vern DePaney and Freeman Clark. Published by J.T. Whyte, Publisher, Seattle, WA. [ca. 1934]. Photo of Franklin D. Roosevelt, facsimile signature. "NRA." Drawings of N.R.A. eagles—"NRA Member, U.S.—We Do Our Part."

FDR-328 Franklin D. Roosevelt March. w.m. Wm. B. Woodin. In: *Boston Sunday Post*, March 12, 1933, page A-6. "Official Tune Composed by Secretary of Treasury Woodin and Played First at Inauguration, chorus of the *Franklin*

D. Roosevelt March, which was dedicated to the President and composed by William H. Woodin, Secretary of the Treasury. The music is copyrighted and published by the Miller Music Company, Inc., 62 West 45th Street, New York City. President Roosevelt calls it, 'My Official March.'"

FDR-329 Mister Roosevelt (We're Sure Proud of You). w.m. Walter Irving. Published by Scholtz Publishing Company, No. 10908 West 6th Street, Los Angeles, CA. 1933. B/w drawing of Franklin Roosevelt, stars. "This song is respectfully dedicated to Franklin D. Roosevelt whose courage and devotion to men defeated and forgot we herein salute and praise." 4pp.

FDR-330 The End Of The New Deal Dream (WPA, AAA, IEC or What Have We?) (A Burlesque). w.m. Charles Hammond Frye. Published by Sunset Song Bureau, Monrovia, CA. 1936. Bl/w photo of child playing with alphabet blocks—"Big AAA house fa' down." Bl/w drawing of Capitol building—"AAA, IEC, WPA, NRA." "There's a dreamer in The White House, building castles in the air, Like a child with lettered blocks, That he piles with greatest care." "Today's Most Popular Song." 4pp. Page 4: "Suggested spoken interludes." [Anti-FDR].

FDR-331 (I Got A) New Deal On Love. w.m. J. Russel Robinson and Bill Livingston. Published by Harry Engel, Inc., No. 1619 Broadway, New York, NY. 1934. Pk/w/bk hearts. B/w photos of Ozzie and Harriet—"As introduced by Ozzie Nelson and Harriet Hilliard." 6pp. Page 2: Blank. Page 6: Advertising.

FDR-332 John Garner. w. W.T. Whaley. m. Beatrice Vance Holmquist. Published by Standard Publications, No. 305 Majestic Theatre Building, Los Angeles, CA. 1932. B/w photo of "John Garner, Our Next President." 4pp. Page 4: Advertising.

FDR-333 There's A New Star In Heaven Tonight. w.m. Jack Kennedy. Published by Lone Star Music Company, No. 1158 North Orange Drive, Hollywood, 28, CA. Sole selling Agents: Pacific Music Sales, 6047 Hollywood Boulevard, Hollywood 28, CA. 1946. Bl/w photo of "Ozzie Waters, The Colorado Ranger." "Ozzie Waters Recorded on Coast Records 2009B." 4pp. Page 4: Advertising.

FDR-334 Bells Of Freedom. w. Edward E. Siebott. m. Daniel W. Sohn. Published by Miracle Music Company, No. 1011 Chestnut Street, Philadelphia, PA. 1941. R/w/b drawing by Harry S. Moskovitz of Franklin D. Roosevelt, stars. 4pp. Page 4: Advertising.

FDR-335 Just South'ard Of The Line. w. Louise Poage. m. Harry Jay. Published by Louise Poage, Ashland, KY. 1936. Gn/w drawing of "Ancestral Poage Home." "Dedicated to President Franklin D. Roosevelt and Vice President John Nance Garner." 6pp. Page 6: Blank.

FDR-336 Let's Go Americans! w.m. Mrs. A.C. Bilbrew. Published Mrs. A.C. Bilbrew, No. 1301 1/2 Commonwealth Avenue, Los Angeles, CA. 1942. Bl/w photo of Mrs. A.C. Bilbrew. Bl/w drawing of Statue of Liberty, flags, geometric design border. "Dedicated to President Franklin D. Roosevelt." 4pp. Page 4: Blank.

FDR-337 We Are New Deal Democratic (A Campaign March Song). w. E.T. Cooke. m. Bert Sams. Published and Distributed by The Young Men's and Women's Democratic Club of Shoshone County, [ID]. [1936]. [8 1/4" × 13 1/2"]. Non-pictorial. "Published and Distributed by The Young Men's and Women's Democratic Club of Shoshone County who endorse the following Nominees for Public Service." Long slate of candidates for Idaho "State Officers" and "County officers." 8pp. Pages 2, 7 and 8: Local advertising. Page 3: B/w drawing of "Franklin D. Roosevelt." Page 6: Blank.

FDR-338 Darling I Am Growing Young (While This White House Man Still Smiles). w. Adelia Edwards Hickman. m. Vernon Leftwich. Published by Aileda Publishing Company, No. 2308 South Union Avenue, Los Angeles, CA. 1933. B/w photo of Franklin D. Roosevelt. Y/w/br drawing of flowers. 4pp. Page 4: Blank.

FDR-339 He! Haw! The Democratic Mule. w.m. M.M. Lyden. Published by M.M. Lyden, Butte, MT. 1932. B/w drawing of donkey kicking elephant. 6pp. Pages 2 and 6: Blank.

FDR-340 There's Something About James A. Farley, That Is Fine, Fine, Fine. w. Franklin Hugh Ellison. Copyright 1933 by Mills Music, Inc. and 1936 by Franklin Hugh Ellison. [8 1/2" × 11"]. B/w photo of James A. Farley. B/w drawing of shield, stars, stripes. 6pp. Page 2: B/w photo of Franklin H. Ellison. Song — **There's Something About A Democrat, That Is Fine, Fine, Fine.** Page 6: Blank.

FDR-341 The Roosevelt March Song. w.m. Wright Barclay. a. Fredric Watson. Published by Wright Barclay, No. 55 West 42nd Street, New York, NY. 1933. Non-pictorial. 4pp. Page 2: "Dedicated to America's 'New Deal.'" Includes a 4 1/2" × 1 1/8" typed insert with "NRA" stamp — "A Great Radio Song in support of the Administration and to make the American people N.R.A. conscious."

FDR-342 Our Star Of Hope (La Stella Della Nostra Speranza). w.m. Emma Talarico. Published by Emma Talarico, No. 313 East County Line Road, Ardmore, PA. 1935. B/w photos of "Franklin D. Roosevelt," "George H. Earle" and "Charles J. Margiotti." Bl/w floral and geometric border. 4pp. Page 4: Blank.

FDR-343 Why Can't We Be Sweet Hearts Again. w.m. Val Holland. Copyright 1933 by A. Holzerlano. [8 1/2" × 11"]. B/w drawings of calendars — "1930-1936." "Dependable Five Year Ref-

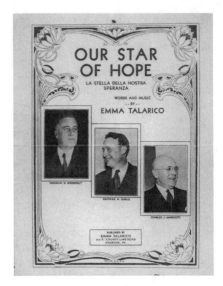

FDR-342

erence Calendar." "Example...Jan. 1932, look at Calendar 'G.'" "Use a new Calendar...Sing a new Song, Let's all help the 'New Deal' along." Various calendars. 4pp. Pages 2 and 3: Music. Page 4: B/w photo of Franklin D. Roosevelt.

FDR-344 We Can, We Will, We Must (The Presidential Fight Song). w.m. Jimmie Berg. Copyright 1942 by Jimmie Berg, Minneapolis, MN. B/w drawing of a U.S. flag, floral design. "Sponsored by the Minneapolis Confederation of Lyrists and Composers." 4pp.

FDR-345 Let's Remember Franklin D. w.m. Jean C. Johns. Published by Nordyke Music Publications, Hollywood, CA. 1948. O/bl drawing of flag, Capitol building. 4pp. Page 4: Advertising.

FDR-346 A Million Thanks To Roosevelt. w.m. Claudia Panneton. Published by Claudia A. Panneton, No. 43 Pine Street, Nashua, NH. 1945. B/w photo of Franklin D. Roosevelt. Bl/w drawing of soldiers, Statue of Liberty, stars. 4pp. Page 4: Blank.

FDR-347 Good-Bye Prohibition. w.m. L.E. Benner. a. Odgard C.

Stemland. Published by Standard Publishing Company, Minneapolis, MN. Copyright 1932 by L.E. Benner. R/w/b drawings of Franklin D. Roosevelt with a donkey eating "(v)oats," a happy man inscribed "The Voter," Herbert Hoover beating an elephant who is hauling a broken wagon inscribed "1920 Model Bootlegger" Wagon, "1932 Democratic Campaign Band" riding in a "1932 Model" wagon with riders labeled "Farmer, Veteran, Labor, Capital, The Women," U.S. Capitol building at the end of a road labeled — "Progress." 6pp. Page 6: "Repeal the 18th Amendment."

FDR-348 December 7, 1941 (A Date That Will Live In Infamy). m. James P. Ployhar. Published by Belwin Mills Publishing Corporation, Melville, NY. 1985. Bl/w/r drawing of Pearl Harbor bombing. "For Band." Full parts set for band. Top of score: "Franklin D. Roosevelt — 'A Date which will live in infamy.'"

FDR-349 Curl The Mo, Uncle Joe. w. Jack Hatch. m. Jack Lumsdaine. Published by J. Albert & Son, Pty. Ltd., Music Publishers, Sydney, Australia. [9 7/16" × 12 3/8"]. 1944. R/w/bk drawing of Franklin D. Roosevelt, Winston Churchill and Joseph Stalin. 4pp.

FDR-350 Victory Banquet [Song Sheet]. March 4, 1937, Riley Room, Claypool Hotel. [4" × 10 1/2"]. B/w drawing of Franklin D. Roosevelt. 2pp. Page 2: Blank.

FDR-351 Roosevelt We Hand The Flag To You! w. William Foster. m. Edna May Foster. Published by Democratic Boosters of Indiana, Gary, IN. 1936. Drawing of Franklin D. Roosevelt, star, shield. 6pp. Page 2: Photo of "M. Clifford Townsend, Democratic candidate for Governor." "You are for Roosevelt! Then Vote for those who are for Roosevelt." Page 6: Photo of "Carroll Holley, Sheriff." "Re-Elect."

FDR-352 The Star Spangled Banner. Published by The United Fund for Refugee Children, No. 233 West 42nd Street, New York, NY. Copyright 1941 by Ben-Horim. [8 1/2" × 9"]. R/w/b litho on silk of "Franklin D. Roosevelt, Thirty Second President," flag. "President Roosevelt's call to Nation to Defend Liberty, Part of President Roosevelt's Fourth of July 1941 Address to Nation." Long quote from speech. "130,000,000, Strong United We Stand." "Compliments of The United Fund for Refugee Children, No. 233 West 42nd Street, New York, NY." 2pp. Page 2: Blank.

FDR-353 Roosevelt For King (Program of the 'Royalist Party' of America). w. Robert Caldwell Patton and Charles King. Published by His Majesty's Ink-Slingers, No. 25 West 43rd Street, New York, NY. 1937. [8 1/2" × 11 1/2"]. R/w/y crown. 36pp. Page 3: "This genial burlesque is dedicated to its hero who we expect will have the loudest laugh of all."

FDR-354 Song Of The Blue Eagle. w. Gerald Vincent Morris. m. Henri E. Cottave. Published by Words & Music Publications, Los Angeles, CA. 1933. Four bl/w NRA eagles — "NRA Member." 4pp. Page 4: Same as page one.

FDR-355 NIRA! NIRA! (March Fox-Trot Song). w. John Harden. m.a. Anotole Bourmann. Published by Harden Music, Inc., Springfield, MA. 1933. Bl/w non-pictorial. "Respectfully Dedicated to The Honorable Franklin Roosevelt, President of the United States of America." "Introduced by John Donoghue and Marion Hoyt Brickett at the N.R.A. Mass Meeting, Springfield, Massachusetts." 4pp. Page 4: Blank.

FDR-356 Franklin Delano Roosevelt (Patriotic March Song). w.m. J. Grayson Jones. a. Len Flemming. Published by Grayson Jones Music, Freeland, PA. 1942. "Professional Copy." Copyright "Warning." 4pp.

FDR-357 Calling For Roosevelt. w.m. Hank Barnes. a. Harold G. Rhoades. a. Len Fleming. Published by Anderson Printing, No. 105 West 4th

Street, Topeka, KS. 1932. Pl/w geometric designs. 6pp. Page 4: "Sponsored by Harry H. Woodring, Gov. of Kansas, Guy T. Helvering, Chair. Demo. State Central Cmte., Chas. E. Miller, Chair. Leavenworth Cnty." Page 6: "Featured by The Purple & White Minstrels."

FDR-358 The Rest Of My Life (With You). w.m. Franklin Roosevelt, Jr. and Kendrick Sparrow. Published by Broadcast Music, No. 580 Fifth Avenue, New York, NY. 1940. Bl/br/w hourglass. 6pp. Page 6: Advertising.

FDR-359 The Handy Andies Of The C.C.C. w.m. Charles Barbara and Gene Cirina. Published by Gene Cirina, No. 652 67th Street, Brooklyn Street, New York, NY. 1936. B/w drawing of Franklin D. Roosevelt, C.C.C. workers. "Dedicated to F.D.R." 6pp.

FDR-360 A Soldier's Prayer For Victory. w.m. Marie Tello Phillips. Published by Success Music, No. 32 S. River Street, Aurora, IL. 1944. R/w/b soldiers, flags, stripes. 4pp. Page 2: "To F.D.R." Page 4: Advertising.

FDR-361 Show-Off Boat [Program and Song Book]. Published by Albany Legislative Correspondent's Association of New York State, Albany, NY. 1936. [8" × 11 3/4"]. N/c drawing of Franklin Roosevelt, politicians, barge — "A Vote-Vamping Voyage and Rollicking Raid into Rustic Regions by Roosevelt Roysters, Featuring the Duke of Dutchess and the Ticker-Tape Twins in that Dashing Drama, 'Farms and the Man,' and Mixed with the Mad Magic of Moonlight on the Democratic Ditch." "'Three Men in a Tub' Departing from Ten Eyck Hotel Terminal, Albany, NY., on the Evening of March 14, 1929, at 7:00 p.m., Hot Time."

FDR-362 Breaks And Outbreaks [Program and Song Book]. Published by Albany Legislative Correspondent's Association of New York State, Albany, NY. 1930. [8" × 11 3/4"]. N/c drawing of Franklin Roosevelt as warden, other politicians in jail — "A Paroxysmic, Penological Panorama, Pillorying Prison Probes, Partisan Pap-Grabbers, Peanut Policies, Phoney Philanthropies, Punctured Pledges and Public Service Piffle, and Redolent with Republican Rebels Riddling Rooseveltian Ruses and Mocking Mogenthau Ministrations and Lehman Loquacities — Topped by That Toothsome Tidbit, 'Cells and Sell-Outs.'" "Detonated at Ten Eyck Hotel Terminal, Albany, NY., On the Evening of March 20, 1930, at 7:00 p.m." [Franklin Roosevelt, Al Smith].

FDR-363 The Scrappy Warriors [Program and Song Book]. Published by Albany Legislative Correspondent's Association of New York State, Albany, NY. 1932. [8" × 11 3/4"]. N/c drawing of Franklin Roosevelt with spear, Al Smith with axe battling in front of Washington skyline — "A Merry, Martial Medley, Mingling Monkey-Wrenches and Muck-Rakers, Presidential Pipe-Dreams, Partisan Perfidies and Prohibition Planks — all Revolving 'Round Convulsive Conclave of Delirious Delegates, Shellshocked

FDR-359

Spellbinders and Rabid Rivals for White House Honors." "Staged at the Ten Eyck Hotel, Albany, the Evening of Thursday, March 3, 1932, at Seven O'clock." [Franklin Roosevelt, Al Smith].

FDR-364 Dealers Choice Or Back-To-Back Biting [Program and Song Book]. Published by Albany Legislative Correspondent's Association of New York State, Albany, NY. 1944. [8" × 11 3/4"]. N/c drawing of Franklin Roosevelt, Thomas Dewey, "Chiang," "Winnie" and "Joe" playing cards — "Featuring the World's Most Exciting Egomaniacs in a Marvelous Musical of Messianic and Mystery: Showing Sinners, Sycophants, Suckers, and Sleuths Saving Civilization with Sound; or Find the Joker!" "Delt Off the Bottom of a Hot Deck — In Three Acts at Ten Eyck, Albany, March 9, 1944. [Franklin Roosevelt, Thomas Dewey].

FDR-365 Sundown At Arlington. w. Lora Campbell. m. Vaughn De Leath. Published by Alfred Music, No. 145 West 45th Street, New York, NY. 1937. B/w drawing of church, sunset, *New York Times* article — "Sept. 25 Fixed as Gold-Star Mother's Day In Proclamation issued by the President, Washington, Sept. 12 — President Roosevelt today designated Sept. 25 as Gold-Star Mother's Day and called upon the nation to pay tribute to the women who lost sons or daughters in the World War…" "Dedicated to the Gold-Star Mothers of the World." 4pp.

FDR-366 Ode To America. w.m. Jules Bledsoe. a. Claude MacArthur. Published by Broadcast Music, No. 580 Fifth Avenue, New York, NY. 1941. [6 7/8" × 10 3/8"]. Non-pictorial. 12pp. Page 3: "Respectfully dedicated to the President Franklin D. Roosevelt."

FDR-367 Rendezvous (FDR) (March/Finale). w. Richard Engquist. m. Jack Gottlieb. Published by Theophilious Music. Sole Agent: Boosey & Hawkes.

1991. [6 7/8" × 10 1/2"]. Non-pictorial. "Presidential Suite, Seven Pieces for Mixed Chorus (SATB) a cappella." 12pp. Page 2: "Presidential Suite is a celebration of America's priceless heritage of liberty. Inspired by the wisdom and whimsy of some of our most colorful presidents, it juxtaposes the eloquence of John F. Kennedy and Franklin Delano Roosevelt, with the journalistic pith of Theodore Roosevelt, Harry S Truman's blunt common sense, Abraham Lincoln's homespun wit and Thomas Jefferson's irony, plus a legendary quip from the taciturn Calvin Coolidge. This patriotic work combines idealism with light-heartedness, inspiration with a dash of salt." Page 3: "For Irene G. Kaplin."

FDR-368 Roosevelt Cheer Song/ Up Salt River. w.m. Anne Barron Donahue. Published by Anne Barron Donahue, No. 816 DeKalb, Norristown, PA. 1936. Pl/w drawing of "Franklin Delano Roosevelt." 4pp. Page 4: Blank.

FDR-369 C.C.C. Follow On (March Song). w. Bernie Grossman. m. Charles Duval. Published by Sam Fox Publishing Company, Cleveland, OH. 1937. R/w/b drawing of mountain, forest. Bl/w photo of two actors. "Sung in *Blazing Barriers* A Monogram Picture." 6pp. Pages 2 and 6: Advertising. Page 3: "Dedicated to the United States Civilian Conservation Corps."

FDR-370 Mother, Heed To OPA! w.m. Iona D. Goins. Published by Iona D. Goins, No. 5510 Columbia Pike, Arlington, VA. 1940. Bl/w drawing of a mother, children at food store with an "OPA" sign. 4pp. Page 4: Blank. [Anti-Franklin Roosevelt, O.P.A.].

FDR-371 Again And Again And Again Or All At Sea [Program and Song Book]. Published by Albany Legislative Correspondent's Association of New York State, Albany, NY. 1945. [8 3/4" × 11"]. N/c drawing of Franklin Roosevelt as pirate, Thomas Dewey as "Black Tom," Henry Wallace, Sidney Hillman, others on ship—"Union Ship C.I.O.-P.A.C." "Black Tom" Dewey walking plank. "Featuring Political Craft and Cunning and Contortions; Also Summoned by Subpoena, or Hit-Toddy and the Shady Lady, the Indestructible Dame Known as Lu-Lu; Together with Mystical Midsummer Mummery of '46, in a Roaring and Raucous and Revealing Racing Scene Entitled 'Hoots and Straddles.'" "All Done with Music, Magic, and Mirrors— In Three Acts at Hotel Ten Eyck, Albany, March 15, 1945."

FDR-372 The Ballad Of Franklin D. w.m. Tom Glazer. Published by Bob Miller, Inc., Music Publisher, No. 1619 Broadway, New York, NY. 1946. B/w non-pictorial geometric border. 4pp.

FDR-373 The Four Freedoms. w. Franklin D. Roosevelt. a. Mary Hallet. m. Roy Ringwald. Published by Shawnee Press, Inc., Delaware Water Gap, PA. 1968. [6 7/8" × 10 1/2"]. B/w drawing of palm branches. "For Mixed Voices (SATB)." 8pp. Page 2: Narrative "From President Franklin Delano Roosevelt's Annual Message to Congress, January 6, 1941."

FDR-374 Four Freedoms. m. Robert Farnon. a. Felton Rapley. Published by Chappell and Company, Ltd., No. 50 New Bond Street, London, England. 1962. [8 1/2" × 11"]. Be/bk/w photo of a statue of Franklin Roosevelt, Four Freedoms monument. "Theme Music from Associated Television's Production *The Four Freedoms*." "Piano Solo." 4pp.

FDR-375 Franklin D. And Prosperity. w.m. Al. Archer. Published by Archer and Sternberg, Mount Pleasant, IA. 1932. [8 1/2" × 11"]. B/w litho of "Franklin Delano Roosevelt, 1932," geometric design border. 4pp. Page 4: Narrative—"What Farmers May Expect From Roosevelt as President—Excerpts from speech at Topeka, Kansas, September 14, 1932."

FDR-376 Smiling With Roosevelt. w.m. Anna Margaret Good. Published by Anna Margaret Good, No. 1105 North Walker Street, Princeton, WV. 1936. R/w/b drawing of trees, geometric designs. Bl/w photo of Franklin Roosevelt. "Dedicated to Franklin D. Roosevelt." 4pp. Page 4: Bl/w eagles, geometric designs.

FDR-377 Our President Celebration Song. w.m. Larkin Craig Chandler. Published by Larkin Craig Chandler, No. 601 West 172nd Street, New York, New York. 1940. B/w Pach Bros. photo of Franklin D. Roosevelt. "Dedicated to all who gave him a glorious victory." [Written] "Tuesday Night (3 A.M.), November 3rd, 1936." 6pp. Page 6: Song—**Oh! Roosevelt.** w.m. L.C. Chandler. m. "Sung to the Tune of *Oh! Susanna* with apologies to the Republican Party of 1936."

FDR-378 FDR's Back Again. w.m. Bill Cox. In: *The New Lost City Ramblers Song Book*, page 246. e.c.a. John Carter, Mike Seger and Holly Wood. Published by Oak Publications, No. 165 West 46th Street, New York, NY. 1964. B/w photo of The New Lost City Ramblers.

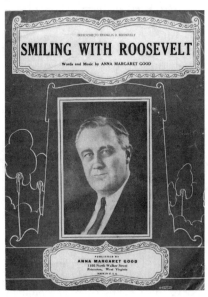

FDR-376

260pp. Page 246: "The master of the commercial recording of this song was cut just one week after FDR was re-elected in 1936 by the greatest plurality in our history. The song attests to [his] popularity...and expresses something of the positive way the nation was feeling as it started to work its way out of the Depression..."

FDR-379 Hurrah For Roosevelt. w. Arlie E. Farmer. m. Katie J. Griffeth. Published by Arlie E. Farmer and Katie J. Griffeth, Athens, GA. 1933. B/w drawing by J.E. Parr of Franklin Roosevelt. 4pp. Page 2: "Dedicated to Franklin Delano Roosevelt, Humanitarian, Patriot, Statesman — Our President." Page 4: Blank.

FDR-380 Keep Going Roosevelt! w.m. Carl Gauthier. Published by Prairie Music Co., Box 752, Williston, ND. 1934. B/w photos of Franklin D. Roosevelt, "Upper Mississippi Band." R/w/b stars and stripes. 4pp. Page 4: Blank.

FDR-381 New Deal. w. Isabelle S. Farrington. In: *Four Songs From Chevy Chase Frantics*, page 2. 1933. [8 1/2" × 11 1/4"]. B/w silhouettes of two women, donkey's head. "A Political Comedy produced by the Chevy Chase Glee Club at the Wardman Park Theatre, Washington, D.C., February 24 & 25, 1933." 20pp.

FDR-382 Democratic Rally [Song Booklet]. Published by [V-1: Butler County Democratic Executive Committee] [V-2: Democratic Women's Club of Oxford, Oxford], OH. 1940. [5 9/16" × 8 9/16"]. B/w photos of "Franklin D. Roosevelt, President" and "Martin L. Davey, Former Governor." [V-2: "Democratic Women's Club of Oxford and Oxford Township, Oxford, Ohio, Friday, Oct. 11, 1940, Music by 'Hink and His Melodiers,' Betty Lundin, Pres., Norma Flanagan, Sec."] [V-2: "Moose Hall, Hamilton, Ohio, Oct. 1, 1940"]. 4pp. Page 4: "Democratic Candidates."

FDR-383 It's V-V-V For Victory. w. Alice Hansen. m. George Rex. Published by Rex Music Publishers, No. 315 Seneca Street, Seattle, WA. 1941. Ma/w photo of Winston Churchill — the Empire's standard bearer. Support him and his efforts and make "V" more than a symbol...let it ring out in song and music with V-V-V for victory." 4pp. Page 3: Ma/w photo of Franklin D. Roosevelt. Page 4: R/w/b drawing of bull dog, "V" symbol — "Everyone should have the "V" spirit of Churchill and Roosevelt."

FDR-384 President Roosevelt March. m. Louis De Francesco. Copyright 1932, 1941. In: *Fox Marches in The American Way* (A Collection of Inspiring Marches for the Piano by American Composers), page 26. Published by Sam Fox Publishing Company, Cleveland, OH. 1941. 52pp.

FDR-385 March On, United Nations. w.m. Ralph Cox, Guido Nadzo and William Livingston. Published by Edwin H. Morris, Inc., No. 1619 Broadway, New York, NY. 1942. R/w/b drawing of sword — "Freedom," globes. "Dedicated to Freedom House." "First Public Performance at Freedom House Reception to Mrs. Eleanor Roosevelt, on May First, Nineteen Hundred Forty-Two." 6pp. Pages 2 and 6: Blank. Pages 2 and 6: Blank.

FDR-386 The Yanks Will Do It Again. w.m. Eddie Foley (Composer of *When The Boys Come Marching Home*). Published by Edward M. Foley, No. 373 Wolverleigh Boulevard, Toronto, Canada. 1945. "Honored by the late Pres. F.D. Roosevelt and U.S. Government." "Song of the hour and hit of the year. The great American Victory song inspired by the Nazi offensive." "A Tribute to the Doughboys." B/w drawing of crossed flags, eagle. 6pp. Page 2: Blank. Page 6: Advertising.

FDR-387 Hello, Americans. w.m. James J. Flannery. a. Walter Moloney. Published by James J. Flannery, Pittsburgh, PA. 1942. R/w/b drawing of

Franklin D. Roosevelt, microphones — "NBC, CBS, MBS, WFIL and WORL." "Dedicated to Franklin Delano Roosevelt, President of the United States of America." 4pp. Page 4: Blank.

FDR-388 Let Us Keep Our President. w.m. Rose Bonavitacola. Published by Shelby Music Publishing Company, Detroit, MI. 1944. R/w/gy/bk drawing of Franklin Roosevelt. 6pp. Pages 2 and 6: Advertising.

FDR-389 Let Gov. Roosevelt Lead The Good Old U.S.A. (Song). w.m. John Young. Published by Frank Harding, Nos. 228-232 East 22nd Street, New York, NY. 1932. Bl/w drawing of Franklin D. Roosevelt, geometric design border. "Respectfully Dedicated to Gov. Franklin D. Roosevelt." 6pp. Page 6: "Turn Out and Vote for Franklin Roosevelt."

FDR-390 The Re-Born American Spirit. w. E.M. Jackson. m. John W. Newton and E.M. Jackson. Copyright 1933 by E.M. Jackson, Box 70, Charleston, WV. R/w/b litho eagle. B/w drawings/photos of Franklin Roosevelt, "Woodrow Wilson — Inaugurated 1913," "Theodore Roosevelt — Inaugurated 1901," "Abraham Lincoln — Inaugurated 1861," "Thomas Jefferson — Inaugurated 1801," "George Washington — Inaugurated 1789." "The Militant March Song Hit of the Day." "Dedicated to Franklin D. Roosevelt, President of the United States, and the millions of American men and women everywhere who have an abiding faith in the future of this great nation, with their faced turned toward the Eastern horizon where glows the golden sunrise of the new-born day that will bring happiness, contentment and prosperity." Newspaper reprints — "What *The Charleston Gazette* had to say about the poem" and "What the Clarksburg Exponent said." 4pp.

FDR-391 We Want Mister Roosevelt. w.m. Vehrl Sager. Published by Vehrl Sager, Woodstock, VA. 1940. B/w photo of Franklin Roosevelt. 4pp. Page 4: Blank.

FDR-392 Why Change? w.m. Robert Thomas Covington. Published by Robert Thomas Covington, No. 1515 North Opal Street, Philadelphia, PA. 1936. Pl/w floral and geometric designs. "A Modern Prophecy — The 1936 Presidential Election." "From The Democratic National Committee: 'Your letter to the White House with reference to the song in which you are interested for possible use in the campaign has been referred to me for attention and I wish to thank you for your loyal support. October 5, 1936.'" 6pp. Page 6: Blank.

FDR-393 Franklin! Winston! Kai-Shek! And Joe!. w.m. Clarence Gaskill (ASCAP). Copyright 1943 by Mills Music Corporation, No. 1619 Broadway, New York, NY. [12 3/8" × 8 15/16"]. Non-pictorial. 2pp. Page 2: Blank.

FDR-394 Gone With The Winner [Program and Song Book]. Published by Albany Legislative Corespondent's Association of New York State, Albany, NY. March 20, 1941. [9" × 11 1/16"]. R/w/bl/y drawing of Franklin Roosevelt and Wendell Willkie riding "A Bicycle Built For Two" labeled — "Roosevelt-Willkie Axis." Wheels — "New Deal" and "Lend Lease Bill." "Or 'Back in the Lap of God.' A Hoosier-Hyde Park Honeymoon Hit, Staring the G. Oomph P.'s Lost Leader and the King of Krum Elbow in 'Lucky Partners.' Says F.D.R. — 'He's My Man.' Says the Republican Party — 'Once a New Dealer, Sometimes a Double- Dealer.' Says the Public — 'Willkie's the Life of the Party, But What Party?" "Served Piping Hot at Hotel Ten Eyck, Albany, New York, Thursday Night, March 20, 1941, at 7:30 O'clock." [Songs on Wendell Willkie and Franklin Roosevelt].

FDR-395 New Deal March. m. Al. Stafford. a. Flo Biart. Published by S&M Music Publishers, Walter Jorgenson, Prof. Mgr., No. 1264 Westlake,

Seattle, WA. 1934. [8 3/4" × 11 1/4"]. B/w drawing by Stan Cook of drum major, geometric designs. "In Commemoration of President F.D. Roosevelt's Visit to the Northwest." "Featured by" listing of various individuals, bands and radio stations. 4pp. Page 4: Blank.

FDR-396 Old Glory Is Calling. w. Henry E. Fries (1942, Winston Salem, NC). m. Mrs. H.E. Fries (1934). Copyright 1936 and 1942. B/w drawing of U.S. flag, tank, airplanes, ship, "V" sign. "Dedicated to President F.D. Roosevelt, Commander in Chief and General Douglas MacArthur." 4pp. 2pp. Insert—Obv: "Victory Review and Rally, Carolina Theatre, Sunday 3 P.M., May 3, 1942." Song Sheet.

FDR-397 Listen, American Voters (A Political Song). w. T. Virginia Waldron. m. Carl Rossini Diton. Published by Virginia Waldron. 1936. Bl/w geometric designs. 6pp. Page 6: Blank.

FDR-398 Row, Row, With Roosevelt. w.m. Norman Kunst and Lester Louis Levin. a. Lester Louis Levin. Published by Edgemere Music Publishing, No. 340 Beach Street, Edgemere, L.I., NY. 1936. R/w/b drawing by E. Diaz of Franklin D. Roosevelt, Capitol dome, stripes, two shields. 4pp. Page 4: Blank.

FDR-399 One For All And All For One. w.m. Frances G. Wise. Published by National Artists Association, No. 1811 North Tamarind, Hollywood, CA. 1933. Bl/w tinted drawing of Franklin D. Roosevelt. "Dedicated to Franklin D. Roosevelt." 4pp. Page 4: Poem—"Stand Fast by Roosevelts Side."

FDR-400 My Country's Flag. w. Henry H. Bennett. m. Herman Katims. Published by Lyric Music Co., Norwalk, CT. 1945. Bk/w/gn drawing of Washington Monument. B/w drawing of "George Washington, Courtesy of Frick Museum, NYC." "In memory of our beloved Franklin Delano Roosevelt, How Excellent is Thy Name In All The Earth, 1882-1945." 8pp. Pages 2 and 8: Blank.

FDR-401 Join The Legion (American Legion Air and March Song). w.m. Al N. Berube. Published by The Plains Music Publishing Company, Nos. 24-42 West Bayaud, Denver, CO. 1937. R/w/b photos and drawings of "George Washington—Revolution," "Abraham Lincoln—Liberty," "Woodrow Wilson—Constitution," and "Franklin D. Roosevelt—Democracy," eagle, two flags—"Yesterday" and "Today," "E Pluribus Unum." Printed verse. 6pp. Page 6: Bl/w photo of "Al N. Berube at the Hammond Electric Organ." Advertising.

FDR-402 Have A Drink, Boys (Here's To You And Yours And Mine). w. Wallace LeGrande Henderson. m. Billy James. Published by New Deal Publishing Company, No. 1420 North 15th Street, Philadelphia, PA. 1933. R/w/b drawing of a Man and The Statue of Liberty with beer mugs, stars. 6pp. Page 2: Blank. Page 3: "Dedicated to President Franklin D. Roosevelt and his 'New Deal.'" Page 6: Advertising.

FDR-403 The Yellow Rose Of Texas (Song for Voice and Piano). a. David W. Guion. Published by G. Schirmer, Inc., New York, NY. 1936. Y/gn/w drawing of a yellow rose, seal of the "Texas Centennial Exposition, 1836-1936." "Written in honor of the One Hundredth Birthday of Texas and Dedicated to President Franklin Delano Roosevelt." 8pp. Page 8: Advertising.

FDR-404 The March Of Victory (The Roosevelt National Campaign Song). w.m. Carl H. Koch. 1936. [10 7/8" × 7 7/8"]. Non-pictorial. "Authorized by the Democrat National Committee." 4pp. Pages 2 and 3: Blank.

FDR-405 (The Dawn Will Bring A) Song Of Peace. w.m. [Lester W. Honen]? [ca. 1945]. Photos of Franklin D. Roosevelt and Composer. "Dedicated to the memory of Franklin D. Roosevelt, an Exponent of International Peace." Under the photo of Roosevelt—

(FDR) FRANKLIN D. ROOSEVELT

"The most good for the greatest number, The Future Belongs to the Children."

FDR-406 Roosevelt (Roosevelt Our President) (Song). w. Edna J. Robinson. m. Charles T. Edwards. Published by Edna J. Robinson, No. 2305 Tatnall Street, Wilmington, DE. 1933. Bl/w drawing of eagle, flag, torch. "Dedicated to Franklin Delano Roosevelt." 4pp. Page 4: Blank

FDR-407 Garner The Sheaves With Garner. w.m. Fran MacAnn. Published by Southern Music Company, No. 112 West Houston Street, San Antonio, TX. 1939. Bl/w photo of "John Nance Garner." R/w/b drawing of eagle, leaf, geometric designs. "Arranged for piano, voice, accordion, guitar, saxophones, trumpets and trombone." 6pp. Page 6: Advertising.

FDR-408 The Democrats Are In Again. W. Katherine De Reeder. M. Max Herschfield. [1936]. [V-1: Handwritten Manuscript] [V-2: Printed song sheet]. Non-pictorial. [V-1: "The right to print, publish and sing this song can only be secured by joint permission of the Authors — Copyright applied for."]. [V-1: 4pp.] [V-2: 2pp. Page 2: Blank.].

FDR-409 The President's Waltz. m. Frances Hamilton. Published by G. Burdette & Co., Publishers, No. 111 West 5th Street, Los Angeles, CA. [ca. 1936]. "Dedicated to our beloved President, Franklin Delano Roosevelt."

FDR-410 God Bless And Keep Our President. w.m. Denver Darling (ASCAP) and Vaughn Horton (ASCAP). Published by Rytvoc, Inc., No. 1585 Broadway, New York 19, NY. 1946.

FDR-411 Viva Roosevelt. w.m. Mollie Wren Whitman. In: *Sing America Sing! An Album of 17 Favorite Patriotic Songs Old And New*, page 54. Published by Edward B. Marks Music Corporation, RCA Building, New York, NY. [ca. 1942]. Br/gn/w drawing of a Minuteman. "Dedicated to the cause of Victory for the United States and the other United Nations." 68pp.

FDR-412 God Bless You. w. Mary Scobbie. m. Luther A. Clark (Arranger of the piano *part When Its Springtime In The Rockies*). Published by Mrs. Mary Scobbie, General Delevery, Greenville, PA. 1934. Y/bl photo of "Franklin D. Roosevelt." 6pp. Pages 2 and 6: Blank.

FDR-413 We're All For You Uncle Sam. w. Sgt. Robert Adler. m. Walter Johns Van Dyke. "Cartoons by S/Sgt. Dave Berger" including a drawing of Franklin D. Roosevelt inscribed "Nation's Friend." In: *Give Out! Songs of, by and for the Men in Service*, page 59. Published by The FRMACK Company, No. 2 East 23rd Street, New York, NY. 1944. [5" × 7 7/16"]. N/c drawing of woman band leader, soldiers marching. 132pp.

FDR-414 The Man Who Wins (The Big Roosevelt March). w. E.K. Arnold. m. P.J. O'Reilly. Published by Golden Heart Music Co., Battle Creek, MI. 1936. Bl/w/bk drawing of trees, geometric designs. "Respectfully dedicated to Hon. Pres. Franklin D. Roosevelt." 6pp. Page 6: B/w drawing of two bushes, geometric designs. "Roosevelt Must Win."

FDR-415 Don't Let Down The Flag (That Never Let You Down). w.m. Billy Arden. Published by Great Lakes Music Publishers, Buffalo, NY. Copyright 1942 by Boleslaw Zielinski. [6 11/16" × 9 1/2"]. B/w litho of eagle, American flag. "Handy A.E.F. Edition." "Keep 'em Fighting Buy War Savings Bonds and Stamps" — B/w litho of a P.T. boat. 6pp. Page 2: Narrative. Page 6: Advertising.

FDR-416 He's A Great American. w.m. R. Magee and John C. Wickes. Published y Santly-Joy-Select, Inc., No. 1619 Broadway, New York, NY. 1940. [8 1/2" × 10 7/8"]. Non-pictorial geometric designs, stars. "SJS Advance Artist Copy." 4pp.

FDR-417 The Old New Deal. w.m. Robert Frank Jarrett. Published by R.F. Jarrett, Jarrett Springs Hotel, Dillsboro, NC. 1934. Litho of couples.

FDR-418 Now That Roosevelt's In. w.m. Mary Alice Mullin. Copyright by Mary Alice Mullin, No. 634 East Third Street, Galesburg, IL. 1934. R/w/b drawing of Capitol dome. 4pp.

FDR-419 Hail! Hail! Our President. w.m. Lewis A. Bedard. 1934.

FDR-420 God Bless Our President. w.m. Grace Wilson. Published by Grace Wilson, No. 625 Warner Avenue, Los Angeles, CA. 1941. Bl/w non-pictorial geometric design border, lyre. "Two Patriotic Songs—1. *God Bless Our President*; 2. *March Away*." 6pp.

FDR-421 God Bless Our President (Roosevelt Victory Song). w. Cal McCarthy. Published as a post card. [1940]. Obv: B/w photos of Franklin D. Roosevelt and Henry A. Wallace. "Roosevelt's Victory Song." Rev: "Franklin D. Roosevelt and Henry A. Wallace, Candidates for President and Vice-President of the Democratic Party." "Macart Series."

FDR-422 Happy Am I. w.m. Henderson & J.E. Marsh. Published by Wilbur Michaux. 1933. Bl/gd litho of sun rising over earth. Globe is ladled "Spiritual." Drawings of five people—Chinese, Country Boy, American, African American, Indian Woman. "Dedicated to Franklin D. Roosevelt on President's Day, April 30, 1933." "Theme Song Of the Church of God." Back Cover: Photo of Franklin D. Roosevelt.

FDR-423 What Would We Do Without President Roosevelt. w.m. Mrs. Max L. Wilson. B/w photo of Mrs. Wilson. 1934. O/w floral decorations.

See also TJ-49; AL-346; JMC-1; JMC-8; CC-53; AES-37; AES-66; AML-9; AML-16; WLW-12; WLW-13; WLW-22; WLW-32; WLW-56; WLW-66; TED-30; TED-31; HST-7; HST-20; HST-22; DDE-9; JFK-61; LBJ-1; HHH-2; HHH-4; MSD-2; HAW-1; HAW-2; HAW-4; HAW-4; MISC-19; MISC-110.

Franklin Pierce

FP-1 President Pierce's March And Quick Step. m. B.R. Lignoski. Published by George Willig, Jr., Baltimore, MD. 1852. B/w litho by P.S. Duval & Company on stone by A. Newsam (from a Daguerreotype by M.A. Root) of Franklin Pierce, Capitol building, hat. "Composed and Arranged for the Piano Forte and Respectfully Dedicated to Miss C.C.P. Learned." "Price 37 _ cents nett [sic]." 8pp. Pages 2, 7 and 8: Blank.

FP-2 Gen. Pierce's Grand March. m. Alonzo Bond. Published by George P. Reed & Company, No. 17 Tremont Row, Boston, MA. 1852. B/w green tinted litho by Tappan and Bradford's of General Franklin Pierce. "As played by Bond's Cornet Band." "Composed and most Respectfully Dedicated to Hon. Franklin Pierce." Price 25 cents nett [sic]." 8pp. Page 2: Blank.

FP-3 Gen'l Franklin Pierce's Grand March. m. Carlo Alboni. Published by J.C. Beckel, No. 22 South 6th Street, Philadelphia, PA. 1852. Non-pictorial. "Composed for the Piano Forte." 4pp. Pages 1 and 4: Blank.

FP-4 A National March. m. T. Moritz Schwale. Published by Lee &

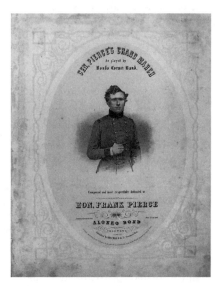

FP-2

Walker, No. 188 Chestnut Street, Philadelphia, PA. [ca. 1853]. Non-pictorial. "Dedicated to Genl. Franklin Pierce, President of the U.S. and in honor of the Granite Club of the Union."

FP-5 Great Democratic Song. m. "Air: *Old Folks At Home*." Published by Thomas M. Scroggy, Publisher, Card and Fancy Job Printer, No. 443 Vine Street, above Twelfth, Philadelphia, PA. [ca. 1852]. [6" × 9 1/2"]. Non-pictorial geometric design border. "Composed and Published in Honor of the recent Democratic Victory." "A Gallant Whig — The following bet was made a few days before the 'Presidential Election,' between a Whig and Democrat, boarding in Arch Street. The loser to purchase, saw and carry into the Chamber of the winner, a half cord of good hickory wood; sawing to commence at 3 o'clock P.M. in front of the house. The loser fully intends to pay the bet in a day or two, for the sake of Gen. Winfield Scott; and a large number of his political and personal friends will be present, to encourage him in his arduous task." 2pp. Page 2: Blank.

FP-6 General Pierce's Presidential Inauguration March And Quick Step. m. George P. Knauff. Published by Miller & Beacham, Baltimore, MD. 1853. "Composed & Dedicated to President Frank Pierce." 4pp. Page 4: Blank.

FP-7 Jordan Is A Hard Road To Travel. m. Old Dan Emmett. Published by David A. Truax, No. 80 Fourth Street, Cincinnati, OH. 1853. Non-pictorial. "The Celebrated Banjo Song as Sung by Young Dan Emmett." "Authorized Edition." 6pp. Pages 2 and 6: Blank. [Verse about Franklin Pierce].

FP-8 Jordan Is A Hard Road To Travel. m. Old Dan Emmett. Published by Oliver Ditson, No. 115 Washington Street, Boston, MA. 1853. B/w engraving of a black minstrel performer. 6pp. Pages 2 and 6: Blank. [Verse about Franklin Pierce].

FP-9 The Presidential Contest (Quickstep). m. George Stimpson, Jr. m.a. "Composed and Arranged as a quickstep by Miss Sarah A. Cheeney. Published by The Ladies at Their Exhibition at Armory Hall, Boston, MA. 1852. Non-pictorial geometric designs. "And Respectfully dedicated to the Successful Candidate." 4pp.

FP-10 President Pierce's March. m. R. Lignoski. In: *Marches Of The Presidents, 1789-1909, Authentic Marches & Campaign Songs*, page 36. A. Carl Miller. Published by Chappell & Co., Inc., No. 609 Fifth Avenue, New York, NY. "By arrangement with Chilmark Press, Inc." 1968. [9" × 12"]. R/w/b litho of eagle, flag. "An Illustrated Piano Folio For All Ages." 72pp.

See also WHT-23; WW-19; FDR-158; DDE-9; LBJ-1; MISC-167.

George H. W. Bush

GB-1 President George Bush March. w. Andrea Fodor Litkei. m. Ervin

GB-1

Litkei. Published by Loena Music Publishing Company, No. 239 West 18th Street, New York, NY. 1988. N/c "Photo by Dave Valdez, The White House," of George Bush, facsimile signature. 4pp.

GB-2 Let's Thank Our Great First Lady. w.m. Judy Atwell Blecha (aka: Judy Weldon). Copyright 1991 by Songrite Creations Productions, [Port St. Lucie, FL]. August, 1989. [8 1/2" × 11"]. Non-pictorial. 2pp. Page 2: Blank.
See also RR-2; RR-7; MISC-110.

GEORGE B. MCCLELLAN

GBM-1 McClellan 1864 (Song). Published by William A. Pond & Company, No. 547 Broadway, New York, NY. 1864. Litho of George B. McClellan — "The President." "No North, No South, No East, No West." "Habeas Corpus, Constitution, White Men, Liberty."

GBM-2 McClellan And Victory! (Or the Battle of South Mountain and the Uprising of the Keystone State). m. "Tune: *Dan Tucker.*" Published by J. Magee, No. 316 Chestnut Street, Philadelphia, PA. 1862. [7 3/8" × 9 7/8"]. Bl/w litho of George B. McClellan, geometric design border. 4pp. Pages 2-4: Lined writing paper.

GBM-3 En Avant! a. G. Baker. Published by A.C. Peters and Brothers, No. 94 West 4th Street, Cincinnati, OH. 1862. B/w litho of General George B. McClellan leading troops on horseback. Page 3: Subtitle: "On to the Field Where Honor Calls Us."

GBM-4 Parade March (Of the Great Potomac Army). m. Charles Fradel. Published by C. Breusing, No. 701 Broadway, New York, NY. 1861. N/c litho by Sherman and Hart of "Major Genl. McClellan," Zouave, Union soldier, cannon, drum, wreath, flags. "Respectfully dedicated to Major Genl. McClellan by Gen. L. Blenker." 8pp. Pages 2 and 8: Blank.

GBM-5 Hail! Glorious Banner Of Our Land. w. Mrs. Mary Farrell Moore. m. Charles Warren (Cincinnati). Published by Lee & Walker, No. 722 Chestnut Street, Philadelphia, PA. Copyright 1861 by Mary Farrell Moore. N/c litho by T. Sinclair's Litho. of Miss Columbia with U.S. flag, ships, eagle and cannon. "Respectfully inscribed to Major General George B. McClellan by Mrs. Mary Farrell Moore, Cincinnati, Ohio, July 4, 1861." 8pp. Pages 2 and 3: Blank. Page 3: Non-pictorial title page. "Hail Glorious banner of our land! Our own red, white, and blue! The starry welkin lends to thee those emblems bright and true, from pole to pole, in every clime, on every land and sea, despot and slave alike revere the banner of the free!" Page 8: Advertising for other Lee & Walker published songs.

GBM-6 General McClellan's Grand March. m. E. Mack. Published by Lee & Walker, No. 722 Chesnut Street, Philadelphia, PA. 1861. N/c litho by T. Sinclair's Litho. of General George B. McClellan. 10pp. Pages 2, 4, 9 and 10: Blank. Page 3: Title page. "Respectfully dedicated to Major General McClellan." Page 5: Start of music.

GBM-7 Give Us Back Our Old Commander. Published by Charles Magnus, No. 12 Frankfort Street, New York, NY. [ca. 1863]. [5" × 8"]. H/c litho of George B. McClellan, other officers on horseback, troops. "500 Illustrated Ballads, Lithographed and Printed by Charles Magnus, No. 12 Frankfort Street, N.Y.; Branch Office: No. 520 7th St., Washington, D.C." 2pp. Page 2: Blank.

GBM-8 Major General McClellan's Grand March. Published by Oliver Ditson & Company, No. 277 Washington Street, Boston, MA. 1861. N/c litho by J.H. Bufford's Litho. of George B. McClellan on horseback. "Arranged for the Piano Forte." 8pp. Pages 2 and 8: Blank.

GBM-9 McClellan For President. w. John C. Cross. m. Air: *Pompey*

Moore. Published by Charles Magnus, No. 12 Franklin Street, New York, NY. [1864]. Litho of George B. McClellan with horse, wreath. "Sung by Cool Burgess of Sam Sharpley's Minstrels." "500 Illustrated Ballads, Lithographed and Printed by Charles Magnus, No. 12 Frankfort Street, New York, Branch Office: No. 520 7th St., Washington, D.C." 4pp. Pages 2-4: Lined note paper. Washington, D.C." 2pp. Page 2: Blank.

GBM-10 The Flag Of Washington (A Song For The People). w. [Handwritten contemporary says Eugene Batchelder]. m. Henry R. Bishop. Published by Oliver Ditson & Company, No. 277 Washington Street, Boston, MA. 1861. Non-pictorial. "The words of this song were written under peculiar circumstances. The name of the Author is a secret." "To Maj. Gen. Geo. H. [sic] McClellan." 4pp. Page 4: Blank.

GBM-11 McClellan Is The Man (Grand Rallying Song with Chorus). w.m. Will S. Hayes. Published by William McCarrell, No. 310 Jefferson Street, Louisville, KY. 1864. Litho of man with hammer atop flag pole, geometric design border. "To the people."

GBM-12 McClellan Schottisch. m. Miss Herminie Seron. Published by Lee & Walker, No. 722 Chestnut Street, Philadelphia, PA. 1863. Non-pictorial. "Composed for the Piano." 6pp. Pages 2 and 6: Blank.

GBM-13 General McClellan's Grand March. m. E. Mack. Published by Lee & Walker, No. 722 Chestnut Street, Philadelphia, PA. 1861. N/c litho by T. Sinclair's Litho. of George B. McClellan, white horse. "To General McClellan." 8pp. Pages 2, 4 and 8: Blank. Page 3: Non-pictorial title page.

GBM-14 M'Clellan Song. m. Air: *Harness Up The Mule*. [ca. 1864]. [4" × 6 1/4"]. Non-pictorial broadside. 2pp. Page 2: Blank.

GBM-15 General McClellan's Farewell. w. E.W.H. m. H. Coyle. Published by Lee & Walker, No. 722 Chestnut Street, Philadelphia, PA. 1863. Non-pictorial. "He that Ruleth his Spirit is better than he that taketh a City." "Respectfully Dedicated to the Army of the Potomac." 6pp. Pages 2 and 6: Blank. Page 3: Title—**Gen. McClellan's Farewell To The Army Of The Potomac**.

GBM-16 Brave McClellan Is Our Leader Now (Or Glory Hallelujah!). w. Mrs. M.A. Kidder. a. Augustus Cull. Published by Horace Waters, No. 481 Broadway, New York, NY. 1862. B/w litho by Stackpole of two Zouave soldiers. "Also the famous *John Brown's Song* Arranged for the Piano." 6pp. Page 5: *John Brown's Song*. Page 6: Advertising for other Horace Waters published songs.

GBM-17 McClellan And The Union (A Grand Rallying Song). w. "From *The Boston Currier*." m. Albert Fleming (Author of *Drummer-Boy, I Keep It Still That Faded Flower*, &c.). Published by William McCarrell, Louisville, KY. 1863. B/w litho of two U.S. flags, two stars, geometric designs. 6pp. Pages 2 and 6: Blank.

GBM-18 Gen. McClellan's Quick Step. m. "A Young Lady of Maryland." Published by Lee & Walker, No. 722 Chestnut Street, Philadelphia, PA. 1862. Non-pictorial. 6pp. Pages 2 and 6: Blank.

GBM-19 McClellan For President. w. John C. Cross. m. "Air: *Pompey Moore*." "Sold at wholesale by Horace Partridge at No. 27 Hanover Street, Boston, MA. [1864]. [5 5/8" × 8 1/4"]. Non-pictorial geometric design border. "Sung by Cool Burgess of Sam Sharpley's Minstrels." 2pp. Page 2: Blank.

GBM-20 Give Us Back Little Mac Our Old Commander. Published by Johnson, Song Publisher, No. 7 North 10th Street, Philadelphia, PA. [ca. 1863]. [5 1/4" × 9 3/8"]. Non-pictorial penny song sheet, geometric design border. "See

Johnson's New Catalogue of Songs." 2pp. Page 2: Blank.

GBM-21 100 Years Hence. w.m. Tony Pastor. Published by Johnson, Song Publisher, No. 7 North 10th Street, Philadelphia, PA. [ca. 1863]. [6 1/4" × 9 1/8"]. Non-pictorial penny song sheet, geometric design border. "See Prof. Brooks' Ball Room Monitor. It will give you more Instruction in Dancing than any book ever Published. Sold by Johnson, No. 7 North 10th Street, Phila." 2pp. Page 2: Blank.

GBM-22 McClellan Will Be President. w. M.J. Million. m. "Air: *Whack, Row De Dow!*" Published by Charles Magnus, No. 12 Frankfort Street, New York, NY. [1864]. [5" × 8"]. B/w litho of George McClellan. Hand Colored litho of two women, ship, wreath. "500 Illustrated Ballads, Lithographed and Printed by Charles Magnus, No. 12 Frankfort Street, N.Y.; Branch Office: No. 520 7th St., Washington, D.C." 4pp. Pages 2-4: Lined note paper.

GBM-23 Democratic Presidential Campaign Songster (No. 1). Published by J.F. Feeks, No. 26 Ann Street, New York, NY. 1864. [3 3/4" × 5 1/2"]. Y/bk litho of George B. McClellan, chain link frame. "McClellan & Pendleton." "Original Campaign Songs, Choruses, &c." 74pp. [M-135, 136].

GBM-24 McClellan Campaign Melodist. c. Sidney Herbert. Published by [V-1 and 2: Benjamin Russel, Boston] [V-3: American News Co., New York, NY] [V-4-7: B.W. Hitchcock, No. 14 Chambers Street, New York, NY]. 1864. [4 3/8" × 6 5/8"]. B/w litho of "McClellan" and "Pendleton." "A Collection of Patriotic Campaign Songs in Favor of the Constitution and the Union, the Election of General McClellan, the Restoration of the Federal Authority, and the Speedy Extermination of Treason." "The Union Must Be Preserved At All Hazards." 34pp. [M-137-143].

GBM-25 M'Clellan's Band. w. "Our Ned." m. "Air: *Gideon's Band.*" Published by Mason & Company, No. 58 North 6th Street, Philadelphia, PA. [ca. 1862]. [5" × 7 13/16"]. B/w litho of General George McClellan, geometric design border. "Clubs and Dealers can have their orders filled for the above, and all other Campaign Songs by addressing Mason & Co., No. 58 North 6th Street, Phila. Dealers in Cartes de Visite, Albumns, Songs, Books, Periodicals, Medals, &c. Catalogues sent Free." 2pp. Page 2: Blank.

GBM-26 Our Ship Moves Proudly On, My Boys (A Union Song). w. E.W. Locke. m. "Air: *A Little More Cider, Too*". Published by E.W. Locke in Maine. 1862. [5 3/4" × 8 1/4"]. Non-pictorial. 2pp. Page 2: Blank.

GBM-27 McClellan Campaign Melodist. e. Sidney Herbert. Published by Benjamin B. Russell, No. 515 Washington Street, Boston, MA. [4 3/8" × 6 11/16"]. 1864. Bl/bk litho of an eagle — "E Pluribus Unum," cotton bales, crops. "A Collection of Patriotic Campaign Songs in Favor of the Constitution and the Union, the Election of General McClellan, the Restoration of the Federal Authority and the Speedy Extermination of Treason." "The Union must be Preserved at all Hazards!" 36pp.

GBM-28 Little Mac! Little Mac! You're The Very Man (Campaign Song). w.m. Stephen C. Foster. Published by J. March, No. 1102 Chesnut Street, Philadelphia, PA. Copyright 1864 by Marion Foster. Non-pictorial.

GBM-29(A) The Chicago Copperhead. w.m. James G. Clark. Published by Horace Waters, No. 481 Broadway, New York, NY. 1864. Non-pictorial geometric design border. 4pp. Page 4: Advertising for other songs including *General Scott's Farewell March* by Mrs. Parkhurst.

(B) The Copperhead of 1864. w. John Holland. m. James Clark. 6pp. Page 2: Blank. Page 6: Advertising.

(C) **The Copperhead Of 1865**.
GBM-30 Give Us Back Our Old Commander. w.m. Sep. Winner. Published by Winner & Company, No. 933 Spring Garden Street, Philadelphia, PA. 1862. Non-pictorial. "To Our Brave Volunteers." "Give us back our old Commander, let him manage, let him plan. With McClellan as our leader we can want no better man." 6pp.

GBM-31 The Noble George McClellan (Song and Chorus). w. Edwin H. Nevin. m. "Adapted to a Favorite Melody." Published by Lee & Walker, No. 722 Chestnut Street, Philadelphia, PA. 1862. Non-pictorial. "Respectfully Dedicated to The Noble George McClellan." "He's young, he's true, he's brave, The Noble George McClellan. His Country he will save — the Noble George McClellan. Hurrah for George McClellan, Old Pennsylvania's son; He'll not give up the battle, 'Till the vict'ry has been won.'" 6pp. Page 2: Blank. Page 6: Advertising for songs.

GBM-32 Benny Haven's O (A McClellan Campaign Song and Chorus). w. Noble Butler. Published by D.P. Faulds, No. 223 Main Street, Louisville, KY. 1864. Non-pictorial geometric design border. "Benny Haven is the name if a man who in other days, dispensed buckwheat cakes, with accompaniments, to such Cadets of West Point as were daring enough to break the regulations and visit his establishment. 'Benny Havens O' has become classic ground to the men of West Point...When General McClellan visited West Point about a year ago the Cadets gathered around him and sung Benny Haven's O, the General joining in the chorus with as much spirit as he had done in other days. It is said that the Cadets made themselves hoarse with shouting 'Hurrah for McClellan!'" 6pp. Pages 2 and 6: Blank.

GBM-33 God Save The Grand Old Stars And Stripes! w. John L. Sullivan, Jr., M.D. m. Mrs. S.G. Knight. Published by Oliver Ditson & Company, No. 277 Washington Street, Boston, MA. 1862. R/w/b flag, Liberty cap; geometric design border. "Dedicated to Gen. Geo. B. McClellan." 6pp. Pages 2, 5 and 6: Blank.

GBM-34 General McClellan's Grand March. m. E. Mack. Published by Lee & Walker, No. 722 Chestnut Street, Philadelphia, PA. 1861. Non-pictorial. 6pp. Pages 2 and 6: Blank.

GBM-35(A) Little Mac's March. m. Carl Muller. Published by A.C. Peters and Bro., No. 94 West Fourth Street, opposite the Post Office, Cincinnati, OH. 1864. B/w oval litho by Ehrgott, Forbriger & Company Lithogr. of General George B. McClellan. "Copy Right Secured." 6pp. Pages 2 and 6: Blank.

(B) **McClellan's Schottisch.**

GBM-36 McClellan Mazurka! m. T.E. Bayley. Published by D.P. Faulds, No. 223 Main Street, Louisville, KY. 1864. R/w/b non-pictorial geometric design border. "To the Friends of the Union Democracy." 6pp. Pages 2 and 6: Blank.

GBM-37 McClellan's Serenade (Quartette). w. Lt. Col. F.S. Nickerson

GBM-35(A)

(Maine 4th Regt). m. S.K. Whiting (Regt. Band, Maine 4th Regt). Published by Oliver Ditson & Company, No. 277 Washington Street, Boston, MA. [ca. 1861]. Non-pictorial. "To the Union Army." 4pp. Page 4: Blank.

GBM-38 Genl. McClellan's March. m. F. Muller. a. "From Donizetti." Published by A.C. Peters and Brother, Cincinnati, OH. 1861. B/w litho from photograph by Eaton and Weber of General George B. McClellan. 6pp. Pages 2 and 6: Blank.

GBM-39 Union. m. L.M. Gottschalk. Published by Wm. Hall & Sons, No. 543 Broadway, New York, NY. 1863. Non-pictorial. "Paraphrase de Concert on the National Airs *Star Spangled Banner*, *Yankee Doodle* and *Hail Columbia*." "To Majr. Genl. Geo. B. McClellan." 20pp. Pages 2 and 20: Blank.

GBM-40 The Nellie Quick Step. m. P. Kalkman (Leader, 2d Regl. Band). Published by Henry Tolman & Company, No. 291 Washington Street, Boston, MA. 1862. Non-pictorial geometric design border. "Most respectfully dedicated to Mrs. Maj. Genl. McClellan by the 2d R.I. Vols." 6pp.

GBM-41 Gen. Geo. B. McClellan's Funeral March. m. H.J. Bennett. Published by White, Smith & Company, Boston, MA. 1885. B/w litho of General George B. McClellan, oak leaves. 6pp. Pages 2 and 6: Blank.

GBM-42 Brave McClellan March. m. James Bellak, Op. 1703. Published by Horace Waters, No. 481 Broadway, New York, NY. 1862. Non-pictorial geometric designs. "The Sunny Side Set for Piano." List of other songs in series. 4pp. Page 4: Blank.

GBM-43(A) Noble George McClellan. w.m. Edwin H. Nevin. Published by Lee & Walker, No. 722 Chesnut Street, Philadelphia, PA. Non-pictorial black border. "National and Patriotic Songs, Ballads, &c., Arranged for Piano." List of songs.

(B) General McClellan's Farewell To The Army Of The Potomac. w.m. H. Coyle.

GBM-44 Mc'Clellan's Farewell (To the Army of the Potomac). m. "Air: *Gay and Happy*." Published by Charles Magnus, No. 12 Frankfort Street, New York, NY. [ca. 1862]. [4 15/16" × 8"]. H/c litho of General George B. McClellan with horse, wreath. Bl/w printing. "500 Illustrated Ballads, lithographed and printed by Charles Magnus, No. 12 Frankfort Street, New York. Branch Office: No. 520 7th St., Washington, D.C." 2pp. Page 2: Blank.

GBM-45(A) McClellan Is The Man (Song). m. Henry Cromwell. Published by G.D. Russell & Company, No. 126 Tremont, opposite Park Street, Boston, MA. 1864. B/w litho by E.N. Carter from a Black and Case photograph of George B. McClellan. 6pp. Pages 2 and 6: Blank

(B) McClellan Is The Man (Schottisch).

GBM-46 Come, At Your Country's Call (Or, Join Brave McClellan's Boys). w. Kate Moncrieff. m. "Adapted to a Favorite Melody." Published by Lee

GBM-45

& Walker, No. 722 Chestnut Street, Philadelphia, PA. 1862. Non-pictorial line border. "Come, come march at your Country's call; Stand to your arms and march in good order. March, march, march at your Country's call; Join Brave McClellan's Boys over the border; See your proud banner spread, waving above your head, With Stars and Stripes so famous in story; Mount and make ready then, Sons of the Mountain glen; Fight neath your flag for Union and Glory." 6pp. Page 6: Advertising.

GBM-47 The Praise Of McClellan. w. S.S. Sanford (of Sanford's Troupe). m. E. Mack. Published by Marsh, No. 1102 Chestnut Street, Philadelphia, PA. 1862. Non-pictorial geometric designs. "As sung by W. Bathlor." 6pp.

GBM-48 Old Abe They Said Was An Honest Man (Song). w. J.W. Jarboe, Esq. m. F. Lafayette. Published by Firth, Son & Company, No. 563 Broadway, New York, NY. 1864. Non-pictorial geometric designs. "Words Composed and Sung with Great Applause by J.W. Jarboe, Esq. at the Great McClellan Union Meeting, Union Square." "To the McClellan Union Clubs." 6pp. Pages 2 and 6: Blank.

GBM-49 McClellan's Farewell To The Army Of The Potomac. m. "Air: *Gay and Happy.*" Published by H. De Marsan, Publisher of Songs, Ballads, Toy-Books, &c., No. 54 Chatham Street, New York, NY. [ca. 1864]. [6" × 10"]. B/w border drawings of military scenes. Quote—"Major General Burnside's Opinion of General George B. McClellan—I have know him most intimately, as students together, as soldiers in the field, and as private students. For years we have lived in the same family, and I know him as well as I know any human being on the face of the Earth, and I know that no more honest, conscientious man exists than Gen. McClellan. I know that no feeling of ambition beyond that of the good and the success of our cause ever enters his breast. All that he does is with a single eye, a single view, to the success of his government, and the putting down of the rebellion. I know that nothing, under the sun, will ever, induce that man to swerve from what he knows to be his duty. He is an honest, Christian-like & Conscientious man; and now let me add one thing; that he has the soundest lead and the clearest military perception of any man of the United States." 2pp. Page 2: Blank.

GBM-50 The Bluebird Echo Polka. m. Mrs. Mary Morrison. Published by Marsh, No. 1102 Chesnut Street, Philadelphia, PA. 1862. Non-pictorial. "To Major Gen. G.B. McClellan." 6pp.

GBM-51 McClellan Campaign Songster. Published by Mason & Company, No. 58 North Sixth Street, Philadelphia, PA. 1864. [2 3/4" × 4 3/4"]. B/w litho of George McClellan. 20pp. "For the use of Clubs, Containing all of the most popular songs."

GBM-51

GBM-52(A) Pendleton's March. m. C.M. Feine. Published by A.C. Peters and Bro. 1863. B/w beige tinted litho of George H. Pendleton. Br/w drawings of vine, woman with anchor, woman with scales. Page 2: Blank.
 (B) **Pendleton's Schottisch.**
GBM-53 The Head Of The Nation McClellan Shall Be. w. C.O. Clayton. m. Air: "Written to the stirring melody *Bonnie Dundee.*" Published by Wm. A. Pond & Company, No. 547 Broadway, New York, NY. 1864. R/w non-pictorial [horizontal format]. "Cordially inscribed to all who revere the Constitution and regard its obligations." 4pp. Page 2: Title—**M'c Clellan And Union** (Campaign Song). Page 4: Blank.
GBM-54(A) Forward March For Little Mac. Published by William A. Pond & Company, No. 547 Broadway, New York, NY. 1864. [6" × 10 1/4"]. [Foldout]. B/w litho of George McClellan, geometric design border. "M'Clellan Campaign Songs." "Sold by American News Company, No. 121 Nassau Street."
 (B) **Little Mac And Pendleton.**
 (C) **The Head Of The Nation McClellan Shall Be** (McClellan and Union). w. C.O. Clayton. 4pp. Page 3: "McClellan Songs, No. 3."
 (D) **Little Mac Is On De Track.**
GBM-55 McClellan Is Our Man (A Union Song). w. E.W. Locke [of Maine]. m. Air: *A Little More Cider Too.* 1862. [6 1/4" × 13 3/8"]. Non-pictorial. 2pp.
GBM-56 Seven Days Fight Before Richmond. Published by H. De Marsan, No. 54 Chatham Street, New York, NY. [ca. 1864]. [6 3/4" × 10 1/4"]. B/w border drawings of military scenes. 2pp.
GBM-57 Major General McClellan's Triumphal March. m. J.C. Beckel. Published by Marsh, No. 1102 Chesnut Street, Philadelphia, PA. 1861. N/c litho of George B. McClellan. Page 3: "Composed and Dedicated to that Gallant Officer."

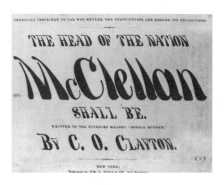

GBM-53

GBM-58 The Union Army March. a. George A. Mietzke, Op. 11. Published by Schuberth & Company, No. 98 Spring Street, New York, NY. 1861. N/c lithos by Shearman and Hart of George McClellan, U.S. and German flags, cannons, Union Generals—"Woll," "Rosencranz," "Siegl," and "Blenker." "Introducing the German National Air—*What is the German's Fatherland?* and the American Patriotic Song—*Columbia the Gem of the Ocean.*" "Dedicated to the Commanders, Officers, and Privates of the Army & Navy." Page 2: Blank.
GBM-59 M'Clellan And Pendleton Polka. m. W.C. Coleman. Published by William M'Carrell, No. 310 Jefferson Street, Louisville, KY. 1864. R/w/b litho of Miss Liberty, flag. 6pp. Pages 2 and 6: Blank.
GBM-60 McClellan's Quickstep. m. Carl Lazare. Published by G.D. Russell & Co., Boston, MA. 1864.
GBM-61 McClellan And Liberty [Song Sheet]. Published by Frank McElroy, No. 113 Nassau Street, New York, NY. 1864. [7" × 17"]. Non-pictorial. "Stand by the Union and I'll Stand by you." "The Work before us; To surpress the Rebellion, To preserve the Union, To maintain the sovereignty of the People!" "Let us apply ourselves to the duty of uniting all the conservative elements of the country, in the effort to place in the Presidential Chair a man who will revere

the Constitution as his highest political authority — Such a man is George B. McClellan." "The following is...from a recent letter of the Hon. Amos Kendall: I am losing my patience in reading Gen. McClellan's report. The injustice to him, and the atrocious wrong to his noble army and the country, are enough to make the blood of honest and patriotic men boil within them." Two songs — **McClellan And Union** and **Hurrah For The Man We Love**. 2pp.

GBM-62 Hurrah For The Man We Love. m. "Air — *Vive L'Amor*." [1864]. [7 3/8" × 14 1/4"]. Non-pictorial. "A McClellan and Union Mass Meeting will be held at Cooper Institute on the beginning of the 17th inst. at which Hon. Amos Kendall, General Jackson's Postmaster General, and President of the 'Conservative Union National Committee' will preside and a large number of our most prominent citizens and military gentlemen have accepted invitations to act as vice-presidents. The exercises will consist of Addresses by eminent speakers interspersed with Patriotic and McClellan songs, by a Glee Club and the whole audience...Old men are especially invited to attend and welcome the venerable Mr. Kendall, and all such will be furnished with tickets admitting them to talk before seven o'clock by sending their names to R.F. Stevens, 105 East 49th Street, by mail or otherwise. The following letter from the Hon. Amos Kendall speaks for itself — Washington, March 24, 1864; Dr. R.F. Stevens, 105 East 49th Street, My Dear Sir: Your letter, informing me that the 17th inst. had been fixed upon for the McClellan Demonstration, came to hand this morning. If the friends of McClellan and the Country, in New York, think it would further the cause for me to preside, you are at liberty to make the announcement. I am losing my patience reading Gen. McClellan's report. The injustice to him, and the atrocious wrong to his noble army and the country, are enough to make the blood of honest and patriotic men boil within them — Yours truly, Amos Kendall." "At the close of this song, A McClellan and Union Flag Raising will take place, with the air *Star Spangled Banner*."

GBM-63 Hail To The Nominee. Published by Charles Magnus, No. 12 Frankfort Street, New York, NY. [1864]. N/c litho of General George McClellan, ornate frame, flags, eagle. 2pp.

GBM-64 Copperhead Minstrel (A Choice Collection of Democratic Poems & Songs). Published by Feeks and Bancker, Wholesale Agents, No. 24 Ann Street, New York. [V-1: 1863] [V-2: 1864]. [4 3/4" × 7 1/4"]. O/bk non-pictorial. "For the use of Political Clubs and the Social Circle." "Price 25 cents." 64pp. [M-133, 134].

GBM-65 McClellan And Victory! (or The Battle of South Mountain and the Uprising of the Keystone State). m. "Tune — *Dan Tucker*." Published by J. Magee, No. 316 Chestnut Street, Philadelphia, PA. 1861. [5" × 7 7/8"]. R/w/b litho of two U.S. flags, border. "Liberty and Union Forever." 4pp. Pages 2-4: Writing paper.

GBM-66 A New Song For The Restoration Of The Constitution. m. "Air — *A Year or Two Ago*." [1864]. [7 7/8" × 12 1/8"]. Non-pictorial. 2pp. Page 2: Blank.

GBM-67 McClellan For President. w. John C. Cross. m. "Air: *Pompey Moore*." Published by H. De Marsan, No. 54 Chatham Street, New York, NY. [1864]. [6 7/8" × 9 7/8"]. B/w litho border of military scenes, soldier, sailor, cannon, ships. 2pp. Page 2: Blank

GBM-68 Ring Merry Bells (The Union Victory). w. M.L. Hofford, A.M. m. M.H. Frank (Author of *The Burnside Expedition*). Published by Marsh, No. 1102 Chesnut Street, Philadelphia, PA. 1862. B/w scroll, geometric designs. "Respectfully inscribed to Major General Geo. B. McClellan, U.S.A." 6pp. Pages 2 and 6: Blank.

GBM-69 McClellan's Dream. [ca. 1862]. [8" × 11 3/8"]. B/w litho of eagle — "E Pluribus Unum," train, crops, plow, flag. "Union Song!" 2pp. Page 2: Blank.

GBM-70 Campaign Document, No. 19: Campaign Songs. Published by *New York Evening Press*, New York, NY. 1864. 12pp. "Sold at 13 Park Row, New York, and at all Democratic newspaper offices, at $1 per 1,000 pages." [M-132].

GBM-71 Little Mac Campaign Songster. Published by E.P. Patten, *The World* Office, New York, NY. 1864. Br/bk litho of George B. McClellan. 16pp. [M-145].

GBM-72 M'Clellan Campaign Songster. Published by Mason & Company, No. 58 North Sixth Street, Philadelphia, PA. 1864. "For the Use of Clubs, Containing All of the Most Popular Song." Y/bk litho of George B. McClellan. [M-146].

GBM-73 Sprague's Campaign Songs For 1868. Published in Cincinnati, OH. 1868. [For George Pendleton's abortive try for President]. 24pp. [M-176].

GBM-74 Little Mac Campaign Songster. Published by T.R. Dawley, New York, NY. 1864. "Price 12 cents." 72pp. [M-144].

GBM-75 Campaign Songs For Christian Patriots And True Democrats, Accompanied With Notes. a. Rev. William D. Potts, M.D. Newark, NJ. Published by Rev. William D. Potts, M.D. Newark, NJ. 1864. [V-1: Gy/bk] [V-2: O/bk] [V-3: Y/bk]. "Single copies, 10 cents. One Hundred $6.00. Address giving Post Office, County, and State in full to Rev. William D. Potts, M.D., Box 5573, New York Post Office." 24pp. [M-147].

GBM-76 McClellan's Richmond March. m. Chas. Degenhard. Published by Sheppard, Cottier & Co., No. 215 Main Street, Buffalo, NY. 1862. B/w non-pictorial geometric designs. "To the 49th Regt. N.Y.S. Volunteers.

GBM-77 Hail! Glorious Banner Of Our Land. w. Mrs. Mary Farrell Moore. m. Charles Warren. Published by Lee & Walker, No. 722 Chestnut Street, Philadelphia, PA. Copyright 1861 by Mary Farrell Moore. B/w geometric design border. "Respectfully inscribed to Major General George B. McClellan by Mrs. Mary Farrell Moore, Cincinnati, Ohio, July 4, 1861." "Hail Glorious banner of our land! Our own red, white, and blue! The starry welkin lends to thee those emblems bright and true, from pole to pole, in every clime, on every land and sea, despot and slave alike revere the banner of the free!" 6pp. Page 2: Blank. Page 6: Advertising.

GBM-78 McClellan's Address To His Army. m. "Air *–Bruce's Address.*" In: Beadle's Dime Knapsack Songster: Containing the Choicest Patriotic Songs, Together with many New and Original Ones, Set to Old Melodies, page 18. Published by Beadle and Company, No. 141 William Street, New York, NY. 1862. [3 3/4" × 5 3/4"]. Litho of coin — "One Dime, United States of America." 74pp.[?].

GBM-80 The General, The Sergeant, And The Flag (Song). w. C. Birch Bagster. m. Stephen C. Massett (Author of *Our Good Ship Sails To-Night, When The Moon On The Lake Is Looming*, etc). Published by H.B. Dodworth, No. 6 Astor Place, New York, NY. 1863. R/w/b non-pictorial geometric designs. "To Mrs. Geo B. McClellan." "Extract from a letter from Gen. McClellan to Mr. Massett: "Expressing my gratification at the manner in which a true incident has been converted into verse. I am Very truly yours, Geo. B. McClellan [facsimile signature]." 8pp. [?]. Page 2, 7 and 8: Blank. Page 3: Narrative on Gen. McClellan.

GBM-81 Brave Little Mac. w. J.H. Taylor. m. "Air *On the Road to Brighton,* Etc." Published by Charles Magnus, No. No. 12 Frankfort Street, New York, NY. [ca. 1862]. H/c litho of

General McClellan and troops. "Sung by J.H. Taylor, the great comic Banjo Soloist, with great applause." "500 Illustrated Ballads, lithographed and printed by Charles Magnus." 2pp. Page 2: Blank.

GBM-82 Antietam. w. Col. Max Langenscwartz. m. "Air *While Everything Is Lovely,* and *The Goose Hangs High.*" Published by Chas. Magnus, No. 12 Frankfort Street, New York, NY. 1864. H/c lithos of General "George Brinton McClellan," "Maj. G. Hooker," and "Maj. Gen. Mansfield." 2pp. Page 2: Blank.

GBM-83 Strike! Ye Sons Of Liberty (Song and Chorus). w.m. C.W.W. Published by Firth, Pond & Co., No. 547 Broadway, New York, NY. 1862. "Respectfully dedicated (by permission) in Gen's. Winfield Scott, & G.B. McClellan."

GBM-84 Little Mac, Little Mac. w.m. Stephen C. Foster. e. Gregg Smith. In: *America's Bicentennial Songs from The Great Sentimental Age, 1850-1900, Stephen Foster to Charles E. Ives,* page 51. Published by G. Schirmer, New York, NY. 1975. [9" × 11 7/8"]. N/c litho of woman with roses, flag, city. 152pp.

GBM-85 Little Mac. w. John L. Davenport. "As Sung by John L. Davenport. In: *John L. Davenport's Own Comic Vocalist,* page 9. Published by H.R. Hildreth, No. 5 Olive Street, St. Louis, MO. 1864. [2 7/8" × 4 1/4"]. B/w non-pictorial double black line border. [18pp?].

See also WS-14; AL-89; AL-357; USG-208; USG-301.

(Stephen) Grover Cleveland

GC-1 Cleveland And Hendricks Grand Victory March. m. Henry Dersch. a. James J. Freeman, Op. 1319. Published by [V-1: R.A. Saalfield, No. 12 Bible House, New York, NY] [V-2 Callender, McAuslan and Troup, Nos. 209 and 211 Westminister Street, Providence, RI] [V-3: R.H. Macy & Company, New York, NY]. 1888. B/w litho of Grover Cleveland and Thomas Hendricks, geometric design border. "Respectfully Dedicated to the Democratic Candidates." [V-3: Advertising for R.H. Macy & Company — "R.H. Macy & Company, 14th Street, Sixth Avenue and 13th Street. We call special attention to our Muslin Underwear for ladies, misses and children. It is all of our own manufacture, and we unhesitatingly say that for variety of design and quality of work it cannot be approached by any other house. Our prices are below all competition. Large assortment of hand embroidered French underwear, our own direct importation, at very attractive prices"]. 6pp. Page 2: Blank. Page 6: Advertising [V-1: Shomer Pianos] [V-2: Adams and Anderson Dry Goods] [V-3: Various New York City retail businesses].

GC-2 Cleveland And Stevenson Songster. Copyright 1892 by W.F. Shaw. [6 13/16" × 8"]. R/w/bl/gn litho of flags, wreath, Grover Cleveland and Adlai Stevenson. 68pp. Pages 2 and 6: Blank. Page 4: Lithos of Grover Cleveland and Adlai Stevenson. Pages 64 and 65: Democratic platform. Page 66: Biographies of candidates. Page 68: Same as page one. [M-298].

GC-3 Cleveland And Thurman Songster. Copyright 1888 by the W.F. Shaw Company. N/c litho of red bandanna, flags, eagle, Capitol building, White House. Br/w photos of Grover Cleveland and Allen Thurman. 68pp. Inside pages misnumbered 1-62. Pages 2 and 67: Advertising for *Winner's Dance Folio.* Page 64: Democratic platform. Pages 65 and 66: Biographies of candidates. Page 68: Same as page one. [M-292].

GC-4 President Cleveland's Grand March. m. E.S. Clark. Published by C.H. Ditson, No. 867 Broadway, New York, NY. Copyright 1884 by Oliver Ditson & Company. B/w litho by J.H. Bufford's Sons of Grover Cleveland. 6pp. Page 2: Blank. Page 6: Advertising.

GC-5 Cleveland's 1892 Campaign March. m. J.W. Lerman. Published by K. Dehnhoff, No. 44 West 29th Street, Between Broadway and 6th Avenue, New York, NY. 1892. B/w litho by Bufford Litho Company of a Hendry drawing of Grover Cleveland. Music trimmed [as made] around Cleveland's head. 4pp. Page 4: Advertising.

GC-6 Cleveland's Inauguration Grand March. m. Clifford Cox. Published by The Saalfield Publishing Company, Printing Rooms, Nos. 794, 796, 798 Tenth Avenue, New York, NY. 1885. B/w litho of Grover Cleveland, geometric design border. "To Hon. Grover Cleveland." 6pp. Page 2: Blank. Page 6: Advertising.

GC-7 Constitutional Centennial March. m. Fred T. Baker. Published by F.A. North & Company, Publishers, No. 1308 Chestnut Street, Philadelphia, PA. 1887. B/w lithos of "James Madison," "President Grover Cleveland," "General Geo. Washington," "Alex. Hamilton," "Hampton L. Carson, Secretary, Constitutional Centennial Committee," "Col. A. Louden Snowden, Marshall, Industrial Parade, Phila., Sept. 15th, 1887," "Amos R. Little, Chairman Executive Committee, Constitutional Centennial Committee," "John A. Kasson, President, Constitutional Centennial Committee." "In Commemoration of the One Hundredth Anniversary of the Adoption of the Constitution of the U.S., Sept. 15th, 16th and 17th." "1787-1887." 4pp.

GC-8 Cleveland's Second Term March. m. L.C. Noles. Published by F. Trifet, Publisher, No. 36 Bromfield Street, Boston, MA., as *The Boston Weekly Journal of Sheet Music*, [V-1: No. 47, March 18, 1896] [V-2: No. 217, June 21, 1999]. [V-1: B/w] [V-2: Br/w] non-pictorial, geometric designs. 6pp. Pages 2 and 6: Advertising.

GC-9 Cleveland's Grand March. m. S.L. Tyler. Published by [V-1: No Publisher Indicated] [V-2: J.W. Linn, No. 322 West Market Street, York, PA]. Copyright 1884 by W.F. Shaw. B/w litho of Grover Cleveland. 6pp. Page 6: Advertising.

GC-10 Hurrah! Hurrah! For Cleve And Steve (Song and Chorus). w. Mrs. Gertie Jones. m. Henri Schoeller. Published by National Music Company, Nos. 215 to 221 Wabash Avenue, Chicago, IL. 1892. B/w drawings by Harry Earl of Grover Cleveland and Adlai Stevenson, geometric designs. 6pp. Page 2: Blank. Page 6: Advertising.

GC-11 The Bandanna Songster. c. Prof. E.B. Cullen (Director of the Waterloo Democratic Glee Club). Published by W.E. Philes, Waterloo, NY. 1888. Br/bk litho of Grover Cleveland and Allen Thurman, eagle, flags, geometric design border. "1888 Campaign 1888." "Compiled for the use of Democratic Glee Clubs with Musical Adaptations by Prof. E.B. Cullen." 32pp.

GC-12 Cleveland & Thurman's Victory March. m. Gustav Lindh. Published by Richard A. Saalfield, No. 41 Union Square, New York, NY. 1888. B/w litho of Grover Cleveland and Allen Thurman. 6[?]pp. Page 2: Blank.

GC-13 Grover Cleveland's

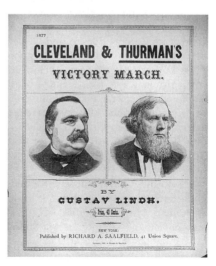

GC-12

Grand March. m. Louis List. Published by C.L. Schuster & Company, Holyoke, MA. 1892. B/w drawing of Grover Cleveland. 6pp. Page 2: Advertising for B.F. Banes copyrighted music. Page 6: Blank.

GC-14 Cleveland Triumphal Campaign March. m. A.J. Davis, Op. 76. Published by M. Stolz & Company, Nos. 26 and 28 Park Place, New York, NY. Copyright 1888 by A.J. Davis. B/w litho by F.A. Ringler & Company of Grover Cleveland. "Most Respectfully Dedicated to His Excellency Grover Cleveland, President of the United States." 8pp. Page 2: Blank. Page 8: Facsimile letter from Grover Cleveland to A.J. Davis.

GC-15 Cleveland's Grand March. m. J.J. Freeman, Op. 1320. Published by [V-1: R.A. Saalfield for R.H. Macy & Company, 14th Street, Sixth Avenue, and 13th Street, New York, NY] [V-2: Callender, McAuslan & Troup, Nos. 209 and 211 Westminister Street, Corner Union, Providence, RI]. 1884. B/w photo engraving of Grover Cleveland, geometric design border. [V-1: Advertising for Macy's underwear — "R.H. Macy & Company, 14th Street, Sixth Avenue and 13th Street. We call special attention to our Muslin Underwear for ladies, misses and children. It is all of our own manufacture, and we unhesitatingly say that for variety of design and quality of work it cannot be approached by any other house. Our prices are below all competition. Large assortment of hand embroidered French underwear, our own direct importation, at very attractive prices"]. "To Hon. Grover Cleveland." 6pp. Page 2: [V-1: Advertising for skin lotion] [V-2: Blank]. Page 6: Advertising.

GC-16 Grover Cleveland's Second Term Triumphal March. m. James J. Freeman, Mus. Doc. Published by S.T. Gordon & Son, No. 13 East 14th Street, New York, NY. 1888. B/w litho of Grover Cleveland. 6pp. Page 6: Advertising for Will H. Bray songs.

GC-17 With Cleveland We Will Win The Day (National Campaign Song). m. J.P. Skelly. Published by Richard A. Saalfield, No. 12 Bible House, New York, NY. 1884. B/w litho of Grover Cleveland, facsimile signature, geometric design border. "To the Hon. Grover Cleveland." 6pp. Page 2: Blank. Page 6: Advertising.

GC-18 Cleveland's Grand March. m. E.S. Clark. Published by C.H. Ditson & Company, No. 843 Broadway, New York, NY. 1882. B/w litho by J.H. Bufford's Sons of Grover Cleveland. "To the Hon. Grover Cleveland." 6pp. Pages 2 and 6: Blank.

GC-19 Grover Cleveland's Campaign March. m. Franz Neumuller. a. [4-hand] P.A. Schnecker. Published by Edward Schuberth & Company, No. 23 Union Square, New York, NY. 1884. Br/w litho of Grover Cleveland. "Staunch and True." 8pp. Page 8: Blank.

GC-20 Cleveland's March Triumphal. m. Phil P. Keil. Published by Phil P. Keil, McKeesport, PA. 1892. Litho of Grover Cleveland. "Respectfully Dedicated to the Democratic Candidate." 6pp. Uncut. "This is our new idea to save turning pages. Open the sheet and have the whole composition before you."

GC-21 Grover Cleveland's Second Term Grand March. m. P.T. Vestvali. [No publisher indicated]. Copyright 1888 by W.F. Shaw. B/w litho of Grover Cleveland. "Respectfully Dedicated to the Democratic Candidate." 6pp. Page 2: Blank. Page 6: Advertising.

GC-22 Grover Cleveland's Grand March. a. William P. Adams. Published by Wm. A. Pond, No. 25 Union Square, Chicago, IL. 1884. B/w litho by H.A. Thomas of Grover Cleveland. "Respectfully Dedicated to His Excellency Gov. Cleveland of New York, the Democratic Nominee for President." 6pp. Pages 2 and 6: Blank.

GC-23 Cleveland & Victory (Campaign Song and Chorus). m.

Thomas P. Westendorf. Published by John Church & Company, No. 66 West Fourth Street, Cincinnati, OH. 1884. B/w litho of Grover Cleveland. 6pp. Page 6: Advertising.

GC-24 Cleveland Is His Name (Song and Chorus). w.m. Mrs. Lula Lloyd Barnum (Author of *Winfield Waltz, Friendship March, Waltz Triumphant*, &c, &c, &c). Published by Mrs. Lula Lloyd Barnum, Louisville, KY. 1885. B/w litho of Grover Cleveland, geometric design border. "Dedicated to President Cleveland." 6pp. Pages 2 and 6: Advertising.

GC-25 Cleveland's Grand March. m. Pere M. Randolph. Published by M.D. Swisher, No. 123 South 10th Street, Philadelphia, PA. 1884. B/w litho by Thomas Hunter of Grover Cleveland, shield, flags, eagle. "For the Piano or Cabinet Organ." 6pp. Pages 2 and 6: Blank. Page 3: Title—**Campaign March**.

GC-26 The Coming Woman (New Military Schottische and Caprice). m. Monroe Rosenfeld (The Composer of many Famous Successes, Author of *The Princes Royal Military Schottisch, With All Her Faults I Still Love Her, The Red Bandanna, Our Cleveland in the Van*, and Hundreds of Popular Campaign Songs). Published by Wenzlik Music and Supply Company, Publishers, Corner 17th Street and Broadway, New York, NY. Copyright 1895 by Monroe Rosenfeld. Gn/w cover. Br/w photo of Grover Cleveland holding Baby Ruth Cleveland. Poem: "I love the Coming Woman, I love her pretty ways, With music and with sweetness, She fills my Fleeting Days; I kiss her Laughing Dimples, And Stroke her hair of Gold, For my Dainty Coming Woman is only four months old." 8pp. Pages 2 and 7: Blank. Page 8: Advertising.

GC-27 The Flag Of Liberty (A Patriotic Anthem). w.m. William B. Gray. Published by Spaulding and Gray, No. 16 West 27th Street, New York, NY. 1896. R/w/b drawing of Miss Liberty, flag, soldier. "There is no calamity which a great nation can invite which equals that which follows a supine submission to wrong and injustice—Grover Cleveland, Dec. 17, 1895." 6pp. Pages 2 and 6: Blank. Page 3: "Respectfully dedicated to the Seventh Regiment, N.G.N.Y."

GC-28 President Cleveland's Wedding March. m. Charles D. Blake (Author of *Clayton's Grand March*, The Most Popular March Ever Published). Published by White, Smith & Company, Boston, MA. 1886. B/w litho of President and Mrs. Grover Cleveland, wedding bells, flowers, cherubs, ribbon—"Hear the Mello Wedding Bells, Golden Bells." 8pp. Page 2: Blank. Page 8: Advertising.

GC-29 Cleveland's Wedding March. m. George Maywood. Copyright 1886 by W.F. Shaw. B/w litho by W.H. Butler of President and Mrs. Grover Cleveland, wedding bells, flowers, flags, shield, eagle. "Most Respectfully dedicated to Grover Cleveland, President of the United States, and wife, Washington, D.C., in Commemoration of their Wedding June 2nd, 1886." 6pp. Page 6: Advertising.

GC-30 Cleveland's Luck & Love (Grand March). m. Miss Ida. Published by P.R. McCargo & Company, Boston, MA. 1888. B/w litho of President and Mrs. Grover Cleveland, eagle, shield, flags, horseshoe, heart, scrolls inscribed "Message: Tariff—Reform." "Dedicated to the Two most popular Democrats." 6pp. Page 6: Blank.

GC-31 Cleveland's Luck And Love (Grand March). m. Miss Ida (Composer of *The March of the Famous Four Hundred* and other well known Compositions). Published by [V-1: Benjamin W. Hitchcock, No. 385 Sixth Avenue, New York, NY] [V-2: Same] [V-3: Hitchcock and McCargo, Publishing Co., No. 385 6th Avenue, New York, NY]. Copyright 1888 by P.R. McCargo of Boston. [V-1: B/w geometric design border at top and sides of flowers and vines; square corners with circle and star design] [V-2: B/w geometric design border all around of leaves; two small classic women's heads in bottom border; square corners with geometric shapes] [V-3: B/w geometric design borders with flower in pots, vines]. "Dedicated to President and Mrs. Cleveland." 6pp. Page 6: Advertising.

GC-32 Folsom March. m. Pierre Latour. Published by F.A. North & Company, No. 1308 Chestnut Street, Philadelphia, PA. 1886. B/w litho by J.H. Camp of Frances Folsom [Mrs. Grover Cleveland]. "Dedicated to Miss Frances Folsom." 6pp. Page 2: Blank. Page 6: Advertising.

GC-33 Wedding March. m. Adam Geibel. Published by F.A. North & Company, No. 1308 Chestnut Street, Philadelphia, PA. 1886. B/w litho by J.H. Camp of Mrs. Frances Folsom Cleveland. "Respectfully Dedicated to the First Lady of our Country." 6pp. Pages 2 and 6: Blank.

GC-34 The Lady Of The White House Grand March. m. E.C. Published by Oliver Ditson & Company, No. 451 Washington Street, Boston, MA. 1886. B/w litho by J.H. Bufford's Sons from a "Photograph used by permission of W.J. Baker, Buffalo, N.Y., owner of the copyright" of Frances Cleveland. "To Mrs. Grover Cleveland." 6pp. Pages 2 and 6: Blank.

GC-35 Ruth Gavotte. m. E.S. Phelps. Published by Jacob Brothers, No. 195 Broadway, Brooklyn, NY. Copyright 1891 by C.G. Hedenberg. Non-pictorial. "Respectfully Dedicated to Miss Ruth Cleveland, Daughter of Ex President Cleveland." 6pp. Page 6: Blank.

GC-36 Baby Ruth (Schottische). m. A. Mirault. Published by Miles and Thompson, Boston, MA. Copyright 1892 by A. Mirault. Non-pictorial geometric designs. "Dedicated to my Friend Fernando de Anguera, Detroit, Mich." 6pp. Pages 2 and 6: Blank.

GC-37 President Cleveland's Reception March. m. George Schleiffarth. Published by National Music Company, Chicago, IL. 1887. B/w litho of Grover Cleveland, geometric designs. 6pp. Page 6: Blank.

GC-38 Ben Slater's Song. w. "A Sixty-Four-Year-Old Jacksonian Democrat." Published in Norwich, NY., November 10, 1884. [5" × 9"]. Non-pictorial broadside. 2pp. Page 2: Blank.

GC-39(A) Hon. Grover Cleveland's March Brilliant. m. Charles D. Blake. Published by White, Smith & Company, Boston, MA. 1884. B/w litho of Grover Cleveland. "Dedicated to the Democratic Party." 6pp. Pages 2 and 6: Blank.

(B) Three Cheers For Cleveland (Song with Male Chorus). w.m. J.M. Munyon. 6pp. Pages 2 and 6: Blank.

GC-40 President Cleveland's Grand Inauguration March. m. E.G. Niklaus. Published by J.M. Hoffmann & Company, No. 537 Smithfield Street, Pittsburgh, PA. 1885. Non-pictorial geometric designs. 6pp. Page 6: Blank.

GC-41 For He Is A Democrat. w. "By a Republican Officeholder in Washington." m. "Air: *Benny Havens, O.*" [1892]. [8 3/4" × 12 9/16"]. Non-pictorial. "The World's $500 Campaign Song, words by a Republican Officeholder in Washington. Winning the prize of $500 paid by the *New York World*." 2pp.

GC-42 Let's Put It Over With Grover. w.m. Richard M. Sherman and Robert B. Sherman. Published by Wonderland Music Company, Inc., No. 800 Sonora Avenue, Glendale, CA. 1967. Copyright 1968 Walt Disney Productions. Bk/w/r drawing of couples dancing, tuba. "Walt Disney Presents *The One and Only Genuine Original Family Band*." 6pp. Page 6: Treble clef symbol.

GC-43 Baby Ruth And Baby McKee. w. George Cooper. m. Adam Geibel. Published for D. McCarthy & Company, Syracuse, NY., by Benjamin W. Hitchcock, No. 385 6th Avenue, New York, NY. 1892. B/w litho of a H. Parsons drawing of Baby Ruth Cleveland with a doll of Grover Cleveland, and of Baby Benjamin Harrison McKee with top hat of Benjamin Harrison, horseshoes. "Presented at New York State Fair, September 8th to 15th, 1892." 8pp. Page 2: Advertising for D. McCarthy & Company's store. Page 7: Song on shopping. Page 8: Advertising for other music.

GC-44 Frances Gavotte. m. Godfrey Carmiencke. Published by Charles W. Held, No. 227 Fulton Street, Brooklyn, NY. 1888. B/w litho by Gagel of a rose. "To Mrs. Grover Cleveland." 6pp. Page 6: Blank.

GC-45 Baby Ruth. w.m. Col. T.L. Weaver. Published by J.S. Ogilvie, No. 57 Rose Street, New York, NY. 1892. B/w litho of Frances Cleveland, Baby Ruth Cleveland and Grover Cleveland, geometric design border. "Dedicated to President and Mrs. Grover Cleveland." 4pp. Page 4: Advertising for Ogilvie book on house building.

GC-46 Cleveland & Hendricks Songster. Copyright 1884 by E.Y. Landis. R/w/bl/gn/br drawing of Grover Cleveland, Thomas Hendricks, George "Washington," Thomas "Jefferson," Andrew "Jackson," ribbons, geometric designs. 64pp. Page 2: Blank. Page 3: Title page. Page 4: Lithos of Grover Cleveland and Thomas Hendricks. Pages 62-64: Narrative: "The Winning Ticket." [M-230].

GC-47 Hon. S. Grover Cleveland's Campaign Grand March. m. G.A. Henry. Published by Lee & Walker, No. 1113 Chestnut Street, Philadelphia, PA. 1884. B/w litho of Grover Cleveland. 8pp. Pages 2 and 7: Blank. Page 8: Advertising.

GC-48 Gov. Cleveland's Grand March. m. Wm. P. Adams. Published by Wm. A. Pond & Company, No. 25 Union Square, Between 15 & 16 Strs., New York, NY. 1882. B/w litho by H.A. Thomas of Grover Cleveland. "Dedicated by Permission to His Excellency Gov. Cleveland of New York." 6pp. Pages 2 and 6: Blank.

GC-49 Waive High The Red Bandana. w.m. Emma Washburn. Published by Edward F. Droop, Washington, DC. Copyright 1888 by Emma Washburn. N/c litho of Grover Cleveland, Allen Thurman. R/w/b drawing of a rooster, shield, flags, bandanna. 6pp. Page 6: Blank.

GC-50 And It Was Not Sung In Vain (Democratic Campaign Song and Chorus). w.m. George M. Vickers. Copyright 1888 by B.F. Banes. B/w litho of Grover Cleveland and Alan Thurman, leaves, bow, facsimile letter from Cleveland to Vickers—"Executive Mansion, Albany, July 21, 1884, Geo. M. Vickers, Esq. Dear Sir: The copy of your campaign song which you sent me was duly received and I thank you for it. I agree with you that it will not be sung in vain, Yours Sincerely, Grover Cleveland." Printed chorus—"This is the song that the victors sang, and it was not sung in vain, with it the valleys and mountains rang and with it we'll win again." 6pp. Pages 2 and 6: Blank.

GC-49

GC-50

GC-51

GC-51 President Grover Cleveland's Wedding March. m. Isidor Witmark. Published by M. Witmark & Sons, No. 402 West 40th Street, New York, NY. Copyright 1886 by Isidor Witmark. B/w litho by Robert Gair of Grover Cleveland. 6pp. Page 6: Advertising.

GC-52 Red Bandana March. m. Gus B. Brigham. Published by National Music Company, Chicago, IL. 1888. R/w/bk litho of Allen G. Thurman on a red bandanna. 6pp. Page 6: Advertising.

GC-53 The Grand Old Red Bandana. w. Hon. E.W. Blaisdell (of Rockford, IL). m. Prof. M.C. Thayer. Published by National Music Company, Chicago, IL. 1888. R/w/bk litho of Allen Thruman on red bandanna. 6pp. Page 2: "Explanatory" narrative — "The sentiment of this song is predicated on the great and memorable struggle in the United States Senate, between the Central Pacific and Union Pacific Railroads and Allen G. Thurman, on the occasion of the brazen attempt of these monster corporations, to avoid and nullify their obligations to the government amounting to two hundred million of dollars. Single handed, and impelled by his own natural honesty, 'The Brave Old Roman' rushed to the rescue, thundered out his denunciations against the giant scheme of inequity and routed the plotters. This song commemorates this noble achievement and should be sung over the whole land." Review of the song by *The Chicago Herald*. "A Great Campaign Song." Page 6: Advertising for other National Music Company published music.

GC-54 The Old Roman March. m. Monroe H. Rosenfeld. Copyright 1884 by P.R. McCargo, Boston, MA. B/w litho by George H. Walker of Allen G. Thurman on r/w bandanna, facsimile signature — "Yours Faithfully." "Dedicated to the Noblest Roman of them all, Hon. Allen G. Thurman." 6pp.

GC-55(A) President Cleveland's Victory March. m. C.A. White. a. B.M. Davison. Published by White, Smith & Company, Publishers, No. 516 Washington Street, Boston, MA. 1884. B/w litho of Grover Cleveland. 6pp. Page 2: Blank. Page 6: Advertising.

(B) President Cleveland's Grand. m. Charles D. Blake.

GC-56 Chicago Galop (Grand Galop de Concert). m. Eduard Holst. Published by Hitchcock's Music Stores, No. 385 Sixth Avenue, New York, NY. 1892. B/w lithos of "Grover Cleveland" and "Adlai E. Stevenson." 10pp. Page 2: Blank. Page 10: Advertising for other Hitchcock published music.

GC-57 Cleveland's Victory March Brillante. m. Frederic E. White, Op. 28. Published by White, Smith Music Publishing Company, Boston, MA. 1892. B/w litho of Grover Cleveland. "Dedicated to Grover Cleveland, Democratic Nominee for President." "4-Hands." Small b/w flower logo inscribed "Marguerite." 10pp. Even pages: "Secundo" part. Odd pages: "Primo" part. Page 10: Advertising for other White-Smith music.

GC-58 The Red Bandanna. w.m. J.F. Mitchell. Copyright 1888 by F. Harding. Non-pictorial. "The Great Democratic Campaign Song." "For sale at all music stores." 6pp. Pages 2 and 6: Blank.

GC-59 Baby Ruth's Slumber Song. m. George Schleiffarth. Published by The S. Brainard's Sons Company, Chicago, IL. 1891. Br/w litho of mother and child, geometric designs. "Most Respectfully Dedicated to Baby Ruth Cleveland." 8pp. Pages 2 and 7: Blank. Page 8: Advertising for other S. Brainard's Sons music.

GC-60 Grover Cleveland's Campaign March. m. Ralph Roland. Copyright 1884 by B.F. Banes. B/w litho by Thomas Hunter of Grover Cleveland, wreath, flags, eagle with ribbon inscribed "E Pluribus Unum." "For the Piano or Cabinet Organ." 6pp. Pages 2 and 6: Blank.

GC-61 Retribution (The Rooshter I Wore on Me Hat) [sic]. w. C.C.H. (In: *The Bloomington Pantagraph*). m. Phil S. Rose. Published by J.R. Bell, Kansas City, MO. 1893. R/w/bk litho of three roosters, geometric designs. "To the Rooster Wearers of Ninety-Two." 4pp. Page 4: Advertising.

GC-62 Cleveland's Campaign March. m. S.L. Tyler. [V-1: Published by J.W. Link, No. 332 West Market Street, York, PA] [V-2: No Publisher Indicated]. Copyright 1884 by W.F. Shaw, Philadelphia, PA. B/w litho by Hofstetter Brothers of Grover Cleveland. "Respectfully Dedicated to the Democratic Candidate." 6pp. Pages 2 and 6: Blank.

GC-63 Cleveland & Hendricks Grand March. m. S.G. Wilson. Published by S. Brainard's Sons, Cleveland, OH. 1884. B/w litho by W.J. Morgan of Grover Cleveland.

GC-64 Song Of 88. [1888]. [5" × 8"]? Non-pictorial broadside. 2pp. Page 2: Blank.

GC-65 Cleveland Is The Man! (Song and Chorus). w.m. Col. Will S. Hays. Published by John F. Ellis & Company, No. 937 Pennsylvania Avenue, Washington, DC. 1892. B/w litho of Grover Cleveland and Adlai Stevenson, geometric designs, facsimile letter to Hays from Cleveland — "Gray Gables, Buzzard's Bay, Mass., July 13, 1892 — Will S. Hays. Dear Sir: I received a copy of the song you have written — to be used, as you say, for an encourager during the approaching campaign. I believe, with you, that the influence of songs and music of the right sort ought not be overlooked as important adjuncts to a political campaign; and in so far as I am able to judge, this latest production of yours must serve a good purpose in that direction. One thing I am certain: The composition of this song by you is a sure demonstration that the Composer is activated by the sort of spirit and enthusiasm which wins elections, Very Truly Yours, Grover Cleveland." "A Stirring and Enthusiastic Campaign Song and Chorus." "Respectfully Inscribed to the Democracy of the United States." 6pp. Pages 2 and 6: Blank.

GC-66 President Cleveland's

Grand March. m. E.S. Clark. Published by Oliver Ditson Company, Boston, MA. [ca. 1905]. O/w/bk non-pictorial floral and geometric designs. "Garland of Melodies, First Series." List of other titles in series.

GC-67   Three Cheers For Cleveland And Thurman (Campaign Song For Male Quartett or Chorus). w.m. C.A. White. Published by White, Smith & Company, No. 516 Washington Street, Boston, MA. 1888. Litho of bandanna, fern branch. "Dedicated to the Democratic Nominees for the Press." 6pp. Page 6: Advertising for other music.

GC-68   Democracy's Ta-Ra-Ra-Boom-De-Ay. w. William H. Peirsol. m. Air: "To The Music of the Chorus of *Ta Ra*." Published in Philadelphia, PA. September, 1892. [4 1/2" × 6"]. B/w litho of Grover Cleveland. 2pp. Page 2: Blank.

GC-69   First In Line For 88 (Grand March and Chorus). w. Phillip F. Sullivan. m. A.G. Lazarus. Published by Rich. A. Saalfield, No. 41 Union Square, New York, NY. Copyright 1888 by A.G. Lazarus. Be/bk litho by Hatch Litho Company of man with parade torch, drum, rooster, building with sign inscribed "Harlem Democratic Club. 1882-1887." "Respectfully Dedicated to the Harlem Democratic Club of the City of New York." 8pp. Pages 2 and 8: Blank.

GC-70   Mary Blaine. w. Ben Warren. m. Air: *Mary Blane.* Published by Hitchcock's Music Store, No. 166 Nassau Street, New York, NY. 1884. Litho of James G. Blaine in woman's dress, slogans—"Side Contracts," "Sentenced to Go Up Salt River, Nov. 6, 1884," "Little Rock RR Bonds," "20 Years in Congress," "Mulligan Letters," "To J.G.B. form the King of the Lobby," "Belmont," "Crooked Paths," "Self." Oriental man with sign inscribed "Blain-E Must-E Go-E." "Utilizing the old air of *Mary Blane* for Patriot Purposes." 4pp. Page 4: Blank.

GC-71   Cleveland's Baby Girl (Song and Chorus). w. Charles M. Ernest. m. George Engelbert Schaller. Published by Oliver Ditson Company, Boston, MA. 1891. Non-pictorial geometric designs. 6pp. Page 6: Advertising for other Oliver Ditson Company published music.

GC-72   Hurrah For Grover Cleveland. w. W. Lovel Eyre. m. Guillaume Sauvlet. Published as a supplement to the *San Francisco Examiner.* [1892]. B/w litho of Grover Cleveland and Adlai Stevenson, cheering crowd, flags. "The *Examiner's* Prize Campaign Songs." "Compliments of the *San Francisco Examiner.*" 4pp. Page 2: B/w litho of woman with flags. Page 3: Song—**Wait Till Next November.** w. S.D. Lount. m. E.M. Rosner.

GC-73   We've Got Him On The List (Male Quartett) (Democratic Campaign Song, 1888). m. Gilbert and Sullivan. a. Yankee Freetrade. Published by S. Brainard's Sons, Cleveland, OH. 1888. R/bk/w geometric designs. B/w litho of Grover Cleveland. 6pp. Pages 2 and 6: Advertisements for S. Brainard music.

GC-74   Cleveland's Triumphal March. m. Henry Werner. Published by Balmer & Weber, Publishers, St. Louis, MO. 1884. B/w litho of Grover Cleveland. "The Nation's Choice" 8pp. Page 2: Blank. Page 3: Title: **President Cleveland's Wedding March.** Copyright 1886. B/w litho of bells and horseshoe at top of music. Page 8: B/w litho of marching bands. Advertising for *Gov. Cleveland's Triumphal March* by Henry Werner and *Gov. Cleveland's Quickstep* by J. Postlewaite.

GC-75   President Cleveland's Grand March. m. E.S. Clark. Published by Oliver Ditson Company, Boston, MA. [1908 edition]. Pk/gn drawing of flowers. "Popular Marches for the Piano." List of other titles in series.

GC-76   Cleveland's March To Victory. m. George Schleiffarth. Published by National Music Company, Nos.

(STEPHEN) GROVER CLEVELAND (GC)

215-221 Wabash Avenue, Chicago, IL. 1884. B/w litho of Grover Cleveland. Title within black line box. 6pp. Page 6: Advertising for other National Music.

GC-77 Cleveland's March To Victory. m. George Schleiffarth. Published by the [V-1: National Music Company, Chicago, IL] [V-2: Huyett Brothers, Managers, Western Temple of Music, No. 321 Felix Street, St. Joseph, MO]. [ca. 188-]. B/w litho of Grover Cleveland. Title within black line box and geometric design. 6pp. Page 6: Blank.

GC-78 Inauguration March. m. Henry C. Timm. Published by Martens Brothers, No. 1164 Broadway, New York, NY. Copyright 1885 by Henry C. Timm. Non-pictorial geometric design. "Respectfully Dedicated (by permission) to Mr. Grover Cleveland, President Elect." "Composed for Military Band and Arranged for the Piano." 10pp. Pages 2 and 10: Blank.

GC-79 Cleveland's March To Victory. m. George Schleiffarth. Published by National Music Company, Chicago, IL. [ca. 188-]. B/w litho of Grover Cleveland. Title formed around head. 6pp. Page 6: Blank.

GC-80 Cleveland's March To Victory. m. George Schleiffarth. Published by National Music Company, No. 113 Adams Street, Corner of Clark, Chicago, IL. 1884. B/w litho of Grover Cleveland, fancy title design formed around head. 6pp. Page 6: Blank.

GC-81 Inaugural March 1893. w.m. H.F. Eberhardt (Formerly of the 4th U.S. Cavalry Band and member of the J.K. Taylor Post 182, G.A.R., Bethlehem, PA). 1892. Non-pictorial geometric designs. "In Honor of and Most Respectfully Dedicated to His Excellency Grover Cleveland." 6pp. Pages 2 and 6: Blank.

GC-82 Red Hot Democratic Campaign Songs For 1892. c. John Bunyon Herbert. Published by The S. Brainard's Sons Company, Chicago, IL. 1892. [5 1/2" × 7 1/4"]. R/bk litho of Grover Cleveland on a banner, Capitol building, marchers, geometric design border. 36pp. Pages 2, 31 and 32: Advertising. Page 3: Contents. [M-299].

GC-83 Souvenirs Of Washington Waltz. m. Manuel Montufar (Charge D'Affaires of Guatemala at Washington). 1888. R/w/b non-pictorial geometric design border. "Respectfully Dedicated to Mrs. Cleveland." 10pp. Pages 2 and 10: Blank.

GC-84 Gov. Hendrick's Quick Step. m. A. Schuman. Litho of Governor Thomas Hendricks.

GC-85 Grover Cleveland Presidential Grand March. m. S. Markstein. Published by T.B. Harms & Company, No. 819 Broadway, New York, NY. 1884. B/w litho by Teller of Grover Cleveland. 6pp. Page 2: Blank. Page 6: Advertising for other T.B. Harms published music.

GC-86 Cleveland's Grand March. m. Will S. Wilcox. Published by S.T. Gordon & Son, No. 13 East 14th Street, New York, NY. 1884. B/w litho of Grover Cleveland. 6pp. Page 6: Advertising for other S.T. Gordon published music.

GC-87 The President's Reception March. m. George Schleiffarth. Published as a supplement to the *Chicago Daily News*, 1887. Non-pictorial. "*Chicago Daily News* Series." "Respectfully Dedicated to Mrs. President Cleveland." 4pp. Pages 2 and 4: blank.

GC-88 Welcome March. m. W.S.B. Matthews. Published as a supplement to the *Chicago Daily News*, October 4, 1887. Non-pictorial. "*Chicago Daily News* Series." "Respectfully Dedicated to Mrs. President Cleveland." 4pp. Page 2: "Dedicated to President and Mrs. Cleveland." Page 4: Blank.

GC-89 The Nation's Chief Grand March. m. W.C.E. Seeboeck. Published as a supplement to the *Chicago Daily News*, October, 4 1887. Non-pictorial. "*Chicago Daily News* Series."

"Respectfully Dedicated to Mrs. President Cleveland." 6pp. Pages 2 and 6: Blank.

GC-90 Our First Citizen Grand March. m. S.G. Pratt. Published as a supplement to the *Chicago Daily News*, October, 4 1887. Non-pictorial. "*Chicago Daily News* Series." "Respectfully Dedicated to Mrs. President Cleveland." 6pp. Pages 2 and 6: Blank.

GC-91 Cleveland's March. m. Noles. Published by Trifet. [ca. 1888]. Non-pictorial geometric design border. "Rondos, Variations, Dances, &c." "Trifet Edition." List of other titles in series.

GC-92 The Broadway Two-Step (March). m. Theodore F. Morse (Composer of *Artful Love Gavotte*). Published by Howley, Haviland & Company, No. 4 East 20th Street, New York, NY. 1895. Pl/bl/w litho by J.E. Rosenthal of Grover Cleveland in police uniform, theater characters in each letter of title. List of other orchestral arrangements available. 6pp. Page 6: Advertising.

GC-93 Columbian March. m. C.M. Ziehrer, Op. 502 (Leader of the Fourth Austrian Infantry Regiment Band). Published by the S. Brainard's Sons Company, Chicago, IL. Copyright 1893 by Marcus Braun. Bk/ma/w drawings of Christopher Columbus, vignettes of discovery, boats. "Respectfully Dedicated to His Excellency Grover Cleveland, President of the United States." "For The Piano-Forte." 6pp. Pages 2 and 6: Blank.

GC-94 President Grover Cleveland's Grand Inauguration March. m. G. Schroeder (Author of *Down the Beautiful Mohawk Waltz, Up & Down The N.Y. Central R.R. Waltz, Gen. Hancock March, My Wife And I Waltz*). Published by Charles Tuttle, No. 83 James Street, Rome, NY. 1885. B/w litho of Grover Cleveland, flowers. "Composed and Respectfully Dedicated to President Grover Cleveland and Mrs. Wm. E. Hoyt."

"Dealer in Pianos, Organs and Instruments of all kind." 6pp. Pages 2 and 6: Blank.

GC-95 We'll Rock Her In The White House Chair. w.m. "From Old Kentuck's Bureau." Published by Lee & Walker, No. 1017 Walnut Street, Philadelphia, PA. Copyright 1888 by William M. Cook. B/w litho of Frances Cleveland, floral wreath. 6pp. Page 6: Blank.

GC-96 Cleveland's Second Term Grand March. m. P.T. Vestvali. Published by W.F. Shaw, Philadelphia, PA. 1888. Y/br non-pictorial geometric design border. 6pp. Page 2: Blank. Page 6: Advertising.

GC-97 And That's How Benny Got In. w.m. Rojamdrof. Published by J.W. Ford, No. 211 Market Street, St. Louis, MO. 1892. Non-pictorial geometric design border. "A Song for the Coming Campaign of 1892." 4pp. Page 4: Blank.

GC-98 Reunion Medley. a. J.A. Bates. Published by Ludden & Bates, Southern Music House, Savannah, GA. 1884. B/w litho of Grover Cleveland, flags, clasped hands, eagle, ribbon inscribed "To Grover Cleveland the People's Choice, 1884." "The Flag of Our Union Forever." "In Commemoration of Reunion Day, Nov. 4, 1884." "The Union of Hearts, The Union of Hands." "Arrangement for Piano and Organ." 8pp. Pages 2 and 8: Blank.

GC-99 President Cleveland's Inauguration Grand March. m. Charles D. Blake. Published by White, Smith & Company, Boston, MA. 1885. B/w litho of Grover Cleveland.

GC-100 The Coming Woman (Military Schottische And Caprice). m. Monroe H. Rosenfeld (Composer of the famous *Kentucky Gallopade, Quityerkiddin Patrol, Journal March, &c., &c., &c.*). Published by Howley, Haviland & Company, No. 4 East 20th Street, New York, NY. 1895. Gd/pl/w cover. Gn/w photo of Ruth Cleveland. 6pp. Page 6: Advertising for other Howley, Haviland Songs.

GC-101 Select Your Candidate [Song Sheet]. Published by Williams & Carleton, Manufacturers, Hartford, CT. [1892]. [13 1/2" × 6 1/2"]. B/w lithos of Benjamin Harrison and Grover Cleveland. One song supporting each candidate, with lyrics boosting Williams Root Beer. "Williams Root Beer is made from 'Williams' Extract' (A highly concentrated extract of roots and herbs). This great family temperance drink is now made at the homes of thousands, and is the safest and best 'hot weather drink' on the market. Williams' Extract is cheap and easily made ready for use. It exceeds all others in purity and strength. Try It. Sold everywhere." 2pp. Page 2: Blank.

GC-102 Campaign Jubilee Song. w.m. Mrs. S.E. Bromwell. Published by F.S. Chandler & Company, Chicago, IL. 1884. B/w litho of Grover Cleveland, clasped hands, geometric design border. "As given by the Spirits to Mrs. S.E. Bromwell, Chicago, Ill., previous to the Democratic Convention." "Published for and by request of the Author's numerous friends." 6pp. Page 2 and 6: Blank.

GC-103 Cleveland's Grand March. m. H. Maylath. Published by M.D. Swisher, No. 115 South 10th Street, Philadelphia, PA. 1884. B/w litho of Grover Cleveland within shield [facing one quarter turn to viewer's right]. "For the Piano or Cabinet Organ." 6pp. Pages 2 and 6: Blank.

GC-104 Cleveland's Grand March. m. H. Maylath. No Publisher Indicated. [1884]. B/w litho of Grover Cleveland in shield [facing one half turn to viewer's right]. "For the Piano or Cabinet Organ." 6pp. Pages 2 and 6: Blank.

GC-105 Cleveland And Victory. w. George Cooper. M. M.H. Rosenfeld. Published by Hitchcock's Music Stores, No. 385 Sixth Avenue, New York, NY. 1892. Lithos of "Grover Cleveland" and "Adlai E. Stevenson." 6pp. Page 2: Blank.

GC-106 When Grover Touched The Button At the Fair (Comic Song and Chorus). W. George C. Edwards. M. Chareles Edwards. Published by Emmanuel Pergament., No. 48 East 4th Street, New York, NY. 1893. R/w/b non-pictorial geometric designs. "Dedicated to the New York Letter Carrier's Assn." ypp. Page 6: Advertising.

GC-107 Hon. Grover Cleveland's March. m. Eben H. Bailey, Op. 58 (Author of Bailey's great *Centennial March, &c*). Published by White, Smith & Company, Boston, MA. 1884. Non-pictorial. "The Democratic Choice." 6pp. Page 6: Advertising.

GC-108 When Grover Cleveland Gets A Baby Boy (Topical Song). w.m. Capt. Jack Crawford (The Poet Scout). Published by Spaulding & Gray, No. 16 West 27th Street, New York, NY. 1895. Non-pictorial geometric designs. "Lew Dockstader's Great Success." 6pp. Page 6: Advertising.

GC-109 The Doctrine Of Monroe (Song and Refrain). w.m. LeRoy F. Lewis. Published by Charles W. Held,

GC-105

Brooklyn, NY. Copyright 1896 by LeRoy F. Lewis. Non-pictorial. "Dedicated to Grover Cleveland, President of the United States." 6pp. Pages 2 and 6: Blank.

GC-110 The White House Bride. w.m. Clara Lewis Moss (Author of *Stand By The Order-Labor Song, My Own Margurette, Don't Forget the Old Folks, The Moonshiner's Daughter*, and Others). a. Henry Graham. Published by Clara Lewis Moss. [ca. 1886]. Bl/w non-pictorial cover. "Dedicated to the Friends and Admirers of Frankie Cleveland." 6pp. Pages 2 and 6: Blank.

GC-111 The Red Bandana Marching Song. m. M.H. Rosenfeld. a. C.E. Pratt. Published by Hitchcock's Music Stores, No. 11 Park Row, Opposite Post Office, New York, NY. 1888. R/w geometric design. 6pp. Page 2: Blank. Page 6: Advertising.

GC-112 To The White House (March). m. George Edw. Jackson. 1884. B/w litho of Grover Cleveland, geometric design border. "To my Friend H.R. Johnson." 6pp. Pages 2 and 6: Blank.

GC-113 President Cleveland's National Grand March m. G.A. Henry. Puglished by Lee & Walker, No. 1113 Chestnut Street, Philadelphia, PA. 1884. B/w litho of Grover Cleveland 8[?]pp. Page 2: Blank.

GC-114 The Man Of Destiny March. m. Anita Owen. Published by National Music Company, Nos. 215-221 Wabash Avenue, Chicago, IL. 1892. B/w litho of Grover Cleveland, geometric designs. "Respectfully Dedicated to Hon. Grover Cleveland." 6pp. Page 2: Blank.

GC-115 Gov. Cleveland's Grand March. m. E.S. Clark. Published by C.H. Ditson, No. 843 Broadway, New York, NY. 1882. B/w litho by J.H. Bufford's Sons of Grover Cleveland. "To His Excellency Grover Cleveland." 6 pp. Pages 2 and 6: Blank.

GC-116 Cleveland And Hendricks Grand March. m. H. Wheeler. Published by D.O. Evans, No. 108 West Federal Street, Youngstown, OH. 1884. B/w litho of "Grover Cleveland For President," Thos. A. Hendricks For Vice President," eagle, flags, wreaths, Capitol building, geometric design border. "Respectfully Dedicated to the Democratic Party." "In Union is Strength." "For Piano or Organ." 6pp. Page 2: Blank. Page 6: Advertising.

GC-117 Cleveland's Second Term Grand March. m. George P. Lyon. Published by The John Church Company, No. 74 West Fourth Street, Cincinnati, OH. 1888. B/w litho of Grover Cleveland. "For Piano." 6pp. Pages 2 and 6: Blank.

GC-118 Bi-Centennial Hymn. w. Howard N. Fuller. m. George E. Oliver (Director of Music, Public Schools, Albany, NY). Copyright 1886 by George E. Oliver. [6" × 7 1/2"]. Non-pictorial. "Dedicated, by Permission, to His Excellency, Grover Cleveland, President of the United States of America." 4pp. Page 3: Song—*America*. Page 4: Song—*American Hymn*.

GC-119 The Banner Ratification

GC-116

Song. [1892]. [4 9/16" × 8 1/2"]. Non-pictorial. 2pp. Page 2: Blank.

GC-120 Cleveland Or Herculean Quick-Step. m. Zaluecus. Published by Richard A. Saalfield, No. 843 Broadway, Between 13th and 14th Streets, New York, NY. [1884]. B/w litho of Grover Cleveland, geometric design border "Composed and Arranged for the Piano Forte." 6pp. Page 6: Advertising.

GC-121 Ruth's Dolly Song. w. David L. Trucksess. m. Ida Virginia Trucksess. Copyright 1903 by David L. Trucksess. B/w photo of Ruth Cleveland. Bl/w flowers. 6pp. Pages 2 and 6: Blank.

GC-122 Good Times Will Come When Grover Goes Out. w.m. R.D. Scott (The Blind Musician) (Author of *Coxey Keep Off The Grass, Strike While the Iron is Hot, &c*). Published by J.R. Bell, Kansas City, MO. 1896. B/w litho of R.D. Scott. Chorus printed to either side of Scott — "Then roll on the Ball, The big Bi-metal Ball, For both Gold and Silver We Sing and Shout, And we'll work like Beavers all Summer and Fall, For good times will come in When Grover goes Out!" 6pp. Pages 2 and 6: Advertising. [Anti-Cleveland Song].

GC-123 Baby Ruth Fantasia Polka. m. B. Kennedy Hance. Published by William A. Pond & Company, No. 25 Union Square, New York, NY. Copyright 1893 by B. Kennedy Hance. B/w ribbon, geometric designs. "Respectfully Dedicated to President Cleveland and Lady." 10pp. Pages 2 and 10: Blank.

GC-124 Homestead Strike And Protection. w. W.A. Robinson. m. D.E. Rudolph. Published by D.E. Rudolph, Coshocton, OH. 1892. B/w non-pictorial geometric designs. 4pp. Page 4: Blank.

GC-125 Notes Of Victory Grand March. m. James E. Magruder. Published by George Willig & Company, Publishers, Baltimore, MD. 1884. B/w non-pictorial geometric designs. "Composed Expressly for His Excellency President Grover Cleveland." 6pp. Pages 2 and 6: Blank.

GC-126 Cleveland And Hendricks Reform (Democratic Campaign March). m. Adolph Pferdner. Published by John Church & Company, No. 66 West Fourth Street, Cincinnati, OH. 1884. Bl/w non-pictorial geometric designs. 8pp Pages 2 and 8: Blank.

GC-127 Cleveland's Popularity Grand March. m. Oliver F. Kauffman. Published by D.W. Crist, Moultrie, OH. 1893. B/w litho of flowers, bird, geometric designs. "For the Piano or Cabinet Organ." 6pp. Page 6: Advertising for other D.W. Crist published music.

GC-128 Ruth, Ester And Marion (Schottische). m. A.M. Cohen. Published by F. Trifet, Publisher, No. 36 Bromfield Street, Boston, MA. as "No. 39, January 22, 1896, *The Boston Weekly Journal of Sheet Music*." Gn/w geometric designs. 4pp. Page 2: "To the Three Graces of the White House." Page 4: Advertising.

GC-129 President Cleveland's Tariff March. m. Mrs. Mollie E. Armstrong. Published for the Author by John F. Ellis & Company, Washington, DC. Copyright 1888 by Mrs. Mollie E. Armstrong. B/w litho of palm branches, ribbon. "Dedicated to my Husband, H.G. Armstrong." 8pp. Page 2: Blank. Page 8: Advertising.

GC-130 Our Country [V-1: "Original Setting in F — National Hymn of the United States of America"] [V-2: "March For Piano — National Military March"] [V-3: "Solo for Soprano, Tenor or Contralto"] [V-4: "Quartette for Mixed Voices — National Hymn of the United States"]. w. Rev. S.F. Smith, D.D. m. Wm. Horatio Clarke. Published by Miles & Thompson, No. 13 West Street, Boston. MA. 1890. B/w litho of eagle, geometric designs. "To the President of the United States." "National Hymn of the United States of America." 6pp.

GC-131 Cleveland's Second-Term

March. m. L.C. Noles. In: *Trifit's Monthly Budget of Music*, page 15. Published by F. Trifit, Publisher, No. 36 Broomfield Street, Boston, MA. 1897. [9 3/4" × 12 1/4"].

GC-132 Stand By Our Leader (Song and Chorus). w.m. George M. Vickers. Copyright 1884 by B.F. Banes. B/w litho by T. Hunter of Grover Cleveland, eagle, angels, stars, flags, arch, geometric designs. 6pp. Pages 2 and 6: Blank.

GC-133 Mama's China Twins. w.m. Lee Johnson. Published by Lee Johnson & Company, St. Ann's Building, San Francisco, CA. 1900. R/w/bl/y/gn/bk drawing by H. Patigian of Chinese scenes. N/c photos of "Chan Wong" and "Ah Fong." Bl/w photo of "Baby Ruth [Cleveland?]." "An Oriental Lullaby by the Author of *Mammy's Carolina* Twins and *My Honolulu Lady*." 6pp. Page 6: Advertising.

GC-134 The National Campaign Band Book. Published by J.W. Pepper, Southwest Corner 8th and Locust Streets, Philadelphia, PA. 1884. [7 1/4" × 5 1/2"]. B/w lithos of "Hon. Grover Cleveland," "Hon Thos. A. Hendricks," "Hon. James G. Blaine" and "Gen. John A. Logan." "Contents" consisting of 36 Marches listed on cover, including **Hail Columbia**. List of full "Instrumentation, 20 Books..." "Price" information. "Complete Catalogue of Parts to the latest Band Music sent for a 3 cent Stamp. Orchestra Music a Specialty." 28pp. Back page — B/w litho of and advertisement for "New Model Band Lamp."

GC-135 Democratic Victory March. m. J.H. Felton. Published by Henry Bollman & Sons, Nos. 1104 and 1106 Olive Street, St. Louis, MO. 1884. B/w litho of "Grover Cleveland," "Thomas A. Hendricks," shield, flags, eagle. "Only Correct and Original Edition." "Millions of Freemen to-day rejoice, Over our Country's defenders, Cleveland and Hendricks proved their choice, In spite of all defamers." 8pp. Pages 2, 7 and 8: Blank.

GC-136 Washington Society (Quadrille) (For The Pianoforte). m. C.A. White. Published by White, Smith & Company, No. 516 Washington Street, Boston, MA. 1887. Gn/w litho of Grover and Frances Cleveland, ribbon inscribed

GC-132

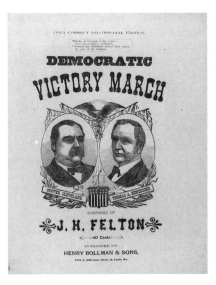

GC-135

"Hear the mellow wedding bells, Golden Bells." R/w geometric design border. "To Professor E. Woodworth Masters, President of National Association of Teachers of Dancing." 8pp. Page 2: Blank. Page 8: Advertising.

GC-137 Cleveland's Grand March To The White House. m. Vernon. Published by F.S. Chandler & Company, Chicago, IL. 1892. B/w litho of Grover Cleveland, geometric design border. 8pp. Pages 2, 7 and 8: Advertising.

GC-138 Cleveland & Thurman Grand March. m. S.G. Wilson. Published by S. Brainard's Sons, Cleveland, OH. 1888. Br/w litho by W.J. Morgan of Grover Cleveland, geometric designs.

GC-139 Schultz & Cos. Cleveland & Hendricks Democratic Campaign Songster. [Published by P.T. Schultz & Co., Cincinnati, OH]. Copyright 1884 by P.T. Schultz & Co. [4 3/8" × 5 7/8"]. Non-pictorial. 34[?]pp. [M-231].

GC-140 Democratic Song Book For The Campaign Of 1888. c. John R. East. Published by John R. East, Bloomington, IN. 1888. [4 1/4" × 5 13/16"]. Bl/bl litho of Grover Cleveland and Allen Thurman. "Price 10 cents, postage prepaid, Liberal Discounts to Dealers." 20pp.

GC-141 Red Hot Democratic Campaign Songs For 1888. e. John Bunyon Herbert. Published by The S. Brainard's Sons Company, Chicago, IL. 1888. [5 3/8" × 7 7/16"]. R/bk geometric designs. 36pp. Pages 2, 31 and 32: Advertising. Page 3: Contents. [M-294].

GC-142 The President's Inauguration March. m. Francis Mueller, Sen. Published by Oliver Ditson & Company, No. 451 Washington Street, Boston, MA. 1885. Non-pictorial geometric designs. 6pp. Pages 2 and 6: Blank.

GC-143 Cleveland And Hendricks Campaign Songster. Published by John Church & Company, Cincinnati, OH. 1884. Gn/bl non-pictorial. Page 3: Subtitle—**Cleveland And Hendricks Campaign Carols.** "Including Biographical Sketches & Constitution for Campaign Clubs." 52pp. [M-228].

GC-144 Hamilton Democratic Glee Club Songster. Published by Democrat Job Rooms, Hamilton, OH. 1884. 36pp. [M-229].

GC-145 Cleveland And Thurman Campaign Songster. Published by The John Church Company, Cleveland, OH. 1888. "The Best and Most Popular Songs." 52pp. O/bk non-pictorial. "Tariff Reform." "Introducing Biographical Sketches and Constitution for Campaign Clubs." [M-291].

GC-146 Our Cleveland in the Van. w.m. Monroe H. Rosenfield. [1884-1895].

GC-147 Gov. Cleveland's Triumphal March. m. Henry Werner. Published by Balmer & Weber, St. Louis, MO. [ca. 1884].

GC-148 Gov. Hendricks' Quickstep. m. J. Postlewaite (Leader of Postlewaite's Great Western Band). Published by Balmer & Weber, St. Louis, MO. [ca. 1884].

GC-149 Politics In Song. Published by Bacon & Doyle, Printers, New Britain, CT. 1888. Non-pictorial. New and Rousing Democratic, Patriotic, and Campaign Songs and Hymns. Adapted to the Presidential Contest of 1888. 16pp. [M-290].

GC-150 Democratic Campaign Songs For 1888. Published by W.A. Vandercook, Los Angeles, CA. 1888. 24pp. [M-293].

GC-151 Democratic Campaign Song Sheet No. 1. Published by Benj. W. Hitchcock, Hitchcock's Steam Printing and Publishing House, No. 385 Sixth Avenue, New York, NY. [1888]. [19 1/8" × 24"]. B/w litho of Grover Cleveland and Allen Thurman. "Cleveland and Thurman." 2pp. Page 2: Blank.

GC-152 Cleveland & Thurman 1888 Campaign Carols. c. W.J. Armstrong, Pittsburg, Indiana (Composer of

Good Bye, Poor Jimmy, Good Bye). 1888. [4 1/4" × 6 3/4"]. Be/bk floral and geometric designs. 20pp.

GC-153 Cleveland's Wedding March. m. Henry Werner. Published by Balmer & Weber, Publishers, St. Louis, MO. 1886. B/w beige tinted litho of Frances and Grover Cleveland, geometric designs. "To President Cleveland and his accomplished Wife." Printed song verse. 8pp. Page 2: Blank. Page 3: B/w litho of wedding bells at top of music. Page 8: Advertising.

GC-154 Lady Cleveland Gavotte. m. Fred. Baker. Published by Balmer & Weber Music House Co., Publishers, Saint Louis, MO. 1887. Sepia Original Painting from the *St. Louis Cronical* [sic] of Grover and Frances Cleveland. Br/w floral designs. "Respectfully Dedicated to Mrs. Frances Cleveland." 8pp. Pages 2 and 8: Blank. Page 3: Geometric designs in title.

GC-155 Cleveland Glide Waltz. m. Horace R. Basler. Published by H.R. Basler, No. 3712 Butler Street, Pittsburg, PA. 1881. B/w non-pictorial.

GC-156 Cleveland And Thurman Grand-March. m. Henry Werner. Published by Balmer & Weber Music House Co., St. Louis, MO. 1888. Non-pictorial geometric and floral designs. "As played at The National Democratic Convention, 1888." "Cheer Boys Cheer, For Cleveland True."

GC-157 Cleveland And Thurman Grand March. m. Th. Thomasi. Published by F.A. Rockar, No. 129 East 125th Street, New York, NY. 1888. B/w lithos of Grover Cleveland and Allan Thurman, cherubs, flag, Capitol, shield inscribed "1889-1893." "To The Harlem Democratic Club."

GC-158 Oh Shoot That Snowy Feather (Democratic Campaign Song). w. Sphinx. m. R. Warner. Published by John F. Ellis & Co., No. 937 Pennsylvania. Avenue, Washington, D.C. 1889. Non-pictorial geometric designs. 6pp.

GC-159(A) Up With The Red Bandanna [sic] (Song and Chorus). w. m. Paul Prescott. Published by Oliver Ditson & Co., No. 451 Washington Street, Boston, MA. 1888. B/w litho by Geo. H. Walker & Co. of "Hon. A.G. Thurman." 6pp. Pages 2 and 6: Blank.

(B) Thurman Grand March. m. Ed. Wincriste.

GC-160 A Democratic Toast. a. Yankee Freetrade. Published by S. Brainard's Sons, Cleveland, OH. 1888. B/w litho of Grover Cleveland. R/w/bk geometric designs. "Democratic Campaign Songs 1888." "Male Quartett." Pages 2 and 6 [?]: Advertisement.

GC-161 Cleveland's Second Term March. m. L.C. Noles. In: *Trifet's Monthly Galaxy Of Music, A Magazine of Vocal and Instrumental Music for the Masses, Volume II*, page 269. Published by F. Trifet, Publisher, No. 408 Washington Street, Boston, MA. July, 1888.

GC-162 Up With The Red Bandanna. w.m. Paul Prescott. In: *Marches Of The Presidents, 1789-1909, Authentic Marches & Campaign Songs*, page 54. A. Carl Miller. Published by Chappell & Co., Inc., No. 609 Fifth Avenue, New York, NY. "By arrangement with Chilmark Press, Inc." 1968. [9" × 12"]. R/w/b litho of eagle, flag. "An Illustrated Piano Folio For All Ages." 72pp.

GC-163 Baby Ruth. w.m. Nick Bachelor. Published by William A. Pond & Co., No. 25 Union Square, New York, NY. 1898. B/w litho of Lydia Yeamans Titus — "Sung with great success by Lydia Yeamans Titus." B/w non-pictorial geometric designs. "Popular Song."

GC-164 Cleveland And Hendricks Grand Victory March. m. A. Wundermann. Published by P.A. Wundermann, No. 145 Third Avenue, New York, NY. 1884. B/w litho of Grover Cleveland and Thomas A. Hendricks, geometric designs.

GC-165 Grover Cleveland March. m. W.S.H. Jones. Published by C.H. Kimball, Manchester, NH. Non-pictorial.

See also GW-134; GW-315; AL-252; JGB-36; JGB-77; BFH-30; BFH-48; BFH-74; BFH-76; WM-48; WM-127; WHT-23; WW-19; FDR-158; HST-16; DDE-9; DDE-71; JFK-53; LBJ-1; LBJ-24; RMN-25; GRF-7; JEC-10; MISC-167.

GEORGE C. WALLACE

GCW-1 All The Way (With Wallace and LeMay). w.m. Joseph Erdelyi, Jr. (October 7, 1968, U.S.A.). Copyright 1968 by Erdelyi Music Publishing Company, Room 600, No. 1697 Broadway, New York, NY. 10019. O/bk Non-pictorial. "Dedicated to the new American political party in the United States, The American Independent Party." "Campaign Song for George C. Wallace, 1968 American Independent Party Candidate for the Presidency of the United States." 2pp. Page 2: Blank.

GCW-2 We're Strong For George Wallace. w. Dr. Julius Radke Finn (Age 87, St. Petersburg, Fla). m. Joe Murphy. Copyright 1950 by Unique Music Publishers, Inc., Toledo, OH. [1976 edition]. [8 1/2" × 11 1/2"]. B/w photo of George Wallace—"His Never-Say-Die Determination Personified." "George Wallace, 'revival' after being shot, shot and shot, proves his physical CONSTITUTION and runs parallel, with his determination to 'revive' the U.S. CONSTITUTION, that has been shot, shot and shot with paralyzing laws." "Oh say can you see, God's work for you and me, He protected George's soul and mind from destruction, this was meant to 'be,' a profound certainty, that George's popular hold will destroy all corruption when election's gray glare dies from the atmosphere, The Almighty will heal George from bullet's raw deal, We will help George establish, a gun-law and restraint on 'bullets.' Our powder is the cause, that usually precedes the 'hearse.'" 4pp. Page 4: Wallace bumper sticker— "Wallace for President-Democrat." Narrative: "When Is A Man A Man?"

GCW-3 Let George Do It. w.m. Joseph Erdelyi, Jr. (July 22, 1968, New York, NY., U.S.A.). Copyright 1968 by Erdelyi Music Publishing Company, Room 600, No. 1697 Broadway, New York, NY. 10019. [8 1/2" × 11"]. Pk/bk non-pictorial. "Dedicated to the four children of George C. and Lurleen Wallace." "Campaign Song for George C. Wallace, 1968 American Independent Party Candidate for the Presidency of the United States." 2pp. Page 2: Blank.

GCW-4 Stand Up For Wallace. w.m. Joseph Erdelyi, Jr. (March 28, 1968, U.S.A.). Copyright 1968 by Erdelyi Music Publishing Company, Room 600, No. 1697 Broadway, New York, NY. 10019. [8 1/2" × 11"]. Y/bk non-pictorial. "Dedicated to Her Excellency, Governor Lurleen Wallace, of the State of Alabama." "Campaign Song for Ex-Governor George C. Wallace of Alabama." "Note: It is suggested that each verse be repeated." 2pp. Page 2: Blank.

GCW-5 Stand Up For Wallace (Campaign Song for George C. Wallace). w.m. Joseph Erdelyi, Jr. Published by Erdelyi Music Publishing Company, Room 600, No. 1697 Broadway, New York, NY. 10019. 1968. Bl/w photo of George Wallace. R/w/b cover. "Win With Wallace." "Courage-Character." 4pp. Page 2: "Dedicated to Her Excellency, Governor Lurleen Wallace, of the State of Alabama." "Campaign Song for Ex-Governor George C. Wallace of Alabama." Page 4: "The Story of George C. Wallace" reprinted from the Liberty Lobby Research Staff Report.

GCW-6 We Need A Change In Washington. w.m. Joseph Erdelyi, Jr. (Aug. 5, 1968, U.S.A.). Copyright 1968 by Erdelyi Music Publishing Company, Room 600, No. 1697 Broadway, New York, NY. 10019. Non-pictorial. "Dedicated to all the Campaign Workers of George C. Wallace." "Campaign Song for George C.

Wallace, 1968 American Independent Party Candidate for the Presidency of the United States." Advertising. 2pp. Page 2: Blank.

GCW-7 Oh, Wallace. w. James Orange, "and other young people." m. "Tune: *Kidnapper*." "I started singing this song during the summer of 1964. When we walked up to the capitol almost a year later — about 40,000 people — it felt good because this made the dream come true. — James Orange, SCLC." In: *Freedom is a Constant Struggle, Songs of the Freedom Movement*, page 168. c.e. Guy Carawan and Candie Carawan. Published by Oak Publications, A Division of Embassy Music Corporation, No. 33 West 60th Street, New York, NY. 10023. 1968. [7" × 10 1/4"]. Br/be slip cover of people singing. Brown had back book with gold title on spine. 232pp.

See also JGS-1; JGS-2; JCS-3; JCS-5.

GERALD R. FORD

GRF-1 President Gerald R. Ford March. w. Andrea Fodor Litkei (ASCAP). m. Ervin Litkei (ASCAP). Published by Loena Music Publishing Company, No. 239 West 18th Street, New York, NY. 10011. 1974. R/w/b drawing of U.S. Capitol building. "Introduced and performed February 15, 1975, in Grand Rapids, Michigan, by the University of Michigan Symphony Band under the direction of George Cavender." 4pp. Page 4: R/w/b Presidential seal.

GRF-2 WIN. w.m. Meredith Willson. Published by Frank Music Affiliates. Sole Selling Agents: Frank Distributing Company, No. 116 Boylston Street, Boston, MA. 02116. Copyright 1974 and 1975. [7 1/2" × 10"]. R/w/bk drawing of a "WIN" [Whip Inflation Now] button. "Special Anti-Inflation Economy-Sized Edition." "Piano Vocal." 4pp. Page 4: Publisher's logo.

GRF-3 President Gerald R. Ford March. w.m. Andrea Litkei and Ervin Litkei. Published by Loena Music Publishing Company, No. 239 West 18th Street, New York, NY. 10011. 1974. [8 1/2" × 11"]. Bl/w photo of Gerald R. Ford. R/w/b cover. 4pp. Page 4: Presidential seal.

GRF-4 This Is Our America. w.m. Wil Rose. Sole selling agent: Words, Inc., Waco, TX. 76703. 1976. N/c photo by Russ Busby of Princess Pale Moon — "As sung by Princess Pale Moon." 4pp. Page 4: Narrative by Wil Rose, President, Nationally, Heritage Foundation, Annondale, VA. on the history of Princess Pale Moon and this song — "During the Bi-Centennial Celebration, Pale Moon has been featured in the New Year's Day parade with the Wagon Train in Washington, D.C., parade July 3, and performed for The President [Gerald Ford] in The Honor America Program — The Republican National Convention this year has scheduled Pale Moon as featured singer and performer for the Convention program, &c."

GRF-5 [A Hunting We Will Go]. m. "Tune: *Farmer in the Dell*." Published by the Illinois Draft Rockefeller Committee. [1964]. [5" × 8"]. Non-pictorial. 2pp. Page 2: Blank.

GRF-6 Go Go Go With Rockefeller. w. Dick DeBrown. m. Chet Gierlach. Published by Leonard Whitcup, Inc., No. 215 East 68th Street, New York, NY. Sole Selling Agents: Cimino Publications, Inc., No. 479 Maple Avenue, Westbury, L.I., NY. 1962. Bl/w photo of Nelson Rockefeller. "Official Song New York Republican State Committee." 4pp.

GRF-7 President Gerald R. Ford March. w. Andrea Fodor Litkei. m. Ervin Litkei. In: *A Tribute To The U.S.A.*, page 23. Published by Loena Music Publishing Company, No. 239 West 18th Street, New York, NY. Copyright 1985 and 1986. N/c drawing by Edward Moran of Statue of Liberty celebration in 1886 — "The Statue of Liberty, standing as an eternal symbol of the friendship of the people of France, was presented to the United States in 1886 by its creator, Frederick Bartholdi." Quotes by "Emma Lazarus (1883)," and by "President Grover Cleveland (1886)."

GRF-8 President Gerald R. Ford March. w. Andrea Litkei. m. Ervin Litkei. In: *The Bicentennial March and Presidential Marches of America*, page 36. Published by Loena Music Publishing Company, New York, NY. 1976. R/w/b drawings of George Washington, Thomas Jefferson, Abraham Lincoln, eagle and flags. "American Revolution Bicentennial, 1776-1976." "Officially Recognized Commorative." 40pp.

GRF-9 Rockefeller Campaign Song. w.m. Bob Saffer (ASCAP). Published by Columbia Advertising Company, No. 133-17 101st Avenue, Richmond Hill 19, NY. [1964]. [6 1/4" × 8 1/4"]. Non-pictorial. 2pp. Page 2: Blank.

GRF-10(A) Having A Time. m. Popular tunes. In: *Thoroughly MADERN Malcolm*, page 12. Published by New York State Legislative Correspondent's Association, Albany, NY. March 16, 1974.

(B) Options Are For Opening, page 14.

(C) Sweet Memories, page 15.

GRF-11 Rock-In For Rocky. w.m. Elizabeth Firestone. [ca. 1964]. [3 1/2" × 5 1/2"]. Obv: B/w photo of Nelson Rockefeller, facsimile signature. Rev: "Lyrics to **Rock-In For Rocky**."

GRF-12 President Gerald R. Ford March. w. Andrea Litkei. m. Ervin Litkei. Published by Loena Music Publishing Company, No. 239 West 18th Street, New York, NY. 10011. 1974. [8 1/2" × 11"]. N/c photo of Gerald R. Ford, facsimile signature. R/w/b cover. 4pp. Page 4: Presidential seal.

GRF-11

GRF-3

George S. McGovern

GSM-1 Let's All Sing (With the

Democratic National Convention Miami Beach) (Official Song Sheet). c. Charles W. Kinzel, "Vice Chairman, National Democratic Committee, Entertainment Subcommittee, Music Director, Miami Douglas MacArthur High School, member of Miami Federation of Musicians Local 655." m. Popular songs. Published by the National Democratic Convention, Miami Beach, FL. 1972. [3 1/2" × 8 1/2"]. B/w litho of Official logo of the convention. 16pp. Inside page: "National Democratic Convention 1972 Song Sheet, compiled by Charles W. Kinzel, Vice Chairman, National Democratic Committee." Page 16: Advertising.

GSM-2 Sgt. Shriver's Bleeding Heart's Club Band. In: *National Lampoon Songbook*. 1976. N/c cover drawing of oddly dressed people on stage. "From Lemmings, a satirical joke-rock mock-concert musical comedy semi-review theatrical production, plus songs from The National Lampoon Radio Hour, The National Lampoon Show and more!"

GEORGE WASHINGTON

GW-1 The Ladies Patriotic Song. m. Air: *Washington's March at the Battle of Trenton*. Printed & sold at G. Gilfert's Musical Magazine, No. 177 Broadway, New York, NY. [ca. 1798]. B/w attached engraving of George Washington. "Sung by Mrs. Hodgkinson with Universal Applause at the Columbia Gardens [New York, July 4, 1798]." 4pp. [S/U, p. 222].

GW-2 General Washington's March. Printed & sold by G. Graupner at his Musical Academy, No. 6 Franklin Street, Franklin Place, Boston, MA. [ca. 1803]. Non-pictorial. "Piano Fortes for sale, to Let, and Tuned in Town & Country at the shortest Notice." Followed by *Yankee Doodle*. Number "114" at top. "Pr. 12 ct." 2pp. [W-9626].

GW-3 Dead March & Monody. w.m. Benjamin Carr. Printed by Joseph Carr, Baltimore, MD. [1799-1800]. B/w attached oval engraving of George Washington. "Performed in the Lutheran Church, Philadelphia, on Thursday the 26th December 1799 being Part of the Music Selected for Funeral Honours to our late illustrious Cheif [sic], General George Washington." "Composed for the occasion and respectfully dedicated to the Senate of the United States by their Obet., humble Servt., B: Carr." Followed on page one by **Monody**. [w.m. Benjamin Carr]. "Sung by Miss. Broadhurst." 4pp. Page 3: "*Dead March* adapted for two Flutes, Violins, Clarinetts [sic] or Guitars [sic]." "*Monody* adapted for two Voices, Violins, Clarinetts [sic] or Guittars [sic]." Bottom of page three: "Printed by J. Carr, Baltimore. Copyright Secured." [S/U, p. 100].

GW-4 Funeral Dirge On The Death Of General Washington. m. P.A. Von Hagen. "Printed & sold at P.A. Von Hagen & Cousin, Musical Magazine, No. 3 Cornhill, [Boston, MA], and to be had of G. Gilfert, New York." [1800]. Non-pictorial. "As sung at the Stone Chapel." "The music composed by P.A. von Hagen, organist of said church." 2pp. [S/U, p. 152].

GW-5 The Victory Of Trenton. w. Major William Jackson. m. George Gillingham. Printed at G. Willig's Musical Magazine, Philadelphia, PA. [1812]. Non-pictorial. "And Sung at the Anniversary Meeting of the Society of the Sons of Washington by A Member, February 22d A.D., 1812." 4pp. [W-3115].

GW-6 Ode. w. Mr. L** [Samuel Low]. m. Air: "*God Save*, &c." 1789. Non-pictorial. "To be Sung on the Arrival of the President of the United States." 2pp.

GW-7 Chorus Sung Before Gen. Washington. w.m. Alexander Reinagle. Printed for the Author, and sold by H. Rice, Market Street, Philadelphia, PA. [1789]. Non-pictorial. "Sung before Gen. Washington as he passed under the Triumphal Arch raised on the bridge at Trenton, April 21st, 1789, set to music and dedicated by permission to Mrs. Washington by A. Reinagle." "Price 1/2 dollar." 8pp. [S/U, p. 63].

GW-8 Ode To Washington [Complete]. w.m. Charles E. Horn. Published by Dubois & Stodart, No. 167 Broadway, New York, NY. 1828. Non-pictorial. "Composed and Dedicated to the Handel and Haydn Society of Boston." "Pr: 2.50." 36p.

(A) **Ode To Washington.** Page 6: **March Funebre** [To Washington].

(B) **O Ne'er To Man.** "Sung by Mr. Horn in *The Ode to Washington.*" Page 11.

(C) **As Some Fond Mother.** "Sung by Mrs. Knight in *The Ode to Washington*, Accompanied on the Violin by Mr. Ostnelli." Page 15.

(D) **The Pearly Drops** (A Duett). "Sung by Mrs. Knight and Miss E. Gillingham in *The Ode to Washington.*" Page 27.

GW-9 Funeral Dirge. a. I. Decker. Engraved by A. Lynn [Alexandria, VA]. [1799-1800]. Non-pictorial. "Adopted for and played by the Alexandria Band at the Funeral of Genl. Geo. Washington." 2pp. [S/U, p. 152].

GW-10 Washington (A Song). w.m. Samuel Holyoke. In: *The Massachusetts Magazine*, page 571, Sept., 1790. Published by Isaiah Thomas and E.T. Andrews, No. 45 Newberry Street, Boston, MA. 1790. Non-pictorial. "Seat of the Muses. For *The Massachusetts Magazine.*" [S/U, p. 449].

GW-11 Brother Soldiers All Hail! (A Favorite New Patriotic Song in Honor of Washington). Printed & sold at B. Carr's Musical Repository, Philadelphia, J. Carr's Baltimore & J. Hewitt's, N. York. [1799]. 4pp. Page 2: [V-1: B/w attached engraving of George Washington] [V-2: Without engraving]. "Heav'n has lent him in love to mankind to add a new grace to the Earth." "To which is added *A Toast* Written and Arranged by F. Hopkinson, Esqr." "Piano Forte, Guittar [sic] and Clarinett [sic]." "Price 23 cents." Page 4: **A Toast.** w.m. Francis Hopkinson. [S/U, p. 50].

GW-12(A) Ode To Columbia's Favorite Son. In: *The Massachusetts Magazine*, page 659, Vol. 1. No. 10, October, 1789. Published by Isaiah Thomas and E.T. Andrews, No. 45 Newberry Street, Boston, MA. Non-pictorial. "Sung by the Independent Musical Society, on the arrival of The President at the Triumphal Arch, in Boston, Oct. 24, 1789." [S/U, p. 312].

(B) **To The President Of The United States.** w. A Lady. m. Mr. Hans Gram. Page 660.

(C) **Ode Upon Arrival Of The President Of the United States.** w. G.R. Page 653.

GW-13 The Favorite New Federal Song [Hail Columbia]. w. Joseph Hopkinson. m. "Adapted to *The President's March.*" Published by B. Carr. 1798. B/w engraving of eagle, shield, sun rays. Attached b/w engraving of George Washington. "For the Voice, Piano Forte, Guittar and Clarinett [sic]." "Sung by Mr. Fox." 4pp. [S/U, p. 173].

GW-14 The Battle Of Prague (A Favorite Sonata For The Piano Forte With Accompaniments). Printed & Sold by Graupner, No. 6 Franklin Street, Boston, MA. [1811?]. B/w engraving of George Washington, drape, floral and geometric designs. "G. Washington, President of the United States." "Price 1 Doll." 8pp. [W-5109].

GW-15 The Battle Of Trenton (A Sonata for the Piano Forte). m. James Hewitt. Printed & Sold by James Hewitt, No. 131 William Street, New York, NY. [1797]. B/w engraving of George Washington, Miss Liberty, drum, flags, angel. "Composed by James Hewitt, who has introduced into his score the music of *Washington's March* and *Yankee Doodle.*" "Dedicated to General Washington. " 14pp. [S/U, p. 309].

**GW-16 Ode For American In-

GW-15

dependence (July 4, 1789). w. Daniel George. m. Horatio Garnet. In: *The Massachusetts Magazine*, page 453, Vol. 1, No. 7, July, 1789. Published by Isaiah Thomas & Company, No. 45 Newberry Street, Boston, MA. 1789. Non-pictorial. [S/U, p. 309].

GW-17 President's March & Ca Ira. m. [Philip Phile]. Published by Carr & Company [Philadelphia, PA]. [1793-1794]. Non-pictorial. "Price 12 Cents." 2pp. Page 2: Blank. [S/U, p. 342].

GW-18 The President's Birth Day Ode. w. A. Stoddard. m. Air: *God Save The King*. In: *The Massachusetts Magazine*, pages 178-179, Vol. III, No. IV, March, 1793. Published by Isaiah Thomas & E.T. Andrews, No. 45 Newberry Street, Boston, MA. 1793. Non-pictorial. "*For The Massachusetts Magazine*." "Performed at Taunton at the Civic Festival, February, 1793."

GW-19 Washington's March. Printed & Sold at G. Willig's Musical Magazine, Philadelphia, PA. [1812?]. Non-pictorial. "As performed at the New Theatre." 2pp. Page 2: *Quickstep*. m. R. Taylor. [W-9617].

GW-20 New Yankee Doodle. Printed & Sold at J. Hewitt's Musical Repository, No. 131 William Street, New York, NY. [1797-1798]. B/w engraving of George Washington. "Sung with great applause at the Theatre by Mr. Hodgkinson." 4pp. "Also sold by B. Carr, Philadelphia & J. Carr, Baltimore." Pages 1 and 4: Blank. [S/U, p. 480].

GW-21 Hail Columbia. In: *Willig's Pocket Companion for Flute or Violin, Containing the most Fashionable Airs [1]*, page 50. Published & Sold by George Willig, No. 171 Chesnut Street, Philadelphia, PA. Gn/bk/be marbled hard covers. Title page: B/w engraving of woman with harp. 106pp. [8 1/4" × 5"]. [See note at W-9963].

GW-22 The President Of The United States March. m. Mr. Sicard. Printed by J. McCulloch, Philadelphia, PA. [ca. 1789]. Non-pictorial. Followed on page one by *Cotillion Minuet*. m. Mr. Sicard. 2pp. Page 2: Blank. [S/U, p. 341].

GW-23 Washington (A Favorite New Song in the American Camp). w. [Jonathan Mitchell Sewell]. m. Air: *British Grenadier*. "Printed and sold next to the Bell-Tavern, in Danvers," [MA]. [1776]. [4 3/8" × 10 5/8"]. B/w engraving of George Washington and General Artemas Ward. "Cash paid for rags."

GW-24 Washington & Count De Grasse (A New Song). m. Air: *The British Grenadiers*. Sold at Russell's Printing Office, near Liberty-Stump, [Danvers, MA]. 1782. B/w wood cut of George Washington & Count De Grasse, other figures. "Great Joy to the Day." 2pp.

GW-25 Wreaths For The Chieftain. w. L.M. Sargent, Esqr. m. Sanderson. a. F. Granger. Published & sold by G. Graupner, at his Music Store, No. 6 Franklin Street, Boston, MA. 1815. Non-pictorial. "Sung by Mr. Huntington in the Stone Chapel, Boston, at the celebration of Peace with Great Britain, and the Birth Day of Gen'l. Washington, Feb. 22, 1815, Adapted to a Favorite air of

Sanderson from the *Lady of the Lake.*" 4pp. Pages 1 and 4: Blank. [W-7827].

GW-26   New President's March. Printed & Sold by G. Willig, No. 185 Market Street, Philadelphia, PA. [1798?]. Non-pictorial. 2pp. Page 2: Blank. [S/U, p. 454].

GW-27   Wreaths For The Chieftain. w.m. L.M. Sargent, Esqr. Printed & sold at Dr. G.K. Jackson's Music Store, Hanover Street, Boston, MA. [1815]. B/w engraving of eagle with scroll. "An Ode for the Anniversary of the Birthday of Washington, Feb. 22, 1815, shortly after the annunciation of peace." 4pp. Pages 1 and 4: Blank. [W-7828].

GW-28   Washington's   Marh [sic]. Published & Sold at G. Willig's' Musical Magazine, Philadelphia, PA. [1812-1814]. Non-pictorial. Followed on same page by **Washington's March At The Battle Of Trenton.** 2pp. Page 2: Blank. [Not listed in Wolfe].

GW-29   Washington's March. m. Jacob Eckhard, Jr. Published by J. Siegling at his Musical Warehouse, [V-1: No. 69 Broad Street] [V-2: No. 109 Meeting Street], Charleston, SC. [V-1: September, 1825] [V-2: 1828-1831]. Non-pictorial geometric designs. "With variations for the Piano-Forte." 2pp. Page 2: Blank. [W-2653].

GW-30   Washington's March. Published by Fiot, Meignen & Company, Philadelphia, PA. [ca. 183-?]. Non-pictorial. Followed on the same page by *Gen. La Fayette's March At Yorktown.* Number "622" at bottom of page. 2pp. Page 2: Blank.

GW-31   Washington's March. Engraved, Printed & Sold by E. Riley, No. 29 Chatham Street, New York, NY. [1818-1826]. Non-pictorial. 2pp. Page 2: Blank. [W-9633].

GW-32   Washington's March. Published by G. Willig's Musical Magazine, Philadelphia, PA. [1812-1826]. Non-pictorial. Followed on the same page by **Washington's March At The Battle Of Trenton.** 2pp. Page 2: Blank. [W-9622].

GW-33   Washington's March. Published by N. Thurston, New York, NY. Non-pictorial geometric designs. 2pp. Page 2: Blank. [W-9634].

GW-34   Washington's   March. Published & Sold by G. Graupner at his Music Store, No. 6 Franklin Street, Boston, MA. [182-]. Non-pictorial. Followed on same page by *Yankee Doodle.* "Sold for G.G. by John Ashton, No. 197 Washington Street." 2pp. Page 2: Blank. [W-9627].

GW-35   Washington's March. Published by G.E. Blake, Philadelphia, PA. [1812-1814]. Non-pictorial. Followed by **Washington's March At The Battle Of Trenton.** 2pp. Page 2: Blank. [W-9621].

GW-36   Washington's March. a. M. Hall. [181-?]. Non-pictorial. "Arranged as a Duett [sic] for the Piano Forte." 2pp. Page 2: Blank.

GW-37   The Baltimore Centennial March. w.m. George F. Cole. Published by John Cole, Baltimore, MD. [1832]. Non-pictorial. "As Performed at the Celebration in 1832 in Honor of The Birth of Washington." "The Music Arranged from the Opera of *Cinderrella* and Dedicated to Col. John Thomas, Chief Marshall." Number "529" at bottom of page. 4pp. Page 4: Blank.

GW-38   Washington's Trenton March. Published & Sold by George Willig, Jr., Baltimore, MD. [ca. 1831]. Non-pictorial. Preceded on page one by *Bazaar.* 2pp. Page 2: Blank.

GW-39   Washington's Assembly. Printed & Sold by G. Graupner at his Musical Academy, No. 6 Franklin Street, Franklin Place, Boston, MA. [ca. 1803-1805]. Non-pictorial. Preceded on page one by *Bounapart's Grand March.* Number "38" at bottom of page. 2pp. Page 2: Blank. [W-945B].

GW-40   Washington's Birthday March (And Quickstep). m. Edward L.

White. Published for the Author by C. Bradlee, No. 164 Washington Street, Boston, MA. Entered according to an Act of Congress the 2nd day of April, 1830. Non-pictorial. "Composed & Arranged for the Piano Forte." "Dedicated to the W.L.J. Company, Newburyport." 4pp. Pages 1 and 4: Blank.

GW-41 Centennial Tribute (A Grand March). m. Edward Richard Hansen. [Published by C. Bradlee, Boston, MA]. [1832]. B/w litho of wreath with "Washington" printed within. "A Grand March Offered to the Memory of the Birth Day of the Immortal Washington." "Parts for a full military band may be had by applying to E.R.H. or C. Bradlee." 4pp. Page 4: Blank.

GW-42 Washington's March. Printed & sold at Carr's Music Store, No. 36 Market Street, Baltimore, MD. [ca. 1812]. Non-pictorial. 2pp. Page 2.

GW-43 Washington's Grand Centennial March. m. Oliver Shaw. Published & Sold by the Author [Oliver Shaw], No. 70 Westminister Street, Providence, RI. 1832. Non-pictorial. "As Performed at the Providence Centennial Celebration of his birth, Feb. 22, 1832, Composed and Inscribed to his friend & Compatriot in arms, General La Fayette." 4pp. Page 1: Blank. Page 4: *Aerial Quick Step*. m. Oliver Shaw.

GW-44 Grand Centennial March. m. Adolph Schmitz. Published by F. Rudolphis, Philadelphia, PA. [ca. 1832]. Non-pictorial. "Composed for the Anniversary of the Immortal Washington and Dedicated to the Philadelphia Band." 4pp. Page 4: Blank.

GW-45(A) President's March. In: *The Instrumental Preceptor, Comprising Instructions for the Clarionett [sic], German Flute, Violin, Bass-Viol and Bassoon; With a Variety of Airs, Minuets, Cotillions, Hornpipes, Marches, Duettes [sic], Rondos, Trios, &c., &c., Original and Selected*, page 35. e. Joseph Herrick. Printed & sold by Ranlet & Norris, Exeter, NH. December, 1807. [8 5/8" × 10 5/8"]. [W-3675].

(B) Washington's March (At The Battle of Trenton). Page 65.

GW-46 The President's March. Published by A. Bacon & Company, No. 11 South 4th Street, Philadelphia, PA. [1816?]. Non-pictorial. 2pp. Page 2: Blank. [W-6990].

GW-47 The President's March. (A New Federal Song). m. [Philip Phile]. Published by G. Willig, Market Street, No. 185, Philadelphia, PA. [1798-1804]. Non-pictorial. 2pp. Page 2: *Yankee Doodle*. [S/U, p. 173].

GW-48 The President's March. Printed & Sold by Mallet & Graupner at the Conservatorio or Musical Academy, Boston, MA. [1802]. Non-pictorial. "For Four Hands." 4pp. Pages 1 and 4: Blank. [W-6989].

GW-49 The President's March. [1795-181-]. Non-pictorial. 2pp. Page 2: Blank.

GW-50 The President's March. Engrav'd, Printed & Sold by E. Riley, No. 29 Chatham Street, New York, NY. [1818-1826]. Non-pictorial. "For the Piano Forte." 2pp. Page 2: Blank. [W-6992].

GW-51 The President's March. m. R.T. Taylor. Engraved & published by William Priest, Philadelphia, PA. [ca. 1795]. Non-pictorial. "Aranged [sic] for two performers on one Piano Forte." "Sold at all the music stores in the United States, and by Preston & Son, No. 97 Strand, London. Price 25 cents." [S/U, p. 342].

GW-52 The New President's March. Printed by B. Carr, [Philadelphia, PA]. [1796]. Non-pictorial. "Price 12 cents." Followed on page one by **Washington's March**. 2pp. Page 2: Blank. [S/U, p. 453].

GW-53 The New President's March. Sold at J. Paff's Musical Store, New York, NY. [1798-1811]. Non-pictorial. Followed on page one by **Washington's**

March. 2pp. Page 2: Blank. [S/U, p. 454] and [W-9618].

GW-54 The New President's March. Printed & Sold by J. Hewitt. No. 23 Maiden Lane, New York, NY. [1799-1800]. Non-pictorial. "Price 1 Shilling." Followed on the same page by **Washington's March**. 2pp. Page 2: Blank. [S/U, p. 454].

GW-55(A) Washington's Reel. In: *A New & Complete Preceptor for the Fife, Together with a Collection of Choice Marches*, page 20. Published by William Williams, No. 60 Genesee Street, Utica, NY. 1819. [14" × 21 1/2"]. 48pp. [W-7212].
(B) **General Washington's March.** Pages 34-35.

GW-56 Washington's Grand March. Published by Keith's Music Publishing, Nos. 67 and 69 Court Street, Boston, MA. [ca. 1834]. Non-pictorial. "Composed for the Piano Forte." 2pp. Page 2: Blank.

GW-57 The President's March. Published by N. Thurston, New York, NY. [1821-1824]. Non-pictorial. 2pp. Page 2: Blank. [W-6993].

GW-58 Hail: Columbia! (The President's March). [m. Philip Phile]. Published & Sold at G. Willig's Musical Magazine, No. 171 Chesnut Street, Philadelphia, PA. [1819?]. Non-pictorial. 4pp. Pages 1 and 4: Blank. [W-6985].

GW-59 Hail Columbia. [m. Philip Phile]. Published by George Willig, No. 171 Chesnut Street, Philadelphia, PA. [1842]. Non-pictorial. "The Celebrated National Air with Variations for the Piano Forte." "Pr. 50." 6pp. Page 6: Blank.

GW-60 Washington's March. Published by Hilbus & Hitz, Washington, DC. [ca. 182-?]. Non-pictorial. Number "10" and "G.H." at bottom of page. 2pp. Page 2: Blank.

GW-61(A) God Save Great Washington. In: *The Gentleman's Pocket Companion for German Flute Or Violin, Consisting of Most Elegant Songs, Airs, Marches, Minuets, Cotillions, Country Dances, &c., No. 1*, page 16. Printed & Sold by G. Willig, No. 12 South 4th Street, Philadelphia, PA. [ca. 1816]. [4 7/8" × 6 3/4"].
(B) **President's March.** Page 8.

GW-62 The President's March. (Or Hail Columbia!). [m. Philip Phile]. Published by [V-1: A. Foit] [V-2: Foit, Meignen & Company, No. 264 Market Street], Philadelphia, PA. [ca. 1830?]. Non-pictorial. Number "56" at the bottom of the page. 2pp. Page 2: Blank.

GW-63 Hail Columbia. Engraved, Printed & Sold by F. [sic] Riley, No. 297 Broadway, New York, NY. [1844-1850]. B/w non-pictorial line border. "A Popular Air, Arranged for the Piano Forte." 4pp. Page 4: Blank.

GW-64 Washington's Favorite March. Published by George Willig, No. 171 Chesnut Street, Philadelphia, PA. [1826-1851]. Non-pictorial. Followed on page one by **March At The Battle Of Trenton**. 2pp. Page 2: Blank

GW-65 Washington's Trenton March. Published by [V-1: John Cole] [V-2: G. Willig], Baltimore, MD. [ca. 183-]. Non-pictorial. Followed on page one by *Yankee Doodle*. Number "626" at bottom of page. 2pp. Page 2: Blank.

GW-66 Washington's Grand March. Published by [V-1: A. Bacon & Company, No. 11 South Fourth Street] [V-2: J.G. Klemm, No. 3 South 3rd Street], Philadelphia, PA. [V-1: 1814-1816] [V-2: 1823-1824]. Non-pictorial. 2pp. Page 2: Blank. [W-9623].

GW-67 Washington's Grand March. Published by [V-1: Firth, Pond & Company] [V-2: Firth & Hall], No. 1 Franklin Square, New York, NY. [1830-1843]. Non-pictorial. Followed on same page by **Washington's March**. Number "2238" at the bottom of page. 2pp. Page 2: Blank

GW-68 Washington's Grand March. Published at Millet's Music Saloon, No. 329 Broadway, New York, NY. [ca. 1840]. Non-pictorial. Followed on same page by *Favorite March* by W.A. Mozart. 2pp. Page 2: Blank.

GW-69 Washington's Grand March. Published by E. Riley, No. 29 Chatham Street, New York, NY. [ca. 1826]. Non-pictorial. Followed on same page by *A Favorite March* by W.A. Mozart. 2pp. Page 2: Blank.

GW-70 Hail Columbia. Published by Wm. Dubois, New York, NY. [1817-1818]. Non-pictorial. "A Favorite Patriotic Song for Piano Forte." 2pp. [W-6983B].

GW-71(A) Washington's March. In: *Complete Fifer's Museum, Or A Collection of Marches of All Kinds, Now in Use in the Military Line, Also a Number of Occasional Tunes for the Actual Service and The Militia with Rudiments and Lessons Complete for the Work*, page 20. c. James Hulbert, Jr. (Philo Musico). Published by Ansel Phelps, Greenfield, MA. [1811?]. [6 1/8" × 10"]. Non-pictorial. 48pp. [W-4389].

(B) **Washington's Favorite**, page 14.

(C) **Lady Washington's Favorite**, page 14.

(D) **President's March**, page 21.

GW-72 Washington's Grand March. a. J.P. L'Hulier. Published by George Willig, No. 171 Chesnut Street, Philadelphia, PA. [1826-1851]. Non-pictorial. "Arranged for the Spanish Guitar." Followed on page by *Sautese*. 2pp. Page 2: Blank.

GW-73 Washington's March. Published by John Cole, Baltimore, MD. [1825?]. Non-pictorial. Followed on page one by **Washington's March At The Battle Of Trenton**. Number "164" at bottom of page. 2pp. Page 2: Blank. [W-9625].

GW-74 Washington's New March. m. Curphew. In: *The Gentleman's Amusement, A Collection of Songs, Duetts, Dances and Marches Properly Adapted for the Flute, Violin and Patent Flageolet*, page 23. Published by W. Dubois, No. 126 Broadway, New York, NY. [1817-1818]. [6 1/2" × 10"]. Non-pictorial. Followed on same page by *A Fancy Troop*. 40pp. [W-2960].

GW-75 The River Patowmac [Sic] (An Epicedium on the Death of the August and Venerable General Washington Late Commander In Chief of the Armies of the United States). w. Mr. Derrick. m. Weizafcker. Printed by G. Willig, No. 185 Market Street, Philadelphia, PA. [ca. 1800]. Non-pictorial. 2pp. [S/U, p. 356].

GW-76(A) Hail Columbia. w. Judge Joseph Hopkinson, L.L.D. a. Francis H. Brown. Published by S.C. Jollie, No. 300 Broadway, New York, NY. 1843. Non-pictorial. "Collection of National Songs of America, No. 2." "The words written by Judge Joseph Hopkinson, L.L.D., the Symphonies & Accomplishments Composed & Arranged and Respectfully Inscribed to the Officers of the Army and Navy of the United States by Francis H. Brown." List of other titles in series. 6pp. Page 2: Narrative on the history of the song. Page 6: Blank.

(B) **Land Of Washington**.

GW-77 Birthday Of Washington (A Bugle Song). w. G.D. Prentice (Louisville). m. W. Nixon (Cincinnati). Published by Dubois & Bacon, No. 167 Broadway, New York, NY. [ca. 1832]. Non-pictorial. "Dedicated to the Senate of the U. States by the Composer." 4pp. Pages 1 and 4: Blank.

GW-78 The President's March. a. C. De Ronceray. Published & Sold by G. Willig, Baltimore, MD. [ca. 1845]. Non-pictorial. "Arranged for the Use of his Juvenile Pupils." 2pp. Page 2: Blank.

GW-79 General Washington's March. In: *Instructor In Martial Music*, page 38. Published by Daniel Hazeltine, Exeter, NH. [1810]. [5 1/8" × 8 7/8"]. 48pp. [W-3575].

GW-80 Hail Columbia (Or The

President's March). [V-1: Published & Sold by George Willig, No. 171 Chesnut Street, Philadelphia, PA. 1826-1850] [V-2: Published by Bourne Depository of Arts, No. 359 Broadway, New York, NY. 1827-1832] [V-3: Published & Sold by Peters, Webb & Company, Louisville, KY. 1849-1856]. Non-pictorial. "As performed at the principal theatres throughout the United States." [V-2: Number "190" at bottom of page one."]. [V-3: Number "26-2" at bottom of page one."]. 4pp. Pages 1 and 4: Blank.

GW-81 A Funeral Elegy On The Death Of General George Washington (Adapted to the 22d of February). m. Abraham Wood. Printed by Thomas & Andrews, Boston, MA. January, 1800. [5 1/2" × 8 11/16"]. Non-pictorial black line border. 8pp. Page 2: Engraving of urn inscribed "G.W. Born Feb. 22, 1732, Died at Mount Vernon, Dec. 14, 1799, Aged 68." "The just shall be had in everlasting remembrance." [S/U, p. 152].

GW-82 The President's March (Or Hail Columbia). Published & Sold at Boswell's Music Store, Baltimore, MD. [ca. 1830?]. Non-pictorial. 2pp. Page 2: Blank.

GW-83 Hail Columbia. In: *American Patriotic Songbook, A Collection of Political, Descriptive, and Humorous Songs of National Character and the Production of American Poets Only, Interspersed with a Number Set to Music*, pages 50-52. Published & Sold by W. M'Culloch, No. 306 Market Street, Philadelphia, PA. 1813. 108pp. Page 3: Title page—*American Patriotic Songbook, A Collection of Political, Descriptive, and Humorous Songs of National Character and the Production of American Poets Only, Interspersed with a Number Set to Music*. "To Hull, and such heroes, a garland we raise, their valour in battle exultingly praise." [W-122].

GW-84 Twenty Second Of February. [ca. 1840]. Non-pictorial. Page 1: Songs—**Twenty Second Of February**, followed by *Island*. Number "12" at bottom of page. 2pp. Page 2: Songs—*The Hero* and *Peter Francisco*.

GW-85 Andre's Request To Washington. w. N.P. Willis, Esq. m. Joseph E. Sweetser. Published by Oliver Ditson, No. 115 Washington Street, Boston, MA. 1847. Non-pictorial. "Composed and Respectfully Dedicated to J. Draper, Esq." 4pp.

GW-86(A) Gen. Washington's March. In: *Massachusetts Collection of Martial Musick [sic], Containing a Plain, Easy & Concise Introduction to the Grounds of Martial Musick [sic], Laid Down in the most Comprehensive Manner, Together with a Large Collection of the most Approved Beats, Marches, Airs, &c., Introducing the Principal Part of the Duties of the Camp, The Evolutions for the Musicians, and Their Signals, A Great Part of Which was Never Before Published, Designed Principally for the Benefit of the Militia of the United States*, page 61. Published by Alvan Robinson, Jr., Exeter, NH. 1820. [W-7521].

(B) Gen. Washington's March [At the Battle of Trenton], page 42.

GW-87 Washington Star Of The West. w.m. R. Loomis. Published by Osbourn's Music Saloon, No. 112 South 3rd Street, Philadelphia, PA. 1846. Non-pictorial. "Composed and sung with great applause by R. Loomis at his concerts." "Respectfully Dedicated to the American People by the Author." Number "535" at bottom of page. 4pp. Page 4: Blank.

GW-88 Hail Columbia (A Favorite Patriotic Song). Published by Firth & Hall, No. 358 Pearl Street, New York, NY. [1827-1831]. Non-pictorial. 4pp. [W-6979B].

GW-89 Hark From The Tombs, &c. And Beneath The Honors. w. "Adapted from Dr. Watts and Set to Music by Samuel Holyoke, A.M." Published by H. Ranlet, Exeter, NH. [1800]. [8 1/2" × 5 3/4"]. Non-pictorial geometric designs. "Performed at Newburyport, 2d. January, 1800. The Day on which the Citizens Unitedly Expressed their Unbounded Veneration for the Memory of Our Beloved Washington." 12pp. [S/U, p. 178].

GW-90 Hail Columbia (Or The President's March). Published by Klemm & Brother, No. 287 Market Street, Philadelphia PA. [ca. 182-]. Non-pictorial. "A National Air Arranged for the Piano Forte." Number "549" at bottom of page. 4pp. Pages 1 and 4: Blank

GW-91 The President's March (Or Hail Columbia). Published by Torp & Viereck, No. 465 Broadway, New York, NY. [ca. 1834]. Non-pictorial. 2pp. Page 2: Blank.

GW-92 The Days Of Glorious Washington. w. J.F. Poole. m. J.N. Sporle. Published by Harding's Music For The Millions, No. 288 Bowery, New York, NY. [ca. 1850]. Non-pictorial. "A New National Song As Sung by Mr. E.H. Harding." "To Edward Bidet, Esq. of New York, as a token of Esteem." 4pp. Page 4: Blank.

GW-93 Washington Crossing The Delaware (A Quartette). w. Seba Smith. w. C. Zeuner. Published by Oliver Ditson, No. 115 Washington Street, Boston, MA. [ca. 1850]. Non-pictorial. 6pp. Page 6: Blank.

GW-94 Mount Vernon. L.M. m. Stephen Jenks. In: *The Musical Harmonist, Containing Concise and Easy Rules of Music Together with a Collection of the Most Approved Psalm and Hymn Tunes Fitted to All the Various Meters*, page 9. Engraved and Printed for the Author by A. Doolittle, New Haven, CT. 1800. Non-pictorial. "Composed on the death of Genl. Washington." 40pp. [S/U, p. 273].

GW-95 Washington's March. [ca. 184-]. Non-pictorial. Preceded on page one by *Pizarro's March*. 2pp. Page 2: Blank.

GW-96 Washington Guards. w.m. John F. Wells (A member of the Third Company of Washington Guards). [1798-1815]. Non-pictorial. 2pp. [S/U, p. 449].

GW-97 President's March. Published by [V-1: William Hall & Son, No. 239 Broadway] [V-2: Firth & Hall, No. 1 Franklin Square], New York, NY. [ca. 1830]. Non-pictorial. 2pp.

GW-98 Gen: Washington's March. In: *The Gentleman's Amusement, A Collection of Songs, Waltzes, Hornpipes, &c., &c., Properly Adapted for the Flute Violin and Patent Flageolet, Book 1*, page 8. Printed & Sold by J. Balls, No. 108 Oxford Street, London, England, and G. Balls, No. 151 Chestnut Street, Philadelphia, PA. [ca. 1815]. Followed on page one by *Life Let Us Cherish* and *La Pipe Ta Bac*. [Not listed in Wolfe].

GW-99 Hail! Columbia, Happy Land (A National Song). w. F. Hopkinson, Esqr. m. Prof. Phile. Published by W.C. Peters, Louisville, KY. [ca. 185-]. Non-pictorial. "Written to *The President's March*." "*The President's March* was composed by Prof. Pfiel and first performed by the Band stationed at Trenton Bridge when Washington passed over to his Inaugeration [sic] at New York, in the year 1789." Number "43" at bottom of page. 4pp. Pages 1 and 4: Blank.

GW-100 Washington's March. Published by C. Bradlee, [V-1: Washington Street] [V-2: 164 Washington Street], Boston, MA. [V-1: 1830-1838] [V-2: 1827-1834]. Non-pictorial. 2pp. Page 2: Blank.

GW-101 Massa Georgee Washington And General La Fayette. w.m. Micah Hawkins. Printed & sold by E. Riley, No. 29 Chatham Street, New York, NY. 1824. B/w engraving of man dressed as George Washington in uniform. "As sung in character by Mr. Roberts with unbounded applause at the theatre, Chatham Gardens." 8pp. Pages 2 and 8: Blank. [W-3475].

GW-102(A) Washington's

March. In: *Riley's Flute Melodies, A Collection of Songs, Airs, Waltzes, Cotillions, Dances, Marches, &c., &c., Arranged for the German Flute, Violin and Patent Flageolet, Second Volume*, page 94. Engraved, Printed & Publised [sic] by the Editor [Edward Riley], No. 23 Chatham Street, New York, NY. [1815-1816]. Preceded on the same page by other songs — *Prague Waltz* and *Roy's Wife of Aldivallo*. Followed on the same page by two other songs — *March in Bluebeard* & *Contradanze*. 100pp. [W-7490].

(B) **President's March**, page 12.
(C) **Gen: Washington's March**, page 21.

GW-103 Washington's Grand March. Published by William Hall & Son, No. 239 Broadway, New York, NY. [1848-1858]. Non-pictorial. Followed one page by **Washington's March**. Number "976" at bottom of page. 2pp. Page 2: Blank.

GW-104 Washington's Grand March. Published by Osbourn's Music Saloon, No. 30 South Fourth Street, Philadelphia, PA. [ca. 1840]. Non-pictorial. Followed on page by **Washington's Quick Step**. m. J.G. Osbourn. 2pp. Page 2: Blank.

GW-105 War Song [Remember the Glories of Brave Washington]. m. Air: "Altered from Moore." In: *The Minstrel, A Collection of Celebrated Songs Set to Music*, pages 248-249. Published by F. Lucas, Jr., No. 138 Market Street, Baltimore, MD. 1812. 316pp. [W-5865].

GW-106 Washington's March. Published by F.D. Benteen, Baltimore, MD. [ca. 183-]. Non-pictorial. Followed on page by **Washington's March At The Battle Of Trenton**. Number "135" at bottom of the page. 2pp. Page 2: Blank.

GW-107 The President's March. a. Ernest von Heeringen, Esq. [ca. 1850]. Non-pictorial. "No. 5." "This March is written with the new Musical Notation of Ernest von Heeringer, Esqr. That gentleman published in the year 1849 an Instruction Book wherein he proposed a very ingenious and simplified notation. Among many approving testimonials we find the names of Henry C. Timm, Esqr., Dr. Edward Hodges, Rev. Dr. Spring, Messrs George Loda, T.F. Montgomery and H.C. Becht. The only real difficulty to introduce it into universal use would be The Music Trade, and the only way to realise [sic] it bye and bye would be the readiness of musical Composers to write at least one page of their new productions in this new shape as that shape facilitates both the reading and printing of music. There are neither sharps no [sic] flats, the white notes being identical with the white keys and the black notes identical with the black keys for a piano forte. Mr. Von Herringen did use for semibreves (whole) and minums (half) the double size! This may confuse some readers and therefore Professor A. Wiener takes the liberty, to propose as an improvement the ancient quadrat shape for semibreves and minums, as that may quicken the conception of the eye! As soon as the reader does understand its plain use, it does not puzzle himself or herself in the least. P.S. Mr. Herringen's semibreve and minums above are not exactly correct for the want of tools." 2pp. Page 2: Blank.

GW-108 Washington Gallop. Published by Henry Tolman, No. 153 Washington Street, Boston, MA. 1853. Non-pictorial. "Introducing the Air of **The Land Of Washington** played by Jullien." 4pp. Pages 1 and 4: Blank.

GW-109 Washington's March. Published by Kretschmar & Nunns, No. 70 South 3rd Street, Philadelphia, PA. [ca. 183-]. Non-pictorial. Followed on page by **Washington's March At The Battle Of Trenton**. 2pp. Page 2: Blank.

GW-110(A) Washington. m. Samuel Holyoke. In: *The American Musical Miscellany, A collection of the Newest and Most Appoved [sic] Songs, Set to Music*, pages 274-277. Printed by Andrew Wright for Daniel Wright & Company,

Northampton, MA. 1798. Gd/br leather with geometric designs on spine and boards. 308pp. Page 5: Title page. Page 7: "To all true lovers of song in the United States of Columbia, this volume is humbly dedicated by their friends and humble servants, the publisher." [S/U, p. 20].

 (B) **Hail Columbia**. Page 122.
 (C) **Song For The Fourth Of July**. w. Daniel George. m. Horatio Garnet. Page 142. [Song praising Washington].

 GW-111 **The Godlike Washington**. m. Air: *My Ain Kind Deary, O*. In: *The Baltimore Musical Miscellany or Columbian Songster, Containing A Collection of Approved Songs, Set to Music, to Which is Prefixed An Essay on Vocal Music, with Directions for Graceful Singing and the Improvement of the Voice, in Two Volumes, Vol. II*, p. 141. Published by Sower & Cole, Baltimore, MD. 1805. [W-3144].

 GW-112 **National Divertimento**. a. A. Clifton. Published by G.E. Blake at his Piano Forte Music Store, No. 13 South 5th Street, Philadelphia, PA. [ca. 1830]. Non-pictorial. "For the Piano Forte, in which are Introduced **Hail Columbia** with a new Trio, and *Yankee Doodle!* with Variations. Composed and Dedicated to Miss Eleanor C. Gittings." "Pr 38 cts. Copy Right." 4pp.

 GW-113 **Hail Columbia**. In: *Riley's Easy Flute Duets (A Collection of One Hundred and Thirty One Favorite Airs)*, page 52. Engraved, Printed & Sold by E. Riley, No. 29 Chatham Street, New York, NY. 1819. [9 3/4" × 6 3/4"]. 98pp. [W-7488].

 GW-114 **Three Marches**. m. Phil Trajetta. Published by J.C. Beckel's Repertory of Music, No. 83 North 2nd Street, Philadelphia, PA. 1841. Non-pictorial. "Three Marches for the Piano Forte with an Accompaniment for the Flute, Composed for the American Conservatorio of Boston, A.D. 1800." "Collection 1, Revised and Improved by the Author [facsimile signature]." 6pp. Page 2: *United States March*. Page 3: **President's March**. Page 4: **Washington's Dead March**. Page 6: Blank.

 GW-115 **Washington's March**. Published by C.H. Keith, Nos. 67 and 69 Court Street, Boston, MA. [1834-1846]. Non-pictorial. Number "82" at bottom of page 1. 2pp. Page 2:

 GW-116(A) **Oh Susanna**. a. Charles Grobe, Op. 30. Published by Lee & Walker, No. 162 Chesnut Street, Philadelphia, PA. 1849. B/w non-pictorial geometric design border. "Salut A' Washington or Gems of the South, Six Favorite Melodies with Variations for the Piano Forte." "A Mademoiselle Emma Virginia Welsh."
 (B) **Dearest Mae**. Op. 125. 8pp.
 (C) **Old Uncle Ned**.
 (D) **Mary Blane**. Op. 127. 6pp.
 (E) **Rosa Lee**.
 (F) **Virginia Rose Bud**. Op. 129. 8pp.

 GW-117 **General Washington's March** [At the Battle of Trenton]. In: *The Fifer's Companion, Containing Instructions for Playing the Fife and A Collection of Music, Consisting of Marches, Airs, &c., With Seconds Added, No. 1*, page 36, Number 76. Printed by Joshua Cushing for Cushing & Appleton, Salem, MA. [1805]. [8 5/8" × 10 3/4"]. 76pp. [W-2790].

 GW-118 **God Bless The Name Of Washington** (Patriotic Song). w. George Cooper. m. J.P. Skelly. Published by J. Schott, No. 52 East Fourth Street, New York, NY. 1889. B/w litho of flowers, geometric designs. 6pp. Pages 2 and 6: Blank.

 GW-119 **The Grave Of Washington**. w. Marshall S. Pike. m. L.V.H. Crosby. Published by Oliver Ditson, No. 115 Washington Street, Boston, MA. 1846. B/w non-pictorial geometric designs. "Respectfully Dedicated to Washington Elliott, Esq. (of Bath, ME)." "Composed and Sung by the Harmoneons." [V-1: Song] [V-2: Quartette]. 6pp. Pages 2 and 6: Blank.

GW-120 The Men Of 76 (Centennial Song and Chorus). w. George Cooper. m. Harrison Millard. Published by W.H. Ewald & Brother, No. 136 Newark Avenue, Jersey City, NJ. 1875. [V-1: Bk/w/gd] [V-2: B/w] lithos of George Washington crossing the Delaware River, monument, flags, eagle, two women, geometric designs. 6pp. Page 2: Blank. Page 6: Advertising.

GW-121 Washington's March (With Brilliant Variations). m. Charles Grobe, Op. 414. Published by Lee & Walker, No. 188 Chesnut Street, Philadelphia, PA. 1854. B/w litho of shield, flag, axes, liberty hat. "Composed and respectfully dedicated to General George Cadwalader." "Semper Honor Nomenque Tuum Landesque Manebunt — Your honor, your name, your praises Shall ever remain." 8pp. Pages 2 and 8: Blank.

GW-122 American Medley. a. Charles Grobe, Op. 1348. Published by Oliver Ditson & Company, No. 277 Washington Street, Boston, MA. 1867. B/w hand Colored litho of George Washington, flags, eagle, sword, two women. "Music of the Union." "A Selection of American National Airs, Arranged for Piano." Price circle — "7 1/2." 10pp. Pages 2 and 10: Blank.

GW-123 American Medley. a. Charles Grobe, Op. 1348. Published by Oliver Ditson & Company, No. 271 Washington Street, Boston, MA. [1861?]. N/c litho of George Washington, flags, eagle, sword, two women. [V-1: "Music of the Union." "A Medley on American National Airs, Arranged for Piano"] [V-2: "American National Airs, Arranged for Piano"]. "6." 10pp.

GW-124 Seven Songs For The Harpsichord Or Forte Piano. w.m. Francis Hopkinson. Publish'd [sic] & sold by J. Dobson, Philadelphia, PA. [1788]. Non-pictorial. 12pp. Page 3: "Dedication: To His Excellency George Washington, Esquire ... F. Hopkinson. Philadelphia, Nov. 20, 1788." [S/U, p. 403].

GW-125 Washington's Call From The Grave (Patriotic Song and Chorus). w.m. C.H. Goldey. Published by William Dressler, No. 927 Broadway, New York, NY. 1863. B/w litho of George Washington. "To the Memory of George Washington." "Ye sons of America hark now to my call, list North, South, East, West, with one mind list ye all. 'Tis the voice of thy Father that calls from the grave, 'Tis the Spirit of Washington comes his Country to save." 6pp. Pages 2 and 6: Blank.

GW-126 George Washington (A Patriotic Song and Chorus). w. John F. Cowan. m. Horatio C. King. Published by Norman L. Munro, No. 74 Beekman Street, New York, NY. [ca. 188-]. B/w litho of floral wreath. "Free with *The New York Family Story*, No. 255." 4pp. Page 2: "To Mr. George Werrenrath." Page 4: Advertising.

GW-127 Sacred Dirges, Hymns And Anthems. m. A "Citizen of Massachusetts" [Oliver Holden]. Printed by I. Thomas & E.T. Andrews, No. 45 Newbury Street, Boston, MA. [1800]. B/w engraving of an urn — "Born Feb. 22, 1732, Died at Mount Vernon, Dec. 14, 1799, Aged 68." "The just shall be had in everlasting remembrance." "Commemorative of the death of General George Washington, the guardian of his country and the friend of man. An original composition." 24pp. [S/U, p. 366].

GW-128 The Washington Quadrilles. m. Mr. P. Brown (Leader and Director of the New York Cotillion Band). Published by Thomas Birch, New York, NY. [184-?]. Non-pictorial geometric designs. "As Danced at All The Grand Balls, Composed and Arranged to the Most Admired Figures and Respectfully Dedicated to the members of the Soiree Society at Concert Hall." Page 2: *Benton Cotillion*.

GW-129   Hail Columbia. In: *Six Military and Patriotic Illustrated Songs, Elaborately Colored in a Novel Form, Series No. 1.* Published by Chas. Magnus, No. 12 Franklin Street, New York, NY. [ca. 1863]. [5 1/2" × 8"]. Hand Colored litho of George Washington. Followed on page one by *America*. Page 12: Advertising.

GW-130(A)   Centennial Hymn (Solo or Chorus). w. William Fenimore. m. W.P. Fenimore. Published by Louis Meyer, No. 1413 Chestnut Street, Philadelphia, PA. 1876. N/c litho of national flags, eagle, shield, George Washington. "The Centennial." 8pp. Pages 2, 7 and 8: Blank. Page 3: "To The American People."

(B)   Grand International Medley (Potpourri Internationale, Containing the National Airs of All the Principal Nations of the World). m. C.F. Blandner. "For Piano."

(C)   Star Spangled Banner (Variations). a. C.F. Blandner.

(D)   Hail Columbia (Variations). a. C.F. Blandner. 8pp. Pages 2 and 8: Blank.

(E)   Columbia The Gem Of The Ocean. a. C.F. Blandner.

(F)   The Heroes Of The Republic (Song and Chorus). w.m. E. Fox.

(G)   Centennial March. m. F. Losse.

GW-131   That Banner A Hundred Years Old. w. B. Devere. m. Eddie Fox. Published by F.W. Helmick, No. 278 West 6th Street, Cincinnati, OH. 1876. N/c litho of George Washington, Continental troops, Miss "Liberty" with flag. "As Sung by Sig. Abecco." 6pp. Page 2: Blank. Page 6: Advertising.

GW-132   The Slow, Passing Bell (Solo and Quartette). w. Mrs. Emily M. Pratt. m. W.J. Landram. Published by Millet & Son, No. 329 Broadway, New York, NY. 1855. Non-pictorial. "As Sung by the National Vocalists." "NOTE: As a testimony of respect to the memory of Washington, the Boats in Passing Mount Vernon toll their Bells." "To the Hon. Charles Morehead of Kentucky and the Friends of the American Union." 6pp. Pages 2 and 6: Blank.

GW-133(A)   The Little Bronze Button. w. Joshua Smith. m. A. Beirly. Published by The S. Brainard's Sons Company, No. 20 East 17th, New York, NY. 1892. R/w/b drawings of George Washington, Ulysses S. Grant, Abraham Lincoln, Phil Sheridan, William T. Sherman. 6pp. Page 2: Blank. Page 6: Advertising.

(B)   The Boys In Blue Are Growing Grey.

(C)   Where Is The Heart Of A Soldier? w.m. E.A. Oakley.

(D)   Unfurl The Grand Old Stars And Stripes. w.m. E. McElroy.

(E)   Just At The Dawn Of Day. w.m. F.K. Van Tassel.

GW-134(A)   American Piano Music Collection. Published by Oliver Ditson & Company, Boston, MA. 1885. N/c litho of George Washington, "Capitol at Washington," "Independence Hall, Phila.," Statue of "Liberty," cherubs representing—"Agriculture," "Music," "Poetry," "Commerce," "Art," "Science." 220pp. [Includes—**Blaine's Grand March** and **Cleveland's Grand March**].

(B)   American Dance Music Collection.

GW-135   Hail Columbia. Published by S.T. Gordon, No. 706 Broadway, New York, NY. 1861. R/w/b litho by P.S. Duval & Son of a Union soldier, night camp scene, flags, eagle—"E Pluribus Unum." "National Melodies by Celebrated Composers." List of other songs in series—"Vocal" and "Instrumental." "3d series."

GW-136   The Virginia Corlitza. m. F. Dollinger. Published by F.D. Benteen, Baltimore, MD. [ca. 1858]. Gd/bk/w litho by A. Hoen & Company of a statue of George "Washington" on horseback, smaller statues of Robert E.

"Lee" and Thomas "Jefferson." "As Performed at C.A. McEvoy's Soirees, Richmond, Va." Page 2: Blank.

GW-137 The Army Of Liberty. m. Air: *I'm Glad I'm in this Army*. In: *Six Military and Patriotic Illustrated Songs, Elaborately Colored in a Novel Form, Series No. 1*. Published by Charles Magnus, No. 12 Franklin Street, New York, NY. [ca. 1863]. [5 1/2" × 8"]. Hand Colored litho of George Washington over a map of the United States. 12pp. [Different songs from GW-129].

GW-138 Mount Vernon Waltz. m. E.L. Ripley. Published by Oliver Ditson & Company, No. 277 Washington Street, Boston, MA. 1857. B/w silver and gold tinted J.H. Bufford's litho of "Mount Vernon," geometric designs. "Composed and Respectfully Dedicated to the Ladies of the Mt. Vernon Association." 10pp. Pages 2 and 10: Blank.

GW-139 Hail Columbia (A National Song). w. Joseph Hopkinson. a. G.J. Webb. Published by Oliver Ditson, No. 115 Washington Street, Boston, MA. [183-?]. B/w litho of George Washington, facsimile signature. Title above litho. 6pp. Page 3: History of the song.

GW-140 The Washington Songster. Published by Turner & Fisher, Chatham Street, New York, NY. [ca. 184-?]. [3 1/8" × 4 1/4"]. Cover Blank? 256pp. Page 5-6: Lithos of George Washington.

GW-141 Hail Columbia (A National Song). w. Joseph Hopkinson. a. G.J. Webb. Published by Oliver Ditson, No. 115 Washington Street, Boston, MA. [1844-1857]. B/w litho of George Washington, facsimile signature but no title on the cover. 6pp. Page 3: History of the song.

GW-142 Virginia Washington Monument Grand March. m. James E. Magruder. Published by Miller & Beacham, Baltimore, MD. 1858. Gd/bk/w litho by A. Hoen & Company of a statue of George "Washington" on horseback, smaller statues of Robert E.

GW-139

"Lee" and Thomas "Jefferson." "Composed in honor of the erection of the Washington statue, Feb. 22, 1858." 6pp. Page 2: Blank. Page 6: Advertising.

GW-143(A) Martha Washington Grand Waltz. m. Rud Aronson. Published by J.E. Ditson & Company, No. 922 Chestnut Street, Philadelphia, PA. 1876. B/w litho of Martha Washington. "To the Ladies of America." 12pp. Pages 2 and 12: Blank.

(B) Martha Washington March. m. E. Mack.

GW-144 Martha Washington (Gavotte). m. Rudolph Aronson. Published by Edward Aronson & Company, Broadway & 39th Street, New York, NY. 1889. B/w litho by Thomas & Wayne of Martha Washington. "To the Ladies of America." 8[?]pp. Page 2: Blank.

GW-145 The Dream Of Washington. w.m. Major J. Barton (Of The Continental Vocalists). Published by J.S. White & Company, Marshall, MI. 1869. Litho by Ehrgott & Forbriger of George Washington, Miss Liberty, Miss Columbia

and Miss Justice. "An American National Song." "Respectfully Inscribed to Bernard Covert, Composer of *The Sword of Bunker Hill*."
GW-146(A) Washington's (Old) March. a. Sep. Winner. Published by J.E. Ditson & Company, No. 922 Chestnut Street, Philadelphia, PA. 1876. B/w litho of George Washington. "Written in Honor of the American Centennial, 1776-1876." 6pp. Pages 2 and 6: Blank.
(B) Washington's (New) March. m. Rud. Aronson.
GW-147 The Bird Of Washington (Song and Chorus). w.m. James G. Clark (Author of *Rock of Liberty, Joys of My Childhood, O Take Me From The Festal Throng*). Published by Henry Tolman, No. 219 Washington Street, Boston, MA. 1857. B/w engraving of Miss "Liberty," eagle, geometric designs. "To my friend Anson G. Chester, Esq." 6pp. Pages 2 and 6: Blank.
GW-148 The Puritan's Mistake. Published by Oliver Ditson, No. 135 Washington Street, Boston, MA. 1844. B/w lithos by Thayer & Company of George Washington, Bishop White[?], Pilgrims landing at Plymouth — "1620." "A Church Adorned With Bishops — A State Without A King." 4pp.
GW-149 Continental March (Sons of 1776). m. James E. Magruder. Published by Miller & Beacham, Baltimore, MD. 1861. B/w sepia tinted litho [horizontal format] by A. Hoen of a reproduction of the painting of George Washington crossing the Delaware River. Page 2: Blank.
GW-150 Vive La Republique. m. Herrman S. Saroni. Published by William Hall & Son, No. 239 Broadway, New York, NY. 1848. [V-1: R/w/bl/be/gd] [V-2: B/w] litho by Sarony & Major of George Washington and General LaFayette, U.S. and French flags, crown, liberty hat — "1776." Banner — "Liberte, Equalite, Fraternite." "An Offering from the United States to the National Republic of France."

GW-150

"1776-1848." "Composed For the Piano Forte." "Price in colors 50 cts. Nett [sic], without 38." 10pp. Page 2: Blank. Page 6: *La Marseillaise*.
GW-151(A) Washington Elm (March). m. Charles Moulton. Published by G.D. Russell & Company, No. 126 Tremont Street, Boston, MA. 1871. B/w litho of elm tree, man and boy, sign inscribed "Under this tree Washington first took command of the American Army, Jan. 31, 1773." "To Francis Peabody." 6pp. Pages 2 and 6: Blank.
(B) Washington Elm (Quickstep).
GW-152 Washington's Centennial Grand March. m. Gustave Lindh. Published by Richard A. Saalfield, No. 41 Union Square, New York, NY. 1889. B/w litho of George Washington, stars, geometric design border. Number "1653" at top of cover. 6pp. Pages 2 and 6: Blank.
GW-153 Washington (Centennial Song). w.m. J.D. McCarthy. a. Alberto Himan. Published by The Washington Souvenir Company, No. 35 Frankfort Street, New York, NY. Copyright 1889 by

J.D. McCarthy. Non-pictorial geometric designs. "To the American people." 4pp. Page 2: "Patriotic Song." Page 4: Blank.

GW-154 The Stamp Galop. m. Arthur O'Leary. Published by Oliver Ditson & Company, No. 277 Washington Street, Boston, MA. 1864. Litho by J.H. Bufford of 43 postage stamps from every country in the world including a George Washington stamp from the United States. 6pp. Pages 2 and 6: Blank.

GW-155 Hail Columbia. Published by S.T. Gordon, No. 706 Broadway, New York, NY. [ca. 186-]. R/w/bl/gd litho of U.S. and French flags. "National Songs." "1st Series." "Sung by Madlle. T. Parodi." List of titles in series.

GW-156 Hail Columbia. Published by Oliver Ditson & Company, No. 277 Washington Street, Boston, MA. 1861. R/w/bl/bk litho of crossed U.S. and French flags. "National Music" List of titles in "Vocal" and "Instrumental" categories.

GW-157 Hail Columbia. a. Ch. K. Published by Lee & Walker, No. 722 Chesnut Street, Philadelphia, PA. [ca. 1860]. R/w/bl/gd litho of crossed U.S. and French flags. "National Songs." "Sung by Madlle. T. Parodi." List of other titles in series. 6pp. Pages 2 and 6: Blank.

GW-158 Hail Columbia. Published by Henry Tolman & Company, No. 291 Washington Street, Boston, MA. 1861. R/w/b litho of U.S. flag. "National Melodies." List of other songs in series.

GW-159 Hail Columbia. a. Albert W. Berg. Published by Firth, Pond & Company, No. 547 Broadway, New York, NY. 1861. R/w/b litho of crossed flags. "National Songs of America." List of other songs in series.

GW-160 Hail Columbia. [V-1: No Arranger noted] [V-2: w. Joseph Hopkinson. a. Thomas Oesten, Op. 148]. Published by Oliver Ditson & Company, No. 277 Washington Street, Boston, MA. 1861. R/w/b litho of crossed U.S. and French flags. "National Music." List of other titles in series. 6pp. [V-1: Page 2: "Note by Publisher: This song written in the summer of 1798, to oblige a young friend of the Author's, who was a singer at the theatre in Philadelphia. It was arranged by a member of the orchestra to the *President's March*, which was the name of the original music. It has since been adopted by common consent as the National Anthem of America. This is the only authentic copy of this song extant, it having been corrected by the Author in the year 1841. Judge Hopkinson died on the 15th of January, 1842." Page 6: Blank. [V-2: Pages 2 and 6: Blank].

GW-161 The Washington Centennial March. m. William C. Rehm. Published by Hitchcock's Music Stores, No. 283 Sixth Avenue, New York, NY. 1889. [V-1: B/w] [V-2: Bl/w] litho of crossed flags, geometric designs. "1789-1889." [V-2: "Arranged for Four Hands" by William Dresser]. 6pp. Pages 2 and 6: Blank.

GW-162 The Resting Place Of Washington (A Monody). w.m. David T. Shaw. Published by Lee & Walker, No. 188 Chestnut Street, Philadelphia, PA. [ca. 1845]. B/w litho by B.W. Thayer & Co. of the tomb of George Washington. "For the Piano Accompaniment to this song, Mr. Shaw is indebted to Mr. F. Weiland." "Composed and arranged for the Piano, Most Respectfully Dedicated to General George Cadwallader." 6pp. Page 6: Blank.

GW-163 Washington! w.m. R.G. Loomis. Published by J.G. Osbourn's Music Saloon, No. 112 South 3rd Street, Philadelphia, PA. [ca. 1832]. B/w litho of George Washington, cherub and geometric border. "The Star of the West." "Price 25 cents nett [sic]." Page 2: Blank.

GW-164 Hyperion Polka. m. Henry T. Oates. Published by Oates & Brothers, Nos. 234 and 236 King Street, Charleston, SC. 1850. B/w litho of "Residence of H.W. Longfellow, Cambridge,

Mass., formerly Washington's Head Quarters." "Composed and Respectfully dedicated to Prof. Henry Wadsworth Longfellow." 6pp. Pages 2 and 6: Blank.

GW-165(A) America's Centennial Grand March. m. D.L. Downing. Published by C.H. Ditson & Company, No. 711 Broadway, New York, NY. 1876. N/c litho of George Washington, Statue of Liberty, Capitol building, Independence Hall, flags, cherubs labeled — "Agriculture, Music, Poetry, Commerce, Art, Science." 6pp. Pages 2 and 6: Blank.

(B) America's Centennial Ode (Chorus). m. Harrison Millard.

(C) Centennial Waltzes. m. H. Fliege, Op. 146. 8pp. Page 8: Blank.

(D) Medley Of National Airs. a. Chas. Grobe.

GW-166(A) Souvenir De Arlington (Polka). m. Hans Krummacher. Published by Hilbus & Hitz, Washington, DC. 1855. B/w beige tinted litho by A. Hoen from a "Daguerreotype by B.P. Paige" of George Washington Park Custis, facsimile signature, geometric designs. "Dedicated to George Washington Park Custis." 6pp. Pages 2 and 6: Blank.

(B) Souvenir De Arlington (Schottishe).

GW-167 Shin-Plaster Jig. m. Jo. Benson. Published by C.D. Benson, Nashville, TN. 1864. Bk/w/gd litho of a "United States Twenty Five Cents Fractional" currency note with a b/w illustration of George Washington. "Exchangeable for Green Backs or any other kind of money." 4pp. Page 4: Blank.

GW-168 Washington (A Patriotic Song and Chorus). w. E.E. Hulfish. m. H. Avery. Published by Lee & Walker, No. 722 Chesnut Street, Philadelphia, PA. 1858. B/w litho of shield, flags, liberty cap, geometric designs. "As sung with applause by J.A. Basquin, Esq. of Sandford's Opera Troupe." 6pp. Pages 2 and 6: Blank.

GW-169 Our Country Now

GW-167

And Ever (A Patriotic Song). w. Reymond J. Cunnynham. m. Karl Merz. Published by Horace Waters, No. 333 Broadway, New York, NY. 1860. B/w litho by Stackpole of banner, cherubs with a portrait of George Washington. "To my friend, William Riddle, Esq." 6pp. Pages 2 and 6: Blank.

GW-170 The Old Pear Tree (Or Washington's Head Quarters) (National Melody). w. George Blake King. m. Charles M. King. Published by Firth & Hall, No. 1 Franklin Square, New York, NY. 1840. B/w litho of house, tree. "Washington tho' Dead in every bosom lives the Breath of Honor — That Virtuous Freedom Lives — Anon." 4pp. Page 2: "The Headquarters of Washington the Liberator is the house occupied by Messers Firth & Hall in the rear of whose premises blooms this old pear tree, a memento of the Father of His Country."

GW-171 If Washington Was Living Now (Centennial Song and Chorus). w. Samuel N. Mitchell. m. Charles E. Prior. Published by F.W. Helmick, No. 278 West 6th Street, Cincinnati, OH. 1876. Gd/w/bl star border. "To Charles

Carroll, Esq., Providence, R.I." 6pp. Page 2: Blank. Page 6: Advertising.

GW-172 **Hail Columbia**. In: *The Black Swan Set*. Published by Winner & Shuster, No. 110 North Eighth Street, Philadelphia, PA. 1855. Non-pictorial. "Winner's Plain Cotillions; These sets have all the proper figures in appropriate places, and are so arranged as to be easily understood, as the music is written out in full to prevent mistakes; also arranged in the easiest possible manner."

GW-173 **Calendar Galop**. m. A. Typo. Published by William A. Pond & Company, No. 547 Broadway, New York, NY. 1875. B/w litho of George Washington, Revolutionary War and Civil War soldier, flags, eagle, bell, Memorial Hall, Centennial Exhibition at Philadelphia, calendar for the year 1876. Chain-link border. "Declaration of Independence Centennial Anniversary 1776-1876." "In Union Is Strength." 6pp. Page 2: Blank.

GW-174 **Hail Columbia**. a. Samuel Jackson and George W. Warren. Published by G. Schirmer, No. 701 Broadway, New York, NY. [ca. 1876].

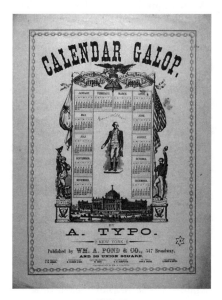

GW-173

B/w litho of flag. "2 American National Songs." List of other titles in series. "Vocal with Piano Accompaniment by Samuel Jackson." "Transcribed for the Piano by George W. Warren."

GW-175 **Young America** (4 Waltzes For The Nation). m. Eugene A. Wiener. Published by Horace Waters, No. 333 Broadway, New York, NY. 1860. B/w litho [horizontal format] by Endicott & Company of George and Martha Washington, "Lord Renfrew," eagle, U.S. and English flags, ribbon—"Let us hope that he may become a true hearted American citizen." Four waltzes: No. 1: *North*— No. 2: *South*— No. 3: *East*— No. 4: *West*. Also: No. 5: **The President's March**—*The President's March* is representing the new musical notation of Ernest Von Herringen." "Dedicated to Lord Renfrew." Page 2: Blank.

GW-176 **Let Washington Rest** (or Washington's Grave). w. J.H. Hewitt, Esqr. Published by F.D. Benteen, Baltimore, MD. 1889. B/w geometric design border. "Composed and Arranged for the Piano Forte." "25 cts. net." 4pp. Page 2: Blank.

GW-177 **The Last Words Of Washington** (Song). w. George P. Morris, Esq. m. J.R. Thomas. Published by Thaddeus Firth, No. 547 Broadway, New York, NY. 1862. B/w sepia tinted litho by Sarony, Major & Knapp of George Washington, stars, wreath frame. "Washington's farewell address will be found on the last page of this song." 6pp. Pages 2 and 6: Blank.

GW-178 **Inauguration March**. m. Albert D. Hubbard. Published by Albert D. Hubbard, No. 162 Ninth Avenue, New York, NY. 1889. Litho of flowers. "To the People of the United States." "In Commemoration of the 100th Anniversary of Washington's Inauguration." 6pp.

GW-179 **Columbia's Son** [V-1: Song] [V-2: March]. w. George Cooper. m. J.P. Skelly. Published by Charles W. Held, Brooklyn, NY. 1889. B/w litho of

George Washington. R/w/b title. "America's Great Centennial Song." 6pp. Pages 2 and 6: Blank.

GW-180 National Colonial Anthem (Of the United States of America). w.m. George K. Hamilton. Published by George K. Hamilton, Ladleton, Ulster County, NY. 1922. R/w/b drawings of "George Washington—1789-1797," "Thomas Jefferson—1801-1809," "Andrew Jackson—1829-1837," "The Colonial Congress," shield—"Declaration of Independence, July 4, 1776," crossed flags. 4pp. Page 4: Blank.

GW-181 Colonial National Anthem (Of the United States of America). w.m. George K. Hamilton. Published by George K. Hamilton, Ladelton, Ulster County, NY. Copyright 1919 and 1922. [Pre-1919 size]. R/w/b drawings of "George Washington—1789-1797," "Thomas Jefferson—1801-1809," "Andrew Jackson—1829-1837," view of the Colonial Congress, shield—"Declaration of Independence, July 4, 1776," crossed flags. 4pp. Page 4: Blank.

GW-182 Our Fathers, Where Were They? (United States of America National Anthem). w.m. Geo. K. Hamilton. Published by Hamilton, Montela, NY. 1919. R/w/b drawings of "George Washington—1789-1797," "Thomas Jefferson—1801-1809," "Andrew Jackson—1829-1837," view of the Colonial Congress, shield—"Declaration of Independence, July 4, 1776," crossed flags. 4pp. Page 4: Blank.

GW-183 Hail Columbia. Published by Oliver Ditson Company, Boston, MA. 1898. N/c drawing of soldier, sailor, flag. "Patriotic Songs." List of titles in the series.

GW-184 The Music That Washington Knew. e. William Arms Fisher. Published by Oliver Ditson Company, Inc., Boston, MA. 1931. [6 7/8" × 10 11/16"]. Bl/bl non-pictorial geometric designs. "A Program of Authentic Music, Vocal and Instrumental, with Historical Data, for Use of Schools, Musical Societies, Music Clubs and Historical Celebrations." 72pp.

GW-185 Hail Columbia. a. Samuel Jackson. Published by G. Schirmer, No. 701 Broadway, New York, NY. 1876. R/w/b crossed flags. "Only Correct Edition of the 2 National Songs." List of titles in series. "Vocal with Piano Accompaniment by Samuel Jackson."

GW-186(A) The Toast To George Washington. w.m. Francis Hopkinson. e. Oliver Strunk. Published by The United States George Washington Bicentennial Commission, Washington, DC. Copyright 1931 by Sol Bloom. Bl/w bust of George Washington. "Music from the Days of Washington." 4pp.

(B) Dance Music. m. Alexander Reinagle and Pierre Landrin Duport. 8pp.

(C) Album Of Military Marches. 12pp.

(D) A Collection Of Patriotic And Military Tunes, Piano And Dance Music, Songs And Operatic Airs. 76pp.

GW-187 The Music Of George Washington's Time [Booklet with Music]. Published by the United States George Washington Bicentennial Commission, Washington, DC. Copyright 1931 by Sol Bloom. [V-1: 6" × 9"] [V-2: 9 1/8" × 12"]. [V-1: B/w] [V-2: Bl/w] drawing of woman at piano, George Washington, flags, geometric designs. [V-1: 108pp] [V-2: 36pp].

GW-188 Music Associated With The Period Of The Formation Of The Constitution And The Inauguration Of George Washington. e. John T. Howard and Eleanor S. Brown. Published by United States Constitution Sesquicentennial Commission, Washington, DC. 1935. Bl/w drawing Miss Liberty, signers of the Constitution—"Washington-Hamilton-Madison-Franklin-Read-Sherman-Pickney-Livingston-Morris-King." "Composed for the Philadelphia Celebration of the Ratification of the

Constitution, July 4, 1788." "We The People, 1787-1937." 40pp.

GW-189 Rule Anglo-Saxia. w. James D. Ross. m. W. Karl Vincent. Published by Coupon Music Publishing Company, Boston, MA. Copyright 1897 and 1898 by James D. Ross. B/w drawings "George Washington," "Joe Howe" and "Gladstone"—"The Anglo Saxon Triumvirate." R/w/b drawing of crossed U.S. and English flags. "We Must Unite to Save the World For Freedom and Fair Trade." 6pp. Page 2: Blank. Page 6: Narrative.

GW-190 For Old Glory (March Song and Chorus). w. J. Cheever Goodwin. m. William Furst. Published by Howley, Haviland & Company, No. 4 East 20th Street, New York, NY. 1897. R/w/b drawing by Syd. Davies of George Washington, flag. 6pp.

GW-191 How Could Washington Be A Married Man (And Never, Never Tell a Lie?). w. Joe Goodwin and Ballard Macdonald. m. Al Piantadosi. Published by Shapiro, Bernstein & Company, Music Publishers, No. 224 West 47th Street, New York, NY. 1916. Bl/w photo of Evelyn Nesbit—"As Introduced by Evelyn Nesbit," geometric designs. 4pp. Page 4: Advertising for other music.

GW-192 Washington For-Ever (March, Two-Step or Song). w.m. C.A. Wicklund. a. Harry J. Lincoln. Published by Harry J. Lincoln Music Company, No. 930 North 19th Street, Philadelphia, PA. Copyright 1932 by C.A. Wicklund. R/w/b drawings of George Washington, U.S. map, Statue of Liberty, stripe corners. "George Washington Bicentennial Number." 6pp. Page 2: "To the American youths of Today and Tomorrow." Page 6: Blank.

GW-193 If I'm As Good As My Old Dad (That's Good Enough for Me). w.m. Cliff Odoms. Published by Longbrake & Edwards, No. 50 North 8th Street, Philadelphia, PA. 1912. R/w/b drawing by Cliff Odoms of George Washington, Abraham Lincoln, child, father, flags. Bl/w photo of "Rose Parker." 6pp. Page 2: "To my father." Page 6: Advertising for other music.

GW-194(A) Song Of Washington's Men (Quartet). w.m. Clark. Published by S. Brainard's Sons, Publishers, Cleveland, OH. 1885. N/c litho by Goes & Quensel of mounted soldiers. "Our National War Songs." List of other songs.

(B) Hail Columbia. a. Bruen.

GW-195 George Washington (A Patriotic Song). w. John F. Cowan. m. Horatio C. King. Published by Norman L. Munro in *The Family Story Paper*, No. 249, No. 74 Beekman Street, New York, NY. [ca. 188-]. B/w litho of George Washington and horse. "Free to all readers." 4pp. Page 4: Advertising for other music.

GW-196 If Washington Should Come To Life. w.m. George M. Cohan. Published by Jerry Vogel Music Company, No. 112 West 44th Street, New York, NY. and F.B. Haviland Publishing Company, No. 114 West 44th Street, New York, NY. 1938. R/w/b drawings by Barbelle

GW-189

illustrating famous George M. Cohen song titles — "*So Long Mary, Guess I'll Have To Telegraph My Baby, You're A Grand Old Flag, Give My Regards To Broadway, The Yankee Doodle Boy.*" Bl/w tinted photo of George M. Cohan. 6pp. Page 6: Advertising for other music.

GW-197 Pictures On The Flag. w. L.A. Barber. m. J. Fred Baldwin. Published by Cahn & Wagenen Music Publishing Company, No. 251 West 42nd Street, New York, NY. 1909. R/w/b drawings by McKinley of George Washington, Abraham Lincoln, Ulysses S. Grant and Robert E. Lee, eagles, flags, stripes. 6pp. Pages 2 and 6: Advertising for other music.

GW-198 By The Bright White Light Of The Moon. w. Beth Slater Whitson (Writer of *Meet Me Tonight, In Dreamland, Let Me Call You Sweetheart,* &c). m. Reuben J. Haskin (Composer of *Pianophiend, &c*). Published by Buckeye Music Publishing Company, New York, NY. 1914. Gy/w photo of Potomac River from a "View taken from Washington's home at Mt. Vernon." 6pp. Pages 2 and 6: Advertising for other Buckeye published music.

GW-199 General Washington's March. m. "Traditional Melody." a. James Hunter. Published by Carl Fischer, Inc., No. 56 Cooper Square, New York, NY. 1932. Gn/w drawing of George Washington, Colonial family. "Washington Bicentennial Series." "For Violin and Piano (First Position) Including a Teacher's Second Violin Part." "Pupil's part printed in large notes." 6pp. Page 6: Advertising.

GW-200 For Old Glory (March Song and Chorus). w. J. Cheever Goodwin. m. William Furst. Published as a "Musical Supplement of *The New York Journal and Advertiser,* Feb. 27, 1898." Copyright 1897 by Howley, Haviland & Company. R/w/b flag design. B/w litho of George Washington crossing the Delaware River. "Sung by Dorothy Morton, Whitney Opera Company, and the Herald Square Theatre, NY." "Selected by Reginold DeKoven." 8pp. Pages 2, 3, 6 and 7: B/w lithos of military scenes. Pages 4, 5 and 8: Bl/w Naval scenes.

GW-201 Washington And Lee Swing. w.m. C.A. Robbins, T.W. Allen and M.W. Sheafe. Published by Robbins Music Corporation, No. 799 Seventh Avenue, New York, NY. 1910. [Edition ca. 193-]. Bl/w drawing of George Washington and Robert E. Lee as part of the University logo — "Washington and Lee University, Virginia, 1782-1871." 6pp. Pages 2 and 6: Blank.

GW-202 Pan-American (March and Two Step). m. James H. Austin. Published as a musical supplement to the *New York Sunday Press,* Sunday, May 26th, 1901, by Richard A. Saalfield, No. 1123 Broadway, New York, NY. Bk/r/w drawing of George Washington and Simon Bolivar, United States, South America, geometric design border. "Respectfully dedicated to the Royal Cycle Club." 4pp.

GW-203 The Flag Of Washington. w.m. W.J. Newton. Published by Henry White, No. 929 "F" Street, Washington, DC. 1899. Non-pictorial. "Written expressly for the children of the Abbott School of Washington, DC., and adapted by them as the Abbott School Flag Song." Published with *Gloria Old Glory,* Written expressly for the children of the Brent School of Washington, DC., and adapted by them as the Brent School Flag Song."

GW-204 The Road To Victory. w.m. Frank Loesser. Published by request of the U.S. Treasury Department in connection with the Third War Loan by Saunders Pubs. Sole selling agent Great Pacific Music Sales, No. 1515 North Vine Street, Hollywood, CA. 1943. Photo of War Bonds with pictures of George Washington, Thomas Jefferson and Abraham Lincoln. "Entire proceeds of this song to be turned over to the National War Fund."

GW-205 Washington's Birthday Entertainment Book (Songs, Drills, Concert Pieces). w. Lizzie De Armond, Belle Kellogg Towne, Laura Roundtree Smith "and others." m. T. Martin Towne, Edward L. Channing and John P. Hamilton. Published by David C. Cook Publishing Company, Elgin, IL. 1908. [6 1/16" × 8 1/16"]. Bk/y drawing of George Washington, flags, eagle floral and geometric designs. "In Honor of Our Nation's Hero." "For Young People of the Day School and the Sunday School." 36pp. Page 36: Advertising.

GW-206 The Flag Of The U.S.A.. (March). w.m. Charles A. Meyers. Published by Charles A. Meyers, No. 145 North Clark Street, Chicago, IL. 1912. R/w/b flag design. Bl/w drawing of Martha Washington. 6pp. Page 6: Advertising for other music.

GW-207 America First (March and Two Step). m. E. Anthony Ryson. Published by Carl Fisher, Nos. 6-12 4th Avenue, New York, NY. 1908. Litho of George Washington on horseback, eagle, crossed flags, anchor, branches. 6pp. Page 6: Advertising for other music.

GW-208 When The World Bows At Washington's Grave. w. E. Chapin Gard. m. A.J. Willey. Copyright 1917 by Chapin Gard and A.J. Willey. Litho of George Washington, flag, city, ships. 6pp.

GW-209 Legionaries March. m. John Philip Sousa. Published by Theodore Presser Company, No. 1712 Chestnut Street, Philadelphia, PA. 1931. Drawings of George "Washington," "La Fayette," "Mt. Vernon." "1776-1931." "Dedicated to the International Overseas Exposition, Paris." "Piano Solo." 6pp. Page 6: Advertising for other John Philip Sousa compositions.

GW-210 The Song Of The Hatchet. w.m. Archibald Humboldt. a. Effie Louise Koogle. Published by March Brothers, Publishers, Nos. 208-210-212 Wright Avenue, Lebanon, OH. 1909. [Post-1919 size]. Gn/w non-pictorial. 6pp. Page 2: Blank. Page 6: Advertising for other March Brothers published music.

GW-211 Just Like Washington Crossed The Delaware, General Pershing Will Cross The Rhine. w. Howard Johnson. m. George W. Meyer. Published as a "War Song" supplement to *The Boston Sunday Advertiser*, June 23, 1918. Copyright 1917 by Leo Feist. [9" × 11"]. B/w photo of General Pershing. B/w reproduction of the painting of George Washington crossing the Delaware River. "Theme Suggested by Elinore and Williams." 4pp.

GW-212 The Bold Volunteer. w.m. Richard Boyle. a. Eric Steiner. Published by Belwin, Inc., Rockville Center, L.I., NY. 1961. Bl/w/s silhouette of George Washington, stars. "Song of the American Revolution, Dedicated to Geo. Washington." "Piano Solo with Words." 4pp. Page 4: Advertising.

GW-213 All About George Washington. w.m. Alan Gray and M. Campbell. Published by Eldridge Entertainment House, Inc., Franklin, OH. 1929. Br/be drawing of three children, soldiers. "Eldridge Entertainment and Action Songs for Children." List of other titles in series. 4pp. Page 4: Blank.

GW-214 When Washington Was A Boy (An Opera for Young People). w.m. John Mokrejs. Published by Clayton F. Summy, No. 64 East Van Buren Street, Chicago, IL. [ca. 1931]. [7 3/4" × 10 3/4"]. Be/bl drawing of hatchet, cherries, geometric design border. 102pp.

GW-215 A Hymn Of Thanksgiving. m. Ira D. Sankey. w. Fanny J. Crosby. Published as a "Supplement to *The New York World*, November 26, 1899. Bl/w photos of Ira D. Sankey and Fanny J. Crosby. Bl/y/w drawing of woman holding banner of song title. "Composed & Written expressly for the Thanksgiving number of the *New York World*." 4pp. Page 4: Narrative on "The

American Thanksgiving" and George "Washington's [Thanksgiving] Proclamation, 1785."

GW-216 Washington Birthday March. w.m. Mary Pickens Opie. Published by E.F. Droop & Sons Company, No. 1300 "G" Street, N.W., Washington, DC. Copyright 1931 by Mary Pickens Opie. R/w/b drawing of flags. Bl/w photo of a sculpture of George Washington. "In Celebration of the 200th Birthday Anniversary of the Father of our Country." "1732-1932." "Arranged for Orchestra and Band." 6pp. Page 2: Blank. Page 3: "To Our First Great Citizen and to Every Loyal American." Page 6: Advertising for other music.

GW-217 Silent Sentinel. w. Chanera. m. Godfre Ray King. a. Vinton and Virginia La Ferrera. Published by Saint Germain Press Company, P.O. Box 1133, Chicago, IL. 1939. N/c drawing of The Washington Monument, cherry blossoms. 16pp. Pages 2, 10, 12 and 15: Blank. Page 11: Dedication. Page 16: Y/bl/w logo — "AIM" and "Music of the Spheres."

GW-218 The Man We Will Always Love. w. Charles Horwitz. m. Fred'k. V. Bowers. Published as the "Music Section, Hearst's *Boston Sunday American*, February 18, 1906." Copyright 1903 by Jos. W. Stern & Company, owners of the copyright. R/w/b drawing of George Washington, woman, flags. "Published by permission of owners of the copyright." 4pp.

GW-219 There's A Million Heroes In Each Corner Of The U.S.A. w. Sam M. Lewis and Joe Young. m. Maurice Abrahams. Published by Kalmar Puck & Abrahams Consolidated, Inc., Music Publishers, No. 1 Strand Theatre Building, Broadway at 47th Street, New York, NY. 1917. Be/bk/w drawings by Barbelle of George Washington and Abraham Lincoln. Be/bk photo of "Belle Barker." 4pp. Page 4: Advertising.

GW-220 Fleur-De-Lis (Song). w. Stanley Murphy. m. Harry Tierney. Published by Jerome H. Remick, New York, NY 1918. R/w/b drawing of George Washington, General Lafayette, French and U.S. solders, fleur-de-lis, stripe border. 4pp. Page 4: Advertising.

GW-221 Tribute To The National Guards, Army And Navy (Patriotic Song and Military March). w.m. B.A. Koellhoffer. Published by B.A. Koellhoffer, No. 550 South 10th Street, Newark, NJ. 1917. R/w/bl/br drawings by Pfeiffer of soldier, sailor, eagle, shield, stars, George Washington. 4pp. Page 4: Advertising.

GW-222 The Flag That Has Never Known Defeat. w. Charles Love Benjamin and George Davison Sutton. m. Mary Dowling Sutton. Published by Jos. W. Stern & Co., No. 45 East 20th Street, New York, NY. 1898. R/w/b flag. B/w photos/drawings of George "Washington — 1776," Winfield "Scott — 1846," Ulysses S. "Grant — 1861," Admirals "Dewey — 1898," "Farragut — 1861" and "Perry — 1812." "The New Star Spangled Banner." 6pp. Page 2: Blank. Page 6: Advertising.

GW-223 America First (Is Our Battle Cry! 'Tis the Land We Love). w. J. Will Callahan. m. Eddie Gray. Published by Frank K. Root & Company, Chicago, IL. 1916. R/w/bk drawing of George Washington — "First in War, First in Peace, First in the Hearts of His Countrymen." 6pp. Pages 2 and 6: Advertising.

GW-224 My Dream Of The U.S.A. w.m. Leonard Chick, Charles Roth and Ted Snyder. Published by Mills Music, Mills Building, Nos. 148-150 West 46th Street, New York, NY. 1931. Bl/bk/w drawing of George Washington, facsimile signature. "Born Feb. 22, 1732 — Died Dec. 14, 1799." 6pp. Pages 2 and 6: Advertising. Page 3: "Dedicated to the memory of Francis Scott Key." Page 6: Advertising.

GW-225 My Washington Grand. w.m. Lawrence Stoddard Graebing. Published by Lawrence Stoddard Graebing, P.O. Box 1907, Washington, DC. 1930. Br/be drawing of George Washington, geometric designs. "Dedicated to the United States of America." 8pp. + insert. Insert is a facsimile letter from Lawrence Stoddard Graebing on George Washington. Pages 2, 7 and 8: Blank.

GW-226 America Rejoice (George Washington Bicentennial Anniversary Song). w.m. Theodore Hoffmann. Published by Theodore Hoffmann, No. 1439 Foxhall Road, NW., Washington, DC. 1932. N/c drawing of George Washington. "1732-1932." 6pp. Pages 2 and 6: Blank.

GW-227 Valley Forge March. w. James Francis Cooke. m. Edwin Franco Goldman. Published by Theodore Presser Company, No. 1712 Chestnut Street, Philadelphia, PA. 1933. Bl/w drawing of George Washington, soldier, stars. List of arrangements available. 6pp. Page 2: "To my friend Dr. James Francis Cooke." Page 6: Advertising.

GW-228 Live On! Washington. w.m. C.C. Chapman. a. Mario Fellom. Copyright 1932 by Loyola University, New Orleans, LA. R/w/b silhouette of George Washington, eagle, shield, star and stripe background. "Dedicated to the Memory of George Washington in Honor of the 200th Anniversary of his Birth." 6pp. Page 6: Blank.

GW-229 If It's Good Enough For Washington (It's Good Enough for Me) (Song). w. Ren Shields. m. Percy Wenrich. Published by Jerome Remick & Company, New York, NY. 1918. Bl/w/gn De Takacs drawing of a Statue of George Washington. 6pp. Page 6: Advertising for other Remick published music.

GW-230 Father Of The Land We Love. w.m. George M. Cohan. Published by The United States George Washington Bicentennial Commission, Washington, DC. Copyright 1931 by Sol Bloom. N/c drawing by "James Montgomery Flagg" of George Washington, map of the United States, stars. "Written for the American people by George M. Cohan to Commemorate the Two Hundredth Anniversary of the Birth of George Washington." 6pp. Page 2: "Story of Washington." Page 6: Vignettes of George Washington's life.

GW-231 George Washington Comes To Dinner. w. George Washington. m. Martin Kalmanoff. Published by Carl Fischer, Inc., Cooper Square, New York, NY. 1950. R/w drawing of table, place settings, stripes. "Text adapted from George Washington's *Rules of Civility and Decent Behaviour in Company & Conversation*." 12pp. Page 2: "To my mother Anna Kalmanoff who made me manners-conscious." Page 12: Advertising for other songs.

GW-232 For France And Liberty. w. J. and A. Flynn. m. Al Piantadosi. Published by Al Piantadosi & Company, Inc., Astor Theatre Building, New York, NY. 1917. [V-1: R/w] [V-2: Bl/w] drawings by Starmer of "George Washington," "LaFayette," Miss "Liberty." 4pp. Page 4: Advertising.

GW-233 Washington's Hacking Hatchet (Song). w. Marie Irish. m. Edna Randolph Worrell. Published by Paine Publishing Company, Dayton, OH. 1922. Br/be drawing of a hatchet. 6pp. Page 6: Advertising for other Paine Publishing Company music.

GW-234 Spirit Of The U.S.A. m. Hazel Cobb. Published by The Willis Music Company, Cincinnati, OH. 1937. R/w/b drawing of George Washington, wagon, flags, plane, ship. "John Thompson's Student Series for the Piano." "Piano Four Hands." List of other titles in series. 6pp. Page 6: Advertising.

GW-235 You're A Grand Old Flag. w.m. George M. Cohan. Published by Maurice Richmond Music Company, No. 145 West 45th Street, New York, NY. 1905. Bl/w drawing by Hauman of George Washington, Jr., eagle, stars, geometric designs. Bl/bl stripes. R/w/b title.

(GW) GEORGE WASHINGTON

"Geo. M. Cohan's Sensational Patriotic Song Originally Introduced in *George Washington, Jr.*" 4pp. Page 4: Adv.

GW-236(A) He Was A Wonderful Man. w.m. George M. Cohan. Published by F.A. Mills, No. 48 West 29th Street, New York, NY. 1906. Bl/w drawing of George Washington, Jr., laurel branch. [V-1: R/w stripes. R/w title on blue background] [V-2: Bl/w stripes. Bl/w title on red background]. "A Song Hit From The Latest Musical Play *George Washington, Jr.*"
    (B)   You're A Grand Old Rag.
    (C)   You're A Grand Old Flag.
    (D)   I'll Be There With Bells On.
    (E)   The Wedding Of The Blue And Grey.
    (F)   All Aboard For Broadway.
    (G)   If Washington Should Come To Life.
    (H)   I've Never Been Over There.
    (I)   You Can Have Broadway.
    (J)   Ethel Levey's Virginia Song.

GW-237 Song Of The U.S.A. (Song with Quartette ad libitum). w.m. Emery C. Stansell. a. "Harmonized" by John Brain. Published by E.K. Stansell, No. 175 Normal Avenue, Buffalo, NY. 1915. Br/w pictures of George Washington and Abraham Lincoln. Bl/w wreath, sunrise, geometric design border. 6pp. Page 6: Blank.

GW-238 America [Song Book]. c. C.E. Smith. Published by Cupples & Leon Company, New York, NY. 1907. [4 3/4" × 6 13/16"]. N/c drawing of George Washington. R/w/b shield. Hard cover. 24pp. Page 14: Photo of Abraham Lincoln. Page 18: N/c photo of Theodore Roosevelt.

GW-239 Ballad Of Valley Forge. w. Alfred Kreymborg. m. Alex North. Published by Edward B. Marks Music Corporation, RCA Building, Radio City, New York, NY. 1942. Ma/o drawing of monument, airplane. 14pp. Pages 2, 12 and 13: Blank. Page 3: "Note: This Ballad was first printed in *Collier's* in February, 1942." Page 14: Advertising.

GW-240 The American Soldier (A Decoration Day March Song). w.m. Arthur S. Josselyn. Published as a "Music Supplement of Hearst's *Chicago American*, Sunday, May 24, 1903," Chicago, IL. Be/bk litho of a statue of George Washington on horseback, soldiers. "Published by permission of The Alpha Music Company, Providence, RI., owners of the copyright." 4pp.

GW-241 Liberty Bell (It's Time to Ring Again). w. Joe Goodwin. m. Halsey K. Mohr. Published by Shapiro, Bernstein & Company, Music Publishers, No. 224 West 47th Street, New York, NY. 1917. Gn/bk/w silhouette drawing by Barbelle of George Washington, Betsy Ross, man, flag. Be/bk/w drawing of The Liberty Bell. 4pp. Page 4: Advertising.

GW-242 The Beginning Of The U.S.A. w. Bartley Costello. m. Max Prival and Billy Vanderveer. Published by Bernard Granville Music Publishing Company, Inc., No. 154 West 45th Street, New York, NY. 1916. R/w/b drawing of George Washington, John Adams,

GW-236(B)

Betsy Ross, eagle, map of the original 13 states, stripes. "Dedicated to our Nation." 6pp. Page 6: Advertising.

GW-243 Lead Us On Washington. w.m. John Richard Mullen, George C. Hofer and Alex P. Werner. Published by Mulwerhof Publishing Company, Wisconson Theatre Building, Milwaukee, WI. 1931. B/w drawing of George Washington. R/w/b drawing of flag, stripes. "In honor of the Two Hundredth Anniversary of the Birth of George Washington, Feb. 22, 1932." 6pp. Page 2: Blank. Page 6: Bl/w drawing of "Mount Vernon, Home of George Washington."

GW-244 Hail Columbia. Published by Firth, Pond & Company, No. 547 Broadway, New York, NY. 1861. R/w/b litho of man holding flag, train, ship. "Our Country's Songs." List of other titles in series.

GW-245(A) Liberty Enlightening The World (Song). w. George Cooper. m. Frederick A. Rothstein. Published by Hitchcock's Music Store, No. 166 Nassau Street, New York, NY. 1885. N/c litho of George Washington, General Lafayette, Statue of Liberty, U.S. and French flags. 6pp. Page 6: Advertising.
- **(B)** **March.**
- **(C)** **Waltzes.**
- **(D)** **Galop.**
- **(E)** **Gavotte.**
- **(F)** **Lanciers.**
- **(G)** **Quadrilles.**

GW-246 General Von Steuben (March-Song). w.m. Peter J. Engles. Published by *The Progressive*, No. 140 Cedar Street, New York, NY. Copyright 1925 by Peter Engles. Br/w drawing "The training grounds at Valley Forge," General Von Steuben, George Washington, troops, laurel branch. "Dedicated to Carl E. Schmidt, President of the Steuben Society of America." "Send for Orchestra and Band Arrangements." "For sale at Steuben Headquarters, 405 Lexington Avenue, New York." 4pp. Page 4: Statue of Von Steuben "In Lafayette Park,

GW-245

Washington, DC., erected by Congress, Albert Saegers, Sculptor."

GW-247 Evacuation Day March. m. James King. Published by Richard A. Saalfield, No. 41 Union Square, New York, NY. 1883. B/w litho of George Washington. 4pp. Page 4: Advertising.

GW-248 Re-Pledging Our Faith. w.m. Unohoo. Published by Unohoo Publishing Company, No. 179 Marcy Avenue, Brooklyn, NY. 1925. R/w/b drawings by Unohoo of eagle, fife and drum players, flag, patriotic and religious vignettes of Moses — "The Ten Commandments on which Christ and Civilization rest," George Washington — "Liberty, Truth, Justice, Brotherhood," Abraham Lincoln — "That Liberty Shall Not Perish From the Face of the Earth," Patrick Henry — "Give Me Liberty or Give Me Death." "For God, Home & Country." 6pp. Page 5: Testimonials.

GW-249 Washington Monument March (Two Step). m. F.P. Ullrich. Published by W.H. Boner & Company, No. 1314 Chestnut Street, Philadelphia,

PA. Copyright 1897 by F.P. Ullrich. B/w photo by Wm. Race of a statue of George Washington. Gn/w geometric designs. "Respectfully Dedicated to the Pennsylvania Society of Cincinnati." 6pp. Pages 2 and 6: Blank.

GW-250 Washington In Massachusetts. w.m. Van Ness Bates. Published by Music Service Company, No. 170-A Tremont Street, Boston, MA. 1932. Litho of "Gilbert Stuart's famous portrait of Washington painted in 1795." "A Patriotic Historical Song Composed for the Massachusetts Washington Bi-Centennial Celebration." "G. Washington [facsimile signature] 1732-1799." 6pp. Pages 5-6: Narrative on "Washington in Mass." Page 6: Song—*Pro Bono Publico* by Van Ness Bates.

GW-251 From Valley Forge To France. w.m. Mary Earl (Writer of *My Sweetheart Is Somewhere in France, Lafayette We Hear You Calling*). Published by Shapiro, Bernstein & Company, Music Publishers, No. 224 West 47th Street, New York, NY. 1918. Br/w/bl/bk Barbelle drawing of George Washington on horseback, WWI soldiers. "This number on all phonograph records and music rolls." 4pp. Page 4: Advertising.

GW-252 I Wonder What George Washington Would Say? w. Ed Gardenier. m. Harry W. Armstrong. Published by Howley, Haviland & Dresser, Nos. 1260-1266 Broadway, New York, NY. 1902. Drawing of George Washington, father, hatchet, cherry tree. Photo of Claude Thardo—"Sung with Immense Success by Mr. Claude Thardo." 6pp.

GW-253 We Will Honor The Mem'ry Of George Washington (A Bicentennial Song). w.m. Julius A. Hansen. Published by Hansen Music Publishing Company, New Brunswick, NJ. 1932. Non-pictorial geometric design border. 6pp. Page 6: Blank.

GW-254(A) Hail Columbia. [V-1: a. George Barker] [V-2: a. Bellak]. Published by J.L. Peters & Brother, No. 49 North 5th Street, St. Louis, MO. 1866. R/w/b litho of flag, title, geometric designs. 6pp. Pages 2 and 6: Blank. Page 3: [V-1: "Arranged with Çhorus"]. "The Melody of *Hail Columbia* is taken from *The President's March* and was composed by Prof. Pfiel and first performed by the band standing at Trenton Bridge when Washington passed over to his Inauguration at New York in the year 1789."

(B) **Washington's March**. a. Bellak.

GW-255(A) Resting-Place Of Washington. Published by Lee & Walker, No. 722 Chestnut Street, Philadelphia, PA. 1863. Non-pictorial black border. "National and Patriotic Songs, Ballads, &c., Arranged for Piano." List of other titles in series.

(B) **Washington's Tomb**. w.m. Carroll Clifford.

(C) **Hail Columbia**.

GW-256 Our Washington. w.m. Charles Gardner. Published by Charles Gardner, Residence, No. 23 Greenville Place, Brighton, Sussex, England. 1876. [9 1/2" × 12"]. R/w/bk geometric designs. "Centennial Jubilee, July 4, 1876." "Dedicated to the Citizens, U.S.A." "Verse I" printed on cover. "For the Piano Forte." "Historical! Patriotic! Instructive! Desceptive! Enthusiastic! And Inspiring! Abounding in Sentiment! And Without Dear or Favour!" 16pp. Page 3: Facsimile letter. Page 16: Advertising.

GW-257 I Dearly Love The Free (A Patriotic Song). w. Jonas B. Phillips, Esq. m. Mr. E.J. Westrop. Published by G. Endicott, No. 359 Broadway, New York, NY. 1838. B/w litho of George Washington. "As Sung with Great Applause by Mr. Morley." 8pp. Pages 2, 7 and 8: Blank.

GW-258 Hail Columbia. a. C. Everest. Published by Lee & Walker, No. 722 Chestnut Street, Philadelphia, PA. Non-pictorial. Geometric design border.

"Musical Echoes, A Collection of Popular Airs Arranged without Octaves for the Piano." List of other titles in series.

GW-259 Song Of Washington's Men (Quartette). w.m. James G. Clark. Published by Russell & Tolman, No. 291 Washington Street, Boston, MA. 1855. B/w litho of floral and geometric designs. "A Collection of Ballads, Duetts and Quartettes Sung by Ossian's Bards." "Poetry and Music Composed and Arranged for the Piano."

GW-260(A) Washington's March. Published by William Hall & Son, No. 239 Broadway, New York, NY. [ca. 185-]. Non-pictorial. "The Flowers of Youth, A Collection of Favorite Airs Arranged in an Easy Manner for Four Hands." List of other titles in series. 4pp. Page 4: Blank.

(B) Hail Columbia.

GW-261 Hail Columbia. Published by Lee & Walker, No. 188 Chesnut Street, Philadelphia, PA. [ca. 1850]. Non-pictorial. "The Sister's, A Collection of Popular and Esteemed Airs Arranged as Duetts [sic] for Two Performers on the Piano Forte, Selected from the Works of the Best Composers." List of other songs in series.

GW-262 Souvenir De Mount Vernon (Grand Valse Brillante). m. Geo. F. Bristow, Op. 29. Published by H.B. Doodworth, No. 6 Astor Place, New York, NY. 1861. Non-pictorial geometric designs. "Dedicated to Miss Emma L. Thompson." 12pp. Pages 2 and 12: Blank.

GW-263 The Glorious Days Of Washington. m. J.N. Sporle. Published by Harding's Music For The Millions, No. 288 Bowery, New York, NY. [ca. 1870]. Non-pictorial. "The Cabinet, A Collection of New and Popular Vocal Music." List of other titles in series.

GW-264 The Flag That's Waved A Hundred Years (Song). w.m. M.H. Rosenfeld. Published by Hitchcock's Music Stores, No. 283 Sixth Avenue, New York, NY. 1889. Br/r/w/bl drawings of George Washington, crossed flags. 6pp. Page 6: Advertising.

GW-265(A) Hail Columbia. a. Barker. Published by J.L. Peters, New York, NY. 1876. B/w litho by Endicott & Company of Miss Liberty, crowd of people in native dress, Washington Monument, Capitol dome, flag. "Columbia's flag is waving a welcome to all." List of other songs in series.

(B) Washington's March. a. Bellak.

GW-266 Hail Columbia. Published by S. Brainard's Sons, Publishers, Cleveland, OH. 1884. O/y/bk/r/w drawing of soldier on horseback. "Our National War Songs." List of titles in series.

GW-267 Hail Columbia. a. Ch. K. Published by Lee & Walker, No. 722 Chestnut Street, Philadelphia, PA. [ca. 1859]. R/w/b crossed flags. "National Songs." "Sung by Madlle. T. Parodi." List of other titles in series. 6pp. Page 2: Blank. Page 6: Advertising.

GW-268 Oh Forge Not A Chain For The Brave. w. Eliza Cook. m. Henry Russell. Published by Musical Bouquet Office, No. 192 High Holborn, London, England. [185-?]. [10" × 13 1/2"]. B/w litho of George "Washington," Louis "Kossuth" [with facsimile signature], and John "Hampden," eagle, branches. "Composed and sung by Henry Russell." 4pp.

GW-269 Hail Columbia (Americanischer Nationalgesang). A. Fred. Beyer. Published by B. Schoff's Sohnen, Mainz, Germany. [ca. 1860]. R/w/b crossed flags. "No. 14." "Vaterlands-Lieder, Chants Patriotiques Fur Das Piano-Forte." 4pp. Page 4: Blank.

GW-270 Washington, He Was A Wonderful Man. w.m. George M. Cohan. Published by George M. Cohan Publishing Company, Inc., No. 1776 Broadway, New York, NY. 1933. R/w/b Barbelle drawing of George M. Cohan, stars and stripes background, "By George M. Cohan" [facsimile handwriting].

"From *George Washington, Jr.*" 8pp. Pages 2 and 8: Advertising for Cohan and Vogel published music.

GW-271 Mr. Yankee Doodle Are We Prepared? w. Joseph J. Barry. m. George H. Taylor and George H. Malmgren. Published by Barry, Malmgren & Taylor, Watertown, CT. 1916. R/w/b drawings of George "Washington — 1776," Andrew "Jackson — 1812," Admiral "Dewey — 1898" and "? — 1917." R/w/b drawings by Starmer of soldier, sailor bugle, shield, four bars of music. 6pp. Pages 2 and 6: Blank.

GW-272 Washington Quickstep. c.a. George C. Gott. In: *Old Familiar Dances With Figures*, page 34. Published by Oliver Ditson Company: Theodore Presser Company, Distributors, No. 1712 Chestnut Street, Philadelphia, PA. Copyright 1918 by George C. Gott. Be/bk drawing of dancers. "For Violin, Flute or Mandolin, and Piano." 56pp.

GW-273 Father Of His Country (March). w. Edwin Wright and Arthur Cleveland Morse. m. E.E. Bagley (Composer of *The National Emblem March*). Published by Walter Jacobs, Inc., Boston, MA. 1931. Bl/w/y drawing of George Washington, flag. "1732-1932 — Commemorating the Bicentennial of the Birth of George Washington." "Published for Band and Orchestra and all Voice Combinations." 6pp. Page 6: Advertising.

GW-274 Mount Vernon (The Mecca of the Free). w.m. C.R. Packard. Published by H.M. Higgins, No. 117 Randolph Street, Chicago, IL. 1864. Non-pictorial geometric design border. 6pp. Page 2: Blank. Page 3: Title: **The Mecca Of The Free**. Page 6: Advertising.

GW-275 It Must Be The Spirit Of 76. w. William Jerome. m. Arthur N. Green. Published by William Jerome Publishing Corporation, Strand Theatre Building, 47th Street and Broadway, New York, NY. 1917. Br/w/bl/bk drawings by Barbelle of George Washington, soldier, sailor in hat marked "Maine." "Introduced by Jos. Howard & Evelyn Clark in *Musical World Revue*." 4pp. Page 4: Advertising.

GW-276 Washington (Patriotic March Song). w.m. Charles H. LaTourette. Published by LaTourette and Mulholland, First Nation Bank Building, Princeton, NJ. 1917. R/w/bl/bk drawings of George Washington, eagle, shield. "The Song with the American Spirit." 4pp. Page 2: "Respectfully Dedicated to the Father of Our Country." Page 4: Blank.

GW-277 George Washington Bicentennial March. m. John Philip Sousa. Published by Sam Fox Publishing Company, Inc., No. 170 N.E. 33rd Street, Ft. Lauderdale, FL. 33334. 1966. R/w/bk drawing of staff with tassels. Package for band. 64 pages.

GW-278 The Home Of Washington. w.m. William F. Sherwood. Published by George W. Fager, No. 12 Union Square, New York, NY. 1902. B/w photo of Mt. Vernon — "Note: This correct and authentic reproduction is given with the object that it may reach every home in the land — The Publisher." R/w geometric design." "Mt. Vernon, memorable as the home of George Washington, is in Fairfax County, Va., on the Potomac River, 15 miles below Washington, D.C. The home is on 200 acres of land purchased in 1858, by The Ladies Mt. Vernon Association for $200,000 and since preserved with great care by that Association which is a national organization with State representatives." 6pp. Page 2: Blank. Page 6: Advertising.

GW-279 The Little Boy Who Never Told A Lie. w. Tommie Conner. m. Manning Sherwin. Published by Francis, Day & Hunter, Ltd., Nos. 138-140 Charing Cross Road, London WC2, England. 1940. [9 7/8" × 12 1/4"]. R/w/b drawing of a small boy, flags, silhouette of George Washington. 4pp. Page 4: Advertising.

GW-280 The Song Of The Hatchet. w.m. Archibald Humbolt. a. Effie Louise Koogle. Published by March Brothers, Publishers, Nos. 208, 210 and 212 Wright Avenue, Lebanon, OH. 1909. R/w/gr/br drawing of little George Washington, father, hatchet. 6pp. Page 6: Advertising.

GW-281 Hail Columbia. James Bellak. Published by Oliver Ditson & Company, [V-1: 277 Washington Street], Boston, MA. 1879. [V-1: B/w litho of Flowers, birds, insects, geometric designs] [V-2: Geometric design border] [V-3: Non-pictorial]. "Leaflets; Fifty Pleasing Duets for the Piano." List of other titles in series.

GW-282 There Will Always Be An Uncle Sammy (On This Side of the Pond). w.m. Rosalia Smith and Ida Smith. Published by F.I.R. Smith, Inc., No. 3039 Huntington Avenue, Baltimore, MD. Copyright 1940 by Ida DeBelle Smith. [9 1/2" × 12 9/16"]. R/w/b drawings of George Washington — "Courage, Determination, Perseverance," Abraham Lincoln — "Discretion, Tolerance, Consideration, Justice," Uncle Sam, Statue of Liberty." "Integrity — Civil Rights." 6pp

GW-283 Washington, Patriotism Among The Young (The Acme Haversack, Song and Patriotic Eloquence: A Monthly Magazine), Vol. 4, No. 1, January, 1890. Published by J.C.O. Reddington, Acme Publishing Bureau, No. 35 University Avenue, Syracuse, NY. [5 1/4" × 7 3/4"]. Gn/bk litho of flag, G.A.R. badge. 68pp.

GW-284 From The Days Of Washington (A Patriotic Score for Toy Orchestra) [Song Folio]. a. J. Lilian Vandevere. Published by C.C. Birchard & Company, Boston, MA. 1932. Bl/gd non-pictorial line border. 14pp. + 7 individual band parts.

GW-285 Father Of The Land We Love. w.m. George M. Cohan. Published by George M. Cohan Music Publishing Company, Inc., No. 1776 Broadway, New York, NY. 1931. Bl/w drawing of George Washington. "Written for the American people by George M. Cohan to Commemorate the Two Hundredth Anniversary of the Birth of George Washington." 6pp. Pages 2 and 6: Advertising.

GW-286 George Washington. w.m. Clancy Hayes and Kermit Goell. Copyright 1947 by Hudson Music Corporation, No. 1650 Broadway, New York, NY. [7 7/8" × 11"]. Non-pictorial "Professional Copy." Copyright "Warning" paragraph. 4pp.

GW-287 The Glorious Star-Spangled Banner. w. Francis Scott Key. a. Theodore Henninger. Published by Theodore Henninger, No. 371 North Smith Avenue, St. Paul, MN. 1912. R/w/bl/bk/gd drawings of George "Washington," Abraham "Lincoln," flag, shield. "Composed and Dedicated to the Patriots of the United States." "In Union there is Life, Strength and Peace." "A modification of its melody and an elaboration of the harmony and bass of our most cherished national song, adapted to the ordinary voice, and especially its successful singing at Public Assemblies, limiting the range of the melody to an octave or eight tones and transforming the 'Solo and Chorus' into a Grand Chorus." 4pp. Page 4: Narrative.

GW-288 Unfurl Old Glory To The Topmast Breeze. w.m. Frank A. Johnson (of Sedgwick Post #8, G.A.R., Spokane, Wash., Department of Washington and Alaska). Published by Frank A. Johnson, Spokane, WA. 1909. B/w drawings/photos of George Washington, Abraham Lincoln and Frank A. Johnson. R/w/bl/y drawing of Uncle Sam — "Welcome," Revolutionary era soldier — "Spirit of '76," ships, G.A.R. badge. 6pp. Page 5: Arranged for Male Quartet. Page 6: Advertising.

GW-289 My Dream Of The USA. w.m. Leonard Chick, Charles Roth and Ted Snyder. Published by Ted Snyder

Company, Inc., Music Publishers, No. 112 West 38th Street, New York, NY. 1908. Bl/w reproduction of the painting of George Washington crossing the Delaware River. R/w/b eagle, shield, geometric designs. 6pp. Page 2: "Quartett Chorus." Page 3: "Dedicated to the Memory of Francis Scott Key." Page 6: Advertising.

GW-290 Just Like Washington Crossed The Delaware (General Pershing Will Cross the Rhine). w. Howard Johnson. m. George W. Meyer. Published by Leo Feist, New York, NY. 1918. R/w/b drawing of George Washington crossing the Delaware River. Br/w tinted photo of General Pershing. "Theme Suggested by Elinore and Williams." 4pp.

GW-291 George Washington Bicentennial (March). m. John Philip Sousa. Published by Sam Fox Publishing Company, Cleveland, OH. 1930. N/c drawing of George Washington, frame, flag. "1732-1932." "Written In Commemoration of the Two Hundredth Anniversary of the Birth of George Washington." 6pp. Page 6: Advertising.

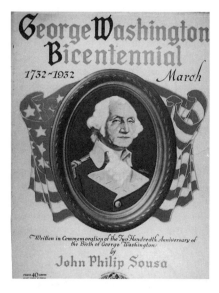

GW-291

GW-292 National Ode To George Washington w.m. Edward L. Bohal. Published by E.L. Bohal & Company, Ashland, OH. 1931. Bl/w drawing by Meyer Both Co. of George Washington, life vignettes. "Father of our Freedom and of our U.S.A." "Solo, Mixed Quartet, Trio, Male Quartet and March for Bicentennial Festivals, Feb. 22, 1932, and Patriotic Occasions." 4pp.

GW-293 Washington's March. a. Ervin Litkei. In: *The Bicentennial March and Presidential Marches of America*, page 6. Published by Loena Music Publishing, No. 239 West 18th Street, New York, NY. 1976. R/w/b drawings of George Washington, Thomas Jefferson, Abraham Lincoln [facsimile signatures], eagle, flags. "American Revolution Bicentennial, 1776-1976." "Officially Recognized Commemorative..." 40pp.

GW-294 A Washington Garland (Seven songs by Francis Hopkinson). w.m. Francis Hopkinson. e. Harold V. Mulligan. Published by Arthur P. Schmidt Company, No. 120 Boylston Street, Boston, MA. [ca. 1917]. Bl/w drawing of George Washington. "Dedicated to George Washington." 52pp. Pages 4 and 5: Facsimile letters from George Washington to Joseph Hopkinson.

GW-295 George Washington (Main Title). m. Laurence Rosenthal. Published by Columbia Pictures Productions, P.O. Box 4340, Hialeah, FL. 1984. B/w photo of actor as George Washington. "From the CBS Entertainment Mini-Series." "A Big 3 Production." 6pp. [Fold Out]. Page 6: Advertising.

GW-296 On Freedom's Shore. w. Gilbert Patten (Author of the famous Frank Merriwell stories). m. Everett Grieve. Published by Mills Music, Inc., Music Publishers, No. 1619 Broadway, New York, NY. 1936. R/w/b drawing by Robert Paterson of George Washington and Abraham Lincoln on flag background. 6pp. Pages 2 and 6: Blank. Page

3: "Dedicated to the Council Against Intolerance In America, Co-Chairmen George Gordon Battle, W. Warren Barbour and William Allen White. *On Freedom's Shore* is dedicated to the Independence Day Ceremony of the Council Against Intolerance In America, in which thousands of American communities has joined to make July Fourth a stirring reaffirmation of those basic principles of liberty and equality set forth in the Declaration of Independence upon which our Country is founded."

GW-297 The American Wedding March. m. Sol Bloom. a. Leo Manfried (Composer of *In His Steps*). Published by Sol Bloom, Randolph and Dearborn Streets, Chicago, IL. 1899. Pk/ma/w drawing of George and Martha Washington, doves, hearts. 6pp.

GW-298 The Star-Spangled Banner (Is the Song That Reached My Heart). w.m. M.T. Bohannon. Published by A.J. Stasny Music Company, New York, NY. 1914. Br/w reproduction of the painting of George Washington crossing the Delaware River. 6pp. Pages 2 and 6: Advertising.

GW-299 Hail Columbia. a. William Dressler. Published by Wm. Hall & Sons, No. 239 Broadway, New York, NY. [ca. 1848]. B/w litho of circle of stars. "National Songs of America Arranged with Accompaniments for the Piano Forte." List of other titles in series. 6pp.

GW-300 Father Of The Land We Love. w.m. George M. Cohan. Published by The United States George Washington Bicentennial Commission, Washington, DC. Copyright 1931 by Hon. Sol Bloom. B/w medallions of George Washington — "George Washington Bicentennial 1732-1932." "Written for the American People." "To Commemorate the Two Hundredth Anniversary of the Birth of George Washington." 2pp.

GW-301 Virginia. w.m. D.A. Barrackman. Published as a "Music Supplement Hearst's *Boston Sunday American*, Sunday, October 30, 1904. Gn/w photo of the "McCoy Sisters." "Sung by The McCoy Sisters." Gn/o/w drawing of Mt. Vernon, Virginia State seal. "Published by permission of the American Advance Music CO., NY., owners of the copyright." 4pp.

GW-302(A) Land Of Washington. a. Francis H. Brown. Published by Oliver Ditson, No. 115 Washington Street, Boston, MA. 1856. B/w litho (Attributed to Winslow Homer) of battle scenes, farm, The White House, Miss Liberty. "National Songs of America Arranged for Piano Forte."

(B) Hail Columbia. 6pp. Page 2: Note by the Publisher: This song written in the summer of 1798, to oblige a young friend of the Author's who was a singer at the theatre in Philadelphia. It was arranged by a number of the orchestras to *The President's March* which was the name of the original music. It has since been adopted, by common consent, as the National Anthem of America. This is the only authentic copy of the song extant, it being corrected by the Author in the year 1841. Judge Hopkinson died on the 15th of January, 1842."

GW-303 Natal Throes (Songs for Home and School). w.m. George Keller DeLong. Published by George Keller DeLong, No. 538 Gordon Street, Allentown, PA. 1916. B/w photos of "George K. Delong" and his mother, "Lucy Keller, nee Bast, 1816-92, mother of fourteen children, grandmother of 106 grandchildren, she is grandmother of George Keller DeLong, who has 11 living brothers and sisters and 82 living first cousins. Cousin George is the Author of numerous songs and poems, the latest publication consists of patriotic airs and folk songs entitled *Natal Throes*. The above picture figures as an illustration for "In Tribute To Mother." "To God, My Mother and My Country." "Part I of

(GW) GEORGE WASHINGTON

Natal Throes Series." 8pp. Page 8: "Hail My Native Land." B/w drawings of George Washington, James Monroe, Abraham Lincoln, flag, the Statue of Liberty. "Panama Girts Up Thy Loins."

GW-304 Natal Throes (Songs for Home and School). w.m. George Keller DeLong. Published by DeLong Publishing Company, Allentown, PA. [ca. 1919]. R/bl/br/be drawing of four U.S. flags. Br/be photo of the "Launching of the Battleship Louisiana. Clinging to a rope-end of an eight man ram, the Author of these songs, hidden behind the dense crowd, is sweating with a 'Whop 'er Up Boys! Whoop 'er Up!' During the entire year of 1904 George Keller DeLong worked on the Battleship Louisiana. On Saturday, August 25th, previous to the launching on August 27th, 1904, the Author originally wrote the song *Launching Day* on the deck of this ship then gallantly poised to take her initial plunge." "To God, my Mother and my Country." "Patriotic Edition." 20pp. Page 20: "Hail My Native Land." R/w/bk/be drawings of George Washington, James Monroe, Abraham Lincoln, flag, Statue of Liberty. "Panama Girts Up Thy Loins."

GW-305 The Sword And The Staff (A National Anthem). w. George P. Morris. m. W. Vincent Wallace. Published by J.L. Hewitt & Company, No. 239 Broadway, New York, NY. 1843. B/w litho by Thayer of building facade, George Washington, Benjamin Franklin, statues of "Peace" and "Victory," eagle, columns, swords, flags. 8pp. Pages 2, 7 and 8: Blank. Page 3: "Dedicated to the American people."

GW-306 Washington Was A Grand Old Man (March Song). w.m. Donald J. Garrison. Published by Donald Garrison, No. 885 Columbus Avenue, New York, NY. 1911. Bl/w drawing of George Washington. R/w stripe cover. 6pp. Page 3: Dedication — "To the Sacred Memory of the 'Father of our Country.'" Pages 2 and 6: Blank.

GW-307 Big Bill The Builder. w.m. Milton Weil, Bernie Grossman and Larry Shay. Published by Milton Weil Music Company, Inc., No. 54 West Randolph Street, Chicago, IL. 1928. B/w photo of Chicago Mayor Bill Thompson — "America First, Big Bill The Builder" [facsimile handwriting]. R/w/b drawings of Big Bill with a portrait of George Washington — "No entangling alliances," Uncle Sam, soldier — "Not for foreign shores," Big Bill Thompson with child and with Charles Lindbergh, boat — "Cape Girardeau." "We are indebted to Corporation Counsel Samuel A. Ettelson for the original suggestion for this song and many of its phrases." "America First." 6pp. Page 3: "Respectfully Dedicated to our dear friend, The Hon. William Hale Thompson." Page 6: Advertising.

GW-308 When Uncle Sam Sings The Marseillaise. w. Earle C. Jones. m. Herman Avery Wade. Published by Jos. W. Stern & Company, No. 102-104 West 38th Street, New York, NY. 1917. R/w/b drawings of George Washington, Lafayette, Uncle Sam, stripe background. Bl/w photo of Henri Leoni — "As Sung by Henri Leoni in *The Parisian Model*, Presenting Anna Held, Management F. Ziegfeld, Jr." 8pp. Pages 2 and 7: Blank. Page 8: Advertising.

GW-309 The Birth Of Washington. w. Lieut. Henry De Wolfe, U.S.A. m. J.M. Bradford. Published by A.M. Leland, Providence, RI. 1855. B/w non-pictorial geometric designs. "A National Song Sung by Mr. Frazer at his Popular Ballad Entertainments." "To The Continentals." 6pp. Pages 2 and 6: Blank.

GW-310 Washington's March. Published by Winner & Schuster, No. 110 North Eighth Street, Philadelphia, PA. [ca. 1850]. Non-pictorial. Followed on page one by *Norma March*. 2pp. Page 2: Blank.

GW-311 On The Steps Of The

Great White Capitol (Stood Martha and George). w. Grant Clarke and Edgar Leslie. m. Maurice Abrahams. Published by Maurice Abrahams Music Company, No. 1570 Broadway, New York, NY. 1914. R/w/bl/br/bk drawing by Pfeiffer of Capitol building, couple embracing. [V-1: Bl/w photo of Bessie Wynn] [V-2: Bl/w photo of Dorothy Brenner]. 6pp. Pages 2 and 6: Blank. Page 8: Advertising.

GW-312 Hail Columbia. w. F. Hopkinson, 1798. Published by Music Department, Emerson Drug Company, Baltimore, MD. [ca. 189-]. Bl/w drawings of instruments, leaves, geometric designs. "Bromo-Seltzer Edition of 171 Popular Selections Complete and Unabridged with Piano and Organ Accompaniment." List of other titles in series. "Compliments of J.S. Carpenter, Giuard, PA." 4pp. Page 4: Advertising for Bromo-Seltzer.

GW-313 Hail Columbia. w.m. F. Hopkinson, 1798. Published by Emerson Drug Company, Baltimore, MD. [ca. 189-]. Bl/w drawings of a bottle of Bromo-Seltzer, cherubs, geometric designs. "The Bromo-Seltzer Collection of 83 Popular Songs Complete & Unabridged with Piano and Organ Accompaniment." List of other titles in series. 4pp. Page 4: Advertising for Bromo-Seltzer.

GW-314 Mount Vernon Polka. m. Hauser. Published by S.T. Gordon, No. 706 Broadway, New York, NY. [186-]. Non-pictorial geometric design border. "Parlor Album Pieces." List of songs in series.

GW-315 Washington's March. a.c. Ervin Litkei (Author of *Presidential Marches of America*). In: *A Tribute To The U.S.A.*, page 8. Published by Loena Music Publishing Company, No. 239 West 18th Street, New York, NY. 10011. Copyright 1985 and 1986. N/c drawing by Edward Moran of the Statue of Liberty celebration in 1886 — "The Statue of Liberty, standing as an eternal symbol of the friendship of the people of France, was presented to the United States in 1886 by its creator, Frederick Bartholdi." Quotes by "Emma Lazarus (1883)," and "President Grover Cleveland (1886)."

GW-316 Hail Columbia. a. John Spindler. Published by Beck & Lawton, SE corner 7th & Chestnut Street, Philadelphia, PA. 1858. Non-pictorial geometric designs. "Golden Melodies Arranged for Piano." List of other titles in series.

GW-317 The Battle Of Prague. m. Francis Kotzwara (Born in Prague, died in London, 1791). a. Charles Grobe. Published by Henry Tolman & Company, No. 291 Washington Street, Boston, MA. 1860. B/w litho of soldiers, geometric designs. "The celebrated *Battle of Prague*, May 5th, 1757, A descriptive Piece for the Piano. "Frederic the Great — Washington commanded his admiration and Mt. Vernon received among its treasures a Prussian sword of honor, forwarded from Potsdam with the words, 'From the oldest general in the world to the greatest.'" "One to destroy is murder by the law, And gibbets keep the lifted hand in awe, To murder thousands take a specious name, War's glorious art, and give immortal fame." 14pp. Page 2: Narrative on the "Battle of Prague." Pages 13 and 14: Blank.

GW-318 America My Sweet Land. w.m. Jacob S. Rosenberg. Published by R.G. Publishing Company, Cleveland, OH. 1918. Bk/pl/w drawing of George Washington, star border. 6pp. Page 6: Biography and photo of Jacob S. Rosenberg.

GW-319 Washington's Birthday. w. Mrs. DeArmond. m. Emma Hemberger. [Published in an unlocated song book, page 8]. [ca. 1900?].

GW-320 Awake America! w.m. Jerry Daly. Published by Maydell Publications, No. 470 Stuart Street, Boston, MA. 1933. Bl/w drawing "From painting by Faed" of George Washington on horseback. R/w cover. 6pp. Page 2: Blank. Page 6: Advertising.

GW-321 Never Say You Didn't When You Did (Motto Song and Chorus). w.m. T.F. Jeffery. Published by White, Smith & Company, Boston, MA. 1885. B/w drawing of George Washington, father — "George and Little Hatchet," cherry tree, couple kissing, boy stealing watermelon, child at school. "Written for and sung by Sam Lucas." 6pp. Page 6: Advertising.

GW-322 You Can Have Broadway. w.m. "Yankee Doodle [George M.] Cohan." Published by F.A. Mills, No. 48 West 29th Street, New York, NY. 1906. B/w photo of George M. Cohan. O/bk/w geometric designs. "Geo. M. Cohan's Sweeping Hit." "As Sung by Himself in *Geo. Washington, Jr.*" 8pp. Pages 2, 7 and 8: Advertising.

GW-323 Hail Columbia. a. Charles Grobe, Op. 386. [V-1 and V-2: Published by Lee & Walker, No. 722 Chestnut Street] [V-3: Edward L. Walker, No. 142 Chesnut], Philadelphia, PA. [V-1: 1854] [V-2: ca. 1867]. [V-3: 1851, 1852, 1853]. Non-pictorial geometric design border. "Melodies of the People." [V-1 and V-3: "New Variations on Old Tunes"] [V-2: "New Variations on New and Old Tunes"]. "Composed for the Piano Forte." List of other songs in series. [V-1 and V-3: "Mademoiselle Kate A. Armstrong, Son aimale Eleve"]. [V-3: 6pp. Page 6: Blank].

GW-324 Hail Columbia. Published by W.H. Boner & Company, No. 1102 Chestnut Street, Philadelphia, PA. 1876. N/c litho of 36 different national flags. "Flags of All Nations Series." List of other titles in series.

GW-325 When Yankees Go Into Battle. w. Antonio Rossi. m. Christian A. Praetorius. Published by Frank Harding, Music Publishers, New York, NY. Copyright 1917 by Antonio Rossi. [9 3/4" × 12 1/2"]. R/w/b flag. Bl/w drawing of "George Washington," soldiers marching. 4pp. Page 4: Blank.

GW-326 Hail The Baltimore & Ohio (Centenary March). w.m. Walter Goodwin and Margaret Talbott Stevens. Published by Walter Goodwin, Inc., No. 156 West 44th Street, New York, NY. 1927. B/w drawing of "Baltimore & Ohio" train — "The President Washington." Bl/w/bk drawing of eagle, geometric designs. "On the Occasion of the Laying of the First Stone of the Baltimore and Ohio Rail Road, July 4th, 1828, several pieces of original music were Composed and Played for the Centenary of the Rail Road, in the fall of 1927. This March was Prepared and rendered by the Bands of Music assembled for the event." 6pp. Pages 2 and 6: Blank.

GW-327(A) Washington He Was A Wonderful Man. w.m. George M. Cohan. Published by Jerry Vogel Music Company, No. 114 West 44th Street, New York, NY. 1933. B/w drawing of a pencil — "Check these Star Spangles hits for your programs." List of other songs in series. Music score background. "Jerry Vogal Presents George M. Cohan's Famous American Songs." "*George Washington, Jr.*" 6pp.

(B) I Was Born In Virginia.
(C) If Washington Should Come To Life.
(D) You're A Grand Old Flag.

GW-328 Hail Columbia. m. Fyles [sic]. In: *Educational Music Course — First Reader*, page 84. Published by Ginn & Company, Publishers. [ca. 1897]. [6 1/4" × 7 3/4"]. Ma/br/gn floral and geometric designs, lyre. 102[?]pp.

GW-329 It Takes A Man To Be A Soldier. w.m. T. Brigham Bishop (Composer of *John Brown's Body*). a. Max Dreyfuss. Published as a "Musical Supplement to *The New York Journal and Advertiser*, March 20, 1898. Copyright 1898 by Primrose and West Music Publishing Company. B/w photo of "Gen. William Tecumseh Sherman" on horseback, girl. R/w/bl/y drawing of George Washington. "Selected by Reginold DeKoven." 4pp.

GW-330 You're A Grand Old Flag. w.m. George M. Cohan. Published by Jerry Vogel Music Company, Inc., No. 112 West 44th Street, New York, NY. [ca. 1950]. Non-pictorial. *"From George Washington, Jr."* 6pp.

GW-331 Gloria Washington (Two-Step March). m. Frederick Neil Innes. Published by Clegg Publishing Company, St. Paul, MN. Copyright 1909 by F.B. Innes. Br/be drawing of George Washington, sun. Br/be photo by Caxton Engravers of Frederick Innes. "The Official March of the Alaska Yukon Pacific Exposition, Seattle, Wash., 1909." 8pp. Pages 2 and 8: Blank.

GW-332 Washington Crossing The Delaware (A New Quartette). w. Seba Smith, Esq. m. C. Zeuner. Published by C. Holt, Jr., Music Publishing Warehouse, No. 156 Fulton Street, New York, NY. 1847. B/w litho by J. Britton of George Washington, troops crossing the Delaware River. "Composed for, and Sung with great effect by The Ilsleys." 8pp. Pages 2, 7 and 8: Blank.

GW-333 An Open Letter To My Teenage Son. w.m. Robert Thompson. Published by ASA Music Company, No. 1556 North La Brea Avenue, Hollywood, CA. 1967. [8 1/2" × 11"]. Bk/w/o drawing of a man, flower. Facsimile handwritten letter with partial song lyrics — "Dear Son, you have asked my [reaction to] long hair [or beards on young people. Some great men have worn long hair and beards], George Washington and Abraham Lincoln..." 8pp.

GW-334 Birth Of A Nation (A Suite of Three Early American Songs). c.a.e. John W. Schaum. Published by Schaum Publications, Inc., No. 2018 East North Avenue, Milwaukee, WI. 1975. R/w/b drawing of George Washington, man ringing bell. "For Piano or Organ." "Based on theme suggested by Alice M. MClullen." 4pp. Page 2: *Liberty Song.* Page 3: **General Washington**. Page 4: *What Grateful Offering?*

GW-335 Federal March. m. Alexander Reinagle. Published by United States Constitution Sesquicentennial Commission, Washington, DC. 1935. Bl/w drawing Miss Liberty, signers of the Constitution including "Washington, Hamilton, Madison, Franklin, Read, Sherman, Pinckney, Livingston, Morris, King — We The People, 1787-1937." "Music Associated with the Period of the Formation of the Constitution and the Inauguration of George Washington. "Composed for the Philadelphia Celebration of the Ratification of the Constitution, July 4, 1788." 2pp. Page 2: Narrative on Alexander Reinagle. Music.

GW-336 Martha Washington Dances. m. W. Otto Miessner. Published by Miessner Institute of Music, No, 1219 Kimball Building, Chicago, IL. 1930. B/w drawing of couple dancing. *"Grand March—Minuet—Gavotte—Mazurka—Reel."* 20pp. Pages 2, 19 and 20: Blank. Page 3: Title page.

GW-337 George Washington Variations. a. Ernest Krenek. Published by Southern Music Publishing Company,

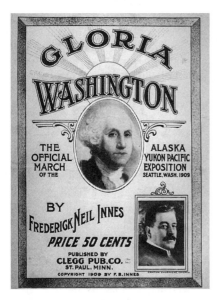

GW-331

Inc., No. 1619 Broadway, New York, NY. 1955. Be/bk non-pictorial. "For Piano." 18pp. Pages 2, 16, 17 and 18: Blank. Page 3: Title page. Page 4: At bottom — "The tunes of the *Grand March* and the *Martial Cotillion* were found in a manuscript book of the Euterpean–Society of Hartford, Conn. about 1800." "Dedicated to Miriam Molin."

GW-338 From The Days Of George Washington (Suite of Marches). a. Adolf Schmid. Published by G. Schirmer, Inc., No. 3 East 43rd Street, New York, NY. 1931. Non-pictorial. "For Free Distribution Only." "Schirmer's Orchestra Miscellany, No. 154 — Violin I." List of other arrangements available. 6pp. Page 2: Forward.

GW-339 Washington Program Songs [Song Book]. Published by Hall & McCreary Company, No. 434 South Wabash Avenue, Chicago, IL. Copyright 1923 and 1932. [5 3/4" × 8 3/4"]. B/w drawing of George Washington. "Order now, Prices 12 cts. a copy, 96 cts. a dozen, or $7.00 a hundred, post paid, $60 a thousand, transportation extra." 32pp. Page 2: Forward and Table of Contents. Pages 31 and 32: Advertising.

GW-340(A) Washington's March. a. T. Bissell. Published by Oliver Ditson & Company, Washington Street, Boston, MA. 1857. Non-pictorial. "The Graces: A Collection of Favorite Melodies Arranged for 3 Performers on One Piano Forte." List of other titles in series."

(B) Hail Columbia.

GW-341 George Washington (The Great Centennial Character Song). w. George Ware. m. Popular Airs. a. Herbert Hersey. In: *Echoes: A Collection of Vocal and Instrumental Music*, Vol. 1, pages 43-48. Published by John F. Perry & Company, No. 538 Washington Street, Boston, MA. 1878. [9 1/2" × 11 3/4"]. Non-pictorial.

GW-342 Washington's Triumph (A Colonial Song). m. "Traditional Melody." a. Henry Fiske. Published by Carl Fischer, Inc., No. 56 Cooper Square, New York, NY. 1932. O/w/bl/bk drawing of Continental soldiers. Bl/w drawing of George Washington — "Washington Bicentennial Series." "For Piano." 4pp. Page 2: Long narrative on the history of the song. Page 4: Advertising.

GW-343 Bow Down To Washington. w.m. Lester J. Wilson, Class of '13. Copyright 1918 and 1934. Selling agents: Capital Music Company, Seattle, WA. Bl/gd/w drawing by Pat Maiorano, '32, of George Washington, drum major, pennants — "Washington" [University of Washington]. 6pp. Page 6: Advertising.

GW-344(A) Hail Columbia (Transcription). a. C. Voss. Published by Oliver Ditson Company, Boston, MA. 1898. R/w/bl/bk/y drawings of woman with sword, Capitol dome, flags, soldiers. List of other titles in series. "Music of the Union."

(B) Hail Columbia (Variations). a. Charles Grobe.

GW-345 The Little Patriots (A Song of Washington's Day). w. John Pepusch. a. Arnold Haynes. Published by Carl Fisher, Inc., No. 56 Union Square, New York, NY. 1932. O/w/bk drawings of Colonial mother and children. B/w drawing of George Washington. "Washington Bicentennial Series." "For Piano." 4pp. Page 2: Long Narrative on how to properly play the song. Page 4: Advertising.

GW-346 Honor To Washington (Song). w. James F. Oates. m. William J. Oates. Published by James F. Oates, No. 1609 "D" Street SE, Washington, DC. 1931. B/w photo of "Home of Washington, Mt. Vernon, Va." B/w drawing of George Washington. 4pp. Page 4: Blank.

GW-347 Washington. w. Nancy Byrd Turner. m. Hoagy Carmichael. In: *Hoagy Carmichel's Songs for Children*, page 20. Published by Simon & Schuster, Rockefeller Center, New York, NY. Copyright 1957 by Carmichael Music

Publications, Inc. [8 1/2" × 11"]. R/w/b hard cover book with a drawing of a drummer on the cover. "A Big Golden Book." All songs illustrated by J.B. Miller. 72pp.

GW-348 Flag Of Liberty. w.m. T.H. Hinton. Published by Charles W. Harris, No. 13 East Fourteenth Street, New York, NY. 1875. B/w litho of U.S. flag, leaves, geometric design's. "Centennial." "1776-1876." "To the Memory of Washington." 6pp. Pages 2 and 6: Blank.

GW-349 The Proud Flag Of Freedom (National Song with Chorus). w. George M. Vickers. m. James C. Beckel. Published by National Music Company, No. 215-221 Wabash Avenue, Chicago, IL. 1879. B/w drawing of George Washington, flags, geometric designs. 6pp. Page 6: Blank.

GW-350 Chips Off The Old Block (March Song). m. Frank Karasek. Published by F. Karasek, Columbus, OH. 1911. Br/w drawing of George Washington, artillery and cavalry soldiers, cannon, flags. 6pp. Pages 2 and 6: Blank.

GW-351 Little Patriot March. m. Bert R. Anthony. Published by Anthony Brothers, Music Publishers, Fall River, MA. 1937. Bl/w drawings of George Washington, Abraham Lincoln, eagle, Boy Scouts. "Anthony Edition, A Symbol of Merit." 6pp. Page 2: Blank. Page 6: Advertising.

GW-352 That's The Flag For Me (Columbia Gem of the Ocean). w. Edw. T. Gahan. m. Edw. A. Jackson. Published by Shantz and Jackson, Music Publishers, Temple Building, Camden, NJ. 1916. R/w/b drawings of George Washington, Abraham Lincoln, flag, geometric design border. 6pp. Page 6: Advertising.

GW-353 George Washington. w.m. George M. Cohen. a. John W. Schaum. Published by Schaum Publications, Inc., No. 2018 East North Avenue, Milwaukee, WI. 1984. R/w/bl/ma drawing of George Washington, flag. "Piano Solo." 4pp. Page 2: "George Washington was truly 'first in war' not from any military disposition of his character, but because of his environment and the times in which he lived. After independence had been won, Washington laid aside his sword and voluntarily returned to the peace of his beloved home. Later he was elected President of the United States, proving that he was first in the hearts of his countrymen." Page 4: Advertising.

GW-354(A) Hail Columbia. In: *The Liberty Bell*, page 6. Published by William A. Pond & Company, No. 25 Union Square, New York, NY. 1876. [6 7/8" × 10 1/8"]. Gn/bk Liberty Bell design made from typed words of the Declaration of Independence, stars, geometric designs. 84pp.

(B) **Land Of Washington**, page 12.

(C) **Grave Of Washington**, page 44.

(D) **Washington's Farewell Address**, page 79.

GW-355 Hail Columbia. In: *War Songs*, page 10. Published by Woolson Spice Company, Toledo, OH. [ca. 1884]. [4 3/4" × 6 7/8"]. N/c litho of war scene, company logos for "Lion Coffee" and "Woolson Spice Co." "Dedicated to the G.A.R., The Woman's Relief Corps and The Sons of Volunteers." 36pp.

GW-356 Washington. w.m. Ireene Wicker (The Singing Story Lady). In: *Sing A Song of History*, page 28. Published by Educational Music Division, Irving Berlin, Inc., No. 799 Seventh Avenue, New York, NY. 1941. R/w/b drawings of historical events and people. "Recorded by Bluebird, Album No. 40." 52pp.

GW-357 Hail Columbia. In: *Wehman's American National Songs,* page 9. Published by Wehman Bros., New York, NY. 1898. [4 11/16" × 7 1/8"]. Bl/w litho of eagle, flag, stars. 64pp. Page 3: "A Choice Collection of American Patriotic and National Songs."

GW-358 The President On The Dollar. w. Bob Hilliard. m. Philip Springer. Published by Shapiro, Bernstein & Company, Inc., Music Publishers, New York, NY. 1956. Gn/w geometric designs. Gn/w photo of "Mitch Miller." 4pp. Page 4: Advertising.

GW-359 Hail Columbia. a. Bissell. Published by S.T. Gordon, No. 538 Broadway, New York, NY. [1850]. Non-pictorial geometric designs. "The Fancy Set for Two Performers on the Piano Forte." List of other titles in series.

GW-360 Hail Columbia. a. C. Everest. Published by Lee & Walker, No. 722 Chestnut Street, Philadelphia, PA. 1863. Non-pictorial geometric design border. "Musical Echoes, a Collection of Popular Airs Arranged without Octaves for the Piano." List of other titles in series.

GW-361(A) Hail Columbia. a. T. Bissell. Published by Oliver Ditson & Company, Washington Street, Boston, MA. 1857. Non-pictorial. "The Melodiana, A Selection of Popular Airs Arranged for the Melodeon and Other Related Reed Instruments." List of other titles in series.

(B) Washington's March.

GW-362 Hail Columbia. a. Johan Spindler. Published by S.T. Gordon, No. 706 Broadway, New York, NY. 1858. Non-pictorial geometric design border. "Golden Melodies Arranged for the Piano."

GW-363 Washington Arch (March). m. Joseph Von Weber. Published by H. Franklin Jones, Publisher, No. 669 Gates Avenue, Brooklyn, NY. 1894. Non-pictorial geometric design border. 6pp. Page 2: Blank. Page 6: Advertising.

GW-364 Washington's Sons. w. W.W. Saunders. m. Julia E. Emmett. Copyright 1943 by W.W. Saunders. B/w drawings by Joe Dolleslager of George Washington, Soldier, Sailor, Marine, Airman. "Washington's Sons will never live to be slaves." "This Song is Dedicated to all branches of the Armed Forces of the United States of America serving at home and abroad." 4pp. Page 4: B/w drawings of four airplanes.

GW-365 Jullien's American Quadrille. a. M. Jullien. Published by S.C. Jollie, No. 300 Broadway, New York, NY. 1853. R/w/b litho of American-like flag with stars in a diamond pattern. 10pp. Page 5: **Land Of Washington**. Page 6: **Hail To The Chief**. Page 12: Advertisement for music related to Jullien's American tour.

GW-366 Jullien's American Quadrille. a. M. Jullien. Published by S.C. Jollie, No. 300 Broadway, New York, NY. 1853. R/w/bl/bk litho by Michelin & Shattuck Company of U.S.-like flag. 10pp. Page 5: **Land Of Washington**. Page 6:. **Hail To The Chief**. Page 12: Blank.

GW-367 Thirty Minutes With Washington. w.m. Traditional. Story by H.L. Bland (Formerly Director of Music, State Teachers College, Clarion, PA). Published by Belwin, Inc., New York, NY. 1939. [6 3/4" × 10 1/2"]. B/w drawing of George Washington. B/w photo of scene from play. R/bk/gn cover. "A Dramatic Musicale Based on the life of our First President." 20pp.

GW-368 We Swear By Washington. w.m. Rodney Powers. Published by Rodney Powers, No. 145 West 45th Street, [New York, NY]. 1912. Br/w drawing of George Washington. 6pp. Pages 2 and 6: Blank.

GW-369 America's Flag. w.m. Nadage Doree. Published by Nadage Doree Society, No. 1947 Broadway, New York, NY. 1925. B/w drawing of "George Washington, The Father of His flag and His Country." R/w/b drawings of four U.S. flags. "Where there is no vision the people perish. A Nation has a soul as well as a body." 6pp. Page 2: "Dedicated to all nations that stand for real justice and a love to all mankind." Poem. Page 6: B/w photo of "Miss Nadage Doree, Born New

Orleans, U.S.A., Feb. 22, author of *Jesus Christianity by a Jewess*, &c." "A Nation has a soul as well as a body. I Prayed and fasted — I prayed to God for the Blessed Soul Privilege — to give All the people of All the World the High Ideals — the Sacred Spirit of America's Flag."

GW-370 Washington's Birthday. w.m. George L. Spaulding. Published by Theodore Presser Company, No. 1712 Chestnut, Philadelphia, PA. 1914. [Edition ca. 1930]. Non-pictorial geometric design border. "Days We Celebrate, Pianoforte Pieces Introducing Popular Melodies." List of other titles in series. 4pp.

GW-371 George Washington Crosses The Delaware. m. Jane Smisor Bastien. Published by General Words & Music Company, Park Ridge, IL. 1945. Gn/bk/w reproduction of the painting of Washington crossing the Delaware River, outline of a piano. "Music through the Piano." [8 1/2" × 11"]. 4pp.

GW-372 Hail Columbia. m. Philip Phile. a. Henry Weber. Published by The Willis Music Company, Cincinnati, OH. 1918. [Edition ca. 1930]. R/w/b geometric designs. "Arranged in the Simplest Manner." 4pp. Page 2: "Written during the threatened war with France, 1798." Page 4: Advertising.

GW-373 A Salute To George Washington And Abraham Lincoln. w.m. Edward and Cecile Edelson. Published by C&E Enterprises, P.O. Box 8159, Haleden, NJ. 07538. 1986. R/w/b silhouettes of George Washington and Abraham Lincoln. Two bars of music. 4pp.

GW-374 The First President (1789). w.m. Helen Cramm. Published by Boston Music Company, Boston, MA. 1920. R/w/b drawing of U.S. map. "The U.S.A. in Rhyme and Lay, To Play and Sing in School and Home." List of other titles in series. 4pp. Page 2: "It is a Great Thing to be the Father of his Country! (Prince Albert of Belgium, at the Tomb of Washington in 1898)."

GW-375 Let George Do It (A Musical For Young Voices). w. Marti McCartney. m. John F. Wilson. Published by Somerset Press, Carol Stream, IL. 1975. [6 7/8" × 10 1/4"]. R/w/bl/bk vignettes of George Washington. 16pp.

GW-376 Washington. w. David Stevens. m. Louis Adolphe Coerne. In: *Folk Songs and Art Songs For Intermediate Grades, Book II*, p. 36. Edited by Teresa Armitage. Published by C.C. Birchard & Company, Boston, MA. 1924. [6 1/2" × 8 7/8"]. Hardback book. Bk/br litho of wreath, lyre. "The Laurel Music Series." 166pp.

GW-377 There Are Just As Many Heroes To-Day. w. Thomas S. Allen. m. Joseph M. Daly. Published by Daly Music Publisher, No. 665 Washington Street, Boston, MA. 1914. R/w/b drawings/photos of George Washington, Abraham Lincoln, Ulysses S. Grant and Admiral George Dewey, shield — "1776-1861," stars. 6pp. Pages 2 and 6: Advertising.

GW-378 Hail Columbia (The President's March). m. J. Failes [sic]. a. M. Greenwald. Published by Century Music Publishing Company, No. 231-235 West 40th Street, New York, NY. 1917. [Edition ca. 1930]. Gn/w drawings of famous composers "Roff," "Wieniawski" and "Spohr," floral design border of lilies with violin. "Duos for Violin and Piano." "Sixteen Transcriptions of Famous American Songs for Violin (In First Position) with Piano Accompaniment." 6pp. Pages 2 and 6: Advertising.

GW-379(A) Hail Columbia. w. Joseph Hopkinson. m. "Attributed to Philip Phile." "The music of this song, originally known as *The Washington March*...It was written in 1789 as an inaugural march for George Washington..." In: *The Golden Book of Favorite Songs*, page 9. Published by Hall and McCreary Company, No. 434 South Wabash Avenue, Chicago, IL. 1923. [5 7/8" × 8 3/4"]. [V-1: Y/bk geometric designs.] [V-2: Bl/w drawing of three women].

(B) Hail To The Chief, page 40. w. Sir. Walter Scott. m. James Sanderson.

GW-380 Hail Columbia. In: *Star Collection of Old Favorite Songs*, page 10. Published by [V-1: C. Kurtzmann & Company, No. 526 Niagara Street, Buffalo, NY] [V-2: Fred W. Peabody, No. 16 Main Street, Amesbury, MA]. [19—]. [5 13/16" × 8 5/8"]. Bl/w photo of woman at a piano. 36pp. [V-1: "Words and Music for 4 Voices and Piano." "These old time songs, like the famous Kurtzmann Piano, are the Favorite of Favorites, in fact, the Kurtzmann Piano is recognized everywhere as the Standard of all Standard Pianos"].

GW-381 Mrs. Washington's Minuet. m. Pierre Landrin Duport. a. W. Oliver Strunk. In: *The Etude Music Magazine*, page 151, March, 1938. "This alluring minuet...was recently brought to life by the United States government in...*Music Associated with the Period of the Formation of the Constitution*. This is reprinted with the consent of the general director, Congressman Sol Bloom. The Minuet was once danced before Mrs. Washington."

GW-382(A) Hail Columbia. In: *The American Songster, Containing a Choice Selection of About One Hundred and Fifty Modern and Popular Songs*, page 4. Published by Cornish, Lamport & Company, No. 267 Pearl Street, New York, NY. 1851. Hardback. "Sterotype Edition." [3" × 4 5/8"]. 272pp.

(B) Immortal Washington, page 173. m. "Tune — *Bunches of Rushes*."

GW-383 Washington's March. In: *Willig's Juvenile Instructor for the Piano-Forte, In Which Rudiments of Music are Simplified to Suit the Youngest Pupil to which is added a Selection of Popular Airs*, page 26. Published by George Willig, Jr., Baltimore, MD. 1835. [6 3/4" × 10 1/4"]. Y/bk non-pictorial.

GW-384 Hail Columbia. w. Joseph Hopkinson. In: *The Florida Chief*, page 1, Vol. VI, No. 50. Published by *The Florida Chief* Publishing Company, Winter Haven, FL. August 30, 1917. B/w drawing of Miss Liberty.

GW-385(A) George Washington (Rote). w.m. Josephine Wolverton. In: *The American Singer, Book 3*, page 144. Published by American Book Company, New York, NY. 1946. [6 5/8" × 8 3/8"]. R/w/b stars, bars of music.

GW-386 Hail Columbia. a. Charles Voss, Op. 242. Published by G. Andre & Company, No. 1104 Chestnut Street, Philadelphia, PA. [1858-1875]. N/c litho of eagle, shield, geometric designs. List of titles in series. "America Transcriptions Brillantes sur des Airs Americains Populairs Composees pour Piano."

GW-387(A) Hail Columbia. Published by S.T. Gordon, No. 706 Broadway, New York, NY. 1861. N/c litho of flag, eagle, shield, rifles, geometric designs. "National Melodies." List of titles in series.

(B) Hail Columbia Rondo. a. Beyer.

GW-388 Andre's Request To Washington. m. Joseph E. Sweetser. Published by Oliver Ditson & Company, No. 277 Washington Street, Boston, MA. [ca. 1850]. Non-pictorial geometric designs. "The Boudoir: A Collection of Favorite Songs." List of titles in series.

GW-389 Hail Columbia. a. E. Mack. Published by Lee & Walker, No. 722 Chestnut Street, Philadelphia, PA. [ca. 1860]. Litho by Sinclair's of woman, children, piano. "The Young Patriots." List of titles in series.

GW-390 George Washington. w.m. George Ware. Adapted by Herbert Hersey. Published by John F. Perry & Company, No. 538 Washington Street, Boston, MA. 1875. B/w litho by J.M. Bufford's Sons from a J.E. Baker drawing of George Washington, Miss Liberty,

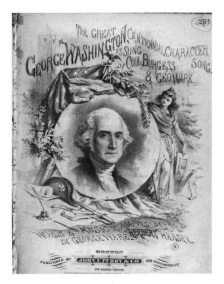

GW-390

flag, Washington Monument. "The Great Centennial Character Song, as Sung by Cool Burgess and Geo. Ware." 8pp. Page 8: Advertising.

GW-391(A) Washington. w. W.W. Caldwell. m. L.B. Marshall. e. Chas. W. Johnson. In: *Songs of the Nation, Patriotic and National College and Home, Occasional and Devotional*, page 127. Published by Silver, Burdett & Company, New York, NY. 1896. [7 1/8" × 9 3/8"]. V-1: R/w/b flag, capitol] [V-2: R/w/b flag].

(B) Hail Columbia, page 18.

GW-392 Washington Monument By Night. w. Carl Sandburg. m. Sam Raphling. Published by Edition Musicus, New York, NY. 1952. B/w drawing of Washington Monument, Capitol Dome. "Music for Voice and Piano." 6pp. Page 2: "To a Fine American, Ruth B. Shipley." B/w drawing of town, sign — "Main Street, U.S.A." Page 6: Adv.

GW-393 A Washington Miscellany (For Double Chorus of Treble Voices). w. George Washington. m. Edwin London. Published by Associated Music Publishers, Inc., New York, NY. Copyright 1963 and 1968. [8 7/8" × 10 3/8"]. Be/bk drawing of George Washington. "Text from the writings of George Washington." "I. Promises, II. Time, III. Potatoes." 16pp. Page 2: "*A Washington Miscellany* is dedicated to Iva Dee Hiatt and the Smith College Glee Club and Choir." "I. Promises. 'Undertake not what you cannot perform but be careful to keep your promise' — Rules of Civility, 82nd, 1745." "II. Time. 'Time is of more importance than is generally imagined' — Letter to James Anderson, Dec. 19, 1799." "III. 'Potatoes of all the improving and ameliorating crops, none are equal to potatoes on stiff and hard bound land' — Letter to Thomas Jefferson, Oct. 4, 1975."

GW-394 Some Rules Of Etiquette According To George Washington. w. George Washington. m. Sol Berkowitz. Published by Elkan-Vogel, Inc., a subsidiary of the Theodore Presser Company, Bryn Mawr, PA. 19010. 1975. [6 7/8" × 10 1/2"]. B/w drawing of George Washington. "Two Part Chorus and Piano." 12pp. Page 2: "Note — When George Washington was a young man of fifteen, he copied a long list of the proper rules of etiquette from a book of his day. A few of these rules have been used in this setting..."

GW-395 Landmarks Of Early American Music, 1760-1800 (A Collection of Thirty-Two Compositions). c.e.a. Richard Franko Goldman and Roger Smith. Published by G. Shirmer, Inc., New York, NY. 1943. [6 3/4" × 10 1/4"]. Be/bk non-pictorial. "For Orchestra or Band or smaller instrumental groups or Mixed Chorus (SATB) with or without Accompaniment." List of arrangements. 20pp. Page 8: **The Toast To General Washington** (1778). w.m. Francis Hopkinson. Page 10: B/w reproduction of the illustrated title portion of **Brother Soldiers All Hail!** Page 11: **Dirge For General Washington** (1799). w.m. Dr. George K. Jackson.

GW-396 Hail Columbia. w. F. Hopkinson, 1798. m. *President's March*. In: *Favorite Songs and Hymns*, page 153. [ca. 1900]. [6 3/4" × 9 3/4"].

GW-397 Washington's Birthday Waltz. m. Adam Preston. Published by McKinley Music Company, Chicago, IL. 1916. O/gn/w floral design. List of titles.

GW-398 Yankee Doodle And Hail Columbia. a. Adolphe Baumbach. Published by Henry Tolman & Company, No. 291 Washington Street, Boston, MA. 1860. B/w non-pictorial geometric designs. "Echoes of the Past, Arranged for the Piano Forte." List of titles in series.

GW-399 Song Of The American Revolution. a. Shirley Munger. Published by Shawnee Press, Inc., Delaware Water Gap, PA. 18397. 1975. [6 7/8" × 10 1/2"]. R/w/b drawing of George Washington crossing the Delaware River. "For Mixed Voices." 12pp. Page 2: Narrative on the various tunes, including *Castle Island Song* and its relationship with John Adams. "Songs of the Revolution was first performed by the West Chester State College Marching Band & Concert Choir at Veterans' Stadium in Philadelphia on November 10, 1974." Page 3: "To Donna Bingham Mungle and in Commemoration of the Bicentennial of the United States of America (1975-1976)."

GW-400 Hail Columbia. a. J. Fayles [sic]. In: *Rubank Holiday Collection, Containing the Best Known and Most Famous National Songs—Folk Songs—Hymns—Ballads and Musical Compositions for Every Occasion*, page 5. e. E. Delamater. Published by Rubank, Inc., Chicago, IL. 1932. 28pp.

GW-401 Hail Columbia. a. Bruen. Published by Russell & Tolman, No. 219 Washington Street, Boston, MA. 1833. B/w engraving by Green & Walker of leaves, vines lattice. "A Collection of Popular Duetts [sic], Songs and Ballads Arranged for the Piano by Various Authors." List of songs in series.

GW-402 Hail Columbia. Published by Frederick Blume, No. 27 Union Square, Broadway, New York, NY. 1870. B/w litho of geometric designs. "Blume's Dance Souvenir." List of songs in series.

GW-403 Hail Columbia. a. Harry Prendiville. In: *The Leaders Joy Band Book*, page 8. Published by Edward A. Samuels, Publisher, Boston, MA. [ca. 1890]. [6 7/8" × 5"]. Non-pictorial. "Containing Sixty-One National and Popular Airs." 32pp.

GW-404 Hail Columbia. In: *Our National Songs*, page 8. Copyright 1889 by Alex L. Van Dyke, Philadelphia, [PA]. Published for White Sewing Machine Company, Cleveland, OH. [4 3/4" × 6 1/8"]. B/w litho of woman with flag. "American Patriotic Melodies with Words." 12pp.

GW-405 Hail Columbia. In: *American Songs*, page 9. [ca. 1893]. Published for Ludwig Piano Company. [5 1/16" × 7 9/16"]. R/bk litho of U.S. flag. "A Collection of National Airs." 12pp.

GW-406 Hail Columbia. Published by John Church, Jr., No. 66 West Fourth Street, Cincinnati, OH. [ca. 1860]. B/w engraving by Greene of a family gathered around a piano. "The Home Circle, A Collection of Standard Melodies." List of songs in series.

GW-407 Follow Washington (Song Of The American Revolution). a. Eric Steiner. Published by Belwin, Inc., Rockville Centre, L.I., NY. 1960. R/w/gn/pk drawing of a silhouette of George Washington on horseback. "Piano Solo with Words." "An Eric Steiner Arrangement." 4pp. Page 4: Advertising.

GW-408(A) Washington. w.m. Richmond K. Fletcher. In: *Tunes and Harmonies (The World of Music)*, page 122. Published by Ginn & Company. 1943. [7" × 9"]. Hard cover book. Bl/gd drawing of globe, music notes, stars. 216pp.

(B) Hail Columbia. w. Joseph Hopkinson. m. Philip Phile.

GW-409 Fifth Regiment March. m. James M. Deems. 1848. B/w litho of monument of George Washington in Baltimore, Maryland. "Dedicated to General Benjamin Chew."

GW-410 Washington — Jefferson College Song. w.m. Bertha Chadwick Trowbridge. Published by Garden Roads Press, P.O.B. 877, New Haven, CT. Copyright 1932 by Mrs. Efford Trowbridge. R/w/bk college logo — "Sigillum Collegii Washingtoniensis Et Jeffersoniensis — MDCCCLXV, Juncta-Juvant, 1802-1806." 6pp. Pages 2 and 6: Blank.

GW-411 Hail Columbia. In: *War Songs*, page 66. Published by The Oliver Ditson Company, Nos. 453-463 Washington Street, Boston, MA. 1890. R/w/bl/y drawings of flag, G.A.R. medal. B/w photos of litho of Ulysses S. Grant, two generals. "The Choruses of all Songs are Arranged for Male Voices." "For anniversaries and gatherings of soldiers." "Dedicated to the G.A.R." 100pp.

GW-412 Hail Columbia. In: *War Songs*, page 66. Published by The Oliver Ditson Company, Boston, MA. 1906. [6 3/4" × 10 3/16"]. N/c photos of Ulysses S. Grant, two other generals, flags. "For Anniversaries and Gatherings of Soldiers. The Choruses of all Songs are Arranged for Mixed Voices." "Dedicated to the G.A.R." 140pp. Page 140: Advertising.

GW-413 Hail Columbia. In: *War Songs*, page 66. Published by The Oliver Ditson Company, Nos. 453-463 Washington Street, Boston, MA. 1890. B/w photo of Ulysses S. Grant, two other generals. Drawing of flag, G.A.R. medal. "The choruses of all songs are arranged for male voices." "For anniversaries and gatherings of soldiers." "Dedicated to the G.A.R." 100pp. Pages 2, 99 and 100: Advertising.

GW-414 Hail Columbia. e. George Root. In: *The Bugle Call*, page 30. Published by Root & Cady, No. 95 Clark Street, Chicago, IL. 1863. 64pp. O/bk non-pictorial line cover.

GW-415 Hail Columbia. w. Joseph Hopkinson. In: *Gospel, Patriotic and Temperance Songster (For Public and Private Song Service)*, page 7. [ca. 1899]. [5 3/8" × 7"]. Be/bk litho of a man. Advertising for up-state New York retail stores. 26pp.

GW-416 Hail Columbia. In: *The Old Songs You Love*, page 28. Published by Kirk, Johnson & Company, No. 16 King Street, Lancaster, PA. Copyright 1925 by W.H. Doyle. [6 1/8" × 9 1/4"]. B/w geometric design border. "Complied Especially for Milton Piano Company, Manufacturers of Milton Pianos, The Distinguished Instrument." 36pp.

GW-417 Hail Columbia. c. Fred. Beyer. Published by Lee & Walker, No. 162 Chesnut Street, Philadelphia, PA. [ca. 185-]. Non-pictorial dark black line and geometric design border. "America, 8 Popular American Melodies Arranged as Rondinos for the Piano." List of other titles in series.

GW-418 Hail Columbia. m.a.c. Ferd. Beyer, Op. 95. Published by A. Foit, No. 196 Chesnut Street, Philadelphia, PA. [ca. 185-]. Non-pictorial black line and geometric design border. "America, 8 Popular American Melodies Arranged as Rondinos for the Piano." List of other titles in series. 6pp. Page 6: Blank.

GW-419 Hail Columbia. c. Fred. Beyer. Published by William Hall & Son, No. 239 Broadway, New York, NY. [ca. 185-]. Non-pictorial floral and geometric design border. "America, 8 Popular American Melodies Arranged as Rondinos for the Piano." List of other titles in series.

GW-420 Hail Columbia (Quartet). In: *America's Song Kit*, page 28. Published by Treasure Chest Publications, Inc., New York, NY. 1941. [6 3/4" × 9 1/2"]. N/c drawing of eagle, Independence Hall, Statue of Liberty, soldiers singing, star and stripe background. Musical notation and verse—"Here's a song to all who love those who love them, the love those that love them that love us." 36pp.

GW-421 The Putnam Phalanx (Song and March). w.m. Felix J. O'Neill. Copyright 1933 by Felix J. O'Neill. Br/w drawing of "Major General Israel Putnam, Beloved by Washington." B/w geometric designs. "The Putnam Phalanx, Hartford, Conn." 4pp. Page 4: "Dedicated to The Putnam Phalanx and kindred organizations designed to keep uncovered the rough trails trod by our forefathers of Colonial Days. Patriotic societies keep the past ever present. They keep the ancient path from being overgrown and hidden by the weed of modern ease. They teach the son that if he will step in the footprints of the sire, from time to time, no weed can thrive in those sacred traces. Especially is this true if the son adopts the very uniform and the tactics and the music used by both sides in our struggle for nationhood. The trail George Washington trod, to win our liberty, will never be overgrown by the weeds and briars and brush of forgetfulness, while such patriotic units as The Putnam Phalanx and The Governor's Foot Guard and The Mattatuck Fife and Drum Corps can swing a scythe.—Felix J. O'Neill."

GW-422 Hail Columbia. In: *Merry Chimes, A Collection of Songs, Duets, Trios and Sacred Pieces For Juvenile Classes, Public Schools and Seminaire*, page 154. e. L.O. Emerson. Published by O. Ditson & Company, No. 277 Washington Street, Boston, MA. [5 3/8" × 7"]. 1865. Gn/bk geometric designs. 224pp.

GW-423 George Washington. w. John Pierpont. m. "Tune—*America*." "For Washington's Birthday." In: *The Sunny Side: A Book of Religious Songs For The Sunday School and The Home*, page 94. e. C.W. Wendte and H.S. Perkins. Published by William A. Pond & Company, No. 25 Union Square, New York, NY. 1895. [5 1/2" × 6 7/8"]. Be/bk drawing of baby angel orchestra, geometric designs. 144pp.

GW-424 Hail Columbia. Published by William Dubois, New York, NY. [ca. 1835]. Non-pictorial geometric designs. "A Favorite Patriotic Song for the Piano Forte." 4pp. Pages 1 and 4: Blank.

GW-425 Hail Columbia. In: *Singer's Own Book, A Well-Selected Collection of the Most Popular Sentimental, Amatory, Patriotic Naval & Comic Songs*, page 34. Published by [V-1 and V-2: Key, Mielke & Biddle, No. 181 Market Street] [V-3: Key & Biddle, No. 6 Minor Street], Philadelphia, PA. 1832. [3 1/8" × 5 1/8"]. [V-1: Bk/gd] [V-2: Gn/gd] [V-3: Br/gd] non-pictorial. [V-2: "New Edition"]. 322[?]pp.

GW-426 Hail Columbia. In: *The Nightingale, A New Juvenile Singing Book*, page 60. e. W.O. and H.S. Perkins. Published by Oliver Ditson & Company, No. 277 Washington Street, Boston, MA. 1860. [7" × 5 3/8"]. Gn/bk litho of bird, branch. 220pp

GW-427 Hail Columbia. In: *The Boston Melodeon: A Collection of Secular Melodies Consisting of Songs, Glees, Rounds, Catches, &c., Including Many of The Most Popular Pieces of The Day (Vol. 1)*, page 108. e. Edward I. White (Teacher of the Piano Forte and Organ). Published by B.B. Mussey & Company, No. 29 Cornhill, Boston, MA. 1846. [10" × 6 7/8"]. Gn/bk geometric designs.

GW-428 How To Close The War. w. George P. Hardwick (Washington, D.C.). m. "Air—*Jordan Is A Hard Road To Travel*." Published by Charles Magnus, No. 12 Frankfort Street, New York, NY. [ca. 186-]. [5" × 8"]. R/w/bl/br/y litho of eagle, flag, George Washington. "500 Illustrated Ballads, Lithographed and Printed by Charles Magnus, No. 12 Frankfort Street, New York; Branch Office: No. 520 7th St., Washington, D.C." 2pp. Page 2: Blank.

GW-429 Washington's March. a. Charles Grobe. Published by Oliver Ditson & Company, Washington Street, Boston, MA. 1855. Non-pictorial. "Melodies of the Day, A Collection of Popular Airs with Easy and Pleasing Variations, Composed for the Piano Forte." List of other titles in series.

GW-430 Hail Columbia. In: *Americana Collection For Band, Orchestra And Chorus*, [V-2: page 4] [V-2: page 5]. Published by Rubank, Inc., Miami, FL. 1942. [V-1: 5 7/8" × 8 3/4"] [V-2: 6 7/8" × 5 1/8"]. Bl/w eagle, stars. [V-1: Vocal Edition] [V-2: Band Edition]. 36pp.

GW-431 Mount Vernon Polka. m. Johann Spindler. Published by S.T. Gordon, No. 706 Broadway, New York, NY. 1861. Non-pictorial geometric design border. "None Such, A Collection of Beautiful And Attractive Piano Forte Pieces." List of other titles in series.

GW-432 For Our Country, Home, And Flag (Patriotic March Song). w.m. Eugene R. Kenney. Published by Eugene R. Kenney, New York, NY. 1917. R/w/b drawing by Pfeiffer of George Washington, Washington crossing the Delaware River, Liberty Bell, eagle, flags, ribbon. 4pp.

GW-433 Hail Columbia. m. Philip Phile. a. Maxwell Eckstein. In: *Let Us Have Music for Piano* (In Two Volumes), page 5. Published by Carl Fisher, New York, NY. 1949. Gn/w drawing of a piano. "Volume Two. Sixty-Nine Famous Melodies. Lyrics are included with most of these numbers." 114pp.

GW-434 Our Noble Washington. w. Edna G. Young. m.a. I.H. Meredith. In: *Merry Songs For Merry Singers, A Collection of Sacred, Secular, Nature and Patriotic Songs for Children*, page 16. e. I.H. Meredith and Grant Colfax Tullar. Published by Tullar-Meredith, No. 265 West 36th Street, New York, NY. 1914. N/c photo of children at flag raising. Gn/w geometric design border. Hardback.

GW-435(A) Hail Columbia. In: *The Army and Navy Fife Instructor: Containing the Calls, Signals, and the Complete Camp and Garrison Duties as Practised in the Army and Navy of the United States, Including the Volunteer and Regular Service, Containing the National Airs, and a Large Collection of Marches, Quicksteps, Waltzes, Polkas, &c.*, page 16. e.a. Elias Howe. Published by Elias Howe, Agt., No. 103 Court Street, Boston, MA. Copyright 1863 by Willard Howe.
  (B) **Washington's March**, page 25.
  (C) **Washington's Grand March**, page 25.
  (D) **March In Memory Of Washington**, page 29.

GW-436 Little Commander (March). m. Robert A. Hellard. "Washington's Birthday seems to call for a patriotic march that everyone can play. Mr. Hellard's snappy 'Little Commander' fills the bill; and we know that thousands of teachers will make this the background for improvised rhythm band, even if the instruments are all homemade from forks, goblets, pie plates, and what have you." "Grade 2 1/2." "Copyright 1946 by Theodore Presser Co." In: *Etude: The Music Magazine*, page 88, Volume LXVII, No. 2, February, 1949.

GW-437 In Honor Of George Washington (Washington's Birthday). w. A.E. Allen. m. Carl Wald. In: *New American Music Reader Number Three (Part Two)*, page 126. e. Frederick Zuchtmann. Published by The MacMillan Company, New York, NY. 1914. Gn/bk lyre. 168pp.

GW-438 Hail Columbia. w. Joseph Hopkinson. "Here is a song strictly American. The tune was composed as a march, probably during the Revolutionary War, and was played at Washington's Inauguration…" In: *Patriotic Songs of America*, page 4. Published by John Hancock Mutual Life Insurance Company, Boston, MA. 1928. R/w/b eagle. 20pp.

GW-439 Washington Grays (March and Two-Step). m. C.S. Grafulla. a. Alfred Roth. Published by Carl Fischer, Cooper Square, New York, NY. 1906. Bl/w drawing of George Washington on horseback, crossed flags, eagle. 6pp. Page 6: Advertising.

GW-440 George Washington (Reading Song). w. Jean Bassett. m. Franz Joseph Hyden. "George Washington and Franz Joseph Hyden were born the same year, 1732." In: *The Music Hour (Third Book)*, page 71. Published by Silver Burdett Company, New York, NY. 1929. 62pp.

GW-441 Hail Columbia. w.m. J. Fayles [sic]. In: *The Radio-Collection of National Songs and Hymns*. Published by Rubank, Inc., Chicago, IL. 1924. [6 7/8" × 10 3/16"]. Non-pictorial. 24pp.

GW-442 Hail Columbia. a. Louis Victor Saar. In: *Five American Songs*, page 7. Published by Art Publication Society, St. Louis, MO. 1935. R/w/b flags. 8pp. Pages 2 and 8: Advertising.

GW-443 Hail Columbia. w. F. Hopkinson. m. *The President's March*. In: *The Abridged Academy Song-Book*, page 4. Published by Ginn & Company, Boston, MA. 1898. [6 5/8" × 9"]. Gn/gd/be geometric designs. 318pp.

GW-444 George Washington. w. Cordelia Brooks Fenno and Frederick H. Martens. m. "Old French Air." a. Humphrey Mitchell. In: *Junior Laurel Songs*, page 42. c. m. Teresa Armitage. Published by C.C. Birchard & Company, Boston, MA. 1917. 164pp.

GW-445 Star Spangled Banner and **Our Flag Is There**. In: *George Washington, Young Folks Library of Choice Literature, Vol. #1*, No. 28, page 29. Published by Educational Publishing Company, Boston, MA. May 1, 1895. [5" × 6 3/4"]. 36pp.

GW-446 Hail Columbia. In: *The Old Glory Song Book, Our Best National Patriotic Songs*, page 4. Published by The Lowell Commercial College. Copyright 1917 by Illinois State Register, Springfield, IL. 20pp.

GW-447 Hail Columbia. w. F. Hopkinson, 1798. In: *The Kranz-Smith Piano Company Song Collection, Vol. #3 — No. 32*, page 8. Published by The Kranz-Smith Piano Company, G. Fred Kranz, President, No. 100 North Charles Street, Baltimore, MD. [4 7/8" × 7 1/8"]. [189-]. Br/bk geometric design. 36pp.

GW-448 Hail Columbia. w. Hopkinson. In: *America's Most Famous Songs*, page 15. Published by Leo Fiest, Nos. 231-235 West 40th Street, New York, NY. [ca. 1918]. [6" × 8 3/4"]. N/c drawing of flowers. 68pp.

GW-449 Hail To Washington. w.m. Robert W. Gibb. Drawing of Mt. Rushmore. In: *Our Land of Song*, page 95. Published by C.L. Birchard & Company, Boston, MA. 1947. [6 7/8" × 8 11/16"].

GW-450 George Washington. w. Annette Waynne. m. Johnny Green. Drawing of Boy Scout and George Washington saluting. Song copyright 1919. In: *New Music Horizons (Fifth Book)*, page 94. Published by Silver, Burdett Company, New York, NY. 1946. [6 3/4" × 8 7/16"].

GW-451 Mansion House March. m. H.C. Hobbs. 1915. Bk/w/gn/br photo of mansion, geometric designs. "Dedicated to The Mansion House, Poland Springs, Maine, Washington's Birthday, February 22, 1915." 6pp. Page 6: Blank.

GW-452(A) President's March, page 8. [ca. 180-]. Non-pictorial handwritten copy book of William Felton, 2d. 28pp.

(B) **General Washington's March**, page 15.

(C) **Lady Washington**, page 15.

GW-453 George Washington. [8 5/8" × 7 1/4"]. Handwritten copy of a song from [Hallis Down?], page 74. Date unknown.

GW-454 George Washington's

Birthday Party. m. C.L. Barnhouse. a. Andy Clark. Published by C.L. Barnhouse Company, No. 205 Cowan Avenue West, Oskaloosa, IA. 52577. Copyright 1998 Birch Island Music Press. N/c picture of George Washington. "Complete Band with Full Orchestra Score."

GW-455 George Washington. w. Louise Stickney. m. Ralph L. Baldwin. In: *Introductory Music*, page 146. Published by Ginn & Company, Boston, MA. 1923. [6 1/2" × 8 3/16"]. Bl/bk hardback book. 184pp.

GW-456 Song Of Washington's Men (Quartette). w.m. James G. Clark. Published by Henry Tolman, No. 153 Washington Street, Boston, MA. 1855. B/w litho of garden trellis, flowers. "A Collection of Ballads, Duetts and Quartettes Sung by Ossian's Bards [sic]." "Poetry and Music Composed and Arranged for the Piano by James G. Clark." 6pp. Pages 2 and 6: Blank. Page 3: "Dedicated to the Continental Vocalists."

GW-457 Virginia. w. Harry Curran Wilber. m. May Walton Kent. Published by May Walton Kent, Apt. 304, No. 1705 Lanier Place, N.W., Chicago, IL. 1911. Bl/w drawing of Virginia state flag. Br/w photos of two statues: "Geo. Washington" and Robert E. Lee." Br/w geometric designs. 6pp + inserts. Page 2: "Dedicated to Capt. Chas. R. Skinner, One of Virginia's bravest Sons." Page 6: Advertising. Two inserts with versions for singers. Small pamphlet advertising the song with a photo of May Walton Kent.

GW-458 The National Shrine (The Temple Songs). w.m. Martha Lee Allison. Published by Martha Lee Allison, Wytheville, VA. 1932. Bl/w drawing of "George Washington National Masonic Memorial." Bl/w litho of George Washington painting. R/w geometric design border. "Dedicated to the George Washington National Masonic Memorial." 6pp. Page 6: Blank.

GW-459 Washington's March. Published by Winner & Shuster, No. 110 North Eighth Street, Philadelphia, PA. [ca. 184-]. Non-pictorial. Followed on page one by *Norma March*. 2pp. Page 2: Blank.

GW-460 Hail Columbia! w. Joseph Hopkinson. In: *The Community Chorus Book*, page 54. Published by The John C. Winston Company, No. 1010 Arch Street, Philadelphia, PA. 1918. [6" × 8 1/2"]. Bk/be logo, geometric design border. "Containing Songs for all Popular, Patriotic, Religious and Classical; Songs for Institute & Community Singing." c. Carroll Dawnes and Logan Marshall. 84pp.

GW-461(A) Washington. m. Percival. In: *The Southern Warbler, A New Collection of Patriotic, National, Naval, Martial, Professional, Convivial, Humorous, Pathetic, Sentimental, Old, and New Songs*, page 315. Published by Babcock & Company, Charleston, SC. 1845. [3 5/8" × 6 7/8"]. Gold imprinting of a lyre, music page, instruments and eagle on brown hard cover. 330pp.

(B) **Hail Columbia**, page 19.

GW-462 Blake's New & Complete Preceptor for the Violin (With a Favorite Selection of Airs, Marches, &c.). Printed & Sold by G.E. Blake, No. 13 South Fifth Street, Philadelphia. PA. [181-?]. 26pp. "Price 75 cents." "Fourth Edition." Inside title: **Blake's Violin Preceptor**. [W-863].

(A) **Hail Columbia**, page 22.
(B) **Washington's March** [At the Battle of Trenton], page 23.

GW-463 Aitken's Fountain Of Music (For Clarinet and Violin). Published & engrav'd [sic] by John Aitken & sold at his musical repository, No. 27 North 2d Street, Philadelphia, PA. [1807-1811]. Title page engraving of monument, trees at Central Square, Philadelphia, crossed instruments and open music book. "Containing an agreeable variety of the most celebrated air's, song's, duett's, dance's, hornpipe's, reel's,

marche's, minuett's, &c., &c. [sic]." 26pp. [W-65].
    (A)   **President's New March**, p. 17.
    (B)   **Washington's March**, p. 24.

GW-464 Dirge For General Washington. m. Dr. G.K. Jackson. In: *New Miscellaneous Musical Works for the Voice and Pianoforte: Consisting of Songs, Serenades, Cantatas, Canzonetts, Canons, Glees, &c., &c.*, page 17. "Printed for the Author." "Copyright Secured." 20pp. [S/U, page 293].

GW-465 Evening Amusement *(Containing fifty airs, song's duetts', dances, hornpipe's, reel's, marches, minuett's, &c., &c., for 1 and 2 German flutes or violins* [sic]." "Price 75 cents." Printed & Sold at B. Carr's Musical Repositories, Philadelphia [PA] & New York [NY] & J. Carr's, Baltimore [MD]. [1796]. 32pp. [S/U, page 127].
    (A)   **God Save The Great Washington**, page 14. [Tune: *God Save The King*].
    (B)   **General Washingtons March**, page 19.

GW-466 Immortal Washington. [No Publisher indicated]. [ca. 1800]. Non-pictorial. 2pp. Page 2: Blank. [S/U, page 204].

GW-467 Instrumental Assistant, Vol. I (Containing instructions for the violin, German flute, clarionett [sic], bass viol and hautboy. Compiled from late European publications. Also a selection of favorite airs, marches, &c. Progressively arranges and adapted for the use of learners.) m. Samuel Holyoke, A.M. "Printed at Exeter, New Hampshire, by H. Ranlet, and sold at his book store." [1800]. [S/U, page 209].
    (A)   **President's March**, page 59.
    (B)   **Washington's March**, page 69.

GW-468 Let Washington Be Our Boast. w.m. Mr. Hodgkinson. Printed & Sold at J. Hewitt's Musical Repository, No. 23 Maiden Lane, New York, NY. [1800]. Non-pictorial. "Sung with great applause at The Theatre at the conclusion of the Ode to the memory of Gen'l G. Washington." "Pr. 25 cents." Arranged for "Guittar" [sic]. [S/U, page 227].

GW-469 Let Washington Be Our Boast. In: *A Collection of New & Favorite Songs*, page 10 "Printed & Sold by B. Carr, Philadelphia; I. Hewitt, New York & J. Carr, Baltimore. Where may be had all the newest musical productions." 220pp. [S/U, page 71].

GW-470 America's Lamentation For Washington. In: *The Easy Instructor, or a new method of teaching sacred harmony, containing the rudiments of music on an improved plan wherein the naming and timing of the notes are familiarized to the weakest capacity....*" e. William Little and William Smith. 1802. [S/U, page 117].

GW-471 The Complete Tutor (For the Fife, Containing ye best & easiest instructions for learners to obtain a proficiency. To which is added a choice collection of ye most celebrated marches, airs, &c. Properly adapted to that instrument, with several choice pieces for two flutes). Printed for & sold by George Willig, No. 12 South Fourth Street, Philadelphia [PA], where also may had a great variety of other music, musical instruments, strings, &c., &c. [ca. 1805]. 30pp. [W-9425].
    (A)   **President's March**, page 21.
    (B)   **Washingtons March**, page 21.

GW-472 President's March. In: *New Instructions for the German Flute, Containing the easiest & most modern method for learners to play. To Which is added a favorite collection of minuets, marches, song-tunes, duets, &c., the method of tongueing* [sic]*, and a complete scale & description of a new invented German flute with the additional keys such as played on by two eminent masters, Fiorio and Tacet*, page[V-1:22] [V-2: 30]. Printed & sold at G. Willig's Musical Magazine, [V-1: No.

165 Market Street, Philadelphia, PA. 1795-1797] [V-2: No. 185 Market Street, Philadelphia, PA. 1801-1804]. 32pp. Followed on page [V-1: 22] [V-1: 30] by **God Save Great Washington**. [W-4492].

GW-473 Military Amusement (A Collection of twenty four of the most favorite marches. Adapted for one or two German flute's, violin's, fife's or oboe's, &c. [sic]. "Printed & sold at B. Carr's Musical Repositories, Philadelphia and New York & J. Carr's, Baltimore. [1796]. 24pp. [S/U, page 98].

    (A)   **President's March**, page 3.
    (B)   **Washington's March**, page 4.
    (C)   **New President's March**, page 5.

GW-474 Washington's Minuet And Gavott. In: *United States Country Dances*, page 1. m. Mr. Pierre Landrin Duport (Professor of dancing from Paris and original composer of cadriels [sic]." "With figures also accompaniments for the piano forte. Composed in America." "Printed for the Author." Engraved by [John] "Roberts, Sc." "Price 1 dol. & fifty cents." [ca. 1800]. 20pp.

GW-475 Washington & Independence (A Favorite Patriotic Song). w.m. Victor Pelissier. Printed & sold by G. Gilfert, No. 177 Broadway, New York, NY. [1797-1801]. Non-pictorial. 2pp. [S/U, page 449].

GW-476 The Village Fifer, No. 1 (Containing Instructions for learning to play the fife and a collection of marches, airs, &c.). "Printed by Norris & Sawyer and sold at their book store, Exeter, N.H." March, 1808. 72 pp. "Sold also by Charles Pierce, Thomas & Tappan, Portsmouth; William Sawyer & Co., Thomas Whipple, Newburyport; Thomas & Andrews, Davis West, John West, Manning & Loring, E. & J. Larking, Boston." [W-9491].

    (A)   **The President's March**, page 28.
    (B)   **General Washington's March**, page 34.

GW-477 General Washington's March [At The Battle of Trenton]. In: *The Drum and Fife Instructor, in two Divisions*, page 31. c. Charles Robbins, Exeter, NH. "Printed by C. Norris & Co.," 1812. 64pp. [W-7506].

GW-478 Washington's Favourite The Brave La Fayette. w.m. "Written by a gentleman of this City to a favorite air." [V-1: Published by John Cole, No. 123 Market Street, Baltimore, MD. [V-1: "21st Aug., 1824"] [V-2: Facsimile published by Musical America, No. 5458 Montgomery Street, Philadelphia, PA. 1956]. B/w engraving of General LaFayette, sun ray-like geometric designs. "Arranged with a chorus in three parts and an accompaniment for the piano forte." 2pp. [V-1: W-8357] [V-2: W-8357A].

GW-479 Washington's March. In: *Riley's New Instructor For The German Flute, Containing the best methods to obtain a proficiency, with compleat scales for four, six and eight key'd patent flute; with a collection of songs, airs, marches, cotillions, &c.* [sic], page 25. Engraved, printed & sold by the Editor [Riley], No. 17 Chatham Street, New York, NY. 1811. 28pp. [W-7491].

GW-480 Washington's Grand March. In: *Riley's Preceptor for the Patent Flageolet, with scales for the English & French Flageolets, containing instructions and a collection of airs, waltzes, songs, rondos, &c.*, page 26. "Engraved, printed & sold by E. Riley, No. 29 Chatham Street, New York, NY. [1818-1822]. [W-7493].

GW-481 A New & Complete Preceptor For The Violin (Together with a choice collection of songs, duets, marches, dances, &c.). Published by Daniel Steele, Sign of the Bible, No. 437 South Market Street, Albany, NY." [1815-1818]. 30pp. [W-7217].

    (A)   **Washington's March**, page 12.
    (B)   **Hail Columbia**, page 12.
    (C)   **Washington's Grand March**, page 19.

GW-482 A New & Complete Preceptor For The German Flute (Together with a collection of airs, hornpipes, marches, waltzes, &c). Published by Daniel Steele & Son, Sign of the Bible, No. 437 South Market Street, Albany, NY." [1824-1826]. 30pp. [W-7215].
  (A) Hail Columbia, page 21.
  (B) Washington's Grand March, page 21.
  (C) March In Memory Of Washington, p. 22. m. Curphew.

GW-483 Two Odes. w. Rev. Samuel Tomb. In: *Oration on the auspicious birth, sublime virtue and triumphant death of General George Washington; pronounced Feb. 22, 1800; in Newbury second parish*. Printed by Edmund M. Blunt, Newburyport, [MA]. 1800. "To which are annexed. Two Odes and an Acrostic, commemorative of the birth and death of that illustrious personage; composed by the same hand." Page 17: "The two following Odes were sung on the occasion with great applause by the musical band under the direction of Mr. Joseph Stanwood, Jr." [S/U, page 313].

GW-484 A New & Complete Instructor For The Piano Forte (To which is added a collection of favorite song's air's prelude's &c [sic]). Printed & sold by G. Gilfert, opposite St. Pauls Church, Broadway, NY. [1802-1803]. 30pp. [W-4495].
  (A) President's March, page 6.
  (B) Washington's March [At The Battle of Trenton], page 8.

GW-485 A Variety Of Marches (Consisting of common tunes, quick steps, double drags, and trios. Likewise a scale of natural notes for the hautboy and a complete gamut for the flute). c. James Hulbert, Jun. Printed at Northampton [MA]. 1803. 12pp. [W-4390].
  (A) Washington's Favorite, page 5.
  (B) Lady Washington's Favorite, page 5.

GW-486 Washington's Grand March. In: *A New & Complete Preceptor For Flageolets of Every Description, particularly for the new and improved patent octave flageolet. With a selection of airs, rondos, waltzes, &c., adapted for the instr.*, page 24. Published by J.G. Klemm, No. 3 South 3d Street, Philadelphia, PA. [1823-1824]. 30pp. [W-7209].

GW-487 Washington's March. In: *A New & Complete Preceptor For The Fife Together with a collection of choice marches, &c, &c.*, page 9 Published by Daniel Steele, Sign of the Bible, No. 472 South Market Street, Albany, NY.". [1815-1818]. Inside title: **The Complete Fife Tutor**. 26pp. [W-7211].

GW-488 Washington's March. In: *Martial Music: A Collection of marches harmorized for field bands on various keys, such as are the most familiar and easy to perform on the clarinet, oboe, bassoon &c. Also a number of easy lessons for young practitioners*, page 10. Published by Daniel Steele, Bookseller, Court Street, Albany, NY. 1807. Printed by Manning & Loring, Boston, MA. 44pp. [W-6660].

GW-489 An Elegy On The Death Of Gen. Washington. In: *The Complete Pocket Song Book*, page 49. c. Eliphalet Mason. Printed by Andrew Wright, Northampton, MA. 1802. [W-2665, 5633].

GW-490 An Ode For The Washington Benevolent Society. Published by E. Riley, Engraver, No. 23 Chatham St., New York, NY. [ca. 1813]. "Written and adapted to music and sung at New York, July 4th, 1812, by Mr. Hill." 2pp. [W-3841].

GW-491 Massa Georgee Washington & General La Fayette (A Cotillion). In: *Riley's Second Sett [sic] of Cotillions*, page 8. Published by E. Riley, No. 29 Chatham Street, New York, NY. 1824. Non-pictorial. "Arranged for the piano." List of six cotillions. page 8: Inside title — **Massa Georgee Washington, &c., &c.** [W-3476].

GW-492 The Dawning Of Music

In Kentucky (Or The Pleasures of Harmony in the Solitudes of Nature). c. Wm. A. Heinrich. Pubd. [sic] by Bacon & Hart, Phila., and by the Author, Kentucky. [1820]. "Opera Prima." "Copyright Secured." 96pp. [W-3596].
  (A) **Hail Columbia**, page 71. m. Phile.
  (B) **The Birthday Of Washington**, page 85.

GW-493 The Instrumental Director (Containing rules for all musical instruments in common use, laid down in a plain & Concise manner. To which is added a variety of instrumental musick [sic] of the richest and most popular kind extant, a part of which was never before published in this country). e.a. Ezekial Goodale. Published by E. Goodale in Hallowell, ME. 1819. 94pp. [W-3168].
  (A) **Hail Columbia**, page 27.
  (B) **Washington's March** [At the Battle of Trenton], page 32.

GW-494 Washington's March. In: *Bacon's Complete Preceptor for the Clarinet, with a selection of airs, marches, &c.*, page 19. Published by A. Bacon, Music Seller & Publisher, No. 11 South 4th Street, Philadelphia, PA. [1818?]. [W-411].

GW-495 Blake's Evening Companion for the Flute, Clarinet, Violin or Flageolet, Vol. [ ], Book 1. Printed & Sold by G.E. Blake, Philadelphia, PA. [1808?]. 26pp. Title page: Engraving of a man, woman with a clarinet, dog, bridge. "Copyright." "Price one dollar." [W-858].
  (A) **Hail Columbia**, page 22.
  (B) **Washington's March** [At the Battle of Trenton], page 23.

GW-496 President's Waltz. In: *Blake's Evening Companion for the Flute, Clarinet, Violin or Flageolet, Vol. [2], Book 8*, page "52". Printed & Sold by G.E. Blake, Philadelphia, PA. [1822-1823]. 32pp. [W-858].

GW-497 Lincoln's Tribute To Washington. w. Abraham Lincoln. m. J.N. Pierce. 1932.

GW-498 Washington's March. In: *The Complete Instructor For The Piano Forte, With the Proper Mode of Fingering Illustrated by a Variety of Examples Consisting of the Most Favorite Airs*, page 11. e.c. James Hewitt. Printed & sold by the Author at his Musical Repository, No. 131 William Street, B. Carr, Philadelphia, and I. Carr, Baltimore. [1797-1799]. "Price [ ]." 18pp. [W-10237].

GW-499 Instructions For The Piano Forte And English And French Flagelets (Also a collection of the newest and most favorite airs, song tunes, marches, &c., Selected and arranged). c.a. G.E. Blake. Printed & sold by G.E. Blake, Philadelphia, PA. [ca. 1807]. Inside title: **Patent Flagelet Preceptor**. 24pp. [W-853].
  (A) **Hail Columbia**, page 22.
  (B) **Washington's March** [At the Battle of Trenton], page 23.

GW-500 Washington's March. In: *A Complete Preceptor for the German Flute, being an introduction to the art of playing on that instrumental explained in the most simple manner. Also a selection of the newest and most favorite airs, songtunes, marches, &c., &c.*, page 23. Printed & sold by the Author [G.E. Blake], No. 13 South 5th Street, Philadelphia, PA. [182-?]. 26pp. Inside title: **Blake's Flute Preceptor**. [W-855].

GW-501 President's March. In: *A. Bacon & Co's Flute Melodies [Book 2].* Printed & sold at A. Bacon & Company, Philadelphia, PA. [1816-1820]. 18pp. "Price 50 cts." Title page engraved with an open music book, instruments, leaves. [W-408].

GW-502 A. Bacon & Co's' Preceptor For The German Flute (With a selection of airs, rondos, waltzes, &c., adapted for the inst.). Printed & sold by A. Bacon & Company, Philadelphia, PA. [1816?]. [W-409].
  (A) **President's March**, page 21.
  (B) **Washington's March** [At the Battle of Trenton], page 22.

GW-503 Lady Washington's Reception (Waltz). w.m. [?] H.T. Schultz. Published by S.T. Gordon & Son, No. 13 East 14th Street, New York, NY. [ca. 187-].

GW-504 The Washington Centennial March (Duet), m. Dressler. In: *Our Monthly Musical Gem, No. 20*. Published by Hitchcock Publishing House, No. 385 Sixth Avenue, New York, NY. [ca. 188-].

GW-505 Mount Vernon Polka. m. Renhart. Published by Lee & Walker, No. 722 Chestnut Street, Philadelphia, PA. [ca. 186-?]. Litho of Mount Vernon?

GW-506 Washington's March. a. Anon. Published by Wm. A. Pond & Company, No. 25 Union Square, Between 15th & 16th Sts., New York, NY. [ca. 188-].

GW-507 Washington Monument. m. Carl Vass. a. Fulton B. Karr. Published by District Publishing Company, No. 808 15th Street, S.E., Washington, DC. 1848. Gn/w "photo by permission of H.H. Rideout" of Washngton Monument at Washington. 4pp.

GW-508 The Washington Remembrance (or Georgetown and Alexandria) Songster's Magazine: A Collection of the Newest and Most Admired Songs, Now Extant. "Selected Impartially." Printed for the Publishers. 1800. 136pp.

GW-509 Hail Columbia. In: *Spicer's Pocket Companion (or The Young Mason's Monitor)*. [ca. 1799]. 64 [?]pp.

GW-510 George Washington (Rote Song). w. Mabel E. Bray. m. Franz Joseph Hayden. N/c drawing of George Washington, crossed flags, trumpets. In: *The Music Hour, First Book*, page 46. Published by Silver Burditt Company, New York, NY. Copyright 1927, 1928, 1936, 1937. 120pp.

GW-511 Washington's Birthday. w.m.George A. Boynton. In: *The American Singer, Book 7*, page 213. Published by American Book Company, New York, NY. 1947. [7 1/2" × 10 1/8"]. R/w/b stars, bars of music. 238pp.

GW-512 Washington The Great. w.m. "Early American Song Sung in Tennessee." In: *The American Singer, Book 5*, page 124. c. John W. Beattie, Josephine Wolverton, Grace V. Wilson, Howard Hinga. Published by American Book Company, New York, NY. 1946. R/w/b stars, bars of music.

GW-513 Hail Columbia (Rote Song). w. Joseph Hopkinson. m. Philip Phyle [sic]. N/c drawing "Copyrighted by J.L.G. Ferris" of "Washington's Inauguration at Independence Hall, 1793." In: *The Music Hour, Fourth Book*. Published by Silver Burdett Company, New York, NY. Copyright 1924 and 1937. [6 1/2" × 8 3/8"]. 184pp.

GW-514 Young George Washington. w.m. Anonymous (Extended by D.S.). B/w drawing of a young George Washington. "Early American Song." In: *We Sing*, page 125. Published by C.C. Birchard aand Company, Boston, MA. [ca. 193-]. [6 7/8" × 8 5/8"]. 200pp.

GW-515 Hail Columbia. In: *The Fourth Music Reader: A Course of Musical Instruction, Containing Musical Theory, Original Solfeggios, A Complete System of Triad Practice, and Scared Music and Songs, with Accompaniment for the Piano*, page 326. Published by Ginn, Heath & Company, Boston, MA. 1882. [6 1/2" × 9 1/8"].

GW-516 Hail Columbia. w. Oliver Wendell Homes (1789) [sic] and F. Hopkinson (1887) [sic]. In: *Songs We Love To So Well: A Complete Collection of all Those Standard songs Which are Known and Loved by English Speaking People the World Over. As Well as the National and Home songs of all the Principal Nations and Peoples*, page 66. Published by Big Four Syndicate, New York, NY. Copyright 1923 by Consolidated Book Publishers. [7" × 9 7/8"]. 278pp. R/bk drawing of Colonial man and woman., rose stem. "Seven Books In One: Patriotic, National, College, Operatic, Love, Home, Sacred."

GW-517 Hail Columbia. In: *The Odeon: A Collection of Secular Melodies, Arranged and Harmonized for Four Voices, Designed for Adult Singing Schools, and for Sacred Music Parties*, page 248. c. G.J. Webb and Lowell Mason. Published by J.H. Wilkins and R.B. Carter, Boston. MA. 1838. [10" × 6 1/2"]. Non-pictorial geometric embossing. Gold title.

GW-518 Washington. w. Nancy Byrd Turner. m. Hoagy Carmichael. In: *New Music Horizons (Sixth Book)*, page 134 Published by Silver Burdett Company, New York, NY. 1946. [6 3/4" × 9 3/8"]. Br/bk hard cover. 246pp.

GW-519(A) Hail Columbia. In: *American Patriotic Songs, A Carefully Selected Collection of the Best and Most Popular American National Lyrics, Words and Music Complete*, page 40. Published by Oliver Ditson Company, Nos. 453-463 Washington Street, Boston, MA. 1893. [6 3/4" 10"]. R/w/b crossed flags, eagle. 92pp.

(B) The Land Of Washington, page 50. w. George P. Morris. a. F.H. Brown and Collin Coe. "Note: The melody of this song was called Drum and Fife March by the Provincial army, and was a great favorite of the American troops, especially as it was played by them at the Battle of Yorktown. As the Publisher is desirous of rescuing from oblivion a spirit-stirring melody, once so familiar in the American camp, it is given anew."

(C) The Land Of Washington, page 60. w. D.B. Dudley. m. W.O. Perkins.

GW-520 Hail Columbia. w. Joseph Hopkinson. m. "Attributed to Philip Phile." a. Bernard Wagness. Bl/w drawing of George Washington, John Adams, others taking oath. "The original version of this song was known as *The Washington March*. Usually, Philip Phile is acknowledged as the composer. It was written in 1789 for use as the inauguration of George Washington as first president of the newly formed United States. A decade later, Joseph Hopkinson wrote the words for a special event. At that time, sympathy in America was divided for England and France who were then at war with one another. Impartial to both countries, *Hail Columbia* was intended to unite all parties and thus retain peace and safety throughout the nation. This idealism has gained a justly deserved place for it among our first rank American songs." In: *I Pledge Allegiance, A Patriotic Album for All Americans*. a. Bernard Wagness. Published by Rubank, Inc., Chicago, IL. 1941. R/w/b drawing of man, woman, eagle, stars, stripes. 16pp.

GW-521 Hail Columbia. Published by Arthur P. Schmidt Company. Br/w drawing of two children dressed as soldiers. "Rank And File, Marches For The Piano Forte."

GW-522 Hail Columbia. w. F. Hopkinson, 1798. In: *America's National Songs*. Published by The Parkview Publishing Company, No. 3943 Market Street, Philadelphia, PA., page 16. 1895. [5 1/2" × 8 1/4"]. Blue and blue drawing of eagle, crossed flags, shield inscribed "E Pluribus Unum," woman. 24pp.

GW-523 Hail Columbia, page 182. w. Joseph Hopkinson, 1798. m. Prof. Phylo [sic]. a. F.E Belden. "Sung for the first time in public at Washington's inauguration in New York in 1789." In: *Uncle Sam's School Songs, for Schools, Colleges, Institutes, and The Home Circle*. Published by [V-1: The Hope Publishing Company, No. 228 Wabash Avenue] [V-2: Hall & McCreary], Chicago, IL. 1897. [5 1/8" × 7 5/8"]. [V-1: R/w/b drawing of crossed flags, shield, Uncle Sam, geometric designs]. [V-2: R/o/bk drawing of mother and children singing, wreath, flags]. [V-1: 196pp] [V-2: 260pp].

GW-524 Hail Columbia, page 30. w. Judge Joseph Hopkinson, 1798. In: *National Melodies and American War Songs, a Collection of National and Patriotic Songs for the Post, the Lodge, the School and the Home, to which are added several songs for occasional and devotional singing*.

Published by The John Church Company, Cincinnati, OH. 1903. 100pp.

GW-525 Ode To Washington. c. Orlando Blackman. In: *Songs and Exercises for High Grammer Grades*, page 16. Published by Chicago Board of Education, Chicago, IL. [6 3/4" × 10"]. 1899. B/w non-pictorial geometric designs. 84pp.

GW-526 Ode For Washington's Birthday. w. Oliver Wendell Holmes. a. P. Heise. "First in war, first in peace, first in the hearts of his countrymen.— Henry Lee." In: *Songs of Purpose, Advanced Music*, page 251. c. Will Earhart and E. Hershey Sneath. Published by Macmillian Company, New York, NY. 1929. [7 1/4" × 10 1/2"]. Gn/o drawing of couple singing, geometric designs. Hardback book. 320pp.

GW-527 Hail Columbia. "The passage of the Alien and Sedition Laws, in 1798, as an outcome of the trouble between France and England, aroused bitter partisan feelings between the Democrats and Federalists of the United States. About this time a Theatre was opened in Philadelphia with a benefit concert for Gilbert Fox, a rising young singer. One Saturday afternoon this young man called upon Joseph Hopkinson, a young lawyer, and asked him to write some patriotic words to the *President's March*, a tune which had been composed at the time of Washington's inauguration. The following day he gave the words to Mr. Fox, who sang them at the concert Monday night. The song at once became popular. President Adams and many notable statesmen came to hear it. It was sung and whistled on the streets. Political differences were forgotten, and in the stanzas of *Hail Columbia*, the people caught new visions of their rights and duties as citizens of a free land." In: *The Golden Book of Favorite Songs, A Treasury of the Best Songs of our People*, page 42. Published by Hall & McCreary Company, Chicago, IL. 1915. [5 5/8" × 8 5/8"]. 132pp.

GW-528 America. Published by Union League Club, Chicago, IL. 1896. [4 15/16" × 6 1/2"]. Bl/bk steel engraving by Metcalf of George Washington. "Virginia gave us this imperial man Cast in the massive mold Of these high-statured ages old, Which into grander forms our metal ran; She gave us this unblemished gentleman: What shall we give her back but love and praise." 4pp. page 2: Union League Club Celebration Washington's Birthday, The Auditorium at 3 P.M., Chicago, Saturday, February twenty-second, 1896." "Commorative address — Hon. Theodore Roosevelt." page 3: Music to *America*. page 4: Washington quotes.

GW-529(A) Washington. w. J.H.Kurzenknabe. m. "Arr. from O, Tannenbaum by J.H.K." In: *American School Songs for Schools, Colleges, Institutes, and The Home Circle*, page 199. Published by Hope Publishing Company, Chicago, IL. 1904. [5 1/4" × 7 1/4"]. R/w/b eagle, shield, crossed flags. Oil cloth cover. 258pp.

(B) Hail Columbia, page 337. w. Joseph Hopkinson, 1798. m. Prof. Phylo. a. F.E. Belden. "Sung [sic] for the first time in public at Washington's inauguration in New York in 1789." "Arrangement copyrighted 1897 by Henry Date."

GW-530 (A) Hail Columbia. w. Joseph Hopkinson. m. "Attributed to Philip Phile." "The music was originally known as the Washington March [sic]. It was written in 1789 as an inaugural march for George Washington by Philip Phile. About nine years later Joseph Hopkinson composed the words, during the days that the American people were being divided by their sympathies for either England or France who were at war. It's purpose was to unite the American People." In: *The True Blue Song Book, Enlarged Edition, The Nation's Choicest Gems*, page 9. Published by Omaha School Supply Company, Publishers, Omaha, NB. 1926. [5 7/8" × 8 3/4"]. 132pp. Bl/w lithos of lyres, geometric designs.

(B) Our Presidents (Our Washington), page 57. W. Lizzie A. Switzer. G.W. Fields.

GW-531 Hail Columbia! w. Joseph Hopkinson. m. J. Fayles [sic]. In: *The Most Popular Songs of Patriotism, Including National Songs of All the World*, page 16. Published by Hinds Hayden & Eldridge, Inc., Publishers, New York, NY. 1916. [7 1/8" × 10 5/8"]. 184pp. R/w/bk drawing of national flags, eagles.

GW-532 14th Regiment Centennial Jubilee. w. Cpt. John A. Esolf [?]. m. Wm. E. Tompkins (Author of *Old Fashion Social Schottisch, Columbian Yacht Club Galop*...). Published by Tompkins Band Office, No. 122 Court Street, Brooklyn, NY. 1876. R/w/b litho of George Washington, flags, Revolutionary and Civil War soldiers shaking hands, "1776-1876." "Dedicated to Johnny Coleman Cann."

GW-533(A) Washington, Chief Of Our Nation. w. Edith S. Tillotson. m. I.H. Meredith. In: *The American Songster, A Collection of Songs Both Old and New for School and Home*, page 79. Published by Tular-Meredith Co., No. 265 West 36th Street, New York, NY. 1907. [6 3/8" × 9 7/8"]. Gn/be non-pictorial cloth cover. 132pp.

(B) Hail, Columbia!, page 90. w. Hopkinson. m. *The President's March*. "Arr. for 1, 2, 3 or 4 Voices."

GW-534 Hail Columbia. "The passage of the Alien and Sedition Laws, in 1798, as an outcome of the trouble between France and England, aroused bitter partisan feelings between the Democrats and Federalists of the United States. About this time a theatre was opened in Philadelphia with a benefit concert for Gilbert Fox, a rising young singer. One Saturday afternoon this young man called upon Joseph Hopkinson, a young lawyer, and asked him to write some patriotic words to *The President's March*, a tune that had been composed at the time of Washington's first [sic] inauguration. The following day he gave the words to Mr. Fox, who sang them at the concert Monday night. The song at once became popular. President Adams and many notable statesmen came to hear it. It was sung and whistled on the streets. Political differences were forgotten, and in the stanzas of *Hail Columbia* the people caught new visions of their rights and duties as citizens of a free land." In: *Uncle Sam's Favorite Song Book, The Song Book of the Nation*, page 42. Published by Hall & McCreary, Chicago, IL. 1919. [5 3/4" × 8 3/4"]. R/w/b drawing of Uncle Sam. 132pp.

GW-535(A) Washington's March. In: *Howe's School For The Violin (Containing New And Complete Instructions For The Violin, With a Large Collection of Favorite Marches, Quicksteps, Waltzes, Hornpipes, Contra Dances, Songs, and Six Setts [sic] of Cotillions, Arranged with Figures, Containing Over 150 Pieces of Music*, page 20. c. Elias Howe, Jr. Published and Sold Wholesale and Retail, by Elias Howe, Jr., No. 7 Cornhill, Boston, MA. 1843. [6 1/2" × 10"]. Y/bk litho of musical instruments, angel, geometric and floral designs.

(B) Washington's Grand March, page 20.

(C) Washington Crossing The Delaware, page 20.

(D) Hail Columbia, page 22.

GW-536 Hail Columbia. In: *Songs of Long Ago, Old Yet Ever New* [Song Book], page 4. Published by Geo. P. Bent, Manufacturer of Crown Pianos & Organs, Chicago, IL. 1903. [4 9/16" × 6 1/2"]. Geometric designs, double blue line border, geometric designs. "Compliments of." 18pp.

GW-537 Hail Columbia! w. Joseph Hopkinson. m. "Attributed to Philip Phile." In: *Victory Song Book for Soldiers, Sailors and Marines*, page 66. e. Hugo Frey. Published by Robbins Music Corporation, No. 799 Seventh Avenue, New York, NY. R/w "V" symbol, stars. [1942]. [6" × 9"]. R/w "V" and star design. 100pp.

GW-538 Hail, Columbia. w.

Joseph Hopkinson. m. Phyla [sic]. In: *Songs of America, A Collection of Patriotic and National Airs Compiled and Arranged Especially for use in the School and Home*, page 14. c. Arthur J. Mealand. Published by Mealand & Parsons, Greenfield, MA. 1910. [6" × 9 1/8"]. R/w/bl/be litho of eagle with ribbon inscribed "E Pluribus Unum," crossed flags, seal inscribed "Exitus acta probat." "For Use on All Public Occasions When we Wish to Sing the Songs of the Land." "With Compliments of The King McLeod Co., Newport, R.I." 36pp.

GW-539(A) The Great Defender (For Washington's Birthday). In: *Bartlett's Music Reader For Day School*, page 142. c. M.L. Bartlett, Mus. Doc. Published by The Echo Music Company, Chicago, IL. [ca. 1890]. [6 1/4" × 8 1/2"]. Be/br geometric designs. 160pp.

(B)   Hail Columbia, page 25.

GW-540 Washington Bi-Centennial March (In Honor Of Our First President). w.m. Eugene Frey. Published by Eugene Frey, No. 1169 Churchill Avenue, St. Paul, MN. 1932. B/w litho of George Washington. "1732-1932." 4pp. Page 4: Blank.

GW-541 Hail Columbia! w. Joseph Hopkinson. m. "Attributed to Philip Phile." In: [V-2: *The New American Song Book], A Century of Progress in American Song*, page 64. c. Marx Oberndorfer and Anne Oberndorfer. Published by Hall & McCreary, Chicago, IL. [V-1: 1933] [V-2: 1941]. [V-1: Pl/s hard cover] [V-2: "Pan American Edition"]. [V-1: 780pp] [V-2: 186pp].

GW-542 Hail, Columbia! In: *Father Kemp and his Old Folks, A History of the Old Folks' Concerts*, page 232. Published by Robert Kemp, Boston, MA. 1868. Gg/bk non-pictorial hard back book. [5" × 7 3/4"]. 270pp.

GW-543(A) Mount Vernon Bells. "Vessels passing Mt. Vernon toll their bells as a perpetual tribute of respect to the memory of Washington." w.m. S.C. Foster. In: *Sovereign Wreath of Song, Third Book for Intermediate and High Schools*, page 107 c. J.D. Luse. Published by J.D. Luse, Columbus, OH. 1899. [7" × 9 3/4"]. Be/bk floral design hard back book. 236pp.

(B)   Hail Columbia, page 110. w. Joseph Hopkinson (Written in 1798). m. Phyla [sic].

GW-544(A) Hail Columbia. In: *The Columbian Songster, Being a Large Collection of Fashionable Songs, for Gentlemen & Ladies in a Series of Numbers*, page 3. Printed by Nathaniel Heaton, Jur., [Wrentham, MA]. 1799. [3 1/2" × 5 3/4"]. Hard cover. 196pp.

(B)   **Ode to Columbia's Favorite Son**, page 8.

(C)   **Hail Godlike Washington**, page 27, Part III. "On the Birth of George Washington, Commander in Chief of the American forces."

GW-545 Hail Columbia. In: *Winner's New Primer For The Flute*. Copyright by William Pond & Company, Washington, DC. 1864. [6 1/2" × 9 3/4"]. Gr/bk litho of musical instruments, geometric design border.

GW-546(A) Hail Columbia, page 20. w. Joseph Hopkinson, 1770-1842. m. "Arr. From *The President's March* by Professor Phyla [sic], which was first played when Washington came to New York to be inaugurated in 1789 [sic]. In: *Patriotic Songs For School and Home* [Song Book], page 20. c.a. John Carroll Randolph. Published by Oliver Ditson Company, Boston, MA. 1899. [6 3/4" × 10 1/4"]. R/w/b flag, geometric border. Hard cover. 208pp.

(B)   **The Land Of Washington**, page 170. w. Geo. P. Morris. m.a. F.H. Brown. "The melody of this song was called the *Drum and Fife March* by the Provincial army, and was a great favorite of the American troops, especially as it was played by them at the Battle of Yorktown. As the Publisher is desirous of rescuing from oblivion a spirit-stirring melody, once so familiar in the American camp, it is here given anew."

(C) Ode For Washington's Birthday, page 172. w. Oliver Wendell Holmes (1809-1894). m. Ludwig van Beethoven [sic] (1770-1827). "From the *Ninth* or *Choral Symphony*."

(D) Mount Vernon Bells, page 163. w. M.B.C. Slade. m. Stephen Collins Foster (1826-1864). "Vessels and steamers going up and down the Potomac, toll their bells in passing Mount Vernon; a perpetual tribute of respect to the memory of Washington."

GW-547 Hail Columbia. In: *The Cantilena*, page 202. e. George F. Bristow. Published by Abbey & Abbot, No. 119 Nassau Street, New York, NY. 1861. [9" × 5 3/4"]. Be/bk non-pictorial hard cover book. 240pp.

GW-548 The Fourth Of July (A Volunteer Song). w. William B. Tappan. m. "Air, *Auld Lang Syne*." "Sung on the 44th Anniversary of American Independence, at the dinner of the First Company Washington Guards of Philadelphia." In: *Songs of Judah and other Melodies*, page 163. w. William B. Tappan (Author of *New England* and other Poems). Published by S. Potter & Co., No. 87 Chesnut Street, Philadelphia, PA. 1820. [3 11/16" × 5 15/16"]. Non-pictorial hard cover. 220pp.

GW-549 Washington, The Brightest Name on History's Page. w.m. Eliza Cook. In: *Old War Songs and New and Old Patriotic and National Songs*. 64pp. [5 1/4" × 6 3/4"]. O/bk litho of flag, soldiers, two men—"C.&J. Scherer, The White House Store," advertising. "Presented as a supplement to the *Acme Haversack of Patriotism and Song*. "This Song Souvenir of, is Presented to the Comrades of the G.A.R. and the Spanish War...St. Joseph, Michigan and Vicinity."

GW-550 Hail Columbia. In: *The American Collection Of War Music, Vocal and Instrumental, Old and New*, page 41. Published by National Music Company, No. 266-268 Wabash Avenue, Chicago, No. 44 East Street, New York, NY. 1898. B/w litho of the American flag, wreath. 80pp.

GW-551 Hail Columbia. In: *Whitney's Improved Easy Method For Parlor Organ*, page 78. Published by J.H. Troup Piano House, No. 15 South Market Square, Harrisburg, PA. Copyright is 1886 by W. W. Whitney. [11 1/2" × 9 3/8"]. Gn/bk geometric designs. Hard Cover. "New and Enlarged Edition." 100 pages.

GW-552 Mount Vernon Bell. A. Stephen C. Foster. "Vessels passing Mount Vernon toll their bells as a perpetual tribute of respect to the memory of George Washington." In: *The Progressive Music Course (In One Book), For Public Schools*, page 118. e. Moro Loomis Bartlett. Published by W.M. Welch Company, Chicago, IL. 1906. [6" × 8 7/8"]. Gn/bk non-pictorial hard cover. 152pp.

GW-553(A) Our Flag Is Floating Today. w. *Youth's Companion*. m.a. S.C. Hanson. In: *Golden Glees*, page 26. e. S.C. Hanson. [8 1/2" × 6 1/8"]. [ca. 1880].

(B) Washington And Liberty, page 92. w. Rose N. Yawger. m. S.C. Hanson.

GW-554(A) The Grave Of Washington. w.m. "Altered from Crosby." In: *Golden Wreath, A Choice Collection of Favorite Melodies, Designed for the Use of Schools, Seminaries, Select Classes, &c.*, page 143. c. L.O. Emerson. Published by Oliver Ditson & Company, No. 277 Washington, Street, Boston, MA. 1857. [V-1: 100th edition, 1857]. [V-2: Edition ca. 1863].

(B) Hail Columbia, page 154.

GW-555 Hail Columbia. w. Joseph Hopkinson. m. "Attributed to Philip Phile." "The music if this song, originally known as The Washington March, is generally attributed to Philip Phile. It was written in 1789 [sic] as an inaugural march for George Washington.

The words were written nine years later by Joseph Hopkinson for a special occasion. At the time, England and France were at war and Americans were being divided by their sympathies for one or the other of these countries. No allusion is made in this song to either of the countries, but its purpose was to keep Americans united. This sentiment has won for *Hail Columbia* a place in our national songs." In: *Everybody's Song Book, A Collection of Favorite Songs of the Nation*, page 6. Published by Frederic J. Haskin, Washington, DC. 1933. [5 3/4" × 8 5/8"]. R/w/b geometric design cover with two music notes. 148pp.

GW-556 Hail Columbia! w. Joseph Hopkinson, 1770-1842. m. Prof. Phyla [sic]. In: *Songs Of Liberty And Patriotism of America And Allies*, page 14. Published by Parlin & Orendorff Company, Canton, IL. Copyright by The J.C. Temple Company, Columbus, OH. 1918. [5 7/8" × 8 3/4"]. N/c litho of Miss Justice holding the American Flag while standing on a globe backed by the flags of the Allied Nations. "Freedom and Justice." "Battle flags of the Allies, Symbols of Unity — Emblems of Freedom — The Standards under which the rights of humanity, the blessings of liberty and lasting peace will be won."

GW-557 Washington (Folk Tune). w.m. Mary Stanhope. In: *Music Education Series Elementary Music*, page 96. Published by Ginn and Company, Boston, MA. 1923. [6 3/8" × 8 3 16"]. Gn/bk geometric designs. Hard cover. 200pp.

GW-558 Washington And Lincoln (Rote). w. Ethel Crowninshield. m. "Belgian Folk Tune." In: *Rhythms And Rimes, The World Of Music*, page 105. Published by Ginn and Company, Boston, MA. 1936. [6 3/8" × 7 15/16"]. Gn/br globe, lyre. Hard cover. 184pp.

GW-559 Hail Columbia. In: *Patriotic Glee Book*. Published by H.M. Higgins, Chicago, IL. 1863. Gn/bk hard cover.

GW-560 Hail Columbia. In: *Winner's Easy System For The Violin*. e. Sep. Winner. Published by Lee & Walker, Chesnut Street, Philadelphia, PA. 1866. [10" × 6 7/8"]. Be/bk geometric designs. 80pp.

GW-561 Hail Columbia! w. Joseph Hopkinson. m. "Attributed to Philip Phile." In: *Songs Of America, for Schools, Assemblies, Music Clubs and Social Groups*, page 7. Published by Robbins Music Corporation, No. 799 Seventh Avenue, New York, NY. 1941. [6" × 9"]. Bl/w non-pictorial. "Robbins Edition." 148pp.

GW-562 Hail Columbia! w. Joseph Hopkinson. m. "Attributed to Philip Phile." In: *America Sings, Community Song Book for Schools, Cluibs, Assemblies, Camps and Recreational Groups*, page 108. Published by Robbins Music Corporation, No. 799 Seventh Avenue, New York, NY. 1941. [6" × 9"]. R/w non-pictorial. "Robbins Edition." 148pp.

GW-563 Hail Columbia. Published by Marsh, No. 1102 Chesnut Street, Philadelphia, PA. 1861. R/w/b crosses U.S. and French flags, geometric designs. "As performed by the United States Brass Band." "National Beauties." List of other tunes in the series.

GW-564(A) The Birthday Of Washington. w. George D. Prentice. m. Mixon. In: *Ye Women's Singing Book for ye use of Ye Daughters and Dames of ye Patriotic Historical Societies of ye United States of America*, page 30. c.a. Thomas G. Shepard. Published by Thomas G. Shepard, New Haven, CT. 1899. [6 3/4" × 10 1/16"]. Bl/be drawing of eagle, geometric designs. Hard cover. 48pp.

(B) Hail Columbia, page 10. w. Joseph Hopkinson, 1770-1842. m. Phyla [sic].

GW-565 Hail Columbia. a. Geo. W. Warren. Published by C. Breusing, New York, NY. R/w/b beige tinted litho by Bouvell Litho of a Union soldier with sword and American flag, U.S. Capitol building, banner at top inscribed with song titles in the series—*Hail Columbia* and *Stars and Stripes Forever*. "Transcribed for the Piano."

GW-566 Hail Columbia. Published by S.T. Gordon, No. 538 Broadway, New York, NY. [ca. 1862]. Non-pictorial. "The Twins, A Collection for two Performers on the Piano Forte."

GW-567(A) March In Memory Of Washington. In: *Musician's Omnibus: Containing the Whole Camp Duty, Calls and Signals Used in the Army and Navy; Forty Setts of Quadrilles, Including Waltz, Polka and Schottische, with Calls; and an Immense Collection of Polkas, Schottisches, Waltzes, Marches, Quicksteps, Hornpipes, Contra & Fancy Dances, Songs, &c., for the Violin, Flute, Cornet, Clarionett, &c, containing over 700 Pieces of Music*, page 29. c. Elias Howe. Published by Elias Howe, No. 103 Court Street, Boston, MA. 1861. [8 1/2" × 11"]. O/bk non-pictorial. "Improved Edition." 100pp.

(B) Washington's March, page 25.
(C) Washington's Grand March, page 25.
(D) Hail Columbia, page 16.

GW-568(A) March In Memory Of Washington. In: *Howe's Diamond School For The Violin: Containing, Complete Instructions and Full Directions in Bowing; to which is added A Large Collection of Popular Polkas, Schottisches, Waltzes, Redowas, Marches, Quicksteps, Dances, Hornpipes, Songs*, page 29. c. Elias Howe. Published by Elias Howe, No. 103 Court Street, Boston, MA. 1861. [8 1/2" × 11"]. Bl/bk non-pictorial. 68pp.

(B) Washington's March, page 25.
(C) Washington's Grand March, page 25.
(D) Hail Columbia, page 16.

GW-569 George Washington (Patriotic Song). w.m. John R. Wolter (Composer of *Our Hero* (Lindbergh) and *Daisy* (Waltz), etc). Published by Dime Song Co., Asbury Park, NJ. Copyright 1931 by John R. Wolter, Ocean Grove, NJ. [5 3/4" × 8 1/2"]. R/w/b litho of George Washington, reverse side of a Liberty Dime. 4pp. page 4: Advertising.

GW-570(A) Hail Columbia. a. Collin Coe. In: *Grand Army War Songs, A Collection of War Songs, Battle Songs, Camp Songs, National Songs, Marching Songs, Etc., as sung by Our Boys In Blue in Camp and Field, to which is added a selection of Memorial Songs and Hymns for use on Decoration Day and other Special Occasions*, page 84. e. Wilson G. Smith. Published by S. Brainard's Sons, Chicago, IL. 1886. [6 9/16" × 10"]. Y/gn/gy litho of a Civil War battle scene. 168pp.

(B) Washington And Lincoln, page 36. w.m. Henry C. Work.

GW-571 Hail Columbia. In: *Patriotic Songs*, page 18. Published by C.A. Gambrill Mfg. Co., Baltimore, MD. [ca. 1918]. [3 15/16" × 6"]. R/w/b eagle, stripes. "Patapsco Choice White Corn Meal." 24pp.

GW-572 Hail Columbia. a. Spindler. Published by S.T. Gordon & Son, No. 13 East 14th Street, New York, NY. 1861. R/w/bl/bk/be litho by P.S. Duval & Son of American flag, shield, eagle, munitions, tents, geometric designs. "National Melodies, 2nd Series." List of other tunes in series.

GW-573 Hail Columbia. Published by Edward Hopkins, No. 30 East 14th Street, New York, NY. [ca. 1876].

GW-574 Hail Columbia. In: *Father Kemp's Old Folks Concert Tunes [V-2: A Collection of the Most Favorite Tunes of Billings, Swan, Holden, Read, Kimball, Ingalls, and others and Choruses and divers patriotic and other songs of the greatest and Best Composers (Revised and Enlarged)]*, [V-1: page 61] [V-2: page 64]. Published by [V-1: Oliver Ditson & Company, No. 277 Washington Street] [V-2: Oliver Ditson Company], Boston, MA. [V-1: 1860] [V-2: 1889]. [V-1: 9 1/2" × 6 1/4"] [V-2: 10 1/8" × 6 3/4"]. [V-1: Gn/bk] [V-2: Be/bk] litho of Father Kemp.

GW-575 Hail Columbia. In: *Fa-*

(GW) GEORGE WASHINGTON

vorite National Songs, page 3. Published by Hallet & Davis Piano Company, Nos. 239-241 Wabash Avenue, Chicago, IL. [ca. 1898]. [6 13/16" × 10 1/8"]. R/w/b lithos of George Washington, Abraham Lincoln, crossed flags, eagle, geometric designs. 20pp.

GW-576 Hail Columbia. w. Judge Joseph Hopkinson, 1798. In: *Standard Patriotic Song Folio*, page 24. Published by Eclipse Publishing Company, No. 136 North 9th Street, Philadelphia, PA. [ca. 1920]. R/w/b litho by Starmer of Civil War soldier, modern soldier and sailor, Uncle Sam ands Miss Liberty, ships, bunting. 52pp.

GW-577 Betsy Ross (Or The Origin Of Our Flag). w. Jessica Moore. m. George L. Spaulding (Writers of *A Joke On The Toymaker, The Spirit Of Christmas, &c)*. Published by M. Witmark & Sons, New York, NY. 1913. [6 3/4" × 10 3 /16"]. Bl/bl drawing of Betsy Ross and children. "An Historical Operetta for Juveniles in Two Scenes." 36pp. [One of the characters is George Washington].

GW-578 America, My America (A National Peace Anthem). w.m. George Thornton Edwards. Published by Underwood Music Co., Portland, ME. Copyright 1914 by George Thornton Edwards. Published as a post card. Obv: N/c litho of Stuart portrait of George Washington. Song. Rev: Narrative on George Washington. "*America, My America* whether recited, or sung to its inspiring music, typifies the spirit of America today."

GW-579 Hail Columbia!. "Written by Judge Hopkinson, and adapted by him to the music of the *President's March.*" In: *War Songs, For Anniversaries and Gatherings of Soldiers, To Which is Added a Selection of Songs and Hymns for Memorial Day, The Choruses of all the Songs are Arranged for Male Voices*, page 66. Published by Oliver Ditson & Company, Boston, MA. 1888. Non-pictorial gn/bk cover. [6 1/2" × 10"]. 100pp.

GW-580 Hail Columbia. In: [Unlocated Songbook], page 10. Published "Compliments Sharood Shoe Corporation, St. Paul, MN. [ca. 1900]. [5 3/4" × 8 5/8"]. "Makers of high grade shoes for the family."

GW-581 Washington's Tomb (Ballad). w. T.P. Coulston. m. Carrol Clifford. a. C. Everest. Published by Wm. H. Coulston, No. 147 North Eighth Street, Philadelphia, PA. 1850. Br/w litho of family at Washington's tomb. "Respectfully inscribed to His Excellency John Letcher, Esq., Governor of Virginia."

GW-582 Hail Columbia. In: *Old Favorite Songs*, page 10. Published by S.W. Miller Piano Co., Sheboygan, WI. [ca. 1900]. [5 3/4" × 8 9/16"]. B/w litho of family playing music inscribed "The Home Quartette." 36pp.

GW-583 Centennial Dirge. m. Francis Johnson. Published by Francis Johnson, Philadelphia, PA. 1832. B/w litho by Chiles & Inmans of Washington's Tomb. "Composed by Francis Johnson. Performed by His band at the Tomb of Washington, During the Visit to That Place by the L.A. Corps of Washington Grays, February 22nd, 1832."

GW-584 Hail Washington (Song). m. Henry Weber. Published by C.D. Benson & Bro., Nashville, TN. 1842. Non-pictorial geometric designs. "Inscribed to the Ladies of the Mount Vernon Association." "With Piano Accompaniment by Henry Weber." 4pp.

GW-585 Martha Washington March. m. H. Schwing. Published by G. Willig, Baltimore, MD. 1854. B/w litho by A. Hoen & Co. of Reverend W.D. Jones—"Very Respectfully, William D. Jones [facsimile handwriting]. 6pp. Pages 2 and 6: Blank. Page 3: "Most Respectfully Inscribed to Revd. W.D. Jones, D.D., President of the Martha Washington College, Abingdon, VA."

GW-586 The Stolen Stars Or Good Old Father Washington. w. Gen.

Lew Wallace. m.a. R. Hastings. Published by A.C. Peters & Bro., Cincinnati, OH. 1863. B/w/ litho of shield with stars and stripes. 6pp.

GW-587 Live Triumphant Or Contending Die (An Ode). w. J.W. Brackett, Esq. m. J. Hewitt. Printed and Sold at J. Hewitt's Musical Repository & Library, No. 59 Maiden Lane, New York, NY. Non-pictorial. "Sung by Mr. Caulfield at the Celebration of the Fourth of July, 1809 by the Washington Benevolent Society." 4pp.

GW-588 Emblems Of Mem'ry Are These Tears. Published by G. Willig, No. 185 Market Street, Philadelphia, PA. 1800. Non-pictorial. "Sung by Mrs. Warrell at the New Theatre in Commemoration of the first Anniversary of General Washington's Birth-Day after his decease, 22d Feby., 1800."

GW-589 Hail Columbia. w. F. Hopkinson, 1798 [sic] and Oliver Wendell Holmes, 1887. "Written, by request, for Centennial of Constitution of United States at Philadelphia, Sept. 17, 1887." In: *The Song Patriot, A Collection of National and Other Songs for School and Home*, page 10. c. C.W. Bardeen, Editor of the School Bulletin. Published by C.W. Bardeen, Publisher, Syracuse, NY. 1892. Non-pictorial. [5 3/8" × 7 1/2"]. "Song Budget Music Series III." 80pp.[?].

GW-590 The Birthday of Washington (Solo and Chorus): w. Miss Lucie Blanchard. m. F. Pannell. Published by H. Pilcher & Son, No. 91 Fourth Street, St. Louis, MO. 1858. Non-pictorial geometric designs. "Sung by the Choir of Christian College, Columbia, Mo." 6pp. Pages 2 and 6: Blank.

GW-591 America (A National Song). w. Lewis Dela. m. Dr. W. P. Cunnington. Published by Lee & Walker, No. 722 Chestnut Street, Philadelphia, PA. 1859. N/c litho of Miss Liberty riding on the back of an eagle while holding an American flag, geometric designs. "Written in the "Washington Pew" in the Hall of Independence." "Respectfully dedicated to the National Guards of Philadelphia." 6pp. Pages 2 and 6: Blank. Page 3: Title—**America Beloved, Revered**.

GW-592 America The Beautiful. w. Katherine Lee Bates, Wellesley, Mass. m. Parke W. Hewins, Wellesley, Mass. Copyright 1917 by Dr. Parke. W. Hewins. B/w litho of a portrait of George Washington. "God Shed His Grace On Thee." R/w/b American flag.

GW-593 Hail Columbia! (Song And Chorus). a. S.T. Gordon. In: *Patriotic Songs For Use In Schools And At Social Gatherings*, page 9. Published by Hitchcock Publishing Company, Nos. 244-246 West 23rd Street, New York, NY. 1898. [5 3/4" × 9"]. R/w/b flags, geometric designs. "Hitchcock Collection, Words and Music." 20pp.

GW-594 The Land of Washington (Quartette & Chorus). w.m. J.H. McNaughton. Published by Oliver Ditson & Co., No. 277 Washington Street, Boston, MA. B/w non-pictorial geometric designs. "To Hon. Joseph Holt, Kentucky." 6pp. Pages 2 and 6: Blank.

GW-595 The Battle Of Trenton (A Favorite Historical Military Sonata). m. James Hewitt (1770-1827). e. Maurice Hinson. 1989. R/w/b drawings of George Washington, Revolutionary troops, Washington crossing the Delaware. "Dedicated to General Washington." 22pp.

GW-596 Washington, Star of the West. Published by Charles Magnus, No. 12 Frankfort Street, New York, NY. [1861-1865]. N/c litho of soldier, woman, Indians looking at a drawing of George Washington. "As sung by Mr. Quale." 2pp. page 2: Blank.

GW-597 Unfurl the Glorious Banner. Published by Charles Magnus, No. 12 Frankfort Street, New York, NY. [1861-1865]. H/c litho of George Washington crossing the Delaware River. "500 Ballads lithographed and printed by Charles Magnus, No. 12 Frankfort Street, New York." 2pp. page 2 Blank.

GW-598 Washington's Tent. In: *Three Sets of Cotillions*, page 6. m. C. Meineke. Published by John Cole, No. 123 Market Street, Baltimore, MD. "30th Oct., 1824." B/w non-pictorial geometric designs. "As Danced at the Grand Ball given at Baltimore, in Honour of Genl. La Fayette." 10pp. [Includes instructions for dance figures].

GW-599 Lafayette's March. m. Eugene Guilbert. Published by J. Siegling at His Musical Ware House, No. 109 Meeting Street, Charleston, SC. [ca. 1824]. "Non-pictorial. "Price 12 cents." Programmatic caption—"He visits the tomb of Washington".

GW-600 Our Flag's the Flag of Washington (Maryland! My Maryland). w. "Union Words & Adaptation by George Barker." Published by A.C. Peters & Bro., Cincinnati, OH. 1863. B/w non-pictorial geometric designs. 6pp. Pages 2 and 6: Blank.

GW-601 Mount Vernon Polka. m. Hauser. Published by Lee & Walker, 188 Chesnut St., Philadelphia, PA.: [ca. 185-]. Non-pictorial geometric designs. "Composed for the Piano." 6pp. Pages 2 and 6: Blank.

GW-602 Hail Columbia. Published by G. Andre & Co., No. 1228 Chestnut Street, Philadelphia, PA. 1876. R/w/b crossed American flags, shield, geometric designs. "American National Airs."

GW-603 Centennial Celebration Of The Inauguration Of George Washington As First President Of The United States Of America [Program and Song Sheet]. "First in War, First in Peace and First In The Hearts of his Countrymen." "Commemorative Exercises held at the Mechanics' Pavilion, San Francisco, California, on the Evening of April 30, A.D., 1889." Br/w/bl drawing of George Washington, crossed flags, military equipment. "1789-1889."

GW-604 The Flag Of Washington (Song and Chorus). w. F.W. Gillett. m. J.E. Gould. Published by Lee & Walker, No. 922 Chestnut Street, Philadelphia, PA. 1869. Non-pictorial geometric design border. "Gould's Miscellany...Songs, duets, trios, quartettes, etc, for Church, the Social, Circle, and Pubic Occasions, for Mixed and Male Voices." 6pp. page 2: Blank. page 6: "To Mr. John K. Mac Gowan, Philadelphia." List of titles in series. Advertisement: ads on front and back covers for Lee & Walker music.

GW-605 Columbia's Plaint. w. H.C. Lewis. m. A.P. Heinrich. Published by Bacon & Hart, Philadelphia, PA. [ca. 182-]? "The music composed by A.P. Heinrich, and Calculated to be Easily Harmonized for Two, or Three Voices, or Simplified 'A Gusto.'" "Respectfully Dedicated to His Masonic Brethren." "It is a fact, that Washington, Hamilton, Perry, Burrows, Rush, and indeed a large majority of the departed officers of the Army and Navy, and of the signers of the Declaration of he American Independence, were members of the Ancient Order." 2pp.

GW-606 Hail Columbia. w. Joseph Hopkins. [sic]. m. "Adapted from *President's March*." In: *Patriotic Songs And Hymns*, page 5. Published by Hope Publishing Company, Chicago, IL. 1918. [6 1/16" × 8 5/8"]. Be/bk litho of soldier, sailor, "Fort McHenry." 48pp.

GW-607 Hail Columbia. In: *The Star Songster, Containing 48 Patriotic, Sentimental and Comic Songs*, page 5. Published by McMullen & Gates, No. 143 Walnut Street, Cincinnati, OH. [ca. 1865]. [3 5/8" × 5 7/8"]. R/w/b star, geometric design frame. 52pp.

GW-608 Hail Columbia. w. Joseph Hopkinson. m. Philip Phile. "The Most popular patriotic air during the early days of America was *The President's March*, which was played at Washington's inauguration in 1789 [sic] and was composed by Philip Phile, of Philadelphia. Nine years later Joseph Hopkinson, of Philadelphia, wrote the words, *Hail Columbia!* to be sung to this march. It was long regarded as the National hymn of America, but of late years, has been supplanted by *The Star Spangled Banner.*" In: *Americanization Songs: Liberty Chorus Song Book for Home, School and Community Singing*, page 6. e. Anne Shaw Faulkner. Published by McKinley Music Company, Chicago, IL. 1920. [7" × 10 3/16"]. Ma/be liberty bell, geometric designs. 116pp.

GW-609 Hail Columbia. Published by S. Brainard & Co., No. 203 Superior Street, Cleveland, OH. [ca. 1858]. R/w/b litho of crossed French and American flags. "National Melodies." List of other titles in series.

GW-610 Our Washington. w. Camilla Sanderson. m. Ernest B. Clifton. In: *The New Era Glee Club Collection For Male Voices*, page 21. E. J.S. Fearis. Published by J.S. Fearis & Bro., No. 4547 North St. Louis Avenue, Chicago, IL. 1920. [6 3/4" × 10"]. Be/bk geometric designs. 70pp.

GW-611(A) Hail Columbia. a. Collin Coe. In: *Our National War Songs, A Complete Collection of our Grand Old War Songs, Battle Songs, National Hymns, Memorial Hymns, Decoration Songs, Quartettes, Etc., With Accompaniment for Piano or Organ*, page 109. Published by The S. Brainard's Sons Co., Chicago, IL. 1884. [9 1/8" × 11 3/4"]. Non-pictorial. 164pp. [?].

(B) Washington And Lincoln, page 81. w.m. Henry C. Work.

GW-612(A) George Washington (Reading Song). w. Jean Bassett. m. Franz Joseph Hyden. "George Washington and Franz Joseph Hyden were born the same year, 1732." In: *The Music Hour (Two Book Course, Upper Grades)*, page 73. Published by Silver Burdett Company, New York, NY. 1938. 208pp.

(B) Hail Columbia! (Study Song). w. Joseph Hopkinson. m. Philip Phile. N/c painting of "Washington's Inauguration at Independence Hall, 1793."

GW-613 Hail Columbia. In: *Patriotic Song Book, For the use of the G.A.R. in their Post-Meeting, Reunions, Camp-Fires, Installation Exercises, Fourth of July Celebrations, and Memorial Service. Also For all Patriotic Occasions*, page 18. Published by Orwell Blake, Des Moines, IA. 1883. [5 15/16" × 9 1/16"]. R/gd litho of a G.A.R. badge. 116pp.

GW-614 Hail Columbia. w. Joseph Hopkinson. m. Philip Phile. "Here is a song American in origin and sentiment. The music was composed by Philip Phile as *The President's March* in 1789 to honor President Washington. In 1798, American parties were dangerously divided over the war in Europe, the Federalists favoring England and the cause of order, the Democrats France and Liberty. Judge Joseph Hopkinson of Philadelphia wrote '*A new Federal Song*' for a friend to sing to *The President's March*, and it swept the country. As Hopkinson wrote, it 'found favour with both parties, for both were American.'" In: *Patriotic Songs Of America*, page 6. Published by John Hancock Mutual Life Insurance Company, Boston, MA. 02117. 1956. [4 3/16" × 6 1/4"]. 20pp.

GW-615 Hail Columbia. In: *Organ At Home.* Published by Ditson & Company, Boston, MA. 1873. Bl/bk geometric design border.

GW-616 Hail Columbia. w. Joseph Hopkinson. m. Philip Phile. "In 1788 the Constitution was ratified and the following year, George Washington was elected first President of the United State. Many perplexing problems, both domestic and foreign, faced the new republic. By 1793, France and Great Britain were again at war. Americans were divided in their sympathies. In 1798, inspired by the need for keeping American united, Joseph Hopkinson wrote the words, *Hail Columbia*, and set them to the tune which had been written as an inaugural march for Washington. nine years before." In: *Minnesota Centennial*

Edition of Our Singing Nation, Songs Americans Have Loved from Early Years to the Present, page 26. [6 5/8" × 9 3/16"]. R/w/b litho of Centennial seal. 172pp.

GW-617 Hail Columbia. w. Joseph Hopkinson. m. Fayles [sic]. In: *Brewers' Collection of National Songs and Hymns*, page 66. Published by The Orville Brewer Publishing Co., Auditorium Building, Chicago, IL. 1904. [6" × 9"]. Bl/s geometric designs. 104pp.

GW-618(A) Washington's March. In: *Marches Of The Presidents, 1789-1909, Authentic Marches & Campaign Songs*, page 4. A. Carl Miller. Published by Chappell & Co., Inc., No. 609 Fifth Avenue, New York, NY. "By arrangement with Chilmark Press, Inc." 1968. [9" × 12"]. R/w/b litho of eagle, flag. "An Illustrated Piano Folio For All Ages." 72pp.

(B) Dead March, page 6. m. B. Carr.

GW-619 The President's March. m. Philip Phile. a. Raynor Taylor (1747-1825). In: *Duets Of Early American Music*, page 10. e. Anne McClenny and Maurice Hinson. Published by Belwin Mills Publishing Company, Rockville Centre, NY. 11571. 1971. R/w/b cover drawing of two women playing piano. "Level Four." "David Carr Glover Piano Library." 36pp.

GW-620 Hail Columbia. w. Philip Phile. m. Joseph Hopkinson. In: *The All-American Patriotic Song Book*, page 39. Published by Creative Concepts Publishing Corp., No. 154 El Roblar Drive, Box 848, Ojai, CA. 93023. R/w/b flag design. "Complete Sheet Music Edition." 100pp.

GW-621 Hail, Columbia ! w. Joseph Hopkinson. m. "Attributed to Philip Phile." In: *Songs Of My Country in Easy Arrangements For Piano*, page 8. c.a. Ada Richter. Published by Theodore Presser Co., No. 1712 Chestnut Street, Philadelphia, PA. 1943. [9 1/4" 11 1/4"]. R/w/b map of the United States. 68pp.

GW-622 George Washington Crosses The Delaware. m. Jane Smisor Bastien. In: *Bastien Favorites*, page 12. Published by General Words & Music Company, Neil A. Kjos, Jr., Publishers, No. 4382 Jutland Drive, San Diego, CA. 92117. 1965. Gn/bk/w litho of child playing piano, animals watching. "Level 3." [8 1/2" × 11"]. 36pp.

GW-623 George Washington. w. Gladys Shelly. m. Ruth Cleary. In: *Little Patriots, A Book Of American Sons For Children*, page 10. Published by ABC Music Corporation, No. 799 7th Avenue, New York, NY. 1941. [6" × 9"]. R/w/b drawing of child. 44pp.

GW-624 Martha Washington Temperance Songster. Published by Nafis & Cornish, No. 270 Pearl Street, New York, NY. [ca. 1850]. [2/1/2" × 4 1/4"]. Pk/r/gn litho of Martha Washington. 64pp.[?].

GW-625 Ode [Recitation]. [179-]. [4 1/2" × 7 1/4"]. Non-pictorial. "An Ode performed at the Oratorio in the Stone Chapel, when the great & immortal Washington visited Boston," 2pp. [Handwritten manuscript].

GW-626 Hail Columbia. In: *Philadelphia And New York Glee Book: Containing 100 Glees, Quartetts, Trios, Songs In Part, Rounds and Catches, Composed, Selected, and Harmonized, with an ad libitum accompaniment for the Piano-Forte*," page 268. c.a. George Loder (Principal of the New York Vocal Institute, and a Member of the Philharmonic and Vocal Societies." Published by Lee & Walker, No. 722 Chestnut Street, Philadelphia, PA. 1857. [10" × 7"]. Gd/br hard cover.

GW-627 Hail Columbia. In: *George Washington, A Booklet Compiled By The English Department Of The Arsenal Technical Schools*, page 46. Published by the Arsenal Technical Schools, Indianapolis, IN. 1932. [6 1/4" × 9 1/2"]. Ma/bk stars, embossed portrait of George Washington. 84pp.

GW-628 What's Good Enough For Washington Is Good Enough For Me. w. Dolph Singer. m. Harry Von Tilzer. Published by Harry Von Tilzer Music Publishing Company, No. 1518 New York, NY. 1926. R/w/b litho of George "Washington," bunting, Washington Crossing the Delaware River. 6pp.

GW-629 Hail Columbia. Published by Russell & Tolman, Boston, MA. [ca. 1861]. R/w/bl/gn litho of U.S., English, Italian and French flags. "National Melodies."

GW-630(A) Hail Columbia. In: *The Red, White And Blue Songster, No. 1, National Patriotic Songs Written To Popular Airs*, page 8. Published by Asher & Co., No. 3 Odd Fellow's Hall. Indianapolis, IN. Copyright 1861 by C.O. Perrine. [3 3/4" × 6"]. R/e/b litho of a thirty-six star American flag, ribbon border.

(B) **Immortal Washington**, page 17.

(C) **Washington's Grave**, page 26.

GW-631 Hail Columbia. In *Songs For Children*, page 142. Published by Amsco Publishing Company, No. 240 West 55th Street, New York 19, NY. 1934. [9" × 12"]. N/c drawing of children, characters from songs. "Everybody's Favorite Series No. 5." 196pp.

GW-632 (A) Yankee Doodle. Reproduction of GW-20. [S/U, page 480]. In: *America's Story In Song (Warner Bros. Salutes The Bicentennial)*, page 10. e. Ronny Schiff. Published by Warner Bros. Publications, Inc., No. 75 Rockefeller Center, New York, NY. 10019. 1975. R/w/b cloud cover. Warner Bros. Logo. 260pp.

(B) **The Favorite New Federal Song** [Hail Columbia], page 12. Reproduction of GW-13 (Variation without the attached engraving of George Washington or John Adams, but with an engraved eagle and shield). [S/U. page 173].

See also JA-4; JA-5; JA-21; JA-25; TJ-8; TJ-40; JQA-6; WHH-23; WHH-47; HC-4; ZT-44; ZT-77; MF-10; JB-5; JB-6; GBM-10; AL-88; AL-89; AL-99; AL-132; AL-192; AL-215; AL-221; AL-292; AL-393; AL-401; AL-479; AL-508; HS-8; USG-104; USG-215; USG-216; JGB-35; BFH-17; GC-7; GC-46; WJB-41; WM-24; WM-47; WM-48; WM-63; WM-90; WM-192; WM-221; TR-153; TR-252; WHT-5; WHT-23; WW-7; WW-8; WW-9; WW-16; WW-19; WW-22; WW-31; WW-41; WW-44; WW-58; WW-65; WW-67; WW-83; WW-85; WW-87; WW-106; WW-150; WW-158; WW-175; WW-203; WW-209; WGH-28; WGH-34; CC-14; AML-9; AML-20; WLW-2; WLW-40; WLW-57; FDR-29; FDR-92; FDR-96; FDR-101; FDR-158; FDR-270; FDR-272; FDR-279; FDR-281; FDR-310; FDR-390; FDR-400' FDR-401; TED-1; HST-18; DDE-9; DDE-50; DDE-52; DDE-76; JFK-15; JFK-51; LBJ-1; LBJ-27; RMN-27; GRF-8; DW-13; JBL-2; JBL-3; WL-1; DAM-32; DAM-54; MISC-7; MISC-36; MISC-46; MISC-76; MISC-77; MISC-78; MISC-79; MISC-90; MISC-94; MISC-97; MISC-101; MISC-112; MISC-120; MISC-126; MISC-127; MISC-130; MISC-138; MISC-146; MISC-150; MISC-157; MISC-167; MISC-167; MISC-168; MISC-169; MISC-171; MISC-186; MISC-187.

Henry A. Wallace

HAW-1 We The People. w.m. Fred Toomey and Frank Toomey. Published by Meltone Music Company, No. 390 Walnut Street, Springfield, MA. 1948. Photo of Henry A. Wallace. "Dedicated to Henry Wallace." Drawing of flags, eagle.

HAW-2 Song Of Peace. w.m. Charles L. Williams. Published by Prediction Music, No. 418 Vine Street, Philadelphia 2, PA. [1948]. Photo of "Henry Wallace." "Crusade For Peace — Henry Wallace." "Souvenir Copy."

HAW-3 Songs For Wallace. Published by People's Song, Inc. for the

HAW-3

National Office of The Progressive Party, No. 39 Park Avenue, New York, NY. 1948. [8 3/8" × 10 1/4"]. B/w drawing of Henry A. Wallace, farm. 12pp. [M-428].

HAW-4 Vote For Henry Wallace. w.m. Carl Leon Eddy. Published by House of Carleon, No. 2439 Park Av-

HAW-4

enue, Indianapolis 5, IN. 1948. Bl/w photos of "Henry Wallace" and "Senator Glen Taylor." O/bl/w geometric designs. 4pp.

HAW-5 Song For A New Party. Copyright 1948 by People's Songs. [3 1/2" × 7"]. Non-pictorial. "Music for these songs in *Songs for Wallace*." "Permission for use on television, newsreel, radio, &c., can easily be obtained from People's Songs by calling WA 9-2356 (NYC)." 16pp. [M-429].

HAW-6 Songs Of The Progressive Party [Song Sheet]. Copyright 1948 by People's Songs, Inc. [7" × 8 1/2"]. B/w geometric design border. "Complete words and music for these songs available in *Songs For Wallace* (25c). Order from Progressive Party, 39 Park Avenue, N.Y.C. Choral arrangements, orchestrations, recordings and film strips available from People' Songs, Inc., 126 West 21st Street, N.Y.C." 4pp.

HAW-7 Wallace For President (The Best Man In The Land). w.m. Toby Dwork and Robert Spencer Douglas. Unpublished manuscript. [1948]. [9 1/2" 12 1/2"]. Non-pictorial. 2pp.

HAW-8(A) Battle Hymn Of '48. w. Bryant M. French. m. "Tune: *John Brown's Body*." In: *People's Songs, Songs of Labor and the American People (Vol. 3, Nos. 1 and 2)*, page 3. Published by People's Songs, Inc., No. 126 West 21st Street, New York, NY. 1948. [8 7/16" × 10 11/16"]. B/w drawing of farmer.

(B) Abraham Lincoln Walks Again. w.m. Lewis Allen. page 14.

HAW-9 National Youth Lobby [Program with Songs]. Published by The Young Progressive Citizens of America. 1947. [8 1/2" × 11"]. B/w drawing of man, the Capitol. "Jobs! Peace! Freedom!." "Hear Henry Wallace Keynote the National Youth Lobby." "Sponsored by Y.P.C.A., Washington, June 15–16, 1947." 30pp. Pages 25–27: Songs.

HAW-10 [Wallace Song Sheet]. [1948]. Bl/bk non-pictorial mimeograph. 4pp. Pages 2 and 4: Blank. [First lines include: "The Donkey is tired and thin," "Everyone Wants Wallace," "I've got a ballot," etc.].

See also FDR-21; FDR-135; FDR-140; FDR-181; FDR-297; FDR-371; HST-20.

HENRY CLAY

HC-1 The Kentucky Gentleman (A Ballad). w.m. John H. Hewitt. Published by John F. Nunns, No. 240 Broadway, New York, NY. 1844. B/w sepia tinted litho by Thayer of Henry Clay, vignettes of eagle, home, Capitol, Ashland, wagon, horse and rider. 8pp. Pages 2 and 8: Blank. Page 3: "Written, Composed and Respectfully Dedicated to Henry Clay, the Farmer of Ashland." Facsimile letter from Henry Clay to John Hewitt.

HC-2 Who Feelith Not A Rapture? (A Whig Banner Song). w. J.A. Shea, Esq. m. Alexander Kyle. Published by John F. Nunns, No. 240 Broadway, New York, NY. 1844. B/w sepia tinted litho of Henry Clay, flags, eagle. 6pp. Pages 2 and 6: Blank.

HC-3 The Ashland Quadrilles. m. W.C. Peters. Published by Peters & Company, Cincinnati, OH. 1844. B/w litho of Henry Clay. Br/w geometric border. "Selected and Arranged for the Pianoforte and Respectfully dedicated to the Friends of the Hon. Henry Clay." "Peters & Company's Collection of Musical Publications for the Pianoforte, Guitar, &c., &c., Containing Songs, Duetts [sic], Rondos, Variations, Quadrilles, Marches, Waltzes, &c." 8pp. Page 2: Blank. Page 3: *The Mill Boy*. Page 4: *The Farmer*. Page 5: *The Senator*. Page 6: *The Patriot*. Page 7: *The Kentucky Gentleman*. Page 8: Catalog of music.

HC-4 The American Marseillaise (A Voice of the People). w.m. B. Cahill. Published by B. Cahill, Boston, MA. July 4, 1844. B/w litho by Thayer & Company of George Washington and Henry Clay, eagle, banner—"Pater et Fili," Bunker Hill Monument, Boston harbor. "A Favorite National Air." "Dedicated to our Country's Weal and Honor." "For sale at the Music Stores throughout the Union." 4pp. Page 4: Blank.

HC-5 A Song For The Man (A Henry Clay Ballad For 1844). w. "By the Author of *A Life on the Ocean Wave*." m. "Adapted to the Popular Air of *The Brave Old Oak*." a. Henry Russell. Published by Firth & Hall, No. 239 Broadway and No. 1 Franklin Square, New York, NY. 1844. B/w beige tinted litho by Thayer of Henry Clay, vignettes of Clay's life. 8pp. Pages 2 and 8: Blank.

HC-6 Clay's Quick Step. m. "From a Favorite French Air." a. E.L. White. Published by Oliver Ditson, No. 135 Washington Street, Boston, MA. 1842. B/w litho by Thayer & Company, of Henry Clay [V-1: Facsimile signature] [V-2: Without facsimile signature]. 4pp. Page 4: Blank.

HC-7(A) Henry Clay's Grand March, Waltz & Quick Step. Published by Oliver Ditson, No. 135 Washington Street, Boston, MA. [1844]. R/w/bl/bk/gd litho "Printed in Colors" by B.W. Thayer & Co. of Henry Clay, women, cherubs, fancy gingerbread frame, home at Ashland. "Arranged for Piano Forte." 8pp. Pages 2 and 8: Blank. Page 3: **Ashland Waltz**. m. E.L. White. Page 4: **Henry Clay's Grand March**. m. Dr. John C. Bartlett. Page 6: **Ashland Quick Step**. m. Dr. John C. Bartlett.

(B) Clear The Tracks For Old Kentucky.

HC-8 Harry Clay And Frelinghuysen. w. Mr. J. Greiner. Published by G.E. Blake, No. 13 South Fifth Street, Philadelphia, PA. 1844. Non-pictorial. "Written by Mr. J. Greiner at the Whig National Convention at Baltimore." 4pp. Pages 1 and 4: Blank.

HC-9 Raising Old Harry (A Whig Song). w.m. "That Same Old Coon." Published by F.D. Benteen, Bal-

(HC) HENRY CLAY

HC-7

timore, MD. 1844. B/w litho of a raccoon holding banner with song title, sign — "Kinderhook & Co." 4pp. Page 2: Title: **Come All Ye Whigs So Gallant And True** (A Clay Song). Page 4: Blank.

HC-10   The National Clay Minstrel. Published by George Hood, No. 15 North 6th Street, Philadelphia, PA. 1843. [3" × 4 1/2"]. Y/bk litho of raccoon sitting on fence, black border. 68pp.

HC-11   The National Clay Minstrel (And True Whig's Pocket Companion for the Presidential Canvass of 1844). Published by [V-1: George Hood, No. 15 North 6th Street, Philadelphia, PA] [V-2: James Fisher, No. 71 Court Street, Boston, MA]. 1843. [3 1/4" × 5 1/8"]. Y/bk litho of raccoon labeled "That Coon" and flag inscribed "Henry Clay," log cabin. "New and Improved Edition." 128pp. Page 10: "To the National Clay Club this work is respectfully dedicated by the Publisher."

HC-12   The Clay Minstrel Or National Songster. c. John Stockton Littell. Published by Turner & Fisher, No. 15 North Sixth Street, Philadelphia, PA. [1842]. Br/bk litho of Henry Clay. "To Which is Prefixed a Sketch of the Life, Pubic Services, and Character of Henry Clay." 168pp. [M-048].

HC-13   The National Clay Melodist (A Collection of Popular and Patriotic Songs, Second Edition, Enlarged and Improved). Published by Benj. Adams, No. 54 Court Street, Boston, MA. 1844. [3" × 5 1/4"]. Inside title page: B/w litho of Henry Clay's home — "O'er Ashland's lawns the skies are bright, From West to East The radiance streams and glows, The land beneath its beams gay beats the heart with joy, Hurrah! Hurrah! Hip! Hurrah!" 108pp. [M-050?].

HC-14   National Clay Minstrel And Frelinghuysen Melodist. Published by George Hood, No. 15 North 6th Street, Philadelphia, PA. [1844]. [2 7/8" × 4 3/16"]. Y/bk litho of Henry Clay, wreath. [V-1: 68pp.] [V-2: 32pp.] [V-1: Page 68: "Miniature biography of Henry Clay."]. [M-051].

HC-15   The Whig Banner Melodist. Published at Philadelphia, PA. 1844. Litho of ship labeled "Ship of State." "Published for the Whigs of the Union and for sale at the Reading Room, Corner of Fifth and Chestnut Streets, and at all Principal Bookstores, June, 1844." 64pp. [M-059?].

HC-16   New Whig Songs (For Clay Glee Clubs). Published by J. Winchester, New World Press, No. 30 Ann Street, New York, NY. [1844]. Non-pictorial. "Arranged in Three and Four Parts by a Professor of Music." "Complete — Price 12 1/2 cents." 24pp.

HC-17   The Kentucky Minstrel And Jersey Warbler [Song Book]. Published by Robinson & Peterson, No. 98 Chestnut Street, Philadelphia, PA. 1844. [2 7/8" × 4 9/16"]. Y/bk litho of Henry Clay and Theodore Frelinghuysen. 68pp. page 3: "Being a Choice Selection of Coon Melodies." Pages 2, 4 and 75: Blank. Page 68: Y/bk litho of Henry Clay and Theodore Frelinghuysen. [M-045].

HC-18   The Clay Minstrel Or

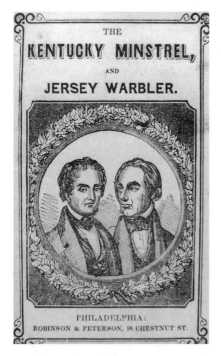

HC-17

National Songster. c. John Stockton Littell. Published by Greeley & M'Elrath, Tribune Building, New York, NY. 1844. [3 1/8" × 4 7/8"]. Non-pictorial. [V-1 & V-2: 288pp.] [V-3: 396pp.]. [V-3: "To Which is Prefixed a Sketch of the Life, Pubic Services, and Character of Henry Clay, by John S. Littell, President of the Clay Club of Germantown." [V-3: page 8: B/w engraving of Henry Clay. Page 396: B/w litho of man climbing flag pole, flag]. [M-046, 047, 049].

HC-19(A) **Here's To You Harry Clay**. w.m. "An Old Coon." Published by Henry Prentiss, No. 33 Court Street, Boston, MA. 1844. B/w litho by Thayer of Henry Clay, top hat, cane. "The Ashland Melodies." "Respectfully Dedicated to J.L. Dimmock, Esq., President of the Boston Clay Club No. 1, by the Publisher." 6pp. Pages 2 and 6: Blank.

(B) **The Origin And Rise Of Prest. Clay**.

(C) **Harry Clay** (We Shall Ne'er See His Like Again) (A New Patriotic Whig Song). w. "By A Member of the Clay Club No. 1, Boston." a. Richard Andrews. "Respectfully dedicated to the several Clay Clubs in The United States."

HC-20 **Here's To You Harry Clay**. w.m. "An Old Coon." Published by Henry Prentiss, No. 33 Court Street, Boston, MA. 1844. B/w litho by Thayer & Co. of Henry Clay, top hat, cane. "A New Song Written by an Old Coon and Respectfully Dedicated to J.L. Dimmock, Esq., President of Boston Clay Club No. 1 by the Publisher."

HC-21 **The Star Of Hope** (A Song Without Words). m. Carl Sahm, Op. 15. Published by M. Schmitz, No. 120 Walnut Street, Philadelphia, PA. 1854. B/w litho of woman playing lyre. "Respectfully dedicated to Miss Lucretia Clay, daughter of Thos. H. Clay, Esq. of Mansfield, and granddaughter of the late Honble. Henry Clay, the Sage of Ashland." 10pp. Pages 2 and 10: Blank.

HC-22 **The Banner Of Clay**. w.m. "By An Old Whig." Published by Oliver Ditson, Washington Street, Boston, MA. 1844. Non-pictorial. "Dedicated to the Portland Clay Club."

HC-23 **Clay And Frelinghuysen** (and) **Clear The Tracks For Old Kentucky**. Published by Oliver Ditson, No. 135 Washington Street, Boston, MA. [1844]. Non-pictorial. "Adapted to a Familiar Air." "Two Popular Whig Songs."

HC-24 **Freedom & Clay** (A New Patriotic Song). Published for the Author by John Cole, Baltimore, MD. 1831. Non-pictorial. "Arranged for the Piano Forte." 4pp. page 4: **Henry Clay's Quick Step**.

HC-25 **Welcome Home**. w. G. Forrester Barstow. m. B. Hime. Published by William Brown, Salem, MA. [1844]. Non-pictorial. "Dedicated to the New England delegates to the Baltimore Whig Convention." 4pp. Page 4: Blank.

HC-26 **The Prize Banner Quick**

Step. Published by F.D. Benteen, Baltimore, MD. 1844. Non-pictorial. "To the Delegates to the Young Men's Whig Convention, May 2d, 1844." 4pp.

HC-27 The Ashland Galop. m. J.C. Lehman. Published by F.D. Benteen, Baltimore, MD. [ca. 1844]. Non-pictorial. "Composed for the Piano Forte and respectfully Dedicated to Miss Georgeanna Spicer." 4pp. page 4: Blank.

HC-28 The Lexington Grand Waltz. m. Wilhelm Iucho. Published by Firth & Hall, No. 1 Franklin Sq, New York, NY. 1834. Non-pictorial. "To Mrs. Henry Clay." 4pp.

HC-29 Henry Clay Grand Funeral March. m. James W. Porter. Published by Winner & Shuster, No. 110 North Eighth Street, Philadelphia, PA. 1852. Non-pictorial. "As performed by the Bands on the occasion of the Funeral of this ever lamented Statesman." 4pp.

HC-30 Henry Clay Grand March. m. "A Citizen of Maryland." Published by John Cole, Baltimore, MD. 1832. Non-pictorial. "Composed and Respectfully Dedicated to him." 4pp.

HC-31 The National Union (Solo and Chorus with Piano Forte Accompaniment). w.m. Charles Collins, Jr. Published by Lee & Walker Music Publishers, No. 162 Chesnut Street, Philadelphia, PA. 1851. Bk/w/gd litho by Thomas Sinclair of "The Capitol at Washington," eagle, flags, gold chain links for each State with the name and the year it entered the Union — "The United States of America Union and Liberty, Forever, One and Inseparable." "In Union's Chain, within its Spell, Freedom & Peace & Safety Dwell." "Respectfully dedicated to the Hon. Henry Clay." Facsimile letter, signature — "Both the sentiments and the poetry are very good, and I yield, with pleasure to your desire to inscribe them to me. With great respect, I am your friend and obedt. Service — H. Clay." 8pp. P. 3: "Most Respectfully Inscribed to the pure Patriot & Statesman."

HC-32 Order Of Exercises (At the Meeting of the Democratic Clay Club of the 10th Ward, City of New York) [Songster]. "Published in behalf of the Ladies of the ward." [1844]. [6" × 9 1/2"]. Y/bk eng. of Henry Clay, star, two women, eagle. "Justice to Harry, the Star of the West." "Held at the Apollo Saloon, 410 Broadway ... for the reception of a ... banner painted by C.E. Weir, to be presented ... by the Hon. Joseph L. White. The President of the Club, N.C. Bradford, Esq., will take the Chair at a quarter before 8 o'clock. William Wood, Esq., will preside at the piano. Music by the Band." 4pp.

HC-33 The Warlike Dead In Mexico. w. Mrs. Balmanno. m. Miss Augusta Browne. Published by C. Holt, Jr., No. 156 Fulton Street, New York, NY. 1848. R/w/bl/bk/gd/gn litho of Henry Clay, eagle, shield, flag, War battle scenes. "*W*e *H*ope *I*n *G*od." [First letter of word each spells — "WHIG"]. "Music Composed and Dedicated (by Special Permission) to the Hon. Henry Clay." "I need not say that the affecting subject of the song, touches me both as a Father and I hope, a Patriot.— H. Clay." 10pp.

HC-34 2 Favorite Funeral Marches. Published by [V-1: Edward L. Walker, No. 142 Chesnut St.] [V-2: Couenhoven, Scull & Co.], Philadelphia, PA. 1852. Non-pictorial. "In memory of Henry Clay." "As performed by Beck's Philad. Band on the evening of the Clay obsequies." "Respectfully Dedicated to the Washington Greys." 6 pp. Page 3: **Henry Clay's Funeral March No. 1.** Page 4: **Henry Clay's Funeral March No. 2.**

HC-36 The Flag Of Henry Clay (A Vocal Quartett). w. A.H. Ryder, Esq. m. C.M. von Weber. a. H.E. Mathews. Published by F. Riley, No. 297 Broadway, New York, NY. [ca. 1844]. Non-pictorial. "For 1st & 2nd tenor and 1st & 2nd bass." "Arranged and Respectfully Inscribed to the Members of the Young Men's Henry Clay Association of the City of New York." 4pp. page 4: Blank.

HC-37 The Reveille (A Prize Song). w.m. John H. Warland. Published by James L. Hewitt, No. 372 Broadway, New York, NY. 1844. Non-pictorial. "For the Young Men's General Clay Club of the City of Brooklyn and dedicated by them to the Whigs of the Union." 4pp. Page 4: Blank.

HC-38 Hurrah For The Clay. w.m. J.G. Osbourn. Published by J.G. Osbourn, No. 112 South 3rd Street, Philadelphia, PA. 1843. B/w litho by T. Sinclair of Henry Clay, four vignettes titled "A Health To The Farmer." Farmer plowing—"How happy the farmer who lives by the Clay;" Home in winter storm—"We'll laugh at the storm when we're sheltered by Clay;" Man and Kids—"He smiles at their sports for he earned them by Clay;" White House at Washington in ruin—"Nothing can save it but filling with Clay." 4pp. Page 2: *Hurrah for the Clay* (by a Philadelphian). Sung with great applause at the Whig Festival at Philad., July 4, 1843, Words and Air Original, Arranged for the Piano Forte." Page 4: Title: **A Health To The Farmer** or Hurrah For Henry Clay.

HC-39 The Kentucky Rally. w. "Poetry by her [M.S. Mortimer] Sister." m. M.S. Mortimer. Published by Firth & Hall, No. 1 Franklin Square, New York, NY. [1844]. Non-pictorial. "Respectfully Dedicated to the Whigs of the United States." 4pp.

HC-40 Clay & Frelinghuysen. w. Quidam. m. Air: *De Boatman's Dance*. Published by Firth & Hall, No. 1 Franklin Square, and No. 239 Broadway, New York, NY. 1844. Non-pictorial. "Property of the Publishers." 4pp. Pages 2 and 4: Blank.

HC-41 A Nation's Farewell To Henry Clay. w. T.E. Garrett, Esq. m. W.W. Rossington. Published by Tripp & Cragg, No. 117 Fourth Street, Louisville, KY. Copyright 1853 by G.W. Brainard & Co. Non-pictorial. 8pp. Page 8: Blank.

HC-42 The Star Of The West (A National Song). w.m. P.W. Sproat. Published by P.W. Sproat, No. 62 Spruce Street, Philadelphia, PA. [1844]. Non-pictorial. "Composed for the Piano Forte." 2pp.

HC-43 Clay's Kentucky Grand March. a. William Ratel. Published by George Willig, No. 171 Chestnut Street, Philadelphia, PA. 1847. Non-pictorial. "Arranged for the Piano Forte and dedicated to the Whigs of Kentucky." 4pp. Pages 1 and 4: Blank.

HC-44 Clay And Frelinghuysen (A Celebrated Whig Song). w. J. Greiner, Esq. m. "The music arranged from a popular American Melody." Published by Atwill's Music Repository, No. 201 Broadway, New York, NY. 1844. B/w litho of woman holding U.S. flag, ships, train, plow, geometric design border with birds. Verse. "The Popular Whig Song." "No. 3—Atwill's Edition of Illuminated Music." "Price 12 1/2 Cents Nett [sic]." 4pp. Page 2: "Arranged for the Piano Forte." Page 4: Advertising.

HC-45 The Whigs Of 76 & 44. w. "A Whig No. 4 Calvert Street." Published by "A Whig," No. 141 Baltimore

HC-44

Street, Baltimore, MD. Copyright 1844 by J. Boswell. Non-pictorial. "As sung with enthusiastic applause by the Ashland Choir." "Written by an eminent Whig, Dedicated to the Whig ladies of Baltimore." 4pp. Pages 1 and 4: Blank.

HC-46 Clay And Frelinghuysen. m. "Set to the Popular Song *Old Dan Tucker*." a. J. Greiner. Published by J.C. Smith's Music Saloon, No. 215 Chesnut Street, Philadelphia, PA. [1844]. Non-pictorial black line border. "Written for the Baltimore Convention." 4pp. Pages 1 and 4: Blank.

HC-47(A) Matty's Lament. w.m. Charles Gapler. In: *That Same Old Coon*, page 1, May 25, 1844, No. 2. Published by R.N. & W.F. Comly, Dayton, OH. B/w litho of a raccoon, wheat, floral designs. Campaign news.

(B) Polk And Dallas. w. Charles Gapler. m. Air: *Dandy Jim from Caroline*. June 15, 1844, No. 5.

(C) Hurrah For Henry Clay. m. Air: *Bob and Joan*. June 22, 1844, No. 6.

HC-48 Frelinghuysen's Grand March. m. W.C. Glynn. Published by H. Prentiss, No. 33 Court Street, Boston, MA. 1844. Non-pictorial geometric designs. 2pp.

HC-49 Clay Convention Quick Step. m. Miss S. Warfield. Published by Samuel Carusi, Baltimore, MD. 1844. Non-pictorial. "As performed by the Independent Blues Band." "Composed expressly for the Great Whig Convention held at Baltimore, May 2d, 1844 and dedicated to the Hon. Henry Clay." 4pp. Pages 1 and 4: Blank.

HC-50 The Whig Chief. w.a. J.B. Warland, Esq. m. Air: *The Brave Old Oak*. Published by W.H. Oakes and for sale by E.H. Wade, No. 197 Washington Street, Boston, MA. 1844. [V-1: Gold trim] [V-2: Silver trim] with n/c litho "Printed in Colors" by B.W. Thayer & Co. of Henry Clay's houses — "Birthplace of Henry Clay, Hanover, Va.," "Ashland, present residence of Henry Clay," and "President's House, future home of Henry Clay." "And Dedicated by Permission to the Hon. Henry Clay by the Boston Clay Club No. 1." "This song received the prize of fifty dollars awarded by the Boston Clay Club for the most approved Clay song." 6pp.

HC-51 Hurrah For Our Own Henry Clay (A National Song). w. Henry F. Penfield. m. A. Lee. Published by Henry F. Penfield, [New York, NY]. 1837. Non-pictorial. "Engraved & Printed by Samuel Ackerman." 4pp.

HC-52 The Farmers And Mechanics (Whig Song). m. "Air — *Lucy Neal*." Published by Atwill, No. 201 Broadway, New York, NY. [1844]. Non-pictorial. "Hurrah for Harry Clay." "As sung with shouts of applause by George W. Dixon, at the meetings of the Nickerbocker Club." 4pp. Pages 1 and 4: Blank.

HC-53 The Capitol Quick Step. m. William C. Glynn. Published by Henry Prentiss, No. 33 Court Street, Boston, MA. 1844. B/w beige tinted litho by Bouve & Sharp of Henry Clay on horseback. "Respectfully dedicated to the

HC-53

Hon. Henry Clay of Kentucky." "Composed and Arranged for the Piano Forte." 4pp. Page 4: Blank.

HC-54 Clay Club Quick Step. m. Charles Grobe. Published by George Willig, No. 171 Chestnut Street, Philadelphia, PA. 1844. Non-pictorial. "Composed for the Piano Forte and dedicated to the Whig ladies of the United States." 4pp. Pages 1 and 4: Blank.

HC-55 Oh Poor Jimmy Polk (A Favorite Patriotic Whig Song and Trio). w.m. "By an eminent Professor." [1844-1848]. Non-pictorial. "Written and adapted for the parlour and public meetings." "Beautifully Arranged with Symphonies and Accompaniments by an eminent Professor." 6pp. Page 6: Blank. [Author's copy has three pages of manuscript verses added].

HC-56 Vive Le Clay! (A New Whig Song). w.m. Seth H. Sweetzer. Published by F.D. Benteen, Baltimore, MD. 1844. B/w litho of Henry Clay being crowned in laurel. By two women. "Written and dedicated to the Whigs of the United States." 6pp. Pages 2 and 6: Blank.

HC-57 Ashland Quick Step. m. Dr. J.C. Bartlett. Published by Oliver Ditson, No. 135 Washington Street, Boston, MA. 1844. Non-pictorial. "Composed for the Piano Forte and Respectfully Dedicated to the Hon. Henry Clay." 4pp. Pages 1 and 4: Blank.

HC-58 O Henry Clay (A Round for Three Voices). w.m. "A Gentleman of Baltimore." Published by F.D. Benteen, Baltimore, MD. 1844. Non-pictorial. 4pp. Pages 1 and 4: Blank.

HC-59 The Grave Of Henry Clay. w. L. Reynolds, M.D. m. Charlie C. Converse. Published by Oliver Ditson, No. 115 Washington Street, Boston, MA. [ca. 1850]. Non-pictorial. "25c. nett [sic]." 6pp. Pages 2 and 6: Blank.

HC-60 Ashland Waltz. m. E.L. White. Published by Oliver Ditson, No. 135 Washington Street, Boston, MA. [1844]. Non-pictorial. "Arranged for the Piano Forte and most Respectfully Dedicated to the Hon. Henry Clay." 2pp. Page 2: Blank.

HC-61 Clay's Grand Quick Step. m. C. Meineke. Published by [V-1: John Cole, Baltimore, MD] [V-2: George Willig, Junr., Baltimore, MD]. 1838. Non-pictorial. "Composed and Respectfully Dedicated to that Great Statesman." 4pp. Page 4: Blank.

HC-62 The Soldier And His Bride. w. George P. Morris, Esq. m. Henry Russell. Published by Firth & Hall, No. 1 Franklin Square, New York, NY. 1841. B/w litho by Thayer of forest scene, Indians, woman being killed, geometric designs. "Accurate view of the scene where the murder of Miss McGrea took place." "Founded on an event in the history of the American Revolutionary War." "The Music Composed and Respectfully Dedicated to Hon. Henry Clay." 8pp. Page 3: At top of music, a long narrative on the incident in which the woman was killed.

HC-63 Clay's Quick Step. m. "From a favorite French air." a. C.L. White. Published by Oliver Ditson, No. 135 Washington Street, Boston, MA. 1842. Non-pictorial. 4pp. Pages 1 and 4: Blank.

HC-64 Come, Come Gallant Whigs. Published by Birch, No. 291 Bowery, New York, NY. [1844]. Non-pictorial geometric design border. "1." 2pp. Page 2: Song —*Life on the Ocean Wave*.

HC-65 Old Kentucky. m. "Adapted to the air of *Old Dan Tucker*." Published by Firth & Hall, No. 239 Broadway, New York, NY. [1844]. Non-pictorial. "As sung by the Henry Clay Clubs." 2pp.

HC-66 Our Clay And Frelinghuysen. Published by Birch, No. 291 Bowery, New York, NY. [1844]. Non-pictorial geometric design border. "7." 2pp. Page 2: Song —*Jullien Polka Dance No. 3 For The Piano Forte*.

HC-67 **Ashland Quick Step**. m. Nathanial Carusi. Published by Samuel Carusi, Baltimore, MD. 1844. Non-pictorial. "Composed & Arranged for the Piano Forte and respectfully dedicated to The Hon. Henry Clay." 4pp. Pages 1 and 4: Blank.

HC-68 **Henry Clay March**. m. F. Miller. a. O. Habersang. Published by Oscar Habersang, No. 52 Springfield Avenue, Newark, NJ. Copyright 1897 by F. Miller. R/w/b drawing of crossed flags, Masonic symbol. "Respectfully dedicated to the Jr. O.U.A.M." 6pp. Page 2: Blank. Page 6: Advertising.

HC-69 **Clear The Way For Henry Clay**. w.m. Thomas Carr. Published by Osbourn's Music Saloon, Philadelphia, PA. [1844]. Non-pictorial. "Arranged for the Piano Forte."

HC-70 **The Whig Banner Melodist**. Published as a newspaper for The Clay Whigs, No. 109 Chesnut Street, Philadelphia, PA. September, 1844 as Vol. 1, Number 1. [19" × 25"]. 4pp. Page 1: Litho of raccoon climbing flag pole with "Henry Clay" flag at top — "It is nailed to the mast!" Songs. Pages 2-4: Lithos & Songs.

HC-71 **The Ashland Quick Step**. m. W. Ratel. Published by George Willig, No. 171 Chesnut Street, Philadelphia, PA. 1844. Non-pictorial. "As Performed before the Clay Club of Lexington, KY., by the Amateur Brass Band at the dedication of the new hall. Composed and dedicated to the Hon. H. Clay." 4pp. Page 4: Blank.

HC-72 **Old Kentucky Quick Step**. In: *Lady's Musical Library, Embracing the Most Popular and Fashionable Music*, page 27, Vol. III, March, 1844. Published by Edmund Ferrett, Publisher's Hall, No. 101 Chestnut Street, Philadelphia, PA. 1844.

HC-73 **The Moon Was Shining Silver Bright** (Or Clear the Track for Old Kentucky). Published by F.D. Benteen, Baltimore, MD. [1844]. Non-pictorial. "Arranged for Piano Forte." 4pp. Pages 1 and 4: Blank.

HC-74 **British Gold**. m. "Tune: *Old Dan Tucker*." [8 3/4" × 3 1/4"]. [1844]. Non-pictorial. 2pp.

HC-75 **The Whig Rally**. w. John H. Hewitt. m. Air: *The Wreckers Daughter*. Published by G. Willig, Junr., Baltimore, MD. 1844. Non-pictorial. "As Sung by Mr. C.S. Duffield, the celebrated Whig Vocalist. Original Words Adapted to the Popular Air of *The Wreckers Daughter*." 4pp. Page 4: Blank.

HC-76(A) **A New Clay Song**. In: *The Clay Bugle*, page 3. Published by C. M'Curdy & J. Knabb, Harrisburg, PA. 1844. "Dedicated to the Clay Club No. 1 of Montgomery County.

(B) **O.K**. (A New Whig Song). w. D. Johnson. m. Air: *Sittin' on a Rail*.

(C) **Voice Of The People**. m. Air: *A Life on the Ocean Wave*.

(D) **Whig Victory Song**. Headed by a b/w woodcut of raccoons singing, dancing and playing musical instruments.

HC-77 **The Ashland March**. m. Philip Burgheim (Professor). Published by F.D. Benteen, Baltimore, MD. 1843. B/w non-pictorial geometric designs, line border, facsimile letter from Henry Clay — "Dear Sir: I received your letter informing me that Mr. Burgheim, Professor of Music, has composed a Grand March which he wishes to publish and dedicate to me, and requesting my assent to the dedication. I yield with pleasure and will thank you to present to him my acknowledgements for the friendly consideration of me, I am, with great respect, your friend and ob. sevt., — H. Clay, Ashland, 25 July, 1843." "Composed and Dedicated by permission to the Hon. Henry Clay (of Kentucky)." Geometric design border. 6pp. Pages 2 and 6: Blank.

HC-78 **Vote For Clay** (A New Whig Song). w. "By the Author of *Here's to you Harry Clay*." m. Thomas Hudson (Of London). Published by Keith's Music Publishing House, Nos. 67 and 69 Court

Street, Boston, MA. 1844. "Dedicated to John L. Dimmock, Esq., President of the Boston Clay Club No. 1." 4pp. Page 4: Blank.

HC-79 Henry's Clay's Grand March. m. C.S. Grafulla (of New York). Published by C.F. Hupfield & Son, Importers of Music & Musical Instruments, No. 12 South 9th Street, Philadelphia, PA. 1847. Non-pictorial. "As performed by the Philadelphia Brass Band." "Composed and arranged for the Piano Forte and Respectfully Dedicated to the Hon. Henry Clay." "Price 19 cts nett [sic]". 4pp. Page 4: Blank.

HC-80 Henry's Clay's Grand March. m. Dr. J.C. Bartlett. Published by Oliver Ditson, No. 135 Washington Street, Boston, MA. 1844. Bk/w/gr tinted litho by Thayer & Co. of Henry Clay. 4pp. Page 4: Blank.

HC-81 The Henry Clay Grand Gallopade. m. Charles Milnor. Published by Osbourn's Music Saloon, No. 112 South 3rd Street, near the Exchange, Philadelphia, PA. [1844?]. Non-pictorial. "Composed and arranged for Piano Forte."

HC-82 The Flag Of Our Union (A National Song). w. General Geo. P. Morris. m. William B. Bradbury. Published by Mark H. Newman & Co., No. 199 Broadway, New York, NY. 1850. Non-pictorial. "To the Honorable Henry Clay this song is most respectfully inscribed by the Author." "Composed for and first sung by F.H. Nash, Esq., with the most Enthusiastic Applause, Broadway Tabernacle, March 13th, 1850." 6pp. Page 6: Blank.

HC-83 [Song Sheet]. w. W. Townsend. m. Popular Airs. [1844]. [6 1/4" × 7 5/8"]. Non-pictorial. Two songs—**The Ashland Farmer** and **Gallant Harry** (A Banner Song). 2pp. Page 2: Blank.

HC-84 Oratorial Grand March (To the Memory of Henry Clay). m. Thomas J. Martin. Published by F. Hartel & Company, New Orleans, LA. 1860. B/w litho by J. Tolti & Ds. Simon Lithography, of a street scene and monument of Henry Clay. 8pp. Pages 2, 7 and 8: Blank.

HC-85 The Ashland Quick Step. m. W. Ratel. Published by George Willig, No. 171 Chesnut Street, Philadelphia, PA. 1844. Litho of soldiers in formation in front of building. "As performed before the Clay Club of Lexington, Ky., by the Amateur Brass Band at the dedication of their new hall composed and dedicated to the Hon. H. Clay." 6pp. Pages 2 and 6: Blank.

HC-86 Ashland Quick Step. m. Philip Burgheim. Published at Boswell's Music Store, No. 109 Baltimore Street, Baltimore, MD. 1843. Non-pictorial floral border. "Composed and Dedicated by permission to the Hon. Henry Clay of Kentucky." Facsimile letter from Henry Clay—"Dear Sir: I duly received and send you my thanks for the copies of the *Ashland Quick Step* which you did me the favor to send to me. It is much admired by better judges than I of music. With great respect, I am your ob. ser.,—H. Clay, Ashland, 3d Jun., 1843." 4pp. Page 4: Blank.

HC-87 Oh, Poor Jemmy Polk. Published by Birch, No. 291 Bowery, New York, NY. [1845]. Non-pictorial geometric design border. "8." 2pp. Page 2: Song—*The Weeping Mother*.

HC-88 Harry Clay (A National Song). m. "Tune—*Hurrah For The Bonnetts of Blue*." [1844]. [3 5/8" × 5 7/16"]? Non-pictorial.

HC-89 The National Clay Almanac, 1845 [Almanac, Songs and Narratives]. Published by Desilver & Muir, No. 18 South Fourth Street, Philadelphia, PA. 1844. [6 13/16" × 7 7/8"]. B/w litho of Henry Clay, ship—"Commerce," plow, crops—"Agriculture."

HC-90 The Same Old Coon. w. Robert E.H. Levering. m. "Air—*Long Tail Blue*." Published at Lancaster, OH.

September 7, 1842. [18" × 5 1/2"]. Bk/pk litho on silk of a raccoon, geometric design border. "Well, Judge, what do you think of the next Campaign?" "I could at one time calculate political results, but who can tell the influence of the d—n-d 'Whig Songs.'" "Why does a certain criminal put the Democrats on the rack? Because it is a Rack Coon!" 2pp. Page 2: Blank.

HC-91 Henry Clay's Funeral March. m. Charles Steinruck. Published by Oliver Ditson, No. 115 Washington Street, Boston, MA. [ca. 1852]. Non-pictorial geometric designs. "Composed for the Piano." 4pp. Pages 1 and 4: Blank.

HC-92 Au Revoir. Published by The Glee Club of the 10th Congressional District. [ca. 1844]. [3 5/8" × 6 3/8"]. Non-pictorial. "To the Washington City Glee Club, on leaving Winchester, by the Glee Club of the 10th Congressional District." 2pp. Page 2: Blank.

HC-93 Life Of Henry Clay And The Clay Minstrel Or National Songster. Published by Greeley & M'Elrath, Tribune Buildings, New York, NY. 1844. [3 1/4" × 5 5/16"]. Bl/gd hardback book with gold imprinting of a wreath and star. 396pp. [M-049].

HC-94 The Ashland Songster. Published by Smith & Raymond, Printers, Rochester, NY. 1844. "Comprising the Most Popular National Songs, for Western New York." 32pp. [M-035].

HC-95 Clay and Frelinghuysen. c. Bemis. 1844. "Whig Songs for the Great Mass Convention on Boston Common, Sept. 19, 1844." 18pp. [M-037].

HC-96 Clay and Frelinghuysen Songster. Published by Turner & Fisher, New York, NY. 1844. 64pp. [M-036].

HC-97 The Clay Club Coon Songster. Published by Santa-Claus, New York, NY. 1844. Litho of raccoon on a fence. 38pp. [M-038].

HC-98 The American Republican Songster (Second Edition). w.m.a. P. De Le Ree. Published and for sale at the Office of the *New York Citizen*, and at American Star House, New York, NY. 1844. 24pp. [M-039].

HC-99 The Native American Songster. e. P. De le Ree. Published by W.H. Graham, New York, NY. 1844. "Dedicated to the American Republican Party." 36pp. [First Edition of HC-98]. [M-040].

HC-100 The Harry Clay Melodist. Published by Benjamin Adams, Boston, MA. 1842. [V-1: Br/bk] [V-2: Gn/bk] [V-3: Pk/bk] litho of Henry Clay. "A Collection of Popular and Patriotic Songs, Respectfully Dedicated to the Friends of Henry Clay Throughout the United States." [M-041].

HC-101 The Clay Songster. Published by [V-1: J. Fisher, Boston, MA] [V-2: Turner & Fisher, New York, NY]. 1842. Litho of Henry Clay. "Henry Clay, The Farmer, The Statesman, The Patriot." 64pp. Inside title—**The Harry Clay Songster (or Melodies for the Whigs and the People).** [M-042].

HC-102 The National Clay Minstrel And True Whig's Pocket Companion For The Presidential Canvass. Published by James Fisher, Boston, MA. 1843. Y/bk litho of a raccoon on log cabin. 126pp. [M-052].

HC-103 Patriotic Songs. For Clay Glee Clubs. Arranged In Three And Four Parts By A Professor Of Music. Part One. Published by J. Winchester, New World Press, New York, NY. 1844. [M-056].

HC-104 Original Clay Songs. Published by W.A. Philomath, Cincinnati, OH. 1842. "Humorous and Sentimental, Designed to Inculcate Just Political Sentiments, to Suit the President Political Crisis and to Advocate the Claims of Henry Clay to the Highest Honors His Country Bestow." [M-057].

HC-105 Whig Songs For The Mendon Clay Club. w. "Written by a Member." Published by J.N. Bradley & Company, Boston, MA. 1844. [M-062].

HC-106 Whig Songs Selected, Sung, And Published By The Choir Of The National Clay Club. Published by Colon & Adriance, Philadelphia, PA. 1844. 32pp. Page 32: Y/bk litho of Henry Clay. [M-063].

HC-107 The Union Clay Glee Book. c. Samuel Withrow. [Published at Gettysburg, PA]. 1844. "A Choice Collection of Original and Select National Airs and Patriotic Songs, Compiled and Dedicated to the Whigs of the Union, by Samuel Withrow." [M-064].

HC-108 The Henry Clay Almanac, For The Year Of Our Lord 1843. Printed and Published by T.K. & P. G. Collins, Philadelphia, PA. 1842. 32pp. "Being the Third Year After Bissextile or Leap Year and, After the 4th of July, the 67th of American Independence. Containing songs and Anecdotes and a Biographical Sketch of Henry Clay, the Illustrious Orator, Statesman, Patriot, and 'Farmer of Kentucky.'" 32pp. [M-043].

HC-109 The Henry Clay Almanac, For The Year Of Our Lord 1844. Printed and Published by T.K. & P. G. Collins, Philadelphia, PA. 1843. 32pp. "Being the Third Year After Bissextile or Leap Year and, After the 4th of July, the 67th of American Independence. Containing songs and Anecdotes and a Biographical Sketch of Henry Clay, the Illustrious Orator, Statesman, Patriot, and 'Farmer of Kentucky.'" 32pp. [M-044].

HC-110 The National Clay Minstrel And True Whig's Pocket Companion For The Presidential Canvass of 1844. Published by George Hood, and sold by all Principal Booksellers throughout the United States, Philadelphia, PA. 1843. Y/bk litho of a raccoon on log cabin. 126pp. [M-053, 054, 055].

HC-111 Torr's Native American Minstrel. c. Joseph Torr. Published by Joseph Torr, Philadelphia, PA. 1844. "Containing Patriotic Native American Songs. And a Complete Account of the Riot." 32pp. [M-058].

HC-112 The Whig Banner Songster. e. Tudor Horton. Published by Tudor Horton, Matchett's Press, Baltimore, MD. 1844. Br/bk litho of Henry Clay. "A Choice Collection of Popular Whig Melodies, to Which is Added a Condensed Sketch of the Life and Public Services of the Hon. Henry Clay, and Many New Songs." 128pp. [M-060].

HC-113 Five Popular Whig Songs. m. Charles F. Heuberer. Published by Oliver Ditson, Washington Street, Boston, MA. 1844. Non-political. "Arramged with Easy Chorus and Dedicated to the Clay Clubs Throughout the Country" 12pp. Page 2: **The Peoples Rally.** Page 4: **Our Candidate.** Page 6: **Justice To Harry Clay.** Page 8: **The Whig Rallying Song.** Page 10: **Baltimore Convention Ratification Song.**

HC-114 The Ashland Waltzes. m. Valentine Dister. Published by Osbourn's Music Saloon, No. 112 South 3rd Street, Philadelphia, PA. [1844]. Non-pictorial. "Composed and Respectfully Dedicated to Miss Augusta Donley." "Osbourn's Music Saloon has removed below the Phila. Exchange." 4pp. Number at bottom of page one through page three reads "11." Page 4: Blank. [Found bound with three other Clay songs.].

HC-115(A) Clear De Way For Ole Kentucky (A Favorite Patriotic Whig Song And Trio). a. "Arranged with Symphonies and Accompaniments by an Eminent Professor." Published by Geo. F. Nesbitt, Tontine Building, Corner of Wall and Water Streets, New York, NY. 1844. B/w litho by Michelin & Cuipers of Henry Clay, desk, chair, geometric design frame. "Lays of Ashland, Favorite Patriotic Whig Songs." List of other songs in series. Page 3: "Written and Adapted for the Parlour and Public Meetings." Last page: **Clare De Way For Ole Kentuck.** Non-pictorial geometric design border.

(B) **Come, Come Gallant Whigs.**

(C) **Van Is A Used Up Man** (A Favorite Patriotic Whig Song and Trio La). a. "Arranged with Symphonies and Piano Accompaniments by an Eminent Professor." [1844]. Non-pictorial geometric designs. "Written and Adapted for the Parlour and Public Meetings." Last page: another song. **Polk is a Used Up Joke.**

(D) **There's Little Mat** (A Favorite Patriotic Whig Song and Trio). a. "Arranged with Symphonies and Piano Accompaniments by an Eminent Professor." [1844]. Non-pictorial geometric designs. "Written and Adapted for the Parlour and Public Meetings." Last page: another song—**There's Jemmy** [sic] **Polk.**

(E) **Huzzah Then For Harry** (A Favorite Patriotic Whig. Song and Trio). a. "Beautifully Arranged with Symphonies and Accompaniments by an Eminent Professor." [1844]. Non-pictorial geometric designs. "Written and Adapted for the Parlour and Public Meetings."

HC-116 Our Nominee (A Clay Canticle). w.m. R.P.N. Published by A. Fiot, Philadelphia, PA. [1844]. Non-pictorial geometric designs. "As Sung by the Allegheny Clay Warblers." "To the Ashland Clay Clubs of Pittsburg." 4pp.

HC-117 Our Clay And Frelinghuysen (A Favorite Patriotic Whig Song And Trio). a. "Beautifully Arranged with Symphonies and Accompaniments by an Eminent Professor." [1844]. Non-pictorial geometric designs. "Written and Adapted for the Parlour and Public Meetings." 4pp.

HC-118 Old Kentucky Quick Step. In: *Twelve Popular Quick Steps, for the Piano Forte.* Published by E. Ferrett & Co., No. 68 South Fourth Street, Philadelphia, PA. 1845. Non-pictorial. 14pp.

HC-119 Incidents In The Campaign Of 1844. c. James T. Hathaway. Published by J.T. Hathaway, No. 287 Crown Street, New Haven, CT. 1905. [5" × 7"]. Bl/gy non-pictorial geometric design border. "Printed for private distribution among old friends." "*Here's to you, Harry Clay*—Old Song." 68pp. [Contains numerous songs].

See also JKP-4; JKP-5; AL-329; AL-476; JBR-2.

HERBERT C. HOOVER

HCH-1 (We're for) Hoover And Curtis. w.m. Albert Gould and Tom Shane. Published by M. Witmark and Sons, New York, NY. 1928. B/w photos of Herbert Hoover inscribed "Cordially Yours" [facsimile handwriting], and Charles Curtis inscribed "Cordially Yours" [facsimile handwriting]. R/w/b drawings of Puritan, Indian, Capitol building. 6pp. Pages 2 and 6: Advertising. Page 3: "Respectfully Dedicated to the Hon. Charles Curtis, Republican Nominee for Vice-President of the U.S. by the Curtis for Vice-President Club of New York."

HCH-2 Prosperity. w. Neil Fitzgerald and Anita Gray Little. m. Anita Gray Little. Published by Anita G. Little, Concord, NH. 1932. Bl/w drawing of map of the United States, city skyline. "Written in response to President Hoover's request for a Prosperity Song." 6pp. Pages 2 and 6: Blank.

HCH-3 Hoover (The Man for Uncle Sam). w.m. L.L. Willis. Publishing Agents—VosBurgh's Orchestration Service, No. 1547 Broadway, New York, NY. Copyright 1928 by "L.L. Willis, Big Stone Gap, Va." Bl/w drawing of Herbert Hoover. R/w/b geometric designs. 6pp. Page 2: "Respectfully Inscribed to Mr. Hoover as part of 'Hoover Day' celebration, Elizbethton, Tenn., October 6, 1928." Page 6: Blank.

HCH-4 Mr. Hoover And Mr. Smith (A Non-Partisan Comedy Song). w. Herb Magidson. m. Robert King.

Published by Shapiro, Bernstein and Company, Music Publishers, Broadway and 47th Streets, New York, NY. "A Non-Partisan Comedy Hit." 1928. Br/w photo of Gus Van and Joe Schenck — "Introduced by Gus Van and Joe Schenck." Bl/br/w geometric designs. 6pp. Page 6: Advertising.

HCH-5 Hoover! We Want Hoover! (The Irresistible Fox Trot Melody). w. "Al" Hegbom and Billy Hunter. m. E.V. "Al" Hegbom. Published by Pacific Music Publishers, No. 1053 Howard Street, San Francisco, CA. 1928. Bl/w photo of Herbert Hoover. 6pp. Page 6: Advertising.

HCH-6 Hoover! We Want Hoover! (The National Campaign Song). w. Al Hegbom and Billy Hunter. m. E.V. "Al" Hegbom. Published by Pacific Music Publishers, No. 1053 Howard Street, San Francisco, CA. 1928. Bl/w photo of Herbert Hoover. R/w/b stripes, eagle. 6pp. page 2: Poem on "Women's Votes." Page 6: Biography of Herbert Hoover.

HCH-7 Hoover The Great. w. Edward Machugh. a. Wilber F. Burleigh.

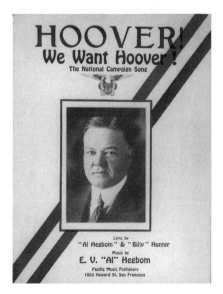

HCH-6

Published by John C. Miller, No. 177 Tremont Street, Boston, MA. 1928. Br/be non-pictorial geometric design border. "Sung by Edward Machugh, The Radio Baritone." "Dedicated to J. Ernest Kerr, Secretary of the Republican Club of Massachusetts." 4pp. Page 4: Advertising.

HCH-8 It's An Elephant's Job (Yes, You Bet It Is). w.m. Eric Karll. Copyright 1932 by Eric Karll, No. 2344 North First Street, Milwaukee, WI. Bl/w photo of "Herbert Hoover." R/w/b drawing of Elephant. "Keep Him On The Job." 6pp. Page 6: "Excerpts From the Address of the President — Hoover Accepting The Republican Nomination for President of the United States."

HCH-9 Mr. Hoover Don't Give Us A Loveless Day. w. Debbie Peterson. m. Ed. W. Penny. Published by Penny and Peterson, No. 1017 Washington Avenue North, Minneapolis, MN. 1918. Gn/w/bl silhouette drawing of lovers, moon, policeman. 4pp. Page 4: Adv.

HCH-10 We're Going To Keep Mr. Hoover (In the White House Chair). w.m. James Wright. Published by James Wright, Music Publisher, No. 313 McBride Avenue, Patterson, NJ. [1932]. Bl/w geometric designs. B/w photo of Herbert Hoover. 4pp. Page 4: Sample ballot for various New Jersey "Republican Candidates."

HCH-11 The Man Who Wins (The Big Hoover March). w. E.K. Arnold. m. P.J. O'Reilly. a. Mima Lee Smoot. Published by Bain, Arnold and McCann Music Company, Louisville, KY. 1928. R/w/b flag, shield, eagle. B/w photo of Herbert Hoover. "Respectfully Dedicated to Hon. Herbert Hoover." 6pp. Page 2: "Highlights In Hoover's Address of Acceptance." Page 6: Blank.

HCH-12 Hoover Rally Song. w.m. Ella A. Cushing. Published by Ella A. Cushing, No. 20 Rawson Road, Wollaston. MA. 1928. Bl/w floral and geometric designs. 6pp. Pages 2 and 6: Blank.

HCH-13 I Thank You Mr.

Hoover (That's the Best Day of the Year). w.m. Clarence Gaskell (Writer of *That's A Mother's Liberty Loan*). Published by M. Witmark and Sons, Witmark Building, New York, NY. 1918. R/w/b drawing of Herbert Hoover, empty dinner table, calendar with days of the week labeled "Meatless," "Lightless," "Wheatless," "Heatless," "Bill-less," "Kiss-less," "Sweetless," "Rideless," and "Wifeless." 4pp. Page 4: Advertising.

HCH-14 President Hoover March (Song). w.m. William Spencer. Published by Triangle Music Publishing Company, No. 1658 Broadway, New York, NY. 1929. B/w photo of "Herbert Hoover," geometric designs. "A Joe Davis Production." 6pp. Page 2: "Respectfuly [sic] Dedicated to Hon. Herbert Hoover." Page 6: Advertising.

HCH-15 Let Hoover Carry On. w. John D. Noble. m. *Glory, Glory, Hallelujah/Battle Hymn of the Republic*. Published by John D. Noble, No. 131 West 23rd Street, New York, NY., as poster with hole at top for hanging. 1928. [10" × 14"]. Obv: B/w photo of Herbert Hoover. Counter stamp — "Window Poster and Campaign Song, Sample Copy." "Campaign Song." Rev: Song.

HCH-16 Hoo Hoo Hoover. w.m. Mary Harriet Morley. Published by Frank Harding, Printers of Music, Poems and Recitations, No. 228 East 22nd Street, New York, NY. 1929. Pl/o/w cover. Pk/o photo by Harris and Ewing of Herbert Hoover. "Dedicated to Our Country and Our President." 4pp. Page 4: Advertising.

HCH-17 On With The Dance! w. Edgar Leslie and Al Dubin. m. Jimmie Monaco. Published by Walter Donaldson, Donaldson-Douglas-Gumble, Inc., Music Publishers, No. 1595 Broadway, New York, NY. 1929. O/w/bk drawing of Capitol dome. B/w photo of Paul Specht. "Chosen as the Official Number for the 'Inaugural Ball' on March 4, 1929, as Featured by Paul Specht and His World Famous Orchestra." 6pp. Pages 2 and 6: Advertising.

HCH-18 Presidential March. w. George Denoyan. m. Harry Mehrab. Published by Mus-Art Company, Music Publishers, No. 980 East 163rd Street, New York, NY. 1928. B/w non-pictorial geometric designs. "Dedicated to Hon. Herbert Hoover." 6pp. Page 6: Blank.

HCH-19 Let's Get Behind Herbert Hoover (Campaign Song). w.m. J.B. Waterfield. Published by J.B. Waterfield, Attleboro, MA. 1932. B/w photo by Bachrach of Herbert Hoover. B/w drawing of palm branches. "Dedicated to the President and the Republican Party." 4pp. Pages 2 and 4: Blank.

HCH-20 Me And The Women Elected Hoover. w.m. Carl C. Countryman. Published by Carl C. Countryman, Canisteo, NY. 1932. R/w/b geometric designs. Bl/w photos of "Herbert Hoover" and "Charles C. Countryman." 4pp. Page 4: Blank.

HCH-21 Our President (Marching Song). w.m. "Doc" Frank. Published by Prof. Joseph Frank Music Publishing Company, Rooms 1131-1136, No. 127 North Dearborn Street, Chicago, IL.

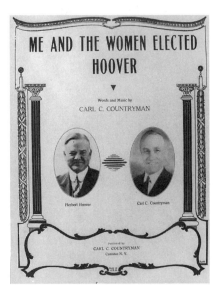

HCH-21

1929. B/w photos of "Herbert Hoover President" and "Prof. Joseph Frank." 6pp. Page 6: Blank.

HCH-22 Spitin' Ol' Mistah' Hoovah! (March, Quickstep, Hoe-Down). w.m. Unohoo. Published by Unohoo Publishing Company, R-321, No. 179 Marcy Avenue, Brooklyn, NY. 1924. Non-pictorial. "Dedicated by The Author and Composer to the memory of his revered Father." List of other publications — "Set of above with memorial cover and songs to old tunes, postpaid anywhere in U.S.A. $1.00." 6pp. Page 6: Advertising.

HCH-23 Who Is Hoover? (Popular Song). w.m. Dayve B. DeWaltoff, M.D., Buffalo, NY. 1928. "Dedicated to Mrs. Herbert Hoover." Advertising.

HCH-24 Hoover Is The Man! (Song). w.m. B.J. McPhee. Published by Louis H. Ross Music Company, No. 288 Tremont Street, Boston, MA. Copyright 1928 by B.J. McPhee. B/w photo of Herbert Hoover. Bl/w geometric designs. 6pp. Page 2: Blank. Page 6: "Arranged for Male Voices by A.M. Beattie."

HCH-25 Hoover Is O.K. (For Thee! For Me!). w. C. Charles Kay. m. C.C. Kuenzig. Published by C.C. Kuenzig, No. 128 Main Avenue, Girard, PA. 1928. Non-pictorial. "The Hoover Campaign Song." 6pp. Pages 2 and 6: Blank.

HCH-26 Your Cause And Mine. w. William Oliver McIndoo. m. Charles L. Johnson. Published by McIndoo Publishing Company, Kansas City, MO. 1928. Photos of Herbert Hoover and Charles Dawes. Drawings of eagle, barge, farm.

HCH-27 Hoover For President (The Hope of Our Nation). w. Anna Lifter. m. Anthony La Paglia. Published by Anthony La Paglia, New York, NY. 1932. Drawing of Herbert Hoover. 4pp.

HCH-28 Hoover (Campaign Song). w.m. E.G. Stone. Published by E.G. Stone, No. 80 Huntington Avenue, Boston, MA. 1928. B/w photo of Herbert Hoover. R/w/b shields, geometric designs. "Introduced by Dora Smith." 4pp. Page 4: Blank.

HCH-29 Salute To The U.S. Flag (March). m. Frank Gradisching. Published by Frank Gradsaching, Ambridge, PA. 1930. Non-pictorial geometric designs. 4pp. Page 3: "Dedicated to President Herbert Hoover and his Citizens."

HCH-30 Big Chief Hoover. w.m. W. Henry Pease. a. Rudy Gunther. Published by The Song Record Publishing and Demonstrating Company, Mt. Vernon, NY. 1928. Photo of Herbert Hoover. "1928." "With Ukulele Arrangement." 6pp. Page 2: Advertising. Page 6: Blank.

HCH-31 Republican March Song. w.m. Paul Hutyan Horvath (Daisytown, PA.). Published by Armand Wiesinger, No. 961 St. Nicholas Avenue, New York, NY. 1928. Bl/w photo of Paul Horvath. R/w/b geometric designs. 6pp. Page 2: "Respectfully Dedicated to the U.S.A. Republican Party." Page 6: Adv.

HCH-32 Prosperity Days Are Near. w. Burton V. Lane. m. Lon F. Stafford. Published by Lon Frederick Stafford and Company, Music Publishers, Syracuse, NY. 1932. B/w photo of Herbert Hoover. R/w/b bunting, eagles, stars. 6pp. Page 2: "Respectfully Dedicated to President Hoover."

HCH-33 Who-oo Who-oo Hoover. w.m. Lucile Manker. Published by Lucile Manker, No. 2200 East 70th Place, Chicago, IL. 1928. Br/w drawing by John Doctoroff of Herbert C. Hoover. Bl/br/w drawing of trees. 6pp. Page 2: Inside Title — **Who-oo-oo-oo Who-oo-oo-oo-Hoover.** "Dedicated to Mrs. Bertha Baur, National Committeewoman for Illinois."

HCH-34 Hoover! We Want Hoover! [w. Al Hegbom and Bill Hunter]. m. [Al Hegbom]. Copyright 1928 by Pacific Music Publishers, No. 1053 Howard Street, San Francisco, CA.

HC-33

[3 1/2" × 6 1/8"]. Non-pictorial. "Who but Hoover?" 2pp. Page 2: Blank.

HCH-35 Hoover Hooverize. w.m. Mrs. Melrose Scales. Published by Scales Music Publishing Company, No. 401 West 10th Street, Dallas, TX. 1918. R/w/b drawing by John Doctoroff of shield, eagle. "Dedicated by Permission to Hon. Herbert C. Hoover." "Approved by United States Food Administration." 4pp. Page 4: Advertising.

HCH-36 Hurrah For Hoover (Song). w. Thomas T. Johnston. m. Rudolph Toll. Published by Thomas T. Johnston, No. 181 Middlesex Avenue, Medford, MA. 1928. Bl/w non-pictorial geometric design border. 4pp.

HCH-37 Hurrah For Hoover (A Campaign Song). w.m. W. Bentley. Published by W.B. Gregg, Peru, IA. 1928. R/w drawing of Herbert Hoover, stripes. 4pp. Page 4: Blank.

HCH-38 Hooverize. w.m. Madelyn Sheppherd. Published by Waterson, Berlin and Snyder Company, Music Publishers, Strand Theatre Building, Broadway at 47th Street, New York, NY. 1918. R/w/gn drawing of military food trucks. "Keep It Coming. We must not only feed our soldiers at the front but the millions of women and children behind our lines — General Pershing." "Dedicated to Mr. Hoover, U.S. Food Commissioner." "Waste Nothing — The U.S. Food Administration." 4pp. Page 4: Advertising.

HCH-39 We're All Good Pals At Last. w.m. Horatio Nicholls. Published by The Lawrence Wright Music Company, Denmark Street, London, W.C.2., England. 1931. [9 3/4" × 12 3/8"]. R/w/bk non-pictorial cover. "A Sweeping Success — The 'Hoover' Song." Many Press Headlines Including — "Hoover War Debt Proposal," "Mr. Hoover's New Statement," "Holding Firm All War Debts," "The World Enjoys A Cheerful Day," "Hoover Asks For Plan, Yes or No," "Holiday from all Debts," "France and her Reparations," "Last Night's Dramatic Moves," "Hitting out at Europe," "Britain's Offer," "Britain's Relief for Dominions." 4pp. Page 4: Advertising.

HCH-40 Hoover Songs [Song Sheet]. w. Sandy Sinclair, Song Writer. [6 1/4" × 9 7/16"]. Non-pictorial. "Hoover Homecoming Meeting, West Branch, IA. August 21, 1928." 4pp.

HCH-41 Hoover And Curtis [Song Sheet]. w. Gene Hanford, Westfield, NJ. m. "Set to good old tunes we can all sing." Published by Gene Hanford, Westfield, NJ. 1928. [9" × 12"]. Bl/w non-pictorial. "Written especially for this campaign." "$1.25 per 100; $7.50 per 1,000." "1928 — 1928." 2pp.

HCH-42 Hooverize. w.m. Cornelius R. Van Rees. Published by Van Rees Press, No. 518-534 West 26th Street, New York, NY. [1918]. Drawing of Uncle Sam giving a loaf of bread to woman [Europe], children.

HCH-43 Victory (Fox Trot Song). w.m. Mary McKee Reisinger. Published by Mary KcKee Reisinger,

Greenwich, CT. 1928. Non-pictorial geometric designs. "Dedicated to the Republican Party." 6pp. Pages 2 and 6: Blank.

HCH-44 Straw Vote (A Community Election Introducing Herbert Hoover and Al Smith). Copyright 1928 by Irving Berlin, Inc., No. 1607 Broadway, New York, NY. [10 5/16" × 6 7/8"]. Non-pictorial. 6pp. Foldout.

HCH-45 We Want Hoover. w.m. Frank S. Johnson. Published by Maranell Publishing Company, Chicago, IL. 1928. B/w drawing of a level and transit — "Construction Boulder Dam, Deep Waterways, Mussel Shoals." "For The People." 4pp. Page 4: Testimonials.

HCH-46 Hoover Over (Republican Campaign Song). w.m. Mary Smyth Davis. Published in Los Angeles, CA. 1928. Br/w photo of Herbert Hoover. R/w/b drawing of flag. "Herbert Hoover Our Standard Bearer." 6pp.

HCH-47 Bonus Blues. [ca. 1932]. [5 1/2" × 11"]. Non-pictorial. "Sold by unemployed Veterans." "Price 10c." 2pp. Page 2: Blank.

HCH-48 President Hoover March. m. Art Gaetke. a. A.E. Gaylord. Published by Art Gaetke, Publisher, No. 1601 2nd Avenue, Wisconsin Rapids, WI. 1929. R/w/b drawing of Herbert Hoover in drum major's uniform, bunting, geometric designs. 6pp. Pages 2 and 6: Blank. Page 3: At top of music — "Dedicated to President Herbert Hoover."

HCH-49 We're For Hoover (Song). w.m. Lawrence Stoddard Graebling. Copyright 1928 by Lawrence Stoddard Graebling, P.O. Box 1907, Washington, DC. [6 3/4" × 10 3/4"]. B/w photos of "Herbert Hoover For President" and "Charles Curtis For Vice President." B/w drawing of an elephant — "Get off and Push," geometric designs. "The Republican Party Standard Bearers." 4pp. Page 4: Blank.

HCH-50 Ballads Of The B.E.F. Published by Coventry House, New

HCH-49

York, NY. 1932. [6 1/8" × 9 1/4"]. Non-pictorial hardback book. 56pp. Page 6: B/w illustration of man praying, bayonets. Illustrated throughout. [Anti-Hoover and anti-MacArthur songs (without musical notation or tunes indicated) in reaction to attacks on World War I Bonus Expeditionary Forces members].

HCH-51 Who's "Who". w. Geo. Cryderman. m. Walter Orion. Published by Cryderman Music Publishing Company, Chicago, IL. 1920. [Pre-1919 size]. Non-pictorial geometric designs. "Dedicated to Herbert Hoover." 4pp.

HCH-52 Hoover And Lindbergh [Song Sheet]. [1928]. [6" × 9 1/2"]. Non-pictorial. 2pp. Page 1: **Hoover And Lindbergh** (Campaign Prize Song). w. William F. Kaiser. m. "Tune of *Auld Lang Syne*." "Winner of prize offered by the American League of Professional Women for best Republican Campaign Song." Page 2: **Hoover There**. w. Henry J. Sayers. m.

"A Republican Campaign Marching Song adapted to the Air, *Over There*." "Dedicated to Our Next President, Hon. Herbert Hoover." Also: **Hoover Campaign Song**. w. Ward Keene. m. Air: *Tramp-Tramp-Tramp, The Boys Are Marching*.

HCH-53 Mr. Hoover And Mr. Smith (A Non-Partisan Comedy Song). w. Herb Magidson. m. Robert King. In: *The Gem Dance Folio for 1929, No. 2, page 30*. Published by Shapiro, Bernstein and Company, Music Publishers, Cor. Broadway and 47th Street, New York, NY. 1929. Song copyright 1928. R/w/bl/bk reproductions of sheet music covers. "Containing the Mid-Season's Musical Comedy and Popular Song Successes, Also the Latest Theme Songs Arranged as Fox-Trots and Waltzes." "Piano Solo Only." 68pp.

HCH-54 Hail To Hoover. w.m. Mary Julia Miller. Copyright 1932 by Mary Julia Miller. B/w photo of Herbert C. Hoover. Bl/w border. 4pp.

HCH-55 [Hoover! Hoover!] [Song Pamphlet] w. Various. m. Popular tunes. [1928]. [3 1/2" × 5 7/8"]. Non-pictorial. 4pp.

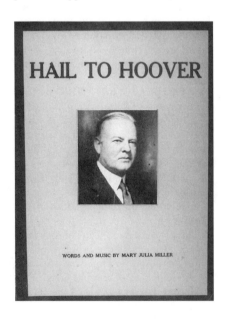

HCH-56 The Herbert Hoover March. m. Peter F. Damm. Published by Peter F. Damm, Dover, NH. 1929. B/w drawing of Herbert Hoover. Bl/w drawing of wreath, eagle, stars, ribbon, blue line border. 6pp. Page 2: **The Herbert Hoover March** (In Two Parts). Page 6: Blank.

HCH-57 White House Blues. In: *The New Lost City Ramblers*, page 245. e.c.a. John Carter, Mike Seger and Holly Wood. Published by Oak Publications, No. 165 West 46th Street, New York, NY. 1964. B/w photo of The New Lost City Ramblers. 260pp. Page 245: "Bob Baker is a young Blue Grass musician around Washington, D.C., and he learned this song from his parents back in Kentucky. It is a modification of a *White House Blues* about Theodore Roosevelt's becoming President after the assassination of President McKinley. This melody has been used for a number of topical songs in the last fifty years. *The Battleship Maine* and *Crazy War* are basically the same tune. Today in Kentucky, patches on clothing are still labeled 'Hoover Badges.'"

HCH-58 Hoover-Curtis (Rhode Island Campaign Song). w.m. Ada Holding Miller and Ruth Tripp. Published for The Woman's Republican Club of Rhode Island. 1928. Bl/w stars and geometric designs. 4pp. Page 2: "Dedicated to Leona Curtis Knight." Page 4: Blank.

HCH-59 My District, 'Tis Of Thee. w. Frederic William Wile. m. "Tune: *America*." In: *A Souvenir of the Inauguration of a President of the United States from Whose Election Half-A-Million American Citizens Were Barred by Constitutional Disfranchisement*, page 6. Published by Citizens' Joint Committee On National Representation for the District of Columbia, Washington, DC. 1929. [4 5/8" × 8"]. Y/bk geometric designs. 8pp.

HCH-60 The Battle Cry (Campaign Songs for 1928, The Home in Action Against the Saloon) [Song Book]. e. Rev. John J. Daniels. Published by Dry

Republicans and Democrats, Minneapolis, MN. [5 3/4" × 8 1/8"]. 1928. Be/bl geometric designs. 36pp. Pages 2, 30-32: Essay—"The Two Candidates" [Smith and Hoover]. [Songs include: **William Jennings Bryan**. w. J.J. Daniels. m. "Tune—*Our Country Will Stay Dry*"].

HCH-61 Help Hoover Win The War. w.m. Ada May Collins. Published by Keystone Music Company, Room 404, Forest Building, Philadelphia, PA. 1918. R/w/b drawing of soldiers at mess, French, English and American flags. 4pp. Page 4: Blank.

HCH-62 Hoover's Who (Song with Violin and Cello Obligato). w.m. Musetta Markland Pearl, L.L.B. (Composer of *O, Come Along And Vote For Hoover* (Negro), *The Happy Farmer Wants Hoover*, Lyric—*God Gave me All But You*). Published by Musetta Markland Pearl, L.L.B., No. 2408 South Harvey Street, Oklahoma City, OK. 1828. Bl/w non-pictorial geometric designs. "Financed by W.E. Ramsey, Oklahoma City, Okla." 6pp. Page 2: "To Dr. J.C. Hubbard and Miss Anna Sechten of Oklahoma City, Okla., whose skill and untiring ministrations enabled me to escape the swath of the Grim Reaper that my song might be completed for my country this number is gratefully dedicated." Page 6: Blank.

HCH-63 O, Come Along And Vote For Hoover (Negro). w.m. Musetta Markland Pearl, L.L.B. Published by Musetta Markland Pearl, L.L.B., No. 2408 South Harvey Street, Oklahoma City, OK. 1928?

HCH-64 The Happy Farmer Wants Hoover. w.m. Musetta Markland Pearl, L.L.B. Published by Musetta Markland Pearl, L.L.B., No. 2408 South Harvey Street, Oklahoma City, OK. 1928?

HCH-65 Vote For Hoover. w. N.B. Herrell. m. Vanna G. Patterson. Copyright 1928 by H.B. Herrell. B/w photo by Underwood & Underwood of "Herbert C. Hoover." B/w drawings of shield, elephant, floral and geometric designs. 4pp. Page 4: B/w photos by Harris & Ewing of "Herbert C. Hoover" and "Charles Curtis." B/w drawings of elephant, shield, eagle, stars.

HCH-66 When Hoover Comes Back To Washington. w. Alice M.P. Newkirk. m. "Tune: *When Johnny Comes Marching Home*." Copyright 1928 by Alice M.P. Newkirk, Tadnor, PA. [3 1/4" × 5 1/2"]. Bl/bk non-pictorial. "Dedicated to Pennsylvania Council of Republican Women." 2pp. Page 2: Blank.

HCH-67 The Next President (Freedom In the Land). w.m. Professor Joseph "DOC" Frank. Published by Prof. Joseph Frank Music Publishing Company, Rooms 1131-1136, No. 127 North Dearborn Street, Chicago, IL. 1928. B/w photos of Herbert Hoover and "Prof. Joseph Frank." R/w/b drawing of crossed flags. "Flag Of The Free, Through Hoover—Herbert Hoover Our President." 6pp. Page 6: Blank.

See also WGH-28; AES-9; FDR-44; FDR-96; FDR-97; FDR-148; FDR-158; FDR-347; DDE-9; LBJ-1; MISC-14.

HORACE GREELEY

HG-1(A) Greeley & Brown's Galop To The White House. m. William Dressler. Published by J.L. Peters, New York, NY. 1872. B/w litho of Horace Greeley and Benjamin G. Brown, crossed flags, eagle, ivy. "To the Friends of Greeley and Brown." 6pp. Pages 2 and 6 Blank. Page 3: "Introducing the Air from Offenbach's *Orpheus*."

(B) Greeley's Grand March. m. Smith.

(C) Greeley's Favorite Polka. m. Strate.

(D) Good Bye Ulysses (or We're Falling Into Line) (Song and Chorus for Male Voices). w.m. A. Templeton Gorham. 6pp. Page 3: "Liberal Republican Campaign Song."

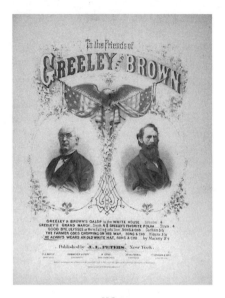

HG-1

HG-2

(E) **The Farmer Goes Chopping On His Way** (Or The Farmer President) (Song and Chorus). w. Harry Miller. m. H.M. Higgins. 6pp. Pages 2 and 6: Blank. Page 3: Adapted to the Melody *The Blue Bird is Singing in the Hill.*

(F) **He Always Wears An Old White Hat** (Song and Chorus). w. Harry Miller. m. Harry Macarty. 6pp. Page 3: "Song and Chorus for Male Voices."

HG-2 The Old White Hat (And the Cincinnati Platform). w.m. H.T. Merrill. Published by H.T. Merrill, Chicago, IL. 1872. [V-1: Br/w attached photo of Horace Greeley] [V-2: Non-pictorial cover]. "Are you a Patriot, or a mere Partisan?" 6pp. Page 6: Advertising.

HG-3 O! What Makes Grant So Fearfully Frown? (Song and Chorus). w.m. The Saint Paul Greeley Club. Published by Weide & Ross, St. Paul, MN. [1872]. B/w engraving of Horace Greeley, geometric design border. "Composed and Sung by the St. Paul Greeley Club and Respectfully Dedicated by them to Horace Greeley." 4pp.

HG-4 Horace Greeley's Grand March. m. William T. Meyer. Published by Lee & Walker, No. 922 Chestnut Street, Philadelphia, PA. 1872. Br/w oval litho of Horace Greeley. 6pp.

HG-5 The Sun's Greeley Cam-

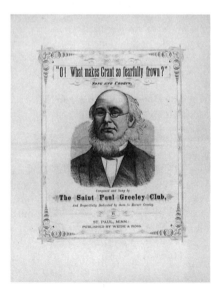

HG-3

paign Songster. c. Amos J. Cumming. Published from *The Sun* Office, New York, NY. 1872. [4 1/8" × 6 1/2"]. Be/bk litho of Horace Greeley, wreath. "He shines for all." 64pp. [M-183].

HG-6 Horace Greeley's Funeral March. m. Pierre Latour. Published by Lee & Walker, No. 922 Chestnut Street, Philadelphia, PA. 1872. B/w litho of Horace Greeley. 6pp. Page 2: Blank. Page 6: Advertising.

HG-7 Oh Horace (Campaign Song and Chorus for 1872). w.m. Harry Birch. Published by White, Smith & Comp'y, Nos. 298, 300 Washington Street, Boston, MA. 1872. B/w litho of Horace Greeley in hat. "Sung by Cool Burgess." 6pp. Pages 2 and 6: Blank.

HG-8 Horace Greeley's March. m. George Wiegand. Published by Horace Waters, Publisher Sheet Music, Music Books, &c., Manufacturer & Dealer in Pianos, Melodians & Organs, No. 481 Broadway, New York, NY. 1872. B/w beige tinted litho by Major & Knapp of Horace Greeley in Hat. "Our Next President." "As played by Grafulla's Seventh Regt. Band." 8pp. Page 2: Blank. Page 3: Non-pictorial title page. Page 8: Advertising.

HG-9 Horace And No Relations (Greeley and Brown Campaign Song). m. W.O. Fiske. Published by Oliver Ditson & Company, No. 277 Washington Street, Boston, MA. 1872. B/w sketch of Horace Greeley reading song title. 6pp. Pages 2 and 6: Blank.

HG-10(A) Greeley's Grand March. m. H. Krummacher. Published by Oliver Ditson & Company, No. 277 Washington Street, Boston, MA. B/w litho of Horace Greeley. "Horace Greeley Campaign Music." 6pp. Pages 2 and 6: Blank.

(B) **Horace And No Relations.** m. Fiske.

(C) **Greeley's Galop.** m. Bela.

HG-11 I Want To Be President. w. Phil E. Buster, Esq. m. Air: *I Want to be an Angel.* In: *The World's Peace Jubilee and Back Bay Bawl*, page 11. Published by New England News Company, No. 41 Court Street, Boston, MA. 1872. 36pp. Y/bl caricature of Horace Greeley holding sheet music to the song *I Want To Be President*, Ulysses S. Grant, dog labeled — "Democracy." "I want to be President and in the White House stand, The nation on my shoulders her fortunes in my hand."

HG-12 Horace Greeley's Grand March. m.a. Charles Glover. Published by William A. Pond, No. 547 Broadway, New York, NY. 1872. B/w beige tinted litho by Robert Teller of Horace Greeley, facsimile signature. "Arranged for the Piano Forte." "Respectfully Inscribed to the Hon. Horace Greeley." 6pp. Pages 2 and 6: Blank.

HG-13(A) Horace Greeley's Waltz. m. Pierre Latour. Published by Lee & Walker, No. 922 Chestnut Street, Philadelphia, PA. 1872. B/w litho by Thomas Sinclair & Son of Horace Greeley, geometric designs. 6pp. Page 2: Blank.

(B) **Horace Greeley's Schottisch.**

(C) **Horace Greeley Grand March.**

HG-14 A Nation Mourns Her Honored Son. w. George Cooper. m. Henry Tucker. Published by William A. Pond, No. 547 Broadway, New York, NY. 1872. B/w litho of Horace Greeley, facsimile signature, black border. "In Memoriam." 6pp. Pages 2 and 6: Blank.

HG-15 Horace Greeley Grand March. m. E. Mack. Published by the S. Brainard's Sons, Cleveland, OH. 1872. B/w litho by W.J. Morgan & Company of Horace Greeley — "Yours" [facsimile signature]. 6pp. Page 6: Blank.

HG-16 Horace Greeley Is On The Track (A Campaign Song). w. William Adolphus Clark. m. F.A. Strauss. Published by Oliver Ditson & Company, No. 277 Washington Street, Boston, MA. Copyright 1872 by William

Adolphus Clark. B/w litho of Horace Greeley. 6pp. Pages 2 and 6: Blank.

HG-17   Horace Greeley's March. m. George Wiegand. Published by Horace Waters, No. 481 Broadway, NY. 1872. Non-pictorial geometric design border. "As played by Grafulla's 7th Regt. Band." 6pp. Page 6: Advertising. [Same as HG-8 without illustrated cover].

HG-18   Hot Corn, Hot Corn (or Katy's Song). w.m. E.H.L. Kurtz (Author of *Crystal Palace Song*). Published by E.H.L. Kurtz, No. 473 Grand Street, New York, NY. 1853. B/w litho of corn stalks. "To Horace Greeley, Esq. and Pastor Pease." "Sold at Griffith's Quadrille Band Office, No. 499, 733, & 843 Broadway, and at the Principal Music and Book Stores in the City." 6pp. Pages 2 and 6: Blank.

HG-19   Hank Monk Schottische. m. J.P. Meder. Published by John G. Fox, Carson City, NV. [ca. 1877]. B/w litho by Thomas Hunter of James Henry "Hank" Monk, mountain, "Pioneer Stage Co. Coach" stage coach with passengers including Horace Greeley—"Keep your seat Horace, I'll get you there on time." "Dedicated to Miss Lillie Swift."

HG-20   After The Election Is Over (A Greeley Campaign Song). m. Air: *After the Opera*. In: *Singer's Journal, No. 81, Vol. II*, page 613. Published by Henry De Marsan, American Music Company, No. 60 Chatham Street, New York, NY. 1892. 36pp.

HG-21   Greeley Campaign Songster. Published by Halpin & McClure, Chicago, IL. 1872. [4" × 5 11/16"]. Pl/bk litho of Horace Greeley, geometric design border. "Chicago: Western News Company, Wholesale Agents." 72pp. [M-187].

HG-22   The Old White Hat (Campaign Song & Chorus). w.m. W. Milton Clarke. Published by S. Brainard's Sons, Cleveland, OH. 1872. B/w litho of a hat. 6pp. Pages 2 and 6: Blank.

HG-23   The Farmer Of "Chappaqua" Songster. Published by Robert M. DeWitt, New York, NY. 1872. Be/bk engraving of Horace Greeley, axe. "Containing a Great Number of the Best Campaign Songs that the Unanimous and Enthusiastic Nomination of the Hon. Horace Greeley, for President, has Produced." "Almost all the Songs in this book can be sung to the music of very popular tunes, and many have Rousing Choruses. Embellished with a splendid steel engraving of the Hon. Horace Greeley, executed by the Celebrated Artist T.C. Buttree, from a fine picture taken in 1854." [M-184].

HG-24   The Greeley & Brown Songster. Published by Fisher & Denison, New York, NY. 1872. Be/bk litho of Horace Greeley. 68pp. "Containing a Large Collection of the Popular Songs as Sung by Leading Glee Clubs." [M-186].

HG-25   The Horace Greeley Campaign Songster. Published by George Munro, New York, NY. 1872. 64pp. [M-188].

HG-26   The Greeley And Brown Campaign Hand-Book For 1972. Sold by The New York News Company, Agents for the Publishers, New York, NY. 1872. Non-pictorial. "Comprising Varied Contents of Interesting Political Facts — Figures — Miscellany — Greeley Anecdotes — Campaign Songs, &c., Together with Valuable Information Relating to The Harmonious Union of the Liberal Republican and Democratic Parties on a United National Platform; On May 1 and July 9, 1872." 64pp [M-185].

HG-27   Horace Greeley's Campaign Songster. Published by Ornum & Co., New York, NY. 1872. Non-pictorial. "A Choice Collection of Campaign Songs, the Most Sparkling of their kind that have ever been Published since the Days of Old Hickory Jackson." [M-189].

HG-28   Hon. Horace Greeley Funeral March. m. J.W. Turner. Published by White, Smith & Company, Boston, MA. [ca. 1885?].

HG-29 The Dying Words Of Little Katy (or, Will He Come). w. Solon Robinson. m. Horace Waters. a. Thomas Baker. Published by Horace Waters, No. 333 Broadway, New York, NY. 1853. B/w litho by S.W. Chandler & Co. of Horace Greeley and little girl. "In the Story of Hot Corn, A New Song." "Published in the *New York Tribune*, Aug. 1853." 8pp. Pages 2 and 8: Blank. Page 3: "Sung by Buckley's Serenaders."

HG-30 Horace Greeley Quickstep. m. C.C. de Nordendorf. Published by C.C. de Nordendorf Musical Exchange, Petersburg, VA. 1872. B/w litho by F. Geese of C.C. de Nordendorf. "To Miss Nannie May."

HG-31 Campaing [sic] Song For 1872. w. A. La Mar. Published by Tripp & Linton, No. 118 Main Street, Louisville, KY. 1872. B/w floral and geometric design frame. Pages 2 and 6: Advertisements for Tripp & Linton music.

HG-32 Hurrah For Horace Greeley! (Campaign Song and Chorus). w. T.C. Harbaugh. m. A.C. Miller Published by J.S. White & Co., Marshall, MI. 1872. "Respectfully Dedicated to Capt. Deville Hubbard, President of the Greeley & Brown Club, Marshall, Mich." Printed verse. Pages 2 and 6: Blank.

See also WHH-91; HC-18; HC-35; HC-93; WS-22; AL-89; USG-200; WM-31.

HUBERT H. HUMPHREY

HHH-1 Hubie Humphrey-We Love You! w.m. Herman (Doc) Silvers (ASCAP). Published by Herman (Doc) Silvers, No. 60 East 14th Street, New York, NY. 10003. 1968. Bl/w photo of Hubert H. Humphrey. 4pp.

HHH-2 Hubert H. Humphrey March. w.m. Mason Mallory. a. Lou Halmy. [8 1/2" × 11"]. 1960. N/c photo of Hubert H. Humphrey. "Eleanor Roosevelt said "In him I see a spark of greatness! Today, Those who know him intimately understand that here is a man fully qualified to lead this nation to new heights in self development and to once again regain the supremacy of respect throughout the World. He will be a great President." 4pp.

HHH-3 Yesterday We Loved You. w.m. Herman (Doc) Silvers. Published by Herman Silvers, No. 60 East 14th Street, New York, NY. 10003. 1968. [8 1/2" × 11"]. Bl/w photo of Hubert H. Humphrey. "A Tribute to Hubert H. Humphrey." 4pp. Page 4: Treble clef.

HHH-4 Sing And Win With Hubert Humphrey. [Song Sheet]. w. Joe Glazer. m. Popular Airs. [1960]. [8 1/2" × 13"]. B/w photo of Hubert H. Humphrey in front of a poster of Franklin D. Roosevelt. "These songs (except for one) were made up by Joe Glazer for the next President of the United States, Hubert Humphrey. *The President for You and Me* was written by Wisconsin's wonderful Lt. Governor and strong Humphrey supporter, Phileo Nash." 2pp.

HHH-4

HHH-5 Hubert H. Humphrey March. w.m. Mason Mallory. a. Lou Halmy. 1960. [6 7/16" × 8 1/2"]. Bl/w photo of Hubert H. Humphrey. 4pp.

HHH-6 Whatever Became Of Hubert? w.m. Tom Lehrer. In: *Tom Lehrer's Second Song Book*, page 34. Published by Crown Publishers, Inc., New York, NY. 1968. [7 1/4" × 10 1/4"]. Gn/w/bk drawing of lyre, musical instruments. 72pp.

See also LBJ-6; JEC-1.

HENRY KRAJEWSKI

HK-1 Farmer Krajewski Campaign Theme Song. m. "The Tune of *Old Grey Bonnet*." [1952]. [8 1/2" × 11"]. Y/bk drawing of pig, stars arranged to spell "Vote For Krajewski." 2pp.

HORATIO SEYMOUR

HS-1(A) The White Man's Banner (Seymour and Blair's Campaign Song). w. M.F. Bigney. m. Thomas von La Hache (Of 10th Ward Club, N.O.). Published by Louis Grunewald, No. 129 Canal Street, New Orleans, LA. 1868. B/w lithos of Horatio Seymour and Francis P. Blair, wreaths. 6pp. Page 6: Blank.
  (B) The White Man's Banner (March).

HS-2(A) Seymour & Blair's March To The White House. m. Dressler. Published by J.L. Peters, No. 198 Broadway, New York, NY. 1868. B/w litho by F. Ratellier of Horatio Seymour and Francis P. Blair, eagle with ribbon inscribed "E Pluribus Unum," flags, shield. "To the Friends of Seymour and Blair."
  (B) Matched! (Song and Chorus). w.m. Mrs. E.H. Pendleton. Page 2: Blank. Page 3: "For President—Horatio Seymour." "Adapted to Mrs. E.H. Pendleton's Beautiful Melody *E Pluribus Unum*."
  (C) Blair's Galop. m. William Dressler.
  (D) Seymour's March. m. Henri Allard.

HS-1

HS-3 Seymour And Blair's Union Campaign March. m. G.W. Lovejoy. Published by Lyon & Healy, Clark and Washington Streets, Chicago, IL. 1868. B/w litho by Chicago Litho Company of Horatio Seymour and Francis Blair, eagle, shield, crossed flags, clasped hands, flowers. 10pp. Pages 2 and 10: Blank. Page 3: Title—**Seymour and Blair's March.**

HS-4(A) Seymour, Blair And Victory! (Song and Chorus). w.m. H. Werner. Published by Balmer & Weber, No. 206 North Fifth Street, St. Louis, MO. 1868. B/w litho by A. McLean of Horatio Seymour, Francis Blair, eagle, flags, wreaths. "To the United Democracy."
  (B) Seymour Schottisch. m. J. Batiste.
  (C) Blair's Favorite Polka. m. F. Mack. 6pp. Pages 2 and 6: Blank.
  (D) Tammany Grand March. m. F. Mack.

HS-5 Seymour & Blair Song Book And Democratic Register. c. By

HORATIO SEYMOUR (HS)

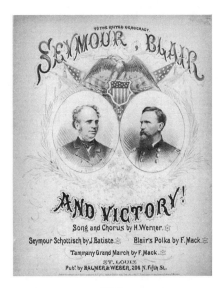

HS-4

an Ex-Staff Officer. Published by V-1: Dick & Fitzgerald, New York, NY] [V-2: Castello & Co., Brooklyn, NY]. 1868. Y/bk litho of Horatio Seymour and Francis P. Blair. 72pp. Inside title — Democratic Campaign Melodist. [M-172].

HS-6 For Seymour, Blair And Liberty (Song and Chorus). w. Joseph C. Hart. m. William Seibert. Published by Lyon & Healy, Clark and Washington Streets, Chicago, IL. 1868. B/w litho by Chicago Litho Company of Horatio Seymour and Francis Blair, flags, eagle, shield, flowers, clasped hands. 6pp.

HS-7 Gov. Seymour's Grand Waltz. m. Mrs. B.F. Cooper. Published by T.S. Berry & Company, No. 297 Broadway, New York, NY. [ca. 1863]. Non-pictorial geometric designs. "Composed and Respectfully Dedicated to Him by Mrs. B.F. Cooper." 6pp. Page 6: Blank.

HS-8 Seymour Campaign Songster. Published by Pattee & Hubbard, Democratic State Committee Rooms, World Building, No. 37 Park Row, New York, NY. 1868. [4" × 5 1/4"]. Gn/bk litho of Horatio Seymour and Francis Blair. "In the spirit of George Washington and the Patriots of the Revolution, Let us take the steps to re-inaugurate our Government, to start it once again on its course to greatness and prosperity — Horatio Seymour." 38pp. [M-173].

HS-9 Governor Seymour's Grand March. m. S. Ehrlich. Published by B.C. Hoff, Syracuse, NY. 1863. Non-pictorial geometric designs. "Respectfully dedicated to His Honor, Horatio Seymour, Governor of the State of New York." 6pp. Pages 2 and 6: Blank. Page 3: Title: **Governor Seymour's Grand Victory March.**

HS-10 Hip! Hip! Hurrah For Seymour And Blair. w. L.J. Blakely. m. Clareton. Published by W.R. Smith, No. 135 North Eighth Street, Philadelphia, PA. 1868. Non-pictorial. "To the Democracy of the U.S." 6pp. Pages 2 and 6: Blank.

HS-11 Matched! (For President Horatio Seymour) (A Campaign Song). m. "Adapted to the Beautiful Melody *E Pluribus Unum* by Mrs. E.H. Pendleton." Published by J.L. Peters, New York, NY. 1868. Non-pictorial. 8pp. Pages 1, 7 and 8: Blank.

HS-12 Not For Grant. m. "Air: *Not for Joseph.*" Published by Johnson, The Great Song Publisher, No. 7 North Tenth Street, Philadelphia, PA. [1868]. [4 3/4" × 8"]. Non-pictorial. 2pp. Page 2: Blank.

HS-13 Seymour's March. m. Henri Allard. Published by J.L. Peters, No. 198 Broadway, New York, NY. 1868. B/w geometric designs and border. "To Horatio Seymour." 8pp. Pages 2, 7 and 8: Advertising.

HS-14 Seymour And Blair Democratic Songster. Published by J. Wrigley, Publisher, No. 61 Chatham Street, New York, NY. 1868. [4 3/8" × 6 7/16"]. Pk/bk litho of Horatio Seymour and Francis P. Blair, leaves. "Wrigley's One Cent Song Books." Table of "Contents" printed on cover. 8pp. Page 8: Blank.

HS-15 Seymour Campaign

(HST) HARRY S TRUMAN

HS-14

Songster. Published and Distributed Free by Paul, the Woolen Remnant Man, Who sells the Best 14oz. All Wool Dollar Cassimeres to be Found, Providence, RI. 1868. [V-1: Y/bk] [V-2: Pl/bk] litho of Horatio Seymour. 8pp. [V-1 and V-2 have different contents]. [M-174, 175].

HS-16 Conny O'Ryan's Campaign Songster. Published by W.S. Haven, Pittsburgh, PA. Copyright 1868 by T. Tramor King. Y/bk litho of an eagle, banner inscribed "Seymour & Blair, The Constitution and Victory." 52pp. "A Choice Collection of Original, General and Local Songs for the Campaign." "For sale by J.A. Chambers, News Dealer, W.S. Haven, Print., Pittsburgh, PA. [M-170].

HS-17 Original Democratic Campaign Songs. w.m. John Kerrigan. e. E.L.G. Published by Craft & Axford, Printers, New York, NY. 1868. Non-pictorial. "Respectfully dedicated to the Democratic Party." "Copyright Secured." 12pp. [M-171].

HS-18 Brick Pomeroy's New Democratic Campaign Song Book. Published in New York, NY. 1868. [M-169].

HS-19 Nasby's Lament Over The New York Nominations. w.m. W.W. Bridewell. Published by [V-1: S. Brainard's Sons, Cleveland, OH] [V-2: Rott and Cady, Chicago, IL]. 1868. Non-pictorial geometric designs. 6pp.
See also USG-205.

HARRY S TRUMAN

HST-1 I'm Just Wild About Harry. w.m. Noble Sissle and Eubie Blake. Published by M. Witmark and Sons, New York, NY. 1921. [Edition 1948]. B/w photo of Harry S Truman — "Victory Smile." O/bk/w cover. "Hit of *Shuffle Along*." "Souvenir Edition." 6pp. Page 2: Special Truman "Victory Version" lyrics. Page 6: Five B/w photos of Truman campaign scenes.

HST-2 Let's Get Behind The President. w.m. George Jessel, Sam Carlton and Dan Dougherty. Published by Leeds Music Corporation, RKO Building, Radio City, New York, NY. 1949. Bl/w photo of Harry S Truman. 4pp.

HST-3 At The Inauguration Ball. w.m. Harry M. Liebermann. Published by Bluebird Music Company, No. 2394 Grand Concourse, New York, NY. 1948. B/w photo of Harry S Truman. R/w/b Barbelle drawing of Capitol building, shield, stars. "Respectfully Dedicated to Our Beloved President Harry S. Truman by the Writer." 6pp. Page 6: Blank.

HST-4 The Democrats Are Winning The Day (Democratic Campaign Song). w.m. Zora Layman and Ethel Bridges. Published by Bob Stephens, Inc., Music Publisher, No. 2263 East Las Tunas Drive, Temple City, CA. 1948. R/w/b drawing of eagle and stripes. 4pp. Page 4: "100 Years of Progressive Liberalism."

HST-5 Harry S. Truman March.

HST-1

w. Andrea Litkei. m. Ervin Litkei. Published by Loena Music Publishing Company, No. 239 West 18th Street, New York, NY. 10011. 1965. Bl/w photo by Fabian Bachrach of Harry Truman. R/w shield background. 4pp. Page 4: Drawing of small flower-like design.

HST-6 Let's Get Behind The President. w.m. George Jessel, Sam Carlton and Dan Dougherty. Published by Leeds Music Corporation, RKO Building, New York, NY. 1949. [8" × 11"]. Bl/w photo of Harry S. Truman. Narrative reprint from *Time* Magazine — "A Democrat Again." "On Thanksgiving Day, The President put in five hours of work before going home at 2 o'clock to eat turkey with his family. Next day, between talks with officials about new housing and labor legislation, he sandwiched in a few minutes with movie Producer George Jessel, who came to present a copy of a song he had written (with two tunesmiths) for Harry Truman. It will be dedicated to the President at a Democratic Rally in Los Angeles next week. Reported Jessel: 'In Hollywood, everyone has decided he's a Democrat again.'" "Artist Copy." 4pp.

HST-7 United Nations Anthem. w.m. Louis Herscher. Published by Clarke Irvine, 4657 Hollywood Blvd., Hollywood, CA. 1945. Bl/w drawings by Henry Goode of Harry Truman, Franklin Roosevelt, Winston Churchill, Charles De Gaulle, Chiang Kai-Shek. 4pp. Page 4: "Souvenir edition, U.N. Conference, San Francisco, CA."

HST-8 Harry Truman. w.m. Robert Lamm. Published by Lamminations Music/Big Elk Music, No. 8600 Melrose Avenue, Los Angeles, CA. 90069. 1975. B/w photo of Harry S Truman. "*CHICAGO*." "Recorded by *CHICAGO* on Columbia Records." 6pp.

HST-9 Truman Flew To Mexico. w.m. Gloria Parker, William Forest Crouch and Barney Young. Published by Winfield Music, Inc., No. 67 West 44th Street, New York, NY. 1947. Bl/w Barbelle drawing of mountains, airplane –named "The Sacred Cow." Bl/w photo of Red River Dave — "Featured by Red River Dave." 4pp. Page 6: Words to ten patriotic songs and other "Red River Dave Favorites."

HST-10 Song Of The Whistle Stop. Published for The Democratic Congressional Wives Forum. [1948]. [8 1/2" × 11"]. 4pp. Page 4: Drawings of and airplane, automobile, train with sign — "Elect Democ."

HST-11 The R-O-A March (Soldiers of the O-R-C). w.m. Lieutenant Colonel Carl J. Koenig, O.R.C.. Published by Carl J. Koenig, No. 1235 Burbank Street, Fair Lawn, NJ. 1949. Bl/w stars and stripes design by Manning. Bl/w photo of "Harry S Truman." "The Official Song of The Reserve Officer's Association." "Dedicated by the Author to the most distinguished and prominent member of the Reserve Officer Association and of the Organized Reserves, Mr. Harry S Truman, President of the United States, Commander-In-Chief of the Armed Forces, and Colonel, Field Artillery Reserve." 6pp. Page 6: Narrative on history of the song.

HST-12 Independence Waltz. w.m. Arthur Whittemore and Jack Lowe. Published by Chappell and Company, Inc., RKO Building, Rockefeller Center, New York, NY. 1950. Bl/bk/w floral designs. 6pp. Pages 2 and 6: Advertising. Page 3: "Dedicated to President Harry S Truman."

HST-13 President Harry S. Truman March. w.m. Clarence Gaskill. Published by Mills Music, Inc., No. 1619 Broadway, New York 19, NY. 1945. R/w/b cover. Handwritten — "Artist Copy Only." "With Vocal Chorus." 4pp. Page 4: Blank.

HST-14 Truman Campaign Song. w. Thomas J. Lillis (Jersey City, NJ). m. "Air: *The Band Played On.*" [1948]. [2 1/2" × 4 1/4"]. Y/bk non-pictorial. 2pp. Page 2: Blank.

HST-15 Our President. w.m. Maurice J. McNellis. Published by Maurice J. McNellis, No. 5304 Tracy Avenue, Kansas City, MO. 1945. B/w photo of Harry S Truman. R/w/bk drawing by L.D. Perkins of Truman's home. 4pp. Page 4: Blank.

HST-16 Harry S Truman March. w. Andrea Fodor Litkei. m. Ervin Litkei. In: *A Tribute To The U.S.A.*, page 23. Published by Loena Music Publishing Company, No. 239 West 18th Street, New York, NY. 10011. Copyright 1985 and 1986. N/c drawing by Edward Moran of the Statue of Liberty celebration in 1886 — "The Statue of Liberty, standing as an eternal symbol of the friendship of the people of France, was presented to the United States in 1886 by its creator, Frederick Bartholdi." Quotes by "Emma Lazarus (1883)," and "President Grover Cleveland (1886)."

HST-17 See The U.S. Thru With Truman. w. Holger C. Lanther. m. Cleda Gray. Published by Radio and Song Scout, "Publisher of the Finest in Song and Poetry," Mobile, AL. 1948. [V-1: Br/w] [V-2: B/w] drawing of Harry S. Truman, map of the United States. "Truman-Truman the Battle Cry of all good Democrats." 4pp. Page 4: Narrative on Truman songwriting contest results.

HST-18 Harry S. Truman March. w. Andrea Litkei. m. Ervin Litkei. In: *The Bicentennial March and Presidential Marches of America*, page 22. Published by Loena Music Publishing Company, New York, NY. 1976. R/w/b drawings of George Washington, Thomas Jefferson, Abraham Lincoln, eagle and flags. "American Revolution Bicentennial, 1776-1976." "Officially Recognized Commorative." 40pp.

HST-19 My Dear Harry Won't You Tarry? w.m. Louis E. Alewel. Published by Louis E. Alewel, St. Louis, MO. 1948. R/w/b flag border. 4pp. Pages 2 and 4: Blank.

HST-20 Alice In Blunderland Or Through The Rooking Class [Program and Songbook]. Published by The Legislative Correspondent's Association of New York State, Albany, NY. 1949. [8 5/8" × 11"]. N/c drawings of Harry Truman, Thomas Dewey, Franklin Roosevelt, Henry Wallace, Harold Stassen, Alben Barkley, Robert Taft, Earl Warren, other politicians. "A Scintillating Satire of Sadistic Surprises and Surprising Successes Featuring a Dramatic Disclosure of How Tom Did Not Go Down to D.C. in Slips; Together with a Give-Away-Nothing Radio Broadcast and Epic Melodrama of the Indian Wars Entitled 'When the Cat's Away the Mice Will Play.'" "Done With Music and Mirrors — Particularly Mirrors in Three Acts at Hotel Ten Eyck, Albany, March 12, 1949." [Songs about Harry Truman, Henry Wallace and Thomas Dewey].

HST-21 We Are Americans Too. w.m. Andy Razaf, Eubie Blake and Charles L. Cooke. Published by Handy Brothers Music Company, Inc., No. 1650 Broadway, New York, NY. 1941. [Edition ca. 1951]. Br/w drawing of Harry Truman on Capitol steps. Br/w photo of Nat King Cole — "As sung by Nat King Cole."

"Featured in Powell Lindsay's *This is America* presented by Panorama of Progress." 8pp. Pages 2 and 8: Adv.

HST-22 Whistle Stop (HST) (Madrigal). w. Richard Engquist. m. Jack Gottlieb. Published by Theophilous Music, Inc. Sole Agent: Boosey & Hawkes, Inc. 1991. [6 7/8" × 10 1/2"]. Non-pictorial. "Presidential Suite, Seven Pieces for Mixed Chorus (SATB) a cappella. 20pp. Page 2: "Presidential Suite is a celebration of America's priceless heritage of liberty. Inspired by the wisdom and whimsy of some of our most colorful presidents, it juxtaposes the eloquence of John F. Kennedy and Franklin Delano Roosevelt, with the journalistic pith of Theodore Roosevelt, Harry S Truman's blunt common sense, Abraham Lincoln's homespun wit and Thomas Jefferson's irony, plus a legendary quip from the taciturn Calvin Coolidge. This patriotic work combines idealism with light-heartedness, inspiration with a dash of salt..." Page 3: "For Sue Klein."

HST-23 Friendly Democratic Relations (1948 Campaign Songs). w. Charles R.H. Johnson. m. Popular tunes. Published by Chariest R.H. Johnson, No. 2603 Jerome Avenue, Dayton 7, OH. 1948. [5 3/8" × 8 1/4"]. R/bk non-pictorial cover. 16pp. Pages 2, 14, 15 and 16: Blank. Page 3: "Friendly Democratic Relations Creed."

HST-24 Harry S Truman March. e. Andrea and Ervin Litkei. In: *The President's March and Other Songs of the Lone Star State*, page 8. Published by Loena Music Publishing Company, No. 239 West 18th Street, New York, NY. 10011. [ca. 1964]. R/w/bl/bk cover, Presidential seal. "Featuring President Lyndon Baines Johnson March and other songs of the Lone Star State." "Pacific Popular Music Books." 36pp. Page 2: Photos of Lyndon Johnson and A. Litkei. Page 35: Photo of Inaugural parade. Page 36: Photo of Lyndon Johnson. Drawings of all presidents.

HST-25 Onward We Must Go (Victory Song). w.m. Mary A. Varallo. [1948]. [8 1/2" 11"]. Non-pictorial. "Dedicated to the Women Voters of Our Country — Presidential Campaign of 1948." "Introduced by Valeria Haggerty." 2pp. Page 2: Blank.

HST-26 The Underdog. w.m. Leslie Leland Dukeshire. Copyright February 16, 1950. B/w photos of Leslie Leland Dukeshire, boy with dog. "Dedicated to President Harry S. Truman, The Greatest Underdog in American Political History. The man who couldn't win but did." 4pp. Page 4: Blank.

HST-27 Help Truman Win (Vote For Him). w.m. Helen Sagstetter. Published by Published by Radio and Song Scout, "Publisher of the Finest in Song and Poetry, Mobile, AL." 1948.

HST-28 A Toast To Harry Truman. w.m. Mrs. Lee Perkins. Published by Published by Radio and Song Scout, "Publisher of the Finest in Song and Poetry, Mobile, AL." 1948.

See also TJ-49; AL-346; TR-343; CC-53; TED-34; FDR-268; FDR-367; DDE-9; DDE-13; JFK-61; LBJ-1.

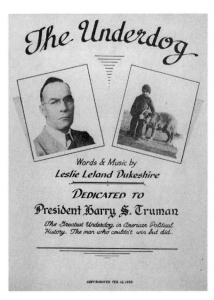

HST-26

John Adams

JA-1 The Favorite New Federal Song. w. Joseph Hopkinson, Esqr. m. "Adapted to the *President's March*." [Published by B. Carr, Philadelphia, PA. 1798]. B/w attached engraving of John Adams. "Behold the Chief who now Commands." "For the Voice, Piano Forte, Guittar [sic] and Clarinett [sic]." "Sung by Mr. Fox." 4pp. Pages 1 and 4: Blank. [S/U, page 172].

JA-2 Adams & Liberty. Printed & sold by G. Gilfert at his Musical Magazine, No. 177 Broadway, New York, NY. [1798-1801]. B/w attached engraving of John Adams. 2pp. [S/U, page 4].

JA-3 Adams March. Printed & Sold at P.A. von Hagen & Cos., Imported Piano Forte Ware House, 3, Cornhill, Boston, MA. [1799-1800]. Non-pictorial. "And to be had at G. Gilfert, New York." "For the pianoforte, German flute or violin." 2pp. [S/U, page 5].

JA-4 Adams & Washington (A New Patriotic Song). m. The music composed by P.A. von Hagen, Jr. Printed & Sold by P.A. von Hagen Jr. & Co. at their Musical Magazine, No. 62 Newbury Street, where also may be had the new patriotic songs of *Washington & Independence*, *Hail, Patriots All*, *Our Country Is Our Ship*, *The Ladies' Patriotic Song*. Also a great variety of single songs, lessons, and an elegant assortment of pianofortes, flutes, haut-boys, clarinets [sic], bassoons, trumpets, French horns, violins and other musical articles of superior quality." [1798-1799]. Non-pictorial. 2pp. [S/U, page 5].

JA-5 Adams & Liberty. w. Thomas Paine, A.M. Printed & Sold by P.A. von Hagen Jr. & Cos., No. 3 Cornhill, Boston, MA. [1799-1800]. Non-pictorial. "Third Edition Corrected." "For the Piano Forte, German Flute or Violin." "Boston, Printed & Sold by P.A. von Hagen & Co. at their Piano Forte Ware House, No. 3 Cornhill; where also may be had, the new Published Songs just Received from London, viz, *Honest Colin*, *How Tedious Alas are the Hours*; *Lilies and Roses*; *Come Buy My Wooden Ware*; *The Little Singing Girl*; *Monseer Nong Tong Paw*; *Megen Oh! Oh! Megen Ee*, *Young Jemmy is a Pleasing Youth*; *As Forth I Rang'd the Banks of Tweed*; *The Favorite Song in Stringer & Answer*. Likewise, *Adams & Washington & To Arms Columbia*, written by Thomas Paine, A.M. The music composed by P.A. von Hagen, Jur. Also a great variety of single songs & lessons, & an elegant assortment of the verry [sic] best kind of Piano Fortes, Flutes, Hautboys, Clarinetts [sic], Bassoons, Trumpets, French Horns, Violins, Bass, Viols & Guitars, also the best Violin & Bass Viol strings just received from Naples & other musical articles at superior quality." 4pp. [S/U, page 3].

JA-6 Adams & Liberty (The Boston Patriotic Song). w. Thomas Paine, A.M. [1798-1799]. 2pp. Page 2: "Engraved by W. Prisson." [S/U, page 4].

JA-7 Canone Funerale (An American National Dirge). m. A.P. Heinrich.

JA-1

In: *The Sylviad [a], No. 3*, page 15. Published by A.P. Heinrich, Boston, MA. 1823. Non-pictorial. "The above is a fragment, from a Manuscript which the Author has not been enabled entitled *The Statesman's Resignation to Death* set to elegant music occasioned by reading the philosophical correspondence between Thomas Jefferson and John Adams, Esqrs., in June 1822, Respectfully dedicated to these gentlemen with an address, verses and the motto Dignum Laude Virtum Musa Vertat mori. *Horace St. Helena*, a universal dirge is contemplated in the series of the *Sylviad*, likewise *The Duke of Reichstadt's March*." [W-10131].

JA-8 Funeral Honors By The Town Of Salem (To Commemorate the Deaths of John Adams and Thomas Jefferson). Printed by W. and S.R. Ives. 1826. Non-pictorial. Page 1: **Voluntary For The Organ** (Hymn for the Occasion). w. Joseph G. Waters. m. Air: *Burford*. **Dirge** (For the Occasion). w. Mr. Jocelyn. m. Air: *Pleyel's Hymn*. "At the North Church in Salem…on Thur., Aug. 10, 1826." 2pp.

JA-9 Adams & Liberty. Published by Russell & Patee, No. 108 Tremont Street, Boston, MA. 1862. Non-pictorial geometric border. "Warblings of Little Birds, For Young Performers." 4pp. Page 2: "Dedicated to Quartr. Sergt. J.M. Rice, 2nd Batt. M.V.M." "As introduced…by Gilmore's Band at Gilmore's Promenade Concerts."

JA-10 Adams & Liberty. w. Thomas Paine. Published by [V-1: G. Graupner] [V-2: C. Bradlee, Washington Street], Boston, MA. [ca. 1827]. Non-pictorial. "Written for and sung at the Fourth Anniversary of the Massachusetts Charitable Fire Society 1789 by Robert T. Paine together with the Ode written by Mrs. Ware and sung on the Fiftieth Anniversary of American Independence." 4pp. Page 3: **Ode**. w. Mrs. Ware.

JA-11 Adams & Liberty. w. Thomas Paine, A.M. Printed & sold at J. Hewitt's Musical Repository, No. 131 William Street, New York, NY. [1798-1799]. Non-pictorial. 4pp. Pages 1 and 4: Blank. Page 2: Music. Page 3: Verses and publisher's address. [S/U, page 4].

JA-12 Adams & Liberty (The Boston Patriotic Song). w. Thomas Paine, A.M. [Published by Thomas & Andrews, Boston, MA]. [1798]. Non-pictorial. 4pp. page 2: Music. Page 3: Verses. [S/U, page 2]. [First Edition].

JA-13 Adams & Liberty. a. Adolph Baumbach. Published by Henry Tolman & Company, No. 291 Washington Street, Boston, MA. 1862. B/w litho of ribbon inscribed "Adams and Liberty." "Popular Melody Played by the Military Bands." "Transcribed for the Piano." 8pp. Pages 2 and 8: Blank.

JA-14 Adams & Liberty. w. Thomas Paine, A.M. Sold by Linley & Moore, No. 19 Marlborough Street, Boston, MA. [1798-1799]. Non-pictorial. "Second Edition Corrected." "Where may be had *Green Mountain Farmer*, A New Patriotic Song." 4pp. Page 3: Engraving of music, flowers and musical instrument. [S/U, p/ 3].

JA-15 Adams & Liberty. w. Thomas Paine. In: *The American Musical Miscellany, A Collection of the Newest and Most Appoved [sic] Songs, Set to Music*, page 211. Printed by Andrew Wright for Daniel Wright & Company, Northampton, MA. [1798]. [S/U, page 16].

JA-16 Mrs. Adams' Hornpipe. In: *Riley's Flute Melodies, A Collection of Songs, Airs, Waltzes, Cotillions, Dances, Marches, &c., &c., Arranged for the German Flute, Violin and Patent Flageolet, Second Volume*, page 79. Engraved, Printed & Publised [sic] by the Editor, No. 23 Chatham Street, New York, NY. [1815-1816]. 100pp. [W-7490].

JA-17 The Green Mountain Farmer (A New Patriotic Song). w. Thomas Paine, A.M. m. Shield. Printed & Sold by J. Hewitt's Musical Repository, No. 121 William Street, New York,

NY. [1798]. Non-pictorial. "Sold also by B. Carr, Philadelphia & J. Carr, Baltimore." "Copy Right Secured." "Price 25 Cents." 4pp. Pages 1 and 4: Blank. [S/U, page 169].

JA-18 Dear Abby (A Musical For Young Voices). w. Grace Hawthorne. m. John F. Wilson. Published by Somerset Press, Carol Stream, IL. 60188. 1985. [6 5/8" × 10 1/4"]. N/c drawings of "Abagail Adams," "John Adams," "First White House," "Signing of the Declaration of Independence." 24pp.

JA-19 Adams Forever (Or Pride of October) (A New Song). w. Jurentus. In: *Columbian Centinel* [sic] *or Massachusetts Federalist*, page 4. Published by Benjamin Russell, New Branch Bank, Boston, MA. Whole Number 1623, No. 11 of Vol. XXXII, Wednesday, October 9, 1799. [No musical notation].

JA-20 Adams & Liberty. m. "Tune—*Anacreon in Heaven.*" [ca. 1800-1810]. [5 1/2" × 12 7/8"]. B/w geometric design at top. 2pp. Page 2: Blank.

JA-21 Adams And Liberty. w.m. R.T. [sic] Paine, Esq. (In 1798). In: *Boston Musical Miscellany (Volume II)*, page 195. Published by J.T. Buckingham, No. 5 Marlbough Street, Boston, MA. 1815. [4" × 6 1/2"]. Be/bk hardback cover with litho of musical instruments, geometric design border. 228pp. [W-954].

JA-22 Adams & Liberty. In: *A Collection of New & Favorite Songs*, page 16 "Printed & Sold by B. Carr, Philadelphia; I. Hewitt, New York & J. Carr, Baltimore. Where may be had all the newest musical productions." 220pp. [S/U, page 71].

JA-23 Adams And Liberty (The Boston Patriotic Song). w. Thomas Paine, A.M. Printed & Sold by W. Howe, organ builder & importer of all kinds of musical instruments, No. 320 Pearl Street, New York, NY. [1798]. "Price 25 cents." 4pp. [S/U, page 3].

JA-24 Adams And Liberty. m. "Tune, *Anacreon In Heaven.*" In: *A Collection of Songs Selected from the works of Mr. Dibdin. To which is added, the newest and most favorite American patriotic songs*, page 315. Published by J. Bioren for H. & P. Rice, and sold by J. Rice, Baltimore, MD. 1799. 328pp. [S/U, page 74].

JA-25 Hail Columbia. a. Wm. Dressler. Published by Wm. Hall & Sons, No. 239 Broadway, New York, NY. [ca. 1848]. B/w attached engraving of John Adams over original circle of stars. "[National] Songs of America Arranged with Accompaniments for the Piano Forte." 6pp. List of other titles in series. [This piece was altered from the original (See GW-299) by someone attaching a cut engraving of John Adams and affixing it to the music directly over the word "National" and the circle of stars found on the original. Added in contemporary handwriting "50th Anniversary of Hail Columbia, composed and first sung in 1798 during the John Adams Administration." Date added to bottom "1848." At Page 3, another cut engraving was added at the top of the music "John Adams." Under this in handwriting, the dates "1797-1801" was added, as was the note "Tune is *President's March* composed by Phile, 1798 Joseph Hopkinson. Portrait on cover is engraving (1925) after Stuart painting of John Adams."

JA-26 Come Genius Of Our Happy Land (A Favorite Patriotic Song). w.m. H.C. Published by Carr's Musical Repository, Baltimore, MD. [1798]. Non-pictorial. 2pp. Page 2: Blank.

JA-27 The Federal Constitution & Liberty For Ever (A New Patriotic Song). w. Mr. Milns. a. J. Hewitt. Printed & Sold at J. Hewitt's Musical Repository, No.131 William Street, New York, NY. [1796-1800]. B/w engraving of eagle, shield, flags. "Sung with great applause by Mr. Williamson." "Sold also by B. Carr, Philadelphia & J. Carr, Baltimore." "Price 25 Cents." 2pp.

JA-28 Pres. Adams' March. In: *Marches Of The Presidents, 1789-1909,*

Authentic Marches & Campaign Songs, page 7. A. Carl Miller. Published by Chappell & Co., Inc., No. 609 Fifth Avenue, New York, NY. "By arrangement with Chilmark Press, Inc." 1968. [9" × 12"]. R/w/b litho of eagle, flag. "An Illustrated Piano Folio For All Ages." 72pp.

JA-29 The Federal Constitution & Liberty For Ever. In: Bound volume of music. [1793-1801]. Handwritten manuscript copy. Copied on the reverse of *O Dearly I Love Somebody*, published by Carr's Musical Repository, Philadelphia. [Lyrics are pro-Adams].

See also GW-242; GW-399; GW-527; GW-534; AL-308; WHT-23; WW-19; FDR-158; FDR-190; DDE-9; JFK-27; LBJ-1; MISC-34; MISC-46; MISC-117; MISC-165; MISC-167; MISC-169; MISC-181.

JAG-1

JAMES A. GARFIELD

JAG-1 Garfield And Arthur Quickstep. m. Harrison Millard. Published by Spear & Dehnhoff, No. 717 Broadway, New York, NY. Copyright 1880 by Harrison Millard. B/w tinted litho by R. Teller of James A. Garfield and Chester A. Arthur, oak wreaths. 8pp. Pages 2, 7 and 8: Blank.

JAG-2 Brave Garfield Is Our Man. Published by John Church & Company, No. 66 West 4th Street, Cincinnati, OH. 1880. B/w litho of James A. Garfield, black line frame. 4pp. Page 4: Blank.

JAG-3 Republican Nomination (Grand March). m. C.W. Wernig. Published by William A. Pond & Company, No. 25 Union Square, Between 15th & 16th Streets, New York, NY. 1880. B/w lithos by H.A. Thomas of James A. Garfield and Chester A. Arthur, geometric designs. "Dedicated to Generals Jas. A. Garfield of Ohio and Chester A. Arthur of New York." 8pp. Pages 2, 7 and 8: Blank.

JAG-4 From The White House To The Sea (Grand March). m. A.H. Rosewig. Published by Lee & Walker, No. 1113 Chestnut Street, Philadelphia, PA. 1881. B/w litho of James A. Garfield. "Respectfully Dedicated to Our President, Gen. James A. Garfield." 6pp. Page 2: Blank. Page 6: Advertising.

JAG-5 While We Are Marching For Garfield. w.m. Thomas D. Story. Copyright 1880 by Thomas D. Story. B/w litho of James A. Garfield, vignettes of Union soldier with flag, U.S. Capitol, voters at polling place. Border of state names. "Campaign Song 1880." 6pp. Pages 2 and 6: Blank.

JAG-6 God Save Our President (The Wish of Every Loyal Heart) (National Hymn). w. Geo. R. Jackson. m. E.H. Bailey. Published by White, Smith & Company, No. 516 Washington Street, Boston, MA. 1881. B/w litho of James A. Garfield, oak and laurel branches. "To Gen. James A. Garfield, President of the United States." 6pp. Page 2: Blank. Page 3: Inside subtitle: "The Voice of the People." Page 6: Advertising for other White, Smith & Company published music.

JAG-7 God Reigns, Our Coun-

try's Safe (Song). w.m. Henry Tucker (Author of *When This Cruel War Is Over, Sweet Genevieve*, &c, &c). Published by William A. Pond & Company, No. 25 Union Square, Broadway between 15th & 16th Streets, New York, NY. 1881. B/w litho of James A. Garfield. 6pp. Page 3: "On receiving news of the death by assassination of President Lincoln (Apr. 15, 1865), Mr. Garfield, then a Congressman, said 'God reigns and the government at Washington still lives.'"

JAG-8 Gen. Garfield's Grand March. m. E. Mack. Published by Oliver Ditson & Company, No. 451 Washington Street, Boston, MA. 1880. B/w litho by J.H. Bufford's Sons of James A. Garfield. 6pp. Pages 2 and 6: Blank.

JAG-9 Pres't. Jas. A. Garfield Grand Inauguration March. m. Richard Stahl, Op. 16. Published by George Willig & Company, Publishers, Baltimore, MD. [V-1: 1881] [V-2: ca. 197-]. [V-1: 8 1/2" × 11"]. [V-1: B/w] [V-2: Be/br] litho of James A. Garfield, facsimile signature. 6pp. Page 2: Title — President James A. Garfield's Grand Inauguration March. Page 6: Blank.

JAG-2

JAG-10 Gen. Jas. A. Garfield's March. m. Adolph Pferdner, Op. 58. Published by John Church & Company, No. 66 West 4th Street, Cincinnati, OH. 1880. B/w litho of James A. Garfield. 6pp. Pages 2 and 6: Blank.

JAG-11 President Garfield's Funeral March. m. L. Hewitt. Published by National Music Company, Chicago, IL. [1881]. B/w litho of James A. Garfield, black border. 6pp. Pages 2 and 6: Blank.

JAG-12 President Garfield's Funeral March. m. Edwin Christie. Published by Oliver Ditson & Company, Boston, MA. 1881. B/w litho by J.H. Bufford's Sons of James A. Garfield, black border. 6pp. Pages 2 and 6: Blank.

JAG-13 Garfield's Funeral March. m. Phil P. Keil. Published by Phil P. Keil, No. 81 Fifth Street, McKeesport, PA. 1881. B/w litho of James A. Garfield, black border. "Composed and Dedicated to the Memory of Gen. James A. Garfield, 20th President of the United States." 6pp. Page 2: Blank. Page 6: Advertising for other Phil P. Keil music.

JAG-14 President Garfield's Inauguration March. m. John Philip Sousa (Bandmaster of the Marine Band, Washington, DC). Published by William A. Pond & Company, No. 25 Union Square, Broadway, bet. 15th & 16th Sts., New York, NY. 1881. B/w non-pictorial geometric border. "Respectfully Dedicated to Gen. Jas. A. Garfield, of Ohio." "As performed during the Inauguration Ceremonies at The Capitol, Washington, D.C., March 4, 1881, and at the Inauguration Ball." 8pp. Page 2: Blank. Page 6: Advertising for other William A. Pond & Company published music.

JAG-15 God Save Our President From Every Harm! (A National Anthem). w.m. Harrison Millard (Author of *The Flag of the Free, Vive L'America*, &c). Published by Spear and Dehnhoff, No. 717 Broadway, New York Hotel, New York, NY. 1881. B/w non-pictorial geometric designs. "1881." "With Accompanied

Recitative and Hymn Chorus." 8pp. Page 2: Blank. Page 3: "New Version." Page 6: Advertising for other Harrison Millard music.

JAG-16 The Verdict March (Fiat Justitia). m. Eugene L. Blake. Published by George D. Newhall, No. 50 West 4th Street, Cincinnati, OH. 1882. B/w lithos of the "Jury that convicted Guiteau," "George B. Corkhill," "J.K. Porter" and "W.S. Cox." 6pp. Page 2: Blank. Page 6: Advertising.

JAG-17 Mother In The Doorway Waiting. w. David Graham Adee. m. James R. Murray. Published by John Church & Company, No. 66 West 4th Street, Cincinnati, OH. 1881. B/w litho of Garfield's mother in a rocking, boy with telegram. "To President Garfield's Mother." 6pp. Pages 2 and 6: Blank. Page 3: Narrative: "President Garfield's aged mother is stopping with her niece at Hiram. She receives frequent messages from Washington, and spends much of her time at the front door of the house anxiously waiting for the messenger who brings her the dispatches. She is much agitated by fears of the worst, yet she clings tenaciously to hope."

JAG-18 Gen. Jas. A. Garfield's Campaign Grand March. w. A.H. Rosewig. Published by Lee & Walker, No. 1113 Chestnut Street, Philadelphia, PA. 1880. B/w litho of James A. Garfield. 8pp. Pages 2 and 7: Blank. Page 8: Advertising for other Lee & Walker published music.

JAG-19 A Nation's Tears In Sorrow Fall (Song and Chorus). w.m. Thomas P. Westendorf. Copyright 1881 by W.F. Shaw. B/w litho of James A. Garfield, black border. "To the Memory of our Beloved President." 6pp. Page 2: Blank. Page 6: Advertising.

JAG-20 Beneath The Dear Old Flag Again (Song and Chorus). w.m. Thomas P. Westendorf. Copyright 1880 by W.F. Shaw. B/w litho of James A. Garfield. "To Garfield and Arthur." Narrative — "The *Cincinnati Gazette* correspondent on the field, W.S. Furay, under date of September 21st, 1863, after describing the perilous conditions of the Union Army, speaks of Garfield's ride and arrival on the battlefield, as follows: Just before the storm broke, the brave and high souled Garfield was perceived making his way to the headquarters of General Thomas. He had come to be present at the formal contest, and in order to do so had ridden all the way from Chattanooga, passing through a fiery ordeal on the road, his horse was shot under him and his orderly was killed by his side. Still he had come through, he scarce knew how, and here he was to inspire fresh courage into the hearts of the brave soldiers, who were holding the enemy at bay, to bring them word of greeting from General Rosecrans, and to inform them that the latter was reorganizing the scattered troops and as fast as possible would hurry them forward to their relief." 6pp. Page 2: Blank. Page 6: Advertising for publications.

JAG-21 Garfield's Funeral March. a. Henry Werner. Published by Balmer & Weber, Publishers, St. Louis, MO. 1881. Non-pictorial geometric designs, black border. "God Reigns and the Government at Washington still lives — Garfield's words on the death of Lincoln." "Arranged and Dedicated to the Memory of the Martyr President, James A. Garfield, 20th President of the United States." 6pp. Pages 2 and 6: Blank. Page 3: Litho of small urn at the top of the music — "Mournfully Inscribed to the Memory of James A. Garfield, Twentieth President of the United States."

JAG-22 Garfield And Arthur (Rally Song). w. Mrs. D. McFalls. m. W.F. Studds. Published by C.H. Ditson & Company, No. 843 Broadway, New York, NY. Copyright 1880 by Oliver Ditson & Co. B/w non-pictorial geometric designs. 6pp. Pages 2 and 6: Blank.

JAG-23(A) President Garfield's

Funeral March. m. Charles D. Blake. Published by White, Smith & Company, Publisher of Sheet Music and Music Books, Nos. 188 and 190 State Street, Chicago, IL. 1881. B/w litho by Charles H. Crosley of James Garfield, leaves, black border. "To the Mother of our Lamented President." 8pp. Page 8: Advertising.

(B) President Garfield's Funeral March. m. D.L. White.

JAG-24 President Garfield's Funeral March. m. Horace R. Basler. Published by Horace R. Basler, No. 3712 Butler Street, Pittsburgh, PA. 1881. B/w litho of James A. Garfield, black border. "To the Memory of Our Martyred President, James A. Garfield." 6pp. Page 2: Blank. Page 6: Advertising.

JAG-25 At Rest. w. B. Herbert. m. Claribel. Published by Munroe's Publishing House, No. 16 Vandewater Street, New York, NY. 1881. Non-pictorial black border. "A Song on the Death of Our Late President, James A. Garfield." "Respectfully Dedicated to Mrs. James A. Garfield." 4pp.

JAG-26 President Garfield's Funeral March. m. Henry Kleber. Published by Wm. A. Pond & Company, No. 25 Union Square, New York, NY. 1881. B/w litho by Major & Knapp of James A. Garfield, geometric designs, black border. "God Reigns, and the Government at Washington still lives." 6pp. Pages 2 and 6: Blank.

JAG-27 Garfield & Arthur Campaign Songster. Published by New York Publishing Company, No. 32 Beekman Street, New York, NY. [1880]. [4" × 6 3/8"]. Hand colored litho of James A. Garfield. 68pp. Pages 2 and 67: Blank. Page 4: Contents. Page 5: Biographies. Pages 60 and 61: Constitution. Pages 64-66: Advertising. Page 68: Hand colored litho of Chester Arthur.

JAG-28 President Garfield's Funeral March. m. L. Hewitt. [1881]. B/w litho by Moss Engraving Company of James A. Garfield, black border. "Delano Edition." 6pp. Pages 2 and 6: Blank.

JAG-29 President Garfield's Funeral March. m. A.H. Rosewig. Published by William H. Boner & Company, No. 1102 Chestnut Street, Philadelphia, PA. Copyright 1881 by T.A. Bacher. B/w litho of James Garfield, black border. 6pp. Page 2: Blank. Page 3: "Introducing the Beautiful Melody *Free as a Bird*." Page 6: Advertising.

JAG-30 President Garfield's Funeral March. m. E. Lagrange. Published by [V-1: W.H. Boner & Company, Agt's., No. 1102 Chestnut Street, Philadelphia, PA] [V-2: Dyer and Howard, No. 148 and 150 East 3rd Street, St. Paul, MN]. Copyright 1881 by W.F. Shaw. B/w litho of James A. Garfield, black border. 6pp. Page 2: Blank. Page 6: Advertising.

JAG-31 President Garfield Died Last Night (Break The Sad News To His Mother) (Pathetic Song and Chorus). w.m. R. Griswold. m. A.H. Rosewig. Published by Lee & Walker, No. 1113 Chestnut Street, Philadelphia, PA. 1881. B/w litho of James Garfield, black border. 6pp. page 2: Blank. Page 6: Advertising.

JAG-32 Funeral March (In Memory of James A. Garfield). m. Theo. H. Klein. Published by W.A. Evans & Bro., Publishers, No. 50 Bromfield Street, Boston, MA. 1881. B/w litho of James Garfield, black border. 4pp.

JAG-33 Our Next President, James A. Garfield. w. Hiram E. Peterson. m. "Air from *Norma*." Published for the Author at Hitchcock's Music Store, No. 32 Park Row, opposite Post Office, New York, NY. 1880. B/w litho of James A. Garfield. 4pp. Page 4: Words to two versions of *The Battle Cry of Freedom* "as sung by the Boys in Blue" and "as sung in Dixie's Land."

JAG-34 The Martyr (or Life and Death of Our Beloved President, James A. Garfield) (Grand Fantasia for the Piano Forte). m. Ludwig W. Harmsen (Author of *The Minstrel's Curse*). Published by the Author [Ludwig W. Harmsen], Minneapolis, MN. 1882. B/w litho by J.R. Rice of James A. Garfield, geometric designs. "To The American People." List of movements by title — "Representing A Noble Life, A Happy Home, The Fiend's Deed, The World's Consternation, The Suffering, A Nation's Prayer (For Piano, Solo or Quartette with words by Rev. Dr. J.H. Tuttle), The End of a Great Man, The Funeral, A Life Eternal." 24pp. Pages 2, 23 and 24: Blank.

JAG-35 Gen. Garfield's Funeral March. m. Carl Renbort. Published by John S. Horner, Everything in the Music Line, No. 430 East 5th Street, Dayton, OH. [1881]. Copyright 1880 by W.F. Shaw. B/w litho of James A. Garfield, black border, black stripe printed over top of **Grand March** in title [see JAG-36]. "Respectfully Dedicated to the Republican candidate." 6pp. Page 2: Title — **Gen. Garfield's Grand March**. Page 6: Advertising.

JAG-36 Gen. Garfield's Grand March. m. Carl Renbort. Copyright 1880 by W.F. Shaw. B/w litho of James A. Garfield. "Respectfully Dedicated to the Republican Candidate." 6pp. Page 6: Advertising for song book.

JAG-37 His Name Is General G. (Republican Campaign Song and Chorus). w. Adele M. Carragues. m. H.B. Roney. Published by White, Smith & Company, No. 516 Washington Street, Boston, MA. 1880. Non-pictorial geometric designs and border. "Dedicated to the Republicans of the United States." Advertising for campaign song *Garfield and Arthur are the Men* by C.A. White. 6pp.

JAG-38 President Garfield's Funeral March. m. E. Gilmore. Published by R.A. Saalfield, No. 12 Bible House, Astor Place (Opposite Cooper Union), New York, NY. 1881. B/w litho of James A. Garfield, black border. "To the American Nation!" 6pp. Pages 2 and 6: Blank.

JAG-39 Dirge For Our Dead Chieftain. w. Mary Bynon Reese. m. Karl Reden. Published by Roseman Gardner, City Music House, Steubenville, OH. 1881. Non-pictorial black border. "To the Memory of Our Martyred President James Abram Garfield." 4pp. Page 4: Blank.

JAG-40 The Veteran's Vote. w. Irenaeus D. Foulon. m. Charles Kunkle. Published by Kunkle Brothers, No. 311 South 5th Street, St. Louis, MO. 1880. [9" × 12 1/4"]. B/w non-pictorial ribbon design border. "The Boys in Blue Series of Republican Campaign Songs for 1880." "Respectfully Dedicated to the Veterans of the War of the Rebellion." 4pp. Page 2 Title: **Die Stimme Des Veteranen**. Text in English and German. "Translated by M. Niedner." Page 4: [V-1: B/w lithos of James A. Garfield and Winfield Scott Hancock — "Under Which Commander?" List of attributes of each: "Garfield" — "Protection to American Labor," "Education Free to All," "Free Ballot and Honest Count," "Peace and Prosperity." "Hancock" — "Burned School Houses," "Andersonville and Libby Prison Keepers," "Ku-Klux Klan," "Diabolism."] [V-2: Advertising].

JAG-41 My Country 'Tis Of Thee Sweet Land Of Liberty Of Thee I Sing (Republican Campaign Song Book 1880). c. L. Foyette Sykes. Published by The Republican Central Campaign Club of New York, Headquarters, Coleman House, No. 1169 Broadway, New York, NY. 1880. [5 13/16" × 9 1/8"]. Gn/bk non-pictorial geometric designs. "For President Gen'l. James A. Garfield of Ohio, For Vice-President Gen'l. Chester A. Arthur of New York." 52pp. Page 2: Table of Contents. Page 3: Title — **Garfield And Arthur Republican Campaign Song Book 1880**. [M-211, 212].

JAG-42 Garfield Is The Man! (Campaign Song). m. C.C. Haskins. Published by John Church & Co., Cincinnati, OH. 1880. Br/w non-pictorial. 6pp. Page 2: "Solo or Quartett." Page 6: Blank.

JAG-43 President James A. Garfield's Funeral. m. J.W. Jost. Published by J.W. Jost & Son, No. 545 North Eighth Street, Philadelphia, PA. 1881. B/w litho of James A. Garfield, geometric designs. "In Memoriam." 6pp. Pages 2 and 6: Blank.

JAG-44 We Mourn Our Country's Loss (National Funeral March). m. Aug. Buechel. Published by P.A. Wundermann, No. 1013 3d Avenue, New York, NY. 1860. [1881 edition]. B/w litho by R. Teller of James A. Garfield, Abraham Lincoln, angels, eagle, flag, Miss Columbia at coffin." 6pp. Page 2: Blank. Page 3: "Copies for Brass Bands can be had by addressing the Publisher." Page 6: Advertising for other Wundermann published music.

JAG-45 Dey's All Put On De Blue (Song and Chorus). w.m. Thomas P. Westendorf. Copyright 1880 by W.F. Shaw. Non-pictorial geometric designs. "To Our Candidate Gen. James A. Garfield." 6pp. Page 6: Blank.

JAG-46(A) Garfield's Triumphal March. m. H. Werner. Published by Balmer & Weber, Publishers, St. Louis, MO. 1880. B/w litho of James Garfield, geographic design border. Bl/bk/w border. German title — **Heil dir Garfield!** "Music for the Million." "English and German Words." 6pp. Page 2: Blank. Page 6: Advertising.

(B) **Hail Brave Garfield** (Song & Chorus). w. John Studdert, Jr. m. Harry A. Saxton.

(C) **Galop.**

JAG-47 Garfield And Arthur Campaign Song Book. Published by Union Book Company, Philadelphia, PA. 1880. [5 7/8" × 8 13/16"]. Y/bk litho of James Garfield and Chester A. Arthur, flags, eagle, geometric designs. 28pp. Page 2: Contents. Page 26: Biographies. Page 27: Electoral vote for 1876.

JAG-48(A) Hail, Brave Garfield! (Song and Chorus). w. John Studdert, Jr. m. Harry A. Saxton. Published by Balmer & Weber, St. Louis, MO. 1880. B/w litho of James A. Garfield. Bl/w titles and geometric designs. "Music for the Million." 6pp. Pages 2 and 6: Blank.

(B) **Garfield's March.**

(C) **Galop.**

JAG-49 The Solid North (Campaign Quartette). w.m. James G. Clark. Published by The Root & Sons Music Company, Chicago, IL. 1880. Non-pictorial geometric designs. "Dedicated to Mr. Frank Lumbard." 6pp. Page 4: "Note: The last line in the Chorus, *In Freedom's Light, &c.*, can introduce the candidates name as follows — 'With Grant to lead us in the Fight,' 'With Washburn to lead us in the Fight,' 'With Garfield to lead us in the Fight.'" Page 6: Blank.

JAG-50 Garfield And Arthur Campaign Songster. Published by John Church & Company, Cincinnati, OH. 1880. [3 13/16" × 8 5/8"]. Bl/w non-pictorial geometric designs. "Including Biographical Sketches & Constitution for Campaign Clubs." 52pp. Inside title: **Garfield And Arthur Campaign Carols**. Pages 2, 51 and 52: Advertising. [M-207].

JAG-51 Slowly & Sadly (Memorial March & Memorial Song) (Song and Quartette). w.m. Miss Arabella Root (Madame De L'Armitage) (Author of the following songs: *Oh, Be Patriotic, My Loving Mother, Far Away By And By, Oh, Dinna Ye Forget, Waiting For Her Sailor Lad, Little Daisy's request, Even Me, Bonnie Sweet Bonnie, True Jessie, When Strolling Thro The Clover*). Published by Chicago Music Company, No. 152 State Street, Chicago, IL. Copyright 1881 by Miss Arabella Root. B/w lithos of "Gen. James A. Garfield;" "The Mother — Mrs. Eliza Garfield;" "The Home — Lawnfield, Mentor, O;" "The Wife — Mrs. Lucretia Garfield;" "The Composer — Miss Arabella Root." "Memorial tribute with deep sympathy, most respectfully dedicated to the bereaved family & friends of the late President Garfield." 6pp. Page 2:

"Biographical Sketch of the Late General Garfield." Narrative. Page 6: Song—**In Memoriam**.

JAG-52(A) Gen. Jas. A. Garfield's Campaign Grand March. m. A.H. Rosewig. Published by Lee & Walker, No. 1113 Chestnut Street, Philadelphia, PA. 1880. B/w litho by Crosscup and West of James A. Garfield. "Chicago's Choice." "Respectfully Dedicated to the National Republican Executive Committee." 8pp. Page 2: Blank.

(B) **With Garfield We'll Conquer Again** (Campaign Song). w.m. George Morley.

JAG-53 Hymn On The Death Of President Garfield. m. Air: *America* or *Olivet*. [1881]. [4 7/8" × 7 9/16"]. Non-pictorial black border. 2pp. Page 2: Blank.

JAG-54 President Garfield's Funeral March. m. Fred T. Baker. Published by Lee & Walker, No. 1113 Chestnut Street, Philadelphia, PA. B/w litho of James A. Garfield, black border. 6pp. Page 2: Blank. Page 6: Advertising for other Lee & Walker music.

JAG-55 His Name Is General G. w. Horace Greeley Knapp. m. G.D. Wilson. Published by Oliver Ditson & Company, No. 451 Washington Street, Boston, MA. 1880. Litho of a spear, clouds, ribbon—"Rally Song 1880," geometric designs. 6pp.

JAG-56 Garfield's At The Front (Song and Chorus). w.m. Charles E. Pratt. Published C.H. Ditson & Company, No. 843 Broadway, New York, NY. Copyright 1880 by Oliver Ditson & Company. Non-pictorial geometric lines. 6pp. Pages 2 and 6: Blank.

JAG-57 With Garfield We'll Conquer Again (Republican Campaign Song). w.m. George Morley. Published by Lee & Walker, No. 1113 Chestnut Street, Philadelphia, PA. 1880. Non-pictorial. "The dark horse wins." 6pp. Pages 2 and 6: Blank.

JAG-58 Garfield's At The Front! (Campaign Song and Chorus). w.m. J. Maurice Hubbard. Published by S. Brainard's Sons, Cleveland, OH. 1880. Non-pictorial geometric design border. "Gen. Garfield proceeded to the Front (Gen. Rosecrans' official report of the battle of Chickamauga)." "Written for, and Inscribed to the Illinois Campaign Glee Club." 6pp. page 6: Blank.

JAG-59 Garfield & Arthur Are The Men (Quartet for Male Voices). w. C.A. White. m. "Melodies from the Operas." 1880. B/w litho of eagle, shield, stars.

JAG-60 Garfield Now Will Lead The Nation (Song and Chorus). w.m. Thomas P. Westendorf. Copyright 1880 by W.F. Shaw. Non-pictorial geometric design border. "Thomas P. Westendorf's Songs." List of other titles in series. 6pp. Pages 2 and 6: Blank.

JAG-61(A) Gen. Garfield's March To The White House. m. C. Hauschild, Op. 70. Published by Oliver Ditson & Company, No. 451 Washington Street, Boston, MA. 1880. B/w litho by J.H. Bufford's Sons of James A. Garfield. 6pp. Pages 2 and 6: Blank.

(B) **Gen. Garfield's Grand March**. m. E. Mack.

JAG-62 Garfield And Arthur Campaign Song Book. Published by The Republican Congressional Committee, Washington, DC. 1880. [5 13/16" × 9 1/16"]. [V-1: Bl/bk] [V-2: Pk/bk] [V-3: Be/bk] [V-4: Gy/bk] litho of James A. Garfield and Chester A. Arthur, palm tree, plants and small animals, geometric designs. 28pp. Page 2: Index. Page 28: "The Electoral Vote for 1880." [M-210].

JAG-63 Garfield's Funeral March. m. [P.S.] Gilmore. Published for R.H. Macy & Company, 14th Street, Sixth Avenue and 13th Street, New York, NY. [ca. 1885]. Non-pictorial geometric design border. "Popular Marches." List of other titles in series. Advertising for R.H. Macy & Company.

JAG-64 God Save The President (Solo and Chorus). w.m. Septimus

(JAG) JAMES A. GARFIELD

Winner. Published by Sep. Winner & Son, No. 1007 Spring Garden Street, Philadelphia, PA. 1881. Non-pictorial black border. "A Nation's Prayer." "Most Respectfully Inscribed to the Mother of our President." 6pp. Page 2: Blank. Page 6: Advertising.

JAG-65 Columbia's Call. w.m. Irenaeus D. Foulon. Harmonized by Charles Kunkel. Published by Kunkel Brothers, No. 311 South Fifth Avenue, St. Louis, MO. 1880. [9" × 12 1/4"]. Non-pictorial line border. "The Boys in Blue Series of Republican Campaign Songs for 1880." "To M.A. Rosenblatt, Esq., the Staunch Republican; A True Friend to his Friends; A True Foe to his Foes, This Song is Respectfully Dedicated by the Author." 4pp. Page 2: L'Appel de la Patrie. "French and English Words and melody by I.D. Foulon. German Translations by N-." Page 4: Advertising.

JAG-66 Fall In! (Song and Chorus). w. Sam Booth. m. D.B. Moody. Published by M. Gray, No. 117 Post Street, San Francisco, CA. 1880. Litho of flags, eagle. "Garfield and Arthur Campaign." "To the Boys in Blue — In my opinion, the best interests of the whole country, North and South, demand the success of this ticket headed by Garfield & Arthur — Ulysses S. Grant." "As sung by the Amphion Quartett." "Bugle or Cornet Obligato ad lib." 4pp.

JAG-67 The Heart Of The Nation Is Sad Today. w. Howard N. Fuller. m. Chopin. a. Arthur Thorne. Published by C.E. Wendell, Albany, NY. 1881. B/w non-pictorial geometric designs. "God Reigns, and the Government at Washington still lives." "Music adapted from Chopin's *March Funebre*." 6pp. Pages 2 and 6: Blank.

JAG-68 Garfield And Arthur Campaign Songs As Sung By The Central Committee. Published by Donnelley, Gasette & Loyd, Chicago, IL. 1880. 16pp. [M-206].

JAG-69 Mr. Garfield. w.m. Ramblin' Jack Elliot. Published by Southwind Music, Inc., Sole Selling Agent: Hill and Range Songs, Inc., No. 1619 Broadway, New York 19, NY. 1965. R/w non-pictorial geometric designs. 4pp. Page 4: Blank.

JAG-70 Guiteau's March To Hades (A Descriptive Piece for the Times). m. H.W. Stratton. Published by Oliver Ditson & Co., Boston, MA. 1881. B/w litho of the Devil and Guiteau.

JAG-71 O [Eye] C [Rebus Title] (Garfield Song, 1880). w. Dr. Daniel Breed. m. "Tune: *Breed's Old Hat* or *John Anderson*." Published by Dr. Daniel Breed, Patent Attorney and Chemist, Corner 8th and "F" Streets, NW., (Opp. Patent Office), Washington, DC. [3 1/8" × 5 1/2"]. B/w litho of an eye in the title. "Breed's Old Hat No. 2." 2pp.

JAG-72 President Garfield's Funeral March. m. Ad. Meyer. Published by Wm. A. Pond & Company, No. 25 Union Square, New York, NY. 1881. B/w litho by Major & Knapp of James A. Garfield, black border. 6pp. Pages 2 and 6: Blank.

JAG-73 Funeral March. m. August Mignon. Published by Edward Schuberth & Company, No. 23 Union Square, New York, NY. 1881. B/w litho by Charles Hart of James A. Garfield, flags, wreath, flowers, black border. "In Memoriam." "In Commemoration of Our Beloved and Illustrious Leader." 8pp. Pages 2, 7 and 8: Blank.

JAG-74(A) His Name Is General G (Republican Campaign Song and Chorus). w. Adele M. Garragues. m. H.B. Roney. "Dedicated to the Republicans of the United States." In: *Folio, A Journal of Music, Drama, Art and Literature*, page 341. Published by White, Smith & Company, No. 516 Washington Street, Boston, MA. 1880.

(B) Gen. James A. Garfield's Grand March. m. A.S. Warren, Op. 66. Page 392. Copyright 1880 by White, Smith & Co.

(C) **God Save Our President** (The Voice of the People). w. G.R. Jackson. m. E.H. Bailey. Page 309. August, 1881.

(D) **Garfield** (A Nation's Tribute of Sorrow for Its Deceased President) (Sacred Quartette for Mixed Voices). m. Frank N. Scott. Page 403. Copyright 1881 by White, Smith & Co.

(E) **President Garfield's Funeral March**. m. D.L. White. Page 440. Copyright 1881 by White, Smith & Co. "N.R.— One by Chas. D. Blake, more difficult, Price 50."

JAG-75 Garfield's Grand March. m. Rosabel. Published by S. Brainard's Sons, Chicago, IL. [V-1: 1884] [V-2: ca. 1897]. [V-1: N/c litho by Orcuft of battle scene] [V-2: Bk/bl/w reprint of V-1 with drawing redone by Harrell]. List of titles in series. "Popular Marches, Battle Pieces, &c. for Piano or Organ."

JAG-76 General Garfield's Grand March. m. E. Mack. Published by Oliver Ditson & Company, Boston, MA. 1880. B/w litho of eagle with ribbon inscribed "E Pluribus Unum," geometric design border. 6pp. Page 2: Blank. Page 6: Advertising.

JAG-77 Funeral March. m. H.T. Knake. Published by Knake & Company, Pittsburgh, PA. 1881. B/w litho of James A. Garfield, flat boat, White House, floral wreath, black border. "In Memory of James A. Garfield, Twentieth President of the United States." 6pp. Page 2: Title — **President Garfield's Funeral March**. Page 6: Advertising.

JAG-78 I'm Wearin' Awa' (Song). m. Lady Nairn. m. Ethel Maud Farnsworth. Published by Richard A. Saalfield, No. 839 Broadway (Opp. Wallacks), New York, NY. 1881. Non-pictorial. "Sung by Emma Abbott. A little girl's tribute to the memory of our late beloved President." "Mama, I want to comfort poor Mrs. Garfield." 6pp. Pages 2 and 6: Blank.

JAG-79 James A. Garfield's Grand March. m. A.E. Warren, Op. 66 (Author of *Love's Return Waltzes, Lass On The Shore March*, &c). Published by White, Smith & Company, No. 516 Washington Street, Boston, MA. 1880. B/w non-pictorial geometric border. Facsimile letter from Garfield to Publisher — "Mentor, Ohio, June 23d, 1880. White, Smith & Co., Boston, Mass., Your favor of the 21st at hand. Thanks for it and the music. Very Truly Yours, J.A. Garfield." 6pp. Page 6: Advertising.

JAG-80 A Funeral Anthem (To Commemorate the Death of James A. Garfield Late President of the United States). m. [Dr.] S. Parkman Tuckerman. Published by Oliver Ditson & Company, No. 451 Washington Street, Boston, MA. 1881. Non-pictorial black border. "Offered as a tribute of respect to the memory and virtues of a great and good man." "The words of this Anthem formed the commencement of the funeral Services at Long Branch, Sept. 20, 1881." "His body is buried in peace, but his name liveth for evermore — Ecclus. XLIV. 14th." "Blessed are the dead which die in the Lord." 6pp. Includes 2 inserts: "Funeral Anthem — *I Heard a Voice From Heaven*" by S. Parkman Tuckerman and *A Christmas Carol*.

JAG-81 The Nation In Tears (A Dirge in Memory of the Nation's Chief, James A. Garfield). w. R.C. m. Konrad Treuer. Published by Oliver Ditson & Company, Boston, MA. 1881. Non-pictorial black border. "In Memoriam." 4pp. Page 4: Blank.

JAG-82(A) Uncle Sam's Summons (Song and Chorus). w.m. A.O. Hand. Published by John Church & Company, No. 66 West 4th Street, Cincinnati, OH. 1880. B/w litho of James A. Garfield, star border. "Republican Campaign Music." "Also ready *The Garfield and Arthur Campaign Songster*, price 10 cts." List of other songs in the series. 6pp. Pages 2 and 6: Blank.

(B) **Three Cheers And A Tiger**

For Garfield. w.m. W.B. Richardson.
    (C) **Garfield Rallying Song**. w.m. C.C. Haskins.
    (D) **Garfield's The Man**. w.m. P.P. Basso.
    (E) **Now Three Times Three**. w.m. A. Hutchington.
    (F) **They Saved Our Flag**. w.m. T.P. Westendorf.
    (G) **Brave Garfield Is Our Man**. w.m. D.C.A.
    (H) **Hurrah For Garfield!** w.m. More Anon.

    JAG-83 We'll Ne'er Forget Our Garfield's Name (Song and Chorus). w.m. J. Calvin Bushey. Published by W.I. Brownell & Company, Akron, OH. 1880. B/w litho of James A. Garfield.

    JAG-84 God Bless The Little Woman (Beautiful Song and Chorus). w. Howard N. Fuller. m. Charlie Baker. Published by F.W. Helmick, No. 180 Elm Street, Cincinnati, OH. Copyright 1881 by Charlie Baker. Non-pictorial geometric designs. 6pp. page 3: Note — "Immediately after President Garfield was shot, he dictated a telegram to his wife informing her of the sad occurrence, remarking, in the most affectionate manner to those beside him, 'God bless the little woman,' &c." Page 6: Advertising.

    JAG-85 Gen'l. Jas. A. Garfield's Grand March. m. Rosabel. Published by S. Brainard's Sons, Cleveland, OH. 1880. B/w litho by W.J. Morgan & Company of James A. Garfield, shield, flowers. 6pp. Pages 2 and 6: Blank.

    JAG-86 The Campaign Songster (Containing a Choice Selection of Songs Suited to all Political Parties). Published by J.P. Coats, Flint, MI. 1880. [3 3/4" × 5"]. Gn/bk non-pictorial. "Compliments of B.F. Cotharin, Wholesale and Retail Furniture, Flint, Michigan." Advertising. 46pp. [Songs for James Garfield and Winfield S. Hancock].

    JAG-87 A Mighty Nation Weeps (A National Hymn of Mourning). w. George Russell Jackson. m. E.H. Bailey. Published by White, Smith & Company, Publisher of Sheet Music and Music Books, Nos. 188-190 State Street, Chicago, IL. 1881. B/w litho by Chas. H. Crosby of James A. Garfield, oak and laurel branches, geometric designs, black border. "To Gen. James A. Garfield, God save our President (The wish of every loyal heart)." "God Reigns and the Government Still Lives." 6pp. Page 2: Blank.

    JAG-88 That Dear Little Church (Song and Chorus). w. John Keynton. m. H.P. Danks. Published by S.T. Gordon & Son, No. 13 East 14th Street, New York, NY. 1881. Litho of church, White House. "During the pealing of the bells..., while the President lay almost at the doors of death, he...whispered 'that dear little church! It has been...bearing a burden for weeks, but when I get up it shall not have cause to regret it.'" "Dedicated to the Rev. F.D. Power, Washington, D.C."

    JAG-89 We Forget Not The Day (Quartette). w. George M. Vickers. m. Adam Geibel. "To the memory of General James A. Garfield." In: *The Welcome Musical and Home Journal*, page 9. Pub-

JAG-85

lished by W.H. Boner & Company, Philadelphia, PA. April 1, 1884. Sheet music copyrighted by W.F. Shaw, 1883."

JAG-90 The Ballad Of Guiteau. w.m. Stephen Sondheim. In: *Assassins*, page 42. Published by Rilting Music, Inc. Sole Agent: WB Music Corp. Copyright 1990 and 1992 by Rilting. Bl/w star cover design by Neal Pozner.

JAG-91 Funeral March. m. Pierre Latour. Published by S. Brainard's Sons, Cleveland, OH. 1881. B/w litho by W.J. Morgan & Company of James A. Garfield. "In Memory of Gen. James A. Garfield." 6pp. Pages 2 and 6: Blank. Page 3: Title—**Jas. A. Garfield Funeral March.**

JAG-92 The Nation Mourns It's Fallen Chief. w. John Keynton. m. G. Operti. Published by T.B. Harms & Company, No. 819 Broadway, New York, NY. 1881. B/w non-pictorial line border. "In Memoriam of Presidential Garfield."

JAG-93 James A. Garfield's Grand March. m. A.E. Warren, Op. 66 (Author *of Love's Return Waltzes, Lass On The Shore March*, &c). Published by White, Smith & Company, No. 516 Washington Street, Boston, MA. 1880. B/w litho of James A. Garfield, leaves. "To the Republican Nominee for President."

JAG-94 Garfield, Arthur And Victory (Campaign Song). w. George Cooper. m. William P. Adams. In: *The Orpheus, Pond's Journal of Music, A Repository of Music, Art and Literature*, page 156. Published by William A. Pond & Company, No. 25 Union Square, New York, NY. August, 1880.

JAG-95 Garfield's Funeral March. m. J.J. Freeman, Op. 1003. Published by Spear and Dehnhoff, No. 717 Broadway, New York, NY. 1881. B/w geometric designs and black border. "In Memory of The Noble Martyr."

JAG-96(A) Gen. Jas. A Garfield's Campaign Grand March. m. A.H. Rosewig. Published by Lee & Walker, No. 1113 Chestnut Street, Philadelphia, PA. 1880. B/w litho by Crosscup & West of James A. Garfield. "Chicago's Choice." "Respectfully Dedicated to the National Republican Executive Committee." 8pp. Page 2: Blank. [Also see JAG-52]

(B) With Garfield We'll Conquer Again (Campaign Song). w.m. George Morley.

(C) We'll Put Garfield In The Chair (Male Quartet). w. Geo. Morley. m. A.H. Rosewig.

JAG-97 President Garfield. w.m. Juliana Hatfield. In: *Become What You Are* [Song Book], page 25. Published by CPP/Belwin, Inc., No. 15800 Northwest 48th Avenue, Miami, Fl. 1993. [9" × 12"]. N/c photo by Atlantic Recording Corporation of a woman sitting in a field of grass. "The Juliana Hatfield Three—*Become What You Are*."

JAG-98 Why Should They Kill My Baby! w. Carlton. m. C.T. De Coenail. Published by Central Music House, Burns & Kaufmann, No. 791 Broadway near 10th Street, Grace Church, New York, NY. Copyright 1881 by C.T. De Coenial. Br/w attached real photo of James A. Garfield. B/w litho geometric designs. "Dedicated in Token of Esteem to Mrs. Anna Garfield, Honored Mother of President James A. Garfield (President of the U.S.A.)." 8pp. Pages 2 and 8: Blank.

JAG-99 Garfield's Funeral March. m. Phil B. Perry. Published by A.W. Perry & Son, Sedalia, MO. 1881. B/w geometric design border. "To the memory of James A. Garfield, who was shot by Chas. J. Guiteau on July 2, '81, and who died from his wounds on Sept. 19, '81." 6pp. Page 2: Blank. Page 6: Advertising.

JAG-100 Elberon To Washington (Funeral March). m. Almon D. Hougas. Published by H.L. Benham & Company, No. 42 Arcade, New York, NY. 1881. Non-pictorial black line border. 6pp. Pages 2 and 6: Blank.

JAG-101 306. [w. T.C. Becker]. **Published in New York. 1880. Pk/bk non-pictorial.** "Campaign Songs Of The 306 For The Garfield and Arthur Campaign." 1880. Litho of flag, banner inscribed "Garfield & Arthur." 28pp. [M-205].

JAG-102 The Most Popular Edition Of Garfield And Arthur Campaign Songster. Published by Popular Publishing Company, A.J. Dick, Manager, New York, NY. 1880. Be/bk litho of James A. Garfield and Chester A. Arthur. "Containing the Largest and Most Complete Collection of Songs, All Written to the Most Popular Airs of the Day." 68pp. [M-208].

JAG-103 National Republican Campaign Songster, 1880, Garfield And Arthur. Published by W.O. Moffitt, Syracuse, NY. 1880. 30pp. [M-209].

JAG-104 Jim Garfield's At The Front. m. G. Elmer Jones.

JAG-105 The Martyr President Sleeps (Song And Chorus). w.m. H.S. Thompson. Published by Blamer & Weber, Publishers, No. 311 North Fifth Street, St. Louis, MO. 1881.

JAG-106 Garfield Memorial Grand March. m. Karl Merz. Published by S. Brainard's Sons, Cleveland, OH. 1881. B/w litho by W.J. Morgan & Co., of James A. Garfield, Mrs. Garfield, burial site, Capitol, home, woman in mourning, geometric designs. 8pp. Pages 2, 7 and 8: Blank.

JAG-107 President Garfield's Funeral March. In: *The Parlor Organ Treasury, Containing the Most Popular Waltzes, Marches, Polkas, Galops, Gavottes, Etc., Including a Choice Section Of Miscellaneous Compositions. Arranged in an Easy And Effective Manner for the Reed Organ.* e.a. W. F. Sudds. Published By Wm. Rohlfing & Sons, Milwaukee, WI. 1882. R/b non-pictorial hard cover.

JAG-108 Programme Of The Public Obsequies Of President Garfield [Program with Songs]. Published by The North Congregational Church, Middletown, CT. 1881. [5 3/4" × 9"]. Be/br non-pictorial line border. "Monday, September 26th, 1881." "Born November 19, 1831, Died President of the United States, September 19, 1881." 4pp.

JAG-109 Garfield (A Republican Campaign Song & Chorus). w. Sam Booth. m. "Air by Worzel." Published by S. Brainard's Sons, Nos. 341 & 343 Euclid Avenue, Cleveland, OH. 1880. B/w non-pictorial geometric design border.

JAG-110 Garfield's Funeral March. m. Henry D. Solge. Published by F.W. Helmick, No. 180 Elm Street, Cincinnati, OH. 1881. B/w litho by C.W. Fleetwood of James A. Garfield, casket lying in State, guards, flags, black border, geometric designs.

JAG-111 On To Victory (Garfield and Arthur Campaign Song and Quartett for Male Voices). w. De Vin. m. D.B. Moody. Published by M. Gray, Steinway Hall, No. 117 Post Street, San Francisco, CA. 1880. R/w/b flags, geometric designs. "Sung by the Amphion Quartett."

JAG-112 President Garfield's Funeral March (Sympathetic). m. L. Hewitt. Published H.R. Basler, No. 3712 Butler Street, Pittsburgh, PA. 1881. B/w geometric design border. "With Sympathy To President Garfield and Family." 6pp. Pages 2 and 6: Blank.

JAG-113 Slowly And Mournfully. m. C. Everest. Published by J.E. Ditson & Co., Philadelphia, PA. 1881. B/w non-pictorial geometric designs and border. "Composed and Revised on the Death of President James A. Garfield." 6pp. Pages 2 and 6: Blank.

JAG-114 Mollie, Dry Thy Tears Away! (Song and Chorus). w.m. Chas. D. Blake. Published by White, Smith & Company, Chicago, IL. 1881. B/w litho by Chas. H. Crosby of Mollie Garfield inscribed "Very Truly Yours, Millie Garfield [facsimile signature]." "To Miss Mollie Garfield, The Daughter of Our

Beloved President." 6pp. Pages 2 and 6: Blank. Page 3: B/w floral and geometric designs in title.

JAG-115 Toll The Bells Slowly. w. W.H. Breese. m. Gomer Thomas. Published by Gomer Thomas, Danville, PA. 1881. B/w non-pictorial black line border, geometric designs. "As Sung by the Mahonning Presbyterian Choir, Daville Penn. Sept. 26th 1881." "Respectfully Dedicated to Mrs. James A. Garfield." 6pp. Pages 2 and 6: Blank.

JAG-116 Wake! Oh Republicans Wake! (Song and Chorus). w. Eugene J. Hall. m. J.W. Reed. Published by S. Brainard's Sons, Cleveland, OH. 1880. B/w non-pictorial geometric design border. "Dedicated to the Success of the Republican Party." Back cover: Advertisement for S. Brainard's Sons catalogue.

JAG-117 From The White House To The Sea. m. A.H. Rosewig. In: *Marches Of The Presidents, 1789-1909, Authentic Marches & Campaign Songs*, page 48. A. Carl Miller. Published by Chappell & Co., Inc., No. 609 Fifth Avenue, New York, NY. "By arrangement with Chilmark Press, Inc." 1968. [9" × 12"]. R/w/b litho of eagle, flag. "An Illustrated Piano Folio For All Ages." 72pp.

JAG-118 President James A. Garfield's Grand Funeral March. m. E. Mack. Published by S.T. Gordon & Son, No. 13 East 14th Street, New York, NY. 1881. B/w litho of James A. Garfield, black drape. "Our Loss His Gain." 6pp. Page 2: Blank. Page 6: Advertising.

JAG-119 Gen. Jas. A. Garfield's Campaign Grand March. m. A.H. Rosewig. Published by Lee & Walker, No. 1113 Chestnut Street, Philadelphia, PA. 1880.Non-pictorial geometric design border. "Chicago's Choice." "Respectfully Dedicated to the National Republican Executive Committee." 8pp. Page 2: Blank.

See also AL-95; USG-200; USG-223; JGB-35; JGB-44; JGB-61; BFH-74; WM-31; WM-96; WM-192; WM-226; WM-254; TR-314; WHT-23; WW-19; WW-58; FDR-158; DDE-9; LBJ-1; MISC-42; MISC-94; MISC-167.

JAMES BUCHANAN

JB-1 Buchanan Schottisch. m. F. Southgate, Op. 30. Published by Henry McCaffrey, Baltimore, MD. 1856. Non-pictorial. 6pp. Pages 2 and 6: Blank.

JB-2 Buchanan's Union Grand March. Published by Nathan Richardson, No. 282 Washington Street, Boston, MA. 1856. B/w sepia tinted litho by J.H. Bufford's Litho. [attributed to Winslow Homer] of James Buchanan, flags, eagle, oak leaves. "Respectfully Dedicated by Special Permission to James Buchanan [facsimile signature]." Page 2: Blank.

JB-3 Buchanan's March. m. James Cox Beckel. [185-]. Non-pictorial. "Composed for the American Conservatorio of Paradise, Lancaster Coy., Penna." 4pp. Pages 1 and 4: Blank.

JB-4 Wheatland Polka. m. Ellen C. Morant. Published by G. Willig, Baltimore, MD. 1857. Non-pictorial geometric designs. "Composed and Respect-

JB-2

fully Dedicated to James Buchanan, President of the United States." 6pp. Pages 2 and 6: Blank.

JB-5 Song Of The Union. w. John M. Crosland (GA). m. George W. Hewitt (NJ), Op. 56. Published by Beck & Lawton, 7th and Chesnut Streets, Philadelphia, PA. 1860. B/w litho of George Washington, eagles, monuments, Capitol. "By a Pennsylvanian, most Respectfully Dedicated to the President and People of the United States by their Fellow Citizen, and Obedient Servant, John M. Crosland, January, 1860." Washington quote — "I shall carry with me to my grave a strong incitement to unceasing vows, that your Union may be perpetual." 8pp. page 2: Version "In the original mountain strain of the Author for the Voice Alone." "Key to symbols on title page — Upper Section, Center: The Union as it is, in all its present and prospective grandeur. On either side — The warning elements of the Slavery question (North and South) stayed by the hand of Patriotism. Middle and Lower Section — The sentiment of division in its first effects — The trampling upon the Glory of our Country, and the firebrands of sectional strife at the Capitol. Note — May be sung to the Scottish Air: *Scots Ha Hake wi Wallace bled*." Page 3: "To revive memories of the past as a guide to the patriotism of the future." Pages 6 and 8: Blank. Page 7: Additional verses.

JB-6 Song Of The Union. w. John M. Crosland (GA). m. George W. Hewitt (NJ), Op. 56. 1860. B/w litho of George Washington, eagles, monuments, Capitol. "By a Pennsylvanian, most Respectfully Dedicated to James Buchanan, President of the United States by his Fellow Citizen and obedient servant, John M. Crosland, January, 1860." George Washington quote — "I shall carry with me to my grave a stirring incitement to unceasing vows, that your Union may be perpetual." 6pp. Pages 2 and 6: Blank.

JB-7 The Constitution (National Anthem). w.m. Frederick Widdows. Published by Firth, Pond & Company, No. 547 Broadway, New York, NY. 1860. Non-pictorial geometric designs. "God Preserve the Union." "The Words and Music Written, Composed and Most Respectfully Dedicated to His Excellency, the President and the People of the United States." "National Anthem." 6pp.

JB-8 Buchanan Polka. m. Eugene Como. Published by David P. Faulds, Main Street, Louisville, KY. 1856. B/w litho of two stars. "To the Friends of Democracy." 6pp. Pages 2 and 6: Blank.

JB-9 Wheatland (Schottisch). m. Frank Emmo. Published by Miller & Beacham, Baltimore, MD. [185-]. Non-pictorial geometric designs. "Composed and Respectfully Dedicated to Hon. James Buchanan." 6pp. Pages 2 and 6: Blank.

JB-10 God Save The Union (National Anthem). w.m. P.S. Gilmore. Published by Russell & Patee, No. 61 Court Street, Boston, MA. 1861. Non-pictorial line border. "Composed in Honor of the Day Set Apart by President Buchanan as a Day of National Fast and Prayer for the

JB-9

Preservation and Peace of the Union, January 4, 1861." "Price 20 cts." 4pp. Page 4: Blank.

JB-11   God Save Our President (National Song). w. Francis De Haes Janvier. m. George Felix Benkert. Published by Oliver Ditson & Company, No. 277 Washington Street, Boston, MA. 1858. Non-pictorial geometric designs. 6pp. Pages 2 and 6: Blank.

JB-12   The Wheelbarrow Polka. w.m. "A Barrel Apples." Published by Oliver Ditson, No. 115 Washington Street, Boston, MA. 1856. B/w litho by J.H. Bufford's Litho. [Attributed to Winslow Homer] of Major Ben. Perley Poore pushing a wheelbarrow loaded with an apple barrel to Boston after losing a wager on the 1856 election between James Buchanan and John C. Fremont. Narrative on event—"Major Ben. Perley Poore of Newbury, made a bet with Col. Robert I. Burbank of Boston, on the Presidential vote in Massachusetts. The bet doomed the loser to wheel a barrel of apples from his house to the house of the winner. The Colonel won the bet, and the Major started the next morning for Newbury (36 miles from Boston) with the apples (notwithstanding the Col. had promptly released him from the conditions of the bet) and arrived at the Tremont House the third day at 2 1/2 o'clock—where in the presence of at least 30,000 enthusiastic spectators the most interesting ceremonies took place between the parties. "Composed and Dedicated to Major Ben. Perley Poore." 6pp. Pages 2 and 6: Blank.

JB-13   Wheatland March. m. Ida T. Reeder. Published by Stayman & Brothers, No. 294 Chesnut Street, Philadelphia, PA. 1852. Non-pictorial. "Dedicated to the Hon. Jas. Buchanan." "Composed and Arranged by Ida T. Reeder in her 14th year." 4pp. Pages 2 and 4: Blank.

JB-14   The White House Chair. w.m. Stephen Collins Foster. In: *The Pittsburgh Dispatch*, Sept. 20, 1885.

JB-15   National Grand March. a. E.B. Saffery. Published by W.C. Peters & Sons, Cincinnati, OH. 1856. B/w star border. "The Union Must Be Preserved." "To the Friends of." 6pp. Pages 2 and 6: Blank.

JB-16   National Democratic Convention Polka. a. Carl Leutner. Published by W.C. Peters & Sons, Cincinnati, OH. 1856. B/w star border. "The Union Must Be Preserved." "To the Friends of The Nominee." 6pp. Pages 2 and 6: Blank. Page 3: Title—**National Democratic Convention Grand March**.

JB-17   Buchanan Galop. m. J.A. Getze. Published by Lee & Walker, No. 120 Walnut Street, Philadelphia, PA. 1846. Non-pictorial. "Arranged for the Piano Forte and Respectfully Dedicated to Miss Emily F. Miller." 4pp. Pages 1 and 4: Blank. [Probably James Buchanan as Secretary of State, Mexican War].

JB-18   The Buck & Breck Campaign Songster. Published by Frost & Dory, Cincinnati, OH. 1856. 32pp. [M-088].

JB-19   National Feeling Song. w. "A Gentleman of Baltimore." m. C.A.S. Published by Th. A. Schmidt, Philadelphia, PA. 1856. B/w litho of a cannon firing out the name "Buchanan." 6pp. Pages 2 and 6: Blank. Page 3: "Dedicated to the Citizens of the United States."

JB-20   Columbia The Gem Of The Ocean. w.m. David T. Shaw. a. T.A. Becket, Esq. Published by Lee & Walker, No. 188 Chestnut Street, Philadelphia, PA. 1843. [Handmade edition 1856]. R/w/b litho by T. Sinclair of crossed flags. "Buck" "and" "Breck" have been hand cut from another document and pasted on the flags. "Sung at the Boston, New York & Philadelphia Concerts, Respectfully Dedicated to John S. Du Solle." 6pp. Pages 2 and 6: Blank.

JB-21   Buchanan's Inauguration March. m. F. Scala (Band Master). Published by George Hilbus, Washington,

DC. 1857. R/w/b flag. "As performed by The United States Marine Band." "Composed and Respectfully Dedicated to Miss Harriet Lane, of Wheatland." 8pp. Pages 2 and 8: Blank.

JB-22 White House Chair, The. w.m. Stephen C. Foster. e. Gregg Smith. In: *America's Bicentennial Songs from The Great Sentimental Age, 1850-1900, Stephen Foster to Charles E. Ives*, page 49. Published by G. Schirmer, New York, NY. 1975. [9" × 11 7/8"]. N/c litho of woman with roses, flag, city. 152pp.

JB-23 Buchanan's Union Grand March. In: *Marches Of The Presidents, 1789-1909, Authentic Marches & Campaign Songs*, page 39. A. Carl Miller. Published by Chappell & Co., Inc., No. 609 Fifth Avenue, New York, NY. "By arrangement with Chilmark Press, Inc." 1968. [9" × 12"]. R/w/b litho of eagle, flag. "An Illustrated Piano Folio For All Ages." 72pp.

See also JCF-8; JCF-25; JCF-27; JCF-35; JCF-39; AL-119; WHT-23; WW-19; FDR-158; DDE-9; LBJ-1; MISC-167.

JOHN BELL

JBL-1 The Bell And Everett Schottisch. m. Francis H. Brown. Published by Firth, Pond & Company, No. 547 Broadway, New York, NY. 1860. B/w beige tinted litho by Sarony, Major & Knapp of John Bell and Edward Everett, eagle, cannon, flags, shield, ships. 8pp. Pages 2 and 8: Blank.

JBL-2 The Tolling Bell (Approaching Mount Vernon). m. Charles Grobe, Op. 1090. Published by Lee & Walker, No. 722 Chesnut Street, Philadelphia, PA. 1859. B/w green tinted litho of "Hon. Edward Everett." "The traveler steaming down the Potomac, some miles below Washington, is startled by a bell, tolling slowly. It is the signal of approach to Mount Vernon, where the greatest of America's sons sleeps his last sleep." "A Musical Delineation for the Piano." 10pp. Page 2: Blank. Page 3: At top of page — "Hark! Hark the bell is tolling! Through every patriot breast emotions strong are rolling, too deep to be repressed."

JBL-3 Honor To Washington (A National Ode). w.m. B.A. Burditt, Esqr. Published by Oliver Ditson & Company, No. 277 Washington Street, Boston, MA. 1859. B/w beige tinted litho of George Washington, flags, hat, women — Miss Columbia and Miss Liberty — eagle, sword. "Inscribed by permission to the Hon. Edward Everett." "Expressly for the Celebration of the 83d Anniversary of American Independence, and Performed before the City Authorities of Boston, in the Music Hall, July 4, 1859." 6pp. Pages 2 and 6: Blank.

JBL-4 John Bell Polka. m. Charles L. Ward. Published by D.P. Faulds & Company, Main Street, Louisville, KY. 1860. Br/w litho of eagle — "E Pluribus Unum," shield, flags, vine border. "To the lovers of the Union." 6pp. Page 6: Blank.

JBL-5 The Union "Bell" Polka. m. Charles Grobe, Op. 1204. Published by Lee & Walker, No. 722 Chesnut Street, Philadelphia, PA. 1860. B/w gray tinted litho by T. Sinclair of John Bell. "Dedicated to the Hon. John Bell of Tenn." 8pp. Pages 2, 7 and 8: Blank. Page 3: Poem at top of music: "Hark the Union Bell is ringing, All the land its echoes hear, listen what its notes are telling, free men hark! For peace is near. All unworthy passions buried by the voice of this great BELL: Brothers rise and live as brothers and loud the Union Chorus swell!"

JBL-6 Gov. Everett's Quick Step. m. George O. Farmer. Published by John Ashton & Company, No. 197 Washington Street, Boston, MA. [1836-1840]. Non-pictorial. "Composed for the Piano Forte." 4pp. Pages 1 and 4: Blank.

JBL-7 Union Bell Schottische. m. James Bellack, Op. 1622. Published

JAMES BIRNEY (JBR)

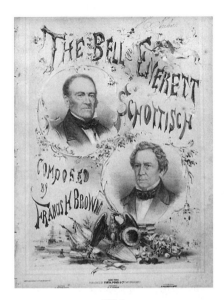

JBL-1

JBL-7

by Ph. P. Werlein, 5 Camp St., New Orleans, LA. 1860. B/w tan tinted litho of John Bell, geometric designs. 8pp.

JBL-8 Gov. Everett's Grand March. m. Charles Zeuner. Published by C. Bradlee, No. 107 Washington Street, Boston, MA. 1836. Non-pictorial designs. "For the Piano Forte." 2pp.

JBL-9 Two Campaign Songs. w. M.F. Bigney. m. Theodore Von La Hatche, Op. 382 & 383 (Author of *Keep Step With The Music*). Published by P.P. Werlein, No. 5 Camp Street, New Orleans, LA. 1860. Bl/w geometrical design border. "No. 1 Dedicated to the Everett Guards." "No. 2 Dedicated to the Young Bell Ringers." Lyrics printed on the cover. 8pp. Pages 2 and 8: Blank. Page 3: **No. #1— Bell & Everett Campaign** (Song and Chorus). Page 6: **No. #2 — Bell & Everett Campaign** (Solo and Chorus in Two Parts).

JBL-10 The Bell And Everett Songster (For The Campaign). Published by A. Winch, Philadelphia, PA. 1860. Y/bk non-pictorial. "The Union, The Constitution, And The Enforcement Of The Laws." "Containing a Large Collection of National and Patriotic Airs as Sung by the Constitutional Glee Clubs." 70pp. [M120].

JBL-11 Everett's Funeral March (In Honor Of Edward Everett). m. B.A. Burditt. Published by Oliver Ditson & Co., No. 277 Washington Street, Boston, MA. 1865. B/w beige tinted litho by J.H. Bufford's of Edward Everett. "As Performed At His Funeral By The Brigade Band." 6pp. Pages 2 and 6: Blank.

See also SAD-10; AL-319.

JAMES BIRNEY

JBR-1 The Liberty Minstrel. e. George W. Clark. Published by George W. Clark, New York, NY. 1844. [4 5/8" × 6 3/4"]. Non-pictorial song book with gold leaf title. "And Sold by Wm. Harned, 22 Spruce St., New York and Baltimore and Marsh, Boston, Mass." 230pp. Page 7: Illustrated title page. B/w litho of lyre, music, trumpet. "When the striving of surges is mad on the main, Like the charge of a column of plumes on the plain, When the thunder is up from his cloud cradled sleep and The tempest is treading the paths of the deep — There is beauty. But where is the beauty to see, like the sun brilliant brow of a nation when free?"

JBR-2 Get Off The Track! m. Jesse Hutchinson, Junr. Published by Jesse Hutchinson, Junr., Boston, MA. 1844. B/w litho by Thayer & Company of a train inscribed "Liberator" and "Immediate Emancipation," second train inscribed "Repealer" and "Liberty Votes and Ballot Boxes, flags inscribed "Herald of Freedom" and "American Standard." Crowd of people. Two wrecked trains in the background, one inscribed "Clay" and the other inscribed "Van." "A Song for Emancipation, Sung by The Hutchinsons, Respectfully Dedicated to Nathl. P. Rogers, as a mark of esteem for his intrepidity in the Cause of Human Rights — By The Author, Jesse Hutchinson, Junr." 6pp. Pages 2 and 6: Blank.

JBR-3 Liberty Song Book. c.a. Thomas N. West and H.E. Calkins. Published and Sold at the Office of *The Spirit of Freedom* Office, Chagrin Falls, OH. 1844. [3 1/2" × 6"]. Non-pictorial. Inside title page subtitle: "Containing Hymns, Odes, Songs, &c. for the Liberty Party." [M-065].

JBR-4 Ode To Birney. w.m. Elizur Wright. "For President of the U. States." "Composed by Elizur Wright and sung by G.W. Clark at the Buffalo Convention. Words and music composed during the meeting." In: *The Liberty Almanac for 1844, Being the 68th and 69th Years of American Independence (So Called)*, page 34. Published by I.A. Hopkins, Townsend Block, Syracuse, NY. 1843. [4 1/16" × 6 3/4"].

JBR-5 Ode To James Birney. w. Elizur Wright, Esq. m. G.W. Clark. Published from J. Barber's Music and Job Printing Office, Townsend Block, Syracuse, New York. [6 3/4" × 10 1/4"]. 1843. Non-pictorial. "Music composed and sung instanter [sic] by G.W. Clark, with great applause, on the nomination of Mr. Birney at the National Convention, held in Buffalo, Aug. 31, 1843." 2pp.

JBR-6 Songs For Freemen [Song Sheet]. Published by George Latimer. [1844]. [7 7/8" × 10 1/4"]. Non-pictorial. 2pp. [14 songs for the Liberty Party].

JAMES B. WEAVER

JBW-1 The Millennium Army. w. George Howard Gibson. m. H.J.W. Seamark. Published by The Alliance Publishing Company, Lincoln, NE. Copyright 1892 George Howard Gibson. B/w non-pictorial geometric design border. "Songs of the People No. 9." "The Voice of the Industrial Classes and Peoples Party of America." "(Mrs. Lease's Favorite of the Songs). 6pp. Pages 2 and 6: Blank.

JBW-2 The Peoples Party Grand March. m. C.L. Keck, Op. 96. Published by National Music Company, Nos. 215-221 Wabash Avenue, Chicago, IL. 1892. B/w hand tinted litho of "James B. Weaver," geometric designs. "Dedicated to Gen'l. James B. Weaver." 6pp. Pages 2 and 6: Blank.

JBW-3 People's Party Song

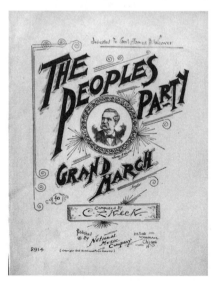

JBW-2

Book. c. Theodore Steele. Published by Theodore Steele, Mt. Vernon, IL. 1892. [3 1/2" × 5 5/16"]. Bl/bk non-pictorial geometric designs. 34pp. [M-320].

JBW-4 National Greenback Labor Songster. c. B.M. Lawrence, M.D. Published by D.M. Bennett, Liberal and Scientific Publishing House, No. 141 8th Street, New York, NY. 1878. [3 3/4" × 6 1/4"]. Gn/bk litho of arm with hammer. 52pp. Page 3: "Original, Practical, Patriotic, Progressive and Stirring Songs, Adapted to the Most Popular Airs in addition to which will be found choice and humorous readings, including 'The Bankers and I Are Out,' 'Men and Monkeys,' 'What We Want,' &c." Page 4: "Contents."

JBW-5 People's National Party Grand March. m. C.L. Keck, Op. 97. Published by Hohmann's Music Company, Lincoln, NE. 1892. Non-pictorial geometric design border. "Respectfully dedicated to its Standard Bearer, Gen. James B. Weaver by F.W. Hohmann." Page 2: Blank. Page 3: Copyright 1892 by National Music Company. Page 6: Adv.

JBW-6 The Political Catechism And Greenback Song-Book. c. J.H. Randall. Published by Rufus H. Darby, Washington, DC. 1880. Gn/r non-pictorial. 36pp. Page 3: "An Honest Money is the noblest work of man and the grandest institute of Government to promote civilization." [M-221].

JBW-7 United States Labor Greenback Song Book. e. Mary Dana Shindler. Published for Mrs. Shindler by Capt. G.W. Loyd, New Rochelle, NY. 1879. [M-222].

JBW-8 Campaign Songs, Anecdotes And Speeches; Facts, Figures And A Full Statement Of How The People Have Been Robbed. Published by C.P. Judd, Hoxie, KS. 1892. "Allow me to sing the songs and the other fellow—Ignatious Donnelly,—may write the platform." [M-319].

JBW-9 The People's Songster For Campaign Purposes And A Jolly Time Generally. e. C.S. White. Published by Vincent Brothers Publishing Company, Indianapolis, IN. 1892. O/bk non-pictorial. "The Economics Library, Vol. 3—No. 3. Monthly. May 15, 1992 [sic]. Subscription $5.00. Price, 10 cents." 266pp. [M-321].

JBW-10 Complete Greenback And Labor Songster (Echoes Of 1880) [Songster]. Published by U. Mulford, Auburn, NY. 1880. "Complete Greenback and Labor Songster." "A Collection of Standard Songs for the Great Industrial Rights Campaign, with Numerous Poems and Readings and Recitations." 104pp. [M-220].

JBW-11 Sentinel Song Book. Published by S.F. Norton, No. 544 Ogden Avenue, Chicago, IL. 1892. [5 3/8" × 7 1/4"]. Non-pictorial. "*The Monthly Sentinel*, Chicago, November, 1892." "*The Monthly Sentinel* will be made up in part of selections from the regular weekly edition of *The Sentinel*,

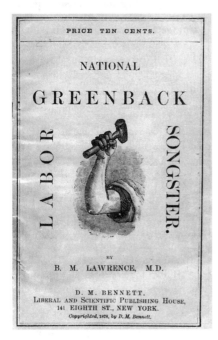

JBW-4

and in part of original and other choice matter-such matter, in fact, as our readers find most suitable and effective for doing missionary work in the People's cause..." 32pp.

JOHN C. BRECKENRIDGE

JCB-1 Breckenridge Schottische. m. Charles Grobe, Op. 1214. Published by Lee & Walker, Chestnut Street, Philadelphia, PA. 1860. B/w beige tinted litho by T. Sinclair of John C. Breckenridge. "Dedicated to the Hon. John C. Breckenridge, floral and geometric designs." 8pp. Pages 2, 7 and 8: Blank.

JCB-2 Gen. Breckenridge's Grand Waltz. m. Charles L. Ward. Published by James A. M'Clure, Nashville, TN. [ca. 1862]. Non-pictorial geometric designs. "Dedicated to the Fifth Kentucky Reg't." [H-3482].

JCB-3 J.C. Breckenridge. a. William Cumming. Published by A.C. Peters & Brother, No. 94 West Fourth Street, opposite the Post Office, Cincinnati, OH. 1860. B/w litho by Ehrgott, Forbriger and Company of John C. Breckenridge. 6pp. Pages 2 and 6: Blank. page 3: Title—**The Breckenridge Schottisch**.

JCB-4 Breckenridge March. m. James Bellack, Op. 1623. Published by Ph. P. Werlein, No. 5 Camp Street, New Orleans, LA. 1860. B/w tan tinted litho by T. Sinclair of John C. Breckenridge, floral and geometric designs. 8pp. Pages 2 and 8: Blank.

JCB-5 Breckenridge & Lane (Campaign Song 1860). m. Air: *Yankee Doodle*. [4 1/8" × 8 1/2"]. Non-pictorial. 2pp. Page 2: Blank.

JCB-6 Breckenridge Polka. m. E.W. Baylor. Published by David P. Faulds, Louisville, KY. 1856. Non-pictorial geometric designs. "To the Friends of Democracy." 6pp. Pages 2 and 6: Blank.

See also JB-18; JB-20; SAD-10; SAD-17; JD-32; JD-37.

JOHN C. FREMONT

JCF-1 Fremont's Great Republican March. a. Nathan Richardson. Published by Nathan Richardson, at the Musical Exchange, No. 282 Washington Street, Boston, MA. 1856. B/w beige tinted litho by J.H. Bufford's Litho. [Attributed to Winslow Homer], of John C. Fremont, Rocky Mountains, facsimile signature. "Arranged from Two Popular Airs and Respectfully Dedicated by Special Permission to J.C. Fremont." 6pp. Pages 2, 7 and 6: Blank.

JCF-2 Fremont And Victory. w.m. SAM. Published by Oliver Ditson, Washington Street, Boston, MA. 1856. Non-pictorial geometric designs. "The Celebrated Republican Campaign Song of 1856." "Words and Music Composed and Sung by SAM." 6pp.

JCF-3 There Is The White House Yonder (or The Fremont Campaign Song). Published by S.T. Gordon, No. 297 Broadway, New York, NY. 1856. B/w beige tinted litho by Sarony & Co. of John C. Fremont, White House, forest

JCB-4

scene with Indian fighting bear, the White House. 6pp. Pages 2 and 6: Blank.

JCF-4   Genl. Fremont's March. m. A.J. Vaas (Author of *Zouave Quickstep*, &c). Published by Root & Cady, No. 95 Clark Street, Chicago, IL. 1861. [V-1: N/c] [V-2: B/w tinted] litho by Ehrgott, Forbriger & Company in oval frame of General John C. Fremont on horseback, marching troops. "To the Army of the Northwest." 8pp. Pages 2 and 8: Blank.

JCF-5(A)   Fremont And Victory. w. E. Vitalis Scherb, Esq. (In Boston). m. Air: *Suoni La Tromba* from *Puritani* by Bellini. a. M. Fenollosa. Published by John J. Jewett & Company, Boston, MA. 1856. Gn/bk litho of John C. Fremont on a mountain peak with U.S. flag, geometric design border. "Freiheitslied Der Deutschen Republikaner." "Preis Lied." 8pp. [German lyrics with English translation]. Pages 2, 7 and 8: Blank.

*****(B)   Fremont And Victory.** w. Charles S. Weyman, Esq. (Of New York). B/w litho of John C. Fremont on a mountain peak with U.S. flag. "Prize Song." 8pp.

JCF-5(A)

JCF-6(A)   The Fremont Polka. m. Alex De Bubna. Published by John Marsh, New Masonic Hall, Philadelphia, PA. 1856. B/w pink tinted litho by L.N. Rosenthal of John C. Fremont. "Composed and Respectfully Dedicated to Col. John C. Fremont." 6pp. Pages 2 and 6: Blank.

(B)   The Fremont March. 8pp. Pages 2, 7 and 8: Blank.

(C)   The Fremont Schottisch. 4pp. Pages 2 and 4: Blank.

(D)   The Fremont Polka, March, And Quick Step (Complete). 14pp.

JCF-7   Freedom Freemen Fremont (Rallying Song). m. Air: *Pop Goes The Weazel*. Published by George R. Reed & Company, No. 13 Tremont Street, Boston, MA. 1856. Non-pictorial. "Dedicated to the Chelsea Fremont Club." 6pp. Pages 2 and 6: Blank.

JCF-8   Hail This Glorious Yankee Land. w. Francis F. Eastlack. m. Air: *Yankee Doodle*. Published by Lemuel Adams, No. 228 North 3rd Street, Philadelphia, PA. 1856. [6" × 9 3/16"]. Non-pictorial geometric design border. "The Song for All Parties." 2pp. [Pro-unity song with lyrics supporting Buchanan, Fremont and Fillmore].

JCF-9   The Pathfinder's Quick Step. m. Andrew Whitney (Author of *Gov. Robinson's Polka*, *Rollstone Polka*, *Fitchburg Polka*). Published by Andrew Whitney, No. 132 Main Street, Fitchburg, MA. 1856. Non-pictorial. "As played by the Fitchburg Cornet Band at the Ratification Convention of the Young America Fremont Clubs (Held at Fitchburg)." "Composed and Arranged for the Piano." 6pp. Pages 2 and 6: Blank.

JCF-10   Tyrants Of '76 And Tyrants Of '56 [Bandanna-Songster]. Published by Shawmut Chemical Printing Company, Boston, MA. [1856]. [10 1/2" × 10 5/8"]. Cloth bandanna printed with eagle, shield. "Fremont and Dayton." Narratives on various issues. Three campaign songs to popular airs. Rev: Blank.

JCF-11 Republican Song 1856. m. "Air: *Star Spangled Banner*." [1856]. [7 13/16" × 9 15/16"]. Non-pictorial. 2pp. Page 2: Blank.

JCF-12 The True Issue [Bandanna-Songster]. Published by the Shawmut Chemical Printing Company, Boston, MA. [1856]. [10 1/4" × 10 3/4"]. Cloth bandanna printed with illustration of John C. Fremont. Narrative to either side. Three campaign songs. Rev: Blank.

JCF-13 Fremont And Victory. m. Air: *La Marseillaise*. Published by Wm. Hall & Son, No. 239 Broadway, New York, NY. 1856. Non-pictorial geometric designs. "Arranged for the Rocky Mountain Fremont Central Club of King's County." "The Fremont Rallying Song for the Campaign of 1856, Adapted to the French National Hymn, *La Marseillaise*." "Free Speech, Free Press, Free Soil, Free Men, Fremont." 6pp. Page 6: Blank.

JCF-14 Huzza, For The Railroad! m. "Air: *Wait For The Wagon*." [1856]. [5 7/8" × 8 5/16"]. B/w litho of railroad train, geometric design border. "Dedicated to the Pacific Railroad Club." 2pp. Page 2: Blank.

JCF-15 Our Chieftain (Campaign Song). w. George William Pettes. m. "Tune: *Scots Wha Hae*." Published by Oliver Ditson, Washington Street, Boston, MA. [1956]. Non-pictorial. 4[?]pp.

JCF-16 The Freeman's Glee Book. Published by Miller, Orton & Mulligan, No. 25 Park Row, New York, NY. [and Auburn, NY]. 1856. [4 15/16" × 6"]. Pk/bk litho of man on mountain peak, music sheets, geometric designs. "A Collection of Songs, Odes, Glees and Ballads with Music, Original and Selected, Harmonized and Arranged for Each. Published under the Auspices of the Central Fremont and Dayton Glee Club of the City of New York, and Dedicated to All, Who, Cherishing Republican Liberty Consider Freedom Worth a Song." 112pp.

JCF-17 Pop! Goes For Fremont (Campaign Song). m. Air: *Pop Goes The Weasel*. Published by the Suffolk Ward & County Committee by Oliver Ditson, Washington Street, Boston, MA. [1856]. Non-pictorial. 4pp. Pages 1 and 4: Blank.

JCF-18 Fremont Songs For The People (Original and Selected) [Songster]. c. Thomas Drew (Editor of *The Massachusetts Spy*). Published by John P. Jewett & Company, Boston, MA. Copyright 1856 by Thomas Drew. [3 5/8" × 5 1/2"]. B/w litho of "J.C. Fremont." "The Campaign of 1856." 68pp. Pages 2 and 6: Blank. Page 5: Dedication.

JCF-19 Gen. Freemont's [sic] **War Song** (Arm. Arm. Victory or Death). m. W. Middleton. Published by H.M. Higgins, No. 117 Randolph Street, Chicago, IL. 1861. Small litho of U.S. shields in title.

JCF-20 Bugle March Of The Fremont Hussars. m. Hermann Shols (Leader of the Band). Published by Beer & Schirmer, No. 701 Broadway, New York, NY. 1862. N/c litho by Sarony, Major & Knapp of a Union soldier with bugle on horseback. "Respectfully Dedicated to Col. George E. Waring, Jr., Commanding the Regiment." "Plain 30¢." "Colored 35¢." 6pp. Page 6: Blank.

JCF-21 Young America Grand March. m. Adolph Baumback. Published by Geo. P. Reed & Company, No. 13 Tremont Street, Boston, MA. 1856. B/w beige tinted litho by J.H. Bufford & Co. of John C. Fremont. "Composed and most respectfully dedicated to Col. J.C. Fremont." 8[?]pp. Page 2: Blank.

JCF-22 The Republican Campaign Songster. Published by Miller, Orton & Mulligan, No. 25 Park Row, New York, NY. 1856. Litho of "Colonel John C. Fremont" facing to viewer's right. "A Collection of Lyrics, Original and Selected, Specially Prepared for the Friends of Freedom in the Campaign of Fifty-Six." [M-098].

JCF-23 General Burnside's Grand Triumphal March. m. G.W. Warren. Published by Clapp & Cory, No. 106 Westminister Street, Providence, RI. 1862. N/c litho of General Burnside, John C. Fremont, other generals. "To Brigadier General A.E. Burnside, Commanding the 3rd Naval and Military Expedition to the South." 10pp. Pages 2 and 10: Blank.

JCF-24 The Republican Campaign Songster. Published by Miller, Orton & Mulligan, No. 25 Park Row, New York, NY. 1856. [3 13/16" × 6"]. Be/bk litho of "Colonel John C. Fremont" facing to viewer's left, black line border. 112pp. Pages 2, 111 and 112: Blank. Page 3: Title page—"A Collection of Lyrics, Original and Selected, Specifically Prepared for the Friends of Freedom in the Campaign of Fifty-Six." Pages 109-110: Contents. [M-097].

JCF-25 [Fremont Song Sheet]. m. Popular Airs. Published by the Fremont Club of Lancaster City, [PA]. Non-pictorial. 2pp. Page 1: Four different songs [made to be cut into individual song sheets]: **Rallying Song, The White-House Race, Fremont** and **Uncle James**. Page 2: Blank.

JCF-26 Fremont And Victory. m. Air: *Marseilles Hymn*. [4 3/16" × 7 3/4"]. [1856]. Non-pictorial broadside. 2pp. Page 2: Blank.

JCF-27 [Fremont Song Sheet]. m. Popular Airs. [1856]. Non-pictorial. 2pp. Page 1: Three different songs [made to be cut into individual penny song sheets]: **Old Buck Going Up Salt River, We're A Band Of Freemen** and **The People's Choice**. Page 2: Blank.

JCF-28 Fremont Grand March. m. E. Krauss. Published by Oliver Ditson, Washington Street, Boston, MA. 1856. Non-pictorial. "To Col. John Chas. Fremont." 6pp. Pages 2 and 6: Blank.

JCF-29 Gen. Fremont's Volunteer Polka. m. Mrs. L.W. Powell. Published by A. Judson Higgins, No. 40 Clark Street, Chicago, IL. 1861. B/w litho of John C. Fremont, vignettes of him giving speech, climbing mountain. "Respectfully dedicated to the Western Volunteers." 6pp. Pages 2 and 6: Blank.

JCF-30 [General] Fremont's March. m. A.J. Vaas. Published by S. Brainard's Sons Company, Chicago, IL. [V-1: 1884] [V-2: ca. 1897]. [V-1: N/c litho by Orcuft of battle scene] [V-2: Bk/bl/w reprint of V-1 with Orcuft drawing redone by Harrell]. List of other titles in series. "Popular Marches, Battle Pieces, &c. for Piano or Organ."

JCF-31(A) Fremont Polka. m. De Bubna. Published by S.T. Gordon, No. 706 Broadway, New York, NY. [ca. 1860]. Non-pictorial geometric design border. "Parlor Album Pieces." List of other titles in series.

(B) Fremont Schottisch. m. De Bubna.

(C) Fremont March. m. De Bubna.

JCF-32 Fremont's Battle Hymn (Quartett). w.m. James G. Clark. Published by Joseph P. Shaw, No. 110 State Street, Rochester, NY. 1863. Non-pictorial. "To Jessie B. Fremont." 8pp. Pages 2 and 8: Blank.

JCF-33 Fremont Polka. m. Pierre Berthoud. Published by Oliver Ditson, Washington Street, Boston, MA. [1856?]. Non-pictorial. 6pp. Pages 2 and 6: Blank.

JCF-34 Fremont Quick Step. m. J. Ascher. Published by Oliver Ditson, Washington Street, Boston, MA. [1856]. Non-pictorial. "Composed for the Piano."

JCF-35 O, Jemmy Bucan! (A Song for the Times). Published by the *New York Musical World* Print, No. 379 Broadway, New York, NY. [1856]. [8 3/4" × 11 1/2"]. Non-pictorial. 4pp. Pages 2-4 numbered 130, 131 and 132.

JCF-36(A) We're Free, We're Free. w.m. Karl Cora. Published by Nathan Richardson at the Musical Exchange, No. 282 Washington Street,

Boston, MA. 1856. Non-pictorial. "The Campaign, 2 Fremont Republican Songs. Words Expressly for the Times." 6pp. Pages 2 and 6: Blank.

(B) **Who'll Follow, Who'll Follow.** w.m. Karl Cora. 6pp.

JCF-37 Freedom And Fremont. m. "Tune: *True Yankee Volunteer.*" Published by Horace Partridge, Nos. 125, 127 & 131 Hanover Street, Boston, MA. [1856]. [6" × 9 5/8"]. Non-pictorial geometric design border. "A Song for the Times." 2pp. Page 2: Blank.

JCF-38 Fremont Glees [Song Sheet]. [1856]. [9 3/4" × 15 1/2"]. Non-pictorial cloth. "As Sung by the Centerville Republican Club." 2pp. Page 2: Blank.

JCF-39 Buchanan And Fremont. m. Air: *Villikins and his Dinah.* Published by Andrews, Printer, No. 38 Chatham Street, New York, NY. [5 1/2" × 9 1/2"]. [1856]. Non-pictorial geometric design border. 2pp. Page 2: Blank.

JCF-40 When Abe Comes Marching Home Again! (Fremont Campaign Song). w. Our Ned. m. Air: *When Johnny Comes Marching Home.* Published by Mason & Company, No. 58 North Sixth Street, Philadelphia, PA. [1864]. [6 1/2" × 9"]. B/w litho of John C. Fremont. "Clubs and Dealers can have their orders filled for the above, and all other Campaign Songs by addressing Mason & Co., No. 58 North Sixth Street, Phila., Dealers in Cartes de Visite, Albums, Songs, Books, Periodicals, Medals, &c. Catalogues sent Free." "Copyright Secured." Advertising. 2pp. Page 2: Blank.

JCF-41 A Fremont Song. w. W.S. Eaton. m. "Tune: *Uncle Sam's Farm.*" Published by W.S. Eaton, East Weare, NH. [1858]. [5 11/16" × 10 1/8"]. Non-pictorial geometric design border. 2pp. Page 2: Blank.

JCF-42 The Fremont Campaign Songster. Published by Frost & Dory, Publishers, No. 140-142 Vine Street, Cincinnati, OH. 1856. [3 1/2" × 5 1/2"]. B/w litho of John C. Fremont. 32pp.

Page 2: "To the Fremont Clubs and the Republican Party throughout the Union, this little volume is Respectfully Dedicated by the Publishers." [M-093].

JCF-43 All Hail, Ye Gallant Freemen True! m. "Tune—*Auld Lang Syne.*" 1856. [6" × 9 5/8"]. Non-pictorial. "For the Mass Meeting at Oyster Bay, September 20, 1856." 2pp. Page 2: Blank.

JCF-44 Fremont And Freedom's All The Go (A Rallying Song). Published by Oliver Ditson, No. 115 Washington Street, Boston, MA. [1856]. Non-pictorial. 2pp. Page 2: Blank.

JCF-45 The Fremont Songster. Published by [V-1: H.S. Riggs & Company, Publishers, No. 4 Cortland Street] [V-2: P.J. Cozans, No. 107 Nassau Street], New York, NY. 1856. [V-1: 3 5/8" × 5 3/4"] [V-2: [3 1/2" × 5 5/8"]. Be/bk litho of wreath, John C. Fremont. "With a current likeness of John C. Fremont, The People's Candidate for the Presidency." 40pp. [M-094, 095].

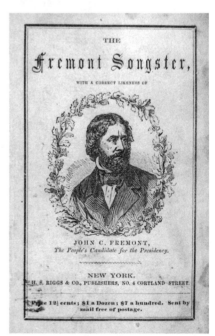

JCF-45

JCF-46 Fremont And Dayton Campaign Songs For 1856. Published by Pinkerton & Company, Printers, Cleveland, OH. 1856. 22pp. [M-092].

JCF-47 Songs For Freemen. Published by H.H. Hawley, Utica, NY. 1856. Be/bk litho of John C. Fremont. "A Collection of Campaign and Patriotic Songs for the People Adapted to Familiar and Popular Melodies, and Designed to Promote the Course of Free Speech, Free Press, Free Soil, Free Men, and Fremont." [M-099].

JCF-48 Rocky Mountain Song Book. Published by Du Dah & Company, Providence, RI. 1856. "Published for the use of the Fremont Flying Artillery of Providence."

JCF-49 The Fremonter. Published by O.R. Patch, Bangor, ME. 1856. "Containing the Lives of Fremont and Dayton, the Republican Platform, Letter of Acceptance of J.C. Fremont, Together with a Full Selection of Songs Adapted to the Campaign of 1856." "Songs for the Campaign." 80pp. [M-100].

JCF-50 The Campaign Of 1856 (Fremont Songs For The People, Original And Selected. c. Thomas Drew (Editor of *The Massachusetts Spy*). Published by John P. Jewitt & Co., Cleveland, OH. 1856. Be/bk litho of John C. Fremont. 64pp.

JCF-51 The Republican Prize Songster. c. Philadelphia Republican Club. Published by the Philadelphia Republican Club. 1856. "Composed of original Songs, by Writers in all parts of the Union, Presented to the Philadelphia Republican Club, in answer to its offer of Prizes for the most meritorious." 96pp. [M-096].

JCF-52 Fremont Barbecue [Song Sheet]. Printed by Stacy & Richardson, Printers, No. 11 Milk Street, Boston, MA. August 26, 1856. [5 1/2" × 7 1/2"]. 2pp. Page 1: **Rallying Song.** "Tune: *The Marseillaise Hymn*." and **The White House Race.** m. "Tune: *Camptown Races.*" Page 2: Blank.

JCF-53 Fremont Hussars March. m. Charles Fradel. Published Beer & Schirmer, No. 701 Broadway, New York, NY. 1862. B/w beige tinted litho by Sarony, Major & Knapp of mounted troops in battle, eagle, floral designs. "Respectfully dedicated to Brig. General Asboth." 8pp. Pages 2 and 8: Blank.

JCF-54 Our Jessie (Waltz). w.m. Published by Oliver Ditson, Washington Street, Boston, MA. [1856]. Non-pictorial geometric designs. "Inscribed to the Republican Ladies." 6pp. Pages 2 and 6: Blank.

JCF-55 Fremont And Freedom (A Rallying Song). w. G.R.C. m. "Popular Melody." Published by Oliver Ditson, Washington Street, Boston, MA. [1856]. Non-pictorial geometric designs. 6pp. Pages 2 and 6: Blank.

See also WS-14; JB-12; USG-208.

JEFFERSON DAVIS

JD-1 President Jefferson Davis Grand March. m. Mrs. Flora Byrne. Copyright 1861 by P.P. Werlein and Halsey. Published in Louisiana. [13 5/8" × 10 3/4"]. Non-pictorial. 6pp. Pages 2 and 6: Blank. [H-3754].

JD-2 Our First President's Quickstep. m. P. Rivinac. Published by Blackmar & Bro., No. 199 Broad Street, Augusta, GA. [ca. 1861]. [11 1/2" × 9 7/8"]. B/w litho by B. Duncan & Co., Columbia, S.C., of Jefferson Davis, oak wreath. "Ninth Edition." 4pp. [H-3720].

JD-3 Jefferson Davis Grand March. m. C.F. Yagle (Pickensville, Ala). Published by Bromberg & Son, No. 46 Dauphin Street, Mobile, AL. 1861. [13 1/2" × 10 3/8"]. B/w engraving of banners—"Constitution" and "Confederation," anchor, cannon, drum, shield, stars. "Our Rights." "Dedicated to the Confederate States of America." 6pp. Pages 2 and 6: Blank. [H-3579].

JD-4 The Southern Wagon. Published by Joseph Block, No. 55

JD-2

Dauphin Street, Mobile, AL. 1862. [13" × 10 1/4"]. Non-pictorial geometric designs. "Respectfully Hitched Up for the President, Officers and Men of the Confederate Army." 6pp. Pages 2 and 6: Blank. Page 5: Verses. [H-3842].

JD-5 Confederacy March. m. Alfred F. Toulmin (of Patapsco Institute). Published by George Willig, Baltimore, MD. 1861. B/w beige tinted litho from a "Photograph by McClees" of Jefferson Davis in oval frame, facsimile signature, geometric designs. "Most Respectfully Dedicated to President Jefferson Davis." 8pp. Pages 2 and 8: Blank.

JD-6 Alabama Secession Galop. m. H. Berge (Wilcox Female Institute, Ala). Published by J.H. Snow, No. 29 Dauphin Street, Mobile, AL. 1861. [13 7/16" × 9 11/16"]. Non-pictorial geometric designs. "Dedicated to the President of the Confederate States of America." 10pp. Pages 2 and 10: Blank. [H-3296].

JD-7 Silver Bells (Mazurka). m. Charles O. Pape. "Copyright secured in the District Clerk's Office for South Carolina." [1861-1864]. [9 1/4" × 12"]. B/w non-pictorial litho by P.L. Valdry, Columbia, S.C., of geometric design frame. "Composed and Respectfully Dedicated to Mrs. Jefferson Davis." 6pp. [H-3802].

JD-8 Jeff Davis March. m. Mary Kelly. Published by George Willig, Baltimore, MD. 1861. [13 7/8" × 10 3/4"]. Non-pictorial geometric designs. "To Jefferson Davis, President of the Confederate States." 6pp. Pages 2 and 6: Blank.

JD-9 Hard Times In Dixie. w. M.K. m. Eugarps. Published by W.W. Whitney, No. 151 Summit Street, Toledo, OH. 1864. Non-pictorial geometric design border. "'Respectfully' Inscribed to Jeff Davis." "10th Thousand, 6th Edition." 6pp. Pages 2 and 6: Advertising.

JD-10 The Last Ditch Polka. m. D'Accacia. Published by Oliver Ditson & Company, No. 277 Washington Street, Boston, MA. 1865. B/w litho of caged rat with the head of Jefferson Davis, eagle, soldier. 6pp. Pages 2 and 6: Blank.

JD-11 Our First President's Quickstep. m. P. Rivinac (Author of *Gen. Bragg's Grand March, Pearl River Polka, &c)*. Published by A.E. Blackmar and Brother, No. 74 Camp Street, New Orleans, LA. 1864. [12 7/8" × 10"]. Non-pictorial. 8pp. Page 2: Blank. Page 8: Advertising for other Blackmar published music. [H-3721].

JD-12 Jeff's Double Quick. m. M.E. Published by Lee & Walker, No. 722 Chestnut Street, Philadelphia, PA. 1865. B/w beige tinted litho of soldier, girl, Jefferson Davis in a woman's dress — "Only my Mother." "The Last Groans of the Confederacy, 'Jeff's War Hoops.'" "Published for the Benefit of the Western Sanitary Fairs of Chicago, Ill., and Milwaukee, Wis." 8pp. Pages 2 and 7: Blank. Page 8: Advertising for other Lee & Walker published music.

JD-13 Our First President's Quickstep. m. P. Rivinac. Published by A.E. Blackmar & Brother, New Orleans, LA. 1861. B/w engraving of Jefferson Davis. 8pp. Page 2: Blank. Page 8: Advertising. [H-3720].

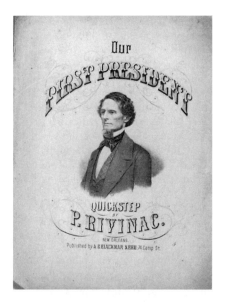

JD-13

JD-14 Jeff's Race For The Last Ditch! w. W. Dexter Smith, Jr. m. Fritz Eustace. Published by G.D. Russell and Company, No. 126 Tremont opp. Park Street, Boston, MA. 1865. "Dedicated to Lieut. Col. D.B. Prichard, 5th Mich. Cavalry." Litho [horizontal format] of soldiers chasing Jefferson Davis in woman's dress. 8[?]pp.

JD-15 Grand March Of The Southern Confederacy. m. J.E. Gleffer. Published by P.P. Werlein and Halsey, Nos. 3 and 5 Camp Street, New Orleans, LA. [ca. 1861]. B/w litho of a woman with a Confederate flag. 6pp. Page 3: "Inscribed to President Davis by the Author." [H-3519].

JD-16 Jeff Davis' Dream (A Serio Comic Song). w.m. Bernard Covert. Published by Henry Tolman & Company, No. 291 Washington Street, Boston, MA. 1862. Non-pictorial geometric designs. "To James T. Franey, Esq." "Written and composed by the Author of the Sword of Bunker Hill." 6pp. Pages 2 and 6: Blank.

JD-17 Poor Old Jeff The Shero. w. E. Rossiter. m. S. Dick. Published by Lee & Walker, No. 722 Chestnut Street, Philadelphia, PA. 1865. B/w beige tinted litho of Jefferson Davis in woman's dress, girl, stars with Black faces inside, drummer, Union soldier—"Only my Ma going for water." "Published for the Benefit of the Soldier's Home Fair, Milwaukee, Wis." 6pp. Page 2: Blank. Page 6: Advertising for other Lee & Walker music.

JD-18 How Do You Like It Jefferson D? w.m. Amos Patton. Published by Oliver Ditson & Company, No. 277 Washington Street, Boston, MA. 1864. B/w litho of black soldier thumbing nose at Jefferson Davis and the devil. 6pp. Pages 2 and 6: Blank.

JD-19 The Sour Apple Tree (Or Jeff Davis' Last Ditch) (Ballad). w. J.W. Turner. Published by Oliver Ditson & Company, No. 277 Washington Street, Boston, MA. 1865. B/w litho by H.F. Greene of Jefferson Davis in a woman's dress with a knife and a bag inscribed "Gold," apple tree with noose. 6pp. Pages 2 and 6: Blank.

JD-20 Jeff In Petticoats (A Song of the Times). w. George Cooper. m. Henry Tucker (Author of *Memory Bells, Its All Up In Dixie, &c, &c*). Published by William A. Pond & Company, No. 547 Broadway, New York, NY. 1865. B/w litho by H.C. Eno of Jefferson Davis in woman's dress, Union soldiers, woman. 6pp. Page 2: Blank. Page 6: Advertising.

JD-21 Jeff's Last Proclamation. w.m. Union. Published by H.L. Story, Burlington, VT. 1865. B/w litho by H.F. Greene of Jefferson Davis in dress hanging from tree, sign inscribed "Jeff's Last Proclamation." 6pp. Pages 2 and 6: Blank.

JD-22(A) Call 'Em Names, Jeff. w.m. R. Thompkins. m. Wurzel. e. George Root. In: *The Bugle Call*, page 14. Published by Root & Cady, No. 5 Clark Street, Chicago, IL. 1863. 64pp. Br/bk geometric designs.

(B) Jefferson D-, Sir. w. "Peace." Page 44.

JD-23 Southern Yankee Doodle. m. Air: *Yankee Doodle*. Published as a penny song sheet (Probably in the South). [ca. 1862]. [3 13/15" × 12 1/16"]. Non-pictorial. 2pp. Page 2: Blank. [Pro-Jeff Davis Lyrics].

JD-24 Goodbye, Jeff! (Song and Chorus). w.m. P.P. Bliss. Published by Root & Cady, No. 67 Washington Street, Chicago, IL. 1865. Non-pictorial geometric designs. 6pp. Page 6: Blank.

JD-25 Call 'Em Names, Jeff. w.m. R. Tompkins. m. Wurzel. Published by Root & Cady, No. 95 Clark Street, Chicago, IL. 1862. Non-pictorial black line border. 6pp. Pages 2 and 6: Blank.

JD-26 Jeff. Davis (A New Irish Song of the Times). w. T.L. Donnelly (Vocalist and Comedian). a. Emil Stadler. Published by Harding's Music for the Million, No. 288 Bowery, New York, NY. 1862. Non-pictorial geometric lines. "Respectfully Dedicated to Capt. W.A. Ketchum, 15th Regt. N.Y.S.V. by the Author." 4pp. Page 4: Blank.

JD-27 Good Bye, Jeff. w.m. George F. Root. Published by Root & Cady, Chicago, IL. 1865. B/w litho of flags — "20 Popular Melodies," geometric design border. "Camps, Tramps and Battle Fields, Arranged as Instrumental Pieces for the Piano-Forte." List of other titles in the series. 4pp. Page 4: Advertising.

JD-28 Beauvoir. w. Mrs. A. Mc.C.-Kimbrough. m. Jean Buckley. Published by The H. Kirkus Dugdale Company, Inc., Washington, DC. 1912. B/w photo of "Beauvoir, Home of Jefferson Davis, Biloxi, Miss." Gn/w drawing of pond, egret. 6pp. Page 2: "Introduction — Beauvoir Yesterday and Today." Page 3: "Affectionately dedicated to the Confederate Veterans of Mississippi by the Author." Page 6: Advertising.

JD-29 Flight And Capture Of Jeff. Davis. w.m. Wolf Erine. Published by J. Henry Whittemore, No. 179 Jefferson Avenue, Detroit, MI. 1865. B/w litho of Jefferson Davis in dress, bag of money inscribed "10,000,000," Union soldiers. Bible quote: "Jeremiah, 13 Chapter, 22 Verse, And if thou say in thine heart, wherefore come these things upon me? For the creatness [sic] of Thine iniquity are the *skirts* discovered, and thy *heels* made bare." "Dedicated to Old Michigan." 10pp. Pages 2 and 10: Blank.

JD-30 Jeff Davis Brought These Hard Times On Me. m. "Tune: *Nell Flaugherty's Drake*." Published by Johnson Song Publisher, No. 7 North 10th Street, Philadelphia, PA. [ca. 1862]. [6 1/4" × 9 9/16"]. B/w non-pictorial geometric design border. Penny song sheet. "See Johnson's New Catalogue of Songs." 2pp. Page 2: Blank.

JD-31 Capture Of Jeff Davis. w. John Forbes. Published by A.W. Auner, Song Publisher, N.E. corner 11th and Market Street, Philadelphia, PA. [1865]. [5 7/8" × 9 1/8"]. B/w penny song sheet with litho of Union soldier chasing Jefferson Davis in dress, geometric design border. "Composed and sung by John Forbes at Long's Varieties, 758 South Third Street, below German, Philadelphia." 2pp. Page 2: Blank.

JD-32 Jeff Davis. Published by Charles Magnus, No. 12 Franklin Place, New York, NY. [ca. 1861]. [5" × 8"]. Hand colored litho of "Jefferson Davis," "Gen. John C. Breckenridge," devil holding map of the "C.S." 2pp. Page 2: Blank.

JD-33 Jeff Davis And His Uncle. w. Isadore Leopold. m. "Air: *Root Hog Or Die*." [V-1: Published by J. Wrigley, No. 23? Chatham Street, New York, NY] [V-2: No publisher indicated]. [186-]. [V-1: 6 3/4" × 9 3/4"] [V-2: 4 1/2" × 6 1/2"]. [V-1: B/w litho border of soldier, sailor, ships, cannon, geometric designs] [V-2: Non-pictorial]. "No. 207." 2pp. Page 2: [V-1: Blank] [V-2: Song: *Happy Be Thy Dreams*].

JD-34 Jeff Davis (Comic). m. Emil Stadler. Published by Harding's Music for the Million, No. 288 Bowery,

New York, NY. [ca. 1870]. Non-pictorial geometric designs. "The Cabinet, A Collection of New and Popular Vocal Music." List of other titles in the series.

JD-35 Oh Jeff! Oh Jeff! (How Are You Now?) (Comic Song and Chorus). w. Henry Schroeder. Published by Charles Magnus, No. 12 Franklin Street, New York, NY. 1865. [5" × 8"]. Hand colored penny song sheet with litho of Jefferson Davis in dress, Union soldiers. "Music published by Firth, Son and Company, No. 563 Broadway, New York, NY." "Ten Illustrated Songs on notepaper, mailed to any address on receipt of 50 cts." 2pp. Page 2: Blank.

JD-36 Jeff Davis In Crinoline. Published by H.M. Higgins, No. 117 Randolph Street, Chicago, IL. [ca. 1966]. Non-pictorial. "25 Prize Songs."

JD-37 Jeff Wants To Get Away. w.m. "By a Lady." Published by Endres and Compton, No. 54 Fourth Street, St. Louis, MO. 1865. B/w litho by A. McLean of J.C. Breckenridge putting blackface on Jeff Davis — "Black me Breckenridge," snake, cotton bales, Black boy holding pan of "Butler's Blacking," devil. Sayings — "Memmingers Funeral Pile," Stack of "CSA Bonds" — "Repudiation," "Butler's Blacking." 6pp. Page 2: Advertising. Page 6: Blank.

JD-38 O! Jefferson Davis, How Do You Do. w. F.B. Scott. m. Charles G. Degenhard. Published by Sheppard Cottier & Company, No. 215 Main Street, Buffalo, NY. 1864. Non-pictorial. 6pp. Page 6: Blank.

JD-39 Jeff Davis Is A Coming (A Song for the Times). w. Richard Hinchcliffe. m. James R. Murray. Published by Russel & Tolman, No. 291 Washington Street, Boston, MA. 1861. B/w litho of ribbon inscribed with song title. "I will carry the war into Massachusetts — Jeff Davis." 6pp. Pages 2 and 6: Blank.

JD-40 How The Veterans Broke Up Jeff Davis' Ball. w. Mrs. G.P. Hardwick, Washington. m. Air: *Lanagan's Ball*. Copyright 1863 by Mrs. G.P. Hardwick. [8 1/4" × 4 1/8"]. Litho of tents, flag, ship, geometric design border. 2pp. Page 2: Lined writing paper.

JD-41 Jeff. Davis' Retreat March. m. F. Albert Kulling. Published by Louis Meyer, No. 1323 Chestnut Street, Philadelphia, PA. 1865. B/w litho of Jefferson Davis in woman's dress carrying a bag of gold and a knife with a Union soldiers in the background. "Don't provoke the President, he might hurt somebody." 6pp. Pages 2 and 6: Blank.

JD-42 Jeff Davis's Retreat. m. E. Mack. Published by Marsh, No. 1102 Chesnut Street, Philadelphia, PA. 1862. B/w vines. "Garden of Roses, A Sett [sic] of New and Easy Arrangement, Arranged for the Piano." List of other titles in the series. 4pp. Page 2: "The Garden of Roses No. 30." Page 4: Blank.

JD-43 Sour Apple Tree (or Jeff Davis' Last Ditch). Published by A.W. Auner's Printing Office, Eleventh and Market Streets, Philadelphia, PA. Copyright by Oliver Ditson & Company, Music Publishers, No. 277 Washington Street, Boston, MA. [1865]. [5" × 8 1/4"]. B/w litho of Jeff Davis in dress carrying a bag of gold and knife, tree with noose, geometric design border. Penny song sheet. 2pp. Page 2: Blank.

JD-44 Jefferson Davis In Prison (Song). w. Rev. J. Baker. m. Alfred Schmidt. Published by William A. Pond & Company, No. 347 Broadway, New York, NY. [186-]. Non-pictorial.

JD-45 The Sour Apple Tree (A Sarcastical Ballad). w.m. James W. Porter. Published by J. Marsh, No. 1029 Chestnut Street, Philadelphia, PA. 1865. B/w litho by G.F. Swain of an apple tree with hanging noose. "As sung by John Forbes at the Principal Concerts." 6pp. Page 2: Blank. Page 3: At top of music — "To be sung in female costume, with knife in hand, not forgetting the Boots." Page 6: Advertising.

(JD) JEFFERSON DAVIS

JD-46   Requiem For Jeff Davis. w.m. Bohemia. Published by Order of The Bohemian Club. Copyright by Saml. Silsbee, [Cincinnati, OH]. 1862. Non-pictorial geometric designs. "Dedicated to Parson Brownlow. 6pp. Pages 2 and 6: Blank. Page 3: At top — "Paraphrase of a toast given at a festival at Adrian, Mo. by an officer in the Union Army."

JD-47   John Merryman. m. "Air: *Old Dan Tucker.*" Published as a penny song sheet (Probably in the South). [ca. 1862]. [4 7/8" × 7 3/4"]. Pk/bk non-pictorial geometric design border. 2pp. Page 2: Blank. [Pro-Davis, Anti-Lincoln Lyrics].

JD-48   Jeff Davis In Crinoline. w. Gen. W.H. Hayward. m. "Air: *Ossawatomie Brown.*" Published by Thomas G. Doyle, Bookseller and Stationer, No. 295 North Gay Street, Baltimore, MD. [1865]. [5 5/8" × 8 3/4"]. Non-pictorial geometric design border. Penny song sheet. 2pp. Page 2: Blank.

JD-49   Johnny Fill Up The Bowl. m. "Tune — *When Johnny Comes Marching Home.*" Published by J.H. Johnson's Card and Job Printing Office, No. 18 North Tenth Street above Market, Philadelphia, PA. [ca. 1862]. [6 1/8" × 9 1/4"]. B/w litho of eagle with ribbon inscribed "United States of America." Advertising at bottom — "Cards, bill heads, circulars, hand bills, labels, envelopes, meeting notices, ball tickets, raffle tickets, party tickets, ladies' invitations, programmes, checks, visiting cards, &c, &c, &c, neatly printed, at prices to suit the times. See *Prof. Brook's Ball Room Monitor.* This little book will give you more instruction in dancing than any book ever published. Price of it is only 25 cents, sold by J.H. Johnson, No. 7 North Tenth Street, Philadelphia." 2pp. Page 2: Blank.

JD-50   All Well, Come To The Rescue (Song). Published as a broadside [Probably in the South]. [ca. 1862]. [4 1/2" × 14 1/8"]. B/w geometric design border. 2pp. Page 2: Blank. [Pro-Jeff Davis lyrics].

JD-51   Capture Of Jeff Davis. w. Eugene T. Johnston. "Air: *The Quilting Party.*" Published by H. De Marsan, Publisher, No. 60 Chatham Street, New York, NY. [1865]. [6 3/4" × 9 3/4"]. B/w penny song sheet with litho border of caricatures of musicians, Black man and children, jesters. 2pp. Page 2: Blank.

JD-52   Jeff Davis (Or The King Of The Southern Dominions). "Air: *The King of the Cannibal Island.*" Published by H. De Marsan, Publisher, No. 54 Chatham Street, New York, NY. [1863?]. [6 3/4" × 9 3/4"]. B/w penny song sheet with litho border of caricatures of musicians, Black man and children, jesters. 2pp. Page 2: Blank.

JD-53   Jeff Davis's Dream. "Air: *Lord Lovel.*" Published by H. De Marsan, Publisher, No. 54 Chatham Street, New York, NY. [1863?]. [6 3/4" × 9 3/4"]. B/w penny song sheet with litho border of caricatures of musicians, Black man and children, jesters. 2pp. Page 2: Blank.

JD-54   Jefferson Davis Grand March. m. William Herz. Published by J.H. Snow, No. 29 Daupin Street, Mobile, AL. 1861. B/w litho of Jefferson Davis. Two other versions indicated on the cover — **Galop** and **Quickstep**. 6pp.[?]. Page 2: Blank. [H-3578].

JD-55   Jeff In Petticoats. In: *Ballads & Songs Of The Civil War,* page 264. c. Jerry Silverman. Published by Mel Bay Publications, Inc., Pacific, MO. 63069. 1998. 276pp.

JD-56   Jeff Davis, Don't You Try To Howl Again. In: *Acme Songs for Grand Army of the Republic and Columbia's Loyal People, Young & Old,* page 12. Published by The Acme Publishing Bureau, J.C.O. Redington, General Manager, No. 35 University Avenue, Syracuse, NY. 1886. [5 1/16" × 6 3/4"]. Y/bk litho of flag, G.A.R. badge, geometric designs. 68pp.

JD-57(A)   His Soldiers To Jefferson D. m. "Air — *Widow Machree.*" In: *Beadle's Dime Knapsack Songster:*

JEFFERSON DAVIS (JD)

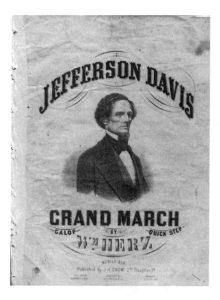

JD-54

Containing the Choicest Patriotic Songs, Together with many New and Original Ones, Set to Old Melodies, page 48. Published by Beadle and Company, No. 141 William Street, New York, NY. 1862. [3 3/4" × 5 3/4"]. Litho of coin—"One Dime, United States of America." 74pp.[?].

(B) **Jeff Davis' Dream**, page 10. m. "Air –*Lord Lovel*."

(C) **Jeff's Lament**, page 16. m. "Air –*The Dismal Swamp*."

JD-58 Jefferson D. a. James Bellak. Published by S.T. Gordon, No. 538 Broadway, New York, NY. 1862. Nonpictorial geometric designs. List of other titles in the series. "The String of Pearls, A Collection of Easy Arrangements for the Piano Forte."

JD-59 Jefferson D. w.m. William B. Justice. Published by S.T. Gordon, No. 538 Broadway, New York, NY. 1861. B/w geometric designs. 6pp. Pages 2 and 6: Blank.

JD-60 How Do You Like It Jefferson D?. In: *Trumpet Of Freedom*. Published by Oliver Ditson & Company, No. 277 Washington Street, Boston, MA. 1864. [6 1/2" × 9 3/4"]. Be/bk litho of Union soldier with trumpet. List of contents. 64pp.

JD-61 Oh Jeff! Oh Jeff! How Are You Now? (Comic Song and Chorus). w.m. Henry Schroeder. Published by Firth, Son & Co., No. 563 Broadway, New York, NY. 1865.

JD-62 Jeff Davis. m. "Air: *Nell Flaugherty's Drake*." Published by H. De Marsan, Publisher, No. 54 Chatham Street, New York, NY [ca. 1863]. [6 3/4" × 9 3/4"]. B/w penny song sheet with litho border of caricatures of musicians, Black man and children, jesters. 2pp.

JD-63 That's Just So! w. E.V. Anress. Published for the Union Soldiers by James D. Gay. [ca. 1864]. H/c lithos of Jefferson Davis, the Devil, Miss Columbia with flag. "Sung by E.V. Anress." 2pp. Page 2: Blank.

JD-64 Jeff Davis (Or, The King Of The Southern Dominions). m. "Air— *The King Of The Cannibal Islands*." In: *The Star Songster, Containing 48 Patriotic, Sentimental and Comic Songs*, page 26. Published by McMullen & Gates, No. 143 Walnut Street, Cincinnati, OH. [ca. 1865]. [3 5/8" × 5 7/8"]. R/w/b star, geometric design frame. 52pp.

JD-65 Les Confederes (Cantate). w. Joachim Duflos. m. D'Alfred Godard, Op. 14. English words by Madme ***. Published by Mr. Alfred Godard, Professor of Piano, No. 5 Rue N.D. de Grace, Paris, France. [1861-1865]. B/w photo of Jefferson Davis—"Estats Confederes Aide Toi Dieu T'Aidera." R/w/b crossed Confederate flags — Battle Flag and the Stars and Bars. Gd/bk floral designs. "A Son Excellence Jefferson Davis, President des Estats Confederes d'Amerique." "Hommage des Auteurs." "Vendue au profit des blesses de L'armee Confederee." "Nota: Cette Cantate deja executee (par ordre) par la Musique Military de la Confederation du Sud." 10pp.

See also AL-64; AL-202; AL-282; AL-295; AL-310; AJN-16; MISC-139.

James E. Carter

JEC-1 Hello Jimmy. w.m. Herman (Doc) Silvers. Published by [V-1: Herman (Doc) Silvers, No. 60 East 14th Street, New York, NY. 10003] [V-3: Passantino Printing Company, No. 311 West 43rd Street, New York, NY. 10036]. 1976. Bl/w photo of Jimmy Carter. [V-1 and V-3: R/w/b flag] [V-2: No flag]. [V-1 and V-3: "One Nation Under God." "1776—1976." "Pray that God will continue to guide our country through our leaders." "As played by Sussio Perrotta and His Orchestra"] [V-2 and V-3: No reference to Perrotta]. 4pp. Page 4: [V-1: Advertising for other Doc Silvers songs including *All the way with L.B.J.*, *Hubie Humphrey*, *Lets Go Lindsey*, and *The LBJ Waltz*] [V-3: Advertising for Passantino Printing Company and for this song as an advertising medium].

JEC-2 Jimmy Carter. w.m. Henry and Bobbie Shaffner. Published by B and H Publishing, One Montgomery Avenue, Bala Cynwyd, PA. 19004. Copyright 1976 and 1977. Br/w photo by Charles Rafshoon of Jimmy Carter. R/w/br drawing of musical instruments. "Inauguration January 20, 1977." 4pp. Page 2: "Based on the traditional song *Rally Round The Flag* original title (*Battle Cry of Freedom*), words and music by George F. Root." "Dedicated to the 39th President of the United States." Page 4: Narrative on "Songs for the President."

JEC-3 Jimmy Who? w.m. Belle Dowdall (The Bard of Buffalo). Published by Bards Music Publishers, Inc., No. 26 Music Square, Nashville, TN. 37203. [1976]. B/w photos of Jimmy Carter, The White House. 6pp.

JEC-4 President Jimmy Carter March. w. Andrea Fodor Litkei. m. Ervin Litkei. Published by Loena Music Publishing Company, No. 239 West 18th Street, New York, NY. 10011. 1977. [8 5/8" × 11"]. Bl/w photo of Jimmy Carter. R/w cover. 4pp.

JEC-5 Born Again (The Man From Plains, Georgia). w.m. Harry Simeone. Published by Shattinger-International Music Corporation, New York, NY. 1977. [V-1: 8 1/2" × 11"] [V-2 and 3: 6 3/4" × 10 1/2"]. Non-pictorial. [V-1: 8pp] [V-2 and V-3: 16pp]. [V-1: Page 2: Extra verses]. [V-2 and V-3: Pages 2, 15 and 16: Advertising]. [V-2: Page 3: "S.S.A. with Piano Accompaniment; Guitar, Bass and Drums Optional"] [V-3: Page 3: "S.A.T.B. with Piano Accompaniment, Guitar, Bass and Drums Optional"] [V-2: Pages 2, 15 and 16: Advertising].

JEC-6 President Jimmy Carter March (Jimmy, Steady On!). w. Andrea Litkei. m. Ervin Litkei. Published by Loena Music Publishing Company, New York, NY. 10011. Distributed by Hansen House, No. 1860 West Avenue, Miami Beach, FL. 33139. 1977. [8 1/2" × 10 7/8"]. Bl/bk drawing of Jimmy Carter. R/w/b flags. 8pp. Pages 2 and 8: Blank.

JEC-7 Plains, Georgia. w.m. Henry and Bobbie Shaffner. Copyright 1977 by Henry and Bobbie Shaffner.

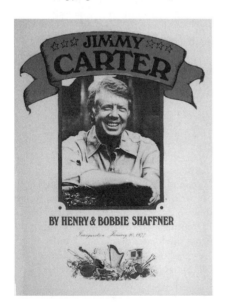

JEC-2

Non-pictorial. Lead sheet format. 4pp. Page 4: Counter stamp: "Keynote Associates, One Montgomery Avenue, Bala-Cynwyd, PA. 19004."

JEC-8 Amy Doesn't Live Here Anymore. w.m. Herman (DOC) Silvers. Published by Passantino Publishing Company, No. 311 West 43rd Street, New York, NY. 10036. 1977. Bl/w photo of Amy Carter. "Dedicated to the President and Mrs. Carter." "As played by Sossio Perrotta and the Senior Citizen's Orchestra." 4pp. Page 4: List of other "Doc" Silvers songs.

JEC-9 Carter For President (Of the U.S.A.). w.m. Ruben Katz and Martin Katz. Copyright 1976 by Eagle Rock Music Company. Background photo of Jimmy Carter. "Souvenir Copy." 2pp. Page 2: Blank.

JEC-10 President Jimmy Carter March. w. Andrea Fodor Litkei. m. Ervin Litkei. In: *A Tribute To The U.S.A.*, page 5. Published by Loena Music Publishing Company, No. 239 West 18th Street, New York, NY. 10011. Copyright 1985 and 1986. N/c drawing by Edward Moran of Statue of Liberty celebration in 1886 — "The Statue of Liberty, standing as an eternal symbol of the friendship of the people of France, was presented to the United States in 1886 by its creator, Frederick Bartholdi." Quotes by "Emma Lazarus (1883)," and "President Grover Cleveland (1886)."

JEC-12 Carter Can Count On Me. w.m. Bob Saffer. [8 1/2" 9 1/2"]. Copyright 1976 by Forward Music Publishing Company, No. 540 Madison Avenue, New York, NY. 10022. Raw-Ann Music Co. Non-pictorial. 2pp. Page 2: Blank.

JEC-11 Switch Off Something (S.O.S., S.O.S., S.O.S.). w. Philip R. Freeman. m. Dick Peters. Published by Philip R. Freeman and Associates, No. 77 Jack London Square, Oakland, CA. 1977. Bl/w cartoon drawing by Al Wiseman of Jimmy Carter switching off a light switch. 6pp. Page 2: Small b/w drawing of a barbershop quartet at top of music.

See also RR-5.

JOHN F. KENNEDY

JFK-1 John F. Kennedy. w.m. Alfred McDermott (Writer of *Wonderful Mother of Mine, Wonderful Daddy of Mine, Old Santa Fe*). Published by Alfred McDermott, Publisher, P.O. Box 601, Green Bay, WI. 1961. Non-pictorial black lines. 4pp. Page 2: "Dedicated to the Kennedys." Page 4: Another song by Alfred McDermott — *One Little Smile.*

JFK-2 John F. Kennedy. w.m. Angela Maria O'Toole. Published by Angela Maria O'Toole, Chicago, IL. 1964. B/w photo of John F. Kennedy. 4pp. Page 4: Blank.

JFK-3 There's A New Man In The White House. w.m. Sid Tepper and Roy C. Bennett. Published by Leeds Music Corporation, No. 322 West 48th Street, New York, NY. 1961. Non-pictorial. 4pp.

JFK-4 In The Summer Of His Years. w. Herbert Kretzmer. m. David Lee. Published by Leeds Music Corporation, No. 322 West 48th Street, New York, NY. 1963. B/w photo by Fabian Bachrach of John F. Kennedy. "Written for a BBC Television tribute to the late President John F. Kennedy." 4pp.

JFK-5 Why? w.m. Ida Young. Published by Intercollegiate Syndicate, Inc., No. 1650 Broadway, New York, NY. 1969. Bl/w non-pictorial geometric designs. "Dedicated to our wonderful President John Fitzgerald Kennedy." 4pp. Page 4: Bl/w photo of John F. Kennedy at White House desk.

JFK-6 The President Kennedy March. m. John T. Boudreau. Published by Bibo Music Publishers, Inc., No. 2444 Wilshire Boulevard, Santa Monica, CA. 1964. Bl/w photo of John Kennedy. R/w/b shield. "Dedicated to our late

(JFK) JOHN F. KENNEDY

President John F. Kennedy." "Piano Solo." 6pp. Page 2: Blank. Page 6: List of arrangements available.

JFK-7 Theme For Jacqueline. m. Russell Faith. Published by Debmar Publishing Company, Philadelphia, PA. Sole selling agent: Criterion Music Corporation, No. 1270 Sixth Avenue, New York 20, NY. 1961. Pk/ma drawing of Jacqueline Kennedy. "*Theme For Jacqueline* Recorded by Russell Faith on Chancellor Records." 4pp. Page 4: Blank.

JFK-8 America America. w.m. Frank Murman. Published by Airy Music Company, R.D. 4, Box 62, Mountain Top, PA. 18707. 1964. [6 1/8" × 9 5/16"]. Bl/w photo of "John Fitzgerald Kennedy." "In Memoriam." "As recorded by Frank Murman on Mur-E-Cord Records." 4pp. Page 4: Elegy by Sen. Mike Mansfield. Quote from John F. Kennedy's Inaugural speech.

JFK-9 The New Frontier. w.m. Doris Knoll. Published by Georgianna Music Publishers, No. 16004 Euclid Avenue, East Cleveland 12, OH. 1960. B/w photo by Fabian Bachrach of John F. Kennedy, facsimile signature. R/w/b flag, Capitol building. "Written & Dedicated for President John Fitzgerald Kennedy on Inaugural day, January 20, 1961." 6pp. Page 6: Advertising.

JFK-10 Profile In Courage. w. Paul Francis Webster. m. Allan Jay Friedman. Published by Webster Music Corporation, Suite 611, No. 1841 Broadway, New York, NY. Copyright 1965 by Paul Francis Webster and Allan Jay Friedman. Non-pictorial gd/bk cover, black line border. "From The ABC-TV Special *The Young Man From Boston* (A Musical Biography of John Fitzgerald Kennedy)." 4pp.

JFK-11 Ask Not. w.m. Baruch J. Cohon (ASCAP). Published by Valley Beth Israel, No. 13060 Roscoe Boulevard, Sun Valley, CA. Copyright 1963 by Baruch J. Cohon. B/w drawing of map of the eastern one-half of the United States. B/w photo of John F. Kennedy. "In memory of John F. Kennedy." 4pp.

JFK-12 Kennedy Memorial March. m. Maurice Briger. [9 1/2" × 12 1/2"]. [ca. 1964]. B/w printing of original manuscript. 8pp. Reverse of each page blank.

JFK-13 P.T. 109. w.m. Marijohn Wilkin and Fred Burch. Published by Cederwood Publishing Company, Inc., No. 815 16th Avenue South, Nashville, TN. Copyright 1961 and 1962. R/w/bk drawing of a P.T. boat. "Recorded by Jimmy Dean on Columbia Records." 4pp.

JFK-14 John Fitzgerald Kennedy. w. Morrie Allen. m. Leonard Whitcup. Published by Music Music Music, Inc., New York, NY. Sole Selling Agent: Cimino Publications, Inc., No. 479 Maple Avenue, Westbury, L.I., NY. Copyright 1966 and 1967. B/w photo "From the John F. Kennedy collection of Aubrey Mayhew" of John F. Kennedy. "Recorded by Jim Ameche on RCA Victor 47-9103." 4pp. Page 4: Advertising.

JFK-15 Five Men On A Mountain. w.m. Dorothy Copeland and Lou Herscher. Published by Accadia Music Company, Beverly Hills, CA. 1963. [6 13/16" × 9"]. Bl/w photo of Mt. Rushmore with John F. Kennedy added. 4pp. Page 4: John F. Kennedy quote.

JFK-16 Four Sad Days. w.m. Corlus Walker and Andrew Spalding. Published by Nordyke Songs and Music Publishers, No. 6000 Sunset Boulevard, Hollywood 28, CA. Copyright 1964 by Corlus Walker and Andrew Spalding. Bl/bk drawing of flag, hand with wreath. 4pp. + 2 page insert. Insert page contains extra verses by Corlus Walker and Andrew Spalding, R.R. #2, Centerville, IN.

JFK-17 Sing Along With Jack [Song Book]. w. Milton M. Schwartz. a. Danny Hurd. Published by Pocket Books, Inc., New York, NY. Copyright 1963 by Bonny Publishing Corporation. [9" × 11 7/8"]. R/w/bk drawing of sheet music "Vive La Dynasty," silhouette of John F. Kennedy in chair with conductor's baton, caricature of Kennedy family. "Hit Songs from the New Frontier." 36pp. Page 3: "Illustrations by David Gantz." Page 36: Drawing of John Kennedy in chair with baton. Song titles.

JFK-18 Special Delivery From Heaven. w. Barbara Jones. m. Hecky Krasnow. Published by Sam Fox Publishing Company, Inc., No. 1841 Broadway, New York 23, NY. 1963. Bl/w/y drawing of sun's rays, clouds. "Narrated by Kathy Dunn on Gallant Record, No. GT 3006." 4pp. Page 4: Narrative — "Special Delivery From Heaven." "Mimeographed copies of the poem dedicated to the memory of President Kennedy."

JFK-19 Kennedy Victory Song. w.m. Felix A. Nolasco. Published by Felix A. Nolasco, No. 1149 Fleley Avenue, Bronx 72, NY. 1960. Bl/w photo of John F. Kennedy, donkey. 4pp. Page 4: Blank.

JFK-20 J.F.K. March. m. Eugene Jelesnik. Published by Mills Music, Inc., No. 1619 Broadway, New York, NY. 1964. Bl/w photo band of marching in a "JFK" formation. 6pp. Page 2: "Introduced by the award winning Tooele High School band at the University of Utah stadium." Page 6: Advertising.

JFK-21 Remembrance (John Fitzgerald Kennedy). w. Fred Wirtz. m. William Steffe. Published by Fred Wirtz, West Bend, IA. 1964. Ma/w photo by Harris and Ewing of John F. Kennedy. 4pp. Page 4: Blank.

JFK-22 We'll Remember. w.m. Eve Golden. Copyright 1963 by Eve Golden. Distributed by the Santa Monica Democratic Women's Club, No. 510 Santa Monica Boulevard, Santa Monica, CA. B/w "Photo by the National Democratic Committee" of John F. Kennedy. "Written, published and donated in blessed memory of our beloved 35th President, John Fitzgerald Kennedy, to benefit the National Cultural Center in Washington, D.C." 4pp. Page 4: "We are forming a chain, down memory lane, with this little song, In memory of the President we loved, A crusader, brave and strong, So please buy some copies and send them to friends, who in turn will kindly see, that this chain never ends."

JFK-23 A Letter From Heaven. w.m. Anna Lee Batt. Published by Anna Lee Batt, Ft. Wayne, IN. [1969]. [8 1/2" × 11"]. Pk/w non-pictorial mimeograph. 2pp. Page 2: Blank.

JFK-24 Everyone's Gone To The Moon. w.m. Kenneth King. Published by Mainstay Music, Inc., No. 101 West 55th Street, New York, NY., as a special supplement in *The Miami Beach Sun*, July 13, 1969 edition. Copyright 1965 by Marquis Music, Ltd., London, England. Pl/o/bk/w photos of John F. Kennedy, Apollo Eleven crew, moon. "Apollo Eleven — No single project in this period will be more impressive to mankind, or more important for the long range exploration of space; and none will be so difficult or expensive to accomplish — President John F. Kennedy." 4pp. Page 4: Additional photos of Apollo crew.

JFK-25 John Fitzgerald Kennedy March. w. Andrea Litkei. m. Ervin Litkei. Published by Loena Music Publishing Company, No. 614 West 51st Street, New York 19, NY. 1964. B/w photo by Fabian Bachrach of John F. Kennedy. 4pp. Page 4: Geometric design.

JFK-26 Kennedy At Dallas. w. Isabelle S. Carter. m. James L. Carter, Jr. Published by J. Lowry Carter, No. 810 North Craige Street, Salisbury, NC. 1964. Bl/w photos of President John F. Kennedy and Jacqueline Kennedy, aerial view of Dallas. 4pp. Page 4: Blank.

JFK-27 Massachusetts Is Our Home. w.m. Lawrence John Stutto. Published by Clickbound Music Company, No. 165 Walnut Street, Chelsea, MA. 1964. Bl/w photos/drawings of "John Fitzgerald Kennedy — 35th President, Jan. 20, 1961," "John Adams — 2nd President, March 4, 1797," "John Quincy

(JFK) JOHN F. KENNEDY

Adams — 6th President, March 21, 1825," and "Calvin Coolidge — 36th President, Aug. 3, 1923." R/w/b drawings of flags, map of the State of Massachusetts. 4pp.

JFK-28 History Repeats Itself. w.m. Buddy Starcher. Published by Glaser Publications, No. 801 16th Avenue South, Nashville, TN. [8 1/2" × 11"]. Copyright 1965 and 1966. Pk/w/bk photo of Buddy Starcher. "Recorded by Buddy Starcher on Boone Records." 4pp. Page 4: B/w geometric designs.

JFK-29 Ask Not. w.m. Meredith Willson. Published by Frank Music Corporation, and Rinimer Corporation. Sole Selling Agents: Frank Distributing Corporation, No. 119 West 57th Street, New York, NY. 10019. 1964. Pk/w drawing of eagle, geometric designs. 12pp. Page 2: Blank. Page 12: Pl/w drawing of treble clef symbols.

JFK-30 Abraham, Martin And John. w.m. Dick Holler. Published by [V-1: Roznique Music Inc., 8th Floor, No. 17 West 60th Street, New York, NY] [V-2: The Goodman Group]. 1968. [V-1: B/w/r/bl] [V-2: Bl/bk] photo/drawing of Mt. Rushmore with busts of John F. Kennedy, Martin Luther King, Robert Kennedy and Abraham Lincoln. [V-2: "Exclusively distributed by Hal Leonard Publishing Corporation, 777 West Bluemound Rd., Milwaukee, WI"]. 6pp. Page 6: Cover photo.

JFK-31 Abraham, Martin And John. w.m. Dick Holler. Published by Roznique Music Inc., West 46th Street, Suite 1200, New York, NY. 10036. 1968. [V-1: 9" × 12"] [V-2: 7" × 10 1/2"]. B/w silhouette of man. [V-1: Quotes by John Kennedy — "Ask not what your country can do for you, Ask what you can do for your country," Martin Luther King — "I have a dream," and Abraham Lincoln — "Of the people, by the people, for the people"] [V-2: "AMLO Choral, The Authentic Record Sound!" "S.A.T.B. with optional Guitar, Bass and Drums"] [V-1: 6pp] [V-2: 8pp].

JFK-32 Sing Along With JFK. m. Hank Levine. Published by Holly-Vine Music Company. Sole Selling Agents: Criterion Music Corporation, No. 150 West 55th Street, New York, NY. 1963. R/w/b drawings of John F. Kennedy, rocking chair, eagle. "Official Version Words and Music as recorded on Reprise Records, R-6083."

JFK-33 Massachusetts My Home State (M-A-Double-S-A-C-H-U-S-E Double-T-S). w.m. John Redmond (ASCAP). Published by Novelty Music Company. Distributed by Wholesome Music Company. No. 315 State Street, Hackensack, NJ. 1958. [Edition 1960]. Bl/w photo of John F. Kennedy. Bl/w drawing of donkey. "With Special Kennedy Version." "Souvenir Copy: John F. Kennedy received the nomination for the Presidency of the United States at the 1960 Democratic National Convention held at Los Angeles, CA." 4pp. Page 4: "Extra Special Choruses...**Kennedy** (K-E-Double-N-E-D-Y)." Bl/w photo of Linda Bowe — "Recorded by Linda Bowe and the Neighborhood Kids. A 20th Century Fox Recording."

JFK-34 My Pony Macaroni. w. Ann Marsters. m. Bill Snyder. a. Mark Nevin. Published by B.F. Wood Music Company, Inc., New York 19, NY. 1963. Bl/bk/w drawing of The White House, pony. "Children's Edition." "Recorded by the Sandpipers, Jim Timmens and Orchestra on Little Golden Record #738." 6pp. Pages 2 and 6: Advertising for B.F. Wood publications.

JFK-35 John Kennedy. w.m. Sidney Faber. Published by Clarence Music Ltd., No. 50 New Bond Street, London, England. 1963. [8 9/16" × 10 7/8"]. R/w/bk drawing of hand, lighted torch. "Recorded by Danny Delmonte on Oriole Records." 4pp.

JFK-36 Walkin' Down To Washington. w.m. Dick Sanford and Sammy Mysels. Published by The Valiant Music Company, No. 1619 Broadway,

JOHN F. KENNEDY (JFK)

JFK-34

New York 19, NY. 1960. R/w photo of Mitch Miller — "Recorded by Mitch Miller on Columbia Records." "We Publish Tomorrow's Standards Today." 4pp. Page 2: "Official Democratic Party Campaign Song for 1960." "Campaign Adaptations by Redd Evans."

JFK-37 Theme From Profiles In Courage (The John F. Kennedy March). m. Nelson Riddle. Published by RSA Music Corp. Sole selling agent Marks Music Corp., No. 136 West 52nd Street, New York, NY. 10019. Copyright 1964 and 1966. B/w photo of John F. Kennedy. R/w/bk cover. "Based on the Concert Band Version by Nelson Riddle." "Arranged for Piano Solo." 4pp.

JFK-38 In The Summer Of His Years. w. Herbert Kretzmer. m. David Lee. Published by Leeds Music Corporation, No. 322 West 48th Street, New York 36, NY. 1963. Non-pictorial. "Written for a BBC Television tribute to the late President John Fitzgerald Kennedy." 4pp.

JFK-39 President Kennedy's Assassination. w.m. Midas Hudson. Published by Midas Hudson, No. 11665 Griggs, Detroit, MI. 48204. 1964. B/w photo of John F. Kennedy. 4pp.

JFK-40 What A Shame. w.m. Dolores Garilli. 1964. Br/w photos of John F. Kennedy and Delores Garilli. "Dedicated to our beloved President John F. Kennedy." 6pp. Pages 2 and 6: Blank.

JFK-41 Walkin' Down To Washington. w.m. Sammy Mysels and Dick Sanford (ASCAP). Published by [V-1 and V-2: The Committee for the Arts, Allen Rivkin, Director, Johnny Green, Musical Director]. Copyright 1960 by Redd Evans Music Company. [5 1/2" × 8 1/2"]. [V-1: R/be] [V-2: R/bk] [V-3: Be/bk] non-pictorial. "Official Democratic Party 1960 Song." [V-1: "The Los Angeles Memorial Coliseum, Edwin H, Knopf and John T. Boudreau, Co-Producers, Joseph Parker, Director." "Hang on to this, you'll be singing it tonight!"] [V-2: "The Committee for the Arts, Allen Rivkin, Director, Johnny Green, Musical Director, John T. Boudreau and His Democratic Brass Band; The Los Angeles Sports Arena, July 12"] [V-3: "Compliments of Thomas Caldarone, Jr., President, Young Democrats of Rhode Island, Leo T. Conners, Outing Committee Chairman, Nicholas DiPietro, Outing Committee Program Chairman"]. 2pp. Page 2: Blank.

JFK-42 Nation's Sorrow. m. George A. Rubisson, Op. 21, No. 9. Published by Presses du temps Present, Nos. 18-20 Rue Fg du Temple, Paris, France. Copyright 1963 by George A. Rubisson, 420 Riverside Drive, New York, NY. [9 1/2" × 12 3/4"]. Non-pictorial. "In Memoriam of John Fitzgerald Kennedy Whom the World Loved." 8pp. Page 3: "En Souvenir de John Fitzgerald Kennedy Les Nations En Deuil." Page 4 and 7: Blank. Page 8: Advertising.

JFK-43 J.F.K. Forever (Memory March). w.m. Vin Bolino. Published by Vin Publishers, P.O. Box 349, Lynn, MA. 1964. B/w photo of President John F. Kennedy. 4pp.

(JFK) JOHN F. KENNEDY

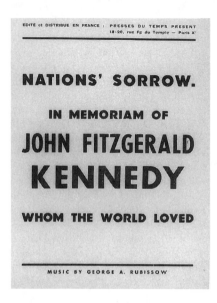

JFK-42

JFK-44 Buddy Mine. w.m. William Andrew Moore, M.D. (Lt. Col., U.S. Air Force Reserve, State Representative 54th District, Illinois). Copyright 1963 by Moore Music, Olney, IL. B/w drawing of rifle, helmet. "In Memoriam To the Memory of our Departed Buddies." "Dedicated to President John F. Kennedy." 4pp. Page 4: Narrative: "Nine reasons to vote for Dr. Wm. A. Moore, M.D. for re-election as State Representative for the 54th District."

JFK-45 The New Frontier. w.m. John Stewart. Published by California Music Press. Sole selling agent: Keys Popular Song Distributors, Inc., No. 128 West 58th Street, New York, NY. 1962. [8 1/2" × 10 15/16"]. Pl/w cover. Bl/w photo of The Kingston Trio. "Recorded by The Kingston Trio." "Capitol Records." 4pp.

JFK-46 President John Kennedy (March). m. Sister M. Rosalina Abejo, R.V.M. Copyright 1963 by Sister M. Rosalina Abejo, R.V.M. Br/be photo of John F. Kennedy. 6pp. Page 6: Blank.

JFK-47 Ask Not. w.m. Mother St. John of the Cross, OSU (An Ursaline Nun). Published by Mount Merici Development Program, Waterville, ME. 1964. B/w photo of John Kennedy. 4pp.

JFK-48 Let's All Sing With Hank [Song Sheet]. w.m. Hank Fort (ASCAP). Copyright 1960 by Gemini Music Company. [5 1/2" × 8 1/2"]. Non-pictorial. Two songs: **Lady Bird** and **Kennedy And Johnson**. 2pp.

JFK-49 The Last Words Of David. w.m. Joseph Freudenthal. Published by Transcontinental Music Publications, New York 19, NY. [ca. 1964]. Pl/w drawing of eternal flame. "In Memory of John F. Kennedy." "He who was chosen to lead — II Samuel 23: 1 to 5." 6pp. Page 2: Blank. Page 3: "Dedicated to John F. Kennedy." Page 6: Advertising.

JFK-50 Who Killed J.F.K., R.F.K., M.L.K., M.J.K? Published by Cutter Designs, Box 1465, Manchester, MA. as a post card. [3" × 5"]. Obv: N/c photo of Rush Harp in front of billboard featuring song title. Five bars of music below — "Not LHO; not JER; not SBS; not EMK not any way." Rev: Description of obverse of post card — "Researcher Rush Harp conducting his Bearsville

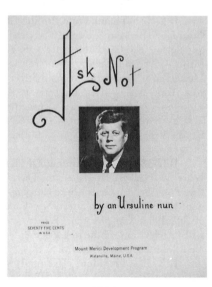

JFK-47

(NY) *Symphonie Conspiracie* in the Vale of Truth and Light along Rte. 28 near Woodstock (NY)."

JFK-51   John Fitzgerald Kennedy March. w. Andrea Litkei. m. Ervin Litkei. In: *The Bicentennial March and Presidential Marches of America*, page 26. Published by Loena Music Publishing Company, New York, NY. 1976. R/w/b drawings of George Washington, Thomas Jefferson, Abraham Lincoln, eagle and flags. "American Revolution Bicentennial, 1776-1976." "Officially Recognized Commorative." 40pp.

JFK-52   Theme From JFK. m. John Williams. Published by Warner Bros. Publications, Inc., No. 265 Secaucus Road, Secaucus, NJ. Copyright 1991 Warner-Tamberlane Publishing Corporation. B/w photos from the movie *JKF* including Kevin Costner, limo scene, Lee Harvey Oswald. "He's a District Attorney. He will risk his life, the lives of his family, everything he holds dear for the one thing he holds sacred...the truth." "Kevin Costner; an Oliver Stone film; *JKF*, The Story that won't go away." Film Credits. 4pp.

JFK-53   John Fitzgerald Kennedy March. w. Andrea Litkei. m. Ervin Litkei. In: *A Tribute To The U.S.A.*, page 12. Published by Loena Music Publishing Company, No. 239 West 18th Street, New York, NY. 10011. Copyright 1985 and 1986. N/c drawing by Edward Moran of the Statue of Liberty celebration in 1886 — "The Statue of Liberty, standing as an eternal symbol of the friendship of the people of France, was presented to the United States in 1886 by its creator, Frederick Bartholdi." Quotes by "Emma Lazarus (1883)," and "President Grover Cleveland (1886)."

JFK-54   New Frontiers. w.m. Bob Saffer and George Mysels. Copyright 1960 by Veronique Publishing Company, No. 250 West 57th Street, New York, NY. Non-pictorial "Professional Copy." 4pp.

JFK-55   Take Him, Earth, For Cherishing (Motet). m. Prudentius (348-413) a. Herbert Howells. Published by H.W. Gray Company, Inc. 1964. [7" × 10 3/8"]. Bl/w photo of the inside of a cathedral. "S.A.T.B. Unaccompanied." 24pp. Page 2: "To the Honoured Memory of John Fitzgerald Kennedy, President of the United States of America."

JFK-56   March Of The Eternal Flame. m. Dave Black. Published by the Alfred Publishing Company, P.O. Box 10003, Van Nuys, CA. 1994. Ma/bl/bk/w drawing of band instruments. "Alfred's Growing Band Series." Complete Band Set. Page 2: "Inspired, and dedicated to, the Memory of John F. Kennedy."

JFK-57   Elegy For J.F.K. (Mezzo Soprano Solo). w. W.H. Auden. m. Igor Stravinsky. Published by Boosey and Hawkes Music Publishers, Ltd., London, England. 1964. 8pp. Pages 2 and 7: Blank. Page 8: Advertising.

JFK-58   Elegy For A Young American. m. Ronald Lo Presti. Published by Theodore Presser Company, Bryn Mawr, PA. 19010. 1967. Non-pictorial. "Full Score." [John F. Kennedy]. 16pp.

JFK-59   J.F.K. In Memoriam (With Optional Narration). w.m. James Curnow. Published by Curnow Music Press, Inc., P.O. Box 142, Wilmore, KY. 40390. 1995. Y/w/bk cover with n/c photo of musical instruments. "Focus on Achievement." "Accolade Series, Grade 3." Parts set for Concert Band.

JFK-60   Abraham, Martin And John. w.m. Richard Holler. a. Anita Kerr. Copyright 1968, 1970 and 1984 by Regent Music Corporation. Non-pictorial. "Pop Choral Showcase." Publisher logos — "The Goodman Group," "Cherry Lane Music Company, Inc.," Jenson Publications, Inc." List of arrangements. Page 2: "S.S.A. Accompanied." 12pp.

JFK-61   Ask Not (JFK) (Anthem). w. Richard Engquist. m. Jack Gottlieb. Published by Theophilious

(JFK) JOHN F. KENNEDY

Music, Inc. Sole Agent: Boosey & Hawkes, Inc. 1991. [6 7/8" × 10 1/2"]. Non-pictorial. "Presidential Suite, Seven Pieces for Mixed Chorus (SATB) a cappella. 12pp. Page 2: "Presidential Suite is a celebration of America's priceless heritage of liberty. Inspired by the wisdom and whimsy of some of our most colorful presidents, it juxtaposes the eloquence of John F. Kennedy and Franklin Delano Roosevelt, with the journalistic pith of Theodore Roosevelt, Harry S Truman's blunt common sense, Abraham Lincoln's homespun wit and Thomas Jefferson's irony, plus a legendary quip from the taciturn Calvin Coolidge. This patriotic work combines idealism with light-heartedness, inspiration with a dash of salt..." Page 3: "For Neil Baudhuin."

JFK-62 Abraham, Martin And John. w.m. Dick Holler. a. Ed Lojeski. Published by [V-1: Roznique Music Inc., No. 1516 Broadway, New York, NY. Distributed by: West Coast Publications, Inc., No. 4423 West Jefferson Boulevard, Los Angeles, CA. 90016. 1968 and 1971. Bk/br/pk/w drawing of Mt. Rushmore with busts of John Kennedy, Martin Luther King, Robert Kennedy and Abraham Lincoln. "SATB For Mixed Chorus with Piano and Optional Percussion, Guitar and String Bass." 16pp.

JFK-63 Ask Not. w. Meredith Willson. a. Howard Cable. Published by Frank Music Affiliates. Sole Selling Agent: Frank Distributing Corp., 122 Boylston Street, Boston, MA. 02116. 1964. [6 7/8" × 10 1/2"]. Bl/w drawing of two eagles, stars. "For Narrator, Speaking Chorus, Four Part Chorus of Mixed Voices (SATB) with Band or Piano." 20pp. Page 2: "The refrain is a quotation from John F. Kennedy's Inaugural Address." Page 20: Logo.

JFK-64 A Dirge. w. Percy Bysshe Shelly. m. Joseph Roff. Published by Hal Leonard Music, Inc., No. 64 East 2nd Street, Winona, MN. 1967. [6 3/4" × 10 7/8"]. R/w/bk non-pictorial geometric design cover. "Hal Leonard Choral Library, Select Series." "Octavo No. R3-101." "S.A.T.B." 6pp. Page 2: "In Memory of the Late President John Fitzgerald Kennedy." "Composed on Nov. 22, 1963."

JFK-65 Little John (Folk Song). w.m. Ellen Anderson. a. George Hunt. Published by Hoffman Press Publications, Wichita 3, KS. 1965. Bl/w drawing by Arthur P. Freeman entitled "A last salute to John F. Kennedy, John F. Kennedy, Jr." of John F. Kennedy and John John Kennedy. "A touching tribute to our late President John F. Kennedy, this song will become American folk lore and through the years will find its rightful place in the heritage of our great land." 4pp. Page 2: "For Treble Voices."

JFK-66 Abraham, Martin And John. w.m. Dick Holler. a. Matt Dennis. Published by Roznique Music Inc., No. 165 West 46th Street, New York, NY. 10036. Copyright 1968 and 1971. [8 1/2" × 11"]. Be/bk drawing of Mt. Rushmore with busts of John F. Kennedy, Martin Luther King, Robert Kennedy and Abraham Lincoln. "Big Note Easy Piano." 4pp.

JFK-67 John Fitzgerald Kennedy March. w.m. Andrea and Ervin Litkei. In: *The President's March and Other Songs of the Lone Star State*, page 4. Published by Loena Music Publishing Company, No. 239 West 18th Street, New York, NY. 10011. [ca. 1964]. R/w/bl/bk cover, Presidential seal. "Featuring *President Lyndon Baines Johnson March* and other songs of the Lone Star State." "Pacific Popular Music Books." 36pp. Page 2: Photos of Lyndon Johnson and A. Litkei. Page 35: Photo of Inaugural parade. Page 36: Photo of Lyndon Johnson. Drawings of all presidents.

JFK-68 Says Kennedy. w.m. Benjamin F. Solis. Published by Nordyke Songs N Music, Hollywood 28, CA. 1963. B/w drawing of President and Mrs. Kennedy and other people walking. 4pp.

JFK-69 Abraham, Martin And John. w.m. Dick Holler. Published by Screen Gems-Columbia Publications, A Division of Columbia Pictures Industries, Inc., No. 6744 N.E. 4th Avenue, Miami, FL. Copyright 1968 and 1972 by Roznique Music Inc., New York, NY. [8 12/2" × 11"]. Pk/br drawings of John Kennedy, Abraham Lincoln and Martin Luther King, piano keyboard. "Bradley Easy Piano Series." 4pp. Page 4: Blank.

JFK-70 Rally Round The Flag (Melody with In The Summer of His Years). a. Milt Okum, Michael Kobluk and William C. Mitchell. w. Herbert Kretzmer. m. David Lee. "*Rally Round the Flag* is a song from the Lincoln years, sung to rally the nation after the assassination. We first sang it after November 22, 1963, when another popular President had been assassinated. In *The Summer Of His Years* came from that special *This Was The Week That Was* program on BBC television after Kennedy's Death..." In: *The Mitchell Trio Song Book*, page 112. Published by Quadrangle Books, Inc., No. 180 North Wacker, Chicago, IL. 50505. 1964. R/w/b drawings of the members of The Chad Mitchell Trio. 146pp.

JFK-71 The Jackie Look. w. Felice Bryant and Boudleaux Bryant. Copyright 1961 by Acuff-Rose Publications, No. 2510 Franklin Road, Nashville, TN. [6" × 9"]. Non-pictorial. "BMI" logo. 4pp.

JFK-72 Armed Forces Song Folio. Published by The Adjutant General of the Department of the Army. September, 1963. [7 3/4" × 10 3/4"]. B/w/pl drawing of John F. Kennedy sitting in a rocking chair. "Special *Mr. President* Issue." 24pp. Page 23: "The Adjutant General of the Department of the Army, wishes to express appreciation to Mr. Irving Berlin for his permission to reproduce the songs contained in this special *Mr. President* issue." Page 24: B/w eagle — "E Pluribus Unum."

JFK-73 The Inaugural Ball Waltz. w. Gloria Ferry Davis. m. Hilda Emery Davis. Published by Empress Music, Inc., No. 119 West 57th Street, New York, NY. 1961. Bl/w photo of Meyer Davis. "Introduced by Meyer Davis and His Orchestra at the Inaugural Ball, 1961." 6pp. Page 6: Bl/w treble clef symbol.

JFK-74 Now The Trumpet Summons Us Again. w. "From the Inaugural Address of John F. Kennedy." m. Daniel Pinkham. Published by C.F. Peters Corporation, No. 373 Park Avenue South, New York, NY. 1965. Bk/gn non-pictorial geometric designs. "Pinkham." "Edition Peters." "High Voice and Piano." 6pp. Page 6: Advertising.

JFK-75 New Frontiers. w.m. Bob Saffer and George Mysels. Selling Agent: Hansen Publications, Inc., No. 119 West 57th Street, New York, NY. Copyright 1960 by Veronique Publishing Company, No. 250 West 57th Street, New York, NY. R/w/b drawing of the Statue of Liberty. 4pp. Page 4: Veronique logo.

JFK-76 Sing Along With Jack [Song Sheet]. w. Milton M. Schwartz. [1963]. [8 1/2" × 11"]. Non-pictorial. 2pp. Page 2: "These lyrics are reproduced from the book *Sing Along With Jack* with permission of Bonny Publishing Corporation."

JFK-77 Badge Of Courage. w. "Based on the inspirational words of President Kennedy when he bestowed the Green Beret on the U.S. Special Forces troops." Published by Music Music Music, Inc., New York, NY. [ca. 196-]. "For S.A.T.B. and Vocal."

JFK-78 Abraham, Martin And John. w.m. Dick Holler. A. John Brimhall. Published by Charles Hansen, Distributor, Educational Sheet Music & Books, No. 1860 Broadway, New York, NY. 10023. Copyright 1968 by Roznique Music Inc., New York, NY. [8 1/2" × 11"]. R/w/b/gn/pl/y drawing of two children,

(JGB) JAMES G. BLAINE

one dressed as Abraham Lincoln. "Brimhall Piano Series." 4pp.

JFK-79 Battle Hymn Of The 60's. w. William Matheson, Union Label Department, International Ladies' Garment Worker's Union. [ca. 1963]. [6 1/4" × 6 5/8"]. B/w photo of John F. Kennedy. "Dedicated to the memory of John F. Kennedy." 2pp. Page 2: Blank.

JFK-80 Ask What You Can Do For Your Country. w.m. Earle F. Olin. Published by Etcetera Music Company, No. 12315 Rye Street, North Hollywood, CA. 1964. Bl/w non-pictorial geometric designs. 4pp.

JFK-81 The Ballad Of John Kennedy. w. Mai O'Higgins. m. Tommy Dando. Published by One Four Two Music Co., Ltd., No. 142 Charing Cross Road, London, W.C.2., England. Sole selling agents: Southern Music Publishing Co., Ltd., 8 Denmark Street, London, W.C.2., England. 1961. [8 15/16" × 11"]. Gn/w non-pictorial. "Featured & Recorded by Peter Tomelty on Fontana Records." 4pp. Page 4: Blank.

JFK-82 Abraham, Martin And John. wm. Dick Holler. In: *Fife 'N' Drums*, page 2. Published by Hal Leonard Publishing Corp., Winona, MN 55987. 1976. [8 1/2" × 11"]. R/w/b litho of Colonial fife and drummers pattern. List of titles. 48pp. Page 3: "Sounder Music Notation copyright 1973 by Hammond Organ Company, Division of Hammond Corporation."

JFK-83 Kennedy & Johnson. w.m. Loyd E. Roberson. Copyright August, 1960, by Pratt Publishing Co., No. 1234 North 5th Street, Abilene, TX. Bl/bl photos of "Sen. John F. Kennedy — "Democratic Nominee for President of The United States of America" and Sen. Lyndon B. Johnson Democratic Nominee for Vice-President of The United States of America" R/w/b printing. 4pp. Page 2: Letter to reader on the nominees. Page 4: R/w/b American flag.

JFK-84 Abraham, Martin &

John. w.m. Dick Holler. In: *The All-American Patriotic Song Book*, page 6. Published by Creative Concepts Publishing Corp., No. 154 El Roblar Drive, Box 848, Ojai, CA. 93023. R/w/b flag design. "Complete Sheet Music Edition." 100pp.

See also TJ-49; AL-346; TR-343; CC-53; FDR-367; HST-22; LBJ-1; MISC-93; MISC-110.

JAMES G. BLAINE

JGB-1 James G. Blaine Grand March. m. G.A. Henry. Published by M.D. Swisher, No. 123 South 10th Street, Philadelphia, PA. 1884. B/w litho by Thomas Hunter of likeness of James G. Blaine on banner hanging from a horn, White House, Capitol building. 6pp. Pages 2 and 6: Blank.

JGB-2 Our Plumed Knight Leads The Way. w. George Cooper. m. Harrison Millard. Published by R.A. Saalfield, No. 12 Bible House, Opposite Cooper Union, New York, NY. Copyright 1884 Harrison Millard. B/w litho of James G. Blaine, facsimile signature, black striped border. 4pp. Page 4: Advertising for Sohmer's Piano Store.

JGB-3 The Blaine Grand March. m. Sidney Ryan. Published by John Church & Company, Cincinnati, OH. 1884. B/w litho of James G. Blaine. 6pp. Page 2: Blank. Page 6: Advertising for other John Church & Company published music.

JGB-4 Blaine's Grand March. m. H. Wagner. Published by [V-1 and V-2: No publisher indicated] [V-3: Callender, McAuslan and Troup, Nos. 209 and 211 Westminister Street, Providence, RI.]. Copyright 1884 by R.AA. Saalfield. B/w litho of James G. Blaine, facsimile signature, geometric designs, black line frame. "To Hon. James G. Blaine." 6pp. Page 2: Blank. Pages 1 and 6: [V-1: Advertising for "R.H. Macy & Company, 14th Street, Sixth Avenue and 13th Street. We call special attention to our Muslin Underwear for ladies, misses and children. It is all of our own manufacture, and we unhesitatingly say that for variety of design and quality of work it cannot be approached by any other house. Our prices are below all competition. Large assortment of hand embroidered French underwear, our own direct importation, at very attractive prices"] [V-2: Advertising for Adam Meldrum and Anderson Dry Goods, Buffalo, NY].

JGB-5 Blaine's Triumphal March. m. Gus. B. Brigham. Published by National Music Company, Chicago, IL. Copyright 1884 and 1892. B/w litho of James G. Blaine, facsimile signature. 6pp. Page 6: Advertising for other National Music songs.

JGB-6 James G. Blaine's Victory March. m. E. Mack. Published by S.T. Gordon & Son, No. 13 East 14th Street, New York, NY. 1884. B/w litho of James G. Blaine. "For Piano." 6pp. Page 2: Blank. Page 6: Advertising for S.T. Gordon song book.

JGB-7 The Dawning Grows To Morn. m. H.E. Peterson. Published by Richard A. Saalfield, No. 12 Bible House, New York, NY. 1884. B/w litho of James G. Blaine, geometric design border. "Rousing Republican Campaign Song." "To Hon. G. Hilton Scrioner [sic]." 6pp. Page 2: "Respectfully dedicated to Hon. G. Hilton Scribner." Page 6: Advertising for Sohmer & Company pianos.

JGB-8 James G. Blaine's Grand March. m. E.G. Nicklaus. Published by J.M. Hoffmann & Company, No. 537 Smithfield Street, Philadelphia, PA. 1884. B/w litho of James G. Blaine. "To the Hon. James G. Blaine." 6pp. Pages 1 and 6: Blank. Loose advertising insert for other J.M. Hoffmann music.

JGB-9 Dinna Ye Hear The Slogan (Campaign Song and Chorus). w. Mrs. D. McFalls. m. W.F. Studds. Published by Mrs. D. McFalls, Gouverneur, NY. 1884. B/w litho by Thomas Hunter of James G. Blaine, axes, eagle, leaves, geometric designs. "A Wide Awake Blaine and Logan Song and Chorus." 6pp. Page 6: Blank.

JGB-10 Blaine's Victory March. m. August Heinrich. Published by George D. Newhall Company, No. 56 West 4th Street Cincinnati, OH. 1884. B/w litho of James Blaine, leaves, geometric designs. 6pp. Pages 2 and 6: Blank.

JGB-11 James G. Blaine Funeral March. m. George Schleiffarth. Published by National Music Company, Nos. 215 to 221 Wabash Avenue, Chicago, IL. 1893. B/w litho of James G. Blaine, facsimile signature, black border. 6pp. Page 6: Advertising for other publications.

JGB-12 Blaine's Grand March. m. W. Rab. Published by Oliver Ditson & Company, No. 451 Washington Street, Boston, MA. 1884. B/w litho by J.H. Bufford's Sons of James G. Blaine. "To the Hon. James G. Blaine." 6pp. Pages 2 and 6: Blank.

JGB-13 Our Good And Glorious Blaine. w. Miss Annie R. Springer. m. C. Raymond. Published by Lee & Walker, No. 1113 Chestnut Street, Philadelphia, PA. 1884. B/w litho of James G. Blaine. Advertising for other Blaine and Logan music. 6pp. Page 2: Blank. Page 6: Advertising.

JGB-14 Jas. G. Blaine's Grand March. m. M.F. Mullin. Published by William Rohlfing & Company, Milwaukee, WI. Copyright 1884 by W.F. Shaw. B/w gray tinted litho by Hofstetter Brothers of James G. Blaine, facsimile signature. "Respectfully Dedicated to the Republican Candidate." 8pp. Pages 2 and 7: Blank. Page 8: Advertising.

JGB-15(A) Hurrah For Blaine & Logan! w.m. Collin Coe. Published by [V-1: S. Brainard's Sons, Cleveland, OH] [V-2: Published by Lee & Walker, No. 1113 Chestnut Street, Philadelphia, PA.]. 1884. B/w litho by W.J. Morgan & Company of James G. Blaine. "Blaine and Logan Republican Campaign Songs." 6pp. Pages 2 and 6: Blank.

(B) **Blaine & Victory.** w.m. G.A.R. 6pp. Pages 2 and 6: Blank.
(C) **Wake, O Republicans, Wake!** m. Reed.
(D) **Hold The Fort For Blaine & Logan.** w. Mary E. Kail. m. P.P. Bliss. 6pp. Pages 2 and 6: Blank.
(E) **Blaine For Our President!** w. Mary E. Kail. m. George F. Root. 6pp. Pages 2 and 6: Blank.
(F) **The Plumed Knight** (Rallying Song). w. Charles Eastman. m. George F. Root. 6pp.
(G) **Rally For The Leader!** w.m.[?] Herrick.
(H) **The Peoples Choice.** w. Collin Coe. m. George F. Root.
(I) **Blaine's Our Banner Man!** m. Rogers.
(J) **Give Blaine And Logan Three Times Three.** w. Rev. Erasmus W. Jones (Hamilton, NY). m. G. Elmer Jones. 6pp. Page 2 and 6: Blank.

JGB-16 James G. Blaine Campaign March. m. Adam Geibel. Published by Thomas P.I. Magoun, Bath, ME. Copyright 1884 by B.F. Banes. B/w litho by Thomas Hunter of parade, banner with picture of James G. Blaine. 6pp. Pages 2 and 6: Blank.

JGB-17 Hon. Jas. G. Blaine's Grand March. m. A.H. Rosewig. Published by Lee & Walker, No. 1113 Chestnut Street, Philadelphia, PA. 1884. B/w litho of James G. Blaine. 8[?]pp. Page 2: Blank.

JGB-18 James G. Blaine's Presidential March. m. M.S. Fredericks. Published by T.B. Harms & Company, No. 819 Broadway, New York, NY. 1884. B/w litho of James G. Blaine. "Dedicated to the Next President." 6pp. Page 2: Blank. Page 6: Advertising.

JGB-19 Blaine's March. m. Irvin J. Heffleu. Copyright 1884 by T.A. Bacher. B/w litho of James G. Blaine. "To Honorable Jas. G. Blaine." 6pp. Page 2: Blank. Page 6: Advertising.

JGB-20 The Rally! (Song for the Blaine Campaign). w.m. Grace Appleton. a. D. King. Published by Wm. A. Pond & Company, No. 25 Union Square, New York, NY. Copyright 1884 by Grace Appleton. Non-pictorial. 6pp. Page 2: Extra verses. Page 6: Blank.

JGB-21 Blaine And Logan Victory March. m. James J. Freeman, Op. 1309. Published by R.A. Saalfield, New York, NY. 1884. B/w lithos of James Blaine and John Logan, facsimile signatures. "To the Republican Candidates." Advertising for "R.H. Macy & Company, 14th Street, Sixth Avenue and 13th Street. We call special attention to our Muslin Underwear for ladies, misses and children. It is all of our own manufacture, and we unhesitatingly say that for variety of design and quality of work it cannot be approached by any other house. Our prices are below all competition. Large assortment of hand embroidered French underwear, our own direct importation, at very attractive prices"] 6pp. Page 2: Blank. Page 3: Title—**Blaine And Logan's Grand Triumphal March**. Page 6: Advertising.

JGB-22 Logan's Gathering. w.m. James G. Clark. Published by C.M. Tremaine, No. 481 Broadway, New York, NY. [1868-]. B/w litho of John A. Logan in uniform. "To Genl. John A. Logan (Commander of the G.A. of R.)." Page 2: Blank.

JGB-23 The Veteran's Last Song (Solo and Chorus). w. Chaplain John Hogarth Lozier. m. Horace Lozier. Published by the Lozier Brothers, Publishers, Mt. Vernon, IA. 1890. Gn/w litho of John A. Logan. "Solo and Chorus for the Home and Loved Ones of the Union Veteran; For Camp Fires, Soldier's Funerals, and Memorial Services." "The Farewell Sentiment of Gen'l. John A. Logan, to Whose Memory it is Dedicated." 6pp. Page 2: Narrative: "General Logan, Father of Memorial Day." Page 6: Advertising.

JGB-24 General Logan's Grand March. w.m. Adam Geibel. Published by

Oliver Ditson & Company, No. 451 Washington Street, Boston, MA. 1884. B/w litho by J.H. Bufford's Sons of John A. Logan. 6pp. Pages 1 and 6: Blank.

JGB-25 The Veteran's Last Song (Solo and Chorus). w. John Hogarth Lozier (Chaplain, First National Encampment G.A.R.). a. Horace Lozier. Published by the Lozier Brothers, Publishers, Mt. Vernon, IA. 1890. Br/w litho of John A. Logan, facsimile signature. "To the Memory of Gen. John A. Logan." "Solo and Chorus for the Home and Loved Ones of the Union Veteran, For Camp Fires, Soldier's Funerals, and Memorial Services." 6pp. Page 2: "Gen. Logan, Father of Memorial Day." Page 6: Advertising.

JGB-26 The Men Of The West (Song and Chorus). w. Edward Willett. m. B.A. Whaples. Published by Belock & Company, No. 110 William Street, New York, NY. 1863. B/w litho of vines and banner—"A New Song." "To Major Genl. John A. Logan." "For The Piano." History of speech "Men of the West"— "In a speech delivered in Illinois by Hon. John A. Logan, when about to take the field as Colonel of the Thirty First Regiment of Volunteers from Illinois, that distinguished patriot and soldier used the characteristic expression that 'The Men of the West' would hew their way to the Gulf, with their swords." 6pp. Pages 2 and 6: Blank.

JGB-27 Only The Old Flag (A Song). w. Mrs. W.W. Case. m. Hattie S. Case. Published by Henry White, No. 935 "F" Street NW., Washington, DC. Copyright 1892 by Hattie S. Case. B/w drawing of flag, eagle, shield, military equipment in the shape of the song title. "Dedicated to Mrs. John A. Logan." 6pp. Page 6: Blank.

JGB-28 The People's Plumed Knight (Republican Campaign Song and Chorus). w. Rev. J.T. Oxtoby. m. H.B. Roney. Copyright 1884 by W.F. Shaw. B/w litho by Hofstetter Bros. of James G. Blaine and John A. Logan. "Respectfully dedicated to the People's Candidates, James G. Blaine and John A. Logan." 6pp. Page 5: "Arrangement for Male Quartett." "As Sung by Roney's Blaine and Logan Glee Club, East Saginaw, Mich." Page 6: Blank. [M-233].

JGB-29 Blaine And Logan Campaign Songster. Published by John Church & Company, Cincinnati, OH. 1884. [4 7/8" × 5 13/16"]. Y/bk non-pictorial geometric design border. "Including Biographical Sketches & Constitution for Campaign Clubs." 52pp. Page 2: Biographies. Page 51 and 52: Blank. [M-233?].

JGB-30 His Name Is Jas. G. Blaine (Republican Campaign Song and Chorus). w. Adele M. Carragues. m. H.B. Roney. Published by White, Smith & Company, Boston, MA. 1884. Non-pictorial geometric design border. "Dedicated to the Republicans of the United States." Advertising for campaign song *Hurrah for Blaine and Logan* by E.H. Bailey. 6pp. Pages 2 and 6: Blank.

JGB-31 Blaine-Blaine-Blaine Of Maine (A Campaign Marching Song). w.m. George Ray. Published by John Church & Company, No. 66 West Fourth Street, Cincinnati, OH. 1884. Non-pictorial geometric designs. 6pp. Pages 2 and 6: Blank.

JGB-32 Blaine And Logan Campaign Song-Book. e. Prof. F. Widdows. Published by The Republican National Committee, New York, NY. 1884. [4 3/8" × 5 11/16"]. [V-1: Bk/y] [V-2: Pk/bk] litho of James G. Blaine and John A. Logan. "From the School—House to the Cabinet, From the Cabin to the Senate." 52pp. Pages 49 and 50: Biographies. Page 51: Index. Page 52: Electoral vote for 1884. [M-251].

JGB-33 Blaine From Maine (Song and Chorus). w.m. Malcolm S. Gordon. Published by John Church & Company, No. 66 West 4th Street, Cincinnati, OH. 1884. Non-pictorial geometric designs. 6pp. Pages 2 and 6: Blank.

JGB-34 The Plumed Knight (Blaine and Logan Campaign Song). w. Lieutenant B.F. Fort. m. Alfred W. Sweet. Published by Alfred M. Church, No. 290 Broad Street, Providence, RI. 1884. [5 7/16" × 8 3/4"]. Be/bk non-pictorial cover. "Dedicated to the Grand Lodge Plumed Knights of Providence, R.I., Fred I. Marcy, Grand Chancellor Commander, I.L. Goff, Colonel Commanding." 2pp. Page 2: Song.

JGB-35 Blaine And Logan Songster. Published by Thomas Hunter, Philadelphia, PA. 1884. [5 1/2" × 7 1/4"]. N/c litho of Abraham Lincoln and James Garfield — "Our Martyred Presidents." Br/w litho of James G. Blaine — "Our Next President," and John A. Logan — "Our Next Vice-President," George Washington, Ulysses S. Grant. 68pp. Page 4: Litho of James G. Blaine and John A. Logan. Pages, 64–66: Biographies. page 68: Same as Page one. [M-237].

JGB-36 Cleveland's Farewell (Song). w.m. J.A. Adams. Published by John Church & Company, No. 66 West 4th Street, Cincinnati, OH. 1884. Non-pictorial. "As Sung by the Great Campaign Singer, J.A. Adams." "Oh! Patriots True and Boys in Blue, Farewell Farewell, A Last Adieu, I now must bid Good Bye of you, Farewell Farewell, A Last Adieu, You Fought for Country, Truth and Right and I opposed with all my Might, and now I must crawl out of Sight, Farewell Farewell, A Last Adieu." 6pp. Pages 2 and 6: Blank.

JGB-37 We'll Follow Where The White Plume Waves. w. Edward M. Tabor. m. John Philip Sousa. Published by John F. Ellis & Company, No. 937 Pennsylvania Avenue, Washington, DC. 1884. Non-pictorial. 6pp. Pages 2 and 6: Blank.

JGB-38 Dinna Ye Hear The S'Logan? (Song and Chorus). w.m. R.A. Dical. Published by Root & Cady, No. 67 Washington Street, Chicago, IL. 1866. Non-pictorial geometric design border. "As Sung by the Lumbards." "Dedicated to Gen. John A. Logan." 6pp. Pages 2 and 6: Advertising.

JGB-39 The White Plume March. m. John Philip Sousa. Published by John F. Ellis, No. 937 Pennsylvania Avenue, Washington, DC. 1884. Non-pictorial. "Introducing the Popular Campaign *Song We'll Follow Where The White Plume Waves*." "To the Republican nominees for President and Vice-President."

JGB-40 Blaine's Grand March. m. H. Wheeler. Published by D.O. Evans, No. 108 West Federal Street, Youngstown, OH. 1884. B/w litho by Thomas Hunter of James G. Blaine, flags. "Respectfully Dedicated to the Young Men's Blaine and Logan Club, Youngstown, Ohio." "For Piano or Organ." 6pp. Pages 2 and 6: Blank.

JGB-41 Beulah's Blaine And Logan Original Campaign Song Book 1884. Printed and Published by Birnie Paper Company, Springfield, MA. 1884. [4" × 5 3/4"]. Gy/bk litho of James G. Blaine and John A. Logan, eagle, flags, shield, line border. 36pp. [M-232].

JGB-42 The Plumed Knight Of Maine (Campaign Chorus for Blaine and Logan 1884). w. J.A.M. Harned (303 Montgomery St., San Francisco, Cal.). m. Walter K. Wheeler (946 Mission St., San Francisco, Cal.). "Printed by Pacific Press, printers and Electrotypers, Oakland and San Francisco." Copyright 1884 by Walter K. Wheeler. Bl/w litho of James Blaine. R/w/b eagle, geometric designs. "For sale at Manvais Music Store, 749 Market St., San Francisco, CA." "Single copies, 25 cents. Ten copies, $1.50. One hundred or more copies at Board of Trade rates." 4pp. "Arranged for Male Voices." "In all large assemblies a cornet should lead the voices."

JGB-43 The Chief We Have Chosen (Song and Chorus). w.m. George Morley. Copyright 1884 by B.F.

Banes. B/w litho by Thomas Hunter of James G. Blaine, eagle and axes. 6pp. Pages 2 and 6: Blank.

JGB-44(A) Blaine And Logan (Song And Chorus). w. Henry Armstrong. m. Henry Harding. Published by John Church & Company, Cincinnati, OH. 1884. B/w litho by Moss Engraving Company of James G. Blaine and John A. Logan. "Republican Campaign Music." "Music is an important element in all Presidential Campaigns." List of other songs in series. Advertising for other Blaine campaign music. 6pp.

(B) A Voice From Garfield's Home. w.m. Westendorf.

(C) Blaine Grand March. m. Ryan.

(D) Blaine From Maine. w.m. Gordon.

(E) Blaine, Blaine, Blaine Of Maine. w.m. Ray.

(F) No Section Lines. w.m. Geo. Root.

(G) Tis Blaine And Logan Now. w.m. Westendorf.

(H) The Nation Loves Its Soldiers Still. w.m. Westendorf.

(I) With Blaine And Jack We'll Clear The Track. w.m. Richardson.

JGB-45 The People's Songs For Blaine & Logan (And the Republican Principles of Good Government). c. "By a comrade of the Grand Army of the Republic." Published by Acme Publishing Bureau, J.C.O. Redington, General Manager, No. 252 Broadway, New York, NY. Copyright 1884 by J.C.O. Redington. [4 7/8" × 6 5/8"]. B/w litho of James G. Blaine. "Adopted by the General Republican Committees in New York City and elsewhere." "Adapted for every Voice in the Glorious Land of Freedom. All the Nation may Sing." "Come, join that Columbia's blessings increase, All Singing for Liberty, Glory and Peace." "Acme Songs." 32pp. Page 32: B/w litho of John A. Logan. [M-246].

JGB-46 James G. Blaine Grand March. m. Jean de Ruver. Published by Knake & Company, Pittsburgh, PA. 1884. B/w litho by Armor Litho. Company of James G. Blaine. 6pp. Page 6: Blank.

JGB-47 The Plumed Knight Songster. Published by The McLaughlin Brothers, New York, NY. 1884. Litho of James G. Blaine, knight's helmet, sword, plume. "Blaine — Logan."

JGB-48(A) Blaine And Logan Grand March. m. Josef Strebinger. Published by Wm. A. Pond & Company, No. 25 Union Square, New York, NY. 1884. B/w litho by Mayer, Merkel and Ottmann of James G. Blaine, John A. Logan, dogwood blossoms. "Republican Nomination." 6pp. Pages 2 and 6: Blank.

(B) Blaine & Logan Are Our Choice (Campaign Song and Chorus for Male Voices). w. W.H. DeShon. m. G. Elmer Jones (Author of *Jim Garfield At The Front, Give Hayes And Wheeler 3 Times Three, &c.*). 6pp. Page 3: "Respectfully Dedicated to the Republican Candidates for President and Vice-President."

JGB-49 James G. Blaine Grand

JGB-44

Patrol March. m. S. Markstein. Published by Willis Woodward & Company, Nos. 842 and 844 Broadway, New York, NY. 1884. R/w/b small silhouettes of children's heads, floral and geometric designs. "Played by the 7th Regiment Band with Great Success." 8pp. Page 8: Advertising.

JGB-50 Republican Campaign Songs. Published by the Bath Republican Glee Club, Bath, ME. 1888. [3 1/3" × 7 1/2"]. B/w litho of eagle. "To James G. Blaine." 4pp. [Foldout].

JGB-51 To Vict'ry He'll Gallantly Lead Us (Song and Chorus). w.m. Ralph Summers. Published by M.D. Swisher, No. 123 South 10th Street, Philadelphia, PA. 1884. B/w litho of James G. Blaine, Miss Liberty with wreath and horn, eagle. 6pp.

JGB-52 Logan Waltz. m. Eduard Holst. Published by Charles W. Held, Brooklyn, NY. 1893. N/c lithos of John A. Logan, Ulysses S. Grant, Winfield Scott Hancock, Sheridan, Sherman and Farragut. "Our American Heroes." "Six Easy Pieces for Piano."

JGB-53 Our Bold Jim Blaine (Campaign Song). w. Sam Booth. m. L. von der Mehden. Copyright 1884 by J.P. Beals. Non-pictorial r/w geometric design border. "The Best Campaign Song Out." 6pp. Pages 2 and 6: Blank.

JGB-54 Jim And John (A Blaine and Logan Campaign Song). w. Derrick Dodd. m. "Air: *Son of a Gambolier.*" 1884. B/w litho by H.S. Crocker & Company of James G. Blaine and John A. Logan, eagle, flags, wreath. "Dedicated to the Blaine & Logan Invincibles." 4pp. Page 4: Blank.

JGB-55 Beneath The Dear Old Flag Again (Song and Chorus). w.m. Thomas P. Westendorf. Copyright 1884 by W.F. Shaw. B/w litho by Hofstetter Brothers of James G. Blaine and John A. Logan. "Dedicated to Blaine and Logan — The People's Choice." 6pp. Page 2: Blank. Page 6: Advertising.

JGB-56 What Would My

JGB-54

Grand-Father Think? (Song and Chorus). w.m. Thomas P. Culier. Copyright 1884 B.F. Banes. B/w litho by Thomas Hunter of James G. Blaine, flags. 6pp. Pages 2 and 6: Blank.

JGB-57 Blaine Club March. m. Michael Brand. Published by Ilsen & Company, Nos. 25 and 27 West Sixth Street, Cincinnati, OH. 1897. B/w litho of James G. Blaine. R/w drawings of flags, wreaths, logo — "Vim — Vigor — Victory, Cincinnati," "Y.M.B.C." "Dedicated to the Young Men's Blaine Club." 6pp. Pages 2 and 6: Blank.

JGB-58(A) Blaine Of Maine And Victory (Campaign Song). w. Dexter E. Chamberlin. m. J. P. Weston. Published by Oliver Ditson & Company, No. 451 Washington Street, Boston, MA. 1884. B/w litho by Bufford of James G. Blaine. "To the Hon. James G. Blaine." 6pp. Pages 2 and 6: Blank.

(B) **Blaine's Grand March.**

JGB-59(A) Blaine's Grand March. m. Stephe. S. Bonbright. Published by the Allen Brothers, No. 30 Arcade, Cincinnati, OH. Copyright 1884 by Stephe. S. Bonbright. B/w litho by Forbriger & Company of James G. Blaine, geometric designs.

(B) **Hurrah For Logan** (Song and Chorus). w.m. Stephe. S. Bonbright, Op. 82 (Author of *Blaine's Grand March, We'll All Vote For Blaine, &c., &c*). 4pp. Page 2: "Grand Campaign Song." Page 4: Blank.

(C) **We'll All Vote For Blaine** (Song and Chorus) m. Stephe S. Bonbright.

JGB-60 The Plumed Knights Waltzes. m. Henry Marsh, Op. 47. Published by Model Music Store, No. 735 Market Street, San Francisco, CA. Copyright 1884 by Henry Marsh. R/W non-pictorial cover. "To Blaine and Logan, Our Plumed Knights." 6pp. Page 6: Blank.

JGB-61 A Voice From Garfield's Home (Song and Chorus). w.m. T.P. Westendorf. Published by John Church & Company, Cincinnati, OH. 1884. B/w facsimile letter from Mrs. Garfield — "Cleveland, O., June 7th — Hon. J.G. Blaine, Our household joins in our great thanksgiving. From the quiet of our home we sent on most earnest wish that, through the turbulent months to follow and, in the day of victory, you may be guarded and kept. Lucretia P. Garfield." "To James G. Blaine." 6pp. Page 6: Advertising.

JGB-62 Blaine's Grand March. m. G.R. Lampard, Op. 61. Published by S. Brainard's Sons, Cleveland, OH. 1884. B/w litho of James G. Blaine, geometric designs. "To Hon. James G. Blaine." 8pp. Pages 2, 7 and 8: Blank.

JGB-63 Memorial Day. w. Jennings. m. Will H. Horsfall. Published by The Smith and Jennings Publishing Company, No. 61 Fairfield Avenue, Bridgeport, CT. 1896. Photo of "Maj. Gen. John A. Logan, Founder of Memorial Day." Drawings of flags, star. "A Fitting Tribute to Our Noble Dead — Wm. E. Disbrow, Past Department Commander, Dept. Conn., G.A.R." "As Sung with Great Success by T.L. Bartholomew, Past Com'd. Elias Howe, Jr. Post No. 3, Dept Conn., G.A.R." Numerous testimonials to the song.

JGB-64 General John A. Logan's Grand March. m. Jennie G. Smith. Published by Carl Hoffman, Leavenworth, [KS]. Copyright 1890 by The John Church Company. Bl/bk/w non-pictorial geometric designs. "For Piano." 6pp. Page 6: B/w litho of "Chickering Hall" in New York City. Advertising.

JGB-65 Facts & Songs For The People. Published by C.E. Bolton, Cleveland, OH. 1884. [5" × 7 1/8"]. R/w/bl drawing of Miss Liberty, flag, scroll — "Vox populi, Vox Dei, 1884." 54pp. Pages 2 and 53: Advertising. Page 3: B/w photo of "Hon. James G. Blaine." Page 4: Photo of "Gen. John A. Logan." Page 5: Title — **Facts & Songs for the People prepared specially for use in the Blaine and Logan Campaign**. [M-239].

JGB-66 The Plumed Knight And Black Eagle (Campaign Song). w. "From *The Cincinnati Commercial*." m.a. F.O. Lio. Published by Knuzenknabe & Sons, No. 1307 North Third Street, Harrisburg, PA. Copyright 1884 by W.F. Shaw. B/w litho by Hofstetter Bros. of James G. Blaine and John A. Logan. "Dedicated to the Republican Nominees." 6pp. Page 2: Blank. Page 6: Adv.

JGB-67 P.T. Schultz & Co's Blaine And Logan Bugle Call. Published by P.T. Schultz & Company, No. 172 Race Street, Cincinnati, OH. 1881. [1884 Edition]. [5 7/8" × 7 5/8"]. Bk/gn litho of James G. Blaine and John A. Logan, flags and eagle, geometric design border. 36pp. Page 36: Advertising. [M-245].

JGB-68 The Bonny Free Flag. w.m. Maj. W.C. Carroll. a. Professor B.A. Whaples. Published by Endres & Compton, No. 52 Fourth Street, St. Louis, MO. 1864. Bk/bl tinted litho of "Maj. Gen. Jno. A. Logan," U.S. flags, cannons, battle scene — "Fort Hill, Vicksburg."

(JGB) JAMES G. BLAINE

JGB-66

Dedicated to Maj. Genl. Jno. A. Logan by a member of his staff." 6pp.

JGB-69 Wait. w. H.E. Gordon. m. No tune indicated. Copyright by H.E. Gordon, Philadelphia, PA. [1884]. [3" × 4 1/2"]. Obv: Br/w drawing of John A. Logan. Rev: Song.

JGB-70 Hurrah For Jimmy Blaine! m. "Air: *Marching Through Georgia.*" [1884]. [2 5/8" × 3"]. Obv: B/w litho by Bufford of John A. "Logan." Rev: Song.

JGB-71 Hurrah! For Blaine Of Maine (Campaign Song and Chorus). w. A.W. Austin. m. L.H. Plogsted. Published by August Rottenbach, 499 Main Street, Buffalo, NY. 1884. Non-pictorial geometric designs. 4pp. Page 4: Blank.

JGB-72 Jim Blaine's Spirit. w. W.O. Fuller, Jr. (La Cygne, Kansas). m. "Tune: *John Brown's Body.*" [3 5/16" × 8 9/16"]. [1884]. Non-pictorial. "Compliments of Kansas City Republicans, who are unanimous for Blaine and Protection." 2pp. Page 2: Blank.

JGB-73 James G. Blaine's Grand Triumphal March. m. E.A. Phelps. Published by The Chicago Music Company, No. 152 State Street, Chicago, IL. 1884. B/w litho of plumes, scroll, geometric designs. "The Plumed Knight." 6pp. Page 6: Blank.

JGB-74 On To Victory. w.m. Julian Jordan. Published by J. Van-Loan & Company, No. 21 East 14th Street, New York, NY. Copyright 1884 by George Molineux. B/w geometric designs. "The Campaign Song." "To the Republican Candidates James G. Blaine of Maine and John A. Logan of Illinois." "As sung by The Republican Glee Club, New York, Julian Jordan and Harold Knox, 1st Tenors; John Van Loan, 2nd Tenor; David Mallory, 1st Bass; S.P. Meigs, 2nd Bass." 6pp. Page 2: Blank. Page 6: Advertising.

JGB-75 Blaine Of Maine (Campaign Song and Male Chorus). [5 7/8" × 9 1/4"]. 1884. Non-pictorial bl/w mimeograph. 2pp. Page 2: Blank.

JGB-76 The Tattoo Is Ended. w.m. Dion De Marbelle. Published by F.S. Chandler Company, Nos. 244-246 Wells Street, Chicago, IL. 1895. Br/w photo of John A. Logan. "In Memory of General John A. Logan, Patriot, Statesman and the Soldier's Friend." 6pp. Page 6: Advertising.

JGB-77 Ma, Ma, Where's My Pa (Up in the White House, Dear!). m. H.R. Monroe. Published by National Music Company, Chicago, IL. [1884]. Non-pictorial. 6pp. Pages 2 and 6: Blank. [Anti-Cleveland].

JGB-78 The Blaine And Logan Collection Of Campaign Songs. Published by J.M. Fernald and W.G. Haskell, Lewiston, ME. 1884. [V-1: Pk/bk] [V-2: Gn/bk] litho of James G. Blaine and John A. Logan. "Have it in your pocket when you go to the Rallies." "All Set to Familiar Tunes." 44pp. [M-235].

JGB-79 Campaign Songs For The Use Of Blaine & Logan Glee Clubs. c. W.D. Pratt. Published by W.D. Pratt, Logansport, IN. 1884. Litho of James G. Blaine and John A. Logan. 20pp. [M-241].

JGB-80 Campaign Songs As Sung By The Blaine & Logan Glee Club Of Logansport, Indiana. Published in Logansport, IN. 1884. Gn/bk litho of James G. Blaine and John A. Logan. 24pp. [M-242].

JGB-81 Champion Blaine And Logan Songster. Published by Republican Music Company, Springfield, IN. 1884. Pk/bk non-pictorial. "These songs can mainly be sung by either mixed or male quartet or chorus. Each piece is properly marked for changeable parts — alto or first base [sic]." 28pp. [M-243].

JGB-82 Campaign Songs For 1884. w.m. John S. Ellis. Published by John S. Ellis, Fostoria, OH. 1884. 4pp. [M-244].

JGB-83 Republican Pocket Monitor And Campaign Song Book. Published by F.S. and C.B. Bartram, New York, NY. 1884. Litho of James G. Blaine. 44[?]pp. [M-248].

JGB-84 Blaine And Logan Campaign Songster. w.m. James Buchanan Siders. Published by American News Company, New York, NY. 1884. "With Biographical Sketches of the Candidates and a Blank Form of Constitution for Campaign Clubs." 32[?]pp. [M-249].

JGB-85 The "Jolly Jubilee" Blaine And Logan Campaign Songster. w.m. William Dennis Stocking. Published by William Dennis Stocking, San Jose, CA. 1884. Be/bk litho of James G. Blaine and John A. Logan. 22pp. "The Author has adapted these songs to familiar and popular airs, for campaign purposes, to avoid the necessity of rehearsing or learning new ones, should the public not have the time or inclination to do so." [M-250].

JGB-86 Blaine And Logan Songster. Published by Arnold Brothers, Canal Dover, OH. 1884. "With Sketches of the Candidates." 16pp. [M-234].

JGB-87 Blaine Of Maine And Logan The Brave. w.m. Jos. Weed. Published by Lee & Walker, No. 1113 Chestnut Street, Philadelphia, PA. 1884.

JGB-88 We'll Vote For Blaine, The Man From Maine (Song). w.m. Thos. O'Neill. Published by Lee & Walker, No. 1113 Chestnut Street, Philadelphia, PA. 1884.

JGB-89 Blaine And Logan Song Book. Published by S. Brainard's Sons, Cleveland, OH. 1884. Gy/r/bl non-pictorial. 56pp. Page 3: "A Collection of Republican Campaign Songs, National Songs, Rallying Songs, &c. Adapted to the Popular Melodies of the Day. Including Marching Through Georgia, Battle Cry of Freedom, Tramp, Tramp, Kingdom Coming, &c." [M-236].

JGB-90 Blaine And Logan Songster. Published by American News Company, New York, NY. 1884. Litho of James G. Blaine and John A. Logan. 76pp. [M-238].

JGB-91 Plumed Knight Campaign Songster, 1884. Published and for sale by C.W. Nevin & Company, Printers, San Francisco, CA. 1884. O/bk non-pictorial. 36pp. Page 2: List of officers of the Plumed Knights of California. [M-240].

JGB-92 The Blaine And Logan Loyal Wreath. c. Hiram E. Peterson. Published by R.A. Saalfield, New York, NY. 1884. 48[?]pp. [M-247].

JGB-93 Honl. James G. Blaine's Quick March To The White House. m. Steven H. Jenko. Published by John F. Ellis & Company, No. 937 Penna. Avenue, Washington, DC. 1884. Non-pictorial geometric designs. 6pp. Page 6: Blank.

JGB-94 James G. Blaine. In: *G.A.R. And Other Popular Songs.* [13 3/4" × 11 1/4"]. [1884]. B/w litho of eagle, flags scroll inscribed "As Sung By Johnny Fitzgerald, Old Fort, Ohio." "Price 10c." 8 pages folded over. 15 tunes.

JGB-95 Logan's Grand March. m. Jno. Mack. Published by White, Smith & Co., Chicago, IL. 1885. B/w litho of John A. Logan, geometric design

(JGS) JOHN G. SCHMITZ

border. "Respectfully Dedicated to Gen. John A. Logan." 6pp. Page 2: Blank. Page 6: Advertising.

JGB-96 The White Plume March. m. John Philip Sousa. In: *The Sousa March Folio*, page 43. Published by The John Church Company, Cincinnati, OH. 1902. B/w litho of John Philip Sousa, geometric and floral designs.

JGB-97 Three Million Marched Out To Save Our Land. "3,335,951 patriots voluntarily left home, family and peaceful pursuits, to defend the flag of our Union. Of these nearly 500,000 perished—Gen. Logan's address May 31, 1886, at the tomb of Gen. Grant." In: *Acme Songs for Grand Army of the Republic and Columbia's Loyal People, Young & Old*, page 47. Published by The Acme Publishing Bureau, J.C.O. Redington, General Manager, No. 35 University Avenue, Syracuse, NY. 1886. [5 1/16" × 6 3/4"]. Y/bk litho of flag, G.A.R. badge, geometric designs. 68pp.

JGB-98 Arlington Funeral March. m. Comrade Henry Fried. Published by John F. Ellis, No. 306 Pennsylvania Avenue, Washington, DC. 1870. B/w litho of column, doves, cross, floral designs. "Written Expressly for the Exercises at National Cemetery Decoration Day, May 30th, 1870 by Comrade Henry Fried." "Respectfully Dedicated to Hon. John A. Logan, Commander in Chief G.A.R." 6pp. Pages 2 and 6: Blank.

JGB-99 James G. Blaine's Grand Victory March. m. Chas. D. Blake. Published by White, Smith & Co., Boston, MA. 1884. B/w litho of James G. Blaine. Advertisement on back cover for C.D. Blake compositions as published by White, Smith & Co.

See also GW-134; USG-34; USG-174; SJT-7; WSH-30; GC-70;GC-134; WM-31; WM-63; WM-189; TR-314.

JOHN G. SCHMITZ

JGS-1 Stand Up For Schmitz. w.m. Joseph Erdelyi, Jr. (March 28, 1968, U.S.A.). Copyright 1968 by Erdelyi Music Publishing Company, Room 600, No. 1697 Broadway, New York, NY. 10019. [1972 Edition]. Y/bk Non-pictorial. Old dedication and text related to George and Lurleen Wallace crossed out—"Name of *John G. Schmitz* substituted for that of George C. Wallace. Schmitz is the American Party candidate for the Presidency of the U.S., Nominated at the American Party Convention in Louisville, Kentucky, August 4, 1972 Campaign Song. For technical reasons, the American Party is known as the Courage Party in New York State." "Dedicated to the Memory of Governor Lurleen Wallace." Advertising. 2pp. Page 2: Blank.

JGS-2 Stand Up For Schmitz And Anderson. w.m. Joseph Erdelyi, Jr. (March 28, 1968, U.S.A.). Copyright 1968 by Erdelyi Music Publishing Company, Room 600, No. 1697 Broadway, New York, NY. 10019. [1972 edition]. Gn/bk non-pictorial. Old dedication and text related to George Wallace crossed out. "Dedicated to the memory of Governor Lurleen Wallace." "Campaign Song for *John G. Schmitz*, Presidential Candidate and *Tom Anderson*, Vice Presidential Candidate of the American Party U.S.A.—Nationwide (In NY State it is called The Courage Party)." Advertising. 2pp. Page 2: Blank.

JGS-3 S-C-H-M-I-T-Z For President. w.m. Joseph Erdelyi, Jr. (August 30, 1972, U.S.A.). Copyright 1972 by Erdelyi Music Publishing Company, Room 600, No. 1697 Broadway, New York, NY. 10019. [8 1/2" × 11"]. Y/bk non-pictorial. "Campaign Song for John G. Schmitz, 1972 American Party Candidate for the Presidency of the United States." "Dedicated to Tom Anderson, 1972 American Party Candidate for the Vice Presidency of the United States." Advertising. 2pp. Page 2: Blank.

JGS-4 S-C-H-M-I-T-Z For

President. w. (In Hungarian) Joseph Erdelyi, Jr., (Songwriter, August 30, 1972, U.S.A.). m. (Hungarian Dance Melody) Joseph Erdelyi, Jr. Published by Erdelyi Music Publishing Company, No. 1697 Broadway, Suite 600, New York, NY. 10019. 1972. [8 1/2" × 11"]. B/w Photo of Joseph Erdelyi, Jr. "Campaign Song for John G. Schmitz, 1972 American Party Candidate for the Presidency of the United States, Dedicated to his running mate, Tom Anderson." Advertising. "For melody, see attached English version" [Probably came together with JGS-3]. [V-1: In Hungarian] [V-2: In English]. 2pp. Page 2: Blank.

JGS-5 Let John Do It. w.m. Joseph Erdelyi, Jr. (July 28, 1968, U.S.A.). Copyright 1968 by Erdelyi Music Publishing Company, Room 600, No. 1697 Broadway, New York, NY. 10019. [1972 Edition]. [8 1/2" × 11"]. Pk/bk Non-pictorial. "Dedicated to the seven children of John and Mary Schmitz." Old dedication and text related to George Wallace crossed out — "Name of *John G. Schmitz* substituted for that of George C. Wallace. Schmitz is American Party Candidate for the Presidency of the U.S. Nominated at the American Party Convention in Louisville, Kentucky, August 4, 1972 — Campaign Song." "For technical reasons, the American Party in New York State is known as the Courage Party." Advertising. 2pp. Page 2: Blank.

JAMES K. POLK

JKP-1 La Polka (or The Way the World is Dancing) (Comic Song). w.m. Peter Morris. Published by A. Foit, No. 196 Chesnut Street, Philadelphia, PA. 1846. Non-pictorial. "Written, Sung & Dedicated to his Philadelphia Friends by Peter Morris." 4pp. Pages 1 and 4: Blank. Page 3: One verse about James K. Polk.

JKP-2 The Coon Exterminator Or Polk And Dallas Songster. Published by *The Democratic Choir*, No. 15 North 6th Street, Philadelphia, PA. 1844. [3 1/4" × 4 1/2"]. Non-pictorial black border. "Adapted by *The Democratic Choir* of Philadelphia and by all the Democratic associations throughout the United States." Page 3: Litho of upside down raccoon — "That same old koon." [M-027].

JKP-3 President's Grand March. m. Ferd. Wagner. Published by Andre & Company, No. 447 Broadway, New York, NY. 1848. "Composed and most Respectfully Dedicated to the President of the United States." 4pp. Page 4: Blank.

JKP-4 Oh, Coony, Coony Clay (A Favorite Democratic Song and Chorus). Published by Atwill, No. 201 Broadway, New York, NY. [1844]. Non-pictorial. "As sung with Unbounded Applause, by the President and members, of the Empire Club." 4pp. Pages 1 and 4: Blank.

JKP-5 The Polka. Published by A. Donally, New York, NY. 1844. B/w litho of politicians talking and dancing *The Polka*, including Andrew Jackson, Martin Van Buren, James K. Polk, Henry Clay, George Dallas, Theodore Frelinghuysen, Lewis Cass, and John Tyler. "A New National Dance Adopted by the Democratic Convention at Baltimore, May 29th, 1844." 2pp. Page 2: Blank.

JKP-6 Governor Polk's Quick Step. a. Samuel Carusi. Published by the Author [Samuel Carusi], Baltimore, MD. 1844. Non-pictorial. "Arranged from a Celebrated Polish Air, and Respectfully Dedicated to The Hon. James K. Polk." "Copy Right." 4[?]pp.

JKP-7 Monterey Waltz. m. J.M. (Professor U.S. Navy). Published by Osbourn's Music Saloon, No. 112 South 3rd Street, Philadelphia, PA. 1846. Non-pictorial. "Composed and Respectfully Dedicated to Mrs. J.K. Polk." 4pp. Page 2: Inside title — **Monterey Grand Waltz**.

JKP-8 Govr. Polk's March & Quick Step. m. F.A. Wagler. Published

(JKP) JAMES K. POLK

JKP-8

by George Willig, Junr., Baltimore [MD] and for sale by Wm. Fischer, Washington City, D.C." 1844. Non-pictorial. "Respectfully Dedicated to the People of the United States." 4pp. Page 1: Blank. Page 4: *Texas Quick March.*

JKP-9 The United States March No. 2 (And A Familiar Quick Step). m. J.E. Jungmann. Published by J.E. Gould, Chesnut Street, Philadelphia, PA. 1845. Non-pictorial. "Composed, Arranged and Respectfully Dedicated to His Excellency, the President of the United States." 4pp. Pages 1 and 4: Blank.

JKP-10 Polk & Dallas Songster. Published by Turner & Fisher, New York, NY. [1844]. Litho of "James K. Polk" within wreath. 32pp. [M-030].

JKP-11 An Original Ode. m. Air: *Auld Lang Syne*. Printed by Dutton & Wentworth, Printers, Transcript Office, Boston, MA. 1845. [5 5/16" × 8"]. B/w blue tinted Non-pictorial geometric design border. "To be Sung at the Inaugural Ball, at Faneuil Hall, March 4, 1845, In the singing of which the whole company are requested to join." "Ode to be sung after *Love Not*." 2pp. Page 2: Blank.

JKP-12 The Democratic Songster. Published by Turner & Fisher, New York, NY. [1844]. Litho of "James K. Polk" within wreath. [M-028].

JKP-13 The Democratic Lute and Polk and Dallas Minstrel. e. John Hickey. Published by H.B. Pierson, Philadelphia, PA. 1844. "Comprising a Great Number of Patriotic, Sentimental, & Comic Political Songs and Duetts [sic], Entirely Original." 36pp. [M-029].

JKP-14 The Polk And Dallas Songster. Published by Andrus, Woodruff & Gauntlett, Ithaca, NY. 1844. "A Collection of Democratic Melodies for Glee Clubs." 8pp. [M-031].

JKP-15 The Polk Songster. Published by Charles D. Hineline, Printer, New Albany, IN? 1844. "Dedicated to the Democratic Association of the Western States, Containing a Choice Selection of Democratic Songs." 32pp. [M-032].

JKP-16 The Western Democratic Melodist. Published by D.M. Dewey, Rochester, NY. 1844. [M-033].

JKP-17 The Young Hickory, and Annexation Minstrel (or Polk and Dallas Minstrel). Published by James M. Davis, Philadelphia, PA. 1844. 32pp. [M-034].

JKP-18 President James K. Polk's Grand March & Quick Step. m. John F. Goneke. Published by G. Willig, No. 171 Chesnut Street, Philadelphia, PA. 1844. Non-pictorial. "Composed and Arranged for the Piano Forte." 2pp.

JKP-19 President James K. Polk's Grand March & Quick Step. m. John F. Goneke. In: *Marches Of The Presidents, 1789-1909, Authentic Marches & Campaign Songs*, page 28. A. Carl Miller. Published by Chappell & Co., Inc., No. 609 Fifth Avenue, New York, NY. "By arrangement with Chilmark Press, Inc." 1968. [9" × 12"]. R/w/b litho of eagle, flag. "An Illustrated Piano Folio For All Ages." 72pp.

See also HC-47; HC-55; HC-115; LC-3; WHT-23; WW-19; FDR-158; DDE-9; LBJ-1; MISC-167.

Joshua Levering

JL-1 Not By My Vote. w.m. Charles M. Fillmore. In: *Fillmore's Prohibition Songs*, page 75. "These four words will answer all arguments on this question — Not By My Vote. If they say to us: Men will have it. We can answer: Not By My Vote. If another say men will sell it. Again we reply, Not By My Vote. I am not bound to abolish the saloon, but only my interest in it. My vote may not hurt the saloon, but I am bound to vote it right all the same. Saloons may go on, like the brook forever. Men may die in them like flies and hell grow fat on drunkards. Girls may be betrayed and boys baited hellward. Faith may be weakened and character dismantled. Homes may be destroyed and women and children beggared. Soldier's Homes may still sell drinks to the old veterans, and Army canteens debauch the young ones. Our national Capitol may have a saloon at either end. Senators and Representatives may be drunk on the floors of Congress, But Not By My Vote." — Hale [Johnson]." Published by Fillmore Brothers Company, No. 421 Elm Street, Cincinnati, OH. 1903. 230pp.

JL-2 Liberty Chimes. e. Will H. Keil. Published by Will H. Keil, Publisher, Senecaville, OH. 1896. Be/bk non-pictorial. 72pp. [M-364].

James M. Cox

JMC-1 League Of Nations (The American Marseillaise) (Song). w.m. George S. Barlow. Published by George S. Barlow, No. 245 East 25th Street, New York, NY. 1920. B/w drawings of "James Middleton Cox For President" and "Franklin Delano Roosevelt — For Vice-President," woman wrapped in U.S. flag, flags from League of Nations' countries — "Allied in Freedom's Cause," dove flying with banner inscribed "Humanity, Peace, Prosperity," eagle. "The Great Campaign Song of Pep, Punch and Slogan Chorus." "Endorsed by the Democratic National Committee." 4pp. Page 2: "Dedicated to the Democratic Party and the Independent Leaguer." "Our Leader has Pledged his Life to Fight for the Triumph of the Right." Page 4: "Campaign Edition: A Song of Endless Chorus."

JMC-2 The Tie That Binds (or Jimmy Is the Man for Us). w.m. Roy L. Burtch (Composer of *We Want a Man Like You, Indiana's Home Rule Song*). Published by Halcyon Publishing Company, Indianapolis, IN. [5 1/2" × 8 1/2"]. 1920. B/w photos of James M. Cox, White House. "Democratic Campaign March Song." 4pp. Page 2: "Copies of this song can be had from all Democratic State Committees." Page 4: Narrative — "Governor Cox's Record of Legislation."

JMC-3 Campaign Circus. w. A.J. Kiser. m. Edouard Hesselberg. Published by A.J. Kiser, Colorado Springs, CO. 1920. B/w drawing by A.J. Kiser of tent inscribed "Campaign Circus-Main Entrance" with James M. Cox riding donkey, small tent inscribed "Side Show" with Warren G. Harding feeding "Peanut

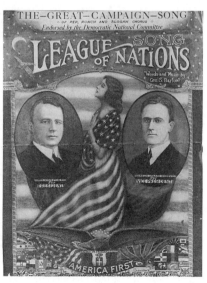

JMC-1

JMC-2

Politics" to an elephant. Warren G. Harding on house porch in background. 6pp. Page 6: "1920 Democratic Campaign Songs" by Kiser: *Jimmy Cox Will Win The Day, Gov'nr. Cox You'll Surely Do, They Can Never Say, I Told You So, A Full Dinner Pail Was Once Their Cry, 38 Senators, We 38 Senators Must Win The Day, Campaign Circus, Give the Devil His Dues, Peace By Resolution,* and *Who Wrecked The League of Nations.*

JMC-4 Gimmie Jimmie Cox (Democratic Campaign Songs). w.m. Inez (Windy) Wilson. Published by Inez (Windy) Wilson, Jenkins, KY. 1920. B/w photo of James M. Cox. Br/w horseshoe, shamrock. 4pp. Page 4: Blank.

JMC-5 Jimmie Cox Will Win The Day. w. A.J. Kiser. m. Edouard Hesselberg. Published by A.J. Kiser, Colorado Springs, CO. 1920. B/w drawing by A.D. Brown of James M. Cox. 6pp. Page 2: Blank. Page 6: "1920 Democratic Campaign Songs" by Kiser including *Jimmy Cox Will Win The Day, Gov'nr. Cox You'll Surely Do, They Can Never Say, I Told You So, A Full Dinner Pail Was Once Their Cry, 38 Senators, We 38 Senators Must Win The Day, Campaign Circus, Give the Devil His Dues, Peace By Resolution,* and *Who Wrecked The League of Nations.*

JMC-6 The League Triumphant. w. Felix Lake. m. Ella Zimmerman. "Issued by the Democratic National Campaign Committee." Copyright 1920 by Felix Lake, No. 2800 Wisconsin Avenue, Washington, DC. Bk/r/w/bl drawing of woman at lectern, soldiers, olive branch. 4pp. Page 4: Advertising.

JMC-7 Rally Democrats (One Step) (Song). w. C.H. Chapman. m. N. Donetelli. Published by Donetelli & Chapman, No. 1457 Dana Street, Los Angeles, CA. 1920. [8 3/4" × 11 7/8"]. Ma/w drawing of convention hall — "Introduced at the Democratic National Convention." 6pp. Pages 2 and 6: Blank.

JMC-8 Democracy (Campaign Song). w.m. Edward P. Favor (Writer of *Jingles, Valley of Visions, &c*). Copyright 1920 by Edward P. Favor, Richmond, ME. Non-pictorial manuscript. 4pp. Pages 3 and 4: Additional verse added so the song could be adapted for the Bishop campaign for Governor of Maine. [Lyrics for Cox and Roosevelt].

JMC-9 Give The Devil His Dues. w. A.J. Kiser. m. Edouard Hesselberg. Published by A.J. Kiser, Colorado Springs, CO. 1920. B/w drawing by A.J. Kiser of Warren G. "Harding" sitting on porch, devil speaking "Give 'em Peace by Resolution." Elephant with man — "Surgeon" saying "This one's gone too! The Nerve is Dead." Quote: "Who is the Devil, I'll Tell You Aloud! Do Your Own Thing, In Spite of the Crowd." 8pp. Includes a 4 page insert for "Male" and "Mixed" Chorus. Page 8: "1920 Democratic Campaign Songs" by Kiser including *Jimmy Cox Will Win The Day, Gov'nr. Cox You'll Surely Do, They Can Never Say, I Told You So, A Full Dinner Pail Was Once*

Their Cry, 38 Senators, We 38 Senators Must Win The Day, Campaign Circus, Give the Devil His Dues, Peace By Resolution, and *Who Wrecked The League of Nations*.

JMC-10 Cox Means Victory. w. Dewey T. Baird. m. Harry T. Myers. Published by Universal Music Company, Louisville, KY. 1920. Photo of James M. Cox.

JMC-11 They Can Never Say, I Told You So. w. A.J. Kiser. m. Edouard Hesselberg. Published by A.J. Kiser, Colorado Springs, CO. 1920. B/w drawing by A.D. Brown of James Cox's head on an Eagle's body sitting on a gravestone and speaking — "Here Lie the dead, Here lie the dead, O'er 'The League of Nations' they lost their head;" gravestone with the inscription — "38 Senators, A.D. 1920." 6pp. Page 6: "1920 Democratic Campaign Songs" by Kiser including *Jimmy Cox Will Win The Day, Gov'nr. Cox You'll Surely Do, They Can Never Say, I Told You So, A Full Dinner Pail Was Once Their Cry, 38 Senators, We 38 Senators Must Win The Day, Campaign Circus, Give the Devil His Dues, Peace By Resolution*, and *Who Wrecked The League of Nations*.

JMC-12 Gov'nr. Cox You'll Surely Do. w. A.J. Kiser. m. Edouard Hesselberg. Published by A.J. Kiser, Colorado Springs, CO. 1920.

JMC-13 A Full Dinner Pail Was Once Their Cry. w. A.J. Kiser. m. Edouard Hesselberg. Published by A.J. Kiser, Colorado Springs, CO. 1920.

JMC-14 We 38 Senators Must Win The Day. w. A.J. Kiser. m. Edouard Hesselberg. Published by A.J. Kiser, Colorado Springs, CO. 1920.

JMC-15 Peace By Resolution. w. A.J. Kiser. m. Edouard Hesselberg. Published by A.J. Kiser, Colorado Springs, CO. 1920.

JMC-16 Who Wrecked The League of Nations. w. A.J. Kiser. m. Edouard Hesselberg. Published by A.J. Kiser, Colorado Springs, CO. 1920.

See also AES-69.

JAMES MADISON

JMD-1 Madison's March. m. Alexander Reinagle. Printed for G. Willig & sold at his Musical Magazine, No. 12 South 4th Street, Philadelphia, PA. [1809?]. Non-pictorial. "As performed at the New Theatre." 2pp. Page 2: Blank. [W-7432].

JMD-2 Madison's March. m. P. Mauro. Printed & Sold at Carr's Music Store, Baltimore, MD. [1809]. Engraving of bow and arrows. "This is the March that the President and his Lady were Serenaded with, by the City Band, the 4th of March, 1809, the day of his Inauguration." 2pp. Page 2: Blank. [W-5649].

JMD-3 Madison's March. m. Alexander Reinagle. Printed & Sold at Carr's Music Store, Baltimore, MD. [1809?]. Non-pictorial. "As played at the New Theatre, Philadelphia and Baltimore." 4pp. Pages 1 and 4: Blank. [W-7433].

JMD-4 President Madison's March. m. Charles Southgate. In: *The Visitor*, page 96, July 15, 1809. Published by Lynch and Southgate, Harris's Building, Richmond, VA. [W-9513].

JMD-5 Mr. Madison's [sic] **March**. In: *The Gentleman's Amusement (Book 1)*, page 2. Printed & sold for Thomas Balls, Richmond, VA. [ca. 1815]. [6 1/2" × 9 1/4"]. Non-pictorial. Followed by *Mr. Gullitan's March* and **Mr. Munroe's** [sic] **March**. 36pp. [W-2962].

JMD-6 Mrs. Madison's Waltz. [m. Clementi]. Printed for G. Willig & sold at his Musical Magazine, No. 12 South 4th Street, Philadelphia, PA. [1810-1812]. Non-pictorial. 4pp. Pages 1 and 4: Blank. [W-901].

JMD-7 President Madison's March. m. P**** W**** [Peter Weldon]. Published by I. & M. Paff, New York, NY. [1809]. "Arranged for the Piano Forte, Flute or Violin." "Copy Right Secured." "Sold by I. & M. Paff and by

JMD-6

G.E. Blake, Philadelphia." 4pp. Pages 1 and 4: Blank. [W-9749].

JMD-8 Mrs. Madison's Waltz. [m. Clementi]. Published by J. and M. Paff, Broadway, New York, NY. [1809-1810]. Non-pictorial. 4pp. Pages 1 and 4: Blank. [W-1900].

JMD-9 Mrs. Madison's Favorite Waltz. m. Clementi. Printed for G.E. Blake, No. 13 South 5th Street, Philadelphia, PA. [1814-1817]. Non-pictorial. 4pp. Pages 1 and 4: Blank. [W-1902].

JMD-10 A Happy New Year To Commodore Rogers (Or Huzza for the President & Congress). Printed by N. Coverly, Jr., [Boston], MA. 1812. [7 5/8" × 9 5/8"]. B/w engraving of American ship and British ship "Belvidera" fleeing under darkness. "A song composed on the arrival of these frigates in Boston, yesterday (Dec. 31, 1812) with a good supply of ready rhino [cash]."

JMD-11 Dolly Madison (Two Step). m. Walter G. Wilmarth. Published by the John Church Company, Cincinnati, OH. 1906. Bk/w/gn/gd drawing of Dolly Madison, social gathering. "Dedicated to the Daughters of the American Revolution." 6pp. Page 6: Blank.

JMD-12 Dolly Madison (March and Two Step). m. Harry Appel. Published by Seminary Music Company., No. 12 East 17th Street, New York, NY. 1906. Pk/gn/w cover drawing of Dolly Madison, White House. 6pp.

JMD-13 Dolly Madison Waltzes. m. Robert Hood Bowers. Published by Jerome H. Remick & Company, New York, NY. 1911. N/c drawing by White of Dolly Madison. "As played in Henry B. Harris' production of *Dolly Madison*." "Popular Edition." 12pp. Pages 2 and 12: Advertising. Page 3: "Dedicated to Miss Elsie Ferguson."

JMD-14 Madison's Whim. In: *The Gentleman's Amusement, A Collection of Songs, Duetts, Dances Properly Adapted for the Flute, Violin and Patent Flageolet, No. 2*, page 8. Published by John Paff, New York, NY. [1812-1815]. Preceded on same page by *The Stralsund Waltze* and *The Italian Momfrina*. [W-2960].

JMD-15 Mrs. Madison's Minuet. m. A. Reinagle. "Printed & sold at Carr's Music Store, Baltimore, [MD]." [ca. 1809]. Non-pictorial. "Danced by Mrs. Green and Mr. Francis." 2pp. Page 2: Blank. [W-7434].

JMD-16 Madison's Quick Step. In: *The Gentleman's Musical Repository (Being a selection from the ancient and modern music of Erin with a number of Scotch and Welsh airs and several original pieces by the compiler. Adapted to violin, flute, flageolet, houtboy and union pipes)*, page 3. c. P.F. O'Hara, New York, NY. Printed for the Author and sold at his new music store, No. 70 William Street, where may be had a great variety of the most ancient and modern single songs; Also a great assortment of flutes, violins, tambarines [sic], drums and all other musical instruments. 1813. [W-6643].

JMD-17 Fashionable Repertory (Being a collection of country dances &

waltzes for the piano forte, flute or violin. Printed & sold at J. Hewitt's Musical Repository & Library, No. 59 Maiden Lane, New York, NY. [1807-1810]. [W-2757].

(A) **Madison's Hornpipe**, page 10.
(B) **Lady Madison's Waltz**, page 17.

JMD-18 Madison's March. m. John M. Bray. In: *Musical Olio, Comprising a selection of valuable songs, duetts [sic], waltzes, glees, military airs, &c., &c. Adapted to the piano forte with an accompaniment for the flute or violin*, page 25. Selected in numbers, No. 3, Oliver Shaw, Providence, RI. September 1814. Printed by H. Mann & Co. [W-1312, 6379].

JMD-19(A) President Madison's March. m. P. Mauro. In: *Marches Of The Presidents, 1789-1909, Authentic Marches & Campaign Songs*, page 10. a. Carl Miller. Published by Chappell & Co., 609 Fifth Avenue, New York, NY. "By arrangement with Chilmark Press." 1968. [9" × 12"]. R/w/b litho eagle, flag. "An Illustrated Piano Folio For All Ages." 72pp.

(B) **Mrs. Madison's Waltz**, page 12.

See also GW-188; GW-335; TJ-44; JMN-14; GC-7; WHT-23; WW-19; FDR-158; DDE-9; LBJ-1; MISC-167.

JAMES MONROE

JMN-1 Monroe's Grand March. m. F.A. Wagler. Published by [V-1: Bacon & Company, No. 11 South Fourth Street] [V-2: J.G. Klemm, No. 3 South 3rd Street], Philadelphia, PA. [V-1: 1821] [V-2: 1823-1824]. Non-pictorial. "For the Piano Forte." "American Musical Miscellany No. 8." 4pp. Pages 1 and 4: Blank. [V-1: W-9556] [V-2: W-9556A].

JMN-2 President Monroe's March. m. Stephen Cristiani. Published by G.E. Blake, No. 13 South 5th Street, Philadelphia, PA. [1819]. B/w engraving of an 8-pointed star with globe in center, maps of Georgia and Maine to either

JMN-1

side. "For the Piano Forte." "No. 27 Blake's Musical Miscellany." 4pp. Pages 1 and 4: Blank. [W-2209].

JMN-3 President Monroe's [sic] Trumpet March. m. I. Briljan. a. P.A. von Hagen. Published & Sold by G. Graupner at his Music Store, No. 6 Franklin Street, Boston, MA. [1817?]. Non-pictorial design. "As performed at his Review of the Garrison of Fort Independence, July 3rd, 1817." "Arranged for the Piano Forte." 4pp. [W-1360].

JMN-4 President Monroe's Waltz. m. An Amateur. Published by Geib & Company, No. 23 Maiden Lane, New York, NY. [1817?]. Non-pictorial. 6pp. [W-110].

JMN-5 Mrs. Monroe's [sic] Favorite (Duo). In: *Riley's Easy Flute Duets, Consisting of A Collection of One Hundred and Thirty One Favorite Airs Arranged For Two Flutes*, page 4. Engraved, printed and sold by E. Riley, No. 29 Chatham Street, New York, NY. [1819]. [9 3/4" × 6 3/4"]. 98pp. [W-7488].

JMN-6 President Monroe's Inauguration March. m. P.K. Moran.

Published by W. Dubois, at his Piano Forte & Music Store, No. 126 Broadway, New York, NY. [1821]. Non-pictorial. "To which is added a Favorite Waltz." "Copy Right Secured." "Price 50 Cents." 6pp. [W-6117].

JMN-7 President Munroe's [sic] **March**. m. Mr. E. Guilbert. Published in Charleston, SC. [ca. 1817]. Non-pictorial. "Harp or Piano-Forte." 2pp. Page 2: Blank. [W-3246].

JMN-8 President Monroe's March. m. M. Gilles, Senr. Published by [V-1: No publisher indicated] [V-2: W. Dubois, No. 126 Broadway, New York, NY]. [1817]. Non-pictorial. "For the Piano Forte with an Acompant. for the Flute or Violin." 2pp. Page 2: Blank. [W-3111A].

JMN-9 President Monroe's March. m. C.F. Hupfeld. Published by [V-1: A. Bacon, No. 11 South 4th Street] [V-2: J.G. Klemm, No. 3 South 3d Street], Philadelphia, PA. [ca. 1817]. Non-pictorial. "For the Piano Forte." 4pp. Pages 1 and 4: Blank. [V-1: W-4430]. [V-2: W-4430A].

JMN-10 Mary's Tears (A Favorite Song). w.m. O. [Oliver] Shaw. Published by O. [Oliver] Shaw at his Musical Repository, Providence, RI. [1817 — 1st Edition]. Non-pictorial. "From *Moore's Sacred Melodies*." "Sung at the Oratorio performed by the Handel and Haydn Society in Boston, July 5th, 1817, in presence of the President of the United States [Monroe]." "Copy Right Secured." 4pp. Pages 1 and 4: Blank. [W-7966].

JMN-11 Mary's Tears (A Favorite Song). w.m. O. [Oliver] Shaw. Published by O. [Oliver] Shaw at his Musical Repository, Providence, RI. [1821?]. "Second Edition." Non-pictorial. "From *Moore's Sacred Melodies*." "Sung at the Oratorio performed by the Handel and Haydn Society in Boston, July 5th, 1817, in presence of the President of the United States [Monroe]." "Copy Right Secured." 4pp. Pages 1 and 4: Blank. [W-7966A].

JMN-12 Mary's Tears (A Favorite Song). w.m. O. [Oliver] Shaw. Published & sold by the Author, No. 70 Westminister Street, Providence, RI. December 4, 1828. "Third Edition." Non-pictorial. "From *Moore's Sacred Melodies*." "Sung at the Oratorio performed by the Handel and Haydn Society in Boston, July 5th, 1817, in presence of the President of the United States [Monroe]." 4pp. Pages 1 and 4: Blank.

JMN-13 Mary's Tears (A Favorite Song). w.m. O. [Oliver] Shaw. Published by O. [Oliver] Shaw, No. 70 Westminister, Providence, RI. 1834. "Fourth Edition." Non-pictorial. "From *Moore's Sacred Melodies*." "Sung at the Oratorio performed by the Handel and Haydn Society in Boston, July 5th, 1817 in presence of the President of the United States [Monroe]." 4pp. Pages 1 and 4: Blank.

JMN-14 Mr. Munroe's [sic] **March**. In: *The Gentleman's Amusement (Book 1)*, page 2. Printed and sold for Thomas Balls, Richmond, VA. [ca. 1815]. [6 1/2" × 9 1/4"]. Non-pictorial. Preceded on same page by **Mr. Maddison's** [sic] **March** and *Mr. Gullitan's March*.

JMN-15 Governor Tompkins's [sic] **Grand March**. m. T. Cooke. Published by W. Dubois at his Piano Forte and Music Store, No. 126 Broadway, New York, NY. [1817-1818]. Non-pictorial. 4pp. [W-2057].

JMN-16 Governor Tompkins's [sic] **New Grand March & Pas Redouble**. m. James Hewitt. Printed & Sold at J. Hewitt's Musical Repository & Library, No. 59 Maiden Lane, New York, NY. [1808-1810]. Non-pictorial. "Arranged for the Piano Forte, Flute or Violin." 4pp. Page 4: Blank. [W-3713].

JMN-17 Governor Tompkins's March. m. C.P.F. O'Hara. In: *The Shamrock or Hibernian Chronicle, Vol. 2, No. 88*, page 4. Published in New York, NY., August 15, 1812. [W-6645]. Followed on the same page by **Governor Tompkins's Quick Step**. m. C.P.F. O'Hara. [W-6646].

JAMES MONROE (**JMN**)

JMN-18 **All Things Fair & Bright Are Thine**. w.m. O. Shaw. Published & Sold the Author by [O. Shaw], No. 70 Westminister Street, Providence, RI. [1835]. Non-pictorial. "Sung at the Oratorio performed by the Handel and Haydn Society in Boston in presence of the President of the U.S. [Monroe]." 4pp.

JMN-19 **Governer** [sic] **Tompkins Grand March Of Salute**. m. Adam Geib. Published by J. & M. Paff, Broadway, New York, NY. [1808?]. Non-pictorial. 4pp. Pages 1 and 4: Blank. [W-2912].

JMN-20 **Govenor** [sic] **Tompkins Parade March**. m. Curphew. In: *The Gentleman's Amusement Book [ ]*, page 25. Published by W. Dubois at his Piano Forte and Music Store, No. 126 Broadway, New York, NY. [ca. 1818]. Preceded on the same page by *Lord Grantham's Whim*. [W-2960].

JMN-21 **The Monroe Doctrine** (March and Two Step). m. M.A. Althouse. Published by M.A. Althouse, No. 30 South 10th Street, Reading, PA. 1908. Bl/w non-pictorial cover. "Dedicated to Frank W. Bartley, Baritone Saxophone, Ringgold Band, Reading, PA." 6pp. Page 6: Blank.

JMN-22 **All Things Fair & Bright Are Thine** (A Favorite Duet). w.m. O. Shaw. Published by Oliver Ditson, Washington Street, Boston, MA. 1835. Non-pictorial. "A Collection of Sacred Songs, Duetts [sic], Trios, &c." List of other songs in series. Note from Oliver Ditson on Copyright Infringement — "Note: The undersigned having purchased the copyrights of all the publications of the late Oliver Shaw hereby notifies parties who have infringed upon said rights, that legal steps will be taken for an adjustment, unless a satisfactory arrangement in relation thereto is made with him — Oliver Ditson." 6pp. Page 2: "From *Moore's Sacred Melodies*, Composed by O. Shaw, Sung at the Oratorio performed by the Handel and Haydn Society in Boston in presence of the President of the United States [Monroe]."

JMN-23 **All Things Fair & Bright Are Thine** (A Favorite Duet). w. "From *Moore's Sacred Melodies*." m. Oliver Shaw. Published by O. [Oliver] Shaw at his Musical Repository, Providence, RI. [ca. 1817]. Non-pictorial. "Sung at the Oratorio performed by the Handel and Haydn Society in Boston, July 5th, 1817, in presence of the President of the United States [Monroe]." "Copy Right Secured." 4pp. [W-7919].

JMN-24 **The Monroe March Song And Two Step**. w.m. Charles E. Lepaige. Published by Lapaige, Dodworth & Company, Nos. 108-110 East 125th Street, New York, NY. 1896. R/w/bl/br drawing of a shield, eagle clutching a scroll inscribed "Monroe Doctrine." 6pp. Page 6: Advertising.

JMN-25(A) **President Monroe's Hornpipe**. In: *Riley's Flute Melodies, Volume 2*, page 1. "Engraved, Printed & Sold by E. Riley, No. 29 Chatham Street, New York, NY. [1817-1820]. [10 1/4" × 6 3/8"]. Hard cover. 102pp. Page 1 inside: B/w engraving of a boy with a flute, two cherubs.

(B) **The President's Welcome To York**, page 1.

(C) **President Munro's** [sic] **March**, page 17.

JMN-26 **The Gentleman's Musical Repository** (Being a selection from the ancient and modern music of Erin with a number of Scotch and Welsh airs and several original pieces by the compiler. Adapted to violin, flute, flageolet, houtboy and union pipes), page 3. c. P.F. O'Hara, New York, NY. "Printed for the Author and sold at his new music store, No. 70 William Street, where may be had a great variety of the most ancient and modern single songs; Also a great assortment of flutes, violins, tambarines [sic], drums and all other musical instruments." 1813. [W-6643].

(A) **Governor Thompkin's Quick Step**. m. O'Hara.

(B) Governor Thompkin's Grand Slow March. m. O'Hara.

JMN-27 President Monroe's March. m. S. Christiani. In: *Marches Of The Presidents, 1789-1909, Authentic Marches & Campaign Songs*, page 14. a. Carl Miller. Published by Chappell & Co., Inc., No. 609 Fifth Avenue, New York, NY. "By arrangement with Chilmark Press, Inc." 1968. [9" × 12"]. R/w/b litho of eagle, flag. "An Illustrated Piano Folio For All Ages." 72pp.

See also GW-303; GW-304; JMD-5; USG-106; GC-109; WHT-23; WW-19; FDR-158; DDE-9; LBJ-1; MISC-42; MISC-167.

JOHN M. PALMER

JMP-1 Our Governors March (Or Two Step) m. Joseph Gearen. Published by Lyon & Healy, Chicago, IL. 1897. Bk/w/gn/br drawings of all Illinois Governors including John M. Palmer, Illinois capitol building, farm scene, law books. 6pp. Page 2: Blank. Page 6: Adv.

JMP-2 Appomattox, April 9, 1865: One Flag Only. w. "Written by Comrade Redington, Editor Acme Haversack, Syracuse, NY. m. "Tune: *America*." "Keep fresh in the hearts of the rising generation a reverence for the Stars and Stripes — the only flag.— Gen. John Palmer, Commander-in-Chief of the G.A.R." In: *Some Rations from The Haversack*, page 5. Published by J.C.O. Redington, of Syracuse, NY. [ca. 1892]. [5 1/4" × 6 3/4"]. Gn/bk litho of flag, G.A.R. badge, geometric designs. 52pp.

JOHN Q. ADAMS

JQA-1 President John Quincy Adams Grand March & Quickstep. m. C. Meineke. Published by John Cole, No. 123 Market Street, Baltimore, MD. [March 4, 1825]. B/w engraving of a feather. "Composed and Arranged for the Piano Forte." 4pp. Page 4: Blank. [W-5804].

JQA-2

JQA-2 President John Quincy Adams Grand March. m. F. Fest. Published by G.E. Blake, No. 13 South 5th Street, Philadelphia, PA. [1825?]. B/w engraving of boy with trumpet. "Composed and arranged for the Piano Forte." "No. 76 of Blake's Musical Miscellany." "Copy Right Secured." 4pp. Pages 1 and 4: Blank. [W-2784].

JQA-3 John Quincy Adams' Funeral March. m. A. Baumbach. Published by G.P. Reed, No. 17 Tremont Row, Boston, MA. 1848. Non-pictorial black border. "Composed and Arranged for the Piano Forte." 2pp. Page 2: Blank.

JQA-4 President J.Q. Adams March. m. M. Higgins. a. P.K. Moran. Published by Firth & Hall, No. 358 Pearl Street, New York, NY. [1827-1828]. Non-pictorial. "Engraved by E. Riley, 29 Chatham Street, New York." "Arranged for the Piano Forte." "Copy Right Secd." "Pr. 25 Cents." 4pp. Pages 1 and 4: Blank.

JQA-5 President John Quincy Adams Grand March & Quick Step. m.

F. Damish. Published & sold by George Willig, Baltimore, MD. February 28, 1925. Non-pictorial. "Composed for the Piano Forte." 4pp. Page 4: Blank. [W-2261].

JQA-6 The Washington Waltz. m. Frederick Damish. Published by John Cole, No. 123 Market Street, Baltimore, MD. [1824-1825]. Non-pictorial. "Respectfully Dedicated to Mrs. President Adams." Number "119" at bottom of page one. 2pp. [W-2262].

JQA-7 Adams' Quick March. m. Miss E******** L*****. [ca. 1825]. Non-pictorial. 2pp. Page 2: Blank.

JQA-8 Order Of Exercises (At the Celebration of the Sixty First Anniversary of American Independence). Published in Newburyport, [MA]. July 4, 1837. [7 1/2" × 13"]. Non-pictorial geometric design border. Various Songs. "1. Voluntary on the organ by Mr. Bailey; 2. Voluntary Music, by The Lafayette Band; 3. National Ode, Air *Adams And Liberty*; 4. Prayer by Rev Thomas B. Fox; 5. Anthem, chorus *Let Us with a Joyful Mind*; 6. Declaration of Independence by Hon. Robert Cross; 7. Hymn, 194 Belknap, music Edward L. While; 8. Oration by Hon. John Q. Adams; 9. Anthem, chorus *Hallelujah*; 10. Benediction." 2pp. Page 2: Blank.

JQA-9 When I Prayed At Mother's Knee (Song). w. Adelaide Arnold. m. Incognito. Published by Adelaide Arnold, No. 258 Columbus Avenue, C.L. Georde Piano Rooms, Boston, MA. 1902. Bl/w drawing of woman and child saying prayers. "To the memory of John Quincy Adams, who always said this prayer." 6pp.

JQA-10 John Quincy Adams. w.m. Rosemary and Stephen Vincent Benet. m. Arnold Shaw. In: *Sing a Song of Americans* [Song Book], page 13. Published by Musette Publishers, Inc., Steinway Hall, New York, NY. 1941. R/w/b drawings by Mollie Shuger of the subjects of several of the songs including Theodore Roosevelt. 84pp.

JQA-11 Funeral March (In Memory of John Quincy Adams, Ex-President of the United States). m. Charles Steinruck, Op. #6. Published by C.G. Christman, No. 404 Pearl Street, New York, NY. 1848. B/w geometric design at top, black border. "As performed by Bloomfield's U.S. Band, March 8th, 1848." "Composed for the Piano Forte." 4pp. Page 4: Blank.

JQA-12 March. m. "By an Officer of Volunteer Corps of Columbian Light Infantry." Published by Henry Stone, Lithographer, Washington, DC. [ca. 1825]. Non-pictorial. "Respectfully inscribed to John Quincy Adams, President of the United States of America, March, 4th, 1825." 4pp. Pages 1 and 4: Blank.

JQA-13 Sweetly Reposing. w.m. Matthias Ward, Esq. a. A.T. Prisson. Published by S.P. Hinds, No. 102 Market Street, Newark, NJ. 1849. Litho by Wm. Endicott & Co., of a man lying under a tree, guitar, angel. "Dream Songs, Dedicated to Hart." 4pp. Page 4: "The Following words by the same Author, adapted [sic] to this music, were sung at the Celebration of the Hon. J.Q. Adams, Funeral in Newark, N.J."

JQA-14 President John Quincy Adams' Grand March. m. F. Fest. In: *Marches Of The Presidents, 1789-1909, Authentic Marches & Campaign Songs*, page 16. a. Carl Miller. Published by Chappell & Co., Inc., No. 609 Fifth Avenue, New York, NY. "By arrangement with Chilmark Press, Inc." 1968. [9" × 12"]. R/w/b litho of eagle, flag. "An Illustrated Piano Folio For All Ages." 72pp.

See also WHT-23; WW-19; FDR-158; DDE-9 JFK-27; LBJ-1; MISC-167.

JAMES R. COX

JRC-1 On To St. Louis With Father Cox. w.m. George W. Bridgeman. Published by Diamond Music Company, Cameo Building, Pittsburgh, PA. 1932.

B/w photo of Father James R. Cox. "The Official 'Blue Shirt' Convention Song." 6pp. Page 2: Narrative on Composer's friendship with Father Cox.

JACOB S. COXEY

JSC-1 Coxey's March To The White House. m. K. Hale. Published by A.W. Perry & Sons' Music Co., Sedalia, MO. 1898. B/w drawing of cherubs, ribbon, oak leaves. "Composed for the Piano or Cabinet Organ." 6pp. Page 3: "To my little niece Kathleen Piper."

JSC-2 Coxey's March To Washington (A Brilliant March). w. John S. Grey (New York, NY). m. Will U. Martin (South Bend, Ind). Published by The Happy Home Publishing Company, South Bend, IN. 1894. Ma/be drawing of spider web, feather, geometric designs. "The Latest Fad!" 4pp. Page 4: Blank.

JSC-3 Coxey's Grand March. m. Max E. Jesse. Published by F. I. Northrup, Wm. Nagel, M.E. Jesse, San Antonio, TX. 1894. [10" × 12 1/4"]. B/w drawing of Miss Liberty, Coxey on horseback, banner inscribed "Peace on Earth, Good will toward man, He [Christ picture], hath risen, But Death to interest on Bonds." "Piano." 6pp. Pages 2 and 6: Blank. Page 3: "Dedicated to his Army."

JSC-4 Coxey Keep Off The Grass! w.m. R.D. Scott (The Blind Musician). Published by J.R. Bell, Kansas City, MO. Copyright 1894 by J.R. Bell.

JSC-5 Coxey's March to Washington (Grand March). m. William F. Held. Published by William F. Held & Co., No. 203 Bouquet Street, Pittsburgh, PA. 1894. B/w non-pictorial geometric design border.

JOHN ST. JOHN

JSJ-1 Hail To St. John, Our Chief! (A Temperance Campaign Song). w.m. Clara Holbrook Smith. Published

JSC-3

by F.S. Chandler & Company, Publishers, Chicago, IL. [1884?]. Non-pictorial geometric design border. 6pp.

JSJ-2 We'll Never Have To License Again! (Song and Chorus). w.m. Joe A. Roff. Published by Oliver Ditson & Company, No. 451 Washington Street,

JSJ-2

Boston, MA. 1881. B/w litho of "Gov. John St. John." "Governor John St. John of Kansas." 6pp. Pages 2 and 6: Blank.

JSJ-3 Prohibition Home Protection Party Campaign Songs. e. Horace B. Durant. Published by Mrs. Horace Abraham Durant, Claysville, PA. 1884. Bl/gn non-pictorial. 50pp. [M-252].

JSJ-4 Prohibition Party Campaign Songs. e. Horace Durant. Published by Mrs. Horace Abraham Durant, Claysville, PA. 1884. Gy/r/w/bl non-pictorial. 84pp. "These songs whilst adapted to the political uses of the party, do not, on that account, make any compromise of moral or religious sentiment or principle." [M-253].

JSJ-5 The Prohibition Songster. c. J.N. Sterns. Published by National Temperance Society and Publication House, New York, NY. 1885. "Words and Music, for Prohibition Campaign Clubs, Temperance Organizations, Glee Clubs, Camp-Meetings, &c., &c." 84pp. [M-254].

JSJ-6 Please Sell No More Drink To My Father (Temperance Song & Chorus). w. Mrs. Frank B. Pratt. m. C.A. White. Published by White, Smith & Co., Boston, MA. 1884. Be/br litho of man, child in bar. "Dedicated to Hon. John P. St. John, the True Friend to the Cause of Temperance." Pages 2 and 6: Advertisements for White, Smith & Co. music. Page 3: "The New Temperance Song."

JOHN TYLER

JT-1 President Tyler's Grand March. m. Mrs. Eleanor B. Redmond. [ca. 184-]. Non-pictorial. "Composed and Dedicated to the Memory of Col. N.W. Smith." 4pp. Pages 1 and 4: Blank.

JT-2 President Tyler's March. m. Charles M. King. Published by Firth & Hall, No. 1 Franklin Square, New York, NY. 1841. Non-pictorial. "A Grand March for the Piano Forte." "Composed and Respectfully Dedicated to John Tyler, President of the United States." "Pr. 50¢." 8pp. Pages 2, 7 and 8: Blank.

JT-3 I Could Not Live Without Thee. w. "Ex President Tyler." m. "Adapted to a Favorite Melody." a. Julius E. Muller. Published by Henry McCaffrey, Baltimore MD. 1855. Non-pictorial geometric design border. "To Mrs. Julia G. Tyler." 6pp. Pages 2 and 6: Blank.

JT-4 Tyler's Quick Step. m. David Perry. a. S.R. Leland. Published by Leland & Putnam, No. 8 Brinley Row, Worcester, MA. 1842. B/w litho by B.H. Thayer & Company of military parade in city street. 4pp. Page 4: Blank. [May not be President Tyler].

JT-5 Virginia. w. "Ex President John Tyler." a. "Arranged and Sung by his daughter, Mrs. Letitia T. Semple." Published by Henry Eberbach, No. 915 "F" Street, Washington, DC. Copyright 1896 by Dr. S. Waggaman. B/w drawing of the Virginia State flag—"Sic Semper Tyrannis." 6pp. Pages 2 and 6: Blank.

JT-6 Aunt Harriet Becha Stowe. w. Charles Soran, Esq. m. John H. Hewitt. Published by Henry McCaffrey, Baltimore, MD. [ca. 1860]. Non-pictorial geometric designs. "Respectfully dedicated to the estimable wife of Ex-President Tyler, and other patriotic and Union loving ladies of Virginia, who so justly rebuked Lady Southerland and the Ladies of England for their uncalled for meddling in the affairs of the people of the United States." "Written expressly for Kunkle's Nightingale Opera Troupe." 6pp. Pages 2 and 6: Blank.

JT-7 Columbia, Freedom's Home Is Thine (A National Song). w. James McHenry, M.D. m. Dr. Wm. Lardner, C.G.P. Published by James G. Osbourn's Piano Forte and Music Saloon, Philadelphia, PA. 1841. Non-pictorial black line border. "Dedicated to his Excellency John Tyler, Prest. U.S." "Nett [sic] 25 cts."

JT-8 Aunt Harriet Beechee Stowe. w. Charles Soran, Esq. m. Charles M. Stephani. Published by J.E. Boswell, Baltimore, MD. 1853. Non-pictorial geometric designs. "Sincerely Inscribed to Mrs. Julia Gardiner Tyler." "Sung by Kunkel's Nightingale Opera Troupe." "The only correct Edition." 6pp. Page 6: Blank.

JT-9 President Tyler's Grand March. m. Geo. O. Farmer. Published by Geo. P. Reed, No. 17 Tremont Row, Boston, MA. [ca. 1841]. Non-pictorial. "For the Piano Forte." 4pp. Pages 1 and 4: Blank.

JT-10 President Tyler's Military Waltz.

JT-11 President Tyler's Grand Quick Step. m. T.H. Vanden Berg. Osbourn's Music Saloon, No. 30 South 4th Street, Philadelphia, PA. 1841. Non-pictorial. "Composed & Arranged For The Piano Forte." 2pp.

JT-12 Grand March. m. F. A. Wagler. Published by Saml. Carusi, Baltimore, MD. [ca. 1842]. Non-pictorial geometric designs. "Respectfully dedicated to John Tyler, President of the United States. 2pp.

JT-13 Texas And Oregon Grand March. m. Anthony Philip Heinrich. Published by C.G. Christman, No. 404 Pearl Street, New York, NY. 1844. "Most respectfully dedicated to His Excellency John Tyler, President of the United States of America."

JT-14 President Tyler's March. In: *Marches Of The Presidents, 1789-1909, Authentic Marches & Campaign Songs*, page 26. A. Carl Miller. Published by Chappell & Co., Inc., No. 609 Fifth Avenue, New York, NY. "By arrangement with Chilmark Press, Inc." 1968. [9" × 12"]. R/w/b litho of eagle, flag. "An Illustrated Piano Folio For All Ages." 72pp.

See also WHH-31; WHH-43; WHH-44; WHH-51; WHH-56; WHH-68; WHH-75; WHH-76; WHH-80; WHH-91; WHH-108; WHH-109; WHH-113; WHH-124; WHH-144; JKP-5; RBH-15; WHT-23; WW-19; FDR-158; DDE-9; LBJ-1; MISC-167.

JOHN W. DAVIS

JWD-1 Davis And Bryan (Democratic Campaign Song). w.m. Mrs. W.D. O'Bannon. a. S.L. Amick. Published by Mrs. W.D. O'Bannon, No. 614 West Broadway, Sedalia, MO. 1924. B/w non-pictorial geometric designs and border. "Respectfully Dedicated to John W. Davis, Chas. W. Bryan and the Democratic Party of the United States of America." "Copies may be obtained by addressing Ms. W.D. O'Bannon, No. 614 West Broadway, Sedalia, MO." 4pp. Page 4: Blank.

JWD-2 March To The White House (March and Two Step). w.m. Charles K. Harris (Author of *After The Ball*). Published by Chas. K. Harris, Columbia Theatre Building, Broadway and 47th Street, New York, NY. 1924. B/w photo by Champlain Studios of John W. Davis, facsimile signature. "Compliments of the Democratic National Committee." 6pp. Page 2: "Respectfully Dedicated to John W. Davis." Page 6: Narrative— "What John W. Davis Believes."

JWD-3 The Slogan Of The Day (Answered). w.m. R.G. Haight. Published by R.G. Haight, No. 304 West 49th Street, New York, NY. 1924. Non-pictorial. "Political History Set To Music—Every Verse A Chorus." "40 cents a copy." 4pp. Page 2: Extra verses. Page 4: Same as page one.

JWD-4 John W. Davis Is The Man. w. T.J. Nicholson (Muskogee, Okla). m. Lillian Green (Muskogee, Oklahoma). Published by Democratic Victory Song Headquarters, No. 910 West Broadway, Muskogee, OK. Copyright 1924 by T.J. Nicholson. Bl/w photos of "John W. Davis—'The Man,' Champion of Democracy" and T.J. Nicholson and

LYNDON B. JOHNSON (LBJ)

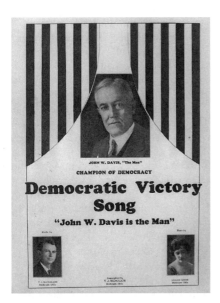

JWD-4

Lillian Green. R/w/b stripes. "Democratic Victory Song." 4pp. Page 4: Bl/w drawing of White House, rooster— "Victory and Prosperity," Dove— "Davis, Peace and Safety." "The Democratic Party favors constructive legislation for the benefit of all the people." "Standard Bearers of Democracy— John W. Davis, West Virginia, Chas. W. Bryan, Nebraska." Advertising.

JWD-5 In Democracy We Trust. m. Air: *Annie Laurie, The Swannee River, Dixie,* or *Auld Lang Syne.* Published by the Democratic National Committee, New York, NY. Copyright 1924 by Francis J. Lowe, N.Y. City. [Approximately 10 1/2" × 9 3/4"]. Hand-held cardboard fan. Obv: R/w/b with photos of seven "Paramount Film Stars: Dorothy Dalton, J. Logan, Agnes Ayres, Pola Negri, Gloria Swanson, Lois Wilson and Beatrice Joy," geometric designs. Rev: Song. "The song of the South and North as follows, can be sung to words of our campaign song above, vis: *Annie Laurie, The Swannee River, The Old Oaken Bucket, My Maryland, Yankee Doodle,*

Dixie using last line only, *Auld Lang Syne* first line only." "Union Made."

JWD-6 The Davis Song (Better Days With Davis). w.m. Frank DelliGatti. Published by E. Morris Publishing Company, No. 694 Madison Avenue, New York, NY. 1924. Bl/w photo of John W. Davis. "Retail Price Fifty Cents." 4pp. See also CC-56; AES-69.

JWD-6

LYNDON B. JOHNSON

LBJ-1 President Lyndon Baines Johnson March. w.m. Andrea and Ervin Litkei. In: *The President's March and Other Songs of the Lone Star State,* page 4. Published by Loena Music Publishing Company, No. 239 West 18th Street, New York, NY. 10011. [ca. 1964]. R/w/bl/bk stripes, Presidential seal. "Featuring *President Lyndon Baines Johnson March* and other songs of the Lone Star State." "Pacific Popular Music Books." 36pp. Page 2: Photos of Lyndon Johnson, A. Litkei. Page 35: Photo of Inaugural parade. Page 36: Photo of Lyndon Johnson. Drawings of all presidents.

LBJ-2 We Shall Overcome. w.m. Zilphia Horton, Frank Hamilton, Guy

Carawan and Pete Seeger. Published by Ludlow Music, Inc., "The Richmond Organization," New York, NY. Copyright 1960 and 1963. B/w photo by Arnold Newman of Lyndon Johnson. "What has happened in Selma is part of a far larger movement what reaches into every section and State of America. It is the effort of American Negroes to secure for themselves the full blessings of American life. This cause must be our cause too. Because it's not just Negroes, but really its all of us who must overcome the crippling legacy of bigotry and injustice. 'And We Shall Overcome.' These are the enemies: Poverty, ignorance, disease. They are our enemies, not our fellow man, not our neighbors, and those enemies too — poverty, disease and ignorance, We Shall Overcome — From President Lyndon B. Johnson's address on voting rights to a joint session of Congress, March 15, 1965." "Dedicated to the Freedom Movement." 4pp. Page 2: "Royalties derived from this song are being contributed to the Freedom Movement under the Trusteeship of the writers." Page 6: Same as cover.

LBJ-3   We The Nation Of The Free. w.m. Bolek Dzikowski. Published by Bolsound Enterprises, No. 250 West 57th Street, New York, NY. Copyright 1965 by Dzikowski. Bl/w drawing of Lyndon B. Johnson, Capitol building. "Dedicated to the Thirty-sixth President of the United States of America August 27th, 1965." 4pp. Page 4: Letters to and from the White House and Bolek Dzikowski.

LBJ-4   Onward, Forward, We Must Go (Johnson's Victory Song). w.m. Mary A. Varallo. Published by The Contemporary Music Press, Philadelphia 28, PA. 1964. R/w/b star, eagle, geometric design border. 6pp. Pages 2 and 6: Blank.

LBJ-5   The Great Society. w.m. Frederick Braun and Bobby Gregory (ASCAP). Published by American Music Publishing Company, No. 14 East 77th Street, New York, NY. 10021. 1965. Bl/w drawing of globe. "Dedicated to our President Lyndon B. Johnson...who envisioned this Great Ideal." 4pp. Page 4: Advertising for song — *That Old White House.*

LBJ-6   These Are The Songs That Were [Song Book]. e. Gerald Gardner (Writer *of Who's In Charge Here?, News-Reals,* and *That Was The Week That Was*). Published by Edwin H. Morris and Company, No. 31 West 54th Street, New York, NY. 10019. 1965. B/w photo of Lyndon B. Johnson, Hubert Humphrey, Everret Dirksen, others. R/w/bk cover. List of contents. 36pp. Pages 8, 23 and 25: Photos of politicians.

LBJ-7   All The Way With L.B.J. w.m. Billy Hays (ASCAP) and Eddie Bonnelly. Published by Arcade Music Company, No. 2733 Kensington Avenue, Philadelphia, PA. 1964. Bl/w photo of Lyndon B. Johnson. 4pp. Page 4: ASCAP logo.

LBJ-8   All The Way...With L.B.J. w. Eli L. Schaff. m. Bee Walker. Published by Zuma Music Company, No. 200 West 54th Street, New York, NY. 10019. 1964. Bl/w photos of Lyndon Johnson and Laura Lane, 5 stars. "As sung by Laura Lane during the Democratic Convention in Atlantic City, N.J., 1964." "Title by Dr. Herman Silvers." 4pp. Page 4: Bl/w treble clef symbol.

LBJ-9   It's Great To Be A Democrat. w.m. Red Mascara and Parke Frakenfield. Published by Sands Music Corporation, No. 1619 Broadway, New York 19, NY. 1964. Bl/w drawing of a donkey dancing on a box. 4pp. Page 4: Blank.

LBJ-10   The Hill Country Theme (From Lyndon Johnson's Texas). m. Glenn Paxton. Published by Alexandra Music, Inc., and Spectacular Music, Inc., New York, NY. Sole selling Agent: Hill and Range Songs, 1619 Broadway, New York, NY. 1966. Br/w/gn photo of L.B.J. ranch scene. 4pp. Page 4: Blank.

LBJ-11 President Lyndon Baines Johnson March. m. Andrea and Ervin Litkei. Published by Loena Publishing Company, No. 614 West 51st Street, New York 19, NY. 1964. [8 1/2" × 11"]. R/w/b drawing of flag, eagles, star border. 4pp. Page 4: Treble clef symbol.

LBJ-12 Everything's OK On The LBJ. w.m. Laughton Williams. Published by Western Hills Music. Sole selling agent: Robert B. Ferguson Music, Inc., Box 391, Nashville, TN. 1964. R/w/bk/gy drawing of cowboy on a horse with a branding iron inscribed "LBJ," cattle, elephant. "Recorded by Laughton Williams on RCA Victor Records." 4pp. Page 4: Advertising.

LBJ-13 The First Lady Waltz. w. Andrea Litkei. m. Ervin Litkei. Published by Loena Publishing Company, No. 239 West 18th Street, New York, NY. 1965. [8 1/2" × 11"]. B/w photo "Used with the permission of the White House" of Lady Bird Johnson. Y/bk/w cover. 4pp.

LBJ-14 Lady Bird Cha Cha Cha. w. Frank H. Keith. m. Samuel D. Starr. Published by De'Besth Music Publishing Company, Hammond, IN. 1968. B/w drawing by Norman Rockwell of Lady Bird Johnson, geometric design border. "Composed by the Authors for the First Lady who cares about the beautification of the United States." 4pp. Page 4: Blank.

LBJ-15 The First Lady Waltz. w. Andrea Litkei. m. Ervin Litkei. Published by Loena Publishing Company, No. 239 West 18th Street, New York, NY. 1965. [8 1/2" × 11"]. B/w photo of Lady Bird Johnson. Y/bk/w geometric design frame. 4pp.

LBJ-16 President Lyndon Baines Johnson March. w. Andrea Litkei. m. Ervin Litkei. Published by Loena Publishing Company, No. 614 West 51st Street, New York, NY. 1964. [8 1/2" × 11"]. Bl/w "photograph used by permission of the White House" of Lyndon B. Johnson. 4pp. Page 4: Treble clef symbol.

LBJ-17 The L.B.J. Waltz. w.m.

LBJ-14

Dr. Herman Silvers. Published by Dr. Herman Silvers, No. 249 Coleridge Street, Brooklyn, NY. 1965. R/w stripes, music notes. 4pp. Page 2: "Dedicated to our President."

LBJ-18 Lyndon Our Boy. w.m. William H. Thomsen. Published by William H. Thomsen, No. 328 East Goulson, Hazel Park, MI. 48023. 1965. Bl/bk/w drawing of The White House. 4pp.

LBJ-19 President Lyndon Baines Johnson March. w. Andrea Litkei. m. Ervin Litkei. Published by Loena Publishing Company, No. 614 West 51st Street, New York, NY. 1964. [8 1/2" × 11"]. R/w/b "Photograph used by permission of The White House" of Lyndon B. Johnson, flag, star border. 4pp. Page 4: Blank.

LBJ-20 Hello Lyndon. [m. Air: *Hello Dolly*]. [1964]. [8 1/2" × 11"]. Nonpictorial. 2pp. Page 2: Blank.

LBJ-21 Happy Democrats Are We. w.m. Bob Saffer. Published by Columbia Advertising Company, No. 133-17 101st Avenue, Richmond Hill 19, NY. Copyright 1964 by The Forward Music

Publishing Company. [8 1/2" × 11"]. Non-pictorial. 2pp. Page 2: Blank.

LBJ-22 LBJ (Presidential Campaign Song). w.m. Bob Saffer and George Mysels. Published by Forward Music Publishing Company, No. 345 West 58th Street, New York 19, NY. 1964. Bl/w non-pictorial. Printed on the reverse of the 45rpm record jacket.

LBJ-23 Hello Lyndon. w. Jerry Herman. m. Air: *Hello Dolly*. 1964. [4 1/4" × 11"]. O/br drawing of eagle, stars, geometric designs. "A Salute to President Johnson, Convention Center, Cleveland Public Auditorium, Thursday, October 8, 1964, 7:30pm." 2pp. Page 2: Blank.

LBJ-24 President Lyndon Baines Johnson March. w. Andrea Litkei. m. Ervin Litkei. In: *A Tribute To The U.S.A.*, page 12. Published by Loena Music Publishing Company, No. 239 West 18th Street, New York, NY. 10011. Copyright 1985 and 1986. N/c drawing by Edward Moran of the Statue of Liberty celebration in 1886 — "The Statue of Liberty, standing as an eternal symbol of the friendship of the people of France, was presented to the United States in 1886 by its creator, Frederick Bartholdi." Quotes by "Emma Lazarus (1883)," and "President Grover Cleveland (1886)."

LBJ-25 Aren't There Black Angels In Heaven Too? w.m. Christopher Smart and Gregory Stone. Published by Credo Music Company, No. 5504 Van Noord Avenue, Van Nuys, CA. 1965. B/w non-pictorial. "Inspired by President Lyndon B. Johnson's Historic Address to Congress on Negro voting rights." "For Voice and Piano." 6pp. Page 6: Blank.

LBJ-26 That Man From Texas. w. Ted Zahn. m. Meyer Davis. Copyright 1964 by Ted Zahn and Meyer Davis. Bl/w photos of Lyndon B. Johnson and "Meyer Davis." "Dedicated to President Lyndon B. Johnson." "Introduced by Meyer Davis and His Orchestra at the President's Birthday Ball at Convention Hall, Atlantic City, N.J., August 27,

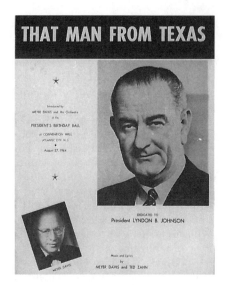

LBJ-26

1964." 4pp. Page 4: Bl/w treble clef symbol.

LBJ-27(A) President Lyndon Baines Johnson March. w. Andrea Litkei. m. Ervin Litkei. In: *The Bicentennial March and Presidential Marches of America*, page 28. Published by Loena Music Publishing Co., New York, NY. 1976. R/w/b drawings of George Washington, Thomas Jefferson, Abraham Lincoln, eagle, flags. "American Revolution Bicentennial, 1776-1976." "Officially Recognized Commorative." 40pp.

(B) *The First Lady Waltz*, page 34.

LBJ-28 Haven On Earth. w.m. Lon F. Stafford. Published by Lon Stafford Music Company, No. 4915 Onondaga Road, Syracuse, NY. 13215. 1965. Non-pictorial. "Dedicated to President Lyndon B. Johnson." 4pp.

LBJ-29 Lyndon Johnson Told The Nation. w.m. Tom Paxton. In: *Politics*, page 24. Published by Cherry Lane Music Company, Inc., P.O. 430, Port Chester, NY. 1989. [9" × 12"]. N/c photo by Jennifer Girard of Tom Paxton. R/w/b flag design. 36pp.

LBJ-30 Lady Bird. w.m. Carl E. Bolte, Jr. (ASCAP), 836 West Terrace, Kansas City 13, MO. a. William F. Nelson, Jr. Copyright 1962 by Holly Record Company. [9" × 12"]. Non-pictorial. 2pp. Page 2: Blank. [Came enclosed in a 45rpm record sleeve of same title.]

LBJ-31(A) Lyndon Johnson Told The Nation. w.m. Tom Paxton. B/w drawing of Lyndon Johnson. In: *Broadside, Volume 2*, page 62. Published by Oak Publications, No. 33 West 60th Street, New York, NY. Copyright 1968 by Broadside Magazine, No. 215 West 98th Street, New York, NY. [8 1/2" 11"]. O/pl/bl/w cover with a b/w photo of folk song gathering. "Songs of our times from the pages of America's foremost topical song magazine." 100pp.

(B) **Mrs. Lady Bird.** w. Norman A. Ross. m. "Tune adapted from the traditional (Mrs. McGrath)." B/w photo of Linda Bird Johnson. Drawing of soldier.

(C) **A President's Prayer.** w. Bob Cohen. m. "Traditional." "Note: Bob Cohen credits the *New York Times* as being co-author of *The President's Prayer*. Bob wrote the song from an article in the *Times* telling how LBJ had confided in his daughter, Lucybird, the he, the president of the U.S., might go down in history as having started World War Three. Lucybird, converted to Catholicism, told her papa not to worry, that she knew some monks who would fix the whole thing up. Bob has not said if he plans to share his royalties."

LBJ-32 Campaign Song. [Tune: *Old MacDonald Had A Farm*]. [1964]. [2" × 3 1/2"]. Non-pictorial. "From *American Purpose Newsletter*." 2pp. Page 2: Blank.

LBJ-33(A) Lyndon Johnson Told The Nation. In: *The Vietnam Songbook*, page 42. c. Barbara Dane and Irwin Silber. Published by The Guardian, No. 32 West 22nd Street, New York, NY. Copyright 1969 by Barbara Dane and Irwin Silber. [7" × 10"]. B/w photo of a protest march. O/y/r/bk cover. 228pp.

(B) **Ladybird's Lullaby**, page 47.
(C) **No More Johnson**, page 129.
(D) **Piss On Johnson's War**, page 126.
(E) **Lyndon's Lullaby**, page 176.
(F) **Do You Believe The Johnson Line?**, page 71.
(G) **Superbird**, page 76.
(H) **Luci Had A Baby**, page 128.
(I) **Mrs. Ladybird**, page 127.
(J) **All The Way**, page 131.
(K) **LBJ Looks After Me**, page 140.
(L) **LBJ, What Do You Say?**, page 136.
(M) **Mister President**, page 162.

See also FDR-53; HST-24; DDE-90; JFK-48; JFK-67; JFK-83; BMG-9; HHH-1; HHH-2; HHH-3; HHH-4; HHH-5; JEC-1.

LEWIS CASS

LC-1 Freedom Of The Seas. w. "From the *Baltimore Republican and Argus*." Broadside. B/w litho of "Funeral of Federal Principles." Animals in a funeral procession, log cabin, raccoon — "That Same Old Coon." Quote: "The remains of the Whig principles of 1840 and 1844, as they appeared when in funeral procession from the National Slaughter House at the Chinese Muse in Philadelphia, June, 1848." 2pp.

LC-2 Cass & Butler Songster. Published by Turner & Fisher, No. 74 Chatham Street, New York, NY. 1848. [2 13/16" × 4 1/4"]. Bl/bk litho of Lewis Cass. 36pp. Pages 2 and 35: Blank. Page 3: B/w litho of Lewis Cass. "A Collection of Original Democratic Songs." Page 34: Contents. Page 36: Advertising for other publications. [M-077].

LC-3 The Boat Horn. w. General William O. Butler. m. C.H. Thornbecke. Published for the Author by A. Foit, also to be had at E.N. Scherr, 266 Chesnut Street, Philadelphia, PA. 1848. B/w litho of General William O. Butler, oak

(LGM) LESTER G. MADDOX

LC-2

wreath. "Most Respectfully Dedicated to Mrs. James K. Polk." 4pp. Page 4: Blank.

LC-4 The Boat Horn. w. General William O. Butler. m. C.H. Thornbecke. Published by G. Willig, Jr., Baltimore, MD. 1849. Non-pictorial. "Composed and Respectfully Dedicated to Miss Frederica Karthaus." "Price 25 cts. net." 6pp. Pages 2 and 6: Blank.

LC-5 The Boat Horn. w. General William O. Butler. m. C.H. Thornbecke. In: *The Cass And Butler Almanac, For 1849*. Published by John B. Perry, No. 198 Market Street, Philadelphia, PA. [1848]. Be/bk litho of Lewis Cass. "Compiled by the Democratic Committee of Publication of the City and County of Philadelphia."

See also JKP-5.

LESTER G. MADDOX

LGM-1 Lester Goes To Ludowici. w.m. Reuben Ware, Sr. Published by Syracuse Music, Inc., No. 806 16th Avenue South, Nashville, TN. 37203. 1970. Bl/w photo of Reuben Ware, Sr.—"Recorded by Reuben Ware, Sr. on Royal American Records." R/w/b cover. "Distributed by Big 3." 4pp. Page 4: Blank.

LGM-2(A) Red, White And Maddox. m. Don Tucker. Copyright 1969 by Sunbeam Music, Inc., No. 22 West 48th Street, New York, NY. Sole selling agent: Valando Music, Inc., "A Metromedia Company," No. 22 West 48th Street, New York, NY. 10036. R/w/bl/y/bk non-pictorial. "Edward Padula presents Theatre Atlanta's Production of *Red, White And Maddox* by Don Tucker and Jay Broad, Staged by Mr. Broad and Mr. Tucker, Set and Costumes by David Chapman, Design Supervision by Richard Casler, Visual Materials by Bill Diehl, Jr., Associate Producers William Domnitz and Authur Miller, Original Cast Album on Metromedia Records." 4pp.

(B) Jubilee Joe. w.m. Don Tucker. 4pp.

MILLARD FILLMORE

MF-1 Eighty Years Ago (A Patriotic Song). w. Charles Sprague. m. J.F. Petri. Published by Wm. Hall & Son, No. 239 Broadway, New York, NY. 1856. B/w beige tinted litho by Sarony & Company of Millard Fillmore, facsimile signature. "The Music Composed and Respectfully Dedicated to the Hon. Millard Fillmore." 8[?]pp. Page 2: Blank. Page 3: Facsimile letter from Fillmore to Petri— "Buffalo, Aug't. 18, 1856. J.F. Petri, Esq., Dr. Sir, Your favor together with the music which you have done me the honor to dedicate to me, came duly to hand, for which I beg you to accept thanks. I have not yet heard the music but as I judge from the beautiful words by Mr. Sprague that it 'keeps step to the Union' it has my most hearty approval. I am truly yours, Millard Fillmore."

MF-1

MF-2 Fillmore Schottisch. m. F. Southgate, Op. 28. Published by Henry McCaffrey, Baltimore, MD. 1856. R/w/bl/bk litho of Miss Liberty, flag, eagle. "Respectfully dedicated to Millard Fillmore." "25 cts nett [sic]." 6pp. Pages 2 and 6: Blank. Page 3: "Performed by the Independent Blues Band."

MF-3 Fillmore Quick Step. m.a. Albert Holland. Published by Miller & Beacham, Baltimore, MD. [V-1: 1856] [V-2: ca. 1970 reprint]. [V-2: 8 1/2" × 11"]. [V-1: B/w] [V-2: Be/br] tinted litho by A. Hoen & Company of Millard Fillmore, chain of States with the abbreviation of each State inside. "If there be those, North and South, who desire an administration for the North as against the South, or for the South as against the North, they are not the men who should give their suffrages to me. For my part, I know only my Country, my whole Country, and nothing but my Country." "To the Citizens of the United States." "As performed by the Independent Blues Band." [V-1: 6pp] [V-2: 4pp]. [V-1: Pages 2 and 6: Blank].

MF-4 No Flag But The Old Flag (Solo and Chorus). w. Jennie M. Parker. m. Charles G. Degenhard. Published by Blodgett & Bradford, Buffalo, NY. 1861. R/w/bl/br litho of eagle, flag. "Dedicated, by permission, to Maj. Millard Fillmore, of the Union Continentals & Corps Under his Command." 6pp. Page 6: Blank.

MF-5 Every Star — Thirty Four (Solo and Chorus). w. G. Simcoe Lee, Esqr. m. Charles C. Degenhard. Published by Blodgett & Bradford, Buffalo, NY. 1861. R/w/bl/br litho of eagle, flag. "Dedicated, by permission, to Maj. Millard Fillmore, of the Union Continentals & Corps Under his Command." 6pp.

MF-6 President Fillmore Waltz. m. G.W. Benson. [ca. 1854]. Non-pictorial. "To Mrs. Francis Prentiss." "Composed for the Piano." 4pp. Pages 1 and 4: Blank.

MF-7 Fillmore Mazurka. m. Joseph C. Foertsch. Published by G. Willig, Baltimore, MD. 1854. Non-pictorial. "Composed and Dedicated to Miss Rowena M. Baldwin of Washington, D.C." 4pp. Pages 1 and 4: Blank.

MF-8 Union Quick Step. m. Gustave Blessner. Published by Lee & Walker, No. 162 Chestnut Street, Philadelphia, PA. 1851. B/w litho of eagle, shield — "E Pluribus Unum." "To his Excellency The Hon. Millard Fillmore, President of the United States of America." "Composed and Arranged for the Piano." "N.B. By applying to the Publisher the score of the above Quick Step arranged for a number of Instruments in use can be obtained." "As a solo, 25 cents; as a duett [sic], 50c nett [sic]." 8[?]pp.

MF-9 Millard Fillmore's Going Home. m. "Tune: *Few Days*." Printed by Johnson's, No. 5 North Tenth Street, Philadelphia, PA. [1856]. [6" × 8 7/8"]. Non-pictorial geometric design border. "You will save 25 per cent by getting your Printing done at Johnson's Cheap Card and Job Printing Office, 5 No. Tenth Street." 2pp. Page 2: Blank.

MF-10 Fillmore And Donelson Songs For The Campaign (Songster). Published by Robert M. De Witt, Nos. 160 and 162 Nassau Street, New York, NY. November 4, 1856. [4 3/4" × 7 1/8"]. Bl/bk litho of George Washington—"July 4, 1776," wreath, geometric design border. "This is the only authorized edition containing Duganne's Songs. Price 6 cts. each, $4 per 100. Discount to trade." Long quote from George Washington's "Farewell Address." 40pp. Page 3: "Union and Peace." [M-101, 102].

MF-11 KN Quickstep. Published by Winner and Schuster, No. 110 North Eighth Street, Philadelphia, PA. 1854. N/c litho of soldiers marching with a skull and crossbones banner, raccoon and rooster hanging from banner, crops, trees, eagle, crossed flags. "Dedicated to the Know Nothings." 6pp. Pages 2 and 6: Blank.

MF-12 Sam's Coming. w.m. William Clifton (Author of *The Banner of the Free, &c., &c.*). Published by Cook and Brother, No. 343 Broadway, New York, NY. Copyright 1855 by Thomas Birch. B/w litho by Stockpole of a young man—"Sam" wearing a large hat. "Inscribed to James W. Barker, Esq., by Permission." "3d Edition." 6pp. Pages 2 and 6: Blank. Page 3: Narrative on "Great Gatherings of Sam's Folks"—An immense number have gathered together in different cities &c., in the different states, to respond to the platform adopted by the late Convention in Philadelphia. The different speakers were listened to with the most earnest attention. Banners were floating in the air, bearing the following inscriptions, Americans, to rule Americans, no North, no South, no East, no West, Americans,—National, not Sectional, The Union must, and shall be preserved. The speakers were; Ex-Governor N.S. Brown of Tennessee, Hon. E.B. Bartlett of Kentucky, F.A. Cole of Georgia, L.C. Lewin of Penna., Judge Hopkins of Geoa., J. Cunningham of S.C., Gen. Pitcher of Keny., Col. W.W. McCall of Ala., The Hon. A.J. Donaldson of Tennessee, the adopted son and heir of General Jackson, and many others."

MF-13 Few Days (or Our Country Now Is Great and Free). w. K.N. a. S.G.A. Published by Oliver Ditson, No. 115 Washington Street, Boston, MA. 1854. Non-pictorial geometric design border. "The Know Nothing Union Song." 6pp. Pages 2 and 6: Blank.

MF-14 The Know Nothing Grand March. m.a. William C. Wright. Published by Berry and Gordon, No. 297 Broadway, New York, NY. 1853. Non-pictorial. "To A.P. Higgins, Esq." "For One or Two Performers." "Composed & Arranged by W.C. Wright." 6pp. Pages 2 and 6: Blank.

MF-15 Have You Seen Sam (Song and Chorus). w.m. Frank Spencer. Published by Berry and Gordon, No. 297 Broadway, New York, NY. 1855. Non-pictorial. "To Sam-." 6pp. Pages 2 and 6: Blank.

MF-16 Sam (Song). w.m. J.B. Bacon. a. H. Bertrand. Published by Horace Waters, No. 333 Broadway, New York, NY. 1855. N/c litho by Sarony & Company of a young man—"Sam," flags. 8pp. Page 2: Blank.

MF-17 Few Days (Or United American's) (Song and Chorus). w.m. George Morris. Published by Faulds, Stone and Morse (Successors to Peters Webb & Company), No. 539 Main Street, Louisville, KY. 1854. Non-pictorial. "The Only Genuine Edition." "Sung by S.C. Campbell, of the Original Campbell Minstrels." [V-1: "Piano"] [V-2: "Guitar"]. 6pp. Pages 2 and 6: Blank.

MF-18 Know Nothing Polka. m. "By Nobody." Published by James Couenhoven, No. 162 Chestnut Street, Philadelphia, PA. 1854. B/w litho of an eye, sun's rays. "Dedicated to Everybody by Nobody." 6pp. Pages 2 and 6: Blank.

MF-19 Know Nothing Polka. m. John P. Ordway. Published by J.P. Ordway,

MILLARD FILLMORE (MF)

MF-16

Ordway Hall, Washington Street, Boston, MA. 1855. B/w litho by L.H. Bradford & Co. of Henry J. Gardner, geometric design border. "Music Composed and Respectfully Dedicated to His Excellency, Henry J. Gardner, Governor of Massachusetts." "As danced by Pike and Pell of Ordway's Aeolians." 6pp.

MF-20 I Don't Know w. Francis F. Eastlack. m. "Air: *Bow, Wow, Wow*." Published by H.J. Kehr, Central Hall, Frankfort Road and Master Streets, and for sale at all Book Stores, [New York, NY?]. [ca. 1855]. [6 1/4" × 9 5/8"]. Non-pictorial geometric design border. "The Great Know Nothing Song." 2pp. Page 2: Blank.

MF-21 The Know Nothing (Song). w.m. Weiss Nicks. Published by Lee & Walker, No. 188 Chestnut Street, Philadelphia, PA. 1854. Non-pictorial. "The Celebrated Know Nothing Song." "Composed and Dedicated to Know Nothing." 6pp. Pages 2 and 6: Blank. Page 3: "Composed by Weis Nichts."

MF-22 Have You Seen 'Uncle Sam,' Boys? w. T. Squires, Esq. m. C.M. Traver. Published by J. Sage & Sons, No. 209 Main Street, Buffalo, NY. 1855. B/w litho of stars, rays, scroll—"A Fine American Song." 6pp. Pages 2 and 6: Blank.

MF-23 Pat's War With The Know Nothings. w. Tom Robinson. m. Air: *Rory O'More*. [ca. 1855]. [5 1/2" × 8"]. Non-pictorial geometric design border. 2pp. Page 2: Blank.

MF-24 Know Nothing Polka. w. William Fisher. Published by G. Willig, Baltimore, MD. 1855. Non-pictorial. "Respectfully Dedicated to SAM." 4pp. Pages 1 and 4: Blank.

MF-25 Know Nothing Password (or Have You Seen Sam?) (Solo and Chorus). w.m. Ossian E. Dodge. Published by G.P. Reed & Company, No. 13 Tremont Street, Boston, MA. 1855. Non-pictorial. "Sung by Ossian's Bards to Thousands of laughter convulsed audiences." "To his friend Jas. G. Clark, Esq." 6pp. Pages 2 and 6: Blank. Page 3: Title: **The Know Nothing Password Or Have** [engraving of an eye] **Seen Sam?**

MF-26 Anti-Know-Nothing Ditty. Published by Quipp's & Company. [ca. 1855]. [6" × 13 1/4"]. B/w litho of two silhouetted people with the devil. "The Famous new Anti-Know-Nothing Ditty, As Sung with Immense Applause by a Distinguished Gent of Philadelphia, at the Grand National Circus and Menagerie, Washington City." "Quipp's & Co's Comic Miscellany No. VIII." 2pp. Page 2: Blank.

MF-27 Few Days (or We Know The Way). w. D.L. a. F. Ferry. Published by J.E. Boswell, Baltimore, MD. 1854. Non-pictorial. "As Sung by Henry Lehr of Kunkel's Nightingale Opera Troupe." 6pp. Pages 2 and 6: Blank.

MF-28 Few Days And Now A'-Days. w.m. Charles G. Mortimer, Jr. Published by William H. Shuster, No. 97 North Eighth Street, Philadelphia, PA. 1854. Non-pictorial. "Adapted to the same Air, and Respectfully Inscribed to W. Chambers, Esqr." 4pp.

(MISC) MISCELLANEOUS

MF-29 Few Days. a. Sep. Winner. In: *Black Swan Set, No. 1*, page 2. Published by Winner and Shuster, No. 110 North Eighth Street, Philadelphia, PA. 1855. Non-pictorial. "Winner's Plain Cotillions; These Sets have all the proper Figures in appropriate places, and are so arranged as to be easily understood, as the music is written out in full to prevent mistakes; also arranged in the easiest possible manner." List of other song sets in series. 6pp. Page 2: **Few Days**. Pages 3-5: Other songs in the *Black Swan Set*.

MF-30 Sam's Know Nothing Quick Step. m. Mary. Published by Firth, Pond & Company, No. 1 Franklin Square, New York, NY. 1855. Non-pictorial. 4pp. Pages 1 and 4: Blank.

MF-31 The Know Nothing Polka. m. James Pierpont. Published by E.H. Wade, No. 197 Washington Street, Boston, MA. 1854. Non-pictorial. 6pp. Pages 2 and 6: Blank.

MF-32 Few Days (Or I'm Coming Home). a. Albert Holland. Published by Miller & Beacham, Baltimore, MD. 1854. "As Sung with great Applause by Christy Minstrels." 6pp. Page 2: Blank. Page 6: Advertising.

MF-33 Know Nothing Waltz. m. Clark. Published by S.T. Gordon, No. 706 Broadway, New York, NY. [ca. 1856]. Non-pictorial. "Twenty Four New and Elegant Polkas, Schottisches, Waltzes, Selected from Favorite Authors." List of other titles in series.

MF-34 Know Nothing Waltz. m. Miss Ellen M. Clarke. Published by John Marsh, New Masonic Temple, Chesnut Street ab. 7th, Philadelphia, PA. 1856. Non-pictorial geometric designs. "Composed & respectfully dedicated to the 6th Ward Council, Washington, D.C." 4pp. Page 4: Blank.

MF-35 Few Days Quick Step. m. Albert Holland. Published by Miller & Beacham, Baltimore, MD. 1854. Non-pictorial. "Introducing '*Tother Side Of Jordan* and *Few Days*.'"

MF-36 Few Days. In: *Golden Wreath, A Choice Collection of Favorite Melodies, Designed for the Use of Schools, Seminaries, Select Classes, &c.*, page 214. c. L.O. Emerson. Published by Oliver Ditson & Company, No. 277 Washington, Street, Boston, MA. 1857. [Edition ca. 1863].

MF-37 Few Days (Our Country Now Is Great And Free). w.m. Anonymous. e. Gregg Smith. In: *America's Bicentennial Songs from The Great Sentimental Age, 1850-1900, Stephen Foster to Charles E. Ives*, page 45. Published by G. Schirmer, New York, NY. 1975. [9" × 11 7/8"]. N/c litho of woman with roses, flag, city. 152pp.

MF-38 Fillmore Quick Step. m. Albert Holland. In: *Marches Of The Presidents, 1789-1909, Authentic Marches & Campaign Songs*, page 34. A. Carl Miller. Published by Chappell & Co., Inc., No. 609 Fifth Avenue, New York, NY. "By arrangement with Chilmark Press, Inc." 1968. [9" × 12"]. R/w/b litho of eagle, flag. "An Illustrated Piano Folio For All Ages." 72pp.

See also ZT-56; ZT-68; Zt-75; JCF-8; WHT-23; WW-19; FDR-158; DDE-9; LBJ-1; MISC-167.

MISCELLANEOUS

MISC-1 We'll Show You When We Come To Vote (The Great Woman's Suffrage) (Song & Chorus). w.m. Frank Howard (Author of *Only A Poor Little Beggar, Out In The Starlight I'm Waiting For Thee, Drunkard's Home, Fairy of the Vail, I'm Happy Little Ned, Grape Vine Swing in the Dell*). Published by W.W. Witney's Palace of Music, Toledo, OH. 1869. B/w litho of women lined up to vote, wall signs reading—"Vote for Susan B. Anthony for President," "For Vice President Mrs. Geo. F. Train," "For Governor of N.Y. Elizabeth Cady Stanton," "For Governor of Mass. Lucy Stone," "Down with Male Rule." "To Mrs. J.M. Ashley."

MISCELLANEOUS (MISC)

MISC-2 Dewey Shall Our Leader Be. w.m. Ferdinand A. Thomson. Published by The International Music Company, No. 53 West 28th Street, New York, NY. 1900. Photo of Admiral George Dewey. Drawing of flowers, geometric designs. "Here is a Democrat!"

MISC-3 They Gotta Quit Kickin' My Dawg Aroun'. w. Webb M. Oungst. m. Cy Perkins. Published by M. Witmark and Sons, New York, NY. 1912. O/bk drawing of a dog. "The Sensational Song Hit." 6pp. Pages 5 and 6: Advertising. [Champ Clark Campaign Theme Song].

MISC-4 Come Back, General Pershing (We'll Make You President). w.m. Dr. Smiles (Composer of *Come On*, &c, &c). Published by Smiles Cartoon Service, No. 532 Lafayette Avenue, Brooklyn, NY. 1919. R/w/bk drawing of "General Pershing." 4pp. Page 4: Advertising.

MISC-5 Pershing For President. w. Mark J. Samuels. m. Jean Harvez. Published by Lyraphone Company of America, New York, NY. 1919. [Pre-1919 size]. Br/w photo by Underwood and Underwood of General John Pershing. 4pp. Page 4: Advertising.

MISC-6 McAdoo And The [Donkey] [Rebus Title]. w.m. R.G. Haight. Published by R.G. Haight, No. 304 West 49th Street, New York, NY. 1924. B/w litho of donkey. "Political History Set To Music — Every Verse A Chorus." 4pp. Page 4: Same as page one.

MISC-7 Our Bonus And Our Beer. w.m. Francis J. Lowe. Published by Soldiers and Sailors Copeland Campaign Committee, GHQ — Fraunces Tavern, No. 101 Broad Street, "Washington's Old Headquarters," New York, NY. 1924. Bl/w photo of Senator Royal Copeland — "Our Choice Copeland For President." R/w border. "Campaign Song Of The Copeland Campaign Club." "Copeland is Our Choice." "Soldiers and sailors Sing It As well As Women who served." "Bonus beer or bust — In Democracy We Trust." 6pp. Page 2: Blank. Page 6: Song — **Copeland's Good Enough For Me** (Campaign Song).

MISC-8 Our Bonus And Our Beer. w.m. Francis J. Lowe. Published by The Soldiers and Sailors Copeland Campaign Committee, New York, NY. 1924. Bl/w photo of Senator Royal Copeland. R/w border. "Remember The Beer Revenues Pay for the Bonus." "Democratic Doctrines." "Bonus Beer or Bust — In Democracy We Trust." 6pp.

MISC-9 Jim Reed From Old Missouri. w.m. Rose Donegan. Published by Topco Publishing Company, No. 1526 Walnut Street, Kansas City, MO. 1928. R/w/bl/o/bk drawing of Uncle Sam, maps of the U.S. and Missouri, Capitol building, banner inscribed "Peoples Choice Jim Reed for President." "From Coast to Coast Campaign March Song." 6pp. Page 6: Bl/w photo of Jim Reed — "Very Sincerely Yours, Jas. B. Reed [facsimile handwriting]."

MISC-10 Song Of The Bunkless Party. w.m. Harry Evans. Published by *LIFE* Publishing Company, New York, NY. 1928. B/w drawing of Will Rogers, cowboy, donkey, elephant. "Campaign Song Will Rogers for President sponsored by *LIFE*." 4pp.

MISC-11 Will Rogers For President (My Big Chief) (Fox-Trot Ballad). w.m. Marvin Burton Gordon. Published by Martin Burton Gordon, No. 360 South Hill Street, Los Angeles, CA. 1931. Non-pictorial. 4pp. Page 4: Blank.

MISC-12 When I'm The President (We Want Cantor). w. Al Lewis. m. Al Sherman. Published by Mack Stark Music Company, Inc., No. 745 7th Avenue, New York, NY. 1931. R/bk photo of Eddie Cantor. R/w/bk drawings of Eddie Cantor. "My Official Campaign Song…Eddie Cantor." 20pp. Pages 2, 18, 19 and 20: Blank. Page 3: "Interview with Eddie Cantor" on election. Pages 6 to 17:

Drawings by Pud Lane illustrating each verse.

MISC-13 When I'm The President (We Want Cantor). w. Al Lewis. m. Al Sherman. Copyright 1931 by Mack Stark Music Company, Inc., No. 745 7th Avenue, New York, NY. Non-pictorial geometric design border. "Eddie Cantor's Official Campaign Song." 4pp.

MISC-14 Hoover Made A Soup Houn' Out O' Me. w.m. F.R. Sawyer. Published by Murray For President, Perrine Building, Oklahoma City, OK. 1932. [6" × 9"]. B/w photo by Hardin Henryetta of "Governor William H. (Alfalfa Bill) Murray — Our Next President, geometric design border." 4pp. Page 4: Advertising.

MISC-15 Wintergreen For President. w. Ira Gershwin. m. George Gershwin. Published by New World Music Corporation, Harms, Inc., Sole Selling Agent, New York, NY. 1932. Pk/w/bl drawing of men with campaign signs inscribed "Wintergreen For President," stars. "Chandler Cowles and Ben Segal Presents *Of Thee I Sing*, Book by George S. Kaufman and Morrie Ryskind, Directed by George S. Kaufman, Dances and Musical Numbers by Helen Tamaris." List of other songs in show. 8pp. Pages 2 and 8: Blank.

MISC-16 Wintergreen For President. w. Ira Gershwin. m. George Gershwin. In: *Of Thee I Sing* (Vocal Score), page 14. Published by Warner Bros. Music, No. 488 Madison Avenue, New York, NY. 10022. 1932. [Edition ca. 196-]. Be/br non-pictorial. "The Pulitzer Prize Musical, Sam H. Harris Presents *Of Thee I Sing*, Book by George Kaufman and Morrie Ryskind, Directed by George Kaufman, Dances and Ensembles by George Hale."

MISC-17 Vote For Gracie. w.m. Charles Henderson. Copyright 1940 by Lehn and Fink Products Corporation, Bloomfield, NJ. Bl/w photo of Gracie Allen. "The Surprise Party's Dark Horse." "A Vote for Gracie is a Vote for Fun." "The Campaign Song for Gracie Allen." 4pp. Page 4: "Gracie's campaign platform planks for everything." Advertising for Hinds' [cold] Cream. Advertising for Burns and Allen show.

MISC-18 Santa Claus For President. w.m. Peter Tinturin. Published by Edwin H. Morris & Company, Music Publishers, No. 1619 Broadway, New York, NY. 1947. Pl/w stripes. Pl/w photo of Sammy Kaye. "Featured by Sammy Kaye and His Orchestra." 4pp. Page 4: Advertising.

MISC-19 Harriman For Me. m. Tune: *Harrigan*. Copyright 1952 by National Committee For Harriman for President, No. 111 East 56th Street, New York 22, NY. [8 1/2" × 11"]. B/w drawings of four donkeys. "Senator Herbert H. Lehman, Hon. Chairman, Congressman Franklin D. Roosevelt, Jr., Chairman." 2pp. Page 2: Blank.

MISC-20 Taft Victory Song. m. "Tune: *Four Leaf Clover*." Published by National Taft-For-President Committee, Clarence J. Brown, Chairman. [1952]. [5 1/2" × 8 1/2"]. Gn/w photo of Robert Taft. Gn/w drawing of clover leaves. "Win With Taft!" 2pp. Page 2: Blank.

MISC-21 Taft Is The Man. w.m. Emma Stephenson. Copyright 1952 by Emma Stephenson. [9 1/2" × 12 1/2"]. B/w photo of Robert Taft. 4pp. Page 4: Blank.

MISC-22 The Senator From Tennessee. w.m. D. Dorney and B. Weinman. Copyright 1952 by Babb Music, No. 824 Fifth Avenue South, Nashville, TN. Non-pictorial. 2pp. Page 2: Blank. [Estes Kefauver for President lyrics].

MISC-23 Song Sheet For Taft Demonstration. [1952]. [8 1/2" × 14"]. Non-pictorial. 2pp. Page 2: Blank.

MISC-24 Elvis Presley For President. w.m. Norman Henry, Ruth Roberts and Bill Katz. Published by Vernon Music Corporation, No. 1619 Broadway, New

York 19, NY. 1956. R/w photo of Elvis Presley. R/w drawing of Capitol dome, cheering crowd with signs inscribed "He's for Kiss-Kiss-Kiss," "Vote for Elvis," "He's for Love-Love-Love," "Vote for Rock and Roll." 4pp.

MISC-25 Underwood March. m. Caroline Westmoreland Dowman (Birmingham, Ala). Published by Roberts and Sons, Birmingham, AL. Copyright 1912 by The Age Herald Publishing Company. Br/w photo of Oscar Underwood. Br/w drawing of leaves. "Dedicated to the Oscar W. Underwood Marching Club of Alabama." 6pp. Page 6: Blank.

MISC-26 March & Chorus In The Dramatic Romance Of The Lady Of The Lake. w. Walter Scott, Esqr. m. Mr. Sanderson. Published by J.G. Klemm, No. 3 South Third Street, Philadelphia, PA. [1823-1824]. Non-pictorial. 4pp. Page 1: Song—*Lady of the Lake*. Pages 2-4: **Hail To The Chief** (Chorus). 4pp. [W-7781B].

MISC-27 Hail To The Chief. a. T. Carr. Printed and Sold at Carrs Music Store, No. 36 Baltimore Street, Baltimore, MD. [1812-1814]. Non-pictorial. "The Much Admired March & Chorus *Hail to the Chief* in the celebrated Melo-Dramatic Romance, The Lady of the Lake, Arranged for the Piano Forte." 2pp. [W-7770].

MISC-28 March And Chorus In The Dramatic Romance Of The Lady Of The Lake. m. Mr. Sanderson. Published by G.E. Blake, Philadelphia, PA. [1812-1814]. Non-pictorial. First page marked in upper right "5." 4pp. Page 2: **Hail To The Chief** (Chorus). w. Walter Scott, Esq. [W-7779].

MISC-29 Hail To The Chief (Lady of the Lake) (Chorus). m. Mr. Sanderson. Published by Wm. Dubois, New York, NY. [1817-1818]. Non-pictorial. [V-1: No number at bottom of page one] [V-2 Number "3" at bottom of page one]. 4pp. Page 4: Blank. [V-1: W-7769A] [V-2: W-7769B].

MISC-30 Hail To The Chief (The Chorus In the Lady of the Lake). w. Sir Walter Scott. m. James Sanderson. Engraved, Printed & Sold by E. Riley, No. 29 Chatham Street, New York, NY. [1818-1826]. Non-pictorial. 4pp. Page 4: Blank. [Not listed in Wolfe].

MISC-31 Hail To The Chief (The Chorus In the Lady of the Lake). w. Sir Walter Scott. m. James Sanderson. Published by Oliver Ditson, No. 115 Washington Street, Boston, MA. [ca. 1860]. Non-pictorial. 4pp. Page 4: Advertising.

MISC-32 Hail To The Chief (Lady of the Lake) (Chorus). w. Sir. Walter Scott. m. Sanderson. Published by Firth & Hall, No. 1 Franklin Square, New York, NY. [ca. 1825]. Non-pictorial. 4pp. [Not listed in Wolfe].

MISC-33 The Minstrel's Vote For President. Published for A.P. Heinrich. [1825-1826]. Non-pictorial. "No. 12 of The Sylviad." 6pp. Page 6: Blank. [W-10145].

MISC-34 Old Independence Hall. w. A. Fletcher Stayman. m. Francis Weiland. Published by Stayman & Brothers, No. 210 Chesnut Street, Philadelphia, PA. 1855. Non-pictorial. "Respectfully dedicated to the Memory of the Signers of the Declaration of Independence." "Fac Simile of their signatures" including John Adams, Sam Adams, Elbridge Gerry, Thomas Jefferson. 8pp. Pages 2 and 8: Blank.

MISC-35 Inauguration Waltz. m. Kallowada. In: *Thirteen Popular Waltzes By Various Composers*, page 3. [ca. 184-]. Non-pictorial. 16pp.

MISC-36 The American Stamp Polka. m. Maria Sequin. Published by William A. Pond & Company, No. 547 Broadway, New York, NY. 1864. Litho by Sarony, Major and Knapp of U.S. postage stamps, including 2-cent Andrew Jackson and 3-cent George Washington. "To my sister Jane."

MISC-37 When A Coon Sits In

The Presidential Chair. w.m. George R. Wilson (of the famous Wilson family). a. Max Hoffman. Published by Chas. K. Harris, Alhambra Theatre Building, Milwaukee, WI. 1898. B/w photo of "The Wilson Family." Bl/w geometric designs. Bl/w photo of Charles K. Harris. "Sung with great success by the Author, George R. Wilson and His Famous Family." 8pp. Pages 2, 7 and 8: Advertising.

MISC-38 Gwine To Change Dat White House Black. w.m. D. Long Miller. Published by Whitney Warner Publishing Company, Detroit, MI. [ca. 1900]. Gn/bk/w/y drawing of White House, black couples. B/w photo of Black man — "Postmaster." "By order of the Postmaster."

MISC-39 Presidents. w. Phil Sheridan. m. Robert Recker. Published by Robert Recker and Company, No. 5 East 14th Street, New York, NY. 1899. Ma/y photos of "Fanny Lewis" and Robert Recker. Ma/y geometric design border. "A Song for the Community." 6pp. Pages 2 and 6: Advertising.

MISC-40 Flatbush Republican Club (March). m. Crosby Mollenhauer. Copyright 1930 by Louis Mollenhauer's Conservatory of Music, No. 71 Malborough Road, Brooklyn, NY. B/w photo of "Hon. F.J.H. Kracke, Executive Member, Twenty-First Assembly District, King's County." "Dedicated to Hon. F.J.H. Kracke." B/w vines, geometric designs. 6pp. Pages 2 and 6: Blank.

MISC-41 Our Presidents. w.m. Frank L. Bristow. Published by The George B. Jennings Company, Cincinnati, OH. 1904. R/w/b drawing of Uncle Sam atop globe. "A Song for the World." 6pp. Page 2: Narrative on "the object of this song [being] to teach the names of our Presidents..." Page 6: Blank.

MISC-42 A Hen In The Nest (A Barnyard Travesty). w.m. George L. Spaulding. Published by Will Rossiter, Publisher, Chicago, IL. 1904. O/bk/w drawing of black men stealing eggs, chicken dressed as a policeman. Border of eggs labeled with historical events — "1823 Monroe Doctrine," "1863 Lincoln's Emancipation Proclamation," "1865 President Lincoln Assassinated," "1881 President Garfield Shot," "1901 President McKinley Shot." "Published for Orchestra, Band, Mandolin and Guitar." 8pp. Page 2: Blank. Page 8: Advertising.

MISC-43 A Cup O' Tea (Japanese Intermezzo). m. Karl Lenox. Published by Lenox Music Company, Boston, MA. Selling Agent: C.W. Thompson & Co., Boston, MA. 1910. Bl/w/gd drawing of "White House Tea" can, White House, cups and saucers. "Compliments of White House Tea, Dwinell-Wright Co., Coffees, Teas, Spices, Boston-Chicago." "Dwinell-Wright Co., Coffees, Teas, Spices, Boston-Chicago." 6pp. Page 6: Bl/w drawing of tea container.

MISC-44 U.S. Marine Band (March And Two Step). m. Ted Browne. Published by Will Rossiter, "The Chicago Publisher," No. 136 West Lake Street, Chicago, IL. 1911. N/c photo of the "United States Marine Band" in front of The White House. O/bk/bl/br/w cover. "As played by United States Military Band." "United States Military Band, William H. Santelmann, Leader." "Published for Band and Orchestra." 6pp. Page 2: Blank. Page 3: "Dedicated to the United States Marine Band, Wm. H. Santlemann, Director." Page 6: Advertising.

MISC-45 In The Candle-Light [V-1: Novelty Song] [V-2: Intermezzo]. w.m. Fleta Jan Brown. Published by M. Witmark & Sons, New York, NY. 1913. Bk/w/o photos of Fannie Ward and John Dean. "Fannie Ward and John Dean in *Madam President*." [V-1: B/w photo of Bessie Wynn. "Sung with great success by Bessie Wynn." "Also published as 'Intermezzo.'". 6pp. Pages 2 and 6: Advertising.

MISC-46 Are You Half The Man, Your Mother Thought You'd Be. w. Leo Wood. m. Harry De Costa. Published by Leo Feist, Inc., New York, NY. 1916. O/br/w drawing of woman and child, presidents and other famous people including Theodore Roosevelt, Ulysses Grant, William H. Taft, Woodrow Wilson, William McKinley, George Washington and John Adams. "The Song You've Been Reading About." 4pp. Page 4: Advertising.

MISC-47 Pride OF The White House (Patriotic March). m. Karl Lenox. Published by Lenox Music Company, Boston, MA. 1916. Br/w drawing of The White House, geometric designs. 6pp. Pages 2 and 6: Advertising. Page 3: "Loyally Dedicated to Our Flag."

MISC-48 The White House Is The Light House Of The World (Song). w.m. Isador Caesar and Alfred Bryan. Published by Jerome H. Remick & Company, New York, NY. 1918. [Post-1919 size]. R/w/b drawing of the White House, shield, eagle. 4pp. Page 4: "Do Your Bit — Food is Ammunition — Don't Waste It — Help Win The War." Advertising.

MISC-49 E.B. Harper Republican Club (March). m. A. Holzmann. Published by A. Holzmann & Company, No. 358 East 123rd Street, New York, NY. 1894. Bl/w litho of "E.B. Harper, President, Mutual Reserve Fund Life Assn." "Respectfully Dedicated to E.B. Hayes." "The E.B. Harper Republican Club, William Porter, President." 6pp. Page 2: Blank. Page 6: Litho of Mutual Reserve Building.

MISC-50 The White House In Washington And The White House In The Lane (Song). w. Alfred Bryan. m. Joseph E. Howard. Published by Jerome H. Remick & Company, New York, NY. 1922. B/w photos of Joseph E. Howard and Ethelyn Clark. "As introduced by Joseph E. Howard and Ethelyn Clark." Y/bk/w/gy drawings of The White House, house. "Operatic Edition." 6pp. Page 2: Blank. Page 6: Advertising.

MISC-51 If I Were In The Old White House. w.m. Angelino Greco. Published by National Manuscript Bureau, No. 333 West 52nd Street, New York, NY. 1932. Pk/bl/w geometric designs. 4pp. Page 4: Advertising.

MISC-52 Please Mister President. w.m. Allie Wrubel and Mose Sigler. Published by De Sylva, Brown and Henderson, Inc., No. 745 Seventh Street, New York, NY. 1933. R/w/bk drawing by Leff of the U.S. Capitol dome, hearts. "Successfully featured by Rudy Vallee." 6pp. Pages 2 and 6: Advertising.

MISC-53 I Don't Want To Be President. w. Lew Brown. m. Harry Akst. Published by M. Witmark & Sons, New York, NY. 1934. Pl/w photos of stars — "Lew Holtz, Phil Baker, Everett Marshall, Jack Whiting, Mitzi Mayfair, Patricia Bowman, Patsy Flick and Gertrude Niesen." Pk/w star background. "Lew Brown's *Calling All Stars!* — Lyrics by Lew Brown, Music by Harry Akst, Dances by Maurice L. Kusell, Sara Mitchel, Strauss Dancers." List of other songs in show. 8pp. Page 8: Advertising.

MISC-54 Republicans Will Win This Fall (Republican Rally Song). w.m. C.P. Siegfried. Copyright 1934 by C.P. Siegfried, Jacksonville, IL. [8 1/2" × 11"]. Bl/w photo of "Woods Brothers, G.O.P. Quartette." Bl/w drawing of elephant. "Successfully introduced and featured at Republican State Convention, Springfield, Ill., Aug. 9, 1934." 4pp. Page 4: B/w photo of Warren E. Wright. "Warren E. Wright for Congress, 20th Congressional District, Illinois." R/w/b flags. Extra verses for Wright.

MISC-55 I Wish I Had A Daddy In The White House. w.m. Bud Burtson. Published by Chappell & Company, Inc., RKO Building, Rockefeller Center, New York, NY. 1951. B/w photo of Kitty Kallen. "As featured by Kitty Kallen on Mercury Record No. 5700."

(MISC) MISCELLANEOUS

Gn/w/bk stripes, geometric designs. 8pp. Page 2: Blank. Page 6: Advertising.

MISC-56   Every Little Boy Can Be President. w. Diane Lampert and Peter Farrow. m. David Saxon. Published by Sam Fox Publishing Company, Inc., No. 1841 Broadway, New York, NY. Copyright 1961 and 1968. R/w/b stripe background. R/w photo of Johnny Whitaker. "Johnny (Jody) Whitaker, on United Artists Record VA 50296." "(Also Appearing as Jody on the CBS TV show *Family Affair*)." "Easy-To-Play Piano and Song Edition." 6pp. Page 6: Advertising.

MISC-57   The President's Lady. w.m. Alfred Newman. Published by Leo Feist, Inc., No. 799 Seventh Avenue, New York 19, NY. 1953. B/w photo of Jackie Gleason. "Recorded on Capitol Record 2515." "Theme Melody from the 20th Century-Fox picture *The President's Lady* Starring Susan Hayward, Charlton Heston with John McIntire, Fay Bainter, Whitfield Conner, Carol Betz, Gladys Hurlburt, Ruth Attaway, Charles Dingle, Produced by Sol C. Siegel. Directed by Henry Levin, Screen Play by John Patrick. Based on a novel by Irving Stone." "A Composition for Piano." 6pp. Pages 2 and 6: Advertising.

MISC-58   The President's Lady. w.m. Alfred Newman. Published by Leo Feist, Inc., No. 799 Seventh Avenue, New York 19, NY. 1953. Non-pictorial. "School Orchestra Series." "Theme Melody from the 20th Century-Fox Picture *The President's Lady*." "Piano Conductor Score." List of parts in full orchestra set. 6pp. Page 6: Blank.

MISC-59   The President's Lady. w.m. Alfred Newman. Published by Leo Feist, Inc., No. 1540 Broadway, New York 23, NY. 1953. Br/w drawing of piano top, keyboard. "Piano Solo." "Theme melody from the 20th Century-Fox picture." 4pp.

MISC-60   We Want A Rock And Roll President. w.m. Robert Colby and Jack Wolf. Published by Redd Evans Music Company, "We Publish Tomorrow's Standards Today," No. 1619 Broadway, New York 19, NY. 1956. R/w photo of The Treniers. "Featured by The Treniers." 4pp. Page 4: Advertising.

MISC-61   Convention   Time (Song). w.m. Josef R. Carnes. Published by Josef R. Carnes, Hillsboro, IN. 1957. B/w photo of "William McMains, 'Official Organist, Democratic and Republican Conventions, 1952-1956.'" "As Featured by William McMains." R/w cover. 4pp. Page 4: Logo of publisher.

MISC-62   Every Little Boy Can Be President. w. Diane Lampert and Peter Farrow. m. David Saxon. Published by Sam Fox Publishing Company, Inc., No. 11 West 60th Street, New York 23, NY. 1961. Gn/bk/w drawing of man, leprechaun, frog. "The original television musical production *Halloran's Luck* Starring Art Carney, Bil Baird's Marionettes and Miss Barbara Cook, Directed by Marc Daniels, Produced by Perry Cross, Book by A.J. Russell, Adapted from the short story by Stephen Vincent Benet, Musical Direction Henri Rene, Choreography Ted Cappy, Art Direction Herb Andrews, Costumes Guy Kent, Executive Producer Henry Jaffe, a Sewanee Production." List of songs in the production. 4pp. Page 2: "From the Original Chevy Show Television Production."

MISC-63   Fall In Line (March). m. George Rosey (Composer of the famous *Honeymoon March, Handicap March, Espanita Waltzes, Maybe,* &c, &c). Published by Jos. W. Stern and Company, No. 34 East 21st Street, New York, NY. 1904. [V-1: Gn/w/bk] [V-2: R/w/bk] [V-3: Bl/bk] drawing of campaign parade. "The Campaign March That Will Stir The Country." "?: The Next President." "Fall in line for the next campaign, Fall in line for parade again, Fall in line to nominate, Fall in line for your candidate, fall in line for a man of note, Fall in line for an honest vote, Fall in line with brooms & tins, Fall in line for the man who wins." 6pp. Page 6: Advertising.

MISC-64 Nomination Quick Step. m. E. Mack. Published by W.R. Smith, No. 135 North Eighth Street, Philadelphia, PA. 1868. Non-pictorial. "Noah's Ark, Easy and Progressive Pieces." List of other titles in series.

MISC-65 The Song Of All Songs. w. Tony Pastor. m. "Air: *The Captain with his Whiskers*." Published by Charles Magnus, No. 12 Frankfort Street, New York, NY. [186-]. [4 13/16" × 7 7/8"]. Hand colored litho of the "President's House." "Written and Sung by Tony Pastor." 2pp.

MISC-66 Campaign March! m. Thomas J. Filas. Published by Will Rossiter, No. 173 West Madison Street, Chicago, IL. 1956. Non-pictorial. "May the Best One Win!" 6pp. Page 2: Blank.

MISC-67 Hail To The Chief. w.a. Bob Saffer and George Mysels. Published by Old Glory Music Publishing Company, No. 345 West 58th Street, New York, NY. 1962. B/w "Seal of the Presidential of the United States." 4pp. Page 4: Blank.

MISC-68(A) It Gets Lonely In The White House. w.m. Irving Berlin. Published by Irving Berlin Music, No. 1650 Broadway, New York, NY. 1962. R/w/b stars. "Leland Howard presents Robert Ryan, Nanette Fabrey in *Mr. President*, A new musical comedy, Music and Lyrics by Irving Berlin, Book by Howard Lindsay and Russel Crouse, Directed by Joshua Logan with Anita Gillette, Jack Haskell, Jack Washburn, Stanley Grover, Jerry Strickle, Wisa D'Orso, Settings & Lighting by Jo Mielziner, Costumes supervised by Theonir Aldredge, Choreographed by Peter Gennaro, Musical Direction by Jay Blackton, Orchestrations by Philip J. Lang, Dance Music arranged and orchestrated by Jack Elliott." 6pp. Page 2: Blank.

(B) The Washington Twist. 6pp. Page 6: Advertising.

(C) The First Lady. 6pp. Page 6: Advertising.

(D) Meat And Potatoes. 6pp. Page 2: Blank. Page 6: Advertising.

(E) Is He The Only Man In The World. 6pp. Page 2: Blank. Page 6: Advertising.

(F) They Love Me. 6pp. Page 6: Advertising.

(G) I've Got To Be Around. 6pp. Page 2: Blank. Page 6: Advertising.

(H) The Secret Service. 6pp. Page 6: Advertising.

(I) This Is A Great Country. 6pp. Page 6: Advertising.

(J) Don't Be Afraid Of Romance. 6pp. Page 2: Blank. Page 6: Advertising.

(K) Empty Pockets Filled With Love. 10pp. Page 2: Blank. Page 10: Advertising.

(L) Let's Go Back To The Waltz. 4pp. Page 4: Advertising.

(M) Glad To Be Home. 6pp. Page 6: Advertising.

(N) In Our Hide Away. 6pp. Page 2: Blank. Page 6: Advertising.

(O) Pigtails And Freckles. 6pp. Page 2: Blank. Page 6: Advertising.

(P) I'm Gonna Get Him. 6pp. Page 6: Advertising.

(Q) Song For Belly Dancer. 6pp. Page 2: Blank. Page 6: Advertising.

(R) Laugh It Up.

(S) Once Every Four Years.

(T) Poor Joe. 6pp. Page 2: Blank. Page 6: Advertising.

MISC-69 Meet The Future President. w. Arthur Swanstrom. m. Mabel Wayne. Published by Popular Melodies, Inc., No. 1619 Broadway, New York, NY. 1936. R/w/b drawing of U.S. Capitol dome, top hat, baby, stripes. 6pp. Pages 2 and 6: Advertising.

MISC-70 Hail To The Chief. w. Albert Gamse. m. James Sanderson. Published by Larrabee Publications, No. 39 West 60th Street, New York, NY. 1964. R/w/b non-pictorial. "Encore Series." 4pp. Page 4: Advertising.

MISC-71 God Save Our President. w. Josephine C. Goodale. m. J.H. Petermann. Published by D. Muller, No. 509 East 76th Street, New York, NY. 1912. B/w drawing of flags, eagle. "Dedicated To the American People." 4pp. Page 2: *My Country 'Tis of Thee*. Page 3: **God Save The President**.

MISC-72 Vote For Mister Rhythm. w.m. Leo Robin, Ralph Rainger, Al Siegel. Published by Famous Music Corporation, No. 1619 Broadway, New York, NY. 1936. B/w drawing of man at piano, music notes. "Featured by Martha Raye in Paramount's 'The Big Broadcast of 1937.'" "Famous Compositions." 4pp. Page 2: "Professional Copy."

MISC-73 Let's Get Together. w.m. Larry Merchant, Bob and Marion Jaqua. Published by The JAQUA Company, Grand Rapids, MI. 1950. Bl/w drawing of elephants. "Stop Confusion, Go Republicans." 6pp. Page 6: Advertising.

MISC-74 The Black Hills Of South Dakota. w.m. Ruth Gammon Brown. Published by Ruth Gammon Brown, No. 128 Wall Street, Lead, South Dakota. 1948. B/w photo of Mt. Rushmore. "Dedicated to Ruth and Web Hill." 4pp. Page 4: Blank.

MISC-75 Hail To The Chief. m. James Sanderson. a. Hugo Frey. Published by Robbins Music Corporation, No. 799 Seventh Avenue, New York, NY. 1942. Pl/w drawing of flowers, geometric design border. "Robbins Royal Edition." 8pp. Pages 2, 6, 7 and 8: Advertising. Page 3: Non-illustrated title page.

MISC-76 Mt Rushmore Memorial March. m. Charles H. Banning (Author of *The Lightning Express*). Published by A.W. Perry's Sons, Sedalia, MO. 1939. B/w photo of partially finished Mt. Rushmore with faces of George Washington, Thomas Jefferson and Abraham Lincoln only. "Upon these Rocks of Ages man has carved Historical Sages." "Dedicated to Mr. Gutzon Borglum." 4pp. Page 4: Advertising.

MISC-77 Look Up America. w.m. Bill Backer, Billy Davis and Rod McBrien. Published by Shada Music, Inc., New York, NY. "Distributed by Big 3." 1974. B/w photos of Mt. Rushmore, Niagara Falls, Grand Canyon, Golden Gate Bridge, Statue of Liberty and the Liberty Bell. "This song was originally featured in the famous commercials for Coca-Cola." 4pp. Page 4: Advertising.

MISC-78 Beautiful Hills Of Dakota. w.m. Benjamin C. Stoller. Published by Nordyke Music Publications, Hollywood, CA. 1949. Be/br photo of George Washington, Thomas Jefferson, Theodore Roosevelt and Abraham Lincoln on Mt. Rushmore, Black Hills Passion Play buildings. Be/br drawing of hills, tree. 6pp. Pages 2 and 6: Advertising.

MISC-79 Spirit Of '76. w. Carl Lertzman. m. Al Delory. Published by United Artists Music Publishing Group. "Distributed by Big 3." Copyright 1975 by United Artists Music Company, Inc. and the Unart Music Corporation, New York, NY. R/w/bl/br/y drawings of flag, two drummers, fife player, rocket, jet, city, Mt. Rushmore carvings. 4pp. Page 4: Publishing data.

MISC-80 Vote For Mister Rhythm. w.m. Leo Robin, Ralph Rainger, Al Siegel. Published by Famous Music, No. 1619 Broadway, New York, NY. 1936. B/w photos of "Jack Benny, George Burns and Gracie Allen, Leopold Stokowski and Symphony Orchestra, Martha Raye, Bennie Goodman and His Orchestra, Shirley Ross, Benny Fields, Eleanore Whitney, Bill Lee, Virginia Weidler, David Holt, Larry Adler, Ray Milland, Frank Forest, Bob Burns." Y/bk/w cover. "Paramount presents *The Big Broadcast of 1937*." List of other songs in film. 6pp. Pages 2 and 6: Advertising.

MISC-81 De Next President Am Gwine Ter Be Er Coon. w. Norman Jefferies. m. Richard Stahl. Published by Oliver Ditson Company, Boston, MA.

1896. Bl/w non-pictorial geometric designs. "The Latest Campaign Song as sung with immense success by Will H. Bray in Chas. H. Hoyt's satirical comedy *A Contented Woman* (Hoyt and McKee Properties)." 6pp. Page 2: Blank. Page 6: Advertising.

MISC-82 Vote! Vote! Vote! w.m. Tommy Johnston. Published by Broadcast Music, Inc., No. 580 Fifth Avenue, New York 19, NY. 1952. Ma/w geometric designs. 6pp. Pages 2 and 6: Advertising.

MISC-83 Let's Have A Party. w. Cliff Friend and Joe Haymes. m. Phil Baxter. Copyright 1932 by Olman Music Corporation, No. 745 Seventh Avenue, New York, NY. [8 1/2" × 11"]. Non-pictorial. "Professional Copy." Copyright "Warning." 4pp. Pages 1 and 4: Extra verses including special 1932 election lyrics. Pages 2 and 3: Original version including musical notation.

MISC-84 I'd Rather Be Mr. Murphy Than The President. w.m. Boyle Woolfolk. Published by Jerome H. Remick and Company, New York, NY. 1907. O/ma/w photos of Murray and Mack—"Very truly yours, Murry and Mack [facsimile handwriting]," and of Boyle Woolfolk. "Murray and Mack In Their New Musical Gaiety *The Sunny Side of Broadway*, Book by Chas. Murray and Eugene Walters." List of other "Musical Numbers" in the show.

MISC-85 President's March. m. Leslie Coward. Published by Chappell & Company, Inc., No. 609 Fifth Avenue, New York, NY. Copyright 1935 and 1967. Bk/bl/w drawing by George Martin of two children at a piano. "For Piano Solo." 4pp. Page 4: Advertisement for the souvenir song folio "Gallant Men." Facsimile of cover of the folio including photographs of Senator Everett Dirksen, Capitol building.

MISC-86 Please Mr. President. w.m. Allie Wrubel and Mose Sigler. Copyright 1933 by De Sylva, Brown and Henderson, Inc., New York, NY. 1933. [8 1/2" × 11"]. Non-pictorial. Copyright "Warning." 4pp. Page 4: Blank.

MISC-87 And Henry's Meant For President When We A-Fordin' Go (Fox Trot). w.m. Roy Pauley. Published by Our Next President Company, Publishers, Detroit, MI. [ca. 1932]. O/w/gn drawing of a Ford Model-A with family, U.S. Capitol building—"Lets Go." 6pp. Page 2 and 6: Blank.

MISC-88 Election Waltz. m. Julie Jervoise. Published by W.A. Evans & Bro., Publishers, No. 1 Columbia Street, Boston, MA. 1884. Non-pictorial geometric designs. 4pp. Page 4: Blank.

MISC-89 Hail To The Chief. m. Air: *Red, White and Blue*. Published by C. Bohn, Washington, DC. [ca. 1862]. [5 1/2" × 8"]. N/c litho of the "Battle of Lexington, Mo., Sep. 16, 1861." Printed on lined note paper.

MISC-90 Pennsylvania. w.m. Joe Francis Weber. Published by Joe Francis Weber, Scranton, PA. 1936. R/w/b drawing of Liberty Bell, keystone, stars—"The First Continental Congress," "Birth Place of Old Glory," "The Declaration of Independence," "Washington at Valley Forge," "Lincoln at Gettysburg." "Official Parade March Song of American Legion Post No. 121." 4pp. Page 4: Logo. Narrative—"Important events in Pennsylvania history."

MISC-91 Something Just Broke. w.m. Stephen Sondheim. Published by Warner Bros. Publications, Inc., No. 265 Secaucus, NJ. 1993. Bl/w stars. "The new song created for the London production of *Assassins*." 16pp. Page 2: Blank.

MISC-92 Mt. Rushmore. w.m. May Kincaid and Beryl Severin. Published by Beryl Severin, Philip, SD. 1939. B/w photo of Mt. Rushmore carvings. Bl/w trees, geometric designs. 6pp. Page 3: Blank. Page 6: Geometric drawings of trees, border.

MISC-93 My Country. w. Jud Strunk. m. Dennis McCarthy. Published by Every Little Tune, Inc., No. 9200

Sunset Boulevard, Los Angeles, CA. Copyright 1974 by Every Little Tune, Inc., Kayteekay Music and Pierre Cossette Music Company — "A Product of the Wes Ferrell Organization." "Multicolor drawings of Abraham Lincoln, John F. Kennedy, Martin Luther King, homes, flag, flute, heart, football game, hamburger, canyon, skyline — "Rock — Jazz — Soul — Country & Western — Folk — Blues." "Recorded by Jud Strunk on Capitol Records." "Distributed by Big 3." 6pp. Page 6: Advertising.

MISC-94 He Used To Be One Of The Boys In Blue. w. Raymond A. Brown. m. Harry Von Tilzer. Published by Harry Von Tilzer Music Publishing Company, No. 42 West 28th Street, New York, NY. 1902. Br/w photos of Raymond A. Brown and of Harry Von Tilzer inscribed "Our Trade Mark." Bk/bl/br/w drawing of a soldier and a sailor, silhouette of battle scene over the names of military leaders including "Washington, Lafayette, Warren, Farragut, John Paul Jones, Sherman, Sheridan, Worden, Scott, Grant, Lincoln, Garfield and McKinley, Dewey, Schley." 6pp. Page 6: Advertising.

MISC-95 Rolling Eggs On Easter Morn. w.m. Raymond A. Sterling. Copyright 1955 by Sterling Music Publishing Company, No. 117 West 48th Street, New York, NY. [8 1/2" × 11"]. Non-pictorial. 4pp. Pages 1 and 4: Blank.

MISC-96 Hail To The Chief. m. James Sanderson. e. William Conrad. Published by Belwin, Inc. New York, NY. [ca. 1930]. N/c photo of pastoral scene. "Edition Beautiful." "E.B. No. 637." 4pp. Page 4: Advertising.

MISC-97 Song Of The Presidents. w.m. Joyce Eilers Bacak. Published by Jenson Publications, Inc., P.O. Box 248, New Berlin, WI. "Exclusively distributed by Hal Leonard Publishing Company, 7777 Bluemound Road, Milwaukee, WI. 53213. 1988. [6 3/4" × 10 9/16"]. R/w/b drawing of George Washington, Theodore Roosevelt, Thomas Jefferson and Abraham Lincoln, stars and stripes design. "2-Part Accompanied." 8pp.

MISC-98 Kisses. w. Ric Harlow. m. Bronislau Kaper. Published by M. Witmark & Sons, New York, NY. 1964. B/w photo of Fred MacMurray in woman's hat, Polly Bergen in the President's chair. "Love Theme from *Kisses For My President*." "Warner Bros. Presents Fred MacMurray, Polly Bergan in *Kisses For My President*, co-starring Arlene Dahl, Edward Andrews and also starring Eli Wallach as Valdez, a Pearlayne Production, Produced and Directed by Curtis Bernhardt." 4pp. Page 4: Narrative — "ASCAP?"

MISC-99 The Commanderess-In-Chief. w. Glen Mac Donough. m. Victor Herbert. Published by M. Witmark and Sons, New York, NY. 1905. Bl/gn/w geometric designs. Bl/w photo of Lew Fields. "Lew Fields' Stock Company presents *It Happened in Nordland*." "Produced under direction [of] Julian Mitchell, Book and Lyrics by Glen MacDonough." "Lew Fields' Theatre, Fred. R. Hamlin, Man'gr." 8pp.

MISC-100(A) Take Care Of This House. w. Alan Jay Lerner. m. Leonard Bernstein. Published by Music of The Times Publishing Corporation, New York, NY. 1976. [8 1/2" × 11"]. N/c drawing of an African-American family, The White House, Statue of Liberty, flag, and eagle. "From the Musical Production *1600 Pennsylvania Avenue*." 8pp. Pages 2 and 7: Blank. Page 8: Advertising.

(B) President Jefferson's Sunday Afternoon Party March.

(C) Bright And Black.

MISC-101 Mt. Rushmore (Tone Poem). m. J. Frederick Muller. Published by Neil A. Kjos Music Company, Park Ridge, IL. 1976. O/w/bk non-pictorial. "On the massive granite face of a mountain in the Black Hills of South Dakota. Gutzon Borglum created the likenesses of

George Washington, Thomas Jefferson, Abraham Lincoln and Theodore Roosevelt. Blasting began in August of 1927 after a dedication speech by President Calvin Coolidge. Each head is approximately 60 feet high… and can be seen from a distance of 60 miles." Parts set for Band.

MISC-102 There's Nothing Like A Democratic Dame (Name). w.m. Carolyn Cline Furr. Published by Casey Music Company, No. 530 Benton Boulevard, Kansas City, MO. 1955. Gn/w drawing of donkey playing a bass drum. 4pp.

MISC-103 Our Presidents (1789-1913). w.m. John J. Cauchois. Published by Uncle Sam Music Publishing Company, New York, NY. 1913. R/w/b drawing of eagle and shield, border. 6pp. Pages 2 and 6: Advertising.

MISC-104 Elected! w.m. Alice Cooper, Michael Bruce, Glen Burton, Dennis Dunaway and Neal Smith. Published by Bizarre Music, Inc. and Alive Enterprises, Los Angeles, CA. 1972. B/w and n/c photo of Alice Cooper taking oath of office for Presidency. "Alice Cooper Elected!" "Recorded by Alice Cooper on Warner Bros. Records." "Distributed by Big 3." 8pp.

MISC-105 The Monkey That Became President. w.m. Tom T. Hall. Published by Hallnote Music and Chappell & Company, Inc. 1972. B/w "Drawing by Gordon Kennedy, Seventh Grade" of a monkey in suit sitting behind a desk, facsimile signature of Gordon Kennedy. "Recorded by Tom T. Hall on Mercury Records." 4pp.

MISC-106 Vote For Names. w.m. Charles E. Ives. Published by Southern Music Publishers, Inc., Peer International Corporation, No. 1619 Broadway, New York, NY. 1912. [1968 Edition]. B/w globe logo — "Peer-Southern Organization Links the World." "For Voice and Piano." 4pp.

MISC-107 Discovering America. w.m. Christopher Bishop and Ben Shelfer. a. Ed Lojeski. Published by Hal Leonard Publishing Company, No. 7777 West Bluemound Road, Milwaukee, WI. 53213. Copyright 1991 by Milwin Music. [7 3/4" × 10 1/2"]. N/c drawings of Mt. Rushmore, "Christopher Columbus — Quincentenary Jubilee 500," space shuttle, Statue of Liberty. "Theme Song for The Christopher Columbus Quincentenary Jubilee." 8pp.

MISC-108 Faces Of Rushmore. w.m. Wm. H. Hill. Published by Gore Publishing Company, No. 314 South Elm, Denton, TX. 76201. 1994. B/w photo of Mt. Rushmore. "Full Score." 20pp. Page 2: "Program Notes and Dedication."

MISC-109 Song Of America. w. Popular Aires. m.a. Mac Huff. Published by Hal Leonard Publishing Company, No. 7777 West Bluemound Road, Milwaukee, WI. 53213. 1984. [7 3/4" × 10 1/2"]. N/c photos of Mt. Rushmore, Statue of Liberty, Monument Valley, flag. "A Choral Review Celebrating Our Home, Our Hope, Our Freedom." "Performance Notes by John Jackson." "SABT Singer's Edition." 56pp.

MISC-110 Our Presidents Speak. w. John F. Kennedy, Franklin D. Roosevelt, Calvin Coolidge, George Bush. m. Eugene Butler. Published by Hinshaw Music, Inc., P.O. Box 470, Chapel Hill, NC. 27514. 1989. [6 11/16" × 10 1/2"]. Bk/gn/w non-pictorial cover. "Four Part Equal Voices (Any Combination), with Piano." 12pp. Page 3: "Commissioned by the Choral Division, South Carolina Music Educators Association."

MISC-111 State Of The Union. w.m. J. Chris Moore. Published by The Heritage Music Press, No. 501 East Third Street, Dayton, OH. 45401. 1973. [7" × 10 1/2"]. B/w/gn litho of logo — "H.M.P." and a horn. "No. W99 (S.A.T.B.)." 12pp. Page 2: "For Daniel Calvin McMillan, April 6, 1972."

MISC-112(A) The Voice Of Freedom. w. Ron Willis. m. Lanny Allen.

Published by Broadman Press, Nashville, TN. 1975. [8" × 10 7/16"]. R/w/b drawings of George Washington, Abraham Lincoln, Ben Franklin, Liberty Bell, church, torch, flag. "Freedom Song Choral Series (SATB)." 16pp.

(B) **America The Beautiful**. w. Katherine Lee Bates. m. Samuel T. Wood. a. David L. Danner. "Genevox Music Group."

(C) **I Care**. w.m. Turner.

(D) **America, You're Beautiful To Me**. w. Allan Davis. m. John Hallett.

(E) **If I Were A Fifer**. w.m. Jacqueline Hanna McNair.

(F) **We Would Remember**. w.m. Philip M. Young.

(G) **To God And Country Let Us Sing**. w.m. Gordon Young.

(H) **This Is My America**. w. David Keith. m. Claude L. Bass.

(I) **America Our Country**. w. Mary Kay Parrish.

MISC-113 **Favorite Son**. w. Betty Comden and Adolph Green. m. Cy Colemen. a. Jay Althouse. Published by CCP Belwin, Inc., No. 15800 N.W. 48th Avenue, Miami, FL. 33014. W.B. Music Corp. Copyright 1991 by Notable Music Company. [7" × 10 5/16"]. Bl/gn/w cover. "From the Tony Award winning show *The Will Rogers Follies*." "Two-Part, Accompanied, with Optional Guitar, Bass and Drums." "Pop Choral Series." Page 2: "Optional Dialogue: Reporter — 'So will you run for President or not, Mr. Rogers?' Will Rogers — 'I sure will...'" Page 16: Advertising.

MISC-114 **Put The Right Man At The Wheel**. w.m. Will S. Hays. e. Gregg Smith. Published by G. Shirmer, New York, NY. [Edition 1974]. [6 7/8" × 10 3/8"]. B/w drawing of Miss Columbia, flag. "America's Bicentennial Songs from the Great Sentimental Age (1850-1900)." "For Four-Part Mixed Voices, Piano Accompaniment." List of other titles in series. 8pp. Page 8: Advertising.

MISC-115 **Shrine Of Democracy**. w.m. Paul Yoder. Published by Loop Music Publishing Company, Park Ridge, IL. 1967. [6 3/4" × 10 1/16"]. Be/bk non-pictorial cover. "SATB Chorus with Piano Accompaniment." "May be performed by the following combinations: Chorus with Piano Accompaniment, Chorus with Band Accompaniment." 8pp. Pages 2 and 7: Blank. Page 3: "To the Rapid City, S.D. Band Festival." Page 8: Advertising. [Mt. Rushmore Tribute].

MISC-116 **Champ! Champ! Champ! The Boys Are Marching**. [1912]. [8 1/2" × 11"]. Pl/w non-pictorial mimeograph. 2pp. Page 2: Blank.

MISC-117 **America** (My Country 'Tis of Thee). w. Samuel F. Smith. m. Henry Carey. a. John Coates, Jr. Published by Shawnee Press, Inc., Delaware Water Gap, PA. 18327. Copyright 1972 and 1984. [V-1: Gn/bk/w] [V-2: Br/bk/w] facsimile of the Declaration of Independence with signatures of John Adams, Thomas Jefferson, &c. [V-1: "For 2-Part Voices (S.A./T.B.)"] [V-2: "For T.B.B. and Piano with Optional Audience Participation"]. 8pp.

MISC-118 **I'm A Member Of The G.O.P.** w.m. Red Mescara and Parke Frankenfield. Published by Sands Music Corporation, No. 1619 Broadway, New York 19, NY. 1964. R/w drawing of an elephant playing banjo sitting on a barrel. 4pp. Page 4: Blank.

MISC-119 **Hail To The Chief**. a. Prendiville. In: *The Leaders Joy Band Book*, page 7. Published by Edward A. Samuels, Publisher, Boston, MA. [ca. 1890]. [6 7/8" × 5"]. Non-pictorial. "Containing Sixty-One National and Popular Airs." 32pp.

MISC-120 **A Trip To Washington** (March Two-Step). m. Walter V. Ullner. Published by Gagle Brothers, Star Publications, No. 1276 Broadway, New York, NY. 1898. R/w/gn drawing of the Washington Monument, The Capitol and "The White House." 8pp. Pages 2, 7 and 8: Advertising.

MISC-121 The Search For A Likely Candidate. w.m. Henry and Bobbie Shaffner and Saul Broudy. Copyright 1991 by Keynote Associates, One Montgomery Avenue, Bala Cynwyd, PA. [8 1/2" × 11"]. Non-pictorial letter paper with words only supporting Mario Cuomo for president. 2pp. Page 2: Blank.

MISC-122 Republican Campaign Song. w.m. Julia M. Rogers. a. George H. Gairclough. Copyright [ca. 1920] by Julia M. Rogers [Minnesota?]. Handwritten manuscript.

MISC-123 Hail To The Chief. m. Sanderson. Published by Lee & Walker, No. 722 Chestnut Street, Philadelphia, PA. [ca. 1963]. Non-pictorial black border. "National and Patriotic Songs, Ballads, &c, Arranged for the Piano." List of other titles in series.

MISC-124 Gary's Got The Big Mo! (The Gary Hart Campaign Song). w.m. Henry and Bobbie Shaffner. Copyright 1994 by Henry and Roberta Shaffner, [One Montgomery Avenue, Bala Cynwyd, PA]. [8 1/2" × 11"]. Non-pictorial letter paper. 4pp. Pages 2 and 4: Blank.

MISC-125 McAdoo'll Do. w. Newt A. Morris. m. "To the Tune of *Battle Hymn Of The Republic*." Published by Times Publishing Company, Marietta, GA. 1924. [4 1/23" × 6"]. Be/bk drawing of William G. McAdoo, two roosters sitting on fences labeled—"Georgia" and "The Nation," crowing—"McAdoo'll Do." "Compliments of Newt A. Morris, Delegate, State at Large, Marietta, Cobb County, Georgia, the birth-place of Hon. Wm. G. McAdoo." 4pp. Pages 2 and 3: Song. Page 4: B/w photo of "Aunt Julia, the old ex-slave mammy, Mr. McAdoo's first nurse, Mr. McAdoo, and Jim Democrat, the old ex-salve darkey who went after and drove Dr. E.J. Setze to the McAdoo home on the night he was born." "This photograph was taken on the steps of the home where Hon. Wm. G. McAdoo was born..."

MISC-126 I Hear America Calling. w.m. Benjamin Edwards Neal. a. Jeffery Marlowe. Published by Neal Publishing Company. Sole Selling Agents: Boston Music Company, Boston, MA. Copyright 1941 by Benjamin Edwards Neal. [6 13/16" × 10 5/16"]. Be/bk drawings of George Washington, Abraham Lincoln and Thomas Jefferson, ribbon border. List of other arrangements available. 8pp. Page 2: Blank. Page 3: "For Four-Part Chorus of Men's Voices with Piano Accompaniment." Page 8: Advertising.

MISC-127 I Hear America Calling. w.m. Benjamin Edwards Neal. Published by Neal Publishing Company. Sole Selling Agents: Boston Music Company, Boston, MA. 1941. R/w/b drawings of George "Washington," Abraham "Lincoln," Thomas "Jefferson," Benjamin "Franklin," "Patrick Henry," "John Paul Jones," Andrew "Jackson" and Commodore "Perry." Bl/w photo of John Charles Thomas—"Featured by John Charles Thomas." "For information regarding the plan of organization to celebrate 'I Am An American Day' in your community, write 'I Am An American Day' Headquarters, Los Angeles, California." 8pp.

MISC-128 A Friend. w.m. Capt. James LeRoy Evans (Capt. Jim). Published by Jim Evans, P.O. Box 663, Bacliff, TX. 77518. 1976. [11" × 14"]. Non-pictorial. "This Song and Poem to be on Ballot for Vote as National." "C & W Ballad." "Wrote 6/21/63." "Century 21 Records and Tapes." [Song contained in a 6 page flyer for James LeRoy Evans for President, Heaven On Earth Party].

MISC-129 Hail To The Chief. m. Sanderson. In: *Willig's Pocket Companion for Flute or Violin, Containing the most Fashionable Airs [1]*, page 41. Published and Sold by George Willig, No. 171 Chesnut Street, Philadelphia, PA. Gn/bk/be marbled hard covers. Title page: B/w engraving of woman with harp. 106pp. [8 1/4" × 5"]. [See note at W-9963].

MISC-130 My Country 'Tis Of Thee [Excerpt]. [ca. 1918] N/c celluloid button with song excerpt, eagle, Capitol building, Liberty Bell, Statue of Liberty, flags, goldenrod, likenesses of George Washington and Abraham Lincoln. N/c photo of a U.S. World War I soldier on horseback. [6" × 8"].

MISC-131 Hail To The Chief. In: *The Army and Navy Fife Instructor: Containing the Calls, Signals, and the Complete Camp and Garrison Duties as Practised* [sic] *in the Army and Navy of the United States, Including the Volunteer and Regular Service, Containing the National Airs, and a Large Collection of Marches, Quicksteps, Waltzes, Polkas, &c.*, page 17. e.a. Elias Howe. Published by Elias Howe, Agt., No. 103 Court Street, Boston, MA. Copyright 1863 by Willard Howe.

MISC-132 Sing A Song Of Friendship [Song Book]. w.m. Irving Caesar. Published by Irving Caesar, No. 1619 Broadway, New York, NY. 1946. Gd/o/bk photos of children, globe. 72pp.

(A) **Thomas Jefferski**, page 17.

(B) **We Address Him As Mr. President**, page 35.

MISC-133 The Man From Tennessee. w. Hampton P. Carter. m. Howard J. Crook. Copyright 1952 by Hampton P. Carter, Madison, NC. [8 1/2" × 11"]. B/w photo of Estes Kefauver. 2pp. Page 2: Blank. [Kefauver for President lyrics].

MISC-134 Mr. President (Have Pity On The Working Man). w.m. Randy Newman. Copyright 1974 Warner-Tamerlane Publishing Corporation. In: *Forest Gump, The Soundtrack*, page 96. Published by Hal Leonard Corporation, No. 7777 West Bluemound Road, Milwaukee, WI. 53203.

MISC-135 The Presidents. w. Randy Rogel. m. Gioacchino Rossini. a. Marty Gold. Copyright 1995 and 1996 by Warner-Tamerlane Publishing Corporation. In: *Animaniacs*, page 33. Published by Warner Bros. Publications, No. 15800 N.W. 48th Avenue, Miami, FL. 33014.

MISC-136 We Need A Man. w.m. George M. Cohan. Published by Famous Music Corporation, No. 719 Seventh Avenue, New York, NY. 1932. B/w photos of George M. Cohan. Pk/bk/w geometric designs. "Paramount presents George M. Cohan in *The Phantom President* with Claudette Colbert & Jimmy Durante — A Paramount Picture." 6pp. Page 6: Advertising.

MISC-137 Dear Mr. ~~President~~ Jesus. w.m. Richard Klender. Published by Hal Leonard Publishing Corporation. Copyright 1985 by Klenco, Inc. R/w/bl/bk drawing of child in Television screen. B/w photo of Richard Klender. "Songwriter, Richard Klender is very concerned for hurting children and adults who have led painful lives. He says, 'I pray that people everywhere will re-experience God's love for children, and that this song will help let out our built up pain and frustration over child abuse incidents, with hopeful tears.'" We all can make an individual difference in overcoming worldwide child abuse, through love, understanding and prayer." "Available on the album Power Source — *Shelter From The Storm*." 6pp.

MISC-138 I'd Rather Be Right. w. Lorenz Hart. m. Richard Rodgers. Published by Chappell & Company, Inc., Rockefeller Center, New York, NY. 1937. O/w/bk drawing of Washington Monument, politician with suitcase inscribed "White House, Washington, DC." "Sam H. Harris Presents Geo. M. Cohan in the New Musical Comedy *I'd Rather Be Right*, Book by Geo. S. Kaufman and Moss Hart, Lyrics by Lorenz Hart, Music by Richard Rogers." 6pp. Page 6: Advertising.

MISC-139(A) We Are Coming Father Abraham. w. William Cullen Bryant. m. L.O. Emerson. In: *The Civil*

War Songbook: Complete And Original Sheet Music For 37 Songs, page 30. e. Richard Crawford. Published by Dover Publications, Inc., New York, NY. 1977. [9" × 11 15/16"]. R/bk/gn drawing of soldier.

(B) **The Grant Pill**, page 66. w. Harriet L. Castle. m. J.C. Beckel.

(C) **Jeff In Petticoats**, page 133. w. George Cooper. m. Henry Tucker.

MISC-140 A Hundred Years From Now. w. William B. Speth. m. Ned Underhill. Published by William B. Speth, No. 1432 Lafayette Street, Denver, CO. 1925. R/w/b drawing of woman in pants suit with a man on a neck chain; Statue of woman — "Erected to commemorate our first woman President, elected A.D. 2025" and holding "Ten Commandments — 1. Husbands obey your wives, 2. Husbands must stay home..." 6pp. Page 6: Advertising.

MISC-141 Hail To Our President. w.m. E. May Glenn Toon. Published by E. May Glenn Toon, Wilmington, NC. 1913. B/w drawing of eagle, ribbon inscribed "In Unity There Is Strength," flags, ribbon inscribed "To Thine high memory and loyal trust our echoes penetrate thy noble dust." "First Anthem respectfully dedicated to the Presidents of the United States — Past — Present and Future." 6pp. Pages 2 and 6: Blank.

MISC-142 O'Reilly For President. w.m. Daniel Lord, S.J. Copyright 1941 by Broadcast Music, Inc., No. 580 5th Avenue, New York, NY. Copyright "Warning." 6pp. Page 6: Blank.

MISC-143 Please Mr. President (Slow Fox Trot). m. Allie Wrubel and Mose Sigler. Copyright 1933 by De Sylva, Brown and Henderson. In: *Supreme Dance Folio for Piano*, page 36. Published by De Sylva, Brown and Henderson, No. 745 Seventh Avenue, New York, NY. 1933.

MISC-144 This Man Was Ment For You And Me. w. James A. Frankus. m. Woody Guthrie. Published by James A. Frankus, No. 8526 S.W. Capitol Highway, Portland, OR. July, 1968. [8 1/2" × 11"]. Non-pictorial mimeograph. "Dedicated to Senator Eugene McCarthy for his 1968 Presidential Campaign." "Instructions for Use" — List of 6 instructions. "This Text is set to W. Guthrie's familiar melody, *This Land Is Your Land*." 4pp. Pages 2 and 3: Sheet music. Page 4: Blank.

MISC-145 This Man Is Your Man — This Man Is My Man. m. Tune — *This Land is Your Land* by Woody Guthrie. Published for rally in Portland, OR. 1970. [5 7/8" × 8 1/2"]. Non-pictorial. 2pp. Page 2: Blank. [Rally song for Robert F. Kennedy].

MISC-146 Hold Firm The American Way. w.m. Clarence E. Cunningham. Published by Mountain States Music Company, Somers, MT. 1952. R/w/b drawings of George Washington — "Put none but Americans on guard tonight," Abraham Lincoln — "If danger ever reaches us, it must spring up amongst us," Theodore Roosevelt — "The man who debauches our public life is a foe to our nation," Douglas MacArthur — "Above all else let us regain our faith in ourselves and rededicated all that is within us to the repair and preservation of our free institutions," eagle, ribbon — "For the boys who died for you, for the living and the unborn too." "Proclaim Today the American Way — Fight For This Land of Ours." 4pp. Page 4: "Hold Firm The American Way, Defeat Socialism and All Other Un-Americanisms and America Will Keep Singing." List of other songs by same composer.

MISC-147 Upon These Grounds. m. John Tatgenhorst. Published by Band Music Press. Distributed by Carl Fischer, No. 62 Cooper Square, New York, NY. 1977. Non-pictorial. "Full Score." 20pp. Page 2: "The musical themes in this special overture for band were originally composed for a

(MISC) MISCELLANEOUS 420

twenty-two minute film score and TV documentary about the White House gardens. The music underscored a brief tour of the White House grounds, its many historical and social changes and special honors for the many Presidents, First Ladies and First Families who have occupied this famous 'Americas' House.'"

MISC-148 **This Man The People Found.** w. James A. Frankus. Published by James A. Frankus, No. 8526 S.W. Capitol Highway, Portland, OR. July, 1968. [8 1/2" × 11"]. Non-pictorial mimeograph. "Dedicated to Senator Eugene McCarthy for his 1968 Presidential Campaign." "Instructions for Use"— List of 6 instructions. Pages 2 and 3: Sheet music. "Dedicated to Senator Eugene McCarthy for his 1968 Presidential Campaign." Page 4: Blank.

MISC-149 **The Long Tall Guy** (In The Coon Skin Cap). w.m. Hank Fort, A.S.C.A.P. Copyright 1952 by Tennessee Music Publishers, Warner Building, Nashville, TN. Non-pictorial. 2pp. [Estes Kefauver].

MISC-150 **That Great American Home!** w.m. Al Sherman, Al Lewis and Allie Wrubel. Published by E. and R. Music Company, No. 299 Broadway, New York, NY. 1933. R/w/b drawing by Barbelle of large family in various ethnic outfits sitting around a table, portraits of George "Washington" and Abraham "Lincoln" on wall. 4pp. Page 4: Advertising.

MISC-151 **Hail To The Chief.** w. Sir Walter Scott. m. James Sanderson. a. Ethel Smith. In: *Stars and Stripes Forever*, page 6. Published by Ethel Smith Corporation, New York, NY. 1953. R/w/bl/bk photos of Ethel Smith, scenes from the movie. "John Philip Sousa arranges by Ethel Smith for pre-set and spinet model Hammond organs. From the Technicolor production *Stars and Stripes Forever* starring Clifton Webb, costarring Debra Paget, Robert Wagner, Ruth Hussey, 20th Century Fox." 36pp.

MISC-152 **Republican Unity Dinner** (Program and Song Sheet). Published by Republican Finance Committee of Pennsylvania, No. 228 South Broad Street, Philadelphia, PA. [ca. 1944]. R/w/b stripe. "In Unity There Is Strength." "Republicans Unite." 4pp.

MISC-153 **Take Care Of This House.** w. Alan Jay Lerner. m. Leonard Bernstein. Published by Music of The Times Publishing Corporation, New York, NY. Charles Hanson Distributor, Educational Sheet Music & Books, Inc., No. 1860 Broadway, New York, NY. Copyright 1976 by Alan Jay Lerner and Leonard Bernstein. [8 1/2" × 11"]. Non-pictorial geometric designs. "From the Musical Production *1600 Pennsylvania Avenue*." 4pp.

MISC-154 **The Good Time Train.** w. Johnny Lehmann. m. Jimmie Driftwood. Copyright 1960 by Worden Music Company, Inc. In: *Welcome To The Jumbo Jamboree* [Program and Song Book]. Published by Republican National Committee, Washington, DC. 1960. [8 1/2" × 11"]. R/w/b drawing of an elephant. "Uline Arena, April 4, 1960, Washington, D.C." 4pp. Page 4: Song.

MISC-155(A) **Hail Columbia.** w. Joseph Hopkinson. m. Phyla [sic]. In: *Songs Every One Should Know*, page 12. Published by American Book Company, New York, NY. Copyright 1908 by Clifton Johnson. 156pp. [6 3/4" × 8 1/2"]. Bl/br geometric cover design.

(B) **Hail To The Chief**, page 20.

MISC-156 **Treasury Of American Song.** a. Elie Siegmeister. Published by Alfred A. Knoff, New York, NY. Copyright 1940 and 1943. [9 7/8" × 10 1/2"]. Blue embossed cover. 424pp.

(A) **Jefferson & Liberty**, page 80.

(B) **Hunters Of Kentucky**, page 106. w. Samuel Woodworth. m. *The Old Oaken Bucket*.

(C) **Lincoln & Liberty**, page 176. w. F.A. Simpson. m. *Old Rosen The Bow*.

(D) **Abraham's Daughter**, page 184. w.m. Septimus Winner.
(E) **Old Abe Lincoln**, page 311.
MISC-157 Abraham Jefferson Washington Lee. w.m. Harry Von Tilzer. 1906.
MISC-158 The President. In: *No. 1 Of A New Sett* [sic] *of Cotilions* [sic], page 5. m. Mr. Pierre Landrin Duport (Professor of dancing from Paris and original composer of cadriels [sic]." "Printed for the Author and Copyright Secured." Engraved by [William] "Rollinson Sct." [ca. 1800]. 20pp.
MISC-159 Hail To The Chief. In: *Bacon's Complete Preceptor for the Clarinet, with a selection of airs, marches, &c.)*, page 26. Published by A. Bacon, Music Seller and Publisher, No. 11 South 4th Street, Philadelphia, PA. [1818?]. [W-411].
MISC-160 Inauguration Waltzes. m. Burrill. Published by S.A. Saalfield, No. 839 Broadway, New York, NY. [ca. 1880].
MISC-161 If I'm Elected (To Be The One You Love). w. Sid Wayne. m. Al Frisch. Published by Bourne, Inc., Music Publishers, No 136 West 52nd Street, New York 19, NY. 1956. Bl/w photo of Eddie Fisher. "Recorded by Eddie Fisher with Hugo Winterhalter and His Orchestra." 4pp. Page 4: Advertising.
MISC-162 That Old White House. w.m. Frederick Braun and Bobby Gregory (ASCAP). Published by American Music Publishing Company, No. 14 East 77th Street, New York, NY. 1965.
MISC-163 The Search For A Likely Candidate. w.m. Henry and Bonnie Shaffner (ASCAP) and Saul Broudy. [ca. 1991]. [8 1/2" × 11"]. Nonpictorial. "For Information Contact (215) 667-4063." 2pp. Page 2: Blank.
MISC-164 Appreciation. w. L.H. Poole. m. George C. Stout. Copyright by Geo. C. Stout and L.H. Poole, Baton Rouge, LA. 1931. [10 13/16" × 151/2"]. R/be/bk drawing of the Louisiana State Capitol building, house—"Night Schools for the older people," books—"Free schools for all children." "Dedicated to Governor Huey P. Long." "Paved Highways and Free Bridges." "Help for the old Confederate veterans they were paid their $212.00 each and their pension was raised to $60.00 per month; New four year farmers road program; Millions of dollars in increased sums of money to save schools of state; Repealed tobacco tax; State medical school; Home for epileptics; Thousands of insane treated humanely who formerly lived in straight jackets and jail cells; Port of New Orleans rescued from financial distress — its charges reduced and sprinkler system installed that lowers insurance rate from $1.04 to 29cts. per $1000.00 on property and cargo; charity hospital death rates reduced 300 per cent living salaries for higher court jurists; New Orleans $3,500,000 overdraft debt paid city placed on cash basis and given $700,000 per year for street improvements; Airport and lakefront improvement and sea wall for New Orleans; Natural gas for New Orleans and Jefferson and St. Bernard parishes; Curbing of carbon black menace." 4pp.
MISC-165 Hail To The Chief, page 9. a. George H. Sanders. In: *Ascher's Zephyr Band Book.* c. George H. Sanders. Published by Emil Ascher, Inc., No. 315 Fourth Avenue, New York, NY. 1937. [6 7/8" × 5 1/4"]. R/gn litho of a train. "Zephyr Band Book." 20pp.
MISC-166 I'll Paint The White House Green. w. Jack Conroy. "Sung by Pat Rooney." In: *Jack Conroy's Wrestling Jack Songster, Containing A Lot of The Liveliest and Most Taking Songs and Sketches Ever Put into One Book*, page 52. Published by Clinton T. De Witt, Publisher, No. 33 Rose Street, New York, NY. 1879. [4" × 6 3/8"]. H/c litho of Jack Conroy, two men wrestling. 68pp.
MISC-167 Presidential Drum & Bugle March Book. m. H.O.

(MISC) MISCELLANEOUS

Wheeler. Published by Geo. Southwell Publishing Co., Kansas City, MO. 1926. [6 11/16"x 4 15/16" Bl/bl drawing of George Washington, soldiers playing drum and bugle. "Dedicated to the Presidents of the U.S.A." "Especially Arranged for following combinations -- Bugles or Cornets alone; Snare Drums alone; or Bugles and Drums together — Bass Drum ad lib." "A March for each President." 20pp.

MISC-168(A) **Hail To The Chief**. w. Sir Walter Scott. m. James Sanderson. In: *357 Songs We Love To Sing, Songs for Every Purpose and Occasion for Home School and Assembly Use*, page 254. Published by Hall & McCreary Company, Chicago, IL. 1938. [5 3/4" × 8 3/4"]. R/w/b non-pictorial. 260pp.

(B) **Hail, Columbia**!, page 232. w. Joseph Hopkinson. m. Philip Phile. "The music of this song, originally known as *The Washington March*, is generally attributed to Philip Phile. It was written in 1789 as an inaugural march for George Washington. The words were written nine years later by Joseph Hopkinson for a special occasion. At the time, England and France were at war and Americans were being divided by their sympathies for one or the other of these countries. No allusion is made in this song to either of the countries but its purpose was to keep Americans united. This sentiment has won for *Hail Columbia!* a place among our national songs."

(C) **We Are Coming Father Abra'am**, page 236. w. Hutchinson. m. L.O. Emerson.

MISC-169 **The American Heritage Songbook**. c.a. Ruth Lloyd and Norman Lloyd. Published by American Heritage Publishing Company, Inc., New York, NY. 1969. R/w/b dust jacket. Red embossed cover.

(A) **The Toast**, page 22. w.m. Frances Hopkinson. Litho of George Washington.

(B) **Hail Columbia**, page 26.

(C) **Adams And Liberty**, page 28. w. Robert Treat Paine. m. John Stafford Smith.

(D) **Hunters Of Kentucky**, page 34. w. Samuel Woodworth.

(E) **Tippecanoe And Tyler Too**, page 112. w. Alexander C. Ross.

MISC-170 **Hail To The Chief**. w. Sir. Walter Scott. m. Sanderson. In: *Uncle Sam's Favorite Song Book, The Song Book of the Nation*, page 28. Published by Hall & McCreary, Chicago, IL. 1919. [5 3/4" × 8 3/4"]. R/w/b drawing of Uncle Sam. 132pp.

MISC-171 **My Country 'Tis Of Thee Flag Songs**. Published by Hansen House, No. 1820 West Avenue, Miami Beach, FL. 33139-9913. Copyright 1991 by Shattinger-International Music Corp. [7" × 9 7/8"]. N/c photo of an American Flag. 100pp.

(A) **God Save Our President**, page 44. w.m. S. Winner.

(B) **Grave Of Washington**, page 47. w.m. Marshall S. Pike.

(C) **Hail, Columbia!**, page 48. w. Joseph Hopkinson. m. Philip Phile.

(D) **Lincoln And Liberty**, page 60.

(E) **Washington And Lincoln**, page 79. w.m. Henry C. Work.

MISC-172 **The White House March And Two-Step**. m. Signorina Peppina Muratori. Published for the Composer by The S. Brainard's Sons Company, 298-300 Wabash Avenue, Chicago, IL. 1905. B/w photos of The White House, Signorina Peppina Muratori. B/w geometric designs. 6pp. Pages 2 and 6: Blank.

MISC-173 **Hail To The Chief**. w. Sir Walter Scott. [m. Sanderson]. In: *The Souvenir Minstrel: A Choice Collection of the Most Admired Songs, Duetts, Glees, Choruses, &c., &c., with Several Originals, and Many Favorites of the Principal Vocalists*, page 212. c. C. Soule Cartee. Published by Marshall, Clark &Company, Boston, MA. 1833. [4" × 6 7/16"]. Br/gd geometric designs. Hard cover. Title on spine. 172pp. [Also contains several American patriotic songs including *Battle Song, The American Star, The Pilgrim Fathers* and *Day of Glory*].

MISC-174 Hail To The Chief. In: *Musician's Omnibus: Containing the Whole Camp Duty, Calls and Signals Used in the Army and Navy; Forty Setts of Quadrilles, Including Waltz, Polka and Schottische, with Calls; and an Immense Collection of Polkas, Schottisches, Waltzes, Marches, Quicksteps, Hornpipes, Contra & Fancy Dances, Songs, &c., for the Violin, Flute, Cornet, Clarionett, &c, containing over 700 Pieces of Music,* pages 7 and 17. c. Elias Howe. Published by Elias Howe, No. 103 Court Street, Boston, MA. 1861. [8 1/2" × 11"]. O/bk non-pictorial. "Improved Edition." 100pp.

MISC-175 [Oh, My Darling Mary Jo]. w. John Biggert. m. Tune— *Oh, my darling Clementine* Published by John Biggert, No. 1875 DuPont Avenue, Memphis, TN. 38127. [ca. 196-]. [2 1/2" × 3 7/8"]. Obv: B/w photo of "Teddy Kennedy"—"Wanted For Murder or President?" Rev: Song. "*Oh, my darling Clementine* was never like this." "Prices for bulk purchase of cards."

MISC-176 Hail To The Chief. w. Thomas Elli. m. James Sanderson. In: *Great Songs Of Peace & Patriotism*, page 92. Published by Warner Bros. Publications, Inc., No. 265 Secaucus Road, Secaucus, NJ. 07-96. 1991. [9" × 12"]. R/w/b flag design. "Piano/Vocal." 132pp.

MISC-177 Hail To The Chief. In: *Singer's Own Book, A Well-Selected Collection of the Most Popular Sentimental, Amatory, Patriotic Naval & Comic Songs*, page 121. Published by Key & Biddle, No. 6 Minor Street], Philadelphia, PA. 1832. [3 1/8" × 5 1/8"]. Br/gd non-pictorial. 322[?]pp.

MISC-178 Hail To The Chief. w. Sir Walter Scott. m. Sanderson. In: *The Song Patriot, A Collection of National and Other Songs for School and Home,*

page 28. c. C.W. Bardeen, Editor of the School Bulletin. Published by C.W. Bardeen, Publisher, Syracuse, NY. 1892. Non-pictorial. [5 3/8" × 7 1/2"]. "Song Budget Music Series III." 80pp.[?].

MISC-179 Ode, For 4th July, 1834. m. "Air, *Adams and Liberty*." 2pp. Obv: "Order of Performance at the Whig Celebration, July 4, 1834." "Original Ode" without musical notation. Rev: "Ode" with musical notation.

MISC-180 Twentieth Century March to the White House. m. Ida L. Newmeyer. Published by Ida L. Newmeyer, Derry Station, PA. 1900. Br/w photo of The White House. Gn/y geometric design border. 8pp.

MISC-181 The Declaration of Independence Of The United States Of North America July 4, 1776. Published by John E. Wilson, Baltimore, MD. 1861. B/w litho of building interior, statues of signers. "Arranged and Adapted for Vocal and Instrumental Music as the Great National Chant and Dedicated to the World." 4pp. Page 4: Facsimile signatures of the "Signers of the Declaration" including John Adams and Thomas Jefferson.

MISC-182 Put The Right Man At The Wheel. w.m. Will S. Hays. e. Gregg Smith. In: *America's Bicentennial Songs from The Great Sentimental Age, 1850-1900, Stephen Foster to Charles E. Ives*, page 54. Published by G. Schirmer, New York, NY. 1975. [9" × 11 7/8"]. N/c litho of woman with roses, flag, city. 152pp.

MISC-183 Hail To The Chief. "Scotch Songs." w. Sir Walter Scott. In: *War Songs of the Blue and the Gray, As Sung by the Brave Soldiers of the Union and Confederate Armies in Camp, on the March and in Garrison, Containing all the favorite Lyrics that are sung with such different feelings of sadness and mirth as they recall the shades and lights of the Great War. There is also included a large variety of old, well known and American Ballads and Songs, both patriotic and sentimental,*

(MSD) MICHAEL S. DUKAKIS

as sung and played during the stirring times of '76 and 1812, page 45. Published by Hurst & Co., Publishers, No. 122 Nassau Street, New York, NY. [ca. 1890].

MISC-184 American Spirit (March And Two-Step). m. Jas. Alvin Feingold. Published by McKinley Music Co., No. 74 Fifth Avenue, New York, NY. Copyright 1904 by Jas. Alvin Feingold. B/w photo of young woman in fire department dress hat. R/w/b geometric designs and printing. "A 1904 Presidential Campaign March." 6pp. Pages 2 and 6: Blank.

MISC-185 The White House. w. Gladys Shelly. m. Ruth Cleary. Bl/w drawing of Abraham Lincoln. In: *Little Patriots, A Book Of American Sons For Children*, page 30. Published by ABC Music Corporation, No. 799 7th Avenue, New York, NY. 1941. [6" × 9"]. R/w/b drawing of child. 44pp.

MISC-186 The District Of Columbia Is My Home. w.m. James L. Dixon. Published by James L. Dixon, No. 1022 Seventeenth Street, N.W., Washington, DC. 1955. Bl/bk/w drawings of Capitol building, Lincoln Memorial, Washington Monument. "Souvenir Copy." 4pp.

MISC-187 The President's Rap (From Washington To Clinton). w. Blaine Selkirk. m. Sara Jordan/ Produced and published by Sara Jordan Publishing, a division of Jordan Music Productions, Inc., Station M, Box 160, Toronto, Canada. 1994. [5 1/4" × 8 1/4"]. R/w/b litho of George Washington, stars. Sara Jordan Presents The President's Rap from Washington to Clinton." "Jordan Music Productions, Inc., Lyrics Book." 56pp. [Packaged with a cassette tape].

MISC-188 White House Serenade. m. Jackie Gleason. Published by Rhapsody Music Co. Sole selling agent Song Smiths, Inc., Music Publishers, No. 870 Seventh Avenue, New York 19, NY., by arrangement with Jagea Music Co. Copyright 1952 and 1953 Jackie Gleason. O/w photo of Jackie Gleason. "Recorded by Jackie Gleason and His Orchestra on Capitol Records." "Piano Edition." 4pp. Page 4: Advertising Leo Talent, Inc., Music Publishers, music.

MICHAEL S. DUKAKIS

MSD-1 Dukakis Has Got It. w.m. Henry and Bobbie Shaffner. [V-1: Published by Keynote Associates, One Montgomery Avenue, Suite #103, Bala Cynwyd, PA. 19004] [V-2: No publisher indicated]. [1988]. [8 1/2" × 11"]. [V-1: Y/bk] [V-2: B/w] drawing of donkey, stars. 2pp. Page 2: Blank.

MSD-2 Dukakis For President. w. Pinky Herman (ASCAP). m. "Parody sung to the tune of *Happy Days Are Here Again*." Published by Pinky Herman, No. 14705 NW 35th Street, #615, Lauderdale Lakes, FL. 33319. [8 1/2" × 11"]. B/w photo of Michael Dukakis—"Democrat for President." Facsimile copy of "Franklin D. Roosevelt Song" record label for *Happy Days Are Here Again*." "Special Parody written by Pinky Herman who was commissioned by Eddie Dowling, Broadway Chairman of The Democratic National Committee to compose words for [a] Franklin D. Roosevelt parody in [the] 1940 President Campaign." "Lets All Now Sing." "Make Xerox copies for friends to sing at rallies." 4pp. Pages 2 and 3: Blank. Page 4: Facsimile letter from General Services Administration to Pinky Herman on song. Narrative on the Bicentennial.

MARTIN VAN BUREN

MVB-1 President M. Van Buren's Grand March. m. John F. Goneke. Printed at the Whig Office, Athens, GA. [ca. 1837]. B/w litho of eagle with ribbon—"E Pluribus Unum," harp, geometric design border. 2pp. Page 2: Blank.

MVB-2 Van Buren Quick Step. m. Miss. Eliza J. Rogers (Bristol, RI).

MARTIN VAN BUREN (**MVB**)

MVB-2

Published for the Author, Boston, MA. Copyright 1836 by Miss. Eliza J. Rogers. Non-pictorial. "Composed and arranged for the Piano Forte." 4pp Pages 1 and 4: Blank.

MVB-3   Free Soil Quick Step. m. J.T. Norton. Published by E.R. Johnson & Company, Peoples Music Store, 6th ab: Chesnut, Philadelphia, PA. 1848. Non-pictorial. "Most respectfully dedicated to Martin Van Buren by the Publishers." 4pp. Pages 1 and 4: Blank.

MVB-4   President Van Buren's Grand March. m. Samuel Carusi. Published & sold at the Author's Music Store cor. 12th Street & Pennsylvania Avenue, Washington, DC. [ca. 1837]. Non-pictorial. 4pp. Pages 1 and 4: Blank. "Composed and Arranged for the Piano Forte."

MVB-5   The Free Soil Minstrel. c. George W. Clark. Published by Martyn & Ely, 162 Nassau Street, New York, NY. 1848. [4 3/4" × 7 1/4"]. Br/br non-pictorial designs, hardback cover. 228pp. Page 3: Litho of lyre, horn, music, ivy. "Go forth with a trumpet's sound, and tell to the nations round — On the hills which our heroes trod, In the shrines of the Saints of God, In the ruler's hall and the captives prison, That the slumber is broke, And the sleepers are risen, That the day of the scourge and the fetter is o'er and Earth feels the tread of the Freeman once more." [M-079].

MVB-6   United States March. m. J.E. Jungmann. Published by G.E. Blake, No. 13 South Fifth Street, Philadelphia, PA. [1837-1841]. Non-pictorial. "Composed and Arranged for the Piano Forte, and Respectfully Dedicated to His Excellency Martin Van Buren, President of the United States." "Property of the Publisher." 2pp.

MVB-7   President Van Buren's Grand March. m. Charles Hutet. Published for the Author by E. Riley & Company, No. 29 Chatham Street, New York, NY. [1839]. "Composed Expressly to Commemorate His Visit to White Plains, West Chester Coty. [County]." 6pp.

MVB-8   Free Soil Songs For The People. Published for sale by Bella Marsh, Wright's Steam Press, No. 36 Cornhill, Boston, MA. 1848. Litho of eagle, clasped hands, geometric design border. Verse — "Cheer up, cheer up, Free Soilers, all, The Time has come for action, For Freedom's cause we must contend, In spite of party faction." "Campaign Of 1848." 36pp. [M-078].

MVB-9   The Sub Treasury Waltz. m. "Composed by A. Jackson." [1837-1840]. Non-pictorial. "As Composed by A. Jackson and Dedicated to Martin Van Buren." Non-pictorial. 2pp. Page 2: Blank.

MVB-10   President Van Buren's Grand Waltz. m. Bruno Held. Published by James L. Hewitt & Co., No. 239 Broadway, New York, NY. [1837-1841]. Non-pictorial. "Composed for the Piano Forte." 4pp. Pages 1 and 4: Blank.

MVB-11   Free Soil Waltzes. m. M.A.C. Published by Stephen W. Marsh, Piano Forte Maker and Music Store Dealer, No. 371 Washington Street, Boston, MA. 1848. Gd/bk/w litho of sunburst design. "Arranged for the Piano Forte." "Respectfully dedicated to Charles Sumner, Esq." "Price 25 cts. nett [sic]." 8pp. Pages 2 and 8: Blank.

MVB-12 The President's Waltz. m. W.A. Newland. Published by W.A. Newland at his Piano Forte and Music Ware Rooms, No. 243 Market Street ab. 6th, Philadelphia, PA. 1840. Non-pictorial. "Composed and Respectfully Dedicated to Miss Harriet Shee." 4pp. Pages 1 and 4: Blank.

MVB-13 Free Soil Songs. w. Messrs. Hutchinson, Jewell, Bates and Foster, of Massachusetts. 1848. [8 1/2" × 13 3/8"]. Non-pictorial. "Composed and sung at the Buffalo Convention, August 9, and 10, 1848." "Printed by R.A. Maynard & Co., Printers Republic Office, Buffalo." 2pp. Page 2: Blank.

MVB-14 Free Soil Songs For The Campaign Of 1848. [10" × 14 1/2"]. B/w litho of eagle. Broadside. 2pp. Page 2: Blank.

MVB-15 The Clarion Of Freedom. c.a. E.D. Howard & J.H. Clark. Published by Smead & Cowles, Cleveland, OH. 1848. "A Collection of Free Soil Songs, Compiled and Arranged by E.D. Howard & J.H. Clark. 40pp. [M-080].

MVB-16 The O.K. Songster: The Democratic Ball; or, Downfall Of Wiggery. [1840?]. 64pp. [M-026].

MVB-17 President Van Burens Grand March. m. J.T. Norton, P.R.A.M. Published by Osbourn's Music Saloon, No. 30 South 4st Street, Philadelphia, PA. [ca. 1837]. Non-pictorial. "Composed and Arranged Expressly for the Piano Forte and Dedicated to Colonel John Thomas of Baltimore." 4pp.

MVB-18 President Van Buren's Grand March. m. J.T. Norton. In: *Marches Of The Presidents, 1789-1909, Authentic Marches & Campaign Songs*, page 20. A. Carl Miller. Published by Chappell & Co., Inc., No. 609 Fifth Avenue, New York, NY. "By arrangement with Chilmark Press, Inc." 1968. [9" × 12"]. R/w/b litho of eagle, flag. "An Illustrated Piano Folio For All Ages." 72pp.

See also WHH-76; WHH-88; WHH-91; WHH-109; HC-47; HC-115; JKP-5; WHT-23; WW-19; FDR-158; DDE-9; LBJ-1; JBR-2; MISC-167.

NATHANIEL BANKS

NB-1 Gov. Banks' Quick Step. m. J.W. Turner. Published by Oliver Ditson & Company, No. 277 Washington Street, Boston, MA. 1857. B/w litho by J.H. Bufford of Nathanial P. Banks, facsimile signature. "Speaker U.S. House of Representatives 1856, Governor of Mass. 1858." "Arranged for the Piano Forte." 6pp. Pages 2 and 6: Blank.

NB-2 Gov. Banks' Grand March. m. J.W. Turner. Published by Oliver Ditson & Company, No. 277 Washington Street, Boston, MA. 1857. B/w litho of Nathanial P. Banks, facsimile signature. "Speaker U.S. House of Representatives 1856, Governor of Mass. 1858." "Arranged for the Piano Forte." 4pp. Page 4: Blank.

NB-3 General Bank's Grand March. m. E. Mack. Published by Lee & Walker, No. 722 Chestnut Street, Philadelphia, PA. 1862. B/w beige tinted litho by T. Sinclair of Nathanial P. Banks. "Respectfully Dedicated to Major General Banks." 6pp. Page 2: Blank. Page 6: Advertising.

See also WS-14.

NEAL DOW

ND-1 Cheers For The Veteran. w.m. Silver Lake Quartette. "Dedicated to Neal Dow, September 28, 1887." In: *Prohibition Bells (And Songs of the New Crusade)*, page 48. Published by Funk and Wagnalls, Publishers, Nos. 18 and 20 Astor Place New York, NY. 1888. [5 7/16" × 6 15/16"]. Gn/bk drawing of bells. 104pp.

ND-2 The Doleful Ballad Of Neal Dow. In: *Neal Dow, The Maine-Law Murderer! and Striped Pig Liquor Dealer: or Beauties of Prohibition*, page 16. Probably published in Maine. [ca. 1850-1870]. [Anti-Dow Song]

ND-3 Dare To Be A Neal Dow. w. Harriet E. Gage Perry. m. "Tune — *Dare To Be A Daniel*." In: *Women's Christian Temperance Union* Songs [Song Book], page 9. Published by Women's Christian Temperance Union of Rhode Island. [ca. 1914]. [5 1/8" × 7 5/16"]. Be/bk photo of young girl with pennant — "The Liquor Traffic Must Go," geometric design border. 22pp.

ND-4 The National Temperance Songster. e. William O. Moffitt. Published by Free Press Publishing House, Beloit, WI. 1878. 40[?]pp. [M-223].

ND-5 The National Temperance Songster. e. William O. Moffitt. Published by O.C. Williams, Providence, RI. 1879. [M-224].

ND-6 The National Temperance Songster, Revised And Enlarged. e. William O. Moffitt. Published by American Temperance Publishing House, New York, NY. 1879[?]. 62pp. [M-225].

PETER COOPER

PC-1 A Battle Song. m. "Air: *Hold The Fort*." Printed by E.D. Slater, Print, No. 147 Fulton Street, New York, NY. 1876. [7 1/2" × 3 1/8"]. Be/bk/r facsimile of dollar bill. Obv: Be/bk/gn/r lithos of "Peter Cooper — For President" and "Sam'l. F. Cary — For V. President." "Peter Cooper, the Friend of the Working Man, the Protector of the Poor and Distressed." "Independent Greenback Party." "The Lord is with the Right." "Be Strong! Be Courageous." "National prosperity cannot be restored by enforcing idleness on a large portion of the people — Peter Cooper." "No Nation can exist with an untaxed monopoly in its midst — Sam'l F. Cary." "1776-1876." "The Bank of Bread." "Pay to the Order of Yourself, By Your honest Days Work by Voting for Peter Cooper and Sam'l F. Cary and against National Banks, Untaxed Bondholders and Monopolies." Rev: Be/gn non-pictorial. Song. Narratives and sample ballot.

PC-2 Greenback And Labor Songs. e. John Young and Daniel McLaughlin. Published by *Greenback News*. Joliet, IL. 1876. Bl/bk non-pictorial. 28pp. [M204].

PC-3(A) Hurrah For Cooper And Cary. w. Julia A. Moore. m. "Air — *Rally 'Round The Flag Boys*." In: *The Sentimental Song Book*, page 32. Published by Julia A. Moore, Grand Rapids, MI. 1876. [4 1/8" × 5 13/16"]. Gn/bk non-pictorial back line border. "Centennial, 1876." 62pp.

(B) The Independent Party, page 50. w. Julia A. Moore. m. "Air — *Perhaps*."

PROHIBITION PARTY

PP-1 The Battle's On (or Prohibitions Bound to Win). w.m. Ella Southworth Clark. Copyright 1910 by Ella Southworth Clark. Gn/w non-pictorial geometric designs. "Dedicated to the Prohibition Party." "Male Quartette and also Arranged for Solo, Duet or Mixed Quartette." 6pp. Page 6: Advertising.

PP-2 The Prohibition Party. m. Air: *The Red, White and Blue*. In: *Water Wagon World Express*, page 4. Published by the Smith-Linsey Company, Hartford, CT. [ca. 1900]. [5 15/16" × 9"]. B/w geometric designs. 8pp.

PP-3(A) The New Exodus. w.m. Silver Lake Quartette. "It is vain to say that the Republican Party must and shall become a Prohibition Party. It must and shall do no such thing. Those who are in it simply to make it so, might as well go at once, for they will not succeed — Cin., O. *Commercial Gazette* (Rep)." In: *Prohibition*

(RBH) RUTHERFORD B. HAYES

Bells (And Songs of the New Crusade), page 16. Published by Funk and Wagnalls, Nos. 18-20 Astor Place New York, NY. 1888. [5 7/16" × 6 15/16"]. Gn/bk drawing of bells. 104pp.

(B) **Republicans And Democrats**, page 40. w.m. Silver Lake Quartette.

(C) **The Coming Hero**, page 42. w.m. Silver Lake Quartette. "A Prohibition President Is Coming."

PP-4 The Town Pump (Characteristic March). m. Frank P. Banta. Published by M. Witmark and Sons, New York, NY. 1912. Gn/bl/w drawing of man at water pump, farm animals, sign inscribed "Vote The Prohibition Ticket." 6pp. Page 6: Advertising.

RUTHERFORD B. HAYES

RBH-1 Hayes And Wheeler Grand March. m. Carl Strandberg. Published by Wm. A. Pond & Company, No. 547 Broadway, New York, NY. 1876. B/w litho by Major & Knapp of Rutherford B. Hayes and William A. Wheeler. "Respectfully Dedicated to Gov. Rutherford B. Hayes of Ohio and Hon. Wm. A. Wheeler of New York." 6pp. Page 2: Blank. Page 6: Advertising.

RBH-2(A) Hayes And Wheeler Grand March. m. Charles Lange. Published by Balmer & Weber, St. Louis, MO. 1876. B/w lithos by F. Welcker Company of Rutherford B. Hayes and William A. Wheeler. "To the Republican Presidential Candidates of 1876." 6pp. Page 2: Blank. Page 6: Advertising.

(B) **The Nation's Choice** (Hayes and Wheeler Song and Chorus). w. Fannie M. Parker. m. John McPeherson. 6pp. Page 2: Blank. Page 6: Advertising.

(C) **Hayes & Wheeler Grand Waltz**. m. Henry Werner[?].

(D) **Hayes & Wheeler Grand March**. m. Henry Werner[?].

RBH-3(A) Hayes And Wheeler Grand March (Song and Chorus). m. C.D. Blake. Published by White, Smith & Company, No. 516 Washington Street, Boston, MA. 1876. B/w litho of Rutherford B. Hayes and William A. Wheeler, gold border. "Dedicated to R.B. Hayes and W.A. Wheeler." 6pp. Page 2: Blank. Page 6: Advertising.

(B) **Our Champions Of The Right** (Song and Chorus). w. Arthur W. French. m. R.S. Walcott. 6pp. Pages 2 and 6: Blank.

RBH-4 Hayes & Wheeler Campaign Songster. Published by John Church & Company, Cincinnati, OH. 1876. [4" × 5 5/8"]. Bl/w litho of Rutherford Hayes and William A. Wheeler. "Including Biographical Sketches & Constitution for Campaign Clubs." 52pp. Page 3: Title—**Hayes & Wheeler Campaign Carols**. [M-194].

RBH-5 Roll Along, Roll Along, Shout The Campaign Battle Song (Republican Campaign Song). w. Thomas Peppergrass. m. Y.D., Esq. Published by Oliver Ditson & Company, No. 451 Washington Street, Boston, MA. 1876. B/w litho by J.H. Bufford's Sons of wagon full of hay inscribed "HAYes," oxen from each state, Capitol, "White House—Honest money paid here," Uncle Sam, flag. Sign on tree—"National Road, Ohio to Washington." Banner on wagon—"A good honest load of HAY[es] on the way to Washington." Large wheel on wagon—"Hard Money Wheeler—Gold Basis." 6pp. Pages 2 and 6: Blank.

RBH-6 The Hayes And Wheeler Campaign Song. w. Jno. C. Pierson. m. C.F. Thompson. Published by C.H. Ditson & Company, No. 711 Broadway, New York, NY. 1876. Nonpictorial geometric designs. "As sung by the Campaign Clubs of the United States to whom it is dedicated." 6pp. Pages 2 and 6: Blank. Page 3: Title—**The Hayes And Wheeler Rallying Song**.

RBH-7 President Haye's [sic] **Grand Triumphal March**. m. Will H. Pontius. Published by F.W. Helmick, No.

50 West Fourth Street, Cincinnati, OH. 1876. B/w litho by Monsch & Company of Rutherford B. Hayes. 6pp. Page 2: Blank. Page 6: Advertising.

RBH-8 Gov. Hayes Grand March. m. Sidney Ryan. Published by John Church & Company, Cincinnati, OH. 1876. B/w litho by MacBrair & Sons of Rutherford B. Hayes, geometric line border. "To Governor Rutherford B. Hayes." 8pp. Pages 2, 7 and 8: Blank.

RBH-9 President Hayes' Grand March. m. C.B. Blake. Published by White, Smith & Company, No. 516 Washington Street, Boston, MA. 1877. B/w litho of Rutherford Hayes, geometric design border. 6pp. Page 2: Blank.

RBH-10 Hayes Is The Man! (Campaign Song) (Solo or Quartett). w.m. C.C. Haskins. Published by John Church & Company, Cincinnati, OH. 1876. Non-pictorial. 6pp. Page 6: Blank.

RBH-11 Hayes & Wheeler Campaign Song Book (For the Centennial Year). Published by the American News Company, Nos. 117, 119, 121, 123 Nassau Street, New York, NY. 1876. [3 7/8" × 6 1/16"]. Y/bk litho of Rutherford B. Hayes and William A. Wheeler, liberty cap, geometric designs. 74pp. Pages 2, 4, 73 and 74: Blank. Page 3: "Containing Over Sixty Original Songs Adapted to Popular Melodies." [M-193].

RBH-12 Republican's Remember. w. James Nicholson. m. Air: *Marching Through Georgia*. [1876]. Non-pictorial. 2pp. Page 2: Blank.

RBH-13 Gov. Rutherford B. Hayes Grand March. m. E. Mack. Published by Oliver Ditson & Company, No. 451 Washington Street, Boston, MA. 1876. B/w litho by J.H. Bufford's Sons of Rutherford B. Hayes. 6pp. Pages 2 and 6: Blank.

RBH-14 Helmick's Republican Campaign Song Book. Published by F.W. Helmick, Music dealer and Publisher, No. 50 West 4th Street, Cincinnati, OH. 1876. [5 1/4" × 7 1/2"]. [V-1:

RBH-11

Y/bk] [V-2: Pl/bk] lithos of Rutherford B. Hayes and William A. Wheeler, geometric design border. "Arranged for Four Voices." "As Sung by the Springfield, (O.) Glee Club." 24pp. [M-198].

RBH-15 Hayes The True And Wheeler Too! (Campaign Song and Chorus). m. "Adapted from the immensely popular Whig song of 1840, *Tippecanoe and Tyler Too*." a. R.E. Publican. Published by Wm. A. Pond, No. 547 Broadway, New York, NY. 1876. Non-pictorial. 6pp. Page 3: "Air, *Tippecanoe and Tyler Too*, The original music, The words as used in the Campaign of 1840." Advertising at bottom of page. Pages 2 and 6: Blank.

RBH-16 Hard Cash And Better Times (Campaign Song and Chorus). w. George Cooper. m. W.F. Heath. Published by John F. Perry & Company, No. 538 Washington Street, Boston, MA. 1876. B/w litho of silver dollar, geometric designs. 6pp. Page 6: Blank.

RBH-17 Hayes And Wheeler Are The Men (Quartet for Male Voices). w. C.A. White. m. "Melodie from the Operas." Published by F.A. North & Company, No. 1308 Chestnut Street, Philadelphia, PA. Copyright 1876 by White, Smith & Company. R/w/bk drawing of eagle, shield, stripe border. 8pp. Pages 2 and 8: Blank.

RBH-18 The Humbug Reform! (Republican Serio-Comic Song and Chorus). m. R.M. Stapp. Published by F.W. Helmick, No. 50 West 4th Street, Cincinnati, OH. 1875. Non-pictorial. 6pp. Page 2: Advertising for F.W. Helmick's organ. Page 6: Advertising for other F.W. Helmick published music.

RBH-19 President Hayes' Grand March. m. E. Mack. Published by Oliver Ditson & Company, No. 451 Washington Street, Boston, MA. 1877. B/w litho by J.H. Bufford's Sons of Rutherford B. Hayes. 6pp. Pages 2 and 6: Blank.

RBH-20 Hayes & Wheeler Song Book. Published by The Union Republican Congressional Committee, Washington, DC. 1876. [5 3/4" × 9 1/4"]. Br/bk litho of Rutherford B. Hayes and William A. Wheeler, shield, geometric design border. "I'll be on hand again shortly." [V-1: Series I" under title on cover] [V-2: Series not indicated on cover]. 52pp. Page 2: Contents. Page 52: State-by-state electoral vote totals for 1876. [M-196, 197].

RBH-21 Hayes Grand March. m. E. Mack. Published by S. Brainard's Sons Music Publishing House, Cleveland, OH. 1876. B/w litho by Armstrong & Company of Rutherford B. Hayes. "To the Hon. Rutherford B. Hayes." "Music Publishing House, Chickering & Sons Celebrated Pianos and Mason & Hamlin Cabinet Organs." 6pp. Pages 2 and 6: Blank.

RBH-22(A) Hold The Fort For Hayes And Wheeler. w. Mary E. Kail. m. "The Music of above songs is Arranged from Popular Songs *Tramp, Tramp, Tramp, Battle Cry Of Freedom, Hold The Fort,* adapted to original words." a. P.P. Bliss. Published by The S. Brainard's Sons, Cleveland, OH. 1876. B/w litho of eagle, flag, geometric design border. 6pp. Page 2: Blank. Page 6: Advertising.

(B) **Grandly The Loyal Hosts Are Marching**. a. George F. Root.

(C) **Hayes For Our President**. w. Mary E. Kail. a. George F. Root. 6pp. Page 2: Blank. Page 6: Advertising.

RBH-23(A) Hurrah For Hayes And Honest Ways (Campaign Song and Chorus). w.m. E.W. Foster. Published by John F. Perry & Company, opposite Boston Theatre, No. 538 Washington Street, Boston, MA. 1876. B/w litho by Armstrong & Company of a J.E. Baker drawing of Rutherford B. Hayes. "The Great Unknown." "Respectfully Dedicated to the Republican Centennial Presidential Candidate, Hon. Rutherford B. Hayes of Ohio." 6pp. Page 6: Advertising for other John F. Perry & Company published music.

(B) **Mack's Grand Centennial March**. m. E. Mack.

RBH-24 Hurrah For Hayes And Honest Ways! (Song and Chorus). w.m. A.O. Hand. Published by John Church & Company, Cincinnati, OH. 1876. Non-pictorial geometric designs. "Admit for the sake of argument that the candidates of both parties are honest men & will go equally for reform and a true currency, it still remains that our opponents cannot elect their men without the Southern vote. Men of all parties, you know what that means! No men nor set of men could resist the claim that such a vote would make & would have, upon the party that it put in power. New Southern war claims and indemnities certainly would be admitted & what other extravagant demands would be pressed it is impossible to say. Fellow citizens, we cannot afford to vote with the party that must pay such a price for success!— A.O.H." "Hand's Campaign Songs No. 1." 6pp. Pages 2 and 6: Blank.

RBH-25 Vote As You Shot Boys (Hayes and Wheeler Campaign Song). w.m. Thomas P. Westendorf. Published by S. Brainard's Sons, Cleveland, OH. 1876. Non-pictorial geometric design border. 6pp. Pages 2 and 6: Blank.

RBH-26 The Boys In Blue Will See It Through (Campaign Song and Chorus). w. S.N. Mitchell. m. H.P. Danks. Published by S.T. Gordon & Son, No. 13 East 14th Street, New York, NY. 1876. B/w lithos of "Rutherford B. Hayes" and "William A. Wheeler," geometric design border. "To the Boys in Blue." Advertising for "Hayes Grand March" by R. Goerdeler. 6pp. Pages 2: Blank. Page 6: Advertising.

RBH-27(A) Gov. Hayes Campaign Grand March. a. Leonard Jennevein. Published by G.D. Russell & Company, No. 126 Tremont Street, Boston, MA. 1876. B/w litho of Rutherford B. Hayes. 6pp. Pages 2 and 6: Blank.

(B) **We'll Vote For The Buckeye Boy.** w.m. Carl Thomas. 8pp.

(C) **Centennial Grand March.** a. Leonard Jennevein. 6pp.

RBH-28 We'll Blow Our Horn For Hayes (Campaign Song and Chorus). w. Samuel N. Mitchell. m. Charles Ed. Prior. Published by F.W. Helmick, No. 50 West Fourth Street, Cincinnati, OH. 1876. B/w litho by Monsch & Company of Rutherford B. Hayes. 6pp. Page 2: Blank. Pages 5 and 6: Advertising.

RBH-29(A) Hayes & Wheeler's Galop To The White House. m. Harry Miller. Published by J.L. Peters, New York, NY. 1876. B/w litho by Snyder and Black of Rutherford Hayes and William A. Wheeler, eagle, flag, ivy. "To the Friends of Hayes and Wheeler." 6pp.

(B) **Hayes & Wheeler's Favorite Polka.** m. Harry Miller. 6pp. Pages 2: Blank. Page 6: Advertising.

(C) **Hayes' Campaign March.**

(D) **Hayes' Campaign Quickstep.**

RBH-30 Valse Imperiale. m. G. Morosini, Op. 24. Published by Spear and Dehnoff, No. 717 Broadway, New York, NY. 1877. Non-pictorial, geometric designs and border. "Pour Piano

RBH-26

RBH-29

Forte, Composee et dediee avec permission speciale a son Excellence Madame La Presidente R.B. Hayes." 12pp. Pages 2 and 12: Blank.

RBH-31 Hayes And Victory. m. George S. Fox. 1876. Non-pictorial.

RBH-32 Our Champions Of The Right (Hayes and Wheeler Campaign Song and Chorus). w. Arthur W. French. m. R.S. Walcott. In: *Folio, A Journal of Music, Drama, Art and Literature*, pages 96-98. Published by White, Smith & Company, No. 516 Washington Street, Boston, MA. September, 1876. [9 1/4" × 12 1/8"]. Bk/w floral border.

RBH-33 Hayes And Wheeler Song Book. 1876. [6" × 9 3/4"]. Non-pictorial. 16pp. [M-195].

RBH-34 Inauguration March. a. Carl Strandberg. Published by Wm. A. Pond & Company, No. 25 Union Square New York, NY. 1877. [V-1: B/w litho of Gotharin & Ball] [V-2: B/w paste-on litho of Lester Wallack], musical instruments, piano, organ. "Latest Compositions." [V-1: Compliments of Edward F. Starin, Proprietor and Manager, Niblo's Garden Theatre]. "Selected by Gotharin & Ball." List of other songs in Series. 6pp. Pages 2 and 6: Advertising for various New York City retail stores.

RBH-35 Hayes And Wheeler Hurrah! Hurrah! w. E.R. Latta. m. W.O. Perkins. Published by Oliver Ditson & Company, No. 451 Washington Street, Boston, MA. 1876. Non-pictorial geometric designs. "Arranged as a Solo and Chorus and Quartett or Chorus for Mixed and for Male Voices." 6pp. Page 6: Blank.

RBH-36 Hayes And Wheeler (Grand March). Published by White, Smith & Company, No. 516 Washington Street, Boston, MA. [ca. 1878]. Non-pictorial black border. "C.D. Blake's Standard Compositions." List of other titles in series — "Solos, No. 1" and "Four Hands."

RBH-37 President Hayes Quickstep. m. G. Stromeyer. a. P. Pfeiffer. Published by Charles F. Escher, Jr., No. 1320 Girard Avenue, Philadelphia, PA. 1877. Non-pictorial geometric designs. 6pp. Pages 2 and 6: Blank.

RBH-38 Hurrah For Hayes & Wheeler (Grand Republican Campaign Song). w. Frank C. Filley. m. "Air: *Sherman's March To The Sea*." [4 1/2" × 9 1/2"]. [1876]. Non-pictorial. "Written and Dedicated to Hayes & Wheeler Blues." 2pp. Page 2: Blank.

RBH-39 Rutherford B. Hayes Song Sheet. w. N.B. Milliken. [1876]. [5 5/16" × 7 1/4"]. Non-pictorial. Two Songs: **For Hayes And Wheeler** and **Yankee Freeman.** 2pp. Page 2: Blank.

RBH-40(A) President Hayes' Inauguration Polka. m. Harry C. Schomaker. Published by Lee & Walker, No. 1113 Chestnut Street, Philadelphia, PA. 1877. B/w litho of Rutherford B. Hayes, chain link border. 6[?]pp.

(B) President Hayes' Grand March.

RBH-41 Hayes' Grand March. m. True Coin. Published by H.S. Mackie, No. 82 State Street, Rochester, NY. 1876. Non-pictorial black lines. "Respectfully Dedicated to 'Our Centennial Candidate,' Hon Rutherford B. Hayes."

RBH-4

RUTHERFORD B. HAYES (**RBH**)

RBH-40

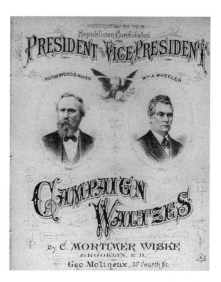

RBH-43

RBH-42 The Hayes And Wheeler Grand March. m. Carl Strandberg. Published by Wm. A. Pond & Company, No. 547 Broadway, New York, NY. 1876. Non-pictorial black line border. "Respectfully Dedicated to Gov. Rutherford B. Hayes, of Ohio, and Hon. William A. Wheeler, of New York." List of other arrangements available. 6pp. Page 2: Blank. Page 6: Advertising.

RBH-43 Campaign Waltzes. m. C. Mortimer Wiske (Brooklyn, E.D.). Published by Geo. Molineau, No. 37 Fourth Street, Brooklyn, NY. 1876. B/w litho of "Rutherford Hayes," and "Wm. A. Wheeler," eagle, geometric designs. "Dedicated to the Republican Candidates for President and Vice-President." 8pp.

RBH-44 Sound The Alarm! w.m. H.E. Gordon. Copyright 1876 by H.E. Gordon. B/w litho of Rutherford B. Hayes and William Wheeler, eagle, flags, geometric design border. "To The Republican Party." 4pp. Page 4: Blank.

RBH-45 The Centennial Meditation of Columbia. w. Sidney Lanier (of Georgia). m. Dudley Buck (of Connecticut). Published by G. Schirmer, No. 701 Broadway, New York, NY. 1876. Non-pictorial. "A Cantata for The Inaugural Ceremonies at Philadelphia, May 10, 1876." "1776-1876." "By Appointment of the U.S. Centennial Commission."

RBH-46 Campaign Lyrics, Songs, And Ballads For The Campaign Of 1876. Published by W.W. Miller, Chicago, IL. 1876. Y/bk litho of Rutherford B. Hayes and William A. Wheeler. 36pp. [M-191].

RBH-47 The Great Centennial Republican Campaign Songster. e. Frank C. Filley. Published by E.T. McLean, Publisher, San Francisco, CA. 1876. 32[?]pp. [M-192].

RBH-48 Republican Campaign Songs. w. James Nicholson. 1876. Non-pictorial. 4pp. [M-200].

RBH-49 Hayes Illustrated Campaign Song And Joke Book. Published by The American News Company, New York, NY. 1876. O/bk litho of Rutherford B. Hayes. "Price Ten Cents." Page 5: Litho of a Goose. "The Democratic Goose looking for Salt River." [M-199].

RBH-50 Hurrah For Hayes And Wheeler (Song And Chorus). w.m. W.F. Studds. Published by Wm. A. Pond & Company, No. 547 Broadway, New York, NY. [1876]. B/w litho of Rutherford B. Hayes and William Wheeler.

RBH-51 Hayes Grand March. m. R. Goerdeler. Published by S.T. Gordon & Son, No. 13 East 14th Street, New York, NY. 1876.

RBH-52 The Hayes And Wheeler Campaign Songster. c. Sam. Booth. a. George T. Evans. Published by San Francisco News Company, San Francisco, CA. 1876. Non-pictorial. "Respectfully dedicated to the Hayes Invincibles of San Francisco." 40pp. [M-190].

RBH-53 Hayes And Wheeler Polka. m. Phil P. Keil. Published by Phil P. Keil, No. 81 Fifth Street, McKeesport, PA. [1876].

RBH-54 Give Hayes And Wheeler Three Times Three. m. G. Elmer Jones.

RBH-55 President Hayes' Grand March. m. M.F. Aledo. Published by Lee & Walker, No. 1113 Chestnut Street, Philadelphia, PA. [ca. 1879].

RBH-56 Campaign Songs. w. Sam Booth. [1876]. [6" × 9 3/8"]. Non-pictorial. "Supplement to *Hayes and Wheeler Songster.*" 4pp. [Verses for local Congressional candidates also, including Horace Davis, Frank Page, Joseph McKenna, Romualdo Pacheco and Dave Kentfield].

RBH-57 Songs Sung At The Reunion Of The 23d Regiment, O.V.I. [Song Sheet]. m. Patriotic airs. Published at Fremont, OH. September 14, 1877. [9 9/16" × 11 13/16"]. B/w non-pictorial line border. 2pp. Page 2: Small b/w eagle litho at bottom of page. "Journal Steam Print." [Rutherford B. Hayes and William McKinley were in attendance at the reunion].

RBH-58 We'll Go For Hayes! (We'll Wheel er in on Time). w. C.N. Fox, Esq. m. "After Hander, (Some time After)." Published by: A.L. Bancroft & Co., No. 721 Market Street, San Francisco, CA. 1876. B/w litho of Abe Lincoln pushing a wheelbarrow with Rutherford B. Hayes sitting inside of it, Capitol, White House, geometric designs. 6pp. Pages 2 and 6: Blank.

RBH-59 Hayes And Wheeler Are Our Choice (Campaign Song and Chorus). w. Samuel N. Mitchell. m. Charles Ed. Prior. Published by Oliver Ditson & Co., No. 451 Washington Street, Boston, MA. 1876. R/w/b non-pictorial. "Respectfully Dedicated to our Candidates." 6pp. Pages 2, 5 and 6: Blank.

RBH-60 The Great Commotion! w. Col. T.K. Presuss. m. "Tune — *Tippecanoe And Tyler Too.*" [1888]. [6" × 9 3/16"]. Non-pictorial. 2pp. Page 2: Blank.

RBH-61 Hurrah For The Hayes Ticket, All. w. Col. T.K. Presuss. m. "Tune — **Good Bye.**" [1888]. [6" × 9 3/16"]. Non-pictorial. 2pp. Page 2: Blank.

RBH-62 Gallant R.B. Hayes. w. Col. T.K. Presuss. m. "Tune — *Lucy Neal.*" [1888]. [6" × 9 3/16"]. Non-pictorial. 2pp. Page 2: Blank.

RBH-63 Vote For Hayes. w. Col. T.K. Presuss. m. "Popular Air." [1888]. [6" × 9 3/16"]. Non-pictorial. 2pp. Page 2: Blank.

RBH-64 In A Few Days, A Few Days. w. Wm. M. Cook. m. "Tune *Shanghai Chicken.*" In: *Marches Of The Presidents, 1789-1909, Authentic Marches & Campaign Songs,* page 47. a. Carl Miller. Published by Chappell & Co., Inc., No. 609 Fifth Avenue, New York, NY. "By arrangement with Chilmark Press, Inc." 1968. [9" × 12"]. R/w/b litho of eagle, flag. "An Illustrated Piano Folio For All Ages." 72pp.

RBH-65 The Grand Republic (Galop Militarre). m. J. Haydn Waud, Op. 90. Published by S.T. Gordon & Son, No. 13 East 14th Street, New York,

NY. 1779. B/w non-pictorial geometric designs. "Respectfully Dedicated to The President Of The United States." "For The Piano." 10pp. Pages 2 and 10: Blank.

See also SJT-7; SJT-13; WHT-23; WW-19; FDR-158; DDE-9; LBJ-1; MISC-167.

ROBERT M. LA FOLLETTE

RML-1 La Follette March Two Step. m. Homer Davis. Published by Marsh Music House, No. 110 Winnebago Street, Decorah, IA. 1905. B/w photos of Robert M. La Follette and Homer Davis. R/w drawing of crossed flags, geometric designs. "Dedicated to the Governor of the State of Wisconsin." 6pp. Pages 2 and 6: Blank.

RML-2 You Bet, La Follette (We're All Set). w.m. Ida Hoyt Treadway. Copyright 1924 Ida Hoyt Treadway. Bl/w photos of Robert M. La Follette, facsimile signature, and Burton K. Wheeler, facsimile signature. R/w/b cover with drawing of Liberty Bell inscribed "Proclaim Liberty." 4pp. Page 2: "Respectfully Dedicated to Senator Robert M. La Follette." Page 4: Narrative "America" by La Follette.

RML-3 Campaign Songs [Song Sheet]. w. Katherine M. Meserole, Bellport, Long Island, NY. m. Popular tunes. [7 1/4" × 10 1/4"]. 1924. Non-pictorial. "Issued 1924, Five Cents." 4pp.

RML-4 Lincoln — La Follette Songster. Published by Warren H. Eddy, No. 205 North Flower Street, Los Angeles, CA. [4" × 7"]. [1924]. Bl/bk drawing of Abraham Lincoln. Bl/bk photo of Robert M. La Follette. 20pp. Page 20: Bl/bk photo of "Burton K. Wheeler."

RML-5 Robert La Follette Is The Man Of My Heart. w.m. Robert Stagg. Published by Robert Stagg, No. 48 East 4th Street, New York, NY. 1924. Portrait of Robert La Follette? "Respectfully Dedicated to Robert La Follette."

See also CC-56.

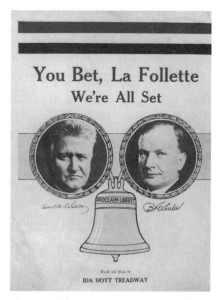

RML-2

RML-4

RICHARD M. NIXON

RMN-1(A)   The White Dove Of Peace. w. Remus Harris. m. Sy Mann and Irving Melsher. Published by Southampton Music Corporation, Charles Hansen Music and Books, No. 1860 Broadway, New York, NY. 10023. Copyright 1945, 1972 and 1973 by Southampton Music Corporation. Bl/w photos of Richard M. Nixon and Jane Langley. "Introduced at the 37th Inaugural Ball for President Richard M. Nixon at The Museum of Natural History and Technology at the Smithsonian Institute on Saturday, January 20, 1973." "Dedicated to President Richard M. Nixon for his ceaseless and untiring efforts to bring America and the world a new generation of peace." "Introduced and dedicated for the Author and Composers by Jane Pickens Langley who made a special appearance at the Inaugural Ball accompanied by Lester Latin's Famous Society Orchestra." 4pp.

(B)   The Voice Of America. w. Remus Harris. m. Abel Baer.

RMN-2   We're Voting For Nixon (To Keep the Country Strong). w.m. Walt Marsh and Dave Thornton. Published by Marsh Publishing Company, No. 711 East "B" Street, Belleville, IL. 1960. [V-1: Standard Size] [V-2: 7" × 10 9/16"]. [V-1: Bl/w] [V-2: B/w] photo of Richard M. Nixon. [V-2: Arranged for 4-part Male Voices]. [V-1: R/w/b] [V-2: B/w] drawing of airplane, truck, ship, rocket, factory, farm, home. 4pp. Page 4: [V-1: Advertising for other Marsh music] [V-2: Piano arrangement].

RMN-3   San Clemente By The Sea. w.m. Marjorie and Walter Botts. 1970. [9 1/2" × 12 1/2"]. N/c photo of the Nixon residence at San Clemente. CA. "President Nixon's home is on the point with beauty all around…" 6pp. Page 6: B/w photo of beach scene, pier.

RMN-4   President Richard M. Nixon March. w. Bert Terhune. m. Ervin Litkei. Published by Loena Pub-

RMN-3

lishing Company, No. 239 West 18th Street, New York, NY. 10011. Distributed by Shapiro, Bernstein and Company, Inc. Copyright 1968 and 1969. B/w photos of the Inaugural parade in Washington, DC., U.S. Capitol. Bl/w cover. 4pp.

RMN-5   Nixon Is The Man For Me. w.m. J. Maloy Roach (ASCAP). Published by Souvenir Songs, No. 5880 Hollywood Boulevard, Hollywood 28, CA. 1962. [4 7/8" × 6 3/4"]. Bl/w photo of Richard Nixon. 4pp. Page 4: "I'm voting for Dick Nixon for Governor because California needs his experienced, decisive leadership." Mailer.

RMN-6   Bring Us Together, Go Forward Together. w. Hal Hackady. m. Larry Grossman. Published by Sunbeam Music, Inc., A Metromedia Company, No. 22 West 48th Street, New York, NY. 10036. 1968. Bl/w drawing of official Inaugural seal inscribed "Nixon/Agnew Inauguration for the President and Vice President." "Official Song Selected by the Inaugural Ball Committee, 1969." 4pp.

RMN-7   Richard Nixon Is The One (Campaign Song). w.m. Raymond J.

Meurer and Raymond J. Meurer, Jr. a. Donn Preston. Copyright 1968 by Richard J. Meurer, Detroit, MI. R/w/b drawing of Richard M. Nixon, shield. 4pp. Page 4: Quartette arrangement.

RMN-8 Nixon Is The Man For Me. w.m. J. Maloy Roach. 1960. Shadow-like photo of Richard M. Nixon behind the music. 2pp. Page 2: Blank.

RMN-9 Humanity With Sanity. w.m. Bill Seiffert. Published by William R. Seiffert, No. 2635 Oceanside Road, Oceanside, Long Island, NY. 1960. Bl/w photos of "Richard M. Nixon" and "Henry Cabot Lodge." "G.O.P." 4pp.

RMN-10 I'm A New Yorker For Nixon. w.m. J. Maloy Roach. Copyright 1960 by J. Maloy Roach, c/o ASCAP, No. 575 Madison Avenue, New York 22, NY. Non-pictorial. 2pp. Page 2: Blank.

RMN-11 Let's Sing For The President [Song Folio]. Published by Henry Tobias Music Company, No. 1255 North Kings Road, Los Angeles, CA. 90069. 1974. Bl/w photo of Richard M. Nixon. R/w/b cover. "Dedicated to President Nixon." "Inspired by Richard Mason."

RMN-9

List of songs in folio. 12pp. Page 2: Song — **Hang In There Mr. President** (Fight! Fight! Fight!). w.m. Henry Tobias. Page 4: Song — **I'm A Democrat For Nixon**. w.m. Henry Tobias and Albert Gamse. Page 6: Song — **Hail To The Chief**. a. Henry Tobias. Page 8: Song — **We're Fixin' A Date With Nixon**. w.m. Henry Tobias and Albert Gamse. Page 12: Blank.

RMN-12 Nixon's The One. Produced by Faillace Productions, Inc. 1968. [8 1/2" × 11"]. Non-pictorial. 2pp. Page 2: Blank.

RMN-13 Stop Pickin' On The President. w.m. Bowen Matthews. Published by Mystique Music Publications, P.O.B. 75982, Sanford Station, Los Angeles, CA. 90005. 1971. Bl/w drawing of dike inscribed "USA" with leaks being plugged with fingers. "And help him guard the dike." 4pp.

RMN-14 Nixon (The Man for Us). w.m. Inez Wilson Clark. 1960. Non-pictorial red line border. "Republican Song." 4pp. Page 4: Blank.

RMN-15(A) Take My Hand. w.m. Jack O'Brien and Bob James. Published by Edwin H. Morris and Company, Inc., No. 31 West 54th Street, New York, NY. Copyright 1971 and 1972. [8 1/2" × 11"]. B/w drawing of an altered Presidential seal inscribed "*The Selling of the President*," television set. "From the Broadway musical *The Selling Of The President*." "John Flaxman in association with Harold Hastings and Franklin Roberts presents Pat Hingle *The Selling of the President*." "Charles Hansen Music and Books, 1860 Broadway, New York, NY. 10023." 16pp. Page 2: Blank. Page 6: Publisher's Logo.

(B) **We're Gonna Live It Together**. 8pp. Pages 2 and 7: Blank. Page 8: Publisher's logo.

(C) **Stars Of Glory**. 6pp. Page 2: Blank. Page 6: Publisher's logo.

RMN-16 Nixon Is The Man For Me. w.m. J. Maloy Roach (ASCAP) (Writer of *One Little Candle*). Copyright

1960 by J. Maloy Roach, %ASCAP, No. 575 Madison Avenue, New York 22, NY. [8 1/2" × 11"]. Bl/bk non-pictorial. "Special Artist Edition." 2pp. Page 2: Blank.

RMN-17 Click With Dick. w. Olivia Hoffman. w. George Stork and Clarence Fuhrman. Published by Elkan-Vogel Company, Inc., No. 1712 Sansom Street, Philadelphia, PA. 1960. [6 7/8" × 10 1/2"]. R/w/b non-pictorial. "Nixon for President Republican Campaign Song 1960." "Recorded by Tom Perkins with Orchestra." 2pp. Page 2: Blank.

RMN-18 Carry On! Carry On! With Nixon! (Siguele! Siguele! Con Nixon!). w.m. Rube Richards. Published by Apex Music Studios, 19146 Twig Lane, Cupertino, CA. 95014. Copyright 1960 & 1972 by E.F. Muss. [8 1/2" × 11"]. B/w photo of Richard Nixon. 4pp.

RMN-19 Forward, Forward, Together. w.m. Jack Arnold Press. Published by Chappell and Company, Inc., No. 609 Fifth Avenue, New York, NY. 1972. R/w/b flag design. 4pp. Page 2: "Dedicated to President Richard M. Nixon." Page 4: Logo.

RMN-20 Hey! Mr. President. w.m. Richie Adams and Mark Barkan. Published by Screen Gems-Columbia Music, 711 Fifth Avenue, New York, NY. 10022. 1969. [8 1/2" × 11"]. R/w/b crossed flags, "?." "Recorded by The Electric Prunes on Reprise Records." 4pp.

RMN-21 Vote For Nixon. w.m. Leonard Keller. Published by Len Art Music Publishing, Inc., No. 1369 Venetian Way, Miami, FL. 1960. Bl/w photo of Richard M. Nixon. R/w/b cover. 4pp. Page 4: "The G.O.P. will have a victory in '60 with Dick Nixon the next President of the U.S.A." Composer's note on Nixon trip to Miami Beach.

RMN-22 Theme From All The President's Men. m. David Shire. Published by Warner Bros. Publications, Inc., No. 75 Rockefeller Plaza, New York, NY. 10019. Copyright 1976 Warner-Tamerlane Publishing Corporation. B/w photo of Dustin Hoffman and Robert Redford. "The Most Devastating Detective Story of This Century. Redford/Hoffman *All The President's Men*." Film Credits — "Robert Redford, Dustin Hoffman, *All*

RMN-18

RMN-21

The President's Men, Staring Jack Warden, Special Appearance by Martin Bakam, Hal Hollbrook and Jason Robards as Ben Bradlee, Screenplay by William Goldman, Based on the book by Carl Bernstein and Bob Woodward, Music by David Shire, Produced by Walter Coblenz, Directed by Alan J. Pakula." "A Wildwood Enterprises production. A Robert Redford-Alan J. Pakula Film." 4pp.

RMN-23 The Richard Nixon Waltz. w. Russell B. Schroeder. a. John Betty. Published by The Blueboy Music Publishing Company, No. 214 North Clark Street, Grand Island, NE. 68801. 1971. Bl/w drawing of "Richard M. Nixon." 4pp.

RMN-24 President Richard M. Nixon March. w. Bert Terhune. m. Ervin Litkei. Published by Loena Publishing Company, No. 239 West 18th Street, New York, NY. 10011. Copyright 1968 and 1969. Bl/w photo of Richard M. Nixon— "The President." R/w cover. "To Ervin Litkei with best wishes, Richard Nixon" [facsimile signature]. 4pp.

RMN-25 President Richard M. Nixon March. m. Ervin Litkei. In: *A Tribute To The U.S.A.*, page 22. Published by Loena Music Publishing Company, No. 239 West 18th Street, New York, NY. 10011. Copyright 1985 and 1986. N/c drawing by Edward Moran of the Statue of Liberty celebration in 1886—"The Statue of Liberty, standing as an eternal symbol of the friendship of the people of France, was presented to the United States in 1886 by its creator, Frederick Bartholdi." Quotes by "Emma Lazarus (1883)," and "President Grover Cleveland (1886)."

RMN-26 President Richard M. Nixon March. w. Bert Terhune. m. Ervin Litkei. Published by Loena Publishing Company, No. 239 West 18th Street, New York, NY. 10011. Copyright 1968 and 1969. Bl/w photo of Richard M. Nixon.

RMN-27 President Richard M. Nixon March. w. Andrea Litkei. m. Ervin Litkei. In: *The Bicentennial March and Presidential Marches of America*, page 30. Published by Loena Music Publishing Company, New York, NY. 1976. R/w/b drawings of George Washington, Thomas Jefferson, Abraham Lincoln, eagle and flags. "American Revolution Bicentennial, 1776-1976." "Officially Recognized Commorative." 40pp.

RMN-28 I'm So Lonely Tonight. m. *Are you Lonely Tonight?* In: *Thoroughly MAD-ERN Malcolm*, page 13. Published by The New York State Legislative Correspondent's Association, Albany, NY. March 16, 1974.

RMN-29 Vote For Nixon. w. Pinky Herman (ASCAP). m. Pinky Herman and Mac Perrin. Published by Manor Music Company, No. 11 Rumsey Road, Yonkers, NY. 1968. Four bl/w photos of Richard M. Nixon. Bl/w drawing of Statue of Liberty, flag. 4pp. Page 4: Bl/w photo of Richard Nixon. "Contributed to the 'Nixon for President' Campaign."

RMN-30 Vote For Nixon. w.

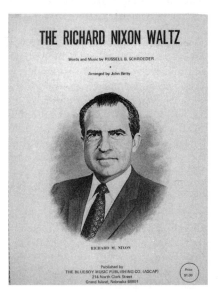

RMN-23

(RMN) RICHARD M. NIXON

RMN-29

Pinky Herman (ASCAP). m. Pinky Herman and Mac Perrin. Published by Manor Music Company, No. 11 Rumsey Road, Yonkers, NY. 1968. [7 7/8" × 11 1/4"]. Non-pictorial lead sheet format. 2pp. Page 2: Blank.

RMN-31 Hang In There, Mr. President (Fight, Fight, Fight). w.m. Henry Tobias (ASCAP). Copyright 1973 by Henry Tobias Music Company, No. 1255 North King Road, Los Angeles, CA. 90069. [8 1/2" × 11"]. Non-pictorial. "Suggested by Richard Mason." 2pp.

RMN-32 Jitterbug Rock. m. Mervin Conn. Published by Pietro Deiro Publications, No. 113 Seventh Avenue South, New York 14, NY. 1959. R/w/bk drawing of couple dancing. 4pp. Page 2: [V-1: "Dedicated to Tricia and Judy Nixon"] [V-2: "Dedicated to Tricia and Julie Nixon"].

RMN-33 Nixon Now. w.m. Ken Sutherland. Copyright 1972 by Colgems Music Corporation. [9" × 12 1/2"]. Non-pictorial. 2pp. Page 2: Blank.

RMN-34 The Ballad Of Spiro Agnew. w.m. Tom Paxton. In: *Politics*, page 7. Published by Cherry Lane Music Company, Inc., P.O. 430, Port Chester, NY. 1989. [9" × 12"]. N/c photo by Jennifer Girard of Tom Paxton. R/w/b flag design. 36pp.

RMN-35 I'm Proud To Be An American. w.m. Robert Taylor. a. Douglas Campbell. [1970]. Non-pictorial. [8 1/2" × 11"]. 2pp. Page 2: Blank. [Dedicated to Spiro Agnew at the Republican State Central Committee Dinner, Detroit, Michigan, June 15, 1970].

RMN-36 Oh, Mr. Nixon. w.m. Herman (Doc) Silvers. [ca. 1970?].

RMN-37 Down At The Old Watergate. w. Congressman William L. Hungate, Democrat, Missouri. Copyright 1973 by Popdraw, Inc., No. 165 West 46th Street, New York, NY. "Recorded by Perception Records, No. 165 West 46th Street, New York, NY." In: *Poor Richard's Watergate*, page 8. e. Roy Kammerman. Published by Price/Stern/Sloan, Publishers, Los Angeles, CA. 1973. [5 1/4" × 6 3/4"]. Bl/w photo of Richard Nixon. 68pp.

RMN-38 I'm Tossing My Hat In The Ring For Mr. Nixon. w.m. Gertrude Goehring and Don Hecht (ASCAP). a. Floyd Bartlett. Published by Dondee Music Prods., No. 3227 Andrita Street, Los Angeles 65, CA. Bk/bl drawing of an elephant. "1960 Republican Presidential Campaign Song." "Price $1.00 Souvenir Edition." 4pp.

RMN-39 Go Go Go Go Republican. w. Joe Martin. m. Al Lamm. Published by Northern Music Corporation, No. 445 Park Avenue, New York, NY Sole selling agent — Keys-Hansen, Inc., 119 West 57th Street, New York, NY. 1960. R/w/b cover drawing of an elephant, flag. Bl/w photos of Dwight D. Eisenhower, Abraham Lincoln, Robert Taft, and Calvin Coolidge. "The Republican Campaign Song." 4pp. Page 4: R/w drawing of a lyre. [Lyrics support Richard Nixon for President].

RMN-40 We Want Dick And

Spiro. w. Alain Peron (A.S.C.A.P.). Published for Central Committee To Re-Elect Richard Nixon And Spiro Agnew, No. 1370 Sunset Cliffs Boulevard, San Diego, CA. 92107. Copyright 1972 by Alain Person. Non-pictorial. Two long narrative paragraphs titled "The Way to Destruction and the Way to Preservation" and "The Way to the Post Office and the Way to Heaven." 4pp. Page 4: Two additional narratives titled "Morning Prayer" and "A Smile."

RMN-41 We Want Dick. w. Alain Peron (A.S.C.A.P.). Published for Central Committee To Re-Elect Richard Nixon And Spiro Agnew, No. 1370 Sunset Cliffs Boulevard, San Diego, CA. 92107. Copyright 1972 by Alain Person. Non-pictorial. Two long narrative paragraphs titled "The Way to Destruction and the Way to Preservation" and "The Way to the Post Office and the Way to Heaven." 4pp. Page 4: Two additional narratives titled "Morning Prayer" and "A Smile."

See also DDE-1; DDE-15; DDE-81; DDE-92.

Ross Perot

RP-1 Rhythm Of Reform: Song Lyrics For Reform Party Volunteers. w. Linda Grant De Pauw. m. Popular Tunes. Published by Peacock Press, 20 Granada Road, Pasadena, MD. 21122. 1996. [5 1/2" × 8 1/2"]. Pl/bk drawing of two bunnies playing drums, musical notes. [Used at the Maryland Reform Party Convention, September, 1996].

RP-2 Ross Perot's Swan Songs. m. Popular tunes. w. Linda Grant De Pauw. In: *Harper's Magazine*, page 20. December, 1996.

Ronald Reagan

RR-1 Thumbs Up, America! w. Sammy Cahn (Director of ASCAP, President Song Writer's Hall of Fame). m. Hon. J. William Middendorf II (Former Secretary of the Navy). Published by The Presidential Inaugural Committee, Washington, DC. 1981. N/c photo of Ronald Reagan. "Inaugural Theme Song for President Ronald Reagan and his First Lady, Nancy, January 20, 1981." B/w Presidential Seal inscribed "Inauguration of The President and The Vice-President." 4pp. Page 2: "Dedicated to the President and First Lady." Page 3: "Music Production Coordinator: Richard A. McCraken." Page 4: Inaugural and song credits. R/w/b drawing of Presidential Seal, fingerprints.

RR-2 Ronald Reagan March. w.m. Sterling Sloan. Published by Country Gospel Music, No. 6406 Carleton Avenue South, Seattle, WA. 98108. 1981. B/w photo of Ronald Reagan. R/w/b flag background. [Publishing data in white on cover]. "The Song of the Year, The Man of the Year, President Ronald Reagan." 4pp. Page 4: Biographies of Nancy and Ronald Reagan. "Bush by his side, and with Nancy his bride, like Clancey they'll lower the boom."

RR-2

RR-3 Ronald Reagan March. w.m. Sterling Sloan. Published by Country Gospel Music, No. 6406 Carleton Avenue South, Seattle, WA. 98108. B/w photo of Ronald Reagan. R/w/b flag background. 4pp. Page 4: Another song— *The Winning Side.* w.m. Bud Sloan.

RR-4 Ronald Reagan He Is The One! w.m. Jimmy Dixon and John Philpott. Published by United Republicans of America, No. 415 2nd Street, N.E., Washington, DC. Copyright July, 1968. [V-1: Br/w] [V-2: Gn/w] photo of Ronald Reagan, music notes. 4pp. Page 4: Long narrative on campaign music and this song.

RR-5 Hello Ronnie, Good-Bye Jimmy. w.m. Herman "Doc" Silvers and Cornel Tanassy. Sole selling agents: Passantino Music Publishing Company, No. 311 West 43rd Street, New York, NY. 1980. [8 1/2" × 11"]. B/w photo of Ronald Reagan. 4pp. Page 4: Blank.

RR-6 Stand Up And Cheer For Ronald Reagan. w.m. E.F. Moss. Published by Apex Music, Cupertino, CA. 95014. Copyright 1970 by E.F. Moss and 1980 by Apex. B/w photo of Ronald Reagan, six U.S. flags. 4pp.

RR-7 Ron For President. w.m. Joseph Erdelyi, Jr. Published by Erdelyi Music Publishing Company, No. 358 51st Street, New York, NY. 1984. [8 1/2" × 11"]. B/w photo of Ronald Reagan wearing hat –inscribed "Democrats Reagan." "Campaign Song for Ronald Reagan, 1984 Republican Party Candidate for President of the United States." "Dedicated to all the volunteer workers of the 1984 Reagan-Bush Campaign." "July 25, 1984." 2pp. Page 2: Blank.

RR-8 Let Ron Do It. w.m. Joseph Erdelyi, Jr. Published by Erdelyi Music Publishing Company, No. 358 West 51st Street, New York, NY. 1980. [8 1/2" × 11"]. B/w photo of Joseph Erdelyi, Jr. "Campaign Song for Ronald Reagan of Los Angeles, California, 1980 Republican Party Candidate for President of the United States." "This song was sung by the Author August 11, 1980, on the NBC-TV Network *Tomorrow Show* hosted by Tom Snyder." Advertising for other Erdelyi songs. 2pp. Page 2: Blank.

RR-9(A) Cowboy From Brooklyn. w. Johnny Mercer (ASCAP). m. Richard A. Whiting (ASCAP). Published by M. Witmark and Sons, New York, NY. 1938. Bl/w photo of Dick Powell and Priscilla Lane. O/w/bl cover. "Warner Bros. Presents *Cowboy From Brooklyn* with Dick Powell, Pat O'Brien, Priscilla Lane, Dick Foran, Ann Sheriden, Johnnie Davis, Ronald Reagan, Directed by Lloyd Bacon, Screen Play by Earl Baldwin, From the play *Howdy Stranger* by Robert Sloane and Louise Pelletier, Jr., Music and Lyrics by Johnny Mercer and Richard A. Whiting—A Cosmopolitan Production—A Warner Bros. Picture." 6pp. Page 6: Advertising.

(B) I'll Dream Tonight. 6pp. Page 6: Advertising.

(C) I've Got A Heartful Of Music.

(D) Ride Tenderfoot Ride. 8pp. Pages 2 and 8: Advertising.

RR-10 President Ronald Reagan March. w. Andrea Fodor Litkei. m. Ervin Litkei. Published by Loena Music Publishing Company, [New York, NY]. 1980. Bl/w photo of Ronald Reagan, facsimile signature. R/w/b border. 4pp. Page 4: R/w/b Presidential Seal.

RR-11(A) I'll Be Loving You. w. Sammy Cahn. m. Vernon Duke. Published by M. Witmark and Sons, New York, NY. 1952. Bk/w photo of Virginia Mayo and Gene Nelson. Pk/bk/w cover. "Warner Bros. Presents *She's Working Her Way Through College*, Color by Technicolor, starring Virginia Mayo, Ronald Reagan, Patrice Wayne, Screen Play by Peter Miline, Directed by Bruce Humberstone, Musical Numbers Staged and Directed by Leroy Prinz, Musical Direction by Ray Heindorf—A Warner Bros. Picture." 4pp. Page 4: Advertising.

(B) **The Stuff That Dreams Are Made Of**. 4pp. Page 4: Advertising.

RR-12(A) **Corn Pickin'**. w. Johnny Mercer. m. Harry Warren. Published by [V-1: Remick Music Corporation, New York, NY] [V-2: Canadian Music Sales Corporation, Ltd., No. 11 Dundas Street, Toronto, Canada]. 1939. Br/w photos of Ann Sheridan, Dick Powell. "Warner Bros. Picture, Inc., Presents *Naughty But Nice* with Dick Powell, Ann Sheridan, Gail Page, Helen Broderick, Ronald Reagan, Allen Jenkins, Zasu Pitts, Maxine Rosenbloom and The National Jitterbug Champions, Directed by Ray Enright, Original Screen Play by Richard Macaula." Br/w couples dancing. 6pp.

(B) **Horray For Spinach**. 6pp. Page 6: Advertising.

(C) **I'm Happy About The Whole Thing**. 6pp. Page 6: Advertising.

(D) **In A Moment Of Weakness**. 6pp. Page 6: Advertising.

RR-13 **Far Away Ireland**. w.m. David Carr Glover. Published by Baldwin-Mills Publishing Corporation. Distributed by Columbia Pictures Publications, a unit of Coca Cola Company. 1986. B/w drawing by Clotfeller of Ronald Reagan. Bk/gy/gn cover. "Dedicated to Ronald Reagan." 4pp.

RR-14 **Bedtime For Bonzo**. w. Ted Berkman and Raphel Blau. m. Ted Berkman. Published by Chappell and Company, Inc., RKO Building, New York, NY. 1951. B/w photo/drawing of Ronald Reagan, Diana Lynn and Bonzo the Chimp in bedroom. Bl/bk/w cover. "*Bedtime For Bonzo* Starring Ronald Reagan, Diana Lynn with Walter Slezak, Jesse White and Introducing Bonzo, Screenplay by Val Burton and Lou Breslow, Directed by Frederick de Cordova, Produced by Michael Kraike, a Universal International Picture." 6pp. Pages 2 and 6: Advertising.

RR-15 **The Girl From Jones Beach**. w.m. Eddie Seiler and Sol Marcus. Published by Harms, Inc., New

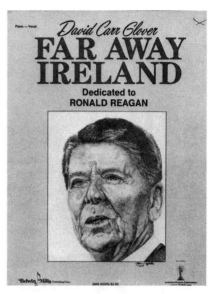

RR-13

York, NY. 1949. O/bk/w photos of Ronald Reagan, Virginia Mayo, Eddie Bracken, beach scene. "Warner Bros. Presents *The Girl From Jones Beach*, starring Ronald Reagan, Virginia Mayo and Eddie Bracken., Directed by Peter Godfrey." 4pp. Page 4: Advertising.

RR-16 **Oh Give Me Time For Tenderness**. w. Elsie Janis. m. Edmund Goulding. Published by The Remick Music Corporation, RCA Building, Radio City, New York, NY. 1939. Br/w photo of "Bette Davis in *Dark Victory*, George Brent, Humphrey Bogart, Geraldine Fitzgerald, Ronald Reagan Henry Travers, Cora Witherspoon, Sung by Vera Van in the motion picture, Directed by Edmund Goulding, Screen play by Casey Robinson, from the play by George Emerson Brewer, Jr., and Bertram Block, Music by Max Steiner, a First National Picture presented by Warner Bros." 6pp. Pages 2 and 6: Advertising.

RR-17 **I Found A Million Dollar Baby** (In a Five and Ten Cent Store). w. Billy Rose and Mort Dixon. m. Harry Warren. Published by Remick Music

(RR) RONALD REAGAN

Corp., New York, NY. 1931. B/w photo of Ronald Reagan, Priscilla Lane, Jeffery Lynn. Gn/w cover. "Warner Bros. Pictures, Inc., Presents Priscilla Lane, Jeffery Lynn, Ronald Reagan in *Million Dollar Baby* with May Robinson, Lee Patrick." 4pp.

RR-18 Heart Of Gold. w. Dave Franklin (ASCAP). m. Lou Forbes (ASCAP). Published by HR Music Corporation, Hollywood, CA. 1955. Bk/w/y photo of woman in bath tub. "From the RKO Motion Picture, Benedict Bogeaus presents John Payne, Ronald Reagan, Rhonda Flemming, Coleen Gray in Bret Harte's *Tennessee's Partner*, print by Technicolor, Superscope." 4pp. Page 4: Blank.

RR-19(A) This Is The Army Mr. Jones. w.m. Irving Berlin. Published by This Is The Army, Inc., Music Publishing Division, No. 799 Seventh Avenue, New York, NY. 1943. Gn/w/y drawing of soldiers as title. "Irving Berlin's *This Is The Army*, Presented by Warner Bros., In Technicolor, Starring men of the Armed Forces with George Murphy, Joan Leslie, Lt. Ronald Reagan and George Tobias Alan Hale, Charles Butterworth and Kate Smith, Directed by Michel Curtiz, Produced by Jack L. Warner and Hal B. Wallis, Screen Play by Casey Robinson and Cpt. Claude Binyon, Based on the Stage Show Irving Berlin's *This Is The Army*." "All profits will be turned over to The Army Emergency Relief Fund."

(B) I Left My Heart At The Stage Door Canteen. 4pp. Page 4: Advertising.

(C) With My Head In The Clouds. 4pp. Page 4: Advertising.

(D) I'm Getting Tired So I Can Sleep. 4pp. Page 4: Advertising.

(E) How About A Cheer For The Navy. 4pp. Page 4: Advertising.

(F) What Does He Look Like (That Boy of Mine). 4pp. Page 4: Advertising.

(G) The Army's Made A Man Out Of Me. 4pp. Page 4: Advertising.

(H) American Eagles. 4pp. Page 4: Advertising.

(I) That's What The Well Dressed Man In Harlem Will Wear. 4pp. Page 4: Advertising.

RR-20(A) This Is The Army Mr. Jones. w.m. Irving Berlin. Published by Chappell, No. 50 New Bond St., London, England. 1942. [6" × 9 1/2"]. Gn/w/y drawing of soldiers as title. "Irving Berlin's *This Is The Army*, Presented by Warner Bros., In Technicolor, Starring men of the Armed Forces with George Murphy, Joan Leslie, Lt. Ronald Reagan and George Tobias Alan Hale, Charles Butterworth and Kate Smith, Directed by Michel Curtiz, Produced by Jack L. Warner and Hal B. Wallis, Screen Play by Casey Robinson and Cpt. Claude Binyon, Based on the Stage Show Irving Berlin's *This Is The Army*." 4pp.

(B) I Left My Heart At The Stage Door Canteen. 4pp.

(C) With My Head In The Clouds.

(D) I'm Getting Tired So I Can Sleep. 4pp.

(E) How About A Cheer For The Navy.

(F) What Does He Look Like (That Boy of Mine).

(G) The Army's Made A Man Out Of Me.

(H) American Eagles.

(I) That's What The Well Dressed Man In Harlem Will Wear.

RR-21(A) Jeepers Creepers. w. Johnny Mercer (ASCAP) m. Harry Warren. Published by M. Witmark and Sons, New York, NY. 1938. Gn/w/br photos of Dick Powell, Anita Louise on horse. "Warner Bros. Pictures, Inc., Presents *Going Places* with Dick Powell, Anita Louise, Allen Jenkins, Louis Armstrong, Maxine Sullivan, Ronald Reagan, Walter Catlett, Directed by Ray Enright, Screen play by Sig Harzig, Jerry Wald & Murice Leo, Based on a play by Victor Mapes and William Collier, Sr. a Cosmopolitan

Production, a First National Picture." 6pp. Page 6: Advertising."
  (B) **Mutiny In The Nursery.** w.m. Johnny Mercer. 10pp. Pages 2 and 10: Advertising.
  (C) **Say It With A Kiss.** w. Johnny Mercer. m. Harry Warren. 6pp. Pages 2 and 6: Advertising.

RR-22 An Open Letter To The President (I Believe In America). w.m. Geoff Morrow, Chris Arnold and Mr. Pomerory. Published by Dick James Music, No. 119 West 57th Street, New York, NY. Exclusive Selling Agent: Warner Bros. Publications, Inc., 75 Rockefeller Plaza, New York, NY. 10019. 1981. Br/w/bl photo of The White House. "Recorded by Hamilton Junior High on Chopper Records." 12pp. Pages 2, 11 and 12: Blank.

RR-23 President Ronald Reagan March. w. Andrea Litkei. m. Ervin Litkei. In: *A Tribute To The U.S.A.*, page 7. Published by Loena Music, 239 West 18th Street, New York, NY. 1986. N/c drawing by Moran of Statue of Liberty celebration, 1886.

RR-24 The Girl From Jones Beach. w.m. Eddie Seiler and Sol Marcus. Published by B. Feldman and Company, 125-7-9 Shaftesbury Avenue, London, England. 1949. [8 1/2" × 11"]. O/bk/w photos of Virginia Mayo, Eddie Bracken, Ronald Reagan. O/w beach scene. "Warner Bros. present *The Girl From Jones Beach* starring Ronald Reagan, Virginia Mayo, Eddie Bracken, Directed by Peter Godfrey. Advertising. 4pp. Page 4: Advertising."

RR-25 Someone To Watch Over Me. w. Ira Gershwin. m. George Gershwin. Published by Chappell and Company, Ltd., No. 50 New Bond Street, London, England. 1926. [ca. 194- edition]. [8 1/2" × 11"]. O/bk/w photos of Ronald Reagan, Patricia Neal, Jack Carson. "From the Warner Bros. film *John Loves Mary* starring Ronald Reagan, Jack Carson, Edward Arnold, Wayne Morris,

RR-25

Virginia Field and Introducing Patricia Neal, Directed by David Butler, produced by Jerry Wald, Screen Play by Phoebe and Henry Ephon, From the hit stage play by Norman Krasna." 6pp. Page 6: Advertising.

RR-26 Let Ron Do It. w.m. Joseph Erdelyi, Jr. Published by Erdelyi Music Publishing Company, 358 West 51st Street, New York, NY. 1980. [8 1/2" × 11"]. Y/bk lead sheet. "Campaign Song for Ronald Reagan of Los Angeles, California, 1980 Republican Party Candidate for President of the United States." 2pp. Page 2: Blank.

RR-27 Unworthy Of Your Love [John Hinkley]. w.m. Stephen Sondheim. In: *Assassins*, page 34. Published by Rilting Music, Inc. Copyright 1990 and 1992 by Rilting. Bl/w star design by Neal Pozner.

RR-28 Say No To Drugs. w.m. Condit Atkinson. Published by Neil A. Kjos Music Company, Distributor, San Diego, CA. Copyright 1987 by Curtis House of Music. [7 7/16" × 10 1/2"]. Pk/r/w drawing of anti-drug symbol inscribed "Drugs" within a circle with slash. "SA (opt. SAB) Accompanied." 8pp. Page 2: "To Nancy Reagan."

RR-29 Montana. m. Louis Forbes. w. Bob Nolan. Published by Ross Jungnickel, Inc. and Bob Nolan Music, Inc. Sole Selling Agent: Hill and Range Songs, Inc., No. 1650 Broadway, NY. 1954. Bl/w drawing of Ronald Reagan, Barbara Stanwyck, Indians. "From the RKO Motion Picture...*Cattle Queen of Montana*, Print by Technicolor with Gene Evans, Lance Fuller, Directed by Allan Dawn, Robert Blees and Howard Estabroo, Produced by Benedict Bogeaus." "Featured by The Sons of Pioneers on Coral Records." 4pp.

RR-30 [**Reagan For President Again**]. w. Mike Folse. Published by Freedom's Ring, Freedom, IN. 47431. 1984 [2 1/4" × 3 1/2"]. Obv: R/w/b stripes. "Reagan for President." Rev: Song. "Sing One For The Gipper." "Compliments of Freedom's Ring."

RR-31 The Battle Hymn Of The Republicans. m. "Sung to the tune of *The Battle Hymn Of The Republic*." Published by Dots Okay, Inc., Annandale, VA. 1982. [9 1/2" × 3 1/4"]. Published with a boxed cloth "Reganomics Doll" with song sheet insert. 2pp. Obv: **The Battle Hymn Of The Republicans**. Rev: Song—**We're In Such A Fixie!** m. "Sung to the tune of *Dixie*." "Every great cause has always had a song to lift and inspire, something to rally 'round before a conflict. The Civil War had opposing 'great causes' that produced two memorial songs, *The Battle Hymn Of The Republic* and *Dixie*. Since the goings-on in Washington these days all too often resemble the Civil War, we thought that these great songs should be revived and revised a bit — as up-to-date calls to arms for supply siders and big spenders. Take your pick, and tune up your vocal chords."

RR-32 This Is The Army (Souvenir Album). w.m. Irving Berlin. Published by This Is The Army, Inc., Music Publishing Division, No. 799 Seventh Avenue, New York, NY. Copyright 1942 and 1943. R/w/bl/gd drawing of soldiers as title. "Irving Berlin's *This Is The Army*." "Illustrated Souvenir Album Complete Words and Music." "The Army Emergency Relief Fund receives all the Proceeds from the sale of this Album." 36pp. Page 18: "*This Is The Army* Program." "Warner Bros. Pictures, Inc., Presents, *This Is The Army* In Technicolor, Starring Soldiers of the U.S Army and George Murphy, Joan Leslie, Lt. Ronald Reagan and George Tobias Alan Hale, Charles Butterworth and Kate Smith, Produced by Jack L. Warner and Hal B. Wallis, Directed by Michel Curtiz, For Army Emergency Relief. Screen Play by Casey Robinson and Cpt. Claude Binyon, Based on the Stage Show, Irving Berlin's *This Is The Army*. Music and lyrics by Irving Berlin."

STEPHEN A. DOUGLAS

SAD-1 Douglass [sic] **Grand March.** m. George L. Walker. Published by [V-1: S.T. Gordon, No. 706 Broadway, New York, NY] [V-2: John Marsh, No. 1102 Chestnut Street, Philadelphia, PA]. 1859. B/w tinted beige litho [V-2:by L.N. Rosenthal] of Steven A. Douglas. "Composed and Respectfully Dedicated to Hon. Stephen A. Douglass [sic]." [V-2: "Copyright secured"]. 8pp. Page 2: Blank.

SAD-2 Douglas Polka. m. A Squire. Published by A.C. Peters & Bro., No. 94 West Fourth Street, Opposite the Post Office, Cincinnati, OH. 1860. B/w litho by Ehrgott, Forbriger & Co. of "Stephen A. Douglas." 6pp. Pages 2 and 6: Blank. Page 3: Title page. Music begins.

SAD-3 Douglas Funeral March. m. H. Grante (Chicago). Published by A. Judson Higgins, Chicago, IL. 1861. B/w beige tinted litho by Charles Shober of Stephen A. Douglas—"Yes, tell them to obey the Laws and support the Constitution of the United States." 6pp. Pages 2 and 6: Blank.

SAD-2

SAD-4 Douglas Polka. Published by J. Church, Jr., No. 66 West Fourth Street, Cincinnati, OH. 1860. B/w litho of by Ehrgott & Forbriger Stephen A. Douglas. 8pp. Pages 2, 7 and 8: Blank.

SAD-5 The Democratic Campaign Songster: Douglas & Johnson Melodies. Published by P.J. Cozans, Publisher, New York, NY. [1860]. [3 7/8" × 6"]. Y/bk litho of an eagle with ribbon — "Douglas & Johnson," train, ships, monument — "Liberty" sitting on rock base — "The Constitution." 40pp. Pages 2 and 39: Blank. Page 40: Advertising. [M-117].

SAD-6 The Douglas Grand March. m. George P. Goulding. Published by Sheppard, Cottier & Company, No. 215 Main Street, Buffalo, NY. 1866. B/w litho of column inscribed "Douglas," church, lake. "A Tribute to the Memory of the Lamented Statesman and Patriot Stephen A. Douglas." "To the Douglas Monument Association." 6pp. Page 2: Blank. Page 6: Advertising.

SAD-7 Douglas Schottisch. m. Charles Grobe, Op. 1212. Published by Lee & Walker, No. 722 Chesnut Street, Philadelphia, PA. 1860. B/w beige tinted litho by T. Sinclair of Stephen A. Douglas. "Dedicated to the Hon. Stephen A. Douglas." 8pp. Pages 2, 7 and 8: Blank. Page 3: At Top — "The Douglas Flag is waving, is waiving in the air and the joyous shout is ringing, we'll have no other there. 'Tis Douglas for the People, Brave Douglas, for us all with Douglas we will fight to win, or with Douglas, to fall."

SAD-8 Douglas Grand March. m. George L. Walker. Published by S.T. Gordon, No. 706 Broadway, New York, NY. [ca. 1860]. Non-pictorial geometric design border. "Parlor Album Pieces." List of other titles in series.

SAD-9 Douglas' Funeral March. m. George W. Hewitt. Published by Lee & Walker, No. 722 Chesnut Street, Philadelphia, PA. 1861. B/w beige tinted litho by T. Sinclair of Stephen A. Douglas. 6pp. Pages 2 and 6: Blank.

SAD-10 Hurra For The Union! w. William Cosgrove. m. "Air: *Wait For The Wagon*." [1860]. [6 1/4" × 9 1/2"]. Non-pictorial geometric design border. "Union Campaign Song." 2pp. Page 2: Blank. [Lyrics also support Breckenridge, Bell and Everett].

SAD-11 The Democratic Campaign Songster, No. #1. Published by American Publishing House, Cincinnati, OH. 1860. Litho of "Stephen A. Douglas." "No. 1" directly above portrait of Douglas.

SAD-12 The Democratic Campaign Songster, No. #1. Published by American Publishing House, No. 60 West Fourth Street, Cincinnati, OH. 1860. [3 7/8" × 5 11/16"]. Pk/bk litho of "Stephen A. Douglas," black line border. At top of cover — "No. 1, Price 10 Cents." 52pp. Pages 2, 4, 50, 51 and 52: Advertising. Page 3: Title page. [M-118].

SAD-13 Douglas Schottisch. m. F.W. Smith Published by Balmer & Weber, No. 56 Fourth Street, St. Louis, MO. 1860. B/w litho of Stephen Douglas. "To The Hon. S.A. Douglas." 8pp.

Pages 2, 7 and 8: Blank. Page 3: Title — **Douglass** [sic] **Schottisch**.

SAD-14 Steph. A. Douglas And H.V. Johnson. m. "Air: *Dandy Jim of Caroline*." Published by H. De Marsan, Publisher of Songs and Ballads — Toy-Books, Paper-Dolls, No. 60 Chatham Street, New York, NY. [1860]. [6 1/2" × 10"]. B/w [hand Colored] litho border of soldier, sailor, geometric shapes. 2pp. Page 2: Blank.

SAD-15 Hon. S.A. Douglas/ Hon. A. Lincoln [Song Sheet]. Published by Geo. G.B. Dewolfe, Olneyville, RI. [1860]. Litho of eagle — "E Pluribus Unum," cotton bales, plow, ship, grain, geometric design border. "The reader can, if he or she pleases, read the lines above containing eight syllables omitting those with six. The same rule will answer for the verses in the next column." "The Steam Machine Poet is frequently asked for his address. Let it be remembered. It is Geo. G.B. Dewolfe, Olneyville, RI. Forty lines will be composed in Ten Minutes." 2pp. Page 2: Blank. [Pro Douglas and Anti-Lincoln lyrics].

SAD-16 Thou Art Far Away. w.m. Harrison Millard (Author of *Viva L'America, Vocalist's Text-Book, &c)*. Published by Firth, Pond & Company, No. 547 Broadway, New York, NY. 1860. Non-pictorial. "To Mrs. Stephen A. Douglas." 6pp. Page 6: Blank.

SAD-17 Gleaner Songbook And Democratic Handbook. Published by Walter H. Shupe, Cleveland, OH. 1860. "Containing a Choice Selection of Original Douglas and Johnson Songs. The Life of Douglas. The Life of Johnson. The Democratic Platform. The Breckenridge Platform. Douglas' letter of acceptance. The amendment to the Constitution, Regulating Election of Vice President. The area and Population of the Slave States; The area and Population of the non-slave States; The popular vote for President in 1848, 1852, and 1856; the result of the Presidential elections from 1790 to 1856." "Price 10 cents." "For sale wholesale and retail by Ingham & Bragg." 64pp. [M-119].

SAD-18 Douglas Polka. m. By Charles L. Ward. Published by D.P. Faulds & Co., Louisville, KY. 1860. Gn/w litho of floral and geometric designs, star. "To the Friends of Democracy." 6pp. Pages 2 and 6: Blank.

See also AL-510.

SILAS C. SWALLOW

SCS-1 Quay=Stone's Quandary. w.m. Charles M. Fillmore. "Respectfully Dedicated to Rev. Dr. S.C. Swallow." In: *Fillmore's Reform Songs No. 1*, page 60. Published by Fillmore Brothers, No. 119 Sixth Street, Cincinnati, OH. 1898. [5 1/2" × 7 7/8"]. R/w geometric designs, flower, birds. "For Temperance, Prohibition, Patriotic, Reform and Special Meetings." 66pp.

SAMUEL J. TILDEN

SJT-1 Tilden And Hendricks' Centennial Reform March. m. R. Goerdeler. Published by S.T. Gordon & Son, No. 13 East 14th Street, New York, NY. 1876. B/w litho of Samuel J. Tilden and Thomas A. Hendricks, geometric and chain link border. "Composed for Piano." Page 2: Blank.

SJT-2 Tilden And Reform (Song and Chorus). w. William H. Long. m. J.G. Kuhn. Published by H.T. Martin, Parkersburg, WV. 1876. Hand colored litho of Samuel J. Tilden and Thomas A. Hendricks, fruit and ribbon border design. 6pp. Pages 2 and 6: Blank.

SJT-3(A) Tilden & Hendricks' Grand March. m. William P. Adams. Published by Wm. A. Pond & Company, No. 547 Broadway, New York, NY. 1876. B/w litho by Major & Knapp of Samuel J. Tilden and Thomas A. Hendricks in oval frames. "Respectfully Dedicated to Gov. Samuel J. Tilden (of New York) and

Hon. Thomas A. Hendricks (of Indiana)." 6pp. Page 2: Blank. Page 6: Advertising.

(B) **National Reform** (Campaign Song and Chorus). w. William Harlow. m. John Harlow. Copyright 1876 by Wm. Harlow. 6pp. Page 2: Blank.

SJT-4 Tilden & Hendricks' Grand March. m. E. Mack. Published by Oliver Ditson & Company, No. 451 Washington Street, Boston, MA. 1876. B/w litho by J.H. Bufford's Sons of Samuel J. Tilden and Thomas Hendricks in oval frames, flags, hat, scroll, law book. 6pp. Pages 2 and 6: Blank.

SJT-5 Tilden's Grand March. m. Charles A. Noel. Published by F.W. Helmick, No. 278 West Sixth Street, Cincinnati, OH. 1874. B/w litho by Monsch & Company of Samuel J. Tilden. "Respectfully Dedicated To Hon. Samuel J. Tilden of New York." 6pp. Page 2: Blank. Page 6: Advertising.

SJT-6(A) Banner Of Tilden & Hendricks (Campaign Song and Chorus). w. J.H. James, Jr. m. J.A. Porter. Published by John Church & Company, Cincinnati, OH. 1876. B/w litho of Samuel J. Tilden. "Honest Sam Tilden." "To the Friends of Tilden and Reform." 6pp. Pages 2 and 6: Blank.

(B) **Tilden & Hendricks' Reform March**.

SJT-7 Tilden and Hendricks' Democratic Centennial Campaign March (With Radical Accompaniments). m. A. Lutz. Published by St. Louis Music Publishing Company, No. 9 North 15th Street, St. Louis, MO. Copyright 1876 by R. Staples. B/w litho of political caricatures including marching rats poking fun at Republican scandals—Benjamin Butler—"Loyal Mashtub." James G. Blaine—"Maine stock jobber $60,000." John A. Logan—"Our Darling." Ulysses S. Grant—"Let Us Have (a) Peace." Rutherford B. Hayes—"The Cooped Chickens." 8pp. Page 2: Blank. Page 3 Title: **Democratic Centinial** [sic] **March**. Page 8: More drawings. List of Republican scandals: Ben Butler as a frog—"Brother-In-Law Casey and the New Orleans Custom House;" James G. Blaine—"A Bird Who Has Lost its Plumage;" "We Heartily Endorse Bab, Belknap & Blaine and Oppose Further Investigation;" "Woman Suffrage in a Horn;" &c.

SJT-8 Tilden Illustrated Campaign Song And Joke. Published by The American News Company, New York, NY. [4 3/4" × 7 1/2"]. 1876. Y/bk litho of Samuel J. Tilden, geometric design border. 50[?]pp. Page 5: Title—**The Illustrated Campaign Tilden Song And Joke Book**.

SJT-9(A) Tilden's Campaign March. m. C. Wiedmann. Published by J.L. Peters, New York, NY. 1876. B/w litho by Snyder & Black of Samuel J. Tilden and Thomas Hendricks, eagle, crossed flags, ivy. "To the Friends of Tilden and Hendricks." 6pp. Pages 2 and 6: Blank.

(B) **Tilden & Hendricks' Galop To The White House**. m. J.R. Wilson.

SJT-4

SJT-9

(C) **Tilden & Hendricks' Favorite Quickstep**. m. J.R. Wilson.
(D) **Put The Right Man At The Wheel** (Song and Chorus). w.m. Will S. Hays. 6pp. Page 2: Advertising. Page 6: Blank.
(E) **The Times Are Out Of Joint** (Song and Chorus). w. Samuel N. Mitchell. m. H.A. Selington.
(F) **Tilden's Campaign Polka**. m. Wallerstein.
(G) **Tilden And Reform** (Song and Chorus). w.m. Will S. Hays. 6pp. Pages 2 and 6: Advertising.

SJT-10 **Tilden And Hendricks Polka**. m. Guiseppe Riano. a. Phil P. Keil. Published by Phil P. Keil, cor. Walnut and Fourth Street, McKeesport, PA. 1877. Non-pictorial geometric designs. 6pp. Pages 2 and 6: Blank.

SJT-11 **Democratic Campaign Songs** [Song Book]. m. "Popular Airs." Published in Madison County, Alabama. [1876]. [3 5/6" × 6 9/16"]. Non-pictorial geometric design border. 4pp. [M-201].

SJT-12 **Tilden's Funeral March**. m. Ernst Markart. Published by Richard A. Saalfield, No. 12 Bible House, New York, NY. 1886. Non-pictorial black border. 4pp. Page 4: Advertising.

SJT-13 **Let No Guilty Man Escape**. w.m. Bab Notguilty. Published by Balmer & Weber, 206 North Fifth Street, St. Louis, MO. 1876. Non-pictorial. "Dedicated to the Young Men's Democratic Clubs for the Presidential Campaign of 1876." "Motto: With Tilden and Hendricks as Chiefs of our Nation, Its liberties rest on a solid foundation; But Rutherford Hayes and Wheeler Elected, Grant's 'Third Term' in principle will be effected."

SJT-14 **Gov. Samuel J. Tilden's Grand March**. m. Eben H. Bailey, Op. 58. In: *Folio, A Journal of Music, Drama, Art and Literature*, pages 100-103. Published by White, Smith & Company, No. 516 Washington Street, Boston, MA. 1876. [4 1/4" × 12 1/8"]. Gn/bk floral border.

SJT-15 **Tilden And Hendricks Grand March**. m. William P. Adam. Published by Wm. A. Pond & Company, No. 547 Broadway, New York, NY. 1876. Non-pictorial advertising.

SJT-16 **The Nation's Declaration** (Or What the People Want and Do Not Want). w. Edward J. Virtue, Jr. (Author of *America's Flag* and *Custer's Last Charge*). m. "Air: *The Wake of Teddy the Tiler*." 1876. [10 1/4" × 13"]. B/w non-pictorial broadside. 2pp. Page 2: Blank.

SJT-17 **Go! Grant, Go!** m. "Tune: *Old Black Joe*." [1876]. [4 11/16" × 8 1/4"]. Non-pictorial. 2pp. Page 2: Blank.

SJT-18 **Gov. Samuel J. Tilden's Grand March**. m. E.H. Bailey, Op. 58 (Author of *Bailey's Great Centennial March*). Published by White, Smith & Company, No. 516 Washington Street, Boston, MA. 1876. B/w litho by J.H. Bufford's Sons of Samuel J. Tilden. 6pp. Page 2: Title—**Gov. Tilden's Grand March**. Page 6: Advertising.

SJT-19 **Put The Right Man At The Wheel** (Song and Chorus). m. Will S. Hays. Published by J.L. Peters, New

York, NY. 1876. Bl/w non-pictorial geometric designs. "Respectfully Dedicated to Gov. Samuel J. Tilden." 6pp.

SJT-20 Centennial Democratic Campaign Song. w. Bab Notguilty. m. Airs: *Hail Columbia, Yankee Doodle,* and *Star Spangled Banner.* Published by Balmer & Weber, No. 206 North 5th Street, St. Louis, MO. 1876. [13 1/2" × 6 3/4"]. Non- pictorial broadside. "Published in Sheet Music." 2pp. Page 2: Blank.

SJT-21 Tilden And Hendricks' Reform Songs (For The Centennial Campaign of 1876). Published by The National Democratic Committee, Box 3637, New York, NY. 1876. [3 7/8" × 5 15/16"]. Gn/bk litho of Samuel J. Tilden and Thomas A. Hendricks, geometric design border. 40pp. Page 2: "Dedicated to the Tilden and Hendricks Campaign Clubs of the United States." Page 40: "Reform Candidates for President, Samuel J. Tilden of New York, For Vice-President, Thomas A. Hendricks of Indiana." [M-203].

SJT-22 Tilden And Hendricks 1876 Reform Grand March. m. C. Romeo. Published by John Church & Company, Cincinnati, OH. 1876. B/w geometric designs. 6pp. Pages 2 and 6: Blank. Page 3: Inside title—**Campaign Grand March.**

SJT-23 Gov. Tilden's Grand March. m. Henry Werner. Published by Balmer & Weber, Publishers, St. Louis, MO. 1876. B/w litho by F. Welcker & Company of Samuel J. Tilden, floral designs. "To the National Democratic Convention of 1876." 8pp.

SJT-24 Gov. Tilden Is Our Man (Campaign Song And Chorus). w. Samuel N. Mitchell. m. Chas. Ed. Prior. Published by F.W. Helmick, No. 50 West Fourth Street, Cincinnati, OH. 1876. B/w litho of Samuel J. Tilden. "Respectfully Dedicated to Hon. Samuel J. Tilden of New York."

SJT-21

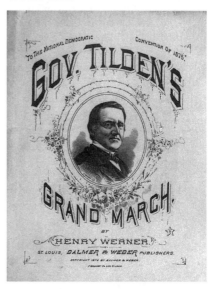

SJT-23

SOCIALIST LABOR PARTY

SLP-1 Workingmen's National Song. w.m. Lewis C. Wegefarth. Published by Oliver Ditson & Company,

Boston, MA. Copyright 1879 by Lewis C. Wegefarth. B/w litho of eagle with ribbon inscribed "E Pluribus Unum," flag, clasped hands, geometric design border. "A Rousing Campaign Song and Adopted by the Workingmen's Party of the United States at their Headquarters, Cincinnati, Ohio, October 6, 1879." "Notice—The Special Committee appointed to Examine into the Merits of your Song, have at last reported Favorably. Our National Executive Committee cheerfully send their approval of the song and recommend it as a proper campaign song—The National Executive Committee, Philip Van Patten, Corresponding Sec'y." 6pp. Page 2: Blank. Page 6: Advertising.

SLP-2 The Internationale and **The March Of The Workers** [Song Sheet]. Published by The Socialist Labor Party of America. [ca. 1930]. [7" × 10 3/8"]. R/w drawing of workers with flag inscribed "SLP America," arm and hammer logo. 4pp. Page 1:. **The Internationale** Page 2:. **The March Of The Workers**. w. William Morris. m. Air: *John Brown's Body*.

SLP-2

SLP-3 Labor Songs. c. Herbert N. Casson. Published by Lynn Labor Press, No. 153 Oxford Street, Lynn, MA. [ca. 1892]. [3 15/16" × 5 13/16"]. Non-pictorial gn/bk cover. 36pp.

SLP-4 L'Internationale. w.m. Eugene Pottier. a. Max Persin. w.a. [English] Chas. H. Kerr. Published by Metro Music, No. 58 Second Avenue, New York, NY. Copyright 1912 by Jos. P. Katz and 1927 by Henry Lefkowitch. R/w drawing of man with horn, flag and banner. "For Voice and Piano." 6pp. Page 6: Advertising in Russian language.

SLP-5 The International. a. Rudolf Liebich. w. Chas. H. Kerr (Translation). Published by Industrial Workers of the World, No. 2422 North Halsted Street, Chicago, IL. 1933. [9 1/2" × 12 3/8"]. B/w drawing of woman with torch—"Torch of Freedom," ribbon inscribed "Organize, I.W.W. One Big Union," globe, workers, union logos. 4pp. Page 4: List of other songs published by the Industrial Workers of the World. Printing of "The Preamble of the Industrial Workers of the World."

SOCIALIST PARTY

SP-1 Socialist Campaign Songs. Published by The Co-Operative Printing Company, No. 5443 Drexel Avenue, Chicago, IL. [ca. 1910]. [7 3/4" × 5 1/4"]. R/br non-pictorial. "Music Fills All Hearts with Fire." "Have your branch get a lot of these matchless, stirring, yet low priced booklets and start the whole community to singing these thrilling Socialist songs. That's the way to make your campaign a glorious success. Do It Now." 18pp. Page 18: Advertising for *Moyer's Songs of Socialism* song book. [M-398, 404].

SP-2 Song Of Freedom. w. Alex W. Grant. m. T.A. Simpson. 1916. Y/w/bk drawing by Perrigard of needy people reaching for sun rising over factories, churches, homes. [V-1: "One half of the net profits from the sale of this song will be contributed to the cause of Socialism"] [V-2: Paste-on Sticker—"One half of the net profits from the sale of this song will be contributed to the Belgium Relief Fund"]. 6pp. Page 2: Verses and narrative. Page 3: "Dedicated to a better civilization." Page 6: Drawing of sun— "For a better civilization." List of socialist principles, including "Government Control, Esperanto, Everybody Working, Preparedness With Righteousness, Early Marriages, &c..."

SP-3 Songs Of The Revolution [Song Book]. Published by Toledo Branch, Socialist Party, No. 213 Michigan Street, Toledo, OH. [ca. 193-]. [5 1/2" × 3 1/2"]. R/bk non-pictorial cover. 4pp. Page 4: "Singing together means— Thinking Together, Striking Together, Acting Together."

SP-4 Socialist Songs With Music. c. Charles H. Kerr. Published by Charles H. Kerr and Company, Chicago, IL. Copyright 1901 and 1902. [5 7/8" × 8 3/4"]. R/bk non-pictorial cover. 50pp.

SP-5 The Dawn Of Freedom (Military March and Two Step). m. J.C. McCabe. Published by Jerome H. Remick & Company, New York, NY. 1913. B/w geometric designs by Starmer. "Introducing *La Marseillaise*." "Dedicated to the Socialist Party of America." "Popular Edition." 6pp. Pages 2 and 6: Advertising.

SP-6 Some Songs Of Socialism. Published by Rochester Socialist Party, Rochester, NY. 1912. 16pp. O/bk non-pictorial. [M-405].

SP-7 Socialism In Song. e. Rev. M.A. Oslin and Rev. S.J. Oslin. Published in Campbell, TX. (and Stigler, OK.). 1916. [M-410].

SP-8 Socialist Song Book. e. Owen Fleischman. Published by The Young People's Socialist League, No. 303 Fourth Avenue, New York, NY. 1959. [8 1/2" × 11"]. B/w drawing of person playing the guitar. 74pp.

Thomas E. Dewey

TED-1 Dewey For President (Campaign Song). w. George Clardy. m. Rocco Colonna. Published by Clardy and Colonna, No. 111 West 49th Street, New York 19, NY. 1944. Photo of "Thomas E. Dewey," "V" symbol. 4pp. Page 4: Quote from George Washington's farewell address.

TED-2 Dewey We Do! w.m. Don Hayes. Published by Bob Miller, Inc., Music Publisher, No. 1619 Broadway, New York, NY. 1944. R/w/b Barbelle drawing of Uncle Sam playing drums, large "V," musical instruments. 4pp. Page 4: Advertising.

TED-3 Date In '48 (1948 Republican Campaign Song). w. Charles Lee. m. Meyer Davis. Published by Campaign Music Publishing Company, No. 119 West 57th Street, New York, NY. 1948. R/w/b drawing of Abraham Lincoln, elephant, flag. "Featured by Meyer Davis and his Band at the 1948 Republican National Convention." 4pp. Page 4: R/w/b design—"Vote Republican."

SP-5

TED-4 Dewey Bricker [Song Sheet]. Published for "Madison Square Garden Rally, Saturday, November 4, 1944." Non-pictorial. Patriotic songs. 2pp. [M-427].

TED-5 Do It With Dewey. w.m. Ruth Carmen. Published by Whitney Blake, Music Publishers, No. 1585 Broadway, New York, NY. 1944. R/w/b border, flag. Bl/w photo of "The White House — Washington, DC." 4pp. Page 4: B/w photo of Herbert Malkin. Advertising — "Send Herbert Malkin to Congress, He will Do It With Dewey-Bricker-Curran, Vote Line A, Rescue America, Vote Straight Republican Ticket."

TED-6 Mister Dewey. w.m. J. Warren Kays. Published by J. Warren Kays, No. 510 Miller Road, Ann Arbor, MI. 1944. B/w drawing of small oak leaf cluster. 4pp. Page 4: Blank.

TED-7 Thomas E. Dewey March. m. Dr. Gorman B. Mance. a. Malcolm Lee. Published by Grand American Freedom Rally Committee and the New York State Fair [Syracuse, NY]. 1952. R/w/b cover. Bl/w photos of "Governor Thomas E. Dewey," "Dr. Gorman B. Mance (Composer-Director)," and the "National Championship American Legion Band, Syracuse Post No. 41 under direction of Dr. Gorman B. Mance." "Dedicated to a great Governor of New York State." 4pp. Page 2: "A Great Governor of New York State, Dedicated at New York State Fair, Sept. 4, 1952." Page 4: Bl/w photo of American Legion officials. Narrative — "Grand American Freedom Rally."

TED-8 We're Marching On To Victory With Dewey. w.m. Franklin Wade. Published by Franklin Wade Publications, No. 1585 Broadway, New York 19, NY. 1944. Ma/w Barbelle drawing of Thomas E. Dewey. 4pp.

TED-9 Republicans Are On The March To Victory! w.m. Grace Louise Bosworth. Published by Allied Arts Publications, No. 232 East Erie Street, Chicago, IL. 1944. R/w/b elephants inscribed "G.O.P.," stars, geometric designs, shields. "We did it before, we'll do it once more in Forty Four!" "Dedicated to the Grand Old Party and the American way of life." 6pp. Page 2: Photo of and advertising for other Grace L. Bosworth music. Page 6: "Buy War Bonds and Stamps for Victory."

TED-10 Victory Is In The Air. w. William G. Adams and Roslyn Wells. m. Roslyn Wells. Published by The Eighth South Republican Club, Inc., No. 157 East 48th Street, New York, NY. 1948. B/w photo of Thomas E. Dewey and Earl Warren. "1948 National Dewey-Warren Campaign Song." "The Eighth South Republican Club, Inc., No. 157 East 48th Street, New York, NY., Dorothy Bell Rackoff and Paxton Blair, Executive Members." 4pp. Page 4: B/w litho of an eagle.

TED-11 Date In '48. w. Charles Lee. m. Meyer Davis. In: *Erie County Republican Banner*, page 1, June 21, 1948, Vol. 4, No. 6. Published by Erie County Republican Committee, Buffalo, NY.

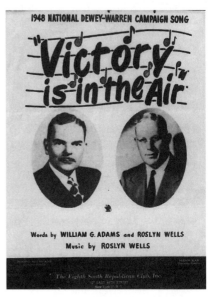

TED-10

Copyright 1948 by Campaign Music Company, New York, NY. "Republican Official Campaign Song."

TED-12   That Grand Old Party. w.m. Perry Alexander and Woody Frisino. Published by Dubonnet Music Publishing, No. 1619 Broadway, New York 19, NY. 1944. B/w drawing of Uncle Sam surrounded by elephants and flags. "G.O.P." 4pp. Page 4: Advertising for other Dubonnet Music.

TED-13   That Grand Old Party. w.m. Perry Alexander and Woody Frisino. Published by Perry Alexander, No. 118 Dubonet Road, Valley Stream, L.I., NY. 1944. R/w/b drawing of Uncle Sam surrounded by elephants and flags, eagle. Flag inscribed "G.O.P." 4pp. Page 4: Blank.

TED-14   Republican Highway. w.m. F.J. Anderson and G.W. Hassler. Published by Republican Headquarters, No. 150 NE 3rd Street, Miami, FL. [1948]. Non-pictorial. [8 7/16" × 6 1/8"]. 4pp.—Foldout. Pages 1 and 4: Blank.

TED-15   Dewey Will Do It (Dewey and Warren Marching On to Victory). w.m. Tom R. Hazard. Published by the Cine-Mart Music Publishers, No. 6912 Hollywood Boulevard, Hollywood, CA. Copyright 1948 by Tom Hazard. Br/w non-pictorial geometric designs. 4pp. Page 4: Blank.

TED-16   We Want Dewey Bricker (In the Presidential Chair). w.m. Carl Mader (B.L.A.E.F. 131st U.S. Inf.). a. Fred Huffer. Copyright 1940 by Carl Mader, Forest Park, IL. [8 1/2" × 11"]. Non-pictorial. 2pp. Page 2: Blank.

TED-17   Dewey For President (Campaign Song). w. Sarah Willis. m. Don R. Colonna. Published by Blue Bell Music Publishing Company, Inc., No. 2030 11th Avenue, South Birmingham 5, AL. Bl/w photo of "Hon. Thomas E. Dewey." R/w/b flags, eagle, stripe border. 4pp. Page 4: Blank.

TED-18   We Want Dewey. w.m. John R. Wolter. Copyright 1944 by John R. Wolter, No. 2029 Arch Street, Philadelphia, PA. [6" × 9"]. Cardboard. Non-pictorial. 2pp. Page 2: B/w photo by Bachrach of "Thomas E. Dewey."

TED-19   Let's All Do-Do-Do-With Dewey. w.m. Russ Lord. Published by Song-Hit Music Publishing Company, No. 1650 Broadway, New York 19, NY. Copyright 1944 by Russ Lord. Bl/w photo of Thomas E. Dewey. R/w/b stripe background. 4pp. Page 4: "12 Good Reasons to Vote For Dewey."

TED-20   Cash Or Carry — On Or It Ain't Hay [Program and Song Book]. Published by Legislative Correspondent's Association of New York State, Albany, NY. 1946. [8 3/4" × 11"]. N/c drawing of Thomas Dewey (MacDewey) and other politicians fighting over "Castle Surplus." "A Stirring Saga Suggesting Scrimping, Scrooging and Spending Twixt the Highlands and Lowlands of State Street Also Looney Left to Luna Looking for Less O'Lockwood, All Pieced Together With A Paralyzing Portrayl of Picket's Putting Pay Ahead of Party." "Hotel Ten Eyck, Albany, NY., March 14, 1946." 28pp.

TED-21   We'll Do It With Dewey. w. G. Jason Long. m. Lee B. Browne. Published by Puritan Publishing Company 1944. Bl/w photo of Thomas E. Dewey. R/w/b drawing of flag, silhouette of The Capitol building. 6pp. Pages 2 and 6: Advertising.

TED-22   That Grand Old Party. w.m. Perry Alexander and Woody Frisino. Published by Perry Alexander Music Publishing, No. 1619 Broadway, New York, NY. Copyright 1944 by Perry Alexander and Woody Frisino. Non-pictorial professional copy. 4pp. Pages 1 and 4: Blank.

TED-23   Dewey-Warren Victory Rally [Program/Songster]. Published by the New York Republican County Committee, New York, NY. 1948. [5 1/4" × 8 3/4"]. Bl/w photos of Thomas Dewey and Earl Warren. Bl/w drawing of two eagles. "Madison Square Garden, Saturday, October 30, 1948." "Gov. Thomas E. Dewey, Lt. Gov. Joe R. Hanley, Sen. Irving M. Ives, Mrs. Preston Davie, Hon. Thomas J. Curran, Hon. George Frankenthaler, Hon. Thos. J. Crawford, Mrs. Lillian Sharp Hunter, Hon. Daniel J. Riesner." 8pp. Foldout. Pages 4 to 7: Songs including: **We All Want Dewey**. w. Douglas D. Ballin.

TED-24   Let Tom E. Dew It (March). Published by Colonial Music House, Bath, ME. Copyright 1948 by N.W.H. R/w/b litho of Uncle Sam marching. 4pp. Page 4: Lyrics.

TED-25   God Bless President Dewey. w.m. The Sheik. Published by the Home Sweet Home Music Publishing Company, Hollywood, CA. 1948. B/w photo of Thomas E. Dewey, facsimile signature. Bl/w cover. 4pp. Page 4: B/w photo of "Earl Warren." "God Bless Dewey God Bless Warren God Bless our Homes Sweet Homes Mother Father You and Me."

TED-26   Dewey Will Do It (Dewey's Victory March). w.m. Tom Hazard and Ernst Adam. Published by Louis Retter Music Company, St. Louis, MO. 1944. Bl/w photo of Thomas E. Dewey. R/w/b "V" symbol, stars 4pp.

TED-27   Better Times Are Coming (Republican Campaign Song). w.m. Perry Bradford. Published by Perry Bradford Music and Periodical Publishing Company, No. 1650 Broadway, Suite 305, New York, NY. 1944. B/w photos of Thomas Dewey and Earl Warren—"The Way Ahead Dewey-Warren." B/w drawing of an elephant making a dollar sign [$] with trunk. "Radio broadcast free." 4pp.

TED-28   Sock-A-Bye-Baby [Program and Song Book]. Published by Albany Legislative Correspondent's Association, Albany, NY. 1938. [8" × 11 3/4"]. N/c drawing Thomas Dewey, other politicians with boxing gloves—"Ace Card for 1938 Golden Gloves Combat." "Legislative Correspondent's Association of New York State Presents Tonight, A No-Punches-Pulled Potpourri, Pillorying Political Palookas on Parade and Set to 'Swing' Time, Plus that Mad Maternal Masterpiece—Labor's Love Lost." "At Ten Eyck Hotel, Albany, N.Y., The Evening of Thursday, March Tenth, 1938, at Seven-Thirty O'clock."

TED-25

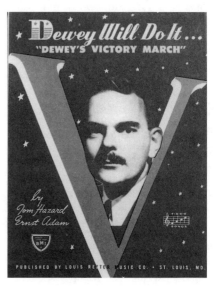

TED-26

TED-29 Vote For Dewey (A Republican Victory Song). w.m. Steve Nelson. Published by Rainbow Music Publishers, No. 1619 Broadway, New York, NY. 1944. Non-pictorial r/w/b cover. 4pp. Page 4: Bl/w drawing of an eagle. "For Close Harmony in Peacetime America Vote for Dewey and Bricker."

TED-30 Knighty-Knighty (Or A Michigan Yankee in King Herbie's Court) [Program and Song Book]. Published by The Legislative Correspondent's Association of New York State, Albany, NY. March 23, 1939. [8" × 11 3/4"]. N/c drawing of Thomas Dewey and Herbert Lehman jousting — "A Bouncing Blend, Mellowly Medieval, of Tangy Tunes, Balmy Buffoons, Flashing Blades and Ravishing Maids, Featuring the Glamour Gink of Gotham and the Caliph of Capitol Hill in 'Let's Tangle Tinware.'" "Thursday, March Twenty-Third, 1939, at Seven-Thirty O'clock. "Ribbingly Ripped Off at Hotel Ten Eyck, Albany, New York. [Songs about Thomas Dewey and Franklin D. Roosevelt].

TED-31 Gulliver's Travelers [Program and Song Book]. Published by The Albany Legislative Correspondent's Association, Albany, NY. March 18, 1943. [9" × 11 3/4"]. O/bl/w drawing of Thomas Dewey as Gulliver and other New York politicians, including Willkie as Lilliputians — "Starring that Astonishing Man from Michigan in a Rip-Roaring Revelation of Magic, or, Out of the Land of Little into the Pastures of Political Preferment, Patronage and Promises — and What Was Found There." "Done in Three Stupendous Acts at Hotel Ten Eyck, Albany, Thursday Night, March 18, 1943, at 7:30 O'clock." [Songs about Thomas Dewey and Franklin D. Roosevelt].

TED-32 Dewey For President (The Best Man In The Land). w.m. Toby Dwork and Robert Spencer Douglas. Unpublished manuscript. [1948]. [9 1/2" × 12 1/2"]. Non-pictorial. 6pp.

TED-33 [Song Sheet For Dewey]. w. Katherine P. Cain. m. Popular Tunes. [1948]. [8 1/2" × 11"]. Non-pictorial mimeograph. 2pp. Page 2: Blank.

TED-34 Visions And Revisions [Program and Song Book]. Published by The Albany Legislative Correspondent's Association, Albany, NY. March 6, 1947. [8 1/2" × 11"]. R/w/gn/y/bk drawing of Thomas "Dewey" as Santa Claus, sign — "Santa's Workshop," other New York politicians. "Revealing in Rhapsodic Revelry of Song and Stunt How a Political Scrooge Became a Political Saint; or, What Happened When Many Paws Raided the Wonderful Workshop of Santa Claus Dewey; Together with Other Strange and Silly Scenes." "Hotel Ten Eyck, Albany, March 6, 1947." 24pp. [Thomas Dewey and Harry Truman songs].

TED-35 A Dewey, Dewey Day. w.m. H. Stanton Sawyer. Copyright 1944 by H. Stanton Sawyer, No. 30 Spring Street, Dexter, ME. Non-pictorial line border. 4[?]pp.

See also FDR-197; FDR-364; FDR-371; HST-20.

Thomas Jefferson

TJ-1 Jefferson's March. Sold & printed by G. Willig, No. 185 Market Street, Philadelphia, PA. 1801. Non-pictorial. "Performed at the Grand Procession at Philadelphia on the 4th of March, 1801." "For Flute or Violin." "For Piano Forte." 2pp. Page 2: Blank. [W-4608].

TJ-2 The People's Friend. w. "A Citizen" [Rembrandt Peale]. m. John J. Hawkins. Printed by G. Willig, Philadelphia, PA. 1801. Non-pictorial. "Written & Composed for the Celebration of the 4th of March, 1801." "Copy Right Secured." 2pp. Page 2: Blank. [W-3471].

TJ-3 Election The People's Right. w.m. John J. Hawkins. [G. Willig], Philadelphia, PA. March, 1801.

Non-pictorial. 2pp. Page 2: Blank. [W-3470].

TJ-4 The Acquisition Of Louisiana (A National Song). w. Michael Fortune. m. "An Amateur." Printed for the Author at George Willig's Musical Magazine, Philadelphia, PA. [1804]. Non-pictorial. 4pp. Pages 1 and 4: Blank. [W-89].

TJ-5 Jefferson And Liberty. m. Air: *The Anacreontic Song*. In: *American Patriotic Song Book, A collection of political, Descriptive, and Humorous Songs of National Character and the Production of American Poets Only, Interspersed With A Number Set to Music*, pages 64-67. Printed & Sold by W. M'Culloch, No. 306 Market Street, Philadelphia, PA. 1813. [3 3/4" × 5 3/4"]. Non-pictorial hard back covers. 108pp. [W-122].

TJ-6 Jefferson's March. m. Alexander Reinagle. Published by John Cole, Baltimore, MD. [1821-1826]. Non-pictorial. "For the Piano Forte." 2pp. Page 2: Blank.

TJ-7 Jefferson's March. Published by G.E. Blake, No. 1 South 3rd Street, Philadelphia, PA. [1804?]. Non-pictorial. Attached label at bottom of page—"From Houston & Tanner's Music & Fancy Store, No. 87, South Third Street, Philadelphia." 2pp. Page 2: Blank. [W-4610].

TJ-8 The Death Of Gen. Washington (With Some Remarks on Jeffersonian Policy). Printed by Nathaniel Coverly, Jun., Milk Street, corner Theatre Alley, Boston, MA. [ca. 1807]. [10" × 11 3/4"]. B/w wood cut of George Washington? 2pp. Broadside. Page 2: Song—*Hull's Surrender or Villany Somewhere*. Small wood cut.

TJ-9 Thomas Jefferson's March. m. J. Womrath. Publish'd [sic] for the Author & sold at all music shops. Norfolk, VA. 1801. Non-pictorial. "Perform'd with universal applause at the Civic Festival, Norfolk, on the 23rd of February, 1801." 2pp. Page 2: Blank. [W-10048].

TJ-10 The Republican Harmonist (Being a Select Collection of Republican, Patriotic, and Sentimental Songs, Odes, Sonnets, &c, American and European: Some of which are Original, and most of the others now come for the first time from an American Press). c. D.E. [Daniel Ebsworth] (A Citizen of the World). Printed "for the People," Boston, MA. 1801. Non-pictorial. 152pp. Page 3: Title—"American and European: Some of which are original, and most of the writers now come for the first time from an American press." "With a Collection of Toasts and Sentimentals."

TJ-11 Monticello Waltz. m. C. Meineke. Published by George Willig, Jr., Baltimore, MD. 1838. Non-pictorial. "Composed and Respectfully Dedicated to Miss Eliza Frick." 4pp. Page 4: Blank.

TJ-12 Burr's Grand March. m. Daniel Marshal. Printed & sold at J & M Paff's Music Store, No. 127 Broadway, New York, NY. [1799-1803]. Non-pictorial. 4pp. Pages 1 and 4: Blank. Preceded on pages one and two by *Ground Ivy*. [S/U, p. 51].

TJ-13 Jefferson's March. m. James Hewitt. [ca. 1801]. Non-pictorial. 2pp. Page 2: Blank. [W-3725].

TJ-14 Jefferson And Liberty. In: *Instructor in Martial Music*, page 21. c. David Hazeltine. Printed by C. Norris & Company, Exeter, NH. 1810. 48pp. [W-3575].

TJ-15 Hail Liberty The Sweetest Bliss (A Quick Step to the New President's March). [V-1: Printed & Sold by G. Willig, No. 185 Market Street, Philadelphia, PA. 1801] [V-2: Facsimile edition by Musical America, No. 5458 Montgomery Street, Philadelphia, PA. 1956]. Non-pictorial. "For One or Two Voices." 2pp. Page 2: Blank. [W-3306].

TJ-16 Freedom And Our President (For The Voice and Piano Forte). w. Clarissa. m. Dr. G.K. Jackson. Printed for the Author by J. Butler, No. 156 Broadway, New York, NY. [1801?]. Non-pictorial.

"The words adapted to a new composition called *Jefferson's March*. Sung by Mr. Hodgkinson." 4pp. Page 3: "The words written extempore by Clarissa." [W-4523].

TJ-17 Jefferson's March. Published & Engravd [sic] by John Aitken & Sold at his Musical Repository, No. 76 North 2nd Street, Philadelphia, PA., "where may be had a veriety [sic] of New Publications." [1801]. Non-pictorial. "And to be had at Charles Taws, Walnut Street, No. 60." "Performed at the Grand Procession at Philadelphia on the 4th of March, 1801." 2pp. Page 2: Blank. [W-4611].

TJ-18 Jefferson's March. m. A. Reinagle. In: *For the Gentleman*, pages 50-51. Published by H. Mann, Dedham, MA. 1807. Non-pictorial. 52pp. [W-7940].

TJ-19 Jefferson And Liberty. In: *The Army and Navy Fife Instructor: Containing the Calls, Signals, and the Complete Camp and Garrison Duties as Practised [sic] in the Army and Navy of the United States, Including the Volunteer and Regular Service, Containing the National Airs, and a Large Collection of Marches, Quicksteps, Waltzes, Polkas, &c.*, page 50. e.a. Elias Howe. Published by Elias Howe, Agt., No. 103 Court Street, Boston, MA. Copyright 1863 by Willard Howe.

TJ-20 The People's March. m. John J. Hawkins. Printed by Geo. Willig, No. 185 Market Street, Philadelphia, PA. March, 1801. "Copy Right Secured." 2pp. Page 2: Blank. [W-3472].

TJ-21 Jefferson's March. m. A. Reinagle. Printed & Sold at Carr's Music Store, Baltimore, MD. [ca. 1805]. Non-pictorial. "As played at the Baltimore and Philadelphia Theatres." 2pp. Page 2: Blank. [W-7429].

TJ-22 Thomas Jefferson March. m. George Emrick. Printed & sold by G. Willig, No. 185 Market Street, Philadelphia, PA. [1801]. Non-pictorial. 2pp. Page 2: Blank. [S/U, p. 428].

TJ-23 Jefferson's March. In: *The Gentleman's Pocket Companion For the German Flute or Violin, Consisting of Most Elegant Songs, Airs, Marches, Minuets, Cotillions, Country Dances, &c.*, page 10. Printed & sold by G. Willig, No. 12 South 4th Street, Philadelphia, PA. [ca. 1816].

TJ-24 Monticello Waltz. m. C. Hommann. In: *Thirteen Popular Waltzes* (By Various Composers), page 12. "Respectfully Inscribed to Miss M. Schriver of York, PA." [ca. 184-]. Non-pictorial.

TJ-25 President Jefferson's March. In: *The Gentleman's Amusement (Book 1)*, page 1. "Printed for and sold by Thomas Balls, Norfolk, VA., and may be had in Richmond, Baltimore, Charleston, Washington, Alexandria and Petersburg." [ca. 1815]. [6 1/2" × 9 1/4"]. Non-pictorial. Followed on same page by **Mr. Burr's Hornpipe**. [W-2962].

TJ-26 Jefferson And Liberty. a. [Paul] Dressler. Published by S. Brainard's Sons, Chicago, IL. [V-1: 1884] [V-2: ca. 1897]. [V-1: N/c litho by Orcuft of battle] [V-2: Bk/bl/w reprint of V-1 with litho redone by Harrell]. List songs. "Popular Marches, Battle Pieces, &c. for Piano or Organ."

TJ-27 Jefferson And Liberty. a. Carl Buchman. e. Richard Franko Goldman. w.m. Anonymous, ca. 1805. Published by the Mercury Music Corporation, New York, NY. 1942. Br/w eagle. Bl/w printing. "*Seven Songs of the Early*

TJ-23

Republic, Edited by Franko Goldman. New Settings by Carl Buchman." "The tune of *Jefferson and Liberty* occurs in many versions during the early and middle 19th century. The one used by Mr. Buchman is taken from a manuscript tune-book compiled by one Silas Dickinson. The character of the melody suggests a folk-music source of perhaps considerable antiquity. The words are taken from the *New York Evening Post* of July 29, 1809, although they too must have been written somewhat earlier. The song enjoyed wide popularity for many years; printed versions are found as late as 1861." 16pp. Page 2: Blank. Page 6: List of other songs in the series.

TJ-28   I Spoke With Jefferson At Guadalcanal. w. Hy Zaret. m. Lou Singer. Published by Leeds Music Corporation, RKO Building, New York, NY. 1943. Non-pictorial. "Leeds Standard Series." 4pp.

TJ-29   Thomas Jefferson's Prayer. m. Joseph Roff. Published by the Willis Music Company, Cincinnati, OH. 1979. [6 7/8" × 10 1/4"]. B/w drawing of Thomas Jefferson. "For S.A.T.B. Chorus Accompanied." 8pp. Page 2: "Dedicated to Caroll Thomas Andrews and the Choir of St. John Vianney Church, St. Petersburg, Florida." Page 8: Advertising for other Willis published song.

TJ-30   Thomas Jefferson March. m. William H. Santelmann (Leader of the Band, U.S. Marine Corps). Published by Carl Fischer, Nos. 6 and 8 Fourth Avenue, New York, NY. 1903. Br/w drawing of Thomas Jefferson, facsimile signature, "Author of the Declaration of Independence." Bl/w drawing of a wreath, stars. "Respectfully Inscribed to the Thomas Jefferson Memorial Association of the United States, George Dewey, Admiral of the Navy, President." 6pp. Page 2: Blank. Page 6: Advertising for other Carl Fischer published songs.

TJ-31   The Declaration Of Independence. w. Thomas Jefferson, Sid Feffer and Pinky Herman. m. Pinky Herman. Published by Manor Music Company, No. 4705 N.W. 35th Street, Lauderdale Lakes, FL. 33319. Copyright 1982 and 1987. [8 1/2" × 11"]. Non-pictorial. Narrative — "What is Bicentennial." "Bicentennial is 200 years of forthright planning by far-sighted men and women for people of all faiths from distant lands, all with a single, common purpose — the Pursuit of Happiness, 'Laissez Faire?' 'Live and let live?' Not exactly. Correction — 'Live and help live! Yes — Bicentennial Is — Re-appraisal of the good life; our way of life; a re-awakening to fundamentals and re-dedication to the principles, courageously created, nurtured and benevolently bequeathed by our Founding Fathers to a grateful America — Pinky Herman, Chairman, Lauderdale Lakes Bicentennial Committee." 4pp. Page 4: Facsimile of the Declaration of Independence.

TJ-32   The Declaration Of Independence. w. Thomas Jefferson, Sid Feffer and Pinky Herman. m. Pinky Herman. Published by Manor Music Company, No. 4705 N.W. 35th Street, Lauderdale Lakes, FL. 33319. Copyright 1982 and 1987. [8" × 10"]. B/w eagle, geometric design border. 4pp. Page 4: Facsimile of the Declaration of Independence.

TJ-33   Tribute To Thomas Jefferson. w. H. Powell. m. E. Abbott. Published by Powell & Abbott, Chickasha, OK. 1913. B/w litho of Thomas Jefferson, Liberty Bell. "Dedicated to the national ownership of his Monticello home." 6pp. Page 2: Blank. Page 6: Advertising.

TJ-34   Thomas Jefferson. In: *Sing A Song of Americans* [Song Book], page 75. Published by Musette Publishers, Inc., Steinway Hall, New York, NY. 1941. R/w/b drawings by Mollie Shuger of song subjects including Theodore Roosevelt. 84pp.

TJ-35   Jefferson's March. a. Ervin Litkei. In: *A Tribute to the U.S.A.*, page 31.

Published by Loena Music Publishing Company, No. 239 West 18th Street, New York, NY. Copyright 1985 and 1986. N/c drawing by Edward Moran of the Statue of Liberty celebration in 1886.

TJ-36 Jefferson's Rondo. In: *The Gentleman's Amusement [Book 2]*, page 5. Printed for & sold by Thos. Balls, Norfolk, VA. [ca. 1815]. Non-pictorial. Followed on page by *Romance*. 36pp. [W-2962].

TJ-37 Spring Is A Wonderful Thing. w. Allan Zee. m. Allan Zee and Sam Jack Kaufman. Published by Halsey Music, No. 1674 Broadway, New York, NY. 1952. B/w photo of the Jefferson Memorial at Washington. 4pp. Page 4: Geometric design.

TJ-38 Monticello Waltz. m. S. Knaebel. Published by Root & Cady, Chicago, IL. 1869. B/w litho of flowers, geometric border. "The Musical Garland, A Collection of Choice Pieces for the Piano." List of titles in series. 6pp. Pages 2 and 6: Blank.

TJ-39 Monticello Suite (Five Compositions For Piano). m. Hans Barth. Published by J. Fischer & Bro., No. 119 West 40th Street, New York, NY. 1946. R/w/bk drawing of "Monticello." "Monticello, located just outside Charlottesville, Virginia, home of Thomas Jefferson, third President of the United States — statesman and gentleman. Jefferson was an accomplished violinist, a good singer and dancer. Designed his own home and before his wife's early death entertained lavishly at Monticello." "Fisher Edition."

(A) **Prelude.** 8pp. Pages 2 and 7: Blank. "Dedicated to Margery Todd." Pages 6 and 8: Blank.

(B) **Minuet.** 4pp. Page 3: "Dedicated to Charlotte Lee." Page 4: Advertising.

(C) **Sarabande.** 4pp. Page 3: "Dedicated to Adelaide V. Reid." Page 4: Advertising.

(D) **Gavotte.** 6pp. Page 2: Blank. Page 3: "Dedicated to Dorothy Powell." Page 6: Advertising.

(E) **Gigue.** 8pp. Page 2: Blank. Page 3: "Dedicated to Glauco D'Attili." Page 8: Advertising.

TJ-40 Jefferson's March. a. Ervin Litkei. In: *The Bicentennial March and Presidential Marches of America*, page 8. Published by Loena Music Publishing, New York, NY. 1976. R/w/b drawings of George Washington, Thomas Jefferson, Abraham Lincoln, eagle, flags. "American Revolution Bicentennial, 1776-1976." "Officially Recognized Commorative." 40pp.

TJ-41 Thomas Jefferson. w.m. Ireene Wicker. In: *Sing A Song of History*, page 37. Published by Educational Music Division, Irving Berlin, Inc., No. 799 Seventh Avenue, New York, NY. 1941.

(A) **Seven Lonely Days.** w.m. Earl Shuman, Alden Shuman and Marshall Brown. Published by Jefferson Music Company, Inc., No. 1619 Broadway, New York, NY. 1953. Photo of singer.

(B) **Dance Ballerina Dance.** w. Bob Russell. m. Carl Sigman.

(C) **Vanity.** w. Jack Manus and Bernard Bierman. m. Guy Wood.

(D) **Are You Livin' Old Man?** w.m. Redd Evans, Irene Higgenbotham and Abner Silver.

(E) **Salt Water Cowboy.** w.m. Redd Evans.

(F) **American Beauty Rose.** w.m. Hal David, Redd Evans and Arthur Altman.

(G) **Light In The Window.** w.m. Redd Evans.

(H) **I'll Still Love You.** w.m. Redd Evans.

(I) **No Moon At All.** w.m. Redd Evans and Dave Mann.

(J) **I've Only Myself To Blame.** w.m. Redd Evans and Dave Mann.

(K) **I Went Down To Virginia.** w.m. Redd Evans and Dave Mann.

(L) **This Is The Night.** w.m. Redd Evans and Lewis Bellin.

(M) **Lillette**. w.m. Jack Gold.
(N) **Too Young**. w. Sylvia Dee. m. Sid Lippman.
(O) **The Melancholy Minstrel**. m. Kay Twomey, Fred Wise and Al Frish. Gn/w cover.
(P) **I Laughed At Love**. w. Benny Davis. m. Abner Silver.

TJ-42 [Jefferson Music Company]. The Jefferson Music Company used a silhouette of Thomas Jefferson as its company logo. The following are a sample of their publications.

TJ-43 March And Quick Step. m. Lewis Krngell. Published by C.G. Christman, No. 404 Pearl Street, New York, NY. [ca. 1830-1840]. B/w litho of Thomas Jefferson, troops marching — "Jefferson Guards." "Respectfully Dedicated to the Battalion of the Jefferson Guards, 38th Regt., N.Y. State Artillery." 4pp.

TJ-44 The Embargo. [ca. 1808]. Non-pictorial broadside. 2pp. [Anti-Thomas Jefferson and James Madison].

TJ-45 The President Jefferson March. w. Alan Jay Lerner. m. Leonard Bernstein. Published by Music of The Times Publishing Corporation, New York, NY. Charles Hanses Distributor. 1976. [8 1/2" × 11"]. Non-pictorial geometric design. "From the Musical Production *1600 Pennsylvania Avenue*." 4pp. Page 4: Blank.

TJ-46 Monticello Montage. m. James Curnow. Published by Hal Leonard Corporation, No. 7777 West Bluemnound Road, Milwaukee, WI. Copyright 1994 by MusicWorks. R/y/w/bk non-pictorial cover. "MusicWorks, Music for Young Bands." "Grade 2." Band Package. On Score — "Program Note: "Thomas Jefferson, 'The Sage of Monticello,' was Congressman, Statesman, Third President...and designer of the Declaration of Independence." "Commissioned by and dedicated to the 1993 Albermarle County Middle School Honors Band, Charlottesville, Virginia..."

TJ-47 The Testament Of Freedom. w. Thomas Jefferson. m. Randall Thompson. Published by [V-1: E.C. Schirmer Music Co., No. 221 Columbus Avenue] [,V-2: C. Schirmer], Boston, MA 1943. [V-1: 1944] [V-2: ca. 1970]. [V-1: 6 7/8" × 10 3/4"] [V-2: 7 7/8" × 10 13/16"]. [V-1: Non-pictorial be/r/y] [V-2: Bl/w wreath]. "A Setting of Four Passages from the Writings of Thomas Jefferson for Men Voices with Piano, Band, or Orchestral Accompaniment." [V-1: Piano-Vocal Score]. 60pp. [V-2: Page 3: "*The Testament of Freedom* was composed in honor of the 200th anniversary of the birth of Thomas Jefferson. The texts, from the writings of Mr. Jefferson, were chosen by the Composer..."]. [V-1: Page 6] [V-2: Page 4]: B/w litho of "Thomas Jefferson, The Pride of America." [V-1: Page 11] [V-2: Page 7]: "To The University of Virginia Glee Club, in Memory of the Father of the University." Page 60: Bl/w litho of "Signet of Thomas Jefferson."

TJ-48(A) Letter To A Daughter. w. Thomas Jefferson. m. Sol Berkowitz. Published by Elkan-Vogel, Inc., A Subsidiary of The Theodore Presser Company, Bryn Mawr, PA. 1979. [6 7/8" × 10 1/2"]. B/w drawing of Thomas Jefferson. "Two Letters From Jefferson." 28pp. Page 2: "An excerpt from a letter by Jefferson to William Carmichael dated Paris, August 9. 1789."

(B) **Letter To A Friend**. 12pp. Page 12: Blank.

TJ-49 No News (Thomas J) (Barbershop Chorale). w. Richard Enqquist. m. Jack Gottlieb. Published by Theophilious Music, Inc. Sole Agent: Boosey & Hawkes, Inc. 1991. [6 7/8" × 10 1/2"]. Non-pictorial. "Presidential Suite, Seven Pieces for Mixed Chorus (SATB) a cappella." 12pp. Page 2: "Presidential Suite is a celebration of America's priceless heritage of liberty. Inspired by the wisdom and whimsy of some of our most colorful presidents, it juxtaposes the eloquence of John F. Kennedy and

Franklin Delano Roosevelt, with the journalistic pith of Theodore Roosevelt, Harry S. Truman's blunt common sense, Abraham Lincoln's homespun wit and Thomas Jefferson's irony, plus a legendary quip from the taciturn Calvin Coolidge. This patriotic work combines idealism with light-heartedness, inspiration with a dash of salt." "Presidential Suite was premiered by the Gregg Smith Singers on October 27, 1990, at St. Peter's Church, Citycorp Center, New York City. It was subsequently recorded by the same group." Page 3: "For Stefan Mengelberg." Pages 10 and 11: Blank. Page 12: Advertising.

TJ-50 Jefferson's Violin. m. "Based on a Rondo by Mozart." In: *The American Singer, Book 5,* page 125. c. John W. Beattie, Josephine Wolverton, Grace V. Wilson, Howard Hinga. Published by American Book Company, New York, NY. 1946. [6 5/8" × 8 3/8"]. R/w/b stars, bars of music.

TJ-51 I Spoke To Jefferson At Guadalcanal. w. Hy Zaret. m. Lou Singer. In: *Sing America,* page 48. c. Annie Allan. Published by Worker's Bookshop, No. 50 East 13th Street, New York, NY. [ca. 1944]. [4 1/2" × 6"]. Non-pictorial. 68pp.

TJ-52 The Sage Of Monticello. w.m. Clinton Cole. Drawing of Monticello. In: *Our Land of Song,* page 98. Published by C.L. Birchard & Company, Boston, MA. 1947. [6 7/8" × 8 11/16"].

TJ-53 Jefferson And Liberty, page 8. [ca. 180-]. Non-pictorial handwritten copy book of William Felton, 2d. 28pp.

TJ-54 Jefferson's March. In: *Blake's Evening Companion for the Flute, Clarinet, Violin or Flageolet, Vol. [ ], Book 1,* page 22. Printed & Sold by G.E. Blake, Philadelphia, PA. [1808?]. 26pp. Title page: Engraving of a man, woman with a clarinet, dog, bridge. "Copyright." "Price one dollar." [W-858].

TJ-55 Jefferson & Liberty. In: *The Village Fifer, No. 1, Containing Instructions for learning to play the fife and a collection of marches, airs, &c,* page 58. "Printed by Norris & Sawyer and sold at their book store, Exeter, N.H." March, 1808. 72pp. "Sold also by Charles Pierce, Thomas & Tappan, Portsmouth; William Sawyer & Co., Thomas Whipple, Newburyport; Thomas & Andrews, Davis West, John West, Manning & Loring, E. & J. Larking, Boston." [W-9491].

TJ-56 Jefferson & Liberty. In: *The Drum and Fife Instructor, in two Divisions,* page 34. c. Charles Robbins, Exeter, NH. "Printed by C. Norris & Co., and sold at their bookstore." 64pp. [W-7506].

TJ-57 Jefferson & Liberty. In: *A New & Complete Preceptor For The Violin Together with a choice collection of songs, duets, marches, dances, &c.,* page 17. Published by Daniel Steele, Sign of the Bible, No. 437 South Market Street, Albany, NY." [1815-1818]. 30pp. [W-7217].

TJ-58 Jefferson's March. In: *New Instructions for the German Flute, Containing the easiest & most modern method for learners to play. To Which is added a favorite collection of minuets, marches, song-tunes, duets, &c., the method of tongueing* [sic], *and a complete scale & description of a new invented German flute with the additional keys such as played on by two eminent masters, Fiorio and Tacet,* page 26. Printed & sold at G. Willig's Musical Magazine, No. 185 Market Street, Philadelphia, PA. [1801-1804]. 32pp. [W-4492].

TJ-59 Jefferson & Liberty. In: *A New & Complete Preceptor For The Fife Together with a collection of choice marches, &c, &c.,* page 9 Published by Daniel Steele, Sign of the Bible, No. 472 South Market Street, Albany, NY." [1815-1818]. Inside title: **The Complete Fife Tutor.** 26pp. [W-7211].

TJ-60 Jefferson's March. In: *Martial Music: A Collection of marches harmonized for field bands on various keys,* *such as are the most familiar and easy to perform on the clarinet, oboe, bassoon &c. Also a number of easy lessons for young practitioners*, page 43. Published by Daniel Steele, Bookseller, Court Street, Albany, NY. 1807. Printed by Manning & Loring, Boston, MA. 44pp. [W-6660].

TJ-61 Jefferson's March. m. James Hewitt. Printed & Sold at J. Hewitt's Musical Repository, No. 59 Maiden Lane, New York, NY. [ca. 1805]. Non-pictorial. Followed on page one by **Jefferson's Quick Step**. 2pp. Page 2: Blank. [W-3725].

TJ-62 Burr's March. Printed & sold at G. Gilfert's Piano Forte Warehouse, No. 177 Broadway [NY], and to be had of P.A. von Hagen, Boston, and G. Willig, Philadelphia. [1802?]. Non-pictorial. 2pp. Page 2: Blank. [W-1406].

TJ-63 Jefferson's Hornpipe. In: *A Collection of Most Favorite Country Dances, Arranged for the piano forte, harp, flute or violin. The figures to be had in a separate book*, page 17. Printed & sold at J. Hewitt's Musical Repository, No. 59 Maiden Street, New York, NY. [1802?]. "Sold also by R. Shw [sic], Philadelphia." 32pp. [W-2008].

TJ-64 Jefferson's March. In: *The Complete Tutor For the Fife, Containing ye best & easiest instructions for learners to obtain a proficiency. To which is added a choice collection of ye most celebrated marches, airs, &c. Properly adapted to that instrument, with several choice pieces for two flutes*, page 22. Printed for & sold by George Willig, No. 12 South Fourth Street, Philadelphia [PA], where also may had a great variety of other music, musical instruments, strings, &c., &c. [ca. 1805]. 30pp.

TJ-65 Jefferson's March. In: *Blake's New & Complete Preceptor for the Violin With a Favorite Selection of Airs, Marches, &c.*, page 22. Printed & Sold by G.E. Blake, No. 13 South Fifth Street, Philadelphia. PA. [181-?]. 26pp. "Price 75 cents." "Fourth Edition." Inside title: **Blake's Violin Preceptor**. [W-863].

TJ-66 Jefferson's March. In: *Instructions For The Piano Forte And English And French Flagelets, Also a collection of the newest and most favorite airs, song tunes, marches, &c., Selected and arranged*, page 22. c.a. G.E. Blake. Printed & sold by G.E. Blake, Philadelphia, PA. [ca. 1807]. Inside title: **Patent Flagelet Preceptor**. 24pp. [W-853].

TJ-67 Jefferson's March. In: *A Complete Preceptor for the German Flute, being an introduction to the art of playing on that instrumental explained in the most simple manner. Also a selection of the newest and most favorite airs, song-tunes, marches, &c., &c.*, page 23. Printed & sold by the Author [G.E. Blake], No. 13 South 5th Street, Philadelphia, PA. [182-?]. 26pp. Inside title: **Blake's Flute Preceptor**. [W-855].

TJ-68 Jefferson & Liberty (A New Song). m. "To the air of *Jefferson's March*." w. "The words by Michael Fortune." Sold at N.G. Dusief's Bookseller, Voltaire's Head, No. 68 South 4th Street, Philadelphia, PA. [1801-1802]. Non-pictorial. "Copy right secured." 4pp. Pages 1 and 4: Blank.

TJ-69 Jefferson & Liberty (Or The Gobby O.). In: *Musician's Omnibus: Containing the Whole Camp Duty, Calls and Signals Used in the Army and Navy; Forty Setts of Quadrilles, Including Waltz, Polka and Schottische, with Calls; and an Immense Collection of Polkas, Schottisches, Waltzes, Marches, Quicksteps, Hornpipes, Contra & Fancy Dances, Songs, &c., for the Violin, Flute, Cornet, Clarionett, &c, containing over 700 Pieces of Music*, page 50. c. Elias Howe. Published by Elias Howe, No. 103 Court Street, Boston, MA. 1861. [8 1/2" × 11"]. O/bk non-pictorial. "Improved Edition." 100pp.

TJ-70 Jefferson & Liberty (Or The Gobby O.). In: *Howe's Diamond School For The Violin: Containing, Complete Instructions and Full Directions in*

Bowing; to which is added A Large Collection of Popular Polkas, Schottisches, Waltzes, Redowas, Marches, Quicksteps, Dances, Hornpipes, Songs, , page 50. c. Elias Howe. Published by Elias Howe, No. 103 Court Street, Boston, MA. 1861. [8 1/2" × 11"]. Bl/bk non-pictorial. 68pp.

TJ-71 Jefferson And Liberty. In: *Songs Of Work And Freedom*, page 188. e. Edith Fowke and Joe Glazer. Published by Roosevelt University, Chicago, IL. 1960. [7 1/2" × 10 1/2"]. Be/bk/w drawing of laborers. Spiral bound. 212pp.

TJ-72 Jefferson And Liberty. w. "Circa 1800." m. "Traditional Irish Tune." a. Walter Russell. "A predecessor of the election songs we sing today, this rousing tune helped spread the promise of a new democracy during Thomas Jefferson's campaign." In: *The People's Songbook*, page 24. Published by [V-1: Boni & Gaer, Inc.] [V-2: Oak Publications], New York, NY. [V-1: 1948] [V-2: 1961]. [V-1: 7" × 10 3/8"] [V-2: 6 15/16" × 9 15/16"]. [V-1: R/w/b musical notes and keyboard] [V-2: Br/bk/w photo of folk singers]. 132pp.

TJ-73 The New President's March Or Jefferson's March. m.a. A. Reinagle. In: *Francis's Ball Room Assistant*, page 14. Published by G. Willig, No. 185 Market Street, Philadelphia, PA. [ca. 1801]. Non-pictorial. "No. 4 Francis's Ball Room Assistant."

TJ-74 Thomas Jefferski. w.m. Irving Caesar. In: *Sing A Song Of Friendship*, page 8. Published by the Anti-Defamation League of B'nai B'rith, No. 212 Fifth Avenue, New York, NY. [ca. 1946].

TJ-75 President Jefferson's March. In: *Marches Of The Presidents, 1789-1909, Authentic Marches & Campaign Songs*, page 8. a. Carl Miller. Published by Chappell & Co., Inc., No. 609 Fifth Avenue, New York, NY. "By arrangement with Chilmark Press, Inc." 1968. [9" × 12"]. R/w/b litho of eagle, flag. "An Illustrated Piano Folio For All Ages." 72pp.

TJ-76 Jefferson's March. In: Bound Volume of music. [[1793-1801]. Handwritten manuscript copy. Copied on the reverse of *The Highland Laddie*, published by Carr & Co.

See also GW-136; GW-142; GW-180; GW-181; GW-182; GW-204; GW-272; GW-282; GW-293; GW-393; GW-410; JA-7; JA-8; WHH-91; AL-202; AL-221; AL-292; AL-346; GC-46; TR-343; WHT-23; WW-19; CC-53; AES-35; WLW-41; WLW-57; FDR-158; FDR-310; FDR-367; FDR-390; HST-18; HST-22; AS-4; DDE-9; DDE-52; DDE-76; JFK-15; JFK-51; JFK-61; LBJ-1; LBJ-27; RMN-27; GRF-8; MISC-34; MISC-76; MISC-77; MISC-78; MISC-79; MISC-97; MISC-100; MISC-101; MISC-109; MISC-117; MISC-126; MISC-127; MISC-132; MISC-156; MISC-157; MISC-167; MISC-181.

THEODORE ROOSEVELT

TR-1 The Treaty Of Peace (A Japanese Intermezzo). m. Wallace A. Johnson. Published by Homer R.S. Klock, Stamford, CT. 1905. Bl/w drawing of Japanese hand fan, lantern, scroll inscribed with Japanese writing. "Dedicated to Our Honored President Theodore Roosevelt Who Was the Means of Bringing About the Treaty of Peace." 6pp. Pages 2 and 6: Blank.

TR-2 Republican Presidential March. m. Edwin F. Kendall. Published by Empire Music Publishing Company, New York, NY. Copyright 1904 by Nathan Goldfinger. Bk/w/y drawing by Frew of oval frame bordered by two axes and eagles. B/w yellow tinted photo by Pach Brothers of "Theodore Roosevelt." 6pp. Pages 2 and 6: Blank.

TR-3 The Loyal American March. m. Ernest Hand. Published by Ernest Hand Publishing Company, Williamsport, PA. 1916. R/w/b striped background, four U.S. flags, oval frame. B/w photo of Theodore Roosevelt.

"Dedicated to the Greatest Living American — Theodore Roosevelt." 6pp. Pages 2 and 6: Blank.

TR-4 A Jolly Good Fellow (Song, Two-Step and March). w. Mortimer Steinfield. m. Herbert Steinfield. Published by W.F. Rossman, Franklin, PA. Copyright 1906 by Herbert Steinfield. Bl/w cover drawing of two goldenrod branches, oval frame. B/w Pach Brothers photo of Theodore Roosevelt. "Dedicated to Juliette Shudmak of Philadelphia, Pa." 6pp. Page 6: Blank.

TR-5 Theodore. w.m. Vincent Bryan. Published by Shapiro, Music Publisher, Corner Broadway and 39th Street, New York, NY. 1904. Be/bk/w Starmer cover design. B/w photos of Theodore Roosevelt and "Jane Elton." 6pp. Page 5: Three additional verses. Page 6: Advertising.

TR-6 Our President (March and Two Step). m. Rudolph Aronson. Published by Chas. K. Harris, New York, NY. 1904. Gy/w clay-like sculpture by T. Sindelar of Theodore Roosevelt, drawing by Davenport of Theodore Roosevelt and Uncle Sam — "He's Good Enough For Me!" Page 3: "Respectfully Dedicated To President Roosevelt." 6pp. Page 6: Blank.

TR-7 Roosevelt March. m. Percy Wenrich. Published by McKinley Music Company, Chicago, IL. 1905. R/w/b flag design. Bl/w photo by Clinedinst of Theodore Roosevelt. 6pp. Page 6: Advertising.

TR-8 The Peacemaker (March). m. Frank Sturtevant. Published by Conservatory Publication Society, Broadway & 37th Street, New York, NY. 1905. Y/bk/w drawing of geometric design frame, eagle, angel with a horn and wreath. Bk/w tinted photo by Pach Brothers of Theodore Roosevelt. "Patriotically Dedicated to His Excellency President Theodore Roosevelt." "Conservatory Edition." 6pp. Pages 2 and 6: Advertising.

TR-9 Strenuous Life (March & Two Step). m. William J. Short (Composer of *American Workingman March*). Published by C.H. Persons Music House, Maynard, MA. 1902. Gd/bl/w cover litho of sun, rays, wreath, frame. B/w photo of Theodore Roosevelt. 6pp. Page 2: Blank. Page 6: Advertising.

TR-10 Our Teddy (March and Two Step). m. Oscar F. Knablin. Published by Oscar F. Knablin, Music Publisher, No. 1113 North Avenue, Bridgeport, CT. 1905. Gd/bk/w drawing by J.H.R. of Theodore Roosevelt on horseback. 6pp. Page 6: Blank.

TR-11 Gov. Roosevelt's Rough Riders (March and Two Step). m. B.W. Phillips (Author of *The Popular Country Club* and *Uncle Sam's Navy Marches, &c*). Published by Finn and Phillips, Scranton, PA. 1898. Br/w geometric designs. B/w photo of Theodore Roosevelt. 6pp. Page 6: Advertising.

TR-12 The Hero Of San Juan. w. Naomi E. Nicholson. m. Victor Arnette. Published by Naomi E. Nicholson, San Diego, CA. 1904. B/w cover drawing of floral and geometric designs. B/w Pach Brothers photo of Theodore Roosevelt. "Respectfully Dedicated to the People of the United States of America." 6pp. Pages 2 and 6: Blank.

TR-13 The Charge Of The Roosevelt Rough Riders. m. Charles Coleman (Composer of *There's A Hero On Every Ship, Fraternity Two-Step, Flitting Fancies, Berlin Polka, New Discovery March*). Published by Charles Coleman, No. 600 Kosciusko Street, Brooklyn, NY. 1941. Bl/w drawing by Teller of Rough Rider charge. "Played by the Leading Bands and Orchestras All Over the Country." 6pp. Pages 2 and 6: Advertising. Page 3: "Inscribed to Ex-President Theo. Roosevelt."

TR-14 Teddy You're A Bear. w. Ring W. Lardner. m. Lee S. Roberts. Published by Jerome H. Remick and Company, Music Publishers, Detroit, MI. 1916. R/w/b flags. Bl/w photo of

Theodore Roosevelt. "Played with Great Success by The Progressive National Band." 6pp. Page 6: Advertising for other Jerome H. Remick and Company music.

TR-15 The Rough Riders (March and Two Step). m. Frederick B. Downing. Published by Brehm Bros., Erie, PA. Copyright 1898 by Frank Brehm, Jr. [V-1: N/c] [V-2: Br/be] drawing of the Rough Riders charging. [V-1: B/w] [V-2: Be/br] drawings of a sword, canteen inscribed U.S.," backpack inscribed "U.S.," and crossed rifles. "Dedicated to Col. Roosevelt's Rough Riders." 6pp. Pages 2 and 6: Blank.

TR-16 Tramp Of Cavalry (Two-Step). m. Rider and Hamilton. Published by the S. Brainard's Sons Company, Chicago, IL. 1898. R/w/bk drawing of Rough Rider cavalry charge. "Dedicated to Col. Roosevelt's Rough Riders." List of arrangements available. 6pp. Page 2: Blank. Page 6: Advertising for other S. Brainard's Sons music.

TR-17 Teddy-Te-Tum-Tay. w.m. Dillon Brothers (Writers of *Put Me Off At Buffalo*). Published by M. Witmark and Sons, New York, NY. 1908. R/w/b drawing of Theodore Roosevelt with Uncle Sam-like beard playing bass drum inscribed "Sung with Great Success by William Dillon in all the Leading Vaudeville Houses." R/w photo of "William Dillon." 6pp. Page 6: Advertising.

TR-18 The American Soldier (March Song and Chorus). w.m. Richard C. Dillmore. Published as a "Music Supplement, Hearst's *Boston Sunday American*, April 23, 1905." Copyright 1904 by Richard C. Dillmore. O/br/w/bk drawing by H.B. Eddy of Theodore Roosevelt in Rough Rider uniform on horseback. "Published by Permission of the North American Music Company, Philadelphia, Pa." 4pp.

TR-19 Our Country (A Patriotic Song). w.m. Theodore Henckels. Published by Carl Fischer, Nos. 6 to 10 Fourth Avenue, New York, NY. 1908. Bl/w drawing of flags, eagle, geometric designs. R/w Pach Brothers photo of Theodore Roosevelt. "To Theodore Roosevelt." 6pp. Pages 2 and 6: Blank. Page 3: Poem — "To Theodore Roosevelt — To you, whose every word and act, New life to loyalty impart, I would, in memory of that fact, Inscribe this tribute of my heart."

TR-20 Dee-Lighted (A Typical Teddy Song). w. James Sprague. m. Wm. F. Braun (Composer of *Coon Song, Money, &c, &c)*. Published by W.F. Braun, Music Publisher, Fox & LaSalle Streets, Aurora, IL. 1910. B/w drawing of Theodore Roosevelt shaking hands with Uncle Sam, Capitol building. 6pp. Page 6: Advertising.

TR-21 The Peacemaker (Characteristic March). m. Harry L. Alford (Composer of *Yankee Boy, Blaze of Glory*). Published by Will Rossiter, Publisher, Chicago, IL. 1905. R/w/b litho of U.S., Japanese and Russian flags, dove. Bl/w photo of Theodore Roosevelt. "Inscribed to the President of the United States." "Introducing Russian and Japanese Battle Songs." 8pp. Pages 2 and 8: Advertising.

TR-22 Parade Of The Teddy Bears (Characteristic March-Two Step). m. George L. Cobb. Published by H.C. Weasner & Company, Music Publishers, No. 244 Genesee Street, Buffalo, NY. 1907. O/bk drawing of marching band of teddy bears holding banner with picture of Theodore Roosevelt inscribed "Delighted," five teddy bear heads at bottom. 6pp. Page 6: Advertising.

TR-23 When Teddy Comes Marching Home. w. Charles Coleman and Lew Evans. m. T. Jay Flanagan Published by Flanagan and Coleman, Music Publishers, No. 136 West 37th Street, New York, NY. 1910. B/w photo of Charles Coleman and Jay Flanagan. R/w/b flags, wreath. Bl/w Pach Brothers photo of Theodore Roosevelt. "By the writers of *Ottawah, When The Fleet*

Comes Sailing Home, Don't Be Angry, Always Remember Mother." 6pp. Page 3: "Respectfully Dedicated to Theodore Roosevelt." Page 6: Blank.

TR-24 The Brave Rough Riders (Ballad). w. J.W. Lieb. m. "Arranged from C.M. v. Webber." a. J.W. Lieb. Copyright 1898 by J.W. Liéb. [V-1: N/c drawing of Rough Riders charge, castle, U.S. and Cuban flags, rifle] [V-2: Cover blank]. "Respectfully Dedicated to Colonel Theodore Roosevelt and the Brave Rough Riders." 6pp. Pages 2 and 6: Blank.

TR-25 Our Teddy (March). m. J.W. Johnston. Published by A.H. Goetting, Springfield, MA. 1904. Bl/w/br drawing of Theodore Roosevelt in Rough Rider uniform, wreath. 6pp. Page 3: "Dedicated to the National Republican Party." Page 6: Blank.

TR-26 G.O.P. (March and Two-Step). m. William Marvin Manzer. a. Fred'k. U. Haines. Published by Manzer's Music Store, No. 4230 Cottage Grove Avenue, Chicago, IL. 1904. Bl/bk/gy/pk/gd/w elephant inscribed "G.O.P." Br/w photo of Theodore Roosevelt. "Respectfully Dedicated to Theodore Roosevelt." In logo: B/w photo of William Manzer "Publisher." 6pp. Page 6: Blank.

TR-27 The Capture Of Santiago (Descriptive). m. Wm. Frederick Peters (Composer of *By The Side of the Girl You Love, Chop Suey, &c*). Published by Howley, Haviland & Company, Nos. 1260-1266 Broadway, New York, NY. 1898. Bl/ma/w geometric design. Ma/w photo of Major General W.R. Shafter. "Respectfully Dedicated to Theodore Roosevelt, An American in the Highest Sense." 8pp. Pages 2 and 8: Blank.

TR-28 Since Bwano Tumbo Came From Jumbo Land. w.m. Francis W. Rivarde. Published by Shapiro, Music, Broadway and 39th Street, New York, NY. 1910. Ma/w geometric designs. Br/w photo of "Theodore Roosevelt." Br/w geometric designs. 6pp. Page 6: Advertising.

TR-29 Moving Day In Jungletown (Song). w. A. Seymour Brown. m. Nat D. Ayer. Published by Jerome H. Remick and Company, New York, NY. 1909. N/c drawing by Starmer of Theodore Roosevelt in safari outfit, elephant, monkeys, hippo, giraffe, ostrich, snake, lion. "Popular Edition." 6pp.

TR-30(A) Moving Day In Jungletown. w. A. Seymour Brown. m. Nat D. Ayer. Published by Jerome H. Remick and Company, New York, NY. 1909. N/c Starmer drawing of Theo. Roosevelt hunting lion, palm leaves, flute players. "Musical numbers from The Ziegfield Review *The Follies of 1909* as presented in The Jardin de Paris, atop the N.Y. Theatre, Book and Lyrics by Harry B. Smith, Music by Murice Levi." List of other songs in Review. 8pp. Pages 2 and 7: Blank. Page 8: Advertising.

(B) That Aero Naughty Girl (Mary Jane And Her Aeroplane). w. Harry B. Smith. m. Maurice Levi. 8pp. Pages 2 and 7: Blank. Page 8: Advertising.

(C) Christy Girl. w. Harry B. Smith. m. Maurice Levi. 8pp. Pages 2, 6 and 7: Blank. Page 8: Advertising.

(D) Linger, Longer, Lingerie. w. Harry B. Smith. m. Maurice Levi. 8pp. Pages 2 and 7: Blank. Page 8: Advertising.

(E) It's Nothing But A Bubble (Bubble Song). w. Harry B. Smith. m. Maurice Levi. 8pp. Pages 2 and 7: Blank. Page 8: Advertising.

(F) The Brinkley Bathing Girl. w. Harry B. Smith. m. Maurice Levi. 8pp. Pages 2 and 7: Blank. Page 8: Advertising.

(G) Take A Tip From Venus. w. Harry B. Smith. m. Maurice Levi. 8pp. Pages 2, 6 and 7: Blank. Page 8: Advertising.

(H) Lyre Birds. w. Harry B. Smith. m. Maurice Levi. 8pp. Pages 2, 6 and 7: Blank. Page 8: Advertising.

TR-31 Teddy Da Roose. w. Ed

Moran. m. J. Fred Helf. Published by J. Fred Helf Publishing Company, No. 136 West 37th Street, New York, NY. 1910. Br/bk/be/bl/o/w drawing by Frew of Theodore Roosevelt, dead elephant, photographer, African natives. 6pp. Page 6: Advertising.

TR-32 I'd Rather Be With Teddy In The Jungle. w. Harry Meyer. m. George J. Levitt (Composer of *The Man Who Swings A Pick At Panama*). Published by Georges Publishing Company, Boston, MA. 1909. Gn/w drawing of Theodore Roosevelt in the jungle. R/w photos of "Robt. Higgins" and "Mae Melville." "Melville & Higgins' Great Tropical Success." 6pp.

TR-33 Teddy's Nig. w.m. Ethelberta Twombly. Published by Vinton Music Publishing Company, Boston, MA. 1910. B/w drawing by Chat. Clark of jungle doll, tropical trees. "Dedicated with due apologies to the African jungle folks." "Trade Mark — Copyright — F.C.A. Richardson." 6pp. Page 2: Blank.

TR-34 The American Hunter (A Characteristic Jungle Symphonie). m. Edwin F. Kendall. Published by Seminary Music Company, No. 112 West 38th Street, New York, NY. 1909. Br/w/o/bk drawing by Frew of Theodore Roosevelt stalking lion. 8pp. Pages 2, 7 and 8: Advertising.

TR-35 When Rough And Ready Teddy Dashes Home. w. ('Red-Fired' by) Ed. Moran. m. ('Patriotic-ized' by) J. Fred Helf. Published by J. Fred Helf Company, No. 136 West 37th Street, New York, NY. 1910. Bl/o/br/w litho of fireworks exploding. Br/w photo of a Theodore Roosevelt look-alike dressed in jungle outfit. "Voltaged by Lew Dockstader." 6pp. Page 6: Advertising.

TR-36 Cannibal Isle. w.m. Olive L. Fields and Harry L. Newman. Published by the Sunlight Music Company, Grand Opera House, Chicago, IL. 1909. Gn/br/r/w drawing of Theodore Roosevelt, monkeys, elephant, lion, tiger, African natives speaking phrases "Oogie Oogie" and "Woogie, Woogie." "Featured by 32 Jake Sternad's Singing Acts." R/w photo of "The Rainbow Sisters — Two Rays of Sunshine." B/w photo of Harry Newman — "Yours truly, Harry L. Newman." 6pp. Pages 2 and 6: Advertising.

TR-37 We're Ready For Teddy Again. w. Harry D. Kerr. m. Alfred Solman. Published by Joe Morris Music Company, No. 130 West 37th Street, New York, NY. 1912. B/w hand tinted Pach Brothers photo of Theodore Roosevelt sitting in chair. 6pp. Page 2: "Respectfully Dedicated to the People's Candidate." Page 6: Advertising for other Joe Morris Music Company published music.

TR-38 When Teddy Comes Marching Home. w. Irving B. Lee. m. W.R. Williams. Published by Will Rossiter, The Chicago Publisher, No. 152 Lake Street, Chicago, IL. 1910. Br/w photo by Clinedinst of Theodore Roosevelt at desk. "Published for Band and Orchestra." 6pp. Insert photograph of Theodore Roosevelt. Page 6: Advertising for other Will Rossiter published song.

TR-39 They Are Calling From The Mountains (We Want Teddy). w. "A West Virginian." m. Dan J. Wall and W.S. Mason. Published by Walter D. Snyder, No. 9 South La Salle Street, Chicago, IL. 1912. B/w drawing of a moose. "As Sung at the National Republican Convention, Chicago, 1912." 6pp. Pages 2 and 6: Blank.

TR-40 He's Coming Back. w. Julie Jones and Alfred Anderson. m. Joe Jordan. Published by Will Rossiter, The Chicago Publisher, No. 136 West Lake Street, Chicago, IL. 1912. Y/br litho of leaves, geometric designs. Br/y photo of Theodore Roosevelt. "The Official Song of Good Times." "3 Cheers for Our Side." 8pp. Page 2: Blank. Pages 7 and 8: Advertising for other Will Rossiter published music.

TR-41 I'm Coming Back. w.m.

Guy Rand. Published by Harold Rossiter Music Company, Chicago, IL. 1909. Gy/w photo of Theodore Roosevelt. 6pp. Pages 2 and 6: Advertising for other Harold Rossiter Music Company published music. Page 3: "Dedicated to Colonel Theodore Roosevelt."

TR-42 My Hats In The Ring. w. Harry Williams. m. Egbert Van Alstyne. a. Brockman. Published by Jerome H. Remick and Company, New York, NY. 1912. Gn/w Gene Buck non-pictorial geometric design. 6pp. Page 2: Blank. Page 6: Advertising for other Jerome H. Remick and Company published music.

TR-43 Teddy's Hat (March Two-Step). m. S. Macaulay. Published by Luckhardt & Belder, No. 10 East 17th Street, New York, NY. 1900. B/w drawing of a Rough Rider hat, wreath inscribed "To Governor Theodore Roosevelt." 6pp. Pages 2 and 6: Blank.

TR-44 My Hat's In The Ring (Song). w. Harry Williams. m. Egbert Van Alstyne. a. Brockman. Published by Jerome H. Remick and Company, New York, NY. 1912. Bl/gd/gn/w Starmer drawing of a Rough Rider hat, geometric designs. 6pp. Pages 2 and 6: Advertising.

TR-45 Teddy After Africa (Humoresque Two-Step). m. Arthur Pryor. Published by Carl Fischer, Nos. 6-10 Fourth Avenue, New York, NY. 1909. R/gn/br drawing by Pfeiffer of elephant, rhino, monkeys and giraffe climbing trees. 6pp. Page 6: Advertising for other Arthur Pryor-Carl Fischer published music.

TR-46 The Big Stick (The American Military March Two-Step). m. Alfred Smith. Published by Black, Smith & Company, Chicago, IL. 1910. R/w/b drawing of Uncle Sam leading a parade band. "Respectfully Dedicated to Theodore Roosevelt." "As Played by All the Leading Bands and Orchestras." 6pp. Page 2: Blank. Page 6: Advertising for National Music Company music.

TR-47 Roosevelt And Fairbanks (March Two Step). m. William P. McBride. Published by The Faulkner Publishing Company, Kane, PA. Copyright 1904 by James G. Faulkner. Bl/w drawing of eagle, shield, oval frames, geometric designs. B/w photos of Theodore Roosevelt and Charles Fairbanks. "Press of Kane Republican Co., Kane, Pa." 6pp. Pages 2 and 6: Blank.

TR-48 American Eagle March. m. John Geo. Bochme (Composer of the *Empire City March*). Published by Ernst Rueffer, No. 109 First Avenue, New York, NY. 1897. [V-1: R/w/bl/gd] [V-2: R/w/bl/y] litho U.S. flags, eagle with ribbon inscribed "E Pluribus Unum," flowers, geometric designs. "Respectfully Dedicated to Our President Theodore Roosevelt." List of other musical arrangements available. 8pp. Pages 2, 6, 7 and 8: Advertising.

TR-49 Bull Moose March. m. E.P. Hartman. Published by Schubert Company, Cleveland, OH. 1912. Gn/w drawing of a moose head. 6pp. Pages 2

TR-47

and 6: Blank. Page 3: "Dedicated to Theodore Roosevelt."

TR-50 Teddy's March. m. Anna Elston Gerrish. Published by Sol Bloom, Chicago, IL. [ca. 1901]. Photo of John Philip Sousa — "Played by Sousa's Band." Drawing of trees, flowers, geometric designs. "Dedicated to Governor Theodore Roosevelt, A Representative American." 6pp. Pages 2 and 6: Blank. Page 3: "Respectfully Dedicated to Governor Theodore Roosevelt, the Ideal American."

TR-51 Roosevelt March And Two-Step. m. Emelie Fricke. Published by Sun Printing Company, Philadelphia, PA. 1900. B/w non-pictorial geometric designs. 6pp. Page 6: Blank.

TR-52 North Dakota (Teddy Roosevelt's West). w.m. Walter Edward Delano. Published by Harold Flammer, Inc., New York, NY. 1925. R/bk/be drawing of sun, rays, cowboy on bucking horse. "Featured by Fletcher Brothers Frederick Hotel Orchestra, Grand Forks, No. Dak." 6pp. Page 2: "Respectfully Inscribed to G.R.J." Page 6: Blank.

TR-53 If We Had A Million More Like Teddy! (The War Would Be Over To-Day). w.m. Charles A. Bayha. Published by Kendis Music Publishing Company, No. 145 West 45th Street, New York, NY. 1917. Gy/bk/w photo of mounted soldiers. "The Song of the Hour." 4pp. Page 4: Advertising for other Kendis music.

TR-54 Marching To Victory (America's Song of Songs). w. Pliny Berthier Seymour. m. Air: "Melody, *Marching Thro' Georgia*" by Henry C. Work. Published by The S. Brainard's Sons, New York, NY. 1905. R/w/bl/y litho of U.S. flag, geometric designs. "Dedicated to Theodore Roosevelt." 6pp. Pages 2 and 6: Blank.

TR-55 We Are With T.R. w. A.W. Loudon (Troy, NY). m. John B. Shirley (Troy, NY). Published by the Progressive Party, Troy, NY. Copyright 1912 by John Shirley. [7 1/4" × 10 1/4"]. B/w photo of Theodore Roosevelt. "Campaign Song of the Progressive Party." 4pp. Page 4: "Progressive Principles."

TR-56 Roosevelt March. m. F. Carl Jahn. Published by Will Wood, No. 233 West 40th Street, New York, NY. 1919. Br/o/w/bk drawing of a Rough Rider [T.R.] on horseback, eagle, shield. B/w photo by Underwood & Underwood of Theodore Roosevelt. 4pp. Page 4: Advertising for Century Music published music.

TR-57 The Trumpet Call. w. Edward Riis. m. Ralph C. Williams. Published by Chandler-Ebel Company, No. 222 Livingston Street, Brooklyn, NY. 1922. B/w litho "Courtesy *Collier's*" of Theodore Roosevelt, four trumpets. "In Memoriam." 4pp. Page 4: Blank.

TR-58 If It Were Not For Dear Old Father (Song). w.m. Nora Bayes and Jack Norworth. Published by Jerome H. Remick & Company, New York, NY. 1909. R/w/bk drawing of a man pointing to a picture on the wall of Theodore Roosevelt. "As Featured in F. Ziegfield Jr's Review *Follies of 1909* at the 'Jardin de Paris' atop the New York Theatre." 6pp. Page 6: Advertising.

TR-59 Emblem Of Freedom. w. Thomas Ostenson Stine. m. C. Blom. Published by Thomas Ostenson Stine, Seattle, WA. 1904. R/w/b crossed flags. Bl/w drawing of Theodore Roosevelt. R/w/b flags, geometric design. "To Theodore Roosevelt — Whereas, that your life has proven to be demonstrative of the sentiment of this song, *Emblem of Freedom*, I therefore Dedicate it to you — Thomas O. Stine." "Arranged for Mixed and Male Voices." 4pp. Page 2: Version for "Mixed Voices." Page 3: Version for "Male Voices." Page 4: Facsimile of song manuscript.

TR-60 He's Good Enough For Me (March Two-Step). m. William R. Haskins and Maurice S. Taube. Published by William Haskins, No. 892

DeKalb Avenue, Brooklyn, NY. 1904. R/w/bl/br drawing of Uncle Sam with his hand on the shoulder of Theodore Roosevelt. "From the famous Davenport cartoon copyrighted and published by the New York Evening Mail whose permission has been obtained to reproduce same." 6pp. Page 6: Advertising for other William Haskins published music.

TR-61   The Call To Camp Roosevelt. w.m. Angus Hibbard. Published by The Camp Roosevelt Association, No. 460 State Street, Chicago, IL. Copyright 1924 by Angus Hibbard. B/w photo of Theodore Roosevelt. B/w silhouette of bugle player, camp scene. "1925 on The Fort Sheridan Military Reservation." 4pp. Page 4: Blank.

TR-62   Sagamore Hill March. w.m. Donald N. Luckenbill. Published by Associated Music Publishers, Inc., New York, NY. Copyright 1954 and 1957. Br/w cover. B/w photos of Theodore Roosevelt and his home at Sagamore Hill. 4pp. Page 2: "Dedicated to TR's home at Oyster Bay, NY." Page 4: Note: "Sagamore Hill is the home of former President Theodore Roosevelt at Oyster Bay, Long Island, N.Y. The Estate was dedicated as a National Shrine on June 14, 1953. *Sagamore Hill March* was premiered in New York by The Goldman Band on June 25, 1954, Edwin Franco Goldman Conducting...Donald Luckenbill is Chairman of the Music Department in the Public Schools of Oyster Bay..."

TR-63(A)   The Great American (Theodore Roosevelt) (One-Step, March, Two-Step). m. Harry J. Lincoln. Published by Vandersloot Music Publishing Company, Williamsport, PA. 1919. [Pre-1919 size]. O/bl/w drawings of Theodore Roosevelt's life events. Br/w/o photo of Theodore Roosevelt. 4pp. Page 2: "To the American Legion and In Memory of the Great American (Theodore Roosevelt)!" Page 4: Advertising.

(B)   The Great American (Theodore Roosevelt) (Song). w. Ray Sherwood. m. Harry J. Lincoln.

TR-64   The Rough Rider's Patrol (March And Two Step). m. Elmer de Lacy Bennett. Published by Gagel Brothers, No. 1276 Broadway, New York, NY. 1898. Gn/w non-pictorial cover. 8pp. Pages 2, 7 and 8: Advertising for other Gagel Brothers published music.

TR-65   Charge Of The Rough Riders (March and Two-Step). m. James W. Casey. Published by Evans Music Company, No. 522 Massachusetts Avenue, Boston, MA. Copyright 1898 by W.A. Evans. Pl/w litho of Theodore Roosevelt and the Rough Riders, bombs bursting. "Dedicated to Col. Theodore Roosevelt." List of arrangements available. 8pp. Pages 2 and 8: Blank.

TR-66   G.O.P. w. Vincent Bryan. m. Gertrude Hoffman. Published by Vincent Bryan Music Company, No. 6 West 28th Street, New York, NY. 1905. R/w/b drawing of an elephant. R/w photo of [V-1: Jeff De Angelis] [V-2: Nat Wills]. 6pp. Page 2: "Dedicated to the Grand Old Party." Page 5: Extra verses. Page 6: Advertising for other music.

TR-67   Rough Riders (Military March). m. H. Engelmann, Op. 328. Published by Theodore Presser, No. 1708 Chestnut Street, Philadelphia, PA. 1898. R/w/b drawing of U.S. flags, geometric designs. 8pp. Pages 2, 4 and 6: Part for Second Piano. Pages 3, 5 and 7: Part for First Piano. Page 8: Advertising for other Presser-Engelmann songs.

TR-68   Rough Riders March (And Two-Step). m. H.A. Fleschler. Published by Star Music Company, Eldred, PA. [1912?]. Bl/w non-pictorial geometric designs. 4pp. Page 4: Advertising for other Star Music Company published music.

TR-69   The Rough Riders (An Equestrian Scene). m. Charles M. Connolly. Published by Witmark and Sons, New York, NY. 1898. O/w/pl drawing of mounted Rough Rider with rope. 12pp. Page 12: Advertising for other Witmark and Sons published music.

TR-70 Teddy's Terrors (March Two-Step). m. Warner Crosby. Published by Hamilton S. Gordon, No. 139 Fifth Avenue, Between 20th and 21st Streets, New York, NY. 1898. B/w drawing of the Rough Riders. "Dedicated to Lieutenant-Colonel Roosevelt." 6pp. Page 6: Blank.

TR-71 Teddy's Dawg. m. Air: *Casey Jones*. Published by the Princeton-Gibbs Advertising Company as a postcard, The Wallace Press, Chicago, IL. 1912. Obv: Drawing of Bulldog, hat in a fight ring with initials —"T.R." "Republican National Convention, Coliseum, Chicago, June, 1912."

TR-72 Rough And Ready (A Yankee March and Two-Step). m. George Lewis. Published by Lewis Music Company, Cleveland, OH. 1907. Bk/gr/w/y/bl drawing of Theodore Roosevelt on horseback with typewriter, telephone, boxing gloves, rifle, &c. 6pp. Page 6: Advertising for other music.

TR-73 Columbia Rules The Waves. w.m. Lala Booke (Author of *While the Wedding Ball Goes On, Just Put The Piano In The Grave With Me*). Published by N. Nelson, Chicago, IL. Copyright 1904 by Lala Booke. Bk/w/pl/gd drawing of Miss Columbia, naval ships, geometric designs. B/w photos of Theodore Roosevelt, Adms. Evans and Dewey, Commodore Schley, two other officers. 8pp. Pages 2, 7 and 8: Blank.

TR-74 The True American (Roosevelt Rag Song). w.m. Edwin E. Downe. Published for the Author by Ted Snyder Company, No. 112 West 38th Street, New York, NY. 1910. R/w/gn drawing of roses, geometric designs. Gn/w photo of Edwin E. Downe. 6pp. Pages 2 and 6: Advertising.

TR-75 For Victory Of Our Country's Flag (Song and Chorus). w.m. Andrew J. Boex. Published by Ilsen & Company, Nos. 25-27 West 6th Street, Cincinnati, OH. 1899. R/w/b U.S. flag. B/w photos of Theodore Roosevelt, Admiral Dewey, Commodore Schley, General Shafter, Eghert, General Miles, Lt. Merritt, Hobson, General Wheeler, General Lee, and General Funston. "Dedicated to the Army and Navy of the United States." 6pp. Page 2: Blank. Page 6: Advertising.

TR-76 The Golden West (A Prediction of Empire). w. William Mullevy. m. Emile E. Mori. Published by Mullevy, No. 1722 Gorooran Street, NW., Washington, DC. 1907. Gd/w cover. B/w photo of U.S. naval ships. "On the landing of the first settlers in Virginia, April 26, 1607." [Handwritten note on cover: "Anniversary April 26th, at Jamestown, 'Mayflower' with President Roosevelt on board at Naval review."]. 6pp. Page 6: Blank.

TR-77 We'll Stand By Our President. w.m. Lee Stuyvesant. Published by Leo Feist, No. 36 West 28th Street, New York, NY. 1912. Bl/w floral and geometric designs. "A Song of the Moment, Respectfully Dedicated to President Theodore Roosevelt." "An American Song for All America." 6pp. Page 2: Blank. Page 6: Advertising for another song.

TR-78 Bull Moose (March). m. Erwin R. Schmidt. Published by The Progressive Music Publishers, Omaha Building, Chicago, IL. 1912. Br/w drawing of moose head. "First and Original March Dedicated to The National Progressive Convention, Chicago, Aug. 5, 1912." 6pp. Page 6: Blank.

TR-79 The Charge Of The Rough Riders (Grand Galop Militaire). m. Eduard Holst (Author of *A Dream of the Battle, Battle of Manila, &c, &c*). Published by Howley, Haviland & Company, Nos. 1260-1266 Broadway, New York, NY. 1898. Br/w/y drawing of charging Rough Riders. Br/w photo by Rockwood of "Col. Theodore Roosevelt" on horseback. List of other arrangements available. 8pp. Pages 2 and 8: Advertising for other Howley, Haviland & Company published music.

TR-80 Raise The Roosevelt

(TR) THEODORE ROOSEVELT

Banner. w. F.B.T. m. "Tune: *Marching Through Georgia*." [1912]. [5" × 7 3/8"]. Non-pictorial broadside. 2pp. Page 2: Blank.

TR-81 Everybody's Teddy (March and Two Step). m. C.H. Prescott. Published by The People's Recreation-Music Company, No. 21 Wellington Avenue, Winter Hill Station, Boston, MA. 1910. R/w/b flags, eagle, shield, sun. B/w photo "Copyright by *Judge* Company, 1901 [and] Courtesy *Leslie's Weekly*" of Theodore Roosevelt on horseback. 6pp. Page 2: Poem by H.C. Williams at top. Page 6: Advertising for other music.

TR-82 Alice Blue Waltzes. m. Abbie A. Ford. Published by National Music Company, No. 339 South Wabash Avenue, Chicago, IL. 1906. Bl/w/gd litho of wedding bells, ribbon. Bl/w photo of The White House. 4pp. Page 4: Advertising for other music.

TR-83 A Daughter Of Uncle Sam. w. John J. Nilan (Composers of *Why Can't A Girl Be A Soldier?*). m. Roger Halle. Published by R. L. Halle, Publisher, No. 202 East 87th Street, New York, NY. 1906. Ma/pk/w Barbelle drawing of Alice Roosevelt, cherubs, roses. Br/w photo of Rose Carlin. "Sung with great success by Rose Carlin, The American Girl." "Respectfully Dedicated to Mrs. Nicholas Longworth." "Jos. W. Stern & Co., Sole Selling Agents." 6pp. Pages 2 and 6: Advertising for other Roger Halle music.

TR-84 Nick And Alice. w.m. Berton J. Maddux. a. J.F. Frazer. Published by Berton J. Maddux, Springdale, OH. 1906. R/w/b drawing of Uncle Sam, eagle, shield with ribbon inscribed "Dedicated to Miss Alice Roosevelt." B/w photos of Nicholas Longworth, Alice Roosevelt, The Capitol. "Photo of Alice complements of *Cinti. Enquirer*." "Photo of Nick courtesy *Cincinnati Post*." 6pp. Pages 2 and 6: Advertising.

TR-85 Alice Roosevelt Waltzes. m. Warner Crosby and Fordyce Hunter. Published by Sol Bloom, New Zealand Building, 37th & Broadway, New York, NY. 1902. B/w photo of Alice Roosevelt. R/w/gn/gd art neuveau design by John Frew. 8pp. Pages 2 and 8: Advertising for other Sol Bloom published music. Page 3: "Dedicated to Miss Alice Roosevelt."

TR-86 Hail To The Nation (March and Two Step). m. Joseph Lacalle (Composer of *Peace Forever March, Hurrah Boys March, &c*). Published by Joseph W. Stern and Company, No. 34 East 21st Street, New York, NY. 1902. R/w/b non-pictorial geometric designs. "Respectfully Dedicated to Miss Alice Roosevelt — Jos. Lacalle [facsimile signature]." 6pp. Page 6: Advertising for other Joseph W. Stern and Company published music.

TR-87 The American Girl (March Two-Step). m. Harold L. Frankensteen. Published by H.A. Sage, Publisher, No. 117 West Fort Street, Detroit, MI. 1905. R/w/b litho of two soldiers with bugles, flags, geometric designs. Bl/w photo of "Miss Alice Roosevelt." "Prize Composition." "Respectfully Dedicated to the First Young Lady of the U.S.A., Miss Alice Roosevelt." 6pp. Page 6: Advertising for other H.A. Sage music.

TR-88 Alice Roosevelt March. m. Walton and Cripe. Published by Victor Kremer Company, Publishers, Chicago, IL. 1902. Gn/w/pl drawing of Alice Roosevelt, ivy. 6pp. Page 2: Blank. Page 3: "Respectfully Dedicated to Mr. Chas. E. Stahl." Page 6: Advertising for other Victor Kremer Company published music.

TR-89 Alice, Where Art Thou Going (March Song). w. Will A. Heelan. m. Albert Gumble (Composer of *Jessamine*). Published by Jerome H. Remick and Company, New York, NY. 1906. O/w/y/r/bl/gn DeTakacs drawing of girl [Alice]. 6pp. [Lyrics mention Alice Roosevelt]. Page 6: Advertising for other Jerome H. Remick and Company published music.

TR-90 The Alice Roosevelt Wedding March. m. Max Bachmann. Published by Max Bachmann, Washington, DC. 1906. B/w drawing of Alice Roosevelt in wedding gown. 6pp. Page 6: Blank.

TR-91 We Stand At Armageddon (The Roosevelt Battle Hymn). w.m. E.H. Purcell. Published by Aubrey Stauffer Company, Music Publishers, Grand Opera House, Chicago, IL. Copyright 1912 by The Schubert Company. Be/br drawing of Theodore Roosevelt, facsimile signature. "We stand for Home & Motherland! And for Our Teddy Too! We've chosen him to lead us for we know he's tried & true. We're fighting for the People's Rights, lead by Brave Theodore. And just Because we know he's true, we want him to lead once more." 6pp. Page 6: Advertising for other Schubert music.

TR-92 Teddy's Coming Back Again (Our Next President). w.m. Capt. A.T. Hendricks. [1912?]. Drawing of Theodore Roosevelt on horseback with banners, Uncle Sam, bucking horse, the White House, title of drawing — "In the stretch, Teddy Wins." "He smiles and fights on, not an experiment but the greatest living American."

TR-93 Roosevelt's Rough Riders. w.m. Sylvester Prout. Published by Mahoney Bros., Washington, DC. 1898. B/w drawing of Rough Rider on horseback. "Dedicated to the Next Governor of New York." "Trade supplied by Henry White, 929 East "F" Street, Washington, DC." 6pp. Pages 2 and 6: Blank.

TR-94 Our Next President (Roosevelt) (March and Two Step). m. Seneca J. Warren. a. Prof. F. Mueller. Published by C.S. Lipschuetz, New York, NY. Copyright 1904 by Seneca J. Warren. B/w Pach Bros. photo of Theodore Roosevelt. Bl/bk/w cover with eagles, geometric designs. "Piano $.50, Mandolin and Guitar $.40, Orchestration $1.00." 6pp. Page 6: Blank.

TR-95 Program Of The Inaugural Grand Concerts. Published by The Inaugural Committee, Pension Building, Washington, DC. 1905. [6" × 9 1/4"]. B/w photo of Theodore Roosevelt and Charles Fairbanks. B/w drawing of shield, eagle, geometric designs. 16pp. Program for the Inaugural ceremonies. Includes two songs written "For the occasion." Page 10: **Union & Liberty** by H. Parker. Page 11: **One Flag And One Country** by F. Fanciulli.

TR-96 The Charge Of The Rough Riders (March Two-Step). m. Anna Russell Simmons. Published by Balmer & Weber Music House Company, St. Louis, MO. 1898. R/w/b non-pictorial stripes. 6pp. Pages 2 and 6: Blank.

TR-97 Our Teddy's Home Coming March. m. R.N. Lombard. Published by The New York and Chicago Music Publishing Company, No. 1529 Broadway, New York, NY. 1912. R/w/bl/br drawing of Theodore Roosevelt and Uncle Sam shaking hands while standing on globe showing Africa and North America, eagle, animals, ships, flags. 6pp. Page 6: Advertising for other music including *Teddy* by W.D. Nesbit.

TR-98 Teddy's For The People. w.m. Benjamin F. Nysewander. Published by National Music Company, No. 425 South Wabash Avenue, Chicago, IL. Copyright 1912 by Benjamin F. Nysewander. B/w photo of Theodore Roosevelt. 6pp. Page 2: "Respectfully Dedicated to Hon. Theodore Roosevelt." Page 6: Advertising.

TR-99 Old Glory, The Blue And The Grey. w.m. Con. T. Murphy. Published by Meyer and Brother, No. 108 Washington Street, Chicago, IL. 1898. Drawing of a flag, flower. "Originally Sung by Charles A. Gardiner." "As Sung by Haverly's Minstrels." "Dedicated to Colonel Theodore Roosevelt." 4pp.

TR-100 The Rough Riders (March). m. Hugo Riesenfeld. Published by Sam Fox Publishing Company,

Cleveland, OH. 1927. O/bl/bk/br/w drawing by Ray Parmelee of Theodore Roosevelt, Rough Riders charging on horseback. "As Played at the Presentation of the Paramount picture *The Rough Riders*." 6pp. Page 6: Advertising for other Sam Fox published music.

TR-101 Roosevelt, We're Glad To Welcome You. w.m. C.F. Potter. Published by F.B. Haviland Publishing Company, New Zealand Building, Broadway and 37th Street, New York, NY. Copyright 1910 by C.F. Potter. Bl/w photos of Theodore Roosevelt and the "Courtney Sisters." Br/w/bl floral and geometric designs. 6pp. Pages 2 and 6: Advertising.

TR-102 Kaiser Bill (Marching Song). w. Captain L.Y. Lenhart. m. Inez Clark-Hall. Published by Bramwell and Ragen, St. Paul, MN. Copyright 1917 by Captain L.Y. Lenhart and Inez Clark-Hall. Non-pictorial geometric designs. "Dedicated to Colonel Theodore Roosevelt." 4pp. Page 4: Blank.

TR-103 Roosevelt's Day At The St. Louis Fair. w.m. Miss Gertie Gray. Published by A.W. Perry & Sons' Music Company, Sedalia, MO. [1904]. Gn/w non-pictorial geometric designs. 6pp. Pages 2 and 6: Blank.

TR-104 The Unpardonable Sin. m. Arthur J. Lamb. m. Frederick V. Bowers. Published by Frederick V. Bowers, Inc., New York, NY. 1919. O/w/pl photo of "Blanche Sweet," daisies. "This Song is founded on the serial story in the *Red Book Magazine*. The Picture of which stars Blanche Sweet at the Broadway Theatre, N.Y.C." 4pp. Page 2: "Respectfully Dedicated to Blanche Sweet." Page 4: "The most soul stirring sensational song hit of the day. You've read the book — You've seen the Picture — Now get the song!" Pl/w photos of "Maj. Rupert Hughes, He Wrote It!; Blanche Sweet, She Starred in it!; Harry Garson, He Produced it!; Marshall Neelan, He Directed it!; Fredk. V. Bowers, He Composed the Song." Pl/w photo of Theodore Roosevelt — "He Liked It."

TR-105 Treaty Of Portsmouth (March and Two Step). m. Simon Sternburg. Published by Amphion Publishing Company, Boston, MA. Copyright 1905 by Simon Sternburg. Bl/o/w non-pictorial design. "Dedicated to President Roosevelt." 6pp. Pages 2 and 6: Blank.

TR-106 Friends. w. Howard Johnson and George W. Meyer. m. Joseph H. Santly. Published by Leo Feist, Inc., New York, NY. 1919. B/w tinted photo of Julian Eltinge. "Successfully introduced by Julian Eltinge." B/w photo of unknown man. Gy/o/w/bk cover of hearts, leaves. 4pp. [Lyrics about death of Theodore Roosevelt]. Page 4: Advertising.

TR-107 Friends. w. Howard Johnson and George W. Meyer. m. Joseph H. Santly. Published by Leo Feist, Inc., New York, NY. 1919. Gy/r/w/bk cover of hearts, leaves. "You can't go wrong with any Fiest song." 4pp. [Lyrics about death of Theodore Roosevelt]. Page 4: Advertising.

TR-108 Col. Roosevelt's March. m. O.R. Farrar. Published by Harry Coleman, Philadelphia, PA. 1898. Bk/be litho by Beck of Theodore Roosevelt on horseback, Rough Riders. "For Piano Forte." "To Roosevelt's Rough Riders." "Also Published for Band and Orchestra." 6pp. Pages 2 and 6: Advertising for other music.

TR-109 My Hat Is In The Ring. w. I.M. Frank. m. U.R. Wright. Published by Kelmayne Publishing Company, St. Louis, MO. 1912. Y/bk drawing of large hat in fight ring inscribed "T.R." 6pp. Pages 2 and 6: Advertising for other music.

TR-110 The Square Deal (March Two Step and Refrain). w.m. H. Maybaum. Published by John Maybaum Music Company, P.O. Box 3452, Station "O," Philadelphia, PA. Copyright 1906 by H. Maybaum. Gn/bk photo of

Theodore Roosevelt. Gn/r/w drawing of U.S. flag, ribbon. "Dedicated to Theodore Roosevelt, President of the United States on the occasion of the marriage of his daughter Alice." 6pp. Pages 2 and 6: Blank.

TR-111 We Want Teddy Four Years More! (Republican Marching Song). w. Frank Abbott. m. Gus Edwards. Published as a "Supplement to the *New York World*, Aug. 28, 1904." Copyright 1904 by M. Witmark and Sons. Br/be Pach Bros. photo of "Theodore Roosevelt." Br/gn/be drawing of eagle, stars. Music begins page one. "Written especially for the *New York World*." 4pp.

TR-111 We Want Teddy Four Years More! (Republican Marching Song). w. Frank Abbott. m. Gus Edwards. Published as a "Supplement to the *New York World*, Aug. 28, 1904." Copyright 1904 by M. Witmark and Sons. Br/be Pach Bros. photo of "Theodore Roosevelt." Br/gn/be drawing of eagle, stars. Music begins page one. "Written especially for the *New York World*." 4pp.

TR-112 Famous Roosevelt (March). m. W.S. Greene. Published by The George Jaberg Music Company, Cincinnati, OH. 1898. B/w photo by Pach Bros. of Theodore Roosevelt. Bl/w geometric designs. "For Piano." 6pp. Page 6: Advertising for other George Jaberg Music Company music.

TR-113 Roosevelt's Grand March. m. D.W. Crist. Published by D.W. Crist, Moultrie, OH. 1905. Bl/w square frame photo of Theodore Roosevelt. R/w/b geometric design border. "For the Piano or Cabinet Organ." 6pp. Page 6: Advertising.

TR-114 Roosevelt's Grand March. m. D.W. Crist. Published by D.W. Crist, Moultrie, OH. 1905. Bl/w oval frame photo of Theodore Roosevelt. R/w/b geometric design border. "For the Piano or Cabinet Organ." 6pp. Page 6: Advertising.

TR-115 Here's To The Noble Rough Riders (Song and Chorus). w. Lila G. Cunningham. m. Mamie A. Reynolds. Published by Thomas Groggan and Brother, Galveston, TX. 1898. B/w photo of Theodore Roosevelt with "Commanding Officers of Roosevelt's Rough Riders." Bl/w geometric designs. 6pp. Page 2: Blank. Page 6: Advertising for other music.

TR-116 Roosevelt March Song (Two-Step). w. Matie Lois Louden. m. Ward Baker. Published by The Donald Publishing Company, New York, NY. 1904. B/w drawing by F.W. Ramsdell of Theodore Roosevelt in Rough Rider uniform, geometric designs. 8pp. Pages 2 and 7: Blank. Page 8: Photo of man [Baker?] with violin.

TR-117 Progressive Battle Hymns [Song Book]. w.c. C.H. Congdon. Published by C.H. Congdon. 1912. Bk/w photos of Theodore Roosevelt and Hiram Johnson. R/w/bk bandanna — "We stand at Armageddon and do battle for the Lord." "For there is neither East now West, Border nor Breed nor Birth, When two strong men stand face to face, Though they come from the ends of the Earth — Kipling." 68pp. Page 2: "Progressive creed." Page 3: "In the spirit of the Chicago Convention." "Authorized as the Official Song Book of the Progressive Party." Page 86: R/w/bk bandanna with moose head. Quotes. [M-403].

TR-118 On The Firing Line (March Two-Step). m. Louis L. Comstock. Published by The Vandersloot Music Publishing Company, Williamsport, PA. 1906. B/w drawing of Theodore Roosevelt, Rough Riders in battle scene. List of arrangements available. 6pp. Page 6: Advertising.

TR-119 Up San Juan Hill (A Descriptive Piece). m. Paul de Longpre, Op. 2. Published by Paul de Longpre, Hollywood, CA. 1905. B/w photo of Theodore Roosevelt (Colonel of the Rough Riders at San Juan Hill), geometric design border. "Dedicated to the American Boys who fought and died like heroes at the storming of San Juan Hill (Cuba 1898)." "It is madness, said the German Attaché, seeing the fearless Americans starting up the hill." "It is splendid, but they will never reach the top alive, said the French Attach." "For the Piano Forte." 6pp. Page 6: Reprint from *The Los Angeles Express*, 9/14/05.

TR-120 The Roosevelt Cavalry March (Two Step). m. George Barker. Published by George Barker, No. 164A Tremont Street, Boston. MA. 1898. R/w/b cover. Bl/w drawing of Cossacks charging. "Dedicated to the American Cossacks." "For the Piano Forte." List of arrangements available. 4pp. Pages 2 and 3: Music for Banjo. Page 4: Advertising.

TR-121 Our National Songs. c. George M. Vickers. Copyright 1904 by George Vickers, Philadelphia, PA. [4 1/2" × 6"]. Litho of an eagle in a shield inscribed "E Pluribus Unum." "A Message to Young Voters." "Campaign of 1904." 8pp.

TR-122 Muck Rake Song. w.m. Joseph H. Hatch. Published by Evans Music Company, Boston, MA. 1908. B/w litho of Theodore Roosevelt. Bl/w cover. "The term 'Muck Rake' was used by President Theodore Roosevelt in speaking of unfair critics." "Respectfully Dedicated to President Theodore Roosevelt." 6pp. Pages 2 and 6: Blank.

TR-123 Cosmopolitan America (March Two Step). m. Helen May Butler (Directoress Helen May Butler's Ladies' Military Band). Published by The Tolbert R. Ingram Company, Denver, CO. 1904. O/bk/w drawings of soldier, men in ethnic dress, skyline. B/w photo of Helen May Butler. "Dedicated to my father, L.M. Butler." "Official Campaign March of National Republican Party for 1904." 8pp. Page 3: Narrative on this song. Page 8: Advertising.

TR-124 Roosevelt March. m. H. Welcker. Published by Adair Welcker, No. 331 Pine Street, San Francisco, CA.

Copyright 1902 by H. Welker. B/w litho of Theodore Roosevelt, two flags, geometric design border. "On receipt of P.O. or express order for fifty cents, the publisher will send the band arrangement for thirty-two instruments to any address. This piece, which is almost daily being asked for by other bands, has already been played by the band of the U.S. Military Academy, West Point, U.S. Naval Academy, Annapolis, by the Golden Gate Park Band, and by other leading and military bands." 6pp. Pages 2 and 6: Blank.

TR-125 The King Of The Sea. w. Charles C. Clark. m. Tony Clark. Published by Charles C. Clark, Proctor, VT. 1900. B/w photos of Theodore Roosevelt, Admiral George "Dewey," Admiral Robley "Evans," Lieutenant "Hobson," Admiral William T. "Sampson," Commodore "Schley," and General William R. "Shafter." R/w/b drawing of a classical archway, flags. "Great National War Song." 6[?]pp.

TR-126 I'm Glad I'm Home Again. w. Ballard Macdonald. m. Harry Carroll. Published by Joseph W. Stern and Company, Nos. 102-104 West 38th Street, New York, NY. 1910. R/w/bl/br litho of on pedestal inscribed "Theodore Roosevelt," eagle, flags. 8pp. Pages 2 and 7: Blank. Page 8: Advertising for other Joseph W. Stern and Company published music.

TR-127 San Juan Hill (Two Step March). m. Juan B. Fuentes, Op. 48. Published by Juan B. Fuentes, Morella, Mish., Mexico. 1904. R/w/bl/gn/o/y litho of U.S. and Cuban flags, hills. "Respectfully Dedicated to the great hero of San Juan Hill, Col. Theodore Roosevelt, President of the United States of America." "Reproduction, arrangements, etc., even in parts, by journals or any kind of printing matter, extrictly [sic] prohibited." 6pp. Pages 2 and 6: Blank.

TR-128 Hon. Theodore Roosevelt. w. Clara Pugh. m. Herbert J. Wrightson. Published by The H. Kirkus

Dugdale Company, Inc., 14th and You Streets, Washington, DC. Copyright 1912 by Clara Pugh. Gn/w drawing of Theodore Roosevelt, lion. 4pp. Page 4: Advertising.

TR-129 The Charge Of The Roosevelt Rough-Riders (March). m. Charles Coleman. Published by Charles Coleman, No. 515 Fulton Street, Brooklyn, NY. 1898. R/w/b flag background. B/w photo of Charles Coleman. "Inscribed to Mr. W.A. Corey of New York City." 6pp. Page 2: Blank. Page 6: Advertising for other Charles Coleman music.

TR-130 Roosevelt, The Peace Victor! (The President's Song). w.m. Irving J. Morgan. Published by I.J. Morgan, No. 308 North 41st Street, Philadelphia, PA. 1905. B/w photo by Bell Photo Company of Theodore Roosevelt. "Special written permission granted at Washington to Irving J. Morgan for use of this photograph by the Bell photo Co." R/w/b cover. "This song is preeminently the first National song composed upon this subject, being written upon the inspiration of the moment and completed by 9 o'clock on the day of the very first morning 'Peace' was publicly declared, Aug. 30th, 1905." "First Public Rendition at the White House by the Marine Band." "On sale at department stores and music stores, all principal cities, or direct order to I.J. Morgan, No. 308 North 41st Street, Philadelphia, Penna., upon receipt of 25 cents." 6pp. Pages 2 and 6: Blank. Page 3: History of lyrics.

TR-131 The Bull Moose Glide. w. J. Will Callahan. m. Will B. Morrison. Published by Henry J. Wiethe, Publisher, Indianapolis, IN. 1912. Ma/o/w drawing of a woman, moose. Advertising — "The sensitive, sentimental ballad *My Dear Old Hoosier Home*." 6pp. Page 6: Advertising.

TR-132 Roosevelt's The Man. w.m. Emma Pauline Sellers. Published by Emma Pauline Sellers, Box 384, Mapleton, MN. 1904. B/w photo of Theodore Roosevelt. Bk/bl/w columns and geometric designs. 6pp. Pages 2 and 6: Blank.

TR-133 George Washington Dasch March. m. Charles Kalitz. Published by George W. Dasch, No. 920 Market Street, Philadelphia, PA. 1905. Br/w photo of "George W. Dasch." Bl/w drawing of the Capitol dome, geometric designs. "As Played with Great Success at the Inauguration at Washington, March 4, 1905, by Kendal's 1st Reg. Band of Phila. and Beal's Municipal Band of Phila. and many others." 6pp. Page 2: Blank. Page 6: Advertising.

TR-134 Heroes Of Today. w.m. Francis Walsh Reid, M.D. Published for Francis Walsh Reid, M.D., by Ariston Music Publishing Company, No. 205 Huntington Avenue, Boston, MA. 1911. R/w/b litho of Spanish-American War vignettes — "Kettle Hill" and "Manila Bay." "Dedicated to Colonel Theodore Roosevelt, Admiral George Dewey, General Leonard Wood and All the Brave Men — Asleep and Awake, who Fought in Our Wars." 8pp. Page 8: Blank.

TR-135 Teddy Come Back! w. W.D. Nesbit. m. R.N. Lombard. Published by New York & Chicago Music Publishing House, No. 1529 Broadway, New York, NY. 1910. B/w photo by Clinedinst of Theodore Roosevelt. R/w silhouette of Theodore Roosevelt in Africa, U.S. Capitol building. 6pp. Pages 2 and 6: Advertising for other music including *Our Teddy's Home-Coming March* and *Teddy* by R.N. Lombard.

TR-136 President Roosevelt's Grand Triumphal March. m. Raphael Fassett. Published by W.H. Willis and Company, Corner 4th and Elm Streets, Cincinnati, OH. Copyright 1894 and 1904. Bl/w drawing of flowers, wreath. B/w photo of Theodore Roosevelt. 6pp. Pages 2 and 6: Blank.

TR-137 Roosevelt He's The Man. w.m. S.M. Hawk. Copyright 1908 by S.M. Hawk, Kankakee, IL. 1908. Bl/w non-pictorial cover. 6pp. Pages 2 and 6: Blank.

TR-138   The Man Of The Moment (March). m. James Swope. Published by M. Witmark and Sons, New York, NY. 1903. Br/w cover of axes, wreaths. Br/w photo by R.W. Thacher "by permission of Albany Art Union" of Theodore Roosevelt. 6pp. Page 6: Advertising.

TR-139   Viva L'America March. m. R. Leoncavallo. Published by Chas. K. Harris, New York, NY. 1906. Br/w drawing of eagle, shield, floral and geometric designs. Br/w photo of R. Leoncavallo. 8pp. Page 3: "Respectfully Dedicated to President Roosevelt."

TR-140   God Save Our President (A New National Hymn). w. Josephine C. Goodale. m. J.H. Peterman. Published as a postcard. Copyright 1902 by J.H. Peterman. Obv: B/w photo of "President Theodore Roosevelt." B/w drawing of crossed flags, eagle. "The melody of this hymn can be used as new music to *My Country 'Tis of Thee.*" "Sung with great success by the N.Y. State Teacher's Association in Convention at Saratoga, July, 23d, 1901, under personal direction of the Composer." "Published for band or orchestra." Rev: Mailing information.

TR-141   The Echo Republican Campaign Songster. e.c. Dr. J.B. Herbert. Published by The Echo Music Company, No. 358 Dearborn Street, Chicago, IL. 1904. [6 3/4" × 9 3/4"]. Lithos of "Theodore Roosevelt" and "Charles W. Fairbanks," eagle, flags. "Republican Nominees." "The Official Songster for 1904." "For Men's Voices." 34pp. [M-389].

TR-142   The Big Stick Blues March (March Song). w.m. W.C. Handy and Charles L. Cooke. Published by Handy Brothers Music Company, Inc., "Publishers Genuine American Music," No. 1650 Broadway, New York, NY. 1951. R/w/b flag and star design. "When you meet your neighbor in the morning speak softly, carry a big stick, this will go far — Theodore Roosevelt." 8pp. Page 2: "Quoting from the 'Theodore Roosevelt Cyclopedia' edited by Albert Busnell Hart, Professor Emeritus, Harvard University, and Herbert Ronald Ferleger, Roosevelt Memorial Association." "Speak softly and carry a big stick — you will go far. If a man continually blusters, if he lacks civility, a big stick will not save him from trouble; and neither will speaking softly avail, if back of the softness there does not lie strength, power. In private life there are a few things more obnoxious than the man who is always loudly boasting; and if the boaster is not prepared to back up his words, his position becomes absolutely contemptible. So it is with the nation. It is both foolish and undignified to indulge in undue self-glorification, and, above all, in loose-tounged [sic] denunciation of other peoples." Page 10: Advertising for the song *Lincoln's Gettysburg Address.*

TR-143   Bull Moose March. m. Brookes C. Peters. Published by Brookes C. Peters, New York, NY. Distributed by T.B. Harms Company, Distributors, New York, NY. 1912. Br/w drawing of moose, geometric designs. "Dedicated to the Progressive Party." 6pp. Pages 2 and 6: Blank.

TR-144   'Twas A Tribute We Paid To Our Country (The Heights of San Juan). w.m. W. Hinton. Published by The S. Brainard's Sons Company, No. 20 East 17th Street, New York, NY. 1899. Br/w photo of woods and stream — "There's a path that winds down by the river to a tryst in the cool, mossy dell." "Dedicated to Col. Theodore Roosevelt and the Heroes of San Juan." Bl/w printing. 6pp. Page 2: Blank. Page 6: Advertising for other S. Brainard's Sons music.

TR-145   Teddy. w. William J. McKenna. m. Ted Snyder. Published by Waterson, Berlin & Snyder Company, Strand Theatre Building, Corner

THEODORE ROOSEVELT (**TR**)

Broadway at 47th Street, New York, NY. 1919. Bk/be/w Barbelle drawing of Theodore Roosevelt. "A Song Version of the Famous Motion Picture of the same name." "Dedicated to the Memory of the Fighting Father of the Fighting Roosevelts." 4pp. Page 4: Advertising.

TR-146 Teddy Is The Man (Song and March). w.m. Charles E. Bernhardt. Published by Charles E. Bernhardt, Indianapolis, IN. 1904. Bl/w photos of Theodore Roosevelt and Charles W. Fairbanks. R/w/b litho of crossed flags. "For Right and Liberty." 6pp. Page 2: "Campaign Song."

TR-147 Two Campaign Songs. Published by The Fountain Music Company, No. 108 East 18th Street, New York City as a "Supplement to *The Daily Record*, Saturday, October 1st, 1904." Bl/w photo of Theodore Roosevelt. R/w/b drawing of two U.S. flags. "Dedicated to the Makers of Presidents — The Voters of the United States." Inside songs: **Roosevelt The Cry**. w.m. Julian Jordan. Also: **Birds Of A Feather**. w.m. Julian Jordan. 4pp.

TR-148 Campaign Songs [Song Pamphlet]. 1912. [5 15/16" × 9"]. Non-pictorial. "Prepared for the Use of the Jane Addams Chorus, First organized and named in Los Angeles, August 26, 1912." "Organize a Rally Committee — Organize a Music Committee." 4pp.

TR-149 We Want Teddy. w. Carla Altstarter and Jennie Rae. m. Homer A. Rodeheaver. Published by The Rodeheaver Company, Music Publishers, No. 14 West Washington Street, Chicago, IL. 1912. [16 1/2" × 18"]. R/w/bk cloth bandanna with a drawing of Theodore Roosevelt — "Our Teddy," and a piece of facsimile sheet music.

TR-150 Battle Hymn Of The National Progressive Party. w. Dr. L.J. McAdam. m. "Tune: *Battle Hymn of the Republic*." [1912]. [5 1/2" × 8 3/4"]. Non-pictorial black frame. "Fully protected for the benefit of the campaign." 4pp.

TR-151 Roosevelt For Mine. w. D.L. Sidler. m. A.W. Ulrich (Writers of *Let The Song Birds Live, The Old Hickory Tree*). Published by D.L. Sidler, Parkville, MI. [1904?]. R/w drawing of flowers. 4pp. Page 4: Blank.

TR-152 Friend Of The World.

TR-146   TR-147

(TR) THEODORE ROOSEVELT

w. Harriet Gaylord. m. Henry Hadley. Published by T.B. Harms and Francis, Day and Hunter, New York, NY. 1919. Br/w photo by Le Gendre of Theodore Roosevelt and baby. "Dedicated to the Memory of Theodore Roosevelt." 8pp. Pages 2 and 8: Blank. Page 3: Poem — "Friend of the World, January Eight, Nineteen Nineteen."

TR-153 Theo. Roosevelt. w.m. David Gardner. Published by David Gardner, No. 1780 1/2 Downey Avenue, East Los Angeles, CA. 1907. Bl/w drawing of floral and geometric designs. 4pp. Page 4: Blank.

TR-154 Charge Of The Rough Riders March Two-Step. m. Louis Morgan. Published by Morgan Music Company, Arkansas City, KS. 1898. Litho of Theodore Roosevelt and charging Rough Riders, geometric designs. "Dedicated to Col. Torrey." List of arrangements available.

TR-155 It's Good Enough For Me. w. Paul Odell. m. Harry Hoyt. Published by Shapiro Music Publishers, corner Broadway and 39th Street, New York, NY. 1910. Photo of Theodore Roosevelt.

TR-156 The Rough Rider (Two Step). m. R.M. Tyrell. Published by Edw. A. Meyer and Company, No. 3439 Marshall Street, Philadelphia, PA. 1899. Non-pictorial geometric designs. "Selected Compositions and Arrangements for the Guitar by Popular Authors." List of other titles in series. "Guitar Solos" and "Guitar Duetts."

TR-157 Park's Republican Campaign Songs (For Male Voices) [Song Book]. Published by J.A. Parks Company, York, NE. 1904. [6 15/16" × 9 3/4"]. Br/br non-pictorial geometric design border. 40pp. [M-390].

TR-158 As Teddy Went Over The Top. w.m. Alfred N. Heroux. 1919. Pl/w litho of roses. 6pp. Page 6: Blank.

TR-159 Republican Songs Campaign Of 1904 [Song Pamphlet]. m. "Adapted to Familiar Airs." 1904. [5 3/8" × 8 3/8"]. Non-pictorial. 8pp. Page 8: At bottom of music — B/w litho of an eagle, ballot box, circle with an "X" inside — "Vote Under the Eagle." [M-392].

TR-160 Sagamore March. w. Adelaide Maibunn-Goldman. m. Edwin Franko Goldman. Published by Carl Fischer, Cooper Square, New York, NY. 1920. Bl/w photo of Edwin Franko Goldman, geometric design border. "Edwin F. Goldman Successes for Piano Solo (Also published for Orchestra and Band)." List of other titles in series. 6pp. Page 2: "Dedicated to the Memory of Theodore Roosevelt." Page 6: Advertising for other Carl Fischer published music.

TR-161 Campaign Songs [Song Sheet]. w. Edwin A. Hartshorn. m. Popular tunes. Printed by McAuliffe & Booth, Printers, New York, NY. 1904. [5 3/16" × 8 1/2"]. Non-pictorial. "Seventh Edition." "1904-1904." 8pp. [M-388].

TR-162 Go And Vote For Teddy Roosevelt and **American Hymn**. w. Hugh Malcolm McCormick. m. Sara Weber-McCormick. Published by McCormick Music Company, Chicago, IL. Copyright 1907 and 1910. B/w litho of eagle, flags. "Price ten cents." 4pp. Page 4: Blank.

TR-163 Rough Riders March Two-Step. m. J.W. Buford (Author of *Moonlight Night Waltzes*). Published by Philip Werlein, Ltd., Nos. 614-616 Canal Street, New Orleans, LA. 1898. Litho of the sun, flag. "Dedicated to Col. Theo. Roosevelt."

TR-164 Rough Riders. w. Hugh Morton. m. Gustave Kerker. Published by T.B. Harms & Company, No. 18 East 22nd Street, New York, NY. 1898. R/w/b non-pictorial designs. "Casino The Extravagant Extravaganza, George W. Lederer and George B. McLellan, Managing Directors." "*Yankee Doodle Dandy*, Book by Hugh Morton; Music by Gustave Kerker; Staged by Geo. W. Lederer." List of other music in the production. 10pp.

Pages 2 and 9: Blank. Page 10: Advertising.

TR-165 Teddy Roosevelt. w.m. Howard Smith. a. Mae Stott. Published by Howard Smith and Son, No. 9019 Commercial Avenue, Chicago, IL. 1899. Photos of Theodore Roosevelt, Howard Smith, graves of soldiers. Drawing of Rough Riders. "His heart was right, his honor bright, as the blade beside his belt, and the bravest gathered round the form of Teddy Roosevelt." "When the Spaniards heard that battle cry and saw old glory fly, they knew that freedom's sons had come to free that land or die." "With one swift blow their work was done and brave those riders are, but left some gallant hearts to sleep, beneath the Southern sun." 6pp[?].

TR-166 When Teddy Comes Marching Home. w.m. Joe Hayden. Published by Will Rossiter, No. 56 5th Avenue, Chicago, IL. 1898. Drawing of Theodore Roosevelt and Rough Riders, cheering crowd, border of stars. "Dedicated to John Guerin (My old partner), Chief of Police, Great Falls, Mont."

TR-167 The Rough Riders March Militaire. m. Philip Browne. Published by E.F. Droop and Sons, No. 925 Pennsylvania Avenue, Washington, DC. 1898. Photos of "Col. Theodore Roosevelt" and "Gen'l. Leonard Wood." Drawing of floral and geometric designs. "Dedicated to the Rough Riders."

TR-168 Charge Of The Rough Riders (March and Two Step). m. James W. Casey (Composer of *No Wedding Bells For Her, Just One Word Of Love, An Old Man's Darling, &c, &c*). Published by Evans Music Company, Boston, MA. 1898. B/w photos of Theodore Roosevelt and the Rough Riders, and James W. Casey. R/w/b drawing of flags, geometric designs. "Played with great success by Sousa's Concert Band." "Dedicated to Col. Theodore Roosevelt." 8pp.

TR-169 Rough Riders March Two Step. m. Rudolph Aronson (Composer of *Sweet and Simple Waltz*). Published by Luckhardt and Belder, No. 10 East 17th Street, New York, NY. 1898. Photo of Theodore Roosevelt. Drawing of horseman charging—"Teddy's Rough Riders," wreath. "Dedicated to Col. Theodore Roosevelt."

TR-170 Rough Riders Two-Step March. m. Jules A. Doucet. Published by I.E. Doucet, Denver, CO. 1898. Drawing of Theodore Roosevelt on horseback, camp scene, geometric designs. "Dedicated to Colonel Roosevelt and His Rough Riders."

TR-171 Col. Roosevelt's Rough Riders (Marche Caracteristique). m. L.P. Laurendeau. Published by Carl Fischer, Nos. 6 and 8 Fourth Avenue, New York, NY. 1898. B/w photo of Theodore Roosevelt. Bl/w drawing of the U.S. flag, flowers, swords. "C. Fischer's Edition."

TR-172 Our Star Spangled Banner. w. Frances Scott Key. m. Air: *Anacreon In Hea*ven. a. Madam Blake. Published by the American Music Company, No. 505 Fifth Avenue, New York, NY. Copyright 1909 by John Henry Blake. B/w photo by Underwood & Un-

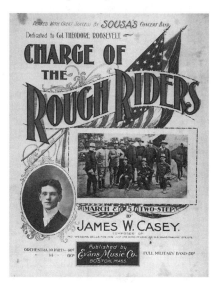

TR-168

derwood of battleships — "American Battleship Fleet leaving Suez, Egypt, on the Round the World Voyage, 1918, 'Connecticut' leading." "Souvenir Edition, Cruise Around the World of American Atlantic Battleship Fleet." Poem. 20pp. Page 2: Photo of Theodore Roosevelt. Page 3: Title page. Pages 16-17: "History of the Origin of the American National Song." Page 19: Photo of a battleship. Page 20: Photo of 1905 the Inaugural parade."

TR-173 Four More Years Of Teddy (A Roosevelt Re-Election Song). w.m. Alice Yarnell. Published by Alice Yarnell, Spokane, WA. 1908. Drawing by Morris of Theodore Roosevelt being tied to the "President's Chair" by Uncle Sam — "By gosh! Theodore, I've got something to say about whether you take this third term or not." "Dedicated to John Lauterback, Editor, *Roosevelt Prevailer*, Kendrick, Idaho."

TR-174 Rough Riders March. m. J.A. Verlander (Author of *Old Glory Two Step*). Published by J.A. Verlander, No. 943 Louisiana Avenue, New Orleans, LA. 1898. Br/w non-pictorial geometric designs. "Dedicated to the Rough Riders." "Fifth Edition." 6pp. Page 2 and 6: Blank.

TR-175 The March Of The Moose. w.m. Vivian Leigh. Published by H.L. Conant, Taunton, MA. 1912. B/w drawing of a moose, geometric designs. "For All Performing Rights, Reproduction, &c., address H.L. Conant, Taunton, Mass." 6pp. Page 6: Blank. [Bull Moose Party].

TR-176 The Rough Riders Two-Step. m. Maie Mead. Published by A.W. Perry & Son, Sedalia, MO. 1899. Litho of a small angel, geometric design border. Page 3: "Dedicated to Governor Roosevelt."

TR-177 March (Rough Riders). m. T.A. Duggan, M.D. Published by T.A. Duggan, New Orleans, LA. 1898. Non-pictorial geometric designs. "Respectfully Dedicated to Col. Theodore Roosevelt." 6pp. Page 6: Advertising.

TR-178 Rough Rider's War-Rally. w.m. N.K. Griggs. Published by The Chicago Music Company, Chicago, IL. Copyright 1898 by N.K. Griggs. Litho of U.S. flag, geometric designs. "Written at the Request of Col. Jay L. Torrey and Dedicated to the Rough Riders of the West."

TR-179 Roosevelt's Rough Riders (Two Step). m. Edward J. Gilbert. Published by The Chicago Music Company, Chicago, IL. 1898. Drawing of Theodore Roosevelt and Rough Riders in mounted charge. "Respectfully Dedicated to Col. Theo. Roosevelt." List of arrangements.

TR-180 Hip-Hip-Hurrah For Teddy Roosevelt. w.m. Dave Richardson. Published by Richardson Music Publishing Company, No. 240 Howard Avenue, Brooklyn, NY. [ca. 1904]. Photo of Theodore Roosevelt. Litho of flowering vine, geometric designs.

TR-181(A) He Rambled Away From His Native Home. w. Joseph McLean. m. E.S.S. Huntington. Published by Knickerbocker Harmony Studios, No. 1545 Broadway, New York, NY. Copyright 1919 by Joseph McLean, Tucson, AZ. Drawing of a woman, Roman column, Pan with flute. "This copy to be used solely for professional demonstrating and exploiting purposes and is not to be exhibited for sale." "To the musical and singing members of the theatrical profession." 4pp. Page 4: Advertising.

(B) Roosevelt Hymn. w. Julius Papa. m. E.S.S. Huntington. Copyright 1921 by Julius Papa.

TR-182 Our President. w.m. Ella M. Boston. Published by Success Music Company, No. 356 Dearborn Street, Chicago, IL. Copyright 1906 by Ella M. Boston. Photo of Theodore Roosevelt, geometric design border. "Sold by all music dealers." 6pp. Page 6: Blank.

TR-183 Young Joshua (Solo and

Chorus). w.m. Dr. J.B. Herbert. Published by Fillmore Brothers, No. 119 West 6th Street, Cincinnati, OH. 1902. Pl/w photo of Theodore Roosevelt. R/w/ma geometric designs. "Solo, Solo and Chorus for Mixed Voices Male Quartet." 6pp. Page 6: Advertising.

TR-184 Roosevelt. w. C.H. Congdon. Published in the September 7, 1912, edition of *The Los Angeles Tribune* newspaper. B/w photo of Theodore Roosevelt. B/w drawing of two moose, stars and stripes background. "As sung by the Jane Addams Chorus." Four page fold-out newspaper size. Page 4: Clip-out coupon: "How to help the Progressive Party."

TR-185 When Teddy Comes Marching Home With His Gun. w.m. Fred Holland Dewey. a. Chris Praetorius. Published by The New Island Music Company, New York, NY. 1910. Photo of Theodore Roosevelt. Drawing of Roosevelt with gun, dead elephants, hippos, cat, dog, chickens, and monkeys. 6pp.

TR-186(A) Oyster Bay (March and Two-Step). m. L.F. Groebl. Published by Groebl Bros., Oyster Bay, NY. 1902. Bl/w photo of "Sagamore Hill, President Roosevelt's Home at Oyster Bay, N.Y.," geometric designs. "Respectfully Dedicated by Permission to Miss Alice Roosevelt." 8pp. Page 2: Blank. Page 8: Advertising.

(B) Sagamore Hill (Waltzes). m. L.F. Groebl. Gn/w photo and geometric designs. 6pp.

(C) Dancing Wave (Polka). m. L.F. Groebl. B/w photo and geometric designs. 6pp.

(D) Merry Students (Galop). m. L.F. Groebl. R/w photo and geometric designs. 6pp.

TR-187 Teddy In The Jungles (Grand March Heroique) (Descriptive). m. Joe W. Phillips. 1909. Photos of "Mayor of Ashland, KY., J.O. Mathewson, Shriner, State Commander R.S. Moses, Knights Templar, Louisville, Ky., Joe Wm. Phillips." Drawing of a boat, sun. "Dirinost Dramatizations to Louisville, Ky., June 9, 1909, Shrine Souvenir Imperial Council of the United States of America, Music Inspirations." "A Toast To T.R. In Africa—When your camp-fire is low in the midnight tropics, where lion, tiger and elephant about your moss-cot frolics, where night-birds, piercing notes through the jungle rings accompanying queer sounding croaks and bleats and rasping of wings, when all else of your camps are in the land of dreams, ar'nt you wistfully 'a'thrill for more sociable themes? [sic]" "Response to Louisville's eruption (1909) of divertissement with the Mystic Shrine." 8pp.

TR-188 Teddy Will Carry It Through. w. Emma G. Cornic. m. E.M. and Anna S. Carlson. Copyright 1903 by Emma Cornic. B/w photo of Teddy Roosevelt, geometric design border. "Dedicated to Theodore Roosevelt, President of the United States." 6pp. Pages 2, 5 and 6: Blank.

TR-189 Oklahoma (The Shining New Star) (March Two Step). m. J.C. Halls. Published by United States Music Company, Williamsport, PA. 1908. Bl/w drawing of Uncle Sam with map of Oklahoma — "The New Star." "To Our President Theo. Roosevelt." 6pp. Page 6: Advertising.

TR-190 Welcome Home Comrade (Song). w.m. Lawrence Monahan, Jr. Published by Lawrence Monahan, Jr., Morris Plains, NJ. 1910. Photo of Theodore Roosevelt. Drawing of flowers, eagle, shield, geometric designs. 6pp. Page 2: Advertising. Page 6: Blank.

TR-191 Teddy (March). m. Charles Kunkel. Published by the Kunkel Brothers, St. Louis, MO. 1903. Non-pictorial geometric designs. "March from the Opera *Roy Bean*." "Book by Hiram W. Hayes." "To Theodore Roosevelt, President of the United States." 10pp. Page 10: Advertising.

TR-192 Teddy The Tried And

True (Teddy's Marching Song). w.m. William M. Wood. Published by Wood Bros., Publishers, Norristown, PA. Copyright 1912 by William M. Wood. B/w photo by Underwood and Underwood of Theodore Roosevelt at desk. Gn/w floral and geometric designs. 6pp. Pages 2 and 6: Blank.

TR-193   The New Campaign (March and Two-Step). m. Will Hardy. Published by Premium Music Company, Publishers, Worcester, MA. Copyright 1904 by Will Hardy. B/w photos of Theodore Roosevelt and Alton B. Parker. [V-1: R/gn] [V-2: Y/bl] drawings by F.P. Dean of the Capitol building, campaign torch, geometric designs. 6pp. Page 6: Blank.

TR-194   Yankee Doodle [Excerpt]. Published as a post card [in Germany?]. [ca. 1904]. [3 1/2" × 5 1/2"]. R/w/b flag design. Br/be attached photo of Theodore Roosevelt. "Glory to the Union." Rev: "Cente Postle-PostKarte-Cartolina Postale-Post Card-Levelczo Lap. Dopisnice. Briefkaart. Weltpostverein."

TR-195   Throw Your Hat Into

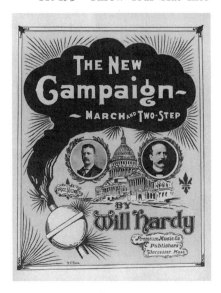

TR-193

The Ring. w.m. Raymond S. Barlow. Published by James A. Rogers, Inc., Nos. 61-65 Cliff Street, New York, NY. Copyright October 1913 by Raymond S. Barlow. Drawing of a Rough Rider hat. 4pp. Page 2: "To Colonel Roosevelt." Page 4: Blank.

TR-196   The Dashing Cavalier. m. John J. McIntyre. Published by The Popular Music Company, No. 179 Warren Street, Brooklyn, NY., as Vol. 1, No. 12, April 11, 1898. B/w non-pictorial geometric designs. "Respectfully Dedicated to Theodore Roosevelt." "For the Piano." "Subscription $100 per year." "Popular music entered as second class matter at the Broadway Post Office." 4pp. Page 4: Advertising.

TR-197   Alice, The Bride Of The White House (Valse). m. Anita Comfort-Brooks (Composer of *Anita Mexican Dance, Monterey Spanish Dance, Remember the Maine Battle Song, Imogene Ballad, &c*). Published by N. Weinstein, Flatiron Building, No. 949 Broadway, New York, NY. 1906. Photos of Alice Roosevelt — "Mrs. Longworth" and "Anita Comfort-Brooks." Drawing of a wedding ceremony — "Marriage of Miss Alice Roosevelt and Mr. Nicholas Longworth, White House, February 17, 1906." Drawing of floral and geometric designs. "Dedicated and Presented to Mrs. Nicholas Longworth." "As played at King Edward's Buckingham Palace and by Prince Louis of Battenberg's Royal Band." "Mrs. Nicholas Longworth sends many thanks for your kind remembrance and good wishes [facsimile signature]." 8pp. Page 8: Advertising for other Comfort-Brooks music.

TR-198   Hands Across The Continent (March, Two-Step with Song Refrain). w.m. Rudolph Aronson (Composer of the Official Campaign Marches for 1904 and 1908). 1912. Non-pictorial geometric design border design. "For there is neither East now West, Border nor Breed nor Birth, When two strong men stand face to face, Though they come from the ends of the Earth — Kipling." "Respectfully Dedicated to Roosevelt and Johnson." 6pp. Pages 2 and 6: Blank.

TR-199 The Praises Of Our Country (A National Hymn). w.m. Enrico Campobello. Published by E. Jonassohn, No. 22 West 8th Street, New York, NY. 1902. Pl/gr/w photo of Theodore Roosevelt. Pl/gn/w drawing of wreath, flowers. "Respectfully Dedicated to Our President." "Sailor — Soldier — Toiler — Statesman." 8pp. Page 8: Blank.

TR-200 The Roosevelt Rally (Song and Chorus). w. Minnie M. Seymour. m. Air: *The Battle Cry of Freedom*. Published by Progressive Publishing Company, East St. Louis, IL. 1912. Photo of "Theodore Rosevelt the People's Candidate." Drawing of flags, shield- "1912."

TR-201 Down In Oyster Bay. w.m. Max Clay. Published by Hirsche & Clay, Music Publishers, No. 18 Boylston Street, Boston, MA. 1914. O/bk/w drawing by Glenn Pierce of a lighthouse, sunset, dancing oysters. 6pp.

TR-202 Fiat Justitia. w.m. Burt G. Wilder. Publisht [sic] for the Author by Oliver Ditson Company, Boston, MA.

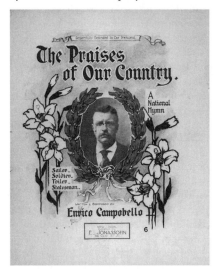

TR-199

1911. Non-pictorial line border. "An International Hymn, Written March, 1905, in Honor of Theodore Roosevelt, Upholder of the 'Square Deal' and Promoter of Peace between Russia and Japan." "Printed for distribution to the members of the First Universal Races Congress, London, July 26 to 29, 1911." 4pp. Page 4: Narrative by "Burt G. Wilder, B.S., M.D., Formerly Surgeon of the Fifty-fifth Mass. Vol. Inf'y., Colored, Emeritus Professor of Neurology and Vertebrate Zoology, Cornell University, Ithaca, N.Y., June 3, 1911," on "The Brain of the Negro." Facsimile letter from Theodore Roosevelt.

TR-203 Rough Rider's Patrol. m. Mrs. J.J. Wolf. Published as an insert? [ca. 1898]. 4pp. Page 1: Blank. Pages 2 and 3: Drawings of Theodore Roosevelt, Rough Rider battle scenes. "Dedicated to Colonel Theodore Roosevelt and the heroes of San Juan Hill."

TR-204 We're Satisfied With Teddy (National Republican Campaign Song). w.m. Monroe H. Rosenfeld. 1904. Non-pictorial. 2pp. Page 2: Blank.

TR-205 We've Put Teddy Up To The Fight. w.m. Eugenie Viles. Published by Lee Anthony and Company, No. 1205 Republic Building, Chicago, IL. 1912. Photos of Theodore Roosevelt and Hiram W. Johnson. "Oyster Bay, Aug. 10th, 1912, 'Win or lose it's a fight worth making.'" 6pp. Pages 2 and 6: Blank.

TR-206 You're All Right Teddy (Republican Campaign Song). w.m. Cole and Johnson (Authors of The Old Flag Never Touched The Ground). Published by Joseph W. Stern and Company, No. 34 East 21st Street, New York, NY. 1904. Bl/w litho of an eagle, geometric designs. "Dedicated to Our Standard Bearers Roosevelt and Fairbanks." 4pp. Page 4: Blank.

TR-207 Cuba Libre. w.m. Frank Byron. Published by Frank Byron, Lockport, NY. 1899. Photo of "Gov.

(TR) THEODORE ROOSEVELT

Theodore Roosevelt." "Descriptive of Roosevelt and the Rough Riders at San Juan." "A Patriotic, Thrilling Song." 4pp. Page 4: Blank.

TR-208 Teddy's Moose (Slow Two Step). m. J.W. Ladd. Published by J.W. Ladd, Bristol, NH. 1912. R/w non-pictorial geometric designs. 4pp. Page 4: Blank.

TR-209 Meteor Waltzer (Meteor Waltz, Valse Meteore). m. Wilhelm Aletter, Op. 200. Published by Fr. Porttius, Leipzig, Germany. 1902. Photo of Alice Roosevelt. Drawing of U.S. and German flags, ship, leaves. "Fur Pianoforte." "Dedicated to Miss Alice Roosevelt." List of arrangements available. 10pp. Page 10: Advertising for other songs.

TR-210 Hip-Hip-Hurrah For Theodore Roosevelt (Song and Chorus). w.m. Dave Richardson. a. J.P. Zimmerman. Published by The Richardson Music Publishing Company, No. 28 Elm Street, New York, NY. 1912. Photo of Theodore Roosevelt, stripe border. "The National Campaign Song Hit." 4pp. Page 4: Blank.

TR-211 Good Bye Teddy Roosevelt (You Were A Real American). w. Alfred Bryan. m. Fred Fisher. Published by McCarthy & Fisher, Inc., Music Publishers, No. 224 West 46th Street, New York, NY. 1919. Br/w photo by Underwood and Underwood Studios of Theodore Roosevelt. Br/w drawing of a phonograph — "This number to be had on all phonograph records and music rolls, Ask your dealer." 4pp. Page 4: Advertising.

TR-212 Our President Roosevelt's Colorado Hunt (March Song). w. Silver Echo Tabor (Author of *Spirits, Love and Likes*, and *In A Dream I Loved You*). m. Professor A.S. Lohmann. Published by Silver Echo Tabor, Denver, CO. 1908. O/bk/w drawing of Theodore Roosevelt. "To the Memory of the Late U.S. Senator H.A.W. Tabor." "Dedicated to my Beloved Father H.A.W. Tabor." 8pp. Pages 2, 7 and 8: Blank.

TR-213 Roosevelt Grand March And Two Step. m. Professor W. Augustus Curry. Published by W.A. Curry, Utica, NY. 1905. B/w photo of Theodore Roosevelt. Bl/w floral and geometric designs. "Respectfully Dedicated to Our President Theodore Roosevelt, Washington, DC." 8pp. Page 8: Blank.

TR-214 They Are Calling From The Mountains. w. "A West Virginian." m. Dan J. Wall. 1912. Non-pictorial line border. "The Song of the West Virginians." "As Sung at the Great Republican National Convention at Chicago 1912 by the Lakeside Quartette." "Our slogan — Hey! Hey! Hey! Come to stay! Fight 'em, fight 'em, fight 'em! West Virginia!" 4pp.

TR-215 Roosevelt's Rough Riders (March Two-Step). m. L.F. Haaren. Published by Thomas Groggan and Brother, Galveston, TX. 1898. B/w photo of Theodore Roosevelt and "Commanding Officers Roosevelt's Rough Riders." R/w floral and geometric designs. 6pp. Pages 2 and 6: Blank.

TR-216 Roosevelt's Grand Triumphal March. m. Lajos von Serly. Published by Lojos von Serly, No. 241 West 137th Street, New York, NY. 1912. O/bl/br/bk/w drawing of Theodore Roosevelt in safari outfit with dead lion. "Dedicated to Ex-President Theodore Roosevelt's Return from Africa and Europe." "Played the first time on Ex-President Theodore Roosevelt's arrival in New York by a band of 64 musicians on Fifth Avenue, June 18, 1910." 6pp. Pages 2 and 6: Blank.

TR-217 They Are Calling From The Mountains. w. "A West Virginian." m. Dan J. Wall. Published by Walter R. Snyder, No. 9 South La Salle Street, Chicago, IL. 1912. [7" × 10 3/8"]. Non-pictorial line border. "The Song of the West Virginians." "As sung at the great Republican National Convention at Chicago, 1912." "The Slogan of the West Virginians — Hey! Hey! Hey! Come to Stay! Fight em! Fight em! Fight em! West Vir-gini-A!" 4pp.

TR-218 Jamestown Dixie (Or Dixie Patrol). a. A. Patricolo. Published by A. Patricolo, Steinway Hall, New York, NY. 1907. Bl/w photos of "A. Patricolo," "Theodore Roosevelt, President of the U.S.A." and Jamestown Exposition officials — "H. St. George Tucker, President; C. Brooks Johnston, Chairman of the Board of Governors; Robt. H. Sexton, Chief of Congresses and Special Events; C.S. Sherwood, Governor, Concessions and Admissions; Barton-Myers, Governor Exploration; J.S. Southgate, Governor of Exhibits; J. Taylor Ellyson, Gov. History and Education; Alvah H. Martin, Governor of Transportation." R/w/b drawing of flag, eagles, flowers, geometric designs. "An Arrangement of *Dixie* Officially Adopted by the Jamestown Exposition." "1607—1907." 8pp. Page 2: "To the American people." Page 8: Advertising for Steinway pianos.

TR-219 Roosevelt A Magical Name. w. S.W. Hook. m. C.J. Stowell. Published by S.W. Hook, New Salem, Franklin County, MA. 1912. [6 1/2" × 10"]. Non-pictorial line border. 4pp. Page 4: Blank.

TR-220 Go Rough Riders, Go! w.m. Jerome Bresler. Published by Roosevelt High School, Chicago, IL. 1931. Bl/y drawing by Gladys Sylvan of face. 6pp. Page 2: "Dedicated to A.J.S." Page 6: Blank.

TR-221 Roosevelt School Song. w. Leland Varley. m. Eliot Smith. Published by the Music Department, Roosevelt School, Eliot Smith, Editor. [19—]. Non-pictorial. 2pp. Page 2: Blank.

TR-222 Turn Out The Light. w.m. A. Hoffman Simms. 1924. Non-pictorial "Professional Copy." "'Turn out the light I'm in for a little sleep'—President Theodore Roosevelt's last words." 6pp. Page 1 and 6: Blank.

TR-223 Oh! What A Difference In The Morning! w. M.C.J. m. Felix McGlennon. Published as a "Musical Supplement, *New York American and Journal*, Sunday, January 29, 1905, pages 5-8." Copyright by Oliver Ditson Company. 1891. Be/br photos of Miss Alice Roosevelt and Countess Cassini. Gn/be/br drawings of Miss Alice Roosevelt and Countess Cassini. News clipping—"Countess Cassini Picked Out Odd Song." "The favorite song of Miss Alice Roosevelt and The Countess Cassini." Br/be photos of Alice Roosevelt and The Countess Cassini. "Published by permission of The Oliver Ditson Company, Boston, owners of the Copyright." 4pp.

TR-224 Is She Dreaming Of Me? w. Dr. E.A. Warren. m. "Tune: *The Star-Spangled Banner.*" Published by E.A. Warren, Sturgis, MI. Copyright January, 1906, by E.A. Warren. [4 1/2" × 6 1/4"]. Non-pictorial. "To Hon. Nicholas Longworth." 2pp. Page 2: Blank.

TR-225 Over Here! (We Are Dreaming Boys of You). w.m. John W. Dick and William D. Howell. Published by Howell, Dick and Nielson, Publishers, New York, NY. 1918. R/w/b drawing by Pfeiffer of man, woman, girl at "Honor Roll" of War dead pointing to the name of "Roosevelt, Q. [Quentin]," church, marching troops, flags, eagle. 4pp. Page 4: "Roll of Honor" logo.

TR-226 A Hundred Million Strong (A War Song for the Nation). w. Rev. Andrew F. Underhill. m. Robert E.S. Olmsted. Published by C.W. Thompson and Company, Boston, MA. [V-2: 6 15/16" × 10 1/2"]. 1917. [V-1: Bl/w litho of eagle, ribbon, sun, axe] [V-2: Non-pictorial]. "Dedicated to Hon. Theodore Roosevelt." [V-2: "Gratis Copy"]. 6pp. Page 6: Advertising for other music.

TR-227 Inno Republicano. w.m. Professor Luigi Romano. Copyright 1905 by Luigi Romano. Photo of Theodore Roosevelt, geometric design border. "A Sua Eccellenza Theodore Roosevelt, Presidente degli Stati Uniti America." 4pp. Page 4: Photo of Luigi Romano.

TR-228 El Caney (Song and Refrain). w.m. W.A. Springer. Published by W.A. Springer, Marboro, MA. 1899. R/w/b drawing of soldier. Photos of Theodore Roosevelt and W.A. Springer? "Inscribed to Col. Theodore Roosevelt." "A Beautiful Ballad Founded on a True Incident." "As sung by Joseph T. Barry with Shea McAuliffe Stock Co." 6pp. Pages 2 and 6: Blank.

TR-229 Teddy's Grand March. m. D.M. Wilcox. a. Helen B. Blahnik. Published by Carrie B. Jennings Music Company, Howard City, MI. [ca. 1924]. Non-pictorial geometric designs. Page 2: "Dedicated to Edna Kimball Wilcox Club, Detroit, Mich."

TR-230 The Ranchman's Hymn To Teddy. w. Lilia Shipman Tromblee. m. Lilian Adele Tromblee. Published by A. Tromblee, No. 35 Excelsior Avenue, Saratoga, NY. 1905. Bl/br drawing of charge of the Rough Riders. 6pp. Pages 2 and 6: Blank.

TR-231 Alice Roosevelt March. m. H.R.W. Miles. Published by Mrs. Kathleen Kastle, Washington, DC. 1905. B/w photo by Pach Bros. Studio of Alice Roosevelt. Bl/w drawing of carnations, geometric designs. 6pp. Pages 2, 7 and 6: Blank.

TR-232 Roosevelt Hymn (Fox Trot). w. Julius Papa. m. Norrie Bernard. Published by the Lenox Company, No. 271 West 125th Street, New York, NY. Copyright 1921 by Julius Papa. Photo by Underwood and Underwood of Theodore Roosevelt. 4pp. Page 4: Blank.

TR-233 When Teddy Comes Marching Home. m. "To the Tune of *When Johnny Comes Marching Home*." [Published by The Progressive National Committee, Forty-Second Street Building, New York, NY]. [5 3/8" × 8 1/2"]. [1912]. Non-pictorial. 2pp. Page 2: Additional Verses.

TR-234 Charge Of The Rough Riders. m. James W. Casey. Published by Evans Music Company, No. 522 Massachusetts Avenue, Boston, MA. 1898. Br/w drawing of Theodore Roosevelt, Rough Riders. "Dedicated to Col. Theodore Roosevelt." 8pp. Pages 2 and 8: Blank.

TR-235 Uncle Sam's Concert (Or The Great Chicago Fair). w.m. Arthur West. a. William Loraine. Published by Frank Harding, Music Printer and Publisher, New York, NY. 1893. [Edition ca. 1912]. R/w/b drawing of Theodore Roosevelt and William H. Taft fighting, Uncle Sam watching—"Uncle Sam: Stop this quarrelling or I'll have to make a change." Alternative Title [?] — *The Bad Boys*. 6pp. Page 6: Advertising.

TR-236 The World Hasn't Anything On Me. w. George B. Somerville. m. Anna B. Somerville. Published by Joseph P. Drew, Philadelphia, PA. 1910. Bl/w drawing of globe with face of Theodore Roosevelt, Saturn, stars. 6pp. Page 6: Blank.

TR-237 If You're An American, Be An American Thru And Thru. w.m. C.F. Potter, No. 383 Woodland Avenue, Woodhaven, NY. 1921. Photo of Theodore Roosevelt. "One Flag, the American Flag." "One Language, the Language of the Declaration of Independence." "One loyalty, loyalty to the American people." "A Man is an American and Nothing else, or He is Not an American at all." "Dedicated To the Memory of Theodore Roosevelt, the First American of his Generation." 6pp. Page 2: Blank. Page 6: Advertising.

TR-238 Our Heroes Of To-Day. w.m. W.H. Pease. Published by Eastern Music Publishing Company, New York, NY. Copyright 1909 by W.H. Pease. Gn/w photos of "Theodore Roosevelt (by I.A. Julee), Admiral Dewey (by Clinedinst), Winfield S. Schley by Pach Bos.), Wilber Wright" and "W.H. Pease." Gn/w drawing of Miss "America," flag, eagle, shield. 6pp. Pages 2 and 6: Blank.

TR-239 Rally 'Round The Hat Boys. w.m. Sylvia Snyder. Published by

Snyder Music Company, Omaha, NE. Copyright 1912 by Sylvia Snyder. Bk/br drawing of Rough Rider hat with "TR" initials. 6pp. Pages 2 and 6: Blank. Page 3: "Dedicated (without permission) to Theodore Roosevelt."

TR-240 Here's To The Stars And Stripes. w.m. Herbert N. Farrar. Published by M. Witmark and Sons, New York, NY. 1901. R/w/b drawing of crossed flags, flag bunting, men toasting at a banquet table. "To Theodore Roosevelt, President of the United States (Who was one of us)." 6pp. Page 6: Advertising.

TR-241 Go And Vote For Teddy Roosevelt. w. Hugh Malcolm McCormick. 1910. [4" × 8"]. Non-pictorial. 2pp. Page 2: Blank.

TR-242 The Charge At San Juan (March and Two Step). m. Lizzie Mae Felker. Published by The General Music Company, No. 15 Courtlandt Street, New York, NY. 1903. Bk/bl/w/o drawing of Theodore Roosevelt, Rough Riders. "Dedicated to Col. Theodore Roosevelt and the Rough Riders." 6pp. Pages 2 and 6: Blank.

TR-243 We Need You, Mr. Roosevelt! (A Campaign Song). w. John Irving Pearce, Jr. 1912. Non-pictorial. "From the June, 1912, issue of *The American Sheep Breeder*." [4 1/2" × 7 1/2"]. 2pp. Page 2: Blank.

TR-244 Bull Moose (Waltz). m. Alfred Walker. Published by Luckhardt and Belder, No. 10 East 17th Street, New York, NY. 1912. Br/be drawing of a moose head. "Inscribed to all lovers of Social Justice." "Waltz for Piano." 10pp. Page 2: Blank. Page 10: Advertising for other music.

TR-245 The Teddy Girl. w. William Jerome. m. Jean Schwartz. Published by Francis, Day and Hunter, No. 15 West 30th Street, New York, NY. 1907. Y/bk/w non-pictorial geometric designs. "Sung by Helen Hale in Henry W. Savage's Production *A Yankee Tourist* Presenting Raymond Hitchcock (Staged by George Marion)." 6pp. Page 6: Advertising.

TR-246 Teddy's In The Ring. w.m. Mildred Hibbs. Published by Charles L. Johnson, Kansas City, MO. 1912. B/w drawing of Teddy Bears shooting pistols, rope circle with hat inside. Hat inscribed "T.R." 6pp. Page 2: Blank. Page 6: Advertising.

TR-247 Teddy Junior (March). m. Sol Wolerstein. Published by Carl Fischer, Inc., Cooper Square, New York, NY. 1923. Br/be drawing of eagle, mountain. Br/be photo of Theodore Roosevelt, Jr. "Respectfully Dedicated to Col. Theodore Roosevelt." "Also Published for Band and Orchestra." 6pp. Page 6: Advertising.

TR-248 [Rose]-Velt [Rebus Title]. w.m. A. Etta Morrill. Published by Omar A. Towne, Franklin Falls, NH. Copyright 1905 by A. Etta Morrill. Gn/pk/w drawing of a rose as part of the title. B/w photo of Theodore Roosevelt. 6pp. Pages 2 and 6: Blank.

TR-249 The Golden Star (A Memorial March). m. John Philip Sousa. Published by Chappell and Company, Ltd., London, England. 1919. Bl/w/gd litho of star. "In memory of the brave who gave their lives that liberty shall not perish." List of other arrangements available. 8pp. Page 2: "To Mrs. Theodore Roosevelt." Pages 6 and 7: Blank. Page 8: Advertising.

TR-250 Golden Rod (The Flower of Our Nation) (Song). w.m. Mabel McKinley. Published by Leo Feist, No. 134 West 37th Street, New York, NY. 1907. O/bl/w drawing of goldenrods. B/w photo of Mabel McKinley. 6pp. Page 2: "Respectfully Dedicated to Honorable Charles W. Fairbanks, Vice President of the United States." Page 6: Advertising.

TR-251 The Roosevelt Campaign March. w.m. Theodore Henckels. a. C.J.H. Published for Theodore Henckels of Middlebury College, Middlebury, VT., by Hatch Music Company,

Philadelphia, PA. 1904. B/w photo of "President Roosevelt." 4pp. Page 4: Facsimile letter from Theodore Henckels to Vermont State Republican Committee.

TR-252 American Heroes (March). m. Joseph J. Kaiser. Published by Jos. J. Kaiser Music Company, New York, NY. 1901. R/w/b drawings of "Heroes" including "Colonel Theodore Roosevelt," George "Washington—1776," "Andrew Jackson," "Winfield Scott," "U.S. Grant," others including "Admiral Schley, Nelson Miles, Admiral Sampson, Admiral Dewey, Anthony Wayne, John Paul Jones, O.H. Perry, William T. Sherman, Robert E. Lee, Admiral Farragut, Stonewall Jackson, Philip Sherman." List of battles. "Let us have peace 1861-65." List of 29 battles—"Bunker Hill" to "Santiago." 6pp. Page 6: Advertising.

TR-253 An Ode To Theodore Roosevelt. w. Carl Rickman. m. Tom Lemonier (Writer of *Just A Word Of Consolation*). Published by Rickman, Lemonier & Johnson, Publishers, No. 3159 South State Street, Chicago, IL. [ca. 1919]. B/w mourning ribbon, black border. 4pp. Page 4: Advertising.

TR-254 Teddy (March Song). w. Ormsby A. Court. m. Walter H. Lewis (Composer of *Yallelly, Honolulu Lou, Blue Eyed Girl in Green, Molly O'Hare, Airy Fairy Floribel, Saladi, Down The Garden Alley, Where The Jasmine Twines, &c, &c, &c*). Published by M. Witmark and Sons, New York, NY. 1904. R/w/b drawing of leaves, geometric designs. 6pp.

TR-255 Teddy Once More (A Patriotic Song and Chorus). w.m. James F. Collins (Wilmerding, PA). Published by The Magbee Music Publishing Company, Pittsburgh, PA. 1907. B/w photo of Teddy Roosevelt. Bl/w star, flag, torch. "Dedicated to the Hon. Theodore Roosevelt." 6pp. Pages 2 and 6 Advertising.

TR-256 The Man In Washington (Song and Chorus). w. S.W. Furst. m. Harry A. Russell. Published by Furst & Haswell, Williamsport, PA. Copyright

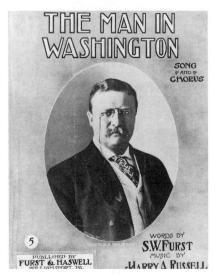

TR-256

1908 by S.W. Furst. B/w photo by Pach Bros. of "Theodore Roosevelt." 6pp.

TR-257 Just For Your Country's Sake. w.m. L.E.W. [Lilian E. Wheeler]. Published by Success Music Company, Star Building, Chicago, IL. 1904. B/w photos of Theodore Roosevelt and

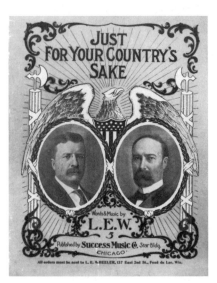

TR-257

Charles Fairbanks. Bk/w/bl drawing of eagle, shield, axes, geometric designs. "All orders must be sent to L.E. Wheeler, No. 137 East 2nd Street, Fond du Lac, Wis." 6pp. Page 2: Blank. Page 3: "Dedicated to my country." Page 6: Advertising.

TR-258 When Yankee Doodle Teddy Boy Comes Marching Home Again. w. Seymour Brown. m. Nat D. Ayer. Published by Jerome H. Remick and Company, New York, NY. 1910. R/w/b drawing by Gene Buck of stylized flowers. "Popular Edition." 6pp. Page 6: Advertising.

TR-259 Bull Moose Romp (March and Two Step). m. Virginia G. Templeton. Published by Globe Music Company, No. 1193 Broadway, New York, NY. 1912. Bl/w photo of Theodore Roosevelt. Br/w/bl/r drawing of two moose. 6pp. Pages 2 and 6: Advertising.

TR-260 The Teddy Girl. w. William Jerome. m. Jean Schwartz. Published by Francis, Day and Hunter, No. 15 West 30th Street, New York, NY. 1907. Bl/w photo of Helen Hale — "Sung by Helen Hale." Bl/gn/w litho by Starmer of floral and geometric designs. "Henry W. Savage Presents Raymond Hitchcock in *The Yankee Tourist*." 6pp. Page 6: Advertising.

TR-261 The Big Stick. w. Will A. Boyd. m. Will T. Pierson. Published by The Columbia Music Publishing Company, The House of Capital Music, Washington, DC. 1908. O/bk/w drawing of man with large stick, boy. 8pp. Pages 2 and 8: Advertising.

TR-262 The Rough Riders (March Song). w. Joseph Maxwell Jones. m. J.E. McClellan. Published by McClellan & Louis Company. Copyright 1904 by Joseph M. Jones. B/w photo of Theodore Roosevelt. R/w/b flags, wreaths labeled inscribed "El Caney — San Juan — Santiago." 6pp. Pages 2 and 6: Blank.

TR-263 Hiram Johnson You're The Man (Campaign Song of 1920).

w.m. Thomas O'Dowd. Published by Thomas O'Dowd, No. 26 8th Avenue, New York, NY. 1920. [8 5/8" × 10 7/8"]. Bl/w litho of flag, geometric designs. 4pp. Page 4: Blank.

TR-264 Triplicity (or The Donkey, MOOSE or Elephant) (Bull Moose Campaign Song). w. H.S. Gillett. m. L. Mae Felker. Published by Maxwell Sales Company, No. 1451 Broadway, New York, NY. Copyright 1912 by H.S. Gillett. R/w/bk litho of a moose, a donkey and an elephant. 4pp. Plus a 2 page insert of extra verses. Page 4: Blank.

TR-265 I Would Still Love You. w. Harry Castling. m. C.W. Murphy. Published by Francis, Day and Hunter, No. 1364 Broadway, New York, NY. 1907. O/pl/w drawing of big stick, flowers. Pl/w photo of Clara Morton. "Sung by Miss Clara Morton of the Four Mortons in the Successful Musical Production *The Big Stick*." 6pp. Page 6: Advertising.

TR-266 I Am For Hiram March. w. T. Shelley Sutton. m. Paul Valtinke. Published by Edgar J. Cook, No. 10 South La Salle Street, Chicago, IL. 1920. B/w shields, stars, geometric designs. "Chorus to be sung the first time as a Solo or Mixed Quartette, and the second time by the audience (Arrangement for Mixed Quartette on back page)." 6pp. Page 6: Arrangement for Mixed Quartette.

TR-267 Teddy We're Glad You're Here. w.m. Vivian I. Russell. Copyright 1910 by Vivian I. Russell, Denver, CO. B/w photos of Theodore Roosevelt and Vivian I. Russell. B/w drawings by Clarence Ellsworth of Theodore Roosevelt riding a camel, elephant, crocodile, ox, sphinx, lion, tiger, monkey, bear, rhino, human hands outstretched towards Roosevelt. R/w/b title and flags. 6pp. Page 2: Copyright data. Page 6: Blank.

TR-268 The Theodore March. m. Marie L. Dorgan. Published by Marie L. Dorgan, No. 211 Fliedner Building,

(TR) THEODORE ROOSEVELT

Portland, OR. 1924. B/w photo by A.L. Ransford of a monument of Theodore Roosevelt on horseback, geometric designs. 6pp. Page 6: Blank.

TR-269 I Am For Hiram (Campaign Songster). w. Edward Johnson Seymour. m. "Popular Tunes." 1920. [9" × 12"]. B/w photo by International Film Service of Hiram Johnson. "Catchy Up-To-Date Songs." "Sing 'em and Help Put Him Over." 4pp. Page 4: Narratives by Edward Seymour.

TR-270 The Triumph Of Old Glory (Our President's March). m. Arthur Pryor. Published by Carl Fisher, No. 8-10 Fourth Avenue, New York, NY. 1907. Drawings of Continental soldiers, flags. Five photos of Arthur Pryor. "Piano Solo." 8pp. Page 2: Blank. Page 8: Advertising and photo of Arthur Pryor.

TR-271 There's Bound To Be A Yankee In The Way. w.m. D'Arcy Blaxall. a. Z.M. Parvin, Mus. Doc. Published by Frederick E. Hunt, Portland, OR. 1904. B/w photo by Pach Bros. of Teddy Roosevelt. R/w geometric designs. "Topical and Campaign Song." "For sale by all music dealers." 8pp.

TR-272 Always Wear That Smile. w.m. Will R. Hoffmann. Published by Will R. Hoffmann, Publisher, No. 271 Broadway, New York, NY. [190-]. Drawing by Starmer of Theodore Roosevelt, two wreaths.

TR-273 He Enlisted With The U.S. Volunteers (A Life's Story). w.m. W.R. Williams (The song writer of *America*, Author of *She's Good Enough For Me, Nola Shannon, The Dying Girl's Request, Somebody's Sweetheart*). a. Lewis Reitermann. Published by Will Rossiter, No. 56 Fifth Avenue, Chicago, IL. 1898. R/w/b drawing of Theodore Roosevelt, marching soldiers, bugle player, couple kissing—"He kissed his girl good-bye." "Over 15 Thousand sold in less than 3 months." List of other titles by Publisher. 6pp. Page 2: Blank. Page 6: Advertising.

TR-274 Sussex By The Sea (Military Marching Song). w.m. W. Ward Higgs. Published by the Anglo-Canadian Music Publisher's Association, Ltd., No. 144 Victoria Street, Toronto, Canada. 1907. [WW-I Edition]. Non-pictorial geometric designs. "Sung with tremendous success by Frank Oldfield at the Roosevelt Victory Loan Meeting at Toronto Armories before an enthusiastic audience of 20,000 people." "A merry heart goes all the day, your sad times in a mile — Shakespeare." 8pp. Page 7: Blank. Page 8: Advertising.

TR-275 Good Bye, Good Bye, Alice Dar-ling (Excerpt). Published as a postcard. Copyright 1905 by Lindemann & Hyman. [3 1/2" × 5 1/2"]. Obv: R/w/b drawing of Alice and Theodore Roosevelt walking up a gang plank to a ship, Arabs waiving good-bye, mosque in skyline. Rev: "Post Card."

TR-276 Our Teddy. w.m. Florence Heath Mitchell. Published by Wulschner-Stewart Music Company, Indianapolis, IN. Copyright 1907 by Mrs. W.B. Mitchell. Bl/w photo of Theodore Roosevelt. R/w/b stripe background. 4pp. Page 4: Blank.

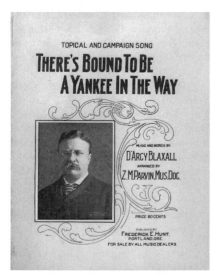

TR-271

TR-277 Daily, Knight Of The Shillaly! w.m. Emma Marie Cass. Published by D. Muller, No. 509 East 76th Street, New York, NY. [ca. 1900]. Non-pictorial geometric designs. "One of Teddy's Terrors." 4pp. Page 4: Advertising.

TR-278 Roosevelt, The Hope Of The Nation. w.m. Ethel May Smith. Published by The O.K. Music Company, Crossley Building, San Francisco, CA. Copyright 1904 by Ethel May Smith. B/w photos of Theodore Roosevelt and Ethel Smith. R/w/b drawing of flag, star border. "Arranged for Band and Orchestra by Nick Brown." 6pp. Pages 2 and 6: Blank.

TR-279 Oh You Teddy! w. Fred. E. Wolff. m. W.T. Buckley. Published by Buckley & Company, Chicago, IL. 1910. Br/be drawing by Kurz and Allesson of Theodore Roosevelt on horseback leading Rough Rider charge, bombs exploding. 4pp. Page 4: Advertising.

TR-280 The Rough Riders In Cuba. w. Frank J. Bonacek Novak. Copyright 1907 Frank J. Bonacek Novak, Omaha. Bl/w drawing of Theodore Roosevelt on horseback leading a Rough Rider charge. "Dedicated to Luther L. Kountze [facsimile handwriting]." "I want my country to be the best for the good of the world — Frank J. Bonacek Novak." 6pp. Pages 2 and 6: Blank.

TR-281 Dee-Lighted. w.m. E. Clinton Keithley and Charles H. Musgrove. Published by Musgrove Music Company, Louisville, KY. 1907. O/w/br litho of Teddy Bear with T.R. smile and big stick. 6pp. Page 6: Blank.

TR-282 Theodore Roosevelt. w.m. Mary E. Casey. Published by The Success Music Company, No. 356 Dearborn Street, Chicago, IL. 1906. Bl/w/bk non-pictorial geometric design. 8pp. Pages 2, 6, 7 and 8: Blank.

TR-283 U.S.W.V. Marcha-Fox (March-Fox). w. Carlos M. del Calvo. m. Mtro. Luis Casas and Solista F. Rojas. Published in Havana, Cuba. 1928. R/w/b drawing of crossed U.S. and Cuban flags. "Dedicata a los Veteranos de la Guerra Hispano-Americana, con motivo de su Trigesima Convencion en la Habana, Cuba." "Dedicated to the Veterans of the Spanish American War, on their 30th Convention, held at Havana (Cuba), October 10th, 1928." 6pp. Page 2: English translation of lyrics [Tribute to T.R. and others]. Page 6: Blank.

TR-284 President Roosevelt's Grand March. m. Monroe M. Oplinger. Published by Monroe Oplinger, Danielsville, PA. [ca. 1904]. Photos of Theodore Roosevelt and Monroe Oplinger — "A Competent Composer."

TR-285 Trip From Washington To Panama (A March and Two Step). m. A. Treumann. Published by Hoffman Brothers, No. 632 Main Street, Joplin, MO. 1906. Photo of Theodore Roosevelt. Drawing of train, naval ship, Capitol building at Washington.

TR-286 Daughter Of The Nation (March and Two Step). m. Charles Kuebler (Composer of *Cupid's Pranks Waltz*, *Vidette March and Two Step*, *Kahkwa Club Two-Step*). Published by Brehm Bros., Erie, PA. 1902. B/w photo by F.B. Johnston of Alice Roosevelt. R/w/b flags, sun rays. "Respectfully Dedicated to Miss Alice Roosevelt." "Published for Orchestra." 6pp. Page 6: Advertising.

TR-287 Keep Time (March and Two Step). m. A. Alvin Myer and Lester C. Riemer. Published by Riemer Music Publishing Company, New York, NY. 1906. R/w/b drawing of soldiers marching and dancing, shield, eagle, flags. Bl/w photos of Alvin Meyer and Lester Riemer. 6pp. Page 2: "Respectfully Dedicated to Theodore Roosevelt." Page 6: Advertising.

TR-288 Strenuous American (March). m. Elizabeth A. Gribbon. Published by Elizabeth A. Gribbon, Swanton, VT. 1908. B/w photo of the battleship

Maine. Bl/w flags, eagle. 6pp. Pages 2 and 6: Blank.

TR-289 America. w. Samuel Francis Smith, D.D. Copyright 1900 by Rockwood, New York, NY. Obv: B/w photo of Teddy Roosevelt. "The President." R/w/b stripes. "Compositions." Rev: Song. [This is a school composition book, with blank, lined pages for writing inside].

TR-290 Sagamore March. m. Edwin Franko Goldman. a. Erik W.G. Leidgen. "Dedicated to the memory of Theodore Roosevelt." In: *The Goldman March Album For Piano*, page 35. Published by Carl Fischer, Inc., No. 62 Cooper Square, New York, NY. 1936. Photo of Edwin Franko Goldman, geometric designs. "His Fifteen Most Popular Marches, Vocal Refrains, For School and General Use." 70pp.

TR-291 Teddy Roosevelt. w. John T. Collins. m. Charles E. Coleman. Published by Hayworth Music Publishing Company, Publishers and Dealers, Washington DC. Copyright 1913 by John Collins. Br/w photo of Theodore Roosevelt in uniform. Bl/w cover. 6pp. Pages 2 and 6: Blank.

TR-292 Do Your Bit Help Send A Kit (For Our Boys In France). w.m. G.F. Bickford. Published by Our Boys In France Tobacco Fund, No. 25 West 44th Street, New York, NY. 1917. R/w/b drawing of a soldier and a sailor smoking. "Soldier's and Sailor's Official Tobacco Song." "SOS—Send Over Smokes." "Endorsed by the Secretaries of the Army and Navy." "Other endorsements Alton B. Parker, The American Red Cross, Cardinal Gibbons, Speaker Champ Clark, Rabbi Wise, Lyman Abbott, Gertrude Atherton, Governor Whitman and the entire nation." "Theodore Roosevelt says—I wish you all possible success in your admirable effort to get our boys in France tobacco." 4pp. Page 4: Narrative: "Gun Smoke Everywhere—But Not a Whiff of Tobacco Smoke to Cheer a Fellow Up."

TR-293 Theodore Roosevelt. w.m. Rosemary and Stephen Vincent Benet. m. Arnold Shaw. In: *Sing A Song of Americans* [Song Book] page 29. Published by Musette Publishers, Inc., Steinway Hall, New York, NY. 1941. R/w/b drawings by Mollie Shuger on cover of Theodore Roosevelt, others. 84pp.

TR-294 Does It Pay To Raise Your Boy To Be A Soldier. w. Fred S. Daniel. m. Wm. Bettmann. Published by Bettmann Bros. & Daniel, New Albany, IN. 1918. R/w/bl/br drawing of mother, soldier son. Facsimile letter from Theodore Roosevelt to Fred Daniel— "Oyster Bay, Long Island, NY; January 29th, 1916, My dear Mr. Daniel, That a very interesting poem. Needless to say, I entirely agree with the sentiment you express. Sincerely yours, Theodore Roosevelt [facsimile signature]." "The Preparedness Song." 6pp. Page 6: Blank.

TR-295 Brain Storms (A Comic Ditty). w.m. Benjamin Hapgood Burt. Published by Jerome Remick and Company, New York, NY. 1907. Br/o/w drawing by DeTakacs of a bald man with drawings on head—"The Big Stick"— "Teddy B"—"Auto"—"Bridge"—"Base Ball"—"Bug."

TR-296 Theodore Roosevelt (The Spanish-American War). w.m. Dorothy Gaynor Blake. Published by Theodore Presser Company, No. 1712 Chestnut Street, Philadelphia, PA. 1925. R/w/b drawing of soldiers from various American wars. "Musical Portraits from American History for the Pianoforte." List of other songs in the series.

TR-297 Yankee Kids (March and Two Step). m. Herbert G. Pulfrey. Published by Charles E. Roat Music Company, Ltd., Battle Creek, MI. 1907. R/w/b flag design, eagle, flags. B/w photos of seven children including "Quentin Roosevelt." 6pp. Page 6: Advertising.

TR-298 Alice Blue Folio. Published by [V-1: The Baldwin Company, Inc., No. 267 Wabash Avenue] [V-2:

National Music Company, State and Quincey Streets], Chicago, IL. [ca. 1906]. [9 7/8" × 13"]. B/w photo of Alice Roosevelt. Bl/w cover. "A Superb Collection of Late Copyright Music." 36pp. Page 2: Song: **Alice Blue Waltzes** by Abbie A. Ford. Page 36: [V-1: B/w photo and drawing of Baldwin factories in Cincinnati and Chicago] [V-2: Advertising].

TR-299 The March Of The Teddy Bears. m. Frank Strawn. Published by A. Hospe Company, Omaha, NE. 1912. O/bk/w drawing of three Teddy Bears marching with rifles. "Dedicated to a Third Term." 6pp. Page 6: Blank.

TR-300 The Man (A March Song). w. E.M. Narramore. m. Clifton Keith. Published by Keith's Music Publishing House, Long Branch, NJ. Copyright 1908 by E.M. Narramore. R/w geometric designs, fleur-de-lis. 4pp. Page 4: Blank.

TR-301 It's A Long Way To Europe, But Teddy Knows The Way. w.m. H.V. Irvine. Published by Irvine Music House, No. 59 East Van Buren Street, Chicago, IL. 1917. Non-pictorial bl/w star border. Facsimile letter from Theodore Roosevelt to Irvine—"H.V. Irvine, Esq., 59 E. Van Buren St., Chicago: My Dear Mr. Irvine: Hearty thanks for *It's A Long Way to Europe*, which I appreciate, and for which I again thank you. Yours faithfully—Theodore Roosevelt." 4pp. Page 4: Blank.

TR-302 When Teddy Got To Jungleville. w. E.J. Burdick. m. W.A. Lampman. Published by Burdick-Lampman Music Company, Lockport, NY. 1909. Gn/w/bk drawing of jungle scene, lion, giraffe, elephant, monkeys. [V-1: Green border with slogan—"Yes! It's the Latest Hit"] [V-2: White border, without slogan]. 6pp. Page 6: Advertising.

TR-303 For Honor, Flag And Nation [Campaign Souvenir]. w.m. Alfred Wooler, Scranton, PA. 1900. Published as a supplement to *The Scranton Tribune*, Saturday, October 20, 1900. [9 1/2" × 12 1/16"]. R/w/b drawing of flag, geometric border. B/w photo of "Hon. Wm. Connell." 4pp. Page 4: Advertising. [Pro William McKinley and Theodore Roosevelt].

TR-304 We All Know The Man Is Theodore Roosevelt. w. Charles D. Craigie. m. "Tune: *When Johnny Comes Marching Home Again*." Published by Chas. D. Cragie and Company, Box 1203, Boston, MA. Copyright 1904 by Helen D.B. Cragie. [3 1/4" × 5 3/8"]. Non-pictorial. 2pp. Page 2: Blank.

TR-305 When Teddy Comes Marching Home. w. Irving B. Lee. m. W.R. Williams. a. Harry L. Alford. Published by Will Rossiter, No. 152 Lake Street, Chicago, IL. 1910. [7" × 10 3/8"]. Bl/w photo of Theodore Roosevelt. "With compliments of 'Will Rossiter Band and Orchestra Club.'" "Positively a 'Knock-Out'—Get Busy!!!" 6pp. [Foldout].

TR-306 Roosevelt. w. C.H. Congdon. m. "Words adapted from *Maryland, My Maryland*." In: *Songs to be Sung at the First National Progressive Convention*, page 1. Copyright 1912 by C.H. Congdon, Chicago. [8" × 11"]. Non-pictorial. "Beginning Monday, August 5th, 1912, Coliseum, Chicago." "Let the Whole Assembly Sing!" 4pp.

TR-307 Roosevelt And Fairbanks (1904 Campaign Song with Ad Lib. Chorus). w.m. T.M. Richards, Canal Dover, OH. 1904. Bl/w non-pictorial geometric designs. 6pp. Page 6: Blank.

TR-308 S.S. Theodore Roosevelt (March and Two Step). m. H.A. Vandercook. Published by The Dixie Music House, No. 134 Van Buren Street, Chicago, IL. 1906. B/w photo by E.C. Clavert of Theodore Roosevelt. B/w photo of the steamship "Theodore Roosevelt." R/w/bk geometric designs. "Featured Daily by the Hadermann Ladies Orchestra on Board the Magnificent Steamship 'Theodore Roosevelt.'" "Respectfully

Dedicated to Manager W.K. Greenebaum." List of Arrangements available. 4pp. Page 4: Blank.

TR-309 While The Battle Ships Are Sailing. w.m. O.Z. Paris. Published by Old Dominion Music Company, No. 14 West 27th Street, S.W. Corner Broadway, New York, NY. 1908. R/w/bk drawing by Welp of floral and geometric designs. "Battle Fleet Starts On Its Historic Cruise: At the Wave of President Roosevelt's Hand Uncle Sam's Magnificent Armada Steams to Sea, With Guns Roaring, Bands Playing and Sailors Singing Jolly Refrains." "The Latest Patriotic March Song Success." 6pp. Page 2: Blank. Page 6: Advertising.

TR-310 The Roosevelt Grand March. m. Elza Lothner Published by C.W. Thompson & Company, No. 13 West Street, Boston, MA. Copyright 1902 by Mrs. E.L. Rahmn. Non-pictorial bl/w cover. "The Original Manuscript Cordially Accepted by the President Roosevelt Family." 6pp. Page 6: Blank.

TR-311 Ho! Ho! For Teddy! w.m. John Howard Craig. Published by M.B. Lyman & Company, Kimball Hall, Chicago, IL. 1910. B/w drawing of wreath, big stick, oak leaves. 8pp.

TR-312 Teddy's Campaign Song. w.m. Byron B. Floyd (Somers Point, NJ). Published by M.D. Swisher, No. 115 South Tenth Street, Philadelphia, PA. 1912. Br/w photo of Theodore Roosevelt. Bl/w geometric designs. 6pp. Pages 2 and 6: Blank.

TR-313 Go Ahead Vote For Teddy Roosevelt. w. Hugh Malcolm McCormick. m. Sara Weber McCormick. Published by The McCormick Music Company, Chicago, IL. Copyright 1910 by Hugh and Sara McCormick. Non-pictorial. "Professional Copy Not To Be Sold." 4pp. Page 2 Song: **Go Ahead Vote for Teddy Roosevelt**. Page 3: Presidential Prayer Song by Hugh and Sara McCormick—**American Hymn**. Copyright 1907. Page 4: Blank.

TR-314 Our Teddy (Valse). m. Oscar Schmoll. Published by The Oscar Schmoll Music Company, Chicago, IL. 1905. B/w photo of Theodore Roosevelt. Bl/w shields, geometric designs. "For Piano." List of arrangements available. "For sale at all music stores." List of other arrangements available. 6pp. Page 6: Testimonials to Oscar Schmoll in German and English with references to songs he composed for Abraham Lincoln, Ulysses S. Grant, John Logan and James Garfield.

TR-315 Teddy Roosevelt Waltz 1906. m. Lillian Macomber. a. Chas. Miller. Published by Lillian Macomber, Princeton, WI. 1906. Bl/w photo of Lillian Macomber. R/w/b drawing of lamps, geometric designs. 6pp. Pages 2 and 6: Blank.

TR-316 Jack Tars March Song (Waltz and Two-Step). w.m. Maria Walker Tumber (San Bernardino, Cal.). Published by Commercial Printing House, Music Publishers, Los Angeles, CA. [ca. 1904]. B/w photos of Theodore Roosevelt, two Naval officers, battleship. R/w/bl/bk drawings of flags, Soldier, Sailor. 6pp. Pages 2 and 6: Blank.

TR-317 O, Why Not Name The Baby Teddy (March Song and Chorus).

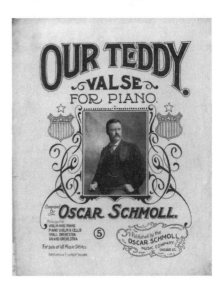

TR-314

w.m. R.E. Edwards. Published by The International Music Publishing Company, Richmond, IN. Copyright 1910 by R.E. Edwards. Drawing of two women, baby, dream-like cloud of Rough Riders in battle scene. 6pp. Page 6: Advertising.

TR-318   Hurrah Again For Teddy. w. B.F. Reed. m. Mrs. C.P. Rieder. Published by B.F. Reed, Saginaw, MI. Selling agents: The New York Sheet Music Clearing House, Nos. 141-147 West 45th Street, New York, NY. 1912. Bl/w drawing of crossed flags. Bl/gn/w geometric and floral designs. "Sung by Charles Wells, in 'Star Theatre,' Bay City, Mich." 6pp. Pages 2 and 6: Blank.

TR-319   Home Again (Song and Chorus). w.m. M.S. Pike. Published by Frank Harding's Music Printing House, New York, NY. [ca. 1910]. B/w photo of Theodore Roosevelt. R/w/b litho of flag, floral and geometric designs. "To the Soldier and Statesman Hon. Theo. Roosevelt." 4pp. Page 4: Advertising.

TR-320   Garryowen. Peno Y. Densari. In: *The Boston Sunday Globe*, September 14, 1902. B/w drawing of woman with harp, shamrocks in title. "President Roosevelt, on his New England tour, said the *Garryowen* is one of his favorite tunes, and that it was a favorite of General Custer."

TR-321   Oh! You Teddy (We're Going to Put You There). w. Dr. Joseph Aarons. Published by Dr. Joseph Aarons, No. 309 Hodges Building, Detroit, MI. 1916. [5 1/32" × 8 1/2"]. Non-pictorial black line border. "The 1916 Campaign Song for the Convention at Chicago." "Respectfully Dedicated to Theodore Roosevelt." 4pp. Page 2: "America First is our slogan in preparedness and efficacy."

TR-322   Let Righteous Peace Preside (Sacred National Song). w. Geo. A. Opharrow, Evangelist. m. William J. Carle. Published by Geo. A. Opharrow, No. 48 West 136th Street New York, NY. 1920. Bl/w photo of Theodore Roosevelt — "The Subject of Col. Theodore Roosevelt's Inauguration speech (March 4th, 1904)." 6pp. Pages 2 and 6: Blank. Page 3: "Dedicated to Hon. Theodore Roosevelt, Jr." "This is done for a life long memory of him who tried to practice what he preached through the Inspiration of Almighty Righteous Justice over All."

TR-323   Roosevelt March. m. Adolph Edgren. Published by the Edgren School of Music Seattle, WA. [ca. 1900]. Bl/w photo of Theodore Roosevelt. Bl/w drawing of eagle, shield, crossed flags, stars. R/w geometric designs. "Respectfully Dedicated to Colonel Theodore Roosevelt by the Composer." 8pp. Pages 2 and 8: Blank.

TR-324   The Peoples Choice (Campaign Song). w.m. Julius. Published by M.D. Swisher, No. 115 South Tenth Street, Philadelphia, PA. Copyright 1912 by M.C. Hutchings. Non-pictorial geometric designs. "Dedicated to Colonel Theodore Roosevelt." 4pp. Page 4: Blank.

TR-325   Teddy, The Jungle Boogie-Man. w.m. Kenneth S. Clark. Published by M. Witmark and Sons, New York, NY. 1908. Gn/w/bk drawing by G. McManus of cartoon bride, groom and baby. "Leffler-Bratton Company Presents *The Newlyweds And Their Baby*, A Comedy with Music Founded on the Cartoons by George McManus by Arrangement with *The New York World*, Book by Aaron Hoffman and Paul West." List of other songs in show.

TR-326   The Jungle King March And Two-Step. m. Joseph Fejer. Published by Ted Snyder and Company, Music Publishers, No. 112 West 38th Street, New York, NY. 1911. Bk/o/w drawing by Frew of a lion. "Respectfully Dedicated to Theodore Roosevelt on his 52nd Birthday." 6pp. Page 6: Advertising.

TR-327   The Bullmoosers. w.m. Captain Fritz Duquesne. Published by Spanuth and Strouse, No. 145 West 45th Street, New York, NY. 1912. Photo of Theodore Roosevelt, two moose heads.

TR-328 The Rider. w. Ben Hur Lampman. m. Ina Rae Seitz. Published by Clayton F. Summy Company, Chicago, IL. 1923. B/w photo of a statue of Theodore Roosevelt inscribed "Theodore Roosevelt, Rough Rider." "To the Memory of Theodore Roosevelt." 6pp. Pages 2 and 6: Blank.

TR-329 [Untitled Song Pamphlet]. [1904]. [4 5/8" × 7 3/16"]. B/w photos of "Theodore Roosevelt" and "Chas. Warren Fairbanks." R/w/b litho of flags, wreath inscribed "E Pluribus Unum." 4pp. Pages 2 to 4: Patriotic songs.

TR-330 March Of The Rough Riders. m. Paul Kruger. Copyright 1898 by W.H. Billing (Hawa, Canada). B/w drawing of a Teddy Roosevelt-like Rough Rider with U.S. Flag and pistol. 4pp.

TR-331 Teddy From Oyster Bay. w. H.K. Williams. m. Greely Henry. Published by H.K. Williams Music Company, Moline, IL. 1912. Gn/w drawing of torch, roses. 6pp. Page 6: Blank.

TR-332 Teddy's Hat Is In The Ring. w.m. George W. Cunningham. Published by State Music House, Chicago, IL. Copyright 1912 by G.W. Cunningham. O/bk/br/w drawing of Teddy Roosevelt, Rough Rider on horseback. 6pp. Page 2: Blank. Page 6: Advertising.

TR-333 My Hat Is In The Ring. w.m. Florence Heath Mitchell. Published by Florence Heath Mitchell, Connersville, IN. 1912. B/w drawing of Theodore Roosevelt and William Howard Taft in boxing ring. 8pp. Page 2: Blank. Page 8: Advertising for another Teddy and Taft song—*Hooligan Twins* by Florence Heath Mitchell.

TR-334 The Triumphal March Of The Rough Riders. m. Sydney Collins. Copyright 1906 by Sydney Collins, St. Joseph, MO. [Post-1919 size]. Bl/w drawing of a Rough Rider holding flag, columns. 6pp. Page 6: Blank.

TR-335 Dainty Butterfly (Intermezzo Characteristique). m. M. Loesch. Published by J. Fisher and Bro., No. 7 and 11 Bible House, New York, NY. 1903. O/gn/w drawing of butterfly, lily pads. "Respectfully Dedicated to Miss Alice Roosevelt." 6pp. Page 6: Advertising.

TR-336 On The Banks Of The Wabash Far Away (Song and Chorus). w.m. Paul Dresser. Published by Howley, Haviland & Company, Nos. 1260-66 Broadway, New York, NY. 1897. [ca. 1898 edition]. Gn/bk/w drawing of trees, river, flower. B/w photo of "Edward Marshall, *The New York Journal* war correspondent, dangerously wounded at Santiago while accompanying the charge of the Rough Riders." Excerpt "From *The NY Sun*, June 29, 1898 — It took thirty-five minutes to catch up with the party, but it seemed like ten years. Marshall was sleeping under the effect of another opiate, but as we changed off at the liter he woke and had another terrible spasm. When he was quieted, he began to sing *The Banks of the Wabash*. This sounds, I know, like an extract from a Rhoda Broughton novel, but it was true none the less. For nearly half of an hour, as we dragged the liter along, Marshall kept repeating the chorus of this song over and over." "Respectfully Dedicated to Miss Mary E. Smith, Terre Houte, Ind." 8pp. Pages 2, 7 and 8: Advertising.

TR-337 Oh! Susanna. w.m. Stephon [sic] C. Foster. In: *The Covered Wagon* [Film Program Booklet], page 17. Published by Famous Players—Lasky Corporation, Adolph Zukor, President, New York, NY. 1923. O/y/gr drawing of covered wagons at sunset. "Jesse L. Lasky...Presents *The Covered Wagon*, A James Cruze Production." "*The Covered Wagon* is a Paramount Picture made by the Famous Players-Lasky Corporation in the regular course of production activities during the year 1923. It was adapted by Jack Cunningham from the novel by Emerson Hough. This booklet has been prepared to present to the public some interesting facts in connection with the production of this Paramount Picture." "A Paramont Picture." 18pp. Booklet. Page 2: "*The Covered Wagon* is a Paramont Picture and is Dedicated to the Memory of Theodore Roosevelt." Page 17: Song.

TR-338 Dee-Lighted (Characteristic March and Two-Step). m. Frank G. Bernhardt. Published by Frank G. Bernhardt, Cincinnati, OH. 1908. Gr/br/w drawing of U.S. Capitol Dome, Teddy Bear carrying a Big Stick and grinning a Teddy Roosevelt-like smile and wearing Theodore Roosevelt-like spectacles. 6pp. Page 2: "Respectfully Dedicated to my Friend, Miss Edna Schoolfield." Page 6: Blank.

TR-339 Peacemaker (The President's March). m. [Frank] Sturtevant. Published by Century Music Publishing Company, No. 1178 Broadway, New York, NY. 1906. Bl/w floral designs. "Standard Marches by Celebrated Composers." List of music in "Series 2." "Century Edition."

TR-340 Uncle Teddy (Marche Pittoresque). m. Julius Fucik, Op. 239. Published by The Whitehall Music Company, No. 31 Charing Cross, SW, London, England. 1910. Drawing by Telemann of Theodore Roosevelt, jungle animals. List of arrangements.

TR-341 A Square Deal (No More No Less). w.m. W.M. Barnes. Published by Harris-Goar Jewelry Company. 1905. B/w litho drawing of Theodore Roosevelt, geometric designs. "One Thousand Dollar Prize Song." 6pp. Page 2: Blank. Page 6: Advertising for Harris-Goar Jewelry Company. [Lyrics are about Harris-Goar Jewelry].

TR-342(A) For Teddy, He's Our President. w.m. Mary V. Hoffner. Published by Success Music Company, Star Building, Chicago, IL. 1904. Bl/w non-pictorial geometric design cover. "Classic Edition of Popular Music." List of other titles in series.

TR-341

(B) **Campaign Song Of 1904**. w.m. Nanna Eline M. Cooper.

(C) **All Vote For Roosevelt**. w.m. Mrs. David Morgan.

TR-343 In The Jungle (Teddy R) (Soundscape). w. Richard Engquist. m. Jack Gottlieb. Published by Theophilious Music, Inc. Sole Agent: Boosey & Hawkes, Inc. 1991. [6 7/8" × 10 1/2"]. Non-pictorial. "Presidential Suite, Seven Pieces for Mixed Chorus (SATB) a cappella. 16pp. Page 2: "Presidential Suite is a celebration of America's priceless heritage of liberty. Inspired by the wisdom and whimsy of some of our most colorful presidents, it juxtaposes the eloquence of John F. Kennedy and Franklin Delano Roosevelt, with the journalistic pith of Theodore Roosevelt, Harry S. Truman's blunt common sense, Abraham Lincoln's homespun wit and Thomas Jefferson's irony, plus a legendary quip from the taciturn Calvin Coolidge. This patriotic work combines idealism with light-heartedness, inspiration with a dash of salt..." Page 3: "For Stephen Sturk."

TR-344 Teddy's Bears (A March For Little Folks). m. William R. Haskins

(Composer of *Twigs and Branches March*). Published by William R. Haskins Company, Music Publishers, No. 51 West 28th Street, New York, NY. 1907. Br/w drawing of five teddy bears including one with a football. 6pp. Pages 2 and 6: Blank.

TR-345 Progressive League Of Burlington County [Song Sheet]. [1912]. [6" × 8 1/4"]. B/w litho of U.S. flag. "For President Theodore Roosevelt, For Vice-President Hiram Johnson, For Congressman Francis D. Potter; For State Senator William B. Shedaker, For Assemblyman Joseph Beck Tyler." "This folder ordered and paid for by the Progressive League of Burlington Co." 4pp.

TR-346 We'll Follow Teddy. w.m. H. Wakefield Smith. 1917. Manuscript. "Dedicated to the Hon. Theodore Roosevelt, one of the Great Presidents of the U.S.A. on the assumption that his offer to lead a Hundred and Fifty Thousand soldiers to fight in France, in the year 1917, would be Accepted." "A Peerless Leader-An Upright Man." 4pp.

TR-347 The Great Adventure. w. "From the Prose of Theodore Roosevelt." m. Maury Madison. Copyright 1932 by Maury Madison. Non-pictorial manuscript. 4pp. Page 4: "Based on selections from *The Great Adventure*, Present Day Studies in American Nationalism." "Excerpts from the Prose of Theodore Roosevelt reprinted by permission of Chas. Scribner's and Sons, and George Roosevelt, Trustee, Roosevelt Estate."

TR-348 De Bull Moose Meet (Male Quartet or Chorus). w. A.W. Loudon. m. John B. Shirley. [1912]. [10 3/4" × 6 5/16"]. Non-pictorial handwritten manuscript. 2pp.

TR-349 The Ballad Of Theodore Roosevelt. w.m. Merrell Chester Dougherty. Copyright 1960 by Merrell Chester Dougherty, No. 13270 Kelowna Street, Arleta, CA. Non-pictorial lead sheet. 2pp.

TR-350 Storming Of El Caney (Marche Hispano-American War). m. Russell Alexander. a. L. Geiger. Handwritten Band Parts. Copyright 1903 by R.L. Barbhouse, Oakaloosa, IA. "Solo Cornet" part subtitle—"To The 3rd and 8th Infantry Regiments and Rough Riders of the 3rd Brigade, 5th Army Corps."

TR-351 The Battle Of San Juan Hill (Grand Descriptive Military Fantasia). m. Albert C. Sweet. Published by Carl Fischer, Inc., Cooper Square, New York, NY. 1909. Non-pictorial conductor's score. List of instrumentation available. Page 2: "The Battle of San Juan Hill (July 7, 1898)." "Synopsis." Page 3: "Conductor."

TR-352 The Gallant Rough Riders (March). m. T.B. Rankine. Copyright 1899 by Oliver Ditson Company, Boston, MA. Non-pictorial band arrangement. "Solo Bb Cornet" part. "Use in public permitted."

TR-353 Teddy, You're A Bear. w. Ring W. Lardner. m. Lee S. Roberts. 1916. [3" × 5 3/16"]. Non-pictorial. Obv: "Official Roosevelt Booster Song." "Join the Chorus of Ten Million Voters." "Regular copies for sale wherever music is sold." "Ask Orchestras and Bands to Play it." Rev: Printed Chorus. "Join in the Chorus with us."

TR-354 Peace (Grand March on the American, Russian and Japanese National Anthems). a. Frederic Mullen. Published by E. Ascherberg and Company, No. 46 Berners Street, W., London, England. 1905. [10 1/4" × 14 1/4"]. B/w photos of "President Roosevelt," "M. White," and "Baron Komura." Gy/pk/w drawing of angel. 8pp. Page 2: Blank. Page 8: Advertising.

TR-355 Our Roosevelt. w.m. Caroline Prentice Kelly. Published by The H. Kirkus Dugdale Company, Inc., 14th and You Streets, Washington, DC. 1912. Gd/w non-pictorial geometric designs. 6pp. Page 6: Advertising.

TR-356 Roosevelt Campaign

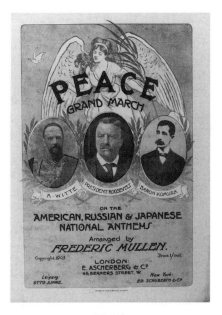

TR-354

Songster 1904 (For Male Voices). c. Logan S. Porter. Published by The Home

TR-356

Music Company, Logansport, IN. 1904. [6" × 9"]. Be/bk photos of Theodore Roosevelt and Charles Fairbanks. Be/bk drawing of a star, geometric designs. "Single Copy 15 cts — $1.60 per Dozen." 36pp. [M-391].

TR-357 The Gallant 71st (A March). m. F. Fanciulli. Published as a "Musical Supplement of *The N.Y. Journal and Advertiser*, July 17, 1898." B/w litho of U.S. soldiers — "The Charge of Company F at San Juan, July 1, 1898." R/w/b litho of shield, geometric designs. "Composed expressly for The Journal by F. Fanciulli, Bandmaster, 71st Regiment Band." 4pp.

TR-358 Would You Rather Be A Tammany Tiger Or A Teddy Bear? w. Jeff T. Branen (Author of *Somebody Lied, You're An Indian, &c*). m. W.R. Williams (Author of *Napanee, When The Moon Plays Peek-A-Boo, &c*). Published by Will Rossiter, No. 152 Lake Street, Chicago, IL. 1908. O/bl/bk/w drawing by Starmer of a tiger and a Teddy bear. "It's Up To You." 6pp. Pages 2 and 6: Blank.

TR-359 Schildkret's Hungarian Waltzes. m. S. Schildkret. Published by S. Schildkret, No. 15 Patomac [sic] Avenue, Chicago, IL. 1907. B/w photo of S. Schildkret. Bl/w cover. 8pp. Page 2: "Respectfully Dedicated to Miss Alice Roosevelt." Page 8: Advertising.

TR-360 My Bandana Rag. w. W.B. Campbell. m. M. Brand. Published by Hot Foot Campbell, Gasden, AL. Copyright 1912 by W.B. Campbell. B/w photos of Theodore Roosevelt and Charles Fairbanks. R/w bandana background of geometric designs. 6pp.

TR-361 Gavotte Debut. m. Prof. R. Neumann, Op. 42. Published by Nau and Schmidt Music Company, No. 309 Grand Avenue, Milwaukee, WI. 1902. Gr/w photo of The White House. Gn/w drawing of floral and geometric designs. "Respectfully Dedicated to Miss Alice Roosevelt, Washington, DC." 6pp.

TR-362 Theodore Roosevelt.

(TR) THEODORE ROOSEVELT   504

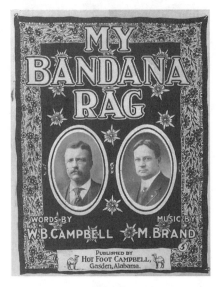

TR-360

w.m. Sidney Rowe. m. Gladys Pitcher. Drawing of airplane. In: *Our Land of Song*, page 99. Published by C.L. Birchard and Company, Boston, MA. 1947. [6 7/8" × 8 11/16"].

TR-363 Golden Rod [V-1: Intermezzo Americana] [V-2: Song]. w.m. Mabel McKinley (Composer of *Anona*, *Karama* and *Feather Queen*). Published by Leo Fiest, New York, NY. 1907. Bk/w/gd/br drawing of woman with golden rods. 6pp. Page 2: "Respectfully Dedicated to Honorable Charles W. Fairbanks, Vice-President of the United States." Page 6: Advertising.

TR-364 Our Ted. w.m. Daniel Simmons. Published by F.B. Haviland Publishing Company, Broadway and 37th Street, New York, NY., as a "Supplement to *The New York Tribune*." 1910. R/w/gn floral drawings. R/w photo of "Inga Orner." 6pp.

TR-365 Pass The Prosperity Around [Song Sheet]. [Published in Colorado]. [1912]. [5 3/8" × 7 9/16"]. Non-pictorial. "Vote for Roosevelt, Johnson and Costigan — They will pass prosperity around." 4pp. [Edward P. Costigan, Candidate for Governor].

TR-366 Songs The Soldiers Sang [Song Book]. Published by Howley, Haviland & Company, Nos. 1260-1266 Broadway, New York, NY. [ca. 1898]. [9" × 11 1/2"]. B/w photos of General "Miles," Admiral "Shafter," Theodore "Roosevelt," and General "Wheeler." R/w/bl/br geometric designs. 36pp.

TR-367 Give Us Teddy (Song & Chorus). w. Will P. Snyder. m. George P. Breigel. Published by Will P. Snyder, Ashland, PA. 1916. B/w non-pictorial geometric design. "Theodore Roosevelt, 'The Spirit of America Incarnate.'" "At his word multitudes will follow wherever he may lead. Fathers and mothers hold him up to their sons as a model of probity, of moral courage and civic achievements; he is their living exemplar of clean manhood, righteous citizenship and devoted public service." 4pp. Page 4: Blank.

TR-368 Where The Healthy Breezes Blow [Theodore Roosevelt song].

TR-369 Up-To-Date Progressive Party Campaign Songs. e. J. Burgess Brown. Published by J. Burgess Brown,

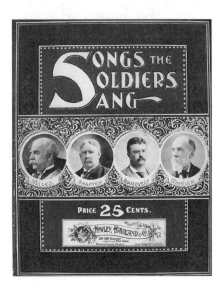

TR-366

Indianapolis, IN. 1912. Be/bk litho of Theodore Roosevelt and Hiram Johnson. "Written And Compiled For The State Progressive Committee by J. Burgess Brown, Leader of the Celebrated Bald-Headed Glee Club." 20pp. [M-402].

TR-370 Hooligan's Twins (Bill And Teddy). w.m. Florence Heath Mitchell. Published by Florence Heath Mitchell, Connersville, IN. 1912.

TR-371 Roosevelt's Grand March. m. D.W. Crist. In: *Banner Melodies*, page 28. Published by D.W. Crist, Moultrie, OH. [ca. 1905].

TR-372 Teddy (Song). m. R.N. Lombard. Published by New York & Chicago Music Publishing House, Suite 612, No. 59 Dearborn Street, Chicago, IL. [1910].

TR-373 A Toast To Roosevelt (Republican Campaign Song). w. Jules Jordan. Copyright October 4, 1904 by Jules Jordan. [5 1/4" × 9 1/4"]. Non-pictorial. "Keep This! This will be sung tonight by Will M. Trafton. Join in the chorus." "Words and Music for sale after this meeting and at all stores. Price 10 cents." 2pp. Page 2: Blank.

TR-374 Marche De Triumphe (Roosevelt March). m. C. Sealsfield Berger. Published by Jas. F. Thompson, No. 403 Scott Street, Covington, KY. Copyright 1902 by Jos. Zeinz. N/c litho of eagle with shield and flags, Capitol building, ships, flowers, geometric designs. "Respectfully dedicated to and accepted by his Excellency Theodore Ro9osevelt, President U.S.A." 6pp. Page 2: Blank. Page 6: Printer's logo.

TR-375 The Heavenly Flag (March And Two Step). m. Sig. Giuseppe Marone. Published by Signor Guiseppe Marone, No. 521 East 12th Street, Indianapolis, IN. 1903. B/w litho of allegorical patriotic scene — "Description: Central group in heaven. The Infant Jesus waving the American Flag, sitting on His Mother's lap, the Holy Father is Crowning Her, and the angels are singing and playing about and holding the table of commandments. On the left is the emancipation of Abraham Lincoln and his cabinet, on the right are angels turning the old world to the new. The U.S. Capitol, the Navy and War Building; on the Avenue are the U.S. Military marching and the Marine Brigade with [Theodore] Roosevelt at the head, his private secretary, the Colonel of the National Park, General F. Lee, and different officers from Illinois, Senator Platt with the silk hat on, Rear Admiral Dewey near Governor Morton's Monument, and the fine monument to Christopher Columbus, showing to the Powers thee greatness of this country. In the river stand a majestic angel with the flower of everlasting peace on the left hand, on the right hand the beautiful American flag sent from heaven to be given to Uncle Sam, Miss Indiana on his right, the favorite state. To help receive the present; the young American boy is ready to defend the matchless flag. The powers of the world with their guns turning towards U.S. are looking with great surprise at the gift. The Author has composed this march to describe in music his painting. The introduction being played by trumpets in heaven, first part is the marching of the soldiers, the trio is the conversation between the angel with Uncle Sam and Miss Indiana." "The painting and music is original, ideal by the noted harpist, Sig. Guiseppe Marone, an American citizen, Indianapolis, Ind." 6pp. Pages 2 and 6: Blank.

TR-376 The White House Waltzes. m. Alice Cary Heiser. Published by The Thompson Music Co., Chicago, IL. 1903. "Respectfully Dedicated to Miss Alice Roosevelt, Washington, D.C. Gn/w/bk litho of White House, geometric designs. Advertisements for Thompson Music Co. stock."

TR-377 The Nation's Bride (Song). w.m. Mary A. O'Connor. Published by B.T. Igo. Bl/w photo by Pach Bros. of Alice Roosevelt Longworth. B/w geometric design frame. 6pp. Page 6: Blank.

TR-378 The American Soldier (March, Song and Chorus). w.m. Richard C. Dillmore. Published by Richard C. Dillmore, Philadelphia, PA. 1904. B/w litho of Theodore Roosevelt on horseback. B/w photo of Richard C. Dillmore inscribed "Sung with great success by Richard C. Dillmore." "There is no honor in the gift of the people too great for the American Soldier." Printed chorus. Back cover: Advertisement for Richard Dillmore's popular songs.

TR-379 God Save Our President (A New National Hymn). w. Josephine C. Goodale. m. J.H. Peterman. Published as a textile. Copyright 1902 by J.H. Peterman. [12 3/8" × 9 1/4"]. Obv: Bl/w eagle, crossed flags, star border. Bl/w photo of "President Theodore Roosevelt." "Sung with great success by the N.Y. State Teacher's Association in Convention at Saratoga, July, 23d, 1901, under personal direction of the Composer." Rev: Blank.

TR-380 Everybody Sing Please [Song Booklet]. Published by the Massachusetts State Committee Progressive Party, No. 70 Devonshire Street, [Boston, MA]. [1912]. [6" × 9 1/16"]. B/w photos of "Progressive Party Standard Bearers — Theodore Roosevelt for President, Hiram Johnson for Vice President, Charles Sumner Bird of Walpole for Governor, Daniel Cosgrove of Lowell for Lieut. Governor." "The power is the people's and only the people's — Roosevelt." "Patriotism and prayers should march hand in hand — Lincoln." 4pp.

TR-381 President Roosevelt's Triumphal March. In: *Marches Of The Presidents, 1789-1909, Authentic Marches & Campaign Songs*, page 4. a. Carl Miller. Published by Chappell & Co., Inc., No. 609 Fifth Avenue, New York, NY. "By arrangement with Chilmark Press, Inc." 1968. [9" × 12"]. R/w/b litho of eagle, flag. "An Illustrated Piano Folio For All Ages." 72pp.

TR-382 He Sure Is Surging On. w. Joseph McLean (Author of *Towser, Duleys Band, All Hands Round, &c*). m. "Tune: *The Battle Hymn Of The Republic*." [1912]. [3 1/2" × 6 7/8"]. Published by Joseph McLean, No. 7 Church Street, South Manchester, CT. Copyright 1912 by Joseph McLean. Br/be litho of moose. "Bull Moose Progressive Campaign Song." 8pp. Foldout.

TR-383 Roosevelt Waltzes. m. Augusta Tobias. Published by L. Grunewald Co., New Orleans, LA. 1906. Bl/w non-pictorial. "Respectfully dedicated to Miss Alice Roosevelt." 6pp. Page 6: Blank.

See also GW-238; GW-528; TJ-34; TJ-49; JQA-10; AJK-42; AL-206; AL-247; AL-346; WM-3; WM-4; WM-5; WM-76; WM-79; WM-84; WM-85; WM-93; WM-95; WM-107; WM-119; WM-122; WM-138; WM-146; WM-173; WM-191; WM-214; WM-216; WM-221; WM-231; WM-238; WM-244; WM-253; WM-324; WM-329; AP-3; AP-5; WHT-6; WHT-12; WHT-23; WHT-27; WHT-36; CEH-7; CEH-8; WW-19; WW-31; WW-35; WW-66; WW-106; WW-155; WW-209; WGH-11; WGH-27; WGH-34; CC-14; CC-53; CC-59; HCH-57; FDR-158; FDR-270; FDR-367; FDR-390; HST-22; DDE-1; DDE-9; DDE-50; DDE-52; JFK-15; JFK-61; LBJ-1; MISC-46; MISC-77; MISC-78; MISC-79; MISC-97; MISC-101; MISC-110; MISC-146; MISC-167.

ULYSSES S. GRANT

USG-1 The Grant And Colfax Campaign March. m. G.W. Lovejoy. Published by Lyon & Healy, Clark and Washington Streets, Chicago, IL. 1868. B/w litho by Chicago Litho Company of Ulysses S. Grant and Shuyler Colfax, eagle, flags, shield, wreath. 8pp. Pages 2 and 8: Blank.

UGS-2 For Grant & Colfax We Will Vote (Song and Chorus). w. Olyn-

ULYSSES S. GRANT (**USG**)

USG-2

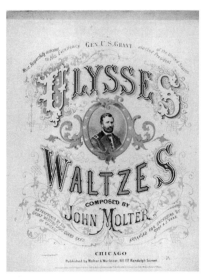

USG-4

thus. m. William Seibert. Published by Lyon & Healy, corner Clark and Washington Streets, Chicago, IL. 1868. B/w litho by The Chicago Litho Company of Ulysses S. Grant and Shuyler Colfax, eagle, flags, shield. 6pp.

USG-3 Grant & Colfax, Our Nation's Choice. w. Paulina. m. William Seibert. Published by Lyon & Healy, corner Clark and Washington Streets, Chicago, IL. 1868. B/w litho by The Chicago Litho Company of Ulysses S. Grant and Shuyler Colfax, eagle, flags. 6pp. Pages 2 and 6: Blank.

USG-4 Ulysses Waltzes. m. John Molter. Published by Molter & Wurlitzer, No. 117 Randolph Street, Chicago, IL. 1868. Bl/w/gd geometric designs. B/w litho by The Chicago Litho Company of Ulysses S. Grant. "As Performed by the Great Western Light Guard Band of Chicago." "Most Respectfully dedicated to His Excellency Gen. U.S. Grant, Elected President of the United States." "For Orchestra by Prof. A.J. Vaas." 12pp.

USG-5 Grant, Our Great Commander (Song and Chorus). w. Maj. J. Barton. m. Bernard Covert (Author of *Dreamland Of My Father, Bright Eyed Little Widdow or There's Danger in her Eye, Sword Of Bunker Hill*, and 100 other popular songs). Published by W.W. Whitney, Palace of Music, No. 173 Summit Street, Toledo, OH. 1868. B/w litho of Ulysses S. Grant, vignettes of Grant's life — "Donelson," "Vicksburg," "Lee's Surrender," "White House in Wash'n." "Adopted by over 100 Grant Organizations." "This Great Campaign Song is Dedicated to the Grand Army of the Republic." "25th Edition." 6pp.

USG-6 Grant & Colfax Grand March. Published by John Church, Jr., No. 66 West 4th Street, Cincinnati, OH. 1868. B/w tan tinted litho [horizontal format] by Bising & Ge of Ulysses S. Grant and Shuyler Colfax, eagle with ribbon inscribed "E Pluribus Unum," flag, wreath. 6pp. Pages 2 and 6: Blank.

USG-7 Lieutenant General Grant's Grand March. m. F.A. Eileman. Published by John Church, Jr., No. 66 West Fourth Street, Cincinnati, OH. 1864. B/w beige tinted litho by Ehrgott, Forbriger & Co. of Ulysses S. Grant. 6pp. Page 3: "Most Respectfully Dedicated to the Hero of Vicksburg."

(USG) ULYSSES S. GRANT

USG-6

USG-8 Grant Is The Man (Campaign Song for 1872). w.m. Harry Birch. Published by White, Smith & Perry, Nos. 294, 300 Washington Street, Boston, MA. 1872. B/w litho of Ulysses S. Grant. 6pp. Pages 2 and 6: Blank.

USG-9(A) We've A Man For Our Leader (A Grant Song) (Song and Chorus). w. Sidney Herbert. m. "Adapted to Hays' Popular Song *Norah O'Neal*." Published by J.L. Peters, New York, NY. 1872. Litho of Ulysses S. Grant. "To the friends of President Grant." 6pp. Pages 2 and 6: Blank. Page 3: "Dedicated to the Grand Army of the Republic."

(B) Grant's Campaign March. m. E. Mack.

(C) Grant's Galop (To the White House). m. William Dressler.

(D) President Grant's Grand March. m. Charles Young (G.R. Herbert).

(E) We've Tested Him In Days Gone By (Song and Chorus). w. Charles B. Harger. m. T. Martin Towne. 6pp. Pages 2 and 6: Blank. Page 3: "To Hon. C.B. Garwell."

(F) The Man Who Saved The Nation (Campaign Song and Chorus). w.m. George Cooper. Page 6: Advertising.

USG-10 President Grant's March. m. P.S. Gilmore. Published by Oliver Ditson & Company, No. 277 Washington Street, Boston, MA. 1869. B/w litho of Ulysses S. Grant. "As performed by Gilmore's Band." "Let us have peace." 8pp. Pages 2 and 8: Blank.

USG-11 Grant's Welcome (March). m. Leon Levoy. Published by John Church, Jr., No. 66 West 4th Street, Cincinnati, OH. 1879. B/w litho of Ulysses S. Grant, geometric designs. 6pp. Pages 2 and 6: Blank.

USG-12 General Grant's Grand March. m. E. Mack. Published by Lee & Walker, No. 722 Chestnut Street, Philadelphia, PA. [186-]. B/w green tinted litho of Ulysses Grant. "Respectfully Dedicated to Major General U.S. Grant." 6pp. Page 2: Blank. Page 6: Advertising.

USG-13 Hurrah! Hurrah For Gen'l. Grant (Campaign Song). w. J.K. Turner. m. "Clareton." Published by W.R. Smith, No. 135 North Eighth Street, Philadelphia, PA. 1868. Non-pictorial geometric designs. "To Union Men." 6pp. Pages 2 and 6: Blank.

USG-14 Gen. Grant's Welcome March. m. J.H. Delaney. Published by Lee & Walker, No. 1113 Chestnut Street, Philadelphia, PA. 1879. Non-pictorial geometric design border. "The good opinion of my Countrymen is dearer to me than the praise of all the world beside — U.S. Grant." 6pp. Page 2: Blank.

USG-15 Inflation Galop! m. W. Stuckenholz. Published by Wm. A. Pond & Company, No. 547 Broadway, New York, NY. 1874. B/w litho [horizontal format] from a cartoon by W.H. Sheldon of Ulysses S. Grant, Ben Butler and other politicians blowing up large balloon labeled "Inflation," "$400,000,000" and "$44,000,000 Legalized." 6pp.

USG-16(A) General Grant's Grand March. m. E. Mack. Published by Lee & Walker, No. 922 Chestnut Street, Philadelphia, PA. 1862. B/w tinted litho of Ulysses S. Grant. 6pp. Page 2: Blank. Page 6: Advertising.

(B) General Grant's Polka. m[?]. Ella V. Young.

ULYSSES S. GRANT (USG)

(C) General Grant's Quickstep. m. E. Mack.

(D) General Grant's Grand March (Four Hands). m. E. Mack.

(E) General Grant's Grand March (Guitar). m. Mack. a. G.W. Brown.

(F) General Grant's Grand March (Violin/Flute). m. Sep. Winner.

USG-17 The President's March. m. Federico Gennari, Op. 44. Published by John F. Ellis, No. 306 Pennsylvania Avenue, Washington, DC. 1869. B/w tan tinted litho by M.H. Traubel of Ulysses S. Grant. "Composed and Dedicated to General U.S. Grant." 6pp. Pages 2 and 6: Blank.

USG-18(A) General Grant's Grand March. m. E. Mack. Published by [V-1 and V-2: Oliver Ditson Company] [V-3: Oliver Ditson Company, No. 449 and 451 Washington Street] [V-4: Oliver Ditson & Co., 451 Washington Street], Boston, MA. [V-1: Copyright 1881 by Oliver Ditson Company] [V-2 and V-3: Copyright 1890 by Mrs. E. Mack] [V-4: ca. 1875?]. B/w litho of Ulysses S. Grant. 6pp. Page 2: Blank. Page 6: Advertising for other songs.

(B) General Grant's Polka. m[?]. Ella V. Young.

(C) General Grant's Quickstep. m. E. Mack. 6pp. Page 6: Advertising.

(D) General Grant's Return Home March.

(E) General Grant's Grand March (Four Hands). m. E. Mack.

(F) General Grant's Grand March (Guitar). m. E. Mack. a. G.W. Brown.

(G) General Grant's Grand March (Violin/Flute). a. Sep. Winner.

(H) General Grant's Grand March. m. J. Gung'l.

USG-19 We'll Vote For Grant Again. w. Capt. Jas. F. Keegan. m. Arthur Percy. Published by C.H. Ditson & Company, No. 711 Broadway, New York, NY. 1872. B/w litho by J.H. Bufford's Litho. of Ulysses S. Grant, flags. List of 17 Grant's battles. "Let Us Have Peace." "Dedicated to the Armies of the Union." 6pp. Pages 2 and 6: Blank.

USG-20 Lieut. Genl. U.S. Grant's Grant March. m. Josef Gung'l, Op. 145. Published by Oliver Ditson & Company, No. 277 Washington Street, Boston, MA. [1862?]. B/w litho by J.H. Bufford's Litho. of Ulysses S. Grant. 6pp. Pages 2 and 6: Blank.

USG-21(A) Grant, A Nation's Hero (Song and Chorus). w.m. William T. Rogers. Published by S. Brainard & Sons, No. 203 Superior Street, Cleveland, OH. 1868. B/w sepia tinted litho by Ehrgott, Forbriger & Co. of Ulysses S. Grant, facsimile signature, floral and geometric design frame. "Respectfully dedicated to the Grand Army of the Republic." 6pp. Pages 2 and 6: Blank.

(B) The Soldier's Chief, The Nation's Chief (Song and Chorus). w. R. Woodhams. m. Wm. T. Rogers.

USG-22 General Grant's Quick Step. m. E. Mack. Published by Lee & Walker, No. 722 Chestnut Street, Philadelphia, PA. 1868. B/w tinted beige litho by T. Sinclair's Litho. of Ulysses S. Grant. "Respectfully Dedicated to General U.S. Grant." 6pp. Page 2: Blank. Page 6: Advertising.

USG-23 Gen. Grant's Funeral March. m. F. Alexander. Published by M.D. Swisher, No. 115 South 10th Street, Philadelphia, PA. Copyright 1885 by B.F. Banes & Company. B/w litho of Ulysses S. Grant, wreath, flags. 6pp. Pages 2 and 6: Blank.

USG-24 General Grant's Funeral March. m. G. Lang. Published by Thomas P.I. Magoun, Bath, ME. Copyright 1885 by W.F. Shaw. B/w litho by Crosscup & West of Ulysses S. Grant, black border. 6pp. Page 2: Blank. Page 6: Advertising.

USG-25(A) General U.S. Grant's Funeral March. m. H. Mullenhaupt. Published by Oliver Ditson & Company, No. 451 Washington Street, Boston, MA.

1885. B/w litho by J.H. Bufford's Sons of Ulysses S. Grant, black border. 6pp. Pages 2 and 6: Blank. Page 3 title: **Ulysses S. Grant Marche Funebre.**

(B) **General U.S. Grant's Funeral March**. m. S.G. Pratt. 6pp. Pages 2 and 6: Blank. Page 3: "To the Memory of Ulysses S. Grant. The Hero, the Statesman, the Citizen."

(C) **General U.S. Grant's Funeral March**. m. Rud. Kramer.

USG-26 Grant-Ed (Campaign Song). w. Mrs. M.A. Kidder. m. Mrs. Duer (Formerly Mrs. E.A. Parkhurst) (Author of *Rally Boys, Sign The Pledge For Mother's Sake, Peace Jubilee, &c., &c.*). Published by William A. Pond & Company, Nos. 547 and 865 Broadway, New York, NY. 1868. B/w litho of Ulysses S. Grant, floral and geometric design border. "With compliments of the Publishers. Please notice and send us a copy of paper. Editors and Publishers of newspapers furnished at $15 per Hundred. Price single copy 15 cts." 6pp. Page 2: Blank. Page 6: Advertising.

USG-27 Lieut. Genl. U.S. Grant's Grand March. m. Josef Gung'l, Op. 145. Published by Oliver Ditson & Company, No. 277 Washington Street, Boston, MA. [1862?]. B/w beige tinted oval litho by Bufford's Litho. of Ulysses S. Grant. 6pp. Pages 2 and 6: Blank.

USG-28 U.S.G. (National Walk Around) (A Song for the Times). w.m. Dan D. Emmett (Author of *Dixie's Land, High Daddy, &c., &c.*). Published by Wm. A. Pond & Company, No. 547 Broadway, New York, NY. 1864. B/w litho of Ulysses S. Grant, eagle, Capitol, flags, geometric designs, "Constitution." "First produced at Bryant's Minstrels, New York, and sung by the whole nation." 6pp. Page 6: Advertising.

USG-29 Grant & Colfax (Song and Chorus). w. K.M. Sherwood. m. George Bowman. Published by S. Brainard & Sons Company, No. 203 Superior Street, Cleveland, OH. 1868. B/w litho of Grant & Colfax, geometric design border. 6pp. Page 2: Blank. Page 6: Advertising.

USG-30(A) Grant's Galop To The White House. m. William Dressler. Published by J.L. Peters, No. 198 Broadway, New York, NY. 1866 and 1868. B/w litho Ulysses S. Grant. "To the Grand Army of the Republic." 6pp.

(B) **We've A Man For Our Leader** (A Grant Song). w. Sidney Herbert. m. "Arranged to Hays' Popular Song *Nora O'Neal*." 6pp. Pages 2 and 6: Blank.

(C) **The Man Who Saved The Nation** (Campaign Song and Chorus). w.m. Geo. Cooper. 6pp. Page 2: Blank. Page 6: Advertising.

(D) **Grant's Campaign March**. m. E. Mack.

USG-31 Gen. Grant's Recovery March. m. Louis Meyer. Published by F.A. North & Company, No. 1308 Chestnut Street, Philadelphia, PA. [1885]. B/w litho by T. Hunter of Ulysses S. Grant. "Composed in commemoration of the Nation's joy at his recovery." 6pp. Pages 2 and 6: Blank.

USG-32 The Grant Songster. Published by Haney & Company, Publishers, No. 119 Nassau Street, New York, NY. 1867. [4 1/4" × 6 3/8"]. Gd/bk litho of "Ulysses S. Grant" smoking a cigar. "American News Company General Agent." 64pp. [M-157].

USG-33 Gone! Brave One, Gone! w.m. Walter A. Perry (Author of *Oh, Where Have The Old Folks Gone?* and *By-Gone Days Recalled*). Published by Perry & Noble, New Bedford, MA. 1885. B/w litho of Ulysses S. Grant, facsimile signature, Union soldier. "A Memorial Tribute to General U.S. Grant." 6pp. Pages 2 and 6: Blank.

USG-34 The American Volunteer's Triumphal March. m. Dr. Edward Clapham (Surgeon 7th Mich. V. Inf., Late of the Army of the Potomac & Tennessee) (Author of *Oh, Where Have The Old Folks Gone?* and *By-Gone Days*

Recalled). Published by H.M. Higgins, No. 117 Randolph Street, Chicago, IL. 1866. B/w sepia tinted litho by Western Engraving Co. of Ulysses S. "Grant," Abraham "Lincoln," eagle with ribbon inscribed "Honor Be To Our Volunteers," flags, columns labeled — "Armies of the Potomac & Cumberland" and "Generals — Sheridan, Sherman, Warren, Griffin, Barlow, Pearson, Mead, Logan, Morrow," battle vignettes. Lists of commands and generals. "Respectfully dedicated to his Friend Gen. H.A. Morrow and his Staff." 6pp. Page 2 title: **The American Volunteer's Grand Triumphal**. Page 6: Blank.

USG-35 The Grant Campaign Song. w.m. William S. Irwin. a. Theo. To Crane. Published by J.L. Carncross & Company, No. 6 North Eighth Street, Philadelphia, PA. [1868?]. Non-pictorial. "Arranged for Piano." "Will be Sung by chorus under the direction of Prof. Theo. T. Crane, before the National Republican Convention at The Academy of Music." 2pp. Page 2: Blank.

USG-36 Maj. Gen. U.S. Grant's Grand March. m. Josef Gung'l, Op. 145. Published by Oliver Ditson & Company, No. 277 Washington Street, Boston, MA. 1863. B/w [V-1: Beige tinted] [V-2: Untinted] litho by J.H. Bufford's Litho. of Ulysses S. Grant on horseback, troops. 6pp. Pages 2 and 6: Blank.

USG-37 Nellie Grant's Wedding March. m. E. Mack. Published by Lee & Walker, No. 922 Chestnut Street, Philadelphia, PA. 1874. B/w litho by Thomas Sinclair & Son of Miss Nellie Grant. 6pp. Page 2: Blank. Page 6: Advertising.

USG-38 Grant Is Gone (A Quartet for Mixed Voices). w.m. Charles McK. Trimmer, Op. 8. Published by White, Smith & Company, Boston, MA. 1886. B/w litho of Ulysses S. Grant, vignettes of Grant's life — "Petersburg, April 3, 1865," "Shiloh Charge of Gen. Grant, April 7, 1862," "Vicksburg," "The Wilderness," "The Battle Above the Clouds," "Appomattox," "Gettysburg." "Written for and sung at the Memorial Services of the Late Lamented Gen. Ulysses S. Grant, August 8th AD, 1885." "Respectfully dedicated to Mrs. Gen. U.S. Grant and family in Memoriam of America's Greatest Soldier." 12pp. Page 2: Blank. Page 12: B/w litho of Ulysses S. Grant. Advertising.

USG-39 All Hail To Ulysses! w. Charles Haynes. m. J.E. Haynes. Published by Root & Cady, No. 95 Clark Street, Chicago, IL. 1864. B/w litho by Ed. Mendel of "Lieut. Genl. U.S. Grant," wreath, eagle, angel, flag. "Our Union Camp Song." "Respectfully Dedicated to the Army of the Union." 6pp. Pages 2 and 6: Blank.

USG-40 Grant Has Passed Away (Song with Chorus ad. lib). w. B.F. Gardner. m. Henry Werner. Published by Balmer & Weber, St. Louis, MO. 1885. B/w litho of Ulysses S. Grant, black border. "A Tribute to the Memory of the Noble Hero, U.S. Grant." 6pp. Page 2: Title: **Our Grant Has Passed Away**. Page 6: Advertising.

USG-41 Gen. Grant's Funeral March. m. A.H. Rosewig. Published by Lee & Walker, No. 1113 Chestnut Street, Philadelphia, PA. 1885. B/w litho by Crosscup and West of Ulysses S. Grant, black border. 8pp. Pages 2 and 7: Blank.

USG-42 General Grant's Funeral March. m. Alberto Himan. Published by R.A. Saalfield, No. 12 Bible House, New York, NY. 1885. B/w litho of Ulysses S. Grant, black border. "The Nation Mourns its Loss." 6pp. Pages 2 and 6: Blank.

USG-43 War Songs [Song Book]. Published by The Oliver Ditson Company, Nos. 453-463 Washington Street, Boston, MA. 1890. R/w/bl/y drawings of flag, G.A.R. medal. Bk/w/y photos of litho of Ulysses S. Grant, two generals. "The Choruses of all Songs are Arranged for Male Voices." "For Anniversaries and

Gatherings of Soldiers." "Dedicated to the G.A.R." 100pp.

USG-44 War Songs [Song Book]. Published by The Oliver Ditson Company, Boston, MA. 1906. [6 3/4" × 10 3/16"]. N/c photos of Ulysses S. Grant, two other generals, flags. "For Anniversaries and Gatherings of Soldiers. The Choruses of all Songs are Arranged for Mixed Voices." "Dedicated to the G.A.R." 140pp. Page 140: Advertising.

USG-45 War Songs [Song Book]. Published by The Oliver Ditson Company, Nos. 453-463 Washington Street, Boston, MA. 1890. B/w photo of Ulysses S. Grant, two other generals. B/w drawing of flag, G.A.R. medal. "The choruses of all songs are Arranged for Male Voices." "For Anniversaries and Gatherings of Soldiers." "Dedicated to the G.A.R." 100pp. Pages 2, 99 and 100: Advertising.

USG-46 General Grant's The Man (A Song and Chorus for the Times). w. George Cooper. m. Henry Tucker (Author of *Dear Mother, I've Come Have To Die, Willow Springs, Memory Bells, &c, &c).* Published by William A. Pond & Company, No. 547 Broadway, New York, NY. 1868. B/w non-pictorial geometric design border. 6pp. Page 2: Blank. Page 6: Advertising for other William A. Pond & Company songs.

USG-47 Grant's March To The White House. m. P.C. Prime. Published by D.S. Holmes, No. 67 Fourth Street, Brooklyn, NY. 1868. B/w litho of the White House, geometric designs. 6pp. Page 6: Blank.

USG-48 Grant At The Head Of The Nation (Song and Chorus). w.m. W.O. Fiske. Published by Oliver Ditson & Company, No. 277 Washington Street, Boston, MA. 1868. Non-pictorial geometric designs. 6pp. Pages 2 and 6: Blank.

USG-49 Gen. U.S. Grant's Grand Reception March. m. S.G. Wilson. Published by S. Brainard's Sons, Cleveland, OH. 1879. B/w litho by W.J. Morgan & Company of Ulysses S. Grant. Quote—"The Good opinion of my countrymen is dearer to me than the praise of all the world besides—U.S. Grant." 6pp. Pages 2 and 6: Blank.

USG-50 Gen. Grant's March. m. Richard Zellner. Published by S. Brainard's Sons Company, New York, NY. Copyright 1862 by Root & Cady. [Undated reprint ca. 1885]. B/w drawing of Fort Donelson battle scene. "Dedicated to the Brave Men who captured Fort Donelson." 6pp. Pages 2 and 6: Blank.

USG-51 Our Old Commander's Gone (Song and Chorus). w. H.G. Wheeler. m. J.W. Wheeler. Published by Oliver Ditson & Company, Boston, MA. 1885. B/w leaves, black line border. "In Memory of Gen. Ulysses S. Grant." 6pp. Page 6: Advertising for other Oliver Ditson & Company songs.

USG-52 U.S. Grant Is The Man. w. J.C.J. m. "Written and Adapted to a Favorite Melody." Published by O. Ditson & Company, No. 277 Washington Street, Boston, MA. 1868. B/w geometric and floral design border. 6pp. Pages 2 and 6: Advertising for other O. Ditson & Company songs.

USG-53 Rally! (A Campaign Song). w. C.C. Haskins. m. W.B. Richardson. Published by John Church & Company, No. 66 West 4th Street, Cincinnati, OH. 1868. Non-pictorial star and stripe title design. "To the Friends of Grant & Wilson." 6pp. Pages 2 and 6: Blank.

USG-54 Grant & Colfax Grand March. Published by I.V. Flager, No. 7 State Street, Auburn, NY. 1868. Non-pictorial geometric designs. 6pp. Page 6: Blank.

USG-55 Grant Our Great Commander! (Song and Chorus). w.m. Bernard Covert (Author of *Dear Land of my Father*, and over 100 other songs). Published by W.W. Whitney, Palace of

Music, No. 173 Summit Street, Toledo, OH. 1868. B/w geometric border design. "This Great Campaign Song is Respectfully Dedicated to the Grand Army of the Republic." 6pp. Page 2: Blank. Page 6: Advertising for other W.W. Whitney music.

USG-56 Presidential Race For 1868 (Campaign Song To the Grant Boys In Blue). w. H.H. Wheeler. m. "Air: *We Won't Go Home Till Morning.*" [1868]. [4 7/8" × 9 7/8"]. Non-pictorial broadside. "Price 10 cents." 2pp. Page 2: Blank.

USG-57 Brave Ulysses Is The Man! (Grant Campaign Song and Chorus). w. Charles Haynes. m. J.E. Haynes. Published by J.A. Butterfield, Drawer 6, 184, Chicago, IL. 1868. B/w geometric design border. "To the Grant Clubs of the United States." 6pp. Page 2: Advertising for other J.A. Butterfield music. Page 6: Blank.

USG-58 Ulysses, Tried And True (Campaign Song and Chorus). w. Thomas F. Winthrop. m. James R. Murray. Published by S. Brainard's Sons, Cleveland, OH. 1872. B/w geometric and floral design border. 6pp. Page 2: Blank. Page 6: Advertising for other S. Brainard's Sons publications.

USG-59 Reception Schottische. m. E.M. Grant. Published by C.M. Tremaine, No. 481 Broadway, New York, NY. 1867. Non-pictorial geometric designs [horizontal format]. "Dedicated to Genl. U.S. Grant." 6pp. Page 6: Blank.

USG-60 Mammoth Ox (Grand March). m. D. Frank Tully. Published by Wm. A. Pond & Company, No. 547 and 865 Broadway, New York, NY. Copyright 1863 by H. Millard. Bl/bk/w/gd litho by Clayton of a large ox. "Sanitary Fair, Boston, Nov., 1864; Sanitary Fair, New York, May, 1864; Sanitary Fair, Chicago, May, 1865; Sanitary Fair, Philadelphia, Nov., 1865." "To Genl. U.S. Grant, President Elect." "Performed at the Central Park Garden during the Exhibition of the Mammoth White Ox — 'Gen: Grant' — of Sanitary Fair Celebrity." 8pp. Page 2: Blank.

USG-61 General Grant's Boys. w. James D. Gay. m. "Air: *Old Virginia Low Lands, Low.*" Published by Charles Magnus, No. 12 Frankfort Street, New York, NY. Copyright 1864 by James D. Gay. [5" × 8"]. Hand Colored litho of Richmond, Virginia skyline. "Respectfully Dedicated to the Army of the Potomac by James D. Gay, 300 North 20th Street, Philadelphia, Pa. All of Gay's Army Songs sent by mail." 2pp. Page 2: Blank.

USG-62 A Grant Song. w. Eugene Batchelder. m. W.H.S. Published by C.H. Ditson & Company, No. 277 Broadway, New York, NY. [ca. 1868]. Non-pictorial geometric designs. 6pp. Pages 2 and 6: Blank.

USG-63 The Grant & Colfax Republican Songster. Published by R.M. Dewitt, Publisher, No. 13 Frankfort Street, New York, NY. 1868. [4" × 6 3/16"]. R/w/b litho of flag. Advertising. 100pp. Pages 2, 99 and 100: Advertising for other publications. Page 3: Title page. "Containing Campaign Songs, Ballads and Choruses. Adapted to the Most Popular and Stirring Tunes. This work also contains the Great Original Song of *General Boum of the C.S.A.*" Adapted to the Immensely Popular Air of *Captain Jenks, of the Horse Marines*, and the Already much played Tanners Chorus, especially arranged for this book — to the Famous tune of *Tippecanoe and Tyler Too!*" Page 4: Index. [M-150].

USG-64(A) Milwaukee Light Guard Quickstep. m. H.N. Hempsted. Published by H.N. Hempstead, No. 410 Main Street, Milwaukee, WI. 1866. B/w tinted litho by Seifert & Lawton of Ulysses S. Grant, Union camp scene, pickets, flags. "Four Popular Marches and Quicksteps." 6pp. Page 6: Blank.

(B) **Garibaldi's Sicilian March**.
(C) **Union Volunteer's Quickstep**.
(D) **Iron Brigade Quickstep**.

USG-65 The Grant & Colfax Spread-Eagle Songster. Published by Beadle & Company, No. 98 William Street, and American News Company, No. 121 Nassau Street, New York, NY. 1868. O/bk litho of a man at political rally with arms in a spread-eagle position. "Beadle's Dime Series." "Songs for the hour!" 68pp. Inside title—**The Grant & Colfax Songster** (Comprising a Choice Selection of New and Popular Songs and Ballads for the Campaign). [M-151].

USG-66 The Tomb Upon The Hill (Song and Chorus). m. M.J. Fitzpatrick (Composer of *Chimes of Trinity, &c, &c*). Published by Howley, Haviland & Company, Nos. 1260-1266 Broadway, New York, NY. 1898. Pl/y/w geometric design cover with pl/w photo of Ulysses S. Grant's tomb in New York City. 6pp. Pages 2 and 6: Advertising for other music.

USG-67 Rally Boys, Rally! (or Reconstruction) (Song and Chorus). w.m. George H. Briggs(Author of *There's Naught So Light As Love, He Came When The Autumn Was Closing, &c., &c.*). Published by A.E. Manning & Company, No. 94 Delaware Street, Leavenworth, KS. 1868. Br/w attached photos of "U.S. Grant" and "Shuyler Colfax." Br/w drawings of eagle, flags, document—"Reconstruction," shield, oak leaves. "To the Union men of the U.S." "Sung for the first time at the Great Republican Convention in Chicago, May, 1868." 6pp. Pages 2 and 6: Blank.

USG-68 The Grant Pill (Or Unconditional Surrender). w. Harriet Castle. m. J.C. Beckel. Published by W.R. Smith, No. 135 North Eighth Street, Philadelphia, PA. [ca. 1864]. Non-pictorial. "To Our Deluded Brothers." Verse.

USG-69 Grant And Wilson Campaign Songster. Published by Frank Eastman, Book and Job Printer, No. 509 Clay Street, San Francisco, CA. [4 1/4" × 5 5/8"]. 1872. Bk/bl geometric design border. 40pp.

USG-67

USG-70 General Grant's Grand March. m. E. Mack. Published by The Jack Snyder Publishing Company, Broadway, New York, NY. [1900-1919]. Drawing of Ulysses S. Grant, sword, wreath.

USG-71 Wilson's Funeral March. m. V. Busch, Op. 251. Published by Oliver Ditson & Company, No. 451 Washington Street, Boston, MA. 1875. B/w litho by J.H. Bufford's Sons of Henry Wilson, black border. "To the Memory of Vice President Wilson." 6pp.

USG-72 We're Brothers True From The North And South (or God Bless Our Dear Old Flag) (Song and Chorus). w. E.C. Center. m. Jackson Gouraud (Son of a veteran 61-65). Published by Howley, Haviland & Company, Nos. 1260-1266 Broadway, New York, NY. 1898. R/w/b litho of Ulysses S. Grant, Robert E. Lee, rifle, eagle, flag design, newspaper clip of speech by Mr. Berry. "Affectionately dedicated to the Blue and the Grey as they are today." 6pp. Pages 2 and 6: Advertising.

USG-73 Shady's Grant And

Wilson Campaign Songster For 1872. Published at Springfield, IL. 1872. [4" × 5 7/8"]. Lithos of Ulysses S. Grant and Henry Wilson. 16pp.

USG-74 **The Nation's Hero** (Funeral March). m. Rudolph Aronson. Published by Edward Aronson & Company, Broadway at 39th Street, New York, NY. 1885. B/w litho by H.A. Thomas of Ulysses S. Grant, black border. "As Performed by Rudolph Aronson's Casino Orchestra." "Tribute to the Memory of Gen. U.S. Grant." 6pp. Pages 2 and 6: Blank.

USG-75 **The Grant Campaign Songster.** Published by Robert M. Dewitt, Publisher, No. 13 Frankfort Street, New York, NY. 1868. [4 1/4" × 5 3/4"]. [V-1: Y/bk] [V-2: Gn/bk] litho of Ulysses S. Grant. 76pp. Inside subtitle: "Containing All the Most Popular Original Songs, Ballads and Recitations that will be most sung during this Presidential Campaign, Adapted to Very Popular and Well-Known Airs and Choruses." 78pp. [M-155].

USG-76 **Gen. Grant's Funeral March.** m. Almon D. Hougas. Printed by John Tanner & Company, No. 206 Race Street, Room 9, by permission of J.C. Groene & Company, Emery Arcade, Owners of the Copyright. [ca. 1885]. B/w litho of Ulysses S. Grant, shield, eagle, flag, geometric design border. "Presented by Knost Brothers & Company, Importers of Toys and Fancy Goods, 137 West Fourth Street, Cincinnati, OH." 4pp. Page 4: Advertising.

USG-77 **Genl. Grant's Triumphal March.** m. Fred Gardner. Published by J. Church, Jr., No. 66 West 4th Street, Cincinnati, OH. [1862?]. B/w Ehrgott, Forbriger & Company of Ulysses S. Grant on horseback, battle scene. 6pp. Pages 2 and 6: Blank. Page 3: Title — **Grant's Grand March.**

USG-78 **Ulysses Is His Name** (Campaign Song and Chorus). w.m. Dexter Smith. Published by S. Brainard & Sons Company, No. 203 Superior Street, Cleveland, OH. 1868. B/w litho of Ulysses S. Grant, geometric design border. 6pp. Page 2: Blank. Page 6: Advertising.

USG-79 **Peace At Last** [Song Folio]. w. Mrs. M.A. Kidder. m. H.P. Danks. Published by Munro's Publishing House, Nos. 24 and 26 Vanderwater Street, New York, NY. Copyright 1885 by Norman L. Munro. B/w litho of Ulysses S. Grant, death bed scene, black drape. "Let us have peace — U.S. Grant." "A Tribute to the Memory of U.S. Grant" [facsimile signature]. 16pp. Page 16: Advertising.

USG-80 **In Memoriam** (On the Death of General U.S. Grant). w. Joseph M. Engard. m. William J. Street. Published by the Author [William J. Street], Camden, NJ. 1885. B/w litho by J.M. Armstrong & Company of Ulysses S. Grant, two flags, wreath. "Sung by Dr. Gilmore, at the Memorial Services at Pitman Grove." 6pp. Pages 2 and 6: Blank.

USG-81 **Requiem** (To the Memory of U.S. Grant). m. C.A. Cappa (Band Master 7th Reg., N.G.S.N.Y.). Published by Wm. A. Pond & Co., 25 Union Square, New York, NY. 1885. B/w litho by H.A. Thomas of Ulysses S. Grant, Miss "Columbia" mourning at tombstone inscribed "Grant," wreaths with state's and nation's names inscribed. 6pp. Pages 2 and 6: Blank.

USG-82 **The Grant Memorial Day March And Two Step.** m. John J. McIntyre. Published by The Duryee Music Company, No. 74 Fifth Avenue, New York, NY. 1897. Pl/w photos of Ulysses S. Grant, tomb, crypt inscribed "His Simplicity Sublime." 6pp. Page 2: Advertising for Kroeger pianos. Page 3: Title — **Grant Memorial March And Two Step.** Page 6: Advertising for this song.

USG-83 **People's Song.** w.m. Converse C.G. Collins. Published by Oliver Ditson & Company, No. 277

Washington Street, Boston, MA. 1868. Non-pictorial geometric designs. "To the Boys in Blue." 6pp. Pages 2 and 6: Blank.

USG-84 We'll Move On The Enemy's Works Again. w.m. Charles St. Denis. Published by Benham Bros., & Company, No. 36 East Washington Street, Indianapolis, IN. 1868. Non-pictorial geometric design border. "Campaign of 1868." "Dedicated to Major W.B. Jacobs, 74th Indiana Volunteer Infantry." 6pp. Pages 2 and 6: Blank.

USG-85 The Great Coming Contest (Song and Chorus for the Campaign of 1868). w. P.M. Sutton. m. Alfred von Rochow (Author of *I Wonder If She Cares For Me*). Published by Balmer & Weber, No. 206 North Fifth Street, Street, Louis, MO. 1868. B/w litho by Scharr and Brother of flags, flowers. "To Gen. Carl Schurz." 8pp. Pages 2 and 8: Blank.

USG-86 Grant Shall Be President (or The Soldier's Campaign Song). w.m. Major J. Barton. Published by Lyon & Healy, No. 116 Washington Street, Chicago, IL. 1868. Non-pictorial geometric design border. "United, like brothers, in heart and in hand; and, Grant shall be President over the land." "Respectfully Inscribed to the Brave Soldiers of America by Their Comrade." 6pp. Page 6: Advertising for other music.

USG-87 Keep The Ball A-Rolling (or Grant in the Chair) (A Campaign Song and Chorus). Published by C.H. Ditson & Company, No. 711 Broadway, New York, NY. 1868. B/w litho of angel with horn. "To the Anderson Brothers of the Union Glee Club." 6pp. Pages 2 and 6: Blank.

USG-88 Ring! Ring The Bell! (Song and Chorus). w. Mrs. Mary E. Kail. m. William T. Rogers. Published by S. Brainard & Sons, No. 203 Superior Street, Cleveland, OH. 1868. B/w non-pictorial geometric design border. 6pp. Page 2 and 6: Blank.

USG-89 Colfax Galop. m. Mrs. Lottie J. Johnson. Published by J.J. Dobmeyer & Company, Cincinnati, OH. 1866. B/w litho of sun, rays, geometric design border. 6pp. Pages 2 and 6: Blank.

USG-90 Let Us Have Peace. w.m. Will S. Hayes. Published by Louis Tripp, Harmony Hall, Louisville, KY. 1869. Non-pictorial. "To the Friends of U.S. Grant, President of the United States." 6pp. Pages 2 and 6: Blank.

USG-91 The Nation's Hero Grand March. m. Edward Hoffman. Published by S. Brainard's Sons, Cleveland, OH. Non-pictorial geometric designs. "Dedicated by Permission to Gen. Ulysses S. Grant, Elected President of U.S., Nov. 3, 1868." 10pp. Pages 2 and 10: Blank.

USG-92 General Grant's Funeral March. m. Phil B. Perry. Published by A.W. Perry & Sons' Music Company, No. 306 Broadway, Sedalia, MO. 1885. [Edition ca. 1902]. B/w litho by Crosscup & West of Ulysses S. Grant, black border. "In Memoriam." 6pp. Pages 2: Advertising for three McKinley funeral songs. Page 3: "For Piano or Cabinet Organ." Page 6: Advertising for other A.W. Perry musical magazine.

USG-93 Hurrah For Grant! w.m. More Anon. Published by John Church & Company, No. 66 West 4th Street, Cincinnati, OH. 1872. Non-pictorial geometric designs. "To the Grant Club of Columbia, Ohio." 6pp. Page 6: Blank

USG-94 Grant Us Another Term (Campaign Song and Chorus). w.m. Mrs. E.A. Parkhurst Duer. Published by C.H. Ditson & Company, No. 711 Broadway, New York, NY. 1872. Non-pictorial geometric designs. 6pp. Pages 2 and 6: Blank. Page 3: "Solo and Quartet."

USG-95 The Fighting Boys In Blue (A Stirring Campaign Song). w. John Caven. m. Zartius. Published by Benham Bros. & Company, Indianapolis, IN. 1868. Non-pictorial geometric designs. 4pp. Page 4: Blank.

USG-96 Grant's The Man. w. C.L. Abdill (Author of *Enlist Again For 3 Years More, By The Lone River Side, &c*). m. J.M. Darling. Published by J. Marsh, No. 1102 Chestnut Street, Philadelphia, PA. 1864. Non-pictorial. "To the Army of the United States." 6pp. Page 2: Blank. Page 6: Advertising for other J. Marsh music.

USG-97 Match Him! w. W.C. Wendell. m. Edgar M. Porter. Published by R. Wittig & Company, No. 1021 Chestnut Street, Philadelphia, PA. 1868. B/w non-pictorial geometric designs. "Grant is on a Mission bent to the White House from the tent; Grant shall be our President, Match Him, if you can." 6pp. Pages 2 and 6: Blank.

USG-98 Bury Me With My Grand Army Badge (On My Breast). w.a. Comrade A. Cantwell. Published by Lozier Bros., Mt. Vernon, IA. "Revised & Copyrighted by Chaplain John Hogarth Lozier, 1891." B/w litho of Ulysses S. Grant, flag, sword, partial black border. "The Gallant Hero's Last Request." 6pp. Page 2: Blank. Page 6: Advertising for other Lozier Brothers music.

USG-99 Grant, The Daring, The Lion Hearted (Shall Be Our Watchword) (Song and Chorus). a. M.A.X. Published by Blamer & Weber, No. 206 North Fifth Street, St. Louis, MO. 1868. Non-pictorial geometric designs. "To E.S. Rowse, Esq." 6pp. Pages 2 and 6: Blank.

USG-100 President Grant's Grand March. m. Henry Sutter (Director of the Conservatory of Music in Jamestown, NY), Op. 16. Published by Cottier & Denton, No. 269 Main Street, Buffalo, NY. 1869. B/w litho of military equipment, cannon, bugle, ribbon inscribed "To His Excellency Gen. Ulysses S. Grant." 6pp. Page 6: Advertising for other Cottier & Denton songs.

USG-101 Grant's Presentation Grand March. m. Pierre Latour. Copyright 1878 by Pierre Latour. B/w litho by Thomas Hunter "from photo by F. Gutekunst" of awards and certificates belonging to Ulysses S. Grant. "Respectfully dedicated to Geo. W. Chiles, Esq." 6pp. Pages 2 and 6: Blank.

USG-102 Grant's Grant March. m. M. Macks. Published by Richard A. Saalfield, No. 41 Union Square, New York, NY. 1882? B/w litho of Ulysses S. Grant, dragonfly, geometric design border. 6pp. Page 6: Advertising for other Richard A. Saalfield songs.

USG-103 All Hail To Ulysses! (Song and Chorus). w. Charles Haynes. m. J.E. Haynes. Published by S. Brainard's Sons, Cleveland, OH. 1864. Non-pictorial. "Song and Chorus In Honor of Maj. Gen. U.S. Grant." 6pp. Pages 2 and 6: Blank.

USG-104 The Grand Centennial Triumphal March (Grand American Medley). m. Fred Wachter. Published by Fred Wachter, Milwaukee, WI. 1875. B/w sepia tinted litho by the Milwaukee Litho & Engraving Company of George Washington, Ulysses S. Grant, Revolutionary and Civil War soldiers, eagle, shield, flags, Liberty cap. "Dedicated to the Memory of the Signers of the Declaration of Independence." "1776-1876." "Containing: *The Grand Centennial, Home Sweet Home, Auld Lang Syne, Star Spangled Banner, Red, White and Blue*." 12[?]pp. Page 2: Blank.

USG-105 General Grant's Funeral March. m. George Maywood. Published by the National Music Company, No. 215-221 Wabash Avenue, Chicago, IL. 1885. B/w litho of Ulysses S. Grant, flags, gun, sword, wreath, black border. 6pp. Page 2: Blank. Page 6: Advertising for other National Music Company music.

USG-106 We'll Go With Grant Again (Song of the Sons of Monroe). w. George Cooper. m. Henry Tucker (Author of *When Fenians FIght For Freedom, Come From Afar, &c., &c.*). Published by Wm. A. Pond & Company, No. 547

Broadway, New York, NY. 1866. Non-pictorial geometric design border. "To my Friend M. Ainsley Scott." 6pp. Page 2: Blank. Page 6: Advertising.

USG-107 General Grant's Richmond March. m. Charles G. Degenhand. Copyright 1865 by George H. Ellis. N/c litho by Henry C. Eno of Ulysses S. Grant and other Union officers on horseback, crossed flags, three shields. 8pp. Pages 2, 7 and 8: Blank. Page 3: "Cordially Inscribed to the Hero of Belmont, Ft. Henry, Richmond, &c."

USG-108 General U.S. Grant's Victory March. m. J.B. Denning. Copyright 1885 by J.D. Barnitz. Non-pictorial geometric designs. "In Commemoration on of his Many Victories Through Life." "Respectfully Dedicated to his Son Hon. Col. Fred D. Grant." 6pp. Page 6: Blank.

USG-109 One Good Turn Deserves Another (Song and Chorus). w. Grace Carelton. m. Eastburn. Published by S. Brainard's Sons, Cleveland, OH. 1872. Non-pictorial geometric design border. 6pp. Page 2: Blank. Page 6: Advertising for other music publications.

USG-110 National Republican Grant And Wilson Campaign Song-Book. Published by The Union Republican Congressional Committee, Washington, DC. 1872. [3 13/16" × 8 9/16"]. Be/bk litho of Ulysses S. Grant. "We'll Sing a Song for U.S. Grant." 100pp. [M-182].

USG-111 Union March Militaire. m. Edgar M. Porter. Published by Charles W.A. Trumpler, No. 926 Chestnut Street, Philadelphia, PA. 1865. Non-pictorial geometric designs. "To Lieut. Gen. U.S. Grant." 8pp. Pages 2 and 8: Blank. Page 3: Title:—**Union Grand March** (Militaire).

USG-112 Grant And Peace (Quartette and Chorus for Male Voices). w.m. G. Edward Bishop. Published by Oliver Ditson & Company, No. 277 Washington Street, Boston, MA. 1868. Non-pictorial geometric designs. "Written & Composed for the Campaign of '68." "Respectfully dedicated to the Grand Army of the Republic." 6pp. Page 6: Blank.

USG-113 The Grant Songster (For the Campaign of 1868). Published by Root & Cady, No. 67 Washington Street, Chicago, IL. 1868. [4 3/4" × 6 3/8"]. O/bk litho of Ulysses S. Grant. "A Collection of Campaign Songs for 1868." 48pp. Page 48: Advertising for Grant Campaign music. [M-158, 159].

USG-114 General Grant's Grand March. m. Joseph Raff [E.A. Daggett]. [New York, NY]. 1864. B/w beige tinted litho by Henry C. Eno of Ulysses S. Grant, battle scenes, banners. List of Grant's 21 battle victories. "Dedicated to Lieutenant General U.S. Grant." 8pp. Page 2: Blank.

USG-115 Gen. Grant's Heroic March. m. Louis Meyer. Published by F.A. North & Company, No. 1308 Chestnut Street, Philadelphia, PA. 1885. B/w litho of Ulysses S. Grant. "For Piano or Parlor Organ." 6pp. Pages 2 and 6: Blank.

USG-116 Lieutenant General Grant's Grand March. m. E. Mack. Published by Lee & Walker, No. 722 Chestnut Street, Philadelphia, PA. 1862. B/w beige tinted litho of Ulysses S. Grant, banner's with lists of Grant's battle victories, crossed swords, tree limbs. "Respectfully Dedicated to Lieutenant General U.S. Grant." 6pp. Page 2: Blank. Page 6: Advertising for other music.

USG-117 Grant A Nation's Hero. w.m. William T. Rogers. Published by S. Brainard's Sons, Publishers, Cleveland, OH. 1885. N/c litho by Goes and Quensel of mounted troops charging in battle. "Our National War Songs." List of other titles in series.

USG-118 The Little Western Man (Song and Chorus). w. Col. E.C. James (of the Sixtieth New York Volunteers). m. T.H. Hinton. Published by

Redington and Howe, No. 2 Wieting Block, Syracuse, NY. 1868. Non-pictorial geometric design border. "To the next President." 6pp. Page 2: Blank.

USG-119 Genl. Grant's Triumphal March. m. George Schleiffarth. Published by The Chicago Music Company, No. 152 State Street, Chicago, IL. 1879. B/w litho of Ulysses S. Grant, eagle, flags, oak branches, military equipment. "Dedicated to Genl. Ulysses S. Grant." 6pp. Page 6: Blank.

USG-120 (Grant Will Do) Four More Years (Quartette for Male Voices). w.m. Pro Phundo Basso. Published by John Church & Company, No. 66 West Fourth Street, Cincinnati, OH. 1872. Non-pictorial geometric design border. "To the *Inter-Ocean*, Chicago." 6pp. Pages 2 and 6: Blank.

USG-121 Grant's Our Banner Man (Song and Chorus). w.m. William T. Rogers. Published by S. Brainard's Sons, Cleveland, OH. 1872. B/w litho of ribbon inscribed with song title, geometric designs. 6pp. Page 6: Blank.

USG-122 Vote For Gen' U.S. Grant (Song and Chorus). w.m. Joe T. Wright. Published by Lee & Walker, No. 722 Chestnut Street, Philadelphia, PA. 1868. Litho of shield, geometric designs. 6pp. Pages 2 and 6: Blank. Page 3: Composer listed as "F.S. Wright."

USG-123 For President Ulysses Grant (A Smoking His Cigar) (Song and Chorus). w. Ason O'Fagun. m. J.P. Webster. Published by Root & Cady, No. 67 Washington Street, Chicago, IL. 1868. Non-pictorial. 6pp. Page 6: Blank.

USG-124 President Ulysses! (Grant Song). w. Miles O'Reilly (Gen. Charles G. Halpine). m. George B. Ayres. Published by Cottier & Denton, No. 269 Main Street, Buffalo, NY. 1868. Non-pictorial geometric designs. "May he rule the country he has saved, And God defend the Right." "Miles O'Reilly's (Gen. Chas. G. Halpine) Grant-Song." 6pp. Pages 2 and 6: Blank.

USG-125 Tanner's Song. m. "Tune: *The Battle Cry of Freedom*." Published by G.G. Byron Dewolfe, Wandering Poet, Nashua, NH. [1868]. [6" × 9 1/4"]. B/w litho of Ulysses S. "Grant." "Grant & Colfax." Poem based on the beginning letters of the alphabet— "Verses Composed for merchants, patent right's men, and the Public generally. Correspondence confidential. Send $1 and have your name there, stating also the particulars of it." 2pp. Page 2: Blank.

USG-126 The Inauguration Quickstep. m. Wilber F. Gale. Published by John Church, Jr., No. 66 West 4th Street, Cincinnati, OH. 1869. Non-pictorial geometric designs. "To President Grant." 8pp. Pages 2, 7 and 8: Blank.

USG-127 General Grant's March. m. E. Mack. Published by [V-1: No Publisher Indicated] [V-2, V-3 and V-4: Eclipse Publishing Company, No. 136 North 9th Street, Philadelphia, PA]. Copyright 1907 by Joseph Morris, Philadelphia, PA. [V-1: Pre-1919 size] [V-2, V-3 and V-4: Post-1919 size]. [V-1: Bl/w, no stripes in shield] [V-2: Bl/w] [V-3: Gn/w] [V-4: Br/w] photo of Ulysses Grant. Bl/w drawing of an eagle, shield without stars, geometric designs. 6pp. Pages 2 and 6: Advertising.

USG-128 General Grant's March. m. E. Mack. Published by Eclipse Publishing Company, No. 136 North 9th Street, Philadelphia, PA. Copyright 1907 by Joseph Morris. [V-1: Pre 1919 Size] [V-2: Post 1919 size]. Bl/w eagle. R/w/b shield. Bl/w photo of Ulysses S. Grant. "Beaux Arts Edition." 6pp. Pages 2 and 6: Advertising for other music.

USG-129 General Grant's March. m. E. Mack. Published by Worch's Piano House, No. 1110 "G" Street N.W., Washington, DC. [ca. 191-]. B/w photo of Ulysses S. Grant. R/w/b shield with three stars, geometric designs, eagle. "Edition De Luxe." 6pp. Pages 2 and 6: Advertising. Bl/w photo of the Worch Piano Building.

USG-130 General Grant's Grand March. m. E. Mack. Published by the Century Music Publishing Company, Nos. 231-235 West 40th Street, New York, NY. [ca. 193-]. Pk/bk/w geometric design border. "Spirited marches (in the third grade), Series One, No. 1109." List of other songs in series. "Century Edition." 6pp. Pages 2 and 6: Advertising for other music.

USG-131 Grant's Grand March. m. E. Mack. Published by the McKinley Music Company, Chicago, IL. [ca. 1909]. Bl/w drawing of the front of a house. "Standard Marches." List of other songs in series. 6pp. Pages 2 and 6: Advertising for other music.

USG-132 Grant's March. m. E. Mack. Published by the McKinley Music Company, Chicago, IL. [ca. 1909]. Gn/w drawing of a girl with flowers. "Standard Marches." List of other songs in series. 6pp. Pages 2 and 6: Advertising.

USG-133 General Grant's March. m. E. Mack. Published by Morris Music Company, No. 1028 Arch Street, Philadelphia, PA. Public Domain. [ca. 1926]. Non-pictorial geometric designs. "Key of F." "Unexcelled Edition." 6pp. Pages 2 and 6: Advertising for other Morris Music Company published music.

USG-134 General Grant's Grand March. m. E. Mack. a. F. Henri Klickmann. Published by Jack Mills, Inc., Nos. 148-150 West 46th Street, New York, NY. 1924. B/w non-pictorial geometric designs. "Edition Supreme." "For Piano." 6pp. Pages 2 and 6: Advertising for other Jack Mills music.

USG-135 General Grant's March (Piano Solo). m. E. Mack. Published by Morris Music Company, No. 1023 Arch Street, Philadelphia, PA. 1933. O/w drawing of cannon, exploding cannon ball. 4pp. Page 4: Advertising for other music.

USG-136 Grant, A Soldier And A Man. m. Will H. Fox. In: *A Soldier and a Man* [Song Folio]. Published by Frank Harding's Music House, New York, NY. 1897. B/w photo of a man [Will Fox?], geometric designs. "Words and music complete."

USG-137 We Are Coming Brave Ulysses (Grant Campaign Song). w. R. Allen, Jr. m. J. Lloyd, Jr. Published and for sale by J.D. Denison, No. 208 Broadway, New York, NY. Copyright 1868 by J. Lloyd. [6 13/16" × 12"]. Non-pictorial broadside. 2pp. Page 2: Blank.

USG-138 Gen. Grant's Funeral March. m. George Edw. Jackson. Published by W.A. Evans and Bro., Publishers, No. 1 Columbia Street, Boston, MA. [1885]. B/w litho by Geo. H. Walker & Company of Ulysses S. Grant, black border. 6pp. Pages 2 and 6: Blank.

USG-139 We'll Fight It Out Here On The Old Union Line (Song and Chorus). w. Rev. John Hogarth Lozier (Late Chaplain 37 Indiana Infantry). m. George F. Root. Published by Root & Cady, No. 67 Washington Street, Chicago, IL. 1868. Non-pictorial geometric designs. "Sung at the Republican National Convention by Chaplain Lozier, Chaplain McCabe and Maj. H.G. Lumbard." 6pp. Pages 2 and 6: Blank.

USG-140 Grant & Colfax Club, Ward 11 [Song Sheet]. m. Popular Airs. Published by Grant & Colfax Club Ward 11, Boston, MA. 1868. [8 5/16" × 16 7/16"]. Non-pictorial broadside. "The audience are prepared to join in singing in good earnest the following songs." Six songs. 2pp. Page 2: Blank.

USG-141 Old Glory And U.S. Grant (Song and Chorus). w. L.J. Bates. m. J.P. Webster. Published by Root & Cady, No. 67 Washington Street, Chicago, IL. 1868. B/w litho of birds, flowers, scroll, geometric design border. "Songs of the Present Time, Melodies of Beauty, Words of Sense, Ideas of Progress." List of other titles in series. 6pp. Pages 2 and 6: Advertising. Page 3: "During the War some of our boys used to call the flag 'Old Glory.'"

USG-142 Grant's March. m. Marks. Published by Richard A. Saalfield, No. 12 Bible House, New York, NY. [ca. 1882]. Non-pictorial geometric design border. "Latest and Most Popular Marches." List of other titles in series.

USG-143 Grant And Wilson Campaign Songster. Published by F. Eastman, San Francisco, CA. 1872. Litho of Ulysses S. Grant. [M-179].

USG-144 Hurrah For General Grant! (Song and Chorus). w. Luke Collin. m. J.P. Webster. Published by Root & Cady, No. 67 Washington Street, Chicago, IL. 1867. B/w litho of the inside of Crosby's Opera House during the Republican Convention. "Dedicated to the Convention that Nominated Gen. Grant for the Presidency at Crosby's Opera House, May 20th, 1868." 6pp. Page 6: Advertising for other music.

USG-145 General Grant's Home Polka. m. Charles Case (Utica, Oneida Co., New York). Published for the Author by William A. Pond & Company, NY. 1865. Non-pictorial geometric designs. "To the Friends of the Union." "For the Piano Forte." 6pp. Page 6: Blank.

USG-146 Grant, A Soldier And A Man (Grant Song). w.m. Will H. Fox. Published by Frank Harding's Music House, No. 1293 Broadway, New York, NY. 1897. Litho of Ulysses S. Grant.

USG-147 Wilson's Battle March. m. Paul J. Bishop. Published by Russell & Tolman, No. 291 Washington Street, Boston, MA. 1861. Bk/y litho by Greene of house, field, fence, trees. 12pp. Pages 2, 9, 10, 11 and 12: Blank. Page 3: Same as page one except b/w. Page 4: B/w sepia tinted litho by J.H. Bufford's of Henry Wilson in uniform. "Respectfully dedicated to the Hon. Henry Wilson."

USG-148 Republican Campaign Melodist And Register. c. Sidney Herbert. Published by Dick and Fitzgerald, New York, NY. 1868. Y/bk litho of Ulysses S. Grant and Shuyler Colfax. "The Register Contains a Full & Concise Report of the Action of the Chicago Convention; Brief Biographies of the Nominees; and their letters of Acceptance. To this is added the names of the National Executive Committee; a Tabular Statement of the popular Vote for President for the last twelve years, and the population, extent, and time holding Annual Elections in the Several States. The Melodist contains a choice selection of original and popular Campaign Melodies, which will be found highly Desirable in giving Increased Power and Intent to the Presidential Contest upon which we are just Entering." [M-160].

USG-149 Grant Campaign Songster. w. Paul (And distributed Free, by Paul, the original woolen remnant man who sells the Best 14 oz. All Wool Dollar Cassimeres to be Found). Published by the Remnant Rooms, No. 51 Dorrance Street, Providence, RI. 1868. [3" x 4 9/16"]. [V-1: O/bk] [V-2: Bl/bk] [V-3: Gn/bk] litho of Ulysses S. Grant. Advertising. "We will fight it out on this line." 8pp. Pages 2, 7 and 8: Advertising. [M-152, 153 — Different contents].

USG-150(A) In Our Own Dear Homes Again! w. John Ross Dix. m. "Air: *The Cottage By The Sea*." Published by Charles Magnus, No. 12 Frankfort Street, New York, NY. 1864. [5" x 8"]. B/w hand Colored litho of woman, children, portrait of Ulysses S. Grant on wall. "500 Illustrated Ballads, lithographed and printed by Charles Magnus, No. 12 Frankfort Street, New York, NY. Branch Office: No. 520 7th St., Washington D.C." 2pp. Page 2: Blank.

(B) The Wife I Left Behind. "Ten Illustrated Songs on note paper, mailed to any address on receipt of 50 cents."

USG-151 Fire Away Galop. m. J. de Jasienski. Published by Wm. Hall & Son, No. 543 Broadway, New York, NY. 1866. R/w/bk/br litho by Eno of cannon firing. "To U.S. Grant." 10pp. Page 10: Blank.

USG-152 General Grant's Grand March. m. E. Mack. Published by Century Music Publishing Company, Nos. 231-235 West 40th Street, New York, NY. [1900-1918]. R/w/gn/br drawing of couples dancing. "Century Edition Sheet Music." 6pp. Pages 2 and 6: Blank.

USG-153 General Grant's Grand March. m. E. Mack. Published by Century Music Publishing Company, Nos. 231-235 West 40th Street, New York, NY. [ca. 193-]. R/w/bk/gn drawing of couples dancing. "Century Certified Edition Sheet Music." 6pp. Pages 2 and 6: Blank.

USG-154 Genl. Grant's Polka. m. Master Ferd. K. Hill. a. R.Z. Salem. Published by Charles W.A. Trumpler, corner 7th and Chestnut Street, Philadelphia, PA. 1865. Non-pictorial geometric designs. "Respectfully Inscribed to Lieut. General Grant by the Author." 6pp. Pages 2 and 6: Blank.

USG-155 Our Ulysses. w. John Ross Dix. m. "Air: *The Groves of Blarney.* "Published by Charles Magnus, No. 12 Frankfort Street, New York, NY. 1864. [5" × 8"]. [V-1: Br/w litho of Ulysses S. Grant, flags] [V-2: litho of view of Richmond, VA]. "500 Illustrated Ballads, lithographed and printed by Charles Magnus, No. 12 Frankfort Street, New York; Branch Office: No. 520 7th St., Washington, D.C." 2pp. Page 2: Blank.

USG-156(A) I Cannot Bid Thee Go, My Boy. w.m. Elbridge G.B. Holder. Published by Wm. Hall & Son, No. 543 Broadway, New York, NY. 1864. Non-pictorial. "Six Gems of War Ballads Composed by Elbridge G.B. Holden." "To Mrs. Genl. U.S. Grant."

    (B) **Kiss Me As Of Old Mother.**
    (C) **Tell Me Mother Can I Go.**
    (D) **Our Boy's A Warrior Now.**
    (E) **Let Me Die, Face To The Foe.** 6pp. Pages 2 and 6: Blank. Page 3: Narrative—"The Last Words of Brigadier Gen. James C. Rice."

USG-157 The Ruler In Peace, And The Leader In War! (Song and Chorus). w. William H. Woodhans. m. J. Maurice Hubbard. Published by Root & Cady, No. 67 Wabash Street, Chicago, IL. 1868. Non-pictorial geometric designs. "Respectfully Inscribed to my Comrades at the Siege of Vicksburg." 8pp. Page 2: Blank. Page 8: Advertising.

USG-158 Match Him. [1868]. [4 1/2" × 10 7/8"]. B/w litho of Ulysses S. Grant, flags, eagle, shield, ribbon inscribed "We will fight it out on this line." 2pp. Page 2: Blank.

USG-159 Wilson's Battle March. m. Paul J. Bishop. Published by S. Brainard's Sons Company, Chicago, IL. [V-1: 1884] [V-2: ca. 1897]. [V-1: N/c litho by Orcuft of battle scene] [V-2: Bk/bl/w reprint of V-1 with Orcuft drawing redone by Harrell]. List of other titles in series. "Popular Marches, Battle Pieces, &c. for Piano or Organ."

USG-160 Grant's March. m. Alexander. Published for R.H. Macy & Company, 14th Street, 6th Avenue and 13th Street, New York, NY. [ca. 1885]. Non-pictorial geometric design border. "Popular Marches." List of other titles in series. Advertising.

USG-161 General Grant's Grand March. m. E. Mack. a. E.F. Derschaky. Published by M.D. Swisher, No. 115 South 10th Street, Philadelphia, PA. 1907. R/w/b drawing of a cannon, flag. Bl/w drawing of Ulysses S. Grant. "The Artists Edition." 6pp. Pages 2 and 6: Advertising. Page 3: "Fingered and edited by E.F. Derschaky."

USG-162 General Grant's Grand March. m. E. Mack. a. E.F. Derschaky. Published by E.B. Swisher, No. 115 South 10th Street, Philadelphia, PA. 1907. [ca. 193-]. Bl/w drawing of Ulysses S. Grant, cannon, flags. "The Artists Edition." 6pp. Pages 2 and 6: Advertising for other E.B. Swisher music.

USG-163 General Grant's March. m. E. Mack. Published by The Morris Music Company, No. 1023 Arch

Street, Philadelphia, PA. 1933. B/w geometric designs. "Unexcelled Edition." 4pp. Page 4: Advertising.

USG-164 General Grant's March. m. E. Mack. Published by Moderne Publications, No. 2611 Indiana Avenue, Chicago, IL. 1936. [V-1: O/w/bk] [V-2: Bl/bk/w] drawing of soldiers marching in formation. [V-1: Piano Solo] [V-2: Piano Accordion Solo]. "Moderne Edition." 6pp. Pages 5 and 6: Advertising.

USG-165 General Grant's Grand March. m. E. Mack. a. Maxwell Eckstein. In: *Let Us Have Music for Marching, 17 Spirited and Famous Marches Arranged for Piano*, page 59. Published by Carl Fisher, Inc., No. 62 Cooper Square, New York 3, NY. 1949. [9" × 12"]. O/w/bk drawing of drum major.

USG-166 General Grant's Grand March. m. E. Mack. In: *Universal March Folio, 25 Marches with Tenor Banjo, Ukulele and Guitar Arrangement*, pages 32-33. Published by Bibo-Lang, Inc., Music Publishers, No. 745 Broadway, New York, NY. 1933. Gn/y geometric designs by Frederick S. Manning. "Twenty Five World Famous Marches by the World's Greatest Composers Adaptable for Schools, Assembly, Play Grounds, Parades, Celebrations, Weddings, Boy and Girl Scouts, Teaching." Contents listed on cover.

USG-167 General Grant's Grand March. m. E. Mack. Published by The Century Music Publishing Company, Nos. 231-235 West 40th Street, New York, NY. [ca. 193-]. [V-1: Bl/bk/br/w] [V-2: Y/w/gn] drawing of flowers. "Century Certified Edition Sheet Music." List of other marches in the series. "Spirited Marches (In the Third Grade) Series One." 6pp. Pages 2 and 6: Advertising.

USG-168 The Storming And Capture Of Fort Donelson (A Military Divertimento). m. J.C. Viereck. Published by Oliver Ditson & Company, No. 277 Washington Street, Boston, MA. [ca. 1862]. B/w litho of Union soldiers in battle, flag. "To Maj. Gen. Grant." 8pp. Page 8: Blank.

USG-169(A) Grant, A Nation's Hero. w.m. William T. Rogers. Published by S. Brainard's Sons, Cleveland, OH. 1884. O/y/r/w/bl/bk drawing of soldier on horseback. "Our National War Songs." List of other titles in series.
(B) Soldier's Chief, The Nation's Chief. w.m. William T. Rogers.

USG-170 General Grant's March. m. E. Mack. a. Mort H. Glickman. Published by Calumet Music Company, No. 201 East 26th Street, Chicago, IL. 1935. Bk/w/y drawing of a man playing a piano. "Piano Solo." 4pp. Page 4: Advertising.

USG-171 General Grant's Grand March. m. E. Mack. Published by Music Sales Corporation, New York, NY. [ca. 193-]. Non-pictorial. "No. 528." "The Master Library of Musical Classics." 4pp. Page 4: Advertising.

USG-172 Here Sleeps The Hero. w. Gerald Carlton. m. Robert F. Walsh. Published by Hitchcock's Music Stores, No. 385 Sixth Avenue, New York, NY. 1892. B/w drawing of "Tomb of General Grant, Riverside Park, New York City." "In Memoriam." 6pp. Page 2: Blank. Page 6: Advertising.

USG-173 Riverside March And Two Step. m. Walter V. Ullner. Published by the Gagel Brothers, No. 1276 Broadway, New York, NY. 1897. B/w photos of "Gen. Grant's Tomb at Riverside," "Temporary Tomb of Gen. Grant," "Riverside Drive, Looking North" and of Walter Ullner. "Respectfully Dedicated to William B. McLewee." "Views by permission of Rand, McNally & Company, Chicago and New York. 8pp. Pages 2, 7 and 8: Advertising.

USG-174(A) Grant March. m. Eduard Holst. Published by Charles W. Held, Brooklyn, NY. 1893. N/c lithos of

Ulysses S. Grant, James Sherman, Phil Sheridan, John Logan, Winfield S. Hancock and Admiral David Farragut. "Our American Heroes." "Six Easy Pieces for Piano."
- (B) Sherman Gavotte.
- (C) Sheridan Waltz.
- (D) Farragut Revere.

USG-175 I Spell Nation With A Great Big N (Song and Chorus). w. Gen. U.S. Grant. m. Charles H. Foster. Published by The Chicago Music Company, No. 152 State Street, Chicago, IL. 1879. B/w non-pictorial geometric designs. "The words and music of this song are the property of The Chicago Music Company, and entered according to the copyright laws of the United States." 6pp.

USG-176 General Grant's Grand March. m. E. Mack. Published by Deluxe Music Company, New York, NY. [193-]. Non-pictorial geometric designs. "For Piano." 6pp. Pages 2 and 6: Advertising.

USG-177 Richmond Is Ours! (Solo or Quartette with Chorus). w. A.J.H. Duganne. m. Mrs. E.A. Parkhurst (Author of *Dey Said We Would'nt Fight, No Slave Beneath The Starry Flag, New Emancipation Song, Soldier's Dying Farewell, O, Send Me One Flower From His Grave, A Home In The Mountains*, 30 cts. each.) Published by Horace Waters, No. 481 Broadway, New York, NY. 1865. Non-pictorial litho border. Chorus — "Richmond is Ours! Richmond is Ours! Hark! to the Jubilant Chorus! Up Through the lips that no longer repress it. Up from the Heart of the People! God Bless it! Swelling with loyal emotion. Leapeth our joy, like an ocean! Richmond is Ours! Richmond is Ours! Babylon fall, and her temples and towers crumble to ashes before us." "To Lieut. Gen. Grant." 6pp. Page 2: Blank. Page 6: Advertising.

USG-178 Gen. Grant's Funeral March. m. Otto Gunnar. Published by S. Brainard's Sons, Cleveland, OH. 1885. B/w litho by W.J. Morgan & Company of Ulysses S. Grant in black frame, shield, drape, laurel branches. "For the Piano." 6pp. Pages 2 and 6: Blank.

USG-179 General Grant's March. m. J.C. Becket. Copyright 1885 by O.V. Greene. B/w litho of Ulysses S. Grant, vignettes of his life. 6pp. Page 6: Advertising.

USG-180 General Grant's March (Funebre). m. J.C. Becket. Copyright 1885 by O.V. Greene. B/w litho of Ulysses S. Grant, vignettes of his life. 6pp. Page 6: Blank.

USG-181 Inauguration Grand March. m. D. Leifluac. Published by John F. Ellis, No. 306 Pennsylvania Avenue, Washington, DC. [1869]. B/w beige tinted litho by H.M. Traubel of Ulysses S. Grant and Shuyler Colfax, eagle with ribbon inscribed "E Pluribus Unum," shield, floral and geometric designs. "Composed in honor of Grant & Colfax." Page 2: Blank.

USG-182 Grant's Birthday (Union of the Blue and Grey). [Program & Song Book]. Published by The Press Club of Chicago, Chicago, IL. 1895. [6

USG-181

3/4" × 9 1/4"]. Br/bl/gn litho of Ulysses S. Grant. "Let Us Have Peace." "Patriotic Celebration The Birthday of General U.S. Grant at the Auditorium, April 27, 8 p.m. under the auspices of the Press Club of Chicago." 28pp. Page 15: **Hail Columbia**.

USG-183   We Will Not Retreat Any More. w. E.W. Locke (Author of *We Are Marching On To Richmond, We Are Marching To Dixie's Land, &c, &c*). a. G. Ascher. Published by S.T. Gordon, No. 538 Broadway, New York, NY. 1863. Non-pictorial geometric design line border. "To Maj. General Grant." 6pp. Pages 2 and 6: Blank.

USG-184   Gen. Grant's Funeral March. m. Louis Meyer. Published by F.A. North & Company, No. 1308 Chestnut Street, Philadelphia, PA. [1885]. B/w litho by Thomas Hunter of Ulysses S. Grant, flags, black border. "Composed in commemoration of a Nation's sorrow at his death." 6pp. Pages 2 and 6: Blank.

USG-185   Campaign Songs! [Pamphlet]. Printed by Crane & Co., No. 533 Clay Street, San Francisco, CA. [1872]. [5 1/2" × 8"]. Non-pictorial. "Dedicated to the 'Grant Invincibles' of San Francisco." 4pp.

USG-186   Shoo Purp Don't Bodder Me (A Capitol Song and Dance). w.m.a. Henry Ward Beecher. Published by [V-1: Louis Tripp, Louisville, KY] [V-2: John F. Ellis & Company, No. 937 Pennsylvania Avenue, Washington, DC]. Copyright 1870 by Louis Tripp. B/w litho of a dog in front of the Capitol at Washington — "A true likeness of the 'Purp' expressed from Cleveland, O. Jan. 27, and refused audience to the President." "Dorgonically [sic] Dedicated to the Rejected Purp." 6pp. Page 6: Advertising.

USG-187   Genl. Grant's Grand Election March. m. A.P. Wyman. Published by S. Brainard & Sons, No. 203 Superior Street, Cleveland, OH. 1868. B/w beige tinted litho of Ulysses S. Grant, facsimile signature. "Respectfully Dedicated to Genl. U.S. Grant, Republican Candidate for President." 8pp. Pages 2 and 8: Blank.

USG-188   Gen. Grant's Welcome Home March. m. Louis Meyer. Published by F.A. North & Company, No. 1308 Chestnut Street, Philadelphia, PA. 1879. Non-pictorial bl/bk/w cover. 6pp. Pages 2 and 6: Blank.

USG-189   Ulysses Leads The Van (A Patriotic Song). w.m. E.W. Locke. a. Dr. W.J. Wetmore. Published by S.T. Gordon, No. 538 Broadway, New York, NY. 1874. Non-pictorial geometric lines. 6pp. Pages 2 and 6: Blank. Page 3: "Arranged for the Piano."

USG-190   Weep For The Brave (Song and Chorus). w. Clara B. Coffey. m. George B. Chase. Published by The John Church Company, No. 74 West Fourth Street, Cincinnati, OH. 1885. B/w litho of Ulysses S. Grant. "In Memory of Gen. Grant and Inscribed to the Boys in Blue." 6pp. Pages 2 and 6: Blank.

USG-191   The Sword Of Ulysses (A Grant Campaign Song). w. Edward Grattan. m. J. Offenbach. Published by C.M. Tremaine, No. 481 Broadway, New York, NY. 1868. R/w/b non-pictorial geometric designs. 6pp. Page 2: "Air: *Sabre de mon Pere. La Grande Duchesse*." Page 6: Blank.

USG-192   General Grant's March. m. E. Mack. Published by Morris Music Company, No. 1025 Arch Street, Philadelphia, PA. 1933. [V-1: Bl/w] [V-2: Ma/w] drawings of a cannon, geometric designs. "Classic M Edition." 4pp. Page 4: Advertising.

USG-193   Grant Memorial March. m. Joseph Bannaker Adger. Published by Joseph Bannaker Adger, Philadelphia, PA. 1897. Bl/w drawing of Ulysses S. Grant. "Introducing the Melody of *Onward Christian Soldiers* Gen. U.S. Grant's Favorite Hymn, which will be sung by 2,000 Public School Children of New York City at the Dedication of the Grant Monument, April

27th, 1897." "Published with the Approval of Rt. Rev. W.B. Derrick, D.D." 6pp. Page 6: Advertising.

USG-194 Memories Of Grant At Shiloh. m. John Russell. Published by H. Bollman & Sons, St. Louis, MO. 1885. B/w non-pictorial geometric designs. "Dedicated to the Heroic Army of the Cumberland." "Composed for Piano or Organ." 8pp. Page 8: Blank.

USG-195 General Grant's Grand March. Published by Century Music Publishing Company, Nos. 231-235 West 40th Street, New York, NY. [ca. 193-]. Gn/bk/w non-pictorial geometric designs. "Century Certified Edition Sheet Music." "No-1109." 6pp. Pages 2 and 6: Blank.

USG-196 My Country Has First Call. w. Joseph H. McKeon. m. W. Lindsay Gordon. Published by The Gordon Music Publishing Company, No. 207 West 34th Street, New York, NY. 1910. N/c drawing of a soldier and woman embracing. Bl/w photo of "W. Lindsay Gordon." "Respectfully dedicated to Major Gen. Fred D. Grant, U.S.A." 6pp. Page 6: Advertising.

USG-197 General Grant's Grand March. m. E. Mack. a. Walter Rolfe. Published by Century Music Publishing Company, No. 235 West 40th Street, New York, NY. 1943 Edition. [V-1: Gn/bl/w] [V-2: B/w] drawings by Erdoes of military symbols from the Revolutionary War to World War II including, sword, drum, flag, parachute, aircraft, eagle, &c. "Transcribed Classics of Lasting Appeal." "Century Certified Edition Sheet Music." "No. 3656." List of other songs in series. 4pp. Page 4: Advertising.

USG-198 General Grant's Grand March. m. E. Mack. Published by Century Music Publishing Company, No. 47 West 63rd Street, New York 23, NY. [194-]. [V-1: R/br/w] [V-2: R/w/br] [V-3: O/gn/w] drawings by Erdoes of military symbols from the Revolutionary War to World War II including, sword, drum, flag, parachute, aircraft, eagle, &c. "Spirited Marches (In the third Grade) Series I." "No. 1109." List of other titles in series. [V-1 and V-3: 4pp] [V-2: 6pp]. [V-1: Page 4: Advertising] [V-2: Page 6: Advertising].

USG-199 The Chieftain Brave (Campaign Song and Chorus). m. A.P. Hand. Published by Henry Tolman & Co., No. 291 Washington Street, Boston, MA. 1868. Non-pictorial geometric designs. "For Mixed or Male Chorus."

USG-200 Gen. Grant's Memorial March. m. A.H.F. Published by White, Smith & Company, No. 516 Washington Street, Boston, MA. 1885. B/w litho of General Ulysses S. Grant. 6pp. Page 6: Advertising for other funeral marches including James G. Garfield, Henry Wilson, Daniel Webster and Horace Greeley.

USG-201 The Chieftain's Return (March). m. Herman Heinze. Published by Reed Meyer, No. 722 Arch Street, Philadelphia, PA. 1868. Non-pictorial geometric designs. "Meyer's Crescent Scale Improved Overstrung Pianos. First Prizes Awarded in Europe and America. Gold Medal Cabinet Organs, Melodeons and Harmoniums." 8pp. Pages 2 and 8: Blank.

USG-202 Hurrah Galop (Pas Redouble de Concert). m. Seven Octaves [Louis M. Gottschalk]. Published by Oliver Ditson & Company, No. 277 Washington Street, Boston, MA. 1863. Non-pictorial geometric designs. "Au General Grant."

USG-203 The Deserted Rebel Mansion (By a Yankee Skirmisher). w.m. I.W. Gougler (Author of *These Charming Scenes, Welcome Merry Spring, The Grave Of My Mother, Mary's Beauty, &c.*). Published by Horace Waters, No. 481 Broadway, New York, NY. 1865. Non-pictorial geometric design border. "To U.S. Grant by permission." 6pp. Pages 2 and 6: Blank. Page 3: At top of music: "On the

5th of September, 1864, a detail of two hundred and fifty men of the 127th N.Y. Vols. Set out from Morris Island on a scouting expedition. Four islands were visited and all were found to be occupied by pleasant but deserted mansions. The sight of one particular suggested the idea of this song, which was written and composed at the time."

USG-204 General Grant Grand March. m. E. Mack. Published by Co-Operative Music Company, Philadelphia, PA. [ca. 188-]. B/w litho of Ulysses S. Grant. 6pp.

USG-205 Not For Seymour (Campaign Song and Chorus). w.m. Dexter Smith. Published by S. Brainard & Sons, No. 203 Superior Street, Cleveland, OH. 1868. Non-pictorial geometric design border. 6pp. Page 2: Blank.

USG-206 Reception To Hon. Shuyler Colfax (At the Opera House) [Song Sheet]. Published at Evansville, Indiana, October 30th, 1868. [18 1/8" × 10"]. Non-pictorial black border. 2pp.

USG-207 In Memoriam General U.S. Grant [Song Sheet]. Published by N.Y. Variety Publishing Company, No. 77 Chatham Street, New York, NY. [1885]. [11 5/8" × 17 1/4"]. B/w litho of Ulysses S. Grant, geometric design border. 2pp. Page 2: Blank.

USG-208 The American Army (Polka or Military Quickstep). m. Edward Clapham. M.D. Published by H.M. Higgins, No. 117 Randolph Street, Chicago, IL. 1864. B/w litho of statue inscribed "Liberty 1776 —1864;" cup with flame, eagle with ribbon inscribed "E Pluribus Unum," swords, scrolls with the names of Union generals including "U.S. Grant," John C. "Fremont," Ben "Butler," George "McClellan" and Nathaniel "Banks." "Composed and Dedicated To the Officers and Privates of that Gallant Army." 8pp. Page 8: Blank.

USG-209 General Grant's Grand March. m. E. Mack. a. William Conrad. Published by Belwin, Inc., New York, NY. [ca. 1950]. Pk/w drawings of famous classical composers — "Schumann, Handel, Mendelssohn, Listz, Mozart, Haydn, Verdi," harps, piano. 6pp. Pages 2 and 6: Advertising.

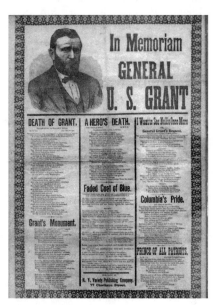

USG-204   USG-207

(USG) ULYSSES S. GRANT

USG-210 The Tanner And The Blue (A Campaign Song and Chorus). w. James Summerfield. m. James R. Murray. Published by Root & Cady, No. 67 Washington Street, Chicago, IL. 1868. Non-pictorial geometric designs. "To the 1st Ward Tanner Club of Chicago & All Tanner Clubs throughout the Union." 6pp. Page 6: Advertising.

USG-211 Rally For The Leader! (Song and Chorus). w. D. McNaughton. m. George O. Herrick. Published by Root & Cady, No. 67 Washington Street, Chicago, IL. 1868. B/w non-pictorial geometric designs. "To Col. Geo. G. Briggs, Prest. of Grant Club, Grand Rapids, Mich." 6pp. Page 6: Blank.

USG-212(A) Grant's Triumphal M'ch. m. Gardiner. Published by John Church, Jr., No. 66 West 4th Street, Cincinnati, OH. [1866?]. Non-pictorial. "XX Beautiful Pieces for the Piano by Eminent Authors." List of other titles in series.

(B) Grant's March. m. Eileman.

USG-213 Grant And Lee At Appomattox. In: *War Songs*, page 1. Published by Woolson Spice Company, Toledo, OH. [ca. 1884]. [4 3/4" × 6 7/8"]. N/c litho of war scene, company logos for "Lion Coffee" and "Woolson Spice Co." "Dedicated to the G.A.R., The Woman's Relief Corps and The Sons of Volunteers." 36pp.

USG-214 General Grant's [Grand] March. m. E. Mack. Published by De Luxe Music Company, No. 233 40th Street, New York, NY. [ca. 193-]. Gn/w drawing of eagle, shield, designs. "De Luxe Edition." 6pp. Pages 2 and 6: Advertising.

USG-215 General Grant's Grand March. m. E. Mack. e. William Conrad. Published by C.C. Church & Company, Hartford, CT. [ca. 193-]. N/c drawing of George Washington, troops, ships in harbor. "Famous Marches for the Piano." List of other songs in series. 8pp. Pages 2, 7 and 8: Blank.

USG-216 Gen. Grant's Grand March. m. E. Mack. Published by C.C. Church & Company, Hartford, CT. [ca. 1930?]. N/c drawing of George and Martha Washington. "Famous Marches for the Piano." 8pp. Pages 2, 7 and 8: Advertising.

USG-217 Three Heroes We Have Lost (Or They Were Loved by All the Nation]. w.m. W. Retisor. Published by Will Rossiter, No. 56 Fifth Avenue, Chicago, IL. 1891. Non-pictorial. "Ulysses S. Grant, 1885; Phil Sheridan, 1888; Wm. T. Sherman, 1891." "An American Song." "Words by, Music by, W.R. Williams (Author of *Sweet Nellie Baun, Nora Malone, A Cute Baby Boy, &c., &c.).* [An apparent incorrect attribution of authorship listed on the cover]. 6pp. Page 6: Advertising.

USG-218 General Grant's Grand March. m. E. Mack. [ca. 1930]. [6 7/8" × 13 15/16"]. Non-pictorial. "By permission, Leo Feist, Inc., New York." 2pp. Page 2: Blank.

USG-219 General Grant's Grand March. m. E. Mack. Published by Century Publishing Company, No. 1178 Broadway, New York, NY. [ca. 1911]. Gn/bl/w drawing of arch, ribbon, geometric designs. "Popular Marches by Celebrated Composers — 2nd Series." "Century Edition." List of other titles in series. 6pp. Pages 2 and 6: Advertising.

USG-220 General Grant's Grand March (Gran Marcha del General Grant). m. E. Mack. a. Henry S. Sawyer. Published by McKinley Publishers, Inc., Chicago, IL. 1922. R/w/b geometric design border. List of other marches in the series. "Popular Marches of Medium Grade (Marchas Populares de Mediana Ejecucion)." "McKinley World Famous Edition (Celebrada Edicion de la Casa McKinley)." 6pp. Pages 2 and 6: Advertising.

USG-221(A) The Turkish Patrol March (Or Turkish Review March). m. Thomas Michaels. a. Louis Bodecker. Copyright 1879 by Dave Wood. B/w litho of men in national dress holding hands around a globe — Uncle Sam, John Bull, &c. "Around the World Popular Melodies." "To Gen. U.S. Grant, and Retinue." 6pp. Pages 2 and 6: Blank. Page 3: Instructions — "This Composition should represent the approach, passing and withdrawal of a company of soldiers."

(B) Around The World Schottische. m. Hennig.

USG-222 Dawley's Campaign U.S. Grant Song Book. Published by T.R. Dawley, Publisher for the Million, Nos. 21 and 23 Ann Street, New York, NY. 1868. [4" × 6 1/4"]. O/bk litho of Ulysses S. Grant, geometric designs and border. 40pp. Page 3: Title – **The Ulysses S. Grant Song Book**. [M-168].

USG-223 General Grant's Requiem March. m. Mrs. Parkhurst Duer (Author of *Lincoln's Funeral March, Garfield's Funeral March, &c., &c.*). Published by Anderson & Company, No. 298 Fulton Street, Brooklyn, NY. 1885. B/w non-pictorial geometric line border. "To the Victorious Leader of the Nation in the Greatest War of Modern Times." 6pp. Page 6: Blank.

USG-224 Take A Glide With Me. w. Maurice E. Marks. m. William H. Smith. Published by George J. Scott Motor Company, Nos. 1720-1722 Broadway, New York, NY. 1906. Bl/w/pk drawing of cupid with "Glide" hat. Bl/w photo of the "Glide" Automobile in front of Ulysses S. Grant's Tomb. "To 'The Smoothest Thing on Wheels.'" "Compliments of Geo. J. Scott Motor Co." 6pp. Pages 2 and 6: Blank.

USG-225 How Sleep The Brave Who Sink To Rest (An Elegy for Soprano Solo with Chorus). w.m. Hugo Pierson. Published by Denton & Cottier, No. 269 Main Street, Buffalo, NY. 1885. Non-pictorial black line border. "As sung at the funeral ceremonies of General U.S. Grant, August 8th, 1885." 6pp. Page 6: Blank.

USG-226 General Grant's Grand March. m. E. Mack. Published by W. Paxton, No. 19 Oxford Street, West., London, England. [ca. 1910]. Non-pictorial black line border. 4pp. Page 4: Advertising for "Famous Pianoforte Pieces by John Pridham, Composer of the *Battle March of Delhi*."

USG-227 General Grant's Grand March. m. E. Mack. a. Maxwell Eckstein. Published by Carl Fisher, Inc., No. 62 Cooper Square, New York 3, NY. 1947. Bl/w non-pictorial cover. "Popular Favorites for Piano." 6pp. Page 2: Blank. Page 4: Advertising.

USG-228 Grant Boys Of 72. w. E.J. Farmer. m. Lydia Hoyt Farmer. Published by J.L. Peters, No. 599 Broadway, New York, NY. 1872. Non-pictorial geometric designs. "Dedicated to Gen'l Grant." 6pp. Pages 2 and 6: Blank.

USG-229 Gen. Grant's March. m. E. Mack. Published by E. Corlett, Publisher, No. 340 Yonge Street, Toronto, Canada. [ca. 1900]. B/w litho of woman in forest. "Instrumental Favorites." List of other titles in series.

USG-230 General Grant's Grand March. m. E. Mack. Published by Theodore Presser Company, No. 1712 Chestnut Street, Philadelphia, PA. [ca. 1920]. B/w pussywillow design border. "Old Popular Favorites for the Pianoforte." List of other titles in series.

USG-231 Keep The Ball A-Rolling (Song and Chorus). w.m. Ossian E. Dodge. Published by Root & Cady, No. 67 Washington Street, Chicago, IL. 1868. Non-pictorial geometric lines. "Dedicated to the 'Little Grant' of Minnesota, Hon. Ignatius Donnelly." 6pp. Page 6: Blank.

USG-232 General Grant (March). m. K.L. King. Published by C.L. Barnhouse Company, Oskaloosa, IA. 1943. [6 7/8" × 10 1/2"]. Non-pictorial. "Conductor" Score. 4pp.

USG-233 Cuba Shall Be Free. w.m. F.A. Werth. Published by F.A.

Werth, No. 916 South Broadway, Los Angeles, CA. May, 1898. B/w litho of shield, geometric designs, eagle with ribbon inscribed "Cuba Liebre." "The Sons of our Heroes of Grant and Lee Are eager to fight, that Cuba be Free!." 6pp. Pages 2 and 6: Blank.

USG-234 General Grant's Grand March (Gran Marcha del General Grant). m. E. Mack. e. Henry S. Sawyer. Published by McKinley Publishers, Inc., Chicago, IL. 1922. Bl/w litho of bell, flags, geometric designs. List of other titles in the series—"Medium Grade Selections." "No. 1004." 6pp. Pages 2 and 6: Advertising.

USG-235 General Grant's Grand March. m. E. Mack. Published by Victor Kremer Company, Chicago, IL. [1907]. Bl/gn/w floral and geometric designs. 6pp. Pages 5 and 6: Advertising.

USG-236 The Blue And The Grey (Song and Chorus). w. Miss Ida Scott Taylor. m. Henry M. Butler (Author of *Hurrah for Grant!, Our Nation's Noble Son, Down in the Dell Where the Primroses Grow, Ho! For California, &c.*). Published by Henry M. Butler, St. Joseph, MO. 1886. B/w litho of U.S. & Confederate flags, military equipment. "U.S. Grant, 1822-1885," and "R.E. Lee, 1807-1870." "We are ane [sic] in our joys, our affections, an A: Sae gi'e me your hand,— We are brethren A." "Let us have Peace." 6pp. Pages 2 and 6: Blank. Page 3: "This song can be sung to *In The Sweet By and By*."

USG-237 Grand Reunion March. m. H.N. Hempsted. Published by H.N. Hempsted, No. 408, 410 and 412 Broadway, Milwaukee, WI. 1880. B/w tan tinted litho by Milwaukee Litho & Engraving Company of Ulysses S. Grant, Phil Sheridan, other Union General, eagle, flags, shield, wreaths, ribbon inscribed "Liberty-Union-Peace." 12pp. Pages 2, 10, 11 and 12: Blank.

USG-238 Gen. Grant's Reception March. m. E. Mack. Published by C.H. Kimball, "Wholesale and Retail Dealer in Music, Books and Cards," Manchester, NH. Copyright 1879 by W.F. Shaw. B/w litho "From a Photograph taken on his arrival at San Francisco, September, 1879" of Ulysses S. Grant. "To the Many Admirers of General Grant." "Sequel to *Gen. Grant's March* by the same Author." 6pp. Page 2: Blank. Page 6: Advertising.

USG-239 Surrender Bill! (Song). w.m. Myles F. Bradley. Published by Harmony Music Company, Flint MI. Copyright 1918 by Myles F. Bradley. Drawing by Myles F. Bradley of hand with club hitting Kaiser Bill—"Ka-Ka-Kamerad!!" Circle with the stripes— "U.S. Club." "Dedicated to The Unconditional Surrender Club of the United States of America." Photo of Ulysses S. Grant. 4pp.

USG-240 General Grant's Grand March. m. E. Mack. In: *The World's Best Album of Marches*, page 78. Published by Amsco Music Publishing Company, Inc., No. 240 West 55th Street, New York 19, NY. 1942. [9" × 12"]. Gd/pl/ma/w drawing by Barbelle of a drum major. "World's Best Music Series No.11." Table of Contents. "Adaptable for Schools, Playgrounds, Parades, Assembly, Teaching." 100pp.

USG-241 Down In Washington (A Grant Campaign Song). m. Air: *Down In A Coal Mine*. In: *Singer's Journal, No. 81, Vol. II*, page 613. Published by Henry De Marsan, American Music Company, No. 60 Chatham Street, New York, NY. 1892. 36pp.

USG-242 Wilson's Funeral March. m. T.P. Ryder. Published by White, Smith & Company, No. 516 Washington Street, Boston, MA. 1875. B/w litho by J.H. Bufford's Litho. of Henry Wilson, black line border. "In Memory of the late Hon. Henry Wilson, Vice President, U.S.A., Who died November 22, 1875." 6pp. Page 2: Blank. Page 6: Advertising.

USG-243 Wilson's Funeral March. Published by White, Smith & Company, Music Publisher, No. 516 Washington Street, Boston, MA. 1876. Non-pictorial black border. "Ryder's Standard Compositions for the Pianoforte." List of other titles in series.

USG-244 Grant's March. a. Sep. Winner. Published by Oliver Ditson Company, Boston, MA. [ca. 1880s]. Non-pictorial geometric designs. "The Evening Hour, A Selection of Popular Melodies." List of other titles in series.

USG-245 President Grant's Polka. m. Ella V. Young. Published by Lee & Walker, No. 922 Chestnut Street, Philadelphia, PA. 1868. B/w geometric designs. "Respectfully Dedicated to General U.S. Grant." 6pp. Pages 2 and 6: Blank.

USG-246 The Huzza Song. Published as a chewing gum wrapper. [1872]. [2 1/8" × 4 1/4"]. Obv: B/w litho of "U.S. Grant." Rev: Song. "For Grant our Noble candidate."

USG-247 General Grant's Boys. w. James D. Gay. [m. Air: *Old Virginia Low Lands, Low*]. Published by James D. Gay, No. 300 North 20th Street, Philadelphia, PA. 1864. [5 1/4" × 8 1/2"]. B/w litho of men at rally, speaker — "Grant's Beverage is Meade," geometric design border. "James D. Gay, the Celebrated Army Song Publisher and Vocalists, No. 300 North 20th Street, Philadelphia, Pa." 2pp. Page 2: Blank.

USG-248 March De Funebre (In Memoriam U.S. Grant). m. Charles Lange. Published by Balmer & Weber, Publishers, St. Louis, MO. 1885. Bl/bk outer wraps with litho of Ulysses S. Grant — Died, July 23d, 1885, Aged, 63 Years," "In Memoriam." Bl/bk litho of arch, angels. 12pp. Pages 2, 4, 11 and 12: Blank. Page 3: B/w litho of Ulysses S. Grant, black line border. Pages 2 and 7: Blank. Page 8: Advertising.

USG-249 General Grant's March. m. [E.] Mack. Published by Century Music Publishers, Nos. 231-235 West 40th Street, New York, NY. [ca. 1930]. Gn/w geometric designs. "Standard Marches." "Series One." List of other marches in series.

USG-250 In Battle We Then Will Defend It (Song & Chorus). w. Alfred B. Street. m. J.A. Butterfield. Published by A.M. Benham & Company, Indianapolis, IN. 1864. Non-pictorial geometric designs. "Respectfully dedicated to America's most successful General U.S. Grant." 6pp. Pages 2 and 6: Blank.

USG-251(A) Re-Joyce McDonald, A-very Crooked Whiskey March (Gallop Burlesque). a. "Sour Mash." Published by Balmer & Weber, St. Louis, MO. 1876. B/w litho of caricatures of Ulysses S. Grant on horseback — "U.S.," other politicians labeled — "*Globe Democrat*," "Crooked Whiskey" and "Vivat Justicia." 6pp. Page 2: Blank. Page 3: Music Marked — "Conspirators' Chorus." Page 5: Music marked "Rogues' March" and "Drummed Out." Page 6: Advertising.

(B) Re-Joyce McDonald, A-very Crooked Whiskey March (Song & Chorus).

USG-252 No Slave Beneath That Starry Flag. w. Rev. George Lansing Taylor. m. Mrs. Parkhurst (Author of *The New Emancipation Song, Little Joe, The Contraband, Sweet Home Of My Early Days, Art Thou Thinking Of Me In My Absence*). Published by Horace Waters, No. 481 Broadway, New York, NY. 1864. B/w geometric design frame. "To the Hon. Henry Wilson, Senator from Massachusetts, to whose distinguished ability, integrity, and firmness for the right, in this and many other instances, humanity and the future are so much indebted, this song is, by his special permission, most respectfully dedicated by the Author." 6pp. Page 2: "The conference committee (of the Senate and the House of Representatives) inserted one very important amendment in the (conscription) bill, when it was before them. Senator Wilson announced to them his firm resolution that no slave should serve the government for one moment 'as a slave' and it was provided that the drafted or enlisted slave shall be free the instant that he enters the service." Page 6: Advertising.

USG-253 Booth Campaign Songster. e. Samuel Booth. Published by Alta California General Printing House, San Francisco, CA. 1871. 36[?]pp. [M-177].

USG-254. The Grant Campaign Songster. Published by J.L. Peters, New York, NY. 1868. O/bk non-pictorial. "A Series of Songs and Choruses Adapted to the Music in the Patriotic Glee Book." Also published by "De Motte Bros., Chicago, IL., J.J. Dobmeyer & Company, Cincinnati, OH., and J.B. Dobmeyer, St. Louis, MO." 34pp. [M-154].

USG-255 Grant Glee Club Book, Buffalo. Published by Sage, Sons & Company, Buffalo, NY. 1868. [V-1: O/bk] [V-2: Be/bk] [V-3 Bl/bk] non-pictorial. [V-1: Litho of flag]. "Price 25 cents." [M-161, 162, 163].

USG-256 The Grant & Wilson Campaign Songster. Published by Fisher & Denison, New York, NY. 1872. Be/bk litho of Ulysses S. Grant. Page 3: "Containing a large Collection of the Popular Songs as Sung by Leading Republican Glee Clubs." [M-180].

USG-257 Holmes' Patriotic Songs For Coming Campaigns. w.m. Samuel N. Holmes. Published by Samuel N. Holmes, Syracuse, NY. 1868.

USG-258 Campaign Songs For The People. w.m. J.A. Kiefer. Published by Douglas & Conner, Indianapolis, IN. 1868. "Grant, Colfax and Victory."

USG-259 Old Glory Song Book. Published by E.F. Rollins, Boston, MA. 1868. Litho of flag. "For The Grant & Colfax Campaign." "For the Use of Grant Clubs, Republican and Grand Army of the Republic Meetings, &c." [M-165].

USG-260 The Union Republican Campaign Glee Book. Published by Hall & Company, Philadelphia, PA. 1868. "Songs of the People: Grant & Colfax." Y/bk non-pictorial. 52pp. [M-166].

USG-261 The Radical Drum Call. e. Henry Tucker. Published by Robert M. DeWitt, New York, NY. 1868. Be/bk non-pictorial. "A Choice Collection of Patriotic Songs Containing All the Well Known "National Airs," Together with Many New and Original Pieces Adapted to the Most Popular Glees and People's Songs. Arranged for & Sung by The Anderson Brothers' Union Glee Club of New York." 100pp. [M-167].

USG-262 The Grant & Wilson Tanner & Shoemaker Melodist. w.m. D.A. De Marbelle. Published by "For the Author, Syracuse, NY. 1872." 16pp. [M-178].

USG-263 Yon Coo Doodle Do [Song Book]. c. Eldridge J. Merick. Published in Rochester, NY. 1872. 8pp. [M-181].

USG-264 Hurrah For General Grant. w. J.A.H. m. C.T. Lockwood. Published by Lockwood and Hoyt, Pontiac, MI. [ca. 1867].

USG-265 Gen. Grant's March. a. P.T. German. Published by Whitney's Palace of Music, No. 173 Summit Street, Toledo, OH. [ca. 186-]. "Collection of Wild Flowers."

USG-266 Who Shall Rule The American Union? (Song And Chorus). w.m. Henry C. Work. Published by Root & Cady, Opera House, No. 67 Washington Street, Chicago, IL. 1868.

USG-267 Columbia's Call (Song And Chorus). w.m. George F. Root. Published by Root & Cady, Opera House, No. 67 Washington Street, Chicago, IL. 1868.

USG-268 Northmen Awake (Quartet). w. S. Fillmore Bennett. m. J.P. Webster. Published by Root & Cady, Opera House, No. 67 Washington Street, Chicago, IL. 1868.

USG-269 The Liberty Bird (Quartet, In Chant Form). w.m. George F. Root. Published by Root & Cady, Opera House, No. 67 Washington Street, Chicago, IL. 1868.

USG-270 All Rights For All (Song And Chorus). w. E.B. Dewing. m. J.P. Webster. Published by Root & Cady, Opera House, No. 67 Washington Street, Chicago, IL. 1868.

USG-271 It Is An Age Of Progress Awake (Quartet). w.m. J.P. Webster. Published by Root & Cady, Opera House, No. 67 Washington Street, Chicago, IL. 1868.

USG-272 Song Of A Thousand Years (Song And Chorus). w.m. Henry C. Work. Published by Root & Cady, Opera House, No. 67 Washington Street, Chicago, IL. 1868.

USG-273 Columbia's Guardian Angels (Song And Chorus). w.m. Henry C. Work. Published by Root & Cady, Opera House, No. 67 Washington Street, Chicago, IL. 1868.

USG-274 Gen. Grant's March. m. R. Zelner. Published by Root & Cady, No. 95 Clark Street, Chicago, IL. [ca. 1862].

USG-275 School Anthem. In: *Commencement U.S. Grant High School* [Program], page 3. Published by Grant High School, Portland, OR. 1941. [Song praising Ulysses S. Grant].

USG-276 President Grant And Political Rings (A Satire). w. P. Ludmore, Esq., Counselor at Law. For sale by P.J. Kennedy, New York, NY. 1880. 92[?]pp. [M-220, 227].

USG-277 Gen. Grant's Funeral March. m. Horace R. Basler. Published by Horace R. Basler, Pittsburg, PA. 1885.

USG-278 The Grant & Colfax Campaign Songster. Published by C.F. Vent & Company, Cincinnati, OH. 1868. Y/bk non-pictorial. "Price 10 cents." [M-149].

USG-279 The Grant Pill. w. Harriet L. Castle. m. J.C. Becket. In: *Ballads & Songs Of The Civil War*, page 250. c. Jerry Silverman. Published by Mel Bay Publications, Inc., Pacific, MO. 63069. 1998. 276pp.

USG-280 General Grant's Grand March. m. E. Mack. In: *The Parlor Organ Galaxy of Instrumental and Vocal Music Including the Most Popular Waltzes, Marches, Polkas, Galops, &c* e. W.F. Studds. Published by Oliver Ditson & Co., Boston, MA. 1886. [8 11/16" × 11 3/16"]. Pk/bk geometric designs. 100pp.

USG-281 General Grant's Grand March. m. E. Mack. a. Rafael Richter. In: *Superior March Album, A Collection of Execellent Marches by Well Known Composers for School, Home and General Use*, page 52. Published by Witmark & Sons, New York, NY. Pl/pk floral designs. 68pp.

USG-282 General Grant's Grand March. B/w drawing of Grant on horseback. 1937. In: *20 Marches*, page 1. Published by Belmont Music Company, Indiana and 26th Street, Chicago, IL. 1938. [6" × 9"]. O/bk/w drawing of a drum major and band. 28pp.

USG-283 General Grant's Grand March. m. E. Mack. Published by C.C. Church and Company, Hartford, CT. [ca. 1935]. N/c drawing of old cabin, lake, sunset. R/w/bk geometric design border. "Edition Beautiful." 6pp.

USG-284 Unfurl The Flag (Patriotic Song And Chorus). w.m. Wm. Whittick. Published by Edward Hopkins, No. 30 East 14th Street, New York, NY. 1876. B/w geometric design border. "Dedicated with great respect to President U.S. Grant." 4pp. Page 4: Advertising.

USG-285 General Grant's Grand March. m. E. Mack. a. Bea Woode. Published by The Willis Music Co., Cincinnati, OH. 1950. Bl/w nonpictorial lines. "Piano Solo." 6pp. Page 2: Blank. Page 6: Advertising.

USG-286 Rally Round Ulysses Boys (Republican Campaign Song). w.

E.H.E. Jameson; m. Charles Carlton. Published by Compton & Dent, No. 205 North Fourth Street, Saint Louis, MO. 1868. B/w non-pictorial geometric designs. 6pp. Pages 2 and 6: Blank.

USG-287 National March. m. A.P. Wyman. Published by C.Y. Fonda, No. 72 West Fourth Street, Cincinnati, OH. 1868. B/w litho by Clayton of Ulysses S. Grant. "Dedicated to Gen. U.S. Grant."

USG-288 Mount McGregor Funeral March. m. Almon D. Hougas. Published by A.W. Perry & Son, Sedalia, MO. 1885. B/w litho by Crosscup & West of Ulysses S. Grant. 6pp. Inside title page: "To the Memory of General U.S. Grant." "For Piano or Cabinet Organ." Page 6: Advertisements for W. Perry & Son music.

USG-289(A) Grant's Grand March. m. Fred. Gardner. Published by John Church & Co., No. 66 West 4th Street, Cincinnati, OH. [186-]. B/w non-pictorial geometric designs. 6pp.

(B) Grant's Grand March. m. F.A. Eileman.

USG-290 Boys in Blue (Song & Chorus). w. W.V. Lawrence. m. J.G. Dunlap. Published by John Church, Jr., No. 66 West 4th Street, Cincinnati, OH. 1868. B/w non-pictorial geometric designs. "Dedicated to the 'Boys in Blue' and Their Supporters." 6pp. Pages 2 and 6: Blank.

USG-291 U.S. Race (Republican Campaign Song With Chorus). w.m. J. William Pope (Author of *Allegheny: An Indian's Lament, Wake From Thy Slumbers, Leave Me Alone In My Sorrow, & c*). Published by C.C. Mellor, No. 81 Wood Street, Pittsburgh, PA. 1868. R/w non-pictorial geometric designs. "Dedicated to the Oakland Glee Club."

USG-292 Grant Polka Briliant. m. J.A.P. Published by G.D. Russell & Company, No. 126 Tremont Street, Boston, MA. 1872. B/w non-pictorial geometric designs. "Composed and Respectfully dedicated to U.S. Grant, Prest. of the United States by J.A.P."

USG-293 General U.S. Grant's Triumphal March. m. Giuseppe Operti, Op. 140. Published by Wm. Hall & Son, No. 543 Broadway, New York, NY. 1869. B/w non-pictorial geometric designs. Respectfully dedicated to Genl. U.S. Grant, President of the United States."

USG-294 General Grant's Grand Victory March. m. G.J. Kredel. Published by Hoffmann & Hoene, No. 53 Fifth Street, Pittsburg, PA. 1864. Bk/w/be floral and geometric design frame. "Respectfully Dedicated to Lieut. General Grant." 4pp.

USG-295 The Firm, The Just & The Brave. w. William Adolphus Clark. m. F.A. Strauss. Published by Oliver Ditson & Co., No. 277 Washington Street, Boston, MA. 1872. Be/bk/w litho of Ulysses S. Grant in oval black line frame.

USG-296 Colfax Polka. Published by Russell, G.D. & Co., No. 126 Tremont St., Boston, MA. [1868]. B/w non-pictorial geometric designs. "To Hon. Schuyler Colfax." 6pp. Page 6: Blank.

USG-297 Victory! (March Triumphal). m. Rudolph Wittig. Published by W.R. Smith, Agt., No. 135 North Eighth Street, Philadelphia, PA. 1864. Non-pictorial geometric designs. "Respectfully Dedicated to Lieut. Gen. Ulysses S. Grant." "Introducing the beautiful melody *Jenny Wade*." 6pp. Pages 2 and 6: Blank.

USG-298 The Firm, The Just And The Brave!. w.m. William A. Clarke and F.A. Strauss. In: *Marches Of The Presidents, 1789-1909, Authentic Marches & Campaign Songs*, page 46. a. Carl Miller. Published by Chappell & Co., Inc., No. 609 Fifth Avenue, New York, NY. "By arrangement with Chilmark Press, Inc." 1968. [9" × 12"]. R/w/b litho of eagle, flag. "An Illustrated Piano Folio For All Ages." 72pp.

**USG-299 War Songs Of The

Blue And The Gray. Published by Hurst & Co., Publishers, New York, NY. [ca. 1880]. [4 3/8" × 6 1/2"]. Bl/k lithos of "Grant," "Robert E. Lee," "Johnston," and "Sherman," 72pp.

USG-300 Grant's The Man. w. C.L. Abdill. m. J.M. Darling. Published by Johnson, Song Publisher, No. 7 10th Street, Philadelphia, PA. 1864. B/w non-pictorial geometric design border. "J. Marsh, 1102 Chestnut Street, All the new popular sheet music, Pianos, Musical Instruments, &c, &c." "See Prof. Brook's Ball Room Monitor, it will give you more instruction in Dancing than any Book ever Published. Sold by Johnson, Song Publisher, No. 7 North 10th Street, Philadelphia, PA. Price 15 cts." 2pp. Page 2: Blank.

See also GW-133; GW-197; GW-222; GW-377; GW-411; GW-412; GW-413; AL-11; AL-72; AL-221; AL-263; AL-272; AL-278; AL-306; AL-350; AL-351; AL-352; AL-507; AL-514; HS-12; HG-1; HG-3; HG-11; SJT-7; SJT-17; WSH-30; JAG-49; JAG-66; JGB-35; JGB-52; JGB-97; BFH-74; WM-96; TR-252; TR-314; WHT-23; WHT-42; WW-16; WW-19; WW-31; WW-58; WW-61; WW-67; WW-85; WW-87; FDR-158; DDE-9; DDE-49; LBJ-1; MISC-46; MISC-94; MISC-139; MISC-167.

WALTER F. MONDALE

WFM-1 All The Way With Mondale. w.m. Joseph Erdelyi, Jr., No. 358 West 51st Street, New York, NY. 10019. 1984. [8 1/2" × 11"]. Non-pictorial. "Campaign Song for Walter Mondale, 1984 Democratic Candidate for President of the United States, with Special adaptation of the song for New York State residents and the Primary Election of April 3, 1984." "Dedicated to the Honorable Governor of the State of New York Mario Cuomo, who encouraged the Author to write a song for the Democrats." 2pp. Page 2: Blank.

WFM-2 We Need A Change In Washington. w.m. Joseph Erdelyi, Jr., No. 358 West 51st Street, New York, NY. 10019. July 18, 1984. [8 1/2" × 11"]. B/w photos of Walter Mondale on a campaign button inscribed "America Needs A Change, Mondale in '84," Joseph Erdelyi, Jr. "Campaign Song for Walter Mondale, 1984 Democratic Candidate for President of the United States." "Dedicated to the Honorable Governor of the State of New York Mario Cuomo, who encouraged the Author to write a song for the Democrats." 2pp. Page 2: Blank

WARREN G. HARDING

WGH-1 Harding (You're The Man For Us). w.m. Al Jolson. w.a. L.L. VosBurgh. 1920. B/w photos of "Warren G. Harding — Republican Candidate for President" and Calvin Coolidge — Republican Candidate for Vice-President." "The Official Republican Campaign Song." 4pp. Page 4: Printer's logo — "Orchestration Service, New York City."

WGH-2 The Man Of The Hour. w.m. Jim C. Madden. Published by Welden Company, Publishers, Philadelphia, PA. 1920. Br/be Clinedinst photo of Warren G. Harding. 4pp. Page 4: Advertising for other Welden Company campaign music.

WGH-3 The Nominee (March Song). w. R. Davidson. m. William A. Peters. Published by A.C. Peters, No. 1068 Park Avenue, New York, NY. 1920. Bl/w design by Pfeiffer of floral and geometric designs. Bl/w Underwood and Underwood photo of Warren G. Harding. 4pp. Page 4: Blank.

WGH-4 Harding March. m. M. Azzolina. Published by Christopher Music Company, DuQuoin, IL. 1920. Br/be drawing of Warren G. Harding. Br/be drawing of bunting, torches, wreaths. 6pp. Page 2: Copyright information. Page 3: "Dedication to the man whose heart beats rhythmic music in accord with what is best for us all — The man who has been chosen to lead this great nation to a more glorious future — The man of destiny, the president-elect, Warren G. Harding, This composition is Respectfully dedicated by the Author." Page 6: Blank.

WGH-5 **(Sink All Your Ships In The Ocean Blue And) Sail On The Ship Of Love.** w. Jack Glogau. m. Fred Fisher. Published by Fred Fisher, Inc., No. 224 West 46th Street, New York, NY. 1921. R/w/b cover. Bl/w photos of Warren G. "Harding" and Charles E. "Hughes." "The Song of the Moment." 6pp. Pages 2 and 6: Advertising for other Fisher music.

WGH-6 **Mr. Harding We're All For You** (Song and Refrain). w.m. John L. McManus. Published by M. Witmark and Sons, Witmark Building, New York, NY. 1920. R/w/b litho of crossed flags, eagle, torches, wreathes. Bl/w photo by Edmonston of Warren G. Harding — facsimile signature. "Endorsed and Approved by the Republican National Committee." "America Always First." 6pp. Page 5: Blank. Page 6: Advertising for other M. Witmark and Sons music.

WGH-7 **President Harding March** (March Song). w.m. Paul Crane. Published by Triangle Music Publishing Company, No. 145 West 45th Street, New York, NY. 1920. Br/w drawings of stars and stripes, eagle. Br/w photo of Warren G. Harding, facsimile signature — "Sincerely Yours, Warren G. Harding." 4pp. Page 2: "Respectfully Dedicated to Hon. Warren G. Harding." Page 4: Advertising.

WGH-8 **O-HI-O!** (He's Every Inch a Man). w.m. Jim C. Madden. Published by Welden Company, Philadelphia, PA. 1920. Br/be drawing of a map of Ohio. Br/w photo of Warren G. Harding with cane. 4pp. Page 4: Advertising for other music.

WGH-9 **"Oh" Harding** (He Is the Man). w. Dewey T. Baird. m. Louis E. Zoeller. a. Harry L. Cook. Published for the Republican State Campaign Committee by The Zoeller Music Company, Louisville, KY. 1920. Br/w/bl eagle. Bl/w Harris and Ewing photo of "Warren G. Harding." 6pp. Page 2: "Dedicated to Warren G. Harding." Page 6: Advertising.

WGH-10 **Harding**. w.m. Jim C. Madden. Published by Welden Company, Philadelphia, PA. 1920. Br/w drawing of elephant — "G.O.P.," suitcase — "Warren G. Harding." Drawing of Capitol dome, flag.

WGH-11 **Harding's The Man For Me** (Song and Male Quartet). w.m. Edward L. Bohal. Published by E.L. Bohal & Company, Music Publishers, Mansfield, OH. 1920. B/w photo of Warren G. Harding. B/w drawings of Theodore "Roosevelt," Abraham "Lincoln," William "McKinley," "Says Uncle Sam and Every Yankee a Rare Good Type Is He, of Roosevelt, Lincoln and McKinley." "He's the Strong Man We Need On This We've Agreed He Shall The Yanks' President Be That's Harding The Good Old Yankee Hurrah, Hurrah for Warren G." 4pp. Page 2: "To Senator Warren G. Harding." Page 4: Advertising.

WGH-12 **The First Lady Of The Land** (Song). w. Eleanor Hope. m. William T. Pierson. Published by W.T. Pierson and Company, Washington, DC. March 4th, 1921. B/w litho of painting "From Miniature Portrait by F.B. Clark" of Mrs. Warren G. Harding, flowers, geometric designs. 6pp. Page 2: Blank. Page 3: "To Mrs. Warren G. Harding." Page 6: Song by John J. Daly.

WGH-13 **Sing On To Victory** [Foldout Song Sheet]. Published by the Republican Bureau, No. 726 Pacific Avenue, Tacoma, WA. 1920. [3 1/8" × 6"]. B/w photos of "Warren G. Harding" [facsimile signature] — "For President" and "Calvin Coolidge" [facsimile signature] — "For Vice President," eagle, flags. "America Always First." 8pp. Fold out. [M-416].

WGH-14 Harding Songs. w. Frank Adams Mitchell (Cheer Master). Assisted by E.K. Orr, J.P. Wahlman and I.H. Christian. m. Popular Tunes. Published for Chicago-Marion Businessmen's Club, September 10-11, 1920. [4" × 7"]. Non-pictorial. 4pp. [M-413].

WGH-15 Harding and Coolidge Campaign [Foldout Song Sheet]. Published by Republican League of Massachusetts. [1920]. [4 1/4" × 9 3/8"]. Non-pictorial. "Everybody Sing" "50,000 members by November!" 6pp. [Contains both popular and political songs]. [M-415].

WGH-16 Wave On Bright Stars And Stripes. w.m. Mrs. Charles Almon Coe. Published by Mrs. Charles Almon Coe, No. 639 Stanford Avenue, Los Angeles, CA. 1921. Bl/w photo of Warren G. Harding. R/w/b flag, facsimile letter—"Los Angeles, Calif., Nov. 10, 1921—This is to certify that I, the undersigned, Mrs. Charles Almon Coe, do hereby transfer and give to the Midnight Mission, the song entitled *Waive On Bright Stars and Stripes*. This is given to the Mission in all its phases, in the Building Fund, or whatever is necessary for the uplifting of humanity." "Dedicated to President Warren G. Harding in honor of his world wide peace propaganda." 6pp. Pages 2 and 6: Blank.

WGH-17 We Want Harding (Song). w. Robert E. Nimmo. m. Burrell Van Buren. Published by Nimmo Publishing Company, No. 527 Elizabeth Street, Sault Ste Marie, MI. 1920. Drawing of vases.

WGH-18 Laddie Boy He's Gone. w. Edna Bell Seward. m. George M. Seward. Published by Harold Rossiter Music Company, Nos. 323-325 West Madison Street, Chicago, IL. 1923. Pl/bk/be drawing of wreaths, ribbons. B/w photo of Warren Harding and his dog Laddie Boy. 6pp. Page 3: "Respectfully Dedicated to the Memory of Warren G. Harding, 29th President of the United States America. Born Nov. 2, 1865 — Died, August 2, 1923." Page 2: "Laddie Boy — Poem." "Ask your dealer for a player-roll or phonograph record of this piece." Page 6: Advertising.

WGH-19 A Man And A Credit To The Nation. m. H.C. Talbert. a. John Stuart. Published by Frank Harding, No. 228 East 22nd Street, New York, NY. 1920. Bl/w photos of Warren Harding, and Calvin Coolidge. Br/w titles. "Upright and honest; Fearless and bold." "Dedicated to the Honorable Senator Warren G. Harding." 4pp. Page 4: Advertising.

WGH-20 Bear Well Our Standard Old Glory (Harding And Coolidge Song) (Prudence, Peace, Prosperity). w.m. Walter E. Peters. Published by Harding's Music House, No. 228 East 22nd Street, New York, NY. Copyright 1920 by W.E. Peters, New Haven, Conn." Ma/w photos of Warren Harding — "For President" and Calvin Coolidge — "For Vice-President." Ma/w drawing of shield, eagle, wreath, axe. "Music adapted from 'Bear well our standard old glory.'" "To Harding, Coolidge and the People of the U.S.A." 4pp. Page 4: Advertising.

WGH-21 Mr. Harding, We Will Vote For You. w.m. Emma Bader. Published by The Lenox Company, Music Publishers, No. 271 West 125th Street, New York, NY. Copyright 1920 by Emma Bader, No. 507 West Arch Street, Pittsville, PA. B/w photos of Warren G. Harding "For President" and Calvin Coolidge "For Vice-President." B/w drawings of shield, eagle, wreath, axe. "A Stirring Song and Chorus." "Prudence. Peace. Prosperity." 4pp. Page 4: Blank.

WGH-22 When Harding's In The White House (In the Presidential Chair). w.m. John J. Bickley. Published by The Lenox Company, Music Publishers, No. 271 West 125th Street, New York, NY. Copyright 1920 by John J. Bickley. Bl/w photos of Warren G. Harding — "For President" and Calvin Coolidge —

WGH-22

"For Vice-President." Bl/w drawings of shield, eagle, wreath, axe. "Prudence. Peace. Prosperity." "A Great Campaign Song." 4pp. Page 4: Blank.

WGH-23 America First (Republican Campaign Song Book). Published for The Republican National Committee, No. 19 West 44th Street, New York, NY., by Weldon Company, No. 119 Walnut Street, Philadelphia, PA. 1920. [6" × 9"]. Br/bk photos of "Warren Harding — For President" and "Calvin Coolidge — For Vice President." 20pp. [M-411].

WGH-24 Harding (March). m. Heck and [Floyd E.] Whitmore. Published by Whitmore Music Publishing Company, Scranton, PA. 1920. Br/be photo by Moffett of Warren G. Harding. 4pp. Page 4: Advertising.

WGH-25 Rah! Rah! Rah! For Warren G. Harding (Harding's Presidential Campaign Song). w.m. W. Reginold Carr. Published by W.R. Carr, Marion, OH. 1920. [Pre-1919 size]. Bl/w drawing of eagles, shield, stars and stripes, geometric designs. 4pp.

WGH-26 O-HI-O (O-My-O). w. Jack Yellen. m. Abe Olman. Special Harding lyrics by Al Jolson. Published by Forster Music Publishers, Inc., No. 235 South Wabash, Chicago, IL. 1920. R/w/bl/bk/br drawing by Van Doon Morgan of a man and a woman sitting under a tree. [V-1: Photos of "Al Jolson, Eddie Cantor, Van and Schenck, Lou Holtz, Jack Strouse, Ted Lewis, Arthur West"] [V-2: Photo of Coleman Goetz — "America's Youngest Songwriter"] [V-3: Photo of "Gus Van and Joe Schenck with Ziegfield's Follies"] [V-4: Photo of Jack Strouse — "Century Promenade Atop The Century Theatre, New York City"] [V-5: Photo of Al Jolson — "Introduced by Al Jolson in *Sinbad*. Al Jolson's Sensational Song Hit"]. 6pp. Page 2: B/w litho of eagle, flags. "President Harding's Inaugural Version." Page 6: Advertising.

WGH-27 Glorious Heroes Of The Great World War! (A World Hymn of Victory and Gratitude for Right and Liberty). w.m. J.F. Curtice. Published for the Americanism National League by American Publishing Company, Indianapolis, IN. 1920. Photos of Warren Harding, Calvin Coolidge, Theodore Roosevelt and Gen. Leonard Wood — "A Pair of 100% Glorious but Unofficial Heroes of Our Great World War." "Americanism Poster — Folder — Help Get It To The People." "The Patriotic Purpose of the American People is 100% Americanism." "This is the trumpet call from American homes."

WGH-28 Home Sweet Home. w.m. John Howard Payne. Published by Harold Rossiter Music Company, Chicago, IL. [ca. 1922]. B/w photos of "Warren G. Harding," "Mrs. Thomas G. Winter, President General Federation of Women's Clubs laying corner stone, Washington, DC., model house," and "Secretary of Commerce Herbert Hoover breaking ground." Gn/bk/w drawings of house, the Washington Monument. "So far as this world knows or can vision there is no attainment more desirable than the happy and contented home — Warren G. Harding." B/w drawing of John Howard Payne, Author of Home Sweet Home." 4pp. Page 4: Photo of and narrative on model house.

WGH-29 Republican Songs. Published by Republican National Committee. 1920. [3 3/8" × 6"]. R/w/b drawing of elephant labeled "G.O.P." 8pp. Page 2: "These songs were complied by The Republican Woman's Club of Minneapolis." Page 8: "Harding and Coolidge — Our Nation Needs Them." Harding and Coolidge quotes.

WGH-30 Harding March. m. John Jones. Published by John Jones, 1936 West 44th St., Cleveland, OH. 1920. Photo of Warren G. Harding in shield frame, eagle.

WGH-31 Harding Campaign Songs [Songster]. Published by The National Republican Committee, Will H. Hays, Chairman. [1920]. [3 3/4" × 6"]. Gy/bk non-pictorial. "As Sung by the Famous Republican Glee Club of Columbus, Ohio, Founded 1872, 100 Voices." 20pp.

WGH-32 Ohio And Warren G. w.m. Effa Lovett. a. Ed J. Lee. Copyright 1920 by Effa Lovett, Columbus, OH. [10 1/2" × 13 1/2"]. Br/w photo of Warren Harding. Br/w drawing of "The Great Seal of the State of Ohio." "A Real March Song." "A Stirring Republican Rally Song." "Respectfully Dedicated to Senator Warren G. Harding, Republican Presidential Candidate." "For sale wherever music is sold." "Printed by Pfeifer Show Print Co., Columbus, Ohio." 6pp.

WGH-33 Way Down On Biscayne Bay.

WGH-34 America Admires Brother Harding. w.m. Charles P. Pavia. Published by Bishop & Pavia Music Publishing Company, Miami, FL. 1921. R/w/b flag, drawings of Warren G. "Harding — The Man of the Hour," George "Washington — Courage," Christopher "Columbus — A Planet of Dreams," Abraham "Lincoln — Emancipator," Benjamin "Franklin — Electricity," Thomas "Edison — Scientist and Inventor," Theodore "Roosevelt — Strenuosity." "Played with Great Success by Mutchler, Piano-Accordion Soloist, Pryor's Band." 6pp. Pages 2 and 6: Blank.

WGH-35 The Dashing G.O.P.'s (Song). w. John Chirgwin. m. Keats Moran. Published by John Chirgwin, Box 453, Iron River, MI. [Pre-1919 size]. 1920. R/w/b drawing of Warren G. Harding, flag, cheering crowd. 4pp.

WGH-36 When Harding's In The White House. w. Jorette Bruce. m. George E. Johnson. Published by George E. Johnson Music Publisher, No. 908 10th Street NE, Washington, DC. 1920. Gn/w litho of water lilies. 4pp.

WGH-37 Marion (March or One Step). m. Lutie Hodder-Wheeler. Published by Rio Grande Publishing Company, Albuquerque, NM. Copyright 1921 by Lutie Hodder-Wheeler. [Pre-1919 size]. B/w photo of Warren G. Harding. R/w/b cover "Designed by L.H. Wheeler." "Dedicated to Warren G. Harding, 29th President, U.S.A." "Piano One-Step, Orchestra, Band." 6pp. Page 6: Advertising.

WGH-38 O-HI-O (O-My-O). w. Jack Yellen. m. Abe Olman. Published by Forster Music Publishing Company, Chicago, IL. 1920. Non-pictorial professional copy. 4pp. Page 4: B/w litho of eagle, flag. "President Harding's Inaugural Version."

WGH-39 Our President. w.m. Roe Pettay. Published by Roe Pettay, No. 7 Church Street, Ashtabula, OH. 1923. B/w photo by Harris and Ewing of Warren G. Harding. "1865 — Warren G. Harding — 1923." 4pp. Page 2: "Dedicated to the Memory of Our Departed President Warren G. Harding."

WGH-40 Tea Pot Blues (Fox Trot Song). w.m. Leona Lovell (Writer of *My Dixie Rose*). Published by Leona Lovell Music Publishing Company, No.

303-4 Melbourne Hotel, St. Louis, MO. 1924. R/w/b drawing of Uncle Sam, arm inscribed "Congress" pouring oil from teapot inscribed "Teapot Dome" onto group of men. 6pp. Pages 2 and 6: Advertising.

WGH-41 The Triumph (A Symphonic Fantasia). m. Francesco Pozzi. Unpublished manuscript — Conductor's score. Copyright 1920 by Francesco Pozzi. [13 1/2" × 10 3/4"]. Non-pictorial. "Dedicated to the Great Victory of Warren G. Harding, President Elect of the United States of America." 32pp.

WGH-42 The Inaugural March. m. Francesco Pozzi. Unpublished manuscript — Conductor's score. [1921]. [13 1/2" × 10 3/4"]. Non-pictorial. "Dedicated to Hon. Warren G. Harding President of the United States of America." 18pp.

WGH-43 G.O.P. Songster. w. Cora Liston. Published by Cora Liston, Galveston, IN. 1920. [4 1/2" × 7 13/16"]. Gn/bk litho of "Sen. Warren G. Harding." 20pp.

WGH-44 Sleep, Soldier Sleep! w.m. Thomasanne Payne. Published by Thomasanne Payne, Grayville, IL. [ca. 1925]. B/w photo by Mason of cross inscribed "The Way of the Cross Leads to God," monument inscribed "Payne," Red Cross woman [Thomasanne Payne], dead soldier with flag, wreath inscribed "The President, Mrs. Harding." "Posed by Thomasanne Payne, Authoress, and Carl Stickleman, Sculptor, beside the first monument dedicated to Peace, November 11, 1918 (By The Authoress). The picture includes the President's wreath and the Gresham flag." "Endorsed by the Evansville Chamber of Commerce, the Service Star Legion, Gresham Chapter, Vanderburg County, Indiana, and Mayor Benjamin Busse, of Evansville, Indiana." "The Hero's Song — Just back to dust at the foot of the cross let my body crumble away — For my soul could find no place so sweet to rise on that last great day; Let me lay up my treasures safely where may be found neither moth nor rust — If my treasures be safe, What need I care that my body turns back to dust — by Thomasanne Payne." 4pp. Page 4: B/w photo of "The Tomb of Lafayette, Paris, France." "Narrative and facsimile of song — *We Have Come Lafayette*" by Thomasanne Payne. Four B/w photos of "James Bethel Gresham — America's First Dead;" "Alice Gresham Hood — Mother of James Bethel Gresham;" "Thomasanne Payne — The Authoress and her only son;" "Mrs. E.E. Hoskinson — Sung 'Sleep, Soldier, Sleep' at Gresham's Funeral;" "Rev. Frank Lenig, Ph.D., Gresham's minister, Simpson M.E. Church, Evansville, Ind." Advertisement; Information on and photo of James Bethel Gresham — "America's First Dead."

WGH-45 Union Memorial Service For Warren Gamaliel Harding [Program Booklet with Songs]. Published by Committee on Arrangements of Union Service, Troy Theatre, August 10th, 1923. [6 7/8" × 10"]. B/w photo of Warren G. Harding — "29th President of the United States, Born 1865, Died 1923." 4pp. Page 4: Songs.

WGH-46 The Boys Of '61 (March Song). w.m. Emma J. Moore-Seamans. Published by Emma J. Moore-Seamans, Yorba Linda, CA. 1928. Bl/w photo of "Dr. George Tryon Harding, Sr., Company I, 136th O.V.I., Father of the Late President Warren G. Harding." Bl/w flags, stars and stripes border. 6pp. Page 2: "Written for and dedicated to my dear friend Dr. George Tryon Harding, Sr." Page 6: Blank.

WGH-47 Patriotic Songs. Published by The Republican Woman's Club of Minneapolis, Minneapolis, MN. 1920. [3 11/16" × 6"]. Bl/bl drawing of elephant. "Republican Campaign 1920." 8pp. Page 2: "Republican Standard Bearers For President — Warren G. Harding of Ohio, For Vice-President Calvin Coolidge of Massachusetts." "America First."

WGH-48 Tumbled In. w. E. Couture. m. G. Glynn. Published by Couture & Glynn, South Bend, IN. 1921. Br/w drawing of a chair, brown line border. "Dedicated to Warren G. Harding." 6pp. Page 6: Blank.

WGH-49 Special Memorial Services In Honor Of The Late President Warren G. Harding [Program Booklet with Songs]. Published by the Salt Lake Tabernacle, [Salt Lake City, UT], "Sunday, August 12th, 1923, at 2 o'clock." [5 1/4" × 8"]. B/w photo of Warren G. Harding, black border. 4pp.

WGH-50 The Man Who Took The Stand (Song). w.m. C.G.L. Dobbins. Published by C.G.L. Dobbins, Rochester, NY. Copyright 1920 and 1921. Bl/w non-pictorial line border. 6pp. Pages 2 and 6: Blank. Page 3: "Respectfully Dedicated to Warren G. Harding."

WGH-51 Keeping Step With The Union. m. John Philip Sousa (Lieut. Commander, U.S.N.R.F.). Published by Theodore Presser Company, No. 1712 Chestnut Street, Philadelphia, PA. 1921. R/w/br/bk/gn drawing by Wm. S. Nortenheim of Americans from all walks of life and professions marching, Capitol dome, sun, flag, spirit of Miss Liberty with torch—"We join ourselves to no party that does not carry the flag and keep step to the music of the Union—From an address by Rufus Choate in 1855." List of arrangements available. "To Mrs. Warren G. Harding." 8pp. Pages 2 and 7: Blank. Page 8: Advertising.

WGH-52 President Elect March. m. Warner E. Bush. Published by Warner E. Bush, No. 136 Main Street, Penn Yan, NY. 1920. B/w non-pictorial geometric design. 6pp. Page 6: Adv.

WGH-53 We'll March To The Polls (Ballad). w. Susie Purcell. m. Frank Ford. Copyright 1920 by Susie Purcell, No. 2012 Arthur Street, Swissvale, PA. Br/bk geometric designs. 4pp. Page 4: Blank.

WGH-54 Republican Campaign Songs For 1920. Published by Ohio Republican State Executive Committee, Geo. Clark, Chairman, No. 187 South High Street, Columbus, OH. 1920. [6" × 9"]. Bk/be geometric design border. 32pp. Page 32: Lithos of "Warren G. Harding "For President," "Harry L. Davis, For Governor," "Frank B. Willis For United States Senator." [M-414].

WGH-55 America First! (Warren G. Harding). w. Philander Johnson. m. Vittorio Gianinni. Copyright 1920 by Philander Johnson. B/w photos of "Warren G. Harding, Republican Candidate, President of the United States" and "Calvin Coolidge, Republican Candidate, Vice President of the United States." Excerpt of "Speech of acceptance at Akron, Ohio, July 22nd, 1920 [of] Warren G. Harding—Possesser of might admits no fear America must stand foremost for the right. We want to help, but we hold to our own interpretation of the American conscience as the very soul of our nationality. America, free, independent, and self-reliant, but offering friendship to all the world." Excerpt of "Speech

WGH-55

of acceptance at Northampton, Mass., July 27th, 1920 [of] Calvin Coolidge — We have been taking council together concerning the welfare of America. Most of the great concourse of people around one hold no public office, expect to hold no public office. Still, in solemn truths, they are the government, they are America. The destiny, the greatness of America lies around the hearthstone." R/w/b cover drawings of U.S. Capitol, man in print shop, farmer with plow, red sunburst background." "Sung by Kelley Streey Business Men's Association, Philadelphia." 4pp. Page 4: "Salutations to the Republican National Committee." List of Committee members.

WGH-56 Republican Women's Committee Campaign Songs. [1920]. [5" × 7"]. B/w litho of two American flags. 4pp.

WGH-57 The G.O.P. Looks Good To Me. W. Hanry F. Wells. M. Dora M. Varney. Published by Suffolk Music Publishing Company, Boston, MA. 1920. B/w photos of Warren G. Harding and Calvin Coolidge.

WGH-58 Our President Passed Away (Song). w. Icil L/ Mingus. Published by Frank Harding, Music Publisher and Printer, No. 228 East 22nd Street, New York, NY. 1924. Gn/y/w non-pictorial geometric designs. 6pp. Pages 2 and 6: Advertising. Page 3: "To the memory of President Warren G. Harding."

WGH-59 President Harding's Grand March. m. Louis Weber. Published by Weber Brothers, No. 622 Minnesota Avenue, Kansas City, KS. Br/w photo by Baker Art Gallery of Warren G. Harding. Br/w photo of "Louis Weber." Br/w drawing of the U.S. flag. 4pp. Page 4: Advertising.

WGH-60 Give Us The Grand Old Party (National Republican Campaign Song!). w.m. Joe Clement (Writer of *You'll Think Of Me, Back To My Alabama Babe*). Copyright 1920 by The Melody Mill, Washington, DC. Non-pictorial. "National Republican Campaign Song!. Page 2: "Dedicated to the Republican Party" Page 4: Advertisement for two more Joe Clement songs.

WGH-61 G.O.P. Songs. Published by Republican Women's Club of Minneapolis, Minneapolis, MN. 1920. Bl/w litho of an elephant, geometric border. "Campaign Of 1920."

See also WW-19; JMC-3; JMC-9; CC-41; CC-59; FDR-158; DDE-9; LBJ-1; MISC-167.

WILLIAM H. HARRISON

WHH-1 The National Whig Song. w. William Hayden, Esq. m. "Adapted to a Popular Air." Published by Parker & Ditson, No. 135 Washington Street, Boston, MA. 1840. B/w litho by B.W. Thayer of William Henry Harrison, facsimile signature. "Respectfully dedicated to the Whigs of the United States." "Price 25 cts. nett [sic]." 4pp. Page 3: Additional verses. Page 4: Blank.

WHH-2(A) Good Hard Cider. Copyright 1840 by Thomas Birch, New York, NY. B/w litho by N. Currier of William Henry Harrison, log cabin, life scenes. "Tippecanoe, the Hero of North Bend." "Respectfully dedicated to the Associations, Partly written and arranged by a member of the Fifth Ward Club." "Six Patriotic Ballads."

    (B)   **The Gallant Old Hero.**
    (C)   **The Buckeye Song.**
    (D)   **The Log Cabin.**
    (E)   **The Tipp's Invitation To Loco.**
    (F)   **The Cincinatus Of The West.**

WHH-3 The Tippecanoe March & Quick Step. m. William Ratel. Published by Geo. W. Hewitt & Company, No. 184 Chestnut Street, Philadelphia, PA. 1840. B/w litho by Thomas Sinclair of William Henry Harrison on horseback. "Dedicated to the Tippecanoe Club of Lexington, Ky." "Pr. 25 cts. Nett." 4pp. Page 4: Blank.

WHH-4 The Whigs Of Columbia Shall Surely Prevail (Harrison Song and Chorus). [Published by the *Daily Journal*, Boston, MA?]. [1840]. [8 5/16" × 12 3/8"]. B/w litho of a log cabin, keg, soldiers, flag inscribed "Harrison And Reform," building with sign inscribed "*Daily Journal*." 2pp. Page 2: Blank.

WHH-5 Bunker Hill (Whig Song). [8 1/8" × 11"]. B/w litho of William Henry Harrison, geometric design border. "September 10, 1840." 2pp. Page 2: Blank.

WHH-6 Tippecanoe Waltz. m. A. Backus (Professor of Music Troy Female Seminary). Published by A. Backus, Troy, NY. 1840. B/w litho by N. Currier from a stone etching by W.K. Hewitt of a man chopping wood, log cabin, cow. "Composed with variations for the Piano Forte and dedicated to Miss Catherine Dodge." 10pp. Pages 2, 9 and 10: Blank.

WHH-7 The Log Cabin Quickstep. Published by George Willig, Jr., Baltimore, MD. 1840. B/w litho of William Henry Harrison, wreath, flags, drums, cannons. 4pp. Page 2: "Dedicated to General Wm. H. Harrison." Page 4: Blank.

WHH-7

WHH-8 Harrison Quadrilles. m. "Popular Airs." Published by Ferd. C. Unger, No. 385 Broadway, New York, NY. 1840. B/w litho by Gimber of William Henry Harrison, log cabin, The White House, eagle flags. "The Hero of Tippecanoe." "Selected from Popular Airs and Arranged for the Piano Forte." "Respectfully dedicated to the Whigs of the United States by the Publisher." "Pr. 50 cts." 10pp. Pages 3-7: Each a different dance. Instructions at bottom.

WHH-9 The Farmer Of North Bend. Published by Charles T. Geslain, No. 357 Broadway, New York, NY. 1840. B/w litho of a log cabin, horse and buggy, steamboat. "The Patriot's Home." "A Very Popular Whig Song Respectfully Dedicated to the Log Cabin Association the United States by the Publisher." "Pr. 50 cts." 6pp. Pages 2 and 6: Blank.

WHH-10 President Harrison's Grand Inauguration March. m. Henry Dielman. Published by F.D. Benteen, Baltimore, MD. 1841. B/w litho by Ed Weber & Company of William Henry Harrison, Inaugural ceremonies, Capitol building. 6pp. Page 2: Blank. Page 3: "As performed by the U.S. Marine Band at Washington City on the 4th March, 1841. Respectfully Dedicated to Wm. Henry Harrison, Prest. U.S." Pages 2 and 6: Blank.

WHH-11 The Tippecanoe Or Log Cabin Quick Step. m. Henry Schmidt (Author of *Hero's Quick Step, &c.*). Published by Henry Prentiss, No. 33 Court Street, Boston, MA. 1840. B/w litho by Thayer of William Henry Harrison, log cabin, vignettes of states. "Composed and respectfully dedicated to Gen. William Henry Harrison (Hero of Tippecanoe and Farmer of North Bend)." 4pp. Page 4: Blank.

WHH-12 When This Old Grey Hat Was New. m. Air: *John Anderson, My Jo*. Printed for the clubs and for sale at the music shops. [1840]. Litho of an eagle, snake. Long narrative on Federalists,

Democrats, &c. "Inscribed to the Republican Societies, throughout the Union."

WHH-13 The Inaugural Ode. Published by Samuel Carusi, Baltimore, MD. 1841. Non-pictorial. "Performed at the Installation of Genl. W.H. Harrison as President of the United States of America, 4 March, 1841, by all the principal choirs in the DC. got-up expressly for the occasion by the Author." Music starts on page one.

WHH-14 Arouse Ye, Patriot Whigs! w. S.H.G. (of Boston). m. B.F. Baker. Published by Geo. P. Reed, No. 17 Tremont Row, Boston, MA. 1840. B/w litho by Thayer of a rally at a log cabin, barrel marked — "Hard Cider;" U.S. flag, eagle with ribbon — "E Pluribus Unum." "Respectfully Dedicated to the Boston Harrison Club." 8pp. Pages 2, 7 and 8: Blank.

WHH-15 Patriot's Quick Step. m. Edward B. Oliver. Published by Henry Prentiss, No. 33 Court Street, Boston, MA. 1840. B/w litho by Moore's Lithography of William Henry Harrison on horseback. "Composed and Arranged for the Piano Forte by Edward B. Oliver and Respectfully dedicated to the delegates of the Bunker Hill Whig Convention." "As performed by the Boston Brass Band, September 10th, 1840."

WHH-16 General Harrison's Grand March. m. Mr. John Bray. Published by G.E. Blake, Philadelphia, PA. [182-]. Non-pictorial. 2pp. Page 2: Blank. [W-1292].

WHH-17 A Drop Of Hard Cider (Or The Tippecanoe Roarer). Published "under the patronage of the Glorious Seventeen Tippecanoe Clubs of the City" by Elton Song-Book Emporium, New York, NY. 1840. Litho of a man carrying a sign inscribed with song title. "Embodying the soul of all the North-Bend melodies, Whig Songs, &c." 36pp. [M-007].

WHH-18 Tippecanoe Club Songster. Published by [V-1: Turner & Fisher, No. 15 North Sixth Street, Philadelphia, PA] [V-2: H.A. Turner, Baltimore, MD]. 1841. [3" × 4 7/16"]. Hand Colored engraving of William Henry Harrison, log cabin. 68pp. Page 2: Blank. Page 66: Table of contents. [M-021, 022].

WHH-19 The Presidents Quadrilles. m. Angele De V. Published by Hewitt & Jaques, No. 239 Broadway, New York, NY. [ca. 1841]. Non-pictorial. "Composed & Arranged for the Piano Forte and respectfully dedicated to Gen. W.H. Harrison." "Pr. 50 cts." 8pp. Pages 2 and 8: Blank. Page 3: Song: **Fort Meigs**. Page 4: Song: **The Farmer Of North Bend**. Page 5: Song: **Tippecanoe**. Page 6: Song: **The Maumee Rapids**. Page 7: Song: **The Battle Of The Thames**.

WHH-20 Harrison's Triumph (A Grand Characteristic Waltz). m. Leopold Herwig (Professor of Music at St. Anns Hall, Flushing, L.I.). Published by Charles G. Christman, No. 404 Pearl Street, New York, NY. 1841. Non-pictorial. "Composed and dedicated to Miss M.C. Bininger." 8[?]pp.

WHH-21 Log Cabin Waltz. m. Charles A. Mintzer. Published by Griffith & Simon, No. 384 North Second Street, Philadelphia, PA. [ca. 1840]. Non-pictorial. "Composed and Respectfully Dedicated to his Friend A.H. Bookhamer, Esqr."

WHH-22 Tippecanoe Dance (or Old Rosin the Beau). Published by Osborn's Music Saloon, No. 30 South 4th Street, Philadelphia, PA. [ca. 1840]. Non-pictorial. "Arranged as an Easy Lesson for Beginners." 2pp. Page 2: Blank.

WHH-23 The Flag Of Washington (A Song). [1840]. [8 1/2" × 11"]. Non-pictorial broadside. "Written for the Concord Barbecue, and to be sung at the Table, July 4, 1840." 2pp. Page 2: Blank.

WHH-24 The Whig Quadrilles. m. B.Mc.C. Published by Geib &

WILLIAM H. HARRISON (WHH)

Walker, No. 23 Maiden Lane, New York, NY. [ca. 1840]. Non-pictorial. "Containing: *La Sarah—Le David—La Forbes—La Eiffe—La Stevenson*." "Composed & Arranged for the Piano Forte and Respectfully Dedicated by Permission to Miss Stevenson." "Price 50¢." 8pp. Pages 2 and 8: Blank.

WHH-25 The Whig Waltz. m. George Hews. Published by Parker & Ditson, No. 135 Washington Street, Boston, MA. 1840. Non-pictorial. "Composed for the Piano Forte." Page 2: Blank.

WHH-26 Harrison's Inauguration Grand March And Quick Step. m. J.C. Beckel. Published by Osbourn's Music Saloon, No. 30 South 4th Street, Philadelphia, PA. 1840. Non-pictorial. "Composed and Respectfully dedicated to W.H. Harrison." 4pp. Pages 1 and 4: Blank.

WHH-27 General Harrison's March. m. C. Mercier. [V-1: Published & sold at George Willig's Musical Magazine, Philadelphia, PA] [V-2: Facsimile published by William C. Gates, Anchorage, KY]. [V-1: ca. 1840] [V-1: 1959]. Non-pictorial. "As Performed at the Circus with great applause in 'Proctors Defeat.'" [V-1: W-5841] [V-2: W-5841A].

WHH-28 Welcome Home. w.m. B. Hime and C. Forrester Barstow. Published by William Brown, Salem, MA. 1840. Non-pictorial. "Dedicated to the New England Delegates to the Baltimore Whig Convention."

WHH-29 The Tippecanoe Club Quick Step. m. Francis H. Brown. Published by Atwill Publisher, No. 201 Broadway, New York, NY. 1840. Non-pictorial. "Composed & arranged for the Piano Forte, and dedicated to New York Tippecanoe Clubs." 4pp. Page 4: Blank.

WHH-30(A) Good Hard Cider. Published by Atwill, No. 201 Broadway, New York, NY. Copyright 1840 by Thomas Birch. B/w litho of log cabin, forest scene, people, flag and a separate litho of William H. Harrison in an oval at top of page—"Tippecanoe the Hero of North Bend, a Series of Favorite Ballads Written and Arranged for the Piano Forte." Page 3: Inscribed title page—"A Favorite Ballad as sung at the Tippecanoe Associations with great applause." "Respectfully written and arranged for the Piano Forte by a Member of the Fifth Ward Club."
(B) **The Gallant Old Hero**.
(C) **The Buckeye Song**.
(D) **The Log Cabin**.
(E) **The Tipp's Invitation to Loco**.
(F) **The Cincinatus Of The West**.

WHH-31 The New Hymeneal Courting Song. m. Air: *Cheer Up My Lively Lads*. Copyright 1841 by A. Smith, New York, NY. Non-pictorial. "Set to the tune sung with so much applause during the late political contest of *Cheer Up My Lively Lads*." "Dedicated to the Tippecanoe and Tyler Too Administration." 4pp. Pages 1 and 4: Blank.

WHH-32 The Whig's Grand March. m. Charles H. Granger. Published by F.D. Benteen, Baltimore, MD. 1840. Non-pictorial. "Respectfully Dedicated to Genl. Harrison." 4pp. Pages 1 and 4: Blank.

WHH-33 Ah! Do Not Forget (Solo and Duett [sic]). w. R.R. Engle. m. J. Travis Quigg. Published by J.E. Winner, No. 545 North Eighth Street, Philadelphia, PA. Copyright 1871 by J. Travis Quigg. Non-pictorial geometric border. "For Mez-Sop and Tenor." "Respectfully Dedicated to Mrs. W.H. Harrison." 8pp. Pages 2 and 8: Blank.

WHH-34 Tippecanoe Hornpipe. m. F.A. Wagler. Published by F.D. Benteen, Baltimore, MD. 1840. Non-pictorial. Followed on page one by **Hard Cider Quickstep**. m. F.A. Wagler. 2pp. Page 2: Blank.

WHH-35 OK Gallopade. m. John H. Hewitt. Published by G. Willig,

Jr., Baltimore, MD. 1840. Non-pictorial. "Composed and respectfully Dedicated to the Whig Ladies of the United States." 4pp. Pages 1 and 4: Blank.

WHH-36 The People Are Rousing (A Harrison Duett [sic] and Chorus). w.m. "A Whig of Providence." Published by Oliver Shaw, No. 70 Westminister Street, Providence, RI. 1840. Non-pictorial. "For the cause of Harrison and Reform." 4pp. Pages 1 and 4: Blank.

WHH-37 Log Cabin Song. w. "The words taken from *The Washington Reporter*, PA." m. Alexander Kyle. Published by C.E. Horn, No. 367 Broadway, New York, NY. 1840. B/w litho by Jenkins Litho. of Log Cabin, men drinking at table. "Respectfully dedicated to the Citizens of the First Ward, New York." 6pp. Pages 2 and 6: Blank.

WHH-38 Up Salt River (A New Whig Song). w. G.B.W. (Toledo, OH). m. "Tune: *All On Hobbies.*" Published by Firth & Hall, No. 1 Franklin Square, New York, NY. 1840. Non-pictorial. "Respectfully Dedicated to the Toledo Tippecanoe Club." "Pr. 25¢ nett [sic]." 4pp.

WHH-39 Nine Cheers For Old Tip (A Favorite Patriotic Ballad). w. "A Member of the Fifth Ward Glee Club." Published by Atwill, No. 201 Broadway, New York, NY. Copyright 1840 by Thomas Birch. Non-pictorial. "As sung by the Tippecanoe Glee Club with great applause, Written, Arranged and Dedicated to the Tippecanoe Associations." 4pp. Page 4: Blank.

WHH-40 Old Tippecanoe. m. "Air: *Rosin The Bow.*" [1840]. [4 3/4" × 10 1/4"]. Non-pictorial broadside. 2pp. Page 2: Blank.

WHH-41 The Log Cabin Song. m. "Adapted to a Popular Air." Published by Parker & Ditson, No. 135 Washington Street, Boston, MA. 1840. B/w litho by B.W. Thayer of log cabin, large U.S. flag, barrels — "Hard Cider —1841." "Respectfully Dedicated to the Whigs of the United States." 4pp. Page 2: Extra verses. Page 4: Blank."

WHH-42 New Haven Whig Song Book. Printed by William Storer, Jr. for the Whig Central Committee, New Haven, CT. 1840. Non-pictorial geometric designs. "Prepared for the New Haven County Mass Convention, Thursday, Oct. 8th, 1840." [4 1/4" × 7 7/16"]. [M-018].

WHH-43 Tip And Ty (A New Comic Whig Glee). Published by Parker & Ditson, Washington Street, Boston, MA. [1840]. Non-pictorial. "Written for and dedicated to the Louisiana Whig Delegation to the Bunker Hill Convention." 4pp. Pages 1 and 4: Blank.

WHH-44 Tip And Ty (A New Comic Whig Glee). Published by Firth & Hall, No. 1 Franklin Square, New York, NY. [1840]. Non-pictorial. "Respectfully dedicated to the Louisiana Whig Delegation to the Bunker Hill Convention." 4pp. Pages 1 and 4: Blank.

WHH-45 The Whig Waltz, 1776. Published by [V-1: Thomas Birch, Music Engraver, Printer & Publisher, Wholesale and Retail, New York, NY] [V-2: No publisher indicated]. [ca. 1840]. Non-pictorial. "Composed and arranged for the Piano Forte." 2pp. Page 2: Blank.

WHH-46 Funeral March. m. J.H. Seipp. Published by Henry Prentiss, No. 33 Court Street, Boston, MA. 1841. B/w litho of a cemetery, woman and child, black border. "In Memory of William H. Harrison, Late President of the United States, performed by the Boston Brigade Band, April 20th, 1841." "Composed and Arranged for the Piano Forte." "Price 25 cts. nett [sic]." 4pp. Page 4: Blank.

WHH-47(A) Hail Columbia (And Hail Forever! Hail The Cause). Published by G.E. Blake, No. 13 South 5th Street, Philadelphia, PA. 1840. [V-1: B/w litho by Sinclair's Litho. of men, cabin, horse, oxen team, flag] [V-2: Page 1: Blank]. "Respectfully inscribed to all true Republicans in the United States." "Blake's Log Cabin Music." 4pp. [V-1 and V-2: Page 2: Litho of man with plow. "In Commemoration of the Two Farmer Presidents Washington, the Father of his Country! and Harrison, The Defender of its Liberty and Laws!" "Adapted and newly Arranged to the American National Anthem." [V-2: Page 4: Blank].

(B) **Turn Out! To The Rescue!** a. T. Carr. Page 2: Litho of men, ball, log cabin, White House. "With heart and soul this ball we roll!" "Inscribed to the patriots of the whole nation."

(C) **Should Brave Old Soldiers Be Forgot?** m. Tune Auld Lang Syne. a. "Newly arranged by T. Carr." Page 2. B/w litho of log cabin with flag inscribed "Tippecanoe." "Respectfully dedicated to The Tippecanoe Associations."

(D) **The Western Steam Boat March**. m. J.C. Beckel. B/w litho of a steamboat. "Dedicated to Genl. Wm. H. Harrison, The Father of the Great West."

(E) **The Brave Old Chief**. w.m. Edward T. Loder. B/w litho of Eagle with ribbon inscribed "The Harrison Song," log cabin, Capitol building. "Adapted to a popular Air."

(F) **Old Tippecanoe's Raisin'**. m.a. Thomas Carr. B/w litho of log cabin, flag inscribed "Tippecanoe." "Sung with Vulcanic effect by the Buckeye Blacksmith." "Dedicated to the friends of Liberty & Reform."

WHH-48 Inaugural Grand March. m. "Authoress of the *Whig Convention March*." Published by Samuel Carusi, Baltimore, MD. 1841. Non-pictorial. "Performed by the Military Band of the Marine garison [sic] at the Installation of Genl. W.H. Harrison, as President of the U.S. of America, 4th March, 1841." 6pp.

WHH-49 Arouse, My Gallant Freemen! (A New Whig Song). w. Thomas F. Adams, Esq. a. Thomas C. Carr. Published by Osbourn's Music Saloon, No. 30 South Fourth Street, Philadelphia, PA. [1840]. B/w litho of cabin, keg, White House, "Kinderhook Hotel." "Respectfully dedicated to Genl. W.H. Harrison." 4pp. Page 4: Blank.

WHH-50 General Harrison's Log Cabin March & Quick Step. Published by Samuel Carusi, Baltimore, MD. 1840. Litho of a log cabin, U.S. flag, music notes, William Henry Harrison, cider keg.

WHH-51 Harrison & Tyler Grand Military Waltz. Published by Osbourn's Music Saloon, No. 30 South 4th Street, Philadelphia, PA. [1841]. B/w litho by Thomas Sinclair of the White House, log cabin, the "Kinderhook Hotel." "Dedicated with respect to President Harrison. Composed in honor of the Grand Ball Given by the Citizens of Phila. by the Publisher." "Price 25 cts. nett [sic]." 8pp.

WHH-52 Ye Jolly Lads Of Ohio. m. Air: *Old Rosin the Beau*. Published by Samuel Carusi, Baltimore, MD. 1840. Non-pictorial.

WHH-53 Lawrence Quadrilles. m. "Selections from Popular Quick Steps." Published by Henry Prentiss, No. 33 Court Street, Boston, MA. 1841. B/w tinted litho by B. Champney, printed by B.W. Thayer, of the 1841 Inaugural Ball. "Selections from Popular Quick Steps as performed at the Grand Inauguration Whig Ball at Faneuil Hall, Mar. 4th, Arranged for the Piano Forte, 1841." 8pp. Pages 2 and 8: Blank. Page 3: *L'Espagnale*. Page 4: *Bigelows*. Page 5: *Wrecker's Daughter*. Page 6: *Harringtons*. Page 7: *Hancock Light Infantry*.

WHH-54 Gen. Harrison's Quick Step. m. "Subject From Herz." a. Charles Zenner. Published by Parker & Ditson, No. 135 Washington Street, Boston, MA. 1840. Non-pictorial. "Arranged for the Piano Forte." 4pp. Pages 2 and 4: Blank.

WHH-55 President Harrison's Funeral Dirge. m. Henry Dielman. Published by Osborn's Music Saloon, No. 30 South Fourth Street, Philadelphia, PA.

1841. B/w litho by Thomas Sinclair of White House, funeral procession, black border. "As performed on the occasion of his burial at Washington City, April, 1841." Inside title: **President Harrison's Funeral March**.

WHH-56 Log Cabin Song Book (A Collection of Popular and Patriotic Songs). Published at *The Log Cabin* office, No. 30 Ann-Street, New York, NY. 1840. [4 7/8" × 7"]. [V-1: Br/bk] [V-2: Y/bk] litho of log cabin, cider barrel, farmer, plow, flag inscribed "Harrison & Tyler," geometric design border. "The Freeman's glittering Sword be Blest, For ever blest the Freeman's Lyre." Page 3: B/w litho of "Major-General William Henry Harrison, of Ohio," facsimile signature. 74pp. [M-020].

WHH-57 The Penitent Loco (A Glee). m. "Adapted to a Popular Melody." [ca. 1840]. Non-pictorial. "Dedicated to the Northampton [Mass] Whig Association." 4pp. Pages 1 and 4: Blank.

WHH-58 Gen. Harrison's Grand March. m. Geo. O. Farmer. Published for the Author by John Ashton & Company, No. 197 Washington Street, Boston, MA. 1840. B/w litho by B.W. Thayer of William Henry Harrison — "The Hero of Tippecanoe," flags, wreath. "Composed and respectfully dedicated to the Boston and Roxbury Whig Associations." 4pp. Page 4: Blank.

WHH-59 Freeman's Quick Step. m. George Hews. Published by Parker & Ditson, No. 135 Washington Street, Boston, MA. 1840. B/w [horizontal format] tinted litho [V-1: Green tint] [V-2: Brown tint] by Sharp & Micheton of a sketch by W. Sharp of soldiers marching at the celebration of the Bunker Hill monument. "As performed on the glorious 10th of September composed and dedicated to the delegates to the Bunker Hill Whig Convention of 1840." "Remarks — As this print will maintain long after all who beheld the brilliant spectacle shall have passed away, it may not be amiss to stamp upon it the interesting fact, that this same '10th of September,' a fair was held by Ladies in the City of Boston, for the purpose of obtaining funds for the completion of the Monument (which is here presented in its unfinished state) the object was entirely successful — This drawing was taken from Mr. Phipps house, South East of the Monument and represents the moment of time when the cavalcade having countermarched, are about returning to the City; which a portion of the Delegates on feet have yet reached the hill." 4pp. Page 4: Blank.

WHH-60 The North Bend (Quick Step). Published by [V-1: F.D. Benteen, Baltimore, MD] [V-2: Geo. Willig, Jr., Baltimore, MD]. 1840. Non-pictorial. "Composed for and Respectfully dedicated to Genl. Wm. H. Harrison." 4pp. Pages 1 and 4: Blank.

WHH-61 Tippecanoe Song-Book (A Collection of Log Cabin and Patriotic Melodies). Published by Marshall, Williams & Butler, Philadelphia, PA. 1840. White on black litho of log cabin, plow, flags, eagle. 180pp. [M-024].

WHH-62 Gen. Harrison's Grand March. m. Edward L. White. Published by C. Bradlee, No. 135 Washington Street, Boston, MA. [1840]. Non-pictorial. "Arranged and Partly Composed by Edward L. White." 4pp. Pages 1 and 4: Blank.

WHH-63 Songs For The People (Or Tippecanoe Melodies) [Songster]. Published for the Authors by James P. Giffing, No. 56 Gold Street, New York, NY. 1840. [3 3/4" × 6"]. Litho of William Henry Harrison, log cabin, flag. "Original and Selected." 76pp. [M-019].

WHH-64 General Harrison's Tippecanoe Grand March. m. Dielman. Published by George Willig, Junr., Baltimore, MD. 1840. B/w litho of William Henry Harrison on horseback. 4pp. Page 2: "Composed and Arranged for the

WHH-63

Forte and Dedicated to the Whigs of the Prize Banner Ward." "Price 25 cts nett [sic]." pp. Page 4: Blank.

WHH-68 The Log Cabin & Hard Cider Melodies (A Collection of Popular and Patriotic Songs). Published by Charles Adams, No. 23 Tremont Street, Boston, MA. 1840. [3 3/4" × 6"]. [V-1: Pk/bk] [V-2: Gn/bk] litho of William Henry Harrison. "The Freemen's glittering Sword be Blest, For ever blest the Freeman's Lyre." 78pp. Pages 2 and 77: Blank. Page 3: Inside title page. B/w litho of log cabin. "Respectfully Dedicated to the Friends of Harrison and Tyler." Page 78: Advertising. [M-012].

WHH-69 Log Cabin Or Tippecanoe Waltz. m. Wm. C. Rayner. Published by John C. Andrews, Troy, NY. 1840. B/w litho by N. Currier of log cabin, cider keg, five men, trees. "Com-

Piano Forte and Respectfully Dedicated to the Young Men's National Convention by Dielman and performed by the military band on the occasion."

WHH-65 Faneuil Hall Grand March. m. Julio Soler. Published by C. Bradlee, Washington Street, Boston, MA. [1841]. Non-pictorial. "Composed for the Inauguration of General Harrison." 4pp.

WHH-66 Genl. Harrison's Grand March. m. J. Tosso. Published by Tosso & Douglass, Music Dealers, No. 24 Fourth Street, Cincinnati, OH. April 1, 1840. B/w litho of an eagle, ribbon with song title inscribed. "Composed and Arranged for the Piano Forte." 4pp.

WHH-67 Prize Banner Quick Step. m. D.H. Haskell. Published by Henry Prentiss, No. 33 Court Street, Boston, MA. 1841. [V-1: B/w green tinted] [V-2: B/w] litho [V-1: by W. & J.C. Sharp] of four men with white flag. "Composed and Arranged for the Piano

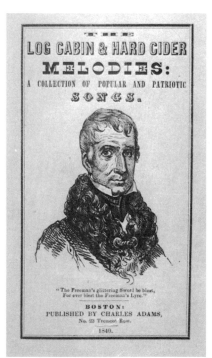

WHH-68

posed and Respectfully Dedicated to Genl. Wm. H. Harrison." 4pp. Page 4: Blank.

WHH-70 The Harrison Waltz. m. I.A. Grohe. Published by G.E. Blake, No. 13 South 5th Street, Philadelphia, PA. 1840. Litho of log cabin labeled "GTW," cider keg, sign inscribed "To Washington." "Dedicated to The Democratic Whigs of Maryland." "Blake's Log Cabin Music." 4pp. Pages 1 and 4: Blank.

WHH-71 Log Cabin Minstrel (or Tippecanoe Songster). c. A Member of the Roxbury Whig Association. Published at the *Patriot and Democrat* Office, Roxbury, [MA]. 1840. [4 1/2" × 6 3/4"]. [V-1:Y/bk] [V-2: Bl/bk] litho of William Henry Harrison, geometric design border. "Old Tip's the boy to swing the flail. Hurrah! Hurrah! Hurrah!" 64pp. Page 3: Title page—"Containing a Selection of Songs Original and Selected Many of them Written Expressly for this Work, Compiled, Published and Arranged by a member of the Roxbury Democratic Whig Association and Respectfully Dedicated to the Log Cabin Boys of the U.S." Page 4: Advertising. Page 64: Y/bk litho of cabin, keg, soldiers. [M-013].

WHH-72 The President's Funeral March (In Memory of William Henry Harrison). m. Anthony Philip Henrich. Published by C.G. Christman, No. 404 Pearl Street, New York, NY. 1841. Non-pictorial. "Composed for the Piano Forte or Organ and designed for Military Bands." Advertising. 4pp.

WHH-73 President Harrison's Dead March. m. Robert Breiter. Published by George Willig, No. 171 Chesnut Street, Philadelphia, PA. 1841. Non-pictorial. "Performed on the day of the Funeral Procession by the Philada. Gray's Brass Band and dedicated to Capt. George Cadwalader." 4pp. Pages 2 and 4: Blank.

WHH-74 Tippecanoe Slow Grand March. m. James M. Deems. Published by James Deems, Baltimore, MD. 1841. B/w litho by Ed. Weber & Company of log cabin, Indians, trees and hills. "Composed, Arranged and most Respectfully Dedicated to William H. Harrison, President of the United States." 6pp. Pages 2 and 6: Blank.

WHH-75 Tip And Tye (A Favorite Patriotic Ballad). a. "A member of the Fifth Ward Glee Club." Copyright 1840 by Thomas Birch. Non-pictorial. "As sung at the Tippecanoe Associations with great applause, Arranged with an Accompaniment for the Piano Forte by a Member of the Fifth Ward Club." 4pp. Page 4: Blank.

WHH-76 The Harrison And Log Cabin Song Book. Published by I.N. Whiting, Columbus, OH. 1840. [3 1/2" × 5 1/2"]. Bl/bk hard cover book with litho of log cabin, flag, eagle. 124pp. Page 8: "Printed at the Straight-out Harrison and Tyler Office." Page 124: Advertising for William Henry Harrison biography. Page 124: Bl/bk litho of eagle. "Go Har-

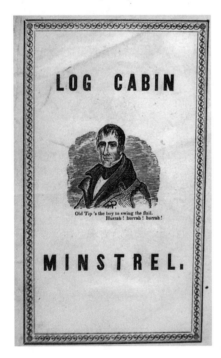

WHH-71

rison, Come it Tyler, and we'll burst Van Buren's biler." Advertising. [M-008].

WHH-77 The Tippecanoe Quick Step. Published by Samuel Carusi, Baltimore, MD. [1840]. B/w litho [horizontal format] of William Henry Harrison, troops fighting Indians.

WHH-78 President Harrison's Grand Military Waltz. Published by Osbourn's Music Saloon, No. 30 South 4th Street, Philadelphia, PA. [1841]. Non-pictorial. 6pp.

WHH-79 Old Tippecanoe (A Patriotic Song). w.m. "A Pennsylvanian." Published by L.D. Meignen & Company, Publishers and Importers of Music, Musical Instruments, Italian Strings, &c., No. 217 Chesnut Street, Philadelphia, PA. 1840. B/w litho by C.S. Duval of nine vignettes of William Henry Harrison's military career, log cabin scene, cannons, William Henry Harrison, crossed flags. Description of each vignette. "Baltimore Convention." "Written, to be sung at Baltimore during the Young Men's Whig Convention and most respectfully inscribed to the Young Ladies of this Monumental City." 4pp. Page 4: Blank.

WHH-81 Baltimore Whig Convention Quick Step. m. Laleueus. Published by Henry Prentiss, No. 33 Court Street, Boston, MA. 1840. B/w litho of monument, street scene. "As performed with great success by the Boston Brigade Band." "Composed and Arranged for the Piano Forte." 4pp. Page 4: Blank.

WHH-80 The Tippecanoe Song-Book. Published by R.S. Elliott & Company, Harrisburg, PA. 1840. [3 3/4" × 5 1/4"]. B/w litho of William Henry Harrison, song lyric. "A Collection of Popular and Patriotic Songs Respectfully Dedicated to the Friends of Harrison and Tyler." 64pp. [M-025].

WHH-82 The Log Cabin Quick Step. Published by Geo. Willig, Jr., Baltimore, MD. 1840. Non-pictorial. "Dedicated to General Wm. H. Harrison." 4pp.

WHH-83 Whig Quick Step. w.m. George O. Farmer. Published by John Ashton & Co., No. 197 Washington Street, Boston, MA. [ca 1840]. Non-pictorial. "Respectfully Dedicated to the Whigs." 4pp. Pages 1 and 4: Blank.

WHH-84 The Inauguration Waltz. m. Kalliwoda. Published by A. Foit, No. 196 1/2 Chesnut Street, Philadelphia, PA. [1841]. Non-pictorial. "Composed for the Piano Forte." "Le Papillion No. 1." "Property of the Publisher." 4pp. Page 4: *Bolero Waltz*.

WHH-85 The Whigs Of Columbia Shall Surely Prevail (A Harrison Song & Chorus). w. "A Whig of Providence." Published by Oliver Shaw, No. 70 Westminister Street, Providence, RI. 1840. Non-pictorial. "For the Cause of Harrison and Reform." 4pp.

WHH-86 Harrison Melodies (Original And Selected). Published by Weeks, Jordan & Co., Boston, MA. 1840. [3 9/16" × 6"]. B/w litho of William Henry Harrison. "Published under the direction of the Boston Harrison Club." 76pp. Page 5: "To William Henry Harrison of Ohio, the gallant soldier, the enlightened statesman, the consistent Republican, and the Honest man..." [M-001, 002, 003].

WHH-87 Dirge (In Four Voices). w.m. John H. Hewitt. Published by Geo. Willig, Jr., Baltimore, MD. [1841]. Non-pictorial. "Written & Composed on the death of William Henry Harrison, Late President of the U. States." 4pp.

WHH-88 A Miniature Of Martin Van Buren (With a Selection of the Best and Most Popular Tippecanoe Songs). 1840. [3 1/2" × 6 1/2"]. [V-1: Br/bk] [V-2: Gn/bk] [V-3: Y/bk] litho of man, chain around neck. Van Buren quote. "Amos Kendall's Veracity — Tom Benton's Honesty — Francis Blair's Beauty." "What is wanting cant be numbered [sic]." 58pp. [M-016].

WHH-89 The Harrison Al-

manac 1841 [Almanac, Campaign Narratives & Songs]. Published by J.P. Griffing, No. 56 Gold Street, New York, NY. 1840. [5" × 8 3/4"]. [V-1: B/w litho of man plowing, symbolic vignettes] [V-2: "Improved." B/w litho of William Henry Harrison sitting on log cabin porch]. 34pp.

WHH-90 The Harrison Medal Minstrel. Published by Grigg & Elliott, Philadelphia, PA. 1840. [3 1/8" × 4 7/8"]. B/w litho of Congressional medal struck for William Henry Harrison with his likeness. "Major General William H. Harrison." 196pp. Page 3: "Comprising a Collection of the Most Popular and Patriotic Songs Illustrative of the Enthusiastic Feelings of a Grateful but Power-Ridden People Towards the Gallant Defender of Their Country. The Hero --The Patriot— the Farmer— the Statesman, and Philanthropist:— oft Weighed in the Balance, and Never found Wanting." Page 196: Reverse side of Congressional medal with facsimile of Congressional Resolution. [M-010].

WHH-91(A) The Farmer Of Tippecanoe. m. Air: *O, Saw Ye the Lass with the Bonny Blue Een!* In: *The Log Cabin*, page 4, Vol. 1, No. 12, July 18, 1840. Published by Horace Greeley & Company, New York, NY. 1840. Non-pictorial.

(B) **The Siege Of Fort Meigs**. m. Air: *Oh,'t Was My Delight of a Shiny Night*. No. 4, May 23.

(C) **The Brave Old Chief**. m. Air: *The Brave Old Oak*. No. 8, July 20. "As sung by Mr. Russell."

(D) **Gathering Song Of The Whigs Of Williamsburgh**, L.I. m. Air: *Bruce's Address*. No. 9, July 27.

(E) **Ode For Log Cabin Raisings**. m. Air: *Kinloch of Kinloch*. No. 16, Aug. 15.

(F) **National Whig Song**. m. H.S. North. No. 23, Oct. 3. "To the Middletown (CT) Tippecanoe Club."

(G) **O! Van Buren!** (A Currency Song). w. N.B.B. m. Air: *Hunters of Kentucky*. No. 14, Aug. 1.

(H) **The Penitent Loco**. No. 6, June 6. "Dedicated to the Northampton (NJ) Whig Club."

(I) **Up Salt River**. w. G.B.W. m. Air: *All On Hobbies*. No. 5, May 30. "Dedicated to the Toledo Tippecanoe Club."

(J) **Come Brothers, Arouse!**. w.m. H. Russell. No. 27, Oct. 31.

(K) **Keep The Ball Rolling** (New Jersey Whig Song). No. 26, Oct. 24.

(L) **Old Tippecanoe**. w. Samuel J. Bayard. m. J.D. Stewart. No. 20, Sept. 12. "For the Montgomery Central Tippecanoe Club."

(M) **Whig Song For The Fourth Of July**. w. H.G. m. Air: *Star Spangled Banner*. No. 10, July 4.

(N) **The Hero Of The West**. m. Air: *Meeting of the Waters*. No. 17, Aug. 22.

(O) **Harrison And Liberty**. m. Air: *Jefferson and Liberty*. No. 19, Sept. 5.

(P) **The Beggars Petition**. m. Air: *All On Hobbies*. No. 13, July 25. "A very pathetic & musical appeal to the Dear People by an Ex-Postmaster General."

(Q) **The Farmer Of Tippecanoe**. m. Air: *O, Saw Ye the Lass wi' the Bonny Blue Een!* No. 21, Sept. 19. "Re-published."

(R) **The March Of The Free** (Whig Song). w. Greeley. m. E. Ives, Jr. No. 24, Oct. 10.

(S) **Whig Rallying Song**. m. Air: *Marseilles Hymn*. No. 15, Aug. 8.

(T) **Hail To The Hero**. m. Air: *Hail to the Chief*. No. 25, Oct. 17.

(U) **The Tippecanoe Gathering**. m. C. Dunton (Kingston, NY). No. 7, June 13. "Dedicated to Thomas Clark ... President of the Kingston Tippecanoe Club."

(V) **Tippecanoe And Tyler Too**. No. 22, Sept. 26.

WHH-92 The Whig Convention Grand March. m. "A Lady of Maryland."

Published by Samuel Carusi, Baltimore, MD. 1840. Non-pictorial. "Composed expressly for the Great Whig Convention held at...Baltimore, May 4th, 1840." 4pp.

WHH-93 Grand March. m. C. Meineke. Published by F.D. Benteen, Baltimore, MD. 1841. Non-pictorial. "Respectfully dedicated to President Harrison." 4pp.

WHH-94 St. Augustine Loco Foco Dance. m. A.F.T. Sold by F.C. Unger, No. 265 Broadway, New York, NY. [ca. 1837-1839]. Non-pictorial. "Composed and Dedicated to the Loco Focos of St. Augustin [sic]." 2pp.

WHH-95 President Harrison's Grand Military Waltz. Published by G.P. Reed, No. 17 Tremont Row, Boston, MA. [1841]. Non-pictorial. "Respectfully Dedicated by the Publisher to the Senators of the U.S." "Pr. 25. Nett [sic]." 4pp.

WHH-96 The Tippecanoe Campaign Of 1840. Published by A.B. Norton, Mount Vernon, OH. 1888. [5 1/2" × 7 1/2"]. Bl/gd book. 496pp. Pages 1-382: Text. Pages 383-485: "Tippecanoe Songs of the Log Cabin Boys and Girls of 1840." [M-276].

WHH-97 The Hard Cider Quick Step. m. J.T.S. Published by S. Carusi, Baltimore, MD. 1840. B/w litho by E. Weber of William H. Harrison, man, log cabin, keg. "Composed and Respectfully Dedicated to the deligates [sic] of the Great Whig Convention Held at Baltimore, May 4, 1840." 4pp.

WHH-98 We've Walloped Them So (A Favorite Patriotic Ballad). w. "By a member of the Fifth Ward Club." Published by Atwill, No. 201 Broadway, New York, NY. 1840. Non-pictorial. "A Favorite Patriotic Ballad as sung by the Tippecanoe Glee Club, with great applause. Written, Arranged and Dedicated, to the Tippecanoe Associations." 4pp. Page 4: Blank.

WHH-99 Harrison And Glory (Or, The Life of The Hero of Tippecanoe!). w. Wm. Goodwin (of New Haven). m. Air: *Ah! Poor Robinson Crusoe*. Printed on silk. [14 3/4" × 9"]. Bl/w litho of William Henry Harrison, cabin, plow, flags, geometric border. "To be sung, said or chanted at all conventions and on all public occasions throughout the States..." "The writer who is a native of London...and impartial reader of history, men, manners, &c., would inquire of the opponents of Gen. Harrison, how and in what way they can justify their feelings by branding the noble and gallant 'Hero' a coward, when history, doings of Congress, and the Nation at large (previous to his becoming a candidate for the Presidency), shows the contrary, and will assuredly rise in judgment against them?" 2pp.

WHH-100 Genl. W.H. Harrison's Grand March. m. J.F. Goneke. Published by George Willig, Baltimore, MD. [1841]. B/w litho of William Henry Harrison. 4pp. Page 3 Title: **Genl. W.H. Harrison's (President of the U.S.) Grand March**. Page 4: Blank.

WHH-101 Gen'l Harrison's Quick Step. Published by E. Riley & Company, No. 29 Chatham Street, New

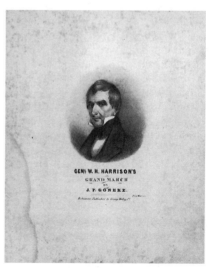

WHH-100

York, NY. [1819-1831]. Non-pictorial. "Dedicated to Miss E.A. Morgan by the Author." 2pp. Page 2: Blank.

WHH-102 Tippecanoe Centennial March. m. M.E. Weinbrecht. Published by Rinker Music Company, Lafayette, IN. 1911. B/w drawings and photos of William Henry Harrison, Tecumseh, battle, monument — "Erected 1908 in honor of the fallen dead heroes." "1812-1912." 6pp. Page 6: Blank.

WHH-103 The Harrison Song. w. Thomas Power, Esq. m. Sporle. Published by Parker & Ditson, No. 135 Washington Street, Boston, MA. 1840. B/w litho by Thayer of William Henry Harrison, Indian battle scene. "Upon one occasion as he (Gen. Harrison) was approaching an angle of the line, against which the Indians were advancing with horrible yells, Lieut. Emmerson of the Dragoons seized the bridle of his horse and earnestly entreated that he would not go there, but the Governor putting spurs to his horse pushed on to the point of attack where the enemy were received with firmness and driven back. (Vide Hist. Battle Tippecanoe)." "Written by Thomas Power, Esq., and Respectfully Dedicated to the Whigs of the United States." 4pp.

WHH-104 Harrison Anthem. w. J.G. Coffin. Published by Henry Prentiss, No. 33 Court Street, Boston, MA. 1840. B/w litho by Thayer of State House, Boston street scene. "As sung by the Boston Tippecanoe Club and at the 4th Ward Festival, &c., &c." 4pp. Page 4: Blank.

WHH-105 The Whigs Triumphant March And Quick Step. m. Mrs. Chater. Published by E. Riley & Company, No. 29 Chatham Street, New York, NY. 1837. Non-pictorial. "Composed & Arranged for the Piano Forte." 4pp. Pages 1 and 4: Blank.

WHH-106 In Days Of Old (A Favorite Patriotic Ballad). a. "A Member of the Fifth Ward Glee Club." 1840. Non-pictorial. "As sung at the Tippecanoe Associations with great applause, Partly Written and Arranged with an Accompaniment for the Piano Forte by a Member of the Fifth Ward Club." 4pp. Page 4: Blank.

WHH-107 Whig Gathering (Song and Chorus). Published by Henry Prentiss, No. 33 Court Street, Boston, MA. 1840. B/w litho by Thayer of a campaign march on a Boston street, banner inscribed "First Cradle of Liberty." "Respectfully Dedicated to the Whigs of the United States." 4pp. Page 4: Blank.

WHH-108 Tippecanoe And Tyler Too! (A Comic Glee). Published in *The Daily Graphic*, Vol. XII, No. 1088, Friday, September 8, 1876, page 475. "Fac-Simile of the Old Campaign Song, *Tippecanoe and Tyler Too*."

WHH-109 Tippecanoe And Tyler Too! (A Comic Glee). Published by G.E. Blake, No. 13 South Fifth Street, Philadelphia, PA. 1840. B/w litho of William Henry Harrison prying Martin Van Buren out of a log cabin made of logs inscribed with Whig states. "A Comic Glee arranged expressly for this work. As sung with thundering applause at the Syracuse Convention." "Some of the Loco Foco party have prepared and paraded a Log Cabin Trap...baited with a barrel of hard cider. By the above it will be seen that the trap has been sprung, and a sly nibbler from 'Hook is looking out through the gratings. An elderly gentleman with a hickory pole is intent on prying him out but it is manifestly no go — The logs are too heavy and growing more so daily." "Blake's Log Cabin Music."

WHH-110 Pittsburgh Brass Band Quick Step, No. 4. m. Henry Kleber. Published by A. Foit, No. 196 Chesnut Street, Philadelphia, PA. 1840. Non-pictorial geometric designs. "Composed for the Piano and Dedicated to the Whig Ladies of Pittsburgh." 4pp. Pages 1 and 4: Blank.

WHH-111 Fort Meig's Grand March. m. Thomas Ayling. Published by Dubois, Bacon and Chambers, No. 285 Broadway, New York, NY. [1840]. Non-pictorial. "For the Piano Forte. Composed and Dedicated to the Whigs of the United States." "Pr. 50 cts." 4pp. Pages 1 and 4: Blank.

WHH-112 Harrison's Grand March. In: *The Army and Navy Fife Instructor: Containing the Calls, Signals, and the Complete Camp and Garrison Duties as Practised* [sic] *in the Army and Navy of the United States, Including the Volunteer and Regular Service, Containing the National Airs, and a Large Collection, of Marches, Quicksteps, Waltzes, Polkas, &c.*, page 26. e.a. Elias Howe. Published by Elias Howe, No. 103 Court Street, Boston, MA. 1863.

WHH-113 Tippecanoe And Tyler Too. w.m. A.C. Ross. In: *The Abridged Academy Song-Book*, page 104. Published by Ginn & Company, Boston, MA. 1898. [6 5/8" × 9"]. Gn/gd/be geometric designs. 318pp.

WHH-114 The Gallant Old Hero (A Favorite Patriotic Ballad). a. "A Member of the Fifth Ward Glee Club." Copyright 1840 by Thomas Birch. Non-pictorial. "As sung at the Tippecanoe Associations with great applause, Partly Written and Arranged, for the Piano Forte by a Member of the Fifth Ward Club." 4pp. Page 4: Blank.

WHH-115 The Cincinatus Of The West (A Favorite Patriotic Ballad). a. "A Member of the Fifth Ward Glee Club." Copyright 1840 by Thomas Birch. Non-pictorial. "As sung at the Tippecanoe Associations with great applause, Partly Arranged and Adapted, to a much Admired Scotch Melody by a Member of the Fifth Ward Club." 4pp. Page 4: Blank.

WHH-116 The Log Cabin (A Favorite Patriotic Ballad). a. "A Member of the Fifth Ward Glee Club." Copyright 1840 by Thomas Birch. Non-pictorial. "As sung at the Tippecanoe Associations with great applause, Partly Written and Arranged, for the Piano Forte by a Member of the Fifth Ward Club." 4pp. Page 4: Blank.

WHH-117 The Buckeye Song (A Favorite Patriotic Ballad). a. "A Member of the Fifth Ward Glee Club." Copyright 1840 by Thomas Birch. Non-pictorial. "As sung at the Tippecanoe Associations with great applause, Partly Written and Arranged, for the Piano Forte by a Member of the Fifth Ward Club." 4pp. Page 4: Blank.

WHH-118 Tipps Invitation To Loco (A Favorite Patriotic Glee). a. "A Member of the Fifth Ward Glee Club." Copyright 1840 by Thomas Birch. Non-pictorial. "As sung at the Tippecanoe Associations with great applause, Written and Arranged for the Piano Forte by a Member of the Fifth Ward Club." 4pp. Page 4: Blank.

WHH-119 Harrison's Song. Unpublished manuscript. 1840.

WHH-120 The Dying Groans Of The Tin Pan. [1840]. [5 1/4" × 15 1/4"]. Non-pictorial. 2pp. Page 2: Blank.

WHH-121 [March, March To Harrison]. w. N.H.C.[?]. [1840]. Unpublished handwritten manuscript. 4pp. Page 1: "To Doc J.W. Ansby, Thompkinsville, Staten Island, [NY]." Folded to use as a mailer. Page 2 and 4: Blank. Page 3: Song.

WHH-122 Original Hymn (On The Death Of President Harrison). w. John H. Sheppard. m. "Air — Mount Vernon." In: *Eulogy, Pronounced at Wiscasset, in the Afternoon of the State Fast, April 22d, 1841, on William Henry Harrison, Late President of the United States*, page 26. "Delivered and Published at the request of a Committee of the Citizens of Wiscasset by John H. Sheppard, Wiscasset. Printed by R.B. Caldwell, 1841. 28pp.

WHH-123 A Collection Of Patriotic Harrison And Tippecanoe Songs, Glees, And Parodies Dedicated

To The Harrison Men Of The United States. Published by J.H. Ginon & Company, Philadelphia, PA. 1840. 32pp. [M-006].

WHH-124 Tippecanoe And Tyler Too. w. A.C. Ross. In: *Marches Of The Presidents, 1789-1909, Authentic Marches & Campaign Songs*, page 24. a. Carl Miller. Published by Chappell & Co., Inc., No. 609 Fifth Avenue, New York, NY. "By arrangement with Chilmark Press, Inc." 1968. [9" × 12"]. R/w/b litho of eagle, flag. "An Illustrated Piano Folio For All Ages." 72pp.

WHH-125 Harrison Melodies: A New Collection of Songs, Glees, and Catches. a. Arranged and Sung by the Harrison Glee Club. Published by The Club Press of Thomas & Company, Buffalo, NY. 1840. 36pp. Page 36: Litho of William Henry Harrison. [M-009].

WHH-126 Harrison's Tippecanoe Songster. Published by Turner & Fisher. New York, NY. 1840. 64pp. [M-011].

WHH-127 Crain's Log Cabin Song Book. Published by J.R. Crain, Springfield, OH. 1840. "Hurrah! Hurrah! Boys, there's no two ways in the fun we'll have at old Tip's raisin'! Hurrah!" 96pp. Inside title: **The Log Cabin Song Book, A Compendious Selection of the Most Popular Tippecanoe Melodies.** [M-014].

WHH-128 Whig Songs 1840. Published by J. & R.C. Wilson, Stubenville, OH. 1840. 66pp. Inside title: **The Log Cabin Songster, Being a Collection of the Most Popular Tippecanoe Songs, Respectfully Dedicated to the Friends of Harrison & Democracy.** [M-015]

WHH-129 [V-1: **Teh** [sic]] [V-2: **The**] **Log Cabin Songster And Straight-Out Harrison Melodies.** Printed at the Straight-Out Harrison and Tyler Office, Columbus, OH. 1840. [M-017].

WHH-130 Genl. W.H. (President Of The United States) Grand March. m. John F. Goneke. Published by G. Willig, Philadelphia, PA. 1840. [See W-3318].

WHH-131 The Tippecanoe Songster. c. J.M. Brown, Vocalist. Printed at the Office of the Log Cabin Herald, Chillicothe, OH. June, 1840. 32pp. [M-005].

WHH-132 The Tippecanoe Song Book. c. "Anon." Published by U.P. James, Cincinnati, OH. 1840. [M-023].

WHH-133 The Brooklyn Tippecanoe Song Book. c. Brooklyn Tippecanoe Glee Club. Published by A. Spooner & Son, Printers, Brooklyn, NY. 1840. "Being a Selection of the Most Approved Songs from the Various Collections Recently Published and Popular Songs, not Included in Other Editions." "For Sale Wholesale and Retail, by S. Culverwell, Hale's News Room, and Folsom's Bookstore." [M-004].

WHH-134 Harrison's Grand March. In: *Howe's School For The Violin (Containing New And Complete Instructions For The Violin, With a Large Collection of Favorite Marches, Quicksteps, Waltzes, Hornpipes, Contra Dances, Songs, and Six Setts [sic] of Cotillions, Arranged with Figures, Containing Over 150 Pieces of Music*, page 24. c. Elias Howe, Jr. Published and Sold Wholesale and Retail, by Elias Howe, Jr., No. 7 Cornhill, Boston, MA. 1843. [6 1/2" × 10"]. Y/bk litho of musical instruments, angel, geometric and floral designs.

WHH-135 Harrison's Grand March. In: *Musician's Omnibus: Containing the Whole Camp Duty, Calls and Signals Used in the Army and Navy; Forty Setts of Quadrilles, Including Waltz, Polka and Schottische, with Calls; and an Immense Collection of Polkas, Schottisches, Waltzes, Marches, Quicksteps, Hornpipes, Contra & Fancy Dances, Songs, &c., for the Violin, Flute, Cornet, Clarionett, &c, containing over 700 Pieces of Music*, page 26. c. Elias Howe. Published by Elias Howe, No. 103 Court Street, Boston,

MA. 1861. [8 1/2" × 11"]. O/bk non-pictorial. "Improved Edition." 100pp.

WHH-136 Harrison's Grand March. In: *Howe's Diamond School For The Violin: Containing, Complete Instructions and Full Directions in Bowing; to which is added A Large Collection of Popular Polkas, Schottisches, Waltzes, Redowas, Marches, Quicksteps, Dances, Hornpipes, Songs,* page 26. c. Elias Howe. Published by Elias Howe, No. 103 Court Street, Boston, MA. 1861. [8 1/2" × 11"]. Bl/bk non-pictorial. 68pp.

WHH-137 Amos Kendall's Lament (A Comic Whig Song). w. G.A. Harington and B.F. Copeland, Esq. m. Geo. O. Farmer. Published by Geo. P. Reed's, No. 17 Tremont Row, Boston, MA. 1840. B/w Thayer litho of "Amos Kendall" at his desk. "Sung with great applause at the Whig Conventions at Roxbury, Randolph, Quincy & other places."

WHH-140 Crow Chapman Crow!! (Or Van Buren's Last Song) (A New Comic Whig Song & Chorus). Published by Atwill. No. 201 Broadway, New York, NY. 1840. Non-pictorial geometric designs. "Arranged for the Piano Forte."

WHH-141 A Favorite March. Published by G.E. Blake, No. 13 South 5th Street, Philadelphia, PA. 1840. B/w litho of American flag, liberty hat. "Selected from Die Puritaner." "And Respectfully Dedicated to Genl. Wm. Henry Harrison."

WHH-142 Patriotic Song. w.m. "By a Citizen." Hand-written manuscript. [1840]. Non-pictorial. "Inscribed to the Tippecanoe Club of Alexandria." 2pp.

WHH-143 The Whig Jubilee Quick Step. m. R.L. Williams. Published by Geib & Walker, No. 23 Maiden Lane, New York, NY. November the 22nd, 1837. Non-pictorial stars. 4pp.

WHH-144 Tip-Tyler Reform! w. A. Sisty. [1840]. [9" × 7"]. Published on silk, Additional patriotic song: *The Star Flag's Streaming In The Breeze.* Obv: Litho of Log Cabin, eagle, flag. Rev: Blank.

See also BFH-23; WHT-23; WW-19; FDR-158; DDE-9; LBJ-1; MISC-167; MISC-169.

WILLIAM H. TAFT

WHT-1 Taft And Sherman Campaign Songster. 1908. [4 1/2" × 6"]. Bl/w photos of "Wm. H. Taft" and "James S. Sherman." Drawing of eagle, flags, shield. "26 Original Songs Set to Familiar and Popular Airs." "1908." 32pp. Pages 2 and 31: Blank. Page 32: R/w eagle, ballot marked "X." Pro-Taft quotes. [M-397].

WHT-2 Oh, William Taft (Song). w. Ellen M. Connolly. m. George Wright. Published by The F.B. Haviland Publishing Company, New Zealand Building, Broadway and 37th Street, New York, NY., as a "Supplement to *The New York Tribune.*" Copyright 1911 by Ellen M. Connolly. Bl/w/br drawing of columns, fountain, stairs, cherubs. Br/w photo of Ellen Connolly. 6pp. Pages 2 and 6: Advertising for other F.B. Haviland music.

WHT-3 Possum (The Latest Craze). w. G.A. Scofield. m. J.B. Cohen. Published by Pease Piano Company, Main Office and Salesroom, No. 128 West 42nd Street, New York, NY. 1909. O/bk/w cover with drawings of a possum in front of the White House and a black man eating possum at dinner table, dog. 6pp. Pages 2 and 6: Advertising for Pease pianos.

WHT-4 Get On The Raft With Taft. w. Harry D. Kerr. m. Abe Holzmann. Published by Leo. Feist, No. 134 West 37th Street, New York, NY. 1912. N/c Pach Brothers photo of William H. Taft, facsimile signature. 6pp. Page 2: "Campaign Song of the People." Page 6: Advertising.

WHT-5 Washington At Valley

Forge. w. George M. Guernsey. m. L.T. Adams. Published by George M. Guernsey, No. 1362 West 27th Street, Indianapolis, IN. 1910. B/w drawing of George Washington. B/w photo of "Earl T. Mott"—"Successfully Introduced by Earl T. Mott." Gn/w cover. 8pp. Page 2: "Respectfully Dedicated to Hon. William Howard Taft, President of the United States." Page 8: Blank.

WHT-6   The Man Of The Hour (March, Two-Step and Song Refrain). m. Rudolph Aronson. Published by Charles K. Harris, New York, NY. 1908. Gy/gy clay-like relief sculpture by Sindelar of William H. Taft. "Respectfully Dedicated to the Hon. William Howard Taft." 6pp. Page 6: Narrative—"President's [Roosevelt] estimate of Taft." History of Taft's career.

WHT-7   Billy Possum March (Billy Taft Chases The Possum). m. Bert Lowe. Published by The New England Music Company, Boston, MA. 1909. O/bk/w drawing of a possum. 6pp. Pages 2 and 6: Advertising for other music.

WHT-8   Taft March. m. Mortimer Wheeler. Published by Frank K. Root & Company, Chicago, IL. 1912. R/w/b flags. Bl/w photo of William H. Taft. 6pp. Pages 2 and 6: Advertising for other Frank K. Root music.

WHT-9   B-I Double L-Bill. w. Monroe H. Rosenfeld. m. Rosie Lloyd. Published by Joseph W. Stern and Company, Nos. 102-104 West 38th Street, Mark Stern Building, New York, NY. 1904. O/w/gy star design with b/w Harris and Ewing photo of William H. Taft—"Very Sincerely Yours, Wm. H. Taft [facsimile signature]." "The Campaign Song for the People." 8pp. Pages 2 and 7: Blank. Page 3: "Dedicated to Wm. Slafer."

WHT-10   Bill? Bill Taft (Campaign Song). w.m. Cecil Marsen. Published by R.W. Heffelfinger, No. 347 South Spring Street, Los Angeles, CA. Copyright 1908 by Cecil Marsen. B/w photo of William H. Taft on telephone. "Dedicated to the Republican Party." 6pp. Pages 2 and 6: Blank.

WHT-11   Taft's Grand March And 2 Step. m. James W. Casey. Published by the Evans Music Company, Boston, MA. Copyright 1909 by W.A. Evans. B/w drawing of William H. Taft, U.S. flags, geometric designs. "Published for Solos, Quartettes, Bands and Orchestra." 8pp. Pages 2 and 8: Advertising. Page 3: "Respectfully Dedicated to our President."

WHT-12(A)   The Nell Brinkley Girl. w. Harry B. Smith. m. Maurice Levi. Published by Cohan & Harris Publishing Company, No. 115 West 42nd Street, New York, NY. 1908. Ma/bl/bk/nc drawing of girl in jester outfit juggling the heads of William H. Taft, Theodore Roosevelt, William J. Bryan, Charles E. Hughes and Charles Fairbanks. "Jardin De Paris (Atop New York Theatre), F. Ziegfield, Jr's New Musical Review," "Book by Harry B. Smith Music by Maurice Levi; Staged by Julian Mitchell; Principals by Herbert Gresham." "*The Follies of 1908.*" 6pp. Pages 2 and 6: Advertising.

(B)   Duchess Of The Table D'hôte. w. Harry B. Smith. m. Maurice Levi. 8pp. Pages 2, 7 and 8: Advertising.

(C)   Society. w. Harry B. Smith. m. Maurice Levi. Pages 2, 6, 7 and 8: Advertising

(D)   The Mosquito Song.

(E)   The Rajah Of Broadway. w. Harry B. Smith. m. Maurice Levi. Pages 2, 6, 7 and 8: Advertising.

(F)   When The Girl You Love Is Loving. w. William Jerome. m. Jean Schwartz. Pages 2, 6, 7 and 8: Advertising.

(G)   Wax Works. w. Harry B. Smith. m. Maurice Levi. Pages 2, 6, 7 and 8: Advertising.

WHT-13   The President Bill Taft (Two Step March). m. Willis McCullough. a. J. Phillips. Published by Joseph W. Phillips (Musical Dir. of the

Philomela Institute of Music Instruction), Ashland, KY. 1909. B/w photos of William H. Taft, "Willis McCullough" and "J.W. Phillips." Bl/w drawing of Treble Clef. "The Leading National Two Step Sensation." "Overture Orchestration by J.N. Phillips — For the Vaudeville Pianist." "Cheerfully Dedicated to Our President." Advertising for J.N. Phillips' Orchestration Services. 6pp. Page 2: "This is Electrically Spontaneous." Page 6: Blank.

WHT-14 I Want A Political Man. w. Bruce Brown. m. F. Henri Klickmann. Published by Frank K. Ruot & Co., Chicago, IL. 1913. O/w/bk/bl drawing of William H. Taft standing in automobile, crowd of people. Bl/w photo of "The Composer." 6pp.

WHT-15 Campaign Song. w.m. Mrs. William Autenrieth. Published by Mrs. William Autenrieth, No. 105 Lincoln Inn Court, Cincinnati, OH. 1908. B/w photo of William H. Taft. Bl/w geometric designs. 6pp. Pages 2 and 6: Blank.

WHT-16 Pennsylvania Republican Campaign Songster. c. Edgar M. Dilley. Published by George J. Brennan, Philadelphia, PA. Copyright 1908 by Edgar M. Dilley. Non-pictorial. "Taft — Sherman 1908." 4pp.

WHT-17 Can't We Call Him Bill (Now That He's President). w.m. Fletcher Stoddard. Published by The Columbia Music Company, "The House of Capitol Music." No. 1301 "G" Street, Washington, DC. 1906. Pk/w/bk/gn flowers, leaves, geometric designs. B/w photo by Harris and Ewing of William H. Taft on telephone. 6pp.

WHT-18 Let Us Have Peace! (A Prayer). w. George Graff, Jr (Author of *Teach Me To Pray, &c*). m. Ernest R. Ball (Composer of *The Crown of Life, The Door of Hope, &c*). Published by M. Witmark and Sons, New York, NY. [V-1: 1911] [V-2: ca. 1925]. Non-pictorial. "Dedicated by Permission to Hon. William H. Taft, President of the United States and the Cause of Peace the World Over." List of arrangements available. [V-2: "Sung by Mme. Schumann-Heink and Mr. David Bispham"]. [V-1: 8[?]pp. Page 2: Advertising. Page 3: Poem "Let Us Have Peace!"] [V-2: 8pp. Pages 2, 7 and 8: Advertising].

WHT-19 On The Avenue (March and Two Step). m. Will T. Pierson. Published by The Columbia Music Company, No. 1301 "G" Street, Washington, DC. 1909. B/w photo of the Inaugural parade down "Pennsylvania Avenue, Washington." Bl/w stars. At top of cover: [V-1: "The Inaugural March for 1909"] [V-2: Without inscription]. 6pp.

WHT-20 God Save Our President (A New National Hymn). w. Josephine C. Goodale. m. J.H. Petermann, No. 115 West 114th Street, New York, NY. 1902. [1909 Edition]. Litho of U.S. flag. "Inauguration Wm. H. Taft. A meeting in the Broadway Tabernacle, N.Y. Compliments of The Brotherhood of Andrew and Philip, March 4th, 1909." "Sung with great success by the New York State Teacher's Association in convention

WHT-14

at Saratoga, July 2nd, 1902, under the personal direction of the Composer."

WHT-21   Will Taft, We're Looking To You. w. Edward Madden. m. Walter H. Cole. Published by Tracy L. Freeman, No. 225 Fifth Avenue, New York, NY. 1908. R/w/b drawing of eagles. Bl/w photos of William H. Taft, The White House. "Distributed by Kent Purchasing Company, 54-56 Stone Street, NY." 6pp. Page 6: Advertising.

WHT-22   Our Good And Honest Taft. w.m. Annie R. Waln Bassett. Published by Annie R. W. Bassett, Norwood, Delaware County, PA. [1908?]. Bl/w photo of "William Howard Taft." B/w drawing of shield, flag, geometric designs. Page 2: Blank.

WHT-23   Star Spangled Banner. w. F.S. Key. a. George Beaverson. Published for Hill and Goodrich Wholesale Foods, Morrisville, VT. [1908]. [7" × 13 1/2"]. Hand-held cardboard fan. Obv: B/w photos of Capitol building, rooster, eagle, all "Presidents of the United States from Washington to Roosevelt" with names and dates of office listed. Large photos of William Taft and William Jennings Bryan — "Who's next?" Rev: **Star Spangled Banner**. Advertising.

WHT-24   He's A Winner. w. Arthur C. Earl. m. Clifford W. Walsh. Published by Gotham-Attucks Music Company, No. 136 West 37th Street, New York, NY. 1911. Br/w photo by Harris & Ewing of Wm. H. Taft. Br/r/w eagle, stars and stripes, geometric designs. "Dedicated to President Taft." 6pp. Page 2: Advertising. Page 6: Blank.

WHT-25   We're Going To Land Big Bill And Sunny Jim. w. David M. Kinnear. m. Frederick W. Mills. Published by D.M. Kinnear, No. 78 State Street, Albany, NY. 1908. B/w drawing of shields. "Republican Campaign Song." 6pp. Page 6: Blank.

WHT-26   William H. Taft March And Two Step. m. C.S. Strange. Published by W.H. Willis and Company, corner 4th and Elm Streets, Cincinnati, OH. 1908. B/w photo of William H. Taft. R/w/bk cover. 6pp. Pages 2 and 6: Blank.

WHT-27   Take Me 'Round In A Taxicab. w. Edgar Selden. m. Melvill J. Gideon. Published by Shaprio Music, Music Publishers, Corner Broadway and 39th Street, New York, NY. 1908. R/w/b drawing by Hy Mayer of girl in jester outfit juggling the heads of William H. Taft, Theodore Roosevelt, Charles E. Hughes, William Jennings Bryan and Charles Fairbanks. "As Introduced at the 'Jardin De Paris' Atop the New York Theatre in F. Ziegfield, Jrs.' New Musical Review *The Follies of 1908*." R/w photo of "Grace Leigh" — "Sung by [Photo of Grace Leigh]." 6pp. Pages 2 and 8: Advertising.

WHT-28   Taft March (From Home To The Capitol). m. Jacob Faigin. Published by Carl Fischer, Cooper Square, New York, NY. 1909. Br/w photo by Underwood and Underwood of William H. Taft. Br/w photo of Jacob Faigin. Bl/w drawing of flags, eagle, leaves. 6pp. Pages 2 and 6: Blank.

WHT-29   Echo   Republican Campaign Songs For 1908. c. Dr. J.B. Herbert. Published by The Echo Music Company, Publishers, No. 358 Dearborn Street, Chicago, IL. 1908. [6 7/8" × 10"]. B/w drawing of "Wm. H. Taft — For President," and "Jas. S. Sherman — For Vice-President," shield, eagle, black line border. "Republican Candidates." "For Male Voices." 36pp. [M-395].

WHT-30   When I Return To The U.S.A. And You (March Song). w. Olivia Fariss Dinkins. m. Myrtle Mae McCay. Published by Proctor-Patterson Music Company, Macon, GA. 1910. R/w non-pictorial. "Second Edition — To our President — William Howard Taft." 6pp. Pages 2 and 6: Blank.

WHT-31   The Taft And Sherman Waltz. m. V.L. Caley. Published for the Composer by Westland Publishing

Company, Los Angeles, CA. 1908. B/w photos by Harris & Ewing of "Wm. H. Taft" and "James S. Sherman." B/w eagles, stars and stripes. Bl/w printing. 6pp.

WHT-32 University Club Banquet. [Song Book]. Published by The University Club, Washington, DC. 1911. Bk/br/w drawing of buildings, grapes, glasses, geometric designs. 30pp. Page 3: "The Seventh Annual Banquet, the New Willard Hotel, Monday, February 27, 1911, 7:00 p.m." Page 5: Menu. Pages 6 to 10: Drawings of Senator Thomas Carter, William H. Taft, Ambassador Bryce, Senator Depew and Hon. Morton Littleton.

WHT-33 The Billy Possum's Barn Dance. m. H.S. Taylor. Published by H.S. Taylor and Company. [ca. 1908]. Drawing of two possums, moon, trees.

WHT-34 March Of The Boy Scouts. m. Howard Kocian. Published by Buck & Lowney, "Publishers of Music that Sells," St. Louis, MO. 1912. N/c drawing by Kissack of Boy Scouts marching. "Dedicated to the Boy Scouts of America." "Also published for band and orchestra." 6pp. Page 6: Bl/w photo — "This photo contains photos of President Taft, Ambassador Bryce, Gen. Baden Powell, Mr. Colin H. Livingston, President of Boy Scouts of America, Mr. A.C. Moses, President of Washington Local Council and Mayor Archibald Butt."

WHT-35 Taft's The Man To Lead The Band (The Tried and True Friend of the People). w. Arthur R. Furnish. m. Glenn W. Ashley. Published by Arthur R. Furnish, No. 630 North Robey Street, Chicago, IL. 1908. Bl/bk photo of "William H. Taft." Bl/bk drawing of shield, geometric designs. "With Quartette Chorus." 6pp. Page 6: Blank.

WHT-36 Voice Of The West. w.m. H.H. Lambert, Eureka, California. Copyright 1908 by H.H. Lambert and W.H. Levasseur. R/w photo of Theodore Roosevelt. Bl/w photo of "Wm. H. Taft." Bl/w drawing of Naval ships sailing through the Panama Canal. 6pp. Pages 2 and 6: Blank.

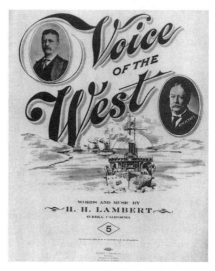

WHT-36

WHT-37 Tariff Bill (A 1910 Song). w.m. George de Romberg and Lewis Elwell. Published by Jerome H. Remick and Company, New York, NY. 1909. B/w photo of William H. Taft. R/w/bk torches, geometric designs. 6pp. Page 6: Blank.

WHT-37

WHT-38 Smiling Bill (Two Step). m. Jack Schuesler. Published by Jack Schuesler, Covington, KY. 1911. Bl/w drawing of William H. Taft. 6pp. Pages 2 and 6: Blank.

WHT-39 Big Bill For Me (A G.O.P. Campaign Song for College Men). w.m. Byron W. Reed (Union '06, Harvard Law '11). Copyright 1908 by B.W. Reed. B/w photo by J.E. Purdy of William Howard Taft. B/w geometric design border. 6pp. Pages 2 and 6: Blank.

WHT-40 President's Greetings. w. Mrs. Wm. P. Toon (Wilmington, N.C.). m. "Tune: *America*." Published as a post card. [ca. 1910]. [3 1/2" × 5 1/2"]. Obv: N/c photos of "Wm. H. Taft," "The Capitol, Washington, D.C." N/c drawings of flags, musical instruments, geometric designs. "First Song Dedicated to Our Presidents." 5 verses. Rev: "Post Card."

WHT-41 Taft-Diaz In El Paso March. m. Ferd. L. Cabello. Published by El Paso Music Publishing Company, No. 191 Newman Street, El Paso, TX. 1910. B/w photos of Presidents Taft and Diaz, Ferd L. Cabello, five U.S. and Mexican scenes and buildings. R/w/bl/gr/bk U.S. and Mexican flags and bunting. 6pp. Page 2: "Respectfully Dedicated to the Honorable Presidents 'Taft and Diaz.'" Page 6: Advertising.

WHT-42 The Blend Of The Blue And The Grey. w.m. J. Alleine Brown. Published by Jerome H. Remick and Company, New York, NY. 1911. Br/be photos of William H. Taft—"A Song with the Right Ring, William H. Taft, March 4, 1911" [facsimile handwriting]; "Gen'l Grant—Let us have peace;" "Gen'l Lee—We are all one now;" "Wm. McKinley—Let us strew flowers alike on the graves of those who wore the blue and those who wore the gray. For American valor is the common heritage of the nation;" "Gen'l Gordon—The American people will forever remain an unbroken brotherhood from sea to sea." "A Reunion Hymn Dedicated to the G.A.R. and U.C.V. Veteran Soldiers & Sailors—1861-1865." 6pp. + 2pp. insert. Page 5: Chorus for Mixed Voices.

WHT-43 Dance Of The Taffy 'Possums. m. Harold Orlob. Published by Jerome H. Remick & Company, New York, NY. 1909. N/c drawing by Starmer of possums dancing, sitting on log, standing behind a fence. "Popular Edition." 6pp. Pages 2 and 6: Advertising.

WHT-44 The Man From Ohio. w. "Tune: *Marching Through Georgia*." [1908]. [5 1/4" × 6 1/2"]. B/w non-pictorial geometric designs. 2pp. Page 2: Blank.

WHT-45 No Matter Who's Elected We Have To Eat To Live (What You Know About It) (Song and Chorus). w.m. Fred W. Clement (of Worcester, Mass). Copyright 1908 by Frank Harding. Bl/bk photo by Harris and Ewing of "Wm. H. Taft." Bl/gn geometric designs, eagle, stars and stripes. 6pp. Pages 2 and 6: Blank.

WHT-46 Taft Two-Step. m. Belle N. Doughty. Published by Belle N. Doughty, Croydon, PA. 1909. B/w photo of William Howard Taft. B/w geometric

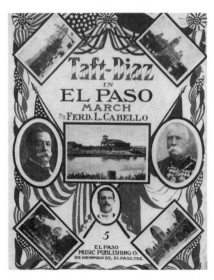

WHT-41

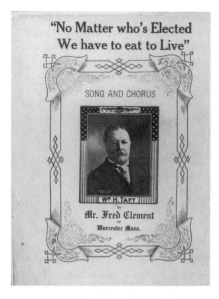

WHT-45

designs. 6pp. Page 6: Advertising for the song *When We Seat Our Mr. Taft.* w.m. Belle N. Doughty.

WHT-47 March No. 2: To The White House. w. Dr. Creamer Peckham. m.a. Major John McCarthy. Published by The A.B. Clinton Company, New Haven, CT. [1908]. B/w photo of William H. Taft. Bl/w geometric designs. "Campaign Songs — Hon. William Howard Taft." 4pp. Page 2: Song: **March No. 2** *(To The White House)*. Page 3: Song: **No. 5.** Page 4: Song: **No. 6.**

WHT-48 Big Bill Taft (Campaign Song for Male Voices). w. Arthur Guiterman. m. S.T. Paul. Published by J. Fisher and Bro., No. 7 and 11, Bible House, New York, NY. [7" × 10 3/4"]. 1908. Non-pictorial black line border. 6pp. Page 2: Blank. Page 6: Advertising.

WHT-49 Taft, Taft. w. Joseph Tait. m. M.C. Hanford. Published by The H. Kirkus Dugdale Company, Inc., 14th and You Streets, Washington DC. Copyright 1912 by Joseph Tait. Bl/w drawing of William H. Taft. 6pp. Page 2: Blank. Page 6: Advertising.

WHT-50 Billy Possum Rag. m. B. Claud Davis. Published by Brit W. Davis, Jr., Valdosta, GA. [ca. 1908]. O/bk/w drawing of a possum.

WHT-51 Park's Republican Campaign Songs (For Male Voices) [Song Book]. Published by The J.A. Parks Company, York, NE. 1908. [6 3/4" × 9 5/8"]. Gn/bk non-pictorial geometric design border. 38p. [M-396, 401].

WHT-52 Won't You Be My Billie Possum. w. William E. Gerow. m. Weston Wilson. Published by Southern California Music Company, Nos. 332-34 South Broadway, Los Angeles, CA. 1909. R/w/br drawing of baby, possum. B/w photo of Bessie Wynn — "Yours, Bessie Wynn" [facsimile handwriting]. "Sung Successfully by [Bessie Wynn]." 6pp.

WHT-53 The Battle Now Is On. w. William J. Applegate. m. William St. Clair. Copyright 1908 by William J. Applegate, No. 18 Alta Vista Terrace, Chicago, IL. B/w litho by Hawlin Engraving Company of William Howard Taft, James S. Sherman, U.S. flag. 4pp.

WHT-54 Billy Possum (March and Two Step). m. Grace D. Schenck-

WHT-53

Henze. Published by Grace D. Schenck-Henze & Company, Kansas City, MO. 1909. Gn/bk/w/o drawing of possum, trees. 6pp. Page 6: Blank.

WHT-55 Inauguration March. m. Abe Holtzman (*Old Faithful, Uncle Sammy, Loveland* and *Love Sparks*). Copyright 1909 by Leo Feist. "Respectfully dedicated to Hon. Wm. H. Taft." In: *Spare Moments, A Monthly Magazine of Inspiration and Progress*, page 2. March, 1909.

WHT-56 Billy Possum. w.m. "Little Miss Fred Dempsey." Published by Thomas Publishing Company, Mercantile Library Building, Cincinnati, OH. Copyright 1909 by L.T. Dempsey. Bl/w photos of "Wm. H. Taft," Miss Dempsey and Mrs. DeForest Allgood, possum. Bl/w printing. "Dedicated to Wm. Taft on his Inauguration as President of the United States and to Mrs. DeForest Allgood, founder of the Billy Possum Club." "Words & Music Composed by Miss Fred Dempsey (Ten years old), Covington, Kentucky." "Also published for band and orchestra." 6pp. Pages 2 and 6: Blank.

WHT-57 Fairbanks' Republican Campaign Songs. Published by Geo. E. Fairbanks, South Cornish, NH. 8pp. "Buy Them, Sing Them, and Taft Will Be Elected." [M-400].

WHT-58 When We Seat Our Mr. Taft. W.m. Belle N. Doughty. 1909. Published by Belle N. Doughty, Croydon, PA.

WHT-59 Big Bill Taft (Popular Campaign Song). w.m. Frederick Hall. Published by The Mather Company, No. 76 East Liberty, Pittsburgh, PA. Copyright 1908 by Frederick Hall. Bl/w photo of William Howard Taft. R/w/b drawing of shield, eagle. 4pp. Page 4: "Special Prices to Political and Glee Clubs, Quartette for in Preparation, Send Request."

WHT-60 Willie Taft. w.m. John R. Boddie, St. Louis, MA. 1908. Gn/w drawing of William H. Taft — "Substitute Bill," "Steamroller Bill," "Injunction Bill." "Dedicated to the Travelling Mens' National Democratic Club." 6pp. Pages 2 and 6: Blank. [Anti-Taft].

WHT-61 Step Into Line For Taft (A Continuation of the Big Stick and Square Deal Policy). w.m. J.M. Hagan. Published by Victor Kremer Company, Chicago, IL. 1908. B/w photo of William H. Taft. 6pp. Page 5: Arranged for "Male Quartette." Page 6: Advertisement for Victor Kremer music.

WILLIAM J. BRYAN

WJB-1 How It Happened (or The Jew of Lombard Street). w. Charles F. Gilbert. m. J.A. Parks. Published by The J.A. Parks Company, York, NE. 1896 B/w photo of William Jennings Bryan, geometric designs. "The Great Silver Song." "Dedicated to Hon. William J. Bryan with compliments of the Bryan Club, York, Neb." 6pp.

WJB-2 The Farmer's Campaign Song. w. Edward W. Kruse. m. A.C. Remie. Published by Balmer & Weber Company, St. Louis, MO. [1896]. Photo of "Hon. Wm. Jennings Bryan." "Played with great success by bands and orchestras, mandolin clubs, &c, &c." "Sung by glee clubs, reunions, political gatherings, &c, &c."

WJB-3 New 1900 Bryan March. m. William H. Penn. Published by Sol Bloom, Corner Randolph & Dearborn Streets, Chicago, IL. 1900. Bl/w photo of William Jennings Bryan. Bl/w/s drawing of a wreath, rays. 6pp. Pages 2 and 6: Advertising for Sol Bloom published music.

WJB-4 Denver Auditorium March. m. Miss Freda Richter. Published by O.H. Richter (Leader of the Orchestra, Orpheum Theatre, Denver, Colo). 1908. B/w drawing by Williamson-Haffner of the Denver "Auditorium." "Dedicated to the National Democratic Convention, Denver, July-1908." 8pp.

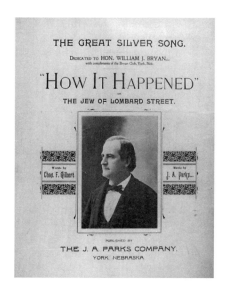

WJB-1

Pages 2 and 7: Blank. Page 8: B/w photo of William Jennings Bryan.

WJB-5 Line Up For Bryan! w.m. George W. Gale. Published by The Gale and Mullane Music Company, Northwest corner 5th and Sycamore Streets, Cincinnati, OH. 1908. B/w photo of William Jennings Bryan. Bl/w drawing of shield, geometric designs. "The Battle Song of Democracy." "Dedicated to the Great Commoner, William Jennings Bryan." 6pp.

WJB-6 Our Willie Of The West. w. Miss Willie Maud Chartrand. m. Dr. William Hooker Vail. Copyright 1896 by William Hooker Vail. Non-pictorial geometric designs, black line border. 4pp. Page 4: Blank.

WJB-7 Bryan's Good-Luck March (Two Step). m. Charles E. Pratt. Published by National Music Company, No. 67 Fifth Avenue, New York, NY. 1896. B/w photo of William Jennings Bryan. [V-1: B/w] [V-2: Bl/w] drawing of horseshoe, 4-leaf clover, house — "Residence of W.J. Bryan at Lincoln, Neb." 6pp. Page 6: Blank.

WJB-8 The National Democratic Song Book For 1900. w. J.J. Kavanaugh. m. W.A. Sullenbarger. Published by The S. Brainard's Sons Company, Chicago, IL. Copyright 1900 by Kavanaugh and Sullenbarger. Be/bk photos of William J. Bryan and Adlai E. Stevenson. Be/bk geometric designs. "No. 1." 20pp. [M-382].

WJB-9 Sixteen To One (Campaign Song). w. S.D. Lount. m. F.W. Reid. Published for the Author by The Chicago Music Company, Chicago, IL. Copyright 1896 by S.D. Lount. Br/w non-pictorial geometric designs. 6pp. Pages 2 and 6: Blank.

WJB-10 Bryan Free Silver March. m. L.M. French (Composer of *Cupid, Students March, &c*). Published by Sol Bloom, Chicago, IL. 1896. B/w photo of William Jennings Bryan, woman, harp. S/w/bk geometric designs. "S.B. 1896.23." 6pp. Pages 2 and 6: Blank.

WJB-11 Democratic Campaign Song Folio. Published by The National Association of Democratic Clubs (Wm. R. Hearst, President), No. 1370 Broadway, New York, NY. 1900. B/w photos of William J. Bryan and Adlai Stevenson. R/w/bl/gn flag design, drawing of woman with harp, wreaths. "Educational Music Series, No. 1, Vol. 1, October, 1900." 16pp. Page 2: Contents. Page 15: Names of "Campaign Prize Song Award" winners. Page 16: R/w/b U.S. flag, star border, songs. [M-380].

WJB-12(A) Shall The People Rule? w.m. J.A. Wallace. Published by Music Publicity Bureau, Pittsburgh, PA. 1908. [9 1/2" × 12 9/16"]. B/w litho of William Jennings Bryan and John W. Kern, geometric designs [V-1: On white background] [V-2: On Black background]. "Four Official Democratic Campaign Songs." "Approved by Norman E. Mack, Chairman, Democratic National Committee." 4pp. Page 4: Campaign issues.

(B) Bryan, Billy Bryan. w. J.A. Wallace. m. Air: *Dixie*.

(C) **The Merry Smile**. w. J.A. Wallace. m. Air: *Merry Widow*. 4pp.

(D) **The People Are Bound To Win**. w.m. J. Adrian. 4pp. Page 4: Narrative on trusts and taxes.

WJB-13 Give Us Silver Jolly Silver (Rousing Campaign Song). w.m. Harold K. Watson. Published by Woodsocket Publishing Company, Woodsocket, RI. 1896. B/w drawing of banner. "Dedicated to Hon. Wm. J. Bryan." 6pp. Pages 2 and 6: Blank.

WJB-14 Bryan, Billy Bryan. w. J.A. Wallace. m. "Tune of *Dixie*." Published by The Sloan Typewriting Bureau, Public Stenographers, Machesney Building, Pittsburgh, PA. [1908]. [5 1/8" × 8"]. O/bk broadside. 2pp. Page 2: Campaign Song touting Johnny Murphy, Mayor of Pittsburgh for Bryan's running mate.

WJB-15 Songs Of The G.O.P. [Song Book]. w. Phi Chi. m. Popular Airs. Published by the Neale Company, Washington, DC. 1900. [5" × 6 7/8"]. Ma/y hardback book with drawing of elephant. 104pp. Pages 93-100: Advertising for other Neale publications. [Anti-Republican]. [M-368].

WJB-16 Star Of The West. w.m. W.C. Piatt. a. G.W. Ashley. Published by The Piatt Music Company, No. 69 Dearborn Street, Chicago, IL. 1908. B/w photo of "William Jennings Bryan." Drawing of a red star. "Illustrated with slides." 6pp. Page 2: At title—"The Nation's Song (Number Two)." Page 5: "Arrangement for Mixed Quartette." Page 6: Poem—"We Trust."

WJB-17 Bryan And Sewall Grand March. m. L.C. Noles. Published by F. Trifet, Publisher, No. 36 Broomfield Street, Boston, MA., as *The Boston Weekly Journal of Sheet Music*, No. 67, August 5, 1896. B/w litho of heron, geometric designs. "For the Piano." "Entered at Post Office at Boston or mail matter of the second class." "Published weekly. Subscription, $1.00 per year in advance." 6pp. Pages 2 and 6: Advertising for other F. Trifet published music.

WJB-18 Red-Hot Democratic Campaign Songs For 1896. c. J.B. Herbert. Published by The S. Brainard's Sons Company, Nos. 151 and 153 Wabash Avenue, Chicago, IL. 1896. [5 1/4" × 7"]. R/be litho of ribbon, geometric designs. 28pp. [M-355].

WJB-19 Democratic National Convention March. m. Warren Beebe. Published by Mark Brothers Music Publishing Company, Suite 1131-1133, No. 153 La Salle Street, Chicago, IL. January, 1896. R/w/b litho of "The White House," shield. "Dedicated to the City of Chicago." 6pp. Page 6: Advertising.

WJB-20 The Bryan Silver March. w. David B. Page. m. William H. Piper. Published by Page and Piper, Kansas City, MO. 1896. "The *Kansas City Times* Edition." Br/w drawing of William J. Bryan. Vignettes of William Jennings Bryan's speeches: Drawing of Bryan and workers—"You shall not press down upon the brow of labor this crown of thorns." Drawing of Bryan and English banker—""You shall not crucify mankind on a cross of gold." Drawing of farmer—"The farmer who goes forth in the morning." Drawing of miners—"The miners who delve in the Earth." Drawing of crown and thorns—"Gold Standard," "No Crown of Thorns, No Cross of Gold." 4pp.

WJB-21 The Silver Regiment (March Two Step). m. Annie G. Pekin (Chicago). 1896. Non-pictorial geometric designs. "Dedicated to Col. W.J. Bryan." 6pp. Page 2: Blank.

WJB-22 Bryan's Democratic Success March. m. George Maywood. Published by P.M. Wolsieffer, No. 201 Clark Street, Chicago, IL. 1896. Photo of William Jennings Bryan. Border of stars, stripes. 6pp. Page 6: Advertising.

WJB-23 Bryan (March Song). w.m. Will J. Conroy. Published by Will J. Conroy, No. 12 Linden Avenue,

Plainfield, NJ. 1908. Bl/w photo of William J. Bryan. R/w/b drawing of an eagle, axe, shield, wreath. 6pp. Pages 2 and 6: Blank.

WJB-24 Bryan Two-Step. m. Minnie Bryan Tucker. Published by Harry E. Tucker, Platte City, MO. 1908. B/w photo of William J. Bryan. Bl/w drawing of an eagle with ribbon inscribed "Equality to All," flags, branches. 6pp. Pages 2 and 6: Blank.

WJB-25 Silver Bill. w. Mary Morrison. m. Edith Morrison. "Respectfully Dedicated to William J. Bryan." In: *Western Rural and Live Stock Weekly*, pages 1332-1333, Vol. 54, No. 41, October 8, 1896. Published by Howard and Wilson Publishing Company, Chicago, IL.

WJB-26 The American Marseillaise (A Song for the People). w.m. Frederic Lowell. Published by Lyon & Healy, Chicago, IL. Copyright 1896 by S.A. Stevens. [7" × 10 1/2"]. R/w litho of William Jennings Bryan, cross inscribed "You shall not press the crown of thorns upon the toilers' brow!," and a crown of thorns, geometric designs. "Dedicated to Hon. Wm. Jennings Bryan." "New Edition Revised and Corrected." "Price 10 cents, per 100, $6.00." 4pp. Page 4: Advertising.

WJB-27 W.J. Bryan's Grand March. m. M.C. Bales. Published by A.W. Perry & Son, Sedalia, MO. 1896. B/w litho of William Jennings Bryan, geometric design border. 6pp. Pages 2 and 6: Advertising for other music. Page 3: "For Piano or Cabinet Organ."

WJB-28 On To Victory 1908. w.m. Helen B. Chamberlin. Published by Helen B. Chamberlin. Copyright 1900 and 1908. B/w photo of William Jennings Bryan. R/w/b flags, shield. "Published for Band and Orchestra by Helen B. Chamberlin." 6pp. Page 6: Blank.

WJB-29 President Bryan's Two-Step March. m. F.W. Gaisberg. Published by M.D. Swisher, No. 115 South 10th Street, Philadelphia, PA. 1896. B/w

WJB-28

photo of William Jennings Bryan, geometric designs. "To Our Silver Hero." 6pp. Pages 2 and 6: Blank.

WJB-30 The Silver Knight Of The West (A Campaign Song for 1896). w.m. Lucius C. West. Published by National Music Company, Nos. 215-221 Wabash Avenue, Chicago, IL. 1896. B/w photo of William Jennings Bryan. Bl/w geometric designs. "Dedicated to Hon. William J. Bryan, Lincoln, Neb." 6pp. Page 2: Blank. Page 6: Advertising.

WJB-31 Democratic Fun (A Campaign Cake Walk). m. Robert Buechel. Published by the Tolbert R. Ingram Music Company, Denver, CO. 1908. O/bk/w cover with a silhouette of a cheering crowd. B/w photo of a child conductor. "Official National Democratic Campaign March." 6pp. Page 2: Blank. Page 3: Two b/w photos of child conductor with comic captions. "Dedicated by permission to the Nominee of the Democratic Party — The next President of our United States."

WJB-32 Sixteen To One (A New Dance Two Step). m. A.F. Jacobs. a. T.A. Holland (Springfield, Mass., Member of

American Society Professors of Dancing of New York). Published by A.F. Jacobs, Springfield, MA. 1896. Gn/w geometric designs. "The Latest." "Sixteen Movements to Complete One Figure." 6pp. Pages 2 and 6: Blank.

WJB-33   Our Pop. Convention (or We'll Be There). w.m. De Forest Harrington. Published by George E. Kessler, White Front Music Store, No. 113 10th Street, Masonic Temple, Sioux Falls, SD. 1900. B/w photo of "The Falls, Souix Falls, S.D." R/w/gn geometric designs. "As sung by the celebrated Min-Ne-Ha-Ha Manskor at the National Peoples Party Convention, Sioux Falls, So. Dak., May 9th, 1900." "Souvenir Edition." 6pp. Pages 2 and 6: Blank.

WJB-34   Sixteen   To   One (Galop). m. T.H. Rollinson. Published by Oliver Ditson Company, Nos. 453-463 Washington Street, Boston, MA. 1896. Bl/gd/sl/w drawing of a scale with a block of silver inscribed "16 oz. value $9.74" and a block of gold inscribed "1 oz. value $18.60." 6pp. Page 2: Blank. Page 6: Advertising.

WJB-35   America. Published by Democratic State Central Committee, Harrisburg, PA. 1900. [4 7/16" × 7 3/16" card]. Obv: B/w photos of William Jennings Bryan and Adlai Stevenson. R/w/b flag, green wreaths. "Democratic Campaign Hymn for 1900." Rev: Speech by William J. Bryan.

WJB-36   The People's Choice. w. Doc Murphy. m. Floyd Thompson. a. Thomas R. Confare. Published by Doc Murphy, No. 1131 Unity Building, Chicago, IL. 1908. B/w photo of "William Jennings Bryan." B/w drawing of shield, wreath, geometric designs. 6pp. Pages 2 and 6: Blank.

WJB-37   Bryan Cocktail (Song). w.m. N.S. Carter and Julia Neibergall. Published by Carlin & Lennox, Indianapolis, IN. 1908. B/w photos of William J. Bryan and John W. Kern. Gn/w geometric designs. 6pp. Page 6: Blank.

WJB-38   Free Silver (The Battle-Cry of Freedom). Published by The Philadelphia Press, Philadelphia, PA. [1896]. Litho of a flag. "The Great Rallying Song of the Silver People — Men, Women and Children." "Compliments of *The Philadelphia Item*."

WJB-39   Public Sentiment (The Original Big Stick). w. E. Watkins. m. V.D. Nirella. Printed by Anchor Press, No. 443 Third Avenue, Pittsburgh, PA. Copyright 1908 by E. Watkins. B/w photos of the "Convention Hall, Denver, Col." and William Jennings Bryan. "For Our President, William J. Bryan, 1909 — 1913." B/w geometric designs. 4pp. Page 4: Blank.

WJB-40   When Bryan Comes To The White House In Nineteen Hundred Nine. w. A.H. Tiffy. m. Glenn W. Ashley. Published by The Victor Kremer Company, Chicago, IL. 1908. Bl/bk/w photos of William J. Bryan and man — "Featured with great success by [photo of unknown man]," geometric designs. 6pp. Page 2: Blank. Page 6: Advertising.

WJB-41   Siemonn's Presidential March. m. George Siemonn. Published by Capitol Publishing Company, Washington, DC. 1900. B/w photos of William Jennings Bryan and Abraham Lincoln. B/w drawings of George Washington, flag. "Dedicated to the Hon. Wm. Jennings Bryan." "Composed by George Siemonn," facsimile signature. List of other orchestrations available. 6pp. Page 6: Blank.

WJB-42   How Can I Make A Dollar. "In German: **Wie Kann Man Geld Verdienen?** (Campaign Song). w.m. Paul G. Zimmerman. Published by Paul G. Zimmerman, Morristown, NJ. 1899. B/w photos of "For President William Jennings Bryan," "For Vice-President Adlai E. Stevenson," and "For Congress Joshua S. Salmon." "For Assembly John Bergen, George Pierson [No photos]." "The 1900 Common Sense Campaign Song." "Respectfully Dedicated to Mrs. Mary B. Bryan." 4pp.

WJB-43 The Rights Of Man (A National Democratic Campaign Ballad). w. T. O'D. O'Callaghan. Published by The Twelfth Assembly District, New York, NY. September 3, 1896. [8 1/2" × 12"]. Non-pictorial. "Written for the Presidential Campaign of 1896." "Dedicated to Freedom and the People." "From *The Brooklyn Citizen*, Sept. 5, 1896." "For Music and Recitation." 2pp.

WJB-44 William Jennings Bryan Of Nebraska (A Democratic Song). w.m. William T. Whelan (Washington, DC). Published by Sanders & Stayman, No. 1327 "F" Street, Washington, DC. Copyright 1900 by William T. Whelan. B/w photo by Bachrach & Brother of William Jennings Bryan. Bl/w drawings of flowers, geometric designs. "Dedicated to the Stainless Young Chieftain and Dauntless Bearer of Democracy." 6pp. Pages 2 and 6: Blank.

WJB-45 The Commoner. w. Josephine B. Craig. m. G.W. Ashley. Published by Victor Kremer Company, Chicago, IL. Copyright 1908 by Josephine B. Craig. Bl/bk photo of William Jennings Bryan. Bl/bk photo of Kasper Weick—"Featured with great success by [photo of Kasper Weick]." Bl/w geometric drawings. 6pp.

WJB-46 Bryan's Victorious March. m. Michael McDonough. Published by Victor Kremer Company, Chicago, IL. 1908. Bl/bl photo of William Jennings Bryan, drawing of woman with U.S. flag. 6pp. Pages 2 and 6: Advertising.

WJB-47 16 To 1 Quickstep (Chicago Convention). m. Mrs. Ala. Bradley. Copyright 1896 by Mrs. Ala. Bradley. B/w drawing of William Jennings Bryan, geometric design border. "Dedicated to W.J. Bryan." "For Pianoforte." 8pp. Page 8: Blank.

WJB-48 Free Silver March. w. J.M. Houk. m. *Marching Through Georgia*. Published by J.M. Houk, Energy, PA. July 20, 1886 [sic]. [4" × 5 1/4"]. 2pp. Page 2: Blank.

WJB-49 William J. Bryan Unser Nachster Prasident. w. Peter J. Felden. m. "Mel: *Die Wacht am Rhein*." Published by Peter J. Felden, No. 73 West Kinzie Street, Chicago, IL. [1900]. [6 1/8" × 10 15/16"]. B/w litho of William

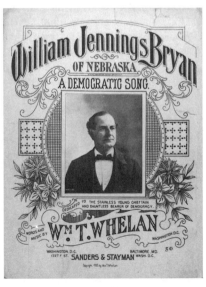

WJB-44

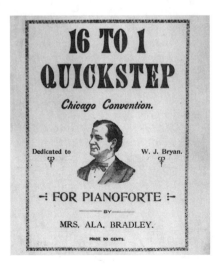

WJB-47

J. Bryan and Adlai E. Stevenson, eagle, flags. 2pp. Page 2: Blank. All lyrics in German language.

WJB-50 Let Us Have Free Coinage, Boys At Sixteen To One! (National Campaign Song with Chorus). w.m. Albert P. Schack. Published by Albert P. Schack, Publisher, No. 809 20th Street, Denver, CO. 1896. B/w drawing of a man waiving hat and holding U.S. flag inscribed "Free Coinage 16 to 1." 10pp. Page 2: Advertising. Page 10: Blank.

WJB-51 Bryan Believed In Heaven (That's Why He's In Heaven To-Night). w. Alfred Dubin and William Raskin. m. F. Henri Klickmann. Published by Jack Mills, Inc., Music Publishers, Jack Mills Building, Nos. 148-150 West 46th Street, New York, NY. 1925. B/w photo of William Jennings Bryan. 6pp. Pages 2 and 6: Advertising.

WJB-52 Bryan And Sewall Grand March. m. L.C. Noles. In: *Trifit's Monthly Budget of Music*, page 12. Published by F. Trifit, Publisher, No. 36 Broomfield Street, Boston, MA. November, 1897. [9 3/4" × 12 1/4"].

WJB-53 When I Get There In The White House Chair. w.m. M.V.H. Smith (Author of *I Am Looking At The Panama Canal*). Published by Sanders & Stayman Company, No. 1327 "F" Street N.W., Washington, DC. Copyright 1907 by M.V.H. Smith. B/w photo of The White House. R/w candles, shield, flags, geometric designs. "Respectfully dedicated to William Jennings Bryan." 6pp. Pages 2 and 6: Blank.

WJB-54 Anti=Expansion March (Two-Step). m. Charles E. Pratt. Published by National Music Company, Nos. 266-268 Wabash Avenue, Chicago, IL. 1896. Bl/w photo of William Jennings Bryan. R/w geometric designs. "Dedicated to Col. W.J. Bryan, The Peoples Choice." 4pp. Page 4: Blank.

WJB-55 Bryan Free Silver Song Book. w. B.M. Lawrence, M.D. Published by Dr. B.M. Lawrence, Mansur

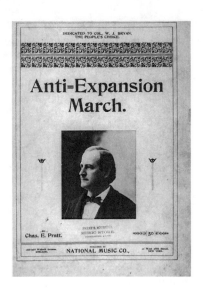

WJB-54

Block, Indianapolis, IN. [2 9/16" × 5 1/2"]. [1896]. B/w litho of an American Flag, geometric design border. "Campaign Songs." "Price 5 cents; 50 cts. Per doz., $2.50 per 100, $25 per $1,000." 16pp.

WJB-56 Parks' Democratic Campaign Songs (For Male Voices). w.m. J.A. Parks. Published by The J.A. Parks Company, York, NE. 1900. Gn/bk non-pictorial. "Respectfully inscribed to Hon. Wm. V. Allen." 40pp. [M-385].

WJB-57 The Liberty Bell Ringing: Songs And Poems. w.m. James G. Clark, A.M. Salyer and J.N. Goodman (Authors *Poetry & Song, Eileen, Hot Shots, &c.*). Published by Salyer and Robinson, Los Angeles, CA. 1896. Gn/bk litho of William Jennings Bryan. 60pp. [M-352].

WJB-58 Silver's Rallying Songs. e. John P. Finkel. Published by John P. Finkel, Columbus, OH. 1896. 16pp. [M-354].

WJB-59 Silver Songs Written For The Bryan Campaign. e. Henry D. Millbank. Published by Silver Songs Publishing Company, Des Moines, IA. 1896. "Adapted to Popular Air." 12pp. [M-357].

WJB-61 Echoes From '76. e.

Charles A. Sheffield (Author of *Songs of the New Emancipation, &c.*). Published by C. St. J. Cole, Minneapolis, MN. 1896. Be/bk non-pictorial. The Nation's Library (May 1, 1896). [M-360].

WJB-60 Bryan Campaign Songster. e. Leontine Stanfield. Published by Stanfield Publishing Company, New York, NY. 1896. 4pp. [M-359].

WJB-61 Echoes From '76. e. Charles A. Sheffield (Author of *Songs of the New Emancipation, &c.*). Published by C. St. J. Cole, Minneapolis, MN. 1896. Be/bk non-pictorial. The Nation's Library (May 1, 1896). [M-360].

WJB-62 New People's Party Songster. e. Theodore Parish Stelle. Published in Mt. Vernon, IL. [ca. 1894]. 32pp. [M-361].

WJB-63 Populist And Silver Songs. w.m. Henry W. Taylor and J.B. Herbert. Published by S. Brainard's Sons Company, Chicago, IL. 1896. Gn/bk non-pictorial. 35pp. [M-362].

WJB-64 The People's Campaign Songster. e. C.S. White. Published by W.L. Reynolds, Chicago, IL. 1896. O/bk litho of the Author. 38pp. [M-363].

WJB-65 Six Red Hot Songs Written And Composed Especially For The Campaign of 1900. w. Dr. T. Wilkins. m.e. Byron J. Bechtel. Published by O.G. Hurser, Chicago, IL. 1900. 16pp. [M-377].

WJB-66 Campaign Prize Songs. Published by *New York Journal*, New York, NY. 1900. "As Published by the *New York Journal* on Behalf of The National Association of Democratic Clubs." [M-378].

WJB-67 Freedom Songs. w.m.c. E.W. Crane. Published by E.W. Crane, Lincoln, NE. 1900. Be/bk non-pictorial. 36pp. Page 3: Litho of William Jennings Bryan. "Endorseded [sic] by the State Central Committee of the Fusion Forces in Nebraska." [M-379].

WJB-68 The Democratic National Campaign Song Book For 1900. e. Harry H. Johnson. Published by Harry H. Johnson, Tacoma, WA. 1900. Gn/bk non-pictorial. "Songs That Will Sing Democratic Principles in Verse to the Latest and Most Popular Melodies as Sung with Great Success by the "Hoi-Polloi" Glee Club of Tacoma, Washington." [M-381].

WJB-69 The Bryan Songster. e. LeRoy Miller. Published by News Printing House, Albia, IA. 1900. Gy/bk litho of William Jennings Bryan. "Dedicated to the Cause of the Great Common People in the Struggle of 1900." [M-383].

WJB-70 Mulligan's Campaign Song Book For 1900. e. John T. Mulligan. Published by John T. Mulligan, Bloomfield, NE. 1900. Be/bk non-pictorial. 28pp. [M-384].

WJB-71 Bryan Campaign Songster For 1900 (For Male Voices). e. Logan S. Porter. Published by Home Music Company, Logansport, IN. 1900. Pk/bk litho of William Jennings Bryan and Adlai E. Stevenson. 36pp. [M-386].

WJB-72 Silver. w.m. Frestone. 1896.

WJB-73 Bryan The Nation's Choice. w.m. Walsemar Malmene. 1896.

WJB-74 Protection and Bimetallism. w.m. Draper. 1896.

WJB-75 Irish Democrat. w.m. Dudley. 1896.

WJB-76 Graduate Of Coin's School. w.m. Roehr. 1896.

WJB-77 Free Coinage. w.m. Foltz. 1896.

WJB-78 Free Silver Marching Song. w.m. C.L. Quellmelz. 1896.

WJB-79 Democratic Victory March. m. H. Werner. 1896.

WJB-80 Harvey's Free Silver March. w.m. Retter. 1896.

WJB-81 The Rooster I Wore On My Hat. w.m. Rose. 1896.

WJB-82 The Silver Ghost. e. T.S.A. [Tom S. Apgar]. Published by Tom

S. Apgar, Robinson, IL. 1896. O/bk cover. 18pp. [M-351].

WJB-83 Silver Party Song Book. e. [Mary Baird Finch]. Published in Pueblo, CO. 1896. 12pp. [M-353].

WJB-84 Free Silver Campaigns Songs And Poems. c. King of Poets. Published in Bedford, IA. 28pp. [M-356].

WJB-85 Sixteen Silver Songs. Published by W.B. Crombie, Lincoln, NE. 1896. 16pp. [M-358].

WJB-86 William The Conqueror. m. Florence Tunison Duncan (Jacksonville, Illinois). Published by Florence Tunison Duncan, Jacksonville, IL. 1908. B/w photo of "William Jennings Bryan." Facsimile letter from Bryan to Duncan: "Mrs. Florence T. Duncan, Jacksonville, Ill., My Dear Madam — Your favor of July 10th has just come to my attention, and I have no objection at all to your dedicating to me the march which you have composed. I shall also take pleasure in ordering a photograph sent you. With best wishes for the success of your composition, I am Very Truly Yours W.J. Bryan" [Facsimile signature]. 6pp. Pages 2 and 6: Blank.

WJB-87 Democratic Campaign Chorus. m. "Tune — *Tammany*." Published as a post card. 1908. Br/be photos of William Jennings "Bryan" and John W. "Kern."

WJB-88 Regular Democratic March Two-Step. m. F.N. Wicker, Jr. (Author of *Sweet Memories Two-Step*). Published by J.A. Verlander, New Orleans, LA. 1900. Br/be litho of rooster within a circle. "Dedicated to Mrs. Robt. Ewing." 6pp. Pages 2 and 6: Blank.

WJB-89 Free Silver & Bryan In 1900. w. Lyman F. George. m. Laurence B. O'Connor. Published L.F. George, No. 45 High Street, Boston, MA. 1897. B/w photo of William Jennings "Bryan." "Sung at the Jefferson Anniversary Banquet, April 13, 1897, by W.T. Miller." "Dedicated to the Massachusetts Democratic Club." 6pp. Pages 2 and 6: Blank.

WJB-90 The First Battle Song. w.m. Stephen Taylor Dekins. Published by Stephen Taylor Dekins, Virginia, IL. 1897. B/w photo of William Jennings Bryan. Bl/w litho of Lady Justice with scales labeled "16" and "1." 6pp. Pages 2 and 6: Blank.

WJB-91 No Crown of Thorns Nor Cross of Gold. w.m. H.O. Nourse. Chicago, IL. 1896. Published by The Chicago Music Co., Chicago, IL. 1896. Bl/gd litho of a cross, crown of thorns. "Embodying Extracts From the Speech of Hon. Wm. J. Bryan, Delivered at the Coliseum, Chicago July 9th 1896 Before the National Democratic Convention." "Dedicated to the Friends and Lovers of American Liberty." 6pp. Pages 2 and 6: Blank.

WJB-92 On To Victory. w.m. Helen B. Chamberlin (Author of *We'll Stand By The Constitution*). Published by Helen B. Chamberlin, Storm Lake, IA. 1900. R/w litho of banner inscribed "For Piano or Organ," laurel wreath. "Respectfully Dedicated to W.J. Bryan." 6pp. Pages 2 and 6: Blank.

WJB-93 William Jennings Bryan Our Next President. w.m. S.M. Hawk. Published by S.M. Hawk, Kankakee, IL. 1908. B/w photo of William Jennings Bryan. B/w litho of shield, geometric designs. "Dedicated to the People." 6pp. Page 6: Advertisement for S.M. Hawk song.

WJB-94 We Will Vote For The Man From Nebraska. w. Frank Finsterbach. 1900. Gn/bk litho of William Jennings Bryan within wreath, ribbon inscribed "To W.J. Bryan," shield, flags, geometric designs. 4[?]pp. Inside title — **The Man From Nebraska**.

WJB-95 [New York Journal Campaign Prize Song Sheet]. Published by *The New York Journal* for National Association of Democratic Clubs. [1900]. 16pp. R/w/b litho of American flag, star border. Songs. Page 15: "Campaign Prize

Song Award — In its examination of over seven hundred campaign songs submitted in competition for the three prizes of $50, $30 and $20 offered by The New York Journal for the National Democratic Clubs, the Committee of Award applied to each these three tests: First — Propriety of sentiment. Second — Musical excellence. Third Elements of Popularity..."

WJB-96 Sixteen to One (Silver March). m. E.T. Blair. Published by A.W. Perry & Sons Music Company, Sedalia, MO. 1898. Bk/w/s geometric design frame. 6pp. Pages 2 and 6: Advertisements for A.W. Perry music.

WJB-97 16 To 1 (A Red Hot Campaign Song). w. C.M. Copp. m. "Adapted to the Melody of *Billy Barlow*." Published by National Music, Nos. 215-221 Wabash Ave., Chicago, IL. 1896. R/w/bk geometric designs. Facsimile coins hanging from eagle in each corner inscribed "Free Coinage 16, 1, 1896."

See also WM-5; WM-37; WM-80; WM-87; WM-105; WM-115; WM-133; WHT-12; WHT-23; WHT-27; WHT-60; WW-85; WW-219; HCH-60.

WILLIAM J. CLINTON

WJC-1 I Am For Clinton And Gore (A Campaign Song). w.m. Dr. Dana R. Dorsey. Published by Dr. Dana Dorsey, P.O. Box 783, Logan, WV. 1992. [8 1/2" × 11"]. B/w photo of Governor Bill Clinton and Senator Al Gore. B/w reproduction of a "Clinton and Gore" campaign bumper sticker, geometric design border. 4pp. Page 4: B/w photo of Governor Bill Clinton — "Putting people first...For a change."

WJC-2 Hello, Billy. w. "Corrupted from Herman by John Burkhardt (Apologies)." m. *Hello Dolly*. Published by John Burkhardt, [Ann Arbor, MI]. [1992]. [8 1/2" × 11"]. Non-pictorial. [Accompanying circular: "Post Inaugural Bash at the Tabard Inn, Sat., Jan. 23, 1993]. 2pp. Page 2: Blank.

WJC-1

WJC-3 President Bill Clinton March. w. Andrea Fodor Litkei. m. Ervin Litkei. Published by Loena Music Publishing Company, No. 239 West 18th Street, New York, NY. 10011. 1992. [8 1/2" × 11"]. B/w photo of Bill Clinton, facsimile signature. R/w/b cover. 4pp.

WJC-4 The First Lady March. w. Andrea Litkei. m. Ervin Litkei. Published by Loena Music Publishing Company, No. 239 West 18th Street, New York, NY. 10011. 1992. [8 1/2" × 11"]. B/w facsimile of the first page of the music with a b/w photo of Hillary Clinton superimposed. 4pp. Page 2: "Dedicated to First Lady Hillary Clinton." Page 4: B/w photo of "Hillary Rodham Clinton."

WJC-5 Happy Days Are Here Again (Gore For President). w. Jack Yellen (ASCAP). m. Milton Ager (ASCAP). Special lyrics by Pinky Herman (ASCAP). Hand made campaign song by Pinky Herman, No. 4705 NW 35th Street, #615, Lauderdale, Lakes, FL. [1988]. B/w photocopy of a cut-and-paste modification of the Warner Bros. Music version of *Happy Days Are Here Again*. "WB Music" logo. "Special Edition." 4pp. Page 2 Subtitle: "Vote for Gore for President." "Special Gore Parody." Pages 2-4: Added lyrics for "Albert Gore for President."

WJC-6 The Search For A Likely Candidate. w.m. Henry and Bobbie Shaffner and Saul Broudy. Copyright 1992 by Keynote Associates, One Montgomery Avenue, Bala Cynwyd, PA. [8 1/2" × 11"]. Letter. Words only supporting Clinton and Gore. 2pp.

WJC-7 Women Light The Way For Change. m. "To the Tune of *Michael Row The Boat Ashore*." 1992. [3 5/8" × 8 1/2"]. Pk/bk drawing of a hand with a torch. 2pp. Page 2: Blank.

WJC-8 Make A Rainbow. w.m. Portia Nelson. Published by Warner Bros. Publications, Inc., No. 265 Secaucus Road, Secaucus, NJ. 07096. Copyright 1969 and 1993 by WB Music Corp. and Dannel Music Publishing. B/w photo of Marilyn Horne — "As sung by Marilyn Horne at President Clinton's Inauguration." R/bl/bk cover. "Recorded on the album *All Through The Night* on BMG Classics." 6pp. Page 6: Blank.

WJC-9 President Bill Clinton March. w. Andrea Fodor Litkei. m. Ervin Litkei. Published by Loena Music Publishing Co. 239 West 18th Street, New York, NY. 10011. 1992. [8 1/2" × 11"]. B/w photo of Bill Clinton. "With best wishes, Bill Clinton [facsimile writing]." R/w/b cover. 4pp. Page 4: "Introduced and Performed at President Bill Clinton's Inauguration, January 20, 1993."

WJC-10 A Salute To The First Lady March. w. Andrea Litkei. m. Ervin Litkei. Published by Loena Music Publishing Company, No. 239 West 18th Street, New York, NY. 10011. 1992. [8 1/2" × 11"]. N/C photo of Hillary Clinton. 4pp. Page 2: "Dedicated to First Lady Hillary Clinton." Page 4: B/w photo of "Hillary Rodham Clinton." "With best wishes, Hillary Rodham Clinton [facsimile handwriting]." R/w/b cover. 4pp. Page 4: "Introduced and Per-

WJC-10

formed at President Bill Clinton's Inauguration, January 20, 1993."

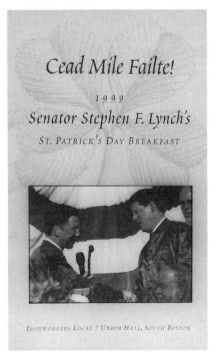

WJC-11

WJC-11 Cead Mile Failte! [Song Book]. Published by Ironworkers Local 7, Union Hall, South Boston, MA. 1999. [5 3/8" × 8 1/2"]. B/w photo of Senator Stephen F. Lynch and Vice President Al Gore. Gn/w drawing of a shamrock. "1999 Senator Stephen F. Lynch's St. Patrick's Day Breakfast." 24pp. Pages 2, 4, 22, 23 and 24: Blank. Page 3: Index.

WJC-12 Hillary, O! Hillary. w.m. Henry and Bobbie Shaffner. Copyright 1999 by Henry and Bobbie Shaffner, One Montgomery Avenue, Bala-Cynwyd, PA. 19004. [8 1/2" × 11"]. [V-1: Non-pictorial black line border. "All Rights Reserved"]. [V-2:Lyrics only]. 6pp. Pages 2, 4 and 6: Blank.

WILLIAM LEMKE

WL-1 Lemke Victory March (Official Union Party March Song). w. Martha Voxland. m. Charlotte Rogers Palmer. Published by The Union Party, National Headquarters, No. 188 West Randolph Street, Chicago, IL. 1936. Bl/w photo of "The Hon. William Lemke." Gn/w drawings of George Washington, Abraham Lincoln, shield. 4pp. Page 4: Blank.

WL-2 Lemke Is The Man! w.m. Dave Peyton. Published by The Union Party, National Headquarters, No. 188 West Randolph Street, Chicago, IL. 1936. Br/w photo of William Lemke on telephone. O/w/bk flags, geometric designs. "Tax Free To Radio Stations." 4pp. Page 4: Blank.

WL-3 Lemke (A Rally Song For Social Justice and the Union Party). w.m. Larkin Craig Chandler (President Unit 27, Congressional District 21). Published by Larkin Craig Chandler, No. 601 West 172nd Street, New York, NY. [1936?]. B/w photos of Father Coughlin and William Lemke. "Dedicated to The Rev. Charles Edward Coughlin."

WENDELL L. WILLKIE

WLW-1 Willkie Victory March. w.m. Ned Brisben, Tom Johnstone and Eva Ulrich. Published by Bob Miller, Inc., Music Publisher, No. 1619 Broadway, New York, NY. 1940. R/w/b drawing of stripes, stars. Bl/w photo of Wendell L. Willkie. "Elwood Souvenir Edition." 4pp. Page 4: Advertising for other Bob Miller music.

WLW-2 G.O.P. March. m. Gust Safstrom (*Writer of Just Remember You Can Smile, Dearest I Always Dream Of You, Mother's Love (Lullaby)*). Published by De Motte Music Company, De Motte, IN. 1940. R/w/b drawing of an elephant playing a drum, eagle, crossed flags, silhouettes of Abraham "Lincoln," George "Washington." "Willkie Official Souvenir Issue." "Notification Ceremonies, Elwood, IN. Aug. 17th, 1940." "Endorsed by Wendell L. Willkie Notification Committee, Homer Caspehart Grand Chairman, George Bonham, Mayor, City of Evansville, Ind., Honorary Grand Chairman." "The Elwood H.S. Band will participate in the proceeds of the sale of the G.O.P. March." 4pp. Page 4: Bl/w drawings of Wendell L. Willkie residence, Capitol building. "A True American," "Like Lincoln From a Humble Home To the White House," "A Business Man to Run the Biggest Business in the World."

WLW-3 The Willkie Hop. w. Thomas J. Jordan, Agnes M. Johnson and Catherine Tyrrell. m. Irving Pietrack. Published by Johnson Music, No. 77 West 46th Street, New York, NY. 1940. Twelve bl/w photos of "Wendell Willkie For President." "Published by special Permission of Republican National Committee." "Have This in your Home." "Let's dance The Willkie Hop." 4pp. Page 4: Bl/w litho of an eagle inscribed "E Pluribus Unum," shield, geometric designs. Song: *The Star Spangled Banner*.

WLW-4 Wendell Willkie Goes To Washington. w.m. Murray Whitman and Noel Bear. Published by Glory Publishing Company, No. 170 Broadway, New York, NY. 1940. R/w/b geometric design border. Bl/w photo of Wendell Willkie. 4pp. Page 4: Verses 3 to 12.

WLW-5 On The Banks Of The Wabash. w.m. Paul Dresser. Special 'Willkie' choruses by John W. Bratton. Published by Paull-Pioneer Music Corporation, No. 1657 Broadway, New York, NY. Copyright 1925, 1932 and 1940. O/br/w drawing of an elephant, sign inscribed "With Special Willkie Choruses." Br/w photo of Wendell Willkie. "Dedicated to Wendell L. Willkie." "Complimentary Copy." 6pp. Page 6: Advertising for other music.

WLW-6 Win With Willkie (The Campaign Song). w. W.S. Campbell. m. F.F. Dugan. a. R.O. McAfee. Published by D. & C. Music Company, No. 907 Akron Savings & Loan Building, Akron, OH. 1940. R/w/b title. Bl/w photo of Wendell Willkie. 4pp. Page 4: "Extracts from Acceptance Speech, Elwood City, Indiana, August 17, 1940."

WLW-7 We'll Win With Willkie. w.m. Maida Townsend. Published by Madia Townsend, No. 7049 Clyde Avenue, Chicago, IL. 1940. R/w/b line border. Bl/w photo of Wendell Willkie. 4pp. Page 4: R/w/b flag. "Dedicated to the Hoosier Willkie Clubs."

WLW-8 We Want Willkie. w. Morrie Ryskind and Bert Kalmer. m. Alexander Steinert. Published by We The People Committee, No. 205 South Beverly Drive, Beverly Hills, CA. 1940. R/w/b stars, stripes. Bl/w photo of Wendell Willkie. 6pp. Page 6: Blank.

WLW-9 Thank God! We've Found The Man. w.m. Robert Crawford. Published by Sprague-Coleman, No. 62 West 45th Street, New York, NY. Copyright 1940 by Robert Crawford. Bl/w photo of Wendell Willkie. R/W/b stripes. "G.O.P. Willkie Song." 4pp. Page 4: R/w/b litho of U.S. flag.

WLW-10 We're On Our Way! (With Willkie). w. Esther Peterson Schleich. m. William Houser. Published by Peterson-Schleich Publishing Company, No. 530 Diversity Parkway, Chicago, IL. 1940. R/w/b drawing of elephant, Capitol building, music notes. 4pp. Page 4: Blank.

WLW-11 We're All Going Out To Vote For Willkie (Campaign Song). w.m. Jock McGraw and Mary Schaeffer. Published by Red Star Songs, Inc., Music Publishers, No. 1619 Broadway, New York, NY. 1940. R/w/b stripes. Bl/w photo of Wendell Willkie. 6pp. Page 2: Blank. Page 6: Advertising for other Red Star music.

WLW-12 I Want To Be A Captain. w. Herbert Teale. m. Harold Healy. Published by J. Meade Publishing Company, No. 258 Western Avenue, Joliet, IL. 1940. 4pp. B/w drawing of soldier in fox hole, pay pouch marked — "$30 — You." 4pp. Page 4: B/w drawing of "Captain Elliott Roosevelt" sitting at desk with feet up, reading newspaper — "A Captain's Pay — Just 23 days before the draft." Pay pouch marked — "$200 + $116," desk labeled — "Confidential Procurement Specialist."

WLW-13 Elliott, I Wanta Be A Cap'n Too! w. C.R. Huff. m. Grace Justus and Jack Maclean. Published by American Music Company, Stahlman Building, Nashville, TN. 1940. R/w/b drawing by Bill Wall of an envious G.I. looking at Cpt. Elliott Roosevelt in new uniform, airplane, hanger in background. 4pp. Page 4: Blank.

WLW-14 Wendell L. Willkie Rally Song Sheet. Published for a Wendell Willkie rally at "Syracuse Municipal Stadium, Monday, October 14, 1940." [5 1/2" × 8 1/2"]. Bl/w eagle. 4pp. Page 2: Instructions for singing at the rally.

WLW-15 We Want Willkie. w.m. Hellen Church and Martha Baird Allen. Published by Barbelle Music Company, No. 145 West 45th Street, New York, NY. Copyright 1940 by Hellen Church and Martha Baird Allen. Bl/w photo of Wendell Willkie. R/w/b cover. "Willkie Campaign Song 1940. Officially sponsored by Associated Willkie Clubs of America." 4pp.

WLW-16 Let Wendell Willkie Spin The Wheel Of Fortune. w. Lelia K. Stair. m. Mary Chatherine Stair and Tommy Wright. Copyright 1940 by Lelia K. Stair. Bl/w photo of Lelia Stair. R/w/b drawing of a large wheel with spokes inscribed "Transportation, Education, Commerce, Agriculture, Communications, Science, Economics, Industry" with a symbol of each — airplane, truck, train, radio, map of Indiana. "Sung by Miss Stair at Elwood Notification." 4pp. Page 2: "Republican Campaign Song of 1940." Page 4: "The Hope of the Country, Willkie and McNary."

WLW-17 Sing For Willkie! [Song Sheet]. m. Popular Tunes. Published by the Associated Willkie Clubs of Pennsylvania, William H. Harrison, Chairman, Land Title Building, Philadelphia, PA. 1940. [5" × 9"]. Non-pictorial. "Vital Campaign Messages, Set to Tunes Everyone Knows and Enjoys." "Everybody Sing! and Win with Willkie." "Used by Permission of Lee Publications, Ardmore, PA." 2pp.

WLW-18 One World. w.m. Harold Simon Dixon. Published by Shattinger Piano and Music Company, St. Louis, MO. 1943. Gd/w/bl drawing of earth, stars. "Inspired by Wendell L. Willkie's book of the same title." 6pp. Page 6: Advertising.

WLW-19 Willkie Is Our Man (Join The G.O.P.). w.m. Margueite T. Phillips. Published by Margueite T. Phillips, No. 1017 Provident Bank Building, Cincinnati, OH. 1936. Bl/w photo of Wendell L. Willkie. R/w/b cover. "Dedicated to Wendell Willkie." 4pp. Page 4: Blank.

WLW-20 Hurrah For Willkie. w.m. Lila Curtis Bates. Copyright 1940 by Lila C. Bates. [7" × 10 1/16"]. Non-pictorial. 4pp. Page 4: Another song by Lila C. Bates — *America, Let Freedom Reign.*

WLW-21 Wendell Willkie. Published by The Peoples Promotional Service Headquarters, Washington, DC. [1940]. Non-pictorial. "Free." 2pp. Page 2: Blank.

WLW-22 Elliott, I Wanna Be A Cap'n Too! w.m. Grace Justus and Jack MacLean. a. C.R. Huff. In: *Chicago Sunday Times*, October 20, 1940. "Songs of the 1940 Campaign!" Copyright 1940 by The American Music Company, Nashville, TN. Non-pictorial. 2pp.

WLW-23 We Are With You Wendell Willkie. w.m. Gene Fifer. a. Frank Rogers. In: *Chicago Sunday Times*, October 27, 1940, Part 8, "Society." "Songs of the 1940 Campaign!" Copyright 1940 by Gene Fifer, No. 5614 Chicago Avenue, Chicago, IL. Non-pictorial. 2pp.

WLW-24 Willkie For President. w.m. Uberto T. Neely. Copyright 1940 by Uberto Neely, Cincinnati, OH. Pl/gy non-pictorial mimeograph. "Dedicated to Wendel [sic] L. Willkie, Republican Presidential Nominee for 1940." 4pp. Pages 1 and 4: Blank.

WLW-25 We Want Willkie (Republican Campaign Song 1940). w.m. R.U. White. a. George Johnson. Published by R.U. White, No. 111 North 49th Street, Philadelphia, PA. 1940. [V-1: 8 3/8" × 11"] [V-2: 8 3/8" × 10 1/2"]. Non-pictorial. [V-1: Large print address in lower left corner — "For additional copies write R.U. White, No. 111 North 49th Street, Philadelphia, Pa."] [V-2: Small print address in lower left corner — "For additional copies write R.U. White, No. 111 North 49th Street, Philadelphia, Pa."]. 2pp. Page 2: Blank.

WLW-26 I'm Going To Vote For Willkie. w.m. Gale Van Deventer. 1940. Non-pictorial. 2pp. Page 2: Blank.

WLW-27 Where There's A Willkie There's A Way. w.m. Andy McCarthy and Janet Folsom. Published by McCarthy & Folsom, No. 505 Costa Rica Avenue, San Mateo, CA. 1940. Four b/w photos of Wendell L. Willkie working. 4pp. Page 4: Blank.

WLW-28 Make Willkie President (Republican Campaign Song). w. Bud Blum. m. Joseph Guinan. Published by Shelby Music Publishing Company, No. 1205 Griswald Street, Detroit, MI. 1940. [6 3/8" × 10 1/16"]. Bl/w photo of Wendell Willkie. R/w/b cover. [V-1: "Elwood Souvenir Edition"] [V-2: "Square Club of Detroit Souvenir Edition"]. 6pp.—Foldout. Page 5: "Greetings to Edward N. Barnard" from "Square Club of Detroit, Grand Republican Testimonial, Thursday Evening, September 5, 1940, Hotel Fort Wayne, Detroit"]. Page 6: Blank.

WLW-29 We Are With You Wendell Willkie (The Willkie Victory March). w.m. Gene Fifer. Published by Gene Fifer, Chicago, IL. 1940. B/w photo of Wendell Willkie. "Dedicated to Wendell Willkie." R/w/b stripes. 6pp. Page 6: Blank.

WLW-30 Win With Willkie. w.m. Lillian Carpenter. Published by H.T. Fitzsimmons Company, No. 23 East Jackson Boulevard, Chicago, IL. 1940. [6 7/8" × 10 1/4"]. B/w photo of "Wendell L. Willkie," geometric designs. 6pp. Page 2: "Dedicated to Wendell Willkie." Page 6: Blank.

WLW-31 When A Third Term Bug Gets Drafted. w.m. J.E. Knight. Published by Westmore Music Corporation, S.W. Ninth at Taylor Avenue, Portland, OR. 1940. Bl/w photo by Gladys Gilbert of Wendell L. Willkie and Charles L. McNary, red stripes. 4pp. Page 4: Blank.

WLW-32 Willkie For President March. Copyright 1940 by P. Giese. Photo of Wendell Willkie. 4pp. Page 2: "Order from Miss Ruth Duncan." Pages 3 and 4: Another Wendell Willkie campaign song: **Franklin Delano Roseveiski** (A Humoristic Campaign Song for 1940). Copyright 1940 by P. Giese.

WLW-33 The SOS Of The USA

WLW-31

Is The GOP. w.m. C.A. Gray. Published by Republican Clubs Publishing Company, No. 621 East Hazel Street, Lansing, MI. 1940. R/w/b drawing of shield. 4pp. Page 4: Drawing of an elephant—"This is a Republican Year!"

WLW-34 Let's All March To Victory With The "G.O.P." w.m. James Wright. Published by Wright and Shaw, No. 242 Broadway, Passaic, NJ. 1936. [8 1/2" × 11"]. B/w photo of Wendell Willkie. R/w/b cover. "For President, Wendell L. Willkie; For Vice President, Charles L. McNary." 4pp. Page 4: Blank.

WLW-35 Work With Willkie And Win The Day. w.m. Horace Lozier. Published by Modern Standard Music Company, No. 54 Randolph Street, Chicago, IL. 1940. B/w photo of Wendell Willkie. Bl/w drawings of farms, factory, ships. 6pp. Page 2: "Quartet Arrangement or Trio for Male or Mixed Voices."

WLW-36 Uncle Sam And Willkie Come To Town. w. E. Jean Nelson Penfield. m. Air: *Yankee Doodle*. In: *Uncle Sammy* [Booklet], page 23. Published by the Government By Law Alliance, No. 280 Broadway, New York, NY., October, 1940. [13 1/2" × 9 1/2"].

R/w/b drawing of Uncle Sam riding a horse jumping "New Deal Hedge"—"Ride With Willkie."

WLW-37 **[Untitled Song Sheet].** m. Air: *Hi-Ho, Hi-Ho*. [1940]. [3 7/8" × 2 3/8"]. Pl/w non-pictorial. 2pp. Page 2: Blank.

WLW-38 **The Willkie March.** w. Douglas D. Ballin. m. Kenneth S. Clark. a. Harold Potter. Published by Paull-Pioneer Music Corporation, No. 1657 Broadway, New York, NY. 1940. Bl/w non-pictorial. 4pp. Page 4: Blank.

WLW-39 **Willkie McNary Rally Songs.** w. Alice Brockett (Music Chairman Women Workers for Willkie). m. Popular Tunes. Published by Whole World, Inc., No. 104 East 56th Street, New York, NY. [1940]. [10 15/16" × 16 15/16"]. B/w drawing of eagle over initials—"WW." 2pp. Page 2: Blank. [M-426].

WLW-40 **Win With Willkie** [Song Pamphlet]. [1940]. [5 1/2" × 8 1/2"]. R/w/b non-pictorial stripes. 4pp. Page 4: Blank.

WLW-41 **That No-3rd Term Tradition.** w. E.B. Leiby. m. Air: *Old Time Religion*. 1940. Non-pictorial. "George Washington and Thomas Jefferson could have had third terms but refused on grounds that this would lead to a dictatorship (The return to a King). Andrew Jackson would not countenance an attempt to give him a third term Americans for the first time in the history of the Republic, are confronted with the dangers and jeopardies of a President in office forcing the people to vote for or against a third term." 2pp.

WLW-42 **Sing And Swing With Willkie** [Song Sheet]. [1940]. Non-pictorial. 2pp. Page 2: Blank.

WLW-43 **Come Rally 'Round** (Republican Rally Song). w.m. Aleta Roberts Slater. Published by Aleta Roberts Slater, No. 2159 High Street, Oakland, CA. 1940. Bl/w photo of Wendell Willkie. "Dedicated to B.L. Richardson." 4pp. Page 4: Song—*Rally For The U.S.A.*

WLW-44 **Off To Work We Go With Wendell Willkie.** m. Tune: *Heigh-Ho*. [1940]. [2 3/8" × 3 7/8"]. Non-pictorial. [V-1: B/w] [V-2: Y/bk]. 2pp. Page 2: Blank.

WLW-45 **The Grand Old Party.** w.m. Alfred Freeman Hobbs. Copyright 1940 by Alfred Hobbs, No. 523 East Chesnut Street, Glendale, CA. R/w/b drawings of Abraham Lincoln, elephant, flag. Bl/w photo of "Hon. A.F. Hobbs." 6pp. Page 3: "Dedicated to the People." Page 6: Blank.

WLW-46 **The Road I Have Chosen.** w. Aaron Kramer. m. Charles Wakefield Cadman. Published by Leeds Music Corporation, Radio City, New York, NY. 1947. Bl/w/br non-pictorial cover. "Leeds Concert Songs." 8pp. Pages 2 and 7: Blank. Page 3: Dedication—"To the Memory of Wendell L. Willkie, Fellow Marcher Toward the One World." Page 8: Advertising.

WLW-47 **G.O.P.** (March Song). 1940. Drawing of an elephant with sign—"Vote for Republicans." "The Grand Old Party."

WLW-48 **We'll Win With Willkie.** w.m. Maida Townsend. In: *Chicago Sunday Tribune*, page 4. November 3, 1940. "Songs of the 1940 Campaign." "Here's another of the original election songs, complete with words and music, which *The Sunday Tribune* has been presenting during the 1940 campaign. Today's song was dedicated by its Author and Composer to the Hoosier Willkie Club." Copyright 1940 by Maida Townsend, No. 7048 Clyde Avenue, Chicago, IL.

WLW-49 **Willkie And McNary** (Is Our Team). Engraved and Printed by Pacific Music Press, Inc., San Francisco, CA. Copyright 1940 by Floris Hudnall. Non-pictorial. "This edition is sponsored by Mrs. Joseph Brown, Jr., Miss Lois Eaken, Mrs. Cecil L. Hudnall, Mrs.

Patrick F. Kirby, Mrs. Jose Renato Lacayo, Mrs. Robert Lee Watson." "May be used without Permission." 2pp. Page 2: Blank.

WLW-50 The Big Boy Who Came From Indiana. w.m. W.R. Williams (ASCAP). Published by Will Rossiter, No. 173 West Madison Street, Chicago, IL. 1940. [8 1/2" × 11"]. Non-pictorial. "Respectfully Dedicated to Mr. Wendell Willkie, A Real American from Elwood, Ind." 4pp. Page 1 and 4: Blank. Page 3: "Writers Note! Tell your audience you are introducing a new Wendell Willkie song and you want them to help you in the Chorus Every time you say Wendell Willkie you want them to shout 'Willkie' immediately after you. Also suggest you sing two choruses after each verse."

WLW-51 Willkie-McNary-Barton Victory Rally [Song Sheet]. Published by the New York Republican County Committee, New York, NY. 1940. [5 1/4" × 8 13/16"]. Bl/w photos of Wendell Willkie, Charles McNary and Bruce Barton. Bl/w drawing of eagles. "Madison Square Garden, Saturday, November 2, 1940." 8pp. Page 2: "Musical Program." Page 8: List of officers and committees.

WLW-52 G.O.P. March. w. J.D. Hosner. m. A.B. Richards. a. Eric Dressel. Published by John D. Hosner, Dearborn, MI. [1940]. Drawing of U.S. flag without stars, elephant, blank music bars. 4pp.

WLW-53 Victory For Willkie. w. Walter I. Sundlun. m. Bert Rose. Published by Chas. W. Homeyer & Company, Inc., No. 498 Boylston Street, Boston, MA. 1940. R/w/b drawings of a working man — "Labor," Naval guns — "Defence [sic]," money — "Prosperity," and an eagle — "Our Emblem." "Official Campaign Song 1940." 6pp. Pages 5 and 6: Blank.

WLW-54 Willkie Campaign Song. m. Air: *Heigh-Ho, Heigh-Ho.* [3 3/8" × 6 1/8"]. Non-pictorial. 2pp. Page 2: Blank.

WLW-55 Surprise Greeting Song For Willkie. m. Tune: *Heigh-Ho, Heigh-Ho.* Directed by Alex Werth, Special Committee Chairman, Coffeyville, KS., September 16, 1940. [3 7/16" × 8 7/8"]. Non-pictorial. 2pp. Page 2: Blank.

WLW-56 Elliott, I Wanna Be A Cap'n Too! w. C.R. Huff. m. Grace Justice and Jack Maclean. Published by 'I Wanna Be A Cap'n' Clubs, No. 1492 Broadway, corner of 42nd Street, Room 904, New York, NY. 1940. R/w/b drawing by Albert Barbelle of Elliot Roosevelt sitting behind a desk with his feet up saying "See Pop," soldiers talking saying "All my training good for what?" — "The beginning of another royal dynasty," "Until now all men were created equal," "Gee! Another indispensable man." 4pp. Page 4: Blank.

WLW-57 Willkie March. w.m. Gust Safstrom. Published by DeMotte Music Company, Publishers, DeMotte, IN.

1940. Bl/w drawing of Wendell L. Willkie. Bl/w photo of Charles McNary. R/w/b drawings of an elephant and a donkey with drums, eagle, crossed flags, silhouettes of George "Washington" and Thomas "Jefferson." "Win with Willkie Business Men's League of America." 4pp. Page 4: Bl/w photo of Willkie talking on telephone—"A business man to run the biggest business in the world." R/w/b facsimile of a membership certificate in "Willkie Business Man's League of America."

WLW-58 We're All Going Out To Vote For Willkie (Campaign Song). w.m. Jock McGraw and Mary Schaeffer. a. Lilly Hyland. Copyright by Red Star Songs, Inc., No. 1619 Broadway, New York, NY. 1940. Non-pictorial. "Professional Copy." Copyright "Warning." 4pp. Page 4: Blank.

WLW-59 Willkie Victory March. w.m. Ned Brisben, Tom Johnstone and Eva Ulrich. [1940]. [8 7/16" × 5 9/16"]. Non-pictorial. 2pp. Page 2: Blank.

WLW-60 Life Begins In '40 (The Peppy Willkie Song). w.m. Hugh Aughinbaugh. Published by Aughinbaugh Music Publishing Company, South Bend, IN. 1940. [7" × 10 1/4"]. B/w photo of a clay statue of an elephant inscribed "Life Begins At '40," geometric design border. "Written by a Hoosier for a Hoosier." 4pp. Page 4: Blank.

WLW-61 Native Hoosier. w. Grace Patterson Lopez-Dias. m. Mae Doelling Schmidt. Published by Clayton F. Summy Company, Chicago, IL. 1940. R/w/b drawing of the State of Indiana with a list of famous Hoosiers—"James Whitcomb Riley, Thomas Marshall, Gene Stratton Porter, Wendell L. Willkie, John T. McCutcheon, George Ade, General Lew Wallace, Booth Tarkington, Meredith Nicholson, Claude Wickard, William Lowe Bryan, Paul McNutt, Kenesaw Mountain Landis, ad-infinitum." 6pp. Pages 2 Blank. Page 6: Advertising.

WLW-62 Yes, Yes, Tomorrow (We'll Be In Again). w.m. Otto W. Kulling. a. Lindsay McPhail. Published by Otto W. Kulling, Meadowbrook, PA. 1940. O/bk/w drawings of elephant with pennant inscribed "G.O.P.," Capitol building, dog inside of a dog house inscribed "New Deal." 6pp. Pages 2 and 6: Blank.

WLW-63 Touchdown With Willkie (Rally Song). w.m. Klaas G. Kuiper. Published by Klaas G. Kuiper, No. 1816 North Third Street, Sheboygan, WI. 1940. Non-pictorial. 4pp. [Foldout]. Page 4: Long quote from "Wendell Willkie's Acceptance Speech, Elwood, Indiana, August 17, 1940."

WLW-64 Theme Song Of The Associated Willkie-For-President Clubs Of New Jersey. w. Ray Ghent, Eleanor Smith and Donald J. Smith. m. Air: *Heigh-Ho, Heigh-Ho*. Published by Associated Willkie-For-President Clubs of New Jersey. [1940]. 2pp. Page 2: Blank.

WLW-65 Wendell Willkie [Song Book]. Published by Willkie For President Club, Plainfield, NJ. 1940. [5 7/16" × 8 7/16"]. B/w photo of "Wendell Willkie," black line frame. 16pp. Page 15: "No Third Term." Page 16: "Win With Wendell Willkie."

WLW-66 The Royal Family Duet. Published as a post card by Northern California Willkie-McNary Campaign Committee, No. 532 Market Street, San Francisco, CA. [1940]. [3 1/2" × 5 1/2"]. Obv: Bl/w caricature drawing by Argens of Franklin and Eleanor Roosevelt singing a song—"We Didn't Raise Our Boys, Privates in the ranks to be," music stand, notes. Rev: Blank.

WLW-67 Republican Campaign Songs. Published by The United Republican Workers of America, Kansas City, KS. 1940. Be/bk litho of Abraham Lincoln. "Let us use our best efforts that government of the people, by the people, for the people, shall not perish from the earth…" [M-425].

(WM) WILLIAM MCKINLEY

WLW-68 Willkie Is The Man. w.m. Clarice A. Baker. a. Jack Lundin. Published by Clarice A. Baker, No. 6437 Glenwood Avenue, Chicago, IL. 1940. B/w photo of Wendell Willkie. R/w/b stripes. "Trade supplied by Carl Fisher, Inc., Chicago, Ill." 4pp. Page 4: Blank.

WLW-69 Awaken America. w.m. Lora Thornhill Jackson. Copyright 1940 by Willkie For President Club, Inc. B/w shadow-like photo of Wendell Willkie behind music. "Compliments of Willkie for President Club, headquarters Sixth Avenue and Union Streets, Washington. Composed by Lora Thornhill Jackson while listening to the radio reports of the Republican National Convention which nominated Mr. Willkie on June 24, 1940." 2pp. Page 2: Blank.

WLW-70 Willkie Will Win. w.m. John Baldwin. [1940]. Pl/w mimeograph. 2pp. Page 2: Blank.

See also TED-31; FDR-285; FDR-394.

WILLIAM MCKINLEY

WM-1 Republican National Convention March. m. Al G. Mark. Published by Mark Bros. Music Publishing Company, No. 3940 Page Avenue, St. Louis, MO. 1896. R/w/b drawings of William McKinley, Levi P. Morton, Thomas Reed, Wm. Allison and "?" [question mark] on flag background, shields. "Dedicated to the City of St. Louis, June 1896." 8pp. Page 2: B/w photos of "Prominent Republicans and Gentlemen who were instrumental in securing the Republican National Convention for St. Louis—Sam M. Kennard, President Business Men's League; Chas. H. Sampson, Chairman Convention Committee; Hon. Chauncey Ives Filley, Chairman Reception Committee; Frank Gaienne, Gen'l. Mgr., St. Louis Exposition; L.S. W. Wall; Chas. F. Wenneker." Page 7: B/w photos of "Merchant's League Club—Wm. H. Hobbs, Vice-President; Louis F. Zipp, Treasurer; Hon. J.A. Talty, President; Theo. D. Kalbfell, Chair., Republican Central Committee; Morris Langsdorf, Sec." Page 8: Blank.

WM-2 McKinley And Hobart March. m. Leopold Kessler. Published by Oliver Ditson Company, Nos. 453-463 Washington Street, Boston, MA. 1896. Gd/w litho of a torch, wreaths. B/w photos of William McKinley and Garret Hobart. 6pp. Page 6: Blank.

WM-3 Mack And Teddy. w. J.B. Robinson, Ph.D. m. T.C. O'Kane. Published by Windsor Music, Nos. 266 and 268 Wabash Avenue, Chicago, IL. 1900. R/w/b flag, liberty cap, geometric designs. B/w photo of William McKinley. B/w drawing of Theodore Roosevelt. 4pp. Page 4: Blank.

WM-4 McKinley & Roosevelt (March). m. Fred Spencer. Published by Howley, Haviland & Company, Nos. 1260-1266 Broadway, New York, NY. 1900. R/w/b crossed flags, wreath. B/w photos of William McKinley and Theodore Roosevelt. "Respectfully Dedicated to William McKinley and Theodore Roosevelt." 6pp.

WM-2

WILLIAM MCKINLEY (**WM**)

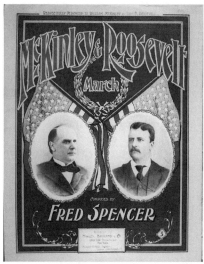

WM-4

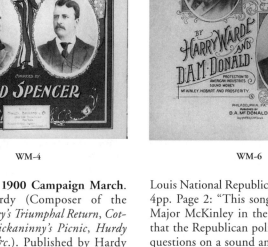

WM-6

WM-5 1900 Campaign March. m. Will Hardy (Composer of the marches, *Dewey's Triumphal Return, Cotton Pickers, Pickaninny's Picnic, Hurdy Gurdy, &c., &c.*). Published by Hardy Music Company, Boston, MA. 1900. R/w/b litho of U.S. flag. B/w photos of William McKinley, Theodore Roosevelt, William Jennings Bryan and Adlai E. Stevenson. "The Original and Best March of the Campaign." "Played by the Leading Bands and Orchestras." 6pp.

WM-6 G.O.P. March (With Vocal Strain). m. Harry Warde and D.A. McDonald. a. Gus. Friedrich. Published by D.A. McDonald, Philadelphia, PA. 1896. B/w photos by Doremus of William McKinley and Garret Hobart. "Dedicated to the Republican Party of the Past, Present and Future." "Protection to American Industries." "Sound Money." "McKinley, Hobart and Prosperity." 6pp. Page 6: Blank.

WM-7 The McKinley Song. w.m. Charles Kunkel. Copyright 1896 by The Kunkel Brothers. R/w/b litho of crossed flags. B/w photo of William McKinley. "As Sung and Played at the St. Louis National Republican Convention." 4pp. Page 2: "This song is dedicated to Major McKinley in the firm conviction that the Republican policy to settle vital questions on a sound and fair basis, will down measures of perfidy and dishonor, advance liberty and prosperity, and lead to the crowning of labor with glory; and that it will also save us from a danger of crucifixion on any cross, whether of Blunder, Bluster and Bluff, or of Blandism and Blarney." "Solo, Quartette and Band Arrangements." Page 4: Blank.

WM-8 President McKinley's Inauguration (Song and Chorus). w.m. J.L. Feeney (Author of *Cuban Liberty, Our Little Home, Boys In Blue, &c.*). Published by Walsh, Godman and Company, No. 26 "I" Street, NW., Washington, DC. 1896. B/w photo of William McKinley. 6pp. Page 3: "Sung by Mr. B.W. Beebe of the McKinley and Hobart Glee Club."

WM-9 The People's Choice March (or Two-Step). m. Harry C. Eldridge. Published by Ilsen & Company, Nos. 25 and 27 West 6th Street, Cincinnati, OH. 1896. Bl/w geometric design.

B/w litho of William McKinley. 8pp. Pages 2 and 8: Blank.

WM-10 Court Of Honor (March and Two Step). m. H. Wannemacher. Published by J.F. Bellois, Philadelphia, PA. 1899. R/w/b litho of flags, eagle, shield. B/w photos by Zabel-Worley of downtown Philadelphia, William McKinley, Admiral George Dewey, General Nelson Miles. "Respectfully Dedicated to the Citizens of Philadelphia in Honor of the Peace Jubilee, October 1898." 6pp. Page 6: Blank.

WM-11 Our War President March. m. George Schleiffarth. Published by P.M. Wolsieffer, No. 201 Clark Street, Chicago, IL. 1898. R/w/bl/gd/bk stripes and stars. B/w photo of William McKinley — "Enlisted June 1, 1861, in Co. E, 23d Ohio. Mustered out with his regiment July 26, 1865, Private, Sergeant, Lieut., Captain, Brevet Major, Staff Officer to Gen. R.B. Hayes and Gen. Geo. Cook." 6pp. Page 3: "Respectfully Dedicated to President William McKinley." Pages 2 and 6: Blank.

WM-12 Presidential March. m. Alex. Brielmayer. Published by Brielmayer & Volmer, South Nyack, NY. 1900. R/w/b flag background, eagle. B/w photos of "William McKinley" and "Alex. Brielmayer — Composed by Alex. Brielmayer." 8pp. Pages 2, 6, 7 and 8: Blank.

WM-13 (The New 1900) McKinley March. m. Leo Friedman. Published by Sol Bloom, corner Randolph and Dearborn Streets, Chicago, IL. 1900. Gd/w drawings by Edgar Keller of eagles, wreath, The Capitol. Bl/w photo of William McKinley. 6pp. Pages 2 and 6: Advertising.

WM-14 The Man Of Destiny March. m. Anita Owen. Published by National Music Company, Nos. 215-221 Wabash Avenue, Chicago, IL. 1892. B/w photo of William McKinley, geometric designs. "Respectfully Dedicated to Hon. William McKinley." 6pp. Page 2: Blank. Page 6: Advertising.

WM-15 The Cabinet Grand March. m. Hans S. Line, Op. 64. Published by National Music Company, Nos. 215-221 Wabash Avenue, Chicago, IL. 1897. R/w cover. B/w photo of William McKinley and eight Cabinet members. "Dedicated to Hon. Lyman J. Gage." 6pp. Page 6: Advertising.

WM-16(A) A True American (Song and March). w.m. N.E. Byers. Published by N.E. Byers and Company, Nos. 1368-1370 Broadway, New York, NY. 1896. B/w photo of William McKinley — "This is Governor McKinly's [sic] latest and best photograph, styled 'The Smiling Face.' I have the exclusive right to use the same on music publications — N.E. Byers." 6pp. Page 6: Blank.

(B) A True American March.

WM-17 Munyon's Liberty Song. w.m. Professor J.M. Munyon, LL.D. (Founder of The Munyon Homeopathic Home Remedy Co). Published by M.D. Swisher, No. 115 South 10th Street, Philadelphia, PA. [ca. 1898]. B/w drawings of Spanish-American War scenes. B/w photos of William McKinley, military leaders — Admiral George "Dewey," Admiral William T. "Sampson," General Nelson "Miles," General William "Shafter," Commodore Winfield Scott "Schley," and Professor Munyon holding song lyrics. B/w litho of battle scenes. 4pp. Page 4: Advertising for Munyon's Emergency Remedy Case.

WM-18 McKinley Two-Step March. m. G.B. Brigham. Published by The Thompson Music Company, Chicago, IL. 1895. Bl/br/be geometric designs. Br/w photo of William McKinley. "Respectfully dedicated to the Hon. Wm. McKinley of Ohio." 6pp. Pages 2, 5 and 6: Blank.

WM-19 Our President (Caprice). m. J. Alex. Silberberg. Published by Brooks & Denton Company, Sixth Avenue and 39th Street, New York, NY.

1896. R/w geometric designs. Bl/w photo of William McKinley. "Dedicated to Hon. William McKinley." 6pp. Page 2: Blank. Page 6: Advertising for other Brooks & Denton music.

WM-20 Our Candidate (March). m. Edward E. Rice. Published by T.B. Harms & Company, No. 18 East 22nd Street, New York, NY. 1896. R/w cover. B/w photo of William McKinley. "Very truly yours, William McKinley" [facsimile handwriting]. "Dedicated to my Friend Mr. Charles A. Hess." 6pp. Page 2: Blank. Page 6: Advertising for other songs.

WM-21 Unity Forever (March Two-Step). m. F.M. Wood. Published by Morris Publishing Company, No. 909 Hamond Building, Detroit, MI. 1901. R/w/bl/gd/gn/bk/y drawing of American, German and English flags, wreath, ships, town. Y/bk photos of William McKinley—"The Home of the Brave," King Edward III—"God Save the King," Emperor William II—"Die Wacht Am Rhein." 8pp. Pages 2, 7 and 8: Blank.

WM-22 The McKinley March. m. J. Rimbault. Published by Hamilton S. Gordon, No. 139 Fifth Avenue, New York, NY. 1896. R/w geometric designs. Gn/w photo of William McKinley. Page 6: Blank.

WM-23 Executive March (Two-Step). m. John H. Flynn. Published by Howley, Haviland & Company, No. 4 East 20th Street, New York, NY. 1898. Bl/w drawing of William McKinley and White House. 6pp. Pages 2 and 6: Advertising. Page 3: Illustrated title—vines.

WM-24 Up With The Stars And Stripes (March Two-Step). m. S.E. Morris. Published by D.O. Evans, Youngstown, OH. 1899. R/w/b drawing of U.S. flag. B/w drawing of William McKinley—"Fraternity;" George Washington—"Liberty;" Abraham Lincoln—"Emancipation." 8pp. Page 2 and 7: Blank. Page 8: Advertising for other D.O. Evans published music.

WM-25 The Plan Of Love. w. Ida E. Jennings. m. Annie P. Lumsden. Published by Boughton's Music Store, Cedar, Corner Halsey Street, Newark, NJ. Copyright 1902 by Ida E. Jennings. Br/w cover. B/w photo of William McKinley—"McKinley's Plan." 6pp. Pages 2 and 6: Blank.

WM-26 McKinley's Grand March. m. Frank Carolina. Published by Frank Harding's Music House, No. 136 East 58th Street, New York, NY. 1896. Gn/w geometric designs, lyre. Gn/w photo of William McKinley. "The Latest Success." 6pp. Page 2: Blank. Page 6: Advertising.

WM-27 McKinley's Grand March. m. M. Rishell. Published by Union Mutual Music Company, No. 265 Sixth Avenue, New York, NY. 1896. Bl/w designs. B/w photo of William McKinley, geometric designs. 6pp. Page 2 and 6: Advertising for other Union Mutual published music.

WM-28 The Nation's Song. w. Palmer Hartsough. m. Dr. J.B. Herbert. Published by Fillmore Brothers, No. 119 West 6th Street, Cincinnati, Ohio, as a supplement to *The Choir*, November, 1901. B/w photo of William McKinley, torches, urn. "Suggested by the dying words of President William McKinley." "As President McKinley was dying I stood behind a screen in his room and heard him say his last words. His wife came into the room and he said to her 'Good-by all; good-by, it is God's way, His will be done, not ours!' About an hour later he said to his wife, 'Nearer My God to Thee, Even tho' it be a cross, it has been my constant prayer.' I wrote the words down at the time so that there can be no question about it—H.D. Mann, M.D., Buffalo, September, 1901." 4pp.

WM-29 Hail To The Chief (Republican Campaign Song). w. A.O. Porter. m. J.S. May. Published by National Music Company, Chicago, IL. 1900. B/w photo of William McKinley.

B/w litho of flags, geometric design border. "Dedicated to the Man of the Hour." 6pp. Pages 2 and 6: Blank.

WM-30 Good-Bye To All, Good-Bye. w.m. J. Reginald MacEachron. Published by C.W. Marvin Publishing Company, Detroit, MI. 1901. Y/r/gn/w drawing of red carnations. "To Mrs. McKinley and the People." 8pp. Pages 2, 6, 7 and 8: Advertising for other music.

WM-31 (McKinley) In Memoriam (March). m. H.L. Heartz. Published by White-Smith Music Company, New York, NY. 1901. B/w photo of William McKinley, geometric designs, black border. 6pp. Page 2: Blank. Page 6: Advertising for other White-Smith funeral marches including "President Garfield (C.D. Balke), Daniel Webster (L. Beethoven), Hon. Horace Greeley (J.W. Turner), Ex-President Arthur's (Thorne), Gen. Logan's (E. Mack)...."

WM-32 Called Home. w. Richard F. King. m. Thomas J. Ryan. Published by George M. Krey, Music Publisher, No. 493 Washington Street, Boston, MA. 1901. B/w photo of William McKinley. B/w drawing of wreath. 6[?]pp. Page 2: Blank.

WM-33 McKinley's Funeral March. m. Otto P. Ikeler (Author of *Eva's Dream Song & Refrain*, *In The Coal Mines Far Away Song & Chorus*, *Mooney Coons*, and *Black Clutch*). Published by Otto Ikeler, Rohrsburg, PA. (Columbus Co.). 1901. R/w/bl/bk drawing of flags, column, drape. B/w photos of William McKinley, Otto Ikeler. 6pp. Page 2: "In Memory of Our President." Page 6: Advertising.

WM-34 President McKinley's Favorite Hymns. Copyright Sept. 25, 1901 by Edwards, Deutsch and Heitmann, Chicago, IL. Ma/w/bk drawing of flags, drape, wreath, eagle and shield. B/w photo of William McKinley, facsimile signature, life data—"Born at Niles, Ohio, Jan. 29, 1843; Died at Buffalo, N.Y., Sept. 14, 1901, Buried at West Lawn Cemetery, Canton, O, Sept. 19, 1901." "His last words! God's will, not ours be done." 4pp. Page 2: Song—**Nearer My God To Thee**. Page 3: Song—**Lead Kindly Light**. Page 4: History of William McKinley's career, songs.

WM-35 There's A Picture Draped In Mourning. w. Frances Corliss. m. James R. Homer. Published by Imperial Music Company, Boston, MA. Copyright 1901 by Frances Corliss. B/w drawing of a woman with wreaths. B/w photo of William McKinley. "Dedicated to Richard Connors." 4pp.

WM-36 McKinley's Memorial March. a. Harry J. Lincoln. Published by The U.S. Music Company, Williamsport, PA. Copyright 1901 by C.A. Mulliner. B/w photo of William McKinley. "Respectfully Dedicated to Our Great Nation." 6pp. Page 2: Poem—"In Memory of Our Late Beloved President." Page 3: Narrative—"This composition may be called a true picture of President McKinley's sad fate. All is peace at the Pan-American where our favorite President spends happy hours, no sooner is he known to be there, till the crowd surround him to take a glimpse at his matured form. He is first seen at the Music Temple, where cheers of joy respond to shake him by the hand. No thought of an anarchist among the throng, he grasps the hand of each and everyone, the assassin approaches as to greet him (Bugles are sounded). President McKinley smiles, bows and extends his hand in that spirit of geniality, the American people so well know (Drums beating). Suddenly the sharp crack of a pistol is heard ringing through the crowd; President McKinley falls by the hand of an anarchist, saying 'Am I Shot?' Great sympathy for our dying President is shown; The hour is come, he is passing away, and as his spirit speaks to the hand on high, he is heard murmuring 'Nearer My God To Thee.'" Page 6: Advertising.

WM-37 McKinley In The Chair (Song and Chorus). w.m. "By The Author of *The Little Dinner Bucket*." [A.M. Bruner]. Published by The L.E. West Publishing Company, Rock Island, IL. 1896. B/w photo of William McKinley, geometric designs. "To the Cause of Protection." 8pp. Page 2: Advertising for L.E. West's Gum and lapel buttons. Page 7: Advertising. Page 8: Advertising for McKinley song—*The Little Dinner Bucket*. Advertising for McKinley and Bryan campaign songs.

WM-38 The McKinley March. m. Louie Maurice (Composer of *The Chicago Athletic Club March*). Published by Will Rossiter, Popular Song and Song Book Publisher, No. 1162 Broadway, New York, NY. 1896. Bl/w photo of William McKinley. 6pp. Pages 2 and 6: Blank.

WM-39 The McKinley Dedication. w.m. John H. Walsh (Composer of *Down in the Bowrey With Sweet Kitty Lowery, Farewell My Little Sweetheart, But Not Forever Dear, We Came Home to Love the Old Folks Once Again, &c.*). Copyright 1908 by John H. Walsh. R/w/b flags, wreath. B/w photo of William McKinley. 6pp. Page 6: Blank.

WM-40 The Favorite McKinley March. m. Richardson Caldwell (Composer of *To The Front March*). Published by White-Smith Music Publishing Company, Boston, MA. 1896. R/w cover. B/w photo of William McKinley standing by small table. "Dedicated to the Winner." 6pp. Page 6: Advertising.

WM-41 Tell Mother I'll Be There (Song and Refrain). w.m. W.W. McCallip. Published by W.W. McCallip, Columbus, OH. 1897. B/w photos of William McKinley (looking to reader's left) and McKinley's mother. [V-1: R/w/b] [V-2: Ma/bl/w] drawings of "The White House" and "The Old Home." "President McKinley's Message to his Dying Mother—In the Dawn of Heaven's Morning." [V-1: "The Hann & Adair Printing Co., Columbus, O"] [V-2: "The Southard Novelty Co., Columbus, O"]. List of arrangements available. l6pp. Pages 2 and 6: Blank.

WM-42 Tell Mother I'll Be There (Song and Refrain). w.m. W.W. McCallip. Published by W.W. McCallip, Columbus, OH. 1897. B/w photos of William McKinley [different photo than WM-41—looking almost straight on] and his mother. R/w/b drawings of "The White House" and of "The Old Home." "President McKinley's message to his dying mother—In the dawn of heaven's morning." 6pp. Pages 2 and 6: Blank.

WM-43 Cantonian March (Two Step). m. Emil Reinkendorff (Musical Director of the Grand Army Band, Canton, Ohio). Published by Emil Reinkendorff, Canton, OH. [ca. 1896]. Bl/w geometric designs. B/w photos of President and Mrs. William McKinley and Mr. and Mrs. Reinkendorff [?]. "For the Piano." 6pp. Pages 2 and 6: Blank.

WM-44 McKinley's Champion Protection March. m. Howard S. Williams. Published by National Music Company, Nos. 215-221 Wabash Avenue, Chicago, IL. 1892. B/w photo of William McKinley [looking to viewer's left], geometric designs. B/w lyre logo—"The Best National Music Co. Edition. The Most reliable published." *"National Home and Music Journal."* "Adams Music Company, Passaic, NJ." 6pp. Page 6: Advertising.

WM-45 McKinley's Champion Protection March. m. Howard S. Williams. Published by National Music Company, Nos. 215-221 Wabash Avenue, Chicago, IL. 1892. B/w photo of William McKinley [Looking to viewer's right]. "Take only the National Edition." 6pp. Page 6: Advertising.

WM-46 A Hymn. w.m. Milton H. Kohn. a. Lee Orean Smith. Published by Vandersloot Music Company, No. 41 West 28th Street, New York, NY. 1901. B/w drawing by A.J. Dewey of William McKinley. 6pp. Page 6: Advertising.

WM-47 A National Paean (A

Popular Chorus Song). w. Walter Allen Rice. m. F.D. Bloomfield. Published by National Paean Company, No. 644 Ellicott Square, Buffalo, NY. 1901. R/w/b litho of crossed flags. B/w drawing of George Washington. B/w photo of William McKinley. "Dedicated to the people of the United States of America." 4pp. Page 4: Narrative on song history.

WM-48 A National Paean (A Popular Chorus Song). w. Walter Allen Rice. m. F.D. Bloomfield. Published by The National Paean Company, No. 644 Ellicott Square, Buffalo, NY. 1901. B/w photo of William McKinley. B/w drawing of George Washington. "Dedicated to the people of the United States of America." 4pp. Page 4: Narrative on letters received including letters from Ex-Presidents Grover Cleveland and Benjamin Harrison.

WM-49 The McKinley Two Step. m. Grace May Roberts. Published by Denton, Cottier & Daniels, No. 269 Main Street, Buffalo, NY. Copyright 1896 by Grace May Roberts. B/w photo of William McKinley, geometric designs. "Dedicated to the McKinley clubs." 6pp.

WM-50 The Republican Two Step And March. m. Ion Arnold. Published by Empire Music Company, No. 1424 Broadway, New York, NY. Copyright 1896 by Ion Arnold. R/w/bl/gn/y/bk drawing of shield, eagle, wreath. B/w photo of "Maj. William McKinley." "Most Respectfully Dedicated to Our Candidate." "Patriotism/Prosperity/Protection." 6pp. Page 6: Advertising.

WM-51 Sacred Hour. m. Leroy Thomas. Published by Marsh Music House, Decorah, IA. 1901. B/w photo of William McKinley, black border. "Our Martyred President, William McKinley." "Printed for Band and Orchestra." 6pp. Page 2: Blank. Page 6: Advertising.

WM-52 Re-United ('Tis God's Way, His Will Be Done). w.m. Pansy A. Lewton. Published by Continental Music Company, Cleveland, OH. Copyright

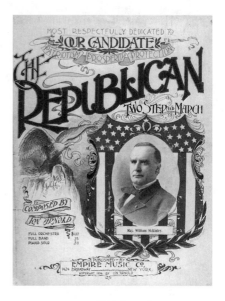

WM-50

1907 by Pansy Lewton. R/w/bk/pk/gn carnations. B/w photos of William McKinley and Ida McKinley. 6pp. Page 2: Statistics on the lives of William McKinley — "Born at Niles, O, Jan. 29, 1843; Enlisted in 23d O.V.I., 1861; Served in Public Office as Prosecuting Attorney of Stark County, Ohio; Member of Congress, Governor of Ohio and Pres. of the United States; Shot by assassin, Buffalo, N.Y., Sept. 6, 1901, and died of his wound thus inflicted, Sept. 14th, 1901" and Ida Saxton McKinley — "Born at Canton, Ohio, June 8th, 1847; Married Major William McKinley, Jan. 25th, 1871; Their martial happiness was clouded by the loss of 2 infant children, Kate and Ida; Since the tragic death of Mr. McKinley, her one wish was that God would permit her to join him; Died at Canton, May 26, 1907." Page 3: Dedication — "In Memory of Hon. and Mrs. Wm. McKinley." Page 6: B/w photo of "McKinley Memorial — Canton, Ohio."

WM-53 Pres. McKinley's Grand March. m. Charles C. Maxwell. Published by National Music Bureau, J. High

Stauffer, President, Allentown, PA. 1896. Pl/w geometric designs. B/w photo of William McKinley. "Respectfully Dedicated to the American Citizen." 6pp. Page 2: "Dedicated to Wm. Maxwell." Page 6: Advertising.

WM-54 Lead Kindly Light (Variations). m. William F. Day. [Published by M.D. Swisher, Philadelphia]. Copyright 1901 William F. Day. B/w drawing of William McKinley, torches. "Dedicated to a Mournful Nation." "The Martyr President." 6pp. Page 6: Another version of **Lead Kindly Light** by Dykes and Cardinal Newman and published by M.D. Swisher, Philadelphia, PA. "President McKinley's Favorite Hymn."

WM-55 McKinley March. m. J.F. Wagner. Published by Gotham Music Company, No. 521 East 13th Street, New York, NY. 1896. B/w photo of William McKinley. Bl/w geometric designs. 6pp. Pages 2 and 6: Blank.

WM-56 Nearer, My God, To Thee. w. Sarah Frances Adams. m. Dr. Lowell Mason. a. T. Bissell. Copyright 1859 by The Mason Brothers, 1887 by Mrs. Lowell Mason and 1901 by Oliver Ditson Company. Published by Will Rossiter, No. 225 Washington Street, Chicago, IL. Br/w geometric designs. Br/w photo of William McKinley, facsimile signature. "Fine Arts Edition." 6pp. Page 2: Blank. Page 6: Advertising for other Will Rossiter published music.

WM-57 McKinley Champion Protection March And Two-Step. m. George Schleiffarth (Maywood) (Composer of *Doris, Officer Porter, &c.*). Published by Sol Bloom, Chicago, IL. 1896. R/w/bk geometric designs. B/w photo of William McKinley. B/w drawing of woman with a breast plate inscribed "I Will." 6pp. Pages 2 and 6: Blank.

WM-58 McKinley's Grand March. m. Frank Carolina. Published by Frank Harding's Music House, No. 136 East 58th Street, New York, NY. [1896]. Bl/w photo of William McKinley, geometric designs. "Dedicated to the Honorable Wm. McKinley." 6pp. Page 2: Blank. Page 6: Advertising for other Harding published music.

WM-59 McKinley's Republican Victory March. m. George Schleiffarth. Published by P.M. Wolsieffer, No. 201 Clark Street, Chicago, IL. 1896. R/w/b litho of two flags, Miss Columbia. B/w photo of William McKinley. "Dedicated to the Marquette Club of Chicago." 6pp. Pages 2 and 6: Advertising for other P.M. Wolsieffer published music.

WM-60 McKinley March (Two-Step). m. W.C. Weeden. Published by Oliver Ditson Company. 1896. Bl/w cover. B/w photo of William McKinley. 6pp. Pages 2 and 6: Blank.

WM-61 McKinley Carnation (March-Two Step). m. William F. Hoffman (Composer of *The Hostess Waltzes, Cinaloa, The Budding Rose Waltzes*). Published by G.W. Mogelberg Company, Publishers, St. Louis, MO. 1905. Br/w/r/bk design by O.E. Hake of carnations. B/w photo of William McKinley. "Dedicated to the McKinley High School at St. Louis." 6pp. Page 6: Advertising.

WM-62 Angels Are Calling Away. w.m. Mrs. A.L. Burdick. Published by Rettmons Music Company, Chicago, IL. Copyright 1902 by A.L. Burdick. R/w columns, angel, torches, geometric designs. B/w photo of William McKinley. "Sold by all Music Dealers." 6pp. Pages 2 and 6: Blank.

WM-63 G.O.P. (March). m. William E. Coleman. Published by Triumph Music Company, Publishers, No. 305 Sycamore Street, Cincinnati, OH. 1915. Br/w drawings of William "McKinley," George "Washington," Abraham "Lincoln," eagle. 6pp. Page 2: "Most Respectfully Dedicated to the Members of the Young Men's Blaine Club, Cin., O." Page 6: Advertising for other Coleman-Triumph song.

WM-64 The White House March

(Two Step). m. Sam Bennett. Published by Frank K. Root & Company, Nos. 307 and 309 Wabash Avenue, Chicago, IL. 1898. Br/w cover. Pl/w photo of The White House. "Dedicated to Wm. McKinley, President of the 'McKinley Music Co.'" Page 2: Blank.

WM-65 McKinley And Hobart Grand March. m. J.W. Turner. In: *The Boston Weekly Journal of Sheet Music* [V-1, V-2 and V-3: No. 63, July 8, 1896] [V-4: No. 225, August 16, 1899]. Published by F. Trifet Publisher, No. 36 Broomfield Street, Boston, MA. [V-1: B/w] [V-2: O/w] [V-3: R/w] [V-4: Gn/w] of geometric designs. "Published weekly. Subscription $1.00 per year, in advance. Catalogue sent free to any address on application." 6pp. Page 2: Advertising for other Trifet published music. Page 6: Advertising for other *Boston Journal* music.

WM-66 A Flag Song. w. John Swinton. m. Kate Vanderpoel. Published under the auspices of the Republican National Committee. Copyright 1896 by Kate Vanderpoel. [7 1/8" × 10 1/16"]. R/w/b flag, geometric designs. "Souvenir Edition, Campaign 1896." "Dedicated to Wm. McKinley." "To be sung on Flag Day, Saturday, October 31, 1896." 4pp. Page 4: Quotes by famous people including Milton, Shakespeare, Beecher, Dix, Hanna and McKinley on flags.

WM-67 Republican Campaign Parodies And Songs [Songster]. Published by Betts and Burnett, South Butler, Wayne County, NY. 1896. [7 3/4" × 5 1/2"]. Be/bk non-pictorial. "McKinley and Hobart." "1896." 28pp. Page 2: Endorsements. Page 3: History of campaign music. Page 4: Table of contents. Page 27: Blank. Page 28: Advertising for this songster. "Republican Campaign Parodies And Songs, Being a Variety of Original and Catchy Verses Adapted to Popular Tunes." [M-340].

WM-68 Hurrah For Bill McKinley (Republican Campaign Song). w. Henry Denver. m. Bertha C. Marshall. Published by Phelps Music Company, Nos. 52-54 Lafayette Place, New York, NY. 1896. Bl/w geometric designs. 8pp. Page 2: Blank. Page 8: Advertising for another Phelps Music Company song— *What's The Matter With Hanna?*

WM-69 Judge's Campaign Song Of The Full Dinner Pail. w. Henry Tyrrell. m. Charles Puerner. Published as a supplement to *Judge Magazine*, No. 992, October 20, 1900. B/w litho of dinner pail inscribed "Four More Years of the Full Dinner Pail." Music begins page one. 4pp.

WM-70 Up Went McKinley (Grand Valse di Concerto Politico Americano). m. E.A. Grireaud, M.D. a. Mae Ayres Sherrey. Published by Legg Brothers, Kansas City, MO. 1895. B/w drawing of eight bars of music. "To His Excellency William McKinley, Governor of the State of Ohio." 8pp. Page 8: Blank.

WM-71 McKinley's Grand March. m. Flora Brockway. Copyright 1895 by Flora Brockway. B/w litho of two birds, branches. 8pp. Page 8: Blank.

WM-72 Shall The Flag Be Taken Down. w.m. W.S. Huslander. Published by J.W. Guernsey, Scranton, PA. Copyright 1900 by W.S. Huslander. R/w/b flag, geometric designs. "Dedicated to the American Voters." 6pp. Pages 2 and 6: Blank.

WM-73 McKinley Is The Man (March and Two Step). w. T.T. Seal. m. Fred C. Meyer. Published by Ohio Music Company, Bellaire, OH. 1896. Bl/w photo of William McKinley. R/w/b flag. List of arrangements available. 6pp. Page 2: "Respectfully Dedicated to Major William McKinley." Page 6: Blank.

WM-74 Our President (March and Two Step). m. Richard L. Weaver. a. H. Engelman. Published by M.D. Swisher, No. 115 South 10th Street, Philadelphia, PA. 1896. B/w drawing of "Hon. Wm. McKinley." Bl/w drawings of flags, shields, geometric designs. 6pp. Page 6: Blank.

WM-75 McKinley Will Save

Our Country (Campaign Song). w. Comrade James T. Cheney. m. W.C. Harris. Published by D.O. Evans, Youngstown, OH. 1896. Photos of William McKinley and James T. Cheney—"Comrade Cheney, Co. A, 5th USC." Geometric border design.

WM-76 McKinley And Roosevelt. w.m. T.M. Richards. Published by T.M. Richards in Ohio. 1900. Litho of William McKinley and Theodore Roosevelt, eagle, shields. "For sale at all principal music houses." "Respectfully inscribed to the G.O.P."

WM-77 In Memoriam (March Funebre). m. Paul B. Armstrong (Composer of *The Choir Boy, Salvation, &c.*). Published by Frank K. Root & Company. Trade supplied by McKinley Music Company, Nos. 307-309 Wabash Avenue, Chicago, IL. Copyright 1901 by Paul B. Armstrong. Non-pictorial, black border. "Lovingly Inscribed to the Memory of Our Martyred President William McKinley." 6pp. Pages 2 and 6: Blank.

WM-78 Ma Li'l Sweet Sunbeam. w.m. Vivian Grey (Miss Mabel McKinley). Published by Leo Feist, New York, NY. 1904. B/w photo of Vivian Grey—"Sincerely yours, Mabel McKinley. Gn/w geometric design frame. "Lovingly Dedicated to my Aunt, Mrs. William McKinley." 6pp. Pages 5 and 6: Advertising.

WM-79 The Administration March. m. Howard Brothers. Published by Jos. W. Stern and Company, No. 34 East 21st Street, New York, NY. 1900. Pl/w photos of William McKinley and Theodore Roosevelt. Gn/pl/w cover. "A Sure Winner." 6pp. Page 6: Advertising.

WM-80 We Want Yer, McKinley, Yes We Do. m. Air: *I Want Yer, Ma Honey, Yes, I Do*. In: *Sound Money—Sound Minds*. Published as a poster, Box 507, Pittsburgh, PA. 1896. [19" × 25"]. Pk/bk drawings of William McKinley, Garret Hobart, anti-Bryan and pro-McKinley stories and caricatures." "Vic-

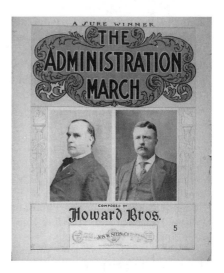

WM-79

tory." "Protection — Prosperity — Patriotism." 2pp. Page 2: Blank.

WM-81 Hurrah For The Major (National Republican League March Song). w.m. Rollin B. Tuller. Published by The Premium Music Company, No. 235 State Street Chicago, IL. Copyright 1896 by Rollin B. Tuller. Br/w litho of William McKinley, geometric design border. "Clubs supplied in quantities at reduced rates. Full military Band Score can be secured as above or at Lyon & Healy." 6pp. Page 2: "March" version. Page 3: "Song" version. Page 6: Blank.

WM-82 McKinley And Hobart Rallying Songs [Songster]. w. Caleb Dunn. Published by J.S. Ogilvie Publishing Company, No. 57 Rose Street, New York, NY. [1896]. [4 7/8" × 7 1/4"]. Pk/bk litho of William McKinley and Garret Hobart. "Protection, Prosperity and Sound Money." 16pp. [M-325].

WM-83 McKinley And Protection (*New York Press* Campaign Song). w. Post Wheeler. m. Louisa Lear Eyre. Published by *New York Press*, New York, NY. 1896. B/w drawing of William McKinley. 6[?]pp.

WM-84 McKinley & Roosevelt

Campaign 1900 [Song Book]. Published for the Wholesale Dry Goods Republican Club, No. 350 Broadway by C.G. Burgoyne, New York, NY. 1900. [4 3/4" × 7"] Y/bk litho of William McKinley and Theodore Roosevelt, eagle, shield. "Meetings daily from 12 Noon until 2 p.m." "A bird that can sing and won't must be made to sing." 20pp. [M-376].

WM-85   Our Nations Choice (or McKinley and Roosevelt's Triumphal March to the White House). m. L.M. French. Published by H.F. Chandler, Chicago, IL. 1899. R/w cover. Photos of William McKinley and Theodore Roosevelt. 8pp. Page 6: Advertising.

WM-86   The Providence Journal March And Two Step. m. John J. Fitzpatrick. Published by the Raymond Music Publishing Company, Providence, RI. [1900]. Bl/w litho of partial front page of the September 10, 1900, edition of *The Providence Journal* with illustration of "President McKinley." 6pp. Pages 2 and 6: Blank.

WM-87   Popular Republican Campaign Songs. w.m. Col. James H. Sprague. Published by Col. James H. Sprague at Norwalk, OH. 1900. N/c drawing of the Capitol, soldiers, flags, eagle. List of song titles. "1861–1899 One Flag, One Country." 4pp. Page 2: Song—**Roll On** (Quartette and Chorus). Page 3: Song—**De Ole Man Bryan** (Coon Song). Page 4: Song—**We'll All Help McKinley Along**. Advertising for Sprague campaign umbrellas.

WM-88   In Memoriam. m. Oscar Jones. Published by George T. Wallau, Nos. 2 and 4 Stone Street, New York, NY. 1901. B/w litho of palm leaves, wreath, shield ribbon inscribed "He Wrought his People Lasting Good," black border. "Respectfully Dedicated to Mrs. McKinley." 4pp.

WM-89   He Bade Us All Good-Bye. w. Walter Van Saun. m. A-Gomez de Fonseca (Composer of *Resting, Quietly Resting*). a. Harry Schminke. Published by A-Gomez de Fonseca, No. 170 Fifth Avenue, New York, NY. [1901]. B/w photo of William McKinley. Bk/w/pl drawing of roses, ribbon. "Dedicated to the Sacred Memory of Our Martyred President." 6pp.

WM-90   The President's March. m. Victor Herbert. Published by Edward Schuberth Company (J.F.H. Meyer), No. 23 Union Square, New York, NY. 1898. R/w/b drawing of a red flag with Presidential seal and stars, The Capitol, Washington Monument. Bl/w drawings of George Washington and Abraham Lincoln. "Schuberth's Popular Edition." 8pp. Pages 2, 7 and 8: Blank. Page 3: B/w litho of eagles, shields—"The general purpose of this march: For a very long time the want has been felt for a musical composition National in flavor and martial in action, which would be identified with the office of the President of the United States, and be played upon all occasions whenever the incumbent of that office approached. Up to this time, *Hail To The Chief* has assumed that purpose. This new march is now presented with that general need in view, and a copy, before publication, was submitted to the White House and approval secured. It is now hoped that the general acceptance of this march will proclaim it the National March of America—*Ladies Home Journal*, July, 1898." "Dedicated with respectful regard to President McKinley by the Composer and *The Ladies Home Journal*."

WM-91   The President At The Pan-American Fair. w.m. May Giltner. Published by Success Music Company, No. 343 Fifth Avenue, Chicago, IL. Copyright 1901 by May Giltner. R/w/b geometric designs. Photo of William McKinley. "Sold by all music dealers." 6pp.

WM-92   Tom Reed Campaign Songs. Published by T.J. Hampton, No. 110 North Broadway, Los Angeles, CA. 1896. Gn/bk litho of Thomas B. Reed

[Speaker of the House], geometric designs. [5 7/8" × 8 3/4"]. "Souvenir." 28pp. Inside advertising, patriotic and pro-McKinley songs. [M-348].

WM-93 Inaugural Ball (Two Step). m. Jay V. Youmans. Published by Jay Youmans, Platteville, WI. 1900. R/w/b drawing of William McKinley and Theodore Roosevelt, couples dancing, flags, eagle. 8pp. Page 2: Blank. Page 6: Advertising.

WM-94 The Buckeye March. m. Arthur S. Josselyn. Published by [V-1: The Alpha Company, No. 131 Mathewson Street, Providence, RI] [V-2: No publisher indicated]. Copyright 1896 by Charles H. Burdick and Arthur Josselyn. Non-pictorial. "For Military, Two-Step and All March Uses." "Played with Great Success by Thayer's Concert Band, of Canton, Ohio." "Respectfully Inscribed to Major McKinley by Comrade C.H. Burdick." "The Alpha Co., 131 Mathewson Street, Providence, RI., Publishers of Copyright music only. No cheap editions. American agents for Monco's songs and Piano Compositions." [V-2: "May 23, 1896"]. 6pp. Page 6: Blank.

WM-95 McKinley And Roosevelt Campaign Glees (And Rough Rider Jingles). Published by J.M. Coe, Richmond, IN. 1900. R/o/bk lithos of William McKinley, Theodore Roosevelt, geometric design border. 16pp.

WM-96 President McKinley's Funeral March. m. M.W. Butler. Published by A.W. Perry Sons' Music Company, Sedalia, MO. 1901. B/w litho of William McKinley, black border. "God's will, not ours, be done." 8pp. Page 3: "For Piano or Organ." Page 6: Advertising for *Garfield's Funeral March* by Phil B. Perry. Page 7: Advertising for *General Grant's Funeral March* by Phil Perry.

WM-97 Boston Journal McKinley March. m. Frank Stammers. In: *The Boston Sunday Journal*, page 3, June 19, 1896. Non-pictorial.

WM-98 William Will (A Republican Campaign Song). m. C.E. Ives. Published by Willis, Woodward and Company, Nos. 842-844 Broadway, New York, NY. 1896. Litho of wreath and ribbon.

WM-99 The Little Dinner Bucket (Song and Chorus). w.m. A.M. Bruner. Published by L.E. West Publishing Company, Rock Island, IL. Copyright 1896 by A.M. Bruner. B/w litho of dinner bucket, geometric designs, facsimile letter from William McKinley to A.M. Bruner. B/w photo of William McKinley. "To the Bread Winners of America." 6pp.

WM-100 Famous McKinley (Two Step March). m. A.A. Knoch. Published by The George Jalberg Music Company, No. 115 West Seventh Street, Cincinnati, OH. 1896. Bl/w/bk/gy photo of William McKinley. B/w geometric designs. "For the Piano." 6pp.

WM-101 McKinley Victory Song. w.m. Charles T. Hoge. Copyright 1900 by Charles T. Hoge. R/w/b drawing of McKinley, shield. [V-1: "Compliments of Thomas A. Carten, Ionia's largest dry goods…house"] [V-2: Matthews Piano Company, Lincoln, NB] [V-3: John Vandersluis…Dry Goods House, Holland, MI] [V-4: "Compliments of Matt J. Dehn, Department Store, Portland, MI"]. 4pp. Advertising throughout.

WM-102 McKinley (Song). w. Andrew Margeson. m. Charles Hughes. Published by Groene Music Publishing Company, No. 32 East Fifth Street, Cincinnati, OH. Copyright 1902 by Margeson and Hughes. Bk/gn/gd/w photo of William McKinley, geometric designs. "Respectfully Dedicated to Mrs. William McKinley." "Respectfully Dedicated to Mrs. Wm. McKinley." 6pp.

WM-103 Lead Kindly Light. w. John P. Newman. m. Air: *Lead Kindly Light— Lux Benigna*. Published by Henry Alte Music, Philadelphia, PA. as a book. 1901. [6 3/8" × 8 3/8"]. B/w photo of McKinley. Bk/w/s cover. "President

McKinley's Favorite Hymn." 26pp. Page 6: Photo of William McKinley. Page 7: "Memorial Edition." "Illustrated." Pages 12-22: Song in illustrated form.

WM-104 The Little Tin Pail Is Empty (Solo and Male Chorus). w. Jno. W. Matthews. m. S.B. Herbert. Published by Fillmore Brothers, No. 119 West 6th Street, Cincinnati, OH. 1896. Bl/w drawing of William McKinley, geometric design border. 6pp.

WM-105 The Political Quartet. m. W.L. Needham. Published by The Cuprigraph Company, No. 404 Fort Dearborn Building, Chicago, IL. 1896. Litho of William McKinley, Garret Hobart, William Jennings Bryan, Arthur Sewall, flag, geometric design. "Four Songs and Chorus for Republican, Democrat, Prohibition and Populist Parties." "Dedicated to the American people."

WM-106 Park's Republican Campaign Songs (For Male Voices). e. James Asher Parks. Published by The J.A. Parks Company, York, NE. 1900. [7" × 9 7/16"]. Bl/bl non-pictorial, geometric design border. "Respectfully Inscribed to Gen. Chas. F. Manderson." 40pp. [M-371].

WM-107 For Right And Dear Old Glory (An Echo of the Grand War for Humanity) (Song and Chorus). w.m. Hofwyl Hoorn. Published by American Publishing Company, Indianapolis, IN. Copyright 1900 by J.F. Curtice. Photos of McKinley—"Prosperity at home, prestige abroad," and Theodore Roosevelt—"Our Flag Once Raised Shall Never Come Down." Litho of man, woman, gun—"The Song of the Old Volunteer." "Souvenir and Ratification Edition." Includes a Half-Tone Supplement—"Charge of the Rough Riders." "To every son and daughter, The Great Republic that never knew defeat and whose destiny is ever onward and upward."

WM-108 Three of the Greatest Republican Campaign Songs of the Season. Published by L.S. Lyman, Lock Box 2841, New York, NY. 1896. [7" × 10 3/4"]. Non-pictorial black line border. "Set to the familiar airs of *The Old Oaken Bucket, Marching Through Georgia,* and *The Battle Cry of Freedom.*" "Republican clubs should order them by the thousand." "They will be sung by the large crowds at Republican meetings in such a manner as to arouse the greatest enthusiasm. Copies of this sheet, containing the 3 songs, may be had for 10 cents each prepaid; $6 per 100 not pre-paid; $40 per 1,000 not pre-paid. Special discount to Campaign Committees and Clubs ordering 100 copies or more. The regular discount will be allowed to music dealers. When large orders are filled C.O.D., 50 cents will be deducted from the bill to pay return charges on the money. Send all orders to L.S. Lyman, Lock Box 2841, New York, NY." 4pp. Page 2: Songs—**Marching With McKinley To Victory**. w. M.C. Dawsey. m. "Tune—*Marching Through Georgia.*" Also **McKinley, Sound Money And Protection**. w. Zacheus. m. "Tune—*The Battle Cry of Freedom.*" Page 3: **The Silver Dollar**. w. M.C. Dawsey. m. "Tune: *The Old Oaken Bucket.* a. L.S. Lyman. [M-347].

WM-109 Sound Money March. m. Waldemar Malmene. Published by The National Music Company, Nos. 215-221 Wabash Avenue, Chicago, IL. 1896. Photo of William McKinley. "Respectfully Dedicated to Wm. McKinley."

WM-110 Nearer My God To Thee. Published as a "Supplement to the *St. Louis Star*, Sunday, September 22, 1901." Litho of "Wm. McKinley," flags. "The Martyr President's Favorite Hymn." "As President McKinley was dying be murmured lines from the hymn *Nearer My God To Thee,* E'n tho' it be a crown that raiseth me, A short pause and then softly came the words, Angels to beckon me—Nearer My God to Thee." "Star Music Album." "Star Series of Old Favorites No. 33." "Used by permission of Balmer & Weber." Page 3: Photo of William McKinley.

WM-111 March On To Victory! (March). m. Kate Vanderpoel. Published by Kate Vanderpoel, No. 1502 Great Northern Boulevard, Chicago, IL. 1896. B/w photo of Mark Hanna. "Dedicated to M.A. Hanna." 8pp. Page 2: "Introducing the well known air *Cheer, Boys, Cheer.*" Page 7: Narrative—"What the Republican Party Stands For." Page 8: Blank.

WM-112 McKinley Inauguration March. m. Victor Herbert. Published by Edward Schuberth & Company (J.F.H. Meyer), No. 23 Union Square, New York, NY. 1897. Ma/w geometric designs. "Dedicated to the Hon. William McKinley." "And played by the 22nd Reg't. Band, N.G.S.N.Y., Under the Composer's direction at the Inauguration Festivities." 8[?]pp. Page 2: Blank.

WM-113 The Shooting Of McKinley. [ca. 1901]. Non-pictorial. 2pp. Page 2: Blank.

WM-114 McKinley's Grand March. m. F. Alexander. Published by A.H. Rosewig, No. 131 South Eleventh Street, Philadelphia, PA. [1896?]. Bl/w litho of William McKinley, geometric designs. 8pp. Pages 2, 7 and 8: Blank.

WM-115 The Farmer's Dream (A Campaign Song). w. Rena N. Sangster. m. Leander Fisher. Published by Leander Fischer, No. 143 Hodge Avenue, Buffalo, NY. 1896. [13 1/4" × 9 3/8"]. Bl/w caricature by Haas Flett of William Jennings Bryan fishing with silver coins for bait, parrot with gold coin—"Say Polly: Why don't the fish bite in this infernal stream, are they dead? Why Mr. Bryan, don't you see you are angling with a silver bait and as there are only Goldfish in this stream, you will find them too blamed smart to bite on nothing; Here's a Gold Dollar Billy, better try it and you'll find it will have in 'Sixteen to One' ten times over and not a free Silver Sucker among them—RNS." "Dedicated to Major and Mrs. McKinley." 6pp. Pages 2 and 6: Blank.

WM-116 Drape The Flag Once More In Mourning. w. Mrs. A.B. Johnson. m. Willard Groom. Published by E.R. Mann Publishing Company, Bergen, NY. Copyright 1901 by A.B. Johnson. Photo of William McKinley. Litho of flag. 6pp. Page 6: Blank.

WM-117 Do We Want Him? Well I Should Say So! (Political Topical Song). w.m. P.J. Meahl. Published by Lyon & Healy, Chicago, IL. Copyright 1896 by P.J. Meahl. Drawing of William McKinley, facsimile signature. "Written for the *Chicago Inter-Ocean.*" "Dedicated to the Republican Party by P.J. Meahl." 4pp. Page 2: "As originally printed in the *Chicago Inter-Ocean*, June 13, 1896." Page 4: Blank.

WM-118 Our Favorite Waltzes. m. Edward F. Denner. Published by J. Fischer and Brother, No. 7 Bible House, New York, NY. Copyright 1896 by Edward F. Denner. B/w photo of Garret Hobart. Bl/w geometric designs. "Respectfully Dedicated to Hon. G.A. Hobart, of New Jersey." 10pp. Pages 2 and 10: Blank.

WM-119 That's The Ticket March. m. Edward E. Rice. Published by Campaign Music Publishing Company, No. 1285 Broadway, New York, NY. 1900. Photos of William McKinley and Theodore Roosevelt. Drawing of stars, stripes, Capitol dome, geometric designs. "Dedicated to McKinley and Roosevelt."

WM-120 Dawn Of Peace (March and Two Step). m. Will T. Pierson, Jr. Published by Henry White, Washington, DC. 1901. B/w photo of a statue of a woman—"Peace," eagle. R/w/bk geometric designs. "Played by United States Marine Band at President McKinley's second Inauguration." 6pp. Page 6: Advertising for other music.

WM-121 Never Till The Old Man Comes. w.m. F.A. Edwards. Published by W.C. Clark, Lincoln, NE. 1896. Drawing of Miss Liberty, Uncle Sam riding camel, ship on fire, Capitol dome, pyramids. "Campaign Song of 1896." 6pp. Page 6: Blank.

WM-122 We Are For Bliss (Campaign Song). m. Harry H. Zickel. 1900. B/w photo of Aaron T. Bliss [Candidate for Governor of Michigan]. R/w/b drawing of Bliss riding elephant inscribed "G.O.P." on the road to The Capitol, cheering crowd, individuals with hats and shirts inscribed "Young Soldier," "Old Soldier," "Farmer," "Business Man," "Clerk," "Working Man." Flags and pennants inscribed "Sound Money," "Full Dinner Pail," "Expansion of Trade," "Protection," "Equal Taxation." 4pp. Page 4: Bl/w drawing of William McKinley and Theodore Roosevelt—"Let Well Enough Alone."

WM-123 American Marseillaise. w. Casimir Michel. a. A. Mirault. Published by Casimir Michel, Lowell, MA. 1898. B/w litho of eagle, crossed flags. "Dedie Respectueusement a son Excellence President McKinley President de la Republique des Etats Unis." 6pp. Page 6: Blank.

WM-124 McKinley's Triumph (March). m. Wilma Mills (The Blind Girl). a. Edward Kloepfer. Published by Edward Kloepfer, Colorado Springs, CO. Copyright 1897 by Wilma Mills. B/w drawing of Wilma Mills, geometric designs. "Dedicated to President Wm. McKinley." 6pp.

WM-125 The Lady Of The White House. m. John Philip Sousa (Composer of *Manhattan Beach, King Cotton, El Capitan Marches, Colonial Dances, Waltzes, &c*). In: *The Ladies Home Journal*, page 16, January, 1898. Published by the Cortis Publishing Company, Philadelphia, PA. B/w litho of John Philip Sousa and The White House. Magazine cover photo of Mrs. Ida McKinley. "Dedicated by *The Ladies Home Journal* and Mr. Sousa to Mrs. William McKinley by special permission granted by the wife of the President."

WM-126 The Coon Dance. m. Amos A.E. Konold. Published by Amos A.E. Konold, Pittsburg, PA. 1898. Bl/w drawing by Bragdon Pitts of four raccoons dancing. "Respectfully Dedicated to the G.O.P." 6pp. Pages 2 and 6: Blank.

WM-127(A) Gathering The Forces. m. "Tune: *Marching Thro' Georgia*." Published by Campaign Company, No. 143 Chambers Street, New York, NY. Copyright 1896 by "Author." [5 1/2" × 11 3/8"]. B/w litho of "William McKinley," "Garret A. Hobart," The Capitol, an eagle with ribbon inscribed "Protection and Sound Money," stars. "1896 Campaign." "Price 10 cents per package." 2pp. Page 2: Blank.

(B) **Baby's Rattle**. m. "Tune: *Yankee Doodle*." 2pp. Page 2: Blank.

(C) **Money Is The Issue**. m. "Tune: *Yankee Doodle*." 2pp. Page 2: Blank.

(D) **Goin' To The Polls**. m. "Tune: *Comin' Thro' The Rye*." 2pp. Page 2: Blank.

(E) **Glory! Glory! Hallelujah!** m. "Tune: *John Brown's Body*." 2pp. Page 2: Blank.

(F) **When David Comes Limping Home**. m. "Tune: *When Johnny Comes Marching Home*." 2pp. Page 2: Blank.

(G) **Good-Eye To Cleveland**. m. "Tune: *Good-Bye, My Lover, Good-Bye*." 2pp. Page 2: Blank.

(H) **Protection**. m. "Tune: *America*." 2pp. Page 2: Blank.

(I) **See The Voters**. m. "Tune: *Hold the Fort*." 2pp. Page 2: Blank.

WM-128 Campaign Songs, 1896 [Song Sheet]. Published by Wholesale Dry Goods Republican Club, New York, NY. 1896. [12" × 18 1/4"]. Non-pictorial. 2pp. [Six songs per page].

WM-129 The Fatal Shot. w.m. Miss Ethel Kelble. Published by The Smith and White Company, Cleveland, OH. 1901. Bk/w/r drawing of William McKinley lying in state, roses, cross inscribed "Thy Will be Done," geometric designs. R/w photo of Miss Ethel Kelble. 6pp. Page 6: Advertising.

WM-130 William McKinley's Dying Words. w. Howard C. Tripp. m. A Sister of St. Joseph, Concordia, KS. 1901. B/w photo of William McKinley. B/w drawing of two women weeping. "Nearer my God to Thee. Nearer my God to Thee." "Good-bye; It is God's way. His will be done." 4pp. Page 4: Blank.

WM-131 Alone. w.m. Sisters of St. Joseph. Published by the Sisters of St. Joseph, Concordia, KS. Copyright 1902 by Nazareth Academy. B/w photo of Mrs. William McKinley. B/w litho of small flower, geometric design border. "Affectionately Dedicated to Mrs. McKinley." 6pp. Pages 2 and 6: Blank.

WM-132 Our Fallen Leader (Song). w.m. Stella L. Woosley. Published by A.W. Perry & Sons Music Company, Sedalia, MO. 1902. B/w drawing of William McKinley, flags, black star border. 6pp. Pages 2 and 6: Blank.

WM-133 A Collection Of Campaign Songs. Published by The Republican State Committee, Columbus, OH. 1899. B/w photo of George K. Nash. "Dedicated to Geo. K. Nash, Our Standard Bearer, Campaign of '99." 12pp. Page 2: Biography of Geo. Nash and "Ohio Republican Platform for 1899." Includes songs—Page 5: **Young Politician** [Anti-Bryan]. Page 9: **We're Marching To Victory** [McKinley and Nash]. Pages 11 and 12: Biographies and photos of local candidates in Williams County, Ohio. [M-367].

WM-134 Republican Campaign Songs. c. J. Burgess Brown. Published for The State Central Committee, Indianapolis, IN. 1896. [5 1/4" × 7 3/8"]. Pk/bk litho of William McKinley and Garret Hobart, eagle, geometric design border. "We love the old Red, White and Blue, That freedom long ago unfurled, We love the glorious Country too, The fairest one in all the World, We love our mines, We love our mills, With fervor that our heart-strings thrills, therefore, 'Tis taken by consent McKinley for Our President." "Up to date." "Second Edition." 24pp. [M-322].

WM-135 The Lady Of The White House (Waltz). m. John Philip Sousa. [ca. 1898]. B/w drawing of John Philip Sousa, geometric designs. "Dedicated to Mrs. McKinley." 4pp. Page 2: At top of music—B/w drawing of women in front of The White House. Page 4: Blank.

WM-136 McKinley March. m. F.W. Green. a. Mrs. E.E. Green. Published by E.E. Green & Son, Elwood, IN. 1896. B/w photo of William McKinley. Bl/w geometric designs. "To my little brother Carl." 8pp. Page 2 and 8: Blank.

WM-137 Illinois No. 2. w. William A. Lamson (of The Marquette Club, for use in the Presidential Campaign of 1896). m. "Air: *Baby Mine*." Published by Clayton F. Summy Company, No. 220 Wabash Avenue, Chicago, IL. [V-1: Copyright 1894 by Clayton F. Summy and 1896 by William A. Lamson]. [V-2: 1896]. [7" × 10 7/8"]. Bl/w drawing of William McKinley [V-2: Bl/w line border]. [V-1 and V-2: "Dedicated to the Marquette Club of Chicago"] [V-2: "Republican Campaign Song—State of Illinois, Campaign of 1896." "One of the best of the (Campaign) songs comes from the Marquette Club of Chicago. It is written by William A. Lamson to the tune *Baby Mine*.— Wm. E. Curtis, in *Chicago Review*, Jan. 22, 1996"]. 4pp. Page 2: "Its sentiments in favor of the Country's Toilers, the Nation's Honor, and the People's Choice, should be known in the home of every Workingman in the State—*Chicago Tribune*, August 17th, '96." Page 4: [V-1: Facsimile letter from William McKinley to William Lamson] [V-1: B/w photo of "Home of the Marquette Club, Chicago"].

WM-138 Prosperity And Protection (Republican Administration). w.m. Revilo Oliver. Published by Oliver

Music Company, Chatsworth, IL. 1900. Bl/w lithos of William McKinley and Theodore Roosevelt, eagle, shield, vines. "Prosperity — Protection." "Dedicated to the Republican Party." 6pp. Page 6: Advertising.

WM-139 Our New President March. m. Juliet S. Norton. Published by Union Mutual Music Company, No. 265 Sixth Avenue, New York, NY. 1896. Bl/w photo of William McKinley. R/w cover. "Dedicated to the Republican Party of America." 6pp. Pages 2 and 6: Blank.

WM-140 Lead Kindly Light. Published as a postcard. [ca. 1901]. [3 7/16" × 5 7/16"]. Obv: Gn/w litho of William McKinley, carnations. Verses. "The Favorite Hymn and Flower of Our Martyred President, William McKinley." Rev: Mailing information.

WM-141 McKinley's Memorial March. a. Harry J. Lincoln. Published by United States Music Company, Cleveland, OH. Copyright 1900 by C.A. Mulliner. Bl/w litho of William McKinley, black border. "Respectfully Dedicated to Our Great Honored Nation." "In Memory of Our Late Beloved President." 6pp. Page 2: Poem by C.A. Mulliner. Page 3: Narrative and music. Page 6: Blank.

WM-142 The Ohio Napoleon (March Two-Step). m. Fred L. Neddermeyer. Published by D.A. McDonald, Columbus, OH. Copyright 1894 by Fred L. Neddermeyer. Bl/w photo by Baker of William McKinley. R/w/b cover. "To His Excellency William McKinley, Governor of Ohio."

WM-143 The New Administration March. m. Prof. Herman Bellstedt. Published by *The Commercial Tribune*. Copyright 1897 by Herman Bellstedt. [7" × 8 1/8"]. Bl/w litho of William McKinley, The White House, wreath. 4pp.

WM-144 Our Leader Is No More. w.m. James O'Dea and Les Friedman. Published by Sol Bloom, Chicago, IL. 1901. Bl/w photo of William McKinley. B/w drawing of Miss Liberty mourning, eagle, book — "In Memoriam the Hon. William McKinley, Late President of the United States." 6pp. Pages 2 and 6: Blank.

WM-145 Columbia My Country (American Anthem). w.m. George M. Vickers (Composer of *Guard the Flag, God Bless Our Land, &c.*). [ca. 1893]. Bl/w litho of Miss Columbia, two women, steamboat. "The New Patriotic Song Approved by People from New England to Alaska." "The sentiment of this song will, I am sure, be indorsed by every true American — William McKinley; Full of Patriotic sentiment, well expressed — Governor Wm. E. Russell, Massachusetts; It is patriotic in sentiment and the music is charming, Governor J.M. Stone, Mississippi; It is a patriotic gem and will probably remain one of the patriotic songs of our country — Governor Elisha P. Petty, Massachusetts; I trust it may be welcomed by an appreciative public with the favour it deserves — Gen. Lyman E. Kemp, Alaska; I regard such music as a important part of the education of the young people of the land — Hon. John Wanamaker, and representative Americans in all parts of the United States." 4pp. Page 2: Facsimile letter releasing copyright. Page 4: Blank.

WM-146 We Are Just From The Mills. w.m. J. Franklin Gill. Published by Danford J. Penfold, Nos. 13-17 Main Street, Lockport, NY. 1896. B/w drawing of "The Full Dinner Quartette" (W.A. Lampan, 1st Tenor; C.J. Clair, Baritone; D.J. Penfold, 2nd Tenor; L. Demachy, Basso)," mill — "Prosperity." "Dedicated to William McKinley...and to Theodore Roosevelt..." 2pp.

WM-147 A Memorial Tribute. w.m. Ida A. Long. Published by Sol Bloom, corner Randolph and Dearborn Streets, Chicago, IL. Copyright 1901 by Ida A. Long. Photo of William McKinley. "Good Bye all it is God's way His will not ours be done." 6pp.

WM-148 McKinley's Dying Words. w. Howard Carleton Tripp. m. Charles E. Smith. Published by the Best Music Company, Kingsley, IA. Copyright 1901 by Composers. Litho of William McKinley, geometric design border. "Good-Bye all, good-bye. It is God's way. His will be done — Wm. McKinley's last words." "Most pathetic song of the day."

WM-149 Lead Kindly Light. w.m. J.B. Dykes. Published by the World Publishing Company, No. 326 North Eighth Street, Philadelphia, PA. [ca. 1901]. B/w photo of William McKinley, black border. "Our late President's favorite hymns." 4pp. Page 2: **Lead Kindly Light**. Page 3: **Nearer My God To Thee**.

WM-150 Brave Jennie Creek. w. Garrett Newkirk. m. Stanley Clayton. Published by National Music Company, Nos. 215 to 221 Wabash Avenue, Chicago, IL. 1895. Ma/w photo of a train. "Beautiful Descriptive Song." "A Railroad Incident of the World's Fair year." 6pp. Page 2: "President Carnot, after corresponding with Governor McKinley, sent her a medal of the Legion of Honor — *New York Tribune*." Page 6: Advertising.

WM-151 Republican Campaign Song-Book 1896. c. Cornelius Higgins. Published by Oliver Ditson Company, Boston, MA. 1896. [7" × 10 1/4"]. B/w litho of "William McKinley" and "Garret A. Hobart." "25,000 of these books have been distributed by the National Republican Committee free." "Single copy for 10 cents." 12pp. [M-329].

WM-152 McKinley's Administration March. m. Clara Bardell Surfluh. 1897. B/w photo of William McKinley. B/w floral and geometric designs. 6pp. Page 6: Blank.

WM-153 Ode To President McKinley. w. Sam Walter Foss. m. Thomas G. Sheppard (Music used by permission of Thomas G. Sheppard of New Haven). In: *Home Market Dinner* [Program of Music During the Dinner], pages 2-3. "Home Market Club Dinner in Honor of President McKinley and members of The Cabinet, Mechanic's Building, Boston [MA], Thursday Evening, February 16, 1899." [6 5/8" × 8 1/2"]. "Stewart's Band, Emil Mollenhauer, Conductor." 4pp. Page 4: Song — *My Country 'Tis Of Thee*.

WM-154 The Hobart March And Two Step. m. Abram Dringer. Published by Abram Dringer, No. 151 Harrison Street, Paterson, NJ. 1896. Bl/w photo of Garret Hobart. B/w litho of leaves, geometric designs. "Dedicated to the Republican Voters of N.J." 6pp. Page 6: Blank.

WM-155 The March Of The Flag Songbook. w. H.D. Tutewiler. Published by H.D. Tutewiler, No. 133 West Market Street, Indianapolis, IN. 1900. [5" × 7 5/8"]. Litho of flag. "The Only Republican Campaign Songs for 1900 Having the Authorized Endorsement [sic] of Both National Republican Committees." 28pp. [M-374].

WM-156 Beautiful Isle Of Somewhere. w. Mrs. Jessie Brown Pounds. m. J.S. Fearis. [V-1: Published by E.O. Excell, Fine Arts Building, Michigan Avenue, Chicago, IL. 6pp.] [V-2: Published by E.O. Excell, Fine Arts Building, Michigan Avenue, Chicago, IL. Heavy cover stock. 8pp.] [V-3: Published by Forster Music Publishing Company, Inc., Chicago, IL. Edition ca. 1918.] [V-4: Forster Music Publishing Company, Inc., Chicago, IL. Post-1919 size]. Copyright 1897 and 1901. B/w photos of William McKinley, "Euterpean Quartette — Harriet Levinger, First Soprano; Fannie Levinger, 2d Soprano; Jeannette Bauhof, First Alto; Katherine Baehrens, Second Alto." "As sung at the funeral of Our Martyred President, Wm. McKinley, by The Euterpean Quartette." 6pp. Page 4 and 5: Arrangements for Men's and Women's Voices.

WM-157 God's Will Not Ours Be Done. w.m. Jennie P. Purviance

(Perryville, Ark). Copyright 1902 by Jennie P. Purviance. B/w photo of William McKinley. B/w drawings of eagle, shield, flowers, black mourning ribbon inscribed with the song title. "Dedicated to the McKinley National Memorial Association." 4pp. Page 2: At top of title: "Last words of William McKinley." Page 4: Blank.

WM-158 Our Nation's Pride. w. W.I. Leggett. m. L. Gertrude Leggett. Published by W.I. Leggett Company, No. 852 South Sawyer Avenue, Chicago, IL. 1904. Bl/w photo of William McKinley. R/w/b drawings of flag, eagle, flowers, geometric designs. "To Our Departed Heroes." "This Spangled Banner e'er will wave, the emblem of the noble free..." 6pp. Page 2: Litho of flag. Music. Page 6: Advertising.

WM-159 The Good Times Candidate Will Win. w.m. Laville. Published by National Music Company, Chicago, IL. [1896]. B/w photo of William McKinley, White House. "With a Rattling, Ringing, Rousing Chorus." "Dedicated to the Army of Good-Times." "The Republican Song of the Campaign." 6pp. Page 6: Blank.

WM-160 The Noblest Of Them All. Photo of William McKinley.

WM-161 The Great McKinley Bill (Campaign Song). w. H.W. Morgan. a. George W. Burgess. Copyright 1896 by H.W. Morgan and George W. Burgess. [7" × 11"]. B/w photo of William McKinley. Bl/w cover. 4pp. Page 4: Advertising.

WM-162 Hail To Our Ohio Man! w.m. Lincoln S. Wyman. Published by Lincoln S. Wyman, Milwaukee, WI. 1896. B/w drawing of "Hon. Wm. McKinley." R/w/bl/bk stripes, geometric designs. "Dedicated to and sung with Great Succes [sic] by the Milwaukee Republican Glee Club." "Members: 1st Tenor — A.L. Pryor, Dr. L. Schiller; 2d Tenor — E.E. Rogers, C.E. Wright; 1st Bass — S.L. Wrightson, C.N. Bowen; 2d Bass — M.A. Potthoff, J.G. Salsman." 6pp. Pages 2 and 6: Blank.

WM-163 Miss Liberty (A Patriotic March-Song). w. Andrew B. Sterling. m. Harry Von Tilzer. Published by Feist and Frankenthaler, No. 1227 Broadway and No. 42 West 30th Street, New York, NY. 1897. Ma/w litho of a facsimile sheet music cover with Miss Liberty, the Statue of Liberty, shield — "Dedicated to the school children of America." "Dedication accepted by President McKinley for the School Children of America." R/w/b flag background. "Patriotic Song." 8pp. Pages 2, 7 and 8: Advertising.

WM-164 President McKinley's Funeral March. m. P.F. Del Campiglio. Published by The George Jaberg Music Company, Cincinnati, OH. 1901. B/w photo of William McKinley, geometric designs. 6pp. Pages 2 and 6: Blank.

WM-165 Victorious Americans (March for Piano). m. G.L. Shaw. Published by Metropolitan Music Company, Nos. 509-511 Nicollet Avenue, Minneapolis, MN. 1898. B/w photos of William McKinley, General Miles and Admiral Sampson. Bl/w geometric designs. "Respectfully Dedicated to the Army and Navy of the U.S." "For Piano." 6pp. Pages 2 and 6: Blank.

WM-166 The Honest Little Dollar. w. Monroe H. Rosenfeld. m. "Melody: *Just Tell Them That You Saw Me*" by Paul Dresser. Published by Howley, Haviland & Company, No. 4 East 20th Street, New York, NY. 1896. O/bk/w geometric designs. "Official Song of the Campaign Endorsed by the Republican National Committee." "First Introduced and Sung by the Queen Regent of Descriptive vocalists, Miss Imogene Comer, As Originally published in *The New York Evening Sun* and *The New York Sun*." 6pp. Page 2: Blank. Page 6: Advertising.

WM-167 Toll The Bells Softly. w.m. Edith T. Atterbury. Published by Richard A. Saalfield, No. 1123 Broadway, Townsend Building, New York, NY., as a

"Musical supplement to the *New York Sunday Press*, Sunday, May 25, 1902." Copyright 1901. B/w drawing of angel ringing bells. R/w wreath, ribbon. 4pp.

WM-168 Safe In The Arms Of Jesus. w. Arthur J. Lamb. m. Hans S. Line. Published by Windsor Music Company, Nos. 266-268 Wabash Avenue, Chicago, IL. 1900. Edition 1901. B/w photo of William McKinley. "His last words — 'God's will, not ours, be done.'" "In Loving Memory of Our Late President, Wm. McKinley." 6pp. Pages 2 and 6: Blank. Page 3: "In Memory of Our Honored President, William McKinley."

WM-169 True Blue Republican Campaign Songs For 1896 [Songster]. c. J.B. Herbert. Published by The S. Brainard's Sons Company, Chicago, IL. 1896. [5 3/8" × 6 7/8"]. R/w/b drawing of crossed flags, wreath, ribbons. Bl/w photo of "Hon. Wm. McKinley." "Protection." 36pp. Pages 2, 35 and 36: Advertising. [M-328].

WM-170 The Philadelphia Press Prize McKinley Inaugural March. m. Joel B. Ettinger. Published by *The Philadelphia Press*, Philadelphia, PA. Sunday, January 17, 1897. [9 3/16" × 12 13/16"]. B/w litho of William McKinley. "Composed December, 1896, by Joel B. Ettinger, Milton, PA., in Competition for Prize Offered by *The Philadelphia Press*." 4pp.

WM-171 Our Leader (Two Step March). m. Gilbert Ashton. Published by B.F. Wood Music Company, Boston, MA. 1896. Sepia litho of William McKinley. 8pp. Page 2: Blank. Page 8: Advertising for other B.F. Wood music.

WM-172 We Know Our Business (National Republican Song Book). Published by W.W. McCallip, Columbus, OH. 1900. [6" × 9"]. Gn/bk cover. B/w photo of William McKinley, geometric designs. "Respectfully Dedicated to The Columbus Republican Glee Club, famous in every campaign since 1872." "Published only by the Author." 24pp.

Page 24: Postlude and index. Photo of children playing "The Megaphono-harp." [M-370].

WM-173 We Know Our Business (National Republican Song Book). Published by W.W. McCallip, Columbus, OH. 1900. [6" × 9"]. Gn/bk cover. B/w photos of William McKinley and Theodore Roosevelt, geometric designs. "Respectfully Dedicated to The Columbus Republican Glee Club, famous in every campaign since 1872." 24pp. Page 24: Postlude and index. Photo of children playing "The Megaphono-harp." [M-370 — Different cover].

WM-174 Old Glory Songster. c. Wilson Imbrie Davenny. Published by the National Music Company, Chicago, IL. 1896. [4 3/8" × 5 11/16"]. R/w/b flag design. "Containing the Latest Campaign Ballads." 20pp. Pages 2, 19 and 20: Blank. Page 3: Title page. Page 4: Advertising.

WM-175 Here's Success To McKinley. w. P.H. Grant. m. Richard R. Trench. Published by The Temple Music Company, No. 241 Wabash Avenue, Chicago, IL. 1896. B/w litho of William McKinley, geometric designs. "Official Republican Campaign Song." "Here's success to Will McKinley that man of great renown, With great shouts of victory, from Maine to Friscotown." 6pp. Page 2: Advertising. Page 6: Blank.

WM-176 Veterans And Sons Of Veterans Campaign Song (Story of the Hour). w. J.H. Wood. m. Professor M.C. Thayer. Published by Lyon & Healy, Chicago, IL. 1896. B/w photo of William McKinley. Bl/w drawing of a shield, crossed swords. "Authors of *Shenadoaha — A Trooper's Song*." 6pp. Page 2: Narrative on history of song. Page 6: Blank.

WM-177 The McKinley March. m. "Winthrop." Published by The John Church Company, Cincinnati, OH. 1896. B/w litho of William McKinley. "For the Piano." 6pp. Page 6: Blank.

WM-178 Song Of Protection (Prosperity and Patriotism). w. I.W. Miner. m. Jo F. Barton. Published by I.W. Miner, No. 422 South 15th Street, Omaha, NE. 1896. B/w photos of "Hon. Wm. McKinley of Ohio," "Hon. John M. Thurston, of Nebraska," "I.W. Miner" and "Jo Barton." "For the McKinley Campaign." "Dedicated to Hon. John M. Thurston, United States Senator, The McKinley Leader." "For sale by all music dealers." 6pp. Pages 2 and 6: Blank.

WM-179 McKinley March Song. w.m. John W. Pratt. Published by The Lyric Music Publishing Company, No. 42 Union Square, New York, NY. Copyright 1900 by John W. Pratt, Seattle, WA. Bl/w litho of William McKinley, geometric designs and border. "For the Campaign of 1900." 6pp. Page 6: Blank.

WM-180 President McKinley And His Golden Chair. w.m. Elizabeth Coyle. Published by Elizabeth Coyle, No. 1117 Germantown Avenue, Philadelphia, PA. 1897. Non-pictorial geometric designs. "Respectfully Dedicated to The Republican Party." 6pp. Pages 2 and 6: Blank.

WM-181 Campaign 1900 March. m. Eva E. Perkins. Published by Sherman, Clay and Company, San Francisco, CA. Copyright 1900 by Eva E. Perkins. Bk/y non-pictorial litho of large shield with title enclosed. "Played by Neale's California Exposition Band, 1900." 8pp. Pages 2, 7 and 8: Blank.

WM-182 McKinley's Grand Protection March. m. W.E. Johnston. Published by A.W. Perry & Sons' Music Company, Sedalia, MO. 1897. B/w litho of William McKinley, birds, geometric design border. 8pp. Pages 2, 7 and 8: Advertising. Page 3: "Respectfully Dedicated to Protection's Champion, Wm. McKinley."

WM-183 McKinley Our Martyred Son. w.m. Ethel Embury Smith. Published by Ethel Embury Smith, Jackson, MI. 1901. B/w photo of William McKinley. B/w litho of flags, black line border. B/w drawing of flags, black border. "A Touching Memorial Song Composed and Respectfully Dedicated to Loyal Americans Everywhere." 6pp. Pages 2 and 6: Blank.

WM-184 Protective Tariff Grand March. m. Will L. Thompson. Published by Will L. Thompson and Company, East Liverpool, OH. 1893. B/w litho by W.J. Morgan and Company of flowers, geometric designs, three factories — "The Knowles, Taylor and Knowles Company — White Granite Works, Decorating Department, and China Works." "Respectfully Dedicated by the Author to the Knowles, Taylor and Knowles Company, American Pottery Manufacturers, E. Liverpool, Ohio." 6pp. Page 6: Advertising.

WM-185 Souvenir For The Occasion. w.m. Mrs. M.A. Ledet (Widow of U.S. Consul). Published in California on a silk ribbon, May 14, 1901. [3 1/2" × 9 3/4"]. Obv: Bk/y litho of William McKinley. Printed song. "Compliments of the Composer." Rev: Blank.

WM-186 President McKinley's March. m. Mary A. Laselle. Copyright 1897 by M.A. Laselle. B/w drawing of flag, flowers. "To Miss Juliette Nelson Childs." 6pp. Page 6: Blank.

WM-187 McKinley Triumphal March. m. Jacob Steuck, Jr. Published by Shattinger Piano & Music Company, No. 10 South Broadway, St. Louis, MO. 1896. B/w photo of William McKinley. Bl/w drawing of dogwood flowers. 6pp. Pages 2 and 6: Blank.

WM-188 President McKinley's Sympathetic March. m. Horace R. Basler. Published by H.R. Basler, No. 128 Sixth Street, Pittsburg, PA. 1901. Bl/w drawing of a woman. B/w photo of William McKinley. "In Honor of Our Martyred President." 6pp. Pages 2 and 6: Advertising for other H.R. Basler copyrighted music.

WM-189 McKinley Is The Man (A Campaign Song and Chorus). w.m. W.T. Porter. Published by [V-1: Fillmore Brothers] [V-2: Geo. B. Jennings Company], Cincinnati, OH. [V-1: 1891] [V-2: 1893]. B/w photo of William McKinley, geometric design border. "To the Republican League of Ohio." [V-1: "Compliments of Hamilton County Republican Executive Committee. Sung at the Great McKinley Meeting in Cincinnati Music Hall, September 19, 1889 by the McKinley Glee Club (Geo. Weitzel, Mgr., Wm. Ehrmann, Sec.) accompanied by the Cincinnati Grand Orchestra, under the Direction of Herman Bellstedt, Jr. The Audience is requested to join in the chorus"]. [V-2: "New and revised edition —1893"]. Advertising. CH&D, Cincinnati, Hamilton & Dayton RR, the Finest on Earth, the only line running Pullman Safety Vestibuled trains with Dining Cars between Cincinnati, Indianapolis, and Chicago, St. Louis, Toledo and Detroit." 6[?]pp. Page 2: "As sung by the Glee Club of the Young Man's Blaine Club of Cincinnati." Advertising.

WM-190 McKinley March (Two Step). a. Paul Jones. [ca. 1900]. B/w photo of William McKinley. "Respectfully Dedicated to President William McKinley."

WM-191 A Collection Of Campaign Songs [Song Book]. 1900. Litho of William McKinley, Theodore Roosevelt, factories, flags, farmer plowing. "For President William McKinley." "For Vice-President Theodore Roosevelt." "Prosperity — Reciprocity." "Dedicated to the Republican Party."

WM-192 United States Of America. w. James Kefford. m. Bert Fulton. Published by The Fulton Music Company, No. 146 Grand Street, Waterbury CT. [ca. 1900]. Litho of William McKinley, James A. Garfield, Abraham Lincoln, George Washington, ship, train, flag, eagle.

WM-193 Our President. w.m. Weaver. Published by M.D. Swisher, No. 115 South 10th Street, Philadelphia, PA. 1898. R/w/b drawing of Uncle Sam raising flag. "Patriotic Gems New and Old." List of other titles in series. "Above Hits for Band and Orchestra 50 cts. each."

WM-194 Our President. w. T.A. Wilkinson. m. Helen A. Wilkinson. Published by H.A. Wilkinson, No. 6 Park Place, Mt. Auburn, Cincinnati, OH. 1900. Bl/w photo of William McKinley, geometric designs. "Dedicated to Wm. McKinley." 6pp. Page 6: Blank.

WM-195 Only A Carnation. w.m. Henry Wersel. a. Charles L. Lewis. Published by Victor Publishing Company, Station "O," Cincinnati, OH. Copyright 1903 by Henry Wersel. B/w photo of William McKinley. R/w/gr drawing by Emerson of red carnations. "Respectfully Dedicated to Mrs. Wm. McKinley and the Carnation League of America." 6pp. Page 6: Advertising.

WM-196 True Blue (March and 2-Step). m. Emma Louise Pearson. Published by C.H. Pearson, New York, NY. 1896. B/w photo of Col. W.C. Brown. Bl/w geometric designs. "Dedicated to Col. W.C. Brown of Governor McKinley's staff, State of Ohio, U.S.A." 6pp. Pages 2 and 6: Blank.

WM-197 The Popocrats Are Coming Boys!! (Campaign Song and Chorus). Published by W.J. Dyer and Brother, Nos. 509-511 Nicollet Avenue, Minneapolis, MN. 1896. Non-pictorial. "Solo for Medium Voice with Unison Refrain or Chorus for Male Voices ad lib." "Great Campaign Success." 4pp. Page 4: Blank.

WM-198 Gold Is The Standard To Win (Campaign Song). w. M.B. Shellman. m. F.S. Pearson. Published by The John Church Company, Cincinnati, OH. 1896. Gd/w drawing of flag-like banner on pole. 6pp. Page 2 and 6: Blank.

WM-199 Blufftonian Waltzes. m. Verdi Karns (Composer of *Guiseppe*

March, *Ragamuffin Two-Step*, *Bluffton Carnival Rag*). Published by The Karns Music Publishing Company, No. 124 West Market Street, Bluffton, IN. 1900. Gn/w non-pictorial cover. "Respectfully Dedicated to the G.O.P. Club." 6pp. Page 6: Advertising.

WM-200 Protection Mac Is Coming! (Campaign Song and Chorus). w.m. A.T. Gorham. Published by The John Church Company, Cincinnati, OH. 1896. B/w litho of William McKinley. "To Wm. McKinley, the Champion of Protection." 6pp. Page 6: Blank.

WM-201 McKinley Is The Man (Song and Chorus for Mixed and Male Voices). w. R.E. Spivey. m. C.H. Anderson. Published by Anderson & Spivey, New Windsor, IL. 1896. Bl/w non-pictorial geometric designs. 6pp. Pages 2, 5 and 6: Blank. Page 3: "For Male Voices." Page 4: "For Mixed Voices."

WM-202 For Country Dear. w. Jack Fay. m. James B. Oliver. Published by The Windsor Music Company, No. 266 Wabash Avenue, Chicago, IL. 1898. R/w/bl/bk drawing by Walt M. DeKalb of Miss Liberty, eagle with shield, naval ships, cavalry. "Dedicated to His Excellency President McKinley." "Trade supplied by National Music Company." 6pp. Page 2: Blank. Page 6: Advertising.

WM-203 The Full Dinner Pail. w. Henry Tyrrell. 1900. [7 1/4" × 10"]. Obv: Br/w photograph of "McKinley Glee Club, Howard, Kans., 1900, 'Full Dinner Pails.'" Listing of club members' names below photograph. Rev: Song. "As Sung by the Republican Glee Club, of Howard Kansas, 1900."

WM-204 Wm. McKinley's Grand March. m. F.M. Steinhauser, Op. 325 (Composer of *Surf Polka*, *Culver Polka*, *Le Chavlier Fantasia*, *&c*, *&c*). Published by F.M. Steinhauser, Omaha, NE. 1896. Non-pictorial. 6pp. Pages 2 and 6: Blank.

WM-205 McKinley's Come To Stay (Republican Campaign Song). w.m. Carolyn Smith. Published by Wm. A. Pond & Company, No. 124 Fifth Avenue, New York, NY. Copyright 1896 by Carolyn Smith. B/w geometric designs. 6pp. Pages 2 and 6: Blank.

WM-206 McKinley's Our Man. w.m. James Stanley. Published by James Stanley, No. 144 41st Street, Brooklyn, NY. 1896. R/w/b flag. "McKinley and Hobart." "Old Glory and Victory." 4pp. Page 4: Blank.

WM-207 The Hand That Held Greeting And Death. w. A. Bowden Doyle. m. R. Joseph Mazza. Published by The Great Eastern Music Publishing Company, No. 193 Main Street, Danbury, CT. 1901. B/w photos of William McKinley — "God's Will be Done," A. Bowden Doyle, "Author," R. Joseph Mazza "Composer" and James Bernardi — "With Barlow and Wilson's Minstrels." "Sung with instantaneous success by the Famous Tenor James Bernardi." "Lovingly Dedicated to our late President Hon. Wm. McKinley, A Song of the Assassination of he whom the whole World loved and shall mourn forever." "If work means success then we should succeed." "By the Author of the Famous song, *To Err is Human, To Forgive Divine*, *The Face in the Moonlight*, *&c, &c*." 6pp. Pages 2 and 6: Advertising.

WM-208 Sinking Of The Merrimac. w.m. John T. Hallett. Published by Press of the Skelton Company, Provo, UT. [ca. 1899]. Bl/w photos of William McKinley, Admiral Dewey, Captain Hobson of the Merrimac, J.T. Hallett and the U.S.S. Merrimac. Bl/w geometric designs. 4pp. Page 4: "Notice to public: Having lost my eye sight and hands through an explosion as recreation in some of the dark hours with an earnest desire to do something in the way of helping myself, I have tried composing and now offer my song *Sinking of the Merrimac*, for sale, feeling confident it will be appreciated by a generous liberty-loving public, Respectfully, J.T. Hallett."

WM-209 McKinley Is His Name (Republican Campaign Song). w.m. John H. Sarchet (Cambridge, Ohio). [1896]. [7" × 10"]. Non-pictorial. 2pp. Page 2: Blank.

WM-210 The Post's McKinley March (Two-Step). m. A.E. Gaylord (Conductor of the Central City Band). Published by *The Syracuse Post* Company, Syracuse, NY. 1896. Non-pictorial. "Dedicated by *The Syracuse Post* to William McKinley." 6pp. Page 6: Blank.

WM-211 You Settled When You Sold Your Wool (Republican Campaign Song). w.m. John H. Sarchet (Cambridge, O). Copyright 1896 by John H. Sarchet. [7" × 10"]. Non-pictorial. 2pp. Page 2: Blank.

WM-212 Gold And McKinley For Me. w. E.G. Hanford. m. "Air: *Bring Back My Bonnie To Me.*" Published by The Wholesale Dry Goods Republican Club, No. 350 Broadway, New York, NY. 1896. [5 7/8" × 9 3/8"]. Non-pictorial. "Compliments Thos. Humphrey, 'Gold Bug' Printer and Stationer, 368 Canal Street." 2pp. Page 2: Blank.

WM-213 When The Gold Reserve Came Tumbling Down (Republican Campaign Song). w.m. John H. Sarchet (Cambridge, O). Copyright 1896 by John H. Sarchet. [7" × 10"]. Non-pictorial. 2pp. Page 2: Blank.

WM-214 Campaign College Songs 1900 [Song Book]. w. Gen. Stillman F. Kneeland. Published for the Wholesale Dry Goods Republican Club, No. 350 Broadway, New York, NY. 1900. [5 7/8" × 9 1/8"]. Y/bk photos of William "McKinley" and Theodore "Roosevelt." Y/bk drawings of eagle, shield, flags. "A bird that can sing and won't sing must be made to sing." 16pp. Page 16: "If any one pulls down the Flag, shoot him on the spot—John A. Dix." "Will you vote for a man who will pull down the American Flag in the Philippines?"

WM-215 McKinley March. m. Glenn Woods. Published by Shattinger Piano and Music Company, No. 910 Olive Street, St. Louis, MO. 1910. B/w non-pictorial star border. 6pp. Pages 2 and 6: Blank.

WM-216 McKinley And Roosevelt Up-To-Date Campaign Song Book. w. Will D. Cobb. Published by Will D. Cobb, c/o: Howley, Haviland & Company, Nos. 1260-66 Broadway, New York, NY. 1900. [5 5/8" × 8 1/16"]. O/bk non-pictorial geometric design border. "Official." "Containing Paraphrases on the Most Popular Songs of the Day, with a Medley of Select Choruses Adaptable for Quartettes." 12pp.

WM-217 The White House (March and Two-Step). m. Annie G. Saddler. Published at Basler's Music House, No. 128 Sixth Street, Pittsburgh, PA. Copyright 1900 by Annie G. Saddler. B/w drawing of William McKinley. B/w "Photo by Claude Minehart" of Annie G. Saddler. R/w geometric designs. "Dedicated to our President William McKinley." 6pp. Pages 2 and 6: Blank.

WM-218 Shenandoah (A Trooper's Song). w. J.H. Wood (A Trooper, Sixth U.S. Cavalry). m. Prof. M.C. Thayer. Published by Oliver Ditson Company, Boston, MA. Copyright 1896 by J.H. Wood. B/w photo of William McKinley. Gr/w drawing of dogwoods. "Set to Music for Bugles." 6pp. + 2 page insert. Page 5: McKinley song—**Confidence And Protection**. Insert—Page 1: **Campaign Songs** [Song Sheet]. Four campaign songs for McKinley set to the tune of *Shenandoah, A Trooper's Song*. Page 6: Blank.

WM-219 McKinley Is The Man (Song). w.m.a. O.E. Henry. Published by O.E. Henry Music Company, Farmdale, OH. 1896. B/w photo of William McKinley. O/w geometric designs. "For Piano or Organ." "No. 4." 4pp. Page 4: Blank.

WM-220 In Canton, Ohio, U.S.A. (McKinley's Old Home Town). w. Harry H. Howard. m. Helen H.

Himes. a. Karl L. King. Published by Howard and McCarty, Canton, OH. [ca. 190-]. Photo of downtown Canton, parade. "Canton's Booster March Song." "Writers of *Two Little Soldier Boys*, In *Buckeye Land, Fame and Honor March, Ohio Rose, Don't Mind The Moonlight Molly, When Dixie Is Dixie Again, Blue Grass Blues*."

WM-221 Inaugural March. m. William A. Haley. Published by Sanders & Stayman Company, No. 1327 "F" Street NW, Washington, DC. 1901. B/w photos of William McKinley, Theodore Roosevelt, members of "Inaugural Executive Committee — Wm. H. Rapley, Chm. Music, J. Joy Edson, Chairman, T.E. Roessle, V. Chairm." R/w/b drawings of flags, White House, The Capitol, The Washington Monument. 6pp.

WM-222 McKinley's Funeral March. m. William Stephens. Published by Wm. Stephens, Milwaukee, WI. Copyright 1901 by Nau and Schmidt Music Company. B/w photo of William McKinley, facsimile signature — "Born, January 29th, 1843, Elected President, 1896, Died, September 14th, 1901," black border. "In Memory of Our Martyred President." 6pp. Pages 2 and 6: Blank.

WM-223 Our Next President (Wm. A. McKinley Song and Chorus). w.m. William A. Ficke (Composer of *They Have Given You To Another, Mabel Schottische*). Published by The Author [William A. Ficke], Cincinnati, OH. 1896. Gd/w drawing of a wreath around a coin inscribed "One." Bl/w geometric designs. 6pp. Page 2: Blank Page 6: Advertising.

WM-224 The President's March. m. Victor Herbert. In: *The Ladies' Home Journal*, July, 1898, p. 12. B/w photo of White House; B/w drawings of eagles, shields. Note: "For a long time the want has been felt for a musical composition, National in flavor and martial in action which would be identified with the office of the President of the United States and be played upon all occasions whenever the incumbent of that office appeared. Up to this time *Hail to the Chief* has answered that purpose. This new march is now presented with that need in view and a copy, before publication was submitted to the White House and approval secured, it is now hoped that the general acceptance of this march will proclaim it the National March of America." "Dedicated with respectful regard to President McKinley by the Composer and *The Ladies' Home Journal*."

WM-225 Safe In Heaven (Sacred Song). w.m. J. Edward A. Dalton. Published by Dalton Music Publishing Company, Boston, MA. 1901. Non-pictorial black lines. "Sung by Miss Julia Maria Blenarhassett." "To my Friend M.H. Dillon." "In Memory of Our Late President, William McKinley." 6pp. Pages 2 and 6: Blank.

WM-226 Down With Anarchy (or The Passing of McKinley). w.m. P. Douglas Bird (English Tenor, Teacher of Voice Culture, Louisville, KY). Published by Finzer and Hamill, Louisville, KY.

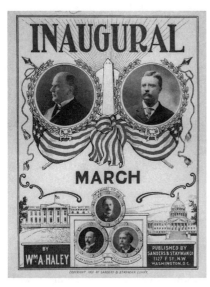

WM-221

Copyright 1901 by P. Douglas Bird. B/w photo of William McKinley. B/w drawings of Abraham Lincoln, James A. Garfield. R/w/bl/bk drawings of crossed flags, eagle, soldier, sailor, coffin. "Our Martyrs." 8pp. Page 3: "Dedicated to Mrs. William McKinley." Pages 2 and 6: Blank.

WM-227 Happiness Awaits Me (Song). w.m. P.M. Haas. Published by D.O. Evans, Youngstown, OH. 1907. B/w photos of President and Mrs. McKinley. Bl/bk/w drawing of sun setting over a village, bird, geometric designs. Quote—"Please God, if it is Thy will, I ask that the remaining days be shortened, happiness awaits me, why defer it? I will wait, I will wait, it cannot be long—Mrs. McKinley." "In Memoriam." 6pp. Page 2: Blank. Page 6: Advertising.

WM-228 Our Chief's Call (March and Two-Step). w.m. Emil Reinkendorff (Musical Director Grand Army Band), Canton, OH). Published by Louis Vitak, Canton, OH. Copyright 1901 by Emil Reinkendorff. R/w/b drawing by W.H. Stough of military officer with bugle, flag, horse. 6pp. Page 2: Narrative by Wm. McKinley—"True Americans Never Shirk Duty." Page 6: Blank.

WM-229 Republican Bugle Blasts (Rally Songs for the Campaign of 1896). a. O.E. Murray, A.M., Ph.D. Published by Norman G. Lenington, No. 308 Dearborn Street, Chicago, IL. 1896. [5 1/2" × 8 3/4"]. Br/bk drawings of William McKinley and Garret Hobart. Advertising. 23pp. [M-335].

WM-230 McKinley's Favorite Flower. w. Ron Moore. m. A.B. Hart. Published by Levi, No. 24 Union Square, New York, NY. as a set of glass slides. ca. 1901. Photograph of William McKinley, drawing of carnations, flag.

WM-231 We'll Vote For McKinley For He's All Right. w.m. Duncan J. Muir. Published by The S. Brainard's Sons Company, No. 20 East 17th Street,

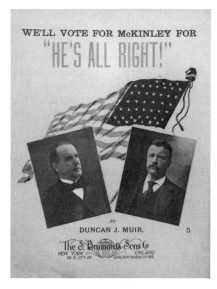

WM-231

New York, NY. 1900. B/w photos of William McKinley and Theodore Roosevelt. R/w/b flag. 6pp.

WM-232 Memorial Services For President McKinley [Program Book with Songs]. 1901. [5 5/16" × 6 7/8"]. Non-pictorial. B/w border. "At Natick, September 19, 1901." "It is God's way, his will be done." 4pp. Page 2: Program and "Double Quartet" membership. Page 3: Songs.

WM-233 Lead, Kindly Light. 1901. [4 13/16" × 12 3/16"]. B/w litho of William McKinley, black border. 2pp. Page 2: Song—**Nearer My God To Thee**.

WM-234 The Ballad Of Czolgosz. w.m. Stephen Sondheim. In: *Assassins*, page 25. Published by Rilting Music, Inc. Copyright 1990 and 1992.

WM-235 Nearer, My God, To Thee (Bethany) (Aspiration). w. Sarah F. Adams. m. Lowell Mason. In: *The Milwaukee Sentinel*, September 20, 1901, page 1. B/w drawings of "Prominent participants in the McKinley Memorial Meeting in the Exposition Building" including "David S. Rose, Casmir Gonski,

Bishop Isaac L. Nicholson, General F.C. Winkler and Judges James G. Jenkins and Eugene S. Elliott."

WM-236 McKinley's Memorial March. a. Harry J. Lincoln. Published by Harry J. Lincoln Music Company, No. 2209 Fairmont Avenue, Philadelphia, PA. Copyright 1901 by C.A. Mulliner. [Post-1919 size]. Non-pictorial. "Respectfully Dedicated to Our Great Honored Nation." "In Memory of Our Late Beloved President." 6pp. Page 3 Note: "This composition may be called a tone picture of President McKinley's sad fate. All is peace at the Pan-American where our favorite President spends happy hours, no sooner is he known to be there, till the crowd surround him to take a glimpse at his matured form. He is first seen at the Music Temple, where cheers of joy respond to shake him by the hand. No thought of an anarchist among the throng, he grasps the hand of each and everyone, the assassin approaches as to greet him (Bugles are sounded). President McKinley smiles, bows and extends his hand in that spirit of geniality, the American people so well know (Drums beating). Suddenly the sharp crack of a pistol is heard ringing through the crowd; President McKinley falls by the hand of an anarchist, saying 'Am I Shot?' Great sympathy for our dying President is shown; The hour is come, he is passing away, and as his spirit speaks to the hand on high, he is heard murmuring 'Nearer My God To Thee.'" Page 6: Advertising.

WM-237 Protection And Gold. w. Mrs. Rose Barton and Sister. m. Miss Edna Cookingham. Published by Mrs. Rose Barton, No. 809 Washington Boulevard, Chicago, IL. 1896. Bl/w photo of William McKinley. "Republican State Central Committee, Great Northern Hotel, Chicago." Facsimile letter to "Mrs. Barton and Sister—"Ladies, This Committee desire [sic] to say that we have examined your song, *Protection and Gold,* and that we find it very fine

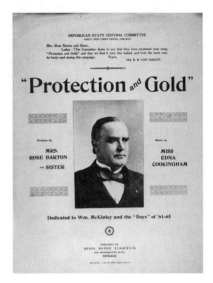

WM-237

indeed, and trust the same may be freely used during the campaign, Yours—Jas. R.B. Van Cleve." "Dedicated to Wm. McKinley and the 'Boys' of '61-65." 6pp.

WM-238 Republican Hot Shot (A Campaign Songster for 1900). e.a. George B. Chase and J.F. Kinsey. Published by Echo Music Company. 1900. [6" × 8 3/4"]. Bk/r lithos of William McKinley and Theodore Roosevelt. "Second Edition." 28pp. [M-365].

WM-239 The Montgomery (March and Two Step). m. Will J. Rickaby. Published by the Canada Company, Quebec, P.Q., Canada. 1899. B/w photos of William McKinley—"Respectfully Dedicated by Authority to the Hon. William McKinley, President of the United States." B/w photos of "Rock where Montgomery Fell, Dec. 31st, 1775," "House where Gen. Montgomery was laid out, Dec. 31st, 1775," "Quebec (from Levis)." Bl/w geometric designs. 6pp. Pages 2 and 6: Blank.

WM-240 McKinley Our Hero, Now At Rest. w.m. Joseph L. Hain. Published by Brehm Bros., Erie, PA. 1901. B/w photo of William McKinley. B/w drawing of angel, wreath. 6pp. Page 6: Advertising.

WM-241 Memorial Service For President Wm. McKinley [Song Sheet]. 1901. [4 15/16" × 10 15/16"]. Non-pictorial. "Thursday, September 19, 1901." 2pp. Page 2: Blank.

WM-242 Memorial Services [Program booklet with Songs]. Published by the Committee on Arrangements, Citizens of Carlisle, PA. 1901. [5 5/8" × 7"]. "Held by the Citizens of Carlisle, Pa., as a Tribute to Our Martyred President, William McKinley at the Hour of the Public Funeral at Canton, Ohio, Thursday, Sept., 19, 1901." B/w photo of William McKinley. 4pp.

WM-243 Shall We Gather At The White House? m. "Air: *Shall We Gather at the River?*" Copyright Sept. 4, 1896 by Joseph Frederick Bickford. [12 5/8" × 9 1/2"]. B/w litho of William McKinley and Garret Hobart, flags, Capitol building, ribbon inscribed "Protection — Prosperity." 2pp. Page 2: Blank.

WM-244 McKinley, Roosevelt And The Whole Republican Ticket [Song Sheet]. Published for The Academy of Music, [Philadelphia, PA]. November 2, 1900. [6" × 11 7/8"]. Bl/w litho of William McKinley and Theodore Roosevelt, two flags. "The Entire Audience will Please Join in Singing These Patriotic Songs." 2pp. Page 2: Blank.

WM-245 In Memoriam [Memorial Program with Music]. Published at Cedar Rapids, IA. September 19, 1901. [5 1/2" × 8 5/8"]. B/w litho of "William McKinley, Born January 29, 1843, Died September 14, 1901," black border. 4pp.

WM-246 The Fatal Shot (Song). w.m. Ethel Kelble. Published by Smith and White Company, Cleveland, OH. 1901. Gn/w cover, flowers, gold cross inscribed "Thy Will Be Done." "A Story of Our Martyred President." 6pp. Page 6: Advertising.

WM-247 The McKinley And Protection Waltz Song. w.m. George W. Sharpe. Published by Willis Woodward and Company, Nos. 842 and 844 Broadway, New York, NY. 1896. Non-pictorial. Pages 2 and 6: Blank.

WM-248 The Dewey Victory. w. Lucy Long. m. F.C. Boeckh (San Diego, Calif.) (Author of *Unity, &c, &c*). Published by Lucy Long, San Diego, CA. June, 1899. R/w/bl/bk/gd drawing of crossed U.S. and English flags — "Patronized by President McKinley and Her Majesty Queen Victoria." R/gd anchor — "Hero." "U.S.N. will Forever Float." 6pp. Pages 2 and 6: Blank.

WM-249 Nearer My God To Thee. Published as a post card. Copyright 1908 by Chas. Rose. [3 7/16" × 5 5/16"]. Obv: N/c photo of William McKinley. Embossed n/c drawings of cherub, carnations. "Last words of McKinley. Born Jan. 29, 1843. Died Sept. 14, 1901." Rev: "Post Card." "Series 11/2."

WM-250 Prosperity, Protection And McKinley (Campaign Song and Chorus). w.m. F.A. Blackmer. Published by F.A. Blackmer, No. 49 Cornhill, Boston, MA. 1896. Bl/w photo of William McKinley. R/w/b litho of a raccoon with U.S. flag inscribed "American Manufacture." "Respectfully Dedicated to the Republican Party." "Arranged for Mixed and Male Voices." "Supplied by Music Dealers and Booksellers." 6pp. Page 6: Advertising.

WM-251 Republican Victory Campaign Songs. c. F.F. Gilbert. Published by Home Music Company, No. 41 East Randolph Street, Chicago, IL. [5 3/8" × 7 3/4"]. 1896. B/w photo of William McKinley. R/w/b drawing of U.S. Flags. 36pp. Page 2: Advertising for the City of Idaho Falls, Idaho. Page 3: Advertising for Keystone Remedy Company. Page 4: Advertising for campaign music. Page 5: Title page. "As sung The Wagner and Leading Quartettes." Page 6 and 35: Advertising for "America Cycle

Mfg. Co." Page 31: Advertising for campaign books. Page 33: Advertising for "Uncle Sam's Toobacco Cure." Page 34: Advertising for "McKinley X-Ray Puzzle." Page 36: Advertising for "Wheeler & Wilson Mfg. Co." Bicycles.

WM-252 That Man From O-HI-O. w.m. Kate Vanderpoel. Published by Kale Vanderpoel, No. 1502 Great Northern Building, Chicago, IL. 1896. B/w photo of William McKinley. B/w litho of leaves, geometric designs. 4pp. Page 4: "Extract from an address by William McKinley, before the Marquette Club, Chicago, February 12, 1896 — What the Republican Party Stands For."

WM-253 Battle At The Polls. w. T.S. Williamson. m. H.G. Neely. Published by Anderson Music Publishing Company, No. 928 Main Street, Anderson, IN. [1900]. [17 5/8" × 17 5/8"]. R/w/b litho on cloth of William McKinley, Theodore Roosevelt, Col. Durbin — "Our Leaders — Our Leaders." "Dedicated to Col. Durbin." Rev: Blank.

WM-254 The Shooting Of Our Presidents. w.m. Seth A. Cook (Composer of *The Broken Hearted Child*). a. F.S. Watson. Published by Cook Publishing Company, Woonsocket, RI. 1901. B/w photo of William McKinley, Abraham Lincoln, James A. Garfield, Seth A. Cook. R/w/b flag. "Dedicated to Chloe E. Cook." 6pp. Page 6: Blank.

WM-255 McKinley And Hobart Grand March. m. J.W. Turner. In: *Trifit's Monthly Budget of Music*, page 22. Published by F. Trifit, Publisher, No. 36 Broomfield Street, Boston, MA. November, 1897. [9 3/4" × 12 1/4"].

WM-256 McKinley And Hobart Song Book. c.w.a. G.E. Treadway. Published by G.E. Treadway, Pittsburgh, PA. 1896. [5" × 6 5/8"]. R/w/b litho of William McKinley and Garret Hobart, flag design. "Now used by the celebrated Tariff Club Quartette of Pittsburgh, Pa." 28pp. Page 28: [M-349].

WM-257 Horray For Bill McKinley And That Brave Rough Rider, Ted. w.m. "Presidential Campaign Song (1900)." In: *No More Booze! And After Ribtickling, Knee Stomping, Gut Busting, High Stepping, Side Splitting, Tow Tapping, Fantastically Funny! Folk*

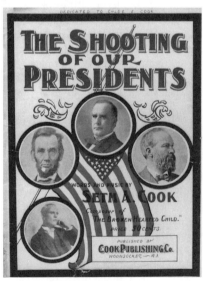

WM-254

WM-256

Songs For Guitar, page 34. c.a. Jerry Shverman. Published by G. Shirmer, New York, NY. 1978. Pl/o/bk/w geometric designs. 68pp.

WM-258 Nearer My God To Thee. Published by *The Daily Republican*, Rochester, IN. [5 1/4" × 10 3/16"]. [1901]. B/w litho of William McKinley, black border. Also on page one: *America*. 2pp. Page 2: Blank.

WM-259 McKinley's Republican Victory March. m. George Schleiffarth (Author of *On Dress Parade, Hesitation, Penitence, &c.*). Published by *The Advertiser*. [3 5/8" × 6 1/16"]. [1896]. B/w photo of William McKinley. "Handsome title page in colors. The publisher claims this is 'the original' McKinley March. It was published two weeks before the St. Louis Convention and is endorsed by Maj. McKinley and Mark Hanna. It is by a popular author and very catchy." 2pp. Page 2: Song. "At present the leading Bands and Orchestras are busy popularizing the *Northwest* and *Northland*, two new March-Two Steps by Ban Terris. Sousa started the *Northwest* on the popular grade and the *Northland* is following closely. They can be obtained at the music store for 40 cts. each.— Advertiser." "Dedicated to the Marquette Club of Chicago."

WM-260 Inauguration March (For The Piano). m. Florence M. Reeves. Published by The John Church Company, Cincinnati, OH. 1896. B/w litho of William McKinley, geometric designs. "To Wm. McKinley, Esq." 6pp.

WM-261 In Memory Of Wm. McKinley. w.m. H.T. Marsh. Published by H.T. Marsh, Springville, NY. 1902. B/w photo of "H.T. Marsh." B/w geometric designs. "Dedicated to Our Nation." 6pp. Pages 2 and 6: Blank. Page 3: B/w photo of William McKinley.

WM-262 McKinley, Hobart And Honor (Campaign Song). w.m. G.F. Perkins. Published by Frank K. Root & Company, Nos. 307 — 309 Wabash Avenue, Chicago, IL. Copyright 1896 by G.F. Perkins. Bl/w litho of eagle, shield, geometric designs. B/w photos of William McKinley and Garret Hobart. "Arranged

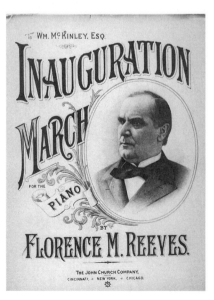

WM-260

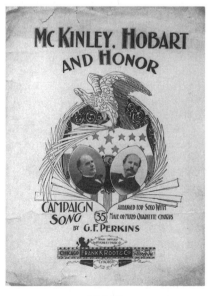

WM-262

for Solo with Male or Mixed Quartette Chorus." "Trade supplied by McKinley Music Co." 4pp.

WM-263 Republican Victory March. m. George Schleiffarth. Published by P.M. Wolsieffer, No. 76 State Street, Chicago, IL. 1898. R/w/bl/gd/bk stripes and stars. B/w photo of William McKinley—"Enlisted June 1, 1861, in Co. E, 23rd Ohio. Mustered out with his regiment July 26, 1865, Private, Sergeant, Lieut., Captain, Brevet Major, Staff Officer to Gen. R.B. Hayes and Gen. Geo. Cook, Elected President United States 1896." 6pp. Pages 2 and 6: Advertising. Page 3: "Note—The only McKinley March played at the St. Louis Nominating Convention in 1896."

WM-264 Faith (A Hymn). w. Capt. Jack Crawford. m. A.D. Liefeld. Published by Song Publishing Company, Mutual Building, Allegheny, PA. Copyright 1907 by Crawford and Liefeld. B/w litho of angel, cross, flowers. "In Memoriam Mrs. McKinley." 6pp. Page 2: Blank. Page 3: "To Mrs. McKinley, In Memoriam." Page 6: Advertising.

WM-265 La Fiesta March 1901 (1902). m. Bernard Berg, Op. 64. Published by Berg Publishing Company, Los Angeles, CA. 1901. R/w/y/gn drawing of Spanish horseman. "Respectfully Dedicated to President William McKinley." 6pp. Page 2: Blank. Page 6: Gn/w drawing of Bernard Berg, listing of his compositions.

WM-266 Nearer My God To Thee and **Lead Kindly Light**. Printed on silk ribbon. [1901]. [1 15/16" × 7 3/16"]. Obv: Bk/pk litho of William McKinley. "President McKinley Memorial." Rev: Blank.

WM-267 Republican Campaign Songs. w.e. A.A. Rowley (Author of Campaign Songs of 1888, 1892 and 1894). Published by *The Topeka Mail*, Topeka, KS. 1896. Litho of geometric designs. "Original Words Set to Popular Airs and Adapted to the National and Kansas State Campaign of 1896." "Address all orders to A.A. Rowley, care *The Topeka Mail*, Topeka, Kas." 32pp. [M-341].

WM-268 To Uncle Sam. m. "Air: *Irish Jaunting Car*." [1896]. [9" × 10"]. Non-pictorial. 2pp. Page 2: Blank.

WM-269 William McKinley's Funeral March. m. J. Marcus H. Winteringer. Published by The Winteringer Music Company Limited, Pittsburg, PA. 1901. B/w photos of "President William McKinley whose death we mourn" and "J. Markus H. Winteringer, Yours truly, The Author." Geometric designs. "Inscribed to the bereaved widow, Mrs. William McKinley, and to the bereaved nation." "Composed for the Piano." 4pp.

WM-270 Grand Victory March. m. Jennie M. Wertheimer (Composer of *Our Colors* and the celebrated *Princess Waltz*.). Published by J.M. Wertheimer, Walnut Hills, Cincinnati, OH. 1896. B/w photo of William McKinley. Bl/w drawing of an eagle. "Dedicated to Hon. Wm. McKinley." 8pp. Page 8: Blank.

WM-271 National Campaigner (Marching Songs Republican Clubs) [Song Book]. Published by Dudley T.

WM-270

Limerick & Company, No. 4031 Locust Street, Philadelphia, PA. 1896. [6 3/8" × 9 3/4"]. Non-pictorial. "The slogan: McKinley is Coming! O! ho! O! ho!" List of contents. Long narrative on marching songs. 24pp. [M-336].

WM-272 McKinley, Hobart And Liberty (Song For Male Voices). w. Harry V. Vogt. m. J. Wesley Hughes. Published by J. Wesley Hughes (New Jersey). 1896. Photos of William McKinley and Garret Hobart.

WM-273 McKinley's Own (March And Two Step). m. H. Clark Thayer. Published by Louis Vitak, Canton, OH. 1899. B/w photograph of soldiers in formation. R/w/b geometric designs. "Respectfully dedicated to the rank and file of the 8th Ohio, U.S.V." 6pp. Pages 2 and 6: Blank.

WM-274 Protection March (or Two Step). m. Howard Kunz. A. Fred Luscomb. Published by Howard Kunz, [Mansfield, OH]. 1896. R/w/b litho of the U.S. flag with "Protection" across the flag. "Dedicated to Hon. Wm. McKinley." 6pp. Page 6: Blank.

WM-275 McKinley Campaign Songster For 1900 (For Male Voices). e. W.G. Thomas. Published by The Home Music Company, Logansport, IN. 1900. Gn/bk litho of "William McKinley for President" and "Theo. Roosevelt For Vice President," eagle, flags, shield. "Send cash with order." "All orders will be promptly filled if accompanied by cash." "Single copy 15 cts. $.50 per dozen." "Note: Our McKinley Campaign Songster No. 2, Entirely Different from this will be issued September 10th. Same Price." 36pp. [M-373].

WM-276 Up To Date Republican Campaign Songster. e. W.H. Higgins. Published by W.H. Higgins, Kokomo, IN. 1896. Pk/bk litho of William McKinley within a horseshoe inscribed "Good Luck." "We want the Best! Sound Money and Protection!" 36pp. [M-330].

WM-277 McKinley Campaign Songster For 1896. e. D.E. Bryer. Published by Home Music Company, Logansport, IN. 1896. Bl/bk litho of William McKinley and Garret Hobart. "All orders will be promptly filled if accompanied by cash." 36pp. [M-323].

WM-278 McKinley And Hobart Campaign Glees. e. Strickland W. Gillian. Published by J.M. Coe, Richmond, IN. 1896. 16pp. [M-326].

WM-279 The Golden Glory! (Republican Songster for 1896). Published by Echo Music Company, LaFayette, IN. 1896. [5 5/16" × 7 3/4"]. Bl/w litho of William "McKinley" and Garret "Hobart." R/w/b geometric designs. 26pp. [M-327].

WM-280 McKinley And Hobart Campaign Songs. e. Clifton Jules. For Sale by Campaign Songs Publishing Company, Kansas City, MO. 1896. 20pp. [M-331].

WM-281 Chaplain Lozier's "Old Glory!" Campaign Songs. e. J.H. Lozier. Published by Lozier Brothers, Mt. Vernon, IA. 1896. "With Greetings from the Tippecanoe Club of Cleveland, O. For Use of Republican Campaign Committees and Glee Clubs." Be/bk litho of William McKinley. 8pp. [M-332].

WM-282 McKinley And Tanner Campaign Songster. Published by J.F. Higgins, Chicago, IL. 1896. [M-334].

WM-283 Republican Campaign Songs With Popular Airs. w.m. O.L. Wullweber and Gustav Kuestermann. c. O.L. Wullweber. 1896. B/w litho of William McKinley and Garret Hobart. "The following 6 campaign songs, Composed by the Undersigned, and the 7th Composed by Mr. Gustav Kuestermann of Green Bay, Wis., are hereby dedicated to the good people of the United States, with the fervent wish, that they may fulfill their mission in aiding to uphold the integrity and honor of our beloved Country, and furthering the general prosperity of our People!—O.L. Wullweber." 4pp. [M-350].

WM-284 Golden Gems. e.

William B. Severe. Published by William B. Severe, Baltimore, MD. 1896. Be/bk non-pictorial. Song verse with the first letters of each line spelling "Silver or Gold." 86pp. [M-342].

WM-285 Six Republican Songs For The Campaign Of 1896. Published by W.H. Pettibone, Chicago, IL. 1896. [M-343].

WM-286 Songs For The Presidential Campaign Of 1896. Published by Merickle Publishing Company, Manufactures and Jobbers of Campaign Supplies, New York, NY. 1896. "McKinley and Hobart, Protection and Sound Money." Gn/bk litho of William McKinley and Garret Hobart. 20pp. [M-344].

WM-287 Sound Money Songs. w. J.A. Fraser, Jr. Published by W. Rossiter, Chicago, IL. 1896. "Issued by Authority of the National Republican Committee." 16pp. [M-345].

WM-288 Campaign Songs. e. James M. Stewart. Published by Robert Hoyt Stewart, Baltimore, MD. 1896. "Dedicated to Hon. Wm. McKinley and Garret A. Hobart." Lithos of William McKinley and Garret Hobart. 8pp. [M-346].

WM-289 William McKinley's Memorial March. m. C.E. Stratton. [1901]. "For Piano or Organ."

WM-290 The Golden Greeting [William McKinley song].

WM-291 Who Shall Rule This Great Republic?. w.m. Lomas. 1896.

WM-292 McKinley Protection. w.m. Shauck. 1896.

WM-293 Major McKinley. w.m. Rojamdorf. 1896.

WM-294 McKinley Our Choice. w.m. Johnson. 1896.

WM-295 McKinley The True And Brave. w.m. Gray. 1896.

WM-296 Little Napoleon March. w.m. Farrar. 1896.

WM-297 Hurrah For McKinley. w.m. Marshall. 1896.

WM-298 McKinley We Endorse. w.m. Greenville. 1896.

WM-299 McKinley And Protection. w.m. W.G. Buehne. 1896.

WM-300 Republican Victory March. m. Ledue. 1896.

WM-301 St. Louis Convention March. m. Herold. 1896.

WM-302 Ohio Governor's March. m. Goodman. 1896.

WM-303 McKinley March. w.m. Shauck. 1896.

WM-304 (Election Day Will Prove To All) McKinley Is The Man! Published by The S. Brainard's Sons Company, No. 20 East 17th Street, New York, NY. 1896.

WM-305 Old Glory Campaign Songs For Republican Clubs And Singers. e. Chaplain J.H. Lozier. Published by Lozier Bros., Publishers, Mt. Vernon, IA. 1896. R/w/b litho of William McKinley and Garret Hobart. 12pp. [M-333].

WM-306 Our Flag Song Book. c. Charles P. Cleaveland (Director of the Republican Campaign Chorus). "Indorsement [sic] of the Republican State Central Committee of Maryland." 12pp. [M-366].

WM-307 McKinley's Triumphal March. m. Joseph Bannaker Adger. Published by James E. Warwick & Company, No. 284 South 11th Street, Philadelphia, PA. [ca. 1897].

WM-308 Its Gods Way. w.m. L. Forrest.

WM-309 The National Republican Song Book. c. W.W. McCallip (Columbus, OH). Published by W.W. McCallip, Columbus, OH. 1900. Gn/bk litho of William McKinley and Theodore Roosevelt. "Respectfully dedicated to the Columbus Republican Glee Club, Famous in Every Campaign Since 1872." 24pp. [M-369].

WM-310 Colonel Joseph H. Sprague's Popular Campaign Songs. Published by Joseph H. Sprague, Norwalk, OH. 1900. [M-372].

WM-311 War And Republican

Campaign Songs. w.c. Harry D. Tutewiler. 1898. "Written for the Marion Glee Club by Harry D. Tutewiler, Indianapolis." "For sale by the Republican State Committee and by the Author, Indianapolis, Ind. Single copies 25 cts." Gy/bk Non-pictorial. 12pp. [M-375].

WM-312 What's The Matter With Hanna? Published by The Phelps Music Company, Nos. 52-54 Lafayette Place, New York, NY. 1896.

WM-313 McKinley Serenade. w.m. Comrade C.H. Burdick. [1896]. "Respectfully inscribed to 'The Nepoleon of Protection.'"

WM-314(A) Our Christian President. w. Palmer Hartsough. m. J.H. Fillmore. In: *Fillmore's Prohibition Songs, A Collection of Songs for the Prohibition Campaign, Patriotic Services and all Meetings in the Interest of Reform*, page 85. Published by Fillmore Bros., No. 119 West 6th Street, Cincinnati, OH. 1900. [5 1/2" × 7 7/8"]. R/w/be flag border. 200pp. [Anti-McKinley]

(B) **We Must Whitewash Him** (Our Idol President), page 126. w. T.C. Johnson. m. Sir Arthur Sullivan. a. J.H. Fillmore. [Anti-McKinley]

WM-315 Lead, Kindly Light. w. John Henry Newman. m. Rev. J.B. Dykes. "One of the late President McKinley's favorite songs." In: *The Temperance Song Banner, A Peerless Collection of Temperance Songs and Hymns for The Woman's Christian Temperance Union, Loyal Temperance Legion, Prohibitionists, Temperance Praise Meetings, Medal Contests, &c.*, page 82. Published by The Temperance Music Company, Rocky Mount, VA. 1909. e. Emmet G. Coleman. [5 1/2" × 7 3/4"]. R/w hard cover song book. 120pp.

WM-316 The Gold Standard (Waltzes). m. Charles Palm (Composer of *Opera Queen Two-Step, &c.*). Published by Howley, Haviland & Company, No. 4 East 20th Street, New York, NY. 1896. Bl/w/gd litho of banner inscribed "Gold Standard," gold coins, horn of plenty. 8pp. Page 2: Blank. Page 8: Advertising.

WM-317 The Largest Flag In The World. w.m. Esther Lunsford. Published by A.E. Lomady, Canton, OH. 1905. N/c hand tinted photo of the Canton McKinley Memorial, large U.S. flag, people gathered around the flag, photo of Arvine E. Lomady — "Dedicated to A. E. Lomady [facsimile signature], The Man Who Helped Put Canton on the Map, Father of the Largest Flag in All the World." 8pp. Pages 2, 6 and 7: Blank. Page 8: B/w photo of Dorothy McCurdy, Soloist, The Largest Flag in All the World, 1212 Sixth Street, N.E., Canton, The City of Diversified Industries."

WM-318 Yellow Metal March. m. H. Butcher. Published by A.W. Perry & Sons, Sedalia, MO. 1896. B/w litho of William McKinley, geometric designs. 6pp. Page 2: "Respectfully dedicated to Ethel Ferguson, Standford, Ind." "For Piano or Cabinet Organ." Page 6: Blank.

WM-319 Memorial Service Upon The First Anniversary Of The Death Of William McKinley [Program]. [1902]. [5 1/2" × 8 3/8"]. Be/bk line border. 4pp. Page 3: *Nearer My God To Thee* and *America*.

WM-320 Our Glorious Union Forever (Medley of National Melodies). a. W.E.C. Howard. Published by Theodore Presser, No. 1708 Chestnut Street, Philadelphia, PA. 1898. R/w/b litho of eagle, flag, torch, geometric designs. 6pp. Page 2: "To the Champion of Liberty, President William McKinley." Page 6: Advertisement for Theodore Presser music.

WM-321 Sound Money and Honesty (Song and Chorus). w.m. Albert M. Bowers. Published Albert M. Bowers, Newark, NJ. 1896. B/w lithos of William McKinley and Garret A. Hobart. R/w/b litho of crossed flags, shield, floral designs. Printed verse. 4pp.

WM-322 Cuckoo! Cuckoo! All Sing Cuckoo! (Republican Campaign Song) (Song and Chorus). w. C. Sharp,

Junior. m. B. Flat, Senior. Published by Emil Wulschner & Son, Indianapolis, IN. 1894. Gn/ma/w cartoon drawings of rooster speaking sayings including "1893-4, Cuckoo Over There!," "1893-4, Yes Sir, Cuckoo, Cuckoo, Cuckoo," "Nov. 1894, I Didn't Cuckoo," and "1897, I C-C-Cant Ck-Ck-Cuckoo, I'm D-D-Dead," Uncle Same saying "Now You Just Get Out Of Here." "To the Indianapolis Bald-Headed Glee Club." 6pp. Includes solo arrangement and arrangement for Male choruses. Page 6: Narrative on the origin of "Cuckoo."

WM-323 McKinley Cyclone (Song & Chorus). w.m. Charles Gibbs. Published by Charles Gibbs, No. 65 Washington Street, Chicago, IL. 1896. B/w non-pictorial geometric designs. 4pp. Page 4: Blank.

WM-324 Hooray For Bill McKinley And That Brave Rough Rider Ted (A Ragtime Campaign Song & Chorus). w.m. Dan Long, Jr. Published by Dan Long Jr., Graham, NC. 1900. Br/be non-pictorial geometric designs. "No Restrictions as to Public Singing."

WM-325 William Will. w. S.B. Hill. m. Charles E. Ives. e. Gregg Smith. In: *America's Bicentennial Songs from The Great Sentimental Age, 1850-1900, Stephen Foster to Charles E. Ives*, page 58. Published by G. Schirmer, New York, NY. 1975. [9" × 11 7/8"]. N/c litho of woman with roses, flag, city. 152pp.

WM-326 McKinley & Hobart March. m. Leopold Kessler. In: *Marches Of The Presidents, 1789-1909, Authentic Marches & Campaign Songs*, page 58. A. Carl Miller. Published by Chappell & Co., Inc., No. 609 Fifth Avenue, New York, NY. "By arrangement with Chilmark Press, Inc." 1968. [9" × 12"]. R/w/b litho of eagle, flag. "An Illustrated Piano Folio For All Ages." 72pp.

WM-327(A) While We Are Booming McKinley. In: [*Handwritten Songbook*], page 14. Manuscript by Magdalina Palmer, No. 447 Blair Street, [city unknown] ca. 1897. [Original? And copied songs].

(B) We've Swiped The West In Football, page 15.

(C) In Honor Of McKinley Boys, page 16.

WM-328 Company A Boys In Blue (Campaign Songs). w. Members of Company A. m. Popular Tunes. Published in Rochester, NY. [1900]. [4" × 6"]. Pl/bk non-pictorial. "Prosperity and the Flag." "Campaign Songs 1880-1900." 16pp

WM-329 California Republican Campaign Songster. c. Sam Booth. Published by Republican State Central Committee, San Francisco, CA. 1900. [5 1/2" × 7 11/16"]. R/w/b lithos of "William McKinley — For President," and "Theodore Roosevelt — For Vice-President." "More McKinley and More Prosperity." 34pp.

WM-330 The Rough Rider (Republican Campaign Song Book). c. J. Burgess Brown. Published by J. Burgess Brown, Indianapolis, IN. 1900. [6" × 9"]. Br/bk non-pictorial. "ROUGH ON DemocRATS." 28pp. Page 3: B/w litho of William McKinley. Page 28: "Republican National Ticket —1900.

See also AL-95; USG-92; RBH-57; TR-250; TR-303; TR-363; WHT-23; WHT-42; WW-19; WW-58; WW-59; WW-106; WGH-11; CC-59; HCH-57; FDR-158; DDE-9; MISC-42; MISC-46; MISC-94; MISC-167.

WINFIELD SCOTT

WS-1 The Soldier's Return (A Song for the People). w. George P. Morris. a. S.O. Dyer. Published by Firth Pond & Company, No. 1 Franklin Square, New York, NY. 1848. N/c litho by Sarony & Major of General Winfield Scott in uniform, horses, soldiers in Mexico. "A Song for the People." 10pp. Pages 2, 9 and 10: Blank.

WS-2 The American Hero's March. m. Francis Barrington. Published

WS-1

by G. Andre & Company, No. 1104 Chestnut Street, Philadelphia, PA. 1861. B/w beige tinted litho by Schnabel & Finkeldey of Winfield Scott. "Composed and Dedicated to Major General Winfield Scott." 6pp. Pages 2 and 6: Blank.

WS-3 The Welcome Home Quick Step. m. James H. Dyer. Published by Firth Pond & Company, No. 1 Franklin Square, New York, NY. 1848. B/w beige tinted litho by Sarony and Major of Winfield Scott, soldiers. "Respectfully Inscribed to Major General Winfield Scott by the Publishers." 4pp. Page 2: Title: **Gen. Scott's Welcome Home Quick Step** (Introducing the air of *On the Banks of the Guadalquiver*).

WS-4 General Scott's Grand Review March. m. Stephen Glover. Published by Oliver Ditson & Company, No. 277 Washington Street, Boston, MA. [ca. 1861]. N/c litho by J.H. Bufford's Litho. of General Winfield Scott in uniform, flag, naval battle scene. 8pp. Pages 2 and 8: Blank.

WS-5 General Scott's Grand March. m. James Hewitt. Published by William Dubois, New York, NY. [ca. 184-]. Non-pictorial. 4[?]pp. Pages 1 and 4: Blank.

WS-6 The Vera Cruz Grand March. m. Francis Buck. Published by F.D. Benteen, Baltimore, MD. 1847. Non-pictorial. "Composed and Respectfully dedicated to Maj. General Winfield Scott, Commanding the forces of the U.S. at the Surrender of the City and Castle of Vera Cruz." 4pp. Pages 1 and 4: Blank.

WS-7 The Army Grand March. m. Charles Grobe, Op. 1358. Published by Oliver Ditson & Company, No. 277 Washington Street, Boston, MA. 1861. Non-pictorial line border. "Introducing the popular melody *Glory, Hallelujah* and *Hail To The Chief*." "To Maj. General Scott." "For Piano." 8[?]pp. Page 2: Blank.

WS-8 Weeping Sad And Lonely (Or When This Cruel War Is Over). m. Henry Tucker. a. Charles Grobe, Op. 1470. Published by Lee & Walker, No. 722 Chestnut Street, Philadelphia, PA. 1863. Non-pictorial. "Brilliant Variations on Henry Tucker's Beautiful Song, *When This Cruel War Is Over*." "Hope On — Hope Ever!" "Dedicated to General Scott." "Hope, though your sun is hid in gloom, and o'er your care-worn Wrinkled brow, Grief spreads his shadow — 'tis the doom That falls on many now." 10pp. Pages 2 and 9: Blank. Page 10: Advertising for other Lee & Walker published music.

WS-9 Hail To The Chieftain & Statesman! (Whig Nomination Quick Step for 1852). a. Charles Grobe. Published by Lee & Walker, No. 188 Chestnut Street, Philadelphia, PA. 1852. Non-pictorial. "Arranged and Respectfully dedicated to Maj. Gen. Winfield Scott and the Hon. W.H. Graham." 6pp. Pages 2 and 6: Blank.

WS-10 The American Flag. w. J.R. Drake. m. Bellini. Published by Lee & Walker, No. 722 Chesnut Street,

Philadelphia, PA. 1861. N/c litho by Thomas Sinclair of Miss Liberty, flag, shield, eagles. "United States of America." "Respectfully dedicated to Major General W. Scott." 8[?]pp. Page 2: Blank. Page 3: Title page and music.

WS-11 Flag Of Our Union Forever (A National Song). "Respectfully Inscribed to Gen. Winfield Scott." In: *Dan Rice's Great American Humorist Song Book*, page 18. 1866. [4 1/8" × 5 3/4"]. Br/bk drawing of an actor. "Containing Original and Selected Songs, Carefully Revised & Corrected." 34pp.

WS-12 Triumphal March. m. J.C. Viereck. Published by J.E. Gould, No. 164 Chesnut Street, Philadelphia, PA. 1847. Non-pictorial line border. "For the Piano Forte." "Composed and Dedicated to Genl. Winfield Scott." List of other titles by the Composer. 6pp. Page 6: Blank.

WS-13 The Chieftain's Daughter (A Ballad). w. George P. Morris, Esq. m. Henry Russell. Published by Firth & Hall, No. 1 Franklin Square, New York, NY. 1841. B/w litho on stone by Fleetwood, of Captain John Smith and Pocahontas, black line border. "Second Edition." "Pr. 30 cts. nett [sic]." 8pp. Pages 2, 7 and 8: Blank. Page 3: Long Narrative on John Smith and Pocahontas.

WS-14 Our General's Grand March m. C.S. Grafulla. Published by E.A. Daggett, New York, NY. 1861. N/c litho [horizontal format] of Union generals, including Winfield Scott, Ben Butler, George B. McClellan, Nathanial Banks, and John C. Fremont. 8pp. Pages 2 and 8: Blank. Page 3: Title — **Our General's Quickstep**. "As Performed by the 7th Reg. National Guard Band."

WS-15 Scott And Graham Melodies (Being a Collection of Campaign Songs for 1852). Published by Huestis & Cozans, Nos. 104 and 106 Nassau Street, New York, NY. 1852. [3 13/16" × 6 1/16"]. B/w litho of Winfield Scott, geometric design border. "As sung by the Whig Clubs throughout the United States." 76pp. Page 2, 4 and 75: Blank. Page 76: Advertising. [M-086].

WS-16 Gen. Scott's Quick Step. Published by Oliver Ditson, No. 115 Washington Street, Boston, MA. 1852. Non-pictorial. "Arranged for the Piano Forte from the celebrated *Sturm March Gallop*." 4pp. Pages 1 and 4: Blank.

WS-17 The Campaign Scott And Graham Songster (A Choice Collection of Original and Selected Whig Songs). w. F.J. Ottarson and E.R. Colston. Published by D.E. Gavit, No. 192 Broadway, New York, NY. August 17, 1852. [3 7/8" × 6 1/4"]. Lithos of Winfield Scott and W.H. Graham, eagle, flags, floral designs. 48pp. [M-081, 085].

WS-18 General Scott & Corporal Johnson. w.m. Bayard Taylor. Published by David A. Warden, No. 1138 Lombard Street, Philadelphia, PA. 1863. Non-pictorial. "Warden's Popular Songs, Duetts [sic], &c." "Authorized Edition." List of other titles in series.

WS-19 The Banner Of The Free. w. Eugene Johnston. m. "Air: *The Sword of Bunker Hill*." Published by Charles Magnus, No. 12 Frankfort Street, New York, NY. [ca. 1861]. [5" × 8"]. Hand Colored litho of General Winfield Scott, wreath, flags. "500 Illustrated Ballads — Illustrated and Printed by Charles Magnus, No. 12 Frankfort Street, N.Y. Branch: No. 520 7th Street, Washington, D.C." 2pp. Page 2: Blank.

WS-20 Fall Of Vera Cruz (And Surrender of the City & Castle of St. Juan D'Ulloa). m. Francis Buck. Published by Frederick D. Benteen, Baltimore, MD. 1847. Non-pictorial. "To the American Forces under Major Genl. Scott (29 March, 1847), a Descriptive Piece, Composed and Respectfully Dedicated to the Officers and Men of the U.S. Army and Navy Engaged in that Glorious Achievement." 10pp. Pages 2 and 10: Blank.

WS-21 Festival March. m. J. Pychowski. Published by Wm. Hall & Son, No. 239 Broadway, New York, NY. [1858?]. B/w beige tinted litho by Sarony and Major of General Winfield Scott. "Performed by the Band of the National Guard, Seventh Regiment, N.Y.S.M." "Composed and Respectfully Dedicated to Genl. Winfield Scott." Page 2: Blank.

WS-22 Quartette. w. F.W.C. m. Air: *Will You Come To The Bower*. Published by John Childe, No. 84 Nassau Street, New York, NY. [ca. 1852]. [21 1/2" × 14"]. B/w litho of General Winfield Scott, William Seward, Horace Greeley and "Whig Chorus." 2pp. Page 2: Blank.

WS-23 Scott And The Veteran. w.m. J.P. Webster. Published by H.M. Higgins, No. 117 Randolph Street, Chicago, IL. 1862. Non-pictorial geometric design border. "Western Gems: 100 Songs Composed by J.P. Webster." List of other titles in series.

WS-24 The Cerro Gordo March And Quick Step. m. "A Lady of Virginia." Published by F.D. Benteen, Baltimore, MD. 1847. Non-pictorial. "Composed & Arranged for Piano." "Dedicated to Major Genl. Winfield Scott and the Officers under his command during the Battle of Cerro Gordo." 4pp. Page 4: Blank.

WS-25 General Scott's Farewell Grand March. m. Mrs. E.A. Parkhurst. Published by C.M. Tremaine, No. 481 Broadway, New York, NY. 1861. B/w litho of shield, flags, eagle. 6pp. Page 6: Blank.

WS-26 The Fall Of Mexico (A Military Divertimento). m. John H. Hewitt. Published by F.D. Benteen, Baltimore, MD. 1847. R/w/bl/be litho of eagle with ribbon inscribed "E Pluribus Unum," geometric design border. "Dedicated to General Winfield Scott, and his Brave Officers and Soldiers." 16pp. Pages 2 and 4: Blank. Page 3: Inside title page. B/w litho by E. Weber & Company of U.S. soldiers, military equipment, eagle, flag, palm tree, view of Mexico City. "Commemorative of the glorious achievements of American arms in the memorable battles of Conteras, Cherubusco, Chapultepec, Molino del Rey, &c., and the final storming of the City of Mexico. Composed and dedicated to Gen. Winfd. Scott and his Brave Officers and Soldiers." Page 16: Advertisement for F.D. Benteen music.

WS-27 Lieut. Greble's Funeral March. m. E. Mack. Published by S.T. Gordon, No. 538 Broadway, New York, NY. 1861. Non-pictorial geometric designs. "Almost the last words of this gallant Officer were, when asked why he did not dodge or retreat as the rest of the troops, he replied, 'I never dodge and when I hear the Bugle sound the retreat, I will leave and not untill [sic] then.'" "Respectfully dedicated to Gen. Winfield Scott." 6pp. Pages 2 and 6: Blank.

WS-28 General Scott's Quick Step. m. F. Rasche. Published by Lee & Walker, No. 188 Chesnut Street, Philadelphia, PA. 1852. Non-pictorial. "Composed for the Piano." 4pp. Pages 1 and 4: Blank.

WS-29 A Grand Slow March. m. Alexander Kyle. Published by E. Riley, No. 29 Chatham Street, New York, NY. 1831. Non-pictorial. "Composed Expressly for the Examination Review of the Cadets U.S.M. Academy, W.P. and dedicated by permission to General Winfield Scott." 4pp. Pages 1 and 4: Blank.

WS-30 Graduating Song. w. "Mrs. Genl. Scott." m. Cadet D.M. Beltzhoover. Published by Firth, Hall and Pond, No. 239 Broadway, New York, NY. 1847. B/w beige tinted litho of a West Point cadet, symbols of various Army branches. "Dedicated to the West Point Graduates of 1846." 8pp. Pages 2, 7 and 8: Blank.

WS-31 The War Song. w. Thomas Mitchell. m. John R. Mitchell (of Lansingburgh, NY). Published by Thomas Mitchell, Lansingburgh, NY. [1861]. R/w/bl/bk litho of crossed American flags. "Cordially Inscribed to Lieut.-

Gen. Winfield Scott, Commanding U.S. Army." 6pp. Page 2: Inside title—**War Song For '61**. Page 6: Blank.

WS-32 Gen. Scott's March. In: *The Army and Navy Fife Instructor: Containing the Calls, Signals, and the Complete Camp and Garrison Duties as Practised in the Army and Navy of the United States, Including the Volunteer and Regular Service, Containing the National Airs, and a Large Collection of Marches, Quicksteps, Waltzes, Polkas, &c.*, page 30. e.a. Elias Howe. Published by Elias Howe, Agt., No. 103 Court Street, Boston, MA. Copyright 1863 by Willard Howe.

WS-33 Vera Cruz Grand March. m. Henry Chadwick. Published by F. Riley & Company, No. 297 Broadway, New York, NY. 1847. Non-pictorial. "Composed & Arranged for the Piano Forte, & Dedicated to Major General Winfield Scott." 4pp. Page 4: Blank.

WS-34 A Word From Long Island. m. "Tune: *Duda Duda Da*." [1852]. [3 3/4" × 10 3/4"]. Non-pictorial. 2pp. Page 2: Blank.

WS-35 Vera Cruz Quick Step. m. E. Nathan. Published by Firth Pond & Company, No. 1 Franklin Square, New York, NY. 1847? Non-pictorial geometric design border. "Dedicated to Major-General Winfield Scott." "Arranged for the Piano Forte." 4pp. Page 4: Blank.

WS-36 Campaign Songs Of Scott & Graham. c. James A. Fraser. Published for the Authors by E. Combs, New York, NY. 1852. "As Composed and Sung by Messrs. Fraser & Missing, Being a New Collection Dedicated to the Whigs of the Union." 48pp. [M-084].

WS-37 The Chippewa Warbler. Published by King and Baird, Philadelphia, PA. 1852. "Containing the Songs of the Chippewa Glee Club as Sung by Messrs. Murphy, Ruth, Poole and Wharton." "Here's to you old Scott." 64pp. [M-082].

WS-38 The Scott Songster. e. True Blue, Esq. Published by Edwards and Goshorn, Cincinnati, OH. 1852. "Compiled Expressly for the Presidential Campaign of 1852. Respectfully Dedicated to the Old Warriors of 1812, and to the Whig Glee Clubs and Chippewa Lodges of the Rank and File of the Whig Party of the United States." 64pp. [M-087].

WS-39 General Scott's Grand March. m. C. Meineke. Printed and Sold at Carr's Music Store, Baltimore. [MD]. [1815?]. "As performed by the band of the 5thRegiment (M.M.)." Non-pictorial. 4pp. Pages 1 and 4: Blank. [W-5777]. [Probably Winfield Scott, War of 1812].

WS-40 General Scott's Grand March. m. James Hewitt. Published by [V-1: John Paff] [V-2: Wm. Dubois], New York, NY. [V-1: 1814?] [V-2: 1818]. Non-pictorial. Followed by **Quick Step**. [W-3702]. [Probably Winfield Scott, War of 1812].

WS-41 Collection Of Scott And Graham Songs. c. J. Covert. Printed for the Author. 1852. "Loco Focos, Stand from Under. The old Hero is Marching on the Capitol." 56pp. [M-083].

WS-42 General Scott's Funeral March. m. Mrs. E.A. Parkhurst (Author of the Popular Funeral March in memory of President Lincoln). Published by Horace Waters, No. 481 Broadway, New York, NY. 1866. Non-pictorial black line border. "Our Lamented Hero." 6pp. Page 2: Blank. Page 6: Advertising.

WS-43 Gen. Scott's March. In: *Howe's School For The Violin (Containing New And Complete Instructions For The Violin, With a Large Collection of Favorite Marches, Quicksteps, Waltzes, Hornpipes, Contra Dances, Songs, and Six Setts [sic] of Cotillions, Arranged with Figures, Containing Over 150 Pieces of Music*, page 19. c. Elias Howe, Jr. Published and Sold Wholesale and Retail, by Elias Howe, Jr., No. 7 Cornhill, Boston, MA. 1843. [6 1/2" × 10"]. Y/bk litho of musical instruments, angel, geometric and floral designs.

WS-44 Gen. Scott's March. In:

Musician's Omnibus: Containing the Whole Camp Duty, Calls and Signals Used in the Army and Navy; Forty Setts of Quadrilles, Including Waltz, Polka and Schottische, with Calls; and an Immense Collection of Polkas, Schottisches, Waltzes, Marches, Quicksteps, Hornpipes, Contra & Fancy Dances, Songs, &c., for the Violin, Flute, Cornet, Clarionett, &c, containing over 700 Pieces of Music, page 25. c. Elias Howe. Published by Elias Howe, No. 103 Court Street, Boston, MA. 1861. [8 1/2" × 11"]. O/bk non-pictorial. "Improved Edition." 100pp.

WS-45 Gen. Scott's March. In: *Howe's Diamond School For The Violin: Containing, Complete Instructions and Full Directions in Bowing; to which is added A Large Collection of Popular Polkas, Schottisches, Waltzes, Redowas, Marches, Quicksteps, Dances, Hornpipes, Songs,* , page 25. c. Elias Howe. Published by Elias Howe, No. 103 Court Street, Boston, MA. 1861. [8 1/2" × 11"]. Bl/bk non-pictorial. 68pp.

WS-46 Hang Out For Scott The Banner. w.m. Gen. Washington Dixon, The Political Poet. Published by Ls. Pessou & B. Simon Lith., No. 175 Chartres Street, New Orleans, LA. [1852]. B/w litho of eagle, shield, flags. "Sung By The Scott Clubs Throughout The Union." 2pp.

WS-47 General Scott's Artillery March (At the Battle of Churubusco). a. W.C. Peters. Published by W.C. Peters & Sons, Cincinnati, OH. 1847. B/w litho by Melodeon of mounted artillery soldiers pulling an artillery field gun. "Arranged for the Piano Forte." "As Performed by the Brass Bands. 6pp. Pages 2 and 6: Blank.

WS-48 Lieutenant General Scott's Grand Funeral March. m. E. Mack. Published Lee & Walker, No. 722 Chestnut Street, Philadelphia, PA. 1866. B/w litho by Sinclair's Litho of Winfield Scott, floral frame with angel at top. Page 6: Advertisement for Lee & Walker music.

See also GW-222; FP-5; GBM-29; GBM-83; AL-297; TR-238; TR-252; MISC-94.

WINFIELD S. HANCOCK

WSH-1 General Hancock's Grand March. m. D.W. Reeves. Published by W.F. Shaw, Philadelphia, PA. Copyright 1880 by W.F. Shaw. [V-1: Bl/w] [V-2: B/w] litho by Crosscup and West of General Winfield Scott Hancock. "Respectfully Dedicated to the Democratic Candidate." 6pp. Pages 2 and 6: Advertising.

WSH-2 The National Democratic Campaign Songster. Printed by The Courier Printing Company, Syracuse, NY. Copyright 1880 by G.N. Harding. [3 3/4" × 5 9/16"]. B/w litho of Winfield S. Hancock and William H. English, eagle, flag. "The right of trial by jury, the habeas corpus, the liberty of the press, the freedom of speech, the national right's of persons, and the right of property, must be preserved — Winfield S. Hancock." "1880 Hancock & English." 52pp. Page 3: Same as cover. Page 5: Dedication. Page 35: Electoral vote. Page 37: Bibliographical sketches. Page 41: "The murder of Mrs. Surratt." Page 47: "General Hancock's Acceptance." [M-218].

WSH-3 When Hancock Takes The Chair. w.m. Thomas P. Westendorf. Published by Wm. H. Sheib, Washington Hall, Wheeling, WV. Copyright 1880 by W.F. Shaw. B/w litho by Crosscup of West of Winfield Hancock. "A Rousing Campaign Song and Chorus." "Respectfully Dedicated to General Winfield S. Hancock of Pennsylvania." "No North! No South! No East! No West! United Everywhere, We'll give our Stalwart Friends a rest, When Hancock Takes the Chair." Page 2: Advertising.

WSH-4 Gen. Winfield S. Hancock's Cincinnati Grand March. m. E. Mack. Published by Lee & Walker, No. 1113 Chestnut Street, Philadelphia, PA.

1880. B/w litho by Crosscup and West of Winfield Scott Hancock. "Cincinnati's Candidate." 8[?]pp. Page 2: Blank.

WSH-5 Hancock The Nation's Choice (Song and Chorus). w. Alex R. Webb. m. Waldemar Malmene. Published by Balmer & Weber, St. Louis, MO. 1880. B/w litho of Winfield S. Hancock. Bk/r geometric designs. "The Great Democratic Campaign Song for North and South!" 6pp. Pages 2 and 6: Blank.

WSH-6 Campaign March And Chorus To Genl. Hancock. w. Mrs. W. Disch. m. Wm. Disch. Published by S.T. Gordon & Sons, New York, NY. 1880. B/w litho of Winfield Scott Hancock, flags, eagle, shield. 6pp. Page 3: Title — **General Hancock's Grand Campaign March** (With Chorus ad. lib.). Page 6: Blank.

WSH-7 Hancock's Victory March. m. W.M. Treloar. Published by John Church & Company, No. 66 West 4th Street, Cincinnati, OH. 1880. B/w litho of Winfield Scott Hancock. "To Every Earnest Democrat in the Land." 6pp. Page 6: Blank.

WSH-8 Hancock's Victory Song. w. Mrs. M.J. Watkins. m. W.M. Treloar. Published by John Church & Company, No. 66 West 4th Street, Cincinnati, OH. 1880. B/w tinted litho of Winfield S. Hancock. 6pp. Page 6: Blank.

WSH-9 The Soldier's Vote. w. M. Niedner. m. Jacob Kunkel. Published by Kunkel Brothers, No. 311 South 5th Street, St. Louis, MO. 1880. B/w nonpictorial geometric design border. "Cock-A-Doodle-Do!! II." "Democratic Campaign Song for 1880." "In response to the Republican Campaign Song, entitled *The Veteran's Vote*." "To Col. John G. Prather, the Staunch Democrat, the Trusted Leader of the Party of Missouri — and Eminent Citizen, most Respectfully Dedicated by the Author." 4pp. Page 4: Blank.

WSH-10 General Hancock's Grand March. m. Sep. Winner. Published by Lee & Walker, No. 922 Chestnut Street, Philadelphia, PA. 1864. B/w tinted litho by Thomas Sinclair of Winfield Scott Hancock. "To Major General Hancock." 6pp. Page 2: Blank. Page 6: Advertising.

WSH-11 Music For The Campaign (A Collection of Original and Selected Songs, Adapted to Familiar Tunes for use at Campaign Meetings, for 1880). [Song Booklet]. Published by The Indianapolis Sentinel as a newspaper supplement, Indianapolis, IN. 1880. [7 3/4" × 10 5/8"]. B/w lithos of Winfield Scott Hancock and William H. English. "This Collection of fifty one first-class Campaign Songs will be sent to any address, postage paid as follows: 25 for 30 cts.; 50 for 60 cts.; 100 for $1.00. Address Sentinel Company, Indianapolis, Ind." 8pp. Foldover.

WSH-12 Trefoil Quick Step. m. T. O'Neill. Published by Lee & Walker, No. 722 Chestnut Street, Philadelphia, PA. 1864. B/w tinted litho by Thomas Sinclair of General Winfield Scott Han-

WSH-12

cock. "To Major General Hancock." 8pp. Page 2: Blank. Page 8: Advertising.

WSH-13 With Hancock, Union, Liberty! (Song and Chorus). w.m. Otto Dresel. Chorus by H. Eckhardt. Published by Oliver Ditson & Company, No. 451 Washington Street, Boston, MA. Copyright 1880 by Otto Dresel. Non-pictorial. "Respectfully dedicated to the great soldier Statesman Gen. Winfield S. Hancock." 6pp. Pages 2 and 6: Blank.

WSH-14 Gen. Hancock's Grand March. m. Sep. Winner. Published by Oliver Ditson Company, Boston, MA. [1908 Edition]. O/w/gn floral cover. "Popular Marches for the Piano." List of other titles in the series. 6pp. Pages 2 and 6: Advertising.

WSH-15 Hurrah For Hancock (Democratic Campaign Song For 1880). Published by John Church & Company, No. 66 West 4th Street, Cincinnati, OH. Non-pictorial geometric designs.

WSH-16(A) Three Cheers For Hancock (Song and Chorus). w.m. J.M. Munyon. Published by White, Smith & Company, No. 516 Washington Street, Boston, MA. 1880. B/w litho of Winfield Scott Hancock, geometric design border. "The Campaign March." "Gen. Winfield S. Hancock's Three Cheers For Hancock." "Solo with Male Chorus." 6pp. Pages 2 and 6: Blank.

(B) Gen. Winfield Scott Hancock's March. m. E.H. Bailey, Op. 98. (Author of *Gov. Samuel J. Tilden's March*). 4pp. Page 4: Advertising.

WSH-17 Hancock Peace And Liberty. w. Hazard. m. "Adapted to a popular melody." Published by Wm. A. Pond & Company, No. 25 Union Square, New York, NY. 1880. Attached photo of Winfield Scott Hancock. B/w geometric designs. 6pp. Pages 2 and 6: Blank.

WSH-18 Hancock And English Union March. m. L.M. French. Published by Ludden and Bates, Savannah, GA. 1880. B/w litho of Winfield Scott Hancock and William H. English, shield,

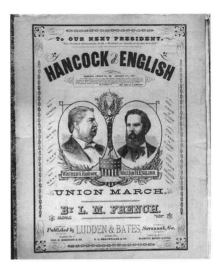

WSH-18

flags, wreath, chain link border. "Gen. Order 40, August 21st, 1867, The right of trial by jury, the habeas corpus, the liberty of the press, the freedom of speech, the natural rights of persons and the rights of property must be preserved. Free institutions, while they are essential to the prosperity and happiness of the people, always furnish the strongest inducements to peace and order — By Command of Maj. Gen. W.S. Hancock." "No North, South, No, East, West, the Union of States, the Union of Hands, the Union of Hearts forever." "To Our Next President — the Soldier Statesman with a Record as Stainless as his Sword." 6pp. Pages 2 and 6: Blank. Page 3: "For Piano or Cabinet Organ."

WSH-19(A) The Banner Of Hancock And English (Quartett or Chorus). w. J.H. James, Jr. m. J.A. Porter. Published by John Church & Company, No. 66 West 4th Street, Cincinnati, OH. 1880. B/w litho of Winfield S. Hancock, star border. "Democratic Campaign Music." List of other songs in series. 6pp. Pages 2 and 6: Blank.

(B) Hurrah For Hancock (Song and Chorus). w.m. Carl.

(C) Around The Hancock Banner Throng Alike The Blue And Grey (Song and Chorus). w.m. Leon Levoy.

(D) Brave Hancock Is The Man. w.m. W.B. Richardson.

(E) Hancock's Victory Song (Song and Chorus). w. Mrs. M.J. Watkins. m. W.M. Treloar.

(F) Gen W.S. Hancock's Grand March.

(G) Hancock's Victory March. m. W.M. Treloar.

WSH-20 Gen. Hancock's Victory March. m. W.A. Fallman, Op. 40. Published by S.T. Gordon & Son, No. 13 East 14th Street, New York, NY. 1880. B/w litho by R. Teller of Winfield Scott Hancock. "Respectfully Dedicated to the Democratic Candidate." "For Piano." 6pp. Page 2: Blank. Page 6: Advertising.

WSH-21 Gen. Hancock's Grand March. m. George Schroeder. Published by Charles Tuttle, No. 83 James Street, Rome, NY. 1880. Non-pictorial. "Composed and Respectfully Dedicated to Major Gen. Hancock." 6pp. Pages 2 and 6: Blank.

WSH-22 Hancock's [Grand] March. m. [M.E.] Walter. Published by Richard A. Saalfield, No. 12 Bible House, New York, NY. [1882]. Non-pictorial geometric design border. "Latest and Most Popular Marches." List of other titles in series.

WSH-23 General Hancock's Grand March. m. Sep. Winner. Published by Oliver Ditson & Company, No. 451 Washington Street, Boston, MA. 1864. B/w litho by [V-1: J.H. Bufford's Sons, Boston] [V-2: T. Sinclair & Son, Philadelphia] of Winfield S. Hancock. "To Major General Winfield S. Hancock." [V-1: Seven co-publishers listed] [V-2: Four co-publishers listed]. 6pp. Page 2: Blank. Page 6: Advertising.

WSH-24(A) Gen. Hancock's Grand March. m. Sep. Winner. Published by Oliver Ditson & Company, No. 451 Washington Street, Boston, MA. 1880. B/w litho by J.H. Bufford's Sons of Winfield Scott Hancock. [V-1: Seven co-publishers listed. Coat buttons in light tones] [V-2: Eight co-publishers listed. Coat buttons dark tone]. [6pp. Pages 2 and 6: Blank].

(B) Gen. Hancock's Campaign March. m. Le Baron.

WSH-25(A) Gen. Hancock's Grand March. m. Sep. Winner. Published by Oliver Ditson Company, Boston, MA. 1880. [Later edition]. B/w litho by J.H. Bufford's Sons of Winfield Scott Hancock. 6pp. Pages 2 and 6: Blank.

(B) Gen. Hancock's Campaign March. m. Le Baron.

WSH-26 The Conscript's Lay. w. George P. Holt. m. Air: *Kingdom Coming*. Published by Charles Magnus, No. 12 Frankfort Street, New York, NY. [ca. 1864]. Hand Colored litho of "Gen. W.S. Hancock." Map — "Country Between Yorktown and Richmond." Followed on same page by *How Are You Conscript?* by G.P. Holt.

WSH-27 For Hancock True And English Too! (Song). w. L.J. Kaufman. m. Air: *Nancy Lee*. Published by S.T. Gordon, No. 13 East 14th Street, New York, NY. 1880. Non-pictorial. "Dedicated to Re-United New York Democracy." "With Piano Accompaniment." 6[?]pp.

WSH-28 General Hancock's Grand March. m. Sep. Winner. Published by Strange & Company, Music Publishers and Imprinters, No. 120 King Street West, Toronto, Canada. [ca. 188-]. [10 3/8" × 14 1/4"]. Non-pictorial. "The Canadian Musical Library." 4pp. Page 4: Advertising.

WSH-30 Hancock Polka. m. Eduard Holst. Published by Charles W. Held, Brooklyn, NY. 1893. N/c lithos of Winfield Scott Hancock, Ulysses S. Grant, John Logan, Sherman, Sheridan and Farragut. "Our American Heroes." "Six Easy Pieces for Piano." 6pp. Page 2:

Blank. Page 6: Advertising.

WSH-31 The Williamsburg Grand Triumph March. m. Professor H. Coyle. Published by Lee & Walker, No. 722 Chesnut Street, Philadelphia, PA. 1862. Non-pictorial. "Respectfully Dedicated to Genl. W.S. Hancock." 6pp. Pages 2 and 6: Blank.

WSH-32 Gen. W.S. Hancock's Grand March. Published by John Church & Company, Cincinnati, OH. 1880. Litho of Winfield Scott Hancock. 6pp. Pages 2 and 6: Blank.

WSH-33 Hancock's Grand March. m. M.E. Walter. Published by Richard A. Saalfield, No. 41 Union Square, New York, NY. 1880. B/w litho of open book with title across pages, geometric border. 6pp. Page 2: Blank. Page 6: Advertising.

WSH-34(A) Ring The Bells For Hancock (Song and Chorus). w. C.C. Northrup. m. H.P. Danks. Published by R.A. Saalfield, No. 839 Broadway, New York, NY. 1880. B/w non-pictorial geometric design border. "The Great Democratic Campaign Song." 6pp. Page 2: Blank. Page 6: Advertising.

(B) Grand Triumphal March. m. J.P. Stockton, Jr.

WSH-35 Hancock And English Campaign Song Book. Published by Union Book Company, Philadelphia, PA. 1880. [5 7/8" × 8 13/16"]. Litho of Winfield Scott Hancock and William H. English. [M-213].

WSH-36 Gen. Winfield Scott Hancock's March. m. E. H. Bailey, Op. 93. In: *Folio, A Journal of Music, Drama, Art and Literature*, page 350. Published by White, Smith & Company, No. 516 Washington Street, Boston, MA. 1880.

WSH-37 The Hancock And English Democratic Campaign Song Book. Published by W.R. Swan & Company, No. 174 Race Street, Cincinnati, OH. 1880. [4 1/2" × 6"]. B/w litho of Winfield Scott Hancock. 36pp. Page 2: Advertising for a book on the "Life of Hancock." Page 3: Blank. Page 4: B/w litho of "Gen. Winfield S. Hancock." Page 5: Title page. Pages 6 and 7: "Our Candidates. "Biographical Sketches of Hancock and English." Page 8: "Preface." Pages 32-36: Advertising. [M-215].

WSH-38 Hancock And English Campaign Songster. Published by John Church & Company, Cincinnati, OH. 1880. [4" × 5 3/4"]. Pk/bk geometric design cover. "Including Biographical Sketches & Constitution for Campaign Clubs." 52pp. Pages 2, 51 and 52: Advertising. Page 3: Title—**Hancock And English Campaign Carols**. Page 5: Title—**Democratic Campaign Carols**. [M-214].

WSH-39 The Hancock And English Democratic Campaign Song Book. Published by W.R. Swan & Company, No. 174 Race Street, Cincinnati, OH. 1880. [4 1/8" × 6"]. B/w litho of "Winfield S. Hancock" and "W.H. English," eagle, shield, flags. 34pp. Page 2: Advertising for a book on the "Life of Hancock." Page 3: Blank. Page 4: B/w litho of "Gen. Winfield S. Hancock." Page 5: Title page. "With portrait and biographical sketches." Pages 6 and 7: "Our Candidates." "Biographical Sketches of Hancock and English." [M-216].

WSH-40 The Hancock And English Campaign Song Book For 1880. w.c. Robert Wm. Wright. Copyright 1880 by R.W. Wright, New York, NY. Litho of Winfield S. Hancock and William H. English. 32pp. [M-219].

WSH-41 The Most Popular Edition Of Hancock And English Campaign Songster. Published by Popular Publishing Company, A.J. Dick, Manager, No. 32 Beekman Street, New York, NY. 1880. Be/bk litho of Winfield Scott Hancock. "Containing the Largest and Most Complete Collection of Songs, All Written to the Most Popular Airs of the Day." 68pp. Page 68: Be/bk litho of William H. English. [M-217].

WSH-42 The Bleached Shirt.

WSH-41

w.m. William M. Pegram. Published by Otto Sutro, Baltimore, MD. 1880. B/w non-pictorial geometric designs. Respectfully dedicated to the Democratic Candidate for the Presidential Campaign of 1880, Maj. Gen. Winfield S. Hancock, The Fearless Soldier, Conscientious Statesman and Noble Gentleman." "The Presidential Campaign of 1880." 6pp. Pages 2 and 6: Blank.

WSH-43 Hancock's Grand March. m. C.A. Noel. Published by O.F.W. Helmick, No. 180 Elm Street, Cincinnati, OH. 1880. Gn/w litho of Winfield S. Hancock.

WSH-44(A) Hancock, The True And Brave (Song and Chorus). w. A. Blue. m. A. Grey. Published by Balmer & Weber, Saint Louis, MO. 1880. B/w litho of Winfield Scott Hancock. R/w/b geometric designs. "To the United Democracy of the United States." Facsimile handwritten from W.S. Hancock. 6pp. Page 2: Blank. Page 6: Advertisements.

(B) **Hancock, The Nation's Choice**. w. A.R. Webb.
(C) **Hancock's Triumphal March**. m. Henry Werner.

WSH-45 The Glory Of A Reunited Nation (Song and Chorus). w. Frank Myrtle. m. Loretz, Jr. Published by Wm. A. Pond & Co., No. 25 Union Square, New York, NY. 1880. B/w litho of Winfield Scott Hancock. "Respectfully Dedicated to Maj. Gen. Winfield S. Hancock by Frank Myrtle." 6pp. Page 2: Blank. Page 6: Advertisement for Wm. A. Pond music.

See also USG-174; JAG-40; JAG-86; JGB-52; GC-94.

WOODROW WILSON

WW-1 March Progressive. m. Amy Titus Worthington. Published by M. Witmark and Sons, No. 10 Witmark Building, New York, NY. 1912. O/w/br cover. B/w tinted photo of Woodrow Wilson, facsimile signature. "By Permission Respectfully Dedicated to Hon. Woodrow Wilson." 6pp. Pages 5 and 6: Advertising.

WW-2 The Man Of The Hour (Wilson Is His Name). w.m. Robert Mortimer. Published by The National Music Publishing Company, New York, NY. 1916. Br/w photo of Woodrow Wilson, eagle with wreaths, flags, geometric designs. "Official Campaign Song adopted by the National Democratic Committee." "I am willing no matter what my personal fortunes may be, to play for the verdict of mankind." 6pp. Page 6: "Wilson and Marshall — Peace, Prosperity and Victory."

WW-3 If You Don't Like Our President Wilson (You Knife the Land That Feeds Us All). w.m. Charles Flagler and W.R. Williams (Writer of The American Tipperary — *We Don't Know Where We're Going But We're On Our Way, Though Duty Calls Its Hard To Say Good-Bye, America To-Day, &c*). Published by Will Rossiter, The Chicago Publisher, No. 71 West Randolph Street, Chicago,

IL. 1917. Br/w Starmer drawing of eagles, geometric designs. N/c photo of Woodrow Wilson. Bl/be photo of "Norma Brandt." "Published for Band and Orchestra." 4pp. Page 4: Advertising.

WW-4 The Woodrow Wilson Inaugural (March and Two-Step). w.m. Newton B. Heims and Jacques Hertz. Published by Newton B. Heims, Music Publisher, Syracuse, NY. 1913. Br/w photo of Woodrow Wilson, facsimile signature. 6pp. Page 3: "Respectfully Dedicated to Hon. Woodrow Wilson, President of the U.S. of A." Page 6: Blank.

WW-5 We're With You Mister Wilson. w.m. Bernie Grossman, Herman Jacobson and Maurice Abrahams. Published by Maurice Abrahams Music Company, No. 1570 Broadway, New York, NY. 1915. O/brbk drawing by Al Barbelle of Woodrow Wilson, Capitol building, cannon, doves. 6pp. Page 6: Advertising.

WW-6 Wilson March. m. Victor LaSalle. Published by Frank K. Root & Company, Chicago, IL. 1912. Bl/w photo of Woodrow Wilson. R/w/b shield design. 6pp. Pages 2 and 6: Advertising.

WW-7 Four Years More In The White House (Should Be the Nation's Gift to You). w. Thomas Hoier. m. Jimmie Morgan. Published by Leo. Feist, Inc., New York, NY. 1916. N/c photo of Woodrow Wilson, facsimile signature. O/bl/w drawings of two eagles with wreaths, Capitol building, Washington Monument. "Portrait of Mr. Wilson used by Permission." 4pp. Page 6: Advertising.

WW-8 We Take Our Hats Off To You — Mr. Wilson. w.m. Blanche Merrill. Published by Leo. Feist, Inc., New York, NY. 1916. N/c photo by Harris and Ewing of Woodrow Wilson, facsimile signature. O/bl/w drawings of two eagles with wreaths, Capitol building, Washington Monument. "Portrait of Mr. Wilson used by Permission." 6pp. Page 6: Advertising.

WW-9 Never Swap Horses When You're Crossing A Stream. w. Harold Robe. m. Jesse Winne. Published by Leo. Feist, Inc., New York, NY. 1916. N/c photo by Harris and Ewing of Woodrow Wilson, facsimile signature. Border drawings of two eagles with wreaths, Capitol building, Washington Monument. "Portrait of Mr. Wilson used by Permission." 4pp. Page 6: Advertising.

WW-10 We'll Vote For The Man Who Kept Us Out Of Was. w. M.A. Jones. m. Phillip Goewey. Published by Jones and Goeway, No. 336 North Street, Pittsfield, MA. 1916. Br/w drawing of U.S. flag. Br/w photo of Woodrow Wilson — "Woodrow Wilson, President of the United States." 4pp. Page 6: Advertising. "Special prices upon application, to Music Dealers, and Democratic Clubs, &c."

WW-11 We Stand For Peace While Others War. w.m. W.R Williams. Published by Will Rossiter, The Chicago Publisher, No. 136 West Lake Street, Chicago, IL. 1914. B/be drawing by Starmer of doves, columns. B/be photo of Woodrow Wilson. 6pp. Page 2: "President Wilson's Appeal To Americans." Long Narrative. Page 3: "Note: This Peace Song was Inspired by President Wilson's Appeal to Americans to remain neutral in thought and deed." Page 6: Advertising.

WW-12 Freedom For All Forever (U.S. War Song and Chorus). w.m. Bertha Haymaker-Dible. Published by Bertha H. Dible, No. 4070 Colonial Avenue, East San Diego, CA. 1918. R/w/b drawing of Uncle Sam, Woodrow Wilson, flags, bell. "Dedicated to the Sammies of Bakerstown, PA." 4pp. Page 4: Blank.

WW-13 Be Good To California, Mr. Wilson (California Was Good to You). w. Andrew B. Sterling. m. Robert A. Keiser. Published by Shapiro, Bernstein and Company, Music Publishers, No. 224 West 47th Street, New York,

NY. 1916. Gy/w photo of Woodrow Wilson. Br/w Starmer drawing of two eagles. "Chorus — Be Good to California, Mr. Wilson, California was good to you, And Don't forget t'was Votes for Women helped to win the Vict'ty too, For when the tide was turning fast against you, she made your dream come true, Be Good to California, Mr. Wilson, California was good to you. 4pp. Page 4: Advertising.

WW-14   We're Going To Celebrate The End Of The War In Ragtime (Be Sure That Woodrow Wilson Leads the Band). w.m. Coleman Goetz and Jack Stern. Published by Shapiro, Bernstein and Company, Music Publishers, No. 224 West 47th Street, New York, NY. 1915. O/w/bl/bk/br drawing by DeTakacs of Woodrow Wilson, band, doves, leaves. Bl/w photo of Nora Bayes — As Introduced by the incomparable Nora Bayes." 6pp. Pages 2 and 6: Advertising.

WW-15   The Hero Of The European War. w. Al Dubin. m. George B. McConnell and Joseph A. Burke. Published by Emmett J. Welch, Music Publisher, Colonial Theatre Building, 15th Street below Chestnut Street, Philadelphia, PA. 1916. Gy/w photo by Harris and Ewing of Woodrow Wilson, facsimile signature. R/w/bl/gy drawing of U.S. flag, eagle, star. 6pp. Pages 2 and 6: Advertising.

WW-16   What A Real American Can Do. w. Roger Graham. m. May Hill and Billy Johnson. Published by Roger Graham, No. 145 North Clark Street, Chicago, IL. 1917. R/w/b drawing of stars and stripes, silhouetted soldier. Bl/w photos and drawings of Woodrow Wilson, George Washington, Ben Franklin, Abraham Lincoln, Ulysses S. Grant, Thomas Edison, Admiral Sampson, Admiral Dewey. 6pp. Page 6: Advertising.

WW-17   When Johnnie Comes Marching Home Again. w.m. Charles B. Weston (Writer of *Over Here*). Published by Charles B. Weston, No. 5819 Fifth Avenue, Brooklyn, NY. 1918. B/w photo of Woodrow Wilson. B/w drawing of soldiers marching. "The Wilson Victory Smile — *New York World*, Sept. 28, 1918." 4pp. Page 4: Blank.

WW-18   When Johnnie Comes Marching Home Again. w.m. Charles B. Weston. Published by Charles Weston, No. 5819 5th Avenue, Brooklyn, NY. 1918. Bl/w photo of Woodrow Wilson. "The Wilson Victory Smile — *New York World*, Sept. 28, 1918." 4pp. Page 4: Advertising.

WW-19   Sail On Victorious, Unseen Sail (A Shorthand History of the U.S.A.). w. J.H. Edwards (Secretary). m. L.H. Hurlburt-Edwards (Director). Published by The Oregon Conservatory of Music, No. 165 1/2 4th Street, Portland, OR. Copyright 1918 by J.H. Edwards. [9 1/2" × 12 3/8"]. Be/bk drawing of ship. Be/bk drawings/photos of all Presidents form George Washington to Woodrow Wilson, shield inscribed "U.S.A. Grand Staff." 8pp. Page 2: "Dedicated to Synocha Partout." Pages 6 to 8: Words to songs for which music is solicited — $10.00 offered for "most Appropriate melody."

WW-20   Get Busy Over Here Or Over There (Work or Fight) (Song). w.m. Edward Laska (Writer of *Do Something*). Published by Jerome H. Remick and Company, New York, NY. 1918. Bl/br/o litho of workers, ship builders, soldiers, ships. "A Song Expression of Provost Marshall Gen. E.H. Crowder Famous 'Work or Fight' Order." "The Song that Predicted this order at the time of President Wilson's Declaration of War." "It is not an Army we must shape and train for war, it is a nation — Woodrow Wilson." 4pp. Page 4: Advertising.

WW-21   The Ace Of Smiles. w.m. Anna May Ross. Published by Ross Music Company, No. 31 Rausch Street, San Francisco, CA. 1919. Br/be/gd floral and geometric designs with photo of Woodrow Wilson waving hat. 4pp. Page 4: Blank.

WW-22 I Think We've Got Another Washington (And Wilson Is His Name). w.m. George Fairman. Published by Kendis Music Publishing Company, No. 145 West 45th Street, New York, NY. 1915. R/w/bl/br drawing of shield, Uncle Sam, George Washington and Woodrow Wilson. "A Popular Patriotic Song." 6pp. Pages 2 and 6: Advertising.

WW-23 Fall In — For Your Motherland. w. President Woodrow Wilson. m. Dr. Frank Black and John L. Golden. Published by T.B. Harms, New York, NY. 1916. [9" × 12"]. Bl/w photo of Woodrow Wilson. R/w/b stars, eagle, facsimile letter — "The White House, Washington, April 17, 1916; My Dear Mr. Golden: Mrs. Wilson and I were greatly pleased to see you and to hear the march, and I am writing to say how sincerely I hope you will have great success in launching it. It quickens the blood and carries a spur which only music, apparently can use and I am sincerely complemented that you should have chosen the words for the song from my speeches. I envy those who can make any great impulse particularly the great impulse of patriotism, move in such strains and accents as will quicken the pulse of a whole people, Cordially yours, Woodrow Wilson." "Music by Dr. Frank Black and John Golden, As sung in the All Soldier Show *The Army Play By Play*, Produced by John Golden and the Second Service Command." 6pp. Page 6: Blank.

WW-24 Row On, Woodrow, Row On. w. Col. M.V.B. Blood. m. Eugene Platzmann. Published by F.B. Haviland Publishing Company, No. 128 West 48th Street, New York, NY. 1918. R/w/b drawing of Woodrow Wilson rowing boat toward Europe and the Kaiser, city skyline burning. Bl/w photo of "Col. M.V.B. Blood." "Dedicated to President Woodrow Wilson." 4pp. Page 4: Blank.

WW-25 Woodrow Wilson, The Whole World's Proud Of You. w.m. Charles T. Keating. Published by Charles T. Keating, Des Moines, IA. 1918. N/c drawing of Woodrow Wilson. 4pp. Page 4: Arrangement for "Male or Mixed Quartette."

WW-26 Woodrow Wilson For President (Song). w. Simon McCullough. m. Carl Seyb. Published by Needham Music Company, St. Louis, MO. 1916. B/w non-pictorial geometric designs. 6pp. Page 6: Blank.

WW-27 Democracy! (Or Allies, Hurrah, Allies!). w.m. Miss Reka Goldberg. Published in "New York, Chicago and San Francisco." 1918. Drawing of a soldier with gun and U.S. and Allied flags. 4pp. Page 2: "Dedicated to President Wilson and all Patriots." Page 4: Blank.

WW-28 We Have The Right Man Now. w. J.F. Smith. m. J.F. Ryan. Published by Smith & Ryan, No. 30 Church Street, New York, NY. 1916. O/bk/w drawing of Woodrow Wilson being carried by soldiers. 6pp. Page 2: Blank. Page 6: Advertising.

WW-29 Wilson Democracy And The Red White And Blue. w.m. Pvt. William H. Hollingsworth, Med. Corps. Published by Haward Publishing Company, Ricksecker Building, Kansas City, MO. 1918. R/w/b drawing of Statue of Liberty, stars and stripes background. Bl/w photo of Pvt. William H. Hollingsworth. 4pp. Page 4: Advertising.

WW-30 Soldiers Of The U.S.A. w.m. Mrs. John Kyle. Published by Mrs. John Kyle, Springfield, OH. 1918. Drawing of "Woodrow Wilson, Commander-in-Chief." 4pp. Page 2: "Dedicated to our President Woodrow Wilson." "Written for Red Cross Day." Page 4: Blank.

WW-31 We're Bound To Win With Boys Like You. w.m. Kendis-Brockman and Nat Vincent. Published by Kendis-Brockman Music Company, Inc., No. 145 West 45th Street, New York, NY. 1918. R/w/b drawings of "Pres. Wilson," Admiral "Dewey," Theodore "Roosevelt," Abraham "Lincoln," Ulysses

S. "Grant," George "Washington," Robert E. "Lee," General "Pershing," soldier, sailor, geometric designs. Bl/w photo of "Ed Martin." 4pp. Page 4: Advertising.

WW-32 Our Wilson Is The Greatest Man The World Has Ever Known. w. Adelbert Reynolds. m. Carl Demangate. Published by Harrington & Reynolds, Publishers, Glens Falls, NY. 1919. [10 2/4" × 13 5/8"]. R/w/b drawing of United States and British flags, eagle, shield. B/w photos of Woodrow Wilson and Adelbert Reynolds, "Adelbert Reynolds, Trumpeter U.S.W.V. Wilson Camp No. 8 Dept., New York." 4pp. Page 4: Blank.

WW-33 Good-Bye, Shot And Shell. w. Lou Spero. m. Gerald Peck. Published by Joseph W. Stern and Company, Nos. 102-104 West 38th Street, New York, NY. 1919. [9 1/8" × 12 1/4"]. Br/w geometric designs. Br/w photo of Woodrow Wilson. "Introduced successfully by Mr. Warwick Williams." "Dedicated to Pres. Wilson and his world famous policy of lasting peace through a concert of power by a League of Nations, the Great and Final enterprise of Humanity." "And back of us is that imperative yearning of the world, to have all disturbing questions quieted, to have just men everywhere come together from a common object. The peoples of the world want peace and they want it now, not merely by conquest of arms but by agreement of minds — From President Wilson's speech at Guildhall, London, Dec. 28, 1918." 4pp. Page 4: Advertising.

WW-34 President Wilson's Wedding March. m. George Fairman. Published by George Fairman, No. 145 West 45th Street, New York, NY. 1915. Y/bl drawing of bell inscribed "Respectfully Dedicated to President Woodrow Wilson and Mrs. Norman Galt," "To the summons of love the whole world sends its greetings." R/w/b silk ribbon attached. 6pp. Pages 2 and 6: Advertising.

WW-35 Wilson Has A Winnin' Way (And a Gosh-Darned Way of Winnin'). w. C.R. Foster. m. I.A. Foster. Published by C.R. Foster Company, No. 845 South Broadway, Los Angeles, CA. 1916. B/w drawing of elephant, moose, feed inscribed "Platitudes, Promises, Criticism," donkey with feed barrel inscribed "8 Hour Day, Child Labor Law, Federal Reserve Bill, Peace, Rural Credits," Uncle Sam, small Teddy Bear with Theodore Roosevelt smile and glasses. "Greatest Comedy Song Sensation." 6pp. Pages 2 and 6: Advertising.

WW-36 Go Right Along Mr. Wilson (And We'll All Stand By You) (Song). w.m. A. Seymour Brown. Published by Jerome H. Remick and Company, New York, NY. 1915. R/w/bl/br Starmer drawing of shield, wreath, eagle. 6pp. Page 6: Advertising.

WW-37 Wilson (You're the Man Behind the Man Behind the Gun) (March Song). w.m. Lee Johnson. Published by Lee Johnson Music Publishing Company, Los Angeles, CA. 1919. [Pre-1919 size]. Bl/bk/w cover, drawing of the Capitol building. B/w photo of Woodrow Wilson." "Endorsed by the County Central Committee, Dan W. Simms, Chairman; F. Ray Graves, Secretary." "Respectfully Dedicated to 'Our President,' the Emancipator of World's Liberty." 4pp.

WW-38 World-Wide Democracy March. m. Wm. C. Rehm. Published by Wm. C. Rehm, New York, NY. 1917. R/w/b flags. B/w Pach Bros. photo of Woodrow Wilson. B/w drawings of a man on a pedestal inscribed "War" and a woman on a pedestal inscribed "Peace," Capitol building, eagle with ribbon inscribed "E Pluribus Unum." "Most Respectfully Inscribed to Woodrow Wilson, President of the United States." "For sale at all principal music stores." 8pp. Pages 2, 7 and 8: Blank.

WW-39 It's Time For Every Boy To Be A Soldier (Song). w. Alfred Bryan.

m. Harry Tierney. Published by Jerome H. Remick and Company, Detroit, MI. 1917. R/br/w drawings of Woodrow Wilson and Abraham Lincoln. R/w/br drawing of a soldier, Capitol building. 4pp. Page 4: Advertising.

WW-40 It's Time For Every Boy To Be A Soldier (Song). w. Alfred Bryan. m. Harry Tierney. Published by Jerome H. Remick and Company, New York, NY. 1917. Bl/w tinted photos of Woodrow Wilson and Abraham Lincoln. O/bl/w/br drawings of a soldier, Capitol building. 4pp. Page 4: Advertising.

WW-41 I Think We've Got Another Washington And Wilson Is His Name. w.m. George Fairman. Published by George Fairman, No. 145 West 45th Street, New York, NY. 1915. B/w litho of hands pointing to a facsimile letter — "New York City, Feb. 22, To The American Public, Dear Friends: I Think We've Got Another Washington and Wilson is his Name, Yours Truly, Geo. Fairman." 6pp. Pages 2 and 6: Advertising.

WW-42 Our Nation's Glory. m. Rev. Herman Benmosche (of Norfolk, Virginia). Copyright 1913 by Rev. Herman Benmosche. R/w/b crossed flags, eagle, shield. Br/w photos of "Our Chief Woodrow Wilson" and Reverend Benmosche. "National Song and Chorus Written in Appreciation of the Patriotism Displayed by the Town of Winthrop, July 4, 1918." 6pp. Pages 2 and 6: Blank.

WW-43 Emblem Of Freedom. w. Thomas Ostenson Stine. m. C. Blom. Published by Thomas Ostenson Stine, Seattle, WA. 1918. R/w/b crossed flags, stripe border. Bl/w photo of Woodrow Wilson. "Dedicated to President Woodrow Wilson." "Third Edition — 1918." 4pp. Page 2: "Mixed Voices." Page 3: "Male Voices." Page 4: Poem by Thomas Ostenson Stine — "Heaven on Earth."

WW-44 Patriotic Songs Of To-Day For Every American Home. Published by Lew Brock Music, Rochester, NY. 1917. R/w stripes. Bl/bk/w photo/drawings of Woodrow Wilson, George Washington and Abraham Lincoln. 8pp.

WW-45 President Wilson U.S.A. (Song). w. Jewell Ellison (Composer of *On To Berlin And Victory, Somewhere In France Tonight, Who's Who In Berlin, I'll Be Waiting Sweetheart, In The U.S.A.*). m. Lee G. Kratz. Published by Jewell Ellison, Lucas, SD. 1918. R/w/b crossed flags, drawing of Woodrow Wilson, wreath, soldier, sailor. "Justice, Love and Honor." "Democracy, the Savior of the World." 4pp. Page 4: Advertising.

WW-46 Meet Me In Dallas (Be Sure and Meet Me). w.m. Jack Gardner. Published by George McBlair, Dallas, TX. 1916. Br/gn/w Kit Ott drawing of two eagles, rooster, man riding a donkey with luggage inscribed "National Democratic Convention 1916." Gn/w photo of downtown Dallas. "Approved by Henry D. Linsley, Mayor of Dallas." 6pp. Page 6: Blank.

WW-47 Flying Fighters For Freedom. w.m. Marion L. Ward. Published by Gordon Publishing Company. Copyright 1918 by Marion L. Ward, Omaha, NE. R/w/b drawing of Uncle Sam in an airplane dropping bombs on a torpedo in the shape of the Kaiser. "Lovingly Dedicated to that Great Leader of Nations, President Woodrow Wilson, Commander-In-Chief of all America's War Forces." 4pp. Page 4: Advertising.

WW-48 Answer Mr. Wilson's Call. w.m. Billy Gould. Published by J. Stasny Music Company, No. 56 West 45th Street, New York, NY. 1917. R/w/bl/br Al. Barbelle drawing of soldier, sailor, ships, eagles. Bl/w tinted photo of Woodrow Wilson. 4pp. Page 4: Advertising.

WW-49 Allies Victorious March. m. C. DeCristoforo. Copyright 1918 by C. DeCristoforo. R/w/b drawing of cheering crowd, eagle, crossed U.S. flags. Bl/w photos of Woodrow Wilson, four Allied leaders. "Democracy, Nov. 11, 1918." 6pp. Pages 2 and 6: Blank.

WW-50 Where Our Wilson Shines Democracy (Patriotic March Song). w.m. Michael Perna. Published by Michael Perna, Boston, MA. 1918. R/w/b silhouette of soldiers marching, sun. "Respectfully Dedicated to His Excellency — The President." 4pp. Page 4: Blank.

WW-51 Give Us A League Of Nations. w.m. Jere De Graff. Published by Jere De Graff, Brooklyn, NY. 1919. [8 5/8" × 11 5/8"]. Br/w drawings of doves, palm branches. "Respectfully Dedicated to Our Great President Woodrow Wilson." "The Free peoples of the world, united to defeat the enemies of liberty and justice, now through their representatives wrought out a plan by which they may remain united in a free partnership of intimate council to promote the cause of justice and of freedom through the beneficent processes of peace and the accords of a liberal policy. It is within the choice of thoughtful men of every nation to enrich the peace of their counsel." 4pp. Page 4: Blank.

WW-52 He's Everybody's President Now. w.m. J.T. Mills, Jr. Published by J.T. Mills, Jr., Music Publisher, Allmondsville, VA. 1915. R/w/b drawing of flag, The White House. B/w photo of Woodrow Wilson in gd/w eagle frame. 6pp. Page 6: Advertising.

WW-53 America's Day (War Song). w.m. Martin J. O'Mahony. Published by *The Patriot* Printing and Publishing Company, Nos. 128-130 Sumpter Street, Brooklyn, NY. 1917. B/w drawing of ribbon, fancy letters — "USA," geometric designs. B/w photo of Woodrow Wilson. "Composed and Dedicated by Permission to Hon. Woodrow Wilson, President of the United States." 6pp. Page 2: "Photographic reproduction of the President's letter of acceptance — Personal, My Dear Sir: The President asks me to acknowledge the receipt of your letter of April 18th, with enclosure, and to thank you for your concern in writing. He deeply appreciates the compliment which you pay him and that sentiment to which you give expression." Page 6: Song verses.

WW-54 Wilson — That's All. w. Ballard MacDonald. m. George Walter Brown. Published by Shapiro Music Publishing Company, Music Publishers, corner Broadway and Thirty-Ninth Street, New York, NY. 1912. O/gy/bk/w Starmer geometric design. B/w Pach Brothers photo of Woodrow Wilson. "Introduced by Julia Ring in *The Yankee Girl* Co." 6pp. Pages 2 and 6: Advertising. Page 3: "Respectfully Dedicated to Hon. James J. Walker, New York."

WW-55 Stand By The President Now! w. Edward Newton Voorhees. m. Susan Schmitt. Published by The Boston Music Company, Boston, MA., as a supplement to *The Boston Sunday Advertiser*, Sunday, August 11, 1918. [9 1/4" × 10 7/8"]. B/w photo of Woodrow Wilson, geometric designs. "War Songs." 4pp. Page 2: "Respectfully Dedicated to President Woodrow Wilson." Page 4: Advertising.

WW-56 League Of Nations March. m. William T. Pierson (Composer of *Sons of America*, *Carry On* and *Just A Song of Home*). Published by W.T. Pierson & Company, Washington, DC. 1919. N/c drawing by Charles Hoover of various League of Nations' flags. Bl/w of "Woodrow Wilson photos (by Underwood and Underwood)," "David Lloyd George (by British Official Photo)," "Georges Clemenceau," "Vittorio Orlando (Central News Photo)" and "Baron Makino (by Harris & Ewing)." 6pp. Page 6: Advertising.

WW-57 In The Beautiful Isle Of Somewhere. w.m. P. Douglas Bird. Published by The Galilean Press, No. 1636 Dale Street, San Diego, CA. 1924. B/w photo of Woodrow Wilson. "This song was sung from M.S. by the Composer at both morning and evening services at the Trinity M.E. Church, San Diego, Calif, on the 3rd February, 1924, Daniel Dundas, Pastor." 4pp.

WW-58 The Man Of The Hour. w.m. Kingsley Hall. Published by National Music Publishing Company, New York, NY. 1916. R/w/bl/bk/br drawing of Woodrow Wilson, Abraham Lincoln, George Washington, Ulysses S. Grant, William McKinley, James Garfield, eagle. 6pp. Pages 2 and 6: Blank.

WW-59 The Beautiful Isle Of Somewhere. w. Mrs. Jessie Brown Pounds. m. J.S. Feraris. In: *The Boston Sunday Post*, October 22, 1911. Copyright 1901 by E.O. Excell. Non-pictorial. "This Hymn was Recently Condemned by Governor Woodrow Wilson of New Jersey. Owing to the Interest of the Discussion Thus Raised, Arrangements have been made to Publish it for the Benefit of *Sunday Post* readers." "Written for the Funeral of President McKinley — Approved by John D. Rockefeller."

WW-60 Our Uncle Sam (March Song). w.m. June Bauer. Published by June Bauer Company, Inc., Judsonia, AR. 1918. R/w/b drawing of Woodrow Wilson as pilot of ship, Uncle Sam helping. 4pp. Page 4: Advertising.

WW-61 Wilson's Inaugural March. m. H. Kirkus Dugdale (Composer of *Alumni March, Ad. Club March, &c*). Published & Sold by The H. Kirkus Dugdale Company, Inc., "The Big Music Publishers," Washington, DC. 1913. R/w/b shield. Bl/w drawing of Woodrow Wilson. 6pp. Pages 2 and 6: Blank.

WW-62 In The Shade Of Shadow Lawn (Ballad). w.m. Maitland S. Wright. Published by the M.S. Wright Publishing Company, Washington, DC. 1916. B/w photo by Underwood and Underwood of house — "Shadow Lawn — The Summer White House." "Trade supplied by E.F. Droop, Washington, D.C." 6pp. Pages 2 and 6: Blank.

WW-63 We Take Our Hats Off To You — Mr. Wilson! w.m. Blanche Merrill. Published by Leo Feist, New York, NY. 1914. Br/w drawing of eagle, geometric designs. Br/w photos of "Woodrow Wilson" [facsimile signature], "Nora Bayes," cheering crowd. "The Great American Peace Song." 6pp. Page 6: Advertising for other music.

WW-64 American Battle Song. w. Ella L. Watts. m. Edward Potjes (of Ward-Belmont School of Music, Nashville, formerly of Royal Conservatory of Ghent, Belgium). Published by Standard Music Company, Nashville, TN. Copyright 1917 by Edward Potjes. Non-pictorial. "Dedicated to Woodrow Wilson, President of the United States." 6pp. Pages 2 and 6: Blank.

WW-65 Columbia (A March). m. Charles Astin, Op. 180. Copyright 1926 by Charles Astin (P.O. Box 90, Atlanta, GA.). R/w/b flag, wreath. Bl/w drawings of Woodrow Wilson and George Washington. "To Betsy Ross — If we would live by the emblems true, Fixed in our flag, The Red, White and Blue, The rest of the world could never undo America — Then let us not worship 'The Golden Calf' Shall Nineveh plead in our behalf In the day when idols are turned to chaff, America? — Oh Michael thou warrior in Heaven above, Aid in our cause with thy sword of love That we may be the peaceful white dove — America." 6pp. Page 2: Title — **Columbia** (Grand March). "To the Memory of Betsy Ross." Pages 4 to 6: Song — **The Star Spangled Banner**. w. Francis Scott Key. a. Charles Astin.

WW-66 For The Honor Of Uncle Sam. w.m. James A. Dillon. Published by Dillon-Praetorius Music Company, No. 1431 Broadway, New York, NY. 1917. R/w/b drawings by Theodore C. Ruehl of Woodrow Wilson shaking hands with Theodore Roosevelt, Uncle Sam, soldier, old man, eagle, ribbon. 6pp. Pages 2 and 6: Blank.

WW-67 There Is Glory In Old Glory. w. Mrs. L.M. Sligh. m. Jack Gardner. Published by Thomas Goggan and Bros., Dallas, TX. 1917. R/w/b shield design. Bl/w drawing by Zeese of military

WW-66

WW-70

camp scene. Bl/w of photos and drawings of Woodrow Wilson, George Washington, Ulysses S. Grant, Abraham Lincoln, Robert E. Lee. 4pp. Page 4: Blank.

WW-68 **Our Flag.** w. Mancle M. Grant. m. Churchill-Grindell. Published by Churchill-Grindell Company, Platteville, WI. 1917. R/w/b drawing of flag, Statue of Liberty, soldier. "Dedicated to President Wilson." Six bars of music. 6pp. Page 6: Advertising for song books.

WW-69 **Everywhere That Wilson Goes**. w.m. Charles R. McCarron, Henry Lewis and Carey Morgan (Writers of *Oh, Hellen, Wait And See, I'm Glad I Can Make You Cry, &c*). Published by Joseph W. Stern and Company, Nos. 102 to 104 West 38th Street, New York, NY. 1919. Bl/w Starmer design cover with bl/w photo of [V-1: Henry Lewis] [V-2: Geo. Jessell], geometric designs. 4pp.

WW-70 **The Ship Named U.S.A.** (Or Wilson's War Cry of Peace). w. James F. Whitehorn and T.F. Ambrose. m. Wm. Loraine. Published by Whitehorn and Ambrose, Publishers, Los Angeles, CA. 1915. Bl/w photo of Woodrow Wilson—"Our President." R/w/b drawing of a battleship. "Dedicated to Woodrow Wilson." 6pp. Pages 2 and 6: Blank.

WW-71 **(Nobody Knows How I Miss You) Dear Old Pals**. w.m. Eddie Dorr and Lew Porter. Published by Meyer Cohen Music, No. 1531 Broadway, New York, NY. 1919. R/w/bk photos of soldier and family — "The departure" and "The return." "Scenes from *Friendly Enemies*, A.H. Wood's Big Success." "Endorsed by President Wilson." "The President said — All that I can say has already been said most admirably about this beautiful play. All the sentiments I Could express have been admirably represented — sentiments that, I hope, will soon grip the world." 4pp.

WW-72 **'Till We Win** (Flag Song and Special Chorus). w.m. George R. Laird. Published by E.F. Droop and Sons, Washington, DC. 1918. Bl/w photo by Harris & Ewing of Woodrow Wilson. "Under freedom's flag we shall fight 'Till We Win — President Wilson speaking at the Capitol." "Respectfully Dedicated to President Woodrow Wilson and all those who will fight with him under freedom's flag 'Till We Win' a lasting peace for liberty and justice." "Now here's to the President, our fearless leader for the Stars and Stripes, a Peerless Leader! With him Old Glory shall new glories win and will fight for our flag, boys, we'll fight 'Till we win!" "The President's March." 4pp. Page 4: Blank.

WW-73 Our Wilson Again. w. Patrick Kane. m. Joseph T. Layton. Published by Joseph T. Layton and Company, No. 6511 South Artesian Avenue, Chicago, IL. Copyright 1916 by Patrick Kane. R/w/b litho of Woodrow T. Wilson, shield, and flags. "Our President Woodrow Wilson." 6pp.

WW-74 Woodrow Wilson March. m. Axie A. Lowthian. Published by Axie A. Lowthian, Camp Verde, AZ. 1914. R/w/b litho of Woodrow Wilson, shield, flags, laurel. 6pp. Pages 2 and 6: Blank.

WW-75 The Man With The Iron Shoe. w.m. Daniel Wilkinson. Published by Daniel Wilkinson, Paris, IL. 1912. R/w/b litho of Woodrow Wilson, shield and flags. "For President." 6pp. Page 4: Arrangement for Mixed Quartet. Page 5: Arrangement for Male Quartet.

WW-76 (Read Between the Stars and Stripes and Spell) Humanity (Song). w.m. I. Della Taylor. Copyright 1918 by Della Taylor, South Orange, NJ. Non-pictorial. "And my dream is this...That America will come into the full light of that day when all shall know she puts human rights above all other rights, and that her flag is the flag, not only of America but the flag of humanity — President Woodrow Wilson, to whom this song is dedicated." 4pp.

WW-77 When I Return To The U.S.A. And You (March Song). w. Olivia Faress Dinkins. m. Myrtle Mae McCay. Published by Proctor-Patterson Music Company, Inc., Macon, GA. Copyright 1910 by Olivia Faress Dinkins. R/w non-pictorial designs. "To Our Honored President — Woodrow Wilson." 4pp. Page 4: Advertising.

WW-78 Woodrow Wilson March. m. F.G. Simpson. Published by A.W. Perry & Sons' Music Company, Sedalia, MO. Copyright 1913 by F.G. Simpson. Br/w litho of acorns, geometric design border. 4pp. Page 4: Blank.

WW-79 The U.S.A. (Patriotic Song). w.m. Henry Champness. Published by Champness and Desmarais, No. 55 Greenwich Avenue, New York, NY. 1917. R/w/bl/br drawing of Woodrow Wilson, flag. "The Honor of Our Nation Must be Upheld Today, The same as when the Spirit of Seventy-six Made the U.S.A." "Dedicated to the man of the hour."

WW-80 Wilson March. m. Blanche A. Roussin. Published by Orpheus Music Publishing Company, Lowell, MA. Copyright 1912 by Blanche A. Roussin. B/w litho of flowers. "Respectfully Dedicated to His Excellency Woodrow Wilson." "For Piano." 6pp. Page 6: Blank.

WW-81 As Our (President Comes/Boys Come) Sailing Home. w. Edith Rojean Orne. m. George Lowell Tracy. Published by C.W. Thompson & Company, Boston, MA. 1919. R/w/b drawing of liberty ship, dove, palm branches. "The National Peace Song." 4pp. Page 4: Advertising for other music.

WW-82 W-I-L-S-O-N Means Wilson With The Good Old U.S.A. At His Command. w. S. Edw. Sanfilippo. m. Billy H. Hickey and Daniel D. Rappaport. Published by James S. White Company, Inc., Music Publishers, No. 224 Tremont Street, Boston, MA. 1917. Bl/w photo by Harris and Ewing of Woodrow Wilson. R/w drawing of cannons. 4pp. Page 4: Advertising.

WW-83 America's President Song. w. E.B. DeLangevin. m. E.S.S. Huntington. Published by T.R. Banks, Tacoma, WA. 1917. R/w/bk drawings of Woodrow T. Wilson, George Washington and Abraham Lincoln. 4pp. Page 4: Blank.

WW-84 Woodrow Wilson's Grand March. m. Fred Kimball Conant. Published by Fred Kimball Conant, Boston, MA. 1913. B/w drawing by Seymour Thomas of Woodrow Wilson. Pl/w geometric designs. "Respectfully Dedicated to Woodrow Wilson, President of the United States of America." 6pp. Pages 2 and 6: Blank.

WW-85 When All The World's At Peace. w. Fleta Jan Brown. m. Charles N. Grant. Published by F.B. Haviland Publishing Company, Strand Theatre Building, Broadway at 47th Street, New York, NY. 1914. R/w/b photos/drawings of George Washington, Abraham Lincoln, Ulysses S. Grant, Robert E. Lee, William Jennings Bryan and Woodrow Wilson, doves, sun. "The International Peace Song." 8pp. Page 2: Blank. Page 8: Advertising.

WW-86 Fall Into Line For Your Motherland (A National Song). w. "The words of Woodrow Wilson." m. John L. Golden. In: *The World Magazine*, August 20, 1916, page 16. Copyright 1916 by T.B. Harms and Francis, Day & Hunter. [10 5/8" × 18"]. B/w photos of "Woodrow Wilson" and "John L. Golden." "On page 12 inside is reprinted a letter from President Wilson commending this song." 12pp.

WW-87 Hurrah! Hurrah! For The U.S.A. (Patriotic March Song). m. George B. Mann. Published by Star Music Company, Eldred, PA. 1917. R/w drawings and photos of George "Washington," Abraham "Lincoln," Ulysses S. "Grant" and Woodrow "Wilson." Bl/w drawing of Uncle Sam, Statue of Liberty. 4pp. Page 4: Advertising for *Rough Riders March* by H.A. Fischler.

WW-88 America's Leader. w. Luke A. Keenan. m. Rubey Cowen. Published by Luke Keenan, No. 475 11th Avenue, Long Island City, NY. 1916. Bl/w photo by Underwood and Underwood of Woodrow Wilson. R/w/b drawings of flag, eagle, star, wreath. "A Statesman, and a Patriot True, America is proud of you Our Leader Woodrow Wilson." 8pp. Page 2: Extra verses. Page 7: "An American Toast." Page 8: Blank.

WW-89 We'll Link His Name With Lincoln. w.m. William Jerome and J.F. Mahoney. Published by F.B. Haviland Publishing Company, Nos. 112-114 West 44th Street, New York, NY. Copyright 1924 by William Jerome. B/w Pach Bros. photo of Woodrow Wilson, geometric design frame. 6pp. Pages 2 and 6: Advertising. Page 3: "To the Memory of Woodrow Wilson, The Hearts of the World Were in his Heart."

WW-90 When Wilson Called The Kaiser's Bluff. w.m. L.F. Newman. Published by Newman, No. 161 West 3rd Street, New York, NY. [ca. 1917]. Photo of L.F. Newman. Drawing of the Kaiser running. Verse. "One of the latest war songs."

WW-91 Good Government March. m. Louis Decker, Op. 2. Published by Louis Decker, Publisher, Glen Falls, NY. 1914. Br/w photo by Harris and Ewing of Woodrow Wilson. Bl/w nonpictorial cover. "To my Classmate Woodrow Wilson, President of the United States." 6pp. Page 6: Advertising for other Louis Decker music.

WW-92 Hail To America! w.m. G. Herb Palin. Copyright 1917 by G. Herb Palin. R/w/bl/br drawings of the U.S. flag and eagle. "Respectfully Dedicated to the Nation's President in the Hour of America's need." 6pp. Pages 2 and 6: Blank.

WW-93 We Will Honor You Forever (March Song). w. M.C. Fekete. m. J. Psota. Published by Music Printing Company, Inc., New York, NY. Copyright 1919 by M.C. Fekete and J. Psota. Bl/w photo of Woodrow Wilson. R/w/b drawing of Capitol dome, allied flags, eagle. "Dedicated to Our President Woodrow Wilson." 6pp. Pages 2 and 6: Blank.

WW-94 We Want Wilson In

The White House Four More Years. w.m. James Kendis. Published by The Kendis Music Publishing Company, No. 145 West 45th Street, New York, NY. 1916. Bl/w drawing of Woodrow Wilson, drawing of Capitol building. 6pp. Page 2: Advertising for other music. Page 6: Blank.

WW-95 Our Wilson Is The Greatest Man The World Has Ever Known. w. Adelbert Reynolds. m. Carl Demangate. Published by The Plattsburg Radio Supply Company, Plattsburg, NY., as a post card. Copyright 1919 by Adelbert Reynolds. [Edition ca. 1924]. [3 1/2" × 5 1/2"]. Obv: N/c photo of Woodrow Wilson—"He wanted peace." Printed chorus of song. "Woodrow Wilson 28th President of the United States, Born at Staunton, Va., Dec. 28, 1856, Died at Washington on Feb. 3, 1924, Aged 67 years." Rev: Long biographical sketch of important life events.

WW-96 Wilson For President (A Campaign Song). w. W.M. Wheatly and C.H. Hitchner. m. Paul Jones. Published by The Praise Publishing Company, No. 46 North 12th Street, Philadelphia, PA. Copyright 1912 by W.M. Wheatly and C.H. Hitchner. B/w photo of "Honor. Woodrow Wilson." R/w floral and geometric designs. 4pp. Page 4: Blank.

WW-97 The Allies March. m. Joseph Biondi. Published by Joseph Biondi, No. 1713 East 2nd Street, Brooklyn, NY. 1918. R/w/b drawing by Pfeiffer of soldiers marching, eagle, shield, Allied flags. Bl/w photo of "President Wilson." 6pp. Pages 2 and 6: Blank. Page 3: "Respectfully Dedicated to Our President, Woodrow Wilson."

WW-98 The Glory Of Peace. w. Henry Kessler. m. Carl A. Egener. Published by Carl A. Egener and Henry Kessler, No. 543 Eighth Avenue, New York, NY. 1914. Bl/bk/w drawing of globe with dove, palm branches. "Respectfully Dedicated to and Accepted by Our President Woodrow Wilson." 6pp. Page 6: Advertising.

WW-99 Bing! Bang! Bing 'Em On The Rhine (Comic Song). w.m. Jack Mahoney and Allan Flynn. Published by Jerome H. Remick and Company, New York, NY. 1918. R/w/bk cover with B/w tinted photo of Blanche Ring—"As sung by Blanche Ring." Slogans—"They won't take a drink of Pilsen, They'll get Haig and Haig and Wilson." "We'll hit Berlin like a Rocket, Get the 'Watch Am Rhine' and hock it;" "And when we all go swimming in the Rhine, We'll hang our clothes on Hindenburg's old line;" "This Sounds ever so much sweeter on a forty-centimeter." 4pp. Page 4: Advertising.

WW-100 President Wilson's Triumphal March. m. Mrs. Olla Hewitt (Composer of *Sweet Echo Waltz, Boys in France, &c*). Published by Mrs. Olla Hewitt, Weed, CA. 1918. R/w/b flag. Photo of Woodrow Wilson. 4pp.

WW-101 The Sammies Are Off To War. w. H. Lionel Broom. m. Eddie Elliott and W. Max Davis. Published by The DuQuesne Music Company, "Publishers of Music," Atlantic City, NJ. 1917. Bl/w photo of Woodrow Wilson. R/w/b drawing by Pfeiffer of a parade of Uncle Sams, soldier, sailor, flag. 4pp. Page 4: Advertising.

WW-102 America Awake! (The Yankee Camp Song). w.m. George Clinton Baker. Published by Liberty Publishing Company, Santa Barbara, CA. 1918. R/w/bl/be drawing of Uncle Sam with gun, marching troops. 6pp. Page 2: Wilson quote—"I summon you, not only to sustain, but to swell the hosts that have their forces now set toward the light..." Page 3: "To Woodrow Wilson, our illustrious President and intrepid Commander-In-Chief, this song is faithfully dedicated."

WW-103 Gone. w.m. Marie Bruck. Published by Marie Bruck, Memphis, TN. 1924. Photo of Woodrow Wilson, leaves. 6pp. Page 2: Blank. Page 3:

"Lovingly Dedicated to the Memory of Woodrow Wilson."

WW-104 Let Us Stand By The President. w.m. B. Anna Rosenberg. Published by American Publishing Company, No. 2832 38th Avenue South, Minneapolis, MN. 1917. R/w/b drawing of Uncle Sam. Bl/w photo of child in military uniform. "Successfully Introduced by Evelyn Harkins." 4pp. Page 4: Blank.

WW-105 At The White House Ball. w.m. Harry Manthal-Lieberman (Writer of *Cause I Like You, &c.*). Published by Independent Music Publishing Company, New York, NY. 1916. Bl/w photo of White House, [V-1: Bl/w photo of "June Mills"—"Sung with Great Success by June Mills." Different editions have different stars. R/w/b drawing of stars and stripes background. 6pp. Page 6: Advertising.

WW-106 United Arms Of Victory. w. Lucy B. Long. m. H.J. Stewart. Published by Lucy B. Long, San Diego, CA. 1919. B/w photos and drawings of Woodrow Wilson, Abraham Lincoln, George Washington, William McKinley, dove. "Faithfully Dedicated to the Victorious Allies, 1918." "Allies Symbol of Peace." Two verses and song refrain printed on cover. 4pp. Page 4: Advertising for other songs including The *Golden Greeting* [William McKinley song]" and *Where The Healthy Breezes Blow* [Theodore Roosevelt song]."

WW-107 Welcome Wilson! w.m. Pietro Marzen. Published by Pietro Marzen, No. 193 Sinclair Avenue, New York, NY. 1913. Bl/w drawing of Uncle Sam welcoming Woodrow Wilson to the White House. "To His Excellency Woodrow Wilson, President of the United States of America—*New York Evening Journal*, November 6, 1912." 4pp. Page 4: Facsimile letter from Woodrow Wilson to Pietro Marzen.

WW-108 Emblem Of Peace (March and Two Step). m. George A. Reeg, Jr. Published by Volkwein Brothers, Pittsburg, PA. 1914. R/w/b shield, star and stripe border. 6pp. Page 2: "Respectfully Dedicated to our President Woodrow Wilson." Page 6: Advertising.

WW-109 It's A Grand Old Flag To Fight For (March Song). w. John H.G. Fraser. m. Duncan E. MacPherson. Published by MacPherson & Fraser, Room 12, No. 164A Tremont Street, Boston, MA. 1918. R/w/b silhouette drawing of soldiers, facsimile letter—"The White House, Washington, 12 February, 1918, Hon. Calvin D. Paige, House of Representatives, My Dear Mr. Paige: May I not thank you for your courtesy in bringing to my attention the song *Its A Grand Old Flag to Fight For* by Mr. Fraser and Mr. MacPherson? It is very delightful to see such assurances of patriotic feeling. Cordially and sincerely yours, (Signed) Woodrow Wilson" [facsimile signature]. B/w photo of Sergt. George "Duddy" Conners—"Successfully introduced by George Conners of Camp Devens." 4pp. Page 4: Advertising.

WW-110 Allies United For Liberty (Military March). m. Paolo Signore. Published by Brooklyn International Conservatory of Music, No. 33 St. John Place, Brooklyn, NY. 1918. Photo of military statue. "By Courtesy of the United Cigar Stores Company." 4pp. Page 2: "Dedicated to Hon. Woodrow Wilson President of U.S.A." Page 4: Photo of Paolo Signore.

WW-111 Come Along Boys (We're with You, Mr. Wilson). w.m. M.L. Jeffords. Published by Columbia Music Company, No. 310 West 95th Street, New York, NY. 1917. R/w/b drawing of the U.S. flag, soldier, sailor, Capitol dome. Bl/w photo of Woodrow Wilson. 4pp. Page 4: Advertising.

WW-112 Administration Waltz. m. Earl McCarthy. Published by Globe Music Company, No. 1193 Broadway, New York, NY. 1913. Bl/w photos of "Woodrow Wilson" [facsimile signature] and "The Capitol, Washington, DC." Bl/gn/w drawing of flowers. 6pp. Page 6: Advertising.

WW-113 The Man Of The Hour. w. Mayme Gehrue. m. Victor Hammond. Published by Royal Music Company, No. 160 West 46th Street, New York, NY. 1918. Pl/w photo of Woodrow Wilson. B/w eagle, wreath, shield, geometric design border. 4pp. Page 4: Advertising.

WW-114 Woodrow Wilson Leader Of The U.S.A. w. Henry Rupprecht. m. Waldemar Maass. Published by Atlantic Music Publishing Company, No. 131 South Eight Street, Lebanon, PA. 1918. B/w photos of Woodrow Wilson, The White House. R/w/b drawing of a soldier with bugle, tents, flags. "Woodrow Wilson Leader Of The U.S.A., To whose genius the whole world pays Tribute." 4pp. Page 4: Blank.

WW-115 Woodrow Wilson (Four Years More). w.m. W.M. Treloar. Published by The Treloar Music Company, St. Louis, MO. 1916. Bl/w photo of "Woodrow Wilson." R/w/b shield, wreaths. 4pp. Page 4: Arrangement for "Mixed and Male Voices."

WW-116 America's Message (A Universal Anthem). w. Harvey Worthington Loomis. m. Arthur Edward Johnstone. Published by The Oliver Ditson Company, [Boston, MA]. 1917. [6 7/8" × 10 3/4"]. R/w/b non-pictorial geometric design border. "Inspired by President Wilson's Memorable Address of April 2, 1917." "Unison Double Chorus To be sung simultaneously with *My Country, 'Tis of Thee*." List of arrangements. 4pp. Page 2: Narrative on the song.

WW-117 When You're All In Down And Out. w. W.R. Williams (Author of *You Were All I Had, After All I've Done For You, I'd Love To Live In Loveland, &c*). m. Ernie Erdman (Composer of *Down At The Barebcue, I'm A Long Way From Tipperary, &c*). Published by Will Rossiter, The Chicago Publisher, No. 136 West Lake Street, Chicago, IL. 1915. O/bk/w drawing of crowd of people. O/w/bk photo of "Billy McKee of Hartkins, McKee & Taylor." "Dedicated to the Democratic Administration." 6pp. Pages 2 and 6: Advertising.

WW-114

WW-118 Let's Rally Boys! (Our Allies' Delight). w.m. George Surrey Barlow. Published by George S. Barlow, No. 245 East 25th Street, New York, NY. 1918. Bl/w drawing of woman wrapped in U.S. flag, English and French flags, ships, dove. "Humanity, Peace, Prosperity." "Allied in Freedom's Cause." 4pp. "Respectfully dedicated to Our Allies." "We are Comrades, dependent on one another — President Wilson." Page 4: "An Historic, Inspiring Song of Freedom and Democracy based upon Wilson's great message." Patriotic verses and narrative.

WW-119 The Man Behind The Hammer And The Plow (A Song Every American Should Learn). w.m. Harry Von Tilzer. Published by Harry Von Tilzer Music Company, No. 222 West 46th Street, New York, NY. 1917. R/w/b Pfeiffer drawing of farmer, blacksmith. 4pp. Page 4: Proclamation by the President.

WW-120 U.S. Rainbow Division (Military March). a. M.L. Lake. Published by Music Printing Company, Inc., No. 59 Bank Street, New York, NY. 1918. B/w litho of Capitol, eagle, wreath, stars. 6pp. Page 2: "Dedicated to the loyal sons of our nation who were first to respond to the command 'Over There.'" Page 6: Endorsement by Woodrow Wilson "of the work of the National Florence Crittenton Mission."

WW-121 Till Over The Top We Go. w.m. Roy L. Burtch (Composer of *When The Bugle Calls*, *Peace On Earth And Liberty*, *Think Of Me*, *Tell Me, The Organ And The Choir*, *Bye Bye Baby Dear*). Published by The Halcyon Publishing Company, Indianapolis, IN. 1918. Drawing of soldier—"U.S. Marine," machine gun. "The Song Our Allies, Lodges and Glee Clubs are Singing." "State Campaign Song—Democratic State Committee, Denison Hotel, Indianapolis, Ind." "Extra copies of this March Song mailed free on request." 4pp. Page 4: Photos of Woodrow Wilson and 13 State Democratic candidates. "The Party with a Purpose." Text on 11 reasons to vote Democratic.

WW-122 The Berlin Special. w.m. T.A. Parrish. Published by T.A. Parrish, No. 409 Eight Street, Oakland, CA. 1918. R/w/b drawing by Jack Lustig of five U.S. soldiers charging two Germans, flag. "Dedicated to the Boys Over There." 4pp. Page 4: R/w/b drawing of flag, eagle, Woodrow Wilson, General Pershing.

WW-123 For The Honor Of The U.S.A. w.m. Walter Lysaght. Published by Walter Lysaght, No. 254 West 46th Street, New York, NY. 1918. R/w/b drawing of soldier, sailor, shield. Photo of Gladys Coverly—"The American Girl." 4pp. Page 4: "Proclamation by the President to the People."

WW-124 We're Waiting For The Call Mr. Wilson. w. J.W. Metrie and S.W. Cloutman. m. George Gerber. a. Billy Williams. Published by Sillaway Publishing Company, Milwaukee, WI. 1917. Gn/w photos by Buck of Woodrow Wilson—"Dedicated to President Wilson." Gn/w photo of soldiers 4pp. Page 4: Advertising.

WW-125 America To Day. w. Herbert Moore. m. W.R. Williams. Published by Will Rossiter, No. 71 West Randolph Street, Chicago, IL. 1917. [V-1 and V-2: R/w/b] [V-3: Gn/bl] Starmer drawing of Statue of Liberty. [V-1: Sheet Music. 4pp.] [V-2 and V-3: Songster. 20pp] [V-3: 8 3/4" × 11 7/16"]. [V-1 and V-2: Bl/w] [V-3: Gn/bl] photo of "President Wilson." "Don't Worry—Uncle Sam's all right!" "Liberty's still standing in the bay."

WW-126(A) Put On Your Old Grey Bonnet. w. Stanley Murphy. m. Percy Wenrich. Published by Remick Music Corporation, New York, NY. 1919. [1944 Edition]. R/w/b photos from the movie *Wilson*. "Darryl F. Zanuck's Production of *Wilson* with Alexander Knox, Charles Coburn, Geraldine Fitzgerald, Thomas Mitchell, Ruth Nelson Sir Cedric Hardeicke, Vincent Price, William Eythe, Mary Anderson, Directed by Henry King, Photographed in Technicolor, Written for the Screen by Lamar Trotti." "A 20th Century-Fox picture." List of other songs in movie. 6pp. Pages 2 and 6: Advertising.

(B) By The Light Of The Silvery Moon.

(C) Madelon. w. Louis Bousquet and Al Bryan. m. Camille Robert.

(D) Smiles. w. J. Will Callahan. m. Lee S. Robert.

(E) Moonlight Bay. w. Edward Madden. m. Percy Wenrich.

WW-127 Just Give Me A Week In Paris. w. Alex Sullivan. m. Lynn Cowan. Published by Shapiro, Bernstein and Company, No. 224 West 47th Street, New York, NY. 1918. [Post-1919 size]. O/bk/w Barbelle drawing of U.S. soldier, two French women, street sign inscribed

"Avenue du President Wilson." B/w photo of "Lynn Cowan." 4pp.

WW-128 I Love My Home Land. w. Joseph H. Hughes. a. Harry Richardson. Published by Joseph H. Hughes, Saginaw, MI. 1917. Bl/w/y litho of U.S. map, sunlight, facsimile telegram to "President Wilson, Washington, D.C.—We are with you 100,000,000 strong." 4pp. Page 4: Advertising.

WW-129 When Woodrow Wilson Takes A Hand. w.m. S.E. Cox. a. J.J. Scull. Published by Dixie Music Company, Twin Building, Nashville, TN. 1918. O/bk/w drawing by Werrbach of Uncle Sam in military uniform choking the Kaiser, battle scene. 4pp. Page 4: "Dedication to the American Red Cross." Long Narrative on the Red Cross.

WW-130 We Will Stand By Our President. w.m. Ada Brown Waggoner. Published by Keith's Music Publishing House, Long Branch, NJ. 1919. Bl/w drawing of roses, lyre, geometric designs. 4pp. Page 4: Blank.

WW-131 Songs Of America. Published by The Ft. Wayne Printing Company, Ft. Wayne, IN. 1917. [6 7/8" × 9 7/8"]. R/w/b flag, geometric designs. "Containing President Wilson's War Message to Congress, Patriotic and National Airs, with words and music from Lincoln's Address at Gettysburg, Extracts from Lincoln's speeches, Eulogy on the flag, &c." "Compliments of the Danford Company, Furniture and Undertaking, Wooster, OH." 36pp.

WW-132 Woodrow Wilson And The U.S.A. w. Frank Seib. m. J.E. Andino. Published by Frank Seib, Jersey City, NJ. 1915. Bl/w photo of Woodrow Wilson. R/w/b drawing of Uncle Sam, shield. 6pp. Pages 2 and 6: Blank.

WW-133 Freedom's Battle Song. w. Katherine Lee Bates. m. L. Camilieri. Copyright 1917 by L. Camilieri (Conductor of the New Singing Society, New York). Non-pictorial. 4pp. Page 1 and 4: Blank. "The Poem used with kind permission of the Author and of *The N.Y. Times*." "Dedicated to the President of the United States, August, 1917." 4pp. Pages 1 and 4: Blank.

WW-134 Then I'll Be Home Again (Song). w.m. Phil Uphardt. Published by Phillip-Gene and Edwards Music Publishing Company, Cincinnati, OH. 1917. Bl/w non-pictorial geometric designs, stars. "This Song is Being Sold for the Benefit of American and Allied War Orphans and Widows Under the Auspices of the Prospect Club of Springfield, Ohio" 4pp. Page 2: "Respectfully Dedicated to Our President Wilson." Page 4: Blank.

WW-135 America Thou Victorious One (A Peace Anthem). w.m. Carrie Hulse-Petrillo (Composer of *Nita Bonita*, *Chanson D'Amour* and *Czardas*, &c). Published by The Reinecke Music Service, Erie, PA. 1919. [Pre-1919 size]. Non-pictorial. "Sung with Great Success by Umberto Sorrentino the Famous Italian Tenor." "Dedicated to Woodrow Wilson Glorious President of a Glorious Nation." Facsimile letter—"The President asks me to thank you warmly for the compliment you have paid him, Joseph Tumulty, Secretary to the President." 4pp. Page 4: Blank.

WW-136 Stand By The President. w.m. Blanche Evans Abrahams. Published by Blanche Evans Abrahams, Pittsburgh, PA. 1917. Bl/w non-pictorial. 4pp. Page 4: Blank.

WW-137 Old Glory (Song). w.m. Susie Powell Hart. Published by Susie Powell Hart, No. 630 Center Street, Henderson, KY. 1917. R/w/b flag, stars. "Respectfully Dedicated to President Wilson." 4pp. Page 4: Advertising.

WW-138 Neutrality. w.m. J. Patrick Doyle. Published by James P. Doyle, Music Publisher, No. 552 East Eagle Street, Buffalo, NY. 1915. R/w/b drawing of Uncle Sam, map of the Western hemisphere, flags. "Dedicated to the person and policy of Woodrow Wilson,

President, U.S.A." 6pp. Pages 2 and 6: Blank.

WW-139 Right On To France (A War Time March). w.m. G. Byron Ulp. a. E.H. Ulp and V.E. Woodrig. Published by Pennsylvania Music Company, Record Building, Renovo, PA. 1918. R/w/b drawing by W.J. Ulp of tents, cannon, rifles. 4pp. Page 2: "Dedicated to President Wilson." 4pp. Page 4: Advertising.

WW-140 Wilson March. m. Blanche A. Roussin. Published by Blanche Roussin, Lowell, MA. "Sales Agents: New York Sheet Music Clearing House, 141 to 147 West 45th Street, New York." 1912. Bl/w photo by Underwood and Underwood of Woodrow Wilson. R/w/b drawing of flowers, geometric designs. "Respectfully Dedicated to His Excellency Woodrow Wilson." "For Piano." 6pp. Page 6: Blank.

WW-141 Our Presidential Chair. w. Anna Ramspacher. m. Jack Stanley. Published by H. Kirkus Dugdale Company, Inc., 14th and You Streets, Washington, DC. 1912. Bl/w non-pictorial geometric designs. 6pp. Page 2: Blank. Page 6: Advertising.

WW-142 America My Country (National Hymn). w. Lena Shackelford Hesselberg. m. Edouard Hesselberg. Published by Edouard Hesselberg, Lincoln, NE. 1918. B/w drawing of eagle, shield. "Dedicated to Woodrow Wilson, Esq., President of the United States of America." "For Unison Chorus with Piano Accompaniment or Mixed Chorus." "Endorsed by Lieut. John Philip Sousa, U.S.N.R.F." 6pp. Page 6: Advertising.

WW-143 We're Glad To See You Back Mr. Wilson.

WW-144 Hope Of The World America. w. Walter Carruth. m. Cal O'-Chortus. Published by Sierra Music Publishing Company, No. 1316 Webster Street, Oakland, CA. 1919. Br/w photo of Woodrow Wilson. R/w/bl/br stripes, flag, geometric designs. "Dedicated to President Woodrow Wilson, Protagonist of the League of Nations." 4pp. Pages 2 and 4: Blank.

WW-145 Wilson's Inaugural March. m. Clara Phillips Cathey. Published by Cathey Music Company, No. 123 West 44th Street, New York, NY. 1913. Gn/o photo of Woodrow Wilson — "Used by permission of the Inaugural Committee, Washington, D.C." Gn/o geometric designs. "Dedicated to Joseph Bishop Phillips, A gallant soldier who gave his life for his country while on duty in Cuba during the Spanish American War." 8pp. Pages 2, 7 and 8: Blank.

WW-146 Wilson And Victory (Campaign of 1912). w.m. Henry C. Daniels. m. Genevieve Scott. Published by The H. Kirkus Dugdale Company, Music Publishers and Dealers, Dugdale Building, Washington, DC. Copyright 1913 by H.C. Daniels. B/w drawing of Woodrow Wilson. B/w photo of Henry Daniels. Br/w shield, geometric designs. 6pp. Page 6: Advertising.

WW-147 The Man Behind The Flag. w.m. Belle Williams. Published by Belle Williams, No. 525 North Madison Street, Stockton, CA. 1917. Bl/w photo of Woodrow Wilson. R/w/b flag frame. 4pp. Page 2: "Dedicated to Woodrow Wilson." Page 4: Blank.

WW-148 (I Wonder If You Really Know) What Wilson's Done For You. w. Carolyn Wolfe. m. Dominick Travaline. Published by Friant Music Company, Camden, NJ. 1916. R/w/b drawing of eagle, shield, geometric designs. 6pp. Pages 2 and 6: Advertising.

WW-149 Fall In Line For Your Motherland (National March Song). w. Woodrow Wilson. m. "Made into a National Song by John L. Golden." Published by T.B. Harms, Inc., New York, NY. 1916. Bl/w photo of Woodrow Wilson. R/w/b drawing of eagle, flag, stars, stripes, facsimile letter — "The White House, Washington, April 17, 1916: My Dear Mr. Golden: Mrs. Wilson and I were greatly pleased to see you and to hear the march, and I am writing to say how sincerely I hope you will have great success in launching it. It quickens the blood and carries a spur which only music, apparently can use and I am sincerely complemented that you should have chosen the words for the song from my speeches. I envy those who can make any great impulse particularly the great impulse of patriotism, move in such strains and accents as will quicken the pulse of a whole people, Cordially yours, Woodrow Wilson, facsimile signature." 6pp. Page 2: "Dedicated to B.M.B." Page 6: Advertising.

WW-150 The American Marseillaise. w. Felix Schreiber (Founder of the Sons and Daughters of Washington, The Family Behind Its Defenders, and The League of Fraternal Democracy). m. Air: *The French Marseillaise*. Published by Felix Schreiber, Blake Block, Oakland, CA. 1919. "Dedicated to the Defenders of Democracy and to the League of Nations." Bl/w circle inscribed "E Pluribus Unum, Sub Lege Libertas," star inscribed "Peace." Bl/w drawings/photos of Woodrow Wilson, George Washington and Abraham Lincoln in triangle design — Triangle inscribed "Liberty, 1776 A.D., Equality 1865 A.D., Fraternity 1918 A.D., The Everlasting triangle of American Democracy." Bl/w photos/drawings of Allied Leaders "Joffre, Foch, Petain, Kitchner, Haig, Frence, Diaz, Brussiloff." Bl/w photo of John Pershing and bl/w drawing of Lafayette — "Lafayette we are here." "Words composed and adapted to the air of *The French Marseillaise* as a token of reverence and devotion to brave and beautiful France." "To be sung and played 1. As a means of self-rededication to the cause of justice and humanity; 2. As a declaration of America's motives, aims and objects in the World War; 3. As an expression of mutual affection and community of ideals between the two sister republics and all free nations." 4pp.

WW-151 All The World Is Proud Of You (Waltz). w. Edward B. Graham. m. A.S. Lohmann. Published by Edward B. Graham, Denver, CO. 1919. B/w photos of Woodrow Wilson, General Pershing, man. R/w/b drawings of Paris scenes, soldiers and sailors marching, eagle. 4pp.

WW-152 American Consecration Hymn. w. Percy MacKaye. m. Francis MacMillen. Published by Carl Fischer, Cooper Square, New York, NY. 1918. Drawing of wreath, geometric design border. "Dedicated by the Author and the Composer to President Woodrow Wilson in response to the Great Incentive of his own words — 'The right is more precious than the peace.'" "Introduced by Miss Margaret Woodrow Wilson.'" 6pp.

WW-153 Liberty For All (March). m. Alfred Francis. Published by Shapiro, Bernstein and Company, Music Publishers, No. 224 West 47th Street, New York, NY. 1918. Br/w/y/g Barbelle drawing of Miss Liberty with wings, sword and shield inscribed "Right," moon. "Respectfully Dedicated to Woodrow Wilson, President of the United States." 6pp. Page 6: Advertising.

WW-154 Mr. Wilson It's Up To You. w. Olivia Phelps. m. Genevieve Scott. Published by The H. Kirkus Dugdale Company, Music Publishers and Dealers, Dugdale Building, Washington, DC. Copyright 1913 by Olivia Phelps. Bl/w drawing of a shield. 6pp. Page 2: Blank. Page 6: Advertising.

WW-155 Woodrow Wilson. w.m. Rosemary and Stephen Vincent Benet. m. Arnold Shaw. In: *Sing A Song of Americans* [Song Book], page 59. Published by Musette Publishers, Inc., Steinway Hall, New York, NY. 1941. R/w/b drawings by Shuger of Theodore Roosevelt, others. 84pp.

WW-156 Soldier's Of Freedom. w. John W. Williams. m. J. William Tussing. Published by Niagara Music Publishing Company, Buffalo, NY.

Copyright 1918 by John W. Williams and J. William Tussing. Gn/gy clay sculpture of globe, torches, soldiers marching. 4pp. Page 2: "Dedicated to Woodrow Wilson, President of the United States, who called our boys Soldiers of Freedom."

WW-157 Wilson's Commemoration March. w. B.M. Petru. m. Quido Petru. Published by Quido Petru, No. 236 Talcott Avenue, Park Ridge, IL. 1924. Br/w drawing of Woodrow Wilson. R/w/b crossed flags, cover. 6pp.

WW-158 Mothers Of Men (Song). w. Willis Robards. m. Gus Edwards. Published by Jos. W. Stern and Company, Nos. 102-104 West 38th Street, New York, NY. 1917. Br/o/w/bk drawing by E.E. Walton of woman with baby, Woodrow Wilson, George Washington, Abraham Lincoln. "Founded upon the Masterful Photoplay of the same name Produced by Robard's Players." 4pp.

WW-159 W-I-L-S-O-N Means Wilson (With the Good Old U.S.A. at His Command). w. S. Edw. Sanfilippo. m. Billy H. Hickey and Daniel D. Rapaport. In: *Come On America! Boston Sunday Advertiser War Songs* [Songster], October 13, 1918, page 6. [9" × 10 5/8"]. Published by The Oliver Ditson Company, Boston, MA. 8pp.

WW-160 Don't Forget That He's Your President (Song). w.m. John P. Hall. Published by Merrimack Music Company, No. 54 7th Street, Lowell, MA. 1916. Bl/w photo of President Woodrow Wilson, geometric design border. 6pp. Page 2: Advertising. Page 6: Blank.

WW-161 The Wilson Era (Inaugural Marching Song). w. Frank A. Humphrey. m. Len Fleming. Published by Len Fleming and Company, Music Publishers, No. 1416 Broadway, New York, NY. 1913. G/w drawing of flowers. 8pp. Page 2: Advertising. Page 8: Blank.

WW-162 The Victory Song (Hearts of America). w.m. Terry O'Donnell. a. E.M. Code. Published by The F.J. Ringley Publishing Company, Chicago, IL. 1918. Y/bk/w drawing by H.W. Jensen of "Winged Victory" statue, airplanes, ships. "Dedicated to the hearts of America, in air, on land and on sea, and to their Commander-in-Chief, Woodrow Wilson." 4pp. Page 4: Advertising.

WW-163 The Spirit Of The U.S.A. w.m. Paull Specht (Composer of *Somewhere To-Night in Dixie*). Published by The Monarch Music Company, Inc., Reading, PA. 1918. R/w/b drawing by Pfeiffer of Uncle Sam, flag background. "Uncle Sam's 'Community Sing' Song." "Commended by President Woodrow Wilson." "Published for Band and Orchestra." 4pp. Page 4: Advertising.

WW-164 Wilson Marching Song. m. "Tune: *Everybody's Doing It*." [1912]. [4" × 6"]. O/bk/w geometric design border. "Parade tonight, June 24, 8 o'clock, Belvedere. Get on line!" 2pp.

WW-165 P-E-A-C-E (Let's Call the Soldiers Home). w.m. James A. Lonergan. Published by James A. Lonergan Publishing Company, Waterbury, CT.

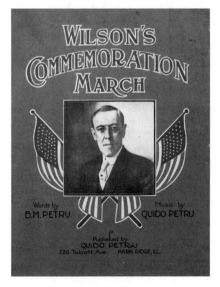

WW-157

1915. Bl/w geometric designs. Bl/w photo of Woodrow Wilson. 6pp. Page 6: Blank.

WW-166 The Spirit Of America 1917 (A Patriotic Song). w.m. Andrew Miller. Published by Andrew Miller, No. 339 10th Street, Brooklyn, NY. 1918. [9" × 12"]. R/w/b ribbon-like border. Bl/w eagle at top. Red cross. R/w/b ribbon border. "America shall ever stand, A bulwark for humanity Till Freedom reigns and every land Shall know the true Democracy." "The proceeds from the sale of this song during the war will be given to The American National Red Cross." 4pp. Page 2: "Respectfully Dedicated to President Wilson." Page 4: Blank.

WW-167 Wilson And California (Song). w.m. Francis H. Boehnlein. Published by Francis Boehnlein, Menesha, WI. 1917. Br/w photo of Francis Boehnlein — "Successfully sung by F. Boehnlein." 6pp. Pages 2 and 6: Blank.

WW-168 Battle Songs Of Seventeen [Song Book]. Compiled and Published for *The Oakland Tribune* by The Rodeheaver Company Press, Chicago, IL. Copyright 1917 by Charles Howard Shaw. [6 7/8" × 10"]. R/w/b drawings of World War I battle scenes, G.A.R. badges. Bl/w photo of "Pres. Wilson, USA." "5 big hits — Words and Music." "Making the World safe for Democracy." List of tunes included. 12pp.

WW-169 Our Buddies. w. Joe Merrick. m. Marian Townsend. Published by Jos. C. Merrick Publishing Company, No. 333 South Dearborn Street, Chicago, IL. 1918. Br/w photo of "President Wilson, Commander-In-Chief of Our Buddies." R/w/bl/br drawings of eagle, crossed flags, soldiers and sailors marching to and from ships, eagle, crossed flags. "Americans Supreme War Song." "Arranged for Band and Orchestra by Harry L. Alford." 4pp. Page 4: Advertising.

WW-170 Wilson, That's All. w. Ballard MacDonald. m. Geo. Walter Brown. Published by Shapiro Music Publishing Company, Broadway and 39th Street, New York, NY. 1912. Non-pictorial. "Professional Copy." "Respectfully dedicated to Hon. Jas. J. Walker, New York." 4pp. Page 4: Blank.

WW-171 The World For Democracy (President Wilson's Call). w. Marks Probasco (Composer of *The Liberty Bells Are Ringing*). m. Metta J. Shoemaker. Published by Marks Probasco, Publisher, Mishawaka, IN. 1917. B/w drawing of two world globes. "The Song that is going around the World!" "Patriotic." "President Wilson's Call." "Dedicated to the Allied Nations." 4pp. Page 4: Blank.

WW-172 The World's Peace Anthem. w.m. W.W. Chapple. Published by W.W. Chapple, No. 9 East Bernard Street, St. Paul, MN. 1916. Non-pictorial geometric design border. "Two sets of words, The first may be sung while the nations are at war, and the second when peace shall be proclaimed." "Respectfully Dedicated to the People of All Nations." "Played by the United States' Marine Band in St. Paul by Command of the President." 4pp. Page 4: Blank.

WW-173 It's A Grand Old Land, Lads (Military March Song). w.m. Louis P. Halling, Jr. Published by Bernard, Scheib and Eldridge, Beckley Building, Rochester, NY. 1918. [Post-1919 size]. Bl/w non-pictorial. "Prize Winning Song, Songwriter's Contest held November 6, 1918, at Family Theatre, Rochester, N.Y., John H.W. Fenyvessy, Resident Mgr." "Respectfully Dedicated to Our Noble President, Woodrow Wilson." 4pp. Page 4: Blank.

WW-174 The Grandest One Of All (Our President Woodrow Wilson). w. G.H. McFarland. m. Frank W. Ford. Published by G.H. McFarland, Elmford, NY. 1918. R/w/b drawing of Uncle Sam, shields, eagle, ribbon border. 4pp. Page 4: Blank.

WW-175 America's Greatest (March). m. David H. Hawthorne

WW-175

(Composer of *The Captive March, The Overland March, The Laurel Waltzes, Only The Moon-Song, Lucille Song, Buffalo Bill's Wild West March, &c., &c*). Published by Hawthorne Music, Buffalo, NY. 1917. Bl/w photo of Woodrow Wilson. Bl/w drawings of George Washington, Abraham Lincoln, eagle, shields, flags, striped border. 4pp.

WW-176   Woodrow Wilson And The Red, White And Blue. w.m. Geo. Hansford and Geo. Wollow. Published by Hansford-Wollow Music Publishing Company, No. 1206½ 5th Street, Sacramento, CA. 1917. Bl/w photos of Woodrow Wilson, George Hansford and George Wollow. B/w geometric designs. "Originally Introduced by Hansford & Wollow." 4pp. Page 4: Quartette Arrangement.

WW-177   Sois Benie O Grande Americque! (Hymne A Wilson). w.m. "Paroles et Musique de M. Bruzzi." Editions Nationales, No. 109 Boulevard Beaumarchais, Paris, [France]. [ca. 1918]. [3 5/8" × 5 1/2"]. 4pp. Postcard. B/w photo of Woodrow Wilson. "Depose Tous Droits Reserves." "Creation de U. Bruzzi, 1st Tenor des Grands Theatres de Paris — Lyon — Marseille — Bruxelles — New York, &c." Page 4: "Republic Francaise Carte Postale." "Imp. Lupu, 117 Rue

WW-176   WW-177

de Turenne-Vise, Paris N. 1287." "Publications de propagande nationale."

WW-178 Parks' Democratic Campaign Songs (For Male Voices). Published by The J.A. Parks Company, York, NE. 1912. [7" × 9 1/2"]. Gn/bl non-pictorial geometric designs. 36pp. [M-399].

WW-179 Three Scirs For The New President Of The U.S.A. (American Military and Naval Marsh) [sic]. m. F.W. Grell. [ca. 1912]. Non-pictorial manuscript. "In Honor Dedicated to His Excellency Wilson, President of the U.S.A." 4pp.

WW-180 Allied Victory (Italian Dance). m. Prof. A. Amato. Published by Prof. A. Amato, Izzo, [Italy]. Copyright 1917 by Prof. A. Amato. R/w/bl/gn/gd drawing of Uncle Same dancing with a woman wearing a crown and a dress in the colors of the Italian flag, German officer watching behind a curtain, Allied Flags, flowers. "To The President of the United States: Woodrow Wilson, The Deliverer." 6pp. Page 6: Music to various national songs.

WW-181 Woodrow Wilson's The Right Man. w. L.M. Martin. m. A.F. Heckle. Published by Bush and Gerts Piano Company, Dallas, TX. Copyright 1912 by L.M. Martin. B/w photo of Woodrow Wilson. Br/w geometric designs. 6pp. Page 6: Counter stamp — "From Woodrow Wilson Campaign Music Distributors, Mrs. L.M. Martin, Mgr., 1304 Elm St., Dallas, Texas."

WW-182 Mister Wilson We Are Grateful To You. w.m. Ray Wilkinson. Published by Bernard-Scheib and Company, Beckley Building, Rochester, NY. 1919. B/w photo of Carrie Gordon. Bl/w shield, geometric designs. "Successfully Introduced by Carrie Gordon." "Prize Winning Song Songwriters Contest-Family Theatre, Rochester, NY." 4pp.

WW-183 Love Law And Liberty (Patriotic Hymn). w.m. Silas G. Pratt.

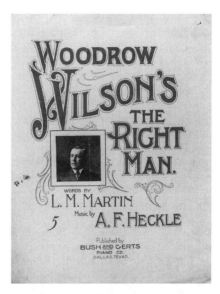

WW-181

Published by Volkwein Brothers, Pittsburgh, PA. Copyright 1915 by Silas G. Pratt. R/w photo of Woodrow Wilson within a red cross. Bl/w drawing of red cross, geometric design border. "Respectfully Dedicated to His Excellency Woodrow Wilson, President of the United States of America." "For Schools and Churches; Words and Music for the Voices only; Two Dollars per Hundred; Orchestra or Military Band One Dollar." "For Sale for the Benefit of the International Red Cross Society." 6pp. Page 6: Blank.

WW-184 Our Flag And Country (Song). w.m. Sohpie Green. Published by Sophie Green, No. 804 East 12th Street, Kansas City, MO. 1917. R/w/b drawing of Woodrow Wilson, U.S. Map and flag, stripe border. 6pp.

WW-185 We're Goin' Daddy Woodrow (A Patriotic March Song). w.m. C.A. Herman and H.D. Herman. Published by Luckhardt and Belder, No. 36 West 40th Street, New York, NY. Copyright 1918 by C.A. Herman. R/w/b drawing of soldiers marching, U.S. flag. 6pp.

WW-186 We Stand For Peace While Others War. w.m. W.R Williams. Postcard. Copyright 1914 by Will Rossiter, No. 136 West Lake Street, Chicago, IL. [3 3/4" × 5 13/16"]. Obv: Y/bk/w drawing by Starmer of doves, Capitol dome. Y/bk photo of "President Wilson." "Help the 'Cause' by Memorizing this Poem." "Suggested by President Wilson's Appeal To the American People to remain neutral in thought and deed which will best safeguard the nation against distress and disaster." Rev: "We Stand For Peace." Space for "Address Only," message and stamp — "Place cent stamp here."

WW-187 Hurrah For Our Leader! (Democratic Campaign Song). m. "To be sung to the tune of *Turkey in the Straw*." Published as a postcard. 1912. [3 1/2" × 5 1/2"]. Obv: Non-pictorial. "Dedicated to Woodrow Wilson, Nominee of the Democratic Party." Rev: B/w photo of "Thomas Scully," facsimile signature. "Private Mailing Card." Space "For Address Only" and stamp — "Put a one cent stamp here."

WW-188 We're Glad We've Got You Mr. Wilson. w.m. J.J. Rosenthal, Jr.

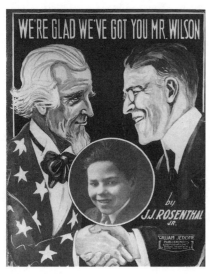

WW-188

Published by William Jerome Publishing Corporation, Strand Theatre Building, 47th Street and Broadway, New York, NY. 1917. Bl/w/br drawing by Barbelle of Woodrow Wilson shaking hands with Uncle Sam. Bl/w photo of J.J. Rosenthal, Jr. 4pp. Page 4: Advertising.

WW-189(A) They Are The Stars In The Service Flag. w. Jack Mason and Al Piantadosi. m. Jack Glogau. Published by Al Piantadosi and Company, Inc., Astor Theatre Building, New York, NY. 1918. Bl/w photos of Woodrow Wilson, 16 military officers in r/w/b drawing of a hat; Bl/w photo of 4 officers; Bl/w photo of "Col. William Allen Phillips, C.O." "The Ordinance Dept. U.S.A. — U.S. Proving Grounds, Aberdeen, Md. Presents by special permission of Col. William Allen Phillips, C.O. The Farce comedy with music entitled *Who Stole The Hat*, Conceived and Staged by Jack Mason." "Committee of Arrangements: Lieut. A.J. Drexel, Chairman, Lieut. L.E. McCann, Lieut. William M. Hough, Lieut. P.J. Degnon." 4pp.

(B) My Salvation Army Girl. w. Jack Mason and Al Piantadosi. m. Jack Glogau.

WW-190 We're All With You Mister Wilson. w.m. Happy Mack. Published by The Lyric Publishing Company, No. 145 West 45th Street, New York, NY. 1918. Br/bl/w drawings of soldier and sailor. Bl/w photo of "Happy Mack" [facsimile signature]. 4pp. Page 2: "Dedicated to The B.P.O. of Elks of America." Page 4: Bl/w litho of German WWI soldier — "W.S.S." Pages 2 and 8: Blank.

WW-191 President Wilson's Inauguration (Intermezzo). m. Rose L. Honeycutt. Published by Erie Music Publishing Company, Erie, PA. Copyright 1917 by Mrs. Rose Button. Bl/w geometric designs. 8pp.

WW-192 The Glory Of Peace (Inter-National War Song). w.m. Mr. and Mrs. Stanley H. Frazier. Published by Stanley H. Frazier, Cainsville, MO.

1919. R/w/b drawing of Woodrow Wilson, other world leaders, angels, soldiers. 4pp. Page 4: Blank.

WW-193 We Are Coming, President Wilson (With Six Hundred Thousand More). Bl/w photo of Woodrow Wilson. "War song of the '60s — *We Are Coming Father Abraham*." In: *The Old Glory Song Book, Our Best National Patriotic Songs*, page 17. Published by The Lowell Commercial College. Copyright 1917 by Illinois State Register, Springfield, IL. 20pp.

WW-194 In Memoriam. w. Anna H.B. Osborn. m. Vivian Brooks. Published by Anna H.B. Osborn, No. 130 South Front Street, Milton, PA. 1915. Bk/gn wreath. Handwritten in ink: "Dedicated to Mrs. Woodrow Wilson — With Compliments of the Author." 6pp. Pages 2 and 6: Blank. [Lyrics on the death of Mrs. Wilson].

WW-195 Song Book. Published by Princeton Alumni Association of the District of Columbia, Washington, DC. March 3, 1913. [4 7/8" × 8"]. R/w/bl/bk/y drawing of eagle with ribbon — "E Pluribus Unum," shield, tiger with Princeton shield. "Reception and Smoker in honor of Woodrow Wilson, '79, given by the Princeton Alumni Association of the District of Columbia, The New Willard, March 3, 1913." 32pp.

WW-196 He Gave Us Wilson. w.m. Charles R. Campbell. Published by Reinecke Music Service, Erie, PA. 1918. Pk/bl photo of Woodrow Wilson. R/w/bl/pk shields, geometric designs. "Respectfully Dedicated to Our President." 4pp. Page 4: Advertising.

WW-197 Peace Made In The U.S.A. w. May I. Trabold. m. William Starke. Published by John T. Hall Music Publishing Company, New York, NY. 1914. R/w/b drawing of Uncle Sam, shield, stars, rings. Bl/w photo of Woodrow Wilson inscribed "Made in the U.S.A." 6pp. Pages 2 and 6: Advertising.

WW-198 We Are Going Father Woodrow (A Swinging Rhythmic Pulsing March Song). w.m. Edmund M. Capen (Writer of *Back Home I'll Come, &c.*). Published by E. Minot Capen, Music Publisher, No. 343 Pleasant Street, Marlboro, MA. 1918. Bl/w drawing of soldier, eagle, stars and stripes. "The Great Song 'Hit' of 1918." 4pp. Page 2: "Respectfully Dedicated to the Armies and Navies of the Allies and the U.S.A." Page 4: Advertising.

WW-199 Hurrah For Our Leader! (Democratic Campaign Song). w. E.H.M. m. (Mrs) Orphella J. Hart. Published by S.A. Moreland, Washington, DC. 1912. Bl/w drawing of torch, flowers. "Dedicated to the Democratic Party." 4pp. + insert.

WW-200 National March. m. Clara Phillips Cathey. Published by Cathy Music Company, Memphis, TN. 1913. Gn/w photo of Woodrow "President Wilson, U.S.A." "Dedicated to Joseph Bishop Phillips, A gallant soldier who gave his life for his country while on duty in Cuba during the Spanish-American War." "For Piano." 6pp. Page 2: Blank.

WW-201 Bust The Trusts (Democratic Campaign Song). w. F.J. Miller. m. Licco I. Liggy. Published by Weiss, MacEachen & Miller, No. 209 West 13th Street, New York, NY. 1912. Bl/w photo of Woodrow Wilson, facsimile signature. R/w/b drawing of flags, star, rays. "Photo published by permission of Woodrow Wilson." 6pp. Pages 2 and 6: Blank. Page 3: "Respectfully dedicated to the Hon. Woodrow Wilson."

WW-202 All For The U.S.A. (A Patriotic Song). w.m. W.S. Madden. Published by Liberty Music Company, No. 1725 Chestnut Street, Philadelphia, PA. 1918. B/w litho of a wreath and scroll — "Dedicated to His Excellency Woodrow Wilson, President of the United States of America." 4pp. Page 4: Blank.

WW-203 We'll Do The Same To-Day. W. Chas. H. Wagner. M. E.

(WW) (Thomas) Woodrow Wilson 650

WW-201

Meinardus. Published by Meinardus Music Company, Kiel, WI. 1918. R/w/b drawings of "George Washington," "Abraham Lincoln," "George Dewey," and "Woodrow Wilson," Revolutionary Soldier, World War I soldier. 4pp. Page 4: Blank.

WW-204 The Wilson-Lincoln Reign. w. Gray. m. C.J.A. Jerrold. 1915.

WW-205 The Ex-President Of The U.S.A. w. Mrs. Rallus Li Vecchi. m. Norrie Bernard. Published by The Lenox Company, Music Publishers, No. 271 West 125th Street, New York, NY. Copyright 1922 by Mrs. Rallus Li Vecchi. Bl/w floral design. 4pp. Page 4: Blank.

WW-206 Woodrow Wilson (Song). w.m. R.M. Halliday. Published by The Marks-Goldman Company, Inc., Music Publishers and Dealers, No. 506 14th Street, N.W., Washington, DC. 1913. Bl/w drawing of shield, geometric designs. 6pp. Page 2: Blank. Page 6: Advertising.

WW-207 Wilson. w. Roland W. Benson. m. E.S.S. Huntington. Published by Knickerbocker Harmony Studios, No. 1545 Broadway, New York, NY. Copyright 1918 by Roland W. Benson, N. 37 Pleasant Street, Bristol. CT. "O/w/b litho of column, Pan with flute, woman reading, geometric designs. "This copy to be used solely for Professional Demonstrating & Exploiting Purposes and is not to be exhibited for sale. Anyone violating this command will be prosecuted under copyright law by the copyright owner. To the Musical and Singing Members of the Theatrical Profession. The performing rights to this song are unconditionally released to those who are selected to have copies submitted to for consideration for professional use." 4pp. Page 4: Advertising.

WW-208 Wilson's Favorite Rag. m. Otto Stock. Published by Otto Stock, Pine Island, MN. 1913. Floral designs. 6pp. [Probably refers to Woodrow Wilson].

WW-209 For Right And Dear Old Glory (Americanism Marching Song And Chorus). w.m. J.F. Curtice. Published by American Publishing Company, Indianapolis, IN. 1918. [6 1/4" × 9 1/16"]. R/w/b crossed flags and print. Bl/w photo of Woodrow Wilson. B/w litho of George Washington and Abraham Lincoln. ""Americanism, Preparedness, 1776-1861-1917." "Help Win The War Patriotic Folder—Americans To The Rescue Or Liberty Will Perish!" "Fight or give to the Red Cross, buy Liberty Bonds, Thrift and War Savings Stamps, to Win the War for Liberty! Aroused, United, Let every Patriot Aid!" "Help distribute this appeal for patriotism, liberty, right and humanity." "Fight and Sing—Give and Pray." 4pp. Page 4: Bl/w photo of Theodore Roosevelt. Long Narrative by Roosevelt. Patriotic sayings.

WW-210 Hymnes Nationaux Des Allies [Song Sheet]. Published in Luxembourg, 1918. [9 1/8" × 11 11/16"]. Br/be drawings of "Le President Wilson" and "Le General Foch." "En souvenir de l'entrée solennelle des troupes allies a Luxembourg, le 21 Novembre, 1918, et a L'honneur de nos sauveurs." "Vendu au profit des Prisionniers allies en sejour dans le Luxembourg." "Prix de vente: fr. 1,25." "Nombre des exemplaires tires: 2000." "Autograph J. Feller, Luxbg.—Litho Fricke, Luxbg." 4pp.

WW-211 The Voice Of The People. w.m. Billy Repaid. Published by House of Repaid, Detroit, MI. 1916. B/w litho of Woodrow Wilson. "Once More He is Our President." "Peace And Prosperity Through His Sincerity." Back cover: Advertisement for House of Repaid music.

WW-212 We Are All Americans (Allegiance). w. Fanny Hodges Newman. m. Carrie Jacobs-Bond. Published at The Bond Shop, by Carrie Jacobs-Bond & Son, Inc., No. 746 Michigan Avenue, Chicago, IL. 1918. N/c litho of three World War I soldiers. Inside page: B/w photo of Margaret Woodrow Wilson. B/w litho geometric design frame. Page 4: "To Miss Margaret Woodrow Wilson." Back cover: Advertisement for Carrie Jacobs-Bond music.

WW-213 Now To The Mercy Seat (Inaugural Anthem). w.m. Wm. C. Shimoneck (Of the G.A.R.). Published by The H. Kirkus Dugdale Co., The Big Music Publishers, Washington, DC. 1912. B/w litho of a shield, geometric designs. "In honor of the National Occasion." 6pp.

WW-214 Fame And Honor Overture. m. M.W. Dent (Author of *World Peace Overature* also *Quick And Easy Step In Music—50 Compositions—for Mandolin and Piano*). Published by M.W. Dent, Scottsville, IL. 1919. Bl/w litho of Woodrow Wilson, angel, eagle with ribbon inscribed "Peace On Earth," globe. "Respectfully dedicated to Woodrow Wilson, President of the U.S.A." 8pp. Pages 2 and 8: Blank.

WW-215 The Presidential Hymn (The Nation's Prayer For The President Of The United States Of America). w. Rev. Benjamin G. Barker. m. "Adapted from *Felice Giardi*ni." Published by Rev. Benjamin George Barker, No. 623 West Vermont Street, Indianapolis, IN. 1915. R/w/b litho of an eagle, flags, stars, ribbon inscribed "E Pluribus Unum." "Justice, Truth, Liberty, Equality, Peace with Honor," "Fraternity." 4pp. Page 3: B/w photo of Rev. Benjamin Barker. Page 4: Blank.

WW-216 Battle Songs Of Liberty. Published and Complied for *The Pittsburgh Leader*, Pittsburgh, PA. Copyright 1918 by Charles Howard Shaw. [6 7/8" 10 1/8"]. R/w/b litho of battle scenes, Statue of Liberty, U.S. and French flags. Bl/w tinted photo of "Pres. Wilson, U.S.A." List of contents.

WW-217 Patriotic Songs Of America For School And Home. Published by U.S. Publicity and Service Co., No. 906 G Street N.W., Washington, DC. 1917. [6 1/4" × 9 1/4"]. R/w/b eagle. B/w photo of Woodrow Wilson. 20pp.

WW-218 On A Little Farm In Normandie. w. Lieut. Ballard MacDonald. m. Nat Osborne. Published by Shapiro, Bernstein & Co., Corner 47th Street & Broadway, New York, NY. 1919. Gd/bk/w DeTakacs drawing of a woman, silhouette of a soldier. "As featured in the Successful Musical Review *Atta Boy* with Captain Frank Tinney and 100 Overseas Soldiers and Sailors. Staged by Dan Dody." "As sung by Priv. John Haw before President Wilson at Polis Theatre, Washington, D.C." 4pp. Page 4: Advertising.

WW-219 Democratic National Hymn (La Paz Para Piano Y Canto). w.m. Professor B.N. Silva. Published by Prof. B.N. Silva, San Luis, CO. 1915. Be/br photos of Woodrow Wilson and William Jennings Bryan. Be/br geometric designs. "Respectfully dedicated tot he first official Congress and the Leaders of the Democratic Party of the U.S.A." 4pp Page 4: Blank.

WW-220 My Pretty Little Indian Maid. w.m. M.J. Fitzpatrick. Published by Fitzpatrick Brothers. R/w/br/bk drawing of an Indian girl. Background of newspaper clippings including headlines "Wilson Love Song Can't Be Stopped" and other Wilson response headlines. Articles include "Despite protest from the White House, the printing presses are busy running off copies of a song dedicated to President Wilson and his bride-to-be, under the title *Pretty Little Indian Maid*." Also "While the name of Mrs. Galt, the President's fiancée, is not mentioned, the reference in the song is unmistakable, because of the fact that Mrs. Galt is descended from Pocahontas, the Indian Princess."

See also FDR-46; FDR-158; FDR-270; FDR-390; FDR-401; DDE-9; LBJ-1; MISC-46; MISC-167.

Zachary Taylor

ZT-1 Major General Zachary Taylor (A Quartett). w. Charles Orphean. m. Jacob Orphean. Published by C. Holt, Jr., No. 156 Fulton Street, New York, NY. 1847. Non-pictorial. "Written by Charles and Adapted to music by Jacob of the Orphean Family and Sung by The Orpheans with unabounded applause." 6pp. Pages 2 and 6: Blank.

ZT-2 President Taylor's Grand Inauguration March. m. Albert Holland. Published by George Willig, Jr., Baltimore, MD. 1849. B/w litho by Ed Weber & Company of The Capitol at Washington. 6pp. Pages 2, 3 and 6: Blank. Page 4: "As performed by the Independent Blues Band. Composed and respectfully dedicated to Genl. Z. Taylor."

ZT-3 General Taylor's Mexican Quick Step. m. "A Lady of Virginia." Published by F.D. Benteen, Baltimore, MD. 1846. Non-pictorial. "Composed and Dedicated to Him [Taylor]." 4pp. Pages 1 and 4: Blank.

ZT-4 General Taylor's Encampment Quick Step. Published by William Vanderbeek, No. 385 Broadway, New York, NY. 1846. Non-pictorial. "As performed by The Bands of the United States Army in Texas." "25¢ nett [sic]." 6pp. Pages 2 and 6: Blank.

ZT-5 Rough And Ready Polka. m. Josef Gung'l, Op. 95. Published by Scharfenberg & Luis, No. 483 Broadway, New York, NY. 1849. Non-pictorial. "As performed at the Inauguration Ball at Washington." "Composed and respectfully inscribed to Robert James, Esq." 6pp. Pages 2 and 6: Blank.

ZT-6 Rough & Ready Polka. m. James Bellak. Published by E.R. Johnson, Peoples Music Store, 6th ab. Chestnut Street, Philadelphia, PA. 1848. Non-pictorial. "Respectfully Dedicated to Gen. Zachary Taylor by the Publisher." 4pp. Pages 1 and 4: Blank.

ZT-7 Rough & Ready (The Bold Soger [sic] Boy). w. H.P. Gratten. a. Adolph Schmitz. Published by Lee & Walker, No. 120 Walnut Street, Philadelphia, PA. Copyright 1848 by Adolph Schmitz. B/w litho by M. Schmitz of soldier, cannon, flags, eagle, monument with Zachary Taylor's military victories listed along with the names of U.S. officers killed.

ZT-8 Grand Triumphal March. m. L. Gabici. Sold by Wm. T. Mayo, Publisher, South Camp Street and J.E. Benoit, Chartres Street, New Orleans, LA. 1847. B/w litho of Zachary Taylor, other military officers in theatre box, orchestra members, eagle." "L. Gabici, Leader of the Orchestra at the Saint Charles Theatre." "Performed on the occasion of the General's visit to that establishment, Decr. 3, 1847."

ZT-9 The Peoples Choice (Song). w. Thomas Williams. Published by William Hall & Son, No. 239 Broadway (cor. of Park Place), New York, NY. 1848. Non-pictorial. "Arranged for the Piano Forte." 4pp.

ZT-10 Monterey (A National Song). w. J.W. Watson. m. Austin Phillips. Published by Firth & Hall, No.

1 Franklin Square, New York, NY. 1847. B/w green tinted litho of soldiers fighting at Monterey, Mexico. R/w/gd litho of eagle, flags. "Respectfully dedicated to Genl. Zachary Taylor." 8pp. Pages 2, 7 and 8: Blank. Page 3: Inside title —**Monterey No. 3**. "New series National songs."

ZT-11 A Little More Grape Captain Bragg (A National Song). w.m. William J. Lemon. Published by Lee & Walker, No. 120 Walnut Street, Philadelphia, PA. 1847. B/w litho by P.S. Duval of Buena Vista battle scene, cannon balls at top. "Composed & Respectfully dedicated to General Zachary Taylor." "Pr. 50 cts net." 8pp. Pages 2 and 8: Blank.

ZT-12 The Battle Of Buena Vista (A Descriptive Fantasie for the Piano). m. Charles Grobe, Op. 101. Published by George Willig, Jr., Baltimore, MD. 1847. [V-1: Hand Colored] [V-2: B/w] litho by E. Weber & Co. of soldiers, drums, eagles, cannons, shields, crossed flags. "Veni, Vidi, Vici." "Composed and most respectfully inscribed to Genl. Z. Taylor, the Hero who never lost a battle." "Price 75 cts net." 14pp. Pages 2 and 14: Blank.

ZT-13 Rough & Ready (A Patriotic Song). w. Major Norton. m. Air: *Old Dan Tucker*. Published by W.H. Oakes & E.H. Wade, No. 197 Washington Street, Boston, MA. 1847. B/w litho of General Zachary Taylor. "Dedicated to Gen. Zachary Taylor, by the Rough & Ready Association." 4pp. Page 4: Blank.

ZT-14 Inauguration Quadrille. m. Josef Gung'l, Op. 96. Published by Scharfenberg & Luis, No. 483 Broadway, New York, NY. 1849. Non-pictorial geometric design litho border. "For the Piano." "As Performed at the Inauguration Ball." "Respectfully dedicated to Mrs. General Z. Taylor, the 5th of March, 1849." Page 2: Blank.

ZT-15 Grand Triumphal Quick Step. m. Edward L. White. Published by Oliver Ditson, No. 115 Washington Street, Boston, MA. 1847. B/w litho by Bufford & Company of Zachary Taylor. "Partly composed and dedicated to Gen. Zachary Taylor." 4pp. Page 4: Blank.

ZT-16 The Battle Of Resaca De La Palma. m. John Schell. Published by George Willig, Jr., Baltimore, MD. 1848. B/w litho by E. Weber of vignettes of Taylor's battles — "Ft. Harrison, Matororas, Palo Alto, Monterey, Resaca de la Palma, Buena Vista." "Price 75 cts nett [sic]." 14pp. Pages 2 — 13: Descriptions of movements — "General Taylor's Grand March; The Mexicans open on the American Advance; Mexican Lancers Advancing to the Charge; They are Repulsed with Great Slaughter by Ridgley's Battery; Hold on Charlie 'till I Draw Their Fire; Capt. May Advances to the Charge; General La Vega Surrenders to Capt. May; Mexicans in Full Retreat; Rejoicing After the Victory; Cries of the Wounded; Burial of the Slain; Yankee Doodle." Page 14: Blank.

ZT-17 Gen. Taylor's Quick Step. m. A.G. Pickins. Published by Oliver Ditson, No. 115 Washington Street, Boston, MA. [ca. 1847]. Non-pictorial. "Composed for the Piano Forte." 4pp. Pages 1 and 4: Blank.

ZT-18 Buena Vista Grand Triumphal March. m. F. Weiland. Published by J.G. Osbourn, No. 112 South 3rd Street, Philadelphia, PA. [1847]. B/w litho by T. Sinclair's Litho. of Buena Vista, Mexico, battle scene. "General Taylor Never Surrenders." "Composed in Honor of Major General Taylor's victory in Mexico, February 23d, 1847." Page 2: "Composed in Honor of Gen: Taylor's recent victory." Page 4: Blank.

ZT-19 General Taylor's Grand March. m. Henry Rohbock. Published by Frederick D. Benteen, Baltimore, MD. [ca. 1846]. Non-pictorial. "Composed & Dedicated to Him and the Officers and Soldiers Under his Command in the Mexican Campaign." "25 cts net." 3pp. [Published with other pieces back-to-back including *Capt. May's Quickstep* (Page 4) and *Capt Walker's Quickstep* (Page 6).]

ZT-20 Grand Inauguration March. m. Professor H. Dielman (of St. Mary's College, MD). Published by George Willig, Jr., Baltimore, MD. 1849. B/w litho by E. Weber of eagle holding a medal with an engraved bust of Zachary Taylor, vignettes of Taylor's battles — "Ft. Harrison, Matororas, Palo Alto, Monterey, Resaca de la Palma, Buena Vista. "Accepted by the President, Adopted by the Committee of arrangements and performed by the Marine Band of the United States On the occasion of the inauguration of Genl. Z. Taylor as President of the United States." "Composed and arranged for the Piano." 6pp. Pages 2 and 6: Blank. Page 3: Inside title — **President Taylor's Inauguration March**.

ZT-21 Rio Grand March. m. Dr. Wozencraft. Published by W.C. Peters, Cincinnati, OH. 1847. Non-pictorial. "Most respectfully dedicated to General Taylor." 4pp. Pages 1 and 4: Blank.

ZT-22 General Taylor's Grand March. m. A. Kurs. Published by Firth & Hall, No. 1 Franklin Square, and Firth, Hall & Pond, 239 Broadway, New York, NY. 1846. Non-pictorial. "Most Respectfully Dedicated to Brigr. Genl. Z. Taylor and His Brave Companions by the Publishers." 4pp.

ZT-23 The Rio Grand Quick March. m. John C. Andrews. Published by Firth & Hall, No. 1 Franklin Square, New York, NY. 1846. B/w litho by Bufford & Company, of Zachary Taylor, battle scene. "Composed and respectfully dedicated to Major Genl. Z. Taylor, Commander of the Army of Occupation." 4pp. Page 4: Blank.

ZT-24 Dream On The Ocean Waltz. m. Josef Gung'l. a. G.F. Bristow. Published by Firth, Pond & Company, No. 1 Franklin Square, New York, NY. 1849. Non-pictorial. "Performed at the Grand Inauguration Ball given at Washington in honor of General Taylor, by Gung'ls Band." 10pp. Page 10: Blank. "3d Edition, To Mrs Col. W. Bliss."

ZT-25 Dream On The Ocean Waltz. m. Josef Gung'l. a. G.F. Bristow. Published by William A. Pond & Company, No. 547 Broadway, New York, NY. 1849. Non-pictorial. "Performed at the Grand Inauguration Ball given at Washington in honor of Genl. Taylor by Gung'l's Band." "To Mrs. Col. W.B. Bliss." [V-1: Duet] [V-2: Solo]. 12pp. Pages 2 and 12: Blank.

ZT-26 Storming Of Monterey (A Descriptive Military Waltz). m. Francis Buck. Published by F.D. Benteen, Baltimore, MD. 1846. B/w litho by E. Weber of the battle scene at Monterey — "September 21st, 22nd, 23rd, 1846." "Composed and dedicated to Genl. Z. Taylor and Officers of the American Army in Mexico." 6pp. Pages 2 and 6: Blank.

ZT-27 Old Zack's Quick Step. m. Air: "Arranged from the Popular Melody of *Rosa Lee*." a. Edward L. White. Published by Oliver Ditson, No. 115 Washington Street, Boston, MA. 1848. Non-pictorial. 4pp. Pages 1 and 4: Blank.

ZT-28 Old Rough And Ready Quick Step. a. Charles Grobe. Published by George Willig, No. 171 Chestnut Street, Philadelphia, PA. 1846. Non-pictorial. "Arranged for the Piano Forte and respectfully Dedicated to General Zac. Taylor." 4pp. Pages 1 and 4: Blank.

ZT-29 The Rough And Ready Songster. Printed by Benham, New Haven, CT. [1848]. [3 11/16" × 5 11/16"]. Bl/bk non-pictorial geometric design border. 22pp. [M-071].

ZT-30 Convention Quick Step. m. D.H. Haskell. Published by Oliver Ditson, No. 115, Washington Street, Boston, MA. 1848. Non-pictorial. "Dedicated to the Taylor Whigs." 4pp. Pages 1 and 4: Blank.

ZT-31 Rest Warrior Rest. m. Orramel Whittlesey [facsimile signature]. Published by Orramel Whittlesey, Salem, [NY]. 1847. Non-pictorial. Facsimile signature of Whittlesey. "Music Composed and Respectfully Dedicated to

Major General Zachary Taylor, U.S.A." 6pp. Pages 2 and 6: Blank.

ZT-32   The Old Zack Songster. Published by William H. Graham, New York, NY. 1848. Litho of U.S. Flag. Ribbon inscribed—"A Little More Grape Mr. Bragg." [M-067].

ZT-33   The Battle Of Buena Vista. m. William Striby. Published by [V-1: David P. Faulds, Louisville, KY] [V-2: D.P. Faulds, No. 165 Fourth Avenue, Louisville, KY] [V-3: H.J. Peters & Co., Louisville, KY]. [ca. 1847]. Non-pictorial geometric design border. "Composed and arranged for the Piano Forte and respectfully dedicated to Major General Zachary Taylor." 12pp. Page 2: Blank. Page 12: **Hail Columbia**.

ZT-34   Gen. Taylor's Quick Step At Monterey. m. J.C. Viereck, Op. 77. Published by A. Foit, Philadelphia, PA. 1846. Non-pictorial geometric design. "Arranged for the Piano and Dedicated to Miss Rebecca Moss." 2pp.

ZT-35   The Soldier's Story. Published by F.D. Benteen, Baltimore, MD. 1847. B/w litho by J.H. Bufford's of Zachary Taylor, battle scene. "Rough and Ready."

ZT-36   Genl. Taylor's Victory March. m. Theodore V. La Hache, Op. 4. Published for the Author by Firth, Hall & Pond, No. 239 Broadway, New York, NY. 1847. Non-pictorial geometric design border. "Respectfully dedicated to the Victorious Army." 6pp. Pages 2 and 6: Blank. Page 3: **Gen. Taylor's Victory March**. Page 4: *Gen. Worth's Quick Step*.

ZT-37   The Death Of Taylor. w.m. John P. Ordway. Published by A. & J.P. Ordway, No. 339 Washington Street, Boston, MA. 1850. Non-pictorial geometric design border. "Sung by Ossian E. Dodge, Esq." "Poetry and Music Composed and Respectfully Inscribed to the Family of the Beloved and Lamented President." "He Departed this Life July 9th, 1850, at half past 10 p.m. Aged 66 years." 6pp. Page 6: Blank.

ZT-38   General Taylor's Old Rough & Ready Songster. Published by Turner & Fisher, New York, NY. [ca. 1848]. [2 7/8" × 4 3/8"]. Litho of Zachary Taylor, camp scene. 32pp.

ZT-39   General Taylor's Quick Step. m. Matthias Keller. Published by Lee & Walker, No. 120 Walnut Street, Philadelphia, PA. 1846. Non-pictorial. "Composed for the Piano and Respectfully Dedicated to General Z. Taylor." 4pp. Pages 1 and 4: Blank.

ZT-40   Taylor's Grand March. m. J. Messemer. Published by H.J. Peters & Company, Louisville, KY. [ca. 1847]. Non-pictorial. "Composed for the Piano Forte, and Respectfully Dedicated to Genl. Z. Taylor." 4pp. Page 4: Blank.

ZT-41   The Rough & Ready Songster. c. By An American Officer. Published by Nafis & Cornish, Publishers, No. 278 Pearl Street, New York, NY. 1848. Bk/gd hardback with title, Taylor likeness and eagle and list of Mexican victories on spine. 266pp. Page 6: B/w engraving of Zachary Taylor. Page 7: B/w engraving of cannon. "Embellished with twenty-five splendid engravings, illustrative of the American victories in Mexico."

ZT-42   Rough And Ready (Song). w. Alfred Wheeler. Published by Firth, Hall & Pond, No. 234 Broadway, New York, NY. 1847. B/w beige tinted litho by Sarony & Major of the members of the singing group "The Alleghanians." "Songs, Duetts [sic], Glees &c. Arranged for the Piano Forte." 6pp. Pages 2 and 6: Blank. Page 5: Arrangement for "Quartette."

ZT-43   Grand National Waltzes. m. Adaline Maxwell Cooper (of London). Published by William Hall & Son, No. 239 Broadway, New York, NY. 1850. Non-pictorial geometric design border. "Dedicated to Genl. Z. Taylor, President of the United States." 12pp. Pages 2 and 12: Blank.

ZT-44   The National Songster. w. "By an American Officer." m. Popular Airs. Published by Cornish, Lamport

& Company, No. 267 Pearl Street, New York, NY. [ca. 1848]. [3" × 4 1/8"]. Bk/gd non-pictorial geometric designed hardback song book with gold imprinted spine. 260pp. Page 3: Litho of George Washington. Page 5: Title page: "The National Songster—Embellished with Twenty-Five Splendid Engravings, Illustrative of the American Victories in Mexico." Page 7: Title: **Rough And Ready Songster**.

ZT-45 Rio Grande March. m. Dr. Wozencraft. Published by W.C. Peters & Sons, Cincinnati, OH. 1858. Non-pictorial geometric designs. "Favorite Marches Selected from Various Authors." List of other songs in series. 4pp. Page 2: "Most respectfully dedicated to General Taylor." Page 4: Blank.

ZT-46 Order Of Exercises. Published for "Funeral Ceremonies in Honor of the Late President of the United States at the Church of the First Parrish, Cambridge, [MA], August 13, 1850." [7 13/16" × 9 7/8"]. Bl/bk non-pictorial. 2pp. Page 2: Blank. [Songs and Eulogy].

ZT-47 Storming Of Monterey (Grand Galop). m. Maurice Strakosch. Published by William Hall & Son, No. 239 Broadway (at Park Place), New York, NY. 1848. Non-pictorial. "For the Piano Forte." "Respectfully dedicated to Major General Zachary Taylor." 10pp. Pages 2 and 10: Blank.

ZT-48 General Taylor's Grand March. a. Charles Grobe. Published by Lee & Walker, No. 120 Chestnut Street, Philadelphia, PA. 1846. Non-pictorial. "Arranged for the Piano." "Most Respectfully Dedicated to General Taylor by the Publishers." 4pp. Pages 1 and 4: Blank.

ZT-49 For Taylor Ho! (A Patriotic Song). w. "By a Lady." m. L.V. Parsons. Published and for sale by Isaac Keagy, and for sale by the Booksellers and Music dealers generally, Harrisburg, PA. [1848]. Non-pictorial. "Arranged for Four Voices." "Respectfully Dedicated to the American People." 4pp. Pages 1 and 4: Blank.

ZT-50 Grand Funeral March. m. Charles Wels. Published by Firth, Pond & Co., No. 1 Franklin Square, New York. 1850. Non-pictorial blank border. "As played by Dodworth's Band on the occasion of the Funeral Solemnities in the City of New York to the memory of General Zachary Taylor (July 23d, 1850)." 4pp. Pages 4: Blank.

ZT-51 Rio Grand March. m. Dr. C.F. Koch. Published by Lee & Walker, No. 120 Chestnut Street, Philadelphia, PA. 1846. Non-pictorial. "Composed and Arranged for the Piano Forte and respectfully dedicated to the Philadelphia Volunteers." 4pp.

ZT-52 Old Rough And Ready. w. HAL. m. Air: *Vive La Compagnia*. [1848]. [11" × 4 1/2"]. Non-pictorial. "Dedicated to the Whigs of the Ward Four." 2pp. Page 2: Blank.

ZT-53 The Battles Of Palo Alto & Resaca De La Palma. m. Charles Grobe, Op. 72. Published by F.D. Benteen, Baltimore, MD. 1846. Non-pictorial. "A Musical delineation, composed for the Piano Forte And dedicated as a tribute of respect to the Officers & Men of the U.S. Army." 10pp. Pages 2 and 10: Blank. Page 3: Narrative to music—"Two o'clock p.m.—General Taylor takes up the line of march in the direction of the enemy..."

ZT-54 Old Zack Must Be Our Man. w. HAL. m. Air: *Mary Blane*. [1848]. [11" × 4 1/2"]. Non-pictorial. "Dedicated to the Whigs of the Ward Four." 2pp. Page 2: Blank.

ZT-55 Camp Taylor March. m. Henry Bellman. Published by F.D. Benteen, Baltimore, MD. 1846. Non-pictorial. "Composed and Dedicated to Genl. Taylor and the Officers and Soldiers under his Command on the Rio Bravo del Norte." 4pp. Pages 1 and 4: Blank.

ZT-56 Taylor And Fillmore Songster. Published by Turner & Fisher, New York, NY. 1848. [2 3/4" × 4 3/8"]. [V-1: Pk/bk] [V-2: Bl/bk] litho of

Zachary Taylor. 34pp. Pages 2 and 33: Blank. Page 3: Subtitle—"An Original Collection of New Whig Songs for the Campaign of 1848." Page 34: Advertising. [M-074, 075].

ZT-57   General Taylor Crossing The Rio Grande. (A Quick Step). Published by Klemm & Brother, No. 275 Market Street, Philadelphia, PA. 1846. Non-pictorial. 4pp. "Arranged for the Piano Forte." Pages 1 and 4: Blank.

ZT-58   Fort Harrison March. m. C.H. Weber. Published by Balmer & Weber, St. Louis, MO. 1848. B/w orange tinted litho by Sarony & Major of Indians attacking Fort Harrison. "Composed and Most Respectfully Dedicated to Genl. Zachary Taylor." "Price 25 cts. nett [sic]." 6pp. Pages 2 and 6: Blank.

ZT-59   Rough And Ready (or Florida Polka). m. J.C. Beckel. Published by Lee & Walker, No. 162 Chesnut Street, Philadelphia, PA. 1851. Non-pictorial. "To James N. Becks, Esq." "Composed and Arranged with Brilliant Variations for the Piano." 8pp. Pages 2 and 8: Blank.

ZT-60   The Hero Who Dares, Is The Hero Who Wins. w. Charles D. Stewart, Esqr. m. Austin Phillips. Published by Willam [sic] Hall & Sons, No. 239 Broadway, New York, NY. 1850. B/w hand Colored litho by Sarony of Major General Zachary Taylor. "Sung at the Grand Complimentary Ball given in honor of Major Genl. Zachary Taylor on the 5th, February, 1850." 8pp. Pages 2, 7 and 8: Blank.

ZT-61   Buena Vista Grand March. a. E. Nathan. Published by Firth, Hall & Pond, No. 239 Broadway, New York, NY. 1847. Non-pictorial geometric litho design. "Respectfully Dedicated to Major Genl. Zachary Taylor." "Subject from *Mercadante*." "Arranged for the Piano Forte." 6pp. Pages 2 and 6: Blank.

ZT-62   Rough And Ready Polka. m. James Bellak. Published by Lee & Walker, No. 188 Chesnut Street, Philadelphia, PA. 1855. B/w litho of

ZT-60

vines and leaves. "Pleasure Train for Two Performers on the Piano." "To Miss Josephine Bowlby." List of other songs in the series. 4pp. Page 4: Blank.

ZT-63   Rough And Ready Quick Step. Published by Klemm & Brother, No. 275 Market Street, Philadelphia, PA. 1847. Non-pictorial. 2pp. Page 2: Blank.

ZT-64   The American Flag. w. J.R. Drake. m. Bellini. Published by Lee & Walker, No. 120 Walnut Street, Philadelphia, PA. 1847. Litho of Miss Liberty holding U.S. flag standing on a globe with a map of the "United States of America." "Respectfully Dedicated to Major General Z. Taylor by the Publishers." 8[?]pp.

ZT-65   The Veteran Polka. m. Carl Eckert. Published by William Hall & Son, No. 239 Broadway, New York, NY. 1854. B/w beige tinted litho by Sarony & Co. of Zachary Taylor in uniform, eagle, flags, cannons. 6pp.

ZT-66   Rough And Ready, The Soldier's Story. Copyright 1847 by F.D. Benteen, Baltimore. Non-pictorial. 4pp.

ZT-67   General Taylor's Quick March At Buena Vista. m. Louis Reimer. Published by Lee & Walker, No.

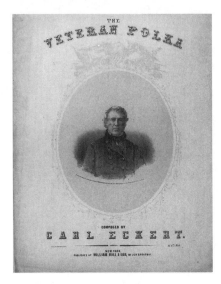

ZT-65

120 Walnut Street, Philadelphia, PA. 1847. Non-pictorial. "Composed for the Piano and Respectfully Dedicated to him." 4pp. Pages 1 and 4: Blank.

ZT-68 Rough And Ready (A Whig Song). w. J.R.I. m. F.F.B. Published by G.P. Reed, No. 17 Tremont Row, Boston, MA. 1848. Non-pictorial. "Dedicated to the Friends of Taylor and Fillmore." "Arranged for the Piano." 4pp. Page 4: Blank.

ZT-69 Rough And Ready Quick Step. In: *The Army and Navy Fife Instructor: Containing the Calls, Signals, and the Complete Camp and Garrison Duties as Practised* [sic] *in the Army and Navy of the United States, Including the Volunteer and Regular Service, Containing the National Airs, and a Large Collection of Marches, Quicksteps, Waltzes, Polkas, &c.*, page 25. e.a. Elias Howe. Published by Elias Howe, Agt., No. 103 Court Street, Boston, MA. Copyright 1863 by Willard Howe.

ZT-70 Ratification Quick Step. m. T. Bricher. Published by O. Ditson, No. 115 Washington Street, Boston, MA. 1848. Non-pictorial. "Composed and Dedicated to Gen. Zack. Taylor." 4pp. Pages 1 and 4: Blank.

ZT-71 Rough And Ready Grand March. m. J. Waterman. Published by Oliver Ditson, No. 115 Washington Street, Boston, MA. 1848. Non-pictorial. "Composed for the Piano Forte with an Accompaniment for the Flute." 4pp. Pages 1 and 4: Blank.

ZT-72 Taylor's Triumph March. m. Josef Gungl. Published by Schuberth & Company, New York, NY. 1848. B/w litho of Josef Gungl. "The Carnival of the United States, Delices for the Piano." List of other music in the series. "Published from the original manuscript of the Author." "Copy-right for every arrangement of these compositions secured by law."

ZT-73 Toe The Mark, 'Tis Taylor Can (A Whig Song). w. Nathaniel P. Willis. m. "Tune: *Dandy Jim of Caroline*." [1848]. 4pp. Handwritten manuscript. Accompanied by a published copy of the song from a newspaper of the time. 2pp. "Note: It was mentioned in one recent account of the battle of Buena Vista, that General Taylor's gray great coat had two bullet-holes through it, when he took it off after the action."

ZT-74 All The Letters Of Major General Zachary Taylor, Anecdotes of Rough And Ready, Songs of Old Zach's Campaigns, &c. "A Little More Grape Captain Bragg." Published by Burgess Stringer & Company, New York, NY. 1848. Br/bk litho of Zachary Taylor. 24pp. [M-066].

ZT-75 The Rough And Ready Melodist. Published by H. Long & Brother, New York, NY. 1848. Br/bk litho of Zachary Taylor. 72pp. "Illustrated O.Z. Edition Containing a Selection of the Best Taylor and Fillmore Songs, with Many Written and Arranged Expressly for This Work." Page 72: Br/bk litho of Millard Fillmore. [M-068].

ZT-76 Rough And Ready Minstrel. Published for the National Rough & Ready Club by King & Baird, Philadelphia, PA. 1848. "A Choice Collection of Songs for the Campaign." [V-1: 32pp.] [V-2: 64pp.]. [M-069, 070].

ZT-77 Washington American Song-Book — Rough And Ready. 1848. 16pp. Pk/bk litho on rear cover of "President Donkey L.L.D." [M-076].

ZT-78 Gen'l Taylor's Quickstep. In: *The Amateur's Quartette Club, No. 2.* Published by Lee & Walker, No. 922 Chestnut Street, Philadelphia, PA. [ca. 186-]. "An easy collection of Instrumental Music. Arranged for and second Violin, Violoncello and Flute, Cornet ad Libitum."

ZT-79 Rough And Ready's Rio Grande Songster. Published by J. Torr, Philadelphia, PA. 1848. "Torr's Superior Editions of Song Books." Vignette of "Grand Jubilee on raising the American Flag in Metamaras." 32pp. [M-073].

ZT-80 Rough And Ready Quickstep. In: *Musician's Omnibus: Containing the Whole Camp Duty, Calls and Signals Used in the Army and Navy; Forty Setts of Quadrilles, Including Waltz, Polka and Schottische, with Calls; and an Immense Collection of Polkas, Schottisches, Waltzes, Marches, Quicksteps, Hornpipes, Contra & Fancy Dances, Songs, &c., for the Violin, Flute, Cornet, Clarionett, &c, containing over 700 Pieces of Music*, page 30. c. Elias Howe. Published by Elias Howe, No. 103 Court Street, Boston, MA. 1861. [8 1/2" × 11"]. O/bk non-pictorial. "Improved Edition." 100pp.

ZT-81 Rough And Ready Quickstep. In: *Howe's Diamond School For The Violin: Containing, Complete Instructions and Full Directions in Bowing; to which is added A Large Collection of Popular Polkas, Schottisches, Waltzes, Redowas, Marches, Quicksteps, Dances, Hornpipes, Songs,* page 30. c. Elias Howe. Published by Elias Howe, No. 103 Court Street, Boston, MA. 1861. [8 1/2" × 11"]. Bl/bk non-pictorial. 68pp.

ZT-82 Honest Zack. m. "Air, *Dearest Mae.*" [1848]. [3 1/2" × 8 1/2"]. 2pp. Page 2: Blank.

ZT-83 Metamoras Grand March. m.a. Henry Chadwick. Published by L. Hjousebery, No. 438 Fulton Street, Brooklyn, NY. 1846. B/w litho by A. Wilson of Zachary Taylor on horseback leading troops in battle scene. "Respectfully dedicated to Major Genl. Z. Taylor." "Composed & arranged for the Piano Forte." 6pp.

ZT-84 The Matamoras Grand March. m.a. W.C. Peters. Published by W.C. Peters, Cincinnati, OH. 1846. Non-pictorial geometric designs. "Arranged & partly composed for the Piano Forte and Most Respectfully dedicated to Major Genl. Z. Taylor." "As Performed by the Brass Bands." 6pp

ZT-85 Major General Taylor's Grand March And Quick Step. m. A.H. Durocher, Balto. M.D. Published by Shaff & Boswell, Baltimore, MD. 1846. B/w litho by Weber & Co of General Taylor on horseback leading troops in battle. "Composed and dedicated with Most distinguished respects to Major General Taylor, U.S. Army." 6pp.

ZT-86 Marche Du General Taylor. m. "Composee Par E. Prevost." Published in New Orleans. [ca. 1848]. "A vendie chez tous les marchand de musique." "Dediee a l'Armee de rio Grande."

ZT-87 Funeral Dirge of Gen. Zachary Taylor (Late President of the United States). m. C.L. Barnes. Published by the C.L. Barnes. New York, NY. 1850. Non-pictorial. "Composed and Arranged As A Quartett." 2pp.

ZT-88 Monterey. m. Austin Philips. In: *Marches Of The Presidents, 1789-1909, Authentic Marches & Campaign Songs,* page 30. a. Carl Miller. Published by Chappell & Co., Inc., No. 609 Fifth Avenue, New York, NY. "By arrangement with Chilmark Press, Inc." 1968. [9" × 12"]. R/w/b litho of eagle, flag. "An Illustrated Piano Folio For All Ages." 72pp.

See also WHT-23; WW-19; FDR-158; DDE-9; LBJ-1; MISC-167.

Appendix
Publishers by City

ABILENE, TX
Pratt Pub. Co., 1234 N. 5th St. JFK-83
AKRON, OH
Browned, W.I. & Co. JAG-83
D&C Music Co., 907 Akron S&L Bldg. WLW-6
ALAMEDA, CA
Buck, R.H., 1008 Central Ave. FDR-260
ALBANY, NY
Andrews, A. & D.R., 85 State St. AL-18
Kinnear, David M., 78 State St. WHT-25
Legislative Correspondent's Association AES-17; AES-65; AES-66; AES-67; AES-68; AES-69; FDR-277; FDR-325; FDR-361; FDR-362; FDR-363; FDR-364; FDR-371; FDR-394; TED-20; TED-28; TED-30; TED-31; TED-34; HST-20; RMN-28; GRF-10
Our Next President Co. AES-41
Riley, Wilson & Co., 30 Chapel St. AES-8; AES-72
Sherman, W.F., 85 State St. AL-69
Steele, Daniel., Court St. GW-488
437 So. Market St. GW-481; GW-482; TJ-57; TJ-59; TJ-60
472 So. Market St. GW-487
Wendell, C.E. JAG-67
ALBIA, IA
News Printing House WJB-69
ALBUQUERQUE, NM
Rio Grande Pub. Co. WGH-37
ALENDALE, CA
Hobbs, Alfred. WLW-45
ALEXANDRIA, VA
Lynn, A. GW-9
Parrott, John H. AL-268

ALLEGHENY, PA
Song Pub. Co., Mutual Building WM-264
ALLENTOWN, PA
DeLong, George Keller, 538 Gordon St. GW-303
DeLong Pub. Co. GW-304
National Music Bureau WM-53
ALLMONDSVILLE, VA
Mills, Jr., J.T. WW-52
AMBRIDGE, PA
Gradischnig, Frank HCH-29
ANAPOLIS, MD
Halpine, Cpt. Chas. Greham, 1 Taney Ave. DDE-7
ANCHORAGE, KY
Gates, William C. WHH-27
ANDERSON, IN
Anderson Music Pub. Co., 928 Main Street WM-253
ANN ARBOR, MI
Burkhardt, John BC-2
Kays, Warren, 510 Miller Rd. TED-6
ANNONDALE, VA
Dots Okay, Inc. RR-31
ARDMORE, OK
Ardmoreite Pub. Co. FDR-279
ARDMORE, PA
Talarico, Emma, 313 County Line Rd. FDR-342
ARKANSAS CITY, KS
Morgan Music Co. TR-154
ARLETA, CA
Dougherty, Merrell Chester, 13270 Kelowna St. TR-349

ARLINGTON, VA
Goins, Iona D., 5510 Columbia Pike FDR-370

ASBURY PARK, NJ
Dime Song Co. GW-569

ASHLAND, KY
Phillips. Joseph W. WHT-13
Poage, Louise FDR-335

ASHLAND, OH
Bohal & Co. GW-293

ASHLAND, PA
Snyder, Will P. TR-367

ASHATABULA, OH
Pettay, Roe, 7 Church St. WGH-39

ATHENS, GA
Farmer, Arlie and Katie J. Griffeth FDR-379

ATLANTIC CITY, NJ
DuQuesne Music Co. WW-101

ATTLEBORO, MA
Waterfield, J.B. HCH-19

AUBURN, NY
Flager, I.V. USG-54
Milford, U. JBW-10

AUGUSTA, GA
Blackmar, A.E. & Bros. JD-13
199 Broadstreet JD-2

AUGUSTA, ME
The Augusta Press AML-22

AURURA, IL
Success Music Co., 32 So. River St. FDR-360
W.F. Braun Music, Fox & Lasalle Sts. TR-20

BACLIFF, TX
Evans, James L., P.O. Box 663 MISC-26

BALA CYNWYD, PA
B & H Publishing, One Montgomery Ave. JEC-2; JEC-7; MISC-124
Keynote Associates, One Montgomery Ave. JEC-7; MSD-1; BC-6; BC-12; MISC-121; MISC-163

BALTIMORE, MD
Benteen, F.D. GW-106; GW-136; GW-176; WHH-10; WHH-32; WHH-34; WHH-60; WHH-93; HC-9; HC-26; HC-27; HC-56; HC-58; HC-73; HC-77; ZT-3; ZT-19; ZT-26; ZT-35; ZT-53; ZT-55; ZT-66; WS-6; WS-20; WS-24; WS-26
Boswell, J.E. JT-8; MF-27
Boswell's Music Store GW-82
C.A. Gambrill Mfg. Co. GW-571
Carr, J. GW-3
Carr's Musical Repository JA-26
Carr's Music Store GW-42; TJ-21; JMD-2; JMD-3; JMD-15; AJK-34; WS-39
Carusi, Samuel WHH-13; WHH-48; WHH-50; WHH-52; WHH-77; WHH-92; WHH-97; JT-12; HC-49; HC-67; JKP-5
Cole, John GW-37; GW-65; GW-73; GW-478; TJ-6; AJK-33; HC-24; HC-30; HC-61; DW-21
123 Market St. GW-598; JQA-1; JQA-6
Cole and Hewes GW-111
Deems, James WHH-74
Doyle, Thomas G., 295 N. Gay St. JD-48
Durocher, A.H. ZT-85
Emerson Drug Co. GW-312; GW-313
Horton, Tudor HC-112
Kranz-Smith Piano Co., 100 N. Charles St. GW-447
Lucas, Jr., F., 138 Market St. GW-105
McCaffrey, Henry JT-3; JT-6; MF-2; JB-1
205 Baltimore St. AL-319
Miller & Beachman GW-142; GW-149; FP-6; MF-3; MF-32; MF-34; JB-9
Robinson, Henry A. AL-469
Severe, William B. WM-284
Smith, F.I.R., 3039 Huntington Ave. GW-282
Stewart, James M. WM-288
Sutro, Otto WSH-42
Turner, H.A. WHH-18
Whig, A., 141 Baltimore St. HC-45
Willig, G. GW-78; GW-585; WHH-7; ZT-12; MF-7; MF-24; JB-4; DW-5; JD-5; JD-8
No. 71 Market St. AJK-27
Willig, George & Co. JAG-9; BFH-67; GC-125
Willig, George, Jr. GW-38; GW-383; TJ-11; JQA-5; AJK-16; AJK-19; AJK-46; WHH-35; WHH-64; WHH-82; WHH-87; WHH-100; HC-61; HC-75; LC-4; JKP-8; ZT-2; ZT-16; ZT-20; FP-1; DW-21
Wilson, John E. MISC-181

BANGOR, ME
Patch, O.R. JCF-49

BATH, ME
Bath Republican Glee Club JGB-50

Appendix

Colonial Music House TED-24
Magoun, P.I. USG-24; JGB-16

BATTLE CREEK, MI
Chas. E. Roat Co., Inc. TR-297
Golden Heart Music Co. FDR-414

BELLAIRE, OH
Ohio Music Co. WM-73

BELLEVILLE, IL
Marsh Pub. Co., 711 East "B" St. RMN-2

BELOIT, WI
Free Press Publishing House ND-4

BERGEN, NY
Mann, E.R. WM-116

BEVERLY HILLS, CA
Accadia Music Co. JFK-15
We The People Committee, 205 S. Beverly Dr. WLW-8
Zoeller Music Co. FDR-157; FDR-281

BIRMINGHAM, AL
Roberts & Son MISC-25

BINGHAMTON, NY
151 Oak St. DAM-17

BLOOMFIELD, IN
Craig, Ira FDR-83
East, John R. GC-140

BLOOMFIELD, NE
Mulligan, John T. WJB-70

BLOOMFIELD, NJ
Lehn & Finks Products Corp. MISC-17

BLOOMINGTON, IL
Henry, C. FDR-83
507 N. Madison St. FDR-193; FDR-257

BLUFFTON, IN
Karns Music Co. WM-199

BOSTON, MA
Adams, Benj. HC-100
54 Court St. HC-13
Adams, Charles.
No. 23 Tremont St. WHH-68
Al Smith Club of Boston AES-61
Amphion Pub. Co. TR-105
Ariston Pub. Co., 205 Huntington Ave. TR-134
Arnold, Adelaide, 258 Columbus Ave. JQA-9
Arrow Music Pub. Co., 24 Warren St. AL-225
Arthur P. Schmidt Co., 120 Boylston St. GW-294

Ashton, John, 197 Washington St. AJK-14; WHH-58; WHH-83; JBL-6
Bach Music Co. DDE-32
Barker, George, 164A Tremont St. TR-120
B.F. Wood Music Co., The WM-171
Birchard, C.C. & Co. GW-284; GW-449; GW-514; TJ-52; AJK-39; AL-370; AL-473; AL-484; TR-362
Blackmer, F.A., 49 Cornhill WM-250
Boston Music Co. GW-374; WW-55; FDR-68; MISC-126; MISC-127
Boston Sunday Advertiser GW-211; WW-159
Boston Sunday American GW-218; GW-301; TR-18
Boston Sunday Globe TR-320
Boston Sunday Journal WM-97
Boston Sunday Post WW-59; FDR-328
Bostonia Pub. Co., 181 Tremont St. AL-206
Bradlee, C. GW-100; JA-10; AJK-12; WHH-72
Washington St. GW-100
107 Washington St. JBL-8
135 Washington St. WHH-62; DW-8; DW-9; DW-10
164 Washington St. GW-40; GW-100; AJK-2; AJK-41; DW-10
Bradley, J.N. HC-105
Buckington, J.T., 5 Marlborough St. JA-21
Cahill, B. HC-4
Clapp, C.C. & Co., 69 Court St. AL-97
Clark, Marshall & Co. MISC-173
Cooper, D.W. Pub. Co., 224 Tremont St. AL-183
Conant, Fred K. WW-84
Conley & Moore, No. 19 Marlborough St. JA-13
Coupon Music GW-189
Coverly, Jr., Nathaniel, Milk Street TJ-8; TJ-10
Cragie, Charles D. & Co., Box 12203 TR-304
Dalton Music Pub. Co. WM-225
Daly Music Publishers, 665 Washington St. GW-377
Ditson and Co. GW-615; AL-23
Ditson, Oliver AL-452
Washington St. JMN-22; HC-22; HC-113; JCF-2; JCF-15; JCF-28; JCF-33; JFC-34; JCF-54; AL-116
115 Washington St. GW-85; GW-93; GW-139; GW-141; GW-119; GW-302;

DWC-3; HC-59; HC-91; ZT-15; ZT-17; ZT-27; ZT-30; ZT-70; ZT-70; MF-13; WS-16; FP-8; JCF-44; JB-12; AJN-11; DW-1; DW-8; DW-17; MISC-31
135 Washington St. GW-94; HC-6; HC-7; HC-23; HC-57; HC-60; HC-63; DW-29
Ditson, Oliver & Co. GW-134; GW-281; GW-340; GW-361; GW-579; AL-23; AL-40; AL-467; AL-495; USG-18; USG-51; USG-280; JAG-12; JAG-70; JAG-76; JAG-81; DW-3; SLP-1
Washington Street GW-429; JCF-55
115 Washington St. GW-80; DW-6
135 Washington St. GW-148
271 Washington St. GW-123; AL-493
277 Washington St. GW-222; GW-138; GW-154; GW-160; GW-156; GW-181; GW-388; GW-422; GW-426; GW-574; GW-594; WS-4; WS-7; JB-11; GBM-8; GBM-10; GBM-33; GBM-37; AL-10; AL-12; AL-25; AL-45; AL-52; AL-66; AL-75; AL-91; AL-100; AL-101; AL-102; AL-104; AL-133; AL-135; AL-141; AL-156; AL-162; AL-195; AL-236; AL-237; AL-291; AL-293; AL-318; AL-493; AJN-4; AJN-7; AJN-10; HG-9; HG-10; HG-16; USG-10; USG-20; USG-27; USG-36; USG-52; USG-48; USG-83; USG-112; USG-168; USG-216; USG-295; DW-19; DW-29; JBL-11; JD-10; JD-18; JD-19; JD-60; NB-1; NB-2; BFB-3; BFB-6
451 Washington St. USG-25; USG-71; SJT-4; RBH-5; RBH-13; RBH-19; RBH-35; RBH-59; WSH-13; WSH-23; WSH-24; JAG-8; JAG-55; JAG-61; JAG-80; JGB-12; JGB-24; JGB-58; GC-34; GC-142;GC-159; DW-2; BFB-5; BFB-7; JSJ-2
Dobbin, G. and Murphy AJK-1
Dutton & Wentworth Printers, Transcript Office JKP-11
E.C. Shirmer Music Co. TJ-47
221 Columbus Ave. AL-356
Educational Pub. Co. GW-445
Evans Music Co. TR-122; TR-168; WHT-11
522 Mass. Ave. TR-65; TR-234
Evans, W.A. & Bro., 1 Columbia St. USG-138; MISC-88
Evans, W.A.& Bros., 50 Bromfield St. JAG-32

Fisher, James HC-101; HC-102
71 Court St HC-11
Fitzwilliam, Edward BFH-94
Frank Music Affiliates, 116 Boylston St. GRF-2
122 Boylston JFK-63
George, L.F., 45 High St. WJB-89
Georges Pub. Co. TR-32
Ginn and Co. GW-443; GW-455; GW-557; GW-558; WHH-113; AL-375; AL-377; AL-474
Ginn, Heath and Co. GW-515
Goullard, Louis P., 108 Tremont St. BFB-15
Grant and Colfax Club, Ward 11 USG-140
Graupner, G. JA-10
No. 6 Franklin St. GW-2; GW-25; GW-34; GW-75; JMN-3
Hardy Music Co. WM-5
Heinrich, P.A. JA-7
Hewitt, James TJ-12
Hewitt, James L. & Co., No. 36 Market St. DW-14
Hirsche & Clay, 18 Boylston St. TR-201
Homeyer, Chas. W. and Co., 498 Boylston St. WLW-53
Howe, Elias, 7 Cornhill Street GW-535; WHH-134; WS-43
103 Court Street GW-435; GW-567; GW-568; TJ-19; TJ-69; TJ-70; AJK-54; AJK-55; WHH-112; WHH-135; WHH-136; ; ZT-69; ZT-80; ZT-81; WS-32; WS-44; WS-45; MISC-131; MISC-174
Hutchinson, Jr., Jesse. and Co. JBR-2
Imperial Music Co. WM-35
Ironworkers Local 7, Union Hall, South Boston BC-11
Isaiah Thomas and Company, No. 45 Newberry St. GW-16
Isaiah Thomas & Ebenezer T. Andrews GW-10; GW-12; GW-81; JA-4; JA-12
No. 45 Newberry St. GW-18; GW-127
Jackson, G.K., Hanover St. GW-27
Jacobs, Walter GW-273
Jas. S. White Co., 224 Tremont St. WW-82
Jewett, John J. & Co. JCF-5
John Hancock Mutual Life Insurance Company GW-438; GW-614
Keith, C.H., 67 & 69 Court St. GW-56; GW-115
Keith and Moore, 67 & 69 Court St. DW-32

Keith's Music Pub. House, 67 & 69 Court St. GW-56; HC-78
Kemp, Robert GW-542
Krey, George M., 493 Washington St. WM-32
L.A. Kennedy Dry Goods Store CC-14
Ladies at their Exposition, Armory Hall FP-9
Lennox Music Co. MISC-43; MISC-47
Lewis H. Ross Music Co., 228 Tremont St. HCH-24
Linley & Moore, No. 19 Marlborough St. JA-14
Mallet & Graupner, Musical Academy GW-48
Marsh, Bella, No. 36 Cornhill MVB-8
Marsh, Stephen W., 371 Washington St. MVB-11
Massachusetts State Committee Progressive Party, 70 Devonshire St. TR-380
Maydell Publications, 470 Stuart St. GW-320
McCargo, P.R. & Co. CAA-4; BFH-4; BFH-5; BFH-61; BFH-72; GC-30; GC-54
McCargo, Pub. Co. BFH-61
MacPherson & Fraser, 164A Tremont St. WW-109
Miles & Thompson GC-36; GC-130
Miller, John C., 177 Tremont St. HCH-7
Music Service Company, 170-A Tremont St. GW-250; FDR-72; FDR-178
Mussey, B.B. and Company, 29 Cornhill GW-427
Neal Pub. Co. MISC-126; MISC-127
New England Music Co. AL-228; WHT-7
New England News Co. HG-11
Oakes, W.H. & E.H. Wade, 197 Washington St. HC-50; ZT-13
Oliver Ditson Company GW-183; GW-184; GW-344; GW-412; GW-546; GW-574; AL-272; AL-351; USG-18; USG-43; USG-44; USG-45; USG-244; WSH-14; WSH-25; BFH-47; GC-66; GC-71; GC-75; WM-60; WM-151; WM-218; TR-202; TR-352; WW-116; WW-159; DW-15; MISC-81
449-451 Washington St. USG-18
453-463 Washington St. GW-411; GW-413; GW-51;9; AL-350; AL-352; USG-43; USG-45; BFH-12; WJB-34; WM-2

Ordway, A. & J.P., 339 Washington St. ZT-37
Ordway, J.P., Washington St. MF-19
Parker & Ditson, Washington St. WHH-43
107 Washington St. AJK-9
135 Washington St. WHH-1; WHH-25; WHH-41; WHH-54; WHH-59; WHH-103
Parker, S.H., 141 Washington St. AJK-7
Partridge, Horace GBM-19; AL-152
125,127 & 131 Hanover St. JCF-37
Peoples Recreation-Music Co., 21 Wellington Ave. TR-81
Perkins, George H., 40 Court St. AES-57
Perna, Michael WW-50
Perry, John F. & Co., 538 Washington St. GW-341; GW-390; RBH-16; RBH-23
Popular Music Co., 181 Tremont St. AES-14
Prentiss, Henry, No. 33 Court St. WHH-11; WHH-15; WHH-46; WHH-53; WHH-67; WHH-81; WHH-104; WHH-107; HC-19; HC-20; HC-48; HC-53; JKP-5
R.D. Row Music Co., 725 Boylston St. FDR-19
Reed, G.P. JCF-7
17 Tremont Row JQA-3; WHH-14; JT-9; ZT-68; DW-17
Reed, G.P. & Co., 13 Tremont St. MF-25; JCF-21
17 Tremont Row WHH-95; WHH-137; FP-2
Richards, Samuel FDR-94
Richardson, Nathan, 282 Washington St. JCF-1; JCF-36; JB-2
Rollins, E.F. USG-259
Russell & Patee, 61 Court St. JB-10
108 Tremont St. JA-9; AL-142
Russell & Tolman GW-629
219 Washington St. GW-401
291 Washington St. AL-134; USG-147; JD-39
Russell, Benjamin B., New Branch Bank JA-19
515 Washington St. GBM-27
Russell, G.D. & Co., No. 126 Tremont St. GW-151; GBM-45; AL-103; AL-146; USG-296; RBH-27; JD-14
Samuels, Edward A. GW-403; MISC-119
Saunders Pubs., Inc., 119 W. 57th St. AL-132
Schirmer Music Company, 221 Columbus Ave. AL-355

Shawmut Chemical Printing Co. JCF-10; JCF-12
Stacy & Richardson, 11 Milk St. JCF-52
Stone, E.G., 80 Huntington Ave. HCH-28
Suffolk Music Publishing Co. WGH-57
Suffolk Ward & County Committee, Washington St. JCF-17
Thayer, A.M. & Co. BFB-12
Thayer & Eldridge AL-8
Thompson, C.W. & Co. AL-390; TR-226; WW-81
13 West St TR-310
Tolman, Henry, 153 Washington St. GW-108; GW-456
219 Washington St. GW-147; GW-148
291 Washington St. JA-13; GBM-40; AL-83; AL-122; AL-161; AL-238; JD-16
Tolman, Henry & Co. AL-33
291 Washington St. GW-317; GW-398; USG-199; DW-24
Trifet, F., 36 Bromfield St. BFH-91; GC-8; GC-128; GC-131; WM-65; WJB-17
408 Washington St. GC-161
Vinton Music TR-33
Veteran Pub. Co., 28 State St. AL-214
Von Hagen, P.A. & Cos., No. 3, Cornhil GW-4; JA-3; JA-5
Von Hagen, P.A., Jr. & Co., No. 62, Newbury St. JA-4
Wade, E.H., 197 Washington St. MF-9; DW-31
Weeks, Jordan & Co. WHH-86
White, Smith & Co. GW-321; GBM-41; USG-38; USG-95; SJT-18; RBH-3; JAG-6; JAG-80; JGB-30; JGB-99; BFH-71; BFH-80; GC-28; GC-39; GC-99; GC-107; BFB-1; JSJ-6
298-300 Washington St. HG-7
516 Washington St. USG-200; USG-242; USG-243; SJT-14; SJT-18; RBH-3; RBH-9; RBH-32; RBH-36; WSH-16; WSH-36; JAG-6; JAG-37; JAG-74; JAG-79; JAG-93; BFH-7; GC-55; GC-67; GC-136
White-Smith Music Pub. Co. GC-57; WM-40; DW-34
296, 300 Washington St. USG-8
White, Smith & Perry, 298-300 Washington St. USG-8
Wilkins, J.H. and R.B. Carter GW-517
Women's Republican Club of Massachusetts, 46 Beacon St. CC-43

BREMERTON, WA
Ward, Henry, Y.M.C.A. Bldg. DDE-39

BRIDGEPORT, CT
Knablin, Oscar F., 1113 North Ave. TR-10
Smith & Jennings Pub. Co., 61 Fairfield Ave. JGB-63

BRISTOL, NH
Ladd, J.W. TR-208; TR-229

BRISTOL, PA
Williams, Mr. & Mrs. John E., RD #2 FDR-174

BRONX, NY
Nolasco, Felix, 1149 Fleley Ave. JFK-19

BROOKLYN, NY
Anderson & Co., 298 Fulton St. USG-223
Beacon Music Pub. Co., 8215 20th Ave. DAM-21
Biondi, Jos., 1713 E. 2nd St. WW-97
Breslow, Ben, 1215 E. 13th St. AES-51
Brooklyn International Conservatory of Music, 33 St. John Place WW-110
Brooklyn Young Republican Club BFH-53
Castell & Co. HS-5
Chandler-Ebel Co., 222 Livingston St. TR-57
Coleman, Charles, 253 Linden Blvd. FDR-45
515 Fulton St. TR-129
600 Kosciusko St. TR-13
DeWaltoff, D.B., 451 47th St. HCH-23; FDR-122
Franks & Tucker, 299 Underhill Ave. AES-22
Graff, Jerry De. WW-51
Grube & Metz., 163 Atlantic St. AL-241
Hager, J.M. BFH-56
Hamilton Music Pub. Co., 419 86th St. AES-44
Haskins, Wm. R., 892 Dekalb TR-60
Held, Charles W. GW-179; USG-174; WSH-30; JGB-52; GC-109
227 Fulton St. GC-44
Henry Peters Co., 7005 Percey Terrace AES-10
Hjousebery, L., 438 Fulton St. ZT-83
Holmes, D.S., 67 Fourth St. AL-499; USG-47; DW-30
Jacob Bros., 195 Broadway GC-35
Jones, Franklin, 669 Gates Ave. GW-363
Louis Mollenhauer's Conservatory of Music, 71 Marlborough Rd. MISC-40

Makhoul & Nahmee, 574 47th St. FDR-142
Miller, Andrew, 339 10th St. WW-166
Molineau, Geo, 37 Fourth St. RBH-43
Patriot Printing & Publishing Co., 128-130 Sumpter St. WW-53
Popular Music Co., 179 Warren St. TR-196
Richardson Music Pub. Co., 240 Howard St. TR-180
Roosevelt "My Friends" Legion, 428 54th Street FDR-309
Silvers, Herman, 249 Coleridge St. LBJ-17
Smiles Cartoon Service, 532 Lafayette Ave. MISC-4
Spaulding & Kornder, 487 Fulton St. BFH-17
Spooner, A. and Son WHH-133
Stanley, James, 144 41st St. WM-206
Unohoo Publishing Company, 179 Marcy Ave. GW-248; HCH-22
Waston, Chas. B., 5819 5th Ave. WW-17; WW-18

BRYN MAWR, PA
Elkan-Vogel, Inc. GW-394; TJ-48; AL-288; AL-326
Theodore Presser Co. AL-343; JFK-58

BUFFALO, NY
Beck, Fred CC-13
Blodgett & Bradford MF-4; MF-5
209 Main St AL-9
Buffalo Times AES-38
Cottier & Denton, 269 Main St. USG-100; USG-124; USG-225
Denton, Cottier & Daniels, 269 Main St. WM-49
Doyle, James P., 552 E. Eagle St. WW-138
Eire County Republican Banner TED-11
Fischer, Leander, 143 Hodge Ave. WM-115
Great Lakes Music Publishers FDR-415
Hawthorne-Wollow Pub. Co. WW-175
Hickey & Tigue, 527 Ellicott Sq. AES-43
Kurtzmann & Co., 526 Niagra St. GW-380
National Paean Co., 644 Ellicott St. WM-47; WM-48
Niagara Music Publishing Company WW-156
Rottenbach, August, 499 Main St. JGB-71

Sage, J. & Sons, 209 Main St. MF-22
Sangster, Urania N., 203 Auburn Ave. CC-5
Sheppard, Cottier & Co., 215 Main St. SAD-6; GBM-76; AL-130; JD-38
Stansell, E.K., 175 Normal Avenue GW-237
Thomas and Company WHH-125
Weasner, H.C. & Co., 244 Genesee St. TR-22

BURLINGTON, VT
Story, H.L. AL-126; JD-21

BUTTE, MT
Lyden, M.M. FDR-339

CAINSVILLE, MO
Frazier, Stanley H. WW-192

CALDWELL, NJ
Bernhardt, Fred C. DDE-64

CAMDEN, NJ
Temperance Gazette Printing House, 131 Federal St. CBF-2

CAMBRIDGE, MA
Coupon Music Pub. Co., Lafayette Sq. BFH-21
Intercollegiate Music League FDR-105
Romney & Donahue AES-4

CAMDEN, NJ
Friant Music Co WW-148
Shantz & Jackson, Temple Theatre Bldg. GW-352
Street, J. USG-80

CAMP VERDE, AZ
Lowthian, Axie A. WW-74

CANAL DOVER, OH
Arnold Brothers JGB-86

CANISTEO, NY
Countryman, Carl C. HCH-20

CANTON, IL
Parlin & Orendorff Company GW-556

CANTON, MA
Bracken, James, 23 Kinsley Place FDR-171

CANTON, OH
Dice, Harold Edwin, 335 Cleveland Ave., NW FDR-301
Howard and McCarthy WM-220
Lomady, A.E. WM-317
McClay, Sam, 1300 25th St. N.W. FDR-42
Reinkendorff, Emil WM-43
Vitak, Louis WM-228; WM-273

CAROL STREAM, IL
Somerset Press GW-375; JA-18

CARSON CITY, NV
Fox, John G. HG-19

CARTARET, NJ
Lennox, Chas. J., 92 Warren St. AES-29

CEDER RAPIDS, IA
WM-245

CHAGRIN FALLS, OH
Spirit of Freedom Office JBR-3

CHAMPAIGN, IL
Allied Arts Publications, 232 E. Eire St. TED-5
Granger & Francis, 107 West University Avenue AES-18
Mark Foster Music Co., Box 4012 AL-341

CHAPEL HILL, NC
Hinshaw Music, Inc., P.O. Box 470 MISC-110

CHARLESTON, SC
Babcock & Co. GW-461; AJK-52
Oates & Bros., 234 & 236 King St. GW-164
Siegling, J., 69 Broad St. GW-29
109 Meeting St. GW-599

CHARLESTON, WV
Honaker, T.J. CC-12
Jackson, E.M., Box 70 FDR-390

CHARLISLE, PA
Committee On Arrangements WM-242

CHARLOTTE, NC
Heritage House AL-481

CHATSWORTH, IL
Oliver Music Co. WM-138

CHELSEA, MA
Clickbound Music Co., 165 Walnut St. JFK-27

CHESTER, PA
Valley Brook Publications, Inc., 112 E. 5th St. DDE-108; DDE-109

CHICAGO, IL
Allied Arts Pubs., 232 E. Erie St. TED-9
Anthony, Lee & Co., 1205 Republic Bldg. TR-295
Applegate, William J., 18 Alta Vista Terrace WHT-53
Arzich Bros. FDR-30
Aubry Stauffer Co., Grand Opera House TR-91

Baker, Clarice A., 6437 Glenwood Ave. WLW-68
Baldwin Co., The, 267 Wabash Ave. TR-298
Barton, (Miss) Rose, 809 Washington Blvd. WM-237
Bent, Geo. P. GW-536
Black, Smith & Co. TR-46
Bloom, Sol GW-98; WJB-10; WM-57; WM-144; WM-147; TR-50
Randolph and Dearborn Streets GW-297; WJB-3; WM-13
Brant, S.B. BFH-105
Buckley & Co. TR-279
Butterfield, J.A. USG-57
Calumet Music Co., 201 E. 26th St. USG-170
Carl Fischer, Inc., 306 S. Wabash Ave. DAM-25
Chandler, F.S. & Co. GC-102; GC-137; JSJ-1
Chandler, H.F. WM-85
Chicago American GW-240
ChicagoBoard of Education GW-525
Chicago Daily News GC-87; GC-88; GC-89; GC-89; GC-90
Chicago-Marion Businessmen's Club WGH-14
Chicago Music Co. BFH-26; WJB-9; WJB-91; TR-178; TR-179
152 State St. USG-119; USG-175; JAG-51; JGB-73
Chicago Sunday Tribune WLW-22; WLW-23; WLW-43; WLW-48
Clayton F. Summy Co. TR-328; WLW-61
220 Wabash Ave. WM-137
Cook, Edgar J., 10 S. La Salle St. TR-266
Co-operative Printing Co., 5443 Drexel Ave. SP-1
Consolidated Speciality Co., 1209 N. LeClaire Ave. FDR-8
Country Music Publishers., 20 E. Jackson Blvd. FDR-28
Cuprigraph Co., 404 Fort Dearborn Bldg. WM-105
Cyderman Music Pub. Co. HCH-51
De Montte Bros. USG-254
De Montte Music Co., 855 E. 75th St. AML-9
Denison, T.S. & Co. AL-222
DeVaigne Music Corp. FDR-134; FDR-248
443 S. Dearborn St. FDR-55; FDR-134

Dixie Music House, 134 Van Buren St. TR-308
Donnelley, Fasette & Loyd JAG-68
Dunn, W.P. and Co. BFH-102
Echo Music Co. GW-539
358 Dearborn St. TR-141; WHT-29
Edwards, Deutsch & Heitmann WM-34
Englewood Music Co., 516 Englewood Ave. FDR-267
Excell, E.O., Fine Arts Bldg., Michigan Ave. WM-156
Felden, Peter J., 73 West Kinzie St. WJB-49
Fifer, Gene WLW-29
5614 Chicago Ave. DAM-26
Fish Music Publications, 3541 W. 62nd St. AL-294
F.J. Ringley Publishing Co. WW-162
Forster Music Publisher, Inc. WM-157; WGH-38
216 S. Wabash Ave. AML-3; FDR-104; DDE-51
235 S. Wabash Ave. WGH-26
F.S. Chandler Co., 244-246 Wells St. JGB-76
Furnish, Arthur R., 630 N. Robey St. WHT-35
Gamble, Gene, 64 E. Jackson Blvd. CC-4
Gamble Hinged Music Co. CC-37; CC-38; CC-39; CC-49; CC-5.
Gibbs, Charles, 65 Washington St. WM-323
Goldberg, Reka WW-23
Graham, Roger, 145 Clark St. WW-16
Great Western Music Co. GW-379
442 Plymouth Ct. FDR-31
Hall & McCreary Company GW-523; GW-534; GW-541; AL-488; MISC-168; MISC-170
434 S. Wabash Ave. GW-339; GW-527
Hallet & Davis Piano Co., 239-241. Wabash Ave. GW-575
Halpin & McClure HG-21
Harold Rossiter Music Co. TR-41; WGH-31
Hart, Joe, 139 Clark St. FDR-209
Harty, Robert E., 443 S. Dearborn St. FDR-323
Haggard, J.M., 121 W. Wacker Dr. DAM-47
Higgins, A. Judson SAD-3
40 Clark St. JCF-29
Higgins, H.M., 117 Randolph St. GW-274; GW-559; WS-23; JCF-19; AL-35; AL-36; AL-39; AL-41; AL-54; AL-56; AL-145; AL-149; AL-168; AL-242; AL-253; AL-265; AL-267; AL-271; AL-277; AL-432; AL-513; AJN-16; USG-34; USG-208; JD-36
Higgins, J.F. WM-282
Home Publishing Co. GW-606
228 Wabash Avenue GW-523
Hope Music Co., 41 E. Randolph St. WM-251
Hope Publishing Co. GW-529
Howard & Wilson Publishing Company WJB-25
H.T. Fitzsimmons Co., 23 E. Jackson Blvd. WLW-30
Hurser, O.G. WJB-65
Irvine Music House, 59 E. Van Buren TR-301
Jacobs-Bond, Carrie & Son, 746 Michigan Ave. WW-212
John Church Co. GW-524
Jos. C. Merrick Publishing Co., 333 S. Dearborn St. WW-169
Joseph Frank Music Pub. Co., 127 Dearborn St. HCH-21
Kent, May Walton, 1705 Lanier Place, Apt. 304 GW-457
Kerr, Charles H. & Company SP-4
Kohl, P.J. and Co. AML-28
Lamb, Isabel, 6530 Lafayette Ave. FDR-289
Layton, Joseph T. & Co., 6511 S. Artesian Ave. WW-73
Lenington, Norman G., 308 Dearborn St. WM-229
Leo. Fiest, Inc. WW-7; WW-8; WW-9
Lozier Bros. BFH-108
Lyman, M.B. and Co., Kenball Hall TR-311
Lyon & Healy WJB-26; WM-117; WM-176; JMP-1
Clark & Washington Sts. AL-67; AJN-1; AJN-3; AJN-13; AJN-19; HS-3; HS-6; USG-1; USG-2; USG-3
114 Clark St. AJN-25
116 Washington St. USG-86
161 State St. BFH-89
Manker, Lucille, 2200 E. 70th Place HCH-33
Manzer's Music Store, 4230 Cottage Grove Ave. TR-26
Maranell Pub. Co. HCH-45
Mark Bros. Music Pub. Co., 153 La Salle St. WJB-19
Maurice Abrahams Music Co., 1570 Broadway WW-5

McCormick Music Co. TR-162; TR-313
McKinley Music Co. GW-397; GW-608; USG-131; TR-7
McKinley Publishers, Inc. USG-220; USG-234
Merrill & Brennan, 91 Washington St. AL-82
Merrill, H.T. HG-2
Meyer & Brother, 108 Washington St. TR-99
Meyers, Chas. A., 145 N. Clark St. GW-206
Miessner Institute of Music, 1219 Kimball Building GW-336
Miller, W.W. RBH-46
Milton Weil Music Co., 54 W. Randolph St. GW-307
Moderne Pubs., 2611 Indiana Ave. USG-164
Modern Standard Music Co., 54 Randolph St. WLW-28
Molter & Wurlitzer, 117 Randolph St. USG-4
Murphy, Doc, 1131 Unity Bldg. WJB-36
Music Products Corp., 28 E. Jackson Blvd. FDR-215
Musical Publicity For Coolidge And Dawes CC-1; CC-31
National Music Co. JAG-11; JGB-5; JGB-77; BFH-62; BFH-63; GC-37; GC-52; GC-53; GC-77; GC-79; WM-29; WM-159; WM-174; WW-4; FDR-131; FDR-196; JBW-2
113 Adams St. GC-77
215-221 Wabash Ave. GW-349; USG-105; JGB-11; BFH-6; BFH-81; GC-10; CG-76; GC-114; WJB-30; WJB-97; WM-14; WM-15; WM-44; WM-45; WM-109; WM-150
266 Wabash Ave. BFH-59; WJB-54
339 S. Wabash Ave. TR-82
425 S. Wabash Ave. TR-98
State & Quincey Sts. TR-298
Neale Wrightman Publishers, 30 W. Washington St. DAM-24
Nelson, N. TR-73
New York & Chicago Pub. House, Suite 612, 59 Dearborn St. TR-372
Noland Commercial Studios, 224 S. Michigan Blvd. AML-2
Norton, S.F., 544 Ogden Ave. JBW-11
Orpheum Pub. Co. FDR-268
Oscar Schmoll Music Co. TR-314
O'Toole, Angela Maria JFK-2

Owen, Delos, 215 East Chestnut St. AML-32; DDE-88
Page, Sr., Pierre, 510 Deming Place FDR-191
Peterson-Scheich Pub. Co., 530 Diversity Pkwy. WLW-10
Pettibone, W.H. WM-285
Piatt Music Co., 69 Dearborn St. WJB-16
Pond, Wm. A., 25 Union Sq. GC-22
Premium Music Co., 235 State St. WM-81
Press Club of Chicago USG-182
Princeton-Gibbs Adv. Co. TR-71
Professor Joseph Frank Music Co., 127 Dearborn St. AES-45; HCH-67
Progressive Pub. Co., Omaha Bldg. TR-78
Protection Pub. Co., South Central BFH-20
Quadrangle Books, Inc., 180 N. Wacker JFK-70
Reed's Temple of Music, 69 Dearborn St. AL-160
Republican Service League, 920 McCormick Bldg. FDR-235
Rettmons Music Co. WM-62
Reynolds, W.L. WJB-64
Rickman, Lemonier and Johnson, 3159 State St. TR-253
Rodeheaver Co. WW-168
14 W. Washington St. TR-149
Roosevelt High School TR-220
Roosevelt Pub. Co., 1741 N. Central Ave. FDR-149
Roosevelt University TJ-71
Root & Cady TJ-38; JD-27
67 Washington St. AL-51; AL-154; AL-160; AL-419; AJN-5; USG-113; USG-123; USG-139; USG-141; USG-144; USG-157; USG-210; USG-211; USG-231; JGB-38; JD-24
95 Clark St. GW-414; JCF-4; AL-62; AL-96; AL-99; AL-127; AL-140; AL-143; AL-256; AL-285; USG-39; JD-22; JD-23; JD-25
Root & Sons JAG-49
Root, Frank K. & Co. GW-223; WW-6; WHT-8
307 & 309 Wabash Ave. WM-64; WM-77
95 Clark St. GW-414; JCF-4; AL-62; AL-96; AL-99; AL-127; AL-140; AL-143; AL-256; AL-285; USG-39; JD-22; JD-23; JD-25

Appendix

Root & Sons JAG-49
Root, Frank K. & Co. GW-223; WW-6; WHT-8
307 & 309 Wabash Ave. WM-64; WM-77; WM-262
Rossiter, Harold WGH-31
323-325 W. Madison St. WGH-18
Rossiter, Will WM-287; TR-21; MISC-42
56 5th Ave. AL-278; USG-217; TR-166; TR-273
71 W. Randolph St. WW-3; WW-125; WW-126; WW-127
136 Lake St. TR-40; WW-11; WW-117; WW-186; MISC-44
152 Lake St. TR-38; TR-305; TR-358
173 W. Madison St. AL-201; WLW-50; DDE-18; MISC-66
225 Washington St. WM-56
Rubank, Inc. GW-400; GW-441; GW-520
Russell, G.D. and Co. GBM-60
S. Brainard's Sons Co. GW-570; GW-611; TJ-26; JCF-30; USG-159; JAG-66; JGB-89; BFH-88; GC-59; CG-82; GC-93; CJ-141; WJB-8; WJB-63; WM-188; TR-16; MISC-172
151 & 153 Wabash Ave. WJB-18
341 & 343 Euclid Ave. JAG-109
Schildkret, S., 15 Patomic Ave. TR-359
Saint Germain Press Co., P.O. Box 1133 GW-217
Smith, Howard & Son, 9019 Commercial Ave. TR-165
Snyder, Walter D., 95 S. La Salle St. TR-39; TR-217
State Music House TR-332
Stewart, Charles W., 439 Arlington Place AES-70
Success Music Co., Star Bldg. TR-257
343 Fifth Ave. WM-91
356 Dearborn St. TR-182; TR-282
Sunlight Music Co., Grand Opera House TR-36
Summy, Clayton F., 64 E. Van Buren St. GW-214
Swisher, M.D., 149 Wabash Ave. BFH-22
Ted Brown Music Co. FDR-108; FDR-148
Temple Music Co. WM-175
Thompson Music Co. WM-18; TR-376
Townsend, Maida, 7049 Clyde Ave. WLW-7

Union League Club GW-528
Union Party Headquarters, 188 W. Randolph St. WL-1; WL-2
Vanderpoel, Kate, 1502 Great Northern Blvd. WM-111; WM-252
Victor Kremer Co. USG-235; WJB-40; WJB-45; WJB-46; TR-88; WHT-61
Volunteers, The, 435 N. Michigan Avenue AML-27
W.I. Leggett Co., 852 S. Sawyer Ave. WM-158
Ward, Dennis A., 516 N. Lockwood Ave. AJK-40
Webster News Co. BFH-64
White, Smith & Co. JAG-114; JGB-95
188 & 190 State St. JAG-23; JAG-87; CAA-1
Windsor Music Co. WM-202
266 & 268 Wabash Ave. WM-3; WM-168
Wolsieffer, P.M., 76 State St. WM-263
201 Clark St. WJB-22; WM-11; WM-59
Zeph Fitz-Gerald Publicity For Coolidge-Dawes, Wrigley Bldg. CC-1
Zodiac Pub. Co. FDR-217

CHICKASHA, OK
Powell & Abbott TJ-33

CINCINNATI, OH
Allen Brothers, 30 Arcade JGB-59
American Publishing House SAD-11; AL-298
No. 60 W. Fourth St. SAD-12; AL-397
Authenrieth, Mrs. Wm., 105 Lincoln Inn Ct. WHT-15
Belmont Music Co., Indiana & 26th St. USG-282
Benham, H.L. & Co., 46 Arcade St. CAA-8
Bernhardt, Frank G. TR-338
Church, John, Jr., 66 W. Fourth St. GW-406; SAD-4; AL-2; AL-4; AL-11; AL-72; AL-173; AL-274; AL-290; AL-463; AJN-2; AJN-24; USG-6; USG-7; USG-11; USG-53; USG-77; USG-126; USG-212
Church, John & Co. SJT-6; SJT-22; WSH-32; WSH-38; RBH-10; RBH-24; JAG-42; JAG-50; JAG-82; JGB-3; JGB-29; JGB-44; JGB-61; GC-143
66 W. Fourth St. AL-138; AL-173; USG-93; USG-120; USG-289;

USG-290; RBH-4; RBH-8; WSH-7; WSH-8; WSH-15; WSH-19; JAG-1; JAG-10; JAG-17; JAG-85; JGB-31; JGB-36; JGB-33; GC-23; GC-126
Dobmeyer, J.J. & Co. AL-283; USG-89; USG-254
Edwards & Goshorn WS-38
Fillmore Bros., 119 W. Sixth St. WM-28; WM-104; WM-314; TR-183; SCS-1
421 Elm St. JL-1
Ficke, William A. WM-223
Fonda, C.Y., 72 W. Fourth St. USG-287
Frost and Dory Publishers, 140-142 Vine St. JCF-42; JB-18
Gale & Mullane Music Co., N.W. cor 5th & Sycamore Sts. WJB-5
Geo. B. Jennings Co. WM-189; MISC-41
George Jalberg Music Co. WM-164; TR-112
115 W. Seventh St. WM-100
Groene Music Pub. Co., No. 32 E. Fifth St. WM-102
Helmick, F.W., 50 W. Fourth St. SJT-24; RBH-7; RBH-14; RBH-18; RBH-28
180 Elm St. WSH-43; JAG-84; JAG-110
278 W. Sixth Street GW-82; GW-131; GW-171; SJT-5
Ilsen & Co., 25 & 27 W. Sixth St. JGB-57; WM-9; TR-75
James, . U.P. WHH-132
John Church Co. GW-524; JMD-11; AL-224; AL-277; JGB-96; CC-145; WM-177; WM-198; WM-200; WM-260; CBF-6
74 W. Fourth St. USG-190; BFH-49; BFH-70; BFH-83; BFH-125; GC-117
Lincoln Centennial Memorial Assn. AL-430
McMullen & Gates, 143 Walnut St. GW-607; AL-497
Neely, Unberto WLW-24
Newhall & Evans Music Co. BFH-74
171 W. Fourth St. BFH-37
Newhall, George D. JGB-10
50 W. Fourth St. JAG-16
Orville Brewer Pub. Co., Auditorium Bldg. GW-617
Peters, A.C. & Bro. GW-586; GW-600; GBM-38; AL-257; AL-286
94 W. Fourth St. SAD-2; GBM-3; AL-73; AL-465

Peters & Co. HC-3; JCB-3
Peters, W.C. ZT-21; ZT-84
Peters, W.C. & Sons ZT-45; WS-47; JB-15; JB-16
Phillip-Gene & Edwards Music Co. WW-134
Phillips, Margueite, 1017 Provident Bank Bldg. WLW-19
Philomath, W.A. HC-104
Rauch, F.W., 82 W. Fourth St. AL-6
Schultz, P.T. & Co., 172 Race St. JGB-67; BFH-97
Success Music Co. TR-342
Swane, W.R. and Co., 174 Race St. WSH-37; WSH-39
Thomas Publishing Company, Mercantile Library Building WHT-56
Tosso & Douglass Music Dealers, 24 Fourth St. WHH-66
Triumph Music Co., 305 Sycamore St. WM-63
Truax, David A., 80 Fourth St. FP-7
Vent, C.F. & Co. USG-278
Victor Pub. Co., Station "O" WM-195
Werthemier, J.M., Walnut Hills WM-270
Whitmore Associates, 16 Ashburton Place DAM-55
Wilkinson, H.A., 6 Park Place, Mt. Auburn WM-194
Willis Music Company GW-234; TJ-29; AL-324; AL-430; USG-285
Willis, W.H. & Co., 4th & Elm TR-136; WHT-26
Wurlitzer, R., 123 Main St. AL-260

CLAYSVILLE, PA
Durant, Horace JSJ-3; JSJ-4

CLEARWATER, FL
Nostalgia U.S.A., Inc., 1502 Pine Circle East AL-197

CLEVELAND, OH
Bolton, C.E. JGB-65
Brainard, S. & Co. AL-38; AL-176
203 Superior St. GW-609; AL-132; AL-272; AL-419; AL-452
Brainard, S. & Sons JAG-106
203 Superior St. USG-207
Continental Music Co. WM-52
Crutchley, D.S. & Co., 182 Superior St. AL-42
Cuyahoga County Republican Party Central Committee BFH-106
Industrial Workers of the World Pub-

Appendix

lishing Bureau, 112 Hamilton Ave. EVD-4
Jewett, John P. & Co. JCF-18; JFC-50
Langdon, James F., 8219 Woodland Ave. FDR-15; FDR-71
Lewis Music Co. TR-72
Ludwig Music Pub. Co., 557-67 E. 140th St. AL-325
Mayflower Music Pub. Co. FDR-244
Pnkerton & Co. JCF-46
R.G. Publishing Co. GW-318
Rosenberg, Jacob, 805 E. 10th St. AL-250; CC-40
S. Brainard's Sons GW-194; GW-266; AL-49; AL-118; AL-175; AL-192; AL-215; HS-19; HG-17; HG-22; USG-49; USG-58; USG-91; USG-103; USG-109; USG-117; USG-121; USG-169; USG-178; RBH-21; RBH-22; RBH-25; RBH-54; JAG-58; JAG-75; JAG-85; JAG-91; JGB-15; JGB-62; BFH-29; BFH-30; BFH-42; BFH-47; BFH-65; GC-63; GC-73; GC-138; GC-141; GC-160
145 & 147 Wabash Ave. BFH-32
203 Superior St. USG-21; USG-29; USG-78; USG-88; USG-187; USG-205
Sam Fox Pub. Co. GW-291; TR-100; FDR-38; FDR-292; FDR-369; FDR-384
Schubert Co. TR-49
Shupe, Walter H. SAD-17
Smeed & Cowles MVB-15
Smith & White Co. WM-129; WM-246
Songwriters League DDE-70
United States Music Co. WM-141
Willis Music Co. GW-372

CODY, WY
Murray & Rotter AML-30

COFFEYVILLE, KS
Werth, Alex WLW-55

COLORADO SPRINGS, CO
Kiser, A.J. JMC-3; JMC-5; JMC-9; JMC-11; JMC-12; JMC-13; JMC-14; JMC-15; JMC-16
Kloepfer, Edward WM-124

COLUMBUS, OH
Finkel, John P. WJB-58
Karasek, Frank GW-350
Lovett, Effa WGH-32
Luse, J.D. GW-543

McCallip, W.W. WM-41; WM-42; WM-172; WM-173; WM-309
McDonald, D.A. WM-142
Murry-McCarty Music, 101 Hoffman Ave. AES-46
Ohio State Campaign Committee CC-58
Republican State Executive Committee WM-133; CEH-10
187 South High St. WGH-54
Smythe, A.H. BFH-23
Straight-Out Harrison and Tyler WHH-129
Ward, Rollin C., 1641 Indianola Ave. DW-20
Whiting, I.N. WHH-76

CONCORD, NH
Little, Anita Gray HCH-2

CONCORDIA, KS
Sisters of St. Joseph WM-130; WM-131

CONNERSVILLE, IN
Mitchell, Florence Heath TR-332; TR-370

COON RAPIDS, IA
Enterprise Print. BFH-98

COSHOCTON, OH
Rudolph, D.E. GC-124

COVINGTON, KY
Thompson, Jas. F., 403 Scott St. TR-374

CROYDON, PA
Doughty, Belle N. WHT-46; WHT-58

CUPERTINO, CA
Apex Music RMN-18; RR-6

DALLAS, TX
Bush and Gerts Piano Co, WW-181
Goggan, Thomas and Bros. WW-67
McBlair, George. WW-46
Scales Music Pub. Co., 401 W. 10th St. HCH-35

DANBURY, CT
The Great Eastern Music Pub. Co., 193 Main St. WM-207

DANIELSVILLE, PA
Opinger, Monroe M. TR-284

DANVILLE, PA
Thomas, Gomer JAG-115

DARLINGTON, MO
Rudy, C.I. AML-21

DAYTON, OH
Comly, R.N. & F.W. HC-47
Heritage Music Press, 501 E. Third St. MISC-111
Horner, John S., 430 E. 5th St. JAG-35
Jean, Billy, 627 Hickory St. DAM-16
Lorenz Publishing Co., 501 E. Third St. AL-337
McAfee Music Corp., 501 E. Third St. AL-323

DAYTON, OH
Johnson, Charlest R.H., 2603 Jerome Ave. HST-23
Paine Pub. Co. GW-233

DE MOTTE, IN
De Motte Music Co. WLW-2; WLW—57

DEARBORN, MI
Hosner, John D. WLW-52

DECATUR, IL
Scott & Scott, 2237 E. Prairie AL-302

DECORAH, IA
Marsh Music House, 110 Winnebago St. WM-51; RML-1

DEDHAM, MA
Mann, H. TJ-18

DELAWARE WATER GAP, PA
Shawnee Press GW-399; AL-327; FDR-373; DDE-21; DDE-24; DDE-40; DDE-72; DDE-73; MISC-117

DENTON, TX
Gore Pub. Co., 314 S. Elm MISC-108

DENVER, CO
Doucet, I.E. TR-170
Graham, Edward B. WW-151
Plains Music Publishing Co., 24-42 W. Bayaud FDR-284; FDR-401

DENVER, CO
Richter, O.H. WJB-4
Russell, Vivian I. TR-267
Schack, Albert P., 809 20th St. WJB-90
Speth, William B., 1432 Lafayette St. MISC-140
Tabor, Silver Echo TR-212
Talbert R. Ingram Co. WJB-31; TR-123

DERRY, NH
Wark, A.B., 86 E. Broadway CC-7

DERRY STATION, PA
Newmwyer, Ida L. MISC-180

DES MOINES, IA
Blake, Orwell GW-613; AL-505
Keating, Chas. T. WW-25
Register Press Printing House BFH-50
Silver Songs Pub. Co. WJB-59

DETROIT, MI
Aarons, Dr. Joseph, 309 Hodges Bldg. TR-321
C.W. Marvin Publishing Company CAA-9
House of Repaid WW-211
Hudson, Midas, 11665 Griggs JFK-39
Madison Music, 965 E. Jefferson Ave. FDR-99; FDR-280
Melody Music Co. AL-367
Morris Pub. Co., 909 Hamond Bldg. WM-21
Our Next President Company MISC-87
Remick, Jerome H. & Co. TR-14; WW-39
Sage, H.A., 117 W. Fort St. TR-87
Shelby Music Pub. Co. FDR-388
Tetreault, Victor A., 3821 Montgomery Ave. FDR-147
Whitney Warner Pub. Co. MISC-38
Whittemore, J. Henry AL-27; ; AL-480; JD-29
Young, William, 1150 Campbell Ave. FDR-237
Zickel Bros. WM-122

DEXTER, ME
Sawyer, H. Stanton, 30 Spring Street TED-35

DILLSBORO, NC
Jarrett, R.F., Jarrett Springs Hotel FDR-417

DOBBS FERRY, NY
Thompson, Thomas H. BFH-84

DONGAN HILLS, NY
Stoffel, Irene M. FDR-274

DOVER, NH
Damm, Peter F. HCH-56
Tremont Music Co. FDR-185

DOVER, NJ
Williams Pub. Co. DDE-27

DOVER, OH
Ohio School of Sales, Box 401 DDE-105

DUQUOIN, IL
Christopher Music Co. WGH-4; CC-41

DURHAM, ME
Robinson, Jr., Alvan GW-86

EAST CLEVELAND, OH
Georgianna Music Publishers, 16004 Euclid Ave. JFK-9

EAST LIVERPOOL, OH
Thompson, Will L. & Co. WM-184

EAST LOS ANGELES, CA
Gardner, David TR-153

EAST SAN DIEGO, CA
Dibble, Bertha Haymaker, 4070 Colonial Ave. WW-18

EAST ST LOUIS, IL
Progressive Pub. Co. TR-200

EAST WEARE, NH
Eaton W.S. JCF-41

EDGEMERE, NY
Edgemere Music Pub. Co., 340 Beach St. FDR-398

EL DORADO, KS
Walnut Valley Times Print BFH-109

EL PASO, TX
El Paso Music Pub. Co., 191 Newman Street WHT-41

ELGIN, IL
David C. Cook Pub. Co. GW-205

ELDRED, PA
Star Music Co. TR-68; WW-87

ELIZABETH, NJ
Gerardo Bros. Pub. Co. FDR-127

ELKINS PARK, PA
Rowe, Tommy & Billy James, 7823 Mill Road FDR-300

ELMFORD, NY
McFarland, G.H. WW-174

ELWOOD, IN
Greene E.E. & Son WM-136

ENERGY, PA
Houk, J.M. WJB-48

ERIE, PA
Brehm Bros. WM-240; TR-15
Erie Music Pub. Co. WW-191
Gallagher, Joseph, Park Theatre Bldg. FDR-212
Reineke Music Service WW-135; WW-196

EVANSTON, IL
Schulze, Ernest A., 1003 Washington St. AES-37

EXETER, NH
Hazeltine, Daniel GW-79; TJ-14
Norris and Sawyer TJ-55
Norris, C. and Co. GW-477; TJ-56
Ranlet, H. GW-89; GW-467
Ranlet and Norris GW-45

FAIR LAWN, NJ
Koenig, Carl, 1235 Burbank St. HST-11

FAIRFIELD, CT
Keeler, Georgina Gordon, 254 Post Rd. FDR-90

FALL RIVER, MA
Anthony Brothers Music Publishers GW-351
Zias, Bernard H. FDR-36

FALLBROOK, CA
Red Mountain Springs, R1, Box 187 FDR-273

FARMDALE, OH
Oliver E. Henry Music Co. WM-219

FARMINGTON MI
Stolz, Elvira A., 21411 Waldron Rd. DDE-63

FITCHBURG, MA
Whitney, Andrew, 132 Main St. JCF-9

FLINT, MI
Coats, J.P. JSG-85
DePaul Publishers, 804 Genessee Bank Bldg. DDE-58
Harmony Music Co. USG-239
Webb, Dollie P., 1506 Jane St. FDR-227

FOREST HILLS, NY
Masson, Korecka, 8902 73rd Ave. FDR-112

FOREST PARK, IL
Mader, Carl TED-16

FOSTORIA, OH
Ellis, John S. JGB-82

FRANKLIN, OH
Eldridge Entertainment House GW-213

FRANKLIN, PA
Rossman, W.F. TR-4

FRANKLIN FALLS, NH
Towne, Omar A. TR-248

FREEDOM, IN
Freedom's Ring RR-30

FREELAND, PA
J. Grayson Jones Music Co. FDR-356
P.O. Box 177 FDR-234

FRIEND, NE
Winkler, Emile, R.F.D. 2 FDR-258

FT LAUDERDALE, FL
Sam Fox Pub. Co., 170 N.E. 33rd. St. GW-277

FT WAYNE, IN
Batt, Anna Lee JFK-23
Ft. Wayne Printing Co. WW-131
Wayne Music Publishers, 115 E. Wayne St. FDR-4

GALESBURG, IL
Smith, Mary Alice, 634 E. Third St. FDR-418

GALVESTON, IN
Liston, Cora WGH-43

GALVESTON, TX
Groggan, Thos. & Bro. TR-115; TR-215

GARY, IN
Calumet Music Publishers FDR-132
Democratic Boosters of Indiana FDR-351

GASDEN, AL
Hot Foot Campbell TR-360

GENEVA, OH
Foster, G. Porter CAA-7

GIRARD, PA
Kuenzig, C.C., 128 Main Ave. HCH-25
Hobbs, Alfred Freeman, 523 Chestnut St. WLW-51
Wonderland Music Co., Inc., 800 Sonora Ave. BFH-43; BFH-45; GC-42

GLENDALE, CA
Alfred Hobbs, 523 East Chesnut St. WLW-45

GLENS FALLS, NY
Decker, Lois WW-91
Harrington & Reynolds WW-32

GLOUCESTER, NJ
Amberger, Marie A., 220 Rosalind Ave. FDR-187

GOUVERNEUR, NY
McFalls, Mrs. D. JGB-9

GRAHAM, NC
Long, Jr., Dan WM-324

GRAND ISLAND, NE
Blueboy Music Pub. Co., 214 Clark St. RMN-23

GRAND LEDGE, MI
Cadwell, M.S. BFB-18

GRAND RAPIDS, MI
JAQUA Co. MISC-73
Moore, Julia A. PC-3
Spencer and Tudor, 547 Umatilla St. S.E. FDR-307

GRAYVILLE, IL
Payne, Thomasanne WGH-44

GREEN BAY, WI
McDermott, Alfred, P.O. Box 601 JFK-1

GREENFIELD, MA
Mealand & Parsons GW-538
Phelps, Ansel GW-71

GREENSBORO, NC
Stanley, R.K. CC-30

GREENVILLE, PA
Scobbie, Mary, General Delivery FDR-412

GREENWICH, CT
Reisinger, Mary McKee HCH-43
Rundle, Adaline P. CC-9; CC-22

HACKENSACK, NJ
Novelty Music Co. JFK-33

HALEDON, NJ.
C & E Enterprises, P.O. Box 8159 GW-373

HALLOWELL, ME
Goodale, E. GW-493

HAMILTON, OH
Democratib Job Rooms GC-144
Dugan Music Service, 244 High St. FDR-164

HAMMOND, IN
De'Besth Music Pub. Co. LBJ-14

HARLAN, IA.
Nelson, Evelyn FDR-98

HARRISBURG, PA
Democratic State Central Committee WJB-35
Elliott, R.S. and Co. WHH-80

J.H. Troup Piano House, 15 South Market St. GW-551
Keagy, Isaac ZT-49
Knuzenknabe and Sons, No. 1307 North Third St. JGB-66
M'Curdy & Knabb HC-76

HARTFORD, CT
Audio Center, 398 Trumbull St. DDE-33
Bickley, John J. and Sons CC-52
Case, Lockwood and Brainard & Co. BFH-104
Church, C.C. & Co. USG-215; USG-216; USG-283
New England Pub. Co. FDR-91
Smith-Linsley Co. PP-2
Williams & Carleton GC-101

HAVERHILL, MA
Clifford and Fuller DDE-89

HAZEL PARK, MI
Thomsen, William H., 328 E. Goulson LBJ-18

HAZELTON, PA
Hazelton Chamber of Commerce FDR-106

HENDERSON, KY
Susie Powell, 630 Center St. WW-137

HIALEAH, FL
Columbia Pictures, P.O. Box 4340 GW-295

HILLSBORO, IN
Carnes, Josef R. MISC-61

HOLLYWOOD, CA
Advance Music, Inc., Markham Bldg. FDR-41
Aeolian Music Pub. Co. DAM-59
ASA Music Company, 1556 N. La Brea Ave. GW-233
Charles Ridgeway Studios FDR-266
Cine-Art Music Publishers, 6912 Hollywood Blvd. TED-15
Crow Music Co., 2220 Vista Del Mar. FDR-100
E.B. DuBain Pub. Co. FDR-27
Edwards, Norman, 9136 Sunset Blvd. FDR-271
Fireside Classics, 1313 No. Highland Ave. FDR-270
Great Pacific Music Sales, 1515 N. Vine. GW-204
Hawaii Conservatory Pub. Co., 5002 Melrose Ave. DAM-28
Herb-Mor Music Pub. Co., 6000 Sunset Blvd. DDE-55
Hollywood Publishers FDR-246
Hollywood Publishing Co., 5426 Sierra Vista Ave. FDR-5
Home Sweet Home Music Pub. Co. TED-25; DAM-23
HR Music Corp. RR-18
Irvine, Clarke, 4657 Hollywood Blvd. HST-7
Jack-Helen Artists Assn., 11204 Huston St. FDR-263
Keyser, Annette, 5337 Sunset Blvd. FDR-67
Laguna Music Prints, 1717 N. Vine St. DAM-44
Lone Star Music Co., 1158 N. Orange Dr. FDR-333
Longpre, Paul de. TR-119
Music City Pub. Co., 219 Taft Bldg. FDR-43
National Artists Ass'n., 1811 N. Tamarind FDR-399
National Music Pub. Co., 312 W. First St. FDR-9
Nordyke Pub. Co. DDE-75; DAM-12
Nordyke Songs & Music Publishers FDR-345; JFK-68; MISC-78
6000 Sunset Blvd. JFK-16
Pacific Music FDR-272
Pacific Music Sales, 1515 N. Vine DAM-35; FDR-272
Pipin, Antun K., 717 N. Van Ness Ave. FDR-231; FDR-233
Pyramid Music Co., 6087 Sunset Blvd. BMG-1
Rainbow Music Co. FDR-239
Saunders Publications, 5617 Hollywood Blvd. FDR-288
Souvenir Songs, 5880 Hollywood Blvd. DDE-106; RMN-5; DAM-50
Stone, Sasha FDR-52
Studio Staff Productions DAM-2; DAM-54
Sweet Music, Inc., 6087 Sunset Blvd. DDE-53

HOLYOKE, MA
Schuster, C.L. GC-13

HONOLULU, HI
George, Don FDR-214
Tongg Pub. Co. DAM-49; DAM-53

HOWARD, KS
Tyrrell, Henry WM-203

HOWARD CITY, MI
Carrie B. Jennings Music Co. TR-229
Americanism National League WGH-27

HOXIE, KS
Judd, C.P. JBW-8

INDIANAPOLIS, IN
American Pub. Co. WM-107; WW-209; CEH-8; WGH-27
Arsenal Technical Schools GW-627
Asher & Co., 3 Odd Fellow's Hall GW-630
Barker, Rev. Benjamin George, 623 West Vermont St. WW-215
Benham, A.M. & Co. USG-250
Benham Bros. & Co. USG-95
36 E. Washington St. USG-84
Bernhardt, Charles E. TR-146
Brown, J. Burgess WM-330; TR-369
Carlin & Lennox WJB-37
Douglas and Conner USG-258
Guernsey, George M., 1362 W. 27th St. WHT-5
Halcyon Pub. Co. WW-121; JMC-2
307 E. North St. CC-10; CC-50
House of Carleon, 2439 Park Ave. HAW-4
Indianapolis Sentinel WHS-11
Lawrence, Dr. B.M., Mansur Block WJB-55
Marone, Guiseppe, 521 E. 12th St. TR-375
Smith, Frank WM-278
St. Claire Music Pub. Co. FDR-77
State Central Committee WM-134
Tutewiler, H.D., 133 W. Market St. WM-154
Vincent Brothers Pub. Co. JBW-9
Wiethe, Henry J. TR-131
Wulschner, Emil BFH-13; WM-322
Wulschner-Stewart Music Co. TR-276

IRON RIVER, MI
Chirgwon, John, Box 453 WGH-35

ITHACA, NY
Woodruff and Gauntlett JKP-14

JACKSON, MI
Smith, Ethel Embury WM-183

JASONVILLE, IN
Kepinger, J.E. FDR-97

JEANNETTE, PA
Guy, Clyde L. FDR-103

JACKSON, TN
Weir, Eva R., 399 S. Royal FDR-293

JACKSONVILLE, IL
Duncan, Florence T. WJB-86
Keplinger, J.F. FDR-97
Siegfried, C.P. MISC-54

JENKINS, KY
Wilson, Inez JEC-4

JERSEY CITY, NJ
Ewald, W.H. & Bro., 136 Newark Ave. GW-120
Seib, Frank WW-132
Star Music, 153 Jackson Ave. DDE-111

JOLIET, IL
Greenback News PC-2
J. Meade Pub. Co. WLW-12
Lee, Ray, 307 Mississippi Ave. FDR-208

JONESBORO, AK
Sammons, LaFayette, P.O. Box 75 BMG-2

JOPLIN, MO
Hardin, Homer FDR-248
Hoffman Bros., 632 Main St. TR-285

JUDSONIA, AR
June Bauer Co., Inc. WW-60

KANE, PA
Faulkner Pub. Co. TR-47

KANKAKEE, IL
Hawk, S.M. WJB-93; TR-137

KANSAS CITY, MO
Barnum, Kenneth R., 926 McGee DDE-104
1001 Linwood Blvd. DDE-91
Bell, J.R. BFH-73; GC-61; GC-122; JCS-4
Bolte, Jr., Carl E., 926 McGee DDE-104; LBJ-30
Campaign Songs Publishing Co. WM-280
Casey Music Co., 530 Benton Blvd. MISC-102
Geo. Southwell Publishing Co. MISC-167
Green, Sophie, 804 E. 12th St. WW-184
Haward Pub. Co., Ricksecker Bldg. WW-29

Jackson County Republican Committee, 1014 Grand Ave. DDE-92
Legg Bros. WM-70
McIndoo Pub. Co. HCH-26
McNellis, Maurice J., 5304 Tracy Ave. HST-15
Metz, Jr., Conrad, 514 Pickwick Bldg. AML-17
Page & Piper WJB-20
Schenck-Henze, Grace D. & Co. WHT-54
Topco Pub. Co., 1526 Walnut St. MISC-9
Townsend Music Publishers, 120 W. 7th St. DDE-36; DDE-52; DDE-61
United Republican Workers of America WLW-67
Weber Brothers, 622 Minnesota Ave. AL-184; WGH-59

KENOSHA, WI
Independent Music Publishers, 6044 8th Ave. AES-60

KEOKUK, IA
Brown, W. Frank, 24 N. Fifth FDR-151; FDR-152; FDR-153

KIEL, WI
Meinardus, E. WW-203

KING CITY, MO
Hall, Geo. W. AL-191

KNOXVILLE, TN
Lyrique Hiroique, P.O. Box 558 AL-187

KOKOMO, IN
Higgins, W.H. WM-276

LA CYGNE, KS
Fuller, Jr., W.O. JGB-72

LACONIA, NH
Bab-El-Bra Pub. Co. DDE-16

LACONIA, NH
O'Shea Bros., 128, 130, 132, 134 & 136 Main St. CAA-2

LADELTON, NY
Hamilton, George K. GW-180; GW-181

LAFAYETTE, IN
Echo Music Co. BFH-115; BFH-123; FH-120; WM-279; CBF-5
Rinker Music Co. WHH-102

LAGUNA BEACH, CA
Laguna Music Prints, 472 Popular St. DAM-29; DAM-44

LAKE FOREST, IL
Tweed Enterprises, Inc., P.O.B. 392 AS-6; AS-8

LAKEWOOD, NJ
Goldberg Music Publishers, Box 113 Cross St. DDE-43

LANCASTER, PA
Fremont Club of Lancaster City JCF-25
Kirk, Johnson and Co., 16 King St. GW-416

LANSING, MI
Republican Clubs Pub. Co., 621 E. Hazel St.

LANSINGBURGH, NY
Mitchell, Thomas WS-31, WLW-33

LAUDERDALE LAKES, FL
Herman, Pinky, 4705 NW 35th St., #615 MSD-2; BC-5
Manor Music Co., 4705 NW 35th St. TJ-31; TJ-32

LEBANON IN
March Bros., 208-210-212 Wright Ave. GW-210

LEBANON, OH
March Bros., 208, 210, 212 Wright Ave. GW-280
School And College Novelty Co. AML-8

LEBANON, PA
Atlantic Music Pub. Co., 131 S. Eight St. WW-114

LEAD, CO
Brown, Ruth Gammon, 128 Wall St. MISC-74

LEVENWORTH, KS
Hoffman, Carl JGB-64
Manning, A.E. & Co., 94 Delaware St. USG-67

LEWISTON, ME
Ferndale, J.M. and W.G. Haskell JGB-78

LINCOLN, ME
Clark, W.C. WM-121

LINCOLN, NE
  Crane, E.W. WJB-67
  Crombie, W.B. WJB-85
  Hesselberg, Edouard WW-142
  Hohmann's Music Co. JBW-5
  United Artists Music Co., 108-114 N. Kickapoo St. AL-266

LOCKPORT, NY
  Burdick-Lampman Music Co. TR-302
  Byron, Frank TR-207
  Penfold, Danforth J., 13-17 Main St. WM-146.

LOGAN, WV
  Dorsey, Dana R., P.O.B. 783 BC-1

LOGANSPORT, IN
  Blaine & Logan Glee Club of Logansport JGB-80
  Home Music Co. WJB-71; WM-275; WM-277; TR-356
  Pratt, W.D. JGB-79

LONG BEACH, CA
  Faith and Freedom Songs, 5901 Rose Ave. BMG-5

LONG BRANCH, NJ
  Keith's Music Pub. House TR-300; WW-130

LONG ISLAND, NY
  Belwin, Inc., Rockville Centre AL-169
  Keenan, Luke A., 475 11th Ave. WW-88

LOS ANGELES, CA
  Aileda Publishing Co., 23098 S. Union Ave. FDR-338
  Allied Publishing Co., 357 S. Hill St. DAM-38
  Anderson and Lawless DAM-31
  ART Music Co., POB 19662, Rimpau Station DDE-3
  1279 Queen Anne Place DDE-81
  B&R Pub. Co., 646 N. Harper Ave. FDR-2
  Berg Publishing Co. WM-265
  Bilbrew, A.C., 1301 1/3 Commonwealth Ave. FDR-336
  Bizarre Music, Inc. MISC-104
  Burdette, G. & Co., 111 W. Fifth St. FDR-39; FDR-409
  California Music Co., 802 W. 8th St. FDR-17
  Caire & Stern, 117 W. 9th St. AML-5
  Charles Lent Publications, 953 W. Seventh St. DAM-4
  Coe, Chas. Almon, 639 Stanford Ave. WGH-16
  Cosmo Publishing Co. DAM-36
  C.R. Foster Co., 845 Broadway WW-35
  Croxton Publishing Co., 659 S. Orange Dr. DAM-5
  Democrats Southern Authority, 608 South Hill St. FDR-64
  Dixie Pub. Co., 2328 W. Seventh St. FDR-182
  Dondee Music Prods., 3227 Andrita St. RMN-38
  Donetelli & Chapman, Dana St. JMC-7
  Eddy, Warren H., 205. N. Flower St. RML-4
  Every Little Tune, Inc., 9200 Sunset Blvd. MISC-93
  Gordon, Marvin B., 360 S. Hill St. MISC-11
  Hampton, T.J., 110 N. Broadway WM-93
  Hawaii Conservatory Pub. Co., 741 S. Western Ave. FDR-175
  Heffelfinger, R.W., 347 S. Spring St. WHT-10
  Henry Tobias Music Co., 1255 N. Kings Rd. RMN-11; RMN-31
  Lamminations Music/Big Elk Music, 8600 Melrose Ave. HST-8
  Lay, H., 1242 Brockton Ave. FDR-265
  Lee Johnson Music Pub. Co. WW-37
  Lee Pub. Co., 717 Majestic Bldg. CEH-11
  Los Angeles Music Pub. Co., 520 Broadway AES-52
  Los Angeles Pub. Co. FDR-253
  Los Angeles Times TR-184; DAM-41
  Morales, Delphina, 159 W. 23rd St. FDR-226
  Mystique Music Pub. Co., POB 75982, Sanford Station RMN-13
  Price/Sterns/Sloan RMN-37
  Scholts Publishing Co., 1008 W. 6th St. FDR-329
  Sinclair Pubs., 2024 S. Vermont Ave. FDR-206
  Slayer & Robinson WJB-57
  Southern California Music Company, 332-34 S. Broadway WHT-52
  Southwest Music Pubs., 5817 S. Arlington Ave. AL-220
  S.S. Publications, 1280 Muirfield Rd. FDR-87

Standard Publishing, 305 Majestic Theatre Bldg. FDR-332
Vandercook, W.A. BFH-114; GC-150
W.A.M. Publishers AS-4
Westland Pub. Co. WHT-31
Whitmore & Ambrose WW-71
Wildau, Franklin, 8932 S. Manhattan Place FDR-216
Wilson, Grace, 625 Warner Ave. FDR-420
Words and Music Pubs. FDR-354

LOUISVILLE, KY
Bain, Arnold & McCann Music Co. HCH-11
Barnam, Lula Lloyd GC-24
Faulds, David P. ZT-33; AL-179; JCB-6; JBL-4
Main St. JB-8; JBL-5
165 Fourth Ave. ZT-33
223 Main St. GBM-32; GBM-36; AL-86
Faulds, D.P. and Co. SAD-18
Faulds, Stone & Morse, 539 Main St. MF-17
Firizer & Hamill WM-226
McCarrell & Mininger, 91 West Jefferson St. GBM-17
McCarrell, Wm., 310 Jefferson St. GBM-11; GBM-59
Peters, H.J. & Co. ZT-40
Peters, W.C. GW-99
Peters, Webb & Co. GW-80
Tripp and Craig, 117 Fourth St. HC-41; AL-316
Tripp and Linton, 118 Fourth St. HG-31
Tripp, Louis AL-76; USG-90; USG-186
Universal Music Co. JMC-10
Werth, F.A., 916 S. Broadway USG-233
Zoeller Music Co. WGH-9

LOWELL, MA
Fredette Music Pub. Co. FDR-236
Merrimack Music Co., 54 7th St. WW-160
Michel, Casimir WM-123
Orpheus Music Pub. Co. WW-80
Roussin, Blanche WW-140
Tanner, T.A., 265 Christian St. AL-227

LUCAS, SD
Ellison, Jewell WW-45

LYNN, MA
Lynn Labor Press, 153 Oxford St. SLP-3
Vin Publishers, P.O. Box 249 JFK-43

MACON, GA
Proctor-Paterson Music Co. WHT-30; WW-77
Southern Music Co., 217 Bibb Bldg. FDR-201

MADISON, WI
Cardinal Press AL-209
Four Lakes Music Co. CC-18

MAHANOY PLANE, PA
Donaghue, Leo and Frank, Bridge St. AES-40

MANCHESTER, NH
Kimball, C.H. USG-238

MANSFIELD, OH
Bohal & Co. WGH-11
Kunz, Howard WM-274

MANTENO, IL
Wright, E. Monroe CC-42

MAPLETON, MN
Sellers, Emma Pauline, Box 384

MARIETTA, GA
Times Publishing Co. MISC-125

MARION, OH
Carr, W.R. WGH-25, TR-132

MARLBORO, MA
Capen, E. Minot, 343 Pleasant St. WW-198
Springer, W.A. TR-228

MARSHALL, MI
White, J.S. & Co. GW-145; HG-32

MAYNARD, MA
C.H. Persons Music House TR-9

MCKEESPORT, PA
Keil, Phil P. GC-20
Walnut & Fourth St. SJT-10
81 Fifth St. JAG-13; RBH-53

MEADOWBROOK, PA
Kulling, Otto W. WLW-62

MEDFORD, MA
Johnson, Thomas T., 181 Middlesex Ave. HCH-36

MELROSE HIGHLANDS, MA
Lang, Mary B., 90 Nowell Rd. AML-13; AML-15

MELVILLE, NY
Belwin Mills Pub. Co. AL-342; FDR-348

MEMPHIS, TN
  Biggert, John, 1875 DuPont Ave. MISC-175
  Bruck, Marie WW-103
  Cathey Music Co. WW-200
  Pace & Handy Music Co. AL-245

MENASHA, WI
  Boehnleim, Francis H. WW-167
  Reid, George L. BFH-118

MEREDOSIA, IL
  Meredosia Wide-Awakes AL-143

MIAMI, FL
  Bishop and Pavia Music Pub. Co. WGH-34
  CCP/Belwin, Inc., 15800 NW 48th Ave. JAG-97; MISC-113
  Congress Music Publications DDE-34
  Democratic National Convention GMG-1
  Len Art Music Pub. Co., 1369 Venetian Way RMN-21
  Republican Headquarters, 150 N.E. 3rd St. TED-14
  Rubank, Inc. GW-430
  Screen Gems-Columbia, 6744 N.E. 4th Ave. JFK-69
  Warner Bros. Pub. Corp., 15800 N.W. 48th Ave. MISC-135

MIAMI BEACH, FL
  Hanson House, 1820 West Ave. MISC-171
  1860 West Ave. JEC-6

MIDDLETOWN, CT
  North Congregational Church JAG-108

MILTON, PA
  Osborn, Anna H.B., 130 S. Front St. WW-194

MILWAUKEE, WI
  Field Art Studio Publishers, 1720 N. 17th St. FDR-66
  Hal Leonard Pub. Co., 7777 W. Bluemound Rd. TJ-46; JFK-30; MISC-97; MISC-107; MISC-109; MISC-134
  Harris, Charles K., Alhambra Theatre Bldg. MISC-31
  Hempsted, H.N., 408, 410 & 412 Broadway USG-237
  410 Main St. AL-136; AL-321; AL-458; USG-64
  Jack Carr, Inc. FDR-314
  Karll, Eric, 2344 N. First St. HCH-8
  Milwaukee Sentinel WM-243
  Mulwerhof Pub. Co., Wisconsin Theatre Building GW-243
  Music Arranging Bureau, 523 Wells St. AES-12
  Paulish, John EVD-2
  Rohlfing, Wm. & Co. JAG-107; JGB-14
  Schaum Publications, Inc. GW-353
  2018 E. North Avenue GW-234; AL-365
  Schmidt & Peterson CC-28
  Sillaway Pub. Co. WW-124
  Stephens, Wm. WM-222
  Violet Music Publishers, 528 Broadway AES-25
  Wachter, Fred USG-104
  Wyman, Lincoln S. WM-162

MINNEAPOLIS, MN
  American Pub. Co., 2832 38th Ave. S. WW-104
  Berg, Jinnie FDR-344
  Cole, C. St. J. WJB-61
  Dry Republicans and Democrats HCH-60
  Dyer, W.J. & Bro., 509-511 Nicollet Ave. WM-195
  Hanes, Layne H., Frontenac Bldg., 435 S. Dearborn St. AML-7
  Harmsen, Ludwig W. JAG-34
  McAllister, P.W. AL-208
  Metropolitan Music Co., 509-511 Nicollet Ave. WM-165
  Nau & Schmidt Music Co., 309 Grand Aveune TR-361
  New Times Socialist Pub. Co. EVD-3
  Penny & Paterson, 1017 Washington Ave. HCH-9
  Republican Woman's Club WGH-47
  Schmitt Music Publications Division, 110 Fifth St. AL-121
  Standard Publishing Co. FDR-348

MISHAWAKA, IN
  Probasco, Marks WW-171

MISSOULA, MT
  Stricker, Will, 1423 Van Buren St. FDR-44

MOBILE, AL
  Block, Joseph, 55 Dauphin St. JD-4
  Bromberg and Son, 46 Dauphin St. JD-3
  Radio and Song Scout HST-17; HST-27; HST-28

Snow, J.H., 29 Dauphin St. JD-6; JD-54

MOLINE, IL
H.K. Williams Music Co. TR-331

MONROEVILLE, IN
Bobilya Pub. House FDR-48

MONROVIA, CA
Sunset Song Bureau FDR-330

MONTICELLO, AR
Patriotic Music Pub. Co. DAM-51

MONTELA, NY
Hamilton, Geo. K. GW-182

MORRIS PLAINS, NJ
Monahan, Lawrence Jr. TR-190

MORRISTOWN, AZ
Pitt, M.D. FDR-35

MORRISTOWN, NJ
Zimmerman, Paul G. WJB-42

MORRISVILLE, VT
Hill & Goodrich Wholesale Foods WHT-23

MOULTRIE, OH
Crist, D.W. GC-127; TR-113; TR-114; TR-371

MT JOY, PA
Druckenmiller AL-515

MT PLEASANT, IA
Archer and Sternberg FDR-375

MOUNT TABOR, NJ
Hughes Pub. House AML-12

MT VERNON, IA
Lozier Bros. USG-98; JGB-23; JGB-25; BFH-90; WM-281; WM-305.

MT VERNON, NY
Song Record Pub. & Demo. Co. HCH-30
Steele, Theodore JBW-3

MT VERNON, OH
Norton, A.B. WHH-96

MOUNTAIN TOP, PA
Airy Music Co., R.D. 4 Box 62 JFK-8

MUSKOGEE, OK
Democratic Victory Song Hqs., 910 W. Broadway JWD-4

NASHUA, NH
Dewolfe, G. Byron USG-125
Panneton, Claudia, 43 Pine St. FDR-347
Thayer, H. BFH-122

NASHVILLE, TN
Acuff-Rose Pub., 2510 Franklin Rd. JFK-71; DAM-14
American Music Co., Stahlman Bldg. WLW-13
Babb Music, 824 Fifth Ave. S. MISC-22
Bards Music Publishers, 26 Music Sq. JEC-3
Beauman, C.T. AL-15
Benson, C.D. GW-167
Benson, C.D. and Bro. GW-584
Broadman Press. MISC-112
Cederwood Pub. Co., 815 16th Ave. S. JFK-13
Dixie Music Co., Twin Bldg. WW-129
Glaser Publications., 801 16th Ave. S. JFK-28
McClure, James A. AJK-50; JCB-2
Standard Pub. Co. WW-64
Syracuse Music, Inc., 806 16th Ave. LGM-1
Tennessee Music Publishers, Warner Building MISC-149
Tree Publishing Company, 8 Music Sq. West DAM-43
Warden Music Co. AJK-45
Western Hills Music LBJ-12

NEW ALBANY, IN
Bettmann Bros. & Daniel TR-294
Hineline, Charles D. JKP-15
Thornton, M.C., 207 Elsby Bldg. FDR-290

NEW BEDFORD, MA
Perry & Noble USG-33

NEW BERLIN, WI
Jenson Pubs., Inc. MISC-97

NEW BRITAIN, CT
Bacon & Doyle GC-149

NEW BRUNSWICK, NJ
Hansen Music Pub. Co. GW-253

NEW HAVEN, CT
A.B. Clinton Co. WHT-47
Benham ZT-29
Capecelatro, Raffaele, 246 Columbus Ave. FDR-22

Doolittle, A. GW-94
Garden Roads Press., P.O.B. 877 GW-410
Geary Brothers BFH-110
Hathaway, James T., 287 Crown St. HC-119
Shepard and Bonney BFH-99
Shepard, Thomas G. GW-564
Storer, William, Jr. WHH-42

NEW ORLEANS, LA
Blackmar, A.E. AL-30; BFB-19
Blackmar, A.E. and Brother JD-13
74 Camp St. JD-11
Duggan, T.A. TR-177
Grunwald, Louis TR-383
129 Canal St. HS-1
Hartel, F. and Co. HC-84
Johns & Co., Charles & Common Sts. AJK-56
Loyola University GW-228
Mayo, Wm. T., So. Camp St. ZT-8
Pessou, Ls. And B. Smith, 175 Chartres St. WS-46
Peters, A.C. and Brother, 94 W. 4th St. JCB-3
Verlander, J.A. WJB-88
943 Louisiana Ave. TR-174
Werlein, Ph. P., 5 Camp Street JCB-4; JBL-7; JBL-9
Werlein, Philip, 614-616 Canal St. TR-163
Werlein, P.P. & Halsey, 3 & 5 Camp St. JD-15

NEW ROCHELLE, NY
Capt. G.W. Loyd JBW-7

NEW SALEM, MA
Hook, S.W. TR-219

NEW WINDSOR, IL
Anderson & Spivey WM-201

NEW YORK, NY
Abbey & Abbot, 119 Nassau St. GW-547
ABC Music Co., 799 7th Ave. GW-623; AL-512; MISC-185
Abilene Music Co., 342 Madison Ave. DDE-56
Abrahams, Maurice, 1570 Broadway GW-311
Acme Music Corp. (Del), 1585 Broadway DAM-11

Acme Pub. Bureau, 252 Broadway JGB-45
Ager, Yellen & Bornstein, Inc., 1595 Broadway AL-226
A.J. Stasny Music Co. GW-298
Al Gallico Music Corp., 65 W. 55th St. AL-301
Alexander Music, Inc. & Spectacular Music, Inc. LBJ-10
Alfred Music Co., 145 W. 45th St. FDR-365
American Baptist Home Mission Society, Inc. AL-198
American Book Co. GW-511; GW-512; TJ-50; AL-371; AL-471; MISC-155
American Heritage Book Co. MISC-169
American Music Co., 505 Fifth Ave. TR-172
American Music Corp., 745 Seventh Ave. FDR-125
American Music Pub. Co., 14 E. 77th St. LBJ-5; MISC-162
American News Co. AL-402; SJT-7; RBH-49; JGB-84; JGB-90
117, 119, 121, & 123 Nassau Street RBH-11
American Protective League BFH-100
American Temperance Publishing House ND-6
Amsco Music Publishing Co., Inc., 240 West 55th Street GW-631; USG-240
Andre & Co., 447 Broadway JKP-3
Andrews, 38 Chatham St. JCF-39
Anti-Defamation League of B'nai B'rith, 212 Fifth Ave. TJ-74
Aronson, Edward & Co., Broadway & 39th St. GW-144; USG -74
Ascher, Emil, 315 Fourth Avenue MISC-165
Associated Music TR-62
Atwill's Music Saloon, No. 201 Broadway WHH-29; WHH-30; WHH-39; WHH-75; WHH-98; WHH-139; HC-44; HC-52; JKP-4; DW-7
Barclay, Wright, 55 W. 42nd St. FDR-341
Barbelle Music Co., 145 W. 45th St. WLW-15
Barlow, Geo. Surrey, 245 E. 25th St. WW-118; JMC-1
Barnes, C.L. ZT-87
Bartram, F.S & C.B. JGB-83
Bedele & Co., 98 William St. USG-65; USG-253
141 William St. GBM-78; AL-489; JD-57; BFB-21

Appendix

Beer & Schirmer, 701 Broadway JCF-20; JCF-53; AL — 26
Belock & Co., No. 110 William St. JGB-26
Belwin, Inc. GW-367; USG-209; MISC-96
Benham, H.L. & Co., 42 Arcade JAG-100
Bennett, D.M., 141 8th St. JBW-4
Bergman, Vocco & Conn., 1619 Broadway AL-202; FDR-86; FDR-296
Bernard Granville Music Pub. Co., 154 W. 45th St. GW-242
Berry & Gordon, 297 Broadway MF-14; MF-15
Berry, T.S. & Co., 297 Broadway HS-7
B.F. Wood Music Co. JFK-34; BMG-4
Bibo-Lang, Inc., 745 Broadway USG-166
Big Four Syndicate GW-516
Birch, Thomas GW-128; WHH-30; WHH-45; WHH-75
50 Howard St. AJK-10
235 Chapple near Canal St. AJK-12
291 Bowery HC-64; HC-66; HC-87
Birch, Thomas and Son, 521 Sixth Ave. AL-451
Blake, Whitney, 1585 Broadway TED-5
Bloom, Sol, New Amsterdam Theatre Building AP-1
New Zealand Bldg., 37th & Broadway R-85
Bluebird Music Co., 2394 Grand Concourse HST-3
Blume, Frederick, 27 Union Sq. GW-402
Bob Miller, Inc., 1619 Broadway AL-182; AML-24; WLW-1; FDR-111; TED-2; DAM-46
Bolsound Enterprises, Inc., 250 W. 57th St. LBJ-3
Boni & Gaer TJ-72
Book Craft, 304-320 E. 45th St. AML-16
Bourne, Inc., 136 Broadway MISC-161
Bourne Depository of Arts, 359 Broadway GW-80
Bowers, Frederick K. TR-104
Brannan Music Pub. Co., 121 W. 42nd St. FDR-128
Breusing, C. GW-565
701 Broadway GBM-4
Broadcast Music, Inc., 580 Fifth Ave. AL-464; FDR-358; FDR-366; MISC-82; MISC-142

Broadway Music Corp., 1600 Broadway AES-7
Brooks & Denton Co., Sixth Ave. & 39th St. WM-19
Bruns & Kaufmann, 791 Broadway JAG-98
Buckeye Music Pub. Co. GW-198
Butler, J., No. 156 Broadway TJ-16
Burgoyne, C.G. WM-84
Byers, N.E. & Co., 1368-1370 Broadway WM-16
Caesar, Irving, 1619 Broadway MISC-132
Cahn and Wagenen Music Pub. Co., 251 W. 47th St. GW-197
Campaign Co., 143 Chambers St. WM-127
Campaign Music Pub. Co., 119 W. 57th St. TED-3
1285 Broadway WM-119
Carl Fisher, Inc., 62 Cooper Sq. GW-345; TR-290; TR-351
Carnegie Music Co., Carnegie Hall AML-6
Cathey Music Co., 123 W. 44th St. WW-145
Cayuga Democratic Club, 2043 Seventh Ave. AES-13; AES-15
Century Music Pub. Co., 231-235 W. 40th St. GW-378; USG-130; USG-152; USG-153; USG-167; USG-195; USG-198; USG-249
1178 Broadway USG-219; TR-339
C.F. Peters Corp. AL-344
373 Park Ave. So. JFK-74
Champness & Desmaris, 55 Greenwich Ave. WW-79
Chandler, Larkin Craig, 601 W. 172nd St. FDR-307; WL-3
Chappell & Co., RKO Bldg. AL-196; FDR-89; FDR-95; FDR-188; HST-12; DDE-15; DDE-45; DDE-46; DDE-54; DDE-85; RR-14; MISC-55; MISC-138
606 Fifth Ave. AL-349
609 Fifth Ave. GW-618; JA-28; TJ-75; JMD-19; JMN-27; JQA-14; AJK-58; MVB-18; WHH-126; WHH-124; JT-14; JKP-19; ZT-88; MF-38; FP-10; JB-23; AL-509; AJN-28; USG-298; RBH-64; JAG-117; CAA-11; GC-162; WM-326; TR-381; RMN-19; MISC-84
Charles Hansen Music & Books, 119 W. 57th St. DAM-8; DAM-9; DAM-58

1860 Broadway RMN-1; RMN-15; MISC-100
Charles Ryan Pub. Co., 136 W. 46th St. FDR-107
Childe, John, 84 Nassau St. WS-22
Christman, Charles G., 404 Pearl Street TJ-43; JQA-11; WHH-20; WHH-72; JT-13
Cirina, Gene, 652 67th St. FDR-359
Clardy & Colonna, 111 W. 49th St. TED-1
Clark, George W. JBR-1
Clayton & Van Norden DWC-8
Cohan & Harris Pub. Co., 115 W. 42nd St. WHT-12
Cohn, Lillian & Samuel English, 1658 Broadway DDE-41
Collins, R.M., 21 Park Row BFH-1
Columbia Advertising Co., 133-17 101st St. GRF-9
Columbia Music Co., 310 W. 95th St. WW-111
Combs, E. WS-36
Committee for the Nomination of Governor Alfred E. Smith, Prudeme Bldg. AES-21
Conejo, Rodolfo, P.O. Box 186 DAM-52
Conservatory Pub. Society, Broadway & 37th St. TR-8
Cook & Brother, 343 Broadway MF-12
Cornish, Lamprot & Co., 267 Pearl St. GW-382; AJK-49; ZT-44
Coventry House HCH-50
Cozans, P.J. SAD-5
107 Nassau St. JFC-45
Craft and Axford HS-17
Crestwood Music Pubs., 1585 Broadway FDR-219
Crown Publishers, Inc. HHH-6
Cupples & Leon Co. GW-238
Curtin, Jas. H. AP-4
Daggett, E.A. WS-14; AL-1
333 Broadway AL-59
Damaso Publishing Co., 47 W. 76th St. FDR-324
Davis, Joe, 1619 Broadway FDR-47
Davis, Meyer, 119 W. 57th St. DDE-74
Dawley, T.R. GBM-74; AL-77
13-15 Park Row AL-74
21 & 23 Ann St. USG-222
Dayton, H., No. 36 Howard St. AL-57
De La Portilla Publications, Inc., 871 7th Ave. DAM-40
De Marsan, H., 54 Chatham St. GBM-50; GBM-56; GBM-67; AL-281; AL-459; JD-52; JD-53; JD-62
58 & 60 Chatham St. AL-116; AL-502
60 Chatham St. SAD-14; AL-112; AL-113; AL-115; USG-241; JD-51
64 Chatham Street AL-114
De Sylva, Brown and Henderson, Inc. MISC-52; MISC-86; MISC-143
De Witt, Robert HG-23; USG-261
160 and 162 Nassau St. MF-10
De Witt, Clinton T., 33 Rose St. MISC-166
Dehnhoff, K., 44 W. 29th St. BFH-57; GC-5
Delaney, William H., 117 Park Row CEH-1
Deluxe Music Co., Broadway & 28th St. USG-176
233 40th St. USG-214
Democratic National Committee JWD-5
Democratic Song Co., 205 W. 75th St. AES-23
Demorest, W. Jennings, No. 39 Beekman St. AL-20; AL-21
Denison, J.D., 208 Broadway USG-137
Dewitt, Robert M., 13 Frankfort St. USG-63; USG-75
Dick & Fitzgerald HS-5; USG-148
Dick James Music, Inc., 119 W. 57th St. RR-22
Dickinson, J.R., 227 W. 22nd St. FDR-33
Dillon-Praetones, 1431 Broadway WW-66
Ditson, C.H. & Co., 277 Broadway USG-62
711 Broadway GW-165; USG-19; USG-87; USG-94; RBH-41
843 Broadway JAG-22; JAG-56; GC-18; GC-115
867 Broadway GC-4
Dodworth, H.B., 6 Astor Pl. GBM-80
Domino Music, Inc., 1674 Broadway DDE-67
Donald Pub. Co. TR-116
Donaldson-Douglas-Gumble, Inc., 1595 Broadway HCH-17
Doodworth, H.B., 6 Astor Place GW-262
Dover Pubs., Inc. MISC-139
Drake-Hoffman-Livingston, 1619 Broadway FDR-194
Dressler, William, 927 Broadway GW-125

Dubois & Bacon, 167 Broadway GW-77
Dubois, Bacon and Chambers, 285 Broadway WHH-111
Dubois & Stodart, 126 Broadway GW-8; DWC-4; DWC-6
Dubois, William GW-70; GW-424; AJK-21; WS-5; MISC-29
126 Broadway GW-74; JMN-6; JMN-8; JMN-15; JMN-20
126 Broadway GW-74; JMN-6; JMN-8; JMN-15; JMN-20
Dubonnet Music Pub., 1619 Broadway TED-12
Duryee Music Co., 74 Fifth Ave. USG-82
E. and R. Music Co., 299 Broadway MISC-150
E. Morris Publishing Co., 694 Madison Avenue JWD-6
Eastern Music Pub. Co. TR-238
Edition Musicus GW-392; AL-378
Edward B. Marks Corp., RCA Bldg. GW-240; AL-181; AL-213; AL-217; AL-218; AL-231; FDR-61; FDR-411
Edwards Music Co., 1619 Broadway FDR-32
Egener, Carl A. and Henry Kessler, 543 Eighth Ave. WW-98
Eighth South Republican Club, 157 E. 48th St. TED-10
Elton, 134 Division St. AJK-38
Elton Song-Book Emporium WHH-17
Empire Music Co. AP-2; TR-2
1424 Broadway WM-50
Empress Music Co., 119 W. 57th St. JFK-73
Endicott, G., 359 Broadway GW-257
Engel, Harry, 1619 Broadway FDR-331
Erdelyi Music Pub. Co., 358 51st St. WFM-1; WFM-2; RR-7; RR-8
1697 Broadway GCW-1; GCW-3; GCW-4; GCW-5; GCW-6; JGS-1; JGS-2; JGS-3; JGS-4; JCS-5
E.T. Paull Music Co., 46 West 28th St. AL-230
Ethel Smith Corporation MISC-151
Fager, George W., 12 Union Sq. GW-278
Fairman, George, 145 W. 45th St. WW-34; WW-41
Fairway Pub. Corp. AL-196
Family Story Paper, No. 74 Beekman St. GW-195
Famous Music Corp., 719 7th Ave. CC-11; CC-16; MISC-136

1619 Broadway FDR-145; DDE-9; MISC-72; MISC-80
Famous Players — Lasky Corp. TR-337
Fantus Bros., 525 S. Dearborn St. CEH-2
F.B. Haviland Co., Broadway at 47th St. TR-364; WW-85
112-114 W. 44th St. WW-89
114 W. 44th St. AML-10
Feeks, J.F., 26 Ann St. GBM-23
Feist and Frakenthaler, 1227 Broadway WM-163
Feist, Leo GW-290; WM-78; TR-106; TR-107; TR-354; WW-63; FDR-10; MISC-46
36 W. 28th St. TR-77
56 Cooper Sq. FDR-1
134 W. 37th St. WHT-4
231-235 W. 40th St. GW-448
799 Seventh Ave. DAM-48; MISC-57; MISC-58
1540 Broadway MISC-59
Fifty Seventh Street Music, 37 W. 57th St. DDE-4
Fine Arts Music Publishers, 113 W. 57th St. FDR-51
Fine Arts Opera Co., 1425 Broadway AES-6
Finger, Jerome, 710 Fairmont Place FDR-57
Firth & Hall, 1 Franklin Sq. GW- 67; GW-97; GW-170; AJK-6; WHH-38; WHH-44; HC-39; HC-40; HC-62; HC-65; ZT-10; ZT-22; ZT-23; WS-1; WS-13; DW-4; DW-18
239 Broadway HC-5
358 Pearl St. GW-385; JQA-4; AJK-47
Firth, Hall & Pond, 234 Broadway ZT-42
239 Broadway ZT-36; ZT-61; WS-30
Firth, Pond & Co. DW-4
1 Franklin Sq. GW-67; ZT-50; MF-30; WS-3; WS-35
547 Broadway GW-159; GW-244; AJK-51; ZT-24; JB-7; SAD-16; GBM-83; AL-357;AL-383; JBL-1
Firth, Son & Co., 563 Broadway GBM-48; AL-150; AL-269; AL-332; JD-61
Firth, Thaddeus, 547 Broadway GW-177
Fisher and Denison HG-24; USG-256
Fischer, Carl GW-433; FDR-243
Cooper Square GW-439
6 & 8 Fourth Ave TJ-30; TR-171
6-10 Fourth Ave TR-19; TR-45

6-12 Fourth Ave. GW-207
Cooper Sq. GW-231; TR-160; TR-247; WHT-28; WW-152; FDR-62
56 Cooper Sq. GW-95; GW-199; GW-342
62 Cooper Sq. AL-478; USG-165; USG-227; DAM-37; MISC-147
Fischer, J. & Bro., 7 Bible House WM-118; TR-335; WHT-48
Fisher, Fred, 224 W. 46th St. WGH-5
Flanagan & Coleman, 136 W. 37th St. TR-23
Flanagan Bros. AES-31
Foley, Edward M., 373 Wolverleigh Blvd. FDR-386
Fonseca, A-Gomez de., 170 Fifth Ave. WM-89
Forward Music Pub. Co. BMG-5
345 W. 58th St. LBJ-22
540 Madison Ave. JEC-12
Fountain Music Co., 108 E. 18th St. TR-147
Francis, Day & Hunter, 15 W. 30th St. TR-245; TR-260
1364 Broadway TR-265
Frank Harding Music Store USG-136; GC-58
136 E. 58th St. WM-26; WM-58
228 E. 22nd St. AES-30
Frank Harding's Music House TR-235
14 Christopher St. TR-319
1293 Broadway USG-146
Frank Music Corp. & Rinimer Corp. JFK-29
Freeman, Tracy L., 225 5th Ave. WHT-21
Friends of the Abraham Lincoln Brigade, 125 W. 45th St. AL-304
FRMACK Co., 2 East 23rd St. FDR-413
Funk & Wagnalls PP-3
18 & 20 Astor Place ND-1
Gagel Bros., 1276 Broadway USG-173; TR-64; MISC-120
Galaxy Music Corp. AL-307
Gallagher Pub. House FDR-6
Galligan, C.H., 1587 Broadway FDR-37
Gardian, The, 32 W. 22nd St. LBJ-33
Garrison, Donald J., 885 Columbus Ave. GW-306
Gavit, D.E., 192 Broadway WS-17
Geib, A. & W., 23 Maiden Lane DWC-7
Geib & Company, 23 Maden Lane DWC-1; JMN-4

Geib & Walker, 23 Maiden Lane DWC-1; WHH-24
Geib, W., No. 219 Broadway AJK-17
General Music Co., 15 Courtlandt St. TR-242
Geo. J. Scott Motor Co., 1720-1722 Broadway USG-224
George M. Cohan Pub. Co., Inc., 1776 Broadway GW-270; GW-285
Geslain, Charles T., 357 Broadway WHH-9
Giffing, James P., No. 56 Gold St. WHH-63; WHH-89
Gilfert, G., 177 Broadway GW-1; GW-462; GW-484; JA-2; TJ-62
Globe Music Co., 1193 Broadway TR-259; WW-112
Glory Pub. Co., 170 Broadway WLW-4
Goodwin, Walter, 156 W. 44th St. GW-326
Gordon, Hamilton S., 139 Fifth Ave. WM-23; TR-70
Gordon, S.T., 13 E. 14th St. GW-503; RBH-51; RBH-65; WSH-27
297 Broadway, JCF-3
538 Broadway, GW-359; GW-566; WS-27; USG-183; USG-189; DW-16; JD-58
706 Broadway GW-135; GW-155; GW-314; GW-362; GW-387; GW-431; MF-33; JCF-31; SAD-1; SAD-8
Gordon, S.T. & Son WSH-6
13 E. 14th St. GW-572; SJT-1; RBH-26; WSH-20; JAG-88; JAG-118; JGB-6; GC-16; GC-86; BFB-10
Gotham-Attucks Music Co., 136 W. 37th St. WHT-24
Gotham Music Co., 521 E. 13th St. WM-55
Government By Law Alliance, 280 Broadway. WLW—36
Graham, William H., HC-99; ZT-32
Greeley & McElrath HC-18; HC-35
Tribune Buildings HC-93
Greeley, Horace & Co. WHH-91
Grey, John A. & Green AL-411
Guild Publications of Art and Music, Inc., 202 E. 44th St. FDR-297
Haight, R.G., 304 W. 49th St. JWD-3
Hall, Wm. & Son. AL-431
No. 239 Broadway GW-97; GW-103; GW-150; GW-260; GW-299; GW-419; JA-25; ZT-9; ZT-43; ZT-47; ZT-60; ZT-65; MF-1; WS-21; JCF-13

Appendix

543 Broadway GBM-42; AL-153; USG-151; USG-156; USG-293
Halle, Roger, 202 E. 87th St. TR-83
Halsey Music, Inc., 1674 Broadway TJ-37
Handy Bros. AL-200
1650 Broadway AL-245; TR-142; HST-21; DDE-1
Haney & Co., 199 Nassau St. USG-32
Hansen, Charles, 1860 Broadway JFK-78
Harcourt, Brace & Company, Inc. AJK-53; AL-476.
Harding, Frank GW-325; AES-53
228 E. 22nd St. WGH-19; WGH-58; HCH-16; FDR-161; FDR-306
228-232 E. 22nd St. FDR-120; FDR-126; FDR-389
Harding's, 228 E. 22nd St. WGH-20; FDR-308
288 Bowery GW-92; GW-263; JD-26; JD-34
Harold Flammer, Inc. TR-52
Harms, Inc. RR-15
Harms, T.B. AL-233; TR-143; WW-23
Harms, T.B. & Co. WW-149
18 E. 22nd St. BFH-69; WM-20; TR-164
819 Broadway JAG-92; JGB-18; GC-85
Harms, T.B. & Francis, Day & Hunter TR-152
Harper's Weekly AL-289
Harriman For President, 111 E. 56th St. MISC-19
Harris, Chas. K. TR-6; TR-139; WHT-6
Columbia Theatre Bldg., Broadway at 47th St. JWD-2
Harris Chas. W., 13 E. 14th St. GW-348
Harry Von Tilzer Music Pub. Co., 42 W. 28th St. MISC-93
1587 Broadway GW-628
Harry Williams Music Company, 154 W. 46th St. AL-213
Harvey Music Corp., 1619 Broadway AL-311
Haviland, F.B., Broadway at 37th St. TR-101
128 W. 48th St. WW-24
Haviland Publishing Company, Broadway at 37th St. WHT-2; TR-354
112 W. 44th St. FDR-12
114 W. 44th St. FDR-24
Haws, Francesca C., 22 E. 31st St. CC-15

Henry Waterson, Inc., 1971 Broadway CC-56
Hewitt, J., 23 Maiden Lane GW-54; GW-468
59 Maiden Lane GW-587; TJ-61; TJ-63; JMD-17; JMN-16
121 William St. JA-17
131 William St. GW-20; JA-1; JA-27
Hewitt & Jaques, 239 Broadway WHH-19
Hewitt, James L., 372 Broadway HC-37
Hewitt, James L. & Co., 36 Market St. AJK-2
137 Broadway AJK-2
239 Broadway GW-305; MVB-10; DW-13
Hill & Range Songs, Inc., 1619 Broadway JAG-69; LBJ-10; RR-29
Hinds, Hayden and Eldredge, Inc. GW-531; AL-229; AL-491
His Majesty's Ink-Slingers, Inc., 25 W. 43rd St. FDR-353
Hitchcock & McCargo Pub. Co. BFH-61
385 Sixth Ave. BFH-61
Hitchcock, Benjamin W., 14 Chambers St. GBM-24
385 Sixth Ave. GC-31; GC-43; GC-151
Hitchcock Pub. Co., 244-246 W. 23rd St. GW-593
Hitchcock Pub. House, 325 Sixth Ave. BFH-3; BFH-19
385 Sixth Ave. GW-504
Hitchcock's Music Store, 11 Park Row BFH-33; GC-111
32 Park Row JAG-33
166 Nassau St. GW-245; GC-70
283 Sixth Ave. GW-161; GW-264
385 Sixth Ave. USG-172; BFH-66; GC-56; GC-105
Hitchcock's Steam Printing and Publishing House, 385 Sixth Ave. BFH-82
Hitt Music Pub. Co., 509 Fifth Ave. FDR-82
Hoffman, W.R., 271 Broadway TR-272
Holt, C., Jr., 156 Fulton St. GW-332; HC-33; ZT-1
Holzmann, A. & Co., 358 E. 123rd St. MISC-49
Hopkins, Edward, 30 E. 14th St. GW-573; USG-284
Horn, C.E., 367 Broadway WHH-37
Howe, W., 320 Pearl St. JA-23
Howell, Dick & Nielson TR-225

Howley, Haviland & Co., 4 E. 20th St. GW-190; GC-92; GC-100; WM-22; WM-166; WM-316
1260-1266 Broadway AL-221; AL-492; USG-66; USG-72; WM-4; WM-216; TR-27; TR-79; TR-336; TR-366
Howley, Haviland & Dresser AL-263
1260-1266 Broadway GW-252
Hubbard, Albert, 162 Ninth Ave. GW-178
Hudson Music Corp., 1650 Broadway GW-286
Huestis & Cozans, 104 & 106 Nassau St. WS-15
Hurst & Co., 122 Nassau St. AJK-57; AL-507; USG-299; MISC-183
Hutchinson, O. AL-387
272 Greenwich St. AL-175; AL-317
I Wanna Be A Cap'n Club, 1472 Broadway, Room 904 WLW-56
Independent Music Pub. Co. WW-105
Intercollegiate Syndicate, Inc., 1650 Broadway JFK-5
International Music Co., 53 W. 28th St. MISC-2
International Music Publishers, 1229 Park Row Bldg. FDR-65
Irving Berlin, Inc., 799 7th Ave. GW-356; TJ-41; AL-194; FDR-180; FDR-179
1607 Broadway AES-9; HCH-44; FDR-63; FDR-204
1650 Broadway DDE-8; DDE-19; DDE-48; DDE-60; DAM-42; MISC-68
J & M Novelty Co., 156 W. 44th St. FDR-13
J & M Paff's Music Store, No. 127 Broadway TJ-13; JMD-4
J. Fred. Helf Publishing Co., 136 W. 37th St. AL-205; TR-31; TR-35
J. Stasny Music Co., 56 W. 45th St. WW-48
Jack Snyder Pub. Co. USG-70
Jefferson Music Co., 1619 Broadway TJ-42
Jerry Vogel Music Co., 112 W. 44th St. GW-196; GW-330
114 W. 44th St. GW-327
Joe Davis Music Co., 1619 Broadway FDR-70; DDE-2
Joe Morris Music, 130 W. 37th St. TR-37
Johnson Music, 77 W. 46th St. WLW-3

Johnstone-Montei, Inc., 1619 Broadway DDE-28
Jollie, S.C., 300 Broadway GW-76; GW-365; GW-366
Jonassohn, E., 22 W. 8th St. TR-199
Jos. J. Kaiser Music Company TR-252
J.S. Ogilvie Pub. Co., 57 Rose St. WM-82
Kalmar Puck & Abrahams, 1 Strand Theatre Bldg. GW-219
Kehr, H.J., Central Hall, Frankford Road & Mastert Streets MF-20
Kelly, Capt. Patrick F., 39 Beekman St. AL-482
Kelton-Romm, Inc., 250 W. 49th St. DDE-35
Kendis-Brockman Music, 145 W. 45th St. WW-31
Kendis Music Pub. Co., 145 W. 45th St. TR-53; WW-22; WW-94
Kennedy, P.J. USG-276
Kenney, Eugene R. GW-432
Keys Popular Song Dist., 128 W. 58th St. JFK-45
Knickerbocker Harmony Studios, 1545 Broadway TR-181; WW-207
Knoff, Alfred A. MISC-156
Kurtz, E.H.L., 473 Grand St. HG-18
L. Dodworth & Co., 108-110 125th St. JMN-24
La Paglia, Anthony HCH-27
Lapham & Townsend, 1607 Broadway AML-1
Larrabee Publications, 39 W. 60th St. MISC-70
Leeds Music Corp., RKO Bldg. TJ-28; WLW-46; FDR-177; HST-2; HST-6
322 W. 48th St. JFK-3; JFK-4; JFK-38
Len Flemming & Co., 1416 Broadway WW-161
Lenox Co., Music Publishers, 271 W. 125th St. TR-232; WW-205; WGH-21; WGH-22
Levi, 24 Union Square WM-230, JMN-23
Liberal Party FDR-242
LIFE Pub. Co. MISC-10
Lincoln Music Corp., 1619 Broadway AL-321; FDR-230
Link, J.W., 332 W. Market St. GC-62
Lipschuetz, C.S. TR-94
Loena Music Publishing Co. GW-294; RR-10
239 W. 18th St. GW-293; GW-315; TJ-35; TJ-40; AL-252; AL-292; FDR-

Appendix

53; FDR-121; FDR-291; FDR-310; HST-5; HST-16; HST-18; HST-24; DDE-44; DDE-71; DDE-76; DDE-90; JFK-51; JFK-53; JFK-67; LBJ-1; LBJ-13; LBJ-15; LBJ-24; LBJ-27; RMN-4; RMN-24; RMN-25; RMN-26; RMN-27; GRF-1; GRF-3; GRF-7; GRF-8; GRF-12; JEC-4; JEC-10; RR-23; GB-1; BC-3; BC-4; BC-9; BC-10
614 W. 51st St. JFK-25; LBJ-11; LBJ-16; LBJ-19
Log Cabin, 30 Ann St. WHH-56
Long, H & Brother ZT-75
Luckhardt & Belder, 10 E. 17th St. TR-43; TR-169; TR-244
36 W. 40th St. WW-185
Ludlow Music, Inc. LBJ-2
Lupal Music Co., 501 Madison Ave. DDE-38
Lyman, L.S. WM-289
Lock Box 2841 WM-108
Lyraphone Company of America MISC-5
Lyric Music Pub. Co., 42 Union Sq. WM-179
Lyric Pub. Co., 145 W. 45th St. WW-190
Lysaght, Walter, 254 W. 46th St. WW-123
Mack Stark Music Co., Inc., 745 7th Ave. MISC-12; MISC-13
MacMillan Company, The GW-437; GW-526; AL-479
Macy, R.H. and Co. USG-160; JAG-63; CAA-2
Magnus, Chas. JD-35
12 Frankfort St. GW-137; GW-129; GW-428; GW-596; GW-597; WS-19; GBM-7; GBM-22; GBM-44; GBM-81; GBM-82; AL-17; AL-111; AL-109; AL-357; AL-366; AL-376; AL-434; USG-61; USG-150; WSH-27; JD-35; BFB-22; MISC-65
12 Franklin Place GBM-9; USG-155; JD-32
Mainstay Music, Inc., 101 W. 55th St. JFK-24
Marks Music Co., 225 W. 46th St. AES-16
Martens Brothers, 1164 Broadway GC-78
Martyn & Ely, 162 Nassau St. MVB-5
Marzen, Pietro, 193 Sinclair Ave. WW-107

Mason Music Co., 1587 Broadway FDR-146
Maurice Richmond Music Co., 145 W. 45th St. GW-235
Mayhams Music Co., 12 W. 117th St. FDR-117
Maxwell Sales Co., 1451 Broadway TR-264
McAuliffe & Booth TR-161
McCarthy & Fischer, Inc., 224 W. 46th St. TR-212
McElroy, Frank, 113 Nassau St. GBM-61
McKinley Music Co., 74 Fifth Ave. MISC-184
McKinley Publishers, Inc., 797 Eighth Ave. DDE-49
McLaughlin Bros. JGB-47
Megan Music Co. AL-190
Mercury Music Corp. TJ-18; TJ-27
Merickle Pub. Co. WM-286
Metro Music Co., 58 Second Avenue SLP-4
Metropolis Music Co., 145 W. 45th St. CEH-6
Meyer Cohen Music, 1531 Broadway WW-71
Meridian Music Corp., 1619 Broadway AS-3
Messier, E.S., 28 Wall St. AJK-21
Microfone Music Publishers, 148 W. 46th St. CC-20
Miller & Shoemaker, 745 7th Ave. AES-3
Miller, Bob, 1619 Broadway FDR-372
Miller Music, 62 W. 45th St. FDR-54
Miller, Orton and Mulligan, 25 Park Row JCF-16; JCF-22; JCF-24
Millet & Son, 329 Broadway GW-132
Millet's Music Saloon GW-68
375 Broadway DW-28
Mills, F.A., 48 W. 29th St. GW-236; GW-322
Mills, Jack, 148-150 W. 46th St. USG-134; WJB-51
Mills Music, Inc. FDR-340
148-150 W. 46th St. GW-224
1619 Broadway GW-296; AL-185; AL-335; FDR-79; FDR-80; FDR-224; FDR-225; FDR-229; FDR-249; FDR-252; FDR-393; HST-13; JFK-20
Mode Music, Inc., 1650 Broadway AS-1
Morris, A. AL-394

Morris, Edw. H. & Co., 31 W. 54th St. LBJ-6; RMN-15
1619 Broadway FDR-385; MISC-18
Muller, D., 509 E. 76th St. TR-277; MISC-71
Munro, George HG-23
Munro, Norman L., No. 74 Beekman St. GW-126; GW-195
Munroe's Pub. House, 16 Vanderwater St. JAG-25
24 & 26 Vanderwater St. USG-79
Mus-Art Pub. Co., 980 E. 163rd St. HCH-18
Musette Publishers, Inc., Steinway Hall TJ-34; JQA-10; AL-247; TR-293; WW-155
Music Mail Co., 225 W. 46th St. FDR-12
Music Music Music, Inc. JFK-14; JFK-77
Music of the Times Publishing Corp. TJ-45; MISC-153
Music Printing Co. WW-93
59 Bank St. WW-120
Music Sales Corp. USG-171
Mutual Music Society, 1270 Sixth Ave. DDE-22; DDE-78
M.V. Smith Pub. Co. CC-19
Nafis & Cornish, 270 Pearl St. GW-624
278 Pearl St. ZT-41
Nadage Doree Society, 1947 Broadway GW-369
National Assn. of Democratic Clubs, 1370 Broadway WJB-11
National Book Co., 505 Fifth Ave. DDE-68
National Citizen Political Action Committee, 205 E. 42nd St. FDR-197
National Democratic Committee, Box 3637 SJT-21
National Manuscript Bureau, 236 W. 55th St. FDR-156
333 W. 52nd St. MISC-51
National Music Co. WW-2; WW-58
44 E. 14th St. GW-550; BFH-60
67 Fifth Ave. WJB-7
National Temperance Society JSJ-5
Nationwide Songs, Inc., 1674 Broadway FDR-123
Nationwide Songs, Inc., 1674 Broadway FDR-123
Nesbitt, Geo. F., Tontine Bldg. HC-115
New Island Music Co. TR-185
New World Music Corp. MISC-15
New World Press, 30 Ann St. HC-16

New York American and Journal TR-223
New York & Chicago Music Pub. Co., 1529 Broadway TR-97; TR-135
New York Citizen HC-98
New York Evening Press GBM-70
New York Journal and Advertiser GW-200; GW-329; WJB-66; WJB-95; TR-357
New York Musical World, 379 Broadway JCF-35
New York News Co. HG-26
New York Press WM-83
New York Popular Publishing Co., 32 Beekman St. WSH-41; JAG-27
New York Republican County Committee WLW-51; TED-23
New York State Committee For The Nomination Of Gov. Alfred E. Smith, Prudeme Building AES-21
New York Sun HG-5
New York Sunday Press GW-202
New York Times Magazine AL-374
New York Tribune AL-388; BFH-44; BFH-68
New York World GW-215; AP-3; TR-111
New York World Press HC-103
Newman, L.F., 161 W. 3rd St. WW-90
Newman, Mark H., 199 Broadway HC-82
Noble, John D., 131 W. 23rd St. HCH-15
470 E. 161st St. CC-36
1966 Broadway CC-34
Nolasco, Felix A. FDR-141
North Eastern Music Co. CEH-3
Northern Music Corp., 445 W. Park Ave. RMN-39
Noteworthy Music Co., 146 W. 54th St. DDE-29
Nunns, John F., 240 Broadway HC-1; HC-2
N.Y. Variety Publishing Co., 77 Chatham St. USG-207
Oak Publications TJ-72; AL-490
165 W. 46th St. HCH-57; FDR-378; LBJ-31; GCW-7
O'Dowd, Thomas, 8 Magaw Place FDR-302
26 8th Ave TR-263
Ogilvie, J.S., 57 Rose St. GC-45
O'Hara, C.J., 111 E. 88th St. AES-24; AES-64
O'Hara, P.F., 70 William St. DWC-9; LMD-16; JMN-26

Appendix

Old Dominion Music Co., 14 W. 27th St. TR-309
Old Glory Music Pub., 345 W. 58th St. MISC-67
Olman Music Corp., 745 Seventh Ave. MISC-83
Opharrow, Geo. A., 48 W. 136th St. TR-322
Orum & Co. HG-27
Our Boys In France Tobacco Fund, 25 W. 44th St. TR-292
Paff, I & M. JMD-7
Paff, J & M. TR-12; JMD-8
Paff, John GW-53; JMD-14; JMN-19; AJK-21; WS-40
Palumbo, Pierina FDR-7
Pan American Music Co., RKO Bldg. FDR-276
Paragon Music Publishers DAM-10
Partee, C.L. AL-193
Passantino Music Pub. Co., 311 W. 43rd St. JEC-1; JEC-8; RR-5
Patricolo, A., Steinway Hall TR-218
Patriotic Songs Publications, 351 W. 52nd St. FDR-203
Patten & Hubbard, World Bldg., 37 Park Row HS-8
Patten, E.P. GBM-71
Paull-Pioneer Music Co., 119 Fifth Ave. AES-1; AES-2; AES-4
1657 Broadway WLW-5; WLW-38; DAM-2
Pearson, C.H. WM-196
Pease Piano Co., 128 W. 42nd St. WHT-3
Peer International Corp. AL-207; AL-262; MISC-106
Penfield, Henry F. HC-51
People's Songs HAW-5
126 W. 21st St. HAW-8
Pergament, Emmanuel, 48 E. 4th St. GC-106
Perry Alexander Music Pub., 1619 Broadway TED-22
Perry Bradford Music and Periodical Publishing Company, 1650 Broadway, Suite #305 TED-27
Peterman, J.H., 115 W. 114th St. WHT-20
Peters, A.C., 1068 Park Ave. WGH-3
Peters, Brooks C. TR-143
Peters, J.L. GW-265; HS-11; HG-1; USG-9; USG-254; SJT-9; SJT-19; RBH-29
198 Broadway USG-30; HS-2; HS-13

599 Broadway USG-228
Phelps Music Co., 52-54 Lafayette Place AL-306; WM-68; WM-312
Piantadosi, Al & Co., Astor Theatre Bldg. GW-232; WW-189
Pickford Music Co., 1674 Broadway DAM-1
Pietro Deiro Publications, 113 Seventh Ave. RMN-32
Pioneer Music Co., 199 Fifth Ave. AES-5
Planetary Music Pub., 1619 Broadway AL-212; DDE-20
Pocket Books, Inc. JFK-17
Pond, Wm. A. & Co. USG-145
25 Union Sq. GW-354; GW-423; GW-506; USG-81; RBH-34; WSH-17; WSH-29; WSH-45; JAG-3; JAG-7; JAG-14; JAG-26; JAG-72; JGB-20; JGB-48; GC-20; GC-48; GC-123; GC-163
547 Broadway GW-173; ZT-25; GBM-1; GBM-54; AL-32; AL-37; AL-46; AL-80; AL-89; AL-90; AL-92; AL-108; AL-171; AL-259; AL-503; AJN-8; AJN-21; HG-12; HG-14; USG-15; USG-26; USG-28; USG-46; USG-60; USG-106; SJT-3; SJT-15; RBH-1; RBH-15; RBH-42; RBH-50; JD-20; JD-44; MISC-36
Popular Melodies, Inc., 1619 Broadway MISC-69
Popular Publishing Co. JAG-102
Powers, Rodney, 145 West 45th St. GW-368
Progressive, The, 140 Cedar St. GW-246
Progressive Party, The, 39 Park Ave. HAW-3
Powers, Rodney., 145 W. 45th St. GW-368
Radio Artists' League of America, 3105 Chrysler Bldg. FDR-16
Rainbow Music Publishers, 1619 Broadway TED-29
RCA Music Corp. JFK-37
Recker, Robert & Co., 5 East 14th St. MISC-39
Red Evans Music Co., 1619 Broadway TJ-42; MISC-60
Red Star Songs, Inc., 1619 Broadway WLW-11; WLW-58
Rehm, Charles AL-3
Rehm, Wm. C. WW-38
Remick, Jerome H. GW-220; WW-36

Publishers by City

Remick, Jerome H. & Co. GW-229; JMD-13; TR-20; TR-29; TR-30; TR-42; TR-44; TR-58; TR-89; TR-258; TR-295; WHT-37; WHT-42; WHT-43; WW-40; WW-99; SP-5; MISC-84
Remick Music Corp. CC-45; RR-12; RR-16; RR-17; MISC-48; MISC-50
Randolph, A.D.F., 683 Broadway AL-359
Republican Central Campaign Club of New York, 1169 Broadway JAG-41
Republican League of the United States, 202 Fifth Ave. BFH-58
Republican National Committee JGB-32
19 W. 44th St. WGH-23
41 E. 42nd St. AML-18
Republican Women In Industry & Professions, 270 Park Ave. DDE-103
Richardson Music Pub. Co., 28 Elm St. TR-120
Riemer Music Pub. Co. TR-287
Riggs H.S. & Co., 4 Courtland St. JCF-45
Riley, E., 17 Chatham St. GW-479
23 Chatham St. GW-102; GW-489; JA-16; AJK-32
29 Chatham St. GW-31; GW-50; GW-69; GW-101; GW-113; GW-480; GW-491; DWC-3; JMN-5; JMN-25; AJK-4; MVB-9; WS-29; MISC-30
297 Broadway GW-63; HC-36
Riley, E. and Co., 29 Chatham St. WHH-101
297 Broadway WS-33
Risky Music Publishing Co., 1674 Broadway FDR-322
Roach, J. Mallory, 575 Madison Ave. RMN-10
Robbins Company, 1619 Broadway DDE-5
Robbins Music Corp., 799 Seventh Ave. GW-201; GW-561; GW-562; FDR-20; DAM-18; MISC-75
Rocker, F.A., 129 E. 125th St. GC-157
Roger Hale Music Co., 173 E. 93rd St. AL-188
Rogers, James A., 61-65 Cliff St. TR-195
Rossiter, Will, 1162 Broadway WM-38
Royal Music Co., 160 W. 46th St. WW-113
Roznique Music, Inc. JFK-78
17 W. 60th St. JFK-30; JFK-31

165 W. 46th St. JFK-66
1516 Broadway JFK-62
Rueffer, Ernst., 109 First Ave. TR-48
Rytvoc, Inc., 1585 Broadway FDR-176; FDR-410
S. Brainard's Sons Co. USG-50; JAG-116; TR-54
20 E. 17th St. GW-133; WM-230; WM-304; TR-144
Saalfield Pub. Co., 794, 796, 798 Tenth Ave. GC-6
Saalfield, Richard A. CAA-3; JGB-21; JGB-92
12 Bible House USG-42; USG-142; SJT-12; JAG-38; WSH-23; JGB-2; JGB-4; JGB-7; GC-1; GC-17; BFB-4
41 Union Sq. GW-152; GW-203; GW-247; USG-102; WSH-33; CAA-6; BFH-24; GC-12; GC-15; GC-69
839 Broadway WSH-34; JAG-78; MISC-160
843 Broadway GC-120
1123 Broadway GW-202; WM-167
Sage, H., 214 Broadway DWC-7
Sam Fox Pub. Co., RCA Bldg. DDE-6
11 W. 60th St. MISC-62
1841 Broadway JFK-18; MISC-56
Sanctuary, E.N., 142 W. 91st St. DAM-32
Sands Music Corp., 1619 Broadway LBJ-9; MISC-118
Santa-Claus HC-97
Santly-Joy-Select, Inc., 1619 Broadway FDR-73; FDR-74; FDR-75; FDR-416
Saunders Pubs., Inc., 119 W. 57th St. AL-216
Scharfenberg & Luis, 483 Broadway ZT-5; ZT-14
Schirmer, Inc., G. GW-395; MF-37; JB-22; GBM-84; AL-234; AL-334; AL-506; WM-257; WM-325; FDR-317; FDR-403; MISC-182
3 East 43rd St. GW-338
701 Broadway GW-174; GW-185; RBH-45
Schlacht, Joseph, 440 E. 6th St. FDR-269
Schneider, Walter E., 1 W. 64th St. DDE-13
Schott, J., 52 E. 4th St. GW-118; BFH-28
Schuberth & Co., 98 Spring St. ZT-72; GBM-58

Appendix

Schuberth, Edward & Co. AJN-20
23 Union Sq. JAG-36; JAG-74; GC-19; WM-90; WM-112
Screen Gems-Columbia Music, Inc., 711 Fifth Ave. RMN-20
Seminary Music Co., 12 E. 17th St. JMD-12
112 W. 38th St. TR-34
Serly, Lajos von., 241 W. 137th St. TR-216
Shada Music, Inc. MISC-77
Shamrock, The JMN-17
Shapiro, Bernstein & Co. GW-358; WW-218; FDR-69; DAM-13
Broadway & 39th St. HCH-4
224 W. 47th St. GW-191; GW-241; GW-251; AL-219; WW-13; WW-14; WW-144; WW-153; HCH-53
666 Fifth Ave. DDE-17
Shapiro Music, Broadway & 39th St. TR-5; TR-28; TR-155; WHT-27; WW-54; WW-170
Shattinger International Music Corp. JEC-5
Silver Burdett Co. GW-391; GW-440; GW-450; GW-510; GW-513; GW-518; GW-612; AL-470
Silvers, Herman, 60 E. 14th St. HHH-1; HHH-3; JEC-1
Simon and Schuster, Rockefeller Center GW-347
Skidmore Music Co., 1270 Sixth Ave. FDR-1
Slater, E.D., 147 Fulton St. PC-1
Smith & Ryan, 30 Church St. WW-28
Song Hit Music Pub. Co., 1650 Broadway TED-19
Soldiers and Sailors Copeland Campaign Committee, 101 Broad St. MISC-7; MISC-8
Song Smiths, Inc., Music Pub. Co., 870 Seventh Avenue MISC-188
Southern Music Pub. Co., 1619 Broadway GW-337; MISC-106
Southwind Music, Inc. JAG-70
Spanuth & Strouse, 145 W. 45th St. TR-327
Spaulding & Gray, 16 W. 27th St. GC-27; GC-108
Spear & Dehnhoff, 717 Broadway RBH-30; JAG-1; JAG-15
Sprague-Coleman, 62 W. 45th St. WLW-8
Stagg, Robert, 48 E. 4th St. RML-5
Stanfield Pub. Co. WJB-60

Stargen Music Corp. DDE-26; DDE-42
Starret System Club FDR-143
Stazny-Lang, Inc., 1619 Broadway AML-25
Stern, Jos. W., 45 E. 20th St. GW-222
Stern, Jos. W. & Co. MISC-63
34 E. 21st St. WM-79; TR-86; TR-206
102-104 W. 38th St. GW-308; TR-126; WHT-9; WW-33; WW-69; WW-158
Stirling Music Pub. Co., 117 W. 48th St. MISC-95
Stolz, M. & Co., 26 & 28 Park Place GC-14
Stratford Music DDE-85
Stringer, Burgess & Co. ZT-74
Sunbeam Music Corp., 22 W. 48th St. RMN-6; LGM-2; LGM-3
1619 Broadway DDE-10
T.B. Harms Company AL-315; DAM-6
Ted Snyder Co., Inc., 112 W. 38th St. GW-289; TR-74; TR-326
This Is The Army, Inc., 799 Seventh Ave. RR-20; RR-32
Thompson's Band Office, 122 Court St. GW-532
Thurston, N. GW-33; GW-57
Tilzer Music Co., 222 W. 46th St. WW-119
Times Pub. Corp. TR-44; MISC-100; MISC-153
Torp and Viereck, 465 Broadway GW-91
Torp, O., 465 Broadway AJK-28
Transcontinental Music Corp. FDR-186; FDR-189; FDR-220; JFK-49
Treasure Chest Publications, Inc. GW-420
Tremaine, C.M., 481 Broadway WS-25; AL-273; AL-402; USG-59; USG-191; JGB-22
Triangle Music Pub. Co., 145 W. 45th St. WGH-7
1658 Broadway CC-6; HCH-14
Triumphant Music, 1472 Broadway FDR-11
Tullar-Meredith, 265 West 36th Street GW-434; AL-360
Turner & Fisher WHH-126; HC-96; HC-101; JKP-10; JKP-12; ZT-38; ZT-56
Chatham St. GW-140
74 Chatham St. LC-2
Twelfth Assembly District WJB-43
Uncle Sam Music Pub. Co. MISC-103

Unger, F.C., 385 Broadway WHH-8; WHH-94
Unicorn Press, Inc., 790 Madison Ave. BMG-13
Union Mutual Co., 265 Sixth St. WM-27; WM-139
Union Music Co. FDR-172; FDR-173
United Fund for Refugee Children, 233 W. 42nd St. FDR-352
Unlimited Artists Music Pub. Co. MISC-79
Valando Music, 22 W. 48th St. LGM-2
Valiant Music Co., 1619 Broadway JFK-36
Van Loan, J. and Co., 21 E. 14th St. JGB-74
Van Rees, Cornelius R., 518-534 W. 26th St. HCH-42
Vanderbeek, Wm., 385 Broadway ZT-4
Vandersloot Music Co., 41 W. 28th St. WM-46
Vernon Music Corp, 1619 Broadway MISC-24
Vernonique Publishing Co., 250 West 57th Street JFK-54; JFK-75
Vicom Press, Inc., 700 Madison Ave. BG-13
Vincent Bryan Music Co., 6 W. 28th St. TR-66
Vincent Youmans Co., 157 W. 57th St. BMG-3
VosBurgh's Orchestration Service, 1547 Broadway HCH-3
Wade, Frank, 1585 Broadway TED-8
Wallau, George T., 2 & 4 Stone St. WM-88
Warner Bros. Music, 488 Madison Ave. CC-47; MISC-16
Warner Bros. Publications, Inc., 75 Rockefeller Plaza RMN-22
Washington Souvenir Co., 35 Frankfort St. GW-153
Waters, Horace, 333 Broadway GW-169; GW-175; MF-10; HG-29
481 Broadway WS-42; GBM-16; GBM-29; AL-24; AL-43; AL-44; AL-98; AL-107; AL-148; AL-169; AL-368; HG-8; HG-17; USG-177; USG-203; USG-252
Waterson, Berlin & Snyder, CC-56
Strand Theatre, 47th & Broadway TR-145; HCH-38
Waterson, Henry, 1971 Broadway CC-56
Webster Music Corp., 1841 Broadway JFK-10

Wehman Bros. GW-357; AL-353
Weinstein, N., 24 W. 23rd St. BFH-31
949 Broadway TR-197
Weir, C.E. HC-32
Weiss, MacEachen & Miller, 209 W. 13th St. WW-201
Wenzlik Music and Supply Co., 17th St. & Broadway GC-26
White Music Pub. Co., 507 W. 50th St. AES-32
Whitecup, Leonard, 215 E. 68th St. GRF-6
White-Smith Music Co. WM-31
Whitney Blake Music Publishers, 1585 Broadway FDR-93
Wholesale Dry Goods Club BFH-85; WM-128
350 Broadway WM-214
Wide World, Inc., 104 E. 56th St. WLW-39
Wiesinger, Armand, 961 St. Nicholas Ave. HCH-31
William Jerome Pub. Corp., Strand Theatre Bldg. WW-188
William Lee Mann Associates FDR-88
William R. Haskins Company, 51 W. 28th St. TR-344
Willis, Woodward & Co., 842 & 844 Broadway WM-98; WM-247
Willson, John, M., 14 Maiden Lane DWC-5
435 Broadway AL-177; AL-178
Winchester, J., 30 Ann St. HC-20
Winfield Music, Inc., 67 W. 44th St. HST-9
Witmark, M. & Sons GW-577; USG-281; TR-17; TR-69; TR-139; TR-240; TR-254; TR-325; WHT-18; HCH-1; FDR-170; FDR-207; HST-1; RR-9; RR-11; RR-21; PP-4; MISC-3; MISC-45; MISC-53; MISC-98; MISC-99
10 Witmark Bldg. WW-1; WGH-6; HCH-13
402 W. 40th St. GC-51
1657 Broadway FDR-34
Witro Music Publishing, 1619 Broadway AL-244
Wm. Jerome Pub. Corp., 47th St. & Broadway GW-275
Wonderland Music Co., 477 Madison Ave. AJK-43
Wood, Will, 223 W. 40th St. TR-56
Woodward, Willis & Co., 842 & 844 Broadway JGB-49; BFH-15

Worker's Book Shop, 50 E. 13th St. AL-333; TJ-51; FDR-221; CP-1; CP-4
Workers Library Publishers, P.O. Box 148, Station D AL-494; CP-3
Worker's Music League CP-2
Wright & Shaw, 242 Broadway WLW-34
Wrigley, J., 61 Chatham St. HS-14; JD-33
Wunderman, P.A., 824 Broadway AL-444
145 Third Ave. GC-164
1013 Third Ave. JAG-44
Young, Barney, 1616 Broadway FDR-60
Young People's Socialist League, 303 Fourth Ave. SP-8
Zuma Music Co., 200 W. 54th St. LBJ-8

NEWARK, NJ
Boughton's Music Store, Ceder, cor. Halsey St. WM-25
Bowers, Albert M. WM-321
Bowman-Burck Music Pub. Co. AL-232
Habersang, Oscar, 52 Springfield Ave. HC-68
Hinds, S.P., 102 Market St. JQA-13
Koellhoffer, B.A., 550 S. 10th St. GW-221
Morrow, Henry, 318 Sanford Ave. FDR-255
Potts, Rev. William D. GBM-75

NEWBURGH, NY
D'Agostino, Giacomo, 235 Washington St. FDR-144

NEWBURYPORT, MA
Blunt, Edmund M. GW-483

NEWCASTLE, DE
Goulbourne, J. Matthew, 127 E. Fourth St. CC-54

NORFOLK, VA
Balls, Thos. TJ-25; TJ-36
Benmosche, Rev. Herman WW-43
Womrath, J. TJ-9

NORRISTOWN, PA
Donahue, A.B., 816 DeKalb St. FDR-368
Wood Bros. TR-192

NORTH HOLLYWOOD, CA
Etcetera Music Company, 12315 Rye Street JFK-80

Jack-Helen Artists Assn., 11204 Huston St. FDR-263

NORTHAMPTON, MA
Wright, Andrew GW-489
Wright, Daniel & Co. GW-110; JA-15

NORWALK, OH
Lyric Music Company FDR-400
Sprague, Jas. H. WM-87; WM-310

NORWOOD, PA
Bassett, Annie R. Waln WHT-22

OAKLAND, CA
Anderson, F. Geary, 1015 MacArthur Blvd. DDE-69
Buck, R.H. FDR-259
Farley, William, 600 16th St. FDR-118
Fraternal Citizens of America, 1634 Telegraph Ave. FDR-46
Freeman, Philip R. and Assocs., 77 Jack London Sq. JC-11
Oakland Tribune WW-168
Parrish, T.A., 409 Eight St. WW-122
Schreiber, Felix, 1st National Bank Bldg. WW-150
Sierra Music Pub. Co., 1316 Webster St. WW-144
Slater, Aleta Roberts, 2159 High St. WLW-43

OCEAN CITY, NJ
Top Tunes Co. DDE-110

OCEANSIDE, NY
Seiffert, Wm. R., National Bank Bldg. AML-4; RMN-9
OJAI, CA.
Creative Concepts Pub. Corp., 154 El Roblar Dr., Box 848 GW-620; JFK-84

OKLAHOMA CITY, OK
Murray For President, Perrine Bldg. MISC-14
Pearl, Musetta Markland, 2408 South Harvey HCH-42; HCH-43; HCH-44

OLNEY, NY
Moore Music JFK-44

OLNEYVILLE, NY
Dewolfe, Geo. G.B. SAD-15

Publishers by City

OMAHA, NE
A. Hospe Co. TR-299
McIntosh, E.W., 3321 Davenport St. AL-516
Miner, I.W., 422 S. 15th St. WM-178
Perfection Pub. Co. FDR-160
Pettengill & Caniglia, 1242 S. 7th St. DAM-33
Snyder Music Co. TR-239
Steinhauser, F.M. WM-204
Watts, Mary S., 833 S. 30th St. FDR-299

ORANGE, NJ
Sordo, Harry del FDR-3

OSKALOOSA, IA
C.L. Barnhouse Co. GW-454; USG-232

OXFORD, OH
Democratic Women's Club of Oxford and Oxford Township FDR-382

OYSTER BAY, NY
Groebl Bros. TR-186

PACIFIC, MO
Mel Bay Pub., Inc. AL-475

PADUCAH, KY
Turner, Jettie W.E., 407 S. 3rd St. AL-287

PARIS, IL
Wilkinson, Daniel WW-75

PARK RIDGE, IL
General Words and Music Company GW-371
Neil A. Kjos Music Company MISC-101
Loop Music Pub. Co. MISC-115
Petru, Quido, 236 Talcott Ave. WW-157

PARKERSBURG, WV
Martin, H.T. SJT-2

PARKVILLE, MI
Sider. D.L. TR-151

PASADENA, MD
Peacock Press, 20 Granada Rd. MISC-160

PASSAIC, NJ
Adams Music Co. WM-44

Feher, Duke FDR-254
Superior Song Studios FDR-84

PATTERSON, NJ
Dringer, Abram, 151 Harrison St. WM-155
Wright, James, 313 McBride Ave. HCH-10

PAWTUCKET, RI
Aspinwall, E.E. AES-20

PENN YAN, NY
Bush, Warner E., 136 Main St. HCH-55

PERU, IA
Gregg, W. Bentley HCH-37

PETERSBURG, VA
C.C. de Nordendorf Musical Exchange HG-30

PHILADELPHIA, PA
Academy of Music WM-244
Ackland, William, 1126 S. 51st St. FDR-85
Adams, A. Lemuel, 228 N. 3rd St. JCF-8
Adjer, Joseph Bannaker USG-193
Aitken, John, 27 No. 2nd St. GW-463
76 No. 2nd St. TJ-17
Amherst Alumni Association of Philadelphia CC-27
Andre, G. & Co., 1104 Chestnut St. GW-386; WS-2; AL-13
1228 Chestnut St. GW-602
Arcade Music Co., 2733 Kensington Ave. LBJ-7
Associated Willkie Clubs of Pennsylvania, Land Title Bldg. WLW-17
Auner, A.W., 11th & Market AL-63; JD-31; JD-43
Bacon, A., No. 11 South 4th St. GW-503
Bacon, A. & Company, No. 11 South 4th St. GW-46; GW-66; GW-501; GW-502; JMN-1; JMN-9; MISC-159
Bacon, A. & Hart GW-605
No. 11 South 4th St. GW-492
Balls, J., 108 Oxford St. GW-98; TJ-18
Balls, Thos. TJ-30
Beck & Lawton, Cor. 7th & Chestnut GW-316; JB-5
Beckel, James C. AJK-8
22 South 6th St. FP-3

Appendix

914 Sansom St. BFH-55; BFH-127
Beckel's Repertory of Music, 83 North 2nd St. GW-114
Bellois, J.F. WM-10
Blake, G.E. GW-35; GW-495; TJ-54; AJK-24; WHH-16; MISC-28
1 South 3rd St. TJ-7
13 South 5th St. GW-112; GW-462; GW-496; GW-499; GW-500; TJ-65; JMD-9; JMN-2; JQA-2; AJK-13; AJK-15; AJK-31; AJK-30; MVB-6; WHH-47; WHH-109; WHH-138; WHH-141; HC-70; DW-11
Boner, William H. & Co. JAG-89
1102 Chestnut St. GW-324; JAG-29; JAG-30; JAG-89
1314 Chestnut St. GW-249; BFH-11
Bradlee, C., Washington St. DW-8
135 Washington St. DW-8
Brennan, Geo. J. WHT-16
Bruce & Bisbee, N. Seventh Ave. AL-240; AL-485
Campaign Pub. Co., 707-709 Filbert St. BFH-2; BFH-76
Carncross, J.L. & Co., 6 N. 8th St. USG-35
Carr & Co. GW-17
Carr, B. GW-52; GW-465; GW-469; GW-473; JA-1; JA-22
Carroll, Joe, 2624 Kensington Ave. FDR-195
Clay Whigs, 109 Chesnut St. HC-70
Coleman, Harry TR-108
228 N. 9th St. BFH-39
Collins, T.K. & P. HC-108; HC-109
Colon and Adriance HC-106
Contemporary Music Press LBJ-4
Co-Operative Music Co. USG-204
Couenhoven and Scull and Co. HC-34
Couenhoven, James, 162 Chestnut St. MF-18
Coulston, T.P., 147 N. Eighth St. GW-581
Coyle, Elizabeth, 1117 Germantown Ave. WM-180
Covington, Robert Thomas, 1515 North Opal St. FDR-392
Curtis Pub. Co. WM-125; WM-225
Dasch, George W., 920 Market St. TR-133
Davis, James M. JKP-17
Day, C.H. AL-69
Debmar Pub. Co. JFK-7
Dilmore, Richard C. TR-378
DeLuca-Niederman-Sarnoff, 2222 S. 5th St. FDR-279

Democratic Choir, 15 N. 6th St. JKP-2
Desilver and Muir, 18 S. Fourth St. HC-88
Ditson, J.E. & Co. JAG-113
922 Chestnut St. GW-143; GW-146
Dobson, J. GW-124
Dresler & Muir, 18 S. Fourth St. HC-77
Drew, Joseph P. TR-236
Duffy, Mary E. FDR-320
Eclipse Publishing Co., 136 N. 9th St. GW-576; USG-127; USG-128; USG-216
Escher, Chas. F., 1242 Girard Ave. BFH-52
1320 Girard Ave. RBH-37
Elkan-Vogel Co., Inc. AL-345; FDR-223
1712 Sansom St. RMN-17
Ferrett, Edmund, Publishers Hall, 101 Chestnut St. HC-72
Ferrett, E. & Co., 68 S. Fourth St. HC-118; DW-36
Foit, A. GW-62; HC-116; LC-3; ZT-34
196 Chestnut St. GW-418; WHH-110; JKP-1; DW-35
196 1/2 Chestnut St. WHH-84
Foit, Meignen & Co. GW-30; GW-62
Frederick, J.L., 53 S. 4th St. AJK-5
Gay, James D., 300 N. 20th above Race St. AL-157; AL-336; AL-385; USG-247; USG-301
George Willig's Musical Magazine, 165 Market St. GW-472
Ginon, J.H. WHH-123
Gordon, H.E. JGB-69
Gould, J.E., Chestnut Street JKP-9
164 Chesnut St. WS-12
Griffith & Simon, 384 North 2nd St. WHH-21
Grigg & Elliott WHH-90
Hall and Co. USG-260
Harry J. Lincoln Music, 930 N. 19th St. GW-192; WM-236; CC-24
Hatch Music Co. TR-251
Henry Altemus Music Co. WM-103
Hewitt, George W. & Co., 184 Chestnut St. WHH-3
Hewitt, James, 131 Williams St. GW-498
Hoffman, J.M. & Co., 537 Smithfield JGB-8
Hood, George HC-102
15 N. 6th St. HC-10; HC-11; HC-14
Hunter, Thomas JGB-35
J.C. Smith's Music Saloon, 215 Chestnut St. HC-46; HC-86

John C. Winston Co., 1010 Arch St. GW-460
John Maybaum Music Co., P.O. Box 3452, Station O. TR-110
Johnson, E.R. & Co., 6th at Chestnut MVB-3; ZT-6
Johnson, Francis GW-583
142 Chesnut St. HC-34
Johnson, J.H., 7 N. 10th St. GBM-20; GBM-21; AL-53; AL-58; AL-60; AL-87; AL-137; AL-174; AL-359; HS-12; USG-300; JD-28; JD-30
No. 18 N. 10th St. JD-49
Johnson's, 5 N. 10th St. MF-9
Jost, J.W. & Son, 545 N. 8th St. JAG-43
Judaic Union, Disraeli Lodge No. 4 FDR-321
Key and Biddle, 6 Minor St. GW-425; MISC-177
Key, Mielke and Biddle, 181 Market St. GW-425
Keystone Music Co., Room 404, Forest Bldg., King & Baird ZT-76; WS-37
Klemm & Brother, 275 Market St. ZT-57; ZT-63
287 Market St. GW-90
Klemm, J.G., 3 So. 3rd St. GW-66; GW-486; JMN-1; MISC-26
Kretschmar & Nunns, 70 S. 3rd. St. GW-109
Lawton, J.W. & Co., 19 So. Eighth St. AL-466
Lee & Walker, Chestnut St. GW-560; JCB-1
162 Chesnut St. GW-116; GW-417; HC-31; ZT-59; MF-8
188 Chestnut St. GW-121; GW-162; GW-261; GW-601; ZT-62; FP-4; MF-21; WS-9; WS-28; JB-20
722 Chestnut St. GW-157; GW-168; GW-255; GW-258; GW-267; GW-323; GW-360; GW-389; GW-505; GW-591; GW-626; WS-8; WS-10; WS-48; SAD-7; SAD-9; GBM-5; GBM-6; GBM-12; GBM-13; GBM-15; GBM-18; GBM-31; GBM-34; GBM-43; GBM-46; GBM-77; AL-7; AL-19; AL-22; AL-29; AL-31; AL-47; AL-64; AL-88; AL-105; AL-128; AL-166; AL-180; AL-235; AL-239; AL-255; AL-299; AJN-9; AJN-12; USG-12; USG-22; USG-116; USG-122; WSH-12; WSH-31; JBL-5; JD-12; JD-17; NB-3; BFB-9; MISC-123

922 Chestnut St. GW-604; ZT-78; AL-276; HG-4; HG-6; HG-13; USG-16; USG-37; USG-245; WSH-10
1113 Chestnut St. USG-14; USG-41; RBH-40; RBH-55; WSH-4; JAG-4; JAG-18; JAG-31; JAG-52; JAG-54; JAG-57; JAG-96; JAG-119; CAA-5; JGB-13; JGB-15; JGB-17; JGB-87; JGB-88; GC-47; GC-113
120 Walnut St. ZT-7; ZT-11; ZT-39; ZT-48; ZT-51; ZT-64; JB-17
1017 Walnut St. BFH-124; GC-95
Liberty Music Co., 1725 Chestnut St. WW-202
Limerick, Dudley T. & Co., 4031 Locust St. WM-271; WM-283
Longbrake & Edwards, 50 N. 8th St. GW-193
Magee, J., 316 Chestnut St. GBM-2; GBM-65; AL-55
Marsh and Bubna, 1029 Chestnut St. AL-270
Marsh, John AL-16
New Masonic Temple. Chestnut Street at 7th MF-34; JCF-6
1029 Chestnut St. AL-106; AL-151; JD-49
1102 Chestnut St. GW-563; SAD-1; GBM-25; GBM-47; GBM-49; GBM-57; GBM-68; JD-42; BFB-20.
Marshall, Williams & Butler WHH-61
Mason & Co. GBM-25; GBM-51; GBM-72
58 N. Sixth St. JCF-40; AL-159
McCulloch, J. GW-22
M'Culloch, W., No. 306 Market St. GW-83; TJ-5
McDonald, D.A. WM-6
McQuaid, J.W. & John, 5311 Larchwood Ave. AES-28
Meignen, L.D. & Co., 217 Chesnut St. WHH-79
Meyer, Edw. A. & Co., 3439 Marshall St. TR-156
Meyer, Louis, 1323 Chestnut St. AL-70; AJN-18; JD-41
1413 Chestnut St. GW-130
Meyer, Reed, 722 Arch Street USG-201
Michael, Maude, 1819 Chestnut St. FDR-205
Miracle Music Co., 1011 Chestnut St. FDR-334
Morgan, Irving J., 308 N. 41st St. TR-130
Morgan and Yeager, Chestnut St. AJK-48

Appendix

Morris, Jos. USG-127
Morris Music Co., 1028 Arch St. USG-133; USG-135; USG-163; USG-192
Murray, Thomas A., 5458 Montgomery St. GW-478
Musical America, 3861 Fairmont Ave. AES-58
National Democratic Convention FDR-319
N.G. Dusief's Bookseller, 68 S. Fourth St. TJ-68
New Deal Pub. Co., 1420 N. 15th St. FDR-402
Newland, W.A., 243 Market St. MVB-12
North, F.A., 1308 Chestnut St. USG-31; USG-115; GC-7; GC-32; GC-33
North, F.A. & Co., 1308 Chestnut St. USG-188; RBH-17; BFH-54
Osbourn, Jas. G., 112 South 3rd St. ZT-18
Osbourn's Music Saloon JT-7; HC-69
112 S. 3rd St. GW-87; GW-163; HC-38; HC-81; HC-114; JKP-7
30 South 4th St. GW-104; MVB-17; WHH-22; WHH-27; WHH-49; WHH-51; WHH-55; WHH-78; JT-11; DW-33
Parkview Publishing Company, 3943 Market Street GW-522
Pepper, J.W., SW cor. 8th & Locust Sts. GC-134
Perry, John B., 198 Market St. LC-5
Philadelphia Item WJB-38
Philadelphia Press WM-170
Philadelphia Record AES-11
Philadelphia Republican Club JFC-51
Pierson, H.B JKP-13
Potter, S. & Co., 87 Chesnut St. GW-548
Praise Pub. Company, 46 N. 12th St. WW-96
Prediction Music, 1418 Vine St. HAW-2
Priest, William GW-51
Presser, Theodore, 1708 Chesnut St. WM-320; TR-67
1712 Chestnut St. GW-210; GW-228; GW-272; GW-370; GW-621; AJK-42; AL-248; TR-296
Republican Finance Committee of Pennsylvania, 228 South Broad St. MISC-152
Republican Song Book Committee BFH-95

Republican State Committee BFH-86
Rice, H., Market St. GW-8
Robinson and Peterson, 98 Chestnut St. HC-17
Rosewig, A.H., 131 So. Eleventh St. WM-114
Rudolphus, F. GW-44; GW-68
Schmidt, Th. A. JB-19
Schmitz, M., 120 Walnut Street HC-21
Scroggy, Thomas M., No. 443 Vine Street FP-5
Shaw, W.F. WSH-1; JAG-9; JAG-19; JAG-20; JAG-35; JAG-60; JGB-29; BFH-3; BFH-16; BFH-51; BFH-103; GC-2; GC-3; GC-9; GC-29; GC-62; GC-96
Shuster, Wm. H., 67 N. Eighth St. MF-28
Smith, W.R., 135 N. Eighth St. AL-258; AL-261; AL-498; HS-8; USG-13; USG-68; USG-297; MISC-64
Sproat, P.W., No. 62 Spruce St. HC-42
Stayman & Bros., 210 Chesnut St. MISC-34
294 Chesnut St. JB-13
Sun Printing Co. TR-51
Sunshine Music Publishing Co. DDE-79
Swisher, E.B., 115 S. 10th St. USG-162
Swisher, M.D. WM-54
115 S. 10th St. USG-23; USG-161; GC-61; WJB-29; WM-17; WM-74; WM-193; TR-312; TR-324
123 S. 10th St. JGB-1; JGB-51; GC-25; GC-103; GC-104
155 10th St. BFH-9
Tin Pan Alley FDR-250; FDR-251
1001 Chestnut St. FDR-36; FDR-228
Theodore Presser Co., 1712 Chestnut St. GW-209; GW-227; USG-230; WGH-51.
Thomas, Chas., 1914 Wilder St. FDR-76
Torr, Joseph HC-111; ZT-79
Trumpler, Chas. W.A., 926 Chestnut St. USG-111
7th & Chestnut St. AL-84; USG-154
Turner & Fisher, 15 North 6th St. WHH-18; HC-12
Union Book Co. WSH-35; JAG-47
Van Dyke, Alex L. GW-404
Walker, Edward L., 142 Chesnut St. GW-323; AJN-23
Warden, David A., 1138 Lombard St. WS-18; AL-158

Warwick, James E. and Co., 284 S. 11th St. WM-307
Welch, Emmett J., Colonial Theatre Bldg. WW-15
Welden Co. WGH-2; WGH-8; WGH-10
1109 Walnut St. WGH-23
White, R.U., 111 N. 49th St. WLW-25
William H. Shuster, 97 N. Eighth St. MF-28
Willig, Geo GW-5; GW-19; GW-28; GW-32; TJ-2; TJ-3; AJK-20; AJK-36; WHH-27; WHH-130
12 So. 4th St. GW-61; GW-113; GW-471; TJ-4; TJ-23; TJ-64; JMD-1; JMD-6
171 Chestnut St. GW-58; GW-59; GW-64; GW-72; GW-80; DWC-2; AJK-3; AJK-11; AJK-18; AJK-22; AJK-29; AJK-35; WHH-73; HC-34; HC-54; HC-71; HC-85; JKP-18; ZT-28; DW-12; DW-25; MISC-129
185 Market St. GW-26; GW-47; GW-588; TJ-1; TJ-15; TJ-20; TJ-22; TJ-58; TJ-73
Winch, A. JBL-10
No. 505 Chestnut St. AL-379
Winner & Co., No. 933 Spring Garden St. GBM-30; AL-167
Winner & Shuster, 110 N. 8th St. GW-172; GW-310; HC-29; MF-11; MF-29
Winner, J.E., 545 N. 8th St. WHH-33
Winner, Sep., 531 N. 8th St. AL-243
933 Spring Garden St. AL-85
Winner, Sep. & Son, 1007 Spring Garden St. JAG-64
Wittig, R. and Co., 1021 Chestnut St. USG-97
Wolter, John R., 2029 Arch St. TED-18
World Pub. Co., 326 N. 8th St. WM-149

PHILIP, SD
Severin, Beryl MISC-92

PINE ISLAND, MN
Stock, Otto WW-208

PITTSBURG, IN
Armstrong, W.J. GC-152

PITTSBURGH, PA
Abrahams, Blanche Evans WW-136
Anchor Press, 443 Third Ave. WJB-39
Arch Press WJB-39
Basler, Horace R., 128 Sixth St. WM-188
3712 Butler St. JAG-24; JAG-112; GC-155
Basler's Music House USG-277
128 Sixth St. WM-217
Campaign Music Pub. Co. BFH-18
Dal E. Haun Co., 2416 Palm Beach Ave. FDR-115; FDR-116
Diamond Music Co., Cameo Bldg. JRC-1
Educational Music Publications DDE-30
Flannery, James J FDR-387
Haven, W.S. HS-16
Held, Wm. F. & Co., 203 Bouquet St. JSC-5
Hoffmann, J.M., 537 Smithfield St. GC-40
Hoffmann and Hoene, 53 Fifth St. USG-294
Knake & Co. JAG-77; JGB-46
Konold, Amos A.E. WM-126
Magee Music Pub. Co. TR-255
Mather Co., 76 East Liberty WHT-59
Mellor, Charles C., 81 Wood St. AL-119; USG-291
Mellor, John & Sons, Inc., 120 to 134 46th St. AES-39
Music Publicity Bureau WJB-12
Pittsburgh Dispatch JB-14
Pittsburgh Leader WW-216
Sloan Typewriting Bureau, Machesney Bldg. WJB-14
Stephenson, R., 1621 Federal St. DDE-101
Tredway, G.E. WM-256
Volkwein Brothers WW-108; WW-183
Volunteers for Stevenson AS-12
Wamelink & Barr AL-14
Winteringer Music Co. Limited WM-269

PITTSFIELD, MA
Jones & Goeway, 336 North St. WW-10

PLAINFIELD, NJ
Conroy, Will J., 12 Linden Ave. WJB-23
Willkie For President Club WLW-65

PLATTE CITY, MO
Tucker, Harry E. WJB-24

PLATTEVILLE, WI
Churchill-Grindell Co. WW-68
Youmans, Jay V. WM-92

Appendix

PLATTSBURG, NY
Plattsburg Radio Supply Co. WW-95

PLYMOUTH, PA
Gilbertson Music Co. AL-210

PLYMOUTH, VT
Home Town Coolidge Club CC-1; CC-3; CC-32; CC-57

PONTIAC, MI.
Lockwood & Hoyt USG-264

PORT CHESTER, NY
Cherry Lane Music Co., Inc., P.O. 430 LBJ-29; RMN-34

PORT ST LUCIE, FL
Songrite Creation Productions GB-2

PORTLAND, ME
Berry and Son, I, 177 Fore AL-94
Underwood Music Co. GW-578
Westmore Music Corporation, SW Ninth Ave. DAM-34

PORTLAND, OR
Dorgan, Marie L., 211 Fliedner Bldg. TR-268
Frankus, James A., 8526 S.W. Capitol Highway MISC-144; MISC-148
Hunt, Frederick E. TR-271
Oregon Conservatory Of Music, 165 1/2 4th St. WW-19
Oregon Publishing Co. FDR-113
Parvin, Z.M., 165 _ Fourth St. AL-477
Westmore Music Corp., S.W. 9th at Taylor WLW-31
Wilson, Daniel H. CEH-6

PRINCETON, IL
Red, White & Blue Productions, Box 341 AL-204

PRINCETON, NJ
LaTourette & Mulholland, First Nation Bank Bldg. GW-276

PRINCETON, WI
Macomber, Lilian TR-315

PRINCETON, WV
Good, Anna Margaret, 1105 No. Walker FDR-376

PROCTOR, VT
Clark, Chas. C. TR-125

PROVIDENCE, RI
Alpha Co., 131 Mathewson St. WM-95
Callender, McAuslan and Troop, 209 and 211 Westminister St. JGB-4
Church, Alfred M., 290 Broad St. JGB-34
Clapp & Cory, 106 Westminster St. JCF-23
Cory, J.R. AL-139
Du Dah & Company JCF-48
Leland, A.M. GW-309
Paul HS-15; USG-149
Raymond Music Co. WM-86
Remnent Rooms, 51 Dorrance St. USG-149
Shaw, Oliver JMD-18; JMN-10; JMN-11; JMN-18
70 Westminister St. GW-43; JMN-12; JMN-23; AJK-18; WHH-36; WHH-85
Williamms, O.C. ND-3
Women's Republican Club of Rhode Island, Butler's Exchange CC-26

PROVO, UT
Skelton Co. WM-208

RAPATEE, IL
Foster, Lawrence L., Box 15 FDR-161

RAPID CITY, SD
Hudspeth, Yvonna CC-22

READING, PA
Hiester Pub. Co., Box 82 FDR-21
Monarch Music Pub. Co. WW-163

RENOVO, PA
Pennsylvania Music Co. WW-139

RICHMOND, IN
Coe, J.M. WM-95; WM-278
International Music Pub. Co. TR-317

RICHMOND, ME
Favor, Edwin P. JMC-8

RICHMOND, VA
Lynch & Southgate, Cor. Harris's Bldg. JMD-4
Thos. Ball. JMD-5; JMN-14

RICHMOND HILL, NY
Columbia Adv. Co., 133-17 101st Ave. BMG-8; BMG-12; LBJ-21

RIVERSIDE, CA
Harvard Book Co., 1523 Main St. FDR-256

ROBIMSON, IL
Apgar, Tom S. WJB-82

ROCHESTER, IN
Daily Republican, The WM-258

ROCHESTER, NY
Bernard-Scheib & Company, Beckley Building WW-182
Bernard, Scheib & Eldridge, Beckley Building WW-173
Central Music Co., 168 Andrews St. BFH-46
Democrat and Chronicle Print BFH-112
Dewey, D.M. JKP-16
Dobbins, C.G. WGH-22
Lew Brock Music WW-44
Mackie, H.S., 82 State Street RBH-41
Merick, Eldridge J. USG-263
Redstone Publishers, 1009 Wilder Bldg. FDR-110
Rochester Socialist Party SP-6
Shaw, Jos. P., 110 State St. JCF-32; AL-48
Smith and Raymond HC-94
WSAY Artist Bureau DDE-80

ROCK ISLAND, IL
L.E. West Pub. Co. WM-37; WM-99

ROCKLAND, MA
Najarian, Mable, 177 E. Water St. FDR-102

ROCKVILLE CENTER, NY
Belwin, Inc. GW-212; GW-407; AL-213; AL-189
Belwin Mills Pub. Co., Rockville Certre GW-619; AJK-59

ROCKY MOUNT, VA
The Temperance Music Co. WM-315

ROHRSBURG, PA
Ikeler, Otto WM-33

ROME, NY
Tuttle, Charles, 83 James St. WSH-21; GC-94

ROXBURY, MA
Patriot Democrat Office WHH-71

RUMSEY, KY
Baker, King W. DDE-96

RYE, NY
Fradkin, James J. FDR-305

SACRAMENTO, CA
Hansford-Wollow Music Pub. Co., 1206 1/2 5th St. WW-176

SAGINAW, MI
Hughes, Jos. H. WW-128

SALEM, MA
Brown, William WHH-28; HC-25
Cushing & Appleton GW-117
Whittlesey, Orramel ZT-31

SALISBURY, NC
Carter, James L. Jr., 810 Craige St. JFK-26

SALT LAKE CITY, UT
Murdock, Orrice DDE-37
Salt Lake City Democratic Committee FDR-210
Salt Lake Tabernacle WGH-49

SAN ANTONIO, TX
FDR-202
Northrup, F.I., Wm. Nagel and M.E. Jesse JSC-3
Southern Music Co. FDR-407; DDE-82

SAN BERNARDINO, CA
Ford, T.J. FDR-25; FDR-26

SAN DIEGO, CA
Allen, Sargent Scotty, 3873 California St. DAM-45
Braune Pub. Co., 505 Watts Bldg. FDR-129
Committee To Re-Elect Richard Nixon And Spiro Agnew, 1370 Sunset Cliffs Blvd. RMN-40; RMN-41
Feenstra, Ronald M., 2184 Tokalon St. BMG-10
Galilean Press, 1636 Dale St. WW-57
Gaughen, James B., 4046 3rd St. AL-312
Kjos, Jr., Neil A., 4383 Jutland Dr. GW-622
Long, Lucy B. WM-248; WW-106
Nichilson, Naomi E. TR-12

SAN FRANCISCO, CA
Alta California General Printing House USG-253
America's Song Pub. Co., 111 Jones St. FDR-264
Bancroft, A.L. & Co., 721 Market St. RBH-58
Booth & Coffey, The Mission Journal BFH-117

Appendix

Boyd, T.C., 228 Montgomery St. AL-329
Broadcast Associates, 431 Clay St. DAM-27
Brook, J.R. & Co., 403 Sansome St. BFH-121
Clark, Milton Francis, 1053 Howard St. FDR-262
Concord Music Pub. Co. FDR-78
Covell, C.D. FDR-119
Crane & Co., 522 Clay St. USG-185
Della Valle Pub. Co., 242 Powell St. FDR-264
Eastman, F. USG-69; USG-143
Grand Army Day May Day Festival Board of Management BFH-75
Grey, M. AL-224
117 Post St. JAG-66; JAG-111
613 Clay St. AL-34; AL-177
Johnson, Lee and Company, St. Ann's Building GC-133
Keen, Crosby E. & John M. Spargur, 1531 Hyde St. DAM-30
McLean, E.T. RBH-47
Model Music Store JGB-60
National Music Publishers FDR-130
Nevin, C.W. & Co. JGB-91
Northern Calif. Willkie-McNary Campaign Committee, 532 Market St. WLW-66
O.K. Music Co., Crosley Building TR-278
Pacific Music, 1053 Howard St. HCH-5; HCH-6; HCH-34; WLW-49
Pacific Press JBG-42
Prince, Meryl, Kress Bldg. FDR-56
Republican State Central Committee WM-329
Ross Music Co, 31 Rausch St. WW-21
San Francisco Examiner GC-72
San Francisco News Company RBH-52
Sherman, Clay & Co. WM-181; FDR-278
Kearny & Sutter Sts. BFH-40
Town and Bacon AL-400
Webster Music Arts, 711 Post Rd. FDR-154
Welcker, Adair, 331 Pine St. TR-124

SAN JOSE, CA
Jay Dee Pub. Co., 204 Auzerais FDR-92
Santarello, Madeline, 303 Hobson St. FDR-312
Stocking, William Stocking JGB-85

SAN LUIS, CO
Silva, Prof. B.N. WW-219

SAN MATEO, CA
McCarthy & Folsom, 505 Costa Rica Ave. WLW-27

SAN PEDRO, CA
Nyvall, Y.J. FDR-318

SANTA BARBARA, CA
Liberty Pub. Co. WW-102

SANTA MONICA, CA
Bibo Music Publishers, 2444 Wilshire Blvd. JFK-6
Santa Monica Democratic Women's Club, 510 Santa Monica Blvd. JFK-22

SARATOGA, NY
Tromblee, A., 35 Excelsior Ave. TR-230

SAULT STE MARIE, MI
Nimmo Pub. Co., 527 Elizabeth St. WGH-17

SAVANNAH, GA
Ludden & Bates, Southern Music House WSH-18; CG-98

SAYVILLE, NY
Gilliam, Wilson J. FDR-275

SCHENECTADY, NY
The Our Next President Company AES-42

SCOTTSVILLE, IL
Dent, M.W. WW-214

SCRANTON, PA
Finn & Phillips TR-11
Guernsey, J.W. WM-72
Weber, Joe Francis MISC-90
Whitmore Music Pub. Co. WGH-24

SEA BRIGHT, NJ
Smack, Cyril A., 30 Beach St. AS-7

SEATTLE, WA
Capitol Music Co. GW-343
Country Gospel Music, 6406 Carleton Ave. So. RR-2; RR-3
Eckmann, Harry N., 521 E. 70th St. FDR-285
Edgren School of Music TR-323
Greenwood, Livingston FDR-199
Hewitt, Dorothy FDR-271
National Music Publishers FDR-169

Rex Music Publishers, 315 Seneca St. FDR-271; FDR-383
Roosevelt Men's Club of King County FDR-154
S&M Music Publishers, 1264 Westlake FDR-395
Stein, Thos. Ostenson TR-59; WW-43
Whyte, J.J. FDR-327

SECAUCUS, NJ
Warner Bros. Publications, Inc., 265 Secaucus Rd. AL-320; BC-8; MISC-91; MISC-176

SEDALIA, MO
A.W. Perry's Sons USG-288; WM-132; WM-182; WM-318; CBF-1; JSC-1; JSC-1; MISC-76
306 Broadway USG-92
Barnum, K.R. CC-21
O'Bannon, Mrs. W.D., 614 Broadway JWD-1
Perry, A.W. & Son JAG-99; WJB-96; WM-96; TR-103; TR-176; WW-78

SHEBOYGAN, WI
Kuiper, Klaas G., 1816 N. Third St. WLW-63
S.W. Miller Piano Co. GW-582

SIOUX FALLS, SD
White Front Music Store, 113 10th St., Masonic Temple WJB-33

SOMERS, MT
Mountain States Music Co. DDE-50

SOUTH BIRMINGHAM, AL
Blue Bell Music Pub. Co., 2030 11th Ave. TED-17

SOUTH BEND, IN
Aughinbaugh Music Pub. Co. WLW-60
Couture and Glynn WGH-48
Happy Home Pub. Co. JSC-2

SOUTH BUTLER, NY
Betts & Burbett WM-67

SOUTH CORNISH, NH
Fairbanks, Geo. E. WHT-57

SOUTH MANCHESTER, CT
McLean, Joseph, 7 Church St. TR-382

SOUTH NYACK, NY
Brielmayer & Volmer WM-12

SOUTH ORANGE, NJ
Martin, Franklin FDR—295
Taylor, I. Della WW-76

SOUTHINGTON, CT
Shanley, Ben AES-50

SPOKANE, WA
Johnson, Frank A. GW-288
Yarnell, Alice TR-173

SPRINGDALE, OH
Maddux, Berton J. TR-84
Republican Music Co. JGB-81

SPRINGFIELD, IL
Carpender, F. AL-340
Illinois State Register GW-446; WW-193
1512 S. 15th St. AL-264
Lincoln Clarion, The AL-393

SPRINGFIELD, IN
Republican Music Co. JGB-81

SPRINGFIELD, MA
Birnie Paper Co. JGB—41
Goetting, A.H. TR-25
Harden Music Co. FDR-355
Jacobs, A.F. WJB-32
Meltone Music Co., 390 Walnut St. HW-1
Republican Phalanx BFH-79
Sangamo Music Pub. Co. CBF-4

SPRINGFIELD, OH
Crain, J.R. WHH-127
New Era Co. JGB-81

SPRINGVILLE, NY
Marsh, H.T. WM-261

ST JOSEPH, MO
Butler, Henry M. USG-236
Collins, Sydney TR-334
F.W. Thomas Music Publishers FDR-29
Huyett Bros., No. 321 Felix St. GC-77

ST LOUIS, MO
Art Publication Society GW-442
Balmer & Weber ZT-58; USG-40; USG-248; USG-251; SJT-16; SJT-20; SJT-23; RBH-2; WSH-5; WSH-44; JAG-21; JAG-46; JAG-48; GC-74; GC-153; GC-154; GC-156; WJB-2; TR-96
56 Fourth St. SAD-13; AL-78; AL-129; AL-147
206 N. Fifth St. HS-4; USG-85; USG-99; SJT-13;
311 N. Fifth St. AL-95; JAG-105
Boddie, John R. WHT-60
Bollman, H. & Sons. USG-194; GC-135
Compton and Dent., 205 North Fourth St. USG-286
Empire Pub. Co., 606 Chestnut St. FDR-134
Endres & Compton, 52 Fourth St. AL-28; AL-93; JGB-68; JD-37

Appendix

Ford, J.W., 211 Market St. GC-97
Glewel, Louis HST-19
G.W. Mogelberg Co. WM-61
H. Pilcher & Son, 91 Fourth St. GW-590
Hanick Music Co., 52 Musical Art Bldg. AES-19
Hildreth, H.R., 5 Olive St. GBM-85
Kelmayne Pub. Co. TR-109
Kennen, Mark, Marquette Hotel AES-35
Kunkel Bros. WM-7; TR-191
311 S. 5th St. WSH-9; JAG-40; JAG-65
Loena Lovell Music Publishing Co., 313-4 Melbourne Hotel WGH-40
Louis Retter Music Co. TED-36
Mann, Delphia Dorothy, 5919 Pershing Ave. DDE-62
Mark Bros. Music Pub. Co., 3940 Page Ave. WM-1
Needham Music Company WW-177
Peters, A.C. & Bro., 94 W. 4th St. GBM-35
Peters, J.L. & Bro., 49 N. 5th St. GW-254
Premier Music, 5013 Margaretta Ave. FDR-245
Shattinger Piano & Music Co. AL-313; WLW-18; FDR-81
10 S. Broadway WM-187
910 Olive St. WM-215
St. Louis Music Co., No. 9 N. 15th St. SJT-7
St. Louis Star WM-110
Treloar Music Co. WW-115

ST PAUL MN
Bramwell & Ragen TR-102
Chapple, W.W., 9 East Bernard St. WW-172
Clegg Publishing Co. GW-331
Dryeer & Howard, 148 & 150 E. 3rd St. JAG-30
Frey, Eugene, 1169 Churchill Ave. GW-540
Henninger, Theodore, 371 N. Smith Ave. GW-287
Sharood Shoe Corp GW-580
Song Publishing Co., 507 Court Block CEH-4
Tufts, H.W. and G.A. Brahy, 1790 Hague Ave. FDR-49
Weide & Ross HG-3

STAMFORD, CT
Klock, Homer R.S. TR-1

STEUBENVILLE, OH
Gardner, Rosemam JAG-3
Wilson, R.C. WHH-128

STOCKTON, CA
Williams, Belle, 525 N. Madison St. WW-147

STORM LAKE, IA
Chamberlin, Helen B. WJB-92

STRONG CITY, KS
Jones, Frank M. BFH-93

STURGIS, MI
Warren, Dr. E.A. TR-224

SUMMERS, MT
Mountain States Music Co. FDR-50; MISC-146

SUN VALLEY, CA
Valley Beth Israel, 13060 Roscoe Blvd. JFK-11

SWANTON, VT
Gribbon, Elizabeth A. TR-288

SWISSVALE, PA
Purcell, Susie, 2012 Authur St. WGH-53

SYRACUSE, NY
Acme Publishing Bureau BFH-27
35 University Ave. GW-283; JGB-97; BFH-25; HD-56
115 S. Clinton St. BFH-14
Bardeen, C.W. GW-589; MISC-178
Benearl Pub. Co., 299 Heffernan Bldg. FDR-158
Coon, H.W., 22S. Salina St. AL-496
De Marbelle, D.A. USG-262
Grand American Freedom Rally Committee TED-7; DDE-11
Heims, Newton B. WW-4
Hoff, B.C. HS-9
Holmes, Samuel Newall USG-257; BFH-107
Hopkins, I.A., Townsend Block JBR-4
J. Barber's Music & Job Printing, Townsend Block JBR-5
Moffitt, W.O. JAG-103
Redington & Howe, No. 2 Wieting Block USG-118
Redington, J.C.O. JMP-2
Stafford, Lon F. and Co., 523 N. Geddis St. FDR-50
Stafford, Lon F. & Co. HCH-21
4915 Onondage Rd. LBJ-28
Syracuse Post Company WM-210

TACOMA, WA
Banks, T.R. WW-83
Johnson, Harry H. WJB-68
Republican Bureau, 726 Pacific Ave. WGH-13

TADNOR, PA
  Newkirk, Alice M.P. HCH-66
TAUNTON, MA
  Conant, H.L. TR-175
TEMPLE CITY, CA
  Bob Stephens, Inc., 2263 E. Las Tunas Dr. HST-4
TERRA HAUTE, IN
  Fudge, Thomas G. EVD-1
TOLEDO, OH
  Socialist Party SP-3
  Unique Music Pubs., Inc. GCW-2
  Whitney, W.W., Palace of Music MISC-1
  151 Summit St. JD-9
  173 Summit St. AJN-6; USG-5; USG-55
  Woolson Spice Company GW-355; AL-303; USG-213; USG-265
TOPEKA, KS
  Anderson Printing Co., 105 W. 4th St. FDR-357
  Crane, Geo. W. and Co. BFH-119
  Topeka Mail, The WM-267
  Stauffer Music Co. AML-19
TROY, NY
  Andrews, John C. WHH-69
  Backus, A. WHH-6
  Progressive Party, The TR-55
UTICA, NY
  Curry, W.A. TR-213
  Dutton, William H., 169 Henesee St. AL-170
  Hawley, H.H. JCF-47
  Williams, William., No. 60 Genesee St. GW-55
VALDOSTA, GA
  Davis, Jr., Brit W. WHT-50
VALLEY STREAM, NY
  Alexander, Perry TED-13
VAN NUYS, CA
  Alfred Publishing Co., P.O. Box 1003 JFK-56
  Credo Music Co., 5504 Van Noord Ave. LBJ-25
VIRGINIA, IL
  Dekins, Stephen Taylor WJB-90
WACO, TX
  Words, Inc. GRF-4
WASHINGTON, DC
  American Free Enterprises, 1025 Vermont Ave. NW AS-2
  Bachmann, Max TR-90

Bohn, C. MISC-89
Breed, Daniel, Cor. 8th & "F" Sts. JAG-71
Canter Pub. Co. CC-8
Capitol Publishing Co. WJB-41
Carusi, Samuel, Cor. 12th St. & Penna. Ave. MVB-4
Citizens' Committee on National Representation for the District of Columbia HCH-59
Columbia Music Co TR-261
1301 "G" St. WHT-17; WHT-19
Darby, Rufus H. JBW-6
District Pub. Co., 808 15th St. S.E. GW-507
Dixon, James L., 1022 Seventeenth St. MISC-186
Droop, Edward F. GC-49
Droop, E.F. & Sons WW-72
925 Penna. Ave. TR-167
1300 "G" St., NW. GW-216
Eberbach, Henry, 915 "F" St. JT-5
Ellis, John F., 306 Penna. Ave. USG-17; USG-181; JGB-98
Ellis, John F. & Co. GC-129
937 Penna. Ave. USG-186; JGB-37; JGB-39; JGB-92; GC-65; GC-158
George Johnson Music Pubs., 908 10th St., NE WGH-36
Graebing, Lawrence Stoddard, P.O. Box 1907 GW-225; HCH-49
Gray & Clarkson BFH-96
H. Kirkus Dugdale Co. WW-213
Dugdale Building AL-362
14th and "U" Sts. TR-128; TR-355; WHT-49; WW-61; WW-141; WW-146; WW-154
Hayworth Music Publishing Co. TR-291
Hilbus & Hitz GW-166; GW-60
Hilbus, George JB-21
Hoffmann, Theodore, 1439 Foxhall Rd., NW GW-226
Inaugural Committee TR-96
Kastle, Kathleen TR-231
Keith, Rosa Belle, 1826 Vernon St. FDR-198
Mahoney Bros TR-93
Marcus-Goodman Co., 506 14th St., N.W. WW-206
Mayflower Music Pub. Co., 100 Maryland Ave. NE FDR-218
Melody Mill WGH-60
Moreland, S.A. WW-199
Mullevy, William, 1722 Gorooran St. TR-76

Appendix

Neale Company WJB-15
Nicol, R.B., 271 Penn. Ave. AL-117
N.S. Wright Pub. Co. WW-62
Oates, James F., 1609 "D" Street GW-346
Peoples Promotional Society WLW-21
Pierson, W.T. and Co. WW-56; WGH-12
Pond, William & Co. GW-545
Republican Congressional Committee JAG-62
Republican National Committee MISC-154
Sanders & Stayman Co., 1327 "F" Street NW WJB-44; WJB-53; WM-221
Sprinkle, Marie O. FDR-101
Stone, Henry JQA-12
Union Republican Congressional Committee USG-110; RBH-20
United Republicans of America, 415 2nd St. RR-4
United States Constitution Sesquicentennial Commission GW-188; GW-335
United States George Washington Bicentennial Commission GW-186; GW-187; GW-230; GW-300
United States Printing Office FDR-167
University Club WHT-32
U.S. Publicity and News Service Co., 906 "G" St. WW-217
Walsh, Goodman & Co., 26 "I" St. WM-8
Washington Cathedral DDE-84
White, Henry WM-120
929 "F" St. GW-203
935 "F" St. JGB-27
Willkie For President Club, Inc., Sixth & Union Streets WLW-69
Worch's Piano House, 1110 "G" St., NW U&SG-129

WATERBURY, CT
Fulton Music Co., 146 Grand St. WM-192
Jas. A. Lonergan Pub. Co. WW-165

WATERLOO, NY
W.E. Philes GC-11

WATERTOWN, CT
Barry, Malgren & Taylor GW-271

WATERVILLE, ME
Mount Merici Development Program JFK-47

WEED, CA
Hewitt, Olla WW-100

WEST BEND, IA
Wirtz, Fred JFK-21

WEST CHESTER, PA
Wide Awake Club No. 1 AL-510

WEST SCRANTON, PA
Davis, Richard, 105 N. Main St. AL-246

WESTFIELD, NJ
HCH-41

WESTERFIELD, OH
The Lincoln-Lee Legion AL-203

WHEELING, WV
Rossi, Jonny P. AES-33
Sheib, William H., Washington Hall WSH-3

WICHITA, KS
Charles Willard Publications FDR-238
Hoffman Press Publications JFK-65

WILLIAMSPORT, PA
Ernest Hand Pub. Co. TR-3
Furst and Haswell TR-256
Souvenir Publishing Co. AL-373
United States Music Co. WM-36; TR-189
Vandersloot Music TR-63; TR-118

WILLIAMSTOWN, KY
Chadsee, Bryan FDR-313

WILLISTON, ND
Prairie Music Co., Box 752 FDR-380

WILMINGTON, DE
Barnes, Edwin H., 404 Delaware Ave. FDR-316
Robinson, Edna J., 2305 Tatnall St. FDR-406

WILMINGTON, NC
Toon, E. May Glenn MISC-141

WILMORE, KY
Curnow Music Press, P.O. Box 142 JFK-59

WINONA, MN
Leonard, Hal JFK-82
64 E. Second St. DDE-59; JFK-64

WINTER HAVEN, FL
The Florida Chief Pub. Co. GW-384

WISCONSIN RAPIDS, WI
Art Gaetke, Publisher, 1601 2nd Avenue HCH-48

WOCHESTER, MA
Leland & Putnam, 8 Brinley Row JT-4
Premium Music Co. TR-193

WOODHAVEN, NY
Potter, C.F., 383 Woodland Ave. TR-237
Tyler & Seagrave, 212 Main St. AL-71

Publishers by City

WOODSOCKET, RI
Cook Pub. Co. WM-254
Woodsocket Pub. Co. WJB-13

WOODSTOCK, VA
Sager, Vehrl FDR-391

WOLLASTON, MA
Cushing, Ella, 20 Rawson Rd. HCH-12

WRENTHAM, MA
Heaton, Jur., Nathaniel GW-544

WYTHEVILLE, VA
Allison, Martha Lee GW-458

YONKERS, NY
Manor Music Co. RMN-29; RMN-30

YORBA-LINDA, CA
Moore-Seamans, Emma J. WGH-46

YORK, NE
J.A. Parks Co. WJB-1; WJB-56; WM-106; AP-6; TR-157; WHT-51; WW-178

YORK, PA
Linn, J.W., 322 W. Market St. GC-9

YOUNGSTOWN, OH
Evans, D.O. WM-24; WM-75; WM-207 108 W. Federal St. JGB-40; GC-116
Evans, Margaret, 35 Brookline FDR-138

BREMEN, GERMANY
Bie Aug. Fr. Cranz AL-280

BRIGHTON, ENGLAND
Charles Gardner, 23 Greenville Place GW-256

HAVANA, CUBA
Grant, Dr. Dick FDR-315

HELSINKI, FINLAND
Kaartinen, Josef DDE-83

IZZO, ITALY
Amato, Prof. A. WW-180

LEIPZIG, GERMANY
Fr. Portius TR-209

LONDON, ENGLAND
Ascherberg, E and Company, 46 Berners St. W. TR-354
Boosey & Hawkes Music Publishers JFK-57
Chappell & Co., Ltd. TR-249; FDR-282 50 New Bond St. FDR-374; RR-20; RR-25
Clarence Music, Ltd., 50 New Bond St. JFK-35
Feldman, B. & Co., 125-9 Shaftesbury Ave. FDR-23; FDR-137; RR-24
Francis, Day & Hunter, Ltd., 138-140 Charing Cross Rd. GW-279; FDR-311
Irving Berlin, LTD., 14 George St. DDE-102
Lawrence Wright Music Co., Denmark St. HCH-39
Musical Bouquet Office, 192 High Holborn GW-268
One Four Two Music Co, 142 Charing Cross JFK-81
Paxton, W., 19 Oxford St. USG-226
Whitehall Music Co., 31 Charing Cross TR-340

MAINZ, GERMANY
Schoff's Sohnen GW-269

MORELLA, MEXICO
Fuentes, Juan B. TR-127

PARIS, FRANCE
Editions Nationales, 109 Boulevard Beaumarchais WW-177
Godard, Alfred, 5 Rue N.D. du Grace JD-65
Presses du Temps Present, 18-20 Rue du Temple JFK-42

SIDNEY, AUSTRALIA
J. Albert & Son FDR-349
Paling, W.H. & Co. DAM-22

TORONTO, CANADA
Anglo-Canadian Music Publisher's Assn, Ltd., 144 Victoria St. TR-274
Canadian Music Sales Corp., Ltd., 11 Dundas St. RR-12
Columbian Music Publishers, Ltd. FDR-165
Corlett, E., 340 Yonge St. USG-229
Foley, Edward M., 373 Waveleigh Blvd. DDE-65
Jordan Music Productions, Station M, Box 160 AL-517
Strange & Co., 120 King St. AL-468; WSH-28

QUEBEC, CANADA
Canadian Company WM-339

Bibliography

American Heritage. *The American Heritage Book of the Presidents and Other Famous Americans*. 12 Vols. New York: Dell Publishing, 1967.

———. *The American Heritage Songbook*. New York: American Heritage Publishing Co., 1969.

APIC. "Come Let Us Sing." Robert M. Goshorn. In: *The Keynoter*, page 4, Vol. 87, No. 2, 1987. Published by the American Political Items Collectors, Inc.

———. "Political Sheet Music (Campaign Music Project — Part 1)." In: *The Keynoter*, page 36, Vol. 86, No. 1, 1986. Published by the American Political Items Collectors, Inc.

———. "Political Sheet Music (Campaign Music Project — Part 2)." In: *The Keynoter*, page 28, Vol. 86, No. 2, 1986. Published by the American Political Items Collectors, Inc.

———. "Sheet Music Project — Part 3." In: *The Keynoter*, page 32, Vol. 87, No. 1, 1987. Published by the American Political Items Collectors, Inc.

———. "Sheet Music Project." In: *The Keynoter*, page 14, Vol. 87, No. 3, 1987. Published by the American Political Items Collectors, Inc.

———. "Sheet Music Project — Continued." In: *The Keynoter*, page 21, Vol. 90, No. 1, 1990. Published by the American Political Items Collectors, Inc.

Bernard, Kenneth A. *Lincoln and the Music of the Civil War*. Caldwell, ID: The Caxton Printers, 1966.

Collins, Herbert Ridgeway. *Threads of History: Americana Recorded on Cloth 1775 to the Present*. Washington: Smithsonian Institution Press, 1979.

Congressional Quarterly. *Congressional Quarterly's Guide to U.S. Elections* (2nd Ed). Washington: Congressional Quarterly, 1985.

Dichter, Harry. *Handbook of American Sheet Music*. Philadelphia: 1947.

———. *Handbook of American Sheet Music*. Philadelphia: 1953.

———, and Elliott Shapiro. *Handbook of Early American Sheet Music: 1768-1889*. New York: Dover Publications, 1977.

French, Tom. *Presidential Sheet Music 1815-1976 Mail Bid Sale #5*. Capitola, CA. 1990.

Fuld, James J. *A Pictorial Bibliography of the First Editions of Stephen C. Foster*. Philadelphia: Musical Americana, 1957.

Fuld, James J. *The Book of World-Famous Music: Classical, Popular and Folk* (3rd Ed). New York: Dover Publications, 1985.

Goshorn, Robert M. "Come Let Us Sing." In: *The Keynoter*, page 4, Vol. 87, No. 2, 1987. Published by the American Political Items Collectors, Inc.

Hartwell, Richard B. *Confederate Belles-Lettres: A Bibliography and a Finding of the Fiction, Poetry, Drama, Songsters, and Miscellaneous Literature Published in the Confederate States of America*. Hattisburg: The Book Farm, 1941.

Heaps, Willard, and Peter W. *The Singing Sixties: The Spirit of the Civil War Days Drawn from The Music of the Times*. Norman: University of Oklahoma Press, 1960.

Hoogerwerf, Frank W. *Confederate Sheet-Music Imprints*. Brooklyn: Brooklyn College, 1984.

Jackson, George Stuyvesant. *Early Songs of Uncle Sam*. Boston: Bruce Humphries, 1933.

Klamkin, Marion. *Old Sheet Music: A Pictor-

Bibliography

ial History. New York: Hawthorn Books, 1975.

Lawrence, Vera Brodsky. "The Harrison Bandwagon." In: *American Heritage Magazine,* page 18, Vol, XXVI, No. 6, 1975. Published by American Heritage Co., Inc.

_____. *Music for Patriots, Politicians, and Presidents: Harmonies and Discords of the First Hundred Years.* New York: MacMillian, 1975.

Levi, Lester. *Flashes of Merriment: A Century of Humorous Songs in America, 1805-1905.* Norman: University of Oklahoma Press, 1971.

_____. *Grace Notes in American History: Popular Sheet Music from 1820-1900.* Norman: University of Oklahoma Press, 1967.

_____. *Picture the Songs: Lithographs from 19th Century America.* Baltimore: Johns Hopkins University Press, 1976.

Marzio, Peter C. *The Democratic Art: Chromolithography 1840-1900— Pictures for a Nineteenth Century America.* London: Scolar Press, 1980.

Melder, Keith. *Hail to the Chief: Presidential Campaigns From Banners To Broadcasts.* Washington: Smithsonian Institution Press, 1992.

Miles, William. *Songs, Odes Glees and Ballads: A Bibliography of American Presidential Campaign Songsters.* Westport: Greenwood Press, 1990.

Milgram, James W. *Abraham Lincoln Illustrated Envelopes and Letter Paper 1860–1865.* Northbrook, Ill.: Northbrook Pub. Co., 1984.

_____. *Presidential Campaign Illustrated Envelopes and Letter Paper 1840–1872.* North Miami: David G. Phillips, 1994.

Moore, Frank. *The Civil War in Song and Story: 1860-1865.* New York: P.F. Collier, 1889.

National Portrait Gallery. *If Elected: Unsuccessful Candidates for the Presidency.* Washington: Smithsonian Institution Press, 1972.

Nathan, John. *Dan Emmett and the Rise of Early Negro Minstrelry.* Norman: University of Oklahoma Press, 1962.

Norton, A.B. *Reminiscences of the Log Cabin and Hard Cider Campaign: The Great Rebellion of 1840.* Mount Vernon: A.B. Norton, 1889.

Papale, Hanry. *Banners, Buttons and Songs: A Pictorial Review and Capsule Almanac of America's Presidential Campaigns.* New York: St. Martin's Press, 1968.

Priest, Daniel B. *American Sheet Music with Prices: A Guide to Collecting Sheet Music from 1775 to 1975.* Des Moines: Wallace-Holmsted Book Co. 1978.

Silber, Irwin. *Songs America Voted By.* Harrisburg: Stackpole Books, 1971.

Sonneck, Oscar G.T. and William T. Upton. *A Bibliography of Early Secular American Music: 18th Century.* Washington: Library of Congress, 1945.

Spaeth, Sigmund. *A History of Popular Music in America.* New York: Random House, 1948.

_____. *Read 'Em and Weep: The Songs You Forgot to Remember.* Garden City: Doubleday, Page, 1926.

Stein, Kurt. *A Select Catalogue of Sheet Music.* Springfield: 1989.

Stutler, Boyd B. "We Are Coming Father Abra'am." In: *Lincoln Herald,* page 2, Vol. 53, No. 2, 1951. Published by Lincoln Memorial University, Harrogate, TN.

Sullivan, Edmund B. *Collecting Political Americana.* New York: Crown, 1980.

Tatham, Davis. *The Lure of the Striped Pig: The Illustration of Popular Music in America 1820-1970.* Barre, Mass.: Imprint Society. 1973.

United States Government Printing Office. *Biographical Directory of the American Congress.* Washington: USGPO. 1971.

Wenzel, Lynn, and Carol J. Benkowski. *I Hear America Singing: A Nostalgic Tour of Popular Sheet Music.* New York: Crown, Inc. 1989.

Westin, Helen. *Introducing the Song Sheet.* Nashville: Thomas Nelson, 1976.

Who Was Who in American History. Chicago: Marquis, 1968.

Wilson, Charles Reagan, and William Feries. *Encyclopedia of Southern Culture.* Chapel Hill: University of North Carolina Press, 1989.

Wolfe, Richard J. *Early American Music Engraving and Printing: A History of Music Publishing in America from 1787 to 1825 with Commentary on Earlier and Later Practices.* Urbana: University of Illinois Press, 1980.

_____. *Secular Music in America 1801-1825: A Bibliography.* New York: New York Public Library, 1964.

Zimmerman, Lawrence. *Catalogue of Fine Sheet Music.* Brooklyn: 1989.

Title Index

A. Bacon & Co's Flute Melodies, Book 2 GW-496
A. Bacon & Co's Preceptor For The German Flute GW-502
Abe Lincoln AL-182; AL-410; AL-490
Abe Lincoln Had Just One Country AL-233; AL-315
Abe Lincoln In Illinois AL-216
Abe Lincoln In The White House AL-517
Abe Lincoln Overture AL-327
Abe Lincoln's Battle Cry AL-385
Abe Lincoln's Union Wagon AL-17; AL-65
Abe-Iad, The AL-268
Abraham AL-194
Abraham Jefferson Washington Lee MISC-157
Abraham Lincoln AL-193; AL-247; AL-248; AL-251; AL-324; AL-347; AL-414; AL-415; AL-450; AL-453; AL-461; AL-462; AL-474; AL-512
Abraham Lincoln And His Books AL-512
Abraham Lincoln And His First Sweetheart Ann Rutledge AL-210
Abraham Lincoln Lives Again AL-356; AL-494
Abraham Lincoln Walks At Night AL-328; AL-478
Abraham Lincoln's Birthday AL-335
Abraham Lincoln's Funeral March AL-27; AL-70; AL-136
Abraham Lincoln's Gettysburg Address AL-311
Abraham Lincoln Jones AL-457
Abraham Lincoln Schottisch AL-403
Abraham Lincoln Song, AN AL-406
Abraham, Martin And John JFK-30; JFK-31; JFK-60; JFK-62; JFK-66; JFK-69; JFK-78; JFK-82; JFK-84
Abraham My Abraham AL-130
Abraham! Our Abraham! AL-69
Abraham The Great And Genl. Grant His Mate AL-72
Abraham's Covenant AL-432
Abraham's Daughter AL-120; AL-163; AL-224; AL-243; AL-281; AL-350; AL-351; AL-352; AL-365; AL-475; AL-495; MISC-156

Abraham's Draft AL-141
Abraham's Tea Party AL-269; AL-489
Abridged Academy Song-Book, The GW-443; WHH-113
Ace Of Smiles, The WW-21
Acme Songs For Grand Army Of The Republic And Columbia's Loyal People, Young & Old JGB-97; JD-56
Acme Songs, Republican Glee Book And Cartridge Of Truth BFH-25; BFH-27
Acme Songs Republican Hand Book For Victory In 1892, The BFH-14
Acquisition Of Louisiana, The TJ-4
Adams & Liberty JA-2; JA-5; JA-6; JA-9; JA-10; JA-11; JA-12; JA-13; JA-14; JA-15; JA-20; JA-21; JA-22; JA-23; JA-24; MISC-169
Adams & Washington JA-4
Adams March JA-3
Adams Forever JA-19
Adams' Quick March JQA-7
Adlai Song Sheet AS-13
Administration March, The WM-79
Administration Waltz WW-112
Advice From Honest Abe AL-346
Aero Naughty Girl, The TR-30
African Hunter, The TR-34
After The Election Is Over HG-20
Again And Again And Again FDR-371
Ah! Do Not Forget WHH-33
Aitken's Fountain Of Music GW-463
Al AES-14
Al! Al! Al! AES-55
Al For All And All For Al AES-8
Al My Pal AES-47
Al S. In Wonderland AES-67
Al Smith AES-20; AES-30; AES-50; AES-58
Al Smith, Al Smith AES-53
Al Smith To Lead Us On AES-61
Al Smith We Are All For You AES-46
Alabama Secession Galop JD-6
Album Of Military Marches GW-186
Alfred E. Smith The Happy Warrior AES-37
Alfred E. Smith The Man You'll Appreciate AES-4

Alice Blue Folio TR-298
Alice Blue Waltzes TR-82; TR-298
Alice In Blunderland Or Through The Rooking Class HST-20
Alice Roosevelt March TR-88; TR-231
Alice Roosevelt Waltzes TR-85
Alice Roosevelt Wedding March, The TR-90
Alice The Bride Of The White House TR-197
Alice, Where Art Thou Going TR-89
All Aboard For Broadway GW-236
All About George Washington GW-213
All American Patriotic Song Book, The GW-620
All For The U-S-A WW-202; DDE-32
All Hail To Our Great Leader FDR-312
All Hail To Ulysses! USG-39; USG-103
All Hail, Ye Gallant Freemen True! JCF-43
All Out For America FDR-190
All Rights For All USG-270
All The Letters Of Major General Zachary Taylor, Anecdotes Of Rough And Ready, Songs Of Old Zach's Campaigns ZT-74
All The Way LBJ-33
All The Way With L.B.J LBJ-7; Bjj-8
All The Way With Mondale WFM-1
All The Way With Wallace And Lemay GCW-1
All The World Is Proud Of You WW-151
All Things Fair & Bright Are Thine JMN-18; JMN-22; JMN-23
All Vote For Roosevelt TR-342
All's For The Best AL-357
All's Well, Come To The Rescue JD-50
Allegiance AL-183; AL-225
Allied Victory WW-180
Allies March WW-97
Allies United For Liberty WW-110
Allies Victorious March WW-49
Aloha To You Mr. Roosevelt FDR-214
Alone WM-131
Always Everywhere Smiling AES-51
Always Wear That Smile TR-272
Amateur's Quartette Club, No. 2, The ZT-78
America GW-238; GW-528; GW-591; BFH-74; WJB-35; WM-319; TR-289; MISC-117
America Admires Brother Harding WGH-34
America Always Will Love You FDR-274
America America JFK-8
America And General MacArthur DAM-4
America Awake! WW-102
America Beloved, Revered GW-591
America First GW-207; GW-223; WGH-23; WGH-55
America, Franklin D! 'Tis For Thee FDR-309
America Is Calling Lincoln AL-443
America Is On Parade FDR-147
America Let's Go! FDR-68
America Marches On FDR-124
America, My America GW-578
America, My Country WW-142
America My Sweet Land GW-318

America, Our Country MISC-112
America Rejoice GW-226
America Sings GW-562
America Sings For Americanism AML-18
America The Beautiful GW-592; MISC-112
America Thou Victorious One WW-135
America To-Day WW-125
America, You're Beautiful To Me MISC-112
American Army, The USG-208
American Battle Song WW-64
American Beauty Rose TJ-42
American Collection For Band GW-430
American Collection Of War Music GW-550
American Consecration Hymn WW-152
American Dance Music Collection GW-134
American Eagle March TR-48
American Eagles RR-19; RR-20
American Flag, The ZT-64; WS-10
American Girl, The TR-87
American Heritage Song Book, The MISC-169
American Hero TR-252
American Hero's March, The WS-2
American Hymn TR-313
American Legends AL-218
American Marseillaise, The HC-4; WJB-26; WM-123; WW-150
American Medley GW-122; GW-123
American Missionary Association Concert Exercise For Lincoln Sunday AL-363
American Musical Miscellany GW-110; JA-14
American Naval And Patriotic Songster AJK-60
American Patriotic Song Book GW-83; TJ-5
American Patriotic Songs GW-519
American Piano Music Collection GW-134
American Republican Songster, The HC-98
American School Songs GW-529
American Singer, The GW-511; GW-512; TJ-50; AL-371; AL-471
American Stamp Polka MISC-36
American Soldier, The GW-240; TR-18; TR-378
American Songbag AJK-53; AL-476
American Songs GW-405
American Songster GW-382; GW-533; AJK-49
American Spirit MISC-184
American Volunteers' [Grand] Triumphal March, The USG-34
American Wedding March GW-297
Americanization Songs GW-608
America's Bicentennial Songs MF-37; JB-22; GBM-84; AL-506; WM-325; MISC-182
America's Centennial Grand March GW-165
America's Centennial Ode GW-165
America's Day WW-53
America's Flag GW-369
America's Greatest WW-175
America's Hero MacArthur DAM-28
America's Lamentation For Washington GW-470

Title Index

America's Leader WW-88
America's Message WW-116
America's Most Famous Songs GW-448
America's National Songs GW-122
America's President Song WW-83
America's Song Kit GW-420
Amherst March Song CC-27
Amos Kendall's Lament WHH-137
Amy Doesn't Live Here Anymore JEC-8
Anchors Aweigh FDR-20
And Henry's Meant For President When We A-Fordin' Go MISC-87
And It Was Not Sung In Vain GC-50
And That's How Benny Got In GC-97
Andre's Request To Washington GW-85; GW-388
Andrew Jackson AJK-42
Andrew Jackson And Long May He Live! AJK-28
Andrew Jackson's March AJK-37
Andy Veto AJN-5
Angels Are Calling Away WM-62
Animaniacs MISC-135
Ann Rutledge AL-313
Anne Rutledge AL-478
Another Roosevelt FDR-162
Answer Mr. Wilson's Call WW-48
Answer To Heflin AES-59
Anthem Of Freedom FDR-246
Antietam GBM-82
Anti-Expansion March WJB-54
Anti-Know-Nothing Ditty MF-26
Apostle Of Peace DDE-30
Appomattox, April 9, 1865 One Flag Only JMP-2
Appreciation MISC-164
Are You Backing Up Your Commander-In-Chief? FDR-197; FDR-221
Are You Half The Man Your Mother Thought You'd Be? MISC-46
Are You Livin' Old Man? TJ-42
Aren't There Black Angels In Heaven Too? LBJ-25
Arlington Funeral March JGB-98
Armed Forces Song Folio JFK-72
Army And Navy Fife Instructor GW-435; TJ-19; AJK-41; WHH-112; ZT-69; WS-32; MISC-131
Army Blue DDE-17
Army Grand March, The WS-7
Army Of Liberty, The GW-137
Army's Made A Man Out Of Me, The RR-19; RR-20
Around The Hancock Banner Throng Alike The Blue And Gray WSH-19
Around The World Schottische USG-221
Around The World With Roosevelt FDR-133
Arouse My Gallant Freemen! WHH-49
Arouse Ye, Patriot Whigs! WHH-14
Arraham's [Sic] Daughter AL-163
As Our (President/Boys Come) Sailing Home WW-81

As Some Fond Mother GW-8
As Teddy Went Over The Top TR-158
Ashland Galop, The HC-27
Ashland Farmer HC-83
Ashland March, The HC-77
Ashland Melodies, The HC-19
Ashland Quick Step HC-7 HC-57; HC-67; HC-71; HC-85; HC-86
Ashland Quadrilles, The HC-3
Ashland Songster, The HC-94
Ashland Waltz HC-7; HC-60
Ashland Waltzes, The HC-7; HC-60; WHH-113
Ask Not JFK-11; JFK-29; JFK-47; JFK-61; JFK-63
Ask What You Can Do For Your Country JFK-80
Assassins AL-309; JAG-90; WM-234; RR-27; MISC-91
Assassin's Vision, The AL-49
At Rest JAG-25
At The Inauguration Ball HST-3
At The White House Ball WW-105
Au Revoir HC-92
Aunt Harriet Beecha Stowe JT-6
Aunt Harriet Beechee Stowe JT-8
Aurora March DDE-83
Awake America GW-320
Awaken America:WLW-69
Away Goes Cuffie AL-135

Baby Ruth GC-36; GC-45; GC-163
Baby Ruth And Baby McKee GC-43
Baby Ruth Fantasy Polka GC-123
Baby Ruth's Slumber Song GC-59
Baby's Rattle WM-127
Bacchanal Of 1919, The AES-65
Back In Hackensack New Jersey AL-321
Back To The Days Of Abraham AL-477
Bacon's Complete Preceptor For The Clarinet GW-494; MISC-159
Bad Boys, The TR-235
Badge Of Courage JFK-77
Ballad Of Abe Lincoln, The AL-231
Ballad Of Booth, The AL-309
Ballad Of Czolgosz, The WM-234
Ballad Of Davy Crockett, The AJK-43
Ballad Of Franklin D FDR-372
Ballad Of Guiteau, The JAG-90
Ballad Of John Kennedy, The JFK-81
Ballad Of Spiro Agnew, The RMN-34
Ballad Of Theodore Roosevelt TR-349
Ballad Of Valley Forge GW-239
Ballads And Songs Of The Civil War AL-475; USG-279; JD-55
Ballads Of The B.E.F HCH-50
Ballet Ballade The Elephant Made, A FDR-237
Baltimore Centennial March, The GW-37
Baltimore Musical Miscellany GW-111
Baltimore Whig Convention Quick Step WHH-81

Title Index

Baltimore Whig Ratification Song WHH-113
Bandanna Songster, The GC-11
Banner Of Clay, The HC-22
Banner Of Hancock And English, The WSH-19
Banner Of The Free, The WS-19
Banner Of Tilden And Hendricks, The SJT-6
Banner Ratification Song, The GC-119
Barry's Boys BMG-4
Barry's Victory March BMG-1
Bartlett's Music Reader GW-539
Bastien Favorites GW-522
Battle At The Polls WM-253
Battle Hymn Of '48 HAW-8
Battle Cry, The HCH-60
Battle Hymn Of The National Progressive Party TR-150
Battle Hymn Of The Republicans RR-31
Battle Hymn Of The 60's JFK-79
Battle Now Is On WHT-53
Battle Of Buena Vista, The ZT-12; ZT-33
Battle Of New Orleans, The AJK-15; AJK-45; AJK-49
Battle Of Prague, The GW-14; GW-317
Battle Of Resaca De La Palma, The ZT-16
Battle Of San Juan Hill, The TR-351
Battle Of The Memorable 8th Of January 1815 AJK-20
Battle Of Trenton, The GW-15; GW-595
Battle Song, A PC-1
Battle Songs Of Liberty WW-216
Battle Songs Of Prohibition CBF-4
Battle Songs Of Seventeen WW-168
Battles Of Palo Alto & Resaca De La Palma, The ZT-53
Battle's On, The PP-1
Be Democrats AS-4
Be Glad You're An American AL-337
Be Good To California, Mr. Wilson WW-13
Beadle's Dime Knapsack Songster GBM-78; AL-469; JD-57; BFB-21
Bear Well Our Standard Old Glory WGH-20
Beautiful Hills Of Dakota MISC-78
Beautiful Isle Of Somewhere WM-156; WW-59
Beauvior JD-28
Become What You Are JAG-97
Bedtime For Bonzo RR-14
Beggar's Petition, The WHH-91
Beginning Of The U.S.A, The GW-242
Believe In Stevenson AS-1
Bell And Everett Campaign JBL-9
Bell And Everett Schottisch, The JBL-1
Bell And Everett Songster For The Campaign, The JBL-10
Bells Of Freedom FDR-334
Ben And Levi BFH-80
Ben Butler BFB-17
Ben Harrison, Hurrah! BFH-6
Ben Slater's Song GC-38
Beneath The Dear Old Flag Again JAG-20; JGB-55

Benjamin & Levi Grand March BFH-15
Benjamin Harrison March BFH-128
Benjamin Harrison's Grand March BFH-10; BFH-11
Benny Butler, Oh BFB-15
Benny Haven's O GBM-32
Berlin Special, The WW-122
Best Known Soldier, The FDR-176
Betsy Ross GW-577
Better Days With Davis JWD-6
Better Times Are Coming TED-27
Better Times With Al AES-9; AES-11
Beulah's Blaine And Logan Original Campaign Song Book BFH-41
B-I Double L-Bill WHT-9
Bi-Centennial Hymn, The GC-118
Bicentennial March, The GW-294
Bicentennial March And Presidential Marches Of America GW-293; TJ-40; AL-292; FDR-310; HST-18; DDE-76; JFK-51; LBJ-27; RMN-27; GRF-8
Big Bill For Me WHT-39
Big Bill Taft WHT-48; WHT-59
Big Bill The Builder GW-307
Big Boy From Indiana, The WLW-50
Big Brown Derby AES-25
Big Chief Hoover HCH-30
Big Stick, The TR-46; TR-261
Big Stick Blues March, The TR-142
Big Three Polka, The FDR-225
Bill? Bill Taft WHT-10
Billy Possum WHT-54; WHT-56
Billy Possum Barn Dance, The WW-33
Billy Possum March WHT-7
Billy Possum Rag WHT-50
Bing! Bang! Bing 'Em On The Rhine WW-99
Bird Of Washington, The GW-147
Birds Of A Feather TR-147
Birth Of A Nation GW-334
Birth Of Washington GW-309
Birthday Of Washington, The GW-77; GW-492; GW-564; GW-591
Black Hills Of South Dakota, The MISC-74
Black Swan Set No. 1 GW-172; MF-29
Blaine And Logan JGB-44
Blaine And Logan Are Our Choice JGB-48
Blaine And Logan Campaign Songster JGB-29; JGB-84
Blaine And Logan Collection Of Campaign Songs JGB-78
Blaine And Logan Grand March JGB-48
Blaine And Logan Loyal Wreath JGB-92
Blaine And Logan Our Plumed Knights JGB-60
Blaine And Logan Song Book JGB-32; JGB-89
Blaine And Logan Songster JGB-35; JGB-86; JGB-90
Blaine And Logan Victory March JGB-21
Blaine And Logan's Grand Triumphal March JGB-21

Blaine And Victory JGB-15
Blaine-Blaine-Blaine Of Maine JGB-31; JGB-44
Blaine Club March JGB-57
Blaine For Our President JGB-15
Blaine From Maine JGB-33; JGB-44
Blaine Grand March, The JGB-3; JGB-44; JGB-62
Blaine Of Maine JGB-75
Blaine Of Maine And Logan The Brave JGB-87
Blaine Of Maine And Victory JGB-58
Blaine's Grand March GW-134; JGB-4; JGB-12; JGB-40; JGB-59
Blaine's March JGB-19
Blaine's Our Banner Man JGB-15
Blaine's Triumphal March JGB-5
Blaine's Victory March JGB-10
Blair's Favorite Polka HS-4
Blair's Galop HS-2
Blake's Evening Companion For The Flute, Clarinet, Violin Or Flageolet, Vol. [ ], Book 1 GW-495; TJ-54
Blake's Evening Companion For The Flute, Clarinet, Violin Or Flageolet, Vol. 2, Book 8 GW-496
Blake's Flute Preceptor GW-500
Blake's New And Complete Preceptor For The Violin GW-462; TJ-65
Blake's Violin Preceptor GW-462; TJ-65
Bleached Shirt, The WSH-42
Blend Of The Blue And The Gray, The WHT-42
Blow, Bugler, Blow Up One Note More CBF-7
Blue And The Grey, The USG-236
Blue Eagle, The FDR-160
Blue Eagle March FDR-236
Blue Eagles Flying High, The FDR-146
Bluebird Echo Polka, The GBM-50
Blufftonian Waltzes WM-199
Boat Horn, The LC-3; LC-4; LC-5
Bobolink Minstrel, The AL-387
Bold Volunteer, The GW-212
Bonny Free Flag, The JGB-68
Bonus Blues HCH-47
Book Of Songs AL-355
Booth Campaign Songster USG-253
Booth Killed Lincoln AL-475
Born Again JEC-5
Boston Journal McKinley March WM-97
Boston Melodeon, The GW-427
Boston Musical Miscellany JA-21
Boundary Quick Step DW-29
Bow Down To Washington GW-343
Boys In Blue USG-290
Boys In Blue Are Growing Grey, The GW-133
Boys In Blue To The Boys In Grey, The AJN-21
Boys In Blue Will See It Through, The RBH-26

Boys Of '61 WGH-46
Boys We Love DAM-40
Brain Storms TR-295
Brave Ben Butler BFB-13
Brave Ben Of Indiana BFH-21
Brave Garfield Is Our Man JAG-2; JAG-82
Brave Hancock Is The Man WSH-19
Brave Jennie Creek WM-150
Brave Little Mac GBM-81
Brave McClellan Is Our Leader Now GBM-16
Brave McClellan March GBM-42
Brave Old Chief, The WHH-91; WHH-138
Brave Rough Riders, The TR-24
Brave Ulysses Is The Man! USG-57
Bread And Butter AJN-19
Breaks And Outbreaks FDR-362
Breckenridge And Lane JCB-5
Breckenridge March JCB-4
Breckenridge Polka JCB-6
Breckenridge Schottische JCB-1
Breckenridge Schottische, The JCB-3
Brewer's Collection Of National Songs And Hymns GW-617
Brick Pomeroy's New Democratic Campaign Song Book HS-18
Bright And Black MISC-100
Bring Us Together, Go Forward Together RMN-6
Brinkley Bathing Girl, The TR-30
British Gold HC-74
Broadside, Volume 2 LBJ-31
Broadway Two-Step, The GC-92
Brooklyn Tippecanoe Song Book, The WHH-133
Brother Soldiers All Hail! GW-11; GW-395
Brown Derby March AES-72
Brown Girl or Fair Eleanor, The AL-476
Bryan And Sewall Grand March WJB-17; WJB-52
Bryan, Believed In Heaven WJB-51
Bryan, Billy Bryan WJB-12; WJB-14
Bryan Campaign Songster WJB-60
Bryan Campaign Songster For 1900 WJB-71
Bryan Cocktail WJB-37
Bryan Free Silver March WJB-10
Bryan Free Silver Song Book WJB-55
Bryan March Song WJB-23
Bryan Silver March, The WJB-20
Bryan Songster, The WJB-69
Bryan The Nation's Choice WJB-73
Bryan Two-Step WJB-24
Bryan's Democratic Success March WJB-22
Bryan's Good Luck March WJB-7
Bryan's Victorious March WJB-46
Buchanan And Fremont JCF-39
Buchanan Galop JB-16
Buchanan Polka JB-8
Buchanan Schottisch JB-1
Buchanan's Inauguration March JB-21
Buchanan's March JB-3
Buchanan's Union Grand March JB-2; JB-23

Title Index

Buck And Breck Campaign Songster JB-18
Buckeye March, The WM-94
Buckeye Song, The WHH-2; WHH-30; WHH-117
Buddy Mine JFK-44
Buena Vista Grand March ZT-61
Buena Vista Grand Triumphal March ZT-18
Bugle Call, The GW-414; AL-140; JD-22
Bugle March Of The Fremont Hussars JCF-20
Bull Moose Glide TR-131
Bull Moose March TR-49; TR-78; TR-143
Bull Moose Romp TR-259
Bull Moose Waltz TR-244
Bullmoosers, The TR-327
Bunker Hill WHH-5
Burial Of Free Trade, The BFH-84
Burr's Grand March TJ-62
Burr's March TJ-12
Bury Me With My Grand Army Badge USG-98
Business Men's Noon Day Meetings At Museum Hall BFH-106
Bust The Trusts WW-201
Butler Campaign Song BFB-16
Butler Quick Step BFB-20
Butler The Beast BFB-21
By The Bright White Light Of The Moon GW-198
By The Light Of The Silvery Moon WW-126
Bye-Bye Landon, Goodbye! FDR-134

Cabinet Grand March, The WM-15
Cactus Jack FDR-104
Cal CC-26
Calendar Galop GW-173
California Republican Campaign Songster WM-329
Call 'Em Names, Jeff JD-22; JD-25
Call To Camp Roosevelt, The TR-61
Called Home WM-32
Calling For Roosevelt FDR-357
Calvin Coolidge Is The Man CC-17
Calvin Coolidge March CC-30
Calvin Coolidge Song CC-30
Calvin's Creed CC-53
Camp Roosevelt TR-61
Camp Songs For The Soldiers And Poems Of Leisure Moments AL-469
Camp Taylor March ZT-55
Campaign, The AL-134
Campaign Butler Song BFB-11
Campaign Circus JMC-3
Campaign College Songs Of 1900 WM-214
Campaign Document No. 19 Campaign Songs GBM-69
Campaign Gavotte BFH-26
Campaign Grand March SJT-22
Campaign Jubilee Song GC-102
Campaign Lyrics, Songs, And Ballads For The Campaign Of 1876 RBH-46
Campaign March GC-25; MISC-66

Campaign March And Chorus To Genl. Hancock WSH-6
Campaign 1900 March WM-181
Campaign Of 1856 – Fremont Songs For The People JCF-50
Campaign Of 1848 Free Soil Songs For The People MVB-8
Campaign Prize Songs WJB-66
Campaign Scott And Graham Songster, The WS-17
Campaign Song AL-144; USG-56; WHT-15; LBJ-32
Campaign Song Book CEH-10
Campaign Song Book For The Republican Party, 1888 BFH-95
Campaign Song For Abraham Lincoln AL-271
Campaign Song Of 1904 TR-342
Campaign Song Of Scott & Graham WS-36
Campaign Song Of 1904 TR-342
Campaign Song Of Scott & Graham WS-36
Campaign Songs USG-185; RBH-56; BFH-44; BFB-77; BFH-85; WM-87; WM-288; TR-148; TR-161; JBW-8; RML-3
Campaign Songs As Sung By The Blaine And Logan Glee Club Of Logansport, Indiana JGB-80
Campaign Songs For 1884:JGB-82
Campaign Songs For The People USG-258
Campaign Songs For The Use Of Blaine And Logan Glee Clubs JGB-79
Campaign Songs 1906 WM-128
Campaign Songs, 1936 AML-33
Campaign Songster, The JAG-86
Campaign Waltzes RBH-42
Campaing [sic] Song For 1872 HG-31
Canners FDR-313
Cannibal Isle TR-36
Canone Funerale JA-7
Can't We Call Him Bill? WHT-17
Cantilena, The GW-547
Cantonian March WM-43
Capitol Quick Step, The HC-53
Capture Of Jeff Davis JD-31; JD-51
Capture Of Santiago, The TR-27
Caroline Gavotte BFH-31
Carpet Bagger, The BFB-2
Carpet Bagger Dance, The BFB-2
Carry On! Carry On! With Nixon! RMN-18
Carry On For General MacArthur DAM-29; DAM-41
Carry On! Old England FDR-270
Carter Can Count On Me JEC-12
Carter For President JEC-9
Cash Or Carry On TED-20
Cass & Butler Songster LC-2
C.C.C. Follow On FDR-369
Cead Mile Failte! BC-11
Celebrated Arion Carnival Festival March, The AJN-20
Centennial Chorus GW-128
Centennial Democratic Campaign Song SJT-20

Title Index

Centennial Dirge GW-583
Centennial Hymn GW-130
Centennial Grand March RBH-27
Centennial March GW-130
Centennial Meditation Of Columbia, The RBH-45
Centennial Ode GW-56
Centennial Tribute GW-41
Centennial Waltzes GW-165
Cerro Gordo March And Quick Step WS-24
Champ! Champ! Champ! They Boys Are Marching MISC-116
Champion Blaine And Logan Songster JGB-81
Chaplain Lozier's Old Glory Campaign Songs BFH-108; WM-281
Charge At San Juan, The TR-242
Charge Of The Roosevelt Rough Riders, The TR-13; TR-129
Charge Of The Rough Riders TR-65; TR-79; TR-96; TR-154; TR-168; TR-234
Charles E. Hughes The American CEH-3
Chasing Depression Away FDR-306
Cheers For The Veteran ND-1
Chicago Copperhead, The GBM-29
Chicago Galop GC-56
Chief We Have Chosen, The JGB-43
Chieftain Brave, The USG-199
Chieftain's Daughter, The WS-13
Chieftain's Return, The USG-201
Chippewa Warbler, The WS-37
Chips Off The Old Block GW-350
Chorus Sung Before Gen. Washington GW-7
Christmas Gifts For A King FDR-315
Christy Girl TR-30
Churchill-Roosevelt Swing, The FDR-311
Cincinatus Of The West, The WHH-2; WHH-30; WHH-115
Civil War Songbook, The MISC-139
Clare De Way For Ole Kentuck HC-115
Clarion Melodist, The "AL-393
Clarion Of Freedom, The MVB-15
Clay And Frelinghuysen HC-23; HC-40; HC-44; HC-46; HC-95
Clay And Frelinghuysen Songster HC-96
Clay Club Coon Songster, The HC-97
Clay Club Quick Step HC-54
Clay Convention Quick Step HC-49
Clay Minstrel Or National Songster, The HC-12; HC-18
Clay Songster, The HC-101
Clay's Grand Quick Step HC-63
Clay's Kentucky Grand March HC-43
Clay's Grand Quick Step HC-61
Clay's Quick Step HC-6; HC-63
Clear De Way For Ole Kentucky HC-115
Clear The Tracks For Old Kentucky HC-7
Clear The Way For Henry Clay HC-69
Cleveland And Hendricks' Campaign Songster GC-143
Cleveland And Hendricks' Grand March GC-63; GC-116

Cleveland And Hendricks' Grand Victory March GC-1; GC-164
Cleveland And Hendricks Reform GC-126
Cleveland And Hendricks' Songster GC-46
Cleveland And Stevenson Songster GC-2
Cleveland And Thurman 1888 Campaign Carols GC-152
Cleveland And Thurman 1888 Campaign Songster GC-145
Cleveland And Thurman Grand March GC-138; GC-157; GC-156
Cleveland And Thurman Songster GC-3
Cleveland And Thurman's Victory March GC-12
Cleveland & Victory GC-23; GC-105
Cleveland Glide Waltz GC-155
Cleveland Is His Name GC-24
Cleveland Is The Man GC-65
Cleveland Or Herculean Quick-Step GC-120
Cleveland Triumphal Campaign March GC-14
Cleveland Wedding March GC-153
Cleveland's Baby Girl GC-71
Cleveland's Campaign March GC-62
Cleveland's 1892 Campaign March GC-5
Cleveland's Farewell JGB-36
Cleveland's Grand March GW-134; GC-9; GC-15; GC-18; GC-25; GC-86; GC-103; GC-104
Cleveland's Grand March To The White House GC-137
Cleveland's Inauguration Grand March GC-6
Cleveland's Luck & Love GC-30; GC-31
Cleveland's March GC-91
Cleveland's March To Victory GC-76; GC-77; GC-79; GC-80
Cleveland's March Triumphal GC-20
Cleveland's Popularity Grand March GC-127
Cleveland's Second Term Grand March GC-21; GC-96; GC-117
Cleveland's Second Term March GC-8; GC-131; GC-161
Cleveland's Triumphal March GC-74
Cleveland's Victory March Brilliant GC-57
Cleveland's Wedding March GC-29; GC-153
Click With Dick RMN-17
Climb On The Adlai Train AS-12
Clinton's Grand March DWC-5
Clinton's Triumph DWC-4
Co. A Original Songs BFH-112
Cockoo! Cockoo! All Sing Cockoo! WM-322
Col. Ellsworth's Funeral March AL-235
Col. Roosevelt's March TR-108
Col. Roosevelt's Rough Riders TR-171
Colfax Galop USG-89
Colfax Polka USG-296
Collection Of Campaign Songs, A WM-191
Collection Of Most Favorite Country Dances TJ-63
Collection Of New And Favorite Songs, A GW-469; JA-22
Collection Of Patriotic And Military Tunes,

Piano And Dance Music, Songs And Operatic Airs, A GW-186
Collection Of Patriotic Harrison And Tippecanoe Songs, Glees and Parodies Dedicated To The Harrison Men Of The United States WHH-123
Collection Of Scott And Graham Songs WS-41
Collection Of Songs, Selected From The Works Of Mr. Dibdin, A JA-24
Colonel Joseph H. Sprague's Popular Republican Campaign Songs WM-310
Colonial National Anthem GW-181
Columbia WW-65
Columbia, Freedom's Home Is Thine JT-7
Columbia Mourns For Our President Lincoln AL-110
Columbia My Country WM-145
Columbia Rules The Waves TR-73
Columbia The Gem Of The Ocean GW-130; JB-20
Columbian Centinel JA-19
Columbian March GC-93
Columbian Songster, The GW-544
Columbia's Call USG-267; JAG-65
Columbia's Guardian Angels USG-273
Columbia's Son GW-179
Come All Ye Whigs So Gallant And True HC-9
Come Along! AML-11
Come Along Boys WW-111
Come, At Your Country's Call GBM-46
Come Back, General Pershing MISC-4
Come Brothers, Arouse! WHH-91
Come, Come Gallant Whigs HC-64; HC-115
Come Genius Of Our Happy Land JA-26
Come To Mammoth Cave In Old Kentucky AL-287
Come Rally, Freemen Rally AL-368
Come Rally 'Round WLW-43
Come, Sons Of Freedom AJK-8
Coming Election, The AL-305
Coming Hero, The PP-3
Coming Woman, The GC-26; GC-100
Commandress-In-Chief, The MISC-99
Commoner, The WJB-45
Community Chorus Book, The GW-460
Company A Boys In Blue WM-328
Complete Fifer's Museum GW-71
Complete Fife Tutor, The GW-471; GW-487; TJ-64
Complete Greenback And Labor Songster JBW-10
Complete Instructor For The Piano Forte GW-498
Complete Pocket Song Book, The GW-489
Complete Preceptor For The German Flute GW-500
Complete Tutor, The GW-471; TJ-59
Confederacy March JD-5
Connecticut Wide-Awake Songster AL-175

Conny O'Ryan's Campaign Songster HS-16
Conscript's Lay, The AL-364; WSH-26
Constitution, The JB-7
Constitutional Centennial March GC-7
Continental March GW-149
Contraband Schottische BFB-9
Convention Quick Step ZT-30
Convention Time MISC-61
Coolidge And Country CC-15
Coolidge And Dawes For The Nation's Cause CC-2; CC-31
Coolidge Campaign Songs CC-43
Coolidge Dawes Rally Song CC-29
Coolidge Song CC-54
Coolidge '24 CC-8
Coon Dance, The WM-126
Coon Exterminator Or Polk And Dallas Songster, The JKP-2
Copeland's Good Enough For Me MISC-7
Copperhead Of 1865, The GBM-29
Copperhead Of 1864, The GBM-29
Corn Pickin' RR-12
Corner-Stone March AMP-1
Cosmopolitan America TR-123
Country's Calling Roosevelt, The FDR-210
Court Of Honor WM-10
Cowboy From Brooklyn RR-9
Cox Means Victory JMC-10
Coxey's Grand March JSC-3
Coxey Keep Off The Grass JSC-4
Coxey's March To The White House JSC-1
Coxey's March To Washington JSC-2; JSC-5
Crain's Log Cabin Song Book WHH-127
Crow Chapman Crow!! WHH-139
Cuba Libre TR-207
Cuba Shall Be Free USG-233
Cup O' Tea, A MISC-43
Curl The Mo, Uncle Joe FDR-349
Cushing Academy March Two Step CC-24

Daily, Knight Of The Shilaly! TR-277
Dainty Butterfly TR-335
Damn The Torpedoes Full Speed Ahead! FDR-19
Dan Rice's Great American Humorist Song Book WS-11
Dance Ballerina Dance TJ-42
Dance Music GW-186
Dance Of The Taffy 'Possums WHT-43
Dancing Wave TR-186
Dare To Be A Neal Dow ND-3
Darling I Am Growing Young FDR-338
Dashing Cavalier, The TR-196
Dashing G.O.P's, The WGH-35
Date In '48 TED-3; TED-11
Dats Whats De Matter Wid De Purps AL-282
Daughter Of The Nation TR-286
Daughter Of Uncle Sam, A TR-83
Davis And Bryan JWD-1
Davis Song, The JWD-6
Dawley's Campaign U.S. Grant Song Book USG-222

Title Index

Dawn Of Freedom SP-5
Dawn Of Peace AJN-27; WM-120
(Dawn Will Bring A, The) Song Of Peace FDR-405
Dawning Day, The EVD-1
Dawning Grows To Morn, The JGB-7
Dawning Of Music In Kentucky, The GW-492
Days Of Glorious Washington, The GW-92
De Bull Moose Meet TR-348
De Next President Am Gwine Ter Be Er Coon MISC-81
De Ole Man Bryan WM-87
De United States Hotel AL-240
Dead March GW-618
Dead March And Monody GW-3
Dead March In Saul AL-299
Dealers Choice Or Back-To-Back Biting FDR-364
Dear Abby JA-18
Dear Mr. President FDR-84
Dear Mr. President Jesus MISC-137
Dear Old Pals WW-71
Dearest Mae GW-116
Death And Patriotism Of Abraham Lincoln AL-58
Death Knell Is Tolling, The AL-67
Death Of Abraham Lincoln AL-246
Death Of Gen. Washington, The TJ-8
Death Of President Lincoln AL-336; AL-395
Death Of Taylor ZT-37
December 7, 1941 FDR-348
Declaration Of Independence, The TJ-31; TJ-32
Declaration Of Independence Of The United States Of North America July 4, 1776 MISC-181
Deed I Do AL-321
Dee-Lighted TR-20; TR-281; TR-338
Deep In The Wildwood AL-334
Democracy WW-27; JMC-8
Democracy On Parade FDR-323
Democracy's Ta-Ra-Ra-Boom-De-Ay GC-68
Democratic Ball, The:MVB-16
Democratic Boat, The BFH-65
Democratic Campaign Carols SJT-38
Democratic Campaign Chorus WJB-87
Democratic Campaign Melodist:HS-6
Democratic Campaign Song FDR-242
Democratic Campaign Song Book For The Campaign Of 1888 GC-140
Democratic Campaign Song Folio WJB-11
Democratic Campaign Song Sheet No. 1 GC-151
Democratic Campaign Songs SJT-11; FDR-232
Democratic Campaign Songs For 1888 GC-150
Democratic Campaign Songs, Poems And Jokes FDR-83
Democratic Campaign Songster Douglas & Johnson Melodies SAD-5
Democratic Campaign Songster No. 1, The SAD-11; SAD-12; GBM-23
Democratic Centenial [Sic] March SJT-7
Democratic Clan BFH-74
Democratic Fun WJB-31
Democratic Lute And Polk And Dallas Minstrel JFK-13
Democratic March, The AS-11
Democratic National Campaign Song Book For 1900 WJB-68
Democratic National Convention March WJB-19
Democratic National Hymn WW-219
Democratic Presidential Campaign Songster No. 1 GBM-23
Democratic Presidential March AP-2
Democratic Rally FDR-382
Democratic Song Book AES-70
Democratic Songs FDR-97
Democratic Songster, The JKP-12
Democratic Toast, A GC-160
Democratic Victory March GC-135; WJB-79; FDR-239
Democratic Whale BFH-74
Democrats, The AES-29
Democrats Are In Again,. The FDR-408
Democrats Are Winning The Day, The HST-4
Denver Auditorium March WJB-4
Deserted Rebel Mansion, The USG-203
Dewey-Bricker TED-4
Dewey, Dewey Day, A TED-35
Dewey For President TED-1; TED-17; TED-32
Dewey Shall Our Leader Be MISC-2
Dewey Victory, The WM-248
Dewey-Warren Victory Rally TED-23
Dewey We Do TED-2
Dewey We Don't FDR-197
Dewey Will Do It TED-15; TED-26
Dewitt Clinton's Grand Canal March DWC-7
Dewitt Clinton's Grand Slow March DWC-9
Dewitt Clinton's Short Troop, Or Waltz DWC-9
Dey's All Put On De Blue JAG-45
Die Stimme Des Veteranen JAG-40
Dinna Ye Hear The Slogan JGB-9
Dinna Ye Hear The S'logan JGB-38
Dirge WHH-87; AL-105
Dirge, A JFK-64; DW-17
Dirge For General Washington GW-395; GW-464
Dirge For Our Dead Chieftain JAG-39
Discovering America MISC-107
District Of Columbia Is My Home, The MISC-186
Dixie Land For Al AES-15
Do It With Dewey TED-5
Do Not Leave Me Mother Darling AL-496
Do We Want Him? Well I Should Say So WM-117
Do You Believe The Johnson Line? LBJ-33

Title Index

Do Your Bit Help Send A Kit TR-292
Doctrine Of Monroe, The GC-109
Does It Pay To Raise Your Boy To Be A Soldier TR-294
Doleful Ballad Of Neal Dow ND-2
Dolly Madison JMD-12
Dolly Madison Two Step, The JMD-11
Dolly Madison Waltzes JMD-13
Don't Be Afraid Of Romance MISC-68
Dont Be Ashamed Of The Name Of Lincoln AL-226
Don't Change Horses FDR-194
Don't Forget That He's Your President WW-160
Don't Let Down The Flag FDR-415
Don't Let 'Em Take It Away! AS-3
Don't Let MacArthur Fade Away DAM-58
Don't Let It Happen Again FDR-266
Don't Worry About That Surplus BFH-74
Doug MacArthur DAM-14
Douglas & Johnson Melodies SAD-5
Douglas Funeral March SAD-3
Douglas Grand March SAD-8
Douglas Grand March, The SAD-6
Douglas Polka SAD-2; SAD-4; SAD-18
Douglas Schottisch SAD-7; SAD-13
Douglas' Funeral March SAD-9
Douglass [Sic] Grand March SAD-1
Douglass [Sic] Schottisch SAD-13
Down At The Old Watergate RMN-37
Down In Oyster Bay TR-201
Down In Washington USG-241
Down With Anarchy WM-226
Draft MacArthur DAM-32
Drape The Flag Once More In Mourning WM-116
Dream Of Washington, The GW-145
Dream On The Ocean Waltz ZT-24; ZT-25
Drop Of Hard Cider, A WHH-17
Drum And Fife Instructor, The GW-477; TJ-56
Duchess Of The Table D'hôte WHT-12
Duets Of Early American Music GW-619; AJK-59
Dukakis For President MSD-2
Dukakis Has Got It MSD-1
Dwight D. Eisenhower March DDE-11; DDE-26; DDE-42
Dying Groans Of The Tin Pan, The WHH-120
Dying Words Of Little Katy HG-31

E' Day DDE-99
Each As Cool As Coolidge CC-13
Easy Instructor, The GW-470
E.B. Harper Republican Club March MISC-49
Echo Republican Campaign Songs For 1908 WHT-29
Echo Republican Campaign Songster, The TR-141

Echoes From '76 WJB-61
Echoes Of Bonneville FDR-113
Echoes Of 1880 JBW-5
Educational Music Course First Reader GW-328
1888 Campaign Songs BFH-122
1861-1899 One Flag, One Country WM-87
Eighty Years Ago MF-1
Eisenhower DDE-51
Eisenhower Centennial DDE-82
Eisenhower March DDE-53
Eisenhower March, The DDE-16
Eisenhower Song Book DDE-23
Eisenhower Songs, The DDE-31; DDE-33
Eisenhower, The Man Of The Hour DDE-62; DDE-66
El Caney TR-228
El Presidente FDR-276
Elberon To Washington JAG-100
Elected! MISC-104
Election Coming, The AL-305
Election Day Will Prove To All, McKinley Is The Man! WM-304
Election, The People's Right TJ-3
Election Waltz MISC-88
Elegy FDR-223
Elegy For A Young American JFK-58
Elegy For J.F.K JFK-57
Elegy On The Death Of Gen. Washington, An GW-489
Elementary Music GW-557
Elliott, I Wanna To Be A Cap'n Too! WLW-22; WLW-56
Elliott, I Wanta To Be A Cap'n Too! WLW-13
Elvis For President MISC-24
Emancipation March AL-42
Emancipation Quick Step AL-238
Embargo, The TJ-44
Emblem Of Freedom TR-59; WW-43
Emblem Of Peace WW-108
Emblems Of Memr'ry Are These Tears GW-588
Empty Pockets Filled With Love MISC-68
En Avanti! GBM-3
Encampment Quick Step AL-238
End Of The New Deal Dream, The FDR-330
Enjoras AL-86
Ethel Levey's Virginia Song GW-236
Etude, The GW-381; GW-436
Evacuation Day March GW-247
Evening Amusement GW-465
Everett's Funeral March JBL-11
Every Little Boy Can Be President MISC-56; MISC-62
Every Star — Thirty Four MF-5
Everybody Sing WGH-15; CC-44
Everybody Sing Please TR-381
Everybody Song Book GW-555
Everybody's Teddy TR-81
Everyone's Gone To The Moon JFK-24
Everything American Is Good Enough For Me AML-20

Title Index 722

Everything Will Be Rosy With Roosevelt FDR-108
Everything's Ding-A-Ling FDR-155
Everything's OK On The LBJ LBJ-12
Everywhere That Wilson Goes WW-69
Ev'rybody Ev'ry Payday FDR-167
Ex-President Arthur's Funeral March CAA-9
Ex-President Of The U.S.A. WW-205
Executive March WM-23

Face On The Dime, The FDR-207
Faces Of Rushmore MISC-108
Facts And Songs For The People JGB-65
Fairbanks' Republican Campaign Songs WHT-57
Faith WM-264
Fall In! JAG-66
Fall In For Your Motherland WW-23
Fall In Line MISC-63
Fall Into Line For Your Motherland WW-86; WRW-149
Fall Of Mexico, The WS-26
Fall Of Vera Cruz WS-20
Fame And Honor Overture WW-214
Famous McKinley WM-100
Famous Roosevelt TR-112
Faneuil Hall Grand March WHH-65
Far Away Ireland RR-13
Farewell Father, Friend And Guardian AL-51; AL-124; AL-215
Farmer Ben's Patriotic Song And March To Washington City CC-5
Farmer Goes Chopping On His Way, The HG-1
Farmer Henry Krajewski Campaign Theme Song HK-1
Farmer Of Chappaqua Songster HG-23
Farmer Of North Bend, The WHH-9
Farmer Of Tippecanoe, The WHH-91
Farmers And Mechanicks [sic], The HC-52
Farmer's Campaign Song, The WJB-2
Farmer's Dream WM-115
Farragut Revere USG-174
Fashionable Repertory JMD-17
Fatal Shot, The WM-129; WM-246
Father Abraham's Reply To The 600,000 AL-215; AL-285
Father Abraham's Reply To The 60,000 AL-192
Father Kemp And His Old Folks GW-542
Father Kemp's Old Folks Concert Tunes GW-574
Father Of His Country GW-273
Father Of The Land We Love GW-230; GW-285; GW-300
Favorite March, A WHH-140
Favorite McKinley March, The WM-40
Favorite National Songs GW-575
Favorite New Federal Song, The GW-13; JA-1
Favorite Son MISC-113
Favorite Songs And Hymns GW-396

F.D.R FDR-72
F.D.R. Jones FDR-95; FDR-282
F.D.R. Way, The FDR-241
FDR's Back Again FDR-378
Federal Constitution & Liberty For Ever JA-27; JA-29
Federal Follies AML-25
Federal March GW-335
Festival March WS-21
Few Days MF-13; MF-17; MF-27; MF-29; MF-32; MF-36; MF-37
Few Days And Now A'days MF-28
Few Days Quick Step MF-34
Fiat Justitia TR-202
Fifer's Companion GW-117
Fifth Regiment March GW-409
Fight On With Mr. Roosevelt FDR-57
Fighin' Doug MacArthur DAM-6
Fighin' Doug MacArthur U.S.A DAM-27
Fighting Boys In Blue USG-95
Fillmore And Donelson Songs For The Campaign MF-10
Fillmore Mazurka MF-7
Fillmore Quick Step MF-3; MF-38
Fillmore Schottisch MF-2
Fillmore's Prohibition Songs WM-314; JL-1
Fillmore's Reform Songs SCS-1
Firm, The Just & The Brave, The USG-295
Fire Away Galop USG-151
First Battle, The WJB-90
First In Line For 88 GC-69
First Lady, The MISC-68
First Lady March, The BC-4
First Lady Of The Land, The WGH-12
First Lady Waltz, The DDE-85; LBJ-13; LBJ-15; LBJ-27
First President, The GW-374
First Reader GW-328
Five Men On A Mountain JFK-15
Five Popular Whig Songs HC-113
Five Star President DDE-10
Five Stars Are Shining DDE-105
Flag Of Henry Clay, The HC-36
Flag Of Liberty, The GW-348; GC-27
Flag Of Our Union HC-82
Flag Of Our Union Forever WS-11
Flag Of The U.S.A., The GW-206
Flag Of Washington, The GW-203; WHH-23; GBM-10
Flag Song FDR-318
Flag Song, A WM-66
Flag That Has Never Known Defeat, The GW-222
Flag That's Waived A Hundred Years, The GW-264
Flatbush Republican Club March MISC-40
Fleur-De-Lis GW-220
Flight And Capture Of Jeff Davis JD-29
Flower From Lincoln's Grave, The AL-412
Flying Fighters For Freedom WW-47
Foam, Sweet Foam FDR-277

Folio SJT-14; RBH-32; WSH-36; JAG-74
Folk Songs And Art Songs For Intermediate Grades GW-376; AL-322
Folk Songs For Conservatives BMG-13
Follow The President FDR-86
Follow Washington GW-407
Folsom March GC-32
For Brave Men Are They From The Mighty U.S.A DAM-16
For Country Dear WM-202
For Eisenhower DDE-4
For France And Liberty GW-232
For God And Country AL-198
For God And Liberty AL-332
For Grant & Colfax We Will Vote USG-2
For Hancock True And English Too WSH-27
For Hayes And Wheeler RBH-39
For He Is A Democrat GC-41
For Honor, Flag And Nation TR-303
For Old Glory GW-190; GW-200
For Our Country, Home, And Flag GW-432
For President Gov. Alfred E. Smith AES-63
For President Ulysses Grant USG-123
For Right And Dear Old Glory WM-107; WW-209; CEH-8
For Seymour, Blair And Liberty HS-6
For Taylor Ho! ZT-49
For Teddy, He's Our President TR-342
For The Gentleman TJ-18
For The Honor Of The U.S.A WW-123
For The Honor Of Uncle Sam WW-66
For Victory Of Our Country's Flag TR-75
Fore, Ike Is On The Tee DDE-12
Forest Gump, The Soundtrack MISC-134
Fort Harrison March ZT-58
Fort Meig's Grand March WHH-111
Forward, Forward, Together RMN-19
Forward March For Little Mac GBM-54
Forward March Republicans BFH-74
Forward With Roosevelt FDR-231; FDR-233
Four Freedoms, The FDR-249; FDR-373; FDR-374
Four More Years USG-120
Four More Years In The White House WW-7
Four More Years Of Teddy TR-173
Four Northern Heroes AL-305
Four Sad Days JFK-16
Four Songs From Chevy Chase Frantics FDR-382
Fourth Internationale AES-66
Fourth Music Reader, The GW-515
Fourth Of July, The GW-548
14th Regiment Centennial Jubilee GW-532
Fox Marches In The American Way FDR-384
FRA Of Uncle Sammy, The FDR-56
Frances Gavotte GC-44
Franklin D. And Prosperity FDR-375
Franklin D. March FDR-107
Franklin D. Roosevelt FDR-221
Franklin D. Roosevelt March FDR-54; FDR-328

Franklin D. Roosevelt He's Our President FDR-238
Franklin D. Roosevelt's Address To His Forces FDR-175
Franklin D. You're Good Enough For Me FDR-212
Franklin D., Winston C., Joseph V., Victory Jones FDR-177
Franklin Delano Roosevelski WLW-32
Franklin Delano Roosevelt FDR-234; FDR-240; FDR-356
Franklin D.R FDR-62
Franklin Roosevelt, Our President FDR-199
Franklin Roosevelt, There's Nothing The Matter With Him FDR-90
Franklin Roosevelt We're With You FDR-205
Franklin! Winston! Kai-Shek! And Joe! FDR-393
Free Coinage WJB-77
Free Silver WJB-38
Free Silver & Bryan In 1900 WJB-89
Free Silver Campaigns Songs And Poems WJB-84
Free Silver March WJB-48
Free Silver Marching Song WJB-78
Free Soil Minstrel, The MVB-5
Free Soil Quick Step MVB-3
Free Soil Songs MVB-13
Free Soil Songs For The Campaign Of 1848 MVB-14
Free Soil Waltzes MVB-11
Freedom And Clay HC-24
Freedom And Fremont JCF-37
Freedom And Our President TJ-16
Freedom For All Forever WW-12
Freedom Freemen Fremont JCF-7
Freedom-Liberty AL-220
Freedom Of The Seas LC-1
Freedom Songs WJB-67
Freedom's Battle Song WW-133
Freedom's Call FDR-46
Freeman's Call AL-134
Freeman's Glee Book, The JCF-16
Freedom's Martyred Chief AL-487
Freeman's Quick Step WHH-59
Freiheitslied Der Deutschen Republikaner JCF-5
Frelinghuysen's Grand March HC-48
Fremont JCF-25
Fremont And Dayton Campaign Songs For 1856 JCF-46
Fremont And Freedom JCF-55
Fremont And Freedom's All The Go JCF-44
Fremont And Victory JCF-2; JCF-5; JCF-13; JCF-26
Fremont Barbecue JCF-52
Fremont Campaign Songster, The JCF-42
Fremont Glees JCF-38
Fremont Grand March JCF-28
Fremont Hussars March JCF-53
Fremont March JCF-6; JCF-31

Title Index

Fremont Polka JCF-6; JCF-31; JCF-33
Fremont Polka, March And Schottisch, The JCF-6
Fremont Quick Step JCF-34
Fremont Schottisch JCF-6; JCF-31
Fremont Song, A JCF-41
Fremont Song Sheet JCF-25; JCF-27
Fremont Songs For The People JCF-18
Fremont Songster JCF-42; JCF-45
Fremonter, The JCF-49
Fremont's Battle Hymn JCF-32
Fremont's Great Republican March JCF-1
Fremont's March JCF-30
Friend, A MISC-26
Friend Of The World TR-152
Friend Roosevelt FDR-3
Friendly Democratic Relations HST-23
Friends TR-106; TR-107
From The City Streets AES-39
From The Days Of Washington GW-284; GW-338
From The Sidewalks Of New York To Washington AES-32
From The White House To The Sea JAG-4; JAG-117
From Valley Forge To France GW-251
Full Dinner Pail, The WM-203
Full Dinner Pail Was Once Their Cry, A JMC-13
Fun During Recession FDR-295
Funeral Anthem, A JAG-80
Funeral Dirge GW-9
Funeral Dirge Of President Lincoln AL-270
Funeral Dirge Of Zachary Taylor ZT-87
Funeral Dirge On The Death Of General Washington GW-4
Funeral Elegy On The Death Of General Washington, A GW-81
Funeral Honors By The Town Of Salem JA-8
Funeral March JQA-11 WHH-46; AL-24; AL-25; AL-37; AL-66; AL-78; AL-98; AL-102; AL-147; AL-150; AL-151; AL-452; USG-71; JAG-32; JAG-77; JAG-91
Funeral March, A AL-26
Funeral March In Honor Of Daniel Webster DW-1; DW-2; DW-3; DW-8; DW-17
Funeral March In Memory Of John Quincy Adams JQA-11
Funeral Procession Of President Lincoln AL-61
Funeral Service For The Hon. Dwight David Eisenhower, 1890-1969 DDE-84

Gallant Harry HC-83
Gallant Old Hero WHH-2; WHH-30; WHH-114
Gallant R.B. Hayes RBH-62
Gallant Rough Riders, The TR-352
Gallant 71st TR-357
G.A.R. Songs And Other Popular Songs JGB-94

Garfield JAG-109
Garfield, A Nation's Tribute Of Sorrow For Its Deceased President JAC-74
Garfield And Arthur JAG-22
Garfield And Arthur Are The Men JAG-59
Garfield And Arthur Campaign Carols JAG-50
Garfield And Arthur Campaign Song Book JAG-47; JAG-62; JAG-68
Garfield And Arthur Campaign Songster JAG-27; JAG-50
Garfield And Arthur Quickstep JAG-1
Garfield And Arthur Rally Song JAG-22
Garfield, Arthur And Victory JAG-94
Garfield Is The Man! JAG-42
Garfield Memorial Grand March JAG-106
Garfield Now Will The Nation JAG-60
Garfield Rallying Song JAG-82
Garfield Songs JAG-101
Garfield's At The Front JAG-56; JAG-58
Garfield's Funeral March JAG-13; JAG-21; JAG-63; JAG-95; JAG-99; JAG-110
Garfield's Galop JAG-46
Garfield's Grand March JAG-75
Garfield's The Man JAG-82
Garfield's Triumphal March JAG-46
Garfield's Triumphal Song & Chorus JAG-46
Garibaldi's Sicilian March USG-64
Garner The Sheaves With Garner FDR-407
Garryowen TR-320
Gary's Got The Big Mo MISC-124
Gathering Song Of The Whigs Of Williamsburgh WHH-91
Gathering The Forces WM-127
Gavotte Debut TR-391
Gen. B.F. Butler's Campaign March BFB-10
Gen. Breckenridge's Grand Waltz JCB-2
Gen. Butler's Grand March BFB-3
Gen. Eisenhower's Triumphant March DDE-27
Gen. Freemont's [Sic] War Song JCF-19
Gen. Fremont's Volunteer Polka JCF-29
Gen. Garfield's Grand March JAG-8; JAG-36; JAG-61
Gen. Garfield's March To The White House JAG-61
Gen. Garfield's Funeral March JAG-35
Gen. Geo. B. McClellan's Funeral March GBM-41
Gen. Grant's Funeral March USG-23; USG-41; USG-76; USG-138; USG-177; USG-184
Gen. Grant's Grand March USG-216; USG-280
Gen. Grant's Grand Reception March USG-49
Gen. Grant's Grand Victory March USG-294
Gen. Grant's Heroic March USG-115
Gen. Grant's March USG-50; USG-229; USG-265; USG-274
Gen. Grant's Memorial March USG-200
Gen. Grant's Reception March USG-238
Gen. Grant's Recovery March USG-31

Title Index

Gen. Grant's Welcome Home March USG-188
Gen. Grant's Welcome March USG-14
Gen. Hancock's Campaign March WSH-24; WSH-25
Gen. Hancock's Grand March WSH-14; WSH-21; WSH-24; WSH-25
Gen. Hancock's Victory March WSH-20
Gen. Harrison's Campaign March BFH-52
Gen. Harrison's Grand March WHH-58; WHH-62
Gen. Harrison's Quick Step WHH-54
Gen. James A. Garfield's Grand March JAG-74
Gen. Jas. A. Garfield's Campaign Grand March JAG-18; JAG-52; JAG-96; JAG-119
Gen. Jas. A. Garfield's March JAG-10
Gen. MacArthur And His Men DAM-52
Gen. McClellan's Quick Step GBM-18
Gen. Pierce's Grand March FP-2
Gen. Scott's March WS-32; WS-43; WS-44; WS-45
Gen. Scott's Welcome Home Quick Step WS-3
Gen. Scott's Quick Step WS-16
Gen. Taylor's Quick Step ZT-17
Gen. Taylor's Quick Step At Monterey ZT-34
Gen. U.S. Grant's Grand Reception March USG-49
Gen Washington's March GW-86; GW-98; GW-102
Gen Washington's March At The Battle Of Trenton GW-86
Gen. Winfield S. Hancock's Cincinnati Grand March WSH-4
Gen. Winfield S. Hancock's March WSH-16; WSH-36
Gen. Winfield S. Hancock's Three Cheers For Hancock WSH-4
Gen. Winfield Scott Hancock's March WSH-36
Gen. W.S. Hancock's Grand March WSH-19; WSH-32
General Andrew Jackson's Presidential Grand March AJK-10
General Banks' Grand March NB-3
General Burnside's Grand Triumphal March JCF-23
General Butler BFB-14
General Dwight D. Eisenhower March DDE-71; DDE-76
General Dwight Eisenhower March DDE-44
General Eisenhower March DDE-18
[General] Fremont's March JCF-30
General Garfield's Grand March JAG-76
General Grant March USG-232
General Grant's Boys USG-61; USG-247
General Grant's Funeral March USG-24; USG-42; USG-92; USG-105
General Grant's Grand March USG-12; USG-16; USG-18; USG-70; USG-114; USG-130; USG-134; USG-152; USG-153; USG-161; USG-162; USG-165; USG-166; USG-167; USG-171; USG-176; USG-195; USG-197; USG-198; USG-209; USG-214; USG-215; USG-218; USG-219; USG-226; USG-227; USG-230; USG-234; USG-235; USG-240; USG-249; USG-280; USG-281; USG-282; USG-283; USG-285; USG-285
General Grant's Grand Victory March USG-294
General Grant's Home Polka USG-145
General Grant's March USG-127; USG-128; USG-129; USG-133; USG-135; USG-163; USG-164; USG-170; USG-179; USG-192; USG-204; USG-220
General Grant's March Funebre USG-180
General Grant's Polka USG-16; USG-18
General Grant's Quickstep USG-16; USG-18; USG-22
General Grant's Requiem March USG-223
General Grant's Return Home March USG-18
General Grant's Richmond March USG-107
General Grant's The Man USG-46
General Hancock's Grand Campaign March WSH-6
General Hancock's Grand March WSH-1; WSH-10; WSH-23; WSH-28; WSH-29
General Harrison's Grand March WHH-16; BFH-12
General Harrison's Log Cabin March & Quick Step WHH-50
General Harrison's March WHH-27
General Harrison's Tippecanoe Grand March WHH-64
General Ike March DDE-49
General Jackson's Favorite March AJK-16
General Jackson's Grand March AJK-13; AJK-21; AJK-34
General Jackson's March AJK-36
General Jackson's New Orleans March AJK-6
General Jackson's Waltz AJK-27
General John A. Logan's Grand March JGB-64
General Logan's Grand March JGB-24
General MacArthur DAM-51
General McClellan's Farewell GBM-15
General McClellan's Farewell To The Army Of The Potomac GBM-43
General McClellan's Grand March GBM-6; GBM-13; GBM-34
General Pierce's Presidential Inauguration March FP-6
General Scott And Corporal Johnson WS-18
General Scott's Artillery March WS-47
General Scott's Farewell Grand March WS-25
General Scott's Funeral March WS-42
General Scott's Grand March WS-5; WS-39; WS-40
General Scott's Grand Review March WS-4
General Scott's Quick Step WS-28; WS-42
General Taylor Crossing The Rio Grande ZT-57

Title Index

General Taylor's Encampment Quick Step ZT-4
General Taylor's Grand March ZT-19; ZT-22; ZT-48
General Taylor's Mexican Quick Step ZT-3
General Taylor's Old Rough & Ready Songster ZT-38
General Taylor's Quick Step ZT-39
General, The Sergeant, And The Flag, The GBM-80
General U.S. Grant's Funeral March USG-25
General U.S. Grant's Triumphal March USG-293
General U.S. Grant's Victory March USG-108
General Von Steuben GW-246
General Washington Variations GW-337
General Washington's March GW-2; GW-55; GW-79; GW-117; GW-199; GW-465; GW-476; GW-477
Gen'l Butler's Grand March BFB-4
Gen'l Franklin Pierce's Grand March FP-3
Genl. Fremont's March JCF-4
Genl. Grant's Funeral March USG-25
Genl. Grant's General Election March USG-187
Genl. Grant's Polka USG-154
Genl. Grant's Triumphal March USG-77; Ugg-119
Genl. Harrison's Grand March WHH-66; BFH-4; BFH-5
Genl. Harrison's Quick Step WHH-101
Genl. Jackson's March To Pensacola AJK-4
Genl. Jackson's Triumph Grand March AJK-30
Gen'l. Jas. A. Garfield's Grand March JAG-85
Genl. McClellan's March GBM-38
Genl. Taylor's Quickstep ZT-78
Genl. Taylor's Victory March ZT-36
Genl. W.H. Harrison's Grand March WHH-100
Genl. W.H. (President Of The United States) Grand March WHH-130
Gentleman's Amusement, The GW-74; GW-98; TJ-25; TJ-36; JMD-14; JMN-14; JMN-20
Gentleman's Musical Repository DWC-9; JMD-16; JMN-26
Gentleman's Pocket Companion For German Flute Or Violin, The GW-61; TJ-23
George Washington GW-126; GW-195; GW-286; GW-295; GW-341; GW-353; GW-356; GW-385; GW-390; GW-440; GW-444; GW-445; GW-450; GW-453; GW-455; GW-510; GW-569; GW-612; GW-623; GW-627
George Washington Bicentennial March GW-277; GW-291
George Washington Comes To Dinner GW-231
George Washington Crosses The Delaware GW-371; GW-522

George Washington Dasch March TR-133
George Washington Variations GW-337
George Washington's Birthday GW-454
Get A Jap Or Two DAM-30
Get Busy Over Here Or Over There WW-20
Get Down On Your Knees O' America AL-308
Get Ike DDE-52; DDE-61; DDE-104
Get Off The Track JBR-2
Get On The Raft With Taft WHT-4
Get On Your Bike And Hike For Ike DDE-79
Get Out And Fight For Ike DDE-110
Get Out And Vote! CC-56
Get Yourself A Nice Brown Derby AES-26
Gettysburg AL-202; AL-342
Gettysburg Address AL-190; AL-222; AL-323; AL-342; AL-369
Gettysburg Hymn, The AL-186; AL-372
Gimmie Jimmie Cox JMC-4
Girl From Jones Beach RR-15; RR-24
Girl I Love Is A Democrat, The FDR-105
Girl With The Paint On Her Face, The FDR-252
Give 'Em Hell MacArthur DAM-46
Give Blaine And Logan Three Times Three JGB-15
Give Hayes And Hayes Three Times Three RBH-54
Give Out! FDR-413
Give The Devil His Dues JMC-9
Give Thanks All Ye People AL-289
Give Us A League Of Nations WW-51
Give Us Back Little Mac Our Old Commander GBM-20
Give Us Back Our Old Commander GBM-7; GBM-30
Give Us Just Another Lincoln AL-221; AL-492
Give Us Silver Jolly Silver WJB-13
Give Us Teddy TR-367
Give Us The Grand Old Party WGH-60
Glad To Be Home MISC-68
Gleaner Songbook And Democratic Handbook SAD-17
Gloom Is Cast O'er All The Land, A AL-169
Gloria Old Glory GW-183
Gloria Washington GW-331
Glorious Days Of Washington, The GW-263
Glorious Heroes Of The Great World War! WGH-7
Glorious Nineteen, The AJN-22
Glorious Star Spangled Banner, The GW-287
Glory CC-48
Glory! Glory! Hallelujah WM-127
Glory Of A Reunited Nation WSH-45
Glory Of Peace, The WW-98; WW-192
Go Ahead Vote For Teddy Roosevelt TR-313
Go And Vote For Teddy Roosevelt TR-162; TR-241
Go Go GoRepublican RMN-39
Go Go Go With Rockefeller GRF-6
Go G.O.P DDE-15; DDE-54

Go! Grant, Go! SJT-17
Go Right Along Mr. Wilson WW-36
Go Rough Riders, Go TR-220
Go With Goldwater BMG-3
God Bless And Keep Our President FDR-410
God Bless Our Late Commander In Chief FDR-118
God Bless Our President FDR-79; FDR-193; FDR-257; FDR-420; FDR-421
God Bless President Dewey TED-25
God Bless President MacArthur DAM-23
God Bless The Little Woman JAG-84
God Bless The Name Of Washington GW-118
God Bless The President AJN-8
God Bless The Soldier BFB-12
God Bless You:.FDR-412
God Bless You MacArthur DAM-5
God Bless You Mr. Roosevelt FDR-307
God Protect Our President FDR-262
God Reigns, Our Country's Safe JAG-7
God Save Great Washington GW-61; GW-465; GW-472
God Save Our President JB-11; JAG-6; JAG-64; JAG-74; TR-140; TR-379; WHT-20; MISC-71; MISC-171
God Save Our President From Every Harm JAG15
God Save The Grand Old Stars And Stripes! GBM-33
God Save The Great Washington GW-465
God Save The Union JB-10
Godlike Washington GW-111
God's Gift To The U.S.A FDR-129
God's Will, Not Ours Be Done WM-157
Goin' To The Polls WM-127
Gold And McKinley For Me WM-212
Gold Is The Standard To Win WM-198
Gold Standard, The WM-316
Golden Book Of Favorite Songs GW-379 GW-527
Golden Gems WM-284
Golden Glees:GW-553; AL-487
Golden Glory, The WM-279
Golden Greeting, The WM-290
Golden Rod TR-250; TR-363
Golden Star, The TR-249
Golden West TR-76
Golden Wreath GW-554; MF-36
Goldwater BMG-5
Goldwater Anthem, The BMG-2
Goldwater-Miller Team BMG-12
Goldwater Presidential Campaign Song BMG-8
Gone WW-103
Gone! Brave One, Gone! USG-33
Gone With The Winner! FDR-394
Good By, Teddy! You Must March! March! AP-3
Good-Bye Cal, Hello Al AES-10; AES-19; AES-23
Good Bye, Good-Bye Alice Darling TR-275

Good-Bye Jeff JD-27
Good-Bye Mr. Hoover FDR-148
Good-Bye Prohibition FDR-347
Good-Bye, Shot And Shell WW-33
Good Bye Teddy Roosevelt TR-211
Good Bye To All, Good Bye WM-30
Good-Bye To Cleveland WM-127
Good Bye Ulysses HG-1
Good Evening, Mr. President DDE-67
Good Government March WW-91
Good Hard Cider WHH-2; WHH-30
Good Luck AES-34; AES-36
Good Morning, Master Lincoln AL-434
Good Neighbor, A FDR-286
Good Old Father Abraham AL-155
Good Old U.S.A., The FDR-92
Good Times Candidate Will Win, The WM-159
Good Times Will Come In When Grover Goes Out GC-122
Good Times With Hoover, Better Times With Al AES-9
Goodbye, Jeff! JD-24
G.O.P TR-66; WLW-52
G.O.P. Looks Good To Me WGH-57
G.O.P. March WM-6; WM-63; TR-26; AML-9; WLW-2; WLW-52
G.O.P. Songs WGH-61
G.O.P. Songster WGH-43
G.O.P. Or Is It Gyp? FDR-222
Gospel, Patriotic And Temperance Songster GW-415
Gov. Bank's Grand March NB-2
Gov. Bank's Quick Step NB-1
Gov. Benjamin F. Butler's Grand March BFB-1
Gov. Cleveland's Grand March GC-48; GC-115
Gov. Cleveland's Triumphal March GC-147
Gov. Everett's Grand March JBL-8
Gov. Everett's Quick Step JBL-6
Gov. Hayes Campaign Grand March RBH-27
Gov. Hayes Grand March RBH-8
Gov. Hendrick's Quick Step GC-84; GC-148
Gov. Roosevelt's Rough Riders TR-11
Gov. Rutherford B. Hayes Grand March RBH-13
Gov. Samuel J. Tilden's Grand March SJT- 14; SJT-18
Gov. Seymour's Grand Waltz HS-7
Gov. Tilden Is Our Man SJT-24
Gov. Tilden's Grand March SJT-18; JT-23
Govenor [Sic] Tompkins Parade March JMN-20
Governer [Sic] Thompkins [sic] Grand March JMN-19
Governer [sic] Thompkins [sic] Grand March Of Salute JMN-19
Governor De Witt Clinton's Grand March DWC-2
Governor Polk's Quick Step JKP-6

Title Index

Governor Roosevelt March FDR-144
Governor Seymour's Grand March HS-9
Governor Seymour's Grand Victory March HS-9
Governor Tomkins's [sic] New Grand March & Pas Redouble JMN-16
Governor Tompkins's Grand March JMN-15
Governor Tompkins's Grand Slow March JMN-26
Governor Tompkins's March JMN-17
Governor Tompkins's Quick Step JMN-17; JMN-26
Gov'nr. Cox You'll Surely Do JMC-12
Govr. Polk's March And Quick Step JKP-8
Graduating Song WS-30
Grand Army War Songs GW-570
Grand Canal March DWC-6
Grand Centennial March GW-44
Grand Centennial Triumphal March USG-104
Grand Funeral March AJK-19; ZT-50; AL-80
Grand Inaugural Polonaise AL-160
Grand Inauguration March ZT-20
Grand International Medley GW-130
Grand March WHH-93; JT-12; RBH-41
Grand March Of The Southern Confederacy JD-15
Grand Marche Des Wide Awakes AL-123
Grand National March AJK-33
Grand National Waltzes ZT-43
Grand Old Party, The BFH-74; WLW-45
Grand Old Red Bandana GC-53
Grand Republic Galop RBH-65
Grand Reunion AL-306
Grand Reunion March USG-237
Grand Slow March, A WS-29
Grand Triumphal March ZT-8; WSH-34
Grand Triumphal Quick Step ZT-15
Grand Victory March WM-270
Grandest One Of All WW-174
Grandly The Loyal Hosts Are Marching RBH-22
Graduate Of Coin's School WJB-76
Grant, A Nation's Hero USG-21; USG-117; USG-169
Grant, A Soldier And A Man USG-136; USG-146
Grant & Colfax USG-29
Grant & Colfax Campaign March, The USG-1
Grant & Colfax Campaign Songster, The USG-278
Grant & Colfax Club, Ward 11 Songsheet USG-140
Grant & Colfax Grand March, The USG-6; USG-54
Grant & Colfax, Our Nation's Choice USG-3
Grant And Colfax Republican Songster, The USG-63
Grant And Colfax Songster, The USG-65
Grant And Colfax Spread-Eagle Songster, The USG-65
Grant And Lee At Appomattox USG-213
Grant And Peace USG-112
Grant And Wilson Campaign Songster USG-69; USG-143; USG-256
Grant And Wilson Tanner And Shoemaker Melodist USG-262
Grant At The Head Of The Nation USG-48
Grant Boys Of 72 USG-228
Grant Campaign Song, The USG-35
Grant Campaign Songster, The USG-75; USG-149; USG-254
Grant-Ed USG-26
Grant Glee Club Book, Buffalo USG-255
Grant Has Passed Away USG-40
Grant Is Gone USG-38
Grant Is The Man USG-8
Grant March USG-174
Grant Memorial Day March And Two-Step USG-82
Grant Memorial March USG-193
Grant Our Great Commander USG-5; USG-55
Grant Pill, The USG-68; USG-279; MISC-139
Grant Polka Brilliant USG-292
Grant Shall Be President USG-86
Grant Song, A USG-62
Grant Songster, The USG-32; USG-113
Grant, The Daring, The Lion Hearted USG-99
Grant Us Another Term USG-94
Grant Will Do Four More Years USG-120
Grant's Birthday USG-182
Grant's Campaign March USG-9; USG-30
Grant's Galop To The White House USG-9; USG-30
Grant's Grand March USG-77; USG-102; USG-131; USG-289
Grant's March USG-132; USG-142; USG-160; USG-212; USG-244
Grant's March To The White House USG-47
Grant's Our Banner Man USG-121
Grant's Presentation Grand March USG-101
Grant's The Man USG-96; USG-300
Grant's Triumphal M'ch USG-212
Grant's Welcome USG-11
Grave Of Henry Clay, The HC-59
Grave Of Washington, The GW-119; GW-354; MISC-171
Great Adventure, The TR-347
Great American, The TR-63
Great Centennial Republican Campaign Songster, The RBH-47
Great Coming Contest, The USG-85
Great Commotion, The RBH-60
Great Defender, The GW-539
Great Democratic Song FP-5
Great McKinley Bill, The WM-161
Great Memorial Day March And Two Step, The USG-82
Great Society, The LBJ-5
Greeley And Brown Campaign Hand-Book For 1872 HG-26

Greeley And Brown Songster HG-24
Greeley & Brown's Galop To The White House HG-1
Greeley Campaign Songster HG-21
Greeley's Favorite Polka HG-1
Greeley's Galop HG-10
Greeley's Grand March HG-1; HG-10
Green Mountain Farmer, The JA-17
Greenback And Labor Songs PC-2
Greenback Quick Step AL-88
Greenback Song Book BFB-18
Greenbacks! AL-90
Grover Cleveland March GC-165
Grover Cleveland's Campaign March GC-19; GC-60
Grover Cleveland's Grand March GC-13; GC-22
Grover Cleveland's Presidential Grand March GC-85
Grover Cleveland's Second Term Triumphal March GC-16
Grover's Lam(O)Ent BFH-74
Guiteau's March To Hades JAG-70
Gulliver's Travelers TED-31
Gwine To Change Dat White House Black MISC-38

Hail, America, Hail GW-110
Hail! Benjamin And Whitelaw FH-12
Hail, Brave Garfield! JAG-46; JAG-48
Hail Columbia GW-13; GW-21; GW-58; GW-59; GW-63; GW-70; GW-76; GW-80; GW-83; GW-88; GW-90; GW-112; GW-129; GW-130; GW-135; GW-139; GW-141; GW-155; GW-156; GW-157; GW-158; GW-159; GW-160; GW-172; GW-174; GW-183; GW-185; GW-194; GW-244; GW-254; GW-255; GW-258; GW-260; GW-261; GW-265; GW-266; GW-267; GW-269; GW-281; GW-299; GW-302; GW-312; GW-313; GW-316; GW-323; GW-324; GW-328; GW-340; GW-344; GW-354; GW-355; GW-357; GW-359; GW-360; GW-361; GW-362; GW-365; GW-366; GW-372; GW-378; GW-379; GW-380; GW-382; GW-384; GW-386; GW-387; GW-389; GW-391; GW-394; GW-398; GW-400; GW-401; GW-402; GW-403; GW-404; GW-405; GW-406; GW-408; GW-411; GW-412; GW-413; GW-414; GW-415; GW-416; GW-417; GW-418; GW-419; GW-420; GW-422; GW-424; GW-425; GW-426; GW-427; GW-430; GW-433; GW-435; GW-438; GW-441; GW-442; GW-443; GW-446; GW-447; GW-448; GW-460; GW-461; GW-462; GW-481; GW-482; GW-492; GW-493; GW-495; GW-499; GW-509; GW-513; GW-515; GW-516; GW-517; GW-519; GW-520; GW-521; GW-522; GW-523; GW-524; GW-527; GW-529; GW-530; GW-531; GW-533; GW-534; GW-535; GW-536; GW-537; GW-538; GW-539; GW-541; GW-542; GW-543; GW-544; GW-545; GW-546; GW-547; GW-550; GW-551; GW-554; GW-555; GW-556; GW-559; GW-560; GW-561; GW-562; GW-563; GW-564; GW-565; GW-566; GW-567; GW-568; GW-570; GW-571; GW-572; GW-573; GW-574; GW-575; GW-576; GW-579; GW-580; GW-582; GW-589; GW-593; GW-602; GW-606; GW-607; GW-608; GW-609; GW-611; GW-612; GW-613; GW-614; GW-615; GW-616; GW-617; GW-620; GW-621; GW-626; GW-627; GW-629; GW-630; GW-631; JA-1; ZT-33; BFH-74; USG-182; MISC-155; MISC-168; MISC-169; MISC-171
Hail Columbia And Hail Forever! Hail The Cause WHH-47
Hail Columbia, Happy Land GW-99
Hail Columbia Rondo GW-387
Hail! Glorious Banner Of Our Land GBM-5; GBM-77
Hail Godlike Washington GW-544
Hail! Hail! Our President FDR-419
Hail Liberty The Sweetest Bliss TJ-15
Hail MacArthur DAM-10; DAM-56
Hail Our Great President FDR-245
Hail Prosperity FDR-259; FDR-260
Hail The Baltimore And Ohio GW-326
Hail The President FDR-196
Hail This Glorious Yankee Land JCF-8
Hail To America WW-92
Hail To Eisenhower DDE-36
Hail To Hoover HCH-54
Hail To Our Ohio Man WM-162
Hail To Our President FDR-158; MISC-141
Hail To St John, Our Chief! JSJ-1
Hail To The Chief GW-365; GW-366; GW-379; WM-29; MISC-26; MISC-27; MISC-28; MISC-29; MISC-30; MISC-31; MISC-32; MISC-67; MISC-70; MISC-75; MISC-89; MISC-96; MISC-119; MISC-123; MISC-129; MISC-131; MISC-151; MISC-155; MISC-159; MISC-165; MISC-168; MISC-170; MISC-173; MISC-174; MISC-176; MISC-177; MISC-178; MISC-183
Hail To The Chieftain & Statesman! WS-9
Hail To The Hero WHH-91
Hail To Hoover HCH-54
Hail To The Nation TR-86
Hail To The Spirit Of Freedom GW-245
Hail To The United Nations DDE-70
Hail To Washington GW-449
Hail Washington GW-584
Hamilton Democratic Glee Club Songster GC-144
Hancock And English Campaign Song Book WSH-35
Hancock And English Campaign Song Book For 1880 WSH-40

Title Index

Hancock And English Campaign Songster WSH-38
Hancock And English Campaign Carols WSH-38
Hancock And English Democratic Campaign Song Book WSH-37; WSH-39
Hancock And English Union March WSH-18
Hancock Peace And Liberty WSH-17
Hancock Polka WSH-30
Hancock The Nation's Choice WSH-5; WSH-44
Hancock The True And Brave WSH-44
Hancock's Grand March WSH-22; WSH-33; WSH-43
Hancock's March WSH-22
Hancock's Triumphal March WSH-44
Hancock's Victory March WSH-7; WSH-19
Hancock's Victory Song WSH-8; WSH-19
Hand That Held Greeting And Death, The WM-207
Hands Across The Continent TR-198
Hands Across The Sea FDR-23
Handy Andies Of The C.C.C., The FDR-359
Handy Andy Polka AJN-23
Hang In There Mr. President RMN-22; RMN-31
Hang Out For Scott The Banner WA-46
Hank Monk Schottische HG-19
Happiness Awaits Me WM-227
Happy Birthday America AL-249
Happy Days Are Here Again BC-5
Happy Days With Landon AML-7
Happy Democrats Are We LBJ-21
Happy Farmer Wants Hoover, The HCH-64
Happy I Am FDR-422
Happy Landin' With Landon AML-5
Happy New Year To Commodore Rodgers, A JMD-10
Happy Warrior, The AES-28
Happy Warrior Al AES-40
Hard Cash And Better Times RBH-16
Hard Cider Quick Step, The WHH-97
Hard Times In Dixie JD-9
Harding WGH-10
Harding And Coolidge Campaign [Songsheet] WGH-15; WGH-20
Harding And Coolidge Song WGH-20
Harding Campaign Songs WGH-31
Harding March WGH-4; WGH-24; WGH-30
Harding Songs WGH-14
Harding You're The Man For Me WGH-1
Harding's The Man For Me WGH-11
Hark From The Tombs GW-89
Harriman For Me MISC-19
Harrison Almanac 1841, The WHH-89
Harrison Anthem WHH-104
Harrison And Glory WHH-99
Harrison And Liberty WHH-91
Harrison And Log Cabin Song Book, The WHH-76

Harrison And Morton Campaign Songster BFH-83
Harrison And Morton Flag March BFH-28
Harrison And Morton Grand March BFH-42
Harrison And Morton Song Book BFH-54; BFH-95
Harrison And Morton Songster BFH-8
Harrison And Morton's Grand March BFH-24
Harrison And Morton's March BFH-91
Harrison And Reid Campaign Song BFH-66
Harrison & Protection BFH-125
Harrison And Reid Campaign Song Book BFH-35; BFH-78
Harrison And Reid Campaign Songster BFH-49; BFH-51
Harrison And Reid Campaign Songster, 1892, The BFH-117
Harrison And Reid Songster BFH-51
Harrison & Tyler Grand Military Waltz WHH-51
Harrison Campaign Songster BFH-87
Harrison Grand March, The BFH-18
Harrison Log Cabin Song Book Of 1840, The BFH-23
Harrison Medal Minstrel, The WHH-90
Harrison Melodies WHH-86
Harrison Quadrilles WHH-8
Harrison Song, The WHH-103
Harrison Waltz, The WHH-70
Harrison's Campaign March BFH-5; BFH-9
Harrison's 1892 Campaign March BFH-57
Harrison's Grand March WHH-112; WHH-134; WHH-135; WHH-136; BFH-12; BFH-127
Harrison's Grand March To The White House BFH-7; BFH-126
Harrison's Inauguration Grand March & Quick Step WHH-26
Harrison's March BFH-13
Harrison's March To The White House BFH-59; BFH-60; BFH-61; BFH-62; BFH-63
Harrison's Second Grand Triumphal March BFH-81
Harrison's Song WHH-119
Harrison's Tariff Campaign March BFH-16
Harrison's Tippecanoe Songster WHH-126
Harrison's Triumph WHH-20
Harrison's Triumphant March BFH-71
Harrison's Victory March BFH-4; BFH-29; BFH-72
Harry Clay HC-88
Harry Clay And Frelinghuysen HC-8
Harry Clay Melodist, The HC-100
Harry Clay Songster, The HC-101
Harry Clay, We Shall Ne'er See His Like Again HC-19
Harry S. Truman March HST-5; HST-16; HST-18; HST-24
Harry Truman HST-8
Harvey's Free Silver March WJB-80
Hats Off To MacArthur DAM-3

Have A Drink, Boys FDR-402
Have You Ever Tried To Count To A Billion
  AML-2
Have You Seen Him AL-349
Have You Seen Sam? MF-15
Have You Seen Uncle Sam, Boys? MF-22
Haven On Earth LBJ-28
Having A Time GRF-10
Hayes And Victory RBH-31
Hayes And Wheeler Are Our Choice RBH-59
Hayes And Wheeler Are The Men RBH-17
Hayes And Wheeler Campaign Song RBH-6
Hayes And Wheeler Campaign Song Book
  RBH-11
Hayes And Wheeler Campaign Carols RBH-4
Hayes And Wheeler Campaign Songster
  RBH-4; RBH-52
Hayes And Wheeler Grand March RBH-1;
  RBH-2; RBH-3; RBH-36; RBH-42
Hayes And Wheeler Grand Waltz RBH-2
Hayes And Wheeler Hurrah; Hurrah! RBH-35
Hayes And Wheeler Are Our Choice RBH-59
Hayes And Wheeler Polka RBH-53
Hayes And Wheeler Rallying Song, The RBH-41
Hayes And Wheeler Song Book RBH-20;
  RBH-33
Hayes And Wheeler's Favorite Polka RBH-29
Hayes And Wheeler's Galop To The White
  House RBH-29
Hayes' Campaign March RBH-29
Hayes' Campaign Quickstep RBH-29
Hayes For Our President RBH-22
Hayes Grand March RBH-21; RBH-41
Hayes Illustrated Campaign Song And Joke
  Book, The RBH-49
Hayes Is The Man RBH-10
Hays Songsheet RBH-39
Hayes The True And Wheeler Too! RBH-15
He Always Wears An Old White Hat HG-1
He Bade Us All Good-Bye WM-89
He Enlisted With The U.S. Volunteers TR-273
He Gave Us Wilson WW-196
He! HAW! The Democratic Mule FDR-339
He Is Surging On TR-382
He May Be Your Man AL-321
He Rambled Away From His Native Home
  TR-181
He Used To Be One Of The Boys In Blue
  MISC-94
He Was A Wonderful Man GW-236
He Was Your Friend And Mine FDR-157
Head Of The Nation McClellan Shall Be, The
  GBM-53; GBM-54
Head-Quarters Republican Glee Book BFH-14
Health To The Farmer, A HC-38
Heart Of Gold RR-18
Heart Of The Nation Is Sad To Day, The
  JAG-67

Heather Bell And Other Poems, The BFH-118
Heaven In My Heart AL-321
Heaven Watch The Philippines DAM-42
Heavenly Flag, The TR-375
Heifer Dance BFB-5
Heil Dir Garfield JAG-46
Hello Americans FDR-387
Hello Billy BC-2
Hello Jimmy JEC-1
Hello Lyndon LBJ-20; LBJ-23
Hello Ronnie, Good-Bye Jimmy RR-5
Helmer's Lincoln Song AL-50
Helmick's Republican Campaign Song Book
  RBH-14
Help Hoover Win The War HCH-61
Help Truman Win HST-27
Helping Hands Across The Seas FDR-322
Hen In The Nest, A MISC-42
Henry Clay Almanac, For The Year Of Our
  Lord 1844, The HC-109
Henry Clay Almanac, For The Year Of Our
  Lord 1843, The HC-108
Henry Clay Grand Funeral March HC-29
Henry Clay Grand Gallppade HC-81
Henry Clay March HC-68
Henry Clay's Funeral March HC-91
Henry Clay's Funeral March No. 1 HC-34
Henry Clay's Funeral March No. 2 HC-34
Henry Clay's Grand March HC-7; HC-30;
  HC-79; HC-80
Henry Clay's Grand March, Waltz & Quick
  Step HC-7
Henry Clay's Quick Step HC-24
Herbert Hoover March, The HCH-56
Here Sleeps The Hero USG-172
Here We Come Mr. President FDR-151; FDR-152; FDR-153
Here's Success To McKinley WM-75
Here's To Doug MacArthur DAM-47
Here's To The Name Of Roosevelt FDR-128
Here's To The Noble Rough Riders TR-115
Here's To The Stars And Stripes TR-240
Here's To You Harry Clay HC-19; HC-20
Here's To You, MacArthur DAM-13
Hero Of San Juan, The TR-12
Hero Of The European War, The WW-15
Hero Of The West, The WHH-91
Hero Who Dares, Is The Hero Who Wins,
  The ZT-60
Heroes Of The Republic, The GW-130
Heroes Of Today TR-134
He's A Great American FDR-75; FDR-416
He's A Winner WHT-24
He's Coming Back TR-40
He's Doing It Now FDR-119
He's Everybody's President Now WW-52
He's Gone To The Arms Of Abraham AL-53;
  AL-162; AL-167; AL-359; AL-366
He's Good Enough For Me TR-60
He's My Uncle FDR-296
He's On Our Side FDR-326

Title Index

He's Our Al AES-7; AES-54
He's The Man Of The Hour AML-19
He's The People's Choice FDR-197
Hey Look Him Over BMG-11
Hey! Mr. President RMN-20
Hi, Ho Hail The New Deal FDR-261
Hi, Ho Hi, Ho WLW-37
Hickory Tree AJK-38
Hickory Twigs AJK-49
Hike With Ike DDE-1; DDE-56; DDE-87
Hill Country Theme, The LBJ-10
Hillary, O! Hillary BC-12
Hills, The Devil And MacArthur, The DAM-18
Hip! Hip! Hurrah For Seymour And Blair HS-10
Hip! Hip! Hurrah For Teddy Roosevelt TR-180; TR-210
Hip, Hip, Hurrah, Harrison! BFH-68
Hip! Hip! Hurray For Roosevelt FDR-112
Hiram Johnson You're The Man TR-263
His Excellency Governor Clinton's Grand March And Quick Step DWC-1
His Name Is General G JAG-37; JAG-55; JAG-74
His Name Is General Jas. G. Blaine JGB-30
His Soldiers To Jefferson D. JD-57
History Repeats Itself JFK-28
Ho! Ho! For Teddy! TR-311
Hoagy Carmichel's Songs For Children GW-347
Hobart March And Two Step, The WM-154
Hold Firm The American Way DDE-50; MISC-146
Hold On Abraham AL-46; AL-174; AL-489; AL-503
Hold That Line For F.D.R FDR-21
Hold The Fort For Blaine And Logan JGB-15
Hold The Fort For Hayes And Wheeler RBH-22
Home Again TR-319
Home Echoes GW-341
Home For The Flag, A BFH-74
Home Of Washington, The GW-278
Home On The Range FDR-317
Home Sweet Home WGH-28
Homes' Patriotic Songs For Coming Campaigns USG-257
Homestead Strike And Protection GC-124
Homage To Roosevelt FDR-248
Hon. Grover Cleveland's March Gg-107
Hon. Grover Cleveland's March Brilliant GC-39
Hon. Horace Greeley Funeral March HG-28
Hon. Jas. G. Blaine's Grand March JGB-17
Hon. S. Grover Cleveland's Campaign Grand March GC-47
Hon. S.A. Douglas/Hon. A. Lincoln SAD-15
Hon. Theodore Roosevelt TR-128
Honest Abe AL-228; AL-473
Honest Abe And Hamlin True AL-300

Honest Abe's Songster AL-77
Honest Little Dollar, The WM-166
Honest Old Abe AL-9
Honest Old Abe's Quick Step AL-45
Honest Zack ZT-82
Honl. James G. Blaine's Quick March To The White House JGB-92
Honor To Our President FDR-93
Honor To Washington GW-346; JBL-3
Honor You Today, Lincoln Oh Lincoln AL-413
Honorable Alfred Smith, The AES-44
Hoo Hoo Hoover HCH-16
Hooligan's Twins TR-370
Hooray For Bill McKinley And That Brave Rough Rider Ted WM-324
Hoosier Johnny AL-476
Hoover HCH-28; HCH-33
Hoover And Curtis HCH-1; HCH-41
Hoover And Lindbergh HCH-52
Hoover Campaign Song HCH-52
Hoover-Curtis Rhode Island Campaign Song HCH-58
Hoover For President HCH-27
Hoover Hoover HCH-55
Hoover Hooverize HCH-35
Hoover Is O.K. HCH-25
Hoover Is The Man HCH-24
Hoover Made A Soup Houn' Out O' Me MISC-14
Hoover Over HCH-46
Hoover Rally Song HCH-12
Hoover Songs HCH-40
Hoover The Great HCH-7
Hoover The Man For Uncle Sam HCH-3
Hoover There HCH-52
Hoover We Want Hoover HCH-5; HCH-6; HCH-34
Hooverize HCH-38; HCH-42
Hoover's Who HCH-62
Hope Of The World America WW-144
Horace And No Relations HG-9; HG-10
Horace Greeley Campaign Songster HG-25
Horace Greeley Grand March HG-13; HG-15
Horace Greeley Campaign Songster HG-25
Horace Greeley Quickstep HG-30
Horace Greeley's Campaign Songster HG-27
Horace Greeley's Grand March HG-4; HG-12; HG-13
Horace Greeley's Is On The Track HG-16
Horace Greeley's March HG-8; HG-17
Horace Greeley's Schottisch HG-13
Horace Greeley's Waltz HG-13
Horray For Bill McKinley And That Brave Rough Rider, Ted WM-257
Horray For Spinach RR-12
Hot Corn, Hot Corn HG-18
How About A Cheer For The Navy RR-19; RR-20
How Are You Conscript? AL-364; WSH-26
How Are You Greenbacks! AL-87; AL-89; AL-376

How Can I Make A Dollar WJB-42
How Could Washington Be A Married Man GW-191
How Do You Like It Jefferson D? JD-18; JD-60
How It Happened WJB-1
How Sleep The Brave Who Sink To Rest USG-225
How The Slave Loved Lincoln AL-516
How The Veterans Broke Up Jeff Davis' Ball JD-40
How To Close The War GW-428
Howe's Diamond School For The Violin GW-568; TJ-70; AJK-55; WHH-136; ZT-81; WS-45; MISC-174
Howe's School For The Violin GW-535; WHH-134; WS-43
Hubert H. Humphrey March HHH-2; HHH-5
Hubie Humphrey — We Love You HHH-1
Hughes And Fairbanks Campaign Song Book CEH-1
Hu-Lah For Hal-Li-Son BFH-92
Humanity WW-76
Humanity With Sanity AML-4; RMN-9
Humbug Reform! RBH-18
Hundred Million Strong, A TR-226
Hundred Years From Now, A MISC-140
Hunter's Of Kentucky, The AJK-11; AJK-23; AJK-25; AJK-49; AJK-53; AJK-60; AL-57; MISC-156; MISC-169
Hunting We Will Go, A GRF-5
Hurra For The Union! SAD-10
Hurrah Again For Teddy TR-318
Hurrah For Bill McKinley WM-68
Hurrah For Blaine And Logan JGB-15
Hurrah For Blaine Of Maine JGB-71
Hurrah For Cooper And Cary PC-3
Hurrah For Garfield JAG-82
Hurrah For General Grant! USG-144; USG-264
Hurrah For Grant! USG-93
Hurrah For Grover Cleveland GC-72
Hurrah For Hancock WSH-15; WSH-19
Hurrah For Hayes And Honest Ways RBH-23; RBH-24
Hurrah For Hayes And Wheeler RBH-38; RBH-50
Hurrah For Henry Clay HC-47
Hurrah For Hoover HCH-36; HCH-37
Hurrah For Horace Greeley! HG-32
Hurrah For Jimmy Blaine! JGB-70
Hurrah For Logan JGB-59
Hurrah For McKinley WM-297
Hurrah For Our Leader WW-187; WW-199
Hurrah For Our Own Henry Clay HC-51
Hurrah For Roosevelt FDR-379
Hurrah For The Clay HC-38
Hurrah For The Hayes Ticket All RBH-61
Hurrah For The Major WM-81
Hurrah For The Man We Love GBM-61; GBM-62

Hurrah For Willkie WLW-20
Hurrah Galop USG-202
Hurrah! Hurrah! For Cleve And Steve GC-10
Hurrah! Hurrah! For Gen'l. Grant USG-13
Hurrah! Hurrah! For The U.S.A WW-87
Hurray, Hurrah For Roosevelt FDR-263
Hush My Baby Go To Sleep BFH-40
Hutchinson's Republican Songster For 1860 AL-317
Huzza, For The Railroad! JCF-14
Huzza Song, The USG-246
Huzzah Then For Harry HC-115
Hymn Of Thanksgiving, A GW-215
Hymn On The Death Of President Garfield JAG-53
Hymnes Nationaux Des Allies WW-210
Hyperion Polka GW-164

I Am A Soldier Of The U.S.A DAM-25
I Am An American FDR-268
I Am For Clinton And Gore BC-1
I Am For Hiram March TR-266
I Am For Hiram Campaign Songster TR-269
I Am Proud To Be An American RMN-35
I Cannot Bid Thee Go, My Boy USG-156
I Cannot Support Him! Can You? USG-301
I Care MISC-112
I Could Not Live Without Thee JT-3
I Dance Alone FDR-252
I Dearly Love The Free GW-257
I Do Not Choose To Run CC-20
I Dont Know MF-20
I Don't Want To Be President MISC-53
I Found A Million Dollar Baby RR-17
I Give You A Song MacArthur DAM-39
I Go For Ike DDE-29
I Got A New Deal In Love FDR-331
I Have A Rendezvous With Life FDR-215
I Hear America Calling MISC-126; MISC-127
I Laughed At Love TJ-42
I Left My Heart At The Stage Door Canteen RR-19; RR-20
I Like Ike DDE-8; DDE-41; DDE-93; DDE-95
I Like My President FDR-290
I Love My Home Land WW-128
I Love You O America FDR-189
I Love You Like Lincoln Loved The Old Red-White And Blue AL-213
I Must Have A Dinner Coat FDR-252
I Pledge Allegiance GW-520
I Spell Nation With A Great Big N USG-175
I Spoke To Jefferson At Guadalcanal TJ-28; TJ-51
I Thank You Mr. Hoover HCH-13
I Think We've Got Another Washington And Wilson Is His Name WW-22; WW-41
I Want A Political Man WHT-14
I Want To Be A Captain WLW-12
I Want To Be President HG-11
I Was Born In Virginia GW-327

Title Index

I Went Down To Virginia TJ-42
I Wish I Had A Daddy In The White House MISC-55
I Wish You Were Jealous Of Me AL-321
I Wonder If You Really Know What Wilson's Done For You WW-148
I Wonder What George Washington Would Say? GW-252
I Wonder What They're Doing To-Night AL-219
I Would Still Love You TR-265
I'd Like To Fish With The President CC-4
I'd Like To Shake The Hand Of General McArthur [Sic] DAM-36
I'd Rather Be Mr. Murphy Than The President MISC-84
I'd Rather Be Right MISC-138
I'd Rather Be With Teddy In The Jungle TR-32
If I Were A Fifer MISC-112
If I Were In The Old White House MISC-51
If I Were President CEH-7
If I'm As Good As My Old Dad GW-193
If I'm Elected MISC-161
If It Were Not For Good Old Father TR-58
If It's Good Enough For Washington GW-229
If Smith Sits In The Presidential Chair AES-43
If Washington Should Come To Life GW-196; GW-236; GW-327
If Washington Was Living Now GW-171
If We Had A Million More Like Teddy TR-53
If You Don't Like Our President Wilson WW-3
If You're An American, Be An American Thru And Thru TR-237
Ike For Four More Years DDE-19; DDE-60
Ike Is A Wonderful Man DDE-14
Ike, Mr. President DDE-24; DDE-40; DDE-72; DDE-97
Ike Will Lead The Way DDE-47
Ike's The Man DDE-63
I'll Be Loving You RR-11
I'll Be There With Bells On GW-236
I'll Dream Tonight RR-9
I'll Paint The White House Green MISC-166
I'll Still Love You TJ-42
Illinois AL-204; AL-340
Illinois No. 2 WM-137
Illustrated Campaign Song And Joke Book, The RBH-49
Illustrated Campaign Tilden Song And Joke Book, The SJT-8
I'm A Democrat For Nixon RMN-22
I'm A Member Of The G.O.P MISC-118
I'm A New Yorker For Nixon RMN-10
I'm Coming Back TR-41
I'm For Barry BMG-10
I'm Getting Tired So I Can Sleep RR-19; RR-20
I'm Going To Vote For Al Smith AES-27
I'm Going To Vote For Willkie WLW-26
I'm Glad I'm Home Again TR-126
I'm Gonna Get Him MISC-68
I'm Happy About The Whole Thing RR-12
I'm Just Wild About Harry HST-1
I'm So Lonely Tonight RMN-28
I'm Tossing My Hat In The Ring For Mr. Nixon RMN-38
I'm Wearin' Awa' JAG-78
Immortal Washington GW-382; GW-466; GW-630
Impeachment Polka AJN-7
Impeachment Song AJN-14
In A Few Days, A Few Days RBH-64
In A Moment Of Weakness RR-12
In Battle Then We Will Defend It USG-250
In Canton, Ohio, U.S.A WM-220
In Days Of Old WHH-106
In Democracy We Trust JWD-5
In Dixie's Sunny Land AL-197
In Honor Of George Washington GW-437
In Honor OfMcKinley [sic] Boys WM-327
In Memoriam AL-66; AL-82; USG-80; JAG-51; JAG-73; WM-31; WM-77; WM-88; WM-245; WW-194
In Memoriam A. Lincoln AL-273
In Memoriam Abraham Lincoln AL-153
In Memoriam General U.S. Grant USG-207
In Memory Of Abraham Lincoln AL-154
In Memory Of Wm. McKinley WM-261
In Our Hide-Away MISC-68
In Our Own Dear Homes Again USG-150
In The Beautiful Isle Of Somewhere WW-57
In The Candle-Light MISC-45
In The Jungle TR-343
In The Shade Of Shadow Lawn WW-62
In The Summer Of His Years JFK-4; JFK-38
In The Woods Of Old Kentucky Long Ago AL-191
Inaugural Ball WM-93
Inaugural Ball Waltz, The JFK-73
Inaugural Grand March WHH-48
Inaugural March WM-221; WGH-42
Inaugural March 1893 GC-81
Inaugural Ode, The WHH-13
Inauguration Grand March AL-10; USG-181
Inauguration March GW-178; RBH-34; GC-78; WM-260; WHT-55; DDE-96
Inauguration Polka RBH-41
Inauguration Quadrille ZT-14
Inauguration Quickstep, The USG-126
Inauguration Waltz, The WHH-84; MISC-35
Inauguration Waltzes MISC-160
Incidents In The Campaign HC-119
Independence Waltz HST-12
Independent Party. The PC-3
Inflation Galop USG-15
Inno Republicano TR-227
Instructions For The Piano Forte And English And French Flagelets GW-499; TJ-66
Instructor In Martial Musick [sic] GW-79; TJ-14

Title Index

Instrumental Assistant Vol. 1 GW-467
Instrumental Director GW-493
Instrumental Preceptor, The GW-45
Internationale, The SLP-2
Intermediate Music AL-474
Introductory Music GW-455; AL 375
Irish Democrat WJB-75
Irish Wide-Awake, The AL-502
Iron Brigade Quickstep USG-64
Iroquois Campaign Song Abp-5
Is He The Only Man In The World MISC-68
Is It True What They Say About Roosevelt FDR-211; FDR-319
Is She Dreaming Of Me? TR-224
Is That You Andy? Or My Policy AJN-4
It Gets Lonely In The White House MISC-68
It Is An Age Of Progress USG-271
It Is Only A Little Way CC-19
It Must Be The Spirit Of 76 GW-275
It Takes A Man To Be A Soldier GW-329
It's A Grand Old Flag To Fight For WW-109
It's A Grand Old Land, Lads WW-173
It's A Long Way To Europe, But Teddy Knows The Way TR-301
It's Al Smith AES-73
It's All In The Game CC-45; CC-46; CC-47
It's An Elephant's Job HCH-8
It's Coolidge CC-21
It's Good Enough For Me TR-155
It's Got To Be G.O.P. DDE-88
It's Great To Be A Democrat LBJ-9
It's Like The Promised Land AL-302
It's No Use Standing There A-Knocking Or My Policy AJN-4
It's Nothing But A Bubble TR-30
It's Time For Every Boy To Be A Soldier WW-39; WW-40
It's Time To Dance FDR-115; FDR-116
It's V-V-V For Victory FDR-383
It's You I Want FDR-252
I've Got A Heartful Of Music RR-9
I've Got Another Day From The NRA FDR-145
I've Got To Be Around MISC-68
I've Never Been Over There GW-236
I've Only Myself To Blame TJ-42

Jack Tars March Song TR-316
Jackie Look, The JFK-71
Jackson At New Orleans AJK-41; AJK-54; AJK-55
Jackson Song AJK-38
Jackson's Duet AJK-59
Jackson's Duett AJK-29
Jackson's Favorite March AJK-1
Jackson's Grand March AJK-9; AJK-22; AJK-56
Jackson's Victory Grand March AJK-24
Jackson's Welcome Home AJK-32
James A. Garfield's Grand March JAG-79; JAG-93

James G. Blaine JGB-54
James G. Blaine Campaign March JGB-16
James G. Blaine Grand March JGB-1; JGB-46
James G. Blaine's Funeral March JGB-11
James G. Blaine's Grand March JGB-8
James G. Blaine's Grand Patrol March JGB-49
James G. Blaine's Grand Triumphal March JGB-73
James G. Blaine's Grand Victory March JGB-99
James G. Blaine's Presidential March JGB-18
James G. Blaine's Victory March JGB-6
Jamestown Dixie TR-218
Jas. A. Garfield Funeral March JAG-91
Jas. G. Blaine's Grand March JGB-14
Jasmine Waltz AL-275
J.C. Breckenridge JCB-3
Jeepers Creepers RR-21
Jeff Davis JD-26; JD-32; JD-34; JD-52; JD-62; JD-64
Jeff Davis And His Uncle JD-33
Jeff Davis Brought These Hard Times On Me JD-30
Jeff Davis, Don't You Try To Howl Again JD-55
Jeff Davis' Dream JD-16
Jeff Davis In Crinoline JD-36; JD-48
Jeff Davis Is A Coming JD-39
Jeff Davis March JD-8
Jeff Davis' Retreat JD-42
Jeff Davis' Retreat March JD-41
Jeff Davis's Dream JD-53; JD-57
Jeff In Petticoats JD-20; JD-55; MISC-139
Jeff Wants To Get Away JD-37
Jefferson And Liberty TJ-5; TJ-14; TJ-19; TJ-26; TJ-27; TJ-53; TJ-55; TJ-56; TJ-57; TJ-59; TJ-68; TJ-69; TJ-70; TJ-71; TJ-72; MISC-156
Jefferson D. JD-58; JD-59
Jefferson D-, Sir JD-22
Jefferson Davis Grand March JD-3; JD-54
Jefferson Davis In Prison JD-44
Jefferson's Hornpipe TJ-63
Jefferson's March TJ-1; TJ-6; TJ-7; TJ-13; TJ-17; TJ-18; TJ-21; TJ-23; TJ-35; TJ-40; TJ-54; TJ-58; TJ-60; TJ-61; TJ-64; TJ-65; TJ-66; TJ-76
Jefferson's Quick Step TJ-61
Jefferson's Rondo TJ-36
Jefferson's Violin TJ-50
Jeff's Double Quick JD-12
Jeff's Lament JD-57
Jeff's Last Proclamation JD-21
Jeff's Race For The Last Ditch! JD-14
Jerico BFH-74
J.F.K. Forever JFK-43
J.F.K. In Memoriam JFK-59
J.F.K. March JFK-20
Jim And John JGB-54
Jim Blaine's Spirit JGB-72
Jim Garfield's At The Front JAG-104

Title Index

Jim Reed From Old Missouri MISC-9
Jimmy Carter JEC-2
Jimmy Cox Will Win The Day JMC-5
Jimmy Who? JEC-3
Jitterbug Rock RMN-32
Jobs, Security, Democracy And Peace CP-1
John Bell Polka JBL-4
John Davenport's Own Comic Vocalist GBM-85
John F. Kennedy JFK-1; JFK-2
John Fitzgerald Kennedy JFK-14
John Fitzgerald Kennedy March JFK-25; JFK-51; JFK-53; JFK-67
John Garner FDR-332
John Kennedy JFK-35
John Merryman JD-47
John Quincy Adams JQA-10
John Quincy Adams' Funeral March JQA-3
John W. Davis Is The Man JWD-4
Johnny Fill Up The Bowl! AL-137; AL-157; AL-254; JD-49
Join The Legion FDR-401
Jolly Good Fellow, A TR-4
Jolly Jubilee Blaine And Logan Campaign Songster JGB-85
Jordan Is A Hard Road To Travel FP-7; FP-8
Jordan Marsh And Company's Latest Instrumental Collection AL-314
Journey's End DAM-44
Juarez And Lincoln AL-279
Jubilee Joe LGM-2
Judge's Campaign Song Of The Full Dinner Pail WM-69
Jullien's American Quadrille GW-365; GW-366
Jungle King, The TR-326
Junior Laurel Songs GW-444; AL-369
Just At The Dawn Of Day GW-133
Just For Your Country's Sake TR-257
Just Give Me A Week In Paris WW-127
Just Like Washington Crossed The Delaware GW-211; GW-290
Just Our Al The Workingman's Pal AES-57
Just South'ard Of The Line FDR-335
Just You And I CC-40
Justice To Harry Clay WHH-113

Kaiser Bill TR-102
Kansas Campaign Songs BFH-119
Keep Cool And Keep Coolidge CC-1; CC-3; CC-32; CC-55; CC-57
Keep Cool-Idge CC-25
Keep Coolidge In The White House CC-52
Keep Cool With Coolidge CC-12
Keep Going Roosevelt FDR-380
Keep Him There In The White House Chair FDR-256
Keep Ike DDE-91
Keep The Ball A-Rolling USG-87; USG-231
Keep The Ball Rolling WHH-91
Keep Time TR-287

Keeping Step With The Union WGH-51
Kennedy And Johnson JFK-48; JFK-83
Kennedy At Dallas JFK-26
Kennedy Memorial March JFK-12
Kennedy Victory Song JFK-19
Kentucky Gentleman, The HC-1
Kentucky Minstrel And Jersey Warbler, The HC-17
Kentucky Rally, The HC-39
King Andrew AJK-7
King Of The Sea, The TR-125
Kiss Me As Of Old Mother USG-156
Kisses MISC-98
KN Quickstep MF-11
Knighty-Knighty TED-30
Know Nothing, The MF-21
Know Nothing Grand March, The MF-14
Know Nothing Password MF-25
Know Nothing Polka MF-18; MF-19; MF-24; MF-31
Know Nothing Waltz MF-33; MF-34
Knox Notification Ceremony AML-28
Kranz-Smith Piano Company Song Collection GW-447

La Follette March-Two Step RML-1
La Fiesta March WM-265
La Polka JKP-1
Labor Songs SLP-3
L'acquilla Blu FDR-7
Laddie Boy He's Gone WGH-18
Ladies Patriotic Song, The GW-1
Lady Bird JFK-48; LBJ-30
Lady Bird Cha Cha Cha LBJ-14
Lady Cleveland Gavotte GC-154
Lady Madison's Waltz JMD-17
Lady Of The White House, The WM-125; WM-135
Lady Of The White House Grand March, The GC-34
Lady Washington's Favorite GW-71; GW-485
Lady Washington's Reception GW-503
Ladybird's Lullaby LBJ-33
Land Of Lincoln AL-294; AL-325
Land That We Adore, The CAA-4
Land Of Washington GW-76; GW-108; GW-302; GW-354; GW-365; GW-366; GW-519; GW-546; GW-594
Landing With Landon AML-13; AML-15
Landmarks Of Early American Music, 1790-1800 GW-395
Landon Boom Song AML-17
Largest Flag In The World, The WM-317
Last Ditch Polka, The JD-10
Last Race Of The Rail Splitter, The AL-472
Last Words Of David, The JFK-49
Last Words Of Washington, The GW-177
Laugh It Up MISC-68
Laughing Waters CBF-1
Lawrence Quadrilles WHH-53
LBJ Looks After Me LBJ-33

Title Index

LBJ Presidential Campaign Song LBJ-22
L.B.J. Waltz, The LBJ-17
LBJ What Do You Say? LBJ-33
Lead Kindly Light WM-54; WM-103; WM-140; WM-149; WM-233; WM-266; WM-315
Lead Us On Washington GW-243
Leaders Joy Band Book, The GW-403; AL-348; MISC-119
League Of Nations' March WW-56
League Of Nation's Song JMC-1
League Triumphant, The JMC-6
Legionnaire:DAM-59
Legionnaires March GW-209
Lemke WL-3
Lemke Is The Man WL-2
Lemke Victory March WL-1
Les Confederes JD-65
Lester Goes To Ludowici LGM-1
Let Coolidge Carry On CC-34; CC-36
Let George Do It GW-375; GCW-3
Let Gov. Roosevelt Lead The Good Old U.S.A. FDR-389
Let Hoover Carry On HCH-15
Let John Do It JGS-5
Let Me Die, Face To The Foe USG-156
Let Me Dream CC-49
Let No Guilty Man Escape SJT-13
Let Righteous Peace Preside TR-322
Let Ron Do It RR-8; RR-26
Let The President Sleep AL-460
Let Tom E. Dew It TED-24
Let Us Have Free Coinage, Boys At Sixteen To One! WJB-50
Let Us Have Music For Piano GW-433
Let Us Have Peace USG-90; WHT-18
Let Us Keep Our President FDR-388
Let Us Stand By The President WW-104
Let Washington Be Our Boast GW-468; GW-469
Let Washington Rest GW-176
Let Wendell Willkie Spin The Wheel Of Fortune WLW-16
Let Your Hair Down With A Bang FDR-252
Let's All Be For Al AES-52
Let's All Do Do Do With Dewey TED-19
Let's All March To Victory With The G.O.P WLW-34
Let's All Sing GSM-1
Let's All Sing With Hank JFK-48
Let's Fight For Ike DDE-75
Let's Get Behind Herbert Hoover HCH-19
Let's Get Behind The President HST-2; HST-6
Let's Get Together MISC-73
Let's Go Americans FDR-336
Let's Go Back To The Waltz MISC-68
Let's Have A Party MISC-83
Let's Land Landon In The White House AML-6
Let's Lend A Hand To Roosevelt FDR-40

Let's Make Al Smith Our President For Nineteen Twenty Nine AES-24; AES-64
Let's Make It Unanimous DDE-109
Let's O-K, I-K-E DDE-34
Let's Put Barry In The White House BMG-12
Let's Put It Over With Grover GC-42
Let's Rally Boys WW-118
Let's Re-Re-Re-Elect Roosevelt FDR-58; FDR-213
Let's Remember Franklin D. FDR-345
Let's Sing CC-59
Let's Sing For Democracy DAM-21
Let's Sing For The President RMN-11
Let's Stand Behind Great Britain FDR-230
Let's Thank Our Great First Lady GB-2
Letter To A Brother AL-288
Letter To A Mother AL-288
Letter From Heaven, A JFK-23
Letter To A Daughter TJ-48
Letter To A Friend TJ-48
Lexington Grand Waltz, The HC-28
Liberty Bird, The USG-269
Liberty Bell GW-241; GW-354
Liberty Bell Ringing Songs And Poems, The WJB-57
Liberty Enlightening The World GW-245
Liberty For All WW-153
Liberty Minstrel, The JBR-1
Liberty Song Book JBR-3
Liberty Under God AL-234
Liberty's Call AL-91
Lick 'Em With Landon AML-22
Lieu. Genl. U.S. Grant's Grant March USG-20; USG-27
Lieut. Greble's Funeral March WS-27
Lieutenant General Grant's Grand March USG-7; USG-116
Lieutenant General Scott's Grand Funeral March WS-48
Life Begins At 40 WLW-60
Life Of Henry Clay And The Clay Minstrel Or National Songster HC-93
Light In The Window TJ-42
Lillette TJ-42
Lincoln AL-187; AL-188; AL-229; AL-320; AL-360; AL-373; AL-377; AL-398; AL-422; AL-423; AL-0428; AL-441; AL-442; AL-445; AL-455; AL-464; AL-470; AL-471
Lincoln Address, A AL-326
Lincoln And Douglas AL-435
Lincoln & Hamlin AL-112; AL-113; AL-515
Lincoln And Hamlin Songster, The AL 382
Lincoln And Hamlin Campaign Songster, The AL 396
Lincoln And Johnson Campaign Song Book AL-408
Lincoln And Johnson Union Campaign Songster AL-379
Lincoln And Liberty AL-365; AL-475; AL-476; AL-510; MISC-156; MISC-171
Lincoln And The Starry Flag AL-391

Lincoln Boys March, The AL-276
Lincoln Campaign Songster AL-79; AL-81
Lincoln Centennial AL-230; AL-427
Lincoln Club March AL-277
Lincoln Day Souvenir Program AL-373
Lincoln Grand March AL-6; AL-73; AL-232
Lincoln, Grant And Lee AL-263
Lincoln Highway March AL-454
Lincoln Highway March Two Step AL-447; AL-448
Lincoln In Memorium [Sic] AL-274
Lincoln Letter, A AL-344
Lincoln Lies Sleeping AL-60; AL-114
Lincoln Lyrics AL-484
Lincoln Medley Quadrille AL-261
Lincoln Memorial March AL-227
Lincoln Memorial Song AL-399
Lincoln On A Rail AL-384
Lincoln Penny, The AL-181; AL-218
Lincoln Polka AL-4
Lincoln Portrait AL-333
Lincoln Quick Step AL-2; AL-7; AL-29; AL-463
Lincoln Schottisch AL-73; AL-149
Lincoln Speaks AL-345
Lincoln Symphony, A A:-417
Lincoln The Great Commoner AL-207; AL-341
Lincoln The Liberator AL-386
Lincoln, The Pride Of Springfield, Illinois AL-264
Lincoln Tune AL-439
Lincoln Two Step AL-314
Lincoln-Union-Victory March AL-265
Lincoln Way Grand March AL-425
Lincoln We're Proud Of You AL-266
Lincoln's Address AL-482
Lincoln's Birthday AL-355; AL-429
Lincoln's Campaign Song AL-153
Lincoln's College Flag AL-205
Lincoln's Dying Refrain AL-258
Lincoln's Face AL-375
Lincoln's Fame, Lincoln's Bright Name AL-440
Lincoln's Funeral March AL-95; AL-257; AL-259; AL-286; AL-331; AL-407; AL-437
Lincoln's Gettysburg Address AL-185; AL-200; AL-262
Lincoln's Grand March AL-260
Lincoln's Grave AL-108
Lincoln's Inaugural Address AL-507
Lincoln's Land AL-322
Lincoln's Log Cabin March AL-184
Lincoln's March AL-291
Lincoln's Reign AL-436
Lincoln's Requiem AL-145
Lincoln's Tribute To Washington GW-467
Line Up For Bryan WJB-5
Linger, Longer, Lingerie TR-30
L'internationale SLP-4
Listen, American Voters FDR-397

Litoria AL-483
Little Boy Who Never Told A Lie, The GW-279
Little Bronze Button, The GW-133
Little Commander GW-436
Little Dinner Bucket WM-99
Little Frog In A Little Pond, A AL-196
Little John JFK-65
Little Mac GBM-85
Little Mac And Pendleton GBM-54
Little Mac Campaign Songster GBM-71; GBM-74
Little Mac Is On De Track GBM-54
Little Mac Little Mac GBM-84
Little Mac! Little Mac! You're The Very Man GBM-28; GBM-84
Little Mac's March GBM-35
Little More Grape Captain Bragg, A ZT-11
Little Napoleon March WM-296
Little Patriot March GW-351
Little Patriots [Songbook] GW-623; AL-513
Little Patriots, The GW-345
Little Star In The Sky, A FDR-6
Little Tad AL-104
Little Tin Pail Is Empty WM-104
Little Western Man, The USG-118
Little White House Down In Georgia, The FDR-201
Little Willie's Grave AL-431
Live But One Moment AL-118
Live On! Washington GW-228
Live Triumphant Or Contending Die GW-587
Log Cabin, The WHH-2; WHH-30; WHH-116
Log Cabin & Hard Cider Melodies, The WHH-68
Log Cabin Minstrel WHH-71
Log Cabin Or Tippecanoe Waltz WHH-69
Log Cabin Quick Step, The WHH-7; WHH-82
Log Cabin Song WHH-37; WHH-41
Log Cabin Song-Book WHH-56; WHH-127
Log Cabin Songster, The WHH-128
Log Cabin Songster And Straight-Out Harrison Melodies, The [sic] WHH-129
Logan Waltz JGB-52
Logan's Gathering JGB-22
Logan's Grand March JGB-95
London Mathews, The AJK-48
Long Live King Franklin The First AML-16
Long Tall Guy, The MISC-149
Look Ahead Neighbor DDE-5
Look Up America MISC-77
Lost On The Sultana AL-93
Love, Law And Liberty WW-183
Loyal Legion Hymn Abraham Lincoln AL-453
Luci Had A Baby LBJ-33
Lyndon Johnson Told The Nation LBJ-29; LBJ-31; LBJ-33

Title Index

Lyndon Our Boy LBJ-18
Lyndon's Lullaby LBJ-33
Lyre Birds TR-30
Ma Li'l Sweet Sunbeam WM-78
Ma Ma Where's My Pa? JGB-77
Mack And Teddy WM-3
MacArthur And His Minute Men DAM-33
MacArthur For America In 1952 DAM-2
MacArthur For America In 1948 DAM-54
MacArthur For President DAM-1
MacArthur The Magnificent DAM-38
MacArthur The Man DAM-31
MacArthur's Hand DAM-43
MacArthur's Here Again DAM-9
MacArthur's Shift DAM-12
MacArthur Victory March DAM-45
MacArthur's March DAM-49
Mack's Grand Centennial March RBH-23
Madelon WW-126
Madison Square Garden Rally AML-26
Madison's Hornpipe JMD-17
Madison's March JMD-1; JMD-2; JMD-3; JMD-18
Madison's Quick Step JMD-16
Madison's Whim JMD-14
Maj. Gen. U.S. Grant's Grand March USG-36
Major General McClellan's Grand March GBM-8
Major General McClellan's Triumphal March GBM-57
Major General Zachary Taylor ZT-1
Major General Zachary Taylor's Grand March And Quick Step ZT-85
Make A Rainbow BC-8
Make Al Smith President AES-49
Make Willkie President WLW-28
Mama's China Twins GC-113
Mamie DDE-21; DDE-73
Mamie And Ike DDE-74
Mammoth Ox USG-60
Man, The TR-300
Man And A Credit To The Nation, A WGH-19
Man Behind The Flag, The WW-147
Man Behind The Hammer And The Plow, The WW-119
Man From Ohio WHT-44
Man From Tennessee, The MISC-133
Man In Washington, The TR-256
Man Of Destiny March GC-114; WM-14
Man Of The Hour WHT-6; WW-2; WW-58; WW-113; WGH-2; DDE-25
Man Of The Hour, General Eisenhower DDE-2
Man Of The Moment, The TR-138
Man We Will Always Love, The GW-218
Man Who Saved The Nation, The USG-9
Man Who Took The Stand, The WGH-50
Man-Who-Wins, The HCH-11; FDR-414
Man With The Iron Shoe WW-75
Mansion House March GW-451

March JQA:12
March And Chorus In The Dramatic Romance Of The Lady Of The Lake MISC-26; MISC-28
March And Quickstep TJ-43
March De Funebre USG-248
March Funebre GW-8; AL-509
March In Memory Of Washington GW-435; GW-482; GW-567; GW-568
March, March To Harrison WHH-121
March No. 2 To The White House WHT-47
March Of Free Men, The FDR-297
March Of The Boy Scouts WHT-34
March Of The Eternal Flame JFK-56
March Of The Flag Songbook WM-155
March Of The Free WHH-91
March Of The Iron Horse AL-189
March Of The Moose TR-175
March Of The Rough Riders TR-330
March Of The 600,000 AL-468
March Of The Teddy Bears, The TR-299
March Of The Workers, The SLP-2
March Of Victory, The FDR-169; FDR-404
March On For F.D.R FDR-87
March On To Victory WM-111
March On, United Nations FDR-385
March On With Adlai & John AS-2
March On With Roosevelt FDR-9
March Progressive WW-1
March Rough Riders TR-177
March To Democracy AES-6
March To Eisenhower, A DDE-45
March To The White House JWD-2
Marche De Truumphe:TR-374
Marche Du General Taylor ZT-86
Marche Funebre AL-102
Marches USG-282
Marches Of The Presidents GW-618; JA-28; TJ-75; JMD-19; JMN-27; JQA-14; AJK-58; MVB-18; WHH-144; JT-14; JKP-119; ZT-88; MF-38; FP-10; JB-23; AL-509; AJN-28; USG-298; RBH-64; JAG-117; CAA-11; BFH-126; GC-162; WM-326; TR-381;
Marching For The NRA FDR-51
Marching To Victory TR-54
Marching With Ike DDE-80
Marching With McKinley WM-108
Marcia Funerale In Memory Of The Late President Of The United States, Abraham Lincoln AL-444
Marion WGH-37
Martha Washington Dances GW-336
Martha Washington Gavotte GW-144
Martha Washington Grand Waltz GW-143
Martha Washington March GW-143; GW-585
Martha Washington Temperance Songster GW-624
Martial Music GW-488; TJ-60
Martyr, The JAG-34
Martyr Of Liberty, The AL-43
Martyred Patriot, The AL-106

Martyr President Sleeps, The JAG-105
Mary Blaine GC-72
Mary Blane GW-116
Mary's Tears JMN-10; JMN-11; JMN-12; JMN-13
Massa Georgee Washington And General La Fayette GW-101; GW-491
Massa Georgee Washington, Etc., Etc. GW-491
Massa Linkum's Boy AL-409
Massachusetts Collection Of Martial Musick [sic] GW-86
Massachusetts Is Our Home JFK-27
Massachusetts Magazine GW-10; GW-12; GW-16; GW-18
Massachusetts My Home State JFK-33
Matamoras Grand March, The ZT-83; ZT-84
Match Him! USG-97; USG-158
Matched! HS-2; HS-11
Matty's Lament HC-47
May Rose AL-275
McAdoo And The [Donkey] MISC-6
McAdoo'll Do MISC-125
McArthur [Sic] DAM-36
McClellan GBM-1
McClellan And Liberty GBM-61
McClellan And The Union GBM-17
McClellan And Union GBM-53; GBM-61
McClellan And Victory! GBM-2; GBM-65
McClellan Campaign Melodist GBM-27
McClellan Campaign Songster GBM-51
McClellan For President GBM-9; GBM-19; GBM-67
McClellan Is Our Man GBM-55
McClellan Is The Man GBM-11; GBM-45
McClellan Mazurka! GBM-36
McClellan Schottisch GBM-12; GBM-35
McClellan Will Be President GBM-22
McClellan's Address To His Army GBM-78
McClellan's Dream GBM-69
McClellan's Farewell To The Army Of The Potomac GBM-44; GBM-49
McClellan's Quickstep GBM-60
McClellan's Richmond March GBM-76
McClellan's Serenade GBM-37
McKinley WM-102
McKinley And Hobart Campaign Glees WM-278
McKinley And Hobart Campaign Songs WM-280
McKinley And Hobart Grand March WM-65; WM-255
McKinley And Hobart March WM-2; WM-326
McKinley And Hobart Rallying Song Book WM-256
McKinley And Hobart Rallying Songs WM-82
McKinley And Protection WM-83; WM-299
McKinley And Protection Waltz Song WM-247
McKinley And Roosevelt WM-76
McKinley And Roosevelt Campaign Glees WM-95
McKinley And Roosevelt Campaign 1900 WM-84
McKinley And Roosevelt March WM-4
McKinley And Roosevelt Up-To-Date Campaign Songbook WM-216
McKinley And Tanner Campaign Songster WM-282
McKinley Campaign Songster For 1896 WM-277
McKinley Campaign Songster For 1900 WM-275
McKinley Carnation WM-61
McKinley Cyclone WM-323
McKinley Dedication WM-39
McKinley Grand March WM-27
McKinley, Hobart And Honor WM-262
McKinley, Hobart And Liberty WM-272
McKinley In The Chair WM-37
McKinley Inauguration March WM-112
McKinley Is His Name WM-209
McKinley Is The Man WM-73; WM-189; WM-201; WM-219; WM-304
McKinley March, The WM-22; WM-38; WM-55; WM-60; WM-136; WM-177; WM-190; WM-215; WM-303
McKinley March Song WM-179
McKinley Our Choice WM-294
McKinley Our Hero, Now At Rest WM-240
McKinley Our Martyred Son WM-183
McKinley, Roosevelt And The Whole Republican Ticket WM-244
McKinley Serenade WM-313
McKinley Song, The WM-7; WM-102
McKinley Sound Money WM-108
McKinley The True And Brave WM-295
McKinley Triumphal March WM-187
McKinley Two-Step March WM-18; WM-49
McKinley Victory Song WM-101
McKinley We Endorse WM-298
McKinley Will Save Our Country WM-75
McKinley, Roosevelt And The Whole Republican Ticket WM-244
McKinley's Administration March WM-152
McKinley's Champion Protection March WM-44; WM-45; WM-57
McKinley's Come To Stay WM-205
McKinley's Dying Words WM-148
McKinley's Favorite Flower WM-230
McKinley's Funeral March WM-33; WM-222
McKinley's Grand March WM-26; WM-58; WM-71; WM-114
McKinley's Grand Protection March WM-182
McKinley's Memorial March WM-36; WM-141; WM-236
McKinley's Our Man WM-206
McKinley's Own WM-273
McKinley's Republican Victory March WM-59; WM-259

McKinley's Triumph WM-124
McKinley's Triumphal March WM-307
M'Clellan And Pendleton Polka GBM-59
M'Clellan Campaign Songster GBM-72
M'Clellan Song GBM-14
M'Clellan's Band GBM-25
Me And The Women Elected Hoover HCH-20
Meat And Potatoes MISC-68
Mecca Of The Free GW-274
Medal Of Honor March DDE-38
Medley Of National Airs GW-165
Meet Me In Dallas WW-46
Meet The Future President MISC-69
Meeting Of The Waters Of Hudson And Erie, The DWC-3
Melancholy Minstrel, The TJ-42
Melody CC-37; CC-38; CC-39; CC-51
Memorial Day JGB-63
Memorial Services WM-242
Memorial Services For President McKinley WM-232
Memorial Services For President Wm. McKinley WM-241
Memorial Services Upon The First Anniversary of The Death Of William McKinley WM-319
Memorial Tribute, A WM-147
Memories Of Grant At Shiloh USG-194
Memories Of Lincoln AL-421
Men Of 76, The GW-120
Men Of The U.S.A.:CEH-11
Men Of The West JGB-26
Merry Chimes GW-422
Merry Smile, The WJB-12
Merry Songs For Merry Singers GW-434; AL-360
Merry Students TR-186
Meteor-Walzer TR-209
Mighty Nation Weeps, A JAG-87
Military Amusement GW-473
Millard Fillmore's Going Home MF-9
Millennium Army, The JBW-1
Million Thanks To Roosevelt, A FDR-346
Milwaukee Light Guard Quickstep USG-64
Miniature Of Martin Van Buren, A WHH-88
Minneapolis Grand March BFH-19
Minnesota Centennial; Edition Of Our Singing Nation GW-616
Minstrel, The GW-105
Minstrel's Return From The War, The DW-18
Minstrel's Vote For President, The MISC-33
Miss Liberty WM-163
Missouri Harmony, The AL-476
Mister Dewey TED-6
Mister Eisenhower DDE-39
Mister Franklin D. And Mr. Winston C FDR-117
Mister President LBJ-33
Mister President We're For You FDR-247
Mister Wilson We Are Grateful To You WW-182

Mister Roosevelt FDR-329
Mitchell Trio Song Book, The JFK-70
Modern Messiah, A FDR-114
Mollie, Dry Thy Tears Away JAG-114
Money Is The Issue WM-127
Monkey That Became President, The MISC-105
Monody GW-3
Monody On The Death Of A. Lincoln AL-283
Monody On The Death Of Abraham Lincoln AL-151
Monody On The Death Of Ellsworth AL-235
Monroe Doctrine, The JMN-21
Monroe March-Song And Two Step JMN-24
Monroe's Grand March JMN-1
Montana RR-29
Monterey ZT-10; ZT-88
Monterey Grand Waltz JKP-7
Monterey No. #3 ZT-10
Monterey Waltz JKP-7
Montgomery March, The WM-239
Monticello Montage TJ-49
Monticello Suite TJ-39
Monticello Waltz TJ-11; TJ-24; TJ-38
Moon Was Shining Silver Bright, The HC-73
Moonlight Bay WW-126
Mosquito Song WHT-12
Most Popular Edition Of Garfield And Arthur Songster JAG-102
Most Popular Songs of Patriotism GW-531; AL-491
Mother Goose's Campaign Melodies BFH-2; BFH-76
Mother Heed The O.P.A FDR-370
Mother In The Doorway Waiting JAG-17
Mothers Of Men WW-158
Mount McGregor Funeral March USG-288
Mount Vernon GW-61
Mount Vernon Bell GW-552
Mount Vernon Bells GW-543; GW-546
Mount Vernon Polka GW-314; GW-431; GW-505
Mount Vernon, The Mecca Of The Free GW-274; GW-505
Mount Vernon Waltz GW-138
Mourn Not! Oh, Ye People, As Those Without Hope AL-44
Moving Day In Jungletown TR-29; TR-30
Mr. Burr's Hornpipe TJ-13
Mr. Garfield JAG-69
Mr. Harding We're All For You WGH-6
Mr. Harding We Will Vote For You WGH-21
Mr. Hoover And Mr. Smith HCH-4; HCH-53
Mr. Hoover Don't Give Us A Loveless Day HCH-9
Mr. Johnson, The Sandman Said Goodnight BMG-9
Mr. Maddison's [Sic] March JMD-5.
Mr. Munroe's [Sic] March JMN-14

Mr. President MISC-134
Mr. President We're A Hundred Percent For You! FDR-111
Mr. Roosevelt Won't You Please Run Again? FDR-41
Mr. Wilson It's Up To You WW-154
Mr. Yankee Doodle Are We Prepared? GW-271
Mrs. Adams' Hornpipe JA-16
Mrs. Lady Bird LBJ-31
Mrs. Ladybird LBJ-33
Mrs. Madison's Favorite Waltz JMD-9
Mrs. Madison's Minuet JMD-15
Mrs. Madison's Waltz JMD-6; JMD-8; JMD-19
Mrs. Munroes [Sic] Favorite JMN-5
Mrs. Washington's Minuet GW-381
Mt. Rushmore MISC-92; MISC-101
Mt. Rushmore Memorial March MISC-76
Mt. Vernon GW-94
Muck Rake Song TR-122
Mulligan's Campaign Song Book For 1900 WJB-70
Munyon's Liberty Song WM-17
Music Associated With The Period Of The Formation Of The Constitution And The Inauguration Of George Washington GW-188
Music Education Series Elementary Music GW-557
Music For The Campaign WSH-11
Music Hour, The GW-440; GW-513
Music Hour Upper Grades, The GW-612
Music Of George Washington's Time, The GW-187
Music Of America, Songs Of The Union AL-365
Music That Washington Knew GW-184
Musical Harmonist, The GW-94
Musical Olio:JMD-18
Musician's Omnibus GW-567; TJ-69; AJK-54; WHH-135; ZT-80; WS-44; MISC-174
Mutiny In The Nursery RR-21
My Bandana Rag TR-360
My Country MISC-93
My Country Has First Call USG-196
My Country 'Tis Of Thee Song Book JAG-41; MISC-171
My Country's Flag FDR-400
My District 'Tis Of Thee HCH-59
My Dear Harry Won't You Tarry? HST-19
My Dream Of The U.S.A GW-224; GW-289
My Fellow Countrymen FDR-269
My Friend Roosevelt FDR-197
My Hat Is In The Ring TR-109; TR-333
My Hats In The Ring TR-42; TR-44
My Heart Is Buried There AL-208
My Land My Flag AL-361
My Policy Or Johnson On The Brain AJN-6
My Pony Macaroni JFK-34
My Pretty Little Indian Maid WW-220

My Salvation Army Girl WW-189
My Washington Grand GW-225

Name Of Lincoln, The AL-226
Nancy Hanks AL-217; AL-218; AL-247; AL-307
Nasby's Lament Over The New York Nomination HS-19
Natal Throes GW-303; GW-304
Nation In Tears, The AL-20; AL-21; JAG-81
Nation Is Weeping, The AL-109
Nation Loves Its Soldiers Still, The JGB-44
Nation Mourns, The AL-111
Nation Mourns Her Chief, A AL-129
Nation Mourns Her Honored Son, A HG-14
Nation Mourns Her Martyr'd Son, A AL-85
Nation Mourns Its Fallen Chief, The JAG-92
Nation Of The People, The DDE-77
Nation Weeps, A AL-100
National Campaigner WM-271
National Campaign Band Book GC-134
National Campaigner Marching Songs – Republican Clubs WM-283
National Clay Almanac, 1845, The HC-88
National Clay Melodist, The HC-13
National Clay Minstrel, The HC-10; HC-11
National Clay Minstrel And Frelinghuysen Melodist HC-14
National Clay Minstrel And True Whig's Pocket Companion For The Presidential Canvass HC-102
National Clay Minstrel And True Whig's Pocket Companion For The Presidential Canvass of 1844 HC-110
National Colonial Anthem GW-180
National Consecration Chant AL-319
National Democratic Campaign Songster WSH-2
National Democratic Convention Grand March JB-15
National Democratic Convention Polka JB-16
National Democratic Song Book For 1900 WJB-8
National Divertimento GW-112
National Feeling Song JB-19
National Funeral March, The AL-84; AL-138
National Grand March JB-15
National Greenback Labor Songster GLP-1
National Greenback Party Songster JBW-3
National Hymn, A AL-255
National Lament FDR-206
National Lampoon Songbook GSM-2
National March WW-200
National March:USG-287
National March, A FP-4
National Melodies And American War Songs GW-524
National Ode To George Washington GW-292
National Paean, A WM-47; WM-48
National Prayer, The FDR-77

Title Index

National Prohibition Lincoln-Lee Legion, The AL-203
National Recovery March Of The USA, The FDR-301
National Reform SJT-3
National Republican Campaign Song Book BFH-56; WM-309
National Republican Campaign Songs BFH-105
National Republican Campaign Songs For 1888 BFH-74
National Republican Campaign Songster, 1880, Garfield And Arthur JAG-103
National Republican Grant And Wilson Campaign Song Book USG-110
National Republican Rally Rhymes BFH-109
National Republican Song Book:WM-307
National Shrine, The GW-458
National Soldiers Reunion Grand March CAA-10
National Songster, The ZT-44
National Temperance Songster ND-4; ND-5
National Temperance Songster, Revised And Enlarged ND-6
National Union, The HC-31
National Whig Song, The WHH-1; WHH-91
National Youth Lobby HAW-9
Nation's Bride, The TR-377
Nation's Chief Grand March, The GC-89
Nation's Choice, The RBH-2
Nation's Declaration, The SJT-16
Nation's Farewell To Henry Clay, A HC-41
Nation's Hero, The USG-74; USG-91
Nation's Honored Dead, The AL-97
Nation's Prayer For The President FDR-98
Nation's Purest Man, Abraham Lincoln, The AL-76
Nation's Song, The WM-28
Nation's Sorrow JFK-42
Nation's Tears In Sorrow Fall, A JAG-19
Native American Songster, The HC-99
Native Hoosier WLW-61
Nearer, My God, To Thee WM-56; WM-110; WM-233; WM-235; WM-258; WM-266; WM-319
Nell Brinkley Girl, The WHT-12
Nellie Grant's Wedding March USG-37
Nellie Quick Step, The GBM-40
Neutrality WW-138
Never Say You Didn't When You Did GW-321
Never Swap Horses When You're Crossing A Stream WW-9
Never Till The Old Man Comes WM-121
New Administration March, The WM-143
New American Music Reader Number Three GW-437
New American Song Book GW-541; AL-488
New And Complete Preceptor For Flageolets Of Every Description, A GW-486
New And Complete Preceptor For The Fife, A GW-487; TJ-59

New And Complete Preceptor For The Fiff [Sic], A GW-55
New And Complete Preceptor For The Piano Forte, A GW-484
New And Complete Preceptor For The German Flute, A GW-482
New And Complete Preceptor For The Violin, A GW-481; TJ-57
New Campaign, The TR-193
New Clay Song, A HC-76
New Collection Of Songs, Glees, And Catches, A WHH-125
New Deal FDR-381
New Deal, The FDR-109; FDR-156
New Deal In Love FDR-331
New Deal March FDR-142; FDR-395
New Deal March Song, The FDR-138
New Deal Review, The AML-21
New Deal Rose With Roosevelt, The FDR-48
New Exodus, The PP-3
New Frontier, The JFK-9; JFK-45
New Frontiers JFK-54; JFK-54
New Haven Whig Song Book WHH-42
New Instructions For The German Flute GW-472
New Miscellaneous Musical Works For Voice And Pianoforte GW 464
New Music Horizons GW-450
New Hymeneal Courting Song, The WHH-31
New Instructions For The German Flute GW-472; TJ-58
New Jackson Song, A AJK-49
New Lost City Ramblers Songbook HCH-57; FDR-378
New Music Horizons (Sixth Book) GW-518
New New Republicans DDE-86
New 1900 Bryan March WJB-3
New 1900 McKinley March, The WM-13
New Patriotic Songs AL-508
New People's Campaign Songster WJB-62
New President's March GW-26; GW-473
New President's March Or Jefferson's March TJ-73
New President's March, The GW-52; GW-53; GW-54
New Song For The Restoration Of The Constitution, A GBM-66
New Star, The TR-189
New Sunrise, The FDR-324
New Whig Songs HC-16
New Yankee Doodle GW-20
New York Jackson Guard's March, The AJK-47
New York Journal Campaign Prize Song Sheet WJB-95
Next President, The AES-45; HCH-67
Nick And Alice TR-84
Nightingale, The GW-426
Nine Cheers For Old Tip WHH-39
1900 Campaign March WM-5
1936 Franklin Roosevelt Song Book FDR-302

Title Index

NIRA Eagle, The FDR-126
NIRA! NIRA! FDR-355
Nixon Is The Man For Me RMN-5; RMN-8; RMN-16
Nixon Now RMN-33
Nixon, The Man For Us RMN-14
Nixon's The One RMN-12
No Blue Eagle Blues FDR-327
No Crown Of Thorns Nor Cross Of Gold WJB-91
No Depression FDR-161
No Flag Beneath That Starry Banner USG-252
No Flag But The Old Flag MF-4
No Matter Who's Elected, We Have To Eat To Live WHT-45
No Moon At All TJ-42
No More Booze WM-257
No More Johnson LBJ-33
No News TJ-49
No. 1 Of A New Sett [sic] Of Cotilions [sic] MISC-158
No Section Lines JGB-44
Noble George McClellan, The GBM-31; GBM-43
Noblest Of Them All, The WM-160
Nobody Knows How Much I Miss You Dear Old Pals WW-71
Nomination Quick Step MISC-64
Nomination Song AL-41
Nominee, The WGH-3
North Bend Quick Step, The WHH-60
North Dakota TR-52
Northland CC-18
Northmen Awake USG-268
Not By My Vote JL-1
Not For Grant HS-12
Not For Grover BFH-111
Not For Seymour USG-205
Notes Of Victory Grand March GC-125
Now To The Mercy Seat WW-213
Now That Roosevelt's In FDR-418
Now The Trumpet Summons Us Again JFK-74
Now Three Times Three JAG-82
N=R=A Song FDR-316
NRA Song, The FDR-303

O Captain! My Captain! AL-479
O, Come Along And Vote For Hoover HCH-63
O-[Eye]-C JAG-71
O Henry Clay HC-58
O! Jefferson Davis, How Do You Do JD-38
O, Jemmy Bucan! JCF-35
O Ne'er To Man GW-8
O! Van Buren! WHH-91
O! What Makes Grant So Fearfully Frown? HG-3
O, Why Not Name The Baby Teddy TR-317
Ode GW-6
Ode For American Independence GW-16
Ode For Log Cabin Raisings WHH-91
Ode For The Canal Celebration DWC-8
Ode For The Washington Benevolent Society, An GW-490
Ode For Washington's Birthday GW-526; GW-546
Ode For 4th July, 1834 MISC-179
Ode To America FDR-366
Ode To Birney JBR-4
Ode To James Birney JBR-5
Ode To Columbia's Favorite Son GW-12; GW544
Ode To Gen Andrew Jackson AJK-50
Ode To General Jackson AJK-48
Ode To Lincoln 362
Ode To President McKinley WM-153
Ode To Theodore Roosevelt, An TR-253
Ode To The President Of The United States GW-12
Ode To Washington GW-8; GW-525
Ode Upon The Arrival Of The President Of The United States GW-12
Odeon, The GW-517
Off To Work We Go With Wendell Willkie WLW-44
Official Republican Campaign Song-Book BFH-110
Oh, Al You Are My Pal AES-38
Oh, Alf Landon AML-30
Oh, Benjamin Harrison BFH-45
Oh, Coony, Coony Clay JKP-4
Oh Forge Not A Chain For The Brave GW-268
Oh Give Me Time For Tenderness RR-16
Oh Harding WGH-9
Oh Horace HG-7
Oh Jeff! Oh Jeff! How Are You Now? JD-35; JD-61
Oh! Look At That Baby AL-321
Oh! Massa's Gwine To Washington AL-132
Oh, Mr. Nixon RMN-36
Oh, My Darling Mary Jo MISC-175
Oh Poor Jimmy Polk HC-55; HC-87
Oh Roosevelt FDR-307
Oh Roosevelt, Oh Roosevelt FDR-258
Oh Shoot That Snowy Feather GC-158
Oh! Speak To Me Once More! AL-103
Oh! Susanna GW-116; TR-337; AML-10; AML-14; AML-31
Oh, Wallace GCW-7
Oh! What A Difference In The Morning! TR-223
Oh What A Man FDR-323
Oh! Why Should The Spirit Of Mortal Be Proud? AL-47; AL-56; AL-171; AL-223; AL-426
Oh, William Taft WHT-2
Oh You Teddy! TR-279; TR-321
O-Hi-O! WGH-8; WGH-26; WGH-38
Ohio And Warren G WGH-32

Title Index

Ohio Governor's March WM-302
Ohio Napoleon, The WM-142
Oily Blues AES-18
O.K. HC-76
OK Gallopade WHH-35
O.K. Songster MVB-16
Oklahoma TR-189
Old Abe Came Out Of The Wilderness AL-476
Old Abe Has Gone & Did It, Boys AL-39; AL-253; AL-504
Old Abe Lies Sick AL-481
Old Abe Lincoln AL-211; AL-297; MISC-156
Old Abe Lincoln Came Out Of The Wilderness AL-475
Old Abe Polka AL-5
Old Abe They Say Was An Honest Man GBM-48
Old Abe's Gallop AL-267
Old Abe's Lament AL-501
Old Buck Going Up Salt River JCF-27
Old Chieftain, The AL-64; AL-166
Old Familiar Dances With Figures GW-272
Old Favorite Songs GW-582
Old Glory AL-199; WW-137
Old Glory And U.S. Grant USG-141
Old Glory Campaign Songs For Republican Clubs And Singers WM-305
Old Glory Is Calling FDR-396
Old Glory Song Book, The GW-446; USG-259; WW-193
Old Glory Songster WM-174
Old Glory, The Blue And The Grey TR-99
Old G.O.P., The FDR-283
Old Hickory AJK-39; AJK-44
Old Hokum Week AES-68
Old Honest Abe For Me AL-383
Old Independence Hall MISC-34
Old Italian Love Song, An AL-321
Old Kentucky HC-65; HC-72
Old Kentucky Quick Step HC-72; HC-118
Old New Deal, The FDR-417
Old Pear Tree, The GW-170
Old Roman March, The GC-54
Old Rough And Ready ZT-52
Old Rough And Ready Quick Step ZT-28
Old Soldiers Never Die DAM-7; DAM-8; DAM-15; DAM-37; DAM-48; DAM 50
Old Songs You Love GW-416
Old Songs We Love To Sing So Well, The GW-516
Old Tippecanoe WHH-40; WHH-79; WHH-91
Old Uncle Ned GW-116
Old Union Wagon, The AL-11; BFH-93
Old White Hat, The HG-2; HG-22
Old War Songs And New And Old Patriotic And National Songs GW-549
Old Zack Must Be Our Man ZT-54
Old Zack Songster, The ZT-32
Old Zack's Quick Step ZT-27

Ole Shady BFB-6; BFB-7
Ole Uncle Abrum's Comin' AL-485
On A Little Farm In Normandie WW-218
On Freedom's Shore GW-296
On, On, On The Boys Are Shouting BFH-74
On The Avenue WHT-19
On The Banks Of The Wabash WLW-5
On The Banks Of The Wabash Far Away TR-336
On The Death Of Abraham Lincoln AL-482
On The Firing Line TR-118
On The Lincoln Highway AL-433
On The Right Road With Roosevelt FDR-13
On The Steps Of The Great White Capitol GW-311
On To St. Louis With Father Cox JRC-1
On To Victory JAG-111; JGB-74; WJB-92
On To Victory March FDR-321
On To Victory 1908 WJB-28
On To Victory We Go FDR-289
On With Roosevelt FDR-5; FDR-14; FDR-26; FDR-27; FDR-39
On With The Dance HCH-17
Once Every Four Years MISC-68
One Flag, One Country WM-87
One For All And All For One FDR-399
One Good Turn Deserves Another USG-109
100 Years Hence GBM-21
One World WLW-18
Only A Carnation WM-195
Only The Old Flag JGB-27
Onward, Forward, We Must Go LBJ-4
Onward We Go HST-25
Onward With Roosevelt FDR-273; FDR-280
Open Door, The CC-11
Open Letter To My Teenage Son, An GW-333
Open Letter To The President, An RR-22
Open The Gates Of The White House AES-33
Options Are For Opening GRF-10
Oration On The Auspicious Birth, Sublime Virtue And Triumphant Death Of General George Washington, An GW-483
Oratorial Grand March HC-84
Order Of Exercises JQA-8; HC-32; ZT-46
Organ At Home GW-615
Origin And Rise Of Prest. Clay, The HC-19
Original Clay Songs HC-104
Original Democratic Campaign Songs HS-17
Original Hymn WHH-122
Original Ode, An JKP-11
O'Reilly For President MISC-142
Our Al AES-3
Our Al From Tammany AES-16
Our Al Is Meant For Pres-I-Dent AES-42
Our Al Smith AES-48
Our Al To Succeed Cal AES-62
Our American Cousin Polka AL-177; AL-178; AL-179; AL-180
Our American Cousin Schottisch AL-180
Our Bold Jim Blaine JGB-53

Title Index

Our Bonus And Our Beer MISC-7; MISC-8
Our Boy Roosevelt He'll Go In FDR-267
Our Boy's A Warrior Now USG-156
Our Brutus AL-30
Our Buddies WW-169
Our Candidate WHH-113; BFH-69; WM-20
Our Campaign Hymn AML-1; AML-27
Our Champions Of The Right RBH-3; RBH-32
Our Chief's Call WM-228
Our Chieftain JCF-15
Our Choice CEH-5
Our Christian President WM-314
Our Clay And Frelinghuysen HC-66; HC-117
Our Cleveland in the Van GC-146
Our Country GC-130; TR-19
Our Country Now And Ever GW-169
Our Country's Flag AL-13
Our Cue For '52 DDE-13
Our Emblem! BFH-94
Our Flag Is Floating Today GW-553
Our Fallen Chief FDR-198
Our Fallen Leader WM-132
Our Fathers, Where Were They? GW-182
Our Favorite Waltzes WM-118
Our First Citizen Grand March GC-90
Our First Lady's Waltz FDR-100
Our First President's Quickstep JD-2; JD-11; JD-13
Our Flag WW-68; CC-33
Our Flag And Country WW-184
Our Flag And You FDR-164
Our Flag Is Floating Free GW-553
Our Flag Is Half-Mast High! AL-34
Our Flag Is There GW-445
Our Flag Our Army And Our President AL-148
Our Flag Shall Wave There AL-498
Our Flag Song Book WM-306
Our Friend FDR-184
Our Friend And President CC-42
Our Generals Grand March WS-14
Our Generals Quickstep WS-14
Our Glorious Union Forever WM-320
Our Good And Glorious Blaine JGB-13
Our Good And Honest Taft WHT-22
Our Governor Still Lives BFB-8
Our Governors March JMP-1
Our Grant Has Passed Away USG-40
Our Guiding Star FDR-202
Our Heroes FDR-181
Our Heroes Of To-Day TR-238
Our Idol President WM-314
Our Jessie JCF-54
Our Land Of Song GW-449; TJ-52; AL-370; TR-362
Our Landon AML-1
Our Leader WM-171; FDR-82; FDR-284
Our Leader Is No More WM-144
Our Lincoln AL-430
Our Lincoln The Hero Of The Nation AL-389
Our Lincoln's Act AL-424
Our Martyr President AL-146
Our Miracle Man DAM-17
Our Monthly Musical Gem GW-504
Our Moses Swinging Round The Circle AJN-16
Our National Songs GW-404; TR-121
Our National Union March AL-3
Our National War Songs GW-611
Our Nation's Captain AL-164
Our Nation's Choice WM-85
Our Nation's Glory WW-42
Our Nation's Pride WM-158
Our New President March WM-139
Our Next President TR-94
Our Next President, James A. Garfield JAG-33
Our Next President, William A. McKinley WM-223
Our Noble Chief Has Passed Away AL-92
Our Noble Chief Washington GW-434
Our Nominee HC-116
Our Old Commander USG-51
Our Own MacArthur DAM-34
Our Pal AES-22
Our Plumed Knight Leads The Way JGB-2
Our Pop. Convention WJB-33
Our President WM-19; WM-74; WM-193; WM-194; TR-6; TR-182; WGH-39; HCH-21; FDR-67; FDR-136; FDR-192; FDR-209; FDR-243; HST-15
Our President Celebration Song FDR-377
Our President Of 1933 FDR-103
Our President Passed Away WGH-58
Our President Roosevelt's Colorado Hunt TR-212
Our President Was Called Away To Heaven FDR-28
Our Presidential Chair WW-141
Our Presidents GW-530; MISC-41
Our Presidents 1798-1913 MISC-103
Our Presidents Speak MISC-110
Our President's Waltz DDE-3
Our Roosevelt TR-355; FDR-15
Our Ship Moves Proudly On, My Boys GBM-26
Our Soldier's Return Grand March CAA-5
Our Star Of Hope FDR-342
Our Star Spangled Banner TR-172
Our Ted TR-364
Our Teddy TR-10; TR-25; TR-276; TR-314
Our Teddy's Home Coming March TR-97
Our Ulysses USG-155
Our Uncle Sam WW-60
Our War President March WM-11
Our Washington GW-256; GW-610
Our Willie Of The West WJB-6
Our Wilson Again WW-73
Our Wilson Is The Greatest Man The World Has Ever Known WW-32; WW-95
Out Of The Wilderness With Ike DDE-52; DDE-61

Title Index

Over Here TR-225; FDR-203
Oyster Bay TR-186

Pan-American March And Two-Step GW-202
Parade March GBM-4
Parade Of The Teddy Bears TR-22
Parks' Democratic Campaign Songs WJB-56; AP-6; WW-178
Parks' Republican Campaign Songs WM-106; TR-157; WHT-51
Parker Campaign Songster, 1904 ABP-7
Parker! Parker! AP-4
Parlor Organ Galaxy, The USG-280
Parlor Organ Treasury, The:JAG-107
Pass The Prosperity Around TR-365
Patent Flagelet Preceptor GW-499
Pathfinder's Quick-Step, The JCF-9
Patriotic Glee Book GW-559
Patriotic Song:WHH-142
Patriotic Song Book GW-613; AL-505
Patriotic Songs AL-330; WGH-47
Patriotic Songs And Hymns GW-606
Patriotic Songs Arranged In Three And Four Parts By A Professor Of Music HC-102
Patriotic Songs For School And Home:GW-546
Patriotic Songs For Use In Schools And At Social Gatherings:GW-593
Patriotic Songs Of America For School And Home WW-217
Patriotic Songs Of America GW-438; GW-614
Patriotic Songs Of To-Day For Every American Home WW-44
Patriot's Quick Step WHH-15
Pat's War With The Know Nothings MF-23
P-E-A-C-E WW-165
Peace At Last USG-79
Peace By Resolution JMC-15
Peace Grand March TR-354
Peace Made In The U.S.A. WW-197
Peacemaker, The TR-8; TR-21 TR-339
Pearly Drops, The GW-8
Pendleton's March GBM-52
Pendleton's Schottisch GBM-52
Penitent Loco, The WHH-57; WHH-91
Pennsylvania MISC-90
Pennsylvania Republican Campaign Songster WHT-16
People Are Bound To Win, The WJB-12
People Are Rousing, The WHH-36
People's Advent, The AL-513
People's Campaign Songster, The WJB-64
People's Choice, The ZT-9; JCF-25; JGB-15; WJB-36; WM-9; TR-324
People's Friend, The TJ-2
People's March, The TJ-20
People's National Party Grand March JBW-5
People's Party Grand March JBW-2
People's Party Song Book JBW-3
People's Plumed Knight, The JGB-28
People's Rally, The WHH-113

People's Song, The USG-83
People's Songbook, The TJ-72; AL-490
People's Songs HAW-8
People's Songs For Blaine And Logan, The JGB-45
People's Songster For Campaign Purposes And A Jolly Time Generally JBW-9
Pershing For President MISC-5
Peter Butternut's Lament AL-310
Phildelphia And New York Glee Book GW-626
Philadelphia Press Prize McKinley Inaugural March WM-170
Pictures On The Flag GW-197
Pigtails And Freckles MISC-68
Piss On Lyndon's War LBJ-33
Pittsburgh Brass Band Quick Step WHH-110
Plains, Georgia JEC-7
Plan Of Love, The WM-25
Play The Game FDR-154
Please Mister President MISC-52; MISC-86; MISC-143
Please Mr. Lincoln AL-438
Please Sell No More Drink To My Father JSJ-6
Plumed Knight JGB-15; JGB-34
Plumed Knight And Black Eagle JGB-66
Plumed Knight Campaign Songster, 1884 JGB-91
Plumed Knight Of Maine JGB-42
Plumed Knight Songster JGB-47
Plumed Knight Waltzes JGB-60
Political Catechism And Greenback Song Book, The JBW-6
Political Quartet WM-105
Politics [Songbook] LBJ-29; RMN-34
Politics In Song GC-149
Polk & Dallas HC-47
Polk & Dallas Songster JKP-10 JKP-14
Polk Is A Used Up Joke HC-115
Polk Songster, The JKP-15
Polka, The JKP-5
Poor Joe MISC-68
Poor Old Jeff The Shero JD-17
Poor Old Lincoln AL-295
Pop! Goes For Fremont JCF-17
Popocrats Are Coming, Boys!, The WM-197
Popular Republican Campaign Songs WM-87
Populist And Silver Songs WJB-63
Possum WHT-3
Post's McKinley March, The WM-210
Potato Party, The AML-12
Praise Of McClellan, The GBM-47
Praises Of Our Country, The TR-199
Prasident Lincoln's Marsch AL-280
Prayer For General Eisenhower And His Men, A DDE-22; DDE-78
Prayer For Peace FDR-224
Prayer Hymn For Those In Active Service, A DAM-55
Pres. Adams' March JA-28

Title Index

Pres. McKinley's Grand March WM-53
President, The MISC-158
President A. Jackson's Inauguration March AJK-46
President Abraham Lincoln's Quick Step AL-290
President Adams Grand March & Quickstep JQA-5
President Andrew Johnson's Grand March AJN-18; AJN-28
President Arthur's Grand March CAA-1; CAA-2; CAA-3; CAA-6; CAA-7; CAA-8; CAA-11
President Arthur's March CAA-6
President At The Pan-American Fair WM 91
President Bill Clinton March BC-3; BC-9
President Bill Taft Two Step March WHT-13
President Bryan's Two-Step March WJB-29
President Cleveland's Grand Inauguration March GC-40
President Cleveland's Grand March GC-4; GC-55; GC-66; GC-75
President Cleveland's Inauguration Grand March GC-99
President Cleveland's National Grand March GC-113
President Cleveland's Reception March GC-37
President Cleveland's Tariff March GC-129
President Cleveland's Victory March GC-55
President Cleveland's Wedding March GC-28
President Coolidge March CC-6; CC-41
President Elect March, The WGH-55
President Fillmore Waltz MF-6
President Garfield JAG-97
President Garfield Died Last Night Break The Sad News To His Mother JAG-31
President Garfield's Funeral March JAG-11; JAG-12; JAG-23; JAG-24; JAG-26; JAG-28; JAG-29; JAG-30; JAG-38; JAG-54; JAG-72; JAG-74; JAG-107; JAG-112
President Garfield's Inauguration March JAG-14
President George Bush March GB-1
President Gerald R. Ford March GRF-1; GRF-3; GRF-7; GRF-8; GRF-12
President Grant And Political Rings USG-276
President Grant's Grand March USG-9; USG-100
President Grant's March USG-10
President Grant's Polka USG-245
President Grover Cleveland's Grand Inauguration March GC-94
President Grover Cleveland's Wedding March GC-51
President Harding March WGH-7
President Harding's Grand March WGH-59
President Harrison's Dead March WHH-73
President Harrison's Funeral Dirge WHH-55
President Harrison's Grand Inauguration March WHH-10; BFB-55; BFH-67
President Harrison's Grand Military Waltz WHH-78

President Harry S. Truman March HST-13
President Hayes' Grand March RBH-9; RBH-19; RBH-40; RBH-55
President Haye's [Sic] Grand Triumphal March RBH-7
President Hayes' Inauguration Polka RBH-40
President Hayes Quickstep RBH-37
President Hoover March HCH-14; HCH-48
President J.Q. Adams March JQA-4
President Jackson's Favorite March AJK-58
President Jackson's Favorite March And Quick Step AJK-3
President Jackson's Grand March AJK-2; AJK-18; AJK-26; AJK-31; AJK-35
President Jackson's Grand March & Quick Step AJK-14
President Jackson's Inauguration March AJK-17
President Jackson's Parade March AJK-5
President James A. Garfield's Funeral March JAG-43
President James K. Polk's Grand March & Quick Step JKP-18; JKP-19
President Jefferson Davis Grand March JD-1
President Jefferson March, The TJ-45
President Jefferson's March TJ-25
President Jefferson's Sunday Afternoon Party March MISC-100
President Jimmy Carter March JEC-4; JEC-6; JEC-10
President John Kennedy March JFK-46
President John Quincy Adams Grand March JQA-2; JQA-14
President John Quincy Adams Grand March & Quickstep JQA-1
President Johnson's Grand March AJN-9; AJN-12
President Johnson's Grand Quick Step AJN-9; AJN-12
President Johnson's Grand Union March AJN-1; AJN-3; AJN-15
President Johnson's March AJN-24
President Johnson's Quick Step AJN-16
President Kennedy March JFK-6
President Kennedy's Assassination JFK-39
President Lincoln Campaign Songster, The AL-74
President Lincoln's Favorite Poem AL-63
President Lincoln's Funeral March AL-14; AL-19; AL-23; AL-28; AL-31; AL-40; AL-52; AL-139; AL-241; AL-418; AL-420
President Lincoln's Grand March AL-1
President Lyndon Baines Johnson March LBJ-1; LBJ-11; LBJ-16; LBJ-19; LBJ-24; LBJ-27
President M. Van Buren's Grand March MVB-1; MVB-18
President Madison's March JMD-4; JMD-7; JMD-19
President McKinley And His Golden Chair WM-180
President McKinley's Favorite Hymns WM-34

Title Index

President McKinley's Funeral March WM-96; WM-164
President McKinley's Inauguration WM-8
President McKinley's March WM-186
President McKinley's Sympathetic March WM-188
President Monroe's Hornpipe JMN-25
President Monroe's Inauguration March JMN-6
President Monroe's March JMN-2; JMN-8; JMN-9; JMN-27
President Monroe's Waltz JMN-4
President Munroe's [Sic] March JMN-7
President Munroe's [Sic] Trumpet March JMN-3
President Munro's [Sic] March JMN-25
President Of The United States March, The GW-22
President Of The USA FDR-287
President On The Dollar GW-358
President Pierce's March FP-10
President Pierce's March And Quick Step FP-1
President Richard M. Nixon March RMN-4; RMN-24; RMN-25; RMN-26; RMN-27
President Ronald Reagan March RR-10; RR-23
President Roosevelt FDR-102
President Roosevelt And The NRA FDR-91
President Roosevelt Humanity March FDR-35
President Roosevelt March FDR-12; FDR-53; FDR-121; FDR-291; FDR-310; FDR-384
President Roosevelt We Greet You FDR-174
President Roosevelt's Grand March TR-284
President Roosevelt's Grand Triumphal March TR-136
President Roosevelt's Smile FDR-33
President Roosevelt's Triumphal March TR-381
President Song, The DDE-9
President Taylor's Grand Inauguration March ZT-2
President Taylor's Inauguration March ZT-20
President Tyler's Grand March JT-1; JT-9
President Tyler's Grand Quick Step JT-11
President Tyler's March JT-2; JT-14
President Ulysses! USG-124
President Van Buren's Grand March MVB-4; MVB-7; MVB-17
President Van Buren's Grand Waltz MVB-10
President Wilson U.S.A WW-45
President Wilson's Inauguration WW-191
President Wilson's Triumphal March WW-100
President Wilson's Wedding March WW-34
Presidential Contest, The FP-9
Presidential Drum & Bugle March Book MISC-167
Presidential Hymn, The WW-215
Presidential March WM-12; HCH-18
Presidential Polonaise BFH-39
Presidential Race For 1868 USG-56
Presidents MISC-39; MISC-135

President's Ball, The FDR-288
President's Birthday Ball, The FDR-179; FDR-180
President's Birth Day Ode GW-18
President's Death, The AL-68
President's Emancipation March, The AL-62
President's Funeral March, The WHH-72
President's Grand March JKP-3
President's Greetings WHT-40
President's Hymn, The AL-96; AL-237; AL-289; AL-358; AL-446
President's Inauguration March, The GC-142
President's Lady, The MISC-57; MISC-58; MISC-59
President's Love Letter, The CC-22
President's March GW-45; GW-61; GW-71; GW-97; GW-102; GW-114; GW-467; GW-471; GW-472; GW-473; GW-484; GW-501; GW-502
President's March, The GW-46; GW-47; GW-48; GW-49; GW-50; GW-51; GW-57; GW-62; GW-78; GW-180; GW-82; GW-91; GW-107; GW-476; GW-619; USG-17; WM-90; WM-224; MISC-85
President's March And Ca Ira GW-17
President's Marches FDR-53; HST-24; DDE-90; LBJ-1
President's Message, The FDR-220
Presidents On Parade CC-16
President's Prayer, A LBJ-31
President's Quadrilles, The WHH-19
President's Rap MISC-187
President's Reception March, The GC-87
President's Turkish March, The AJK-12
President's Waltz GW-496
President's Waltz, The MVB-12; FDR-409
President's War, Victory And Marching Song FDR-94
President's Welcome To York JMN-25
Pres't. Jas. A. Garfield Grand Inaugural March JAG-9
Prest. Lincoln's Funeral Dirge AL-270
Pride Of The White House MISC-47
Prize Banner Quick Step WHH-67; HC-26
Pro Patria AL-499
Profile In Courage JFK-10
Program Of The Inaugural Grand Concerts TR-95
Programme Of The Public Obsequies Of President Garfield JAG-108
Progressive Battle Hymns TR-117
Progressive League Of Burlington County Song Sheet TR-345
Progressive Music Course GW-552
Prohibition Bells Nd-1; PP-3
Prohibition Campaign Songs CBF-5
Prohibition Campaign Songster CBF-6
Prohibition Home Protection Party Campaign Songs JSJ-3
Prohibition Party, The PP-2
Prohibition Party Campaign Songs JSJ-4

Title Index

Prohibition Song CBF-3
Prohibition Songster, The:JSJ-5
Prosperity HCH-2; FDR-131
Prosperity And Hughes CEH-4
Prosperity And Protection WM-138
Prosperity Days Are Here FDR-50
Prosperity Days Are Near HCH-32
Prosperity Is Coming Thanks To Franklin D FDR-227
Prosperity Is Returning FDR-150
Prosperity March FDR-127
Prosperity, Protection And McKinley WM-250
Prosperity Song FDR-191
Protection WM-127
Protection And Bimetallism WJB-74
Protection And Gold WM-237
Protection Bugle, The BFH-99
Protection Campaign Songs And Recitations BFH-94
Protection Collection Of Campaign Songs For 1888 BFH-96
Protection Mac Is Coming WM-200
Protection March WM-274
Protective Tariff Grand March WM-184
Proud Flag Of Freedom, The GW-349
Providence Journal March And Two Step WM-86
P.T. 109 JFK-13
P.T. Schutz & Co's Blaine And Logan Bugle Call JGB-67
Public Sentiment WJB-39
Pull Together Boys AP-1
Puritan's Mistake, The GW-148
Put On Your Old Grey Bonnet WW-126
Put The Right Man At The Wheel SJT-9; SJT-19; MISC-114; MISC-182
Putnam Phalanx, The GW-421

Quartette WS-22
Quay-Stone's Quandary Scs-1

Radical Drum Call, The USG-261
Radio Collection Of National Songs And Hymns GW-441
Rah Rah! Rah! For Warren G. Harding WGH-25
Rail Splitter's Polka AL-131; AL-236
Raise The Roosevelt Banner TR-80
Raising Old Harry HC-9
Rajah Of Broadway, The WHT-12
Rally! USG-53
Rally, The JGB-20
Rally Boys, Rally! USG-67
Rally Democrats JWD-7
Rally For The Leader USG-211; JGB-15
Rally Round The Cause Boys! AL-159
Rally Round The Hat Boys TR-239
Rally Round The Flag JFK-70
Rally Round Ulysses Boys USG-286

Rally The Standard Of Abe Lincoln CC-10; CC-50
Rallying Song JCF-25; JCF-52
Ranchman's Hymn To Teddy, The TR-230
Rank And File GW-521
Ratification Quick Step ZT-16
Raw Recruit AL-120; AL-195
Read Between The Stars And Stripes And Spell Humanity WW-76
Reagan For President RR-30
Real American, A AL-201
Real Depression Buster, A FDR-43
Rebel Songster AL-481
Re-Born American Spirit, The FDR-390
Reception March BFH-75
Reception Schottisch USG-59
Reception To Hon. Shuyler Colfax USG-206
Red Bandana, The GC-58
Red Bandana March, The GC-52
Red Bandana Marching Song GC-111
Red Hot Democratic Campaign Songs For 1888 GC-141
Red Hot Democratic Campaign Songs For 1892 GC-82
Red Hot Democratic Campaign Songs For 1896 WJB-18
Red, White And Blue Songster No. 1, The GW-630
Red, White And Maddox LGM-2
Regina Gavotte BFH-37
Regular Democratic March Two-Step WJB-88
Re-Joyce McDonald, A–very Crooked Whiskey March USG-251
Re'lection Day! FDR-96
Remember F.D.R FDR-32
Remembrance JFK-21
Rendezvous FDR-367
Re-Pledging Our Faith GW-248
Republican [sic] Campaign Songs RFH-115
Republican Bugle Blasts WM-229
Republican Campaign March Of 1888 BFH-73
Republican Campaign Melodist And Register USG-148
Republican Campaign Music JGB-44
Republican Campaign Parodies And Songs WM-67
Republican Campaign Song AL-159; MISC-122
Republican Campaign Song Book CC-35
Republican Campaign Song Book 1896 WM-151
Republican Campaign Song Book, With Music, 1892 BFH-107
Republican Campaign Song Sheet No #1 BFH-82
Republican Campaign Songs RBH-48; JGB-50; BFH-41; BFH-64; BFH-100; BFH-102; BFH-121; BFH-123; BFH-129; WM-134; WM-267; WLW-67
Republican Campaign Songs For 1888 BFH-1; RFH-114

Republican Campaign Songs For 1920 WGH-54
Republican Campaign Songs With Popular Airs WM-283
Republican Campaign Songster, The JCF-22; JCF-24
Republican Campaign Songster For 1860, The AL-57
Republican Campaign Songster For 1904, The TR-159
Republican Campaign Songster No. #1 AL-298
Republican Campaign Songster No. #2 AL-397
Republican Club Campaign Song Book For 1888 BFH-20
Republican Club Songs BFH-79
Republican Glee For Lincoln & Hamlin AL-115
Republican Harmonist, The TJ-10
Republican Highway TED-14
Republican Hot Shot WM-238
Republican League Campaign Song Book, The BFH-58
Republican League Campaign Song Book 1888, The BFH-113
Republican League Harrison And Morton Song Book BFH-50
Republican March Song HCH-31
Republican National Convention March WM-1
Republican Nomination JAG-3
Republican Pocket Monitor And Campaign Song Book JGB-83
Republican Presidential March TR-2
Republican Prize Songster JCF-51
Republican Rallying Song AL-500
Republican Song Book AL-8; BMG-6
Republican Song 1856 JCF-11
Republican Songs For The People AL-390
Republican Songs For The Campaign Of 1888 BFH-104
Republican Song Review Of 1916 CEH-2
Republican Songs WGH-29
Republican Songster For The Campaign Of 1864 AL-405
Republican Two Step And March WM-50
Republican Unity Dinner MISC-152
Republican Victory Campaign Songs WM-251
Republican Victory March WM-263; WM-300
Republican Victory Songs AML-23
Republican Women's Committee Campaign Songs WGH-56
Republican Yell Raiser, The BFH-120
Republicans And Democrats PP-3
Republicans Are On The March To Victory TED-9
Republicans-Our Country Needs You DDE-58
Republican's Remember RBH-12

Republicans Will Win This Fall MISC-54
Requiem AL-83; USG-81
Requiem For Jeff Davis JD-46
Requiem March In Honor Of President Lincoln AL-52
Rest, Noble Chieftain AL-128
Rest, Martyr, Rest AL-54
Rest Of My Life, The FDR-358
Rest Spirit Rest AL-32
Rest Warrior Rest ZT-31
Resting Place Of Washington, The GW-162; GW-255
Retreat Of The Sixty Thousand Lincoln Troops, The AL-296
Retribution GC-61
Return Franklin D. Roosevelt FDR-254
Reunion Medley GC-98
Re-United WM-52
Reveille, The HC-37
Rhythm Of Reform Song Lyrics For Reform Party Volunteers MISC-160
Rhythms And Rimes GW-558
Richard Nixon Is The One RMN-7
Richard Nixon Waltz, The RMN-23
Richmond Is Ours USG-177
Ride 'Em Cal CC-7
Ride Tenderfoot Ride RR-9
Rider, The TR-328
Right On To France WW-139
Rights Of Man, The WJB-43
Riley's Easy Flute Duets JMN-5
Riley's Flute Melodies GW-102; JA-16; AJK-32
Riley's Flute Melodies, Vol. 2 JNM-25
Riley's New Instructor For The German Flute GW-479
Riley's Preceptor For The Patent Flageolet GW-480
Riley's Second Sett [sic] Of Cotillions GW-491
Ring Merry Bells GBM-68
Ring! Ring The Bell! USG-88
Ring The Bells For Hancock WSH-34
Rinka Tinka Man FDR-252
Rio Grand March ZT-21; ZT-45; ZT-51
Rio Grand Quick March, The ZT-23
River Patowmac [sic], The GW-75
Riverside March And Two Step USG-173
R-O-A March, The HST-11
Road I Have Chosen, The WLW-46
Road Is Open Again, The FDR-34
Road To Victory, The GW-204
Robert La Follette Is The Man Of My Heart RML-5
Rock-In For Rocky GRF-11
Rockefeller Campaign Song GRF-9
Rocky Mountain Song Book JCF-48
Roll Along, Roll Along, Shout The Campaign Battle Song RBH-5
Rolling Eggs On Easter Morn MISC-95
Ron For President RR-7
Ronald Reagan He Is The One RR-4

Ronald Reagan March RR-2; RR-3
Roose Franklin FDR-165
Roosevelt TR-184; TR-306; FDR-120
Roosevelt A Magical Name TR-219
Roosevelt And Fairbanks TR-47; TR-307
Roosevelt And The Four Freedoms FDR-221
Roosevelt At The Throttle FDR-42
Roosevelt Campaign March, The TR-251
Roosevelt Campaign Songster For 1904 TR-356
Roosevelt Cavalry March, The TR-120
Roosevelt Cheer Song FDR-368
Roosevelt Day FDR-185
Roosevelt Est Un Peu La FDR-298
Roosevelt For King FDR-353
Roosevelt For Mine TR-151; FDR-99
Roosevelt, Garner And Me FDR-63; FDR-204
Roosevelt Glide FDR-4
Roosevelt Grand March, The TR-310
Roosevelt Grand March And Two Step TR-213
Roosevelt, Guffey And Earle FDR-320
Roosevelt Here We Come FDR-2
Roosevelt He's The Man TR-137
Roosevelt Hymn TR-181; TR-232
Roosevelt I'm For You FDR-85
Roosevelt Is In We're Bound To Win FDR-216
Roosevelt Is On The Job FDR-10; FDR-18
Roosevelt Is The Man FDR-31
Roosevelt Lullaby FDR-16
Roosevelt March TR-7; TR-56; TR-124; TR-323. FDR-16
Roosevelt March And Two Step, The TR-51
Roosevelt March Song TR-116; FDR-78; FDR-341
Roosevelt NRA March Song FDR-49
Roosevelt Rally, The TR-200
Roosevelt (Roosevelt Our President) FDR-406
Roosevelt School Song TR-221
Roosevelt Song FDR-141; FDR-171
Roosevelt Song, The FDR-52
Roosevelt Songs Campaign Of 1904 TR-159
(Roosevelt=Stalin=Churchill And Company) Canners FDR-313
Roosevelt The Cry TR-147
Roosevelt, The Hope Of The Nation TR-278
Roosevelt, The Peace Victor TR-130
Roosevelt Victory Song FDR-143
Roosevelt-Wallace Campaign Song FDR-140
Roosevelt Waltzes TR-383
Roosevelt We Are Following You FDR-264
Roosevelt We Do Our Part FDR-244
Roosevelt We Hand The Flag To You! FDR-132; FDR-351
Roosevelt We're All For You FDR-218
Roosevelt We're For You FDR-149
Roosevelt, We're Glad To Welcome You TR-101
Roosevelt, You're The Pride Of The U.S.A. FDR-308

Roosevelt's Campaign Song FDR-30
Roosevelt's Day At The St. Louis Fair TR-103
Roosevelt's Grand March TR-113; TR-114; TR-371
Roosevelt's Grand Triumphal March TR-216
Roosevelt's Rough Riders TR-93; TR-179; TR-215
Roosevelt's The Man TR-132
Roosevelt's Victory Campaign Song FDR-122
Rooster I Wore On My Hat, The WJB-81
Root-Root-Root For Roosevelt FDR-88; FDR-304
Rosa Lee GW-116
[Rose]-Velt TR-248
Ross Perot's Swan Songs MISC-161
Rough & Ready ZT-7; ZT-13; ZT-42; ZT-68; TR-72
Rough And Ready Campaign Songs BFH-101
Rough And Ready Grand March ZT-71
Rough & Ready Or Florida Polka ZT-59
Rough And Ready Melodist ZT-75
Rough And Ready Minstrel ZT-76
Rough And Ready Polka ZT-5; ZT-6; ZT-62
Rough And Ready Quick Step ZT-63
Rough And Ready Quickstep ZT-69; ZT-80; ZT-81
Rough And Ready Songster, The ZT-29; ZT-41; ZT-44
Rough And Ready, The Soldier's Story ZT-66
Rough And Ready's Rio Grande Songster ZT-79
Rough Rider, The WM-330; TR-156
Rough Riders TR-164
Rough Riders, The TR-15; TR-69; TR-100; TR-176; TR-262
Rough Riders In Cuba TR-280
Rough Riders March TR-68; TR-174
Rough Riders March Two Step TR 163; TR-169
Rough Riders March Militaire, The TR-167
Rough Riders Military March TR-67
Rough Rider's Patrol, The TR-64; TR-203
Rough Riders Two-Step, The TR-176
Rough Riders Two Step March TR 170
Rough Riders War Rally TR-178
Roundups And Showdowns AES-69
Row On, Woodrow, Row On WW-24
Row, Row, Row With Roosevelt FDR-38; FDR-292
Row, Row With Roosevelt FDR-398
Royal Family Duet, The WLW-66
Rubank Holiday Collection GW-400
Rule Anglo-Saxia GW-189
Ruler In Peace And The Leader In War, The USG-157
Ruth, Ester And Marion GC-128
Ruth Gavotte GC-35
Rutherford B. Hayes Song Sheet RBH-39
Ruth's Dolly Song GC-121

Sacred Dirges, Hymns And Anthems GW-127

Sacred Hour WM-51
Safe In Heaven WM-225
Safe In The Arms Of Jesus WM-168
Sage Of Monticello, The TJ-52
Sagamore Hill March TR-62
Sagamore Hill Waltzes TR-186
Sagamore March TR-160; TR-290
Sail On The Ship Of Love WGH-5
Sail On Victorious, Unseen Sail WW-19
Salt Water Cowboy TJ-42
Salute To Eisenhower DDE-57
Salute To George Washington And Abraham Lincoln GW-373
Salute To The First Lady March BC-10
Salute To The U.S. Flag HCH-29
Sam MF-16
Same Old Coon, The HC-90
Sammies Are Off To War, The WW-101
Sam's Coming MF-12
Sam's Know Nothing Quick Step MF-30
San Clemente By The Sea RMN-3
San Juan Hill TR-127
Santa Claus For President MISC-18
Saule-Pleurer AL-339
Save Our Flag AL-480
Savior Of Our Country, The AL-16
Say It With A Kiss RR-21
Say No To Drugs RR-28
Says Kennedy JFK-68
Schildkret's Hungarian Waltzes TR-359
S-C-H-M-I-T-Z For President JGS-3; JGS-4
School Anthem USG-275
School Where Lincoln Went, The AL-206
Schultz & Cos Cleveland & Hendricks Democratic Campaign Songster GC-139
Scott And Graham Melodies WS-15
Scott And The Veteran WS-23
Scott Songster, The WS-38
Scrappy Warriors, The FDR-363
Search For A Likely Candidate BC-6; MISC-121; MISC-163
Secret Service, The MISC-68
Secretary Chase's Grand March And Quickstep AL-88
See The U.S. Thru With Truman HST-17
See The Voters WM-127
See You In Malila DAM-53
Select Your Candidate GC-101
Senator From Tennessee, The MISC-22
Senior Loyal Temperance Legion Song Book CBF-7
Sentimental Song Book, The PC-3
Sentiments For Franklin D. Roosevelt FDR-187
Sentinel Song Book JBW-11
Serenade Of The 300,000 Federal Ghosts, The AL-172
Seven Days Fight Before Richmond GBM-56
Seven Lonely Days TJ-42
Seven Songs For The Harpsichord Or Piano Forte GW-124

Seymour And Blair Democratic Songster HS-14
Seymour And Blair Song Book And Democratic Register HS-5
Seymour And Blair's Union Campaign March HS-3
Seymour And Blair's March To The White House HS-2
Seymour, Blair And Victory HS-4
Seymour Campaign Songster HS-8; HS-15
Seymour March HS-2
Seymour Schottisch HS-4
Seymour's March HS-13
Sgt. Shriver's Bleeding Heart's Club Band GSM-2
Shady's Grant And Wilson Campaign Songster For 1872 USG-73
Shall The Flag Be Taken Down WM-72
Shall The People Rule? WJB-12
Shall We Gather At The White House? WM-243
Shenandoah WM-218
Sheridan Waltz USG-174
Sherman Gavotte USG-174
Shin-Plaster Jig GW-167
Ship Named U.S.A., The WW-70
Ship Of State, The AL-143
Shrine Of Democracy MISC-115
Shoo Purp Don't Bodder Me USG-186
Shooting Of McKinley, The WM-113
Shooting Of Our Presidents, The WM-254
Shout The Battle Cry BFH-74
Show-Off Boat FDR-361
Show Us The Way, Blue Eagle FDR-278
Sidewalks Of New York, The AES-1; AES-2; AES-5; AES-71
Siege Of Fort Meigs, The WHH-91
Siemonn's Presidential March WJB-41
Siguele! Siguele! Con Nixon RMN-18
Silent Sentinel GW-217
Silver WJB-72
Silver Bells JD-7
Silver Bill WJB-25
Silver Dollar WM-108
Silver Ghost WM-82
Silver Knight Of The West, The WJB-30
Silver Party Song Book WJB-83
Silver Rallying Songs WJB-58
Silver Regiment, The WJB-21
Silver Songs Written For The Bryan Campaign WJB-59
Silverspoons, Schottisch BFB-19
Since Bwano Tumbo Came From Jumbo Land TR-28
Sing A Song Of Americans TJ-34; JQA-10; AL-247; TR-293; WW-155
Sing A Song Of Friendship TJ-74; MISC-132
Sing A Song Of History GW-356; TJ-41
Sing Along With Jack JFK-17; JFK-76
Sing Along With JFK JFK-32
Sing America AL-356; FDR-221

Title Index

Sing America Sing FDR-411
Sing And Swing With Willkie WLW-42
Sing And Win With Hubert Humphrey HHH-4
Sing For Willkie! WLW-17
Sing On To Victory WGH-13
Sing To The Tune Of The Old Grey Mare [Song Sheet] FDR-283
Singer's Own Book, The GW-425; MISC-177
Sink All Your Ships In The Ocean Blue And Sail On The Ship Of Love WGH-5
Sinking Of The Merrimac WM-208
Sin Hundred Thousand More AL-497
600,000 More We Are Coming Father Abram! AL-38
Six Military & Patriotic Illustrated Songs GW-129; GW-137
Six Patriotic Ballads WHH-2
Six Red Hot Songs Written And Composed Especially For The Campaign Of 1900 WJB-65
Six Republican Songs For The Campaign Of 1896 WM-285
Sixteen Silver Songs WJB-85
Sixteen To One WJB-9; WJB-32; WJB-34; WJB-96
16 To 1 WJB-97
16 To 1 Quickstep WJB-47.63 Is The Jubilee AL-127
Skip-Hop Dance AL-196
Sleep, Soldier Sleep! WGH-44
Slogan Of The Day, The JWD-3
Slow, Passing Bell, The GW-132
Slowly And Mournfully JAG-113
Slowly And Sadly JAG-51
Smiles WW-126
Smiling Bill WHT-38
Smiling With Roosevelt FDR-376
Socialism In Song SP-7
Socialist Campaign Songs SP-1
Socialist Song Book SP-8
Socialist Songs With Music SP-4
Society WHT-12
Sock-A-Bye Baby TED-28
Sois Benie, O Grande Amerique! WW-177
Soldier And His Bride, The HC-62
Soldier's Chief, The Nation's Chief, The USG-21
Soldiers Of Freedom WW-156
Soldiers Of The U.S.A WW-30
Soldier's Prayer For Victory, A FDR-360
Soldier's Return, The WS-1
Soldier's Story, The ZT-35
Soldier's Vote, The WSH-9
Solid North, The JAG-49
Some Rules Of Etiquette According To George Washington GW-394
Some Songs Of Socialism SP-6
Someone To Watch Over Me RR-25
Someone You Know AL-196
Something Just Broke MISC-91

Son Of Protection WM-178
Song Book WW-195
Song Book Of The Campaign Of 1916 CEH-2
Song For Belly Dancer MISC-68
Song Of A Thousand Years USG-272
Song For Republican Rally, Nov. 1, 1864 AL-71
Song For The Fourth Of July GW-110
Song For The Man, A HC-5
Song Of All Songs MISC-65
Song Of America MISC-109
Song Of Democracy, The AJK-40
Song Of '88 GC-64
Song Of Freedom SP-2
Song Of Heroes DDE-68
Song Of Peace FDR-405; HAW-2
Song OF Lincoln AL-404
Song Of Protection WM-178
Song Of The Abraham Lincoln Battalion AL-304
Song Of The Blue Eagle FDR-354
Song Of The Bunkless Party MISC-10
Song Of The Hatchet GW-210; GW-280
Song Of The Legionaire [sic] FDR-125
Song Of The Presidents MISC-97
Song Of The Union JB-5; JB-6
Song Of The U.S.A. GW-237
Song Of The Whistle Stop HST-10
Song Of Washington GW-194
Song Of Washington's Men GW-452
Song On The Death Of President Abraham Lincoln AL-55; AL-284
[Song Pamphlet For Theodore Roosevelt] TR-329
Song Patriot, The GW-589
[Song Sheet For Dewey] TED-33
Song Sheet [For Henry Clay] HC-83
Song Sheet For Taft Demonstration MISC-23
Song To Eisenhower DDE-89
Songs And Exercises For High Grammar Grades GW-525,
Songs Everyone Should Know MISC-155
Songs For A New Party HAW-5
Songs For America AL-494
Songs For Children GW-631
Songs For Freemen JCF-47; JBR-16
Songs For Landon Day AML-29
Songs For 1924 CC-58
Songs For Political Action FDR-197
Songs For Republican Rallies DDE-103
Songs For The Campaign Of '88 BFH-116
Songs For The Campaign Of 1888 BFH-36
Songs For The Great Campaign AL-374
Songs For The Great Campaign Of 1860 AL-388
Songs For The People WHH-63
Songs For The Presidential Campaign Of 1888 BFH-34
Songs For The Presidential Campaign Of 1896 WM-286
Songs For The Union AL-411
Songs For Wallace HAW-3

Songs Of America GW-538; GW-561; WW-131
Songs Of Judah And Other Melodies GW-548
Songs Of Liberty And Patriotism Of America And Allies GW-556
Songs Of Long Ago GW-536
Songs Of My Country GW-621
Songs of Purpose, Advanced Music AL-479
Songs Of Republican Sing To Victory AML-32
Songs Of Struggle CP-4
Songs Of The American Revolution GW-399
Songs Of The G.O.P WJB-15
Songs Of The Nation GW-391; GW-542
Songs Of The People CP-3
Songs Of The Progressive Party HAW-6
Songs Of The Revolution SP-3
Songs Of Victory DAM-34
Songs Of Work And Freedom TJ-71
Songs Sung At The Reunion Of The 23d Regiment, O.V.I. RBH-57
Songs The Soldiers Sang TR-366
Songs To Be Sung At The First National Progressive Convention TR-300
S.O.S. Of The U.S.A. Is The G.O.P WLW-33
Sound Money And Honesty WM-321
Sound Money March WM-109
Sound Money Songs WM-287
Sound The Alarm RBH-16
Soung [sic] From McClellan GBM-379
Sour Apple Tree JD-43
Sour Apple Tree, The JD-19; JD-45
Sousa March Folio, The JGB-96
Southern Warbler, The GW-461; AJK-52
Southern Wagon, The JD-4
Southern Yankee Doodle JD-23
Souvenir De Arlington GW-166
Souvenir De Mount Vernon GW-262
Souvenir For The Occasion WM-185
Souvenir Minstrel, The MISC-173
Souvenirs Of Mount Vernon GW-262
Souvenirs Of Washington GC-83
Sovereign Wreath Of Song GW-543
Spare Moments WHT-55
Special Delivery From Heaven:JFK-18
Special Memorial Services In Honor Of The Late President Warren G. Harding WGH-49
Spicer's Pocket Companion GW-509
Spirit Of America 1917 WW-166
Spirit Of Gene Debs EVD-2
Spirit Of Roosevelt The Great FDR-268
Spirit Of '76 MISC-79
Spirit Of The N.R A., The FDR-130
Spirit Of The U.S.A GW-234; WW-163
Spirits Of Our Dead Heroes, The BFH-74
Spitin' Ol' Mista' Hoover! HCH-22
Sprague's Campaign Songs For 1868 GBM-73
Spring Is A Wonderful Thing TJ-37
Square Deal, A TR-341
Square Deal, The TR-110

S.S. Theodore Roosevelt TR-308
St. Augustine Loco Foco Dance WHH-94
St. Louis Convention March WM-301
Stamp Galop, The GW-154
Stand By Our Leader GC-132
Stand By Our President FDR-195
Stand By The Grand Old Party BFH-74
Stand By The President AL-140; WW-136
Stand By The President Now WW-55
Stand Fast Americans FDR-272
Stand! Father Abraham AL-133
Stand Up And Cheer For Ronald Reagan RR-6
Stand Up For Schmitz JGS-1
Stand Up For Schmitz And Anderson JGS-2
Stand Up For Wallace GCW-4; GCW-5
Standard Patriotic Song Folio GW-577
Star Collection Of Old Favorite Songs GW-380
Star Of Hope, The HC-21
Star Of The West, The HC-42; WJB-16
Star Songster, The GW-608; AL-497; JD-64
Star Spangled Banner GW-130; GW-298; GW-445; BFH-74; WHT-23; CC-14; FDR-1; FDR-21; FDR-158; FDR-352
Stars And Stripes Forever!, The DAM-22
Stars Of Glory RMN-15
State Of The Union MISC-111
Statues And Statuettes AES-17
Step Into Line For Taft WHT-61
Step Up And Meet The New Champ FDR-300
Steph. A. Douglas And H.V. Johnson SAD-14
Stevenson AS-5
Still Their Hearts Are Young BFH-89
Still We Lead The Nation BFH-74
Stolen Stars Or Good Old Father Washington, The GW-586
Stop Pickin' On The President RMN-13
Storming And Capture Of Fort Donelson, The USG-168
Storming Of El Caney TR-350
Storming Of Monterey ZT-26; ZT-47
Straw Vote HCH-44
Strenuous American March TR-288
Strenuous Life TR-9
Strike For The Right! AL-94; AL-101
Strike Hard, America FDR-89
Strike Ike AS-9
Strike Ye Sons Of Liberty GBM-83
Stuff That Dreams Are Made Of, The RR-11
Sub-Treasury Waltz MVB-9
Sundown At Arlington FDR-365
Sun's Greeley Campaign Songster, The HG-5
Sunny Side, The GW-423
Superbird LBJ-33
Superior March Album USG-281
Sure Al Is Meant For Pres-I-Dent AES-41
Surprise Greeting Song For Willkie WLW-55
Surrender Bill! USG-239
Sussex By The Sea TR-274

Title Index

Sweet Memories GRF-10
Sweetly Reposing JQA-13
Swinging Around The Circle AJN-26
Swinging 'Round The Circle AJN-25
Switch Off Something JEC-11
Sword And The Staff, The GW-305
Sword Of Ulysses, The USG-191
Sylviad, The JA-7

Taft And Sherman Campaign Songster WHT-1
Taft And Sherman Waltz, The WHT-31
Taft-Diaz In El Paso March WHT-41
Taft Is The Man MISC-21
Taft March WHT-8
Taft March From Home To The Capitol WHT-28
Taft, Taft WHT-49
Taft Two-Step WHT-46
Taft Victory Song MISC-20
Taft's Grand March And 2 Step WHT-11
Taft's The Man To Lead The Band WHT-35
Take A Glide With Me USG-180
Take A Tip From Venus TR-30
Take Care Of This House MISC-100; MISC-153
Take Good Care Of My Heart DDE-69
Take Him, Earth, For Cherishing JFK-55
Take Me Back To My Daddy FDR-25; FDR-26
Take Me 'Round In A Taxicab WHT-27
Take My Hand RMN-15
Tammany Grand March HS-4
Tanner And The Blue, The USG-210
Tanner's Song USG-125
Tariff And Campaign Rhymes, The BFH-100
Tariff Bill WHT-37
Tattoo Is Ended, The JGB-76
Taylor And Fillmore Songster ZT-56
Taylor's Grand March ZT-40
Taylor's Triumph March ZT-72
Tea Pot Blues WGH-40
Tears, Idle Tears AJK-51
Tears On Lincoln's Face, The AL-301
Teddy TR-145; TR-191; TR-254; TR-372
Teddy After Africa TR-45
Teddy Come Back TR-135
Teddy Da Roose TR-31
Teddy From Oyster Bay TR-331
Teddy Girl, The TR-245; TR-260
Teddy In The Jungles TR-187
Teddy Is The Man TR-146
Teddy Junior TR-247
Teddy Once More TR-255
Teddy Roosevelt TR-165; TR-291
Teddy Roosevelt Waltz 1906 TR-315
Teddy-Te-Tum-Tay TR-17
Teddy, The Jungle Boogie-Man TR-325
Teddy The Tried And True TR-192
Teddy We're Glad You're Here TR-267
Teddy Will Carry It Through TR-188
Teddy You're A Bear TR-14; TR-353

Teddy's Bears TR-344
Teddy's Campaign Song TR-312
Teddy's Coming Back Again TR-92
Teddy's Dawg TR-71
Teddy's For The People TR-98
Teddy's Grand March TR-229
Teddy's Hat TR-43
Teddy's Hat Is In The Ring TR-332
Teddy's In The Ring TR-246
Teddy's March TR-50
Teddy's Moose TR-208
Teddy's Nig TR-33
Teddy's Terrors TR-70
Tell Eisenhower DDE-106
Tell Her I'm A Soldier And Not Afraid To Die AL-278
Tell Me Mother Can I Go USG-156
Tell Mother I'll Be There WM-41; WM-42
Temperance Song Banner, The WM-315
Testament Of Freedom, The TJ-47
Texas And Oregon Grand March JT-13
Texas Waltz, The FDR-65
Thank God For Franklin Roosevelt FDR-275
Thank God I Am An American DW-20
Thank God! We've Found The Man WLW-9
Thank You, Mr. President FDR-73
Thank You, Mr. Roosevelt FDR-314
Thanks, Mister President DDE-57
Thanks, Mister Roosevelt FDR-137
That Aero Naughty Girl TR-30
That Banner A Hundred Years Old GW-131
That Dear Little Church JAG-88
That Grand Old Party TED-12; TED-13; TED-22
That Great American Home MISC-150
That Man From O-Hi-O WM-252
That Man From Texas LBJ-26
That Man In The White House FDR-197
That No-3rd Term Tradition WLW-41
That Old White House MISC-162
That Same Old Tune AL-504
That's Just No So! JD-63
That's The Flag Of Flags For Me GW-352
That's The Spirit Of G.O.P DDE-43
That's The Ticket WM-119
That's What The Well Dressed Man In Harlem Will Wear RR-19; RR-20
Thats Whats The Matter With The Purps AL-282
Theme For Jacqueline JFK-7
Theme From Abe Lincoln In Illinois AL-216
Theme From All The President's Men RMN-22
Theme From JFK JFK-52
Theme From Profiles In Courage JFK-37
Theme Song Of The Associated Willkie-For-President Clubs Of New Jersey WLW-64
Then I'll Be Home Again WW-134
Theo. Roosevelt TR-153
Theodore TR-5
Theodore March, The TR-268

Theodore Roosevelt TR-282; TR-293; TR-296; TR-362
There Are Just As Many Heroes To-Day GW-377
There Is Glory In Old Glory WW-67
There Is The White House Yonder JCF-3
There Was A Man From New York Town CEH-6
There Will Always Be An Uncle Sammy GW-282
There'll Be A Big Brown Derby In The White House AES-25
There'll Never Be A Stain On Old Glory FDR-281
There's A Million Heroes GW-219
There's A New Man In The White House JFK-3
There's A New Star In Heaven Tonight FDR-333
There's A Picture Draped In Mourning WM-35
There's A Roosevelt In The Chair FDR-265
There's An 'FDR' In Freedom FDR-123
There's Bound To Be A Yankee In The Way TR-271
There's Jemmy Polk HC-115
There's Little Mac HC-115
There's Nothing Going Wrong AL-507
There's Nothing Like A Democratic Dame MISC-102
There's Something About Franklin D. Roosevelt That Is Fine, Fine, Fine FDR-139
There's Something About James A. Farley That's Fine, Fine, Fine FDR-340
There's Something About John N. Garner That's Fine, Fine, Fine FDR-163
There's Still Time Brother DDE-20
These Are The Songs That Were LBJ-6
They Are Calling From The Mountains TR-39; TR-214; TR-217
They Are The Stars In The Service Flag WW-189
They Asked For It And Now They're Gonna Get It FDR-228
They Can Never Say I Told You So JMC-11
They Gotta Quit Kickin' My Dawg Around MISC-3
They Like Ike DDE-48; DDE-102
They Love Me MISC-68
They Saved Our Flag JAG-82
Things Look Rosy With Roosevelt FDR-255
Thirteen Popular Waltzes TJ-24; MISC-35
Thirty Minutes With Washington GW-367
This Country Of Ours FDR-219
This Is A Great Country MISC-68
This Is My America MISC-112
This Is Our America DDE-101; GRF-4
This Is The Army RR-32
This Is The Army Mr. Jones RR-19; RR-20
This Is The Night TJ-42
This Man Is Your Man MISC-145

This Man The People Found MISC-148
This Man Was Meant For You And Me MISC-144
Thomas E. Dewey March TED-7
Thomas Jefferski TJ-74; MISC-132
Thomas Jefferson TJ-34; TJ-41
Thomas Jefferson March ; TJ-22; TJ-30
Thomas Jefferson's March TJ-9
Thomas Jefferson's Prayer TJ-29
Thoroughly Mad-Ern Malcolm RMN-28; GRF-10
Thou Art Far Away SAD-16
Three Cheers And A Tiger For Garfield JAG-82
Three Cheers For Cleveland GC-39
Three Cheers For Cleveland And Thurman GC-67
Three Cheers For F.D.R FDR-60
Three Cheers For General Ike DDE-64
Three Cheers For Hancock WSH-16
Three Cheers For Our President FDR-47; FDR-70
Three Cheers For President IKE:DDE-111
Three Heroes We Have Lost USG-217
357 Songs We Love To Sing MISC-168
301 JAG-101
Three Hundred Thousand More AL-329
300,000 More! AL-48; AL-170
Three Long Years AML-24
Three Marches GW-114
Three Million Marched Out To Save Our Land JGB 97
Three Of The Greatest Republican Campaign Songs Of The Season WM-289
Three Scirs For The New President WW-179
Three Sets Of Cotillions GW-598
3 Shots More! BFH-90
Throw Your Hat Into The Ring TR-195
Thumbs Up, America! RR-1
Thurman Grand March GC-159
Tie That Binds, The JMC-2
Tilden And Hendricks' Centennial Reform March SJT-1
Tilden And Hendricks' Democratic Centennial Campaign March SJT-7
Tilden And Hendricks' 1876 Reform Grand March SJT-22
Tilden And Hendricks' Favorite Quickstep SJT-9
Tilden And Hendricks' Galop To The White House SJT-9
Tilden And Hendricks' Grand March SJT-3; SJT-4; SJT-15
Tilden And Hendricks' Polka SJT-10
Tilden And Hendricks' Reform March SJT-6
Tilden And Hendricks' Reform Songs SJT-21
Tilden And Reform SJT-2; SJT-9
Tilden Illustrated Campaign Song And Joke Book SJT-8
Tilden's Campaign March SJT-9
Tilden's Campaign Polka SJT-9

Title Index

Tilden's Funeral March SJT-12
Tilden's Grand March SJT-5
Till Over The Top We Go WW-121
Till We Win WW-72
Times Are Out Of Joint, The SJT-9
Tip And Ty WHH-43; WHH-44
Tip And Tye WHH-75
Tip-Tyler Reform WHH-144
Tippecanoe And Morton Too BFH-33; BFH-44; BFH-144
Tippecanoe And Tyler Too WHH-91; WHH-108; WHH-109; WHH-113; WHH-124; MISC-169
Tippecanoe And Victory Too BFH-70
Tippecanoe Campaign Of 1840, The WHH-96
Tippecanoe Centennial March WHH-102
Tippecanoe Club Quick Step, The WHH-29
Tippecanoe Club Songster WHH-18
Tippecanoe Dance WHH-22
Tippecanoe Gathering, The WHH-91
Tippecanoe Hornpipe WHH-34
Tippecanoe March & Quick Step, The WHH-3
Tippecanoe Or Log Cabin Quickstep WHH-11
Tippecanoe Quick Step, The WHH-77
Tippecanoe Slow Grand March WHH-74
Tippecanoe Song-Book WHH-61; WHH-80; BFH-97
Tippecanoe Songster WHH-131; BFH-103
Tippecanoe Waltz WHH-6; WHH-12
Tipp's Invitation To Loco, The WHH-2; WHH-30; WHH-118
Tis Blaine And Logan Now JGB-44
To Arms! Freemen To Arms! AL-142
To Arms! To Arms! April 15th, 1861 AL-451
To Canaan AL-176
To God And Country MISC-112
To Our President FDR-294
To The Man Of The Hour FDR-29
To The Memory Of Abraham Lincoln AL-252; AL-292
To The White House BFH-3; GC-112
To Thee America FDR-186
To Uncle Sam WM-268
To Vict'ry He'll Gallantly Lead Us JGB-51
To You Roosevelt FDR-55
Toast, A GW-11
Toast, The MISC-169
Toast To General MacArthur, A DAM-19
Toast To George Washington, The GW-186; GW-395
Toast To Harry Truman, A HST-28
Toast To Roosevelt, A TR-373
Toll The Bell Mournfully AL-22
Toll The Bells Slowly:JAG-115
Toll The Bells Softly WM-167
Tolling Bell, The JBL-2
Tom Lehrer's Second Song Book HHH-6
Tom Reed Campaign Songs WM-92

Tomb Upon The Hill, The USG-66
Torr's Native American Minstrel HC-111
Tory, Tory, Hallelujah FDR-325
Touchdown With Willkie WLW-63
Toward The Sun FDR-188
Town Pump, The PP-4
Train Time FDR-252
Tramp Of Cavalry TR-16
Treasury Of American Song MISC-156
Treaty Of Peace TR-1
Treaty Of Portsmouth TR-105
Trefoil Quick Step WSH-12
Tremaine Brothers' Lincoln And Johnson Campaign Song-Book AL-402
Tribute To President Lincoln, A AL-28
Tribute To The National Guards, Army And Navy GW-221
Tribute To The U.S.A. GW-315; TJ-35; AL-252; FDR-291; HST-16; DDE-71; JFK-53; LBJ-24; RMN-25; GRF-7; JEC-10; RR-23
Tribute To Thomas Jefferson TJ-33
Trifit's Monthly Budget Of Music GC-131; WJB-52; WM-255
Trifit's Monthly Galaxy Of Music GC-161
Trip From Washington To Panama TR-285
Trip To Washington, A MISC-120
Triplicity TR-264
Triumph, The WGH-41
Triumph Of Old Glory, The TR-270
Triumphal March WS-12
Triumphal March Of The Rough Riders, The TR-334
True American, The AL-250; WM-16; TR-74
True Blue BFH-88; WM-196
True Blue Republican Campaign Songs For 1888 BFH-32
True Blue Republican Campaign Songs For 1892 BFH-47
True Blue Republican Campaign Songs For 1896 WM-169
True Blue Song Book GW-530
True Issue, The JCF-12
Truly I Do AL-321
Truman Campaign Song HST-14
Truman Flew To Mexico HST-9
Trumpet Call, The TR-57
Trumpet Of Freedom AL-493; JD-60
T.S.A. WJB-82
Tumbled In WGH-48
Tuning In AL-377
Turkish Patrol March, The USG-221
Turkish Review March USG-221
Turn Out The Light TR-222
Turn Out! To The Rescue! WHH-47
Twas A Tribute We Paid To Our Country TR-144
Twelfth Battalion Song — Campaign 1916 CEH-9
Twelve Popular Quick Steps HC-118; DW-36
Twentieth Century March To The White House MISC-180

Title Index

20 Marches USG-282
Twenty Second Of February GW-84
Two Campaign Songs TR-147; JBL-9
2 Favorite Funeral Marches HC-34
Two Funeral Marches DW-17
Two Odes GW-483
Tyler's Quick Step JT-4
Tyrants Of '76 And Tyrants Of '56 JCF-10

Ulysses Grant Marche Funebre USG-25
Ulysses Is His Name USG-78
Ulysses Leads The Van USG-189
Ulysses, Tried And True USG-58
Ulysses Waltzes USG-4
Ump-Um Ump! BFH-74
Uncle Abe's Rebellious Boys AL-168
Uncle Abe's Republican Songster For Uncle Abe's Choir AL-400
Uncle Abe's Songster AL-400
Uncle Abram, Bully For You! AL-35
Uncle James JCF-25
Uncle Joe's Hail Columbia AL-256
Uncle Sam And Willkie Come To Town WLW-36
Uncle Sam We Promise You FDR-271
Uncle Sam's Concert TR-235
Uncle Sam's Favorite Song Book GW-534; MISC-170
Uncle Sam's Menagerie AL-119
Uncle Sam's Songs GW-523
Uncle Sam's Summons JAG-82
Uncle Teddy TR-340
Under The Banner Of Protection BFH-86
Under The Big Blue Eagle FDR-66
Underwood March MISC-25
Unemployment Blues, The FDR-44
Unfurl The Glorious Banner GW-597
Unfurl Old Glory To The Topmast Breeze GW-288
Unfurl The Flag USG-284
Unfurl The Grand Old Stars And Stripes GW-133
Union GBM-39
Union And Liberty TR-95
Union Army March GBM-58
Union Bell Polka, The JBL-5
Union Bell Schottische JBL-7
Union Clay Glee Book, The HC-107
Union Forever, The DW-35
Union Grand March DW-31
Union Grand March Militaire USG-111
Union March AL-318
Union March Militaire USG-111
Union Memorial Service For Warren Gamaliel Harding WGH-45
Union Quick Step MF-8
Union Republican Campaign Glee Book USG-260
Union Volunteer's Quickstep USG-64
United Arms Of Victory WW-106
United Nations Anthem HST-7

United Republican Dinner DDE-98
United States Country Dances GW-474
United States Labor Greenback Song Book JBW-7
United States March MVB-6
United States March No. 2 JKP-9
United States Of America WM-192
Unity Forever WM-21
University Club Banquet Program And Song Book WHT-32
Unpardonable Sin, The TR-104
Until That Rising Sun Is Down DAM-24
Until The End AL-321
Untitled Song Sheet TR-329; WLW-37
Untitled Song Sheet For Eisenhower And Nixon DDE-92
Unworthy Of Your Love RR-27
Up Salt River WHH-38; WHH-91; FDR-368
Up San Juan Hill TR-119
Up The Stars And Stripes BFH-12
Up-To-Date Progressive Party Campaign Songs TR-369
Up To Date Republican Campaign Songster WM-276
Up Went McKinley WM-71
Up With The Banner BFH-22; BFH-48
Up With The Red Bandanna GC-159; GC-162
Up With The Stars And Stripes WM-24
Upidee AL-483
Upon These Grounds MISC-147
U.S. Flag Is Waving In Heaven FDR-293
U.S. Grant Is The Man USG-52
U.S. Marine Band March & Two Step MISC-44
U.S. Race USG-291
U.S. Rainbow Division WW-120
U.S.A., The WW-79
U.S.A.'s MacArthur DAM-20
U.S.G USG-28
U.S.W.V TR-283

Valley Forge March GW-227
Valse Imperiale RBH-30
Van Buren Quick Step MVB-2
Van Is A Used Up Man HC-115
Vanity TJ-42
Variety Of Marches, A GW-485
Vera Cruz Grand March, The WS-6; WS-33
Vera Cruz Quick Step WS-35
Verdict March, The JAG-16
Veteran Polka, The ZT-65
Veterans And Sons Of Veterans Campaign Song WM-176
Veteran's Last Song, The JGB-23; JGB-25
Veteran's Vote, The JAG-40
Veto Galop!, The AJN-17
Vice President Andrew Johnson's Grand March AJN-2
Victorious Americans March WM-165
Victory USG-297; HCH-43

Title Index 760

Victory Banquet FDR-350
Victory For Democracy FDR-226
Victory For Willkie WLW-53
Victory In '56 DDE-35
Victory Is In The Air TED-10
Victory Jones FDR-177
Victory Of Trenton, The GW-5
Victory Song, The WW-162
Victory Song Book For Soldiers, Sailors And Marines GW-537
Vietnam Songbook, The LBJ-33
Village Fifer No. 1, The GW-476; TJ-55
Violet Waltz AL-275
Virginia GW-301; GW-457; JT-5; FDR-22
Virginia Corlitza, The GW-136
Virginia Rose Bud GW-116
Virginia Washington Monument Grand March GW-142
Visions And Revision TED-34
Visitor, The JMD-4
Viva L'America March TR-139
Viva Roosevelt FDR-61; FDR-411
Vive L'America BFB-22
Vive La Republique GW-150
Vive Le Clay! HC-56
Voice From Garfield's Home, A JGB-44; JGB-61
Voice From The Army, A AL-117
Voice Of America, The RMN-1
Voice Of Freedom MISC-112
Voice Of The People HC-76; WW-211
Voice Of The West WHT-36
Voluntary For The Organ JA-7
Vote As You Shot Boys RBH-25
Vote For Abraham AL-126
Vote For Clay HC-78
Vote For Dewey TED-29
Vote For Eisenhower DDE-107
Vote For Gen. C.B. Fisk CBF-2
Vote For Gen' U.S. Grant USG-122
Vote For Gracie MISC-17
Vote For Hayes RBH-63
Vote For Henry Wallace HAW-4
Vote For Hoover HCH-65
Vote For Mister Rhythm MISC-72; MISC-80
Vote For Names MISC-106
Vote For Nixon RMN-21; RMN-29; RMN-30
Vote On! Pennsylvania! FDR-166
Vote! Vote! Vote! MISC-82

Wait JGB-69
Wait Till Next November GC-72
Wait Till The Votes Are Counted BFH-74
Waive High The Red Bandana GC-49
Wake, O Republicans, Wake! JGB-15; JAG-116
Walkin' Down To Washington JFK-36; JFK-41
Wallace For President HAW-7
Wallace Song Sheet HAW-10
War And Republican Campaign Songs WM-311
War Song GW-105; WS-31

War Songs GW-355; GW-411; GW-412; GW-413; GW-529; AL-579; AL-303; AL-350; AL-351; AL-352; AL-495; USG-43; USG-44; USG-45; USG-213
War Songs Of The Blue And The Gray AJK-57; AL-507; USG-299; MISC-183
War Veteran's Parade March BFH-46
Warlike Dead In Mexico, The HC-33
Washington GW-10; GW-23; GW-110; GW-153; GW-163; GW-168; GW-276; GW-347; GW-376; GW-391; GW-408; GW-461; GW-518; GW-557
Washington American Song-Book – Rough & Ready ZT-77
Washington And Count De Grasse GW-24
Washington & Independence GW-475
Washington And Lee Swing GW-201
Washington And Liberty GW-553; GW-553
Washington And Lincoln GW-558; GW-570; GW-611; AL-99; AL-192; AL-215; AL-479; MISC-171
Washington Arch GW-363
Washington At Valley Forge WHT-5
Washington Bi-Centennial March GW-540
Washington Birthday March GW-216
Washington Centennial March, The GW-161; GW-504
Washington, Chief Of Our Nation GW-533
Washington Crossing The Delaware GW-93; GW-332; GW-535
Washington Elm March GW-151
Washington Elm Quick Step GW-151
Washington Et Lincoln AL-401
Washington For-Ever GW-192
Washington Gallop GW-108
Washington Garland, A GW-294
Washington Grays GW-439
Washington Guards GW-96
Washington, He Was A Wonderful Man GW-270; GW-327
Washington In Massachusetts GW-250
Washington-Jefferson College Song GW-410
Washington, Lincoln And Franklin D FDR-279
Washington March GW-260
Washington Miscellany, A GW-393
Washington Monument GW-507
Washington Monument By Night GW-392
Washington Monument March GW-249
Washington, Patriotism Among The Young GW-283
Washington Program Songs GW-339
Washington Quadrilles, The GW-128
Washington Quickstep GW-272
Washington Remembrance (or Georgetown And Alexandria) Songster's Magazine, The GW-508
Washington Songster, The GW-140
Washington Society GC-136
Washington Star Of The West GW-87; GW-596

Title Index

Washington The Brightest Name On History's Page GW-549
Washington The Great GW-512
Washington Twist MISC-68
Washington Waltz JQA-6
Washington Was A Grand Old Man GW-306
Washington's Assembly GW-39
Washington's Birthday GW-319; GW-370; GW-511
Washington's Birthday Entertainment Book GW-205
Washington's Birthday March GW-40; GW-370
Washington's Birthday Waltz GW-397
Washington's Call From The Grave GW-125
Washington's Centennial Grand March GW-152
Washington's Centennial Inaugural March BFH-17
Washington's Dead March GW-114
Washington's Farewell Address GW-354
Washington's Favorite GW-71; GW-485
Washington's Favorite March GW-64
Washington's Favorite The Brave La Fayette GW-478
Washington's Grand Centennial March GW-43
Washington's Grand March GW-56; GW-66; GW-67; GW-68; GW-66; GW-69; GW-72; GW-103; GW-104; GW-435; GW-480; GW-481; GW-482; GW-486; GW-535; GW-567; GW-568
Washington's Grave GW-630
Washington's Hacking Hatchet GW-233
Washington's March GW-19; GW-28; GW-29; GW-30; GW-31; GW-32; GW-33; GW-34; GW-35; GW-36; GW-42; GW-45; GW-52; GW-53; GW-54; GW-60; GW-67; GW-71; GW-73; GW-95; GW-100; GW-102; GW-103; GW-106; GW-109; GW-115; GW-121; GW-146; GW-254; GW-265; GW-293; GW-310; GW-315; GW-340; GW-361; GW-383; GW-429; GW-435; GW-462; GW-467; GW-471; GW-473; GW-479; GW-481; GW-484; GW-487; GW-493; GW-495; GW-494; GW-498; GW-499; GW-500; GW-503; GW-506; GW-535; GW-567; GW-568; GW-618
Washington's March At The Battle Of Trenton GW-28; GW-32; GW-35; GW-64; GW-73; GW-106; GW-109
Washington's Marh [Sic] GW-28
Washington's Minuet And Gavott GW-474
Washington's New March GW-74; GW-146
Washington's Old March GW-146
Washington's Quick Step GW-104
Washington's Reel GW-55
Washington's Sons GW-364
Washington's Tent GW-598
Washington's Tomb GW-255; DW-13
Washington's Trenton March GW-38; GW-65; GW-581
Washington's Triumph GW-342
Water Lily Waltz AL-275

Water Wagon World Express AL-125; PP-2
Wave On Bright Stars And Stripes WGH-16
Way Down On Biscayne Bay WGW-33
We Address Him As Mr. President MISC-132
We All Know The Man Is Theodore Roosevelt TR-304
We All Want Dewey TED-23
We Are All With You Wendell Willkie WLW-35
We Are Americans WW-212
We Are Americans Too HST-21
We Are Coming Brave Ulysses USG-137
We Are Coming Father Abra'am AL-125; AL-158; AL-467; AL-495; MISC-168
We Are Coming Father Abra'am, 600,000 More AL-107; AL-466
We Are Coming Father Abra'am, 300,000 More AL-75; AL-121; AL-165; AL-293; AL-506
We Are Coming Father Abraham AL-158; AL-166; AL-192; AL-215; AL-303; AL-330; AL-350; AL-351; AL-352; AL-353; AL-365; AL-488; AL-489; AL-505
We Are Coming Father Abraham, 600,000 More AL-122; AL-173 AL-456
We Are Coming Father Abraham, 300,000 More AL-33; AL-36; AL-161; AL-239
We Are Coming Father Abrah'm AL-491
We Are Coming Father Abr'am AL-475
We Are Coming Father Abram, Full 600,000 More AL-465
We Are Coming President Wilson, Six Hundred Thousand More WW-193
We Are For Bliss WM-122
We Are Going Father Wilson WW-198
We Are Just From The Mills WM-146
We Are New Deal Democratic FDR-337
We Are With TR TR-55
We Are With You Wendell Willkie WLW-23; WLW-29
We Can, We Will, We Must FDR-344
We Can Win With Roosevelt FDR-135
We Forget Not The Day JAG-89
We Have Another Lincoln And Edwards Is His Name AL-486
We Have The Right Man Now WW-28
We Know Our Business WM-172; WM-173
We Like Ike's Leadership DDE-81
We Love Our President Of America FDR-17
We Love The Sunshine Of Your Smile DDE-28; DDE-59
We Mourn Our Country's Loss AL-444; JAG-44
We Mourn Our Fallen Chieftain AL-416
We Must Whitewash Him WM-314
We Need A Man MISC-136
We Need A Change In Washington WFM-2; GCW-6
We Need You Franklin D FDR-250; FDR-251
We Need You, Mr. Roosevelt TR-243
We See The Break Of Day AL-134
We Shall Overcome LBJ-2
We Sing AL-473
We Stand At Armageddon TR-91

Title Index

We Stand For Peace While Others War WW-11; WW-186
We Swear By Washington GW-368
We Take Our Hats Off To You Mr. Wilson WW-8; WW-63
We The Nation Of The Free LBJ-3
We The People HAW-1
We 38 Senators JMC-14
We Want A Man Like Roosevelt FDR-45
We Want A Rock And Roll President MISC-60
We Want Adlai AS-10
We Want Al Smith For The Presidential Chair AES-60
We Want Dewey TED-18
We Want Dewey-Bricker TED-16
We Want Dick RMN-41
We Want Dick And Spiro RMN-40
We Want Eisenhower For President DDE-6; DDE-94
We Want Franklin D FDR-59
We Want Goldwater BMG-7
We Want Harding WGH-17
We Want Hoover HCH-45
We Want Ike DDE-55; DDE-108
We Want Mister Roosevelt FDR-391
We Want Roosevelt FDR-37; FDR-64
We Want Teddy TR-149
We Want Teddy Four Years More TR-111
We Want Willkie WLW-8; WLW-15; WLW-25
We Want Wilson In The White House WW-94
We Want Yer, McKinley, Yes We Do WM-80
We Will Follow Brave Debs To The End EVD-3
We Will Honor The Mem'ry Of George Washington GW-253
We Will Honor You Forever WW-93
We Will Not Retreat Any More USG-183
We Will Stand By Our President WW-130
We Will Vote For The Man From Nebraska WJB-94
We Will Win With Ike DDE-37
We Would Remember MISC-112
Webster's Funeral March DW-15; DW-16; DW-24; DW-26; DW-30; DW-34
Webster's Grand March DW-5; DW-33
Webster's Grand March And Quick Step DW-14
Webster's Quick Step DW-4; DW-6; DW-7; DW-9; DW-10; DW-11; DW-12; DW-16; DW-19; DW-21; DW-22; DW-23; DW-25; DW-27; DW-28; DW-32; DW-36
Wedding March GC-33
Wedding Of The Blue And Grey GW-236
Weep For The Brave USG-190
Weep Not For The Slain, O Columbia AL-242
Weeping Sad And Lonely WS-8
Wehman's American National Songs GW-357; AL-353
Welcome Coolidge CC-28
Welcome Home WHH-28; HC-25
Welcome Home Comrade TR-190
Welcome Home Quick Step WS-3
Welcome March GC-88
Welcome Mr. Roosevelt FDR-200
Welcome To The Jumbo Jamboree MISC-154
Welcome Wilson WW-107
We'll All Be In The Money Now FDR-299
We'll All Go Vote For Blaine JGB-59
We'll All Go Voting For Al AES-21
We'll All Help McKinley Along WM-87
We'll Blow Our Horn For Hayes RBH-28
We'll Carry On, On To Victory FDR-159
We'll Do It With Dewey TED-21
We'll Do The Same To-Day WW-203
We'll Fight For Uncle Abe AL-156; AL-475; AL-493; AL-506
We'll Fight It Out Here On The Old Union Line USG-139
We'll Follow MacArthur DAM-11
We'll Follow Teddy TR-346
We'll Follow Where The White Plume Waves JGB-37
We'll Go For Hayes RBH-58
We'll Go With Grant Again USG-106
We'll Link His Name With Lincoln WW-89
We'll March To The Polls WGH-53
We'll Move On The Enemy's Works Again USG-84
We'll Never Forget Our Garfield's Name JAG-83
We'll Never Have To License Again JSJ-2
We'll Put Garfield In The Chair JAG-96
We'll Remember JFK-22
We'll Rock Her In The White House Chair GC-95
We'll Show You When We Come To Vote MISC-1
We'll Stand By Our President TR-77
We'll Vote For Blaine, The Man From Maine JGB-88
We'll Vote For Grant Again USG-19
We'll Vote For McKinley For He's All Right WM-231
We'll Vote For The Buckeye Boy USG-27
We'll Vote For The Man Who Kept Us Out Of War WW-10
We'll Win The Race Again BFH-12
We'll Win Through — We Always Do FDR-74
We'll Win With Willkie WLW-7; WLW-48
Wendell L. Willkie WLW-14
Wendell Willkie WLW-21; WLW-65
Wendell Willkie Goes To Washington WLW-4
We're A Band Of Freemen JCF-27
We're All For Eisenhower DDE-7
We're All For You Uncle Sam FDR-413
We're All Going Out To Vote For Willkie WLW-11; WLW-58
We're All Good Pals At Last HCH-39
We're All With You Mister Wilson WW-190
We're All With You Oh Doug MacArthur DAM-26

Title Index

We're Bound To Win With Boys Like You WW-31
We're Brothers True From The North And South USG-72
We're Comin' Inauguration! FDR-101
We're Coming Fodder Abraham AL-15; AL-316
We're Free, We're Free JCF-36
We're Fixin' A Date With Nixon RMN-22
We're For Adlai AS-7
We're For Al AES-42
We're For Hoover HCH-49
We're For Hoover And Curtis HCH-1
We're For Roosevelt FDR-8
We're For You Mr. Smith AES-12
We're Glad To See You Back Mr. Wilson WW-143
We're Glad We've Got You Mr. Wilson WW-188
We're Goin' Daddy Woodrow WW-185
We're Going Big For That Big Blanket Code FDR-36
We're Going To Celebrate The End Of The War In Ragtime WW-14
We're Going To Keep Mr. Hoover HCH-10
We're Going To Land Big Bill And Sunny Jim WHT-25
We're Gonna Live It Together RMN-15
We're In Such A Fixie! RR-31
We're Keepin' F.D.R FDR-208
We're Madly For Adlai AS-6; AS-8
We're Marching On To Victory With Dewey TED-8
We're On Our Way! WLW-10
We're On The March FDR-168; FDR-170
We're Over Here FDR-253
We're Ready For Teddy Again TR-37
We're Ridin' To Glory On A Mule FDR-182; FDR-183
We're Rolling AL-244
We're Satisfied With Teddy TR-204
We're Strong For George Wallace GCW-2
We're Voting For Nixon RMN-2;
We're Waiting For The Call Mr. Wilson WW-124
We're With Al Smith AES-35
We're With You Mr. President FDR-81
We're With You Mr. Wilson WW-5
West O The Wide Missouri BFH-43
Western Democratic Melodist, The JKP-16
Western Taps BFH-98
We've A Man For Our Leader USG-9; USG-30
We've Got Him On The List GC-73
We've Got The Right Man In The White House Now FDR-71
We've Put Teddy Up To Fight TR-205
We've Swiped The West In Football WM-327
We've Tested Him In Days Gone By USG-9
We've Walloped Them So WHH-119
What A Man FDR-24
What A Real American Can Do WW-16
What A Shame JFK-40
What Are You Going To Do In 1932 FDR-178

What Does He Look Like RR-19; RR-20
What Does Old Glory Say To The Rest Of The World AL-312
What Would My Grand-Father Think? JGB-56
What Would We Do Without Roosevelt FDR-423
Whatever Became Of Hurbert? HHH-6
What's Good Enough For Washington Is Good Enough For Me GW-628
What's Up With Hanna? WM-312
Wheatland March JB-13
Wheatland Polka JB-4
Wheatland Schottisch JB-9
Wheelbarrow Polka JB-12
When A Coon Sits In The Presidential Chair MISC-37
When A Third Term Bug Gets Drafted WLW-31
When Abe Comes Marching Home JCF-40
When All The World's At Peace WW-85
When Bryan Comes To The White House WJB-40
When Douglas Mac Comes Marching Back DAM-35
When David Came Limping Home WM-127
When Grover Cleveland Gets A Baby Boy GC-108
When Grover Goes Marching Home BFH-30
When Grover Touched The Button At The Fair GC-106
When Hancock Takes The Chair WSH-3
When Harding's In The White House WGH-22; WGH-36
When Hoover Comes Back To Washington HCH-66
When I Am The President MISC-12; MISC-13
When I Get There In The White House Chair WJB-53
When I Prayed At Mother's Knee JQA-9
When I Return To The U.S.A. And You WHT-30; WW-77
When Johnnie Comes Marching Home Again WW-17; WW-18
When Rough And Ready Teddy Dashes Home TR-35
When Teddy Comes Marching Home TR-23; TR-38; TR-166; TR-233; TR-305
When Teddy Comes Marching Home With His Gun TR-185
When Teddy Got To Jungleville TR-302
When The Boys Come Marching Home DDE-65
When The Gold Reserve Came Tumbling Down WM-213
When The World Bows At Washington's Grave GW-208
When The Yankees Go Into Battle GW-326
When This Old Grey Hat Was New WHH-12
When Uncle Sammy Sings The Marseillaise GW-308
When Washington Was A Boy GW-214
When We Seat Our Mr. Taft WHT-58

Title Index

When Wilson Called The Kaiser's Bluff WW-90
When Woodrow Wilson Takes A Hand WW-129
When Yankee Doodle Teddy Boy Comes Marching Home Again TR-258
When Yankees Go Into Battle GW-325
When You're All In Down And Out WW-117
Where Did You Get That Hat? FDR-235
Where Graves Outnumber The Flowers AL-214
Where Is Our Moses? AJN-10
Where Is The Heart Of The Soldier GW-133
Where Our Wilson Shines Democracy WW-50
Where The Healthy Breezes Blow TR-368
Where There's A Willkie There's A Way WLW-27
Which Nobody Can Deny BFH-74
Whig Banner Melodist, The HC-15; HC-70
Whig Banner Songster, The HC-112
Whig Chief, The HC-50
Whig Convention Grand March WHH-92
Whig Gathering WHH-107
Whig Rallying Song WHH-91
Whig Song For The Fourth Of July WHH-91
Whig Songs For 1844 HC-35
Whig Songs For The Mendon Clay Club HC-105
Whig Songs Selected, Sung And Published by The Choir Of The National Clay Club HC-106
Whig Quadrilles, The WHH-24
Whig Quick Step WHH-83
Whig Rally, The HC-75
Whig Rallying Song, The WHH-113
Whig Songs 1840 WHH-128
Whig Victory Song HC-76
Whig Waltz, The WHH-25
Whig Waltz 1776, The WHH-45
Whig's Grand March, The WHH-32
Whigs Of Columbia Shall Surely Prevail, The WHH-4; WHH-85
Whigs Of '76 & '44 HC-45
Whigs Triumphant March And Quick Step WHH-105
While The Battle Ships Are Sailing TR-309
While We AreBooming McKinley WM-327
While We Are Marching For Garfield JAG-5
Whistle Stop HST-22
White Dove Of Peace, The RMN-1
White House, The:MISC-185
White House Blues HCH-57
White House Bride, The GC-110
White House Chair, The JB-14; JB-22
White House Flower, The CC-23
White House In Washington And The White House In The Lane, The MISC-50
White House Is The Light House Of The World MISC-48
White House March, The WM-64; WM-217
White House March Two-Step, The MISC-172
White House Race, The JCF-25; JCF-52
White House Serenade MISC-188
White House Waltz, The DDE-46

White House Waltzes, The:TR-376
White Man's Banner, The HS-1
White Plume March, The JGB-39; JGB-96
White's School For The Reed Organ DW-34
Whitney's Easy Method For Parlor Organ GW-551
Who Feelith Not A Rapture? HC-2
Who Is Hoover? HCH-23
Who Killed J.F.K., R.F.K., M.L.K., M.J.K.? JFK-50
Who Shall Rule This American Union? USG-267
Who Shall Rule This Great Republic? WM-291
Who Whipped? BFH-74
Who Will Care For Old Abe Now? AL-449; AL-459
Who Wrecked The League Of Nations JMC-16
Who'll Follow, Who'll Follow JCF-36
Who-Oo Who-Oo Hoover HCH-33
Who's Hoo HCH-51
Why? JFK-5
Why Can't We Be Sweet Hearts Again FDR-343
Why Change? FDR-392
Why Should They Kill My Baby! JAG-98
Wide-Awake Two-Step AL-367
Wide-Awake Quick Step, The AL-18
Wide Awake Vocalist, The AL-59
Wide Awakes, The AL-116
Wie Kann Man Geld Verdienen? WJB-43
Wife I Left Behind, The USG-150
Wigwam Grand March, The AL-12
Will Rogers For President MISC-11
Will Taft, We're Looking To You WHT-21
William H. Taft March And Two Step WHT-26
William J. Bryan Unser Nachster Prasident WJB-49
William Jennings Bryan HCH-60
William Jennings Bryan Of Nebraska WJB-44
William Jennings Bryan Our Next President WJB-93
William McKinley's Dying Words WM-130
William McKinley's Funeral March WM-269
William McKinley's Dying Words WM-130
William The Conqueror WJB-86
William Will WM-98; WM-325
Willie Taft WHT-60
Williamsburg Grand Triumphal March WSH-31
Willig's Pocket Companion For Flute Or Violin GW-21; MISC-129
Willig's Juvenile Instructor For The Piano-Forte GW-383
Willkie And McNary Is Our Team WLW-49
Willkie Campaign Song WLW-54
Willkie For President WLW-24
Willkie For President March WLW-32
Willkie Hop, The WLW-3
Willkie Is Our Man WLW-19; WLW-68
Willkie March, The WLW-38; WLW-57
Willkie-McNary-Barton Victory Rally WLW-51
Willkie-McNary Rally Songs WLW-39
Willkie Should Stay In Wall Street FDR-285
Willkie Victory March WLW-1; WLW-59

Title Index

Willkie Will Win WLW-70
Wilson WW-37; WW-207
Wilson And California WW-167
Wilson And Victory WW-146
Wilson Democracy And The Red, White And Blue WW-29
Wilson Era, The WW-161
Wilson For President WW-96
Wilson Has A Winnin' Way WW-35
Wilson-Lincoln Reign, The WW-204
Wilson March WW-6; WW-80; WW-140
Wilson Marching Song WW-164
W-I-L-S-O-N Means Wilson With The Good Old U.S.A. At His Command WW-82; WW-159
Wilson — That's All WW-54; WW-170
Wilson's Battle March USG-147; USG-159
Wilson's Commemoration March WW-157
Wilson's Favorite Rag WW-208,
Wilson's Funeral March USG-71; USG-242; USG-243
Wilson's Inaugural March WW-61; WW-145
Win GRF-2
Win With Landon AML-3; AML-8
Win With Roosevelt FDR-110
Win With Willkie WLW-6; WLW-30; WLW-40
Winner's Easy System For The Violin GW-560
Winner's New Primer For The Flute GW-545
Wintergreen For President MISC-15; MISC-16
Wisconsin Forward Forever AL-209
With A Roosevelt In The White House FDR-122
With Blaine And Jack We'll Clear The Track JGB-44
With Cleveland We Will Win The Day GC-17
With Garfield We'll Conquer Again JAG-52; JAG-57; JAG-96
With Hancock, Union, Liberty! WSH-13
With My Head In The Clouds RR-19; RR-20
With Roosevelt As The Skipper FDR-217
W.J. Bryan's Grand March WJB-27
Wm. McKinley's Grand March WM-204
Women Light The Way For Change BC-7
Women's Christian Temperance Union Songs Nd-3
Won't You Be My Billie Possum WHT-52
Woodrow Wilson WW-155; WW-206
Woodrow Wilson And The Red White And Blue WW-176
Woodrow Wilson And The U.S.A WW-132
Woodrow Wilson For President WW-26; WW-96
Woodrow Wilson Four Years More WW-115
Woodrow Wilson Inaugural WW-4
Woodrow Wilson Leader Of The U.S.A WW-114
Woodrow Wilson March WW-78; WW-74
Woodrow Wilson, The Whole World Is Proud Of You WW-25
Woodrow Wilson's Grand March WW-84
Woodrow Wilson's The Right Man WW-181
Word From Long Island, A WS-34

Work For The N.R.A FDR-106
Work With Willkie And Win The Day WLW-30
Workers Of The World Awaken EVD-4
Workers Song Book 1934-1 CP-2
Workingmen's National Song SLP-1
World For Democracy WW-171
World Hasn't Anything On Me, The TR-236
World-Wide Democracy March WW-38
World's Best Album Of Marches USG-240
World's Peace Anthem, The WW-172
Wotta Price Amen FDR-305
Would You Rather Be A Tammany Tiger Or A Teddy Bear? TR-358
W.P.A FDR-69
Wreath, The AJN-11
Wreaths For The Chieftain GW-25; GW-27

Yankee Dood-Al AES-13
Yankee Dood'l Do CC-9
Yankee Doodle GW-20; GW-398; TR-194
Yankee Doodle And Hail Columbia GW-398
Yankee Doodler, The FDR-229
Yankee Freeman RBH-39
Yankee Kids TR-297
Yanks Will Do It Again, The FDR-386
Ye Jolly Lads Of Ohio WHH-52
Ye Tailor Man AJN-13
Ye Women's Singing Book GW-564
Year Of Jubilee Is Here, The FDR-76
Yellow Metal March WM-318
Yellow Rose Of Texas, The FDR-403
Yes, Yes, Tomorrow WLW-62
Yesterday AL-321
Yesterday We Loved You HHH-3
Yon Coo Doodle Do USG-263
You Are The Reason FDR-80
You Bet, La Follette RML-2
You Can Have Broadway GW-236; GW-322
You Can't Keep A Good Man Down AES-31
You May Be Lonesome AL-321
You Must Be There AS-14
You Settled When You Sold Your Wool WM-211
Young Abe Lincoln AL-212; AL-371
Young America GW-175; JCF-21
Young Blood Of The G.O.P. DDE-100
Young George Washington GW-514
Young Hickory And Annexation Minstrel, The JKP-17
Young Joshua TR-183
Young Men's Republican Vocalist, The AL-394
Young Republican Campaign Song Book BFH-53
Your Cause And Mine HCH-26
Your Mission AL-272
Your Roosevelt And Mine FDR-11
Youth's Companion GW553
You're A Grand Old Flag GW-235; GW-236; GW-327; GW-330
You're A Grand Old Rag GW-236
You're All Right Teddy TR-206
You're Ev'rything Sweet AL-321
You're The Hit Of The Season FDR-252

Composer Index

Aarons, Dr. Joseph TR-321
Abbott, E. TJ-33
Abbott, Frank TR-111
Abdill, C.L. USG-96; USG-300
Abejo, Rosalina JFK-46
Ablamovicz, Dina FDR-14
Able, F.L. AJK-30
Abrahams, Blanche E. WW-136
Abrahams, Maurice GW-219; GW-31; WW-5
Ackley, B.D. AL-441
Ackland, William FDR-85
Adair, Tom FDR-167
Adam, Ernst TED-36
Adam, William P. SJT-15; GC-22; GC-48
Adams, J.A. JGB-36
Adams, John AL-368; FDR-190
Adams, L.T. WHT-5
Adams, Ray L. FDR-25; FDR-311
Adams, Richie RMN-20
Adams, Sarah F.rancis WM-56; WM-243.
Adams, S.J. AL-33
Adams, Thomas F. WHH-49
Adams, William G. TED-10
Adams, Wm. P. SJT-3; WSH-29; JAG-94
Adee, David Graham JAG-17
Adger, Jos. Bennaker USG-193; WM-307
Adler, Robert FDR-413
Adrian, J. WJB-12
A.F.T. WHH-94
Ager, Milton BC-5
A.H.F. USG-200
Akey, C. AES-25
Akin, Blanche C. BFH-40

Akst, Harry MISC-26
Alban, Theodore FDR-146
Alboni, Carlo FP-3
Aldrich, A.E. CBF-4
Aledo, M.F. JAG-55
Alegro, Johnny FDR-93
Alerrer, Wilheim TR-209
Alexander. USG-160
Alenander, Dorothy FDR-210
Alewel, Louis E. HST-19
Alexander, F. USG-23; WM-114
Alexander, Jerry AES-32
Alenander, Perry TED-12; TED-13; TED-22
Alexander, Russell TR-350
Alford, Harry L. TR-21; TR-305; AML-19
Alfred, Roy AL-212
Allen, Lewis AL-494; FDR-197
Allard, Henry HS-2- HS-13
Allen, A.E. GW-437
Allen, Anne AL-356; FDR-221
Allen, Lanny MISC-112
Allen, Lewis AL-156; AL-333; AL-494; FDR-188; FDR-221
Allen, Martha B. WLW-15
Allen, Morrie AS-5; JFK-14
Allen, Jr., R. USG-137
Allen, Sargent S. DAM-45
Allen, Thomas S. GW-377
Allen, T.W. GW-201
Allison, William D. DAM-38
Alstarter, Carla TR-149
Althouse, Jay MISC-113
Althouse, M.A. JMN-21
Altier, Riley FDR-148
Altman, Arthur TJ-42
Amato, A. WW-180

Amberger, Marie A. FDR-187
Ambrose, T.F. WW-70
Americas, S.J.P. BFH-42
Amick, S.L. JWD-1
Anderson AJK-36
Anderson, Alfred TR-40
Anderson, C.H. WM-202
Anderson, Ellen JFK-65
Anderson, F.J. TED-14
Anderson, Fred BFH-59; BFH-60; BFH-61; BFH-62; BFH-63
Anderson, Geary F. DDE-69
Anderson, Hilding FDR-54
Anderson, Rudolph TR-169
Andino, J.E. AL-443; WW-132
Andrews, John C. ZT-23
Anness, E.V. JD-63
Anonymous. GW-506; TJ-27; MF-37; AL-475
Anthony, Bert R. GW-351
A.O.H. USG-199
Apgar, Tom S. WJB-82
Appel, Harry JMD-12
Applegate, William J. WHT-53
Appleton, Grace JGB-20
A.R. GW-12
Archer, Al FDR-375
Archer, C. AL-128
Archer, T.F. AJK-28
Arden, Billy FDR-415
Armand, E.B. AL-30
Armitage, Teresa GW-376; GW-444; AL-369
Armstrong, Harry W. GW-252
Armstrong, Henry JGB-44
Armstrong, Mollie E. GC-129
Armstrong, Paul B. WM-77
Armstrong, W.J. GC-152

Composer Index

Arnette, Victor TR-12
Arnold, Adelaide JQA-9
Arnold, Chris RR-22
Arnold, E.K. HCH-11; FDR-414
Arnold, Ion WM-50
Arnstein, Ira B. FDR-114
Aronson, Rudolph GW-143; GW-144; GW-146; USG-74; TR-6; TR-198; WHT-6
Artman, (Mrs) S.R. CC-10; CC-50
Arzich, J.H. FDR-30
Ascher, G. USG-183
Ascher J. JCF-34
Ashley, Glenn W. WJB-16; WJB-40; WJB-45; WHT-35
Ashton, Gilbert WM-171
Aspinwall, E.E. AES-20
Astin, Charles WW-65
Atkinson, Condit RR-28
Atterbury, Edith T. WM-167
Auden, W.H. JFK-57
Aughinbaugh, Hugh WLW-60
Augusta, Kay AML-17
Auner, A.W. AL-63; AL-254
Austin, A.W. JGB-71
Austin, James H. GW-202
Authenrieth, (Mrs) Wm. WHT-15
Auvray. AJK-36
Avery, H. GW-168
Ayer, Nat D. TR-29; TR-30; TR-258
Ayling, Thomas WHH-111
Ayres, George B. USG-124
Azzolina, M. WGH-4; CC-41

Babbit, Edwin S. AL-419
Bacak, Joyce Eilers MISC-97
Bach, Charles H. AL-160; AL-321
Bach, E.H. AL-136
Bachelor, Nick GC-163
Bachmann, Max TR-90
Backer, Bill MISC-77
Backus, A. WHH-6
Bacon, J.B. MF-16
Bader, Emma WGH-2
Baer, Abel RMN-1
Bagley, E.E. GW-273
Bagster, C. Birch GBM-80
Bailey, Eben H. SJT-14; SJT-18; WSH-36; JAG-6; JAG-75; JAG-87; GC-107
Bailey, H.B. JAG-74
Bain, Donald AES-37

Baird, Dewey T. JMC-10; WGH-9
Baker. AL-192
Baker, B.F. WHH-14; AL-122
Baker, Billy GW-284
Baker, Charlie JAG-84
Baker, Clarice WLW-68
Baker, Fred T. JAG-54; GC-7; GC-154
Baker, G. GBM-3
Baker, George TR-120
Baker, George C. WW-102
Baker, Herbert AS-11
Baker, Rev. J. JD-44
Baker, King W. DDE-96
Baker, Thomas AL-177; AL-178; HG-29
Baker, Ward TR-116
Baker, W.C. USG-271
Baldwin, J. Fred GW-197
Baldwin, John WLW-70
Bales, M.C. WJB-27
Ball, Douglas WLW-51
Ball, Ernest R. WHT-18
Baldwin, Ralph L. GW-455
Ballard, L.W. AL-238
Ballantine, Eddie DDE-18
Ballin, Douglas D. WLW-38; TED-23
Balmanno, (Mrs) HC-33
Bamber, Ed. FDR-55
Bandre, Antionette FDR-315
Banes, James DDE-82
Bankert, Geo. Felix JB-11
Banning, Charles H. MISC-76
Banta, Frank P. PP-4
Barber, Bert FDR-136
Barber, L.A. GW-197
Barclay, Wright FDR-341
Barker. GW-265
Barker, (Rev) Benjamin G. WW-215
Barker, George GW-254; GW-600
Barker, (Rev) J. JD-43
Barker, J.H. AJK-15
Barker, L.A. GW-197
Barker, Nathan AL-465
Barkan, Mark RMN-20
Barlow, George S. WW-118; JMC-1
Barlow, Raymond S. TR-195
Barnam, K.R. CC-21
Barnard, J.C. AL-37
Barnes. AL-455
Barnes, A.L. BFH-68
Barnes, C.L. ZT-87
Barnes, Edwin H. FDR-316
Barnes, Hank FDR-357

Barnes, W.M. TR-341
Barney, James A. AL-93
Barnhart, Roscoe DAM-32
Barnhouse, C.L. GW-454
Barnum, Kenneth R. DDE-52; DDE-61; DDE-91; DDE-104
Barnum, Lula Lloyd GC-24
Barone, William D. DDE-14
Barrackman, D.A. GW-301
Barrington, Francis WS-3
Barry, Joseph J. GW-271
Barstow, Forrester WHH-28; HC-25
Bartenstein, F. AL-268
Barth, Hans TJ-39
Bartlett, John C. HC-7; HC-57; HC-80
Bartlett, M.L. GW-539; GW552
Barton, Jo. F. WM-178
Barton, Major J. GW-145; USG-5; USG-86
Barton, (Mrs) Rose WM-237
Baskette, Billy FDR-146
Basler, Horace R. USG-277; JAG-24; GC-155; WM-188
Bastein, Jane Smisor GW-371; GW-622
Bassett, Annie R. WHT-22
Bassett, Jean GW-440; GW-612
Bass, Claude L. MISC-112
Basso, P.P. JAG-82
Bassvecchi, P.O. AJK-51
Batchelder, Eugene USG-62
Bates. MVB-13
Bates, J.A. GC-98
Bates, Katherine L. GW-592; WW-133; MISC-112
Bates, Lila C. WLW-20
Bates, L.J. USG-141
Bates, Van Ness GW-250
Batiste, J. HS-4
Batt, Anna Lee JFK-23
Battle, Edgar FDR-60
Baum, Louise AL-375; AL-474
Baumback, Adolphe GW-398; CF-21
Baxter, Phil MISC-83
Baur, June WW-60
Bayard, Samuel J. WHH-91
Bayha, Charles A. TR-53
Bayley, T.E. GBM-36
Baylor, E.W. JCB-6
Bayes, Nora TR-58
Bayha, Charles AL-321
Beall, B.B. AL-210

Composer Index

Bear, Noel WLW-4
Beattie, A.M. HCH-23
Beattie, John W. GW-385; AL-371
Beaverson, George WHT-23
Bebe. AL-410
Bechtel, Byron J. WJB-65
Beck, C.L. BFH-59; BFH-60; BFH-61; BFH-62; BFH-63
Beck, Fred CC-13
Beck, N.P. AES-12
Beckel, James C. GW-349; AJK-8; WHH-26; ZT-59; JB-3; GBM-57; AL-151; AL-235; AL-283; US-68; BFH-22; BFH-48; BFH-111; DW-33; MISC-139
Becker, T.C. JAG-101
Becket, J.C. USG-179; USG-180; USG-279
Becket, T.A. JB-20
Becklaw, L.W. DDE-17
Bedard, Lewis A. FDR-419
Beebe, Warren WJB-19
Beecher, Henry Ward USG-186
Beethoven, Ludwig V. GW-546; DW-1; DW-2; DW-3; DW-8; DW-15; DW-16; DW-26; DW-30; DW-34
Beirly, A. GW-133
Belden, F.E. GW-523; GW-529
Bell, Bill BMG-2
Bell, Irving TR-305
Bell, J.C. AL-199
Bell, Nora DDE-34
Bella. HG-10
Bellak, James GW-254; GW-265; GW-281; GW-310; ZT-6; ZT-62; GBM-42; JCB-4; JBL-7
Bellin, Lewis TJ-42
Bellini. ZT-64; WS-10; JCF-5
Bellman, Henry ZT-55
Bellstedt, Herman WM-143
Beltzhoover, D.M. WS-30
Bemis. HC-95
Benet, Rosemary TJ-34; JQA-10; AL-217; AL-247; TR-293; WW-155
Benet, Stephen V. TJ-34; JQA-10; AL-247; TR-293; WW-155
Ben-Horim, Nabum DDE-68
Benjamin. AL-424
Benjamin, Chas. Love GW-222

Benmosche, Herman WW-42
Benner, L.E. FDR-347
Bennett, Elmer de L. TR-64
Bennett, Henry H. FDR-400
Bennett, H.J. GBM-41
Bennett, Roy C. JFK-3
Bennett, R.R. AL-461
Bennett, S. Fillmore AL-39; AL-505; USG-268
Bennett, Sam WM-64
Benson, G.W. MF-6
Benson, Jo. GW-167
Benson, Roland W. WW-207
Bent, Geo. P. GW-536
Berardini, Sam FDR-17
Berg, Albert W. GW-159
Berg, Bernard WM-265
Berg, Jimmie FDR-344
Berg, T.H. Vanden ZT-11
Berge, H. JD-6
Berger, C. Sealsfield TR-374
Bergerson, Baldwin FDR-252
Bergman, Samuel A. AES-13; AES-15
Berkman, Ted RR-14
Berkowitz, Sol GW-394; TJ-48; AL-288
Berlin, Irving AL-194; AES-9; AES-11; AES-21; FDR-179; FDR-180; DDE-8; DDE-19; DDE-48; DDE-60; DDE-102; JFK-72; RR-19; RR-20; RR-32; DAM-42; MISC-60
Berman, Polly FDR-288
Bernard, Norrie TR-232; WW-205
Berneker, F. AL-264
Bernhardt, Charles E. TR-146
Bernhardt, Frank G. TR-338
Bernhardt, Fred C. DDE-64; DDE-111
Bernstein, Leonard TR-45; MISC-100; MISC-153
Berry, Catherine E. DDE-36
Berthoud, Pierre JCF-33
Bertrand, H. MF-16
Berube, Al N. FDR-401
Bessinger, Frank CC-56
Bettmann, Wm. TR-294
Betty, John RMN-23
Beuchel, Robert WJB-31
Bevier, Alvin FDR-323
Beyer, Fred GW-269; GW-387; GW-417; GW-418; GW-419

Bibo, Irving AL-227
Bickley, John J. WGH-22; CC-52
Beirman, Bernard TJ-42
Biart, Flo FDR-395
Bigney, M.F. HS-1; JBL-9
Bilbrew, A.C. FDR-336
Biondi, Joseph WW-97
Birch, Harry USG-8; HG-7; BFH-80
Bird, Douglas WM-226; WW-57
Bisbee, M.C. AL-240
Bishop. USG-159
Bishop, Christopher MISC-107
Bishop, (Mrs) E.M. CC-23
Bishop, G. Edward USG-112
Bishop, Henri R. GBM-10
Bishop, (Mrs) M.J. AL-97
Bishop, Paul J. USG-147; USG-199
Bishop, T. Brigham GW-329; AL-72
Bissell, T. GW-340; GW-359; GW-361; WM-56
Black, Dave JFK-56
Black, Frank WW-23
Blackburn, Tom AJK-43
Blackman, Orlando GW-525
Blackmer, F.A. WM-250
Blackstone, Dorothy DAM-21
Blackstone, Sigmund DAM-21
Blahnik, Helen B. TR-229
Blair, E.T. WJB-96
Blaisdell, E.W. GC-53
Blake, Charles D. AJN-7; RBH-3; RBH-9; JAG-23; JAG-114; CAA-1; JGB-99; BFH-7; BFH-126; GC-28; GC-39; GC-99; BFB1
Blake, Dorothy G. AJK-42; AL-248; TR-296
Blake, Eubie HST-1; HST-21
Blake, Eugene L. JAG-16
Blake, G.E. GW-499
Blake, James W. AES-1; AES-2; AES-5
Blakely, L.J. HS-10
Blamphin, C. AL-462
Blanchard, (Miss) Lucie. GW-590
Blanchard, W.S. AL-91
Blanchet, Eliza E. FDR-156
Bland, H.L. GW-367
Blandner, C.F. GW-130
Blau, Raphel RR-14
Blaxall, D'Arcy TR-271

Composer Index

Blecha, Judy Atwell GB-2
Bledsoe, Jules FDR-366; DAM-59
Blessner, Gustave MF-8
Bliss, P.P. RBH-22; JGB-15; JD-24
Block, Joseph JD-4
Blom, C. TR-59; WW-43
Blondell, William AJK-11; AJK-23; AJK-25
Blood, M.V.B. WW-24
Bloom, Sol GW-297
Bloomfield, F.D. WM-47; WM-48
Blue, A. WSH-44
Blue, True WS-38
Bobilya, Clarence L. FDR-48
Bochme, John Geo. TR-48
Boddie, John R. WHT-60
Bodecker, Louis USG-221
Boeckh, F.C. WM-248
Boehnlein, Francis H. WW-167
Boex, Andrew J. TR-75
Bohal, Edward L. GW-292; WGH—11
Bohannon, M.T. GW-298
Bohemia. JD-46
Boland, Clay A. FDR-225
Bolduc, Madame Ed. FDR-298
Bolino, Vin JFK-43
Bona, Mrs. J. BFH-73
Bonavitacola, Rose FDR-388
Bonbright, Stephie S. JGB-58
Bond, Alonzo FP-2
Bonnelly, Eddie LBJ-7
Booke, Lala TR-73
Boorn, Hal FDR-147
Booth, Sam USG-253; RBH-52; RBH-56; JAG-66; JGB-53; JAG-109; BFH-117; WM-329
Boston, Ella M. TR-182; CC-29
Bosworth, Grace L. TED-9
Botts, Marjorie RMN-3
Botts, Walter RMN-3
Boudreau, John T. JFK-6
Bourmann, Anotole FDR-355
Bousquet, Louis WW-126
Boutelje, Phil FDR-229
Bowers, Albert M WM-321
Bowers, E. AL-89
Bowers, Fred V. GW-218; AL-201; TR-104
Bowers, Robert H. JMD-13

Bowman, S.L. AL-232; USG-29
Boyd, Bill FDR-28
Boyd, Will A. TR-261
Boyle, Richard GW-212
Boynton,George A. GW-511; AL-471
Boynton, Irene AL-145
Bracken, James FDR-171
Brackett, J.W. GW-587
Bradbury, B. AL-46
Bradbury, William B. HC-82; AL-174; AL-503
Bradford, J.M. GW-309
Bradford, Perry TED-27
Bradley, (Mrs) A. WJB-47
Bradley, Myles F. USG-239
Bragg, Ralph F. DAM-9
Brahy, Gertrude H. FDR-49
Brainard, Charles S. AL-132; AL-176
Brain, John GW-237
Braine, Robert AL-229
Braley, Berton AL-209
Brand, M. TR-360
Brand, Michael JGB-57
Brandrik, Paul AL-121
Branen, Jeff T. TR-358
Brannan, Barrington FDR-128
Bratten, John W. AP-3; WLW-5; FDR-86
Braun, Frederick LBJ-5; MISC-162
Braun, George B.L. FDR-78
Braun, Mr. AJK-14
Braun, William F. TR-20
Bray, John JMD-18; WHH-16
Bray, Mabel E. GW-510
Breed, Daniel JAG-71
Breese, W.H. JAG-115
Breigel, George P. TR-367
Breiter, Robert WHH-73
Bresler, Jerome TR-220
Breslow, Ben AES-51
Briar. AL-415
Bricher, T. DW-29; ZT-70
Brickford, G.F. TR-292
Bridewell, W.W. HS-19
Bridgeman, George W. JRC-1
Bridges, Ethel HST-4
Bridges, J.F. AML-2
Brielmayer, Alex. WM-12
Briger, Maurice JFK-12
Briggs, George H. USG-67
Brigham, Gus. B. JGB-5; GC-52; WM-18
Briljan, I. JMN-3
Brimhall, John JFK-78

Brinley, Jessie AL-463
Brisben, Ned WLW-1; WLW-59
Bristow, F.L. BFH-74
Bristow, Frank L MISC-41
Bristow, Geo. F. GW-262; GW-547; ZT-24; ZT-25
Bristow, P.H. BFH-50
Broadway, William B. AL-76
Brockett, Alice WLW-39
Brocki, Buster FDR-280
Brockman. TR-42
Brockway, Flora WM-71
Brodsky, Rubin FDR-110
Bromby, George Hayden AP-1
Bromwell, (Mrs) S.E. GC-102
Brookens, E. DAM-11
Brooks, Janet B. FDR-165
Brooks, Vivian WW-194
Broom, Lionel WW-101
Broudy, Saul BC-6; MISC-121
Brown, A. Seymour TR-29; TR-30; WW-36
Brown, Bruce WHT-14
Brown, Eleanor S. GW-188
Brown, Fleta Jan WW-85; MISC-45
Brown, Francis H. GW-76; GW-302; GW-519; GW-546; WHH-29; JBL-1
Brown, Frank FDR-151; FDR-152; FDR-153
Brown, G.A. AL-460
Brown, G.W. USG-16; USG-18
Brown, George W. WW-54; WW-170
Brown, J. Alleine WHT-42
Brown, Jessie Burgess WM-134; WM-330; TR-369
Brown, Lew MISC-53
Brown, Marshall TJ-42
Brown, P. GW-128
Brown, Phillip TR-167
Brown, Raymond A. MISC-94
Brown, Ruth Gammon MISC-74
Brown, Seymour TR-258; AES-7; AES-54
Brown, T.M. AL-28
Browne, Augusta HC-33
Browne, Lee B. TED-21
Browne, Ted MISC-44
Broza, Jack FDR-321
Bruce, E.M. AL-466
Bruce, Jorette WGH-36
Bruce, Michael MISC-104

Composer Index

Bruck, Marie WW-103
Bruen. GW-194; GW-401
Brumbach, A. JQA-3
Bruner, A.M. WM-37; WM-99
Bruzzi, M. WW-177
Bryan, Alfred WW-39; WW-40; WW-126; MISC-48; MISC-50
Bryan, Charles F. AJK-39
Bryan, Vincent TR-5; TR-66
Bryant. AL-293
Bryant, Boudleaux JFK-71
Bryant, Felice JFK-71
Bryant, Gerard FDR-311
Bryant, William C. AL-75; AL-158; AL-465; AL-466; AL-467; MISC-139
Bryer, D.E. BFH-87; WM-277
Buchholts, Johann BFH-18
Buck, Dudley RBH-45
Buck, Francis ZT-26; WS-6; WS-20
Buck, Robert FDR-259; FDR-260
Buckley. AL-386
Buckley, Fred AL-156; AL-475; AL-506
Buckley, Jean JD-28
Buckley, W.T. TR-279
Buckman, Carl TJ-27
Buckner, Elliott FDR-326
Buechel, Aug. AL-444; JAG-44
Buehne, W.G. WM-299
Buford, J.W. TR-163
Bugbee, (Mrs) E.J. AL-82
Bullinger, Ethelbert William DAM-55
Bungay, George Washington AL-387
Bunting, Marie Louise FDR-84
Buntz, Ila D. FDR-2
Burch, Fred JFK-13
Burdick, (Mrs) A.L. WM-62
Burdick, C.H. WM-313
Burdick, E.J. TR-302
Burdick, S.C. AL-133
Burditt, B.A. JBL-3; JBL-11
Burditt, L.S. AL-93
Burgess, George W. WM-161
Burgheim, Philip HC-77
Burke, Joseph A. WW-15
Burke, J.F. AL-389
Burkes, E.A. AL-391
Burleigh, Wilber F. HCH-7
Burleigh, W.H. AL-57
Burnam, Edna Mae AL-324

Burns, George AJK-43
Burrill. MISC-160
Burt, Benjamin H. TR-295
Burtch, Roy L. WW-121; CC-10; CC-50
Burton, Glen MISC-104
Burton, Nat DAM-13
Burtson, Bud MISC-55
Busch, V. USG-71
Bush, George MISC-110
Bush, Warner E. HCH-55
Bushey, J. Calvin JAG-83
Buster, Phil E. HG-11
Butcher, H. WM-318
Butler, Eugene MISC-110
Butler, Evelyn AES-32
Butler, Helen May TR-123
Butler, Henry M. USG-236
Butler, M.W. WM-96
Butler, Noble GBM-33
Butler, William O. LC-3; LC-4; LC-5
Butterfield, J.A. AL-145; BFH-89
Buttner, Oauline H. FDR-154
Byers, N.E. WM-16
Byers, S.H.M. AJN-25
Byrne, Flora JD-1
Bryon, Alfred TR-211
Byron, Frank TR-207
Byron, Thomas BFH-20

Cabello, Ferd. L. WHT-41
Cable, Howard JFK-63
Cadman, Charles W. WLW-46
Caesar, Irving TJ-74; FDR-54; FDR-211; FDR-319; MISC-132
Caesar, Isador MISC-48
Cahill, Mary Ryan AES-55
Cahill, S. HC-4
Cahn, Sammy RR-1; RR-11
Cain, Katherine TED-33
Caire, Sid AML-5
Caldwell, Richardson WM-40
Caldwell, W.W. GW-391
Cleaveland, Charles P. WM-306
Caley, V.L. WHT-31
Califin, Emeka TR-301
Calkins, H.E. JBR-3
Callahan, J. Will GW-223; TR-131
Callinan, Gale W. DDE-47
Cameron, Alita Braun FDR-129
Cameron, Ray FDR-16
Camilieri, L. WW-133

Camp, Henry BFH-53
Campaign, R. BFH-30; BFH-65
Campbell. GW-213
Campbell, Alan DAM-37
Campbell, Charles R. WW-196; FDR-212; DAM-37
Campbell, Douglass RMN-35
Campbell, Lora FDR-365
Campbell, W.B. TR-360
Campbell, W.S. WLW-6
Campobello, Enrico TR-199
Caniglia, Lewis K. DAM-33
Canterbury, H. Webster AL-508
Cantwell, A. USG-98
Capano, Frank FDR-228; FDR-250; FDR-251
Capecelatro, Raffaele FDR-22
Capen, Edmund M. WW-198
Cappa, C.A. USG-81
Carawan, Candie GCW-7
Carawan, Guy LBJ-2; GCW-7
Carelton, Grace USG-109
Carey, Henry MISC-117
Carey, Tommy FDR-290
Carl. WSH-19
Carlberg, C. CAA-3; CAA-6
Carle, Wm. J. TR-322
Carlin, E.N. AL-392
Carling, Fos FDR-229
Carlo, Monte FDR-79; DDE-77
Carlson, Anna S. TR-88
Carlson, E.M. TR-188
Carlton, Charles USG-286
Carlton, Gerald USG-172
Carlton, Sam HST-2; HST-6
Carman, Bliss AL-322
Carman, Ruth TED-5
Carmen, Ted FDR-5
Carmichael, Hoagy GW-347; GW-518
Carmiencke, Godfrey GC-44
Carnes, Josef R. MISC-61
Carolina, Frank WM-26; WM-58
Carpender, Lillian WLW-30
Carpino, Louis FDR-148
Carr, Benjamin GW-3
Carr,   Thomas WHH-47; WHH-49; HC-69
Carr, W. Reginold WGH-25

Carragues, Adele M. JAG-30; JGB-37
Carrol, Joe FDR-195
Carroll, Grace FDR-287
Carroll, Harry TR-126
Carroll, Maj. W.C. JGB-68
Carruth, Walter WW-144
Carter, Hampton P. MISC-133
Carter, Isabelle S. JFK-26
Carter, James L. JFK-26
Carter, John FDR-378
Carter, N.S. WJB-38
Carson, Roy CC-6
Carusi, Nathanial HC-67
Carusi, Samuel MVB-4; JKP-6
C.A.S. JB-19
Case, Charles USG-145
Case, Hattie S. JGB-27
Case, (Mrs) W.W. JGB-27
Cases, Luis TR-283
Casey, James W. TR-65; TR-168; TR-234; WHT-11
Casey, Mary E. TR-282
Cashen-Lippert, Ruth AES-38
Cass, Emma Marie TR-277
Cassell, Irwin M. DDE-34
Casson, Herbert N. SLP-3
Casting, Harry TR-265
Castle, Harriet L. USG-68; USG-279; MISC-139
Cathey, Clara Phillips WW-145; WW-200
Catts, Jr., Sidney J. FDR-283
Cauchois, John J. MISC-103
Caulfield, T.N. AJN-21
Cavanagh, Dennis J. FDR-262
Cavanaugh, James DDE-2
Caven, John USG-95
Caven, John USG-95
C.C.H. GC-61
Center, E.C. USG-71
Chadsee, Bryan FDR-313
Chadwick, Henry ZT-83; WS-33
Chamberlin, C.H. AL-340; BFH-105
Chamberlin, Dexter E. JGB-59
Chamberlin, Helen B. WJB-28; WJB-92
Chambreau, Edward AML-11
Champness, Henry WW-79
Chandler, Larkin C. FDR-307; WL-3
Chanera. GW-217
Channing, Edward L. GW-205

Chanslor, Hal FDR-198
Chapman, C.C. GW-228
Chapman, C.H. JMC-7
Chapple, W.W. WW-172
Charles, Victor FDR-82
Chartrand, Willie M. WJB-6
Chase, George B. USG-190; WM-238
Chater, (Mrs) WHH-105
Chawa, Sami FDR-142
Cheeney, Sarah A. FP-9
Cheney, James T. WM-75
Chick, Leonard GW-224; GW-289
Chirgwin, John WGH-36
Chopin. JAG-67
Christian, I.H. WGH-14
Christian, Pass CBF-2
Christiani, S. JMN-27
Christie, Catherine AL-337
Christie, Edwin JAG-12
Church, Hellen WLW-15
Churchill-Grindell WW-68
Cirina, Charles FDR-359
Cirina, Gene FDR-359
Citelle. AL-445
Citizen of Mass. GW-127
Civis, George W. AL-388
C.J.H. TR-251
Clapham, Edward USG-34; USG-208
Clardy, George TED-1
Clareton. HS-10; USG-13
Claribel. JAG-25
Clarissa. TJ-16
Clark. GW-194; MF-33
Clark, Andy GW-454
Clark, Charles C. TR-125
Clark, Ella S. PP-1
Clark, E.S. GW-134; GC-4; GC-18; GC-66; GC-75; GC-115
Clark, Freeman FDR-327
Clark, George Arthur DAM-55
Clark, George W. MVB-5; JBR-1; JBR-4; JBR-5
Clark-Hall, Inez TR-102
Clark, Inez W. RMN-14
Clark, James G. GW-147; GW-452; JCF-32; GBM-29; AL-513; JAG-49; JGB-22; WJB-57
Clark, Kenneth S. TR-325; WLW-38
Clark, Luther A. AML-21; FDR-299; FDR-412
Clark, Milton F. FDR-262
Clark, Tony TR-125
Clark, William A. HG-16; USG-295

Clarke, Ellen M. MF-34
Clarke, Grant GW-311
Clarke, James G. AL-43; AL-513
Clarke, W. Milton HG-22
Clarke, William A. USG-298
Clarke, William H. GC-130
Clay, Max TR-201
Clayton, C.D. GBM-53
Clayton, Stanley WM-150
Cleary, Ruth AL-513; MISC-185
Clement, Fred W. WHT-45
Clement, Joe WGH-60
Clementi. JMD-6; JMD-8; JMD-9
Clements, B.S. AJK-22
Clements, Otis BMG-3
Cleveland, E. FDR-209
Cliff, Charles J. AS-2
Clifford, Carroll GW-255; GW-581
Clifton, A. GW-112
Clifton, W. AL-395
Clifton, William MF-12
Cline, Earl L. DDE-105
Closkey, J.W. AL-398
Cloutier, John E. FDR-71
Cloutman, S.W. WW-124
Coates, Jr., John MISC-117
Cobb, George L. TR-22
Cobb, Hazel GW-234
Cobb, Will D. WM-216
Code, E.M. WW-162
Code, Margaret FDR-14
Cody, H.H. AL-67
Coe, (Mrs) Charles A. WGH-16
Coe, Collin GW-519; GW-570; GW-611; JGB-15
Coe, J.M. WM-94
Coe, S.L. AL-170
Coerne, Louis A. GW-376
Coffey, Clara B. USG-190
Coffin, J.G. WHH-104
Cohen, Bob LBJ-31
Cohan, George M. GW-196; GW-230; GW-235; GW-236; GW-270; GW-285; GW-300; GW-322; GW-327; GW-330; GW-353; FDR-24; FDR-303; MISC-136
Cohen, A.M. GC-128
Cohen, J.B. WHT-3
Cohen, Lemmy DDE-18
Cohn, Lilian DDE-41
Cohon, Baruch J. JFK-11
Coin, True RBH-41
Colby, Carlton L. CC-4

Composer Index 772

Colby, Robert MISC-60
Cole. TR-206
Cole, Clinton TJ-52
Cole, F. AJK-38
Cole, George F. GW-37
Cole, Walter H. WHT-21
Coleman, Charles TR-13; TR-23; TR-129; TR-291; FDR-45
Coleman, Cy MISC-113
Coleman, W.C. GBM-59
Coleman, William E. WM-63
Collin, Luke AJN-6; AJN-19; USG-144
Collins, Ada May HCH-61
Collins, Jr., Chas. HC-31
Collins, Converse USG-83
Collins, Glenn AL-374
Collins, James F. TR-255
Collins, John T. TR-291
Collins, L.S. AL-399
Collins, Sydney TR-334
Colonna, Don Rocco FDR-107; TED-1; TED-17
Colonna, Harold CC-15
Copp, C.M. WJB-97
Colson, Jessie AL-197
Colston, E.R. ZT-17
Comellas, J. AL-401
Comfort-Brooks, Anita TR-197
Como, Eugene JB-8
Comden, Betty DDE-85; MISC-113
Comstock, Louis L. TR-118
Conant, Fred Kimball WW-84
Congdon, C.H. TR-117; TR-184; TR-306
Conigla, Lewis K. DAM-33
Conn, Mervin RMN-32
Conner, Tommie GW-279; FDR-137
Connolly, Charles M. TR-69
Connolly, Ellen M. WHT-2
Conrad, William USG-215; MISC-96
Conroy, Jack MISC-167
Conroy, Will J. WJB-23
Converse, Charlie C. HC-59
Cook, Charles L. TR-142; HST-21
Cook, Eliza GW-268; GW549
Cook, E.T. FDR-334
Cook, Harry L. WGH-9
Cook, James Franco GW-227
Cook, John H. AL-76
Cook, Seth A. WM-254

Cook,Wm. Marshall. RBH-64; BFH-124
Cooke, T. JMN-15
Cookingham, Edna WM-237
Coolidge, Calvin MISC-110
Coolidge, Grace CC-11
Cooper, A. AL-205
Cooper, Adeline M. ZT-43
Cooper, Alice MISC-104
Cooper, B.F. HS-6
Cooper, George GW-118; GW-120; GW-179; GW-245; AL-92; HG-14; USG-9; USG-30; USG-46; USG-106; RBH-16; JAG-94; JGB-2; GC-43; GC-105; JD-20; JD-55; MISC-139
Cooper, M. BFH-66
Cooper, Nanna E.M. TR-342
Cooperman, J. AL-517
Cooperman, S. AL-517
Coots, J. Fred FDR-38; FDR-292
Copeland, Aaron AL-333
Copeland, B.F. WHH-137
Copeland, Dorothy JFK-15
Coppock, W.R. DW-18
Cora, Karl JCF-36; AL-134
Corbett, Jim AS-13
Cordell, Henry E. FDR-217
Corliss, Frances WM-35
Cornejo, Rodolfo DAM-52
Cornic, Emma C. TR-188
Cosgrove, William SAD-11
Costello, Bartley GW-242; CC-6
Cottave, Henri E. FDR-354
Coulston, T..P. GW-581
Countryman, Carl C. HCH-20
Court, Ormsby A. TR-254
Couture, E. WGH-48
Covell, C.D. FDR-119
Covert, Bernard USG-55; JD-16
Covert, J. WS-41
Covington, Robert T. FDR-392
Cowan, John F. GW-126; GW-195
Coward, Leslie MISC-84
Cowen, Lynn WW-127
Cowen, Rubey WW-88
Cox, Bill FDR-378
Cox, Clifford GC-6
Cox, Ralph FDR-385
Cox, S.E. WW-129
Coyle, Elizabeth WM-180

Coyle, H. GBM-15; GBM-43; WSH-31
Craig, Ira FDR-83; FDR-97
Craig, John Howard TR-311
Craig, Josephine B. WJB-45
Craige, Charles D. TR-304
Craine, Paul WGH-7
Craine, Theo. T. USG-35
Cramer, Anna T. AL-277
Cramer, Bruce DDE-33
Cramm, Helen GW-374
Crane, E.W. WJB-67
Crawford, Jack GC-108; WM-264
Crawford, Richard MISC-139
Crawford, Robert WLW-9
Cripe. TR-88
Crist, D.W. TR-113; TR-114; TR-371
Cristiani, Sephen JMN-2
Cromwell, Henry GBM-45; AL-103
Crook, Howard J. MISC-133
Crorkin, Andrew FDR-175
Crosby. GW-554
Crosby, A. Melvin AL-193
Crosby, Fanny J. GW-215
Crosby, L.V.H. GW-119
Crosby, Warner TR-70; TR-85
Crosland, John M. JB-6
Cross, John C. GBM-9; GBM-19; GBM-33
Croswell, Anne AS-1
Crouch, William F. HST-9
Crum, George CC-12
Crowninshield, Ethel GW-558; AL-377
Cryderman, Geo. HCH-51
Cugat, Xavier FDR-61
Culier, Thomas P. JGB-56
Cull, Augustus GBM-16; AL-107
Cullen, E.B. GC-11
Cullinan, Gene AES-10
Cumming, Amos J. HG-5
Cumming, William JCB-3
Cummings, E.S. AL-403
Cunningham, Clarence DDE-50; MISC-146
Cunningham, Geo. W. TR-332
Cunningham, Kitty FDR-31
Cunningham, Lila G. TR-115
Cunningham, W.P. GW-591
Cunningham, Paul DAM-3
Cunnynham, Reymond J. GW-169

Curnow, James TJ-46; JFK-59
Curphew. GW-74; JMN-20
Curry, Lawrence AL-345
Curry, W. Augustus TR-213
Curtice, J.F. WW-79; WW-209; WGH-27
Curtis, Mann FDR-230; DDE-29
Cushing, Ella A. HCH-12
C.W.W. GBM-83

Dabney, Gene FDR-9
D'Accacia. JD-10
Dacoscos, Benny DAM-49
D'Agostino, Giacome FDR-144
Dahlin, Carl FDR-71
Daifotis, John DDE-3; DDE-81
Dale. William P. AL-394
Dallafield, Henry DDE-32
Daly, George AES-10
Daly, Isaac S. BFB-10
Daly, Joseph M. GW-377
Daly, Jerry GW-320
Dalton, J. Edward A. WM-225
Damish, Frederick JQA-5; JQA-6
Damn, Peter F. HCH-56
Damrosch, Walter AL-406
Danderson, James MISC-96
Dando, Tommy JFK-81
Dane, Barbara LBJ-33
Daniels, F.M. AL-471
Daniels, Henry G. WW-146
Daniels, Rev. John J. HCH-60
Danks, H.P. USG-79; RBH-26; WSH-34; BFH-12
Danner. MISC-112
Danziger, I. Dan AS-2
Darling, Denver FDR-176; FDR-410
Darling, J.M. USG-96; USG-300
Darnell, Shelby AML-24; DAM-46
Davalos, Marcos L. FDR-231; FDR-233
Davenny, Wilson I. WM-174
Davenport, John L. GBM-85
David, Hal TJ-42
David, Mack DDE-93
Davidson, R. WGH-3
Davis, Allen MISC-112
Davis, A.J. GC-14
Davis, Benny TJ-42
Davis, Billy MISC-77

Davis, Claud WHT-50
Davis, E.C. AL-78; AL-95; AL-147
Davis, Frank A. AML-20
Davis, Frank J. FDR-183
Davis, Frank M. AL-496
Davis, Gloria Ferry JFK-73
Davis, Hilda Emery FDR-80; JFK-73
Davis, Homer RML-1
Davis, Joe FDR-47; FDR-70
Davis, Katherine K. AL-307
Davis Mary Smith HCH-46
Davis, Meyer TED-3; TED-11; DDE-35; DDE-5; DDE-74; LBJ-26
Davis, Richard AL-246
Davis, Rummy FDR-105
Davis, W. Max WW-101
Davison, Archibald AL-355
Davison, B.M. GC-55
Dawnes, Carroll GW-460
Dawes, Charles G. CC-37; CC-38; CC-39; CC-45; CC-46; CC-47; CC-49; CC-51
Dawn, L.M. AL-51; AL-124
Dawsey, M.C. WM-108
Day, Bob FDR-285
Day, C.H. AL-65
Day, William F. WM-54
D.C.A. JAG-82
De Armond, Lizzie GW-205
De Brown, Dick GRF-6
De Bubna, Alex JCF-6; JCF-31
De Coenial, C.T. JAG-98
De Costa, Harry MISC-46
De Fonseca, A-Gomez WM-89
De Francesco, Louis FDR-384
De Graff, Jere WW-51
De Jasienski, J. USG-151
De le Re, P. HC-98; HC-99
De Leath, Vaughn FDR-365
De Longpre, Paul TR-119
De Luca, Eddie FDR-279
De Marbelle, Dion USG-262; JGB-76
De Mars, Helen FDR-15
De Paney, Vern FDR-327
De Paul, Vincent DDE-58
De Pauw, Linda Grant MISC-160; MISC-161
De Reeder, Katherine FDR-408
De Ronceray, C. GW-78
De Ruver, Jean JGB-46
De Tore, Emillo FDR-61
De Vin. JAG-111

De Wolf, Geo. G.B. SAD-15
De Wolf, Henry GW-309
De Waltoff, Dayve B. AES-73
DeAlwis, Jivaraj FDR-192
DeArmond, Mrs. GW-319
Decker, I. GW-9
Decker, Louis WW-91
DeCristoforo, C. WW-49
Dee, Sylvia TJ-42
Deems, James M. GW-409; WHH-74
Degenhard, Chas. G. MF-4; MF-5; GBM-76; AL-130; JD-38
Dekins, Stephen Taylor WJB-90
Del Calvo, Carlos M. TR-283
Del Campiglio, P.F. WM-164
Del Sordo, Enrico FDR-3
Del Sordo, Harry FDR-3
Dela, Lewis GW-591
Delamater, E. GW-400
Delaney, J.H. USG-14; USG-107
Delangevin, E.B. WW-83
Delano, Walter E. TR-52
Delli-Gotti, Frank JWD-6
DeLong, George Keller GW-303; GW-304
Delory, Al MISC-79
Demangate, Carl WW-32; WW-95
Demsey, Jack FDR-309
Demsey, (Miss) Fred WHT-56
Dempsey, Tom FDR-281
Dempsey, Wm. (Jack) FDR-309
Denner, Edward F. WM-118
Denniker, Paul AL-321
Denning, J.B. USG-108
Dennis, Matt JFK-66
Dennis, Tom CC-20
Denny, Inez AML-22
Denoyan, George HCH-18
Densari, Peno Y. TR-320
Dent, M.W. WW-214
Denver, Henry WM-68
Derschaky, E.F. USG-161
D'erson, Rene AES-34
Derrick, (Mr) GW-75
Dersch, Henry GC-1
DeShon, W.H. JGB-48
Devere, B. GW-131
DeVol, Herm FDR-42
DeWaltoff, Dayve B. HCH-23; FDR-122
Dewey, Fred H. TR-185

Composer Index

Dewing, E.B. USG-270
Dewitt, Robert M. USG-75
DeWolfe, Henry GW-310
Dibble, Bertha H. WW-12
Dical, R.A. JGB-38
Dice, Harold Edwin FDR-301
Dick, John W. TR-225
Dick, S. JD-17
Dickinson, J.R. FDR-33
Dielman, Henry AJK-3; AJK-58; WHH-10; WHH-55; WHH-64; ZT-20
Dilley, Edgar M WHT-16
Dillmore, Richard C. TR-18; TR-378
Dillon. TR-17
Dillon, James A. WW-66
Dilworth, Ella M. FDR-287
Dinkins, Olivia F. WHT-30; WW-77
Disch, (Mrs) W. WSH-6
Disch, William WSH-6
Dister, Valantine WHH-114
Diton, Carl Rossini FDR-397
Dix, John Ross USG-150; USG-155
Dixon, Harold S. WLW-18
Dixon, James L. MISC-186
Dixon, Jinny RR-4
Dixon, Mort RR-17
Dixon, (Gen) Washington WS-46
D.L. MF-27
Doane, W.H. BFH-74
Doar, Bil DDE-99
Dobbins, C.G.L. WGH-50
Dochez, L.A. AJN-14
Dodd, Derrick JGB-54
Dodd, Jimmy DDE-21; DDE-73
Dodge, Marshall J. BG-13
Dodge, Ossian E. MF-25; USG-231
Dolane, Walter A. BFH-17
Dollinger, F. GW-136
Dolph, Jack DDE-24; DDE-40; DDE-72; DDE-97
Donaghue, Frank J. AES-40
Donaghue, Leo AES-40
Donahue, Anne Barron FDR-368
Donaldson, Rosa DDE-79
Donegan, Rose MISC-9
Donetelli, N. JMC-7
Donizetti. AL-25; AL-102
Donnahoo, Shelden DAM-27

Donnelly, T.L. JD-26
Donovan, Henry J. AES-20
Doree, Naadage GW-369
Dorgan, Marie L. TR-268
Dorney, D. MISC-22
Dorr, Eddie WW-71
Dorsey, Dana R. BC-1
Dorsey, D.W. FDR-92
Dotzler, C. AL-267
Doucet, Jules TR-170
Dougherty, Dan HST-2; HST-6
Dougherty, Merrell C. TR-349
Doughty, Belle N. WHT-46; WHT-58
Douglas, Robert S. HAW-7; TED-32
Douglas. AL-413
Douglass. BFH-12
Dowdall, Belle JEC-3
Dowling, Eddie FDR-38; FDR-111; FDR-292
Dowman, Caroline W. MISC-25
Downe, Edwin E. TR-74
Downing, D.L. GW-165
Downing, Frederick B. TR-15
Downing, Mary GW-223
Downey, Morton FDR-168
Doyle, A. Bowden WM-207
Doyle, J. Patrick WW-138
Drago, Frank CC-52
Drake, J.R. ZT-64; WS-10
Draper. WJB-74
Draper, Twila AML-19
Drayton, Frank BFH-55
Dressel, Otto WSH-13
Dresseli, Eric WLW-52
Dressler. GW-504
Dresser, Paul AL-221; AL-263; AL-492; AP-4; TR-336; WLW-5
Dressler, William GW-161; GW-299; JA-25; HS-2; HG-1; TJ-26; USG-9; USG-30
Drew, Frank AL-179
Drew, Thomas JCF-18; JFC-50; AL-8; AL-390
Drews, Barry DAM-7; DAM-8
Dreyfus, Max GW-329
Driftwood, Jimmy AJK-45; MISC-154
Dringer, Abram WM-154
Druckenmiller. AL-515
D'Sandie, A.C. AL-485,
Dubin, Alfred WJB-51; WW-15; HCH-17

Dudley. WJB-75
Dudley,D.B.. GW-519
Dudley, James T. AL-148
Duer, (Mrs) Parkhurst WS-25; WS-42; AL-24; AL-98; AL-368; USG-26; USG-94; USG-223
Duffy, Mary E. FDR-320
Duflos, Joachim JD-65
Dugan, Anna FDR-164
Dugan, F.F. WLW-6
Duganne, A.J.H. USG-177
Dugdale, Kirkus WW-61
Duggan, T.A. TR-177
Duke, Vernon RR-11
Dunaway, Dennis MISC-104
Duncan, Florence Tunison QJB-86
Dunlap, J.G. USG-290
Dunn, Caleb WM-82
Dunn, Charles FDR-82
Dunne, John FDR-58; DDE-25
Dunton, C. WHH-91
Duport, Pierre Landrin GW-187; GW-381; GW-474; MISC-158
Duquesne, (Cpt) Fritz TR-327
Durand, L.B. AL-404
Durant, Horace JSJ-3; JSJ-4
Durban, Edward M. CC-27
Durkee. BFH-91
Durocher, A.H. ZT-85
Duval, Charles FDR-369
Dwork, Toby HAW-7; TED-32
Dwyer, Tom FDR-222
Dyer, James H. WS-3
Dyer, S.O. WS-1
Dykeman, Charles E. FDR-108
Dykes, J.B. WM-149; WM-315
Dzikowski, Bolek LBJ-3

Eager, Edward AL-349
Earhart, Will AL-479
Earl, Arthur C. WHT-24
Earl, Mary GW-251
East, John R. CG-140
Eastburn. USG-109
Eastlack, Francis F. MF-20; JCF-8
Eastman, Charles JGB-15
Eastman, L.W. AJN-2
Eaton, W.S. JCF-41
Eberhardt, H.F. GC-81
Ebsworth, Daniel TJ-10
Eckhard, Jacob GW-29
Eckhardt, H. WSH-13

Composer Index

Eckhart, Carl ZT-65
Eckmann, Harry N. FDR-285
Eckstein, Maxwell GW-433; USG-227
Ecton, Bob DDE-55
Eddie, Rrod FDR-32
Edelson, Cecile GW-373
Edelson, Edward GW-373
Eddy, Carl Leon HAW-4
Eddy, Carl Leon HAW-4
Edwards, Charles T. FDR-406
Edwards, F.A. WM-121
Edwards, George C. GC-106
Edwards, George Thornton GW-578
Edwards, Gus TR-111; WW-158
Edwards, Jack FDR-32
Edwards, J.H. WW-19
Edwards, R.E. TR-317
Edwards, Warren H. RML-4
Egener, Carl L. WW-98
E.H.M. WW-199
Ehrich, S. HS-9
Eileman, F.A. USG-7; USG-212; USG-289
Elderidge, Harry C. WM-9
Eldred, Raymnond B. AL-334
E.L.G. HS-18
Eliscu, Edward FDR-197; FDR-221; FDR-249
Elli, Thomas MISC-176
Elliott, Eddie WW-101
Elliot, Jack JAG-69
Ellis, John JGB-82
Ellison, Franklin H. FDR-139; FDR-309; FDR-340
Ellison, Jewell WW-45
Elwell, Herberts AL-464
Elwell, Lewis WHT-37
Emerson, L.O. GW-422; GW-554; AL-75; AL-351; AL-491; AL-475; AL-495; MISC-139; MISC-168
Emmett, Dan FP-7; FP-8; AL-90; USG-28
Emmett, Julia E. GW-364
Emmett, Tony AL-243
Emmo, Frank JB-9
Emrick, George TJ-22
Engard, Joseph USG-80
Engelman, H. WM-74; TR-67
Engle, R.R. WHH-33
Engles, Peter GW-246
Engquist, Richard TJ-49; AL-346; TR-343; FDR-367; HST-22; JFK-61

Erdelyi, Jr., Joseph WFM-1; WFM-2; RR-7; RR-8; RR-22; GCW-1; GCW-3; GCW-4; GCW-5; GCW-6; JGS-1; JGS-2; JGS-3; JGS-4; JGS-5
Erdman, Ernie WW-117
Erickson, Jack FDR-168
Erine, Wolf JD-29
Ernrst, Charles M. GC-71
Escher, Charles F. BFH-52; BFH-88
Esolf, John A. GW-532
Ettinger, Joel B. WM-170
Eugarps. JD-9
Eustace, Fritz JD-14
Evans, George T. RBH-52.
Evans, Harry MISC-10
Evans, James L. MISC-26
Evans, Lew TR-23
Evans, Margaret D. FDR-138
Evans, Redd TJ-42
Everest, C. GW-258; GW-360; GW-581; AL-22; AL-47; AL-84; AL-255; JAG-113
Eyre, Louisa Lear WM-83
Eyre, Lovel GC-72

Faber, Sidney JFK-35
Faigin, Jacob WHT-28
Failes, Philip GW-379
Fain, Sammy FDR-34
Fairman, George WW-22; WW-34; WW-41
Faith, Russell JFK-7
Fallman, W.A. WSH-20
Fanciulli, F. TR-95; TR-357
Fantus, Felix CEH-2
Fararis, J.S. WW-59
Fargo, J.F. AL-67
Farl, Rex FDR-322
Farley, William FDR-118
Farmer, Arlie E. FDR-379
Farmer, E.J. USG-228
Farmer, George O. AJK-26; WHH-58; WHH-83; JT-9; JBL-6
Farmer, Lydia Hoyt USG-228
Farnon, Robert FDR-374
Farnsworth, Ethel M. JAG-78
Farrar. WM-296
Farrar, Herbert N. TR-240
Farrar, O.R. TR-108
Farrell, Mary GBM-5
Farrow, Peter MISC-56; MISC-62
Fassett, Raphael TR-136

Faulkner, G.W. FDR-242
Faust, Carl AJN-20
Favor, Edward P. JMC-8
Fawcett, George E. AL-62
Fay, Jack WM-203
Fayles, J. [sic: Phile] GW-400; GW-441; GW-531; GW-617
F.B.T. TR-80
Feeney, James L. WM-8; CEH-1
Feenstra, Ronald M. BMG-10
Feffer, Sid TJ-31; TJ-32
Feher, Duke FDR-254
Feine, C.M. GBM-52
Fiengold, Jas. Alvin MISC-184
Fejer, Joseph TR-326
Fekete, M.C. WW-93
Felden, Peter J. WJB-49
Felker, Lizzie M. TR-241; TR-264
Fellom, Mario GW-228
Felton, J.H. GC-135
Fenalllosa, M. JCF-5
Fenno, Cordelia B. GW-444
Fensimore, Wm. GW-130
Ferris, J.S. WM-156
Ferry, F. MF-27
Fest, F. JQA-2; JQA-14
F.F.B. ZT-68
Ficke, William A. WM-223
Field, Carl FDR-168
Field, George C. FDR-66
Fields, Bernice FDR-197
Fields, Olive L. TR-36
Fifer, Gene WLW-23; WLW-29; DAM-26
Fifer, G.W. GW-530
Filas, Thomas J. MISC-66
Filley, Frank C. RBH-38; RBH-47
Fillmore, Charles M. JL-1; SCS-1
Fillmore, J.H. WM-314
Finch, Mary Baird WJB-83
Findet, George BFH-74
Finger, Ben FDR-57
Finkel, John P. WJB-58
Finn, Julius R. GCW-2
Finnerty, John DDE-66
Finsterbach, Frank WJB-94
Firestone, Elizabeth GRF-11
Fischer, G.L. FDR-44
Fischoff, George AL-216
Fish, Forrest AL-294
Fisher, C.J. AL-407
Fisher, Fred WGH-5; CC-16
Fisher, Leander WM-115
Fisher, William MF-24

Composer Index

Fisher, William A. GW-184
Fisk, Clinton B. CBF-1
Fiske, Henry GW-342
Fiske, W.O. AL-52; HG-9; HG-10; USG-48
Fitzgerald, Neil HCH-2
Fitz-Gerald, Zeph CC-2; CC-31
Fitzpatrick, J. USG-66
Fitzpatrick, John J. WM-86
Fitzpatrick, M.J. WW-220
Fitzwilliam, Edward BFH-94
Flagler, Charles WW-3
Flanagan, Jay TR-24
Flanagan, Michael AES-31
Flannery, James J. FDR-387
Flat, B. WM-322
Fledderman, Jack FDR-259; FDR-260
Fleer, William AES-33
Fleischman, Owen SP-8
Fleming, Len WW-161
Flemming, Albert GBM-17
Flemming, A. Len FDR-356
Fleschler, H.A. TR-68
Fletcher, E.O. AP-2
Fletcher, Jay Gould AL-464
Fletcher, Richmond K. GW-408
Fliege, H. GW-165
Flohr, Kathryn S. FDR-166
Floyd, Byron B. TR-312
Flynn, A. GW-232
Flynn, Allan WW-99
Flynn, J. GW-232
Flynn, John H.. WM-23
Foerch, Ole B.J. DAM-18
Foertsch, Joseph C. MF-7
Foley, Eddie FDR-386; DDE-65
Folse, Mike RR-30
Folsom, Janet WLW-27
Foltz. WJB-77
Forbes, John JD-31
Forbes, Louis RR-29
Ford, Abbie A. TR-82; TR-298
Ford, Frank WGH-53
Ford, Frank W. WW-174
Ford, T.J. FDR-25; FDR-26
Formes, Karl AL-154
Forrest, L. WM-308
Forsblad, Leland AL-327; AL-328
Fort, B.F. JGB-34
Fort, Hank JFK-48; MISC-149
Fortune, Michael TJ-4
Foster. MVB-13
Foster, Charles H. USG-175

Foster, C.R. WW-35
Foster, Edna Mae FDR-132; FDR-351
Foster, E.W. AJN-13; RBH-23; BFH-12
Foster, Fay FDR-68
Foster, I.A. WW-35
Foster, Lawrence L. FDR-161
Foster, Stephen C. GW-543; GW-546; GW-552; JB-14; JB-22; GBM-28; GBM-84; AL-121; AL-506; TR-337; AML-10; AML-25
Foster, Warren C. CC-8
Foster, William FDR-132; FDR-351
Foulon, Irenaeus D. JAG-40; JAG-65
Fowke, Edith TJ-71
Fowler, L. Ray DDE-108; DDE-109
Fox, C.N. RBH-58
Fox, E. GW-130
Fox, Eddie GW-131
Fox, George S. RBH-31
Fox, Jack FDR-104
Fox, James M. AL-193
Fox, Will H. USG-136; USG-146
Fox, William P. AL-274
Frances, Alfred WW-153
Francis, Raymond AES-18
Fradel, Charles JCF-53; GBM-4
Fradkin, James J. FDR-305
Frank, I.M. TR-109
Frank, Jewel M. DDE-15; DDE-45; DDE-54
Frank, Joseph "Doc" AES-45; HCH-21; HCH-67
Frank, M.F. GBM-68
Frankenfield, Parke LBJ-9; MISC-118
Frankensteen, Harold TR-87
Franks, Harry R. AES-22
Frankus, James A. MISC-144; MISC-148
Fraser, H.G. WW-109
Fraser, J.A. WM-287
Frazer, James A. WS-36
Frazer, J.F. TR-84
Frazier, S.H. (Mrs) WW-192
Frazier, Stanley H. WW-192
Frazzini, Al AES-14
Freeman, James J. JAG-95; JGB-21; BFH-19; BFH-24; GC-2; GC-16; BFB-4
Freeman, Jason E. FDR-263
Freeman, Phil JC-11
Fredericks, M.S. JGB-18
Fredette, T. Joseph FDR-236

Freetrade, Yankee GC-160
French, Maj. B.B. AL-319
French, Bryant M. HAW-8
French, D.A. AL-127
French, L.M. WSH-18; WJB-10; WM-85
Frestone. WJB-72
Freudenthal, Josef JFK-49
Frey, Eugene GW-540
Frey, Hugo GW-537; DAM-48
Fricke, Emelie TR-51
Fried, Henry JGB-98
Friedman, Allan Jay JFK-10
Friedman, Leo WM-13
Friedman, Les WM-144
Friend, Cliff MISC-83
Fries, Henry E. FDR-396
Fries, (Mrs) Henry E. FDR-396
Frisch, Al TJ-42; MISC-161
Frisino, Woody TED-12; TED-13; TED-22
Fritsch-Modrejewska. AL-361
Frye, Charles H. FDR-330
Fuchs, Richard AL-342
Fucik, Julius TR-340
Fudge, Thos. G. EVD-1
Fuentes, Juan B. TR-127
Fuhrman, Clarence RMN-17
Fuller, Frank R. FDR-92
Fuller, Howard N. JAG-67; JAG-84; GC-118
Fuller, James R. DDE-89
Fuller, W.O. JGB-72
Fulton, Bert WM-192
Furnish, Arthur R. WHT-35
Furr, Carolyn Cline MISC-102
Furst, S.F. AL-373
Furst, S.W. TR-256
Furst, William GW-190; GW-200
Fyles. GW-328

Gabici, L. AJK-56; ZT-8
Gaetke, Art HCH-48
Gahan, Edw. T. GW-352
Gairclough, George H. MISC-122
Gaisberg, F.W. WJB-29
Gale, Diana FDR-161
Gale, George W. WJB-5
Gale, Wilber F. USG-126
Gallagher, Elizabeth FDR-6
Gallagher, Joseph J. FDR-56; FDR-212
Galligan, Charles H. FDR-37
Gamse, Albert RMN-11; MISC-70

Gannon, Robert L. CC-11
Ganter, F. BFH-67
Gapler, Charles HC-47
Gard, E. Chapin GW-208
Gardenier, Ed GW-252
Gardiner, M. USG-212
Gardner, B.F. USG-40
Gardner, Charles GW-256
Gardner, David TR-153
Gardner, Fred USG-77; USG-289
Gardner, Gerald LBJ-6
Gardner, Jack WW-46; WW-67
Garille, Dolores JFK-40
Garnet, Horatio GW-16; GW-110
Garragues, Adele JAG-74
Garrett, T.E. HC-41; BFB-2
Garrison, Donald J. GW-306
Garvey, Ev DDE-66
Gaskill, Clarence HCH-13; FDR-393; HST-13
Gaughen, James B. AL-312
Gauthier, Carl FDR-380
Gay, Helen DDE-87
Gay, James D. AL-17; AL-336; USG-61; USG-247
Gaylord, A.E. WM-210; HCH-48
Gaylord, Harriet TR-152
G.B.W. WHH-38; WHH-91
Gearen, Joseph JMP-1
Gehrue, Mayme WW-13
Geib, Adam JMN-19
Geibel, Adam JAG-89; JGB-16; JGB-24; BFH-16; GC-33; GC-43
Geiger, L. TR-350
Gennari, Federico USG-17
George, Charles AL-222
George, Daniel GW-16; GW-110
George, Don FDR-214
George, Lyman F. WJB-89
Gerardo, D. Carl FDR-127
Gerber, George WW-124
Gerhard, Irene Ryan AES-55
Gerish, Val FDR-239
German, P.T. USG-265
Gerome, Wm. GW-276
Gerow, William E. WHT-52
Gerrish, Anna E. TR-50
Gershwin, George RR-25; MISC-15; MISC-16
Gershwin, Ira RR-25; MISC-15; MISC-16
Getze, J.A. JB-17; AL-166; AL-239; AL-480
Ghent, Ray WLW-64

Gianinni, Vittorio WGH-55
Gibbons, John S. AL-31; AL-33; AL-75; AL-106; AL-456; AL-475
Gibbbs, Charles WM-323
Gibbs, Robert W. GW-449
Gibbs, Sally FDR-80
Gibson, George H. JBW-1
Gideon, Melville J. WHT-27
Gierlach, Chet GRF-3
Gilbert. GC-73
Gilbert, Charles F. WJB-1
Gilbert, Edward J. TR-179
Gilbert, F.F. WM-251
Gilbertson, W.H. AL-210
Gilfert, C. DWC-6
Gill, J. Franklin WM-146
Gillam, Wilson J. FDR-275
Gilles, M. JMN-8
Gillett, F.W. GW-604
Gillett, H.S. TR-264
Gilliam, Strickland W. WM-278
Gillingham, Geo. GW-6
Gilmore. JAG-63
Gilmore, E. JAG-38
Gilmore, P.S. JB-10; AL-165; USG-10
Gilpin, Charles FDR-205
Giltner, May WM-91
Gipner, George AJN-20
Gipson, Ben FDR-161
Girard, E.N.E. FDR-106
Glasco, George DDE-79
Glass, James E. AL-54
Glasser, Samuel DAM-19
Glazer, Joe TJ-71; HHH-4
Glazer, Tom FDR-372
Gleason, Jackie MISC-188
Gleffe, J.E. JD-15
Glogau, Jack WW-189; WGH-5
Glover, Charles AL-89; HG-12
Glover, David C. RR-13
Glover, Stephen WS-4
Glynn, G. WGH-48
Glynn, William C. HC-48; HC-53; DW-18
Godard, D'Alfred JD-65
Godfrey, Kathryn M. DDE-38
Goehring, Gertrude RMN-38
Goeldner, Otto J. BFH-26
Goell, Kermit GW-286
Goerdeler, R. SJT-1; RBH-51
Goetz, Coleman WW-14
Goewey, Phillip WW-11
Goins, Iona D. FDR-370

Gold, Jack TJ-42
Gold, Marty MISC-135
Goldberg, Reka WW-27
Goldberg, Sam DDE-43
Golden, Eve JFK-22
Golden, John L. WW-23; WW-86; WW-149
Goldey, C.H. GW-125
Goldman, Edwin Franco GW-228; GW-395; TJ-27; TR-160; TR-290
Goldsmith, Beatrice AL-231
Goneke, John F. AJK-18; MVB-1; WHH-100; WHH-130; JKP-18; JKP-19
Gonzalez, Lupe FDR-65
Good, Anna Margaret FDR-376
Goodale, Ezekial. GW-493
Goodale, Josephine C. TR-140; TR-379; WHT-20; MISC-71
Goodman. WM-302
Goodwin, Ida Cheever CC-1; CC-3; CC-32; CC-57
Goodwin, J. Cheever GW-190; GW-200
Goodwin, Joe GW-191; GW-241
Goodwin, Walter GW-326; AES-26
Goodwin, Wm. WHH-99
Gordon, Anna Adams. CBF-7
Gordon, H.E. JGB-69; BFH-95
Gordon, Malcolm S. JGB-33; JGB-44
Gordon, Marvin B. MISC-11
Gordon, S.T. GW-593
Gorham, A.T. HG-1; WM-200
Gorman, Olive FDR-160
Gorney, Jay FDR-41; FDR-197; FDR-221; FDR-249
Gott, George C. GW-272
Gottlieb, Jack TJ-49; AL-346; TR-343; FDR-366; HST-22; JFK-61
Gottschalk, L.M. GBM-39; USG-202
Gougler, Isaiah W. AL-108; USG-203
Goulborne, J. Matthew CC-54
Gould, Albert HCH-1
Gould, Billy WW-48
Gould, Jack DDE-1; DDE-56
Gould, J.E. GW-604

Composer Index

Goulding, Edmund RR-16
Goulding, George P. SAD-6
Gouraud, Jackson USG-72
Gradisching, Frank HCH-29
Graebing, Lawrence S. GW-225; HCH-49
Graeser, Louise FDR-39
Graff, Jr., George WHT-18
Graff, George P. AL-54
Grafulla, C.S. GW-439; HC-79; WS-14
Graham, Edward B. WW-151
Graham, Henry GC-110
Graham, Roger WW-16
Gram, Hans GW-12
Granger, A.A. AES-18
Granger, Charles H. WHH-32
Granger, F. GW-25
Grannis, S.M. AL-272
Grant, Alexander SP-2
Grant, Charles N. WW-85
Grant, Dr. Dick FDR-315
Grant, E.M. USG-59
Grant, F.W. FDR-185
Grant, Mancie M. WW-68
Grant, P.H. WM-175
Grant, Ulysses S. USG-175
Grante, H. SAD-3
Gratten, Edward USG-191
Gratten, H.P. ZT-7
Gray. WM-295;WW-204
Gray, Alan GW-213
Gray, C.A. WLW-33
Gray, Cleda HST-17
Gray, Eddie GW-223
Gray, Gertie TR-103
Gray, John S. JSC-2
Gray, William B. GC-27
G.R.C. JCF-55
Greco, Angelino MISC-51
Greeley, Horace WHH-91
Green, Adolph DDE-85; MISC-113
Green, Arthur N. GW-275
Green, Mrs. E.E. WM-136
Green, F.W. WM-136
Green, Grant AL-220
Green, J.L. AL-127
Green, Johnny GW-450; AL-371; AS-11
Green, Lillian JWD-4
Green, Sophie WW-184
Green, W.S. TR-112
Greenville. WM-298
Greenwald, M. GW-378
Greenwood, Livingston FDR-199
Gregg, W. Bentley HCH-37

Gregory, Bobby LBJ-5; MISC-162
Greiner, J. HC-8; HC-44; HC-46; HC-86
Greive, Everett GW-296
Grell, F.W. WW-179
Grever, Maria DAM-40
Grey, A. WSH-44
Grey, Vivian WM-78
Gribbon, Elizabeth A. TR-288
Grierson, B.H. AL-144
Griffeth, Katie J. FDR-379
Griffin, Duane N. AL-125
Griffin, G.W.H. AL-89
Griffin, Vashti R. FDR-192
Griggs, N.K. TR-178
Grireaud, E.A. WM-70
Griswold, W.R. JAG-31
Grobe, Charles GW-116; GW-121; GW-122; GW-123; GW-165; GW-317; GW-344; GW-429; HC-54; ZT-12; ZT-28; ZT-48; ZT-53; WS-7; WS-8; WS-9; SAD-7; AL-7; AL-29; JCB-1; JBL-2; JBL-5
Groebl, L.F. TR-186
Grohe, I.A. WHH-70
Groom, Willard WM-116
Grossman, Bernie AL-219; WW-5; FDR-369
Grossman, Larry RMN-6
Grossman, Sy W. GW-307
Grube, Louis AL-241
Gruss, Charles H. FDR-273
Gruss, Frieda FDR-273
Guernsey, George M. WHT-40
Guerrero, Pastor AES-3
Guest, James AJK-44
Guilbert, E. GW-599; JMN-7
Guion, David W. FDR-317; FDR-403
Guiterman, Arthur WHT-48
Gulesian, Grace W. FDR-19
Gumble, Albert TR-89
Gumpert, G. AL-13
Gungl, Josef ZT-5; ZT-14; ZT-24; ZT-45; ZT-72; USG-18; USG-20; USG-27; USG-36
Gunnar, Otto USG-178
Gunther, Rudy HCH-30
Gurnsey, L.T. WHT-5
Guthrie, Woody MISC-144; MISC-145
Gutterson, A.C. AL-446
Guy, Clyde L. FDR-103
Guyheen, Patrick FDR-199

Haaren, L.F. TR-215
Haas, P.M. WM-227
Haase, F. AL-66
Habersang, O. HC-68
Hackady, Hal RMN-6
Hadley, Henry AL-369; TR-152
Hagan, J.M. WHT-61
Hagen, P.A. Von GW-4; JA-4; JMN-3
Hager, J.M. BFH-56; BFH-58
Haggard, John M. DAM-47
Haight, R.G. JWD-3; MISC-6
Haines, Frederick U. TR-26
Hain, Joseph L. WM-240
Hainy, Lou HHH-2
Hakel, Fred L. AL-312
Hal. ZT-52; ZT-54
Hale, Clifford BFH-4; BFH-5; BFH-72
Hale, K. JSC-1
Haley, Wm. A. WM-221
Hall, Eugene J. JAG-116
Hall, Frederick WHT-59
Hall, George W. AL-191
Hall, John P. WW-160
Hall, Kingsley WW-58
Hall, M. GW-36
Hall, Tom T. MISC-105
Halle, Roger AL-188; TR-83
Hallet, Mary FDR-373
Hallett, John MISC-112
Hallett, John T. WM-208
Halliday, R.M. WW-206
Halling, Jr., Louis WW-173
Halls, J.C. TR-189
Halmy, Lou FDR-52; HHH-5
Halpine, Charles G. USG-124; DDE-7
Halter, August FDR-267
Hamilton. TR-16
Hamilton, Frances FDR-409
Hamilton, Frank LBJ-2
Hamilton, George K. GW-180; GW-181; GW-182
Hamilton, Irving DDE-53
Hamilton, John P. GW-205
Hamlin, Baird FDR-265
Hamm, J.V. BFB-3
Hammerstein, Oscar AL-223; AL-315
Hammond, Victor WW-113
Hampton, T.J. WM-92
Hance, Kennedy GC-123
Hancox, Henry A. AL-214
Hand, A.O. USG-199; RBH-24; JAG-82

Composer Index

Hand, Ernest TR-3
Hanes, Layne H. AML-7
Handley, A.J. AES-34; AES-36
Handy, W.C. AL-200; AL-245; TR-142
Hanford, E.G. WM-212
Hanford, M.C. AL-410; WHT-49
Hanfors, Gene HCH-41
Hanger, Dave AL-266
Hanick, Florence AES-19
Hanks. AL-428
Hansen, Alice FDR-383
Hansen, Edward R. GW-41
Hansen, Julius A. GW-253
Hansford, Geo. WW-176
Hanson, S.C. GW-553
Harbach, Otto AL-233; AL-315
Harbaugh, T.C. HG-32
Harbour, Homer H. AL-355
Harden, John FDR-355
Hardin, Homer FDR-247
Harding, G.N. WSH-2
Harding, Henry JGB-44; BFH-125
Hardwick, G.P. GW-428
Hardwick, (Mrs) G.P. JD-40
Hardy, Will AL-206; WM-5; TR-193
Harger, Charles B. USG-9
Haring, Robert C. FDR-1
Harlow, Ric MISC-98
Harlowe, John SJT-3
Harlowe, William SJT-3
Harmon, A.W. AL-110
Harmsen, Ludwig W. JAG-34
Harned, J.A.M. JGB-42
Harper, Bruce CC-2; CC3; CC-32; CC-57
Harries, John BFH-96
Harrington, De Forest WJB-33
Harrington, G.A. WHH-137
Harris, Charles K. JWD-2
Harris, Ellis B. EVD-3
Harris, Remus RMN-1
Harris, W.C. WM-75
Hart, A.B. WM-230
Hart, Joey FDR-209
Hart, Joseph C. HS-5
Hart, Lorenz MISC-138
Hart, Orphella J. WW-199
Hart, Susie P. WW-137
Hartman, E.P. TR-49
Hartshorn, Edwin A. TR-161
Hartsough, Palmer WM-28; WM-314

Harty, Robert E. FDR-323
Harvez, Jean MISC-5; MISC-22
Haskell, D.H. WHH-67; ZT-30
Haskin, Reuben J. GW-198
Haskins, C.C. USG-53; JAG-42; JAG-82; RBH-10
Haskins, O.N. AL-242
Haskins, William R. TR-60; TR-344
Hassler, G.W. TED-14
Hassler, Simon CAA-5
Hasting, R. GW-586
Hatch, Jack FDR-349
Hatch, Joseph H. TR-122
Hatfield, Juliana JAG-97
Hathaway, James T. HC-119
Haubrich, Earl AL-321; FDR-30
Hauschild, C. JAG-61
Hauser. GW-314; GW-601
Hawk, S.M. WJB-93; TR-137
Hawes, Charlotte W. BFB-12
Hawkins, John J. TJ-2; TJ-3; TJ-20
Hawkins, Micah GW-101
Hawkins, Naomi DAM-34
Haws, Francesca C. CC-15
Hawthorne, Alice AL-85
Hawthorne, David H. WW-175
Hawthorne, Grace JA-18
Hayden, Joe TR-166
Hayden, William WHH-1
Hayes, Alford AL-182; AL-490
Hayes, Arnold GW-345
Hayes, Clancy GW-286
Hayes, Don TED-2
Hayes, Will S. GBM-11; USG-90
Haymes, Joe MISC-83
Haynes, Arnold GW-353
Haynes, Charles AL-41; AL-164; AJN 16; USG-39; USG-57; USG-103
Haynes, Edward AL-164
Haynes, James E. AL-41; AL-271; AJN-16; USG-39; USG-57; USG-103
Hays, Billy FDR-36; FDR-251; LBJ-7
Hays, Will S. SJT-9; SJT-11; GC-65; MISC-114; MISC-182
Hayward, Gen. Wm. H. AL-469; JD-48
Hazard. WSH-17
Hazard, Tom R. TED-15; TED-36

Hazel, John BFH-28
Hazeltine, David TJ-14
H.C. JA-26
Healy, Harold WLW-12
Heartz, H.L. WM-31
Heath, W.F. RBH-16
Hebel, Emil FDR-109
Hecht, Don RMN-38
Hecht, Sig. G. FDR-79
Heckle, A.F. WW-181
Heed, J.C. AL-234
Heelan, Will A. AL-205; TR-89
Heeringer, Ernest Von GW-107
Heffleu, Irvin J. JGB-19
Hegbom, Al HCH-5; HCH-6; HCH-34
Heifetz, Vladimir FDR-220
Heims, Newton B. WW-4
Heinrich, Anthony P. GW-605; JA-7; JT-13; MISC-33
Heinrich, August JGB-10
Heinrich, William A. GW-492
Heinze, Herman USG-201
Heise, P. GW-526
Heiser, Alice Cary TR-376
Held, Bruno MVB-10
Held, William F. JSC-5
Helf, J. Fred AL-205; TR-31; TR-35
Hellard, Robert A. GW-436
Helmick, F.W. RBH-14
Helmsmuller, F.B. AL-1; AL-280
Hemberger, Emma GW-319
Hempsted, H. N. USG-64; USG-237
Henckels, Theodore TR-19; TR-251
Henderson, Charles MISC-17
Henderson, Wallace LeGrand FDR-402
Hendricks, A.T. TR-92
Hennig. USG-221
Henninger, Theodore GW-287
Henry, Cordelia FDR-193; FDR-257
Henry, Edwin AL-64; AL-166
Henry, G.A. JGB-1; GC-47; GC-113
Henry, Greely TR-331
Henry, Norman MISC-24
Henry, O.E. WM-219
Henton, W. TR-144
Herbert, Arthur DDE-55

Herbert, B. JAG-25
Herbert, G.R. AJN-1; AJN-3; AJN-15; USG-9
Herbert, J.B. WJB-18; WJB-63; WM-28; WM-169; TR-141; TR-183; WHT-29
Herbert, S.B. WM-104
Herbert, Sidney GBM-24; GBM-27; USG-9; USG-30
Herbert, Victor WM-90; WM-112; WM-224; MISC-99
Herina, Michael BMG-7; BMG-9
Herman, C.A. WW-185
Herman, H.D. WW-185
Herman, Jerry LBJ-23; BC-2
Herman, Pinky TJ-31; TJ-32; FDR-111; RMN-29; RMN-30
Herold. WM-301
Heroux, Alfred N. TR-158
Herrell, N.B. HCH-65
Herrer, Lazaro FDR-276
Herrick. JGB-15
Herrick, George O. USG-211
Herscher, Louis HST-7; JFK-15
Hersey, Hubert GW-341; GW-390
Hertz, Jacques WW-4
Hervey, Robert AL-498
Herwig, Leopold WHH-20
Herz, William JD-54
Hess, Charles AL-257; AL-286
Hesselberg, Edouard WW-142; JMC-3; JMC-5; JMC-9; JMC-11, JMC-12; JMC-13, JMC-14; JMC-15; JMC-16
Hesselberg, Lena S. WW-142
Heuberer, Charles F. WHH-113
Hewins, Parke W. GW-592
Hewitt, Dorothy FDR-271
Hewitt, George W. JB-5; JB-6; SAD-9
Hewitt, James GW-15; GW-498; GW-587; GW-595; JA-27; TJ-13; TJ-61; JMN-16; WS-5; WS-40
Hewitt, J.H. GW-176
Hewitt, John H. WHH-35; WHH-87; JT-6; HC-75; WS-26; DW-35
Hewitt, L. JAG-11; JAG-33; JAG-112

Hewitt, Olla WW-100
Hews, George WHH-25; WHH-59; HC-1; DW-4; DW-6; DW-7; DW-9; DW-10; DW-11; DW-16; DW-19; DW-21; DW-25; DW-27; DW-28; DW-32; DW-36
Hibbard, Angus TR-61
Hibbeler, Ray AL-288
Hibbs, Mildred TR-246
Hickey, Billy H. WW-82; WW-159
Hickey, John JKP-13
Hickey, Robert AES-43
Hickok, H.W. AL-291
Hickman, Adelia E. FDR-338
Hicks, George E. BFH-21
Hiester, Vernie FDR-21
Higgenbotham, Irene. TJ-42
Higgins. HG-1
Higgins, Cornelius WM-151
Higgins, H. JQA-4
Higgins, W.H. WM-276
Higgins, H. JQA-4
Higgs, Ward TR-274
Hill, Ferd. K. USG-154
Hill, Joe EVD-4
Hill, S.B. WM-325
Hill, William H. MISC-108
Hill, Jr., Al FDR-5
Hillard, Bob GW-358
Hille, Waldemar AL-517
Himan, Alberto GW-153; USG-42
Hime, B. WHH-28; HC-25
Himelman, J.M. AL-314
Hines, Helen H. WM-220
Hinga, Howard GW-385
Hinson, Maurice GW-595; GW-619
Hinton, T.H. GW-348
Hirsch, Walter DAM-48
Hirsh, Hiram D. DDE-15; DDE-45; DDE-54
Hitchner, C.H. WW-96
Hitt, James FDR-82
Hobbs, Alfred F. WLW-45
Hodgkinson, Mr. GW-468
Hodder-Wheeler, Lutie WGH-38
Hofer, George C. GW-243
Hoffman, Edward AL-32; USG-91
Hoffman, Gertrude TR-66
Hoffman, Jack DDE-28; DDE-59
Hoffman, Max MISC-37
Hoffman, Olivia RMN-17
Hoffman, Theodore GW-226

Hoffman, William F. WM-61
Hoffmann, Adolph G. CC-37
Hoffmann, Flodoard AL-280
Hoffner, Mary V. TR-342
Hofford, M.L. GBM-68
Hofman, Al FDR-194
Hoge, Charles T. WM-101
Hoier, Thomas WW-7
Holberton, J. AL-412
Holden, Oliver GW-12; GW-127
Holder, Elbridge, G. USG-156
Holiner, Mann DDE-5
Holland, Albert ZT-2; MF-3; MF-32; MF-34; MF-38
Holland, John GBM-29
Holland, T.A. WJB-32
Holler, Dick JFK-31; JFK-60; JFK-62; JFK-66; JFK-69; JFK-78; JFK-82; JFK-84
Hollingsworth, Wm. H. WW-29
Holloway, John DW-31
Holmes, Oliver W. GW-516; GW-526; GW-546; GW-589; GW-589; AL-176
Holmes, Samuel Newall USG-257; BFH-107; BFH-113
Holmquist, Beatrice FDR-332
Holst, Eduard USG-174; WSH-30; JGB-52; BFH-31; GC-56; TR-79
Holt, George P. AL-364; WSH-26
Holyoke, Samuel GW-10; GW-89; GW-110; GW-467
Holzmann, Abe WHT-4; WHT-55; MISC-49
Homer, James R. WM-35
Hommann, C. TJ-24
Honaker, T.J. CC-12
Honen, Lester W. FDR-405
Honeycutt, Rose L. WW-191
Honn, Margaret J. FDR-246
Hook, S.W. TR-219
Hooper, O.C. BFH-23
Hoorn, Hofwyl WM-107; CEH-8
Hope, Eleanor WGH-12
Hopkins [sic], Joseph GW-606
Hopkinson, Francis GW-76; GW-83; GW-99; GW-

Composer Index

124; GW-129; GW-186; GW-294; GW-312; GW-313; GW-323; GW-324; GW-395; GW-396; GW-443; GW-447; GW-448; GW-516; GW-589; MISC-169
Hopkinson, Joseph GW-13; GW-112; GW-139; GW-141; GW-160; GW-379; GW-384; GW-408; GW-415; GW-438; GW-460; GW-513; GW-520; GW-522; GW-523; GW-524; GW-529; GW-530; GW-531; GW-533; GW-536; GW-537; GW-538; GW-541; GW-543; GW-546; GW-555; GW-556; GW-559; GW-560; GW-561; GW-562; GW-563; GW-579; GW-589; GW-608; GW-612; GW-613; GW-614; GW-615; GW-616; GW-617; GW-620; GW-621; JA-1; MISC-155; MISC-168; MISC-171
Horn, Charles E. GW-8
Hornberger, James DDE-27
Horner, Wilson G, AL-319
Horsfall, Will H. JGB-63
Horton, Tudor HC-112
Horton, Vaughn FDR-176; FDR-410
Horton, Zilphia LBJ-2
Horvath, Paul H. HCH-31
Horwitz, Charles GW-218
Hoschina, K.L. AL-413
Hosmer, F.I. AL-347
Hosmer, J.D. WLW-52
Hotlen, Adolf CC-18
Hougas, Almon D. USG-76; USG-288; JAG-100; CAA-8
Houk, J.M. WJB-48
Houser, William WLW-10
Howard. WM-79
Howard, Frank MISC-1
Howard, Henry H. WM-220
Howard, John T. GW-188
Howard, Joseph E. MISC-50
Howard, Monte O. FDR-136
Howard, W.E.C. WM-320
Howe, Elias GW-435; GW-535; TJ-19; AJK-41; WHH-112;WHH-134; ZT-69; WS-32; WS-43; MISC-131
Howell, William D. TR-225
Howells, Herbert JFK-55

Hoyt, Harry TR-154
Hoyt, Mildred DDE-46
Hubbard, Albert D. GW-178
Hubbard, J. Maurice USG-157; JAG-58
Hudson, Midas JFK-39
Hudson, Thomas HC-78
Hudspeth, Yvonne CC-23
Huff, C.R. WLW-13; WLW-23; WLW-56
Huff, Mac MISC-109
Hughes. CEH-12
Hughes, Charles WM-102
Hughes, J. Wesley. WM-272
Hughes, Joseph H. WW-128
Hughes, W.M. AML-12
Hulbert, Jr., James GW-71; GW-485
Hulfish, E.E. GW-168
Hulse-Petrillo, C. WW-135
Humbolt, Archibald GW-210; GW-280
Hummel, Herman A. FDR-164
Humphrey, Frank A. WW-161
Hungate, William L. RMN-37
Hunt, Ev FDR-307
Hunt, George JFK-65
Hunter, Billy HCH-5; HCH-6; HCH-34
Hunter, Fordyce TR-85
Hunter, James GW-199
Huntington, E.S.S. TR-181; WW-83; WW-207
Hupfeld, C.F. JMN-9
Hurd, Danny JFK-17
Hurlburt-Edwards, L. WW-19
Huslander, W.S. WM-72
Hutchinson. MVB-13; MISC-168
Hutchinson, Jesse JBR-2; AL-365; AL-475
Hutchinson, John W. AL-175; AL-317
Hutchington, A. JAG-82
Hutchington, Joshua AJN-4
Hutet, Charles MVB-7
Hyden, Franz Joseph GW-440; GW-612

Ibach, F. BFH-9
Ida, Miss GC-30; GC-31
Ikeler, Otto P. WM-33
Innes, Frederick N. GW-331
Irish, Marie GW-233
Irving, H.V. TR-301
Irving, A.B. AL-31
Irving, J.B. AL-505

Irving, James H. DAM-36
Irving, M. BFH-11
Irving, Walter FDR-329
Irwin, William S. USG-34
Iucho, Wilhelm HC-28
Ives, Charles E. AL-207; AL-341; WM-98; WM-325; MISC-106
Ives, Jr., E. WHH-91
Ives, Wally AES-57

Jackson, Edw. A. GW-352
Jackson, E.M. FDR-390
Jackson, George E. USG-138; BFH-3; GC-112
Jackson, George K. GW-395; GW-464; TJ-16
Jackson, George R. JAG-6; JAG-74; JAG-87; CAA-4
Jackson, Lara Thornhill WLW-69
Jackson, Samuel GW-174; GW-185
Jackson, Wm. GW-5
Jacobs, A.F. WJB-32
Jacobs-Bond, Carrie WW-212
Jacobson, Herman WW-5
Jaffe, Moe FDR-225
J.A.H. USG-264
Jahn, F. Carl TR-56
James, Billy FDR-300; FDR-402
James, Bob RMN-15
James, E.C. USG-118
James, Jr., A.L. FDR-261
James, Jr., J.H. SJT-6; WSH-19
Jameson, E.H.E. USG-286
Janis, Elsie RR-16
Janvier, Francis JB-11
J.A.P. USG-292
Jaqua, Bob MISC-73
Jaqua, Marion MISC-73
Jarboe, J.W. GBM-48
Jarden, Samuel AJN-27
Jarrett, Robert Frank FDR-417
Jarvis, Charles AL-180
Javits, Joan AL-196
Jay, Harry AL-210; FDR-335
Jean, Billy DAM-16
Jecko, Steven H. JGB-92
Jefferies, Norman MISC-81
Jefferson, Thomas TJ-31; TJ-32; TJ-46; TJ-48
Jeffery, T.F. GW-321
Jeffords, M.L. WW-111
Jelesnik, Eugene JFK-20
Jenks, Harry DAM-39

Composer Index

Jenks, Stephen GW-94
Jennevein, Leonard RBH-27
Jennings, Ida E. WM-25
Jepson, Benjamin AL-175
Jerome, William GW-275; AL-213; TR-245; TR-260; WW-89
Jerrod, C.J.A. WW-204
Jervoise, Julie MISC-88
Jesse, Max E. JSC-3
Jessel, George HST-2; HST-6
Jeunehomme, Lazare FDR-284
Jewell. MVB-13
J.M. JKP-7
Jocelyn, (Mr) JA-8
John, Pilgrim AL-499
Johns, Jean C. FDR-345
Johnson. WM-294; TR-206
Johnson, (Mrs) A.B. WM-116
Johnson, Agnes M WLW-3
Johnson, Billy WW-16
Johnson, Charles L. HCH-26
Johnson, Charles W. GW-391
Johnson, Charlest HST-23
Johnson, D. HC-76
Johnson, Eugene WS-19
Johnson, Francis GW-583
Johnson, Frank A. GW-288
Johnson, Frank S. HCH-45
Johnson, George WLW-25
Johnson, George E. WGH-36
Johnson, Harry H. WJB-68
Johnson, Howard GW-211; GW-290; AL-226; TR-106; TR-107
Johnson, Lee GC-133; WW-37
Johnson, Lottie J. AL-275; USG-89
Johnson, Mae Hill WW-16
Johnson, Mike AS-14
Johnson, Philander WGH-55
Johnson, Robert B. AL-496
Johnson, Roland DAM-14
Johnson, T.C. WM-314
Johnson, Thomas T. HCH-36
Johnson, Wallace A. TR-1
Johnson, Wayne FDR-247
Johnston, Eugene T. JD-51
Johnston, J.W. TR-25
Johnston, Tommy MISC-82
Johnston, W.E. WM-182
Johnstone, Arthur E. WW-116

Johnstone, Thomas R. AML-6; WLW-1; WLW-59
Jolson, Al WGH-1; WGH-26
Jones, Barbara JFK-18
Jones, Earl C. GW-308
Jones, Erasmus W. JGB-15
Jones, Frank M. BFH-93
Jones, G. Elmer RBH-54; RBH-54; JAG-104; JGB-15; JGB-48
Jones, Gertie GC-10
Jones, J. Grayson FDR-234; FDR-356
Jones, Joseph M. TR-262
Jones, Julie TR-40
Jones, M.A. WW-10
Jones, Margaret W. FDR-201
Jones, Oscar WM-88
Jones, Paul WM-190; WW-96
Jones, Roy L. FDR-248
Jones, W.H.S. GC-165
Jordan, Joe TR-41
Jordan, Jules TR-373
Jordan, Julian JGB-74; TR-147
Jordan, Ray CC-40
Jordan, Sara MISC-187
Jordan, Thomas J. WLW-3
Josselyn, Arthur S. GW-240; WM-94
Jost, J.W. JAG-43
J.R.I. ZT-68
J.T.S. WHH-97
Jules, Clifton WM-280
Jullien, M. GW-365; GW-366
Julius. TR-324
Jungmann, J.E. MVB-6; JKP-9
Jurentus. JA-19
Jurist, Irma FDR-197
Justice, Wm. B. JD-59
Justus, Grace WLW-13; WLW-22; WLW-56

K., Chas. GW-267
Kaartinen, Josef DDE-83
Kablish, Ruth AL-308
Kahal, Irving FDR-34
Kail, Mary E. USG-88; RBH-22; JGB-15
Kaiser, Joseph J. TR-252
Kaiser, William F. HCH-52
Kalitz, Charles TR-133
Kalkman, P. GBM-40
Kalliwoda. WHH-84; MISC-35
Kalmanoff, Martin GW-231

Kalmer, Bert WLW-8
Kamholtz, S. FDR-216
Kampe, H.F. AL-414
Kane, Patrick WW-73
Kaper, Bronislau MISC-98
Kapustka, Bruce FDR-240
Kapustka, Stan FDR-240
Karasek, Frank GW-350
Karll, Eric HCH-8; FDR-200; FDR-314
Karns, Verdi WM-199
Karr, Fulton B. GW-507
Katims, Herman FDR-400
Katz, Martin JEC-9
Katz, Ruben JEC-9
Katz, William DDE-9; MISC-24
Kaufman. Jacob TJ-37
Kaufman. L.J. WSH-27
Kaufman, Oliver F. GC-137
Kaufman, Sam J. TJ-37
Kavanaugh, J.J. WJB-8
Kay, Charles HCH-25
Kaylor, Hurley AML-17
Kay, Ulysses AL-344
Kays, J. Warren TED-6
Keating, Charles T. WW-25
Keck, C.L. JBW-2; JBW-5
Keefer, Arrety 'Rusty' DDE-108; DDE-109
Keegan, James F. USG-19
Keeler, Georgina G. FDR-90
Keen, Toby DAM-30
Keene, Ward HCH-52
Kefford, James WM-192
Kegley, Carl S. FDR-27
Keil, Phil P. SJT-10; RBH-53; JAG-13; GC-20
Keiser, Robert A. WW-13
Keith, David MISC-112
Keith, Frank H. LBJ-14
Keith, Rosa Belle FDR-198
Keithley, E. Clinton TR-281
Kelble, Ethel WM-129; WM-246
Keller, Leonard RMN-21
Keller, M. AL-83; AL-153
Keller, Matthias ZT-39
Kelly, Caroline P. TR-355
Kelly, Clarence FDR-123
Kelly, Frankie DAM-32
Kelly, Mary JD-8
Kelly, Patrick F. AL-482
Kendall, Edwin F. TR-2; TR-34
Kendis, James WW-94
Kennan, Luke WW-88
Kennedy, John F. JFK-29; JFK-74; JFK-77; MISC-110

Kennedy, M.G. AES-39
Kenney, Eugene R. GW-432
Kenney, Jack FDR-333
Kenney, Mark AES-35
Kenny, Charles CC-20
Kent, Walter DAM-13
Kepinger, J.E. FDR-97
Kerker, Gustave TR-164
Kern, Jerome AL-233; AL-315
Kerr, Anita JFK-60
Kerr, Charles H. SP-4; SLP-4
Kerr, Harry D. TR-37; WHT-4
Kerrigan, John HS-17
Kessler, Leopold WM-2; WM-326
Kesler, Lew FDR-252
Key, Francis Scott GW-287; TR-172; CC-14; FDR-1; FDR-21; FDR-158
Keynton, John JAG-88; JAG-92
Keyser, Annette FDR-67
Kidder, (Mrs) M.A GBM-16; AL-44; USG-26; USG-79
Kiefer, J.A. USG-258
Kiefer, Joseph CC-24
Kiely, James F. FDR-134
Kieselmann, Jacob H. FDR-245
Killikelly, Patrick DDE-100
Kimball, George A. AL-71
Kimbrough, (Mrs) A. JD-28
King, Charles FDR-353
King, Charles M. GW-170; JT-2
King. D. JGB-20
King, Geo. Blake GW-170
King, Godfre Ray GW-217
King, Horatio C. GW-126; GW-195
King, James GW-247
King, Kenneth JFK-24
King, K.L. USG-232
King, Laura DAM-40
King of Poets WJB-84
King, Richard F. WM-32
King, Robert HCH-4; HCH-53
Kincaid, May MISC-92
Kinnear, David M. WHT-25
Kinsey, J.F. WM-238
Kinzel, Charles W. GM-1
Kirke, Edmund AL-132
Kirkwood, Jack FDR-327
Kiser. AL-422
Kiser, A.J. JMC-3; JMC-5; JMC-9; JMC-11, JMC-12; JMC-13, JMC-14; JMC-15; JMC-16
Kittredge, Walter AJN-4
Kleber, Henry WHH-110; JAG-26
Klein, Lew AL-226
Klein, Theodore JAG-32
Kleinsinger, George AL-231
Klender, Richard MISC-137
Klickmann, Henri USG-134; WJB-51; WHT-14
Kloeper, Edward WM-124
K.N. MF-13
Knaebel, S. TJ-38; AJK-9
Knablin, Oscar F. TR-10
Knake, H.T. JAG-77
Knapp, Horace G. JAG-55
Knauff, George P. FP-6
Kneeland, Stillman F. WM-214
Knight, J.E. WLW-31
Knight, (Mrs) S.G. GBM-32
Knight, Vic DDE-51
Knoch, A.A. WM-100
Knoll, Doris JFK-9
Knox, William AL-223; AL-426
Kobluk, Michael JFK-70
Koch, Carl H. FDR-130; FDR-169; FDR-404
Koch, C.F. ZT-51
Kocian, Howard WHT-34
Koellhoffer, B.A. GW-221
Koenig, Carl J. HST-11
Konold, Amos A.E. WM-126
Koogle, Effie L. GW-210; GW-280
Koppell, Al FDR-111
Kotzwara, Franz GW-14; GW-317
Kountz, R. AL-415
Kramer, Aaron WLW-46
Kramer, Rud. USG-25
Kramer, Sylvia FDR-197
Krasnow, Hecky JFK-18
Kratz, Harvey H. FDR-301
Kratz, Lee G. WW-45
Krauss, E. JCF-28
Kredel, G.J. USG-294
Krenek, Ernest GW-337
Krestermann, Gustav K. WM-283
Kretzmer, Herbert JFK-4; JFK-38; JFK-70
Kreymborg, Alfred GW-239; AL-181
Krngell, Lewis TJ-43
Kruger, Paul TR-330
Krummacher, Hans GW-166; HG-10
Kruse, Edward W. WM-2

Kuebler, Charles TR-286
Kuenzig, C.C. HCH-25
Kuffner, J. AJK-9; AJK-12
Kuhn, J.G. SJT-2
Kuiper, Klaas G. WLW-63
Kulling, F. Albert JD-41
Kulling, Otto W. WLW-62
Kunkel, Charles JAG-40; JAG-65; WM-7; TR-191; FDR-81
Kunkel, Jacob WSH-9
Kurzenknabe, J.H. GW-529
Kunst, Norman FDR-398
Kunz, Howard WM-274
Kurs, A. ZT-22
Kurtz, E.H.L. HG-18
Kyle, Alexander WHH-37; HC-2
Kyle, (Mrs) John WW-30

La Ferrera, Vinton GW-217
La Ferrera, Virginia GW-217
La Hache, Theodore V. ZT-36; HS-1; JBL-9; BFB-19
La Mer, A. HG-31
La Paglia, Anthony HCH-27
Lacey, George D. AES-49
Lacille, Joseph TR-86
Ladd. USG-301
Ladd, Gertrude I. AL-273
Ladd, M.B. AL-258; AL-416
Ladd, J.W. TR-208
Lady, A. GW-12
Lafayette, F. GBM-48
Lagrange, E. JAG-30
Laird, George R. WW-72
Lake, Felix JMC-6
Lake, Mayhew FDR-190; DDE-6
Lake, M.L. WW-120
Laleueus. WHH-81
Lamb, Arthur J. WM-168; TR-104
Lamb, Henry BFH-37
Lamb, Isabel FDR-289
Lambert, Diane MISC-56; MISC-62
Lambert, H.H. WHT-36
Lamm, Al RMN-39
Lamm, Robert HST-8
Lamont, E.W. AJN-8
Lampard, G.R. AL-35; JGB-62
Lampman, Ben Hur TR-328
Lampman, Rex FDR-104
Lampman, W.A. TR-302
Lamson, William A. WM-137
Landram, W.J. GW-132
Lane, Burton V. HCH-32

Composer Index

Lang, Charles RBH-2
Lang, G. USG-24
Lang, Mary Bush AML-13
Lang, Phil FDR-276
Langan, James F. FDR-71
Lange, Charles USG-248
Lagenschwarz, Max GBM-82; AL-434
Langworthy, Speed CC-4
Lanier, Sidney RBH-45
Lanther, Holger C. HST-17
Lapham, Claude AML-1
Laraway, Cynthia DDE-14
Lardner, Ring W. TR-14; TR-353
Lardner, William JT-7
Laroque, Philip AJK-20
Lasalle, Victor WW-6
Laselle, Mary A. WM-186
Laska, Edward WW-20; AES-23
Laszio, Alexander FDR-297
Latour, Pierre HG-6; HG-13; USG-101; JAG-91; GC-32
LaTourette, Charles H. GW-276
Latta, E.R. RBH-35
Laugeson, L.L. FDR-192
Laurendeau, L.P. TR-171
Lavalle, Paul DDE-26; DDE-42
Laville. WM-159
Lawler, Charles B. AES-1; AES-2; AES-5
Lawrence. AL-412
Lawrence, B.M. WJB-55; JBW-4; GLP-1;
Lawrence, David FDR-151; FDR-152; FDR-153
Lawrence, W.V. USG-290
Lawson, Elliot JFK-77
Lawson, Jimmie FDR-206
Layman, Zora HST-4
Layton, Joseph T. WW-73
Lazare, Carl GBM-60
Lazarus, A.G. GC-69
Le Baron. WSH-24
Leaman, Lou DAM-58
Leavitt, Ezekiel FDR-189
Ledet, (Mrs) M.A. WM-185
Leduc. WM-300
Lee, Allen TJ-37
Lee, Charles TED-3; TED-11
Lee, David JFK-4; JFK-38; JFK-70
Lee, Ed. J. WGH-32
Lee, Irving B. TR-38
Lee, Malcolm TED-7; DDE-11

Lee, Ray FDR-208
Lee, G. Simcoe MF-5
Leftwich, Vernon FDR-338
Leggett, L. Gertrude WM-158
Leggett, W.I. WM-158
Lehrer, Tom HHH-6
Lehman, J.C. HC-27
Lehman, Johnny MISC-154
Leiby, E.B. WLW-41
Leidgen, Eric W.G. TR-290
Leifluac, D. USG-181
Leigh, Vivian TR-175
Leland, S.R. JT-4
Lemon, William J. ZT-11
Lemonier, Tom TR-253
Lengfeld, Helen F. DDE-12
Lenhart, L.Y. TR-102
Lennox, Charles J. AES-29
Lenox, Karl MISC-43; MISC-47
Leoncavallo. TR-139
Leont, Charles DAM-4
Leopold, Isadore JD-33
Lepaige, Chas. E. JMN-24
Lerman, J.W. GC-5
Lerner, Alan Jay TR-45; MISC-100; MISC-153
Lertzman, Carl MISC-79
Lesher, Mary Ann GBM-79
Leslie, Edgar GW-311; HCH-17
Lessner, George FDR-16
Leutner, Carl JB-16
Levering, Robert E.H. HC-90
Levi, Maurice TR-30; WHT-12
Levin, Lester L. FDR-398
Levine, Hank JFK-32
Levitt, George J. TR-32
Levitt, Helen S. AL-375
Levoy, Leon USG-11
Levy, (Mrs) David DDE-94
Lewis, Al FDR-63; FDR-125; FDR-204; MISC-12; MISC-13; MISC-150
Lewis, A.V. AL-361
Lewis, Bob FDR-43
Lewis, Charles L. WM-195
Lewis, Evie FDR-43
Lewis, George TR-72
Lewis, H.C. GW-605
Lewis, Henry WW-69
Lewis, Hugh AL-301
Lewis, Le Roy GC-109
Lewis, Sam M. GW-219
Lewis, Vic FDR-4
Lewis, Walter H. TR-254
Lewton, Pansy A. WM-52
Ley, H. FDR-265

Leyeless, A. FDR-186
L'Huilier, J.P. GW-72
Lieb, J.W. TR-24
Lieberman, Edwin AL-202
Lieberman, Harry M. WW-105
Liefeld, A.D. WM-264
Lifter, Anna HCH-27
Liggy, Licco I. WW-201
Lignoski, B.R. FP-1; FP-10
Lillard, James FDR-112
Lillis, Thomas J. HST-15
Lincoln, Abraham GW-497; AL-56; AL-182; AL-185; AL-186; AL-190; AL-220; AL-222; AL-262; AL-288; AL-311; AL-323; AL-326; AL-333; AL-342; AL-343; AL-344; AL-345; AL-369; AL-372; AL-452
Lincoln, Harry J. GW-192; AL-447; WM-36; WM-141; WM-236; TR-63
Linden, Oscar AL-146
Lindh, Gustave GW-152; GC-12
Lindsay, Vachel AL-478
Line, Hans S. WM-15; WM-168
Lio, F.O. JGB-66
Lippman, Sid TJ-42
List, Louis GC-13
Liston, Cora WGH-43
Litkei, Andrea GW-293; FDR-53; FDR-121; FDR-291; FDR-310; HST-5; HST-16; HST-18; HST-24; DDE-42; DDE-71; DDE-76; DDE-90; JFK-25; JFK-50; JFK-53; JFK-67; LBJ-1; LBJ-11; LBJ-13; LBJ-15; LBJ-16; LBJ-19; LBJ-24; LBJ-27; GRF-1; GRF-3; GRF-7; GRF-8; GRF-12; JEC-4; JEC-6; RR-10; RR-23; GB-1; BC-3; BC-4; BC-9; BC-10
Litkei, Ervin GW-294; GW-315; TJ-35; TJ-40; AL-252; AL-292; FDR-53; FDR-121; FDR-291; FDR-310; HST-5; HST-16; HST-18; HST-24; DDE-42; DDE-71; DDE-76; DDE-90; JFK-25; JFK-50; JFK-51; JFK-67; LBJ-1; LBJ-11; LBJ-13; LBJ-15; LBJ-16; LBJ-19; LBJ-24; LBJ-27; RMN-4; RMN-24; RMN-25; RMN-26; RMN-27; GRF-1; GRF-3;

GRF-7; GRF-8; GRF-12; JEC-4; JEC-6; JEC-10; RR-10; RR-23; GB-1; BC-3; BC-4; BC-9; BC-10
Little, Anita G. HCH-2
Little, John S. HC-12; HC-18
Little, William GW-470
Livingston, Milton FDR-385
Livington, Bill FDR-331
Livington, Jerry FDR-194
Livington, Milton FDR-194
Lloyd, Anita DAM-5
Lloyd, Jr., J. USG-137
Lloyd, Norman MISC-169
Lloyd, Rosie WHT-9
Lloyd, Ruth MISC-169
Lo Presti, Ronald JFK-58
Locke, E.W. GBM-26; GBM-55; AL-94; AL-101; AL-143; AL-372; AL-500; AJN-26; USG-183; USG-189
Locke, Harry S. CEH-4
Lockwood, C.T. USG-264
Loder, Edward T. WHH-138
Loder, George GW-626
Loesch, M. TR-335
Loesser, Frank GW-204
Lojeski, Ed JFK-62; MISC-107
Lohman, A.S. TR-212; WW-151
Lomas. WM-291
Lombard, R.N. TR-97; TR-135; TR-372
London, Edwin GW-393
Lonergan, James A. WW-165
Long, Jr., Dan WM-324
Long, G. Jason TED-21
Long, George "Jeb" AS-10
Long, Ida A. WM-147
Long, J. AJK-28
Long, Lucy WM-248
Long, Lucy B. WW-196
Long, William H. SJT-2
Loomis, Harvey W. WW-116
Loomis, R.G. GW-87; GW-163
Loon, Gerard W. Van AL-234
Lopez-Dias, Grace P. WLW-61
Loraine, William TR-235; WW-70
Lord, Daniel MISC-142
Lord, Russ TED-19
Lorenz. WSH-45
Lorenz, Ellen Jane AL-337
Losekamp, George FDR-256

Losse, F. GW-130; AL-13
Loth, L. Leslie DDE-43
Lothner, Elza TR-310
Lottman, George D. FDR-20
Loubet, Francis P. AES-6; FDR-51
Loudon, A.W. TR-55; TR-348
Louden, Matie Lois TR-116
Lount, S.D. WJB-9
Lovejoy, G.W. USG-1; HS-3
Lovejoy, Leon WSH-19
Lovell, Leona WGH-40
Lovett, Effa WGH-32
Low, Samuel GW-6
Lowe, Bert AL-228; WHT-7
Lowe, Francis J. MISC-7; MISC-8
Lowe, Jack HST-12
Lowell, Frederic WJB-26
Lowthian, Axie A. WW-74
Lozier, Horace JGB-23; JGB-25; WLW-35
Lozier, John H. AL-11; USG-139; JGB-23; JGB-25; BFH-108; WM-281; WM-305
Luckenbill, Donald N. TR-62
Ludmore, P. USG-276
Lumsdane, Jack FDR-349
Lumsden, Annie P. WM-25
Lundberg, C.O. AL-265
Lundin, Jack WLW-68
Lung, Wilma R. FDR-158
Lunsford, Esther WM-317
Luse, J.D. GW-543
Luther, H.W. AL-34
Lutz, A. SJT-7
Lutz, G.B. AL-448; SJT-7
Lyden, M.M. FDR-339
Lyle, Tom FDR-113
Lyman, L.S. WM-108
Lynn, George AL-343
Lyon, Geo. P. GC-117
Lyons, Anna FDR-15
Lysaght, Walter WW-123

M., J. AL-449
Maass, Walsemar WW-114
MacAnn, Fran FDR-07
MacArthur, Claude FDR-365
MacArthur, Douglas DAM-7; DAM-8
Macarty, Harry HG-1
Macaulay, S. TR-43
Macdonald, Ballard GW-191; TR-126; WW-54; WW-170; WW-218

MacDonald, Jim DDE-59; BMG-3
MacDonald, Jimmy DDE-28
Macdonald, William J. AES-14
MacDonough, Glen MISC-99
MacEachron, Reginald WM-30
Machugh, Edward AES-62; HCH-7
Mack and Ceil AL-457
Mack, E. GW-143; GW-389; WS-27; WS-48; GBM-6; GBM-13; GBM-34; GBM-47; AL-19; AL-23; AL-31; AL-40; AL-88; AL-105; AL-272; AL-299; AJN-9; AJN-12; HG-15; USG-9; USG-12; USG-16; USG-18; USG-22; USG-30; USG-37; USG-70; USG-102; USG-116; USG-127; USG-128; USG-129; USG-130; USG-131; USG-132; USG-133; USG-134; USG-135; USG-152; USG-153; USG-161; USG-162; USG-163; USG-164; USG-165; USG-166; USG-167; USG-168; USG-170; USG-171; USG-176; USG-192; USG-195; USG-198; USG-204; USG-209; USG-214; USG-215; USG-216; USG-218; USG-219; USG-220; USG-226; USG-227; USG-229; USG-230; USG-234; USG-235; USG-238; USG-240; USG-249; USG-280; USG-281; USG-285; SJT-4; RBH-13; RBH-19; RBH-20; RBH-23; WSH-4; JAG-8; JAG-61; JAG-76; JGB-6; JD-42; BFB-20; NB-3; MISC-64
Mack, F. HS-4
Mack, Happy WW-190
Mack, Jno. JGB-95
Mack, Robert FDR-172; FDR-173
MacKaye, Percey WW-152
MacLean, Jack WLW-13; WLW-22; WLW-56
Macks, M. USG-102
MacMillen, Francis WW-152

Composer Index

Macomber, Lillian TR-315
MacPherson, Duncan E. WW-109
MacWilliams, Tommy FDR-157
Madden, Edward WHT-21; WW-126
Madden, Jim C. WGH-2; WGH-8; WGH-10
Madden, W.S. WW-202
Maddux, Berton J. TR-84
Mader, Carl TED-16
Madison, Maury TR-347
Magee, Roger J. FDR-75; FDR-416
Magidson, Herb HCH-4; HCH-53
Magliano, M.P. DDE-7
Magnus, Charles AL-111; AL-434
Magruder, James E. GW-142; GW-149
Maharon, Jack AES-16
Mahoney, Charlie FDR-36; FDR-251
Mahoney, Jack WW-99
Mahoney, J.F. WW-89
Maibunn-Goldman, A. TR-160
Malgren, George H. GW-271
Mallory, Mason HHH-2; HHH-5
Malmene, Walsemar WJB-73; WM-109
Maloney, E.J. BFB-16
Maloof, A. AML-6
Maluo, Joseph FDR-286
M.A.M. BFH-125
Mana-Zucca DDE-34
Mance, Gorman B. TED-7; DDE-11
Manfried, Leo GW-297
Manker, Lucile HCH-33
Mann, Dave TJ-42
Mann, Delphia D. DDE-62
Mann, George B. WW-87
Mann, Sy RMN-1
Mann, William L. FDR-88; FDR-304
Manthal-Lieberman, H. HST-3
Manus, Jack TJ-42
Manzer, Wm. Marvin TR-26
Marcus, Sol RR-15; RR-24
Maretzek, Max AJN-23
Margeson, Andrew WM-102
Mario, Don FDR-276
Mark, Al G. WM-1
Markam, Edwin AL-207;
AL-341; AL-484
Markart, Ernst SJT-12
Marks. USG-141
Marks, Maurice E. USG-224
Markstein, S. JGB-49; GC-85
Marlow, Jeffery MISC-126
Marone, Giuseppe TR-375
Marrow, Geoff RR-22
Marsh, Henry JGB-60
Marsh, H.T. WM-261
Marsh, Walt RMN-2
Marshal, Daniel TJ-12
Marshall. WM-297
Marshall, Bertha C. WM-68
Marshall, L.B. GW-391
Marshall, Logan GW-460
Marshall, Louis FDR-324
Marsen, Cecil WHT-10
Marsters, Ann JFK-34
Martens, Frederick GW-444
Martin, Franklin FDR-295
Martin, Joe RMN-39
Martin, L.M. WW-181
Martin, Thomas J. HC-84; AL-42
Marvin, C.E. BFH-74
Mary. MF-30
Marzen, Pietro WW-107
Mascara, Red LBJ-9
Mason, D.G.. AL-417
Mason, Ed. AES-10
Mason, Eliphalet GW-489
Mason, Jack WW-189
Mason, Lowell GW-517; WM-56; WM-243
Mason, W.S. TR-39
Massett, Stephen C. GBM-80
Masson, P. Korecka FDR-112
Massy, Gerald AL-513
Masters, Edgar Lee AL-313
Matesky, Ralph FDR-224
Matheson, William JFK-79
Mathews, Bowen RMN-13
Mathews, H.E. HC-36
Matthews, Bob FDR-123
Matthews, Jno. W. WM-104
Matthews, W.S.B. GC-88
Maurice, Louie WM-38
Mauro, P. TJ-3; JMD-19
M.A.X. USG-99
May, J.S. WM-29
Maybaum, H. TR-110
Mayer, Charles N. AL-214
Mayer, Ferdinand AL-161
Mayer, Henry AL-80
Mayham, Morris FDR-117
Maylath, H. GC-103; GC-104
Mayo, Max AL-18
Maywood, George USG-105; BFH-88; GC-29; WJB-22
Maxwell, Charles C. WM-53
Mazza, R. Joseph WM-207
McAdams, L.J. TR-150
McAfee, R.O. WLW-6
McAllister, P.W. AL-208
McBride, William P. TR-47
McBrien, Rod MISC-77
McCabe, J.C. SP-5
McCallip, W.W. WM-41; WM-309
McCann, Charles A. CEH-5
McCarron, Charles R. WW-69
McCarthy, Andy WLW-27
McCarthy, Cal FDR-421
McCarthy, Dennis MISC-93
McCarthy, Earl WW-112
McCarthy, J.D. GW-153
McCarthy, John WHT-47
McCartney, Marti GW-375
McCarty. HG-1
McCarty, James AES-46
McCauley, Jack AES-42
McCauslin, G.W. FDR-126
McCay, Myrtle Mae WHT-30
McC.-Kimbrough, A. JD-28
McClay, Sam R. FDR-42
McClellan, J.E. TR-262
McClenny, Anne GW-619
McConnell, George B. WW-15
McCormick, Hugh M. TR-162; TR-241; TR-313
McCormick, Sara W. TR-162; TR-313
McCullough, Simon WW-177
McCullough, Willis WHT-13
McCutcheon, Ernest L. FDR-91; FDR-185
McDermott, Alfred JFK-1
McDonald, D.A. WM-6
McDonnell, Tom BMG-3
McDonough, M. CC-26
McDonough, Michael WJB-46
McFalls, (Mrs) D. JAG-22; JGB-9
McFarland, G.H. WW-174
McGlennon, Felix TR-223
McGrane, Paul FDR-252
McGraw, Jock WLW-11; WLW-58
McGruder, James E. GC-125
McHenry, James JT-7

Composer Index

McIndoo, Wm. Oliver HCH-26
McIntyre, John J. USG-82; TR-196
McKay, George F. AL-370; AL-484
McKinley, Mabel WM-78; TR-250; TR-363
McLauchlin, Russell DAM-18
McLaughlin, Daniel PC-2
McLean, Joseph TR-181; TR-382
McManus, John L. WGH-6
McNair, Jacqueline MISC-112
McNaughton, D. USG-211
McNaughton, J.H. GW-594; AL-269
McNellis, Maurice J. HST-15
McPhail, Lindsey WLW-62
McPhee, B.J. HCH-24
McPherson, John RBH-2
McQuaid, John AES-28
McQuaid, J.W. AES-28
McRae, William FDR-8
McRebel, J.P. AL-268
Mead, Maie TR-176
Meahl, P.J. WM-117
Mealand, Arthur J. GW-538
Meder, J.P. HG-19
Mehden, L. Van Der JGB-53
Mehrab, Harry HCH-18
Meinardus, E. WW-203
Meineke, C. GW-598; TJ-11; JQA-1; AJK-27; AJK-33; WHH-93; HC-61; WS-39
Mel, Lee FDR-28; FDR-290
Meline, F. DWC-2
Mellor, John AES-39
Melsher, Irving RMN-1
Menaker, Alice DDE-22; DDE-78
Menken, Alan AL-320
Mercer, Johnny RR-9; RR-12; RR-21
Merchant, Larry MISC-73
Mercier, C. WHH-27
Meredith, I.H. GW-434; GW-533
Meredith, Jack CEH-11
Merick, Eldridge USG-263
Merrick, Joe WW-169
Merrill, Blanche WW-8; WW-63
Merrill, H.T. AL-82; HG-2
Merry, Paul AL-266
Merz, Karl GW-169; AL-418; JAG-106

Mescara, Red MISC-118
Meserole, Katherine RML-3
Messemer, J. ZT-40
Methot, Phil DDE-86
Metrie, J.W. WW-124
Metz, A. AJK-19
Metz, Theodore A. FDR-12
Meurer, Raymond J. RMN-7
Meurer, Jr., Raymond RMN-7
Meyer, Ad. JAG-72
Meyer, Fred C. WM-73
Meyer, George W. GW-211; GW-290; TR-106; TR-107
Meyer, Harry TR-32
Meyer, Henry AL-259
Meyer, Louis USG-31; USG-115; USG-184; USG-188
Meyer, Pauline AL-474
Meyer, William T. HG-4
Meyers, Charles A. GW-206; AES-60
Meyers, Henry FDR-197; FDR-221
Michael, Maud FDR-205
Michaels, Thomas USG-221
Michaud, Dan DDE-55
Michaux, Wilbur FDR-422
Michel, Casimir WM-123
Middendorf II, J. Wm. RR-1
Middleton, W. JCF-19
Miessner, Otto GW-336
Mietzke, George A. GBM-58
Mignon, August JAG-73
Milan de Lalande, C. FDR-16
Miles, H.R.W. TR-231
Mill, George D. FDR-133
Millard, H. AL-332
Millard, Harrison GW-120; GW-165; SAD-16; JAG-1; JAG-15; JGB-2
Millbank, Henry D. WJB-59
Miller, Ada HCH-58
Miller, A.C. HG-32
Miller, A. Carl GW-618; JA-28; TJ-75; JMD-19; JMN-27; JQA-14; AJK-58; MVB-18; WHH-124; JT-14; JKP-19; ZT-88; MF-38; FP-10; JB-23; AL-509; AJN-28; USG-298; RBH-64; JAG-117; CAA-11; BFH-126; GC-162; WM-326; TR-381
Miller, Andrew WW-166
Miller, Bob DAM-46; DAM-59

Miller, Charles TR-315
Miller, C.H.R. AL-306
Miller, D. Long MISC-38
Miller, F. HC-68
Miller, F.J. WW-201
Miller, Harry HG-1; RBH-29
Miller, L.B. AL-419
Miller, LeRoy WJB-69
Miller, Mary Julia HCH-54
Milliken, N.B. RBH-39
Million, M.J. GBM-22
Mills, Frederick W. WHT-25
Mills, J.T. WW-52
Mills, Wilma WM-124
Milnor, Charles HC-81
Milns, Mr. JA-27
Miner, I.W. WM-178
Mingus, Icil L. WGH-58
Minton, T.H. USG-118
Mintzer, Charles A. WHH-21
Mirault, A. BFH-15; GC-36; WM-123
Misuraca, Antonio DAM-25
Mitchell, Florence Heath TR-276; TR-332; TR-370
Mitchell, Frank WGH-14
Mitchell, Humphrey GW-444
Mitchell, Jack DAM-30
Mitchell, J.F. GC-58
Mitchell, John R. WS-31
Mitchell, Samuel N. GW-171; SJT-9; SJT-24; RBH-26; RBH-38; RBH-59
Mitchell, Thomas WS-31
Mitchell, William C. JFK-70
Mizzy, Vic FDR-74; DDE-29
M.K. JD-9
Moelling, Theo. BFH-128
Moffitt, Wm. O. ND-4; ND-5; ND-6
Mohr, Halsey K. GW-241
Mokrejs, John GW-214
Mollenhaur, Crosby MISC-40
Moloney, Walter FDR-387
Monahan, Lawrence TR-190
Monaco, Jimmie HCH-17
Moncrieff, Kate GBM-46
Monroe, H.R. JGB-77
Montemayor, G.R. DAM-49; DAM-53
Montufar, Manuel GC-83
Moody, D.B. JAG-66; JAG-111
Moore, Herbert WW-125

Moore, J. Chris MISC-111
Moore, Jessica GW-577
Moore, Julia A. PC-3
Moore, Mary Farrell GBM-5; GBM-77
Moore, R.J. "Dinty" AES-56
Moore, Ron WM-229
Moore, Wm. A. JFK-44
Moore-Seamans, Emma WGH-46
Morales, Fina FDR-226
Moran, Ed TR-31; TR-35
Moran, Keats WGH-36
Moran, P.K. JMN-6; JQA-4
Morant, Ellen C. JB-4
More Anon JAG-82
Morgan, Carey WW-69
Morgan, (Mrs) David TR-342
Morgan, H.W. WM-161
Morgan, Irving J. TR-130
Morgan, Jimmie WW-7
Morgan, Louis TR-154
Mori, Emile E. TR-76
Morley, George JAG-52; JAG-56; JAG-96; JGB-43
Morley, Mary H. HCH-16
Morosini, G. RBH-30
Moross, Jerome AL-349
Morrell, C.B. BFH-74
Morrill, Etta TR-248
Morris, Duke AES-42
Morris, Edward L. BFH-6
Morris, George MF-17
Morris, George P. GW-177; GW-305; GW-519; GW-546; HC-62; HC-82; WS-1; WS-13
Morris, Gerald V. FDR-354
Morris, J.J. DDE-86; DDE-87
Morris, Newt A. MISC-128
Morris, Peter JKP-1
Morris, S.E. WM-24
Morrison, Edith WJB-25
Morrison, Marion FDR-120
Morrison, Mary GBM-49
Morrison, Will B. TR-131
Morrow, Henry FDR-255
Morse, Arthur C. GW-273
Morse, Theodore F. GC-92
Mortimer, Jr., Chas. MF-28
Mortimer, M.S. HC-39
Morton, Franklin FDR-296
Morton, Hugh TR-164
Moss, Clara L. GC-110
Moss, E.F. RR-6
Mossesson, D.S. FDR-297
Motzart. TJ-50
Moulton, Charles GW-151
Moxley, James DAM-56

Mueller, F. AL-420; TR-94
Mueller, Francis GC-142
Muhlenberg, Rev. Dr. AL-96; AL-289; AL-446
Muir, Duncan J. WM-231
Mullan, James J. AES-58
Mullen, John R. GW-243
Mullen, Frederic TR-354
Mullen, M.F. JGB-14; BFH-12
Mullenhaupt, H. USG-25
Muller, Carl GBM-35
Muller, F. GBM-38
Muller, J. Frederick MISC-101
Muller, Julius E. JT-3
Mullevy, William TR-76
Mulligan, Harold V. GW-294
Mulligan, John T. WJB-70
Mullin, Mary Alice FDR-418
Mullin, James J. AES-59
Munger, Shirley GW-399
Munyon, J.M. WSH-16; GC-39; WM-17
Muratori, Peppina MISC-172
Murdock, Orrice L. DDE-37
Murman, Frank JFK-8
Murphey, Doc WJB-36
Murphy, Con. T. TR-99
Murphy, C.W. TR-265
Murphy, Stanley GW-220; WW-126
Murray, F.E. AML-30
Murray, James R. USG-58; USG-210; JAG-17
Murray, O.E. WM-23
Murray, Thomas A. AES-46; AES-58
Musgrove, Chas. H. TR-281
Musico, Philo GW-71
Myer, A. Alvin TR-287
Myers, Harry T. JMC-10
Myers, Henry FDR-41; FDR-249
Myrtle, Frank WSH-45
Mysels, George AL-311; JFK-54; JFK-75; LBJ-22; MISC-67
Mysels, Sammy JFK-36

Nadzo, Guido FDR-385
Nagel, Clotilde FDR-202
Najarian, Mabel FDR-102
Naramore, E.M. TR-300
Nares, Owen L. AJK-34
Narin, Lady JAG-78
Nathan, E. ZT-61; WS-35
N.B.B. WHH-91

NcNaughton, J.H. AJN-10
Neal, Benjamin E. MISC-126; MISC-127
Neddermeyer, Fred L. WM-142
Neldinger, W.H. AL-421
Needam, W.L. WM-105
Neely, H.G. WM-253
Neely, Uberto T. WLW-24
Nelson, Evelyn FDR-51; FDR-98
Nelson, Jack T. FDR-10; FDR-18
Nelson, Steve TED-29
Nelson, Portia BC-8
Nelson, Violet FDR-51; FDR-98
Nesbit, Jacqueline FDR-158
Nesbit, W.D. TR-135
Neuman, A. AL-236
Neumann, R. TR-361
Neumuller, Franz GC-19
Nevin, Edwin H. GBM-31; GBM-43
Nevin, Mark JFK-34
Newkirk, Alice M.P. HCH-66
Newkirk, Garrett WM-150
Newkirk, Lena CC-21
Newland, W.A. MVB-12
Newman, Alfred MISC-57; MISC-58; MISC-59
Newman, Charles FDR-296
Newman, Fanny Hodges WW-212
Newman, Harry L. TR-36
Newman, John H. WM-315
Newman, John P. WM-103
Newman, L.F. WW-90
Newman, Randy MISC-134
Newmeyer, Id L. MISC-180
Newton, John W. FDR-390
Newton, W.J. GW-203
Nicholls, Robert FDR-64
Nichols, Alberta DDE-5
Nichols, Horatio HCH-39
Nicholson, James AL-255; RBH-12; RBH-48
Nicholson, T.J. JWD-4
Nickerson, F.S. GBM-37
Nickerson, Naomi E. TR-12
Nicklaus, E.G. JGB-8
Nicks, Weiss MF-21
Nicol, R.B. AL-117
Niebergall, Julia WJB-38
Niederman. FDR-279
Niedner, M. WSH-9
Niklaus, E.G. GC-40
Nilan, John J. AL-188
Nimmo, Robert E. WGH-17
Nirella, V.D. WJB-39

Composer Index

Nitram, Edward A. FDR-155
Nixon, W. GW-77
Noble, John D. CC-34; CC-36; HCH-15
Noel, Charles A. SJT-5; WSH-43
Nolan, Bob RR-29
Nolasco, Felix A. FDR-141; JFK-19
Noles, L.C. CAA-2; GC-8; GC-91; GC-131; GC-161; WJB-17; WJB-52
Notguilty, Bab SJT-13; SJT-20
Nordendorf, C.C. de HG-30
Norman, Pierre FDR-145
Norman, Ruth AL-335
North, Alex GW-239
North, H.S. WHH-96
Northrup, C.C. WSH-34
Northrup, Theo. H. BFH-75
Norton, A.B. WHH-96
Norton, Juliet S. WM-139
Norton, J.T. AJK-31; MVB-3; MVB-17; MVB-18
Norton, Maj. ZT-13
Norton, Nancy T. DAM-39
Norworth, Jack TR-58
Nourse, H.O. WJB-91
Novak, Frank Boncek TR-280
Nuccio, Joe FDR-219
Nunn, Earl DAM-14
Nysewander, Benjamin TR-98
Nyvall, Y.J. FDR-318

Oakley, E.A. GW-135
Oates, Henry T. GW-164
Oates, James F. GW-346
Oates, William J. GW-346
O'Bannon, W.D. JWD-1
Oberndorfer, Anne GW-541
Oberndorfer, Max GW-541
O'Brien, Edward D. AL-186; AL-372
O'Brien, Jack AES-61; RMN-15
O'Callaghan, T. O'D. WJB-43
O'Chortus, Cal WW-144
O'Conner, Laurence B. WJB-89
O'Conner, Mary A. TR-377
O'Dea, James WM-144
Odoms, Cliff GW-193
O'Donnell, Daniel P. FDR-135
O'Donnell, Terry WW-162

O'Donoughe, K. AL-130
O'Downey, Derby AL-203
O'Dowd, Thomas TR-263; FDR-302
Oesten, Th. GW-160
O'Fagun, Ason USG-123
Offenbach, J. USG-191
O'Hara, C.J. AES-24; AES-64
O'Hara, P.F. DWC-9; JMN-16; JMN-17; JMN-26
O'Hara, Geoffrey FDR-215
O'Higgins, Mai JFK-81
O'Kane, T.C. WM-3
Oldfield, F.H.H. AL-224
O'Leary, Arthur GW-154
Olin, Earle JFK-80
Oliver, Edward B. WHH-15
Oliver, George E. GC-118
Oliver, James B. WM-203
Oliver, Revilo WM-138
Olman, Abe WGH-26; WGH-38
Olmstead, Robert E.S. TR-226
Olympus. BFH-100
Olynthus. USG-2
O'Mahony, Martin J. WW-53
O'Neill, Felix J. GW-421
O'Neill, T. WSH-12
O'Neill, Thomas. JGB-88
Operti, Giuseppe USG-293; JAG-92
Opharrow, George A. TR-322
Opie, Mary Pickens GW-216
Oplinger, Monroe M. TR-284
Orange, James GCW-7
Ordway, John P. ZT-37; MF-19
Orefice, Luigi D. DAM-10
O'Reilly, P.J. HCH-11; FDR-414
O'Reilly, Miles USG-124
Orlob, Harold WHT-43
Orne, Edith R. WW-81
Orphean, Charles ZT-1
Orphean, Jacob ZT-1
Orr, E.K. WGH-14
Osborn, A.M. AL-58
Osborn, Anna H.B. WW-194
Osborne, Charles FDR-58; DDE-25
Osbourn, Jas. G. GW-104; HC-38
Osbourn, Nat WW-218
Ossman, Wesley FDR-11
Ostermeyer. AL-450

O'Toole, Angela M. JFK-2
Ottarson, F.J. ZT-17
Otten, W.F. AL-451
Oungst, Webb M. MISC-3
Our Ned. JCF-40; AL-159
Overgard, Graham T. DAM-18
Owen, Anita GC-114; WM-14
Owen, Delos DDE-88
Owk, Mr. GW-75
Oxtoby, J.T. JGB-28

Pace, Joy DAM-50
Packard, C.R. GW-274
Page, David B. WJB-20
Page, Estelle B. FDR-191
Page, Eugene FDR-272
Page, Sr., Pierre FDR-191
Page, Sara FDR-272
Paine, John K. AL-26
Paine, Thomas JA-5; JA-6; JA-10; JA-11; JA-12; JA-14; JA-15; JA-17; JA-21; JA-22; JA-23; JA;24; JA-25
Palin, Herb WW-92
Palm, Charles WM-316
Palmer, Charlotte R. WL-1
Palmer, Harry M. AL-502
Palumbo, Pierina FDR-7
Panella, Louis J. FDR-103
Pannell, F. GW-590
Papa, Julius TR-232
Pape, Charles O. JD-7
Paris, Leo FDR-197
Paris, Oz TR-309
Parker. AL-409
Parker, Fannie M. RBH-2
Parker, Gloria HST-9
Parker, H. TR-95
Parker, Jennie M. MF-4
Parkhurst, (Mrs) E.A. WS-25; WS-42; AL-24; AL-98; AL-368; USG-26; USG-94; USG-223; USG-252
Parkinson, Louis J. FDR-96
Parks, James A. AL-422; WJB-1; WJB-56; WM-106
Parmentel, Jr., Noel BG-13
Parrish, Mary Kay MISC-112
Parrish, T.A. WW-122
Parsons, L.V. ZT-49
Partello, Charles BFH-10
Parvin, Z.M. AL-477; TR-271
Pastor, Tony GBM-21; MISC-65
Pater, Jas. W. AL-261
Patouhas, Harry FDR-117
Patricolo, A. TR-218

Composer Index

Patten, Gilbert GW-296
Patterson, Vanna G. HCH-65
Patton, Amos JD-18
Patton, Robert C. FDR-353
Paul. USG-149
Paul, S.T. WHT-48
Paulina. USG-3
Paulish, John EVD-2
Paull, E.T. AL-230
Pauley, Roy AES-41; MISC-87
Pauly, Francis DDE-3; DDE-81
Pavia, Charles P. WGH-34
Payne, John H. WGH-28
Payne, Norma FDR-266
Payne, Thomasanne WGH-44
Paxton, Glenn LBJ-10; LBJ-31
Paxton, Tom LBJ-29; RMN-34
Peale. DDE-10
Peale, Rembrant TJ-2
Pearce, Charlie FDR-105
Pearce, Jr., John I. TR-243
Pearl, Musetta Markland HCH-62; HCH-63; HCH-64
Pearson, Emma Louise WM-196
Pearson, F.S. WM-198
Pearson, George C. AL-56
Pease, Henry HCH-30
Pease, Wm. H. TR-238; CEH-3
Peck, Gerald WW-33
Peckham, Creamer WHT-47
Pegram, Wm. M. WSH-42
Peile, Mr. AJK-2
Peirsol, William H. GC-68
Pekin, Annie G. WJB-21
Pelissier, Victor GW-462
Pelkonen, Matt FDR-28
Pendleton, (Mrs) E.H. HS-2; HS-11
Penfield, E. Jean N. WLW-36
Penfield, Henry HC-51
Penn, Margaret S. FDR-218; FDR-244
Penn, William H. WJB-3
Penney, William Edward. BFH-99
Penny, Ed W. HCH-9
Pepper, Irma DDE-110
Peppergrass, Thomas RBH-5
Pepusch, John GW-345
Perez, Alfred FDR-286
Perkins, Cy MISC-3

Perkins, Eva E. WM-181
Perkins, George H. AES-57
Perkins, G.F. WM-262
Perkins, H.S. GW-423; GW-426
Perkins, (Mrs) Lee HST-28
Perkins, Walton FDR-108
Perkins, W.O. GW-426; GW-519; RBH-35
Perlman, Morris FDR-11
Perna, Michael WW-50
Peron, Alain RMN-40; RMN-41
Perrin, Mac RMN-29; RMN-30
Perry, Bill B. USG-92
Perry, David JT-4
Perry, Harriet Gage FDR-148
Perry, Lester FDR-148
Perry, Oscar FDR-148
Perry, Phil B. JAG-99
Perry, Walter A. USG-33
Perry, William H. AL-148
Persichetti, Vincent AL-326
Persin, Max SLP-4
Peschau, F.W.E. AJK-50
Peterman, J.H. TR-140; TR-379; WHT-20; MISC-71
Peters, Brookes C. TR-143
Peters, Dick JC-11
Peters, Jack AL-304
Peters, Walter E. WGH-20
Peters, William A. WGH-3
Peters, W.C. HC-3; ZT-84; WS-47
Peters, Wm. Frederick TR-27
Peterson, Debbie HCH-9
Peterson, Hiram E. JAG-28; JGB-7; JGB-92
Petri. J.F. MF-1
Petros, Andrew J. FDR-268
Petru, B.M. WW-157
Petru, Quido WW-157
Pettee, W.E.M. AL-139
Pettengill, Robert DAM-33
Pettes, George W. JCF-15
Pettey, Roe WGH-39
Peyers, Billy AES-8
Peyton, Dave WL-2
Pfeiffer, P. RBH-37
Pferdner, Adolph JAG-10; GC-126
Phelps, E.A. JGB-73
Phelps, E.S. GC-35
Phelps, Olivia WW-154
Philadelphia Republican Club JFC-51
Phile, Philip GW-13; GW-17; GW-47; GW-55; GW-58; GW-59; GW-62; GW-63; GW-82; GW-105; GW-106; GW-107; GW-108; GW-112; GW-129; GW-160; GW-330; GW-335; GW-360; GW-379; GW-408; GW-433; GW-492; GW-513; GW-520; GW-530; GW-531; GW-536; GW-537; GW-538; GW-541; GW-543; GW-555; GW-556; GW-559; GW-560; GW-561; GW-562; GW-563; GW-608; GW-612; GW-613; GW-614; GW-615; GW-616; GW-617; GW-619; GW-621; GW-622; JA-1; AJK-59; MISC-155; MISC-168; MISC-171
Phillips, Austin ZT-10; ZT-60; ZT-88
Phillips, B.W. TR-11
Phillips, Joe W. TR-187; WHT-13
Phillips, Jonas B. GW-257
Phillips, Margueite WLW-19
Phillips, Marie T. FDR-360
Philpott, John RR-4
Phyla. GW-538; GW-543; GW-546; GW-556; MISC-155
Phylo, Prof.. GW-523
Piantadosi, Al GW-191; GW-232; AL-219; WW-189
Piatt, W.C. WJB-16
Pickens, A.G. ZT-17
Pickford, William DAM-1
Pierce, J.N. GW-497
Pierpont, James MF-9; MF-31
Pierpont, John GW-423
Pierson, Hugo USG-225
Pierson, Jno. C. RBH-41
Pierson, Will T. WM-120; TR-261; WHT-19; WW-56; WGH-12
Pietrack, Irving WLW-3
Pike, Marshall S. GW-119; MISC-171
Pike, M.S. TR-319
Pinkham, Daniel JFK-74
Piper, William H. WJB-20
Pipin, Antun K. FDR-231; FDR-233
Pitcher, Gladys TR-362
Pitt, M.D. FDR-35
Platzmann, Eugene WW-24; FDR-127

Pleyel. DW-18
Poage, Louise FDR-335
Poelman, Clasina L. FDR-131
Polla, W.C. AML-10
Pollack, Lew FDR-296
Polyhar, James P. FDR-348
Pomerory, Mr. RR-2
Pontius, Will H. RBH-7; CBF-7
Poole, J.F. GW-92
Poole, L.H. MISC-164
Pope, J. William AL-119; USG-291
Porray, Eddie CC-56
Porter, A.O. WM-29
Porter, Edgar M. USG-97; USG-111
Porter, J.A. SJT-6; WSH-19
Porter, James W. HC-29; AL-106; JD-45
Porter, Lew WW-71
Porter, Logan S. WJB-71; ABP-7; TR-356
Porter, W.T. WM-189
Portnoff, Mischa DDE-4
Portnoff, Wesley DDE-4
Posford, George FDR-26
Postlewaite, J. GC-148
Potjes, Edward WW-64
Potter, C.F. TR-101; TR-237
Potter, Harold WLW-38; FDR-32
Pottier, Eugene SLP-4
Potts, Rev. Wm. D. GBM-75
Poulton, George R. AL-48; DDE-17
Pounds, Jessie B. WM-156; WW-59
Powell, Glen AL-321
Powell, H. TJ-33
Powell, L.W. JCF-9
Power, Thomas WHH-103
Powers, Rodney GW-368
Pozzi, Francesco WGH-41; WGH-42; CC-48
Praetorius, Chris GW-325; TR-185
Pratt, Charles E. AL-156; AL-475; AL-506; JAG-56; GC-111; WJB-7; WJB-54
Pratt, Emily M. GW-132
Pratt,Frank B. JSJ-5
Pratt, John W. WM-179
Pratt, S.G. USG-25; GC-90
Pratt, Silas G. WW-183
Prendiville, Harry GW-403; MISC-119
Prentice, G.D. GW-77
Prescott, Paul GC-159; GC-162

Prescott, C.H. TR-81
Press, Jack A. RMN-19
Pressey, Miriam S. DAM-20
Preston, Adam GW-397
Preston, Donn RMN-7
Presuss, Col. T.K. RBH-60; RBH-61; RBH-62; RBH-63
Prevost, E. ZT-86
Preziosi, Remo DAM-10
Price, R.M. AL-424
Prima, Louis FDR-60
Prime, E. Rose BFH-57
Prime, P.C. USG-47
Prior, Charles E. GW-171; SJT-24; RBH-36; RBH-59
Prisson, A.T. JQA-13
Prival, Max GW-242
Probasco, Marks WW-171
Prout, Sylvester TR-93
Provis, Charles AL-423
Prudentius. JFK-55
Pryor, Arthur TR-45; TR-270
Psota, J. WW-93
Publican, R.E. RBH-15
Puener, Charles WM-69
Pugh, Clara TR-128
Purcell, E.H. TR-91
Purnell, Fritz BMG-6
Purnell, Susie WGH-53
Purviance, Jennie P. WM-157
P.W. JMD-7
Pychowski, J. WS-21

Quellmelz, C.L. WJB-78
Quidan. HC-40
Quigg, Travis WHH-33

Rab, W. GW-134; JGB-12
Rae, Jennie TR-149
Raff, Joseph USG-114
Raffelin, A. AJK-24
Rainey, Carrie AL-191
Rainger, Ralph MISC-72; MISC-80
Ralphing, Sam GW-392
Ram, Buck DAM-6
Ramspacher, Anna WW-141
Rand, Guy TR-41
Randall, J.H. JBW-6
Randolph, Pere M. GC-25
Rankin, J.E. CBF-7
Rankine, T.B. TR-352
Rapee, Erno AL-189
Rapley, Felton FDR-374
Rappaport, Daniel D. WW-82; WW-159
Raskin, William WJB-51
Ratel, William WHH-3; HC-43; HC-71; HC-85

Rauch, F.W. AL-6
Rautenberg, Gene AES-12
Ray, George JGB-31; JGB-44
Raymond, C. JGB-13
Rayner, Wm. C. WHH-69
Razaf, Andy AL-321; FDR-47; FDR-70; HST-21
R.C. AL-20; AL-21
Rebere, Paul AML-3
Recker, Robert MISC-39
Reden, Karl JAG-39
Redington, J.C.O. JMP-2
Redmond, Eleanor B. JT-1
Redmond, John DDE-2; JFK-33
Reed. JGB-15
Reed, B.F. TR-318
Reed, Bill W. WHT-39
Reed, Fred E. FDR-259; FDR-260
Reed, J.W. JAG-116
Reed, Leslie O. CC-4
Reed, L.P. AL-425
Reeder, Ida JB-13
Reese, Mary B. JAG-39
Reeves, D.W. WSH-1
Reeves, Florence M. WM-260
Regas, Belle FDR-93
Regg, Jr., Geo. A. WW-108
Rehm, Charles AL-2
Rehm, William C. GW-161; WW-38
Reichner, Bickley FDR-225
Reid, Francis W. WJB-9; TR-134
Reid, George L. BFH-118
Reinagle, Alex GW-7; GW-187; GW-335; TJ-6; TJ-21; TJ-73; JMD-1; JMD-2
Reinkendorff, Emil WM-43; WM-228
Reisinger, Mary McK. HCH-43
Reiss, B. DW-5
Reitermann, Lewis TR-273
Reizner, June BMG-4
Remak, (Mrs) G. AL-235
Remie, A.C. WJB-2
Rems, Jr., Joseph E. DAM-11
Renbort, Carl JAG-35; JAG-36
Renhart. GW-505
Rennie, Thomas FDR-71
Repaid, Billy WW-211
Retisor, W. USG-217
Retter. WJB-80
Rex, George FDR-272; FDR-383
Reynolds, Adelbert WW-32; WW-95

Composer Index

Reynolds, H.J. AML-2
Reynolds, L. HC-59
Reynolds, Mamie A. TR-115
Rhoades, Harold G. FDR-357
Riano, Guiseppe SJT-10
Rice, Edward E. BFH-69: WM-20; WM-119; BFB-5
Rice, Gitz FDR-86
Rice, Walter Allen WM-47; WM-48
Rice, WIlliam T. AL-264
Richard, Leo FDR-187
Richards, A.B. WLW-52
Richards, Rube RMN-18
Richards, Samuel FDR-94
Richards, T.M. WM-76; TR-307
Richards, V.M. FDR-143
Richardson JGB-44
Richardson, Dave TR-180; TR-210
Richardson, Harry WW-128
Richardson, Mary J. DDE-4
Richardson, Nathan JCF-1
Richardson, W.B. USG-53; WSH-19; JAG-82
Richner, J.B. FDR-124
Richter, Ada GW-621
Richter, Freda WJB-4
Richter,Rafael USG-281
Rickaby, Will J. WM-339
Rickman, Carl TR-253
Riddle, Nelson JFK-37
Rider. TR-16
Ridgway, Arthur FDR-2
Rieder, (Mrs) C.P. TR-318
Riemer, Lester C. TR-287
Riesenfeld, Hugo TR-100
Riis, Edward TR-57
Riley, Edward GW-83; GW-84; GW-86; GW-479; GW-480; JA-16; AJK-32
Riley Peter C. AES-72
Rimbault, J. WM-22
Rinck, C.H. AL-377
Ringwald, Roy FDR-373
Ripley, E.L. GW-138
Rishell, M. WM-27
Rivarde, Francis W. TR-28
Rivinac, P. JD-2; JD-11; JD-13
Roach, J. Maloy RMN-5; RMN-8; RMN-10; RMN-16
Roat. JGB-44
Robards, Willis WW-158
Robbins, C. GW-477; TJ-56
Robbins, C.A. GW-201
Robe, Harold WW-9

Roberson, Loyd E. JFK-83
Robert, Camille WW-126
Robert, Lee S. WW-126
Roberts, D.C. AL-149
Roberts, Grace May WM-49
Roberts, Lee S. TR-14; TR-353
Roberts, Ruth DDE-9; MISC-24
Robin, Leo MISC-72; MISC-80
Robinson, Earl AL-182; AL-490; FDR-188; FDR-197
Robinson, Edna J. FDR-406.
Robinson, J.B. WM-3
Robinson, J. Russel FDR-331
Robinson, Salon HG-29
Robinson, Tom MF-23
Robinson, W.A. GC-124
Robisson, George A. JFK-42
Robjohn, W.J. AL-27
Robyn, A.J. AL-426
Roca, Ignace AJ-47
Roche, A.C. AL-477
Rochow, Alfred Von USG-85; BFB-2
Rodeheaver, Homer A. TR-149
Roden. AL-438
Rodgers, Richard MISC-138
Roehr. WJB-76
Roff, Jos. A. JSJ-2
Roff, Joseph TJ-29; JFK-64
Rogel, Randy MISC-135
Rogers. USG-169; JGB-15
Rogers, C.E. AL-452
Rogers, Bernard FDR-223
Rogers, Eliza J. MVB-2
Rogers, Frank WLW-23
Rogers, H.M. AL-453
Rogers, Julia M. MISC-112
Rogers, William T. USG-21; USG-88; USG-117; USG-121
Rohbock, Henry ZT-19
Rojamdrof. GC-97; WM-293
Rojas, Solistra F. TR-283
Roland, Ralph GC-60
Rollinson, T.H. WJB-34
Romano, Luigi TR-227
Romberg, George de WHT-37
Rome, A.D. FDR-312
Rome, Harold J. FDR-95; FDR-177; FDR-197; FDR-207; FDR-282
Romeo, C. SJT-22
Ronch, Isaac E. AL-517

Roney, H.B. JAG-37; JAG-75; JGB-28; JGB-30
Rooney, James AES-30
Roosevelt, Franklin FDR-224; FDR-373; MISC-110
Roosevelt, Jr., F.D. FDR-358
Roosevelt, Theodore TR-347
Root, Arabella JAG-51
Root, George F. GW-414; AL-51; AL-124; AL-140; AL-192; AL-215; AL-285; AL-468; AL-479; USG-139; USG-267; USG-269; RBH-22; JGB-15; JD-22; JD-27
Rosabel. JAG-75; JAG-86
Rose. WJB-18
Rose, Bert WLW-53
Rose, Billy RR-17
Rose, Phil S. GC-61
Rose, Wil GRF-4
Rosenberg, B. Anna WW-104
Rosenberg, Jacob S. GW-318; AL-250; CC-40
Rosenfeld, Monroe H. GW-264; BFH-1; BFH-33; GC-26; GC-54; GC-100; GC-105; GC-111; GC-146; WM-166; TR-204; WHT-9
Rosenthal, J.J. WW-188
Rosenthal, Laurence GW-295
Rosewig, A.H. USG-41; JAG-4; JAG-18; JAG-29; JAG-31; JAG-52; JAG-96; JAG-117; JAG-119; CAA-7; JGB-16
Rosey, George MISC-63
Ross, Alexander C. WHH-113; WHH-124; MISC-169
Ross, Anna May WW-21
Ross, James D. GW-189
Ross, Norman A. LBJ-31
Rossi, Antonio GW-325
Rossi, Johnny AES-33
Rossini, Gioacchino MISC-135
Rossington, W.W. HC-41
Rossiter, E. JD-17
Roth, Alfred GW-439
Roth, Charles GW-224; GW-289
Roth, Fred AL-244
Rothstein, Frederick GW-245
Rotter, Etta AML-30
Rourke, Thomas BFH-101

Roussin, Blanche A. WW-80; WW-140
Rowe, Sidney TR-362
Rowe, Tommy FDR-300
Rowell, Sylvia FDR-150
Rowley, A.A. BFH-64; BFH-102; BFH-119; WM-267
Rozelle, Dick FDR-9
R.P.N. HC-116
Rudolph, D.E. GC-124
Rudy, C.I. AML-21
Rundle, Adaline P. CC-9; CC-22
Rupprecht, Henry WW-114
Russell, Bob TJ-42
Russell, Henry GW-268; WHH-91; HC-5; WS-13; DW-13
Russell, Henry A. TR-256
Russell, John USG-194
Russell, Vivian I. TR-267
Russell, Walter TJ-72
Ryan, Charles FDR-107
Ryan, Gordon FDR-40
Ryan, J.F. WW-28
Ryan, Sidney JGB-3; JGB-44
Ryan, Thomas J. WM-32
Ryder, A.H. HC-36
Ryder, T.P. USG-242
Rynder, Rose AL-270
Ryskind, Morrie WLW-8
Ryson, Anthony GW-207

Saar, Louis Victor GW-442
Sacco, John AL-232
Saddler, Annie G. WM-217
Saffer, Bob JFK-54; JFK-75; BMG-8; BMG-12; LBJ-21; LBJ-22; GRF-9; JEC-12; MISC-67
Saffery, E.B. JB-15
Safstrom, Gust AML-9; WLW-2; WLW-57
Sager, Vehrl FDR-391
Sagstetter, Helen HST-27
Sahm, Carl HC-21
Salem, R.Z. USG-154
Salis, P.G. AJN-25
Sammons, Lafayette BMG-2
Sams, Bert FDR-334
Samuels, Mark J. MISC-5; MISC-22
Sanburg, Carl GW-392 AJK-53; AL-476
Sanctuary, E.N. DAM-32
Sanders, Alma DDE-77
Sanders, George H. MISC-165
Sanderson, James GW-25; GW-27; MISC-26; MISC-28; MISC-29; MISC-30; MISC-31; MISC-32; MISC-43; MISC-75; MISC-129; MISC-151; MISC-168; MISC-170; MISC-176; MISC-178
Sanfilippo, S. Edw. WW-82; WW-159
Sanford, Dick JFK-36; JFK-41
Sanford, Lee AL-427
Sanford, S.S. GBM-47
Sangster, Rena N. WM-115
Sangster, Urania N. CC-5
Sankey, Ira D. GW-215
Santarello, John FDR-312
Santarello, Madeline FDR-312
Santlemann, Wm. H. TJ-23
Santly, Joseph H. TR-106; TR-107
Sarchet, John H. BFH-74; WM-209; WM-211; WM-213
Sargent, L.M. GW-25; GW-27
Sarnoff. FDR-280
Saroni, Herrman S. GW-150
Saunders, Joseph FDR-324
Saunders, W.W. GW-364
Sauvlet, Guillaume GC-72
Sawyer, F.R. MISC-14
Sawyer, H. Stanton TED-35
Sawyer, Henry USG-220; USG-234
Saxton, David MISC-56; MISC-62
Saxton, Harry A. JAG-47; JAG-48
Sayers, Henry J. HCH-52
Scala, F. JB-21; AL-318
Scales, Mrs. Melrose HCH-35
Schack, Albert P. WJB-50
Schaefer, Dawnmarie AL-308
Schaeffer, Mary WLW-11; WLW-58
Schaff, Eli L. LBJ-8
Schaller, George E. GC-71
Schaum, John W. GW-234; GW-353; GW-365
Scheiber, I.B. FDR-297
Schell, John ZT-16
Schenck-Henze, Grace WHT-54
Scherb, Vitalis JCF-5
Schildkret, S. TR-359
Schlacht, Joseph FDR-269
Schleiffarth, Geo. USG-119; JGB-11; BFH-29; GC-37; GC-59; GC-76; GC-77; GC-79; GC-80; GC-87; WM-11; WM-57; WM-59; WM-259; WM-263
Schmid, Adolf GW-338
Schmidt, Alfred JD-44
Schmidt, Erwin R. TR-78
Schmidt, Henry WHH-11
Schmidt, Mae Doelling WLW-61
Schmidt, Susan WW-55
Schmidt, William J. CC-28
Schminke, Harry WM-89
Schmitz, Adolph GW-44; ZT-7
Schmoll, Oscar TR-314
Schnecker, P.A. GC-19
Schneider, Walter E. DDE-13
Schniedt, Dorothy E. DAM-34
Scobbie, Mary FDR-412
Schoeller, Henri GC-10
Schomaker, Harry C. RBH-41
Schonacker, J.E. AL-138
Schraeder, George WSH-21; FDR-46
Schrag, Belle FDR-290
Schreibert, Felix WW-150
Schroeder, G. WSH-21; GC-94
Schroeder, Henry AL-169; JD-35; JD-61
Schroeder, Russell B. RMN-23
Schrogin, Joseph AL-517
Schubert, Hugh W. FDR-93
Schuesler, Jack WHT-38
Schultz, H.T. GW-503
Schultz, L. Frederick FDR-196
Schuman, A. GC-84
Schuster, Ira DAM-3
Schutze, Ernest A. AES-37
Schwale, T. Moritz FP-4
Schwartz. AL-428
Schwartz, Arthur CC-26
Schwartz, Jean AL-213; TR-245; TR-260
Schwartz, Milton M. JFK-17; JFK-76
Schwing, Henry GW-585; AJN-11
Sciver, Esther Van DAM-46
Scofield, G.A. WHT-3
Sconcia, Giovanni AL-142
Scotese, Constantino DAM-28

Composer Index

Scott, Ed AS-1
Scott, Eddie AL-302
Scott, F.B. JD-38
Scott, Frank N. JAG-74
Scott, Genevieve WW-146
Scott, (Mrs) General WS-30
Scott, R.D. GC-122; JSC-4
Scott, Sir. Walter MISC-26; MISC-28; MISC-29; MISC-30; MISC-31; MISC-32; MISC-151; MISC-168; MISC-170; MISC-178; MISC-183
Scotus, Edmundu AL-86
Scull, J.J. WW-129
Seal, T.T. WM-73
Seaman, Gertrude S. AS-7
Seamark, H.J.W. JBW-1
Sedgwick, A. AL-171
Seeboeck, W.C.E. GC-89
Seeger, Pete LBJ-2
Segal, Jacob DDE-20
Seger, Mike FDR-378
Sequin, Maria MISC-36
Segura, T. AJK-35
Seib, Frank WW-132
Seibert, William USG-2; USG-3; HS-6
Seiffert, William R. AML-4; RMN-9
Seiler, Eddie RR-15; RR-24
Seipp, J.H. WHH-46
Seitz, Ina Roe TR-328
Selden, Edgar WHT-27
Selfer, Ben MISC-107
Selington, H.A. SJT-9
Selkirk, Blaine MISC-187
Sellers, Emma P. TR-132
Semola, Al AL-202
Semple, Letitia T. JT-5
Sence, Frank EVD-1
Serly, Lajos Von TR-216
Seron, Herminie GBM-12
Seven Octaves USG-202
Severe, William B. WM-284
Severin, Beryl MISC-92
Sewall, Jonathan M. GW-23
Seward, Edna B. WGH-18
Seward, George M. WGH-13
Seyb, Carl WW-177
Seyman, Rudolph C. FDR-88; FDR-304
Seymour, Edward J. TR-269
Seymour, E.J. BFH-35; BFB-78
Seynour, Minnie M. TR-200
Seymour, Pliny B. TR-54
S.G.A. MF-13
Shaffner, Bobbie JEC-2; JEC-7; MSD-1; BC-6; BC-12; MISC-121; MISC-124; MISC-163
Shaffner, Henry JEC-2; JEC-7; MSD-1; BC-6; BC-12; MISC-121; MISC-124; MISC-163
Shane, Tom HCH-1
Shanley, Ben AES-50
Sharp, C. WM-322
Sharp-Minor, C. DAM-2; DAM-54
Sharpe, George W. WM-247
Shauck. WM-292; WM-303
Shaw, David T. GW-162; JB-20
Shaw, G.L. WM-165
Shaw, Oliver GW-43; JMN-10; JMN-11; JMN-12; JMN-13; JMN-18; JMN-22
Shay, Larry GW-307
Shea, J.A. HC-2
Sheafs, M.W. GW-201
Shear, Lester FDR-87
Shear, W. BFB-13
Sheff, Julia Belle FDR-306
Sheff, William H. FDR-306
Sheffield, Charles A WJB-61
Sheik, The TED-25; DAM-23
Shelly,Gladys AL-512; MISC-185
Shelly, Percy B. JFK-64
Shelton, James FDR-252
Sheldon, Jimmy FDR-100
Shellman, M.B. WM-198
Sheppard, John H. WHH-122
Sheppard, Thomas G. WM-153
Sheppherd, Madelyn HCH-38
Sheridan, Phil MISC-39
Sherman, Al FDR-63; FDR-125; FDR-204; FDR-270; MISC-12; MISC-13; MISC-150
Sherman, Richard M. BFH-43; BFH-45; GC-42
Sherman, Robert B. BFH-43; BFH-45; GC-42
Sherwin, Manning GW-279
Sherwood, Edgar H. BFH-46
Sherwood, K.M. USG-29
Sherwood, Ray TR-63
Sherwood, William F. GW-278
Sherrey, Mae Ayres WM-70
Shindler, Mary Dana LBW-7
Shield. JA-17
Shields, Ren GW-229
Shimoneck, Wm. C. WW-213
Shire, David RMN-22
Shirley, John B. TR-55; TR-348
Shoemaker, Bobby AES-3
Shoemaker, Metta WW-171
Shols, Hermann JCF-20
Short, William J. TR-9
Shrighey, Cleveland AML-16
Shure, R.D. AL-455
Shuman, Alden TJ-42
Shuman, Earl TJ-42
Sibley, Mary O'Brien AML-25
Sicard, (Mr) GW-22
Sickles, Walter E. FDR-115; FDR-116
Sider, D.L. TR-151
Siders, James Buchanan JGB-84
Sieb, Frank WW-132
Siebott, Edward E. FDR-334
Siegal, Arsene DDE-49
Siegel, Al MISC-72; MISC-80
Siegfried, C.P. MISC-54
Siegmeister, Elie AL-181; AL-217; AL-218; AL-478; MISC-156
Siemonn, George WJB-41
Sigler, Mose MISC-52; MISC-86; MISC-143
Sigman, Carl TJ-42; CC-45; CC-46; CC-47
Signore, Paolo WW-110
Sigourney, (Mrs) L.H. DW-13
Silber, Irving LBJ-33
Silberberg, J. Alex WM-19
Sillman, June FDR-252
Silva, Prof. B.N. WW-219
Silver, Abner TJ-42; AL-212; FDR-230
Silverman, Jerry AL-475; WM-257
Silvers, Herman LBJ-17; HHH-1; HHH-3; RMN-36; JEC-1; JEC-8; RR-5
Simeone, Harry DDE-40; JEC-5
Simmons, Anna R. TR-96
Simmons, Cyrus AL-187
Simmons, Daniel TR-364
Simes, Virginia M. DAM-12
Simms, Hoffman TR-222
Simon, D. AES-48
Simon, Nat DDE-2

Composer Index

Simpson, F.A. MISC-156
Simpson, F.G. WW-78
Simpson, T.A. SP-2
Singer, Al FDR-253
Singer, Dolph GW-628
Singer, Lou TJ-28; TJ-51
Sissle, Noble HST-1
Sisters of St. Joesph WM-130; WM-131
Skelly, J.P. GW-118; GW-179; GC-17
Slade, Carrie E. AES-52
Slade, M.B.C. AES-52
Slater, Aleta R. WLW-43
Slater, Samuel FDR-228
Sligh, L.M. WW-67
Sloan, Sterling RR-2; RR-3
Smack, Cyril A. AS-7
Smart, Christopher LBJ-25
Small, Mary FDR-73
Smiles, "Dr." MISC-4
Smith. HG-1
Smith, Alfred TR-46
Smith, Carolyn WM-205
Smith, C.E. GW-238
Smith, Charles E. WM-148
Smith, Clara H. JSJ-1
Smith, Chris AL-457
Smith, Dexter USG-205
Smith, Donald J. WLW-64
Smith, Eleanor AL-470; WLW-64
Smith, Eliot TR-221
Smith, Ethel MISC-151
Smith, Ethel E. WM-183
Smith, Ethel Mae TR-278
Smith, F.W. SAD-13
Smith, Georgia DDE-93
Smith, Gregg MF-37; JB-21; GBM-84; AL-506; WM-325; MISC-114; MISC-182
Smith, H. Wakefield TR-346
Smith, Harry B. TR-30; WHT-12
Smith, Herbert J. FDR-158
Smith, Howard TR-165
Smith, M.V.H. WJB-53
Smith, Ida GW-282
Smith, James G. AL-341
Smith, Jennie G. JGB-64
Smith, J.F. WW-28
Smith, John S. FDR-1; MISC-169
Smith, Joshua GW-133; BFH-89
Smith, Julia AL-183; AL-225
Smith, Laura R. GW-205
Smith, Lee Orean WM-46
Smith, Leroy "Stuff" FDR-60

Smith, Mal DAM-56
Smith, Maria V. CC-19
Smith, Martha J. FDR-89
Smith, Neal MISC-104
Smith, Roger GW-395
Smith, Rosalia GW-282
Smith, Samuel F. TR-289; CC-14; MISC-117
Smith, Seba GW-93; GW-332
Smith, (Rev) S.F. GC-130
Smith, W. D. AL-392
Smith, W. Dexter AL-146; AL-103; AL-153; JD-14
Smith, William GW-470
Smith, Wilson G. GW-570
Smith, Wm. H. USG-224
Smith, Jr., Dexter USG-78; USG-207
Smith, Jr., J. AL-35
Smoot, Mima Lee HCH-15
Sneath, E. Hershey AL-479
Snow, Blanche R. FDR-150
Snyder, Bill JFK-34
Snyder, Sylvia TR-239
Snyder, Ted GW-224; GW-289; TR-145
Snyder, Will P. TR-367
Sofge, Henry D. JAG-110
Sohl, Frank B. DDE-99
Sohn, Daniel W. FDR-334
Soler, Julio WHH-65
Solis, Benjamin F. JFK-68
Solman, Alfred TR-37
Sommerville, Anna B. TR-236
Sommerville, Geo. B. TR-236
Sondheim, Stephen AL-309; JAG-90; WM-234; RR-27; MISC-91
Soran, Charles JT-6; JT-8
Sour Mash. USG-251
Sour, Robert AS-3
Sousa, John Philip GW-209; GW-277; GW-291; AL-209; AL-223; JAG-14; JGB-37; JGB-39; JGB-96; BFH-39; WM-125; WM-135; TR-249; WGH-51; DAM-22
Southgate, Charles TJ-4
Southgate, F. MF-2; JB-1
Spalding, Andrew JFK-16
Spaulding, George L. GW-370; GW-577; AL-429; MISC-42
Spaulding, Hector AL-322
Sparrow, Kendrick FDR-358
Specht, Paul WW-163; AML-3

Spencer, Frank MF-15
Spencer, Fred WM-4
Spencer, William HCH-14
Speth, William B. MISC-140
Spindler, Johann GW-316; GW-362; GW-431; GW-572
Spink, George FDR-37
Spinx. GC-158
Spiro, Lou WW-33
Spivey, R.E. WM-202
Sporle, J.N. GW-92; GW-263; AL-456; WHH-103
Sprague, James H. WM-87; TR-20
Sprague, Joseph H. WM-310
Springer, Annie R. JGB-13
Springer, Philip GW-358
Springer, W.A. TR-228
Springs, G.H. AL-140
Sprague, Charles MF-1
Sprinkle, Marie O. FDR-101
Sproat, P.W. HC-42
Sprole, N.J. AL-467
Spruance, W.D. DAM-27
Squire, A. SAD-2
Squires, T. MF-22
St. Claire, F.J. AL-454
St. Claire, Louis FDR-77
St. Claire, William WHT-53
St. Dennis, Charles USG-84
St. John, Mother JFK-47
Stadler, Emil JD-26; JD-34
Stafford, Al FDR-395
Stafford, Lon F. HCH-32; FDR-50; LBJ-28
Stagg, Robert RML-5
Stahl, Richard JAG-9; CAA-4; MISC-81
Stair, Lelia K. WLW-16
Stair, Mary C. WLW-16
Stammers, Frank WM-97
Stanfield, Leontine WJB-60
Stanhope, Mary GW-557
Stanley, Jack WW-141
Stanley, James WM-206
Stanley, Rufe K. CC-30
Stansell, Emery K. GW-237
Stanton, Frank H. FDR-123
Stapp, R.M. RBH-18
Starcher, Buddy JFK-28
Starke, Lee DAM-34
Starke, William WW-197
Starkweather, L.B. AL-91; AL-135
Starr, Samuel D. LBJ-14
Stauffer, Aubrey DAM-29; DAM-41; DAM-44
Stauffer, Richard B. AML-19
Stayman, A. Fletcher MISC-34

Steele, Silas S. AL-55; AL-284
Steele, Theodore WJB-62; JBW-3
Steffe, William JFK-21
Stein, Hertha Ann FDR-4
Stein, Jeannie FDR-87
Steiner, Eric GW-212; GW-407; Al-211
Steinert, Alexander WLW-8
Steinfield, Herbert TR-4
Steinfield, Mortimer TR-4
Steinhauser, F.M. WM-204
Steinruck, Charles JQA-11; HC-91
Stemland, Odgard C. FDR-347
Stephani, Charles M. JT-8
Stephens, William WM-222
Stephenson, Emma MISC-21
Stephenson, Isabella DAM-55
Stephenson, R. DDE-101
Sterling, Andrew B. WM-163; WW-13
Sterling, Raymond A. MISC-95
Sterling, Robert FDR-13
Stern, Henry DDE-70
Stern, Jack WW-14; AML-5
Stern, Robert DDE-16
Sternburg, Simon TR-105
Sterns, J.N. JSJ-5
Stevens. AL-398
Stevens, A. AS-4
Stevens, David AJK-39; GW-376
Stevens, Lizzie Beach AL-367
Stevens, Margaret T. GW-326
Stevenson, T.E. FDR-184
Stewart. AL-460
Stewart, Charles D. ZT-60
Stewart, H.J. WW-106
Stewart, J. Calvin AES-60
Stewart, James M. AL-155
Stewart, J.D. WHH-91
Stewart, John JFK-45
Stewart, John M. WM-288
Stickney, Louise GW-455
Stillman, Al FDR-61
Stillman, J.M. AL-133
Stimpson, Jr., George FP-9
Stine, Thomas O. TR-59; WW-43
Stock, Laurence DDE-22; DDE-78
Stock, Otto WW-208
Stocking, William Dennis JGB-85

Stockton, Jr., J.P. WSH-34
Stoddard, A. GW-18
Stoddard, Fletcher WHT-17
Stoddon, R.S. FDR-23
Stoffel, Irene M. FDR-274
Stoller, Benj. C. MISC-78
Stolz, Elvira A. DDE-63
Stone, E.G. HCH-28
Stone, Gregory LBJ-25
Stone, Jesse FDR-69
Stone, Sasha FDR-52
Stor, Jean AL-200
Stork, George RMN-17
Story, H.L. JD-21
Story, Nelson E. FDR-136
Story, Thomas D. JAG-5
Stott, Mae TR-165
Stout, George C. MISC-164
Stowell, C.J. TR-219
Strakosch, Maurice ZT-47
Stranberg, Carl RBH-1; RBH-34; RBH-42
Strange, C.S. WHT-26
Strate. HG-1
Stratton, C.E. WM-289
Stratton, H.W. JAG-70
Strauss, F.A. HG-16; USG-298
Stravinski, Igor JFK-57
Strawn, Frank TR-299
Strebiringer, Josef JGB-48
Street, William J. USG-80
Striby, William ZT-33
Striker, Will FDR-44
Stromeyer, G. RBH-37
Strunk, Jud MISC-93
Strunk, W. Oliver GW-381
Stuart, John WGH-19
Stuart, J.W. FDR-192
Stuckenholz, W. USG-15
Studdert, Jr., John JAG-48; JAG-48
Studds, W.F. USG-280; RBH-50; JAG-22; JAG-90; JAG-107; JGB-9
Sturtevant, Frank TR-8; TR-339
Stutto, Lawrence J. JFK-27
Stuyvesant, Lee TR-77
Styne, Jule DDE-85
Sullenbarger, W.A. WJB-8
Sullivan, Alex WW-127
Sullivan, Arthur GC-73; WM-314
Sullivan, J.H. AL-142
Sullivan, Jr., John GBM-32
Sullivan, Phillip F. GC-69
Sullivan, Will. FDR-267
Summerfield, James USG-210
Summers, Allen D. FDR-149

Summers, Franklin AES-44
Summers, Ralph JGB-51
Sundgaard, Arnold AL-196
Sundlun, Walter I. WLW-53
Sunshine, Marion FDR-278
Surdo, J. AL-430
Surette, Thomas W. AL-355
Surfluh, Clara B. WM-152
Sutherland, Ken RMN-33
Sutter, Henry USG-100
Sutton, Frederick J. FDR-99
Sutton, G. Davison GW-222
Sutton, Glenn AL-301
Sutton, Mary D. GW-222
Sutton, P.M. USG-85
Sutton, T. Shelly TR-266
Swanstrom, Arthur MISC-69
Sweet, Albert C. TR-351
Sweet, Alfred W. JGB-34
Sweetser, Joseph E. GW-85; GW-388
Sweetzer, Seth H. HC-56
Swindells, James H. DWC-1
Swinton, John WM-66
Switzer, Lizzie A. GW-530
Swope, James TR-138
Sykes, L. Foyette JAG-41
Szigeti, Joseph AES-48

Tabor, Edward M. JGB-37
Tabor, Silver Echo TR-212
Taft, Madge DDE-75
Tail, Joseph WHT-49
Talarico, Emma FDR-342
Talbert, H.C. WGH-19
Talbert, Wen FDR-112
Tanassy, Carnel RR-5
Tanner, Tom A. AL-227
Tapen, William B. GW-548
Tarr, Florence FDR-67
Tatgenhorst, John MISC-147
Tatnall, Harry L. AL-131
Taube, Maurice S. TR-60
Taylor, Bayard WS-18
Taylor, George GW-271
Taylor, (Rev) Geo. Lansing USG-252
Taylor, H.S. WHT-33
Taylor, I. Della WW-76
Taylor, J.H. GBM-81
Taylor, Henry W. WJB-63
Taylor, (Mrs) Ida S. USG-236
Taylor, Irving FDR-74
Taylor, Raynor GW-619; AJK-59
Taylor, Robert RMN-35
Taylor, R.T. GW-51
Taylor, (Mrs) Walter Q. AML-33

Composer Index

Taylor, William DWC-4
Taylor, William W. FDR-124
Teale, Herbert WLW-12
Templeton, Virginia TR-259
Tenney, Dennis DDE-36
Tepper, Sid JFK-3
Terhune, Bert RMN-4; RMN-24; RMN-25; RMN-26
Tetreault, Victor A. FDR-147
Thall, Peter M. AL-190
Thayer, Charles FDR-238
Thayer, M.C. GC-53; WM-176; WM-218
Thayer, H. BFH-122
Thayer, H. Clark WM-273
Thomas, Benny FDR-294
Thomas, Carl RBH-27
Thomas, Charles FDR-76
Thomas, F.W. FDR-29
Thomas, Gomer JAG-115
Thomas, J.R. GW-177; AL-92; AL-431
Thomas, Leroy WM-51
Thomas, W.G. WM-275
Thomsai, Th. GC-157
Thompkins, R. JD-22; JD-25
Thompkins, Wm. E. GW-532
Thompson, C.F. RBH-41
Thompson, Floyd WJB-36
Thompson, H.S. AL-129; JAG-105
Thompson, Mary A.V. AJK-6
Thompson, Randall TJ-47
Thompson, Robert GW-233
Thompson, Thomas M. BFH-83
Thompson, Will L. WM-184
Thomsen, William H. LBJ-18
Thomson, Ferdinand A. MISC-2
Thornbecke, C.H. LC-3; LC-4; LC-5
Thorne. CAA-9
Thorne, Arthur JAG-67
Thornton, M.C. FDR-290
Tierney, Harry GW-220; WW-39; WW-40
Tiffy, A.H. WJB-40
Tigue, Harry AES-43
Tillotson. AL-441
Tillotson, Edith S. GW-533
Tilzer, Albert Von AES-7; AES-54

Tilzer, Harry Von GW-628; WM-163; WW-119; MISC-93
Timm, Henry C. GC-78
Tinturin, Peter AL-185; MISC-18
Tischendorf, Carl AES-43
Tobey, A.B. AL-432
Tobias, Augusta TR-383
Tobias, Charlie FDR-145
Tobias, Henry H. FDR-145; RMN-11; RMN-31
Tobin, Lew DAM-20
Toll, Rudolph HCH-36
Toom, (Rev) Samuel GW-504
Toomey, Frank HAW-1
Toomey, Fred HAW-1
Toon, E. May Glenn MISC-141
Toon, (Mrs) Wm. P. WHT-5
Toroni, Ann FDR-347
Torr, Joseph HCC-111
Tosso, J. WHH-66
Toulmin, Alfred F. JD-5
Tourgee, A.W. AL-483
Towne, Belle Kellog GW-205
Towne, T. Martin GW-205; AL-458; USG-9
Townsend, Maida AML-1; WLW-7; WLW-48
Townsend, Marian WW-169
Townsend, Robert AML-22
Townsend, W. HC-83
Trabold, May I. WW-197
Travaline, Dominick WW-148
Traver, C.M. MF-22
Trayne, John H. FDR-178
Tredway, G.E. WM-256
Tredway, Ida Hoyt RML-2
Tredway, W.T. BFH-54
Treloar, W.M. WSH-7; WSH-8; WSH-18; WW-115
Trench Richard R. WM-175
Treuer, Konrad AL-20; AL-21; JAG-81
Treuman, A. TR-285
Trimmer, Chas. McK. USG-38
Tripp, Harvey E. AES-52
Tripp, Howard C. WM-130; WM-148; TR-332
Tripp, Ruth HCH-58
Tromblee, Lilia S. TR-230
Tromblee, Lilian A. TR-230
Trowbridge, Bertha C. GW-410
Trucksess, David L. GC-121

Trucksess, Ida V. GC-121
Tucker, Don LGM-2
Tucker, Henry WS-8; HG-14; USG-46; USG-106; USG-261; JAG-7; JD-20; JD-55; MISC-139
Tucker, Minnie B. WJB-24
Tuckerman, Parkman JAG-80
Tudor, Stanley M. FDR-307
Tufts, Hellen Witt FDR-49
Tuller, Rollin B. WM-81
Tully, D. Frank USG-60
Tumber, Maria Walker TR-316
Turner, Elliott AL-287
Turner, J.K. USG-13
Turner, J.W. AL-49; AL-97; AL-100; AL-104; AL-118; AL-141; AL-237; HG-28; WM-65; WM-255; JD-19; NB-1; NB-2
Turner, Nancy Byrd GW-347; GW-518
Tutewiler, Harry D. WM-155; WM-311
Twomblee, Leilia S. AL-362
Twombly, Ethelberta TR-33
Twomey, Kay TJ-42
Tyler, John JT-3; JT-5
Tyler, S.L. GC-9; GC-62
Typo, A. GW-173
Tyrajetta, Phil GW-114
Tyrel, R.M. TR-156
Tyrrell, Catherine WLW — 3
Tyrrell, Henry WM-69; WM-203

Uhl, Dick FDR-167
Ullner, Walter V. USG-173; MISC-120
Ullrich, F.P. GW-249
Ulp, E.H. WW-139
Ulp, G. Byron WW-139
Ulrich, Eva WLW-1; WLW-59
Underhill, Ann. GW-470
Underhill, Andrew F. TR-226
Unger, Stella CC-16
Unohoo. GW-248; HCH-22
Upham, Louise S. AL-109
Upham, Nathan AL-60; AL-114
Uphardt, Phil WW-134

Vaas, A.J. JCF-4; JCF-30; USG-4
Valle, James D. FDR-264
Vallee, Art AL-202

Composer Index

Valtinke, Paul TR-266
Van Allen, J.H. DDE-67
Van Alstyne, Egbert TR-42
Van Buren, Burrell WGH-17; AML-12; FDR-6; FDR-96
Van Deventer, Gale WLW-26
Van Dyke, Walter Johns FDR-413
Van Ess, Mable AL-433
Van Rees, Cornelius HCH-42
Vance, Paul S. DDE-20
Vanden Berg, T.H. JT-111
Vandercook, H.A. TR-308
Vanderpoel, Kate WM-66; WM-111; WM-252
Vanderveer, Billy GW-242
Vanderweyde. AL-451
Vandevere, J. Lillian GW-284; AL-473
Varallo, Mary A. HST-25; LBJ-4
Varley, Leland TR-221
Varney, Dora M. WGH-57
Vass, Carl GW-507
Vecchi, (Mrs) Rallus WW-205
Venable, Douglas FDR-206
Verlander, J.A. TR-174
Vernon. GC-137
Vestvali, P.T. GC-21
Vickers, George M. GW-349; JAG-89; GC-50; GC-132; WM-145; TR-121
Victor. AL-123
Viereck, J.C. ZT-34; WS-12; USG-168
Viles, Eugenie TR-205
Villanueva, N.C. DAM-49; DAM-53
Vincent, Jimmy FDR-253
Vincent, Karl GW-189
Vincent, Nat WW-31
Virtue, Edward J. SJT-16
Voccoli, Toni FDR-122
Vogt, Harry V. WM-272
Vollmer, Laura DAM-38
Volunteer, A. AL-38
Volz, Henry J. DDE-30
Voorhees, Edward N. WW-55
VosBurgh, L.L. WGH-2
Voss, Charles GW-344; GW-386
Voxland, Martha WL-1

Wachter, Fred USG-104
Wade, Franklin TED-8
Wade, Herman A. GW-308
Waggoner, Ada Brown WW-130
Wagans, Edward USG-166
Wagler, F.A. JMN-1; AJK-1; AJK-16; AJK-46; WHH-34; JT-12; JKP-8; ZT-12
Wagner, Chas. H. WW-203
Wagner, Ferd. JKP-3
Wagner, H. JGB-4
Wagner, Harry FDR-155
Wagner, J.F. WM-55
Wagness, Bernard GW-520
Wahlman, J.P. WGH-14
Wald, Carl GW-437
Waldron, T. Virginia FDR-397
Walker, Alfred TR-244
Walker, Bee LBJ-8
Walker, Cora DAM-34
Walker, Corlus JFK-16
Walker, George L. SAD-1; SAD-8
Walker, Leslie DAM-34
Walker, Wm. Stearns AL-323
Wall, Dan J. TR-39; TR-214; TR-217
Wall Street CEH-7
Wallace, Burt AL-362
Wallace, Gen. Lew GW-586
Wallace, J.A. WJB-12; WJB-14
Wallace, M.E. WSH-33
Wallace, Wm. R. AL-431
Wallace, W. Vincent GW-305
Wallerstein. SJT-9
Walsh, Clifford W. WHT-24
Walsh, John J. WM-39
Walsh, Robert F. USG-172
Walter, Julius H. FDR-130
Walter K. JGB-42
Walter, M.E. WSH-22; WSH-33
Waltner, P. FDR-216
Walton. TR-88
Walz, Jean AJK-40; FDR-217
Wamelink, J.T. AL-14
Wanger, Sam AES-8
Wannemacher, H. WM-10
Ward, Charles L. SAD-18; JCB-2; JBL-4
Ward, Dennis A. AJK-40
Ward, Henry DDE-39; DAM-34
Ward, Marion L. WW-47
Ward, Matthias JQA-13
Ward, Rollin C. DW-20
Warde, Henry WM-6
Wardell, Kenneth FDR-45
Warden, David A. AL-158
Warden, Jettie AL-287
Ware, George GW-341; GW-390
Ware, Sr., Reuben LGM-1
Warfield, S. HC-49
Waring, Fred DDE-24; DDE-40; DDE-72; DDE-97
Wark, Alexander B. CC-7
Wark, Emma Viau CC-7
Warland, J.B. HC-50
Warland, John H. HC-37
Warner, J. AL-475
Warner, R. GC-158
Warren, A.E. JAG-74; JAG-79; JAG-93
Warren, Ben GC-70
Warren, Charles GBM-5; GBM-77
Warren, David A. AL-158
Warren, E.A. TR-224
Warren, George W. GW-174; GW-185 JCF-23
Warren, Harry RR-12; RR-17; RR-21
Warren, Seneca J. TR-94
Washburn. AL-430
Washburn, Emma GC-49
Washington, George GW-231; GW-393; GW-394
Waterfield, J.B. HCH-19
Waterman, J. ZT-71
Waters, Horace HG-29
Waters, Joseph G. JA-8
Watkins, E. WJB-39
Watkins, Mrs. M.J. WSH-8; WSH-19
Watson, F.S. WM-254
Watson, Fredric FDR-85
Watson, Gilbert S. AS-6; AS-8
Watson, Harold K. WJB-13
Watson, J.W. ZT-10
Watts, Dr. GW-89
Watts, Ella L. WW-64
Watts, Mary S. FDR-299
Wayne, Bernie AL-262; AS-3
Wayne, Don DAM-43
Wayne, Mabel MISC-69
Wayne, Sid MISC-161
Waynne, Annette GW-450
Waud, J. Haydn RBH-65
Weaver. WM-193
Weaver, A. AJN-6; AJN-19
Weaver, Richard L. WM-74
Weaver, T.L. GC-45
Web, Maron AS-4
Webb, Alex R. WSH-5; WSH-44
Webb, Dollie FDR-227
Webb, G.J. GW-139; GW-141; GW-517
Weber, Carl M. Von HC-36; TR-24
Weber, C.H. ZT-58
Weber, Henry GW-372; GW-584

Composer Index

Weber, Joe Francis MISC-90
Weber, Joseph von GW-363
Weber, Lawrence A. FDR-59
Weber, Louis AL-184; WGH-59
Webster, J.P. AL-39; AL-253; USG-141; USG-143; USG-268; USG-270
Webster, Paul F. JFK-10
Weed, Jos. JGB-87
Weeden, W.C. WM-60
Weelock, M.O. AL-16
Weestrop, E.J. GW-155
Wegefarth, Lewis C. SLP-1
Wegelin, C. BFH-74
Weil, Milton GW-307
Weiland, Francis MISC-34
Weiler, Louis BFH-21
Weinburg, Jacob DDE-68
Weinbrecht, M.E. WHH-102
Weiner, Henry RBH-2
Weiner, Lazar FDR-186
Weinman, B. MISC-22
Weir, Eva R. FDR-293
Weir, George FDR-290
Weise, Charles Von FDR-232; FDR-233
Weisser, Samuel FDR-189
Weizafcker. GW-75
Welcker, H. TR-124
Weldon, Judy GB-2
Weldon, Peter JMD-7
Welland, F. ZT-18
Welling, Frank CC-58
Wellman, Frances AL-481
Wells, Charles ZT-50
Wells, Hank BMG-6
Wells, Henry F. WGH-57
Wells, John F. GW-96
Wells, Roslyn TED-10
Wels, Charles AL-150
Wendell,·W.C. USG-97
Wendte, C.W. GW-423
Wenrich, Percy GW-229; TR-7; WW-126
Wentworth, D. AL-9
Werner, Alex P. GW-243
Werner. WJB-79
Werner, Henry HS-4; SJT-23; USG-40; WSH-44; JAG-21; JAG-46; GC-74; GC-147; GC-153; GC-156
Wernig, C.W. JAG-3
Wersel, Henry WM-195
Werth, F.A. USG-233
Wertheimer, Jennie M. WM-270
Wesner, Wilber S. AES-49
West, Arthur TR-235
West, Lucius C. WJB-30
West, Paul AP-3

West, Thomas N. JBR-3
Westendorf, Thos. P. RBH-25; WSH-3; JAG-19; JAG-20; JGB-44; JAG-45; JAG-60; JGB-55; JGB-61; GC-23
Weston, Charles B. WW-17; WW-18
Weston, J.P. JGB-59
Wetmore, W.J. USG-189
Westrop, E.J. GW-257
Weyman, Chas. S. JCF-5
Whaples, B.A. AL-339; JGB-26; JGB-68
Whear, Paul W. AL-325
Whatley, W.T. FDR-332
Wheatly, W.M. WW-96
Wheeler, Alfred ZT-42
Wheeler, H. JGB-40; GC-116
Wheeler, H.G. USG-51
Wheeler, H.H. USG-56
Wheeler, H.O. MISC-167
Wheeler, J.W. USG-51
Wheeler, Lilian E. TR-257
Wheeler, Mortimer WHT-8
Wheeler, Post WM-83
Wheelock, O. AL-105
Whelan, William T. WJB-44
Whilom, A. BFH-70
Whitcup, Leonard JFK-14; DAM-3
White, C.A. RBH-11; JAG-59; GC-55; GC-67; GC-136; JSJ-6
White, C.L. HC-6; HC-63
White, C.S. WJB-64; JBW-9
White, Charles E. AJN-8
White, D.L. JAG-74
White, Edward I. GW-427
White, Edward L. GW-40; WHH-62; HC-7; HC-60; ZT-15; ZT-27
White, Frederic E. BFH-71; GC-57
White, Isobel C. AJK-44
White, Lee AES-32
White, R.U. WLW-25
Whitehorn, James F. WW-70
Whiting, Richard A. RR-9
Whiting, S.K. GBM-37
Whitman. AL-406; AL-421
Whitman, Mollie W. FDR-62; FDR-243; FDR-411
Whitman, Murray WLW-4
Whitman, Walt AL-479
Whitmore, Floyd E. WGH-24
Whitmore, Heck WGH-24
Whitney, (Mrs) A.H. AL-276
Whitney, Andrew JCF-9
Whitney, W.W. JD-9
Whitson, Beth S. GW-198
Whittemore, Arthur HST-12

Whittick, Wm. USG-284
Whittier. AML-27
Whittnesey, Orramel ZT-31
W.H.S. USG-62
Wicker, Jr., F.N. WJB-88
Wicker, Irene GW-356; TJ-41
Wickes, John C. FDR-75; FDR-416
Wicklund, C.A. GW-192
Widdows, Frederick JB-7; JGB-32
Wiedmann, C. SJT-9
Wiegand, George HG-8; HG-17
Wiener, Eugene A. GW-175
Wilcox, D.M. TR-229
Wilcox, Will S. GC-86
Wildau, F. FDR-216
Wile, Frederic W. HCH-59
Wilkin, Marijohn JFK-13
Wilkin, Marijohn JFK-13
Wilkins, Dr. T. WJB-65
Wilkinson, Helen A. WM-194
Wilkinson, Ray WW-182
Wilkinson, T.A. WM-194
Wilkinson, W.O. AL-347
Willett, Edward JGB-26
Willey, A.J. GW-208
Williams, Belle WW-147
Williams, Billy WW-124
Williams, Charles L. HAW-2
Williams, Edgar DDE-27
Williams, Emma FDR-85
Williams, H.K. TR-331
Williams, Howard S. BFH-81; WM-44
Williams, (Mrs) J.E. FDR-174
Williams, John JFK-52
Williams, John E. FDR-174
Williams, John W. WW-156
Williams, Thomas ZT-9
Williams, Harry TR-42
Williams, Laughton LBJ-12
Williams, Ralph C. TR-57
Williams, Vincent T. AL-313
Williams, W.R. AL-201; AL-278; USG-217; TR-38; TR-273; TR-306; WW-3; WW-117; WW-125; WW-186; WLW-50
Williamson, T.S. WM-253
Willis, L.L. HCH-3
Willis, R. DWC-7
Willis, Ron MISC-112
Willis, Sarah TED-17
Willson, J. DWC-5
Willson, Lester GW-343
Wilson (Mrs) Max L. FDR-423
Willson, Meredith FDR-278; JFK-29; JFK-63; GRF-2
Wilmarth, Walter G. JMD-11

Composer Index

Wincriste, Ed GC-159
Wilson. AL-435; AL-436
Wilson, Daniel H. CEH-6
Wilson, Don C. CC-4; CC-49
Wilson, G.D. JAG-55
Wilson, George R. MISC-37
Wilson, Grace FDR-420
Wilson, Grace V. GW-385
Wilson, Inez JMC-4
Wilson, John F. GW-375; JA-18
Wilson, J.R. SJT-9
Wilson, Lester GW-345
Wilson, Westen WHT-52
Wilson, Woodrow WW-23; WW-86; WW-149
Wilson, S.G. USG-49; GC-63; GC-138
Wilstach, Claxton CAA-10
Winkler, Emile FDR-258
Winne, Jesse WW-9
Winner, Septimus GW-146; GW-560; MF-29; GBM-30; AL-53; AL-85; AL-162; AL-167; AL-359; AL-475; USG-16; USG-18; USG-244; WSH-10; WSH-14; WSH-23; WSH-24; WSH-25; WSH-28; JAG-64; BFB-9; MISC-156; MISC-171
Winstead, S.E. FDR-50
Winteringer, Marcus WM-269
Winthrop. WM-177
Winthrop, Thomas F. USG-58
Wires, P.J. AL-437
Wirtz, Fred JFK-21
Wise, Frances G. FDR-399
Wise, Fred TJ-42
Wiske, Mortimer RBH-42
Witham, Betty FDR-108
Witham, Mitz FDR-108
Withrow, Samuel HC-107
Witmark, Isador GC-51
Witt, Max S. AL-438
Wittig, Rudolph USG-297
Wolerstein, Sol TR-247
Wolf, Charles FDR-323
Wolf, Fred E. TR-279
Wolf, Jack MISC-60
Wolf, J.J. TR-203
Wolfe, Carolyn WW-148
Wolfe, Hugh J. DAM-17
Wollow, Geo. WW-176
Wolsieffer, J. Henry AJN-18; AJN-28
Wolsieffer, William AL-70
Wolter, John R. GW-569; TED-18
Wolverton, Josephine GW-385
Wolverton, (Mrs) Sara AL-480

Womrath, J. TJ-9
Wood, Abraham GW-81
Wood, C. AL-439
Wood, F.M. WM-21
Wood, Guy TJ-42
Wood, Holly FDR-378
Wood, J.H. WM-176; WM-218
Wood, Leo MISC-46
Wood, Samuel T. MISC-112
Wood, William M. TR-192
Woode, Bea USG-285
Woodin, William H. FDR-53; FDR-54; FDR-328
Woodhams, R. USG-21
Woodhams, William H. USG-157
Woodward, E.H. FDR-113
Woodworth, Samuel DWC-3; DWC-8; MISC-156; MISC-169
Woodrig, V.E. WW-139
Woods, Glenn WM-215
Woolcott, Francis AL-274
Woolen, Irma W. FDR-77
Wooler, Alfred TR-303
Woolfolk, Boyle MISC-84
Woollett, J. BFH-50
Woolsley, Stella L. WM-132
Woolworth, S. AJK-11; AJK-23; AJK-25
Work, Henry C. GW-570; GW-611; AL-99; AL-192; AL-215; AL-256; AJN-5; USG-266; USG-272; USG-273; TR-54; CEH-4; MISC-171
Worrell, Ednas R. GW-233
Worsley, J. AJK-12
Worthington, Amy T. WW-1
Worzel. JAG-109
Wozencraft, Dr. ZT-21; ZT-45
Wrenrich, Percy GW-230
Wright. AL-440
Wright, Edwin GW-273
Wright, Elizur JBR-4; JBR-5
Wright, Frank CC-56
Wright, F.S. USG-122
Wright, George WHT-2
Wright, James HCH-10; WLW-34
Wright, Joe T. USG-122
Wright, Maitland S. WW-62
Wright, Monroe CC-42
Wright, Robert Wm. WSH-40
Wright, Tommy WLW-16
Wright, U.R. TR-109
Wright, William C. MF-14
Wrightman, Neale DAM-32
Wrightston, Herbert TR-128
Wrubel, Allie MISC-52;

MISC-86; MISC-143; MISC-150
Wuest, Charles N. FDR-202
Wullweber, O.L. WM-283
Wundernamm, A. GC-164
Wurzel. JD-22; JD-25
Wyman, A.P. USG-187; USG-287
Wyman, Lincoln S. WM-162

Yagle, C.F. JD-3
Yarnell, Alice TR-173
Yawger, Rose N. GW-553
Yellen, Jack WGH-26; WGH-38; BC-5
Yoder, Paul MISC-115
Youmans, Jay V. WM-93
Young, Barney FDR-60; HST-9
Young, Bill FDR-237
Young, Charles USG-9
Young, Edna G. GW-434; AL-360
Young, Ella V. USG-16; USG-18; USG-245
Young, Gordon MISC-112
Young, Ida JFK-5
Young, Joe GW-219; AL-213
Young, John PC-2; FDR-389
Young, Morrey FDR-105
Young, Philip M. MISC-112
Young, Tibby FDR-105
Yung, De BFH-92

Zahn, Ted LBJ-26
Zais, Bernard H. FDR-36
Zaluecus. GC-120
Zanig, Augustus D. AL-355
Zaret, Hy TJ-28; TJ-51
Zartius USG-95
Ziedler, Frank EVD-2
Zee, Allan TJ-37
Zellner, Richard USG-50; USG-274
Zeuner, Charles GW-93; GW-332; WHH-54; AMP-1; JBL-8
Zickel, Harry H. WM-122
Ziehrer, C.M. GC-93
Zimmerman, Charles A. FDR-20
Zimmerman, Ella WW-6
Zimmerman, J.P. TR-210
Zimmerman, Paul G. WJB-42
Ziskin, Victor AL-196
Zoeller, George AL-86
Zoeller, Louis E. WGH-9; FDR-157; FDR-281
Zuchtmann, Frederick GW-437